THE PROPHET

A Book of the Praises of Saint Francis by Bernard of Besse
(1277–1283)

The Versified Life of Saint Francis by Henri d'Avranches
Additions, Amplifications in Light of *The Major Legend*
(after 1283)

A Collection of Sayings of the Companions of Blessed Francis
(Late 13th–Early 14th Century)

The Tree of the Crucified Life of Jesus
Book Five (Excerpts) by Ubertino Da Casale
(1305)

A Mirror of the Perfection, *Rule,* Profession, Life, and True Calling of a Lesser
Brother (The Lemmens Edition, 1901)
(1318)

A Mirror of the Perfection of the *Status* of a Lesser Brother
(The Sabatier Edition, 1928)
(1318)

The Book of Chronicles or of the Tribulations of the Order of Lesser Ones
(Prologue and the First Tribulation)
by Angelo Clareno
(1323–1325-6)

The Deeds of Blessed Francis and His Companions
by Ugolino Boniscambi of Montegiorgio
(1328-1337)

The Little Flowers of Saint Francis
(A Translation and Re-Editing of The Deeds of Saint Francis and His
Companions by an Anonymous)
(After 1337)

Liturgical Texts for the Feast of the Stigmata of Saint Francis
(1337–1340)

The Kinship of Saint Francis by Arnald of Sarrant
(1365)

Related Documents
(1261–1323)

A three-volume series

FRANCIS OF ASSISI: EARLY DOCUMENTS

THE PROPHET

A Book of the Praises of Saint Francis by Bernard of Besse
The Versified Life of Saint Francis by Henri d'Avranches Additions,
Amplifications in Light of *The Major Legend*
A Collection of Sayings of the Companions of Blessed Francis
The Tree of the Crucified Life of Jesus Book Five (Excerpts) by Ubertino Da Casale
A Mirror of the Perfection, *Rule,* Profession, Life, and True Calling of a Lesser
Brother (The Lemmens Edition, 1901)
A Mirror of the Perfection of the *Status* of a Lesser Brother (The Sabatier
Edition, 1928)
The Book of Chronicles or of the Tribulations of the Order of Lesser Ones
(Prologue and the First Tribulation) by Angelo Clareno
The Deeds of Blessed Francis and His Companions by Ugolino Boniscambi of
Montegiorgio
The Little Flowers of Saint Francis (A Translation and Re-Editing of The Deeds
of Saint Francis and His Companions by an Anonymous)
Liturgical Texts for the Feast of the Stigmata of Saint Francis
The Kinship of Saint Francis by Arnald of Sarrant
Related Documents

Volume III of:
Francis of Assisi: Early Documents

Edited by
Regis J. Armstrong, O.F.M. Cap.
J. A. Wayne Hellmann, O.F.M. Conv.
William J. Short, O.F.M.

New City Press

New York   London   Manila

Published in the United States, Great Britain, and the Philippines by
New City Press, 202 Cardinal Rd., Hyde Park, New York 12538
New City, 57 Twyford Ave., London W3 9PZ and
New City Publications, 4800 Valenzuela St. Sta Mesa, 1016 Manila

Cover design by Nick Cianfarani
Cover art by an unknown artist of Emilia or Lombardia, Italy
in the Baptistry of the Duomo of Parma, Italy
Photograph by William R. Cook. Used with permission.
The painting offers an unusual portrait of Francis and the six-winged seraph.
Since the seraph's hands are not visible and his feet show no wounds,
scholars suggest that the reception of the stigmata was not intended by the artist
as much as a portrait of Francis "who seemed to everyone a person of another
age" (1C 36) or "like the angel ascending from the rising of the sun" (Lmj Prol 1).
Maps ©1998, Franciscan Friars of California

British Library Cataloguing-in-Publication Data
A Catalogue record for this book is available
from the British Library

ISBN cloth 0-904287-66-1
ISBN paper 0-904287-65-3

Printed in Canada

Translators:

Regis J. Armstrong, O.F.M. Cap.
Paul Barrett, O.F.M. Cap
Canisius Connors, O.F.M.+
Stephen Cordova
Ewert H. Cousins, Ph.D.
Eric Doyle, O.F.M.+
Edward Hagman, O.F.M. Cap.
J. A. Wayne Hellmann, O.F.M. Conv.
Claude Jarmak, O.F.M. Conv.
Timothy Johnson, S.T.D.
Dominic Monti, O.F.M.
Peter Nickels, O.F.M. Conv.
Timothy Noone, Ph.D.
Gregory Shanahan, O.F.M.
William J. Short, O.F.M.
Jaime Vidal, Ph.D.

Contributors and Consultants:

John and Vicki Chiment
Joseph Chinnici, O.F.M.
Lorenzo Di Fonzo, O.F.M. Conv.
Jay Hammond III, Ph.D.
Conrad Harkins, O.F.M.
Eileen Haugh, O.S.F.
Ingrid Peterson, O.S.F.
Cyprian Rosen, O.F.M. Cap.
Oktavian Schmucki, O.F.M. Cap.
Philippe Yates, O.F.M.

Technical and Research Assistants:

Kevin Hester
John Isom
Daniel Michaels
Donald Patten
Noel Riggs
Daniel Van Slyke
Keith Warner, O.F.M.

Contents

A Book of the Praises of Saint Francis by Bernard of Besse
(1277–1283)

The Versified Life of Saint Francis by Henri d'Avranches
Additions, Amplifications in Light of *The Major Legend* (after 1283)

A Collection of Sayings of the Companions of Blessed Francis
(Late 13th–Early 14th Century)

The Tree of the Crucified Life of Jesus
Book Five (Excerpts) by Ubertino Da Casale (1305)

A Mirror of the Perfection (1318)

The Book of Chronicles or of the Tribulations of the Order of Lesser Ones (Prologue and the First Tribulation) by Angelo Clareno (1323–1325-6)

The Deeds of Blessed Francis and His Companions by Ugolino Boniscambi of Montegiorgio (1328-1337) and The Little Flowers of Saint Francis (A Translation and Re-Editing of The Deeds of Saint Francis and His Companions by an Anonymous) (After 1337)

Liturgical Texts for the Feast of the Stigmata of Saint Francis (1337–1340)

The Kinship of Saint Francis by Arnald of Sarrant (1365)

Related Documents (1261–1323)

Appendix

General Introduction

The prophet: in a period of history buzzing with talk of prophets, prophecy, and signs,[1] Bonaventure presented such an image of Francis of Assisi in the opening passages of his *Major Legend* of the saint.[2] It became a leitmotif for the next generations of Lesser Brothers, one that brought to the fore a concern for their role in the unfolding events of the world. The biblical images of Francis offered by Bonaventure resonated deeply with the apocalyptic views of Joachim of Fiore and prompted many of Francis's followers to declare the dawning of a new age of salvation history. In its context the Saint was situated squarely in the framework of history and unmistakably portrayed as ushering in a climactic turn of events, coming in the spirit of Elijah, as another John the Baptist, God's herald, and prophetically calling all peoples to change their lives. Appearing as the apocalyptic "angel ascending from the rising of the sun," Bonaventure portrayed the Founder as marking his followers with the Tau, the sign of salvation given to the poor and humble, and denied to the rich and powerful.[3]

Bonaventure's portrait of Francis in the *Major Legend* must be seen within his evolving theology of history. His last major work, *The Collations on the Six Days of Creation* (1273), broke in a striking way from the traditional interpretation of the Genesis narrative.[4] Following Augustine, medieval Christians had seen in the account of the six days of creation an allegorical description of six ages of salvation history, from Adam until the end of time. For Augustine, God's salvific work culminated in the "sixth age" with the creation of the "new Adam," Jesus Christ. But in His death and resurrection, Christ also inaugurated the seventh age, the "Sabbath rest" of the Heavenly Jerusalem. Augustine maintained that history's goal, achieved in Christ, was no longer to be awaited in the waning sixth age, but in the salvation of the full number of God's elect. Bonaventure's own allegorical interpretation of the "week" of creation offers a radically different vision. Following Joachim of Fiore, he sees not one, but two parallel dispensations of salvation history. The first, beginning with Adam, culminated with the coming of Christ. But salvation history does not end in this manner. For Bonaventure, Christ is the center of the ages. His Mystical Body, the Church, must live through another six ages until his Second Coming. From this perspective, Bonaventure saw Francis – and his Order – playing a critical role in salvation history. Francis, the perfect imitator of Christ, ushered in the sixth age of church history, and was thus a prophetic figure who would lead those Christians struggling to live Christ's Gospel in the midst of apocalyptic tribulations.[5]

Bonaventure's *Major Legend*, distributed to every Franciscan house in Europe for annual table reading to the brothers on the occasion of Francis's feast,[6] demonstrably influenced art and literature. Giotto's fresco cycle in Assisi's Upper Basilica of Saint Francis[7] and a recast version of Henri d'Avranches's *Versified Life* bear witness to this.[8] Still, fascination with their founder impelled his brothers to "go beyond" this compelling portrait mandated by the General Chapter of 1260 and made official six years later in the General Chapter of 1266.[9] Several were interested in supplementing the information it conveyed about Francis. Shortly after Bonaventure's death, Jerome of Ascoli, his successor as General Minister, added details to the *Major Legend*,[10] and, in a request reminiscent of that of Crescentius of Iesi,[11] requested the brothers in 1276 to send him information about the deeds of Francis and his companions.[12] The immediate result of that request is not known, for in 1288, Jerome became Pope Nicholas IV. In his *Book of The Praises of Blessed Francis,* Bernard of Besse, Bonaventure's secretary and traveling companion, added new details about Francis's companions that were not found in the earlier literature.[13]

But by the end of the thirteenth century, tensions within the Lesser Brothers prompted an exchange of stories that accentuated the prophetic dimensions of Bonaventure's portrait of Francis – the saint's vehement defense of poverty, his outspoken, fearless call to Gospel truth, and his troubled predictions of trials.[14] Bonaventure's theology of history later found a voice in the writings of his student, Peter of John Olivi (1248-1298),[15] who, in turn, influenced Ubertino da Casale (+ c. 1325) and Angelo Clareno (+1337). The fourteenth century compilations in this third volume of *Francis of Assisi: Early Documents* reflect the Parisian-based theology of history in down-to-earth, easily comprehended stories. In the wake of Jerome of Ascoli's request for new information about Saint Francis and his companions, the phenomenon of these new compilations satisfied the brothers' eagerness to supplement Bonaventure's portrait and, at the same time, to promote their particular views of his Gospel way of life.

The crises of fourteenth century Europe

Within Franciscan literature, considerations of the years encompassed by these compilations generally focus on the internal problems of the Order of Lesser Brothers.[16] The larger dramas of fourteenth century Europe are generally overlooked, yet the prophetic consciousness of the Lesser Brothers might best be understood in the larger context of the world in which those internal conflicts were unfolding. Three chains of events were symptomatic of the undercurrents moving fourteenth century European history: the Avignon Papacy (1308-73), the Great Famine (1315-17), and the Black Death (1347-50). These situations were symptomatic of a time of profound crises in church and society in which the espoused values of the Lesser Brothers were tried.[17]

For men bound by their *Rule* to promise obedience to the Roman Pontiff, the tumultuous events leading to the Avignon Papacy clearly indicated the apocalyptic crises foreshadowed by the writings of Bonaventure were upon them.[18] The papacy had been increasing in both power and moral prestige since the Gregory Reform in the latter half of the eleventh century. Two centuries later, it was becoming a victim of its own success. As more and more aspects of church governance became centralized in the Papal court, the Western church became ever more aware of the papacy's use of this vast spiritual authority for narrow political ends within Italy. As a consequence, the papal office itself became politicized. Long vacancies were increasingly common following the death of a pope, as contending factions jockeyed to secure the position.

After a two-year interregnum, the Franciscan pope, Nicholas IV (1288-92) was succeeded by Celestine IV whose pontificate lasted only six months. The legacy of Celestine's successor, the tempestuous Boniface VIII (1294-1303) was filled with conflicts: within the College of Cardinals, between the papacy and the French monarchy, and among Europeans in general. After Boniface's death, the cardinals elected Benedict XI (1303-4) whose pontificate lasted only ten months. Two years later the French Archbishop of Bordeaux, Bertrand de Got, became Pope Clement V (1305-14). Because of the unstable political situation in the Papal States, Clement decided not to travel to Rome, but settled in Avignon. Eventually, the whole Papal court reached their apogee. Its intrusive bureaucracy, oppressive taxation, and opulent life-style made many Western Christians increasingly view the papacy, not as a vehicle of church reform, but its obstacle. Already at the Council of Vienne in 1311, one bishop was calling for "the re-formation of the Church *in head* and in members."[19]

For the Lesser Brothers, such criticism of the papacy was particularly poignant. Their very existence as a worldwide brotherhood, in large measure exempt from local control, was dependent on a centralized church government. Early Franciscan history manifests any number of papal interventions. Innocent III (1198-1216) and Honorius III (1216-27) are clearly central figures in the life of the saint and founder, Francis himself. In *Quo elongati,* Gregory IX (1227-41) not only described his intimate relationship with Francis, but powerfully interpreted his mind and, in doing so, altered the way of life he left for his followers,[20] a path continued by Innocent IV (1243-54).[21] But papal interventions following Bonaventure's death in 1274 were both decisive and divisive. Nicholas III (1277-80), following his predecessors, attempted to promulgate a definitive interpretation of Francis's *Rule.*[22] Yet controversy over its implementation led the saintly Celestine V, in his brief pontificate, to permit its first division by establishing the Poor Hermits. Boniface VIII heavy-handedly attempted to stifle any division within the Order and, with the promulgation of *Olim Caelestinus,* April 8, 1295, stripped the fledgling group of papal protection. In that same year, Boniface removed Raymond Gaufredi as general minister, replaced him with John of Murrovalle, whom he viewed as more sympathetic to his views, and encouraged him to curb the *zelanti,* especially Peter of John Olivi.

In light of this contentious history, the Avignon Papacy and all that it symbolized furthered an already divided and demoralized Order of Lesser Brothers. The "official" portraits of Thomas of Celano and Bonaventure con-

vey the sense that the Church—in the persons of Popes Innocent III and
Honorius III, Cardinal Hugolino, and Bishop Guido of Assisi—"saved" Francis and his Order. At the same time, they also suggest that Francis and his Order "saved" the debilitated, aging Church. In the apocalyptic climate of the
fourteenth century, however, it seemed appropriate for the Franciscan *zelanti*
to focus more intently on Francis's vision and mission.[23] The urgency of this
consciousness became more pressing as the socio-economic conditions in
which they found themselves grew increasingly dismal. By the beginning of
the fourteenth century, the population of Europe had reached an unprece-
dented height, so much so that the land could barely provide sufficient resources to support it. There was no longer any margin for crop failures or even
harvest shortfalls. In an economy driven by profit, prices rose to twenty times
their normal level. In Venice alone, the rate of inflation was 1200 percent.
Strikes and riots became commonplace, as ordinary workers protested their
dismal living conditions.

To compound this precarious situation, the weather patterns of Western
Europe were changing: summers were far more cool and wet, autumns were
plagued with early storms. The spring of 1315, for example, was so extraordinarily wet that it was impossible to plow the fields; that summer was inun-
dated with heavy rains rotting much of the seed before it could germinate. The
same conditions prevailed in 1316 as a series of unusual storms pounded the
Atlantic coast and brought severe flooding to usually fertile lands. With bad
harvests, prices of grain quadrupled, and famine was prevalent. The poor
were desperate to eat but had no money, while the rich bought up whatever
food was available and stored it away. Animals normally used for the fields
were slaughtered, seed grain was eaten, young children were abandoned, and
many of the old voluntarily stopped eating so that younger members of their
families might live to till the fields. There were even numerous reports of can-
nibalism. By the winter of 1317, historians estimate that between ten and fifteen percent of Europe's population had died from disease or starvation.[24]

The number of the poor increased dramatically, as did their ever-worsen-
ing living conditions. Plagues became common-place. Florence endured a
devastating plague in 1340, another in 1344, and yet another in 1346. One
chronicler wrote that the years 1343-54 were among the most tragic in the history of Venice.[25]

Crisis became catastrophe as the Black Death, spread by the fleas of infected rats, struck Italy in 1347 and ravaged Europe over the next two years.
Historians estimate the mortality rate at one-quarter to one-third of the population. Jacques LeGoff deftly sketches how "the fall in population, aggravated
by the plague, cut down the number of the workforce and the consumers."[26]

In the profit economy of fourteenth century Europe, economic forces
shifted in their traditional manner: "only the most powerful, the most skilled
or the luckiest benefitted; others were hit."[27] All of these forces—famine, rise
in prices, plague, and diminution of the workforce—brought into focus the
tragedy of the Hundred Years War that further exacerbated Europe's demoralized state between 1338 and 1453. Its fundamental cause was the anomaly

by which the Plantagenet kings of England held an immense fief in southern France, the remains of the heritage of Eleanor of Aquitaine (+1122-1204).[28] The Hundred Years War, however, may be seen as a war of the English and French nobility who demanded war as an answer to their economic and social difficulties. "But," as LeGoff observes, "as always, war accelerated the process and brought to birth a new economy and society by way of deaths and ru- ins."[29] The Hundred Years War certainly fed an already frenzied apocalyptic mood and convinced much of Christian Europe that the end was at hand.

During this period the Lesser Brothers played a role of paramount impor- tance in the religious life of Western European Christians. By this time, their ministerial efforts were concentrated in the urban centers where the effects of these social and economic crises were most acute. The preaching of the men- dicant orders provided a critical perspective on both the land-based wealth of the secular church and the emerging profit economy, challenging its very foundations.[30] But the economic hardships of the times also breathed life into the otherwise sterile intra-mural debates about Franciscan poverty evident in the final papal interpretation of the *Rule* by Clement V (1305-14).[31] The *usus pauper* of the Lesser Brothers, defended by Peter of John Olivi in his interpre- tation of poverty, was seen and experienced by the poor as providing "a moral response as the courageous free choice for what the fate of the socio-economic forces [of the late thirteenth, early fourteenth centuries] had decreed."[32] In light of the crop failures and famines of the time, the protests of the Spirituals against the accumulation of stores of grain by the brothers can be seen as an act of solidarity with the suffering poor. With Pope John XXII's 1323 condem- nation of the ideal of apostolic poverty, *Cum inter nonnullos,*[33] the Church was deprived of a Gospel response to the difficult challenge of the times in which it found itself.

In these last days . . .

The texts of this third volume undoubtedly reflect the internal problems of the Order of Lesser Brothers. They reveal the struggles of the brothers to un- derstand their way of life and their role in the unfolding saga of four- teenth-century Europe. The heritage of Francis was threatened, as they perceived it, by papal interventions and their own compromising interpreta- tions.

Ubertino da Casale's *Tree of the Crucified Life of Jesus* undoubtedly follows in the apocalyptic tradition highlighted by Bonaventure's portrait of Francis and Peter of John Olivi's commentary on the Apocalypse.[34] Personal experience within the courts of Popes Boniface VIII and Benedict XI had already prompted Ubertino to see the Church of his day as "Babylon the Whore," the carnal Church. Its only hope, he maintained, was the "re-formation of the life of Christ," especially the poor Christ found in the life of Francis. Ubertino's *Tree of the Crucified Life of Jesus* is a consideration of history underscoring Fran- cis's prophetic role. In its Fifth Book, Ubertino weaves biblical and apocalyptic images together with those of the earlier portraits of Francis into a tapestry that fired the imagination of the more zealous of Francis's followers. More practically, however, in 1311 Ubertino alerted them to the existence of the lost *rotulli* or scrolls containing the reminiscences of Brother Leo and his companions, preserved "in the cupboards of the brothers in Assisi."[35]

This discovery produced a number of compilations that included, among other items, editions of the *rotuli* or scrolls, selected writings of Saint Francis, carefully chosen passages from earlier biographical sources, e.g. the works of Thomas of Celano, and, in some cases, stories or statements of famous and holy confreres, e.g. Conrad of Offida. The most famous of these is, undoubtedly, the *Assisi Compilation,* which was transcribed in 1311 shortly after Ubertino's announcement.[36] Shortly thereafter, two new compilations appeared, both using the image of the mirror in their titles: one containing only forty-five paragraphs,[37] the other containing one hundred and twenty-four paragraphs.[38] Both texts adopt different approaches to the *rotuli.* The longer edition reveals, in particular, attempts at sharpening the contours of Francis's prophetic character. The humble Francis of the scrolls, for example, becomes "the most humble Francis;" his austerity becomes outstanding, as does his poverty.

Six years later, Angelo Clareno wrote his *Book of Chronicles or of the Tribulations of the Order of Lesser Ones.*[39] Like Peter of John Olivi and Ubertino da Casale, Angelo describes history in apocalyptic terms and employs their same vocabulary of the *status* of history.[40] Angelo, however, described seven additional periods of history that unfold with the appearance of Francis, each burdened with its own tribulations. The Prologue to Angelo's work is a pessimistic description of the increasing diminishment and decline of the Order. Those who remain faithful to Francis's *Rule* and especially his *Testament,* Angelo maintains, are called to suffer, to undergo the trials and tribulations endured by Christ Himself. As one who struggled for a rigorist interpretation of the *Rule* of Saint Francis, Angelo writes from a troubled point of view. In his attempt to tell the stories of the heroes and villains of his life, Angelo offers a revisionist interpretation of history in which significant events are perceived through the lens of his paranoia.

The Deeds of Blessed Francis and His Companions may well have been a written response to the seemingly forgotten request of Jerome of Ascoli in 1276 for information concerning the saint and his first followers.[41] Written in its present form between 1328-37, *The Deeds* reveals more than one hand in its composition, although that of Ugolino Boniscambi appears to be primary. Like the date of Ugolino's birth, that of his death is unknown. *The Deeds* reveals his knack for remembering and narrating stories, especially those originating in his own Province of the Marches. Four, possibly five, of these stories contain questionable details; many other details are clearly mistaken. Thus, there is need for a critical eye in judging the historical accuracy of this work. Throughout *The Deeds,* however, its authors add colorful details that provide light and often humor.

The earliest manuscript of its Italian translation, *The Little Flowers,* bears the date 1398.[42] Practically speaking, it is far more popular than its source, *The Deeds.*

Every translation is an interpretation. In any language, words assume a variety of meanings and shades of nuance that make their precise translation difficult. *The Little Flowers* is no exception. The translator divides the chapters of *The Deeds* differently, undoubtedly to make them more manageable. He inverts the order of certain chapters and, within chapters, changes the order of certain paragraphs and sentences. At a later date, another translator re-arranged chapters nine, thirty-nine, eighteen, and thirty-eight of *The Deeds* to form four of the five *Considerations on the Sacred Stigmata.* Translated and edited more than one hundred and seventy-five years after the death of Francis, *The Little Flowers* has had an enormous impact on shaping the popular image of Francis of Assisi. For many it has been their only contact with him.

The final work of this third volume, *The Kinship of Saint Francis,* is generally unknown.[43] Of its author, Arnald of Sarrant, little is known. He served his brothers as Provincial Minister sometime in the second half of the fourteenth century; nothing is recorded about his ministry among them. Luke Wadding states that Pope Gregory XI sent Arnald to Spain between 1373-5. *The Chronicle of the Twenty-Four General Ministers*—from Saint Francis to Leonard di Giffoni (1376-78)—is generally recognized as his work.

At the outset Arnald is clear about the purpose of *The Kinship:* to gather together in a more easily followed manner "those things that touch on the same material in other different legends, scattered in the scrolls and sayings of the companions—things that lord Bonaventure omitted totally or in part because everything could not come to his awareness."[44] Since the two manuscripts of this text are poorly preserved and filled with large gaps, it is impossible to determine how successful he was in achieving his purpose.[45] Arnald's text does place him in the apocalyptic line of Bonaventure, Peter of John Olivi, Ubertino da Casale, and Angelo Clareno. "At last," he writes, "in the sixth age, almost on the sixth day, came a human being, Francis, made in God's image and likeness." Once again, the Saint and the Founder is understandably portrayed as a prophet appearing in eschatological terms. This is understandable given Arnald's references to the Black Plague, his awareness of the Avignon papacy, and his allusion to the "community"—the first such reference in this literature.

More importantly, *The Kinship of Saint Francis* is dedicated to identifying nine "conformities" between the lives of Saint Francis and Christ. As such, it paves the way for Bartholomew of Pisa's massive encyclopedic study of forty conformities in his *The Conformity of the Life of Blessed Francis to the Life of the Lord Jesus,* a work begun in 1385 and presented to the friars fourteen years later. *The Kinship* thus marks the end of one period in the history of Franciscan literature and the beginning of another.

Conclusion

With the possible exception of Bernard of Besse's *Book of Praises*, the texts of this third volume have been generally categorized as "unofficial."[46] For the most part these are texts that were never commissioned or formally approved by a pope or by a general chapter of the Order of Lesser Brothers. Through the prism of the post-Bonaventure period of the Order's history, they reveal the intense and multi-dimensional spirituality of Francis of Assisi, as well as the shape and ideals of his early followers. As such, these texts reflect the Order's struggle to reform itself, a struggle intensified by the tragic movements that divided it.[47] From the earliest days, the brothers tended to see Francis in the image of Cardinal Thomas of Capua, the *Forma Minorum,* the form or paragon of their life.[48] Thus it was only logical that their "form," Francis, whom Thomas of Celano had described as conforming perfectly to Christ, should become for his disillusioned, ideologically divided followers the model of reform. Papal documents had focused on the *Rule* as the embodiment of perfection, as had the commentaries of many of the Order's intellectuals.[49] These texts directed their readers to Francis himself.

Although they do reveal Francis in a more personal rapport with his followers, the texts add little to our knowledge of Francis. They do contribute, however, to an increased awareness of the primitive fraternity in which the unique personalities and, at times, idiosyncratic behaviors of Francis's brothers come into focus. With the exceptions of Ubertino da Casale and Angelo Clareno, the rich biblical texture that is so much a part of the writings of Thomas of Celano, Julian of Speyer, and Bonaventure is missing. Biblical quotations used in the compilations seem more contrived and, in the case of Arnald of Arrant, forced. The broad theology of virtue offered by Thomas, and systematized and refined by Bonaventure, is overlooked, replaced by the repetitive descriptions of those virtues accentuated in the struggles of the fourteenth century. The powerful theology of grace implicit in Thomas's portraits and symbolically presented as the underpinning of Bonaventure's legends is set aside.[50] In its place is a moralistic spirituality typical of the fourteenth century *devotio moderna* with its accents on asceticism, the individual, and an "other-worldly" spirituality. A significant addition to the translation of *The Deeds, The Little Flowers,* expresses a devotionalism that soon pervaded Franciscan literature, that is, the formula found at the conclusion of each chapter: "To the praise of Jesus Christ and the little poor man Francis." Besides underscoring the intimate bond between Jesus and Francis, the phrase placed devotion to Francis on a level with that to Christ.[51]

Awareness of these texts, presented in the chronological and inter-textual methodology of these volumes, raises questions about the effectiveness of the decree of the General Chapter of 1266. Were the earlier portraits of Francis as thoroughly *deleantur* [deleted] as modern historians suggest?[52] If so, why and how did the compilers so effectively quote the works of Thomas of Celano? And if Bonaventure's *Major Legend* was held in such disdain, why was it ac-

knowledged, quoted, and respected by those whom modern historians por-
tray as Bonaventure's malingerers?

The Prologue to a fourteenth-century compilation written in Saxony may
offer a key to understanding the dynamic of many of these texts:

> *"Do it exactly according to the* exemplar *[pattern] that was shown to you on
> the mountain* (Ex 25:40). The highest perfection . . . has illumined the
> earth, that is, Christ, who according to the Prophet is a generous and
> fruitful mountain, a mountain that God chose for his dwelling; for
> there the Lord dwells forever . . . The great and high mountain is,
> therefore, the Lord himself; but among his people are other moun-
> tains around Him. That we should raise our eyes to those mountains
> and so be helped by the pattern of a perfect life, Christ our God has
> raised up our blessed father Francis among the holy mountains of his
> exalted Church . . . In him He has shown us the image of His holy life
> and of every perfection according to the Gospel."[53]

These were texts intended to keep the *Forma Minorum,* Francis, continually
before the minds of his followers, texts that were intended to complement or
supplement the "official" documents of the Church and the Order. Their editors carefully crafted stories attributed to their heroes—"we who were with
him," Leo, Conrad of Offida, et al.—and used them to recast Francis in their
own image as a Spiritual and a prophet of tribulation for their time. As such,
these are texts that reveal more about the Order than about Francis himself,
texts that need to be read with a critical eye so that the fundamentalism they
convey will not seduce the reader into accepting a fourteenth-century, biased
portrait of Francis. Nevertheless, the prophetic images of Francis presented in
many of the texts of this volume offer contemporary readers of the
twenty-first century a challenge: to be not only admirers of The Saint and followers of The Founder, but also, in their own time, place, and circumstance, to
be emulators of The Prophet.

Notes

1. Cf. Marjorie Reeves, *The Influence of Prophecy in The Later Middle Ages: A Study of Joachimism* (Oxford: Oxford at The Clarendon Press, 1969); *Joachim of Fiore and The Prophetic Future* (London: SPCK,
1976). *Prophecy and Millenarianism: Essays in Honour of Marjorie Reeves,* ed. Ann Williams (Harkow,
Essex: Longman House, 1980); Bernard McGinn, *Visions of the End: Apocalyptic Traditions in the Middle
Ages* (New York: Columbia University Press, 1979).

2. Cf. *Francis of Assisi: Early Documents,* Vol. 2 *The Founder,* 725-8 (hereafter FA:ED I, II, or III respectively).

3. For excellent studies, see Stephen Bihel, "S. Franciscus fuitne Angelus Sexti Sigili?"
Antonianum 2 (1927): 59-90; Stanislao da Campagnola, *L'Angelo del Sesto Sigillo e L'Alter Christus:
Genesi e Sviluppo dei Due Temi Francescani nei Secoli XIII e XIV* (Rome: Laurentianum, 1971).

4. Cf. Joseph Ratzinger, *The Theology of History in St. Bonaventure,* trans.Zachary Hayes (Chicago:
Franciscan Herald Press, 1971).

5. For a thorough background, see Bernard McGinn, *The Calabrian Abbot: Joachim of Fiore in the
History of Western Thought* (New York: Macmillan, 1985), esp. 207-36; and especially Ratzinger, *Theology of History.*

6. Duncan Nimmo notes the effect of the decision of the 1266 Chapter of Paris to favor
Bonaventure's *Major Legend of Saint Francis* by pointing out: "the Franciscan editors knew of 179

manuscripts of Bonaventure's life; they knew less than a score for Celano's first biography, *The Life of Saint Francis*, most of which had belonged apparently to the Cistercians, not to the brothers at all; and for his Second Life the number of complete copies known at present is two." Cf. Duncan Nimmo, *Reform and Division in the Medieval Franciscan Order: From Saint Francis to the Foundation of the Capuchins*. Bibliotecha Seraphico-Capuccina 33 (Rome: Capuchin Historical Institute, 4 1987), 73-4.

7. Cf. Gerhard Ruf, *San Francesco e San Bonaventura: Un Interpretazione Stofico-salvifica degli Affreschi delta Navata nella Chiesa Superiore di San Francesco in Assisi alla Luce delta Teologia di San Bonaventura* (Assisi: Casa Editrice Francescana, 1974); William Cook, *Images of Saint Francis of Assisi in Painting, Stone, and Glass: From the Earliest Images to c. 1320 in Italy. A Catalogue*. (Florence: L.S. Olschki, 199). Richard Emmerson and Ronald Herzman, *The Apocalyptic Imagination in Medieval Literature* (Philadelphia: University of Pennsylvania Press, 1992).

8. Cf. infra 78-105.

9. Cf. FA:ED II 500-5.

10. Cf. FA:ED II 548.

11. Cf. FA:ED II 61ff.

12. Cf. infra 25.

13. Infra 31-74.

14. Cf. infra 114-137.

15. The earliest Latin sources refer to him as Petrus Johannis Olivi. Apparently his father was John Olivi; thus making him Peter of John Olivi, or, in French, Pierre Déjean Olieu.

16. Cf. Nimmo, *Reform*, 1-429; John R.H. Moorman, *A History of the Franciscan Order—From Its Origins to the Year 1517* (Oxford at The Clarendon Press, 1968), 177-368; Lazaro Iriarte, *Franciscan History: The Three Orders of St. Francis of Assisi*, translated by Patricia Ross, with introduction by Lawrence C. Landidi (Chicago: Franciscan Herald Press, 1982), 51-83; Gratien Baden of Paris, *Histoire de la Fondation e de I'Evolution de I'Ordre des Freres Minuers au XI11e Siecle* (Paris: Societè de Libraire S. François d'Assise, 1928), 321-509; Raphael M. Huber, *A Documented History of the Franciscan Order* (Milwaukee, Washington, D.C.: The Nowing Publishing Apostolate, Inc., 1944), 167-253; Heribert Holzapel, *The History of the Franciscan Order* (Teutopolis: St. Joseph Seminary, 1948), 35-70. Of these works, only Nimmo provides an understanding of the majority of the texts in FA:ED III in a historical context.

17. For an overview of these crises see *The Cambridge Illustrated History of the Middle Ages, Vol. III: 1250-1520*, ed. Robert Fossier (Cambridge: Cambridge University Press, 1987), 1-191. For an evocative description see Barbara Tuchmann, *A Distant Mirror: The Calamitous 14th Century* (New York: Knopf, 1978).

18. For a thorough understanding of this period, cf. Robert Brentano, *Rome Before Avignon: A Social History of Thirteenth Century Rome* (Berkeley and Los Angeles: University of California Press, 1990).

19. Cf. Joseph Lynch, *The Medieval Church: A Brief History* (London: Longman, 1992), 317-35. For the best history of the period see Chester Oakley, *The Western Church in the Late Middle Ages* (Ithaca: Cornell University Press, 1979).

20. FA:ED I 570-5.

21. FA:ED II 774-9.

22. Nicholas III, cf. *Exiit Qui Seminat*, infra 739-64.

23. As Bernard McGinn notes: "it would be almost impossible to discern a writer concerned with apocalyptic themes during this time who was not touched by the 'sign' of the papacy's withdrawal from its established home. Perhaps John XXII was just that much more an Antichrist to the Franciscan Spirituals because he was no longer a Roman pope, and surely the predictions of John of Rupescissa that the pope and the curia would return to Rome before the outbreak of the final events was not a solitary hope." Cf. Bernard McGinn, *Visions of the End: Apocalyptic Traditions in the Middle Ages* (New York: Columbia University Press, 1979), 239.

24. Cf. *Cambridge Illustrated History*, 39-51.

25. For further background, see Michel Mollat, *The Poor in the Middle Ages: An Essay in Social History*, trans. Arthur Goldhammer (New Haven and London: Yale University Press, 1978), 158-64.

26. Cf. Jacques LeGoff, *Medieval Civilization 400-1500*, trans. Julia Barrow (Oxford, UK & Cambridge, USA: Blackwell, 1988), 108.

27. Ibid.

28. For a synthesis of the background to and events of the Hundred Years War, see Charles W. Dunn's introduction to Jean Froissant, *The Chronicles of England, France, and Spain*, introduction by Charles W,. Dunn (New York: Dutton, 1961). Cf. LeGoff, *Medieval Civilization*, 109.

29. Cf. Heiko Augustinus Oberman, *The Dawn of the Reformation. Essays in Late Medieval and Eariy Reformation Thought* (Edinburgh: T. & T. Clark, Ltd. 1986).

30. Cf. Odd Langholm, "The Economic Ethics of the Mendicant Orders: A Paradigm and A Legacy," *Etica e Politica: Le Teorie dei Frati Mendicanti nel Due e Trecento*, Atti del XXVI Convegno Internazionale, Società Internazionale di Studi Francescani (Spoleto: Centro Italiano di Studi sull'Alto Medievo, 1999), 153-72.

31. Cf. Clement V, *Exivi,* infra 767-83.

32. For a thorough study of the controversies concerning poverty and Olivi's interpretation, see David Burr, *Olivi and Franciscan Poverty: The Origins of the Usus Controversy* (Philadelphia: University of Pennsylvania Press, 1989).

33. John XXII, *Cuminter nonnulls,* Cf. infra 789-90.

34. Infra 146-203.

35. For a thorough study of this point and the manuscripts involved, see *Scripta Leonis, Rufini et Angeli Sociorum S. Francisci: The Writings of Leo, Rufino and Angelo Campanions of St. Francis,* edited and translated by Rosalind B. Brooke, (Oxford: Oxford at the Clarendon Press, 1970), 3-78.

36. For background on this text and a discussion of the editors' decision to place it in FA:ED II, see FA:ED II 113-7.

37. Edited and published in modern times by Leonard Lemmens, cf. infra 214-52.

38. Edited as well in modern times by Paul Sabatier but published posthumously in 1928, cf. infra 254-372.

39. Infra 380-426.

40. Because of publishing constraints, the editors have chosen to publish only the Prologue and First Tribulation of Angelo's Book, that is, only those sections that touch directly on his portrait of Francis. For a description of the remaining tribulations, see infra 376-77. Other insights into Angelo's knowledge of Francis, that is, those coming from his *Exposition on the Rule of the Lesser Brothers,* are published in Related Documents, infra 818-22.

41. Infra 435-565.

42. Infra 466-658.

43. Infra 678-733.

44. Cf. infra 679.

45. Should other manuscripts surface, it will be interesting to discover how Arnald deals with the evangelization efforts of Francis and the first generation of his followers, a theme largely overlooked in the fourteenth-century documents.

46. It is important to note that the *Assisi Compilation* (hereafter AC), cf. FA:ED II 111-230, has been categorized in the same manner and, as has been said, could justifiably have been placed in this volume.

47. Cf. Nimmo, *Reform,* 51-108.

48. Cf. FA:ED I 331.

49. Cf. infra 818.

50. Cf. François de Beer, *La Conversion de Saint François selon Thomas de Celano* (Paris: Éditions Franciscaines, 1963); Regis J. Armstrong, "Toward an Unfolding of the Structure of Bonaventure's *Legenda Major,*" *The Cord* 39 (1989): 3-17.

51. Cf. Introduction, *I Fioretti di San Francesco.* L'Anima del Mondo 14. Edited with introduction by Felice Accroca (Asti: Edizioni Piemme, 1997), 5-27.

52. Cf. FA:ED II 22.

53. Cf. "Compilation Franciscaine D'Avignon." *Revue d'Histoire Franciscaine* 1 (1924) 430.

Abbreviations

Writings of Saint Francis

Adm	The Admonitions	LtL	A Letter to Brother Leo
BlL	A Blessing for Brother Leo	LtMin	A Letter to a Minister
CtC	The Canticle of the Creatures	LtOrd	A Letter to the Entire Order
CtExh	The Canticle of Exhortation	LtR	A Letter to Rulers of the Peoples
1Frg	Fragments of Worchester Manuscript	ExhP	Exhortation to the Praise of God
2Frg	Fragments of Thomas of Celano	PrOF	A Prayer Inspired by the Our Father
3Frg	Fragments from Hugh of Digne	PrsG	The Praises of God
LtAnt	A Letter to Brother Anthony of Padua	OfP	The Office of the Passion
1LtCl	First Letter to the Clergy (Earlier Edition)	PrCr	The Prayer before the Crucifix
		ER	The Earlier Rule (*Regula non bullata*)
2LtCl	Second Letter to the Clergy (Later Edition)	LR	The Later Rule (*Regula bullata*)
		RH	A Rule for Hermitages
1LtCus	The First Letter to the Custodians	SalBV	A Salutation of the Blessed Virgin Mary
2LtCus	The Second Letter to the Custodians	SalV	A Salutation of Virtues
1LtF	The First Letter to the Faithful	Test	The Testament
2LtF	The Second Letter to the Faithful	TPJ	True and Perfect Joy

Franciscan Sources

1C	The Life of Saint Francis by Thomas of Celano	ScEx	The Sacred Exchange between Saint Francis and Lady Poverty
2C	The Remembrance of the Desire of a Soul	AP	The Anonymous of Perugia
		L3C	The Legend of the Three Companions
3C	The Treatise on the Miracles by Thomas of Celano	LP	The Legend of Perugia
		AC	The Assisi Compilation
LCh	The Legend for Use in the Choir	UChL	An Umbrian Choir Legend
Off	The Divine Office of Saint Francis by Julian of Speyer	1-4Srm	The Sermons of Bonaventure
		LMj	The Major Legend by Bonaventure
LJS	The Life of Saint Francis by Julian of Speyer	LMn	The Minor Legend by Bonaventure
		BPr	The Book of Praises by Bernard of Besse
VL	The Versified Life of Saint Francis by Henri d'Avranches	IntR	The Intention of the Rule
1-3JT	The Praises by Jacopone da Todi	OL	An Old Legend
DCom	The Divine Comedy by Dante Alighieri	WSF	The Words of Saint Francis
		WBC	The Words of Brother Conrad
TL	Tree of Life by Ubertino da Casale	DBF	The Deeds of Blessed Francis and His Companions
1MP	The Mirror of Perfection, Smaller Version	LFl	The Little Flowers of Saint Francis
2MP	The Mirror of Perfection, Larger Version	KnSF	The Kinship of Saint Francis
HTrb	The Book of Chronicles or of the Tribulations of the Order of Lesser Ones by Angelo of Clareno	ChrTE	The Chronicle of Thomas of Eccleston
		ChrJG	The Chronicle of Jordan of Giano

Other Sources

AF	Analecta Franciscana	DEC	Decrees of the Ecumenical Councils
AFH	Archivum Franciscanum Historicum	DMA	Dictionary of the Middle Ages
AM	Annales Minorum	GR	Greyfriars Review
BFr	Bullarium Franciscanum	PL	Patrologia Latina
CCSL	Corpus Christianorum, Series Latina	PG	Patrologia Graeca
CSEL	Corpus Scriptorum Eccles. Latinorum	TM	Testimonia Minora Saeculi

Scripture abbreviations are from *The New American Bible*; the Psalms follow the modern numbering sequence. Scripture references accompanying non-italicized text imply *confer*, or cf. References to the volumes in *Francis of Assisi: Early Documents* will be abbreviated FA:ED I, II.

A BOOK OF THE PRAISES OF SAINT FRANCIS

BY

BERNARD OF BESSE

(1277–1283)

Introduction

In 1276, less than two years after the death of Bonaventure, the Lesser Brothers gathered in Padua for a General Chapter. Although the General Minister, Jerome of Ascoli, was absent because of a papal commission sending him to Constantinople, he wrote a letter to the capitulars that eventually entered into the Chapter's record:

> All [provincial ministers] are hereby charged to carry out diligently the provisions of the letter sent to the ministers assembled in chapter at Padua by the Reverend Father General Minister, entitled "To the venerable brothers, beloved in Christ, etc." The intent of this letter is to have them conduct an investigation into any additional information worthy of remembrance concerning the deeds of the blessed Francis and of other holy brothers, which may have occurred in their provinces. Such instances are to be reported to the general minister in exact language and under the oath of witnesses.[1]

The first known result of that initiative may well be *A Book of the Praises of Blessed Francis* by Bernard of Besse.

Little is known of Bernard. The date of his birth is unknown; that of his death is generally accepted as 1283, but, curiously, it is uncertain. In his *Chronicle of the Twenty-Four Generals*, written between 1369 and 1374, Arnald of Sarrant indicates that Bernard belonged to the Province of Aquitaine, France.[2] In the sixteenth century, Luke Wadding refined Arnald's information by stating that Bernard was a member of the Custody of Cahors that was part of the Province of Aquitaine.[3] In his study of the friary of Lomousin, France, Ferdinand Delorme discovered a document of January 3, 1250, concerning the nearby friary of Allois, written by a certain Brother Bernard.[4] Delorme suggested that this was Bernard, a native of the now defunct town of Besse in the southwestern region of France. At the time, according to Delorme, he lived in Lomousin, had signed the 1250 document, and was, therefore, a member of the Province of Aquitaine by that date.[5] That Bernard was a writer is confirmed by Arnald's *Chronicle*:

> He also published some devotional books. One was about the purpose of the *Rule*. This was written to silence the envious, and to instruct the brothers to live according to the *Rule* at the time when Brother Bonaventure was General Minister. Another of

25

his books, intended to instruct the novices, is called *The Mirror of Discipline*.[6]

In an autobiographical passage in *A Book of the Praises of Blessed Francis*, Bernard himself tells us of his journeys with the General Minister, Saint Bonaventure.[7] As a result, even the devotional books he composed, which Arnald of Sarrant identifies, have been confused and regularly attributed to Bernard's mentor, Bonaventure.[8] A marginal note in an early manuscript of Arnald's *Chronicles* indicates that Bernard wrote a biography of his confrere of the same French Custody, Christopher of Romagna (+1272), an early companion of St. Francis.[9]

It is difficult to know the origins of *A Book of the Praises of Blessed Francis*. In his *Chronicle*, Arnald suggests that it was part of a much larger trilogy:

> Brother Bernard of Besse from the Province of Aquitaine wrote
> . . . a third work containing three principal parts: a life of Saint
> Francis with many miracles, chronicles of the General Minis-
> ters, and some miracles and divine testimony in approbation of
> the Three Orders of St. Francis, i.e., the Lesser Brothers, the Pen-
> itents, and the Poor Ladies.[10]

The incipit at the beginning of Bernard's *Chronicle of Fourteen or Fifteen General Ministers* seems to confirm this: *Fuerunt igitur post transitum sancti Patris hi eius successores in ministerio generali* . . . [After the passing of the holy father, there were, then, these, his successors, in the general ministry . . .]. Thus the first six chapters of *A Book of the Praises* may well have been taken from a larger work.[11] This is also re-enforced by Arnald's identification of a third consideration, "some miracles and divine testimony in approbation of the Three Orders of St. Francis, i.e., the Lesser Brothers, the Penitents, and the Poor Ladies," that is the seventh chapter of *A Book of the Praises*. Arnald offers no insights, however, as to Bernard's reasons for undertaking such a threefold work, and the work itself offers few, if any, clues.

"In this work," Bernard states in the Introduction, "a few other and, occasionally, the same things are considered, when the occasion demands it, to the praise and honor of the saint." Curiously, a laudatory mood eludes Bernard's work. The word *laus* [praise] in any of its forms appears rarely and usually with God or Christ as its object.[12] Bernard appears more intent on describing, in the first place, exemplary aspects of the founder's life. In doing so, he provides an insight into a difficulty he may have had with his mentor's "definitive" portrait of Francis. "First," Bernard writes, "is the example we should imitate which, if we cannot imitate it perfectly, we should revere."

In the sermon he preached on Francis's feast in 1255, Bonaventure had stated Francis was "more to be praised and wondered at than imitated." Within eight years, however, in the Prologue to his *Major Legend*, he taught that Francis was "worthy of love by Christ, imitation by us, and admiration by the world." The change may seem subtle, but its implications are daunting.

Were Francis's followers obliged to follow his *Rule,* which seemed difficult enough, or his example? "For who," Bernard, Bonaventure's secretary, asks, "could fully follow the footsteps of blessed Francis and of his companions who assisted him?" And he immediately proposes as a resolution of the problem the distinction between Francis, the "inspired" author of the *Rule,* and the *Rule* itself:

> For this reason, even [Francis] did not impose the same kind of rigorous poverty and perfection that he himself observed. Instead, he was instructed by a divine oracle to establish a most perfect rule, that could nevertheless be observed by all at all times. In observing it, one never departs from the discipline of our holy father, although some customs change with the change of climate. On the other hand, careful examination of the perfection of the saints possesses the power to incite virtue and to direct our behavior with their light.[13]

Bernard's portrait, in other words, strives to find a middle path in which Francis is presented as a "formator" eagerly setting the ideals of the *Rule,* his Gospel vision of life, before his followers and, in all his actions, exemplifying them.

Only the first and seventh chapters of *The Book of Praises* provide new information: the first concerning Francis's early companions, the seventh concerning the growth of the Three Orders. The remaining six chapters, two through six and eight, are brief and, for the most part, a collage of passages from the earlier works of Thomas of Celano, Julian of Speyer, John of Perugia, and the "three companions," Leo, Angelo, and Rufino. For the most part, Bernard's recollection of Francis's miracles are greatly abbreviated and based almost entirely on those narrated by Thomas of Celano but omitted by Bonaventure. Were Bernard's purpose to respond to the request of the Chapter of 1276 for new information concerning Francis, he contributes little. Were his intention to acquaint—or reacquaint—the brothers with the insights of those earlier authors whose writings were subsumed into Bonaventure's portraits, Bernard's choice of passages is extremely limited. The chapters that consider the formation of Francis's first disciples and his self-emptying, poverty, humility, and employment, reveal little that is new and offer few insights into the developing tensions within the Order. What, then, motivated Bernard's portrait of Francis?

To answer the question, it is useful to delve into Bernard's "devotional" works, as Arnald of Sarrant describes them, in which he pays considerable attention to the cultivation of the interior spirit. Examination of these "devotional books" reveals the paradoxically lofty yet practical idealism of Bernard, someone steeped in the thought of the twelfth century Victorines and Cistercians, and of their insightful synthesizer, Bonaventure. The *Mirror of Discipline,* for example, begins with a quotation from the Prologue to Hugh of St. Victor's *The Training of Novices:*

> The use of discipline guides the spirit to virtue, while virtue itself
> leads to beatitude. For this, there must be a beginning to the
> practice of discipline, the perfection of virtue, and the reward of
> virtue in eternal beatitude.[14]

From this starting point, Bernard's *Mirror* develops a two-part treatise on
self-discipline in which he considers its nature, scope, and practice. With each
paragraph Bernard conveys his sensitivity to the tension between the spirit
and the law and approaches Gospel life with remarkable insights into the
struggles of human nature. A thread stitching together the thoughts of the
Mirror is a quote from Hebrews 13:9: "It is best that the heart be stabilized
with grace;" with it, Bernard encourages his readers to look deeply into the
role of grace in their lives.[15]

This is clear in the second chapter of Bernard's *Book of Praises* as Bernard
describes Francis's formation of his followers. The chapter draws attention to
many of those attitudes described in Bernard's *Mirror of Discipline:* respect for
one another, patience, avoidance of hypocrisy, and a simplicity that promotes
unity. At the conclusion of the third chapter, moreover, Bernard underscores
an attitude that permeates his portrait of Francis, his ability to look deeply
into another's heart. "He was truly endowed with outstanding discernment
and the grace of simplicity," he writes, "so that with a true *dove-like simplicity,*
he possessed *the prudence of a serpent.*"[16]

A similar attitude emerges in the chapters describing Francis's approach to
poverty, humility, and use of time. Throughout these surprisingly straightforward descriptions, the compiler seems eager to walk a middle road between a
rigid interpretation of Francis's lofty ideals and one that is more flexible.
From this more moderate perspective, Bernard weaves his sources together so
that the towering characterizations of the Gospel life are clearly evident; at
the same time, however, he gently prods each reader to discover an interpretation best suited for daily life. In light of this, Bernard emerges as an interpreter
of Franciscan hagiography conscious of the extremes, of the literalism of "we
who were with him," and their successors who used the saint's life for their
own purposes.

In another way, the first and seventh chapters of Bernard's *Book of Praises*
provides different lenses for examining the early history of the movement.
Brothers are mentioned in the first chapter whose names have never
appeared: Brother Soldanerio, John de Laudibus, Leo, the Archbishop of
Milan, Simon, William of England, and Christopher. Moreover, Bernard provides some insights into their ministries and identifies their resting places. In
doing so, his *Book of Praises* is a prelude to future works such as *The Deeds of
Blessed Francis and His Companions* and *The Chronicle of the Twenty-Four General
Ministers,* both of which devote sections to detailing the exploits of these newly
mentioned disciples of Francis. The seventh chapter, moreover, concisely
describes the purpose of each of the three Orders. Understandably, Bernard
devotes most of this chapter to the Lesser Brothers; his lengthy description of
"miracles and divine approbation" has a twofold purpose: to revive them in

peoples' memory, and, through them, "to demonstrate very plainly the perfection of this way of life."

Bernard's work may well have been overshadowed by a papal declaration: Pope Nicholas III's *Exiit qui seminat* issued on August 14, 1279.[17] Nicholas's lengthy, detailed interpretation of the *Rule* of the Lesser Brothers, like that of Innocent IV, *Ordinem Vestrum*,[18] directed the attention of the Lesser Brothers away from the figure of their founder and fostered debate about the values he proposed for their way of life. Once again Francis's followers struggled with the very question Bernard seems repeatedly to have addressed: observance of Francis's *Rule* or of his own example.

Nonetheless, Bernard of Besse's *Book of the Praises of Saint Francis* makes significant contributions. This is the first text to focus on four distinct traditions, two from Italy: the works of Thomas of Celano and of a mysterious notary John;[19] and two from France: the works of Julian of Speyer, and of Bonaventure.[20] While differing in their identification of the authors, both Angelo Clareno and Arnald of Sarrant followed Bernard's example, the latter suggesting that Francis's four biographers underscore his conformity to the life of Jesus.[21]

Moreover, Bernard provides information that appears for the first time concerning the first generation of Francis's followers, e.g., names, activities, burial places, probably in response to the request of Jerome of Ascoli.

Bernard's repeated use of earlier texts, most specially that of Thomas of Celano, sheds new light on the "destruction" of these texts mandated by the Chapter of Paris in 1266. At the same time, Bernard's comment about the difficulty of following the example of Francis while maintaining the benefit of his *Rule* offers new insights into the struggles of the Lesser Brothers in the period following Bonaventure's generalate. From one perspective, *The Book of Praises* casts a broad beam of light onto the future search for information about not only Francis, but also his companions. It also foreshadows the manipulation of much of that knowledge in defending the varying interpretations of the rule and life Francis proposed.

Notes

1. Andrew George Little, "Definitiones Capitulorum Generalium Ordinis Fratrum Minorum 1260-1282," AFH 7 (1914): 681. Unfortunately, the text of Jerome's letter has not survived.

2. Arnald of Sarrant, "Tempora Fratris Bonagratiae (1279-1283)," *Chronica Generalium Ministrorum Ordinis Fratrum Minorum*, in *Analecta Franciscana sive Chronica Aliaque Varia Documenta ad Historiam Fratrum Minorum Spectantia* (hereafter AF), t. III, ed. Patres Collegii S. Bonaventurae (Ad Claras Aquas, Quaracchi: Collegium S. Bonaventurae, 1897), 377.

3. Cf. Wadding, *Annales* V, 60-1.

4. Ferdinand Delorme, "Les cordeliers dans le Lomousin au XIIIe-XIVe siècle," AFH 32 (1939): 201-59; 33(1940): 114-160; idem, "Codicillo di Alice di Roma," *Studi Franciscani* 11(1925): 126-8.

5. Ferdinand Delorme, "À propos de Bernard de Besse," *Studi Franciscani* 13(1927): 217-28.

6. Arnald, *Chronicles,* 377.

7. Cf. infra 54.

8. The *Speculum disciplinae*, found in St. Bonaventure, *Opera Omnia*, t. III, ed. Patres Collegii S. Bonaventura (Ad Claras Aquas, Quaracchi: Collegium S. Bonaventurae, 1898), 583-622, is identified as a work of Bernard of Besse, although the editors indicate that many incipits have attributed

the work to Bonaventure. After a thorough study, Baldwin Distelbrink came to the same conclusion, cf. *Bonaventura Scripta: Authentica Dubia vel Spuria Critice Recensita,* Subsidia Scientifica Franciscalia 5 (Rome: Istituto Storico dei Cappuccini, 1975), 193. In his introduction to the *Liber de Laudibus* in the *Fonte Francescani,* Giuseppe Cremascoli maintains the *Speculum* is actually the work referred to as *de proposito regulae* [about the purpose of the Rule], but is a work aimed at novices. The same may be said of the *Epistola ad Quendam Novitium Insolentem et Instabilem* [A Letter to An Unfamiliar and Unstable Novice]. At times, it too has been attributed to Bonaventure, but because of its similarity with the *Speculum* both in approach and in teaching, it has been identified also as a work of Bernard. Cf. Distelbrink, *Bonaventura,* 135; Cremascoli, *Fontes,* 1247.

9. Christopher of Romagna was sent to the Province of Aquitaine where he became renowned for his holiness and miracles. He was buried in Cahors, which undoubtedly inspired Bernard to write his life. Cf. AF III, 161, n.1.

10. Arnald, *Chronicles,* 377.

11. Only one manuscript of the work exists, that of the Università di Torino I, VI, 33, ff. 95a-118a, dated at the end of the fourteenth or beginning of the fifteenth century. Cf. AF III, xxvi-vii. It also contains a copy of *The Major Legend of Saint Francis* by Bonaventure of Bagnoregio (hereafter LMj) and a *Legend of Saint Clare for the Choir.*

12. Cf. infra VI where twice the word is directed to God; VII to Christ; Prol, to Francis; VII, to the Order; and II, IV where it is used in general.

13. Cf. infra 32.

14. Hugh of St. Victor, *De institutione novitiorum,* Prologus. See Bonaventure of Bagnoregio, *Opera Omnia* VIII (Ad Claras Aquas, Quaracchi: Collegium S. Bonaventurae, 1938), 583.

15. Bernard uses the same approach in his *Letter to an Unfamiliar and Unstable Novice.* "For a little while you may consider it a joy that you have taken up the habit of holy religion. How I wish that, at the same time, you had assumed the spirit of religion! For the religious habit is of little profit if it is worn with a worldly spirit." In both instances, the author articulates an understanding of religious life that looks deeply into the human heart and into the workings of grace. This same approach is evident in Bernard's portrait of Brother Christopher of Romagna. At first, it is difficult to understand why Bonaventure's secretary would undertake writing the biography of someone who appears for the first time in his own portrait of Francis. The fact that they were both of the same Province of Aquitaine provides the clearest motive, as does the lengthy list of miracles attributed to him. A simple statement following Bernard's description of his confrere's austerity is most telling: "The love of his heart made the affliction of his body sweet." Christopher, in other words, exemplified Bernard's approach to religious life as an expression of the heart and, at a time when externals were becoming increasingly debated, challenged the confreres to look into themselves. And, from this perspective, it is understandable that his writings have frequently been considered as those of his mentor, Bonaventure.

16. The scriptural allusion is to Mt 10:16.

17. Cf. infra 737-64.

18. Cf. FA:ED II 774-9.

19. Cf. infra 832-3.

20. In his *Chronicle* Jordan of Giano writes only of Thomas of Celano and Julian of Speyer, cf. Jordan of Giano, *Chronicle,* in *XIIIth Century Chronicles,* translated by Placid Hermann, with introduction and notes by Marie-Therese Laureilhe (Chicago: Franciscan Herald Press, 1961), 37, 59. Salimbene de Adam writes of Thomas of Celano and Bonaventure, cf. Salimbene de Adam, *The Chronicle of Salimbene de Adam,* trans. Joseph L. Baird, Giuseppe Baglivi, and John Robert Kane (Binghamton, NY: Medieval & Renaissance Texts and Studies, 1986), 166.

21. Unlike Bernard Besse who identifies Thomas, John, Julian, and Bonaventure, cf. *The Book of Praises,* Intro 1-3 (hereafter BPr); Angelo of Clareno identifies Thomas, John, Bonaventure, and Leo, cf. *The History of the Seven Tribulations* Prol 1 (hereafter HTrb). Arnald of Sarrant differs from both by identifying Thomas, Julian, Leo, and Bonaventure, cf. *The Kinship of Saint Francis* I 9 (hereafter KnSF).

A Book of the Praises of Saint Francis

(1277–1283)

Introduction[a]

[1]In Italy, Brother Thomas, a man of exquisite eloquence, at the command of Pope Gregory IX, wrote a Life of Saint Francis;[b] it is said that John, a venerable man who was a Notary of the Apostolic See, wrote a life which begins: *Quasi stella matutina*[c]

[3]In France, there was Brother Julian, famous for his learning and holiness, who also wrote a Life of Saint Francis.[d] He also composed the words and music for the Night Office of Saint Francis, besides some hymns, some antiphons and responses which the Supreme Pontiff himself and some of his Cardinals published in praise of the saint.[e] Lastly, the General Minister, Brother Bonaventure, an admirable vessel of graces and a storehouse of knowledge and virtue—formerly an outstanding Master of Theology in Paris and later a Cardinal of the Holy Roman Church and Bishop of Albano; a man of such authority, discernment, and character that the world acclaimed him most worthy of the highest prelate's office—described more

---

a. This translation is based on Bernardi de Bessa, *Liber de Laudibus beati Francisci*, in AF, t. III, ed. Patres Collegii S. Bonaventurae (Ad Claras Aquas, Quaracchi: Collegium S. Bonaventurae, 1897), 666-92. The numbering of paragraphs is based on that of the edition found in *Fontes Franciscani*, ed. Enrico Menestó, Stefano Brufani, Giuseppe Cremascoli, Emore Paoli, Luigi Pellegrini, Stanislao da Campagnola, with apparatus by Giovanni M. Boccali (S. Maria degli Angeli-Assisi: Edizioni Porziuncola, 1995), 1253-96.
b. Cf. FA:ED I 171-308.
c. Cf. infra 832-3.
d. Cf. FA:ED I 363-420.
e. Cf. FA:ED I 327-60.

fully the whole course of his life in words that are entirely authentic and discerning, as God provided for this worthy herald of the saint's heavenly merits.[a]

[6]In this work a few other and, occasionally, the same things are touched upon, as the occasion demands, concerning the deeds of the saint and his followers, especially signs revealed after his passing. Many of these were omitted earlier for the sake of brevity, which everyone welcomes; things that apostolic authority recommended are included as much for their authority as for their praise.

[7]First is the example we should imitate which, if we cannot imitate it perfectly, we should revere. For who could fully follow the footsteps of blessed Francis and of his companions who assisted him? For this reason, even he did not impose the same kind of rigorous poverty and perfection that he himself observed. Instead, he was instructed by a divine oracle to establish a most perfect rule that could nevertheless be observed by all at all times. In observing it, one never departs from the discipline of our holy father, although some customs fluctuate with the change of climate. On the other hand, careful examination of the perfection of the saints possesses the power to incite virtue and to direct our behavior with their light.

---

a. Cf. FA:ED II 525-683.

Chapter I
THE CONVERSION OF SAINT FRANCIS, AND HIS FIRST DISCIPLES

2C 3

[1]Blessed Francis, like the rising sun, brightened the world by his life, his teaching and his miracles. He had a father intent on worldly affairs, but a very upright mother. Like another Elizabeth, at the sacred font she called him John, and, in spirit,[a] she predicted that, by the grace of his merits, he would become a son of God. The boy grew and conducted himself in a worldly way by his outward manner of life until he was twenty-five years old. Then he left all things and followed the footsteps of Christ. He renewed the old life of the Apostles by reliving their deeds, and he founded the house of his religion not on the sands of temporal things, but on a rock, Christ, and on the perfection of evangelical poverty.[b]

[5]The first stone of this building, after him, was that very ardent man in the Lord, Brother Bernard of Quintavalle,[c] who gave away the abundance that he possessed not to his relatives but to the poor. He was resplendent in a life that was sacred and in a death that was glorious in miracles. The second was Brother Peter[d] who completely renounced the world, and likewise *dispersed* his possessions and *gave them to the poor.* The third was Brother Giles, a man of admirable holiness who, through a gift said to be given by the Lord, when called upon offers whatever pertains to the good of the soul.[e] That devout general minister and cardinal mentioned above, a zealous investigator of such revelations, taught this to us. Brother Philip[f] was added to

Ps 112:9

---

a. Codex B adds to "in spirit" the adjective *prophetali* [prophetic].

b. Here codex B adds: "In all his deeds he conformed himself with Christ. For just as the blessed Christ in the beginning of his public life chose twelve apostles who left all things, so blessed Francis had twelve select companions who chose the most exalted poverty. And just as one of the twelve Apostles hanged himself by the neck, so one of the twelve companions of Saint Francis, Brother John de Capella, hanged himself with a halter. And just as these holy Apostles were objects of admiration for the whole world and were filled with the Holy Spirit, so these companions were men of such holiness that the world did not possess such men since the time of the Apostles. One of these companions, Brother Giles, was enrapt to the third heaven; one, such as Brother Philip the Long, was touched on the lips with a burning coal; one, such as Brother Sylvester, spoke with Christ as friend to friend; one, such as the very humble Brother Bernard of Quintavalle, flew like an eagle to the light of divine wisdom; and one, such as Brother Rufino who was admired for his holiness, was sanctified by the Lord and canonized in heaven while he was still alive."

c. Cf. FA:ED I 203 d.

d. Cf. FA:ED I 204 a.

e. Cf. FA:ED I 204 b. Bernard of Besse changes the tense of the verb "offer" from the perfect to the present to suggest, even after death in 1262, Giles's continuing miraculous powers.

f. Cf. FA:ED I 204 c.

Is 6:6,7 three others.[a] The Lord *touched his lips* with a cleansing *coal* so that, even though he was a lay brother, he understood and interpreted Scripture, uttering words about Jesus that flowed with honey. We have heard that of Francis's first twelve disciples, for whom he also wrote a rule[b] and almost the same mandates that Christ gave to his Apostles, all were holy men except one.[c] Leaving the Order he became leprous and, like another Judas, died by hanging, so that even in his disciples the similarity of Francis to Christ might not be wanting.

[12]It was no insignificant grace that, when he had only six brothers, there was infused in him such certitude of the Order's spreading throughout the world, that he saw the future as though it were present. And he said to the brothers: "I saw the roads filled with the multitude of those coming to us. **They are** 1C 13 **coming from France; Spaniards are hurrying, Germans and English are running, and a huge crowd speaking other languages is rapidly approaching."**[d] He differentiated the brothers of the early and late periods of time under the metaphor of fruit that is more or less sweet.

[15]Holy brothers and fathers, renowned for great virtue, flourished even among the first brothers: such as, Brother Soldanerio,[e] Brother Roger,[f]

---

a. *The Anonymous of Perugia* 17 (hereafter AP) identifies these as Sabbatino, Morico, and John de Capella, which is confirmed by *The Legend of the Three Companions* 35 (hereafter L3C). Little is known of these three beyond the implication of L3C 35 that they were from Assisi where they had relatives. AP 17 refers to Morico as "Morico the Short"; he should not be confused with the Morico mentioned by Bonaventure, LMj, who was a religious of the Crosiers before meeting Francis. For background on John de Capella see FA:ED II 88 a.

b. Cf. *The Life of Saint Francis* by Thomas of Celano 13 (hereafter 1C); L3C 12; LMj III. However, there is a discrepancy about whether Francis wrote this *propositum vitae*, which Bernard calls a rule, for himself and twelve followers or for eleven with himself as the twelfth.

c. Bernard does not identify this Judas-like brother. His name is not revealed until the *De Cognatione S. Francisci* [The Kinship of Saint Francis] in 1365.

d. Passages placed in a bold font indicate sentences or phrases that the author takes directly from an earlier text. The translation of these passages corresponds with that found in earlier editions of *Francis of Assisi: Early Documents*.

e. Brother Soldanerio (+1241) about whom little is known beyond the references of Bernard of Besse, cf. infra, that is, his place among the first brothers, his burial in Viterbo, and the formative value of his character and teaching.

f. In his *Annales Minorum*, which Luke Wadding began publishing in 1625, the author points out that "*Rogerio viro santo* [the holy man Roger] is confused with *Rigerium*. Gregory IX," Wadding continues, "called Roger a saint and ordained that his memory be celebrated." Cf. Luke Wadding, *Annales Minorum seu Trium Ordinum a S. Francisco Institutorum*, t. I (1208-1220), 3rd ed., (Ad Claras Aquas, Quaracchi, 1931), 372. In a 1236 entry, Wadding provides further information: Roger was a noble from the Marches of Ancona who later became provincial minister of that province. Cf. Wadding, *Annales*, t. II (1221-1237), 469.

Brother Rufino,[a] and Brother John de Laudibus,[b] who merited to touch the mortal wounds of the stigmata impressed on Francis's flesh while he was living.[c] Brother Angelo, who was close to Saint Francis;[d] Brother Leo, the saint's confessor;[e] another Brother Leo, who later, as Archbishop, energetically governed the Church at Milan;[f] and Brother James, who merited to observe the holy father's soul ascending into heaven like a star as brilliant as the sun.[g] And there were the holy fathers, Brother Anthony,[h] Brother Nicholas,[i] Brother Simon,[j] Brother Ambrose, Brother John,[k] and so many others, whom it would take too long to mention individually. They brought light to the early times with the light of their virtues. Their *bodies are buried in peace* and in sacred places for veneration. The bones   Sir 44:14 of Brother Bernard, Brother Rufino, Brother Leo, and Brother Angelo were venerably buried in the Church of Saint Francis in Assisi; those of Brother Giles, in Perugia; of Brother Soldanerio, in the church of the brothers in Viterbo; but those of Brother Juniper[l] are buried in the Church of Saint Mary on the Capitolio in Rome.

---

a. Cf. infra 687-8.

b. The author of *Chronicle of The Twenty-Four General Ministers* (written roughly between 1327 and 1377), probably Arnald of Sarrant, states that John de Laudibus (+1266) was buried in Aquasparta, cf. Patres Collegii S. Bonaventurae, ed. AF, t. III, *Chronica XXIV Generalium Ordinis Minorum cum pluribus appendicibus inter quas excellit hucusque ineditus Liber de Laudibus S. Francisci Fratris Bernardi a Bessa* (Ad Claras Aquas, Quaracchi: Collegium S. Bonaventurae, 1897) (hereafter ChrXXIVG); while Bartholomew of Pisa maintains he was buried in Bittoni, cf. Bartholomew of Pisa, *De Conformitate Vitae Beati Francisci ad Vitam Domini Iesu, Analecta Franciscana sive Chronica Aliaque Varia Documenta ad Historiam Fratrum Minorum Spectantia*, t. III, (Ad Claras Aquas, Quaracchi: Collegium S. Bonaventurae, 1906), 243.

c. Little is known about these followers. Arnaldo Fortini identifies Rufino as Rufino di Scipione di Offreduccio, a first cousin of Saint Clare, cf. Arnaldo Fortini, *Nova Vita di San Francesco* II (Assisi: Edizioni Assisi, 1959), 383-387. He was with Francis on LaVerna in 1224, and died on November 14, 1278 and is buried near Francis's tomb. Cf. ChrXXIVG, 225, nn. 3, 4, and 7, and pp. 46 and 252.

d. Cf. FA:ED II 67 a.

e. This is the first reference to Brother Leo as Francis's "confessor," suggesting that he was a priest, although whether he was ordained before he entered the Order or afterwards is not known. Fortini notes: "The only Leo in Assisi records is a 'Domino Leone'—a title sometimes used for priests," cf. Arnaldo Fortini, *Francis of Assisi*, trans. Helen Moak (New York: Crossroad, 1981), 324f. In addition to his role as confessor, he was his frequent companion and secretary. He died possibly on November 15, 1278, and is buried near the tomb of Saint Francis. cf. ChrXXIVG, 65; 226, n. 2, for Brother James, 226, n. 3.

f. Bartholomew of Pisa writes that Brother Leo was Archbishop of Milan from 1244 till his death in 1263, was "a man of *strenuae* [vigorous] holiness," and was buried in Legnano. Cf. Bartholomew of Pisa, Conformitate VIII 302, 363; XI 526.

g. Cf. 1C 110, FA:ED I 278b; LMj XIV 6, FA:ED II 644.

h. Possibly a reference to Saint Anthony of Padua, cf. FA:ED I 107 a.

i. Arnald of Sarrant writes in the ChrXXIVG 225 that Nicholas was a most holy man, renowned for his miracles, and buried in Bologna. A marginal note in manuscript B of the ChrXXIVG indicates that Nicholas was of Rhenish origin, a priest and lawyer, and died in 1225.

j. Cf. infra 36, 538-40; 633-5.

k. Nothing is known of either Ambrose or John.

l. Cf. infra 36.

[21]Brother Soldanerio, like the sun giving light to the world, shed light by his behavior and learning. Brother Juniper shone with such a gift of patience that no one ever saw him disturbed even when he was enduring many difficulties. Brother Roger glittered such evident holiness that Pope Gregory IX approved and confirmed him as a saint, and granted that his memorial be celebrated at Todi where his relics lie. But he did not proclaim a feast with solemnity as is customary is such cases; because of this, we have heard that the cult of this holy man is now being neglected.

[24]Brother Anthony of Padua does not cease to abound in new prodigies. It is said, among other things, that the most holy Brother Nicholas, seeing a dead man being carried out, raised him from his bier and restored new eyes to someone who had had them torn out. He rests in the brothers' church in Bologna. The ancient City venerates Brother Ambrose, famous for many miracles there.[a]

[27]Brother Simon, endowed with the grace of virtues, enriches with many gifts of healing the city of Spoleto, where he rests. In the Spoleto valley we saw a dead man brought back to life by his prayer. The truth of this miracle and of many others was approved and disclosed by the Bishop of Spoleto, who by Apostolic authority inquired into these miracles with remarkable zeal and diligence. Brother John and Brother Nicholas were men of outstanding holiness. One of these, Brother John, went to the Lord while in the office of guardian and, by his miracles, has already distinguished the German territories.[b]

[30]Nearby Brother Augustine and Brother William, in examples of a holy way of life, which we observed, showed us the paths of the holiest perfection. Their virtuous holiness is also remembered as shining through signs while they were still living in the flesh. Venerable Brother Hugh,[c] who was filled *with the spirit of wisdom and understanding,* was sublime in his life and marvelous in the efficacy of his learning. He rests at Marseilles where he affirms his holiness with signs. Brother Christopher, of dove-like simplicity, was placed with

Sir 15:5

---

a. The Latin is *Urbs vetus . . . conditum* [The ancient city . . . found] a pun on the phrase *ab Urbe condita* [from the founding of the city], the reckoning from the founding of Rome in 753 B.C.

b. Brother John of Penna who, according to *The Chronicle of Jordan of Giano* 5 (hereafter ChrJG), was one of the first to be sent to Germany, where he suffered abuse because of his ignorance of German. When he returned to the Province of The Marches in about 1247, he was named guardian, a post he held until his death in 1274. Cf. infra *The Deeds of Saint Francis and His Companions* LVIII 17 (hereafter DBF).

c. Hugh of Digne or, according to Salimbene of Adam, of Barjols (+c. 1257), a native of Provence, whom Salimbene considered "one of the great clerics of the world, an eminent preacher, beloved of the clergy and the people, excellent in controversy and competent in everything," a close friend of John of Parma and "a great Joachimite." Cf. Salimbene of Adam, *The Chonicle of Salimbene of Adam,* trans. Joseph L. Baird, Giuseppe Baglivi, John Robert Kane (Binghamton, NY: Medieval & Renaissance Texts and Studies, 1986), 224, 228.

fitting honor in the brothers' church in Cahors and shines with the brilliance of many signs.[a] Brother Stephen was a man of virtue and grace, formerly an abbot and an important person in the Order of Saint Benedict. Though he chose to be lesser for Christ, he was made Inquisitor against the heretics, and deserved being lifted on high by the crown of martyrdom and the glory of miracles. He lies in the brothers' church at Toulouse.[b] On a par with him was Brother Raymond, who was also crowned with martyrdom, and has been honorably buried there.[c] Brother Benvenuto[d] and Brother Peter, former provincial minister of Calabria,[e] shine with so many miracles that it has been verified as a divine grace, which it truly is.

[36]It would take too long to mention each of the confessors and glorious martyrs who suffered for the faith of Christ and in defense of the Church under the Saracens as well as under supporters of the heretics, while these brothers, at the command of the Apostolic See, were inquiring into the irregularities of these heretics, suffered for the faith of Christ and the defense of the Church.

---

a. The ChrXXIVG states: Brother Christopher was born in the vicinity of Romagna, became a diocesan priest and later, during Francis's lifetime, a brother who "enjoyed an intimate association with St. Francis as long as the saint was alive." His life was spent mostly in France, especially Acquitaine. He died in Cahors in 1272. Cf. ChrXXIVG, 161.

b. Brother Stephen of Narbonne or, according to John Moorman, of Saint-Thibéry, cf. John Moorman, *A History of the Franciscan Order* (Oxford: Oxford at The Clarendon Press, 1968), 302. He was martyred by the Albigensians in 1242 and beatified in 1862 by Pope Pius IX. Cf. Wadding, *Annales*, t. III (1238-1255) 1242, n.3.

c. Raymond of Carbone, companion of Stephen of Narbonne with whom he was martyred and canonized.

d. There are four brothers bearing the name, Benvenutus: the brother who died in Mantua in 1230, cf. Bartholomew of Pisa, *De conformitate* XI 525; Benvenutus of Recanati (+1289), ibid; Benvenutus of Gubbio (+1232), Wadding, *Annales*, 1232, 18; and Benvenutus, Bishop of Auxerre (1282). The ChrXXIVG suggests that this is a reference to Benvenutus of Gubbio "who, after many miracles in that diocese, was canonized," cf. ChrXXIVG, 498.

e. Little is known of Peter of Calabria beyond a description found in Bartholomew of Pisa, *De conformitate* VIII 296; XI 532, that he was a man renowned for holiness.

Chapter II
THE FORMATION OF THE FIRST DISCIPLES

[1]After blessed Francis returned from the Supreme Pontiff from whom he received the authority to preach, he gathered his brothers around him near the city of Assisi in an abandoned hut that was so confined that these most vigorous scorners of large and beautiful homes were hardly able to sit or rest in it. They were in such want that, for lack of bread and to assuage their hunger, they were very often content with turnips which they sought in the fields of Assisi. Their relatives pursued them and others ridiculed them, because at that time no young person could be found who would relinquish all his possessions for the Lord's sake and seek alms from door to door.

AP 36; L3C 52
LMj III 10; LM

IC 42; L3C 55
LMj IV 3; LM

[4]There was no complaining about this;
no grumbling,
but with peaceful heart,
the soul filled with joy, preserved patience.
Under the tutelage of the holy father,
the increased number of brothers
later grew in perfection.
They were truly lesser,
in name as in humility of mind,
who,
while living subject to others,
always sought a place and position of humility,
and, burning with the spirit of charity,
they loved one another in a remarkable way,
even in what might seem an injury.
Whenever they came together,
in that place a shoot of spiritual love sprang up.
What more?
There were
chaste embraces, delightful affection, a holy kiss,
sweet conversation, moderate laughter, joyful looks
and hands untiring for service.

1C 42

1C 38

⁹Since they looked down on all earthly things and never loved themselves selfishly, they poured out all their loving affection in common, hiring themselves out to provide for the others' need, seeking *not their own* interests *but those of Christ* and of their neighbors.

¹⁰Once when a simpleton was throwing stones at the brothers, one brother placed himself in front of them, rejoicing that he would be struck rather than his companion.^a

¹¹*Rooted in charity* and humility, one respected the other as if he were his master. Whoever among them excelled because of a position or grace seemed even more humble and self-effacing than the others. If anyone happened to say something that displeased another, he would not rest until, with the greatest humility, he confessed his fault to that brother. They gathered together out of desire, and were delighted to stay together; but they found separation hard, parting bitter. But truly obedient soldiers, they never dared to place anything before holy obedience, knowing nothing about distinguishing precepts. They almost ran headlong, to carry out what they were asked with no thought of contradicting it.

¹⁶Whatever they were ordered, they considered to be the Lord's will. Thus it was pleasant and easy for them to fulfill everything. They eagerly asked not be sent to the lands of their origin so that they might observe the words of the Prophet: *I have become an outcast to my brothers, a stranger to my mother's sons.*

¹⁸They always found themselves in the Spirit's joy, because they did not possess the stuff of turmoil. They exulted in tribulations as those placed at a great advantage, and they prayed to God for their persecutors. Seeing this, many were converted to them.

²⁰When the rich of the world went out of their way to visit them, they received them quickly and kindly, and would invite them to call them back from evil, and prompt them to penance. Wherever they met men on the roads or in the piazzas, the brothers would encourage them to love and to fear their Creator. They would more willingly accept hospitality among priests than among other seculars. But when they could not obtain lodging, they would inquire who in that place was God-fearing with whom they could be more suitably lodged. And although they were extremely poor, they were always generous in giving to all who asked of them, sharing the alms given to them.

²⁵They so spurned earthly things that they barely accepted the most basic necessities of life. They were content with a single tunic,

---

a. In order to indicate parallel texts, the editors have chosen to use the symbol //.

1C 39

AP 26//L3C 42

AP 26//L3C 42

1C 39

AP 26

L3C 45//AP 29

AP 29

AP 15

L3C 59//AP 40

AP 41//L3C 60

AP 27//L3C 43

1C 41

1C 39

Phil 2:4,21

Eph 3:17

Ps 69:9

often patched inside and out, with crude trousers, and with a piece
of common rope for a belt. Nothing about it was refined, rather it
appeared lowly and rough. Often, when they needed a place to stay
at night, they would stay concealed in crypts or bake-ovens. During the day, those who knew how, worked in suitable places with
their own hands, and would incite all who were with them to an
example of humility and patience. The virtue of patience so envel-   1C 40
oped them that, they were often mocked and made objects of
insult, beaten, stripped naked, and, not defending themselves
with anyone's protection, they endured all these things so humbly,
that from their mouths came only the voice of praise and
thanksgiving.

[29]They never or hardly ever stopped praying and praising God.
Instead, in ongoing discussion, they recalled what they had done.
They gave thanks to God for the good done and, with groans and
tears, paid for what they neglected or did carelessly. They would
have thought themselves abandoned by God if they did not experience in their ordinary prayers that they were constantly visited by
the spirit of piety. For when they felt like dozing during prayer,
they would hold themselves up with various props, so that furtive
sleep would not disturb their prayer.

[32]If one of them took some food or drink, as normally happens   1C 40
out of weariness from travel or for some other reason, they punished
themselves severely with many days of fasting. They strove to restrain the burning of the flesh by such harsh treatment, that they
frequently did not hesitate to strip their bodies naked on ice, or to
cover themselves in blood from gashing them with sharp thorns.
They would inflict so much discomfort on themselves that it   AP 39
seemed they hated themselves. As they practiced peace and gentle-   L3C 58
ness towards all, they avoided all scandal with the greatest zeal.

[36]They thought humbly about themselves, piously about others,   1C 46//LJS 28
especially about priests. When a priest told a brother: "Watch out
that you're not a hypocrite," the brother thought that he was a hypocrite and said: "It was a priest who said it. A priest can't lie, can
he?" He was grieving, dejected and troubled, until the saint wisely
excused the priest's statement.

[39]With a remarkable zeal for silence, these brothers curbed their
tongue. They hardly spoke even when necessary, nor did anything   1C 41
harmful or useless come out of their mouths. All their senses were
so subdued that they scarcely allowed themselves to hear or see
anything except what the purpose of religion required. In them

there was a simple appearance, a modest bearing, and, with their eyes fixed on the ground, their minds were set on heaven.

1C 43   [42]The saint taught them they must mortify not only the vices of the flesh, but also their exterior senses through which *death enters* into Jer 9:20 the soul. When the emperor Otto passed through that area with great pomp to receive the crown of the empire, the most holy father was staying with the others in that small hut next to the parade route. He did not go outside to look, and did not allow anyone else, except for one, that he might continually remind him that this glory would be only short-lived. Apostolic authority resided in him; so he altogether refused to flatter kings and princes.

1C 42
1C 51
1C 42
1C 45   [45]He also used to engage carefully in a daily examination of the brothers. If he found something inappropriate was done, he did not leave it unpunished and he drove from their hearts any negligence. The brothers strove diligently to fulfill not only what he told them as by brotherly advice or by fatherly command, but also what by some sign they recognized he wanted. To bring them to perfection, he used to say that true obedience is not just about a prelate's word, but also about recognizing his will, and in doing what a subject perceives, by a sign, a prelate wants.

1C 46

[48]In this way holy simplicity filled them,

purity of life so possessed them,

that they were totally ignorant of duplicity of heart.

For just as there was in them one faith,

so there was one spirit,

one will, one charity, continual unity of spirit,

harmony in living, cultivation of virtues,

agreement of minds, and piety in action.[49]

1C 41

These are the lessons of the devoted father

by which he instructed his new sons

not so much in words and speech,

but in deed and in truth,

and in which he renewed

the purpose and zeal of an apostolic life.

[50]To show what had been approved was approved in heaven, it was revealed in a vision to a holy man in the beginning of the novitiate that the holy Apostles Peter and Paul gave thanks to God each day for the renewal of their lives, and they were praying for the preservation of that religion. When he made this known to blessed Francis, he said: "If the blessed Peter and Paul are daily praying for us, it is only right that we venerate them daily with reverence." Therefore, it

was decided that in the remembrance of the Apostles that is made in each Hour of the Office of the Blessed Virgin, these two Apostles be mentioned by name, even though previously according to the custom of the Roman Church there was only the general mention of all the Apostles in these prayers. At this time there was added to the orations: *Protect, O Lord,* and: *Hear us, O God* the words *of your Apostles, Peter and Paul,* where previously it read: and *of all your Apostles,* etc.

Chapter III
THE SELF-EMPTYING OF BLESSED FRANCIS

2C 118

[1]The holy man expressed great joy over the brothers' progress, while never looking down on the sick or the tempted. At one time when a tempted brother asked Francis to pray for him, the holy man said: *"Believe me, son,* I believe you are even more *a servant of God* because of this." "No one," he said, **"should consider himself a servant of God until he has** passed through temptations and tribulations. A temptation overcome is like a ring with which the Lord betroths the **soul of his servant. Many flatter themselves over their many years of merit and rejoice at never having suffered any temptations. But sheer fright would knock them out before a battle even started. So they should know that the Lord has kept in mind their weakness of spirit. Hard fights are rarely fought except by those with the greatest strength."**

Jn 4:21; Acts 16:17

2C 110

1C 64

[6]**Another brother was vexed for a long time by a temptation of the spirit, which is worse** and more subtle **than the prompting of the flesh. He came to Saint Francis and** *threw himself at his feet;* overflowing with bitter tears, he could say nothing, prevented by deep sobs. The saint, however, realized that he was tormented by wicked spirits. *"I command you,* demons," he said, "from this moment stop assailing my brother." And immediately **the brother** became **free** of all temptation. In this both the saint's piety for a son and his power over demons appeared.

Ru 3:7-8; Mt 15:30

Jn 14:14

2C 115

2C 117

[10]Tempted himself, he learned to suffer with those who were sometimes tempted. For at times he endured a very great temptation of the flesh and, to put this temptation to flight, he would scourge himself unmercifully. But when this spirit would not depart despite the severe discipline, he would cast himself naked into the snow. It was by this chastisement of his flesh that he expelled the spiritual wound from his breast.

2C 115//AC 63

[12]**At another time a very serious temptation of spirit came upon him, surely to embellish his crown. Because of it he was** *filled with anguish and sorrow;* he *afflicted* and chastised his body, he prayed and wept bitterly. He was under attack in this way for several years, until one day while praying at Saint Mary of the Portiuncula, he heard in spirit a voice: "Francis, *if you had faith like a mustard seed, you would tell*

Heb 11:37

Mt 17:20

the mountain to move from here, and it would move." The saint replied: "Lord, what is the mountain that I could move?" And again he heard: "The mountain is your temptation." And he said, sobbing: *"Lord, be it done to me as you have said!"* At once, after the whole temptation was driven away, he was set free.

Lk 1:38

[17]His spirit emptied itself with humility, cherishing everyone, deferring to everyone. **He used to revere priests of the Church; would respect the elderly, and honored the noble and the wealthy. He loved the poor intimately, however,** and, while preserving peace with people of all rank, he urged his brothers eagerly to this. **He used to tell them: "As you announce peace with your mouth, may you keep it in your heart, thus no one will be provoked to anger or scandal, but rather to kindness and gentleness. For we have been called to this: to cure the wounded, to bind up the broken, and to recall the erring. Many who seem to us to be members of the devil, will yet be disciples of Christ."**

AP 37//L3C 57

AP 38 //L3C 58

[21]To his brothers he would speak compassionately, not as a judge, but as a father to his children and a doctor to the sick, so that the word of the Apostle might be fulfilled in him: *Who is weak that I am not weaker?* **Great was his compassion toward the sick and great his concern for their needs. He conducted himself toward all as he would toward individuals.** As he scrutinized with dignified honor any revered person coming to the Order **and respectfully gave to each his due, he wisely considered in all matters the dignity of rank of each one.** He was truly endowed with outstanding discernment and the grace of simplicity, so that with a true *dove-like simplicity,* he possessed *the prudence of a serpent.*

2 Cor 11: 29

2C 175

1C 57

Mt 10:16

2C 24

Chapter IV
POVERTY

LR XII 5

[1]Among other characteristics, Francis's zeal to observe **poverty and humility** and to be continually engaged with virtuous things was unusual. He rejoiced in poor little dwellings, in cells of wood

AC 23

rather than of stone. He often stayed with a few in hermitages, where an enclosure of thorn bushes sufficed for a wall, and small huts for dwellings. In cities, however, neither people's maliciousness nor the large number of brothers allowed it to be so.

2C 69

[5]He detested a brother with a great deal of clothes, made of refined, soft cloth. Two layers of clothing do not seem to belong to a poor man, since expenses are reduced by clothing that is old and mended. While cheap cloth is certainly rougher, heavier, and less warm, the pious purpose of religion demands this, and, with use, difficulty is easily overcome by grace. Whoever was forced by necessity to wear a softer inner tunic, he would support, **as long as rough and cheap clothing was kept on the outside,** for we have been given to people as an example of poverty and penitence. **As for "necessity" not based on reason but on pleasure, he declared that it was a sign of a** *spirit that was extinguished.* "Not bearing patiently with need," he said, **"is the same as** *returning to Egypt."*

1 Thes 5:19
Nm 14:2-4

2C 62//AC 25

[11]He wanted few books kept, ones not notable for elegance or expense, **and available to the brothers who needed them.** He did not want the brothers to have money or handle it even out of consideration of piety. Therefore, with a remarkable chastening, he punished

2C 66

a brother whom he once found touching a coin. Even though his companion and the saint's word forbade it, another brother took a coin he found carelessly left on the road, and wanted to give it to the lepers. He immediately *gnashed his teeth* and lost **the power of speech. At last, he threw away** the coin, and his penitential lips were set free to give praise.

Ps 35:16

1C 51

[16]**In order to avoid the superfluous,** the holy man **would not even permit a small plate to remain in the house if, without it, he could avoid dire need. He said it was impossible to satisfy necessity without bowing to pleasure.** He depended on the divine foresight according to the word he spoke to the Lord Pope who argued

AP 34

that it was difficult to live without possessions. **"My Lord, I trust in** my Lord Jesus Christ. Since he has promised to give us life and glory in heaven, He will not deprive us of our bodily necessities when we need them on earth." Proposing a parable to him, he said: AP 35//L3C 50, "There once was a king who contracted marriage with a poor but beautiful woman. While he married her because of her beauty, he fathered by her very handsome sons. As adults, they were sent to the king by their mother that he would take care of them. When the king recognized that they looked like him, he embraced them as his sons. And he said: 'You are *sons and heirs. Do not be afraid!* If strangers are fed at my table, I feed those to whom by right an inheritance is due. The brothers are Christ's poor and the sons of a poor religion.' "

Rom 8:17;
Mt 14:27; 17:7

²²He was well aware that the Lord cared for him even in the smallest matters. When he was weak from a very serious illness, while returning from Spain, on the way he told Brother Bernard that he would have eaten a bit of a bird if he had one. Just then someone came riding across the field carrying an exquisite bird and said to him: "Servant of God, take what divine mercy sends you." Accepting it, *he blessed* Christ *for everything,* seeing how He cared for him.

3C 34

Tb 13:1

²⁶He did not want to be involved with the world through temporal things. When the Bishop of Assisi told him that to possess nothing in this world seemed to be a very rough life, he responded: "Lord, if we had any possessions, we would need to have arms to protect them, because they cause many disputes and lawsuits. Possessions usually impede the love of God and neighbor."

AP 17//L3C 35

²⁸He would frequently say: "As far as the brothers will withdraw from poverty, that far will the world withdraw from them. They owe the world an example, and the world owes the food they need. When the brothers withdraw good example, the world withdraws from them its support."

2C 70

³¹Concerned about poverty, *the man of God* feared large numbers and he used to say: "Oh, *if it were possible,* I wish the world would only rarely get to see Lesser Brothers, and should be surprised at their small number!"

2 Kgs 1:9

Mk 14:35; Gal 4:15

³²He wanted the brothers to be content with a few things, and not to possess these few things, whether places or things, as their own. He wanted *to own nothing* so that he could possess everything more fully in the Lord.

2 Cor 6:10

1C 44

Chapter V
HUMILITY

[1]With the greatest zeal he cultivated poverty's companion, the virtue of humility.

[2]Because of this he wanted the brothers to be clothed in a humble habit, girt with a rope, to be called Lesser Brothers, and never to be exalted in this world. When he was asked by the Lord of Ostia about promoting his brothers to ecclesiastical dignities, he would in no way consent, but replied they should be kept in humility.

[4]Blessed Dominic was also present and likewise opposed the promotion of his brothers. He clung to Blessed Francis by such devotion that he most devotedly wore under his inner tunic a cord which he had given him, said that he wished that Francis's religion and his own could be one, and stated that he should be imitated for his holiness by other religious. Oh, how this humility and mutual charity of their Fathers must be imitated by their sons! Truly, it would be profitable to them and to God's Church.

[8]He wanted such great deference shown to prelates and priests, that, because of reverence for their dignity and spiritual power, the brothers would consider not only their hands but also their feet worthy of being kissed. **He used to say: "We have been sent to help clerics for the** *salvation of souls*[a] **so that we may make up whatever may be lacking in them.** *Each shall receive a reward,* not *on account of* authority, but because of the *work* done. Know then, brothers, that the *good of souls* **is what pleases God most, and this is more easily obtained through peace with the clergy than fighting with them. If they should stand in the way of the people's salvation,** *revenge is* for God, *and he will repay* them *in due time."* And he would say: **"Be subject to prelates so that as much as** *possible on your part* no jealousy arises. How is it too much to be subject to superiors, *when, for God's sake, we* must be subject to all human creatures?"*

[14]As he thought humbly of himself, he was, in his own eyes, a great sinner, while actually he was in every way **a mirror of holiness,** and also a virgin in the flesh, as he revealed to that very holy man, Brother Leo, his confessor, and then disclosed to the General

---

a. Cf.FA:ED II 133 b.

(margin references:)
1C 38; 2C 148
AC 49; 2C 148
AC 49; 2C 148
AC 50; 2C 150
AP 37; L3C 57
2C 146//AC 19
2C 123; AC 65
2C 140

1 Pt 1:9
1 Cor 3:8
Wis 3:13
Dt 32:35
Rom 12:18
1 Pt 2:13

Prv 18: 17 Minister.[a] For *as the just one is his own first accuser,* while Blessed Francis accused himself in public of being the greatest of sinners, in private he never confessed the sin of bodily fornication. His confessor was astonished, and piously wanted to know whether he was untainted in his flesh, something he could not obtain from the saint by repeated entreaty. But, because he was a simple man of the greatest purity, he merited to secure from God that he was a virgin. This was revealed and shown to him by a special sign. For while he was praying, he saw blessed Francis standing in a high prominent place which no one could approach and no one could touch. He was told in spirit that this indicated the prominence of the virginal purity found in blessed Francis.

[17]Virginal purity was fitting for flesh adorned with the sacred stigmata. If some ordinary people of the world, by the working of grace and nature, preserve the integrity of the flesh even to old age, who would wonder that Francis preserved it, when God was disposed to exalt him with such a grace? Therefore, a greatly humble man was exalted by the greatest exaltation.

---

a. This is the first explicit mention of Francis's virginity. Whereas Bonaventure implies this in LMj V 4, neither he nor any other biographer states this as does Bernard of Besse.

Chapter VII
THE THREE ORDERS

[1]Francis's teaching produced fruit especially in the three Orders that he established.[a]

[2]The first is the Order of Lesser Brothers whose purpose is to serve the Lord according to the Gospel in poverty and humility, and to preach penitence. Innumerable signs in the professed testify that this is acceptable to God, Who is capable of recounting with how many miraculous signs in and through them the Lord embellished this state!

[5]I will come, however, to the visions, to the expressed callings or few revelations that faithful people now drop from memory. Through these the Lord deigned to demonstrate very plainly the perfection of this way of life. Father Brother Haymo,[b] a former general minister of holy memory, told of a prelate in England who, while taken up in a vision to the heavenly mansions, saw no Lesser Brothers there among the other religious. While he was wondering about this, the most beautiful of ladies, the most blessed Mother of God, came to him and asked what he was turning over in his mind. When the Bishop told her that he was wondering why he saw in that blessedness no Lesser Brothers, whom the Church Militant esteemed so highly, the Blessed Mother responded: "Come with me and I will show you where they are staying." She showed him brothers who were joined to Christ on intimate terms. "See," she said, "they are under the wings of the Judge. Save your soul with them." The Bishop, considering the grace of the vision and on the salutary counsel of the Mother of God, entered the Order of Lesser Brothers with the approval of lord Pope Gregory IX.[c]

[10]Some religious are said to have been shown under the mantle of the Blessed Virgin. Thus the Mother of God herself showed brothers

---

a. This chapter presents the first explicit description of the three "Orders" established by Francis. While Julian of Speyer writes of "the mysterious, ulterior signifance" of the rebuilding of the three churches, i.e. the "three famous Orders" (*The Life of Saint Francis* by Julian of Speyer 14 [hereafter LJS]); and Bonaventure, quoting Thomas of Celano (1C 37) writes of the "triple army of those being saved" (LMj II 7), Bernard of Besse provides an overview of the characteristics of each of the three.

b. Cf. FA:ED II 61.

c. This may be a reference to Ralph, Bishop of Hereford. Cf. infra 54 a.

to be under the protection of the wings of the Son of God, each like those of the two Cherubim.

[11]That prelate is believed to have been Ralph whose entry into the Order has been established; he was a Master of Theology and the Bishop of Hereford.[a] Besides him, there were two other Ralphs, both doctors of theology, one of whom entered the Order at Paris in this way.[b] One time while he was studying, he fell asleep at his book. The devil appeared to him and threatened to take away his sight: "I will blind you with dung." He woke up but fell asleep again, when the devil again appeared to him and repeated the same words. He drove him away by putting his fingers to his eyes. "You will not blind me," he said, "I will blind you." On the following day, while he was sitting in the professor's chair, he received from England a thick letter from a bishop offering him revenue. Interpreting the money as the dung with which the devil wanted to blind him, he entered the Order of Lesser Brothers, scorning everything.

[17]Some time ago, I was traveling with the then celebrated general minister throughout parts of Germany and Flanders.[c] After many years I again had another meal with the brothers, one of whom had been a canon, a very venerable man, and who had been led to enter the Order by means of a remarkable cure and a vision. Perhaps I do not remember all the circumstances after what is now a long time, but I have no doubt about the entry and the cure of the person. I relate the probable fact just as I recall it.

[19]That canon was also a noble and respected person, who feared God and had a special devotion to the virgin saint, Euphemia.[d] Although he was, at that time, weak and advanced in age, yet he was concerned about the salvation of his soul which was accustomed to

---

a. Before his entrance into the Order in 1239, Ralph of Maidstone had been Bishop of Hereford since 1234. He renounced his seat on December 17, 1239 and died, as a Brother, on January 8, 1246. Thomas of Eccleston tells of his entrance into the Order in these circumstances: "[Brother Haymo, provincial minister of England] clothed with the habit of the Order the lord bishop of Hereford, Ralph of Maidstone, in accordance with a vision he had of him while he was still archdeacon of Chester; namely, that a certain boy came while he was seated and arranging the clergy in a synod and threw water into his face, whereupon the boy was immediately changed into a miserable young man. And Ralph came to the bed where Brother Haymo lay, and he asked him to let him lie there; and this he did," *The Chronicle of Thomas of Eccleston* 14 (hereafter ChrTE).

b. The first of these is Ralph de Corbrigge, a Master of Theology at Paris and, later, Lector at Oxford, see A.B. Emden, *A Biographical Dictionary of the University of Oxford to A.D. 1500* (Oxford: Oxford at the Clarendon Press, 1957), I 484. The other may be Ralph of Rheims who, in 1232, was sent by Pope Gregory IX to the German Archbishop of Constantinople with Haymo of Faversham and two others. According to Luke Wadding, it is not certain that he was a Master of Theology, cf. *Annales Minorum*, ad annum 1233, n. 8. See AF III 221, n. 1.

c. A reference to Bernard's travels as secretary with the general minister, Bonaventure of Bagnoregio.

d. A fourth-century martyr under Diocletian in c. 303. Her cult spread rapidly due to the description of her passion and mention of her example by authors such as Peter Chrysologus. Cf. L. Vereecke, "St. Euphemia," *New Catholic Encyclopedia*, Vol. V (Washington, D.C.: The Catholic University of America, 1968), 632.

being jeopardized by his wealth. While wishing to put his hand to more heroic deeds, he desired to be shown the path of salvation, according to the words of the Prophet: *Your ways, O Lord, make known to me; teach me your paths. Show me the way in which I should walk, for to you I lift up my soul.* Through that virgin whom he had taken as his advocate, he begged with continual supplication to be directed to a state suitable for his salvation. Finally, the Lord poured into his heart to renounce the world completely in the Order of Saint Francis.

Ps 25: 4
Ps 143: 8

²⁵He was sick, however, and had an ugly tumor on his throat. Because of this, the minister of the brothers delayed receiving him and, as cautiously as he could, he withdrew from his intention. He recommended his state as honorable, wholesome, fruitful, one that was capable of doing good works for many persons. While he recognized the dismissal, and was deeply saddened because of it, he once more gave himself to prayer, and then fell into a light sleep. Then blessed Euphemia, to whom he was devoted, appeared to him in a vision with a brilliant company of virgins, and urged his entrance into the Order of Lesser Brothers, removed the obstacle to his reception by curing him, and gave him an unequivocal sign that he could easily endure the Order. "Let this be a sign for you," she said, "that I am curing you of all infirmity."

³⁰Soon after the place of the swelling opened and every bit of that tumor was expelled, she closed the place of the tumor by the touch of her hand, and perfectly restored the man to complete health. When he awoke, that lord found himself perfectly cured. And he was received to vows in the Order, and he was transformed there in a most holy way. He is said to have grown in such virtue before the Lord, that, impeded neither by age nor by usual weaknesses, he easily endured the hardships of the Order, and could travel longer on foot than he had been accustomed to do on horseback.

³⁴The most illustrious emperor of Constantinople, Jean, was advised by a divine revelation to take the habit of blessed Francis.[a] Some claim that he alone was left without an inheritance while the

a. A reference to Jean of Brienne (c. 1148-1237), King of Jerusalem (1210-1225) and co-emperor of Constantinople (1228-1237), who was a personal friend of Francis and a tertiary. According to Luke Wadding's *Annales Minorum*, 1210, no. 5: "Jean of Brienne, count of Vienne, was the son of Erardus II, count of Brienne le Chateau in Gaul." Salimbene extols Jean with the greatest praise: "John, king of Jerusalem, an extraordinary, noble, and wise man, a man of great faith and discretion . . . He became a Friar Minor, and would have rendered invaluable service to the Order, if God had not cut him off in his prime. It was Brother Benedict of Arezzo, a holy man and Provincial Minister of Greece, who received King John into the Order." Cf. Salimbene de Adam, *The Chronicle of Salimbene of Adam*, trans. Joseph L. Baird, Giuseppe Baglivi, and John Robert Kane (Binghamton, NY: Medieval & Renaissance Texts & Studies, 1986), 8, 18. Whether Salimbene is correct in his assertion that John became a Lesser Brother is debatable; others maintain he became a member of the Third Order. He was present at Francis's canonization and brought expensive gifts to his tomb. At his death in 1237, he was buried in a habit and interred in the Basilica of Saint Francis in Assisi.

court was left to his fraternal peers, and that he was destined for the Knight Templars or Hospitalers. Since he was a young man, as noble in birth as he was conspicuous in behavior, he attained, with the help of God, the dignity of the kingdom of Jerusalem, and then to that of the Empire. He was renowned for many honors, since his son-in-law was the Roman Emperor. He was a very great defender of the true faith and an adversary of non-believers.

[37]Towards the end of his life, when he was seriously reflecting on how many gifts God had bestowed on him during his life, the greatest desire was sent to him from heaven, some believe, to know beforehand what kind of death he would have. He remained for some time with this desire and, because of it, persisted in his constant supplication of God. One night while he was sleeping, a dignified man appeared to him dressed in white, carrying in his hands the habit, cord, and sandals of the Lesser Brothers. "John," the man said, calling the emperor by name, "since you anxiously desire to know the manner of your death, you should know that you will die in this habit and that this is the will of God." The emperor, awake and terrified at such a future humiliation that, according to the man, was his, aroused with a scream those who by royal custom rested near him. When they came running, however, he would not reveal the reason for his cry.

[42]The following night two men similarly dressed in white appeared to him in his sleep, carrying the same habit, cord and sandals and repeating that it was the divine will that he should die in that habit. Just as before, his spirit shuddered and, awake, he shouted but, again, he would not reveal the reason to the those running to him from their beds.

[44]The third night three men likewise appeared to him in a vision, dressed in white like the others, carrying the same habit, cord, and sandals, and, as before, repeating that his passing would be in them. They added: "Do not believe that this is an illusion or an empty dream. What we say will truly be fulfilled."

[46]The disturbed emperor ordered that his confessor, Brother Angelo, be called immediately. When he arrived, he found the emperor in bed, weeping. He said to him: "I know why you have called me. The same vision which you had was revealed to me." After a few days a tertian fever gripped the emperor and, with full deliberation, he entered the Order and happily finished his days there according to the vision's intent.

[48]But while he was still living, he was impeded by the gravity of his infirmity and debility from exercising the usual duties of humility in the Order. He is said to have expressed the devout attitude of

his soul in a memorable passage: "O my most sweet Lord, Jesus Christ, would that I who have lived elegantly in the pomp of the world, clothed in priceless garments, could, as a truly poor and humble man, follow you, who are poor and humble, by seeking alms in this habit with a sack hanging from my neck!"

[50]In this a very excellent man left us a very great example, that neither the great nor the ordinary nor much less others would be ashamed of what pertains to poverty and humility. He achieved in this vow what nobles usually win for themselves in this Order, that is, to be more humble, more gentle and more simple. Indeed, the sobriety of gentleness and humility is a distinguishing mark of nobility. Grace often ennobles the ignoble, and the fault of pride or sloth makes the noble ignoble. What is more worthless than for a noble to become a boor? Not to be shunned are the lowest in birth, to whom it has been given to serve the Lord as a knight; there is nothing greater than to be a knight of Christ.

[55]But let me continue what I have begun. Brother William of happy memory, former minister of Aquitaine, related that there was a man, once a master in the city of Chartres, bound by a vow to enter the Order of Lesser Brothers.[a] He missed the time, however, determined by brothers for entering the Order. While he was playing checkers outside in front of the Church of the Blessed Virgin Mary, he suddenly lost his sight. When he realized this, he overturned the game with his hand so that the bystanders would notice it. Then calling a boy, putting his hand on his shoulder, he entered the church where, prostrate before the altar of the Virgin, he promised the Mother of God with tears and devotion that, should she restore his sight, he would enter the Order of Lesser Brothers without delay.

[59]When he recovered his sight, he came to the brothers and named the day when he would enter the Order. But once again he went back on his word. He was again playing checkers in the same place as before, and again was made blind. He entered the church as before, and, after many tears, he made a promise to the Blessed Virgin that, if he regained his sight, he would no longer put off entering the Order. At last he recovered his vision, but not as quickly as the first time. Nevertheless, once again he lied by neglecting and delaying his promise of entering the Order.

[62]A third time he became blind as before, entered the church as before, and wept very devoutly before the altar of the Mother of God. Once more, after he repeated his promise to enter the Order, he

---

a. A reference to William of Bayonne, provincial minister of Aquitaine sometime during the tenure of Bonaventure as general minister (1257-1274).

regained his sight, although even more slowly. Seeing that out of necessity he would have to fulfill his vow that had been proven by so
many tests to be pleasing to God and the blessed Virgin, he told the
brothers all that had happened to him, and entered the Order according to his promise.

Eph 4:22   [64]After his entrance into the Order, he did not entirely *put off the
old man,* and did not want to follow the common life of the Order.[a]
Under the pretext of need, he wanted to wear shoes at all times, to
eat in the infirmary, and always to sleep on a mattress. During the
winter, he hurried to the kitchen to warm himself after Mass.

[66]The brothers tolerated his living as one of the sick for almost two
years—not without great dislike, especially since he had been an
honorable person in the world. One night Saint Francis appeared to
him in a vision and said to him: "My son, carry me a little while." But
the brother refused: "I cannot carry you," he said. "You are a large
and heavy person, while I am weak and feeble." But since the saint
asked to be carried by him just the same, grabbing his shins, he
dragged the saint's head on the ground. Blessed Francis cried out:
"You're hurting me, you're hurting me! You're carrying me poorly."
"I can't carry you any other way," he replied. The saint complained
loudly that he was dragged in this way.

[69]The next morning after Mass, he entered the kitchen as usual,
and there told of his dream. A discerning brother listening to this
said to him: "It is as you have seen. For you do hurt and carry blessed
Francis poorly, that is, his Order which you are dragging through the
dirt because of the worldly and degrading life you lead by living excessively and according to the flesh." When he heard the brother's
interpretation of the dream and knew it was true, he took it to heart.
He took off his fur cloak and shoes, and lost interest in the infirmary
and the feather bed. Instead, taking up the common life of the Order
that he had neglected, he turned into another man, completely spiritual and religious, and later became an outstanding preacher. Even
though he had been negligent because of procrastination, he did not
seem to have altogether turned away from his intention.

[73]The venerable father, Brother John of England, who became
Archbishop of Canterbury after being a Master of Theology at Paris,[b]
told of a frightful example of those ungrateful for a vocation to the

---

a. This is the first time the concept of the "common life of the Order" enters into the vocabulary of these
   documents. While in 2C 14 Thomas of Celano maintains that Francis "loved doing what was
   common," neither he nor Bonaventure write of the common life of the Lesser Brothers.
b. John Pecham (c. 1220-92) studied at Paris in the faculty of arts (1245-50), entered the Order in
   1250, returned to Paris, and became a master in 1269. He taught in Oxford between 1271-72, was
   elected provincial minister of the English friars in 1276 and, in 1279, Archbishop of Canterbury. He
   died December 8, 1292.

II 10; LR II 13

Order and who look back with hardened hearts. He said that a cleric at Paris had promised to enter the Order of Lesser Brothers. But when he was about to be invested, he received a letter from his homeland, saying that he had been made a canon of a cathedral church. Withdrawing from entering the Order, he was in his church for nearly half a year, when he contracted a serious illness. Warned by the canons to confess his sins, he refused as though in despair. Then the canons asked the Lesser Brothers to come to the sick man to persuade him to confess his sins.

[77]When the brothers arrived, they found him extremely weak and warned him, with as much diligence as they could, to make a confession of all his sins as a good Christian and a true Catholic. He replied: "Brothers, do not warn me about this. For I am damned and cannot confess. Before you came to me, I was taken into the sight of God Who showed me His awfully terrifying countenance and said: 'I called, and you refused; go, then, to your eternal punishment.' " And when he had said this, at once he ended his last day before them all.

[81]Truly, *the judgments of God are like the mighty deep* and no one can know why He mercifully sets one free and justly condemns another. Because *the Lord is the weigher of spirits,* however, He judges not only externals, as humans do, but perceives the interior of the heart infallibly.[a]

Ps 36:7

Prv 16:2

[83]What I heard had happened at Paris should not, I think, be kept hidden, because it was a sign of approval of this state of life and praise for perseverance in it. A Master at Paris entered the Order of Lesser Brothers. His mother had nourished him on alms and had solicitously reared him despite her poverty. After he entered the Order, his mother grieved over the loss of what she considered a temporal good, her son. She came to visit him but only in order to persuade him to return to his former state of life. She showed him her breasts that gave him suck while repeatedly crying out how she had nourished him throughout a time of very great misery. She set forth many other reasons which might provoke him to leave the Order. The brother felt great compassion for his mother and was crushed in spirit, and he was so tempted by all this that he decided to leave the Order on the next day. Yet because he had not acted out of malice, but was rather deceived by the hidden malice of the devil into thinking that he was only doing his duty, he gave himself to prayer. As had been his custom, he sought out the image of the Crucified. "I do not

---

a. Cf. Bernard of Besse, *Epistola ad Quendam Novitium Insolentem et Instabilem* 1, in Bonaventure, *Opera Omnia* VIII, ed. Patres Collegii a S. Bonaventura (Ad Claras Aquas, Quaracchi: Collegium S. Bonaventurae, 1898), 663.

want to leave you, O Lord," he said, "but I should provide whatever is necessary for my mother who lovingly nurtured me while she was living in poverty." While he was praying in this way and looking at the image of the Crucified, he saw blood flowing from the wound in the Crucified's side, and he heard the voice of the Lord saying: "I have nurtured you more dearly than your mother has and I have redeemed you with this blood. You should not leave me because of your mother." The brother was speechless when he saw the blood and heard the voice. As a result he conquered his temptation and remained in the Order. He placed Christ before his mother since Christ said in the Gospel: *Whoever loves father or mother more than me is not worthy of me.*

Mt 10: 37

[91]Gunther of Brabant, a monk of the Order of Saint Benedict, was not able to live the kind of life in his monastery that he wished. Therefore, he had himself transferred to another monastery. But even there he did not find the spiritual peace for which he hoped. He gave himself up to prayer, reading the Psalter every day and fasting, and beseeching the Lord to point out to him a way to salvation by which he could faithfully serve him. After several days spent in prayer and fasting, he saw blessed Francis in his sleep. Francis had before him the text of the Gospel and also the *Rule* which he had placed under the Gospel. The monk wondered about all this and was made to understand what he saw. He wondered too about the *Rule* being placed under the Gospel. "The *Rule* is under the Gospel because it has been based on the Gospel," the saint said. The monk prayed and fasted for many days, striving to know whether the state of life, portrayed by the vision, was pleasing to God. He suppliantly asked that, if it were so, this vision might be given to him again. Blessed Francis appeared to him again as before with the Gospel and the *Rule*. Nevertheless, for a third time the monk repeated the usual praying and fasting, and in all his prayers he strove more and more to discover more surely whether the state of life shown to him was acceptable to God. Blessed Francis appeared to him in the same way as before and seemed to be receiving the monk into the Order. But the monk was suffering from a serious malady in his leg, and he said to blessed Francis: "The brothers will not have confidence in me, and therefore will not accept me." The saint replied: "Your leg has been cured, and this will be a proof of your sincerity." Aroused from sleep, he found himself cured just as he had experienced it in his dream. When the monk sought admission into the Order, he was put off by the minister as not being quite suitable. Then he recounted his vision and the manifestation of the favor which had been given to him. After he had been received into the Order, he lived in a religious and

holy manner in the Province of Cologne. The brothers from that region told us this story.

[103]I heard the following story from brothers who had it from a brother religious who, we know, was well thought of in the Order. A Cistercian brother from a monastery in the diocese of Toulouse came to him and begged to be received into the Order of blessed Francis. The Cistercian told the brother that a deceased brother of his monastery, who during his life the Cistercian had as a beloved companion, had come one night and called him to a chapter of lay-brothers. During the sufferings of his final illness this brother had promised to do this with the permission of God. When the living brother out of a feeling of affection wanted to embrace him, the deceased brother said: "You will not be able to see or touch me." When the deceased man was asked how he was and what he had to say, he replied: "I will be fine. It is living that is dangerous." "But are you doing well now?" he was asked. "Not yet," was the reply. He pointed out that he yet had to be purged, and that he needed prayers.

[108]The [Cistercian] brother again asked about the state of his Order and about that of some other Orders, and about some religious and seculars known to him. The deceased brother replied that many, especially of some Religious Orders, were damned, and that all of those people about whom he had asked by name were also damned. While he was explaining the reasons for the condemnation of some, he revealed some very personal things. I am not going to reveal the circumstances and the reasons which he indicated about the condemnation of many, because everything that disparages others would better be kept hidden, unless there is a very urgent reason for making it known. All Orders are good, if their Rules are heeded. But when the Cistercian asked about the Lesser Brothers, he said that he had seen none damned, and that those who went to purgatory were quickly purged and soared to heaven. The deceased man admonished his former companion to persevere, and he warned him to beware of certain evils with which he came into contact.

[113]Thus it was that in a few words the deceased man particularly extolled the present state of the Order of blessed Francis. If the purity of a state in life is weighed in the light of the best of ends freely pursued, then the end proves the merit that precedes it. No one, therefore, should he amazed to hear that those brothers were quickly purged, for they purged themselves in this life by living in purity and in extreme poverty, in cold and nakedness, and in many other hardships for the sake of their Lord.

[116]We have now had unexpected testimony concerning a man's ill-will or his unmerited approbation. Such testimony was given to

the Order from the underworld, just as testimony was given from heaven in other visions.

[117]It is said that in Navarre a very beautiful girl, who was remarkable in features and adornment, appeared to a Cistercian brother of great virtue while he was praying very devoutly. He was a native of Spain and was first named Gonsalvo and later Anthony. The girl of the vision invited him to marry her, but he vigorously refused, saying that since he was a monk who professed chastity, he was not allowed to take a wife. "But you have to take me as your wife," she said. "I tell you this in the name of the Order of Lesser Brothers whose beauty and image I bear. If you espouse this Order to yourself by entering it, you will find salvation there." With words such as this she disappeared.

[121]At another time this Anthony saw blessed Francis, and with him he saw another holy brother, William, whose bones, made known by miracles, rest in the Church of Saint Francis.[a] At the same time he saw a very beautiful bed. Anthony asked that saintly brother William whose bed it was, and was told that it was the bed of blessed Francis. Anthony said: "I want to lie upon it that I might be able to say that I have lain on such a beautiful bed." Some time after this vision, when the monks wanted to make him their Abbot, he entered the Order of Lesser Brothers because of the bed of Saint Francis. The monks earnestly sought to bring him back through the instrumentality of the Roman Curia. They alleged among other things that the austerity of their Order was greater than that of the Lesser Brothers. Anthony is said to have responded: "These men did not come to the Roman Curia as I did on foot and begging." The request of the monks was refused by the Supreme Pontiff, and Anthony remained as a brother in the Order. It is said that he possessed such devotion that he shed tears even in the hustle and bustle of people who pressed around him.

[127]He never spoke idle words. Instead, he spoke continually of God so fervently that sometimes he seemed to be intoxicated even though he drank wine only in the Sacrifice of the Mass. In fact, he never drank anything else that could intoxicate a man. He burned with such zeal for souls, that he was untiring in preaching and hearing confessions. He taught the brothers to make sincere confessions, to pray fervently, and to avoid idle words. He added that if they did

---

a. A reference to William of England about whom little is known except that he was famous for his miracles and, at his death in c. 1232, he was buried in the Basilica of Saint Francis in Assisi. Cf. Andrew George Little, "Brother William of England, Companion of St. Francis, and Some Franciscan Drawings in The Matthew Paris Manuscripts," *Franciscan Papers, Lists, and Documents* (Manchester: Manchester University Press, 1943), 16-24.

this, they would progress in virtue beyond their expectations. The deeds of this man and graces done for him demand time.

[131]The following theme now concerns a vocation. But it has been proved that this religion, accepted by God, to which He calls people by means of a special sign, and which He first founded on perfect men as though *on holy mountains,* He adorned with most illustrious people as though with polished stones. Bishops, abbots, archdeacons, and established Masters of Theology entered the Order. So too did princes, nobles, and innumerable others who were noted for their dignity, their nobility, and their knowledge. They were the flower of nobility and learning. If an example is needed, we can omit all others and take Brother Alexander who is remembered to have been the greatest cleric or theologian in the world at that time.[a] There was also Lord John, a soldier valiant in arms, a king and an emperor. He became a brother when he was emperor, in order that the Lord might fulfill the prophesy in Francis: *I will go before you and humble the great men of the earth.*[b]

[134]Who could count the number of brothers of the Order, who were approved and celebrated Doctors of Theology? We should not be silent in our praise for Christ who exalted the humble and wonderfully saw to it that just as a soldier of great dignity and goodness was found in the Order of Minors, so too there was found a very great Master of Philosophy and Theology who was also a great preacher. He was Brother John de La Rochelle who was renowned for his reverence for God, for his knowledge, and for his discernment.[c] He possessed such talent that he added to the subtlety of his teachers and handed down the art and the excellent ways of preaching, and of lecturing in the Faculty of Theology. Both he and Brother Alexander were the authors of formal and useful writings.

[138]After him there came the venerable Father, Brother Odo Rigaldi, who was illustrious in birth but more so in character.[d] He was a Master of Theology, Archbishop of Rouen, and a most famous

Ps 86:1

Is 45: 2

---

a. Alexander of Hales (1185-1245), born in Hales Owen, Shropshire, England, studied in Paris, and became master of theology in 1210 and later regent master. He entered the Order in 1231 and, at Paris, taught Brothers John de La Rochelle, Odo Rigalus, and Bonaventure of Bagnoregio. Known as the *Doctor irrefragabilis* [The Irreffutable Doctor] and the *Doctor doctorum* [The Doctor of Doctors], he died on August 25, 1245.

b. A reference to Jean de Brienne, l cf. supra 55 a, 55-7.

c. John of La Rochelle (c. 1190) is first listed among the friars and masters of theology in Paris. He is noted for his close association with Alexander of Hales and contributed to his *Summa theologica,* cf. Alexander of Hales, *Summa theologica* (Ad Claras Aquas, Quaracchi: Collegium S. Bonaventurae, 1948). He died in Paris in 1245.

d. Odo Rigaldus (+1275) entered the Order in 1236, studied at the University of Paris between 1240-41, and collaborated on the *Exposition of the Rule of the Four Masters.* He was consecrated Archbishop of Rouen in 1248, a post he held until his death on July 2, 1275.

preacher. He was urged to become a member of the Curia and, just as he was illustrious for his life and teaching before in the Order, so now he was so excellent in guidance that he was considered a model for prelates.

[140]The Second Order founded by blessed Francis is that of virgins and continent married women, whose proposal is to serve God in the enclosure, in perpetual silence, and in mortifying the flesh.[a] The first member of this Order was the blessed Clare, a most devout disciple of blessed Francis. Seeing them living in a most holy way according to his teaching under the profession **of the most exalted poverty,** he promised her and the other women professing poverty in a similar way of life his counsel and assistance and that of the other brothers. Blessed Clare and her monastery have always observed this same proposal of poverty up to the present day.

LR VI 4

[144]The Third Order is of the Brothers and Sisters of Penance, shared by clerics, laity, virgins, widows, and married couples. Their purpose is to live uprightly in their own homes, to devote their attention to works of piety, and to flee the world's allurements.[b] Therefore, you might see among them nobles, and even knights, and other people great in the world's estimation, dressed in proper cloaks of black fur,[c] humble in both their clothing and mounts, so modestly associating with the indigent, that you would not doubt they are truly God-fearing. From the beginning a brother was assigned to them as a minister, but now, in each region, they are released to their ministers, but who, as confreres begotten by the same father, are still encouraged by the brothers with counsel and assistance.[d]

---

a. Bernard provides an insight into the *propositum* [purpose] of the Second Order, officially called "the Order of Saint Clare" in a rule given to these women by Pope Urban IV in 1263. (For *propositum*, cf. FA:ED I 189 d). Their life of serving God, in Bernard's terms, is "to serve God *sub clausura perpetuo in silentio et carnis maceratione* [in the enclosure, perpetual silence, and starving the flesh]." While *sub clausura* [under the enclosure] appears in the *Rule* of Urban, the other phrases do not and seem to be expressions of the author alone.

b. As with the Second Order, Bernard now identifies the *propositum* of the Third Order, now known as the Secular Franciscan Order: *in domibus propriis honeste vivere, operibus pietatis intendere, pompam saeculi fugere* [in their own homes, to live honorably, to concentrate on works of piety, and to flee the world's allurements].

c. A reference to Nicholas IV, *Supra montem* (1289), Chapter III: "The brothers may also have cloaks or furred coats without an open neck, either sewed or uncut, or at least laced up as decent people should, and the sleeves should be clothed. The sisters should wear a mantle and a tunic made from the same common cloth, or they should at least wear a mantle with a black or white skirt or petticoat, or an ample gown of hemp or linen, sewn without any pleats."

d. Ibid., Chapter 15: "Let each member devoutly undertake and faithfully execute the office of minister or any other duty mentioned in this document, when such might be laid upon them." Further information on the background of this expression of government can be found in Raffaele Pazzelli, *St. Francis and the Third Order* (Chicago: Franciscan Herald Press, 1989), 149; Octavian Schmucki, "The Third Order in the Biographies of St. Francis," in *Greyfriars Review* 6 (1992): 94-6 (hereafter GR).

¹⁴⁷In composing the rules or forms of living for their Order, Lord Pope Gregory of holy memory, at that time in a lesser capacity, united with blessed Francis through an intimate closeness, devoutly supplied what the holy man lacked in knowledgeable judgment.^a But not content with just these Orders, the saint was busy giving to every class of people a way of penance and salvation. One time when a parish priest told him that he wanted to be his brother while still retaining the church, after he gave him a way of living and acting, he is said to have told him that each year, when the income of the church had been collected, he should give for God whatever was left over from the preceding year.

¹⁵⁰Thus the Lord *made* his servant, Francis, grow *into a great nation,*   Dt 30:1; Sir 44:21
thus *He gave him the blessing of all nations.*

---

a. Cf. Gregory IX, *Quo elongati* 3: ". . . while we held a lesser rank, we stood by him both as he composed the aforesaid *Rule* and obtained its confirmation from the Apostolic See." FA:ED I 571.

Chapter VIII

THE DEATH AND TRANSFERAL OF THE BODY OF SAINT FRANCIS

[1]When the time of Francis's warfare in this life finally came to an end, the holy father **departed happily to Christ in the year of the Incarnation of the Lord, one thousand, two hundred and twenty-six.** He was forty-five years old. It was about twenty years since he turned away from the way of the world. For two years he wore the habit of a hermit, but in the third year of his conversion he began the new Order of Lesser Brothers in the basilica of the holy Mother of God and ever virgin, Mary, **which from ancient times was called Saint Mary of the Angels.** Inspired by heaven, Francis assumed a habit under the protection of her whom he cherished with a particular devotion. It was in this Order that he completed the rest of his life in all holiness, and in the same place where he started the Order he perfected that most auspicious beginning by a most blessed death. He not only knew beforehand the time of his release from this life, but he also predicted nearly the very day that it would happen.

[5]In the very hour of his passing away, he appeared to—among others who saw him ascending into heaven—a holy **brother** who was **absorbed** in prayer. He was dressed **in a purple dalmatic,**[a] accompanied **by an innumerable crowd** of followers like the greatest of princes in the wonderful beauty of glory. Arriving **at a very beautiful place, a palace of amazing size and of a singular abundance of special delights,** he entered there with a glorious company of brothers.

[7]A most illustrious Roman matron, Lady Jacoba dei Settesoli,[b] very devoted to the man of God, came to visit him with a very large retinue as befitted such a great lady. She administered whatever seemed necessary for his funeral. He, who had taught her in Christ and had named her Brother Jacoba because of the vigor of her virtues, wished to see her before he died. He therefore had her summoned. But before the messenger left, there was a great clamor

2C 220a; LJS

LMj II 8

2C 219

AC 8; 3C 37-39

---

a. Cf. FA:ED II 389 a. This vision became the inspiration for the image of the Glory of Saint Francis that was painted at the beginning of the fourteenth century in the four vaults of the Lower Basilica of Saint Francis.

b. For background information on Lady Jacoba dei Settesoli, see FA:ED II 122 b.

outside the door, caused by the horses and attendants of this devoted disciple. She had arrived to visit her most illustrious father and teacher. When the saint saw her, he rejoiced that, as he had hoped, she had been sent by God. After recovering a little in the joy of seeing her, it was thought that the saint would live longer. Lady Jacoba, therefore, decided to send back a part of her retinue, so that she might await the saint's end with fewer attendants. But the saint forbade this. "I will depart on Saturday evening," he said. "You can leave with your retinue on the following day."

¹³On the day and at the hour which he predicted, the saint was gathered to the Lord to live with Him in His eternal mansion. The brothers, bereft of their holy Father, wept. So too did those virgins of Christ, who had followed in his footsteps. With tearful voices they said: "O Father, why are you abandoning us poor women? To whom are you leaving your desolate daughters?"[a]

¹⁵His most holy body was buried at Assisi in the Church of Saint George, where the Monastery of Saint Clare now stands.[b] After a few years a church was built in the saint's honor near the walls of the city and by the authority of Pope Gregory IX who laid the first stone of the foundation.[c] The site of the church is called the Hill of Paradise. Here his body was brought with great pomp and veneration. So great a multitude of people had come together for the celebration that the city was not able to contain them, and they camped all around the field like sheep. The aforementioned Lord Pope Gregory, whose personal presence for the celebration of his translation was anticipated as certain, at that time was prevented owing to certain other urgent business of the Church. He sent nuncios for the purpose with a personal letter which not only explained as necessary the cause of his unexpected absence, but also announced for sure to his sons, whom he comforted with a fatherly affection, that a certain dead man had been brought back to life by blessed Francis.[d]

¹⁹Also, through the same nuncios, he sent a gold cross, priceless owing to its work in gems, but containing wood from the cross of Our Lord more precious than all the gold and gems. Besides this, he sent ornaments and several vessels which pertained to the ministry of the altar, and also vestments which were most fitting for solemn uses. He also sent other considerable donations for the

_{3C 138}

_{2C 143}

_{1C 117}

_{LMj XV 5}

_{LJS 76}

_{LJS 75}

---

a. Cf. FA:ED I 285 a.

b. The body of Saint Francis remained in the crypt of San Giorgio for four years. At her death in 1253, Clare's body was also interred there and, on the site, a basilica was begun in her honor in 1255 and completed in 1265.

c. Cf. FA:ED I 419 c.

d. Cf. FA:ED I 419 b.

expenses connected with the construction of the same building
and for the coming celebration.

[21]The solemnity of this solemn transferal was enacted on the
eighth of the kalends of June, in the year of the Lord one thousand,
two hundred and thirty.[a]

---

a. That is, May 25, 1230.

Chapter IX
CERTAIN MIRACLES

[1]As in Francis's life, so after his passing, the Lord did not cease to magnify his saint by miraculous signs. Some instances of these are offered here.

i
THE CRIPPLES MADE UPRIGHT

C 127; 3C 160

[1]A young girl was brought to his tomb, who, for over a year, had suffered a deformity in her neck so hideous that her head rested on her shoulder and she could only look sideways. She put her head for a little while beneath the coffin in which the treasure of the saint's body rested, and through the merits of that most holy man she was immediately able to straighten her neck, and her head was restored to its proper position. At this the girl was so overwhelmed at the sudden change in herself that she started to run away and to cry. There was a depression in her shoulder where her head had been when it was twisted out of position by her prolonged affliction.

1C 129; 3C 162

[2]Niccoló of Foligno was so crippled in his left leg that it caused him extreme pain, and because of it his neighbors could not sleep at night because of his cries. When medicine did not help, dedicating himself to Saint Francis, he had himself carried to his tomb. After spending a night there in prayer, his crippled leg was cured and, overflowing with joy, he returned home without a cane.

1C 130; 3C 163

[3]A boy had one leg so deformed that his knee was pressed against his chest and his heel against his buttocks. He was carried to the tomb of the blessed Francis, and suddenly his health was fully restored.

1C 132; 3C 165

[4]There was also a little girl in Gubbio; her hands and all her limbs were so crippled that for over a year she lost total use of them. Carrying a wax image, she was brought to the tomb of Saint Francis. After she had been there for eight days, one day all her limbs were restored to their proper functions.

1C 133; 3C 166

[5]There was another boy from Montenero lying for several days in front of the doors of the church where the body of Saint Francis

rested. Since he was completely paralyzed from the waist down, he could not walk or sit up. One day, when he was brought into the church to touch the tomb, he was completely cured. He said that a young man in the habit of the brothers was on top of the tomb with his hands pointing to a pear which he seemed to offer to him. He stood up taking his extended hand and, leading him outside, he was cured.

[6]There was another citizen from Gubbio. When he brought his crippled son, so crippled and deformed that his legs were completely withered and drawn up under him, to the tomb of the glorious father, he received him back whole and sound. 1C 134; 3C 16

[7]A girl of Norcia appeared listless for some time and it was eventually clear she was troubled by a devil. For she would often gnash her teeth and tear at herself. She would not avoid dangerous heights nor did she fear any hazard. Then she lost her speech and was deprived of the use of her limbs, and became totally irrational. Her parents were tormented by the confusion of their offspring; they tied her on a stretcher mounted on a draft-animal and took her to Assisi. During the celebration of Mass on the feast of the Lord's Circumcision, she lay prone before the altar of the saint. Suddenly she vomited, I can't say what, and then got up on her feet. She kissed the altar, and fully free of her illness she shouted in praise of God and the saint. 3C 153

[8]In the diocese of Volterra, Riccomagno could scarcely drag himself along the ground with his hands. His own mother had abandoned him on account of his monstrous swelling. He humbly vowed himself to blessed Francis and was instantly healed. 3C 168

[9]Two women from the same diocese were so crippled that they could not move about unless carried by others. They had stripped the skin from their hands attempting to move themselves. By their vow alone were they restored to health. 3C 169

[10]Giacomo from Poggibonsi was so pitiably bent and crippled that his mouth touched his knees. His widowed mother took him to an oratory of blessed Francis and poured out her prayer to the Lord for his recovery; she brought him home healthy and whole. 3C 170

[11]A woman from Vicalvi with a withered hand had it restored to match the other through the merits of the holy father. 3C 171

[12]In the city of Capua a woman vowed to visit in person the tomb of Saint Francis. Because of the press of household matters she forgot her vow, and suddenly lost the use of her right side. On account of pinched nerves she was unable to turn her head or arm in any direction. She had so much pain that she wore her 3C 172

neighbors out with her constant wailing. Two of the brothers happened to pass by her home, and at a priest's request they stopped to visit the pitiful woman. She confessed to them her unfulfilled vow, and when she received their blessing she at once arose healthy. And now that she was made wiser by punishment, she fulfilled her vow without delay.

C 135; 3C 173
[13]Bartolomeo from Narni was sleeping in the shade of a tree when he lost the use of a leg and a foot. Since he was a very poor man, the lover of the poor, Francis *appeared to him in a dream* and ordered him to go to a certain place. He set out to drag himself there, but had left the direct route when he heard a voice saying to him: *"Peace be with you! I am the one to whom you vowed yourself."* Then leading him to the spot, it seemed that he placed one hand upon his foot and the other upon his leg, and thus restored his crippled limbs. This man *was advanced in years* and had been crippled for six years.

Mt 1:20
Jn 20:21; Dn 10:19
Jos 13:1

C 128; 3C 161
[14]In the district of Narni there was a boy whose leg was bent back so severely that he could not walk at all without the aid of two canes. He had been burdened with that affliction since his infancy; he had no idea who his father and mother were, and had become a beggar. This boy was completely freed from that affliction by the merits of the blessed Francis so that he could go freely where he wished without a cane.

1C 131; 3C 164
[15]In the city of Fano there was a man who was crippled with his legs doubled-up under him. They were covered with sores that gave off such a foul odor that the hospice staff refused to take him in or keep him. But then he asked blessed Francis for mercy and, through his merits, in a short time he rejoiced in being cured.

3C 80
[16]In the city of Narni there was a woman who for eight years had a withered hand with which she could do no work. Blessed Francis appeared to her in a vision, and stretching her hand, healed it and made it able to work as well as the other.

ii
THE BLIND WHO RECEIVED THEIR SIGHT

1C 136; 3C 130
[1]A woman named Sibilla suffered from blindness in her eyes for many years. She was led to the tomb of the man of God, blind and dejected. She recovered her sight and, rejoicing and exulting, returned home.

3C 131
[2]In the village of Vico Albo in the diocese of Sora, a girl who had been born blind was taken by her mother to an oratory of blessed Francis. Invoking the name of Christ, and through the merits of

blessed Francis, she deserved to receive the sight that she never had.

[3]At the tomb of the holy body, a blind man from Spello recovered his sight, which he had lost long before.   1C 136; 3C 13

[4]In the city of Arezzo, in the church of blessed Francis built near the city, a woman who had not been able to see for eight years recovered the sight she had lost.   3C 132

[5]In the same city the son of a poor woman was granted sight by blessed Francis when the mother vowed him to the saint.   3C 133

[6]In Poggibonsi of the diocese of Florence there was a blind woman who, because of a revelation, began to visit an oratory dedicated to blessed Francis. When she was brought there and lay pitiably before the altar, she suddenly received her sight and found her way home without a guide.   3C 135

[7]Another woman, from Camerino, was totally blind in her right eye. Her parents covered the damaged eye with a cloth that the blessed Francis had held. After making a vow, she recovered her sight.   1C 136; 3C 13

[8]Another woman of Gubbio, after making a similar vow, received her sight.   1C 136; 3C 13

[9]A blind man from Assisi, after losing his sight for five years, was cured as soon as he touched his tomb.   1C 136; 3C 13

[10]Albertino from Narni was blind, for his eyelids hung down over his eyes. Vowing himself to the blessed Francis, he merited to regain his sight and to be healed.   1C 136; 3C 13

iii
THE CURING OF THE DUMB AND THE DEAF

[1]A woman in the region of Apulia had long ago lost the ability to speak and to breathe freely. One night while she slept the most blessed Virgin Mary appeared to her and said, "If you want to be cured, go to the church of blessed Francis in Venosa; there you will receive the cure you desire." The woman went to that church of the saint where she poured out her heartfelt request, immediately vomited a mass of flesh, and was marvelously healed in the sight of all.   3C 126

[2]In the town of Nicosia, a priest became deranged and mute. At the invocation of Blessed Francis, he regained his speech and was freed of his madness.   3C 145

[3]A woman in the diocese of Arezzo mute for seven years asked God with a great desire to loosen her tongue. While she slept two brothers appeared and warned her to vow herself to Blessed Francis.   3C 127

She willingly took their advice and vowed in her heart, since she could not speak. She was soon roused, and on waking her speech returned.

1C 149; 3C 140

⁴A young man named Villa, could neither walk nor speak. His mother made a wax image for him and carried it with great reverence to the saint's tomb. When she returned home, she found her son walking and talking.

1C 149

⁵There was a man in the diocese of Perugia who was unable to utter a word. His mouth was always open, and he gaped and

3C 141

gasped horribly, for his throat was swollen and inflamed. He came to the tomb of Blessed Francis and wanted to touch it, when he vomited a great deal of blood. And he was entirely cured and began to speak, opening and closing his mouth as necessary.

1C 150; 3C 142

⁶A woman had a stone in her throat. Due to a violently feverish condition, her tongue stuck to her palate. She could neither speak nor eat, nor drink. After many medicines were tried she felt no comfort or relief. She made a vow to Blessed Francis in her heart, and suddenly the flesh opened and she spat the stone from her throat.

3C 143

⁷Bartholomew from the village of Ceperani had been deaf for seven years and recovered his hearing by invoking blessed Francis.

1C 147-8

⁸In Città della Pieve, a man, deaf and mute from birth, about whom you have accounts elsewhere, was immediately cured by his host's prayer. Looking up he said among other things: "I see Saint Francis standing above me, and he has granted me speech. You shall praise God, and you shall save many people." Thus he uttered definite words, as if he had heard and spoken all the time. People who had known the youth previously crowded together and, filled with the greatest wonder, praised God and the saint.

iv

THOSE WITH DROPSY AND THE PARALYTICS

3C 70

¹In the city of Fano a man suffering from dropsy obtained a complete cure of his illness through the merits of blessed Francis.

1C 142; 3C 71

²A woman of Gubbio lying paralyzed in bed invoked the name of blessed Francis three times for her healing and was restored to health.

3C 72

³A girl from Arpino in the diocese of Sora, miserably oppressed by a paralytic illness of her limbs, was brought to the church of blessed Francis near Vicalvi, There, after she poured out prayers and tears, she was freed from every danger of illness.

3C 73

⁴A young man of the same town was bound by a paralysis that held his mouth shut and distorted his eyes. Since he was unable to move, he was brought by his mother to the church mentioned above. She prayed fervently for him, and, he recovered his original health before they reached their home.

3C 75

⁵Pietro Mancanella lost the use of an arm and hand to paralysis and his mouth was twisted back to his ear. When he submitted to the advice of doctors, he lost both his sight and his hearing. Finally he dedicated himself to blessed Francis, and was completely freed from that illness.

v

THOSE WITH RUPTURES AND EPILEPSY

3C 111

¹Someone from the town of Cisterna in Marittima was horribly burdened with a rupture of the genitals and no device could hold back his intestines. For the truss, which usually helps such cases, caused many new ones. His grief-stricken father and mother, when every remedy and cure had been tried without any success, took him to the church at Velletri built in his honor. Placing the sick boy before the saint's image and, making their vows along with a crowd of many others, offered many tears for him. When the gospel was read, at the passage *what you have hidden from the learned you have revealed to the merest children,* his truss suddenly snapped, and the useless remedies fell away. A scar quickly formed and the full health desired was restored. A great cry went up from those *praising the Lord* and venerating his saint.

Mt 11:25

Lk 2:13

3C 114

²Giovanni from the diocese of Sora was afflicted by an intestinal hernia and could not be helped by any medicine. At the advice of a brother, his wife encouraged him to vow himself to blessed Francis, and to make the sign of the cross on his rupture. When he had devotedly done both, his intestines immediately returned to their proper place, and he was amazed *at the suddenness of his unexpected healing.*

Wis 5:2

THE VERSIFIED LIFE OF SAINT FRANCIS

BY

HENRI D'AVRANCHES

ADDITIONS, AMPLIFICATIONS IN LIGHT OF

THE MAJOR LEGEND

(after 1283)

Introduction

A manuscript in the Municipal Library of Versailles written during the late thirteenth or early fourteenth century contains what seems at first glance to be *The Versified Legend* of Henri d'Avranches (+1262/3). Unfortunately, the manuscript has been poorly preserved: many pages are difficult, if not impossible, to decipher; others are simply missing so that the work ends abruptly with the fifty-fourth verse of its ninth book. This is more lamentable when it becomes apparent that the work is, in many ways, a rewriting of Henri's masterpiece recast in light of Bonaventure's *Major Legend*.

The last addition to Henri's work, an incident involving Brother Raymond, a writer, that took place in Cahors, suggests that the author was a member of the Lesser Brothers of the Province of Aquitaine or close to them.[1] The anonymous author may well have followed Matthew of Vendôme's *Ars Versificatoria*, a twelfth century work providing guidelines for putting works of prose into poetic verse.[2] His attempts are evident in the reworking of the titles of each book of the *Versified Legend*. Instead of Henri's usual four-line verse, his follower reduces each title to two, crafting each title to reflect not the theology of Thomas of Celano but that of Bonaventure of Bagnoregio. Throughout the nine books of his work, he transposes some of Henri's passages, changes others, and omits and adds still more. While some passages reveal a clever hand, the overall set of additions and variations do not offer the brilliance of breadth of knowledge as Henri's earlier *Versified Legend*. They do provide, however, an insight into the influence of Bonaventure's *Major Legend*.

Since the Prologue to his work contains references not only to Bonaventure but to his becoming a cardinal, the work was obviously undertaken after 1273. The fact that it contains passages taken directly from Bernard of Besse's *Book of Praises* places the work after 1283, a date confirmed by the age of the Versailles manuscript.

Notes

1. Cf. AF X, liv.
2. Matthew of Vendôme, *Ars Versificatoria* [The Art of the Versemaker], translated with an introduction by Roger P. Parr (Milwaukee: Marquette University Press, 1981).

The Versified Life of Saint Francis
Additions, Amplifications in Light
of *The Major Legend*

Prologue

Any number of virtuous and **knowledgeable** men, motivated by devotion to the saint and by his distinguished achievements, have taken the trouble **to write** the story of **the most blessed** father Francis, Christ's standard-bearer and Levite, and object of wonder for signs and miracles of power. **With a fuller** discovery of facts, however, **Brother Bonaventure, General Minister** of the Order of Lesser Brothers, is one who assumed the task. A man of good name, privileged as he was with varied graces, he was devoted to God, and the world respected him highly for his knowledge and religious spirit. **Formerly an outstanding master of theology at Paris, he afterwards became a cardinal bishop of the holy Roman Church,** and to this day his teachings and writings illumine the universal Church. In a truly original prose, he wove **the** historical **course of the saint's** entire **life,** and his commendable celebration of a saint is **a worthy praise of God, who gave him the grace.**

Now it appears that Master Henry, a man of profound learning, as his style shows, at a prelate's insistence produced this *life* in verse; with certain additions, derived mostly from the aforesaid cardinal's words, an altered form of it gives it completion. **Many things** included by others find **no mention** in Henry, while he does cite some things they omit; just as in the gospels, what one of the Evangelists passes over, is mentioned by another. He dedicates his work, as to a high dignitary, to the most holy father, the lord pope Gregory IX, of whom, among so many other things, it is told that, with utmost dignity and purpose and exceptional courage, he washed the feet of lepers and paupers, disguising his papal identity in the habit of a Lesser Brother, and that when he was dying he was found wearing a chain and a hair shirt. Henry forms the pope's name out of the initial letters of the fourteen divisions of the work.

When it was pointed out to him that the word "charity" was awkward in a metric system,[a] he maintained that the pagan poets, whose

---

a. Cf. *The Versified Life of Saint Francis* by Henri d'Avranches III 141, FA:ED I 428-520 (hereafter VL).

poetry had no place for that word, were quite ignorant of its inherent value. So, he freely employed "trinity," "unity," and the like,[a] regarding it as improper that the use of words with religious signification should be subject to the rules of the poets.[b] The Vicar of Christ approved of the honest argument in this response and ordered that it be given his authority. Accordingly, this *Versified Life* has been called "Charity" by some, on account of the treatment given this particular word. The work, to be sure, has **examples of imitation** and wonderful points **of veneration;** it contains what could shape **one's conduct** and stimulate one's purpose. Nor does it lack buoyant parts for the uncultivated; so that in it everyone's individual capacity finds provision.

The First Book treats of the blessed Francis's **behavior in secular garb** and of the apparition of Christ under the appearance of the crucified.

The Second: his battle against moral failings; the voice he heard from the cross; his being thought mad as he sold everything.

The Third: persecution by his father; **how he, disinherited** and **stripped, exulted in his own homeland.**

The Fourth: **how** he fell among thieves and served **the lepers and the repairing of three churches.**

The Fifth: **how** he took from the Gospel a form of living; the conversion of the first brothers.

The Sixth: the brothers he had sent through the world to preach all return together immediately, in answer to his prayer; **the approval of the rule.**

The Seventh: how **he taught the brothers to pray and the confirmation of the formerly approved rule. The spirit of prophecy** and the multiplicity of his virtue.

The Eighth: multiplication of foodstuffs on board ship; how he preached the faith of Christ to the Sultan.

The Ninth: creatures obey him; **the grace of healing.**

The Tenth: preaching before the lord **Pope** Honorius; **the affective piety** towards creatures.

The Eleventh: the invitation to **all** creatures **to the praise** of their Creator; his representation **of Christ's Nativity.**

The Twelfth: the revealing of his passing from life; the sacred stigmata and **Christ appearing** in the form of a Seraph.

The Thirteenth: his patience, and all that preceded his happy passing.

---

a. Cf. "Trinity": VL III 141; "Unity": VL X 51; "Truth": VL III 106.

b. An obvious reference to the writings of the Roman poets Virgil, Ovid, Horace and others that are quoted by Henri d'Avranches.

The Final Section: his glorious passing, solemn canonization, and translation; the miracles in general, which, in the prose book on his virtues, are dealt with in particular.[a]

This work of Henry's let no enemy's envy rend,
So well he penned the praises of his amazing friend.

The First Book

THE BLESSED FRANCIS'S BEHAVIOR IN SECULAR GARB, AND THE APPARITION HE HAD OF CHRIST CRUCIFIED.

Addition
[33]**His merchant father violent and sly!**[b]

Lk 1:41-45, 60

A virtuous mother gave birth to a boy, like another Saint Elizabeth   2C 3
endowed with an heir and a prophet;
For when he was brought **to the sacred font** she called him **John,**
And indicating by this name his **ministry** of herald,
She foretold the boy's **future** of sanctity and renown.
Here is the reason, they say, he was later called Francis:
That the French tongue was given to him by heaven above;
In his fervent praising of God he was wont to use it.
And thus, God prompting, it was rather **his father who called him**
A new **name** by which he'd be best known all over the world.
A "Francis" indeed who, converting those heading for death,   1C 120
Enfranchised the French from enslavement to sin, and carried
Within him a heart wondrously frank, noble, that is, and true.
And although father and kinsfolk, who'd delicately raised   LMj I 1
The child surrounded by opulence and in ways that were **vain,**
Towards a transitory world's excesses and gains would haul him,
They could not do so fully, however, nor finish their work.
Yet, his father craving for trade with every breath he drew,
Francis is forced to involve himself in the same concerns.
Withdrawn from studies, he must put his mind to common pursuits.
From now on, he's taught, forget letters and think about wealth.

---

a. A reference to LMj V-XIII, cf. FA:ED II 560-639.

b. In order to make these additions and variations more understandable, the numbering of the translation follows that of FA:ED I 428-520. When appropriate, the verses preceding and/or following those inserted or added have been highlighted. Other words or phrases that have been made bold refer to specific words from the source identified as, in this instance, *The Remembrance of the Desire of a Soul* 3 (hereafter 2C).

Nor is he allowed to turn to his mother's simple ways.
³⁴**O what a monster we've fashioned! Fickle nature's bad, consisting**

Variation and Addition
⁴⁹**Downward we slide; any skyward ascent is with effort.**[a]

So, for long *the youth* is like *a crooked bow*,   Ps 78:57
Terrestrial his heart's yearning, gainful dealings his concern,
And what appears to be, rather than is, good he pursues.
Yet his character, naturally good, was with evil unalloyed;
But his conduct made good habits ugly rather than the ugly
Conform to the good; however, being gentle, generous, kindly,
Affable, amid those wild preoccupations he retained some
⁶⁹Traces of virtue, forecasting a meritorious future.

He so flourished in these, that in the world's whirlwind itself
He was verdant with the flower of chastity, like a rose
Among thorns undamaged; and *he grew in pity* for the wretched,   Jb 31:18
Always wanting to help them, nor ever turn any away.
Indeed ever from childhood mercy grew up alongside him,
So that he merited to heap up goods of a higher kind.
Ever increasing rewards does the virtue **of piety** reap[b]
And manifold is the harvest it yields to its workers.

But contrary to wont—and this was to be a lapse that brought
Forth fresh good, he happened once to upbraid a man in need.
Then, recalling that it was in the King's great name the beggar
Humbly had asked for so little by way of alms, he was sorry
For not granting the request; and lest one bad act beget more,
This in his heart he resolved and vowed to cling to forever,
That if there was anything more he could give to someone
Who begged in Christ's name, he should never be driven away.
He would never allow this vow to depart from his heart;
And that the hand dare not resist the command of the heart,
The mental record of his intentions he sealed with his acts.

So it is that one who's just, with capacity to learn,
A divine vocation furthers, through conflicting occasions.
For one who is just profits from his mistakes; though reckless
The fall, haughty the excesses, that led him to wickedness:
For, once contrite, the rash recklessness turns to fruition,

LMj 1 1

---

a. The following verses are added to VL after VL I 49. Verses 55-63 are then omitted, so that verses 50-70 may express the spirit of *The Major Legend* by Bonaventure.

b. The influence of Bonaventure's theology of *pietas* [piety] is clearly present in these verses, although the editor of these verses employs his own poetic style. Cf. FA:ED II 531 a.

Falling to climbing upward, haughtiness to concession,
Excess to acts of merit, wickedness to doing of good.
    So was it in Francis, these opposing poles were at work.
The doubled strength he got from falling, like that of Antaeus,
Fought all the better, the moment it seemed already lost;
And Francis's own example was an instruction in how
To repulse all sinful ways, for those whom one lapse convicted.
    But since it is difficult to attend both to God and world—   LMj I 2
For to be sure, there is no one who can serve two masters,
The more eagerly Francis worked at things outside himself,
So much feebler was his rising to things of the spirit.
It is not easy to avoid sin, involved in trading;
Indeed business is the cause of many kinds of evil.
Amid opulence, pomp, and high living, who is unblighted?
Who touches pitch or mud and does not get his hands all stained?
In a word, dregs defile, filthy things foul their handlers;
It is a world where decent men find flawless living hard.
Therefore Francis, albeit by the graver sort of sin
Not affected, nonetheless by involvement in all these
Things mundane, in many ways fell in with a sinful world.
[70]For near years five and twenty his youth passed in such wise

Addition
[203]Resisted when pressured, of his own will now might obey.
Now when after the sickness Francis had recovered his strength   LMj I 2
And had fashioned for himself, as was his wont, elegant clothes,
One noble by birth though now needy, dressed in a pauper's garb[a]

Addition
[233]And as refuse regards the goods to which he was used.
Dismounting, he swiftly ran to him, and most tenderly touched   LMj I 5
The leper with kisses, heaping upon him money as well.
Soon upon his horse again, but! leper had vanished and gone,
Nowhere to be seen on all the plain that spread from end to end,
In amazement and in gladness to God did he sing in praise,
From that moment aspiring to soar high to still greater things.
Places remote would hence be his sole seeking wherein to weep,
Wherein the divine pity one day would hear his pleading prayer.
[234]An old grotto, abandoned for years (you find them in Italy),

---

a. Because of a difficulty with the manuscripts, it is difficult to ascertain how these verses were placed
   in the VL. Cf. The manuscript variants indicated in AF X 497.

Addition

²⁴³His foe, and no longer crave for transient things.ᵃ

LMj I 5
Upon a certain day, while deeply absorbed in his prayers
And totally engaged in contemplating godly things,
Christ Jesus appeared to him as though He were nailed to a cross.
As he gazed upon the vision, the love he felt for Him
And for His cross, the Passion now imprinted on his heart
And firmly fixed even to the very marrow of his soul,
Were such that, as often thenceforth the crucifixion of Christ
Came to mind, with difficulty could he restrain his tears.
He now knew this to be the form of the gospel given him
By Christ, who taught that whoever had a mind *to come after*   Mt 16:24
Him, *to deny* himself *and,* having taken up *the cross,*
His undeviating footprints with devotion *follow.*

LMj I 6
Thence his chief concern was to discern the cross within
Himself and to be more personally humble, poor, and pious.
There was a time when in horror from lepers he would recoil
And even from a long way off could scarcely bear their sight;
But now that he was humbled for the sake of Christ crucified,
Who Himself became leper-like, as the prophet testified,
Despised and rejected, he would minister to lepers,
To them be bountiful, and to other needy merciful.
Moreover, his own garments he took off to give away,
And unstitched or tore them for others, not himself, to have.
With reverence he came to the aid of churches and of priests,
Lavish was he with all that worship of the altar lacked,
And in those sacred mysteries his longing was to share.

To Saint Peter's in Rome around that time he made his way,
And saw, on his devotional visit to that holy abode,
A multitude of paupers sitting at the temple's doors.
At that moment, poverty and pity both stirring his love,
He delivered his garments to one he saw to be poorer
Than the rest, and in their stead the other's torn and wretched
Rags he put on; a pauper in a pauper's company.
So, he spent the day the happiest of men among the poor,
Hoping that, thus scorning mundane pride, he might by degrees
Up to those levels of greatest loftiness be transported.
From middle courses to summit is progress wont to be made,
And step by step does heightened virtue receive its vigor;
The mightiest of rivers originate as humble streams.

---

a. The following verses were added as a conclusion in the tradition of LMj.

The Second Book
HIS BATTLE WITH SINFUL WAYS; THE VOICE FROM THE CROSS;
HE IS THOUGHT TO BE MAD FOR SELLING ALL HIS GOODS.

Addition

¹⁴⁷**To the figure of Christ, to deposit this useless load?**
In further ways the Lord touched Francis in his inmost soul.   LMj II 1
Now, close to Assisi there stood, old and precarious,
The church of Saint Damian which, in order to say a prayer
One day Francis entered; and there, while to the Crucified
And to His cross he turned attention, panting in his prayers,
Thrice to him, from heaven and from the cross, came a voice:
"Go, and repair my house, Francis, for it is in ruins."
On hearing the voice, amazed and astonished, beyond himself
He was snatched away; but, returning to himself again,
He took this mandate to mean the material repair
Of the church, which he could see in such a wrecked condition.
Whereas the message was referring rather to that church
That Christ, by shedding His own blood as ransom-price, redeemed,
As to him later, when God revealed the meaning, was made known.
¹⁴⁸**These worries occupy him, when lo! He comes upon the church**

The Third Book
PERSECUTION BY HIS FATHER; DISINHERITED,
HE IS A STRIPPED OUTCAST IN HIS HOMELAND.

Addition

¹⁶⁵**His clothes, he lays them down, including his trousers.**
To be entirely stripped bare he declined not, out of love   LMj II 4
Of Him who upon the cross was willing to hang naked.
And so, departing naked from the world, he left all things,
And being naked, followed the naked Christ crucified.
¹⁶⁶**Without a stitch, stark naked he stands, for all the world like Adam.**

Addition

[179]He accepts some old clothes offered him by a pauper.

LMj II 4   Servant of the bishop, that is to say, a single mantle,
That the prelate, moved by pity, ordered he should be given.
The sign of the cross Francis marked on this; and from that place
[180]He went on his way with nothing but himself; just as an exile

The Fourth Book
HOW HE FELL AMONG THIEVES AND MINISTERED
TO THE LEPERS; THE REPAIRING OF THREE CHURCHES.

Expansion

[129]And forces to the task his fugitive feelings.

LMj II 6   On this account he could claim a great purifying power
Over bodies and minds. Of many cases I tell but one.
That of a certain member of a group of Spoletans,
Whom a malady of a wretched and horrible kind
Had so eaten into and rotted his mouth and his jaw,
That doctors were quite unable to offer him help.
It happened that, returning from Rome, whither as a pilgrim
He had journeyed in order to commend himself to the Saints,
Wandering over the places sacred to the Apostles,
He encountered Francis. The man, having done him homage,
Was now intent upon kissing his feet devoutly, until
The Saint, not allowing him, in no wise countenanced this;
To one who begged for feet to kiss he gave his mouth, and pressed
With inner strength, kisses on those half-eaten leprous lips.
But as soon as the disease was touched by the holy mouth
Of blessed Francis, full healing to the sick man was given.
Harmonized were a humble act and a miracle sublime:
Where there is humble kindness, there arises marvelous power.
[134]Nor were the lepers his sole concern, for indeed he was fully of pity

Addition

[207]Springs forth from the ugly, and profit is made from loss.

LMj II 8   So it was that he built up the fabric of three churches,
Thereby indicating the spiritual construction
Of the three Orders by which he renovated the Church.
To the chapel of God's Mother attachment was enduring,
There his whole self he entrusted to the Mother of Mercy.

Here under her patronage he won increase in virtue,
Here he got to know more surely the things that he must do,
Here, under her, happily began the Order of Minors,
And a light beamed, a world's gloomy blemishes chasing away.
This is the place of a vision shown to a devoted brother,
Before his conversion, a vision well worth the telling:
He saw innumerable people who had been blinded
All crowded round about the hallowed walls of this very church,
Upon their bended knees, their faces and their palms lifted up
To the Lord, as they begged in tears for mercy and for sight.
And there came this great splendor from heaven upon them all,
Bestowing the sight and health they all had so much longed for.
This chapel therefore, above all others, the saint did love,
And wished his disciples to dwell there in perpetuity.

The Fifth Book
HOW HE ADOPTED FROM THE GOSPEL A FORM OF LIVING.

Expansion
¹Francis, most loved to inhabit; nor did he often leave it,
There, immobile, settled, he prolonged the sojourn, restoring
The building, planting the gardens, and on scanty rations
Sustaining life; not like the kind he was used to wearing
Were the clothes he wore, but like those that belonged to hermits.
Whilst he stayed there, continuous were the prayers he offered   LMj III 1
To her who conceived the Savior, that she, whom he had chosen
As his very own guardian and his own patroness,
Would ever be at hand to help him. It was by her merits
That he conceived the grace of the evangelical life.
So it was that once, while he was hearing Mass, the Gospel
⁷That was read one day: Jesus sent out his disciples—after

Addition
¹⁰³Attracts others as followers of what was done in their sight.
Ardent, then, became Bernard, burning well and as boon nard   BPr 1
Of Francis, fragrant; if he was the first in time to be   LMj III 3
His son in Christ, with spiritual merit, too, he was first
To be endowed; since a holy life testified that he was
Ps 115:15   Saintly, as did signs that his *death was precious to the Lord.*
¹⁰⁴Another from the city is converted by his zeal,

Addition

[113]**Of his tribulations.**

LMj III 4   This man[a] was leading Martha's life at first, then that of Mary,   Lk 10:42
Spouse to Leah in action, in contemplation to Rachel.   Gn 29
But in the end, cleaving totally to the *better part*,   Lk 10:42
Inwardly he surged to heavenly things so intensely
That his external bodily functioning was suspended
Oftentimes, and he remained utterly unresponsive;
Totally absorbed in the Lord was the spirit of the man.

LMj III 5   There was then in Assisi a priest called Sylvester, hating
What Francis and his brothers stood for, who was won over thus
By a vision. In apparition he saw a dragon huge
And black, that laid siege to the whole city of Assisi.
It was so big that, if any danger were to threaten it,
It would bring vast destruction upon the entire region.
Thereupon there was seen as it were coming forth from the mouth
Of Francis a cross of brilliant gold: the cross's upper part
Touched the skies, and its arms the boundaries of the world.
When he had thrice seen this, deeming it a divine presage,
He reported it and, following the saint, became himself
A holy man, an outstanding mirror of the perfect life.

LMj III 6   Consequently the cross of life, doctrine's voice, rout our foe;
These were the things that by Francis were renewed in the world.
[113]After another joined those above, a sixth to arms
Had recourse, it was Brother Philip; on his very entry
He was to undergo a total inward transformation,

LP 1   From layman to doctor. The Divine Doctor teaching him
Sacred Scripture's secret words and teaches
[116]**Things he has never studied. All whose hearts he warms, whose
ears**

Addition

[133]**His ranks. In all-out pleading,**

LM III 6   And while over sins committed he prayed the longer,
With this wonderful besprinkling of heavenly sweetness,
Revealed to him was the full remission of his every fault.

1C 26   Also restored to him was the confidence to go on.
At length is completed the prayer that pierces
[134]**the heavens, and his simple soul gazes on God present to him.**

---

a. "This man": a reference to Giles of Assisi.

The Sixth Book
The brothers he had sent through the world
to preach, all return together immediately,
in answer to his prayer;
the approval of the rule.

Addition

⁹⁶**The Pope readily grants in favor. Everything yields**
Ground to the requests and nothing whatever is refused.
Indeed at first the Pope had doubts about giving his blessing   LMj III 9
To such poverty of the most extraordinary kind.
Finally, turning towards the holy man, he said: "Pray, son,
That whatever is the divine will may be made clear to us."
Francis prayed, for what he obtained, that the Pope would kindly   2C 16
Favor him and that he himself might know what would be helpful.
Hence he used a heavenly inspired parable, and said:
"A rich king, attracted by the loveliness of a woman   LMj III 10
Who was poor as well as beautiful, took her in marriage.
By her he had children. But when they had grown, their mother
Sent them to their father to be looked after. The king, noticing
How handsome they were and bore his own likeness, lovingly
Mt 14:27   Embraced them and said: *'Have no fear,* for it is you who are
Rom 8:17   My *heirs;* and if many are the strangers that find feeding
From my table, greater is your right to be supported,
You to whom I allot my whole kingdom for your possession.'
"So," he concluded, "There is no doubting that God will feed
Those children that were borne Him by an Order that is poor.
For poor was the spouse Christ the King especially made His own,
And it was to the poor that He promised His kingdom; therefore
He will give to subjects what He denies not to enemies."
       The Pope marveled at the Lord speaking in one of His servants;   2C 17
Moreover a vision he himself had had at that time   LMj III 10
He now saw, God urging him, find fulfillment in this man.
Gn 28:12   The Pope *had seen in a dream,* he reported, the Lateran
Basilica threatening to fall when, there placing his own
Back underneath it, was this little, poor, and humble man
Supporting it. "This is Francis," he exclaimed, "the one who
By the life he leads, together with his doctrine, will the whole
Church strengthen." From that moment the Pope was favorable, and
Approved the Order's standing and the rule of Francis; also
He charged him to preach, and on the lay brothers who followed him,

To facilitate their preaching, he had tonsures conferred.
[102]**Thus having obtained all that they came to petition,**

Variation
[175]**Its very poverty was comfort to the men that loved her:**

IC 42   Men for whom once it was common to live in fine and spacious
Dwellings, within this place of the most restricted conditions
IC 44   Now were contained, as they rejoiced in the Lord; nor could so
Cramped a spot constrict hearts that were expanded by virtues.
But still, because the passing crowd was disturbing the peace
He had wished for them, Francis now retreating from that place,
[184]**To places not vexed by travelers' pert words,**
Where habitual peace finds a home.

The Seventh Book
HOW HE TAUGHT THE BROTHERS TO PRAY;
CONFIRMATION OF THE FORMERLY APPROVED RULE;
HIS SPIRIT OF PROPHECY; HIS MANY VIRTUES.

Addition
[19]**By the cruel cross you healed our wounds,**

By your death our mortal race, praise be to you throughout
LMj IV 3   The Church and may honor be shown to you in every place!
He instructed them to praise God in all things, and to obey
The faith, so that through it all glory would be given Him.
IC 45   Priests, too, in special manner, and ministers of the faith
He bade them venerate, and wherever there were churches
They came across, he wished the brothers to bow down before them.
[29]**Through these and other prayers, which implore the most high**

Addition
[55]**Its intense flame on the eyes of those brothers in full view,**

LMj IV 4   A flame that in its splendor made the night as bright as day.
They alerted one another: those awake and those who had
Been asleep, all rose: immense bewilderment gripped them all.
But empowered by this fresh light, a new light shone within them,
And they could feel its effect inwardly and outwardly.
It was while they were all looking into one another's hearts,
And all were of one accord, together in their awareness,
And all with a perception of the others' souls, they were aware
That Francis their father, under such a shape and form as this,

Was being made present to his children. If he were absent
In body, always, however, was he present by desire.
His transformation into this figure of the fiery sun,
Meant that he himself had become *a burning and shining lamp,*
To all who were true Israelites the spiritual
Chariot and horseman; Francis, like another Elijah,
After whom it was safe for seekers of the Lord to go.
Credible indeed it is that in answer to Francis's prayer
Christ courteously willed to open for these simple brothers
The perception of their mental and of their bodily eyes,
To see the meaning of this wonderful sign from the Lord.
It was He who made *Elisha's servant see* the encampment
And the chariots of fire, when his *eyes* had been *opened.*
And so, they noted the soul of the saint, as the sphere showed,
Perfect, as the chariot, fleet, as the radiance, blissful.
    After this, Francis went back to the chapel of the Virgin,
Set upright by his efforts, with the brothers who numbered twelve,
That the new Order which began under the Mother of God,
Might, under her, advance in merit and have many join it,
And that she who gave its beginnings might assist its increase.
Hereupon Francis, evangelic messenger, of Him
Who drives away darkness of soul and inspires it to act
Asked, with determined prayer, what was His will in his regard:
To instruct others, or live silently for himself alone?
The teacher in him doubted not; and yet he prayed and pressed
For the Lord's good pleasure to be made more fully known to him.
Reverence in a just man always forbids him to presume.
From what the Lord revealed, therefore, the holy man recognized
That for this was he sent, *to bring back to the fold the sheep*
That wandered, and regain for God souls snatched away from Him.
To preaching he totally applied himself; he went about
Cities, villages and townships, and everywhere the word
Of salvation purposefully preached. *Unflinching* were his *words,*
Burning like a torch, setting the cold-hearted on fire,
Penetrating, not flattering, simple, at the same time stern,
Incredibly empowered to pierce, and sharper *than every*
Two-edged sword; words that had power to move the hardest hearts.
Gladness and joy were what filled out the soul of Francis when
Someone approached to join combat and declare the war on sin.
No matter what one's condition, one's fortune was, or age,
No one got refused. Admission was gained by every type,
Nor was there any levy; the good, the bad, the high, the low,
The rustic and the knight, commoner and man of noble blood,

Marginal references:
Jn 5:35
2 Kgs 2:12
2 Kgs 6:17
LMj IV 5
LMj IV 2
Jn 10:16
LMj IV 5
1C 36
2 Tm 2:11
LMj XII 7
Sir 48:1
LMj XII 8
Hb 4:12

Cleric and layman, the raw and the refined, the pauper,
The rich man, the serf and freeman, the healthy and the sick.
And Francis to one and all, a kind and loving welcome gave.
The pattern he set attracted them, his *exemplary,*   Ti 2:7,8
Blameless life, all that lent authority to his *words.*

LMj IV 6   But because discernment makes for wholeness in a holy proposal,
BPr VII   It is into three Orders he gathered all those converted.
LMj IV 6   One Order got its name from the penance its members practiced:
In it both sexes and every state of life were retained,
Cleric and lay person, man, woman, married and single.
Nor did one have to change one's home; in one's own each one
Knew what rules of life to observe, what was to be carried out.
Already this Order's adherents radiate miracles,
Which goes to show how great in the Lord's eyes is its status.

      Of the second Order—the special order for virgins,
Though it did not turn away virtuous married women—
The first was the most holy virgin Clare; hers was a splendor
Clear shining from virtues, and from her signs and miracles.
Already the Church celebrates a feast in her honor
That was instituted solemnly by the Supreme Pontiff.

Mj IV 7; BPr VII   The third, surpassing the others, is the Order of Lesser Ones,
Which more perfectly cleaves to the counsels of the Gospel,
Under whose banner so many followed the camp of Francis,
Leaving all things, and setting out for the heights with fervor.

LMj IV 8   There was at that time near Assisi a religious in vows,
A member of the Crosiers, and his name was Morico.
The man was suffering from a severe illness, so badly
That death was not far off, in the opinion of the doctors.
He sent a message to Francis, humbly entreating him
To offer up prayers to the Lord to succor him and cure him.
Francis complied with his wish and, as well as praying for him,
Taking some oil from the lamp, that before the Virgin's altar
Burned, soaked some crumbs of bread in it, and sent it to him.
"Bring this medicine," he said, to our brother Morico,
"By means of it the power of Christ will restore him to full
Health, and on top of it give us the gift of a fighter!"
As soon as the sick man tasted of the present sent to him,
He got from it so much corporal and mental vigor,
That not long afterwards in the Order of Francis, which he
Entered, a single tunic only would he have for clothing,
Wearing for a very long time a hair shirt next to his skin.
Bread and wine he never would have, and he ate only

Things that were raw, partaking of vegetables, herbs or fruit.
Yet he remained in good condition and strong in body.
    Since the sun, a star, or a mountain cannot be concealed,   LMj IV 9
So Francis's reputation attracted many from afar
Who wished to see him; he was like another Solomon,
Mustering to himself those from far away his fame had reached.
Among these was a man who, in the composing of poems
And songs, had achieved such proficiency that he was named,
By the Emperor himself, King of Verse, and also had been
Crowned as such by him. Although he never had an idea
Of what Francis looked like, the moment he caught sight of him
He recognized him, on being pointed out by a special sign.
For as God's herald instructed the people as usual,
The man could see him marked with the sign of the cross, in the
Form of two swords spread transversely, up and down and across.
These symbolic swords were flashing with incredible brilliance.
One went from his head to his feet, the other touched each hand.
Intent upon the word of God, that sword of the spirit,
Is how the holy man was heard by his new disciple,
And bidding him renounce all mundane display and concerns.
And all intent upon the word of God, which is the sword
Of the spirit, was the holy man, as his new pupil heard
How he should renounce the pomp of the world and all its cares.
Taking the habit and the vows of the holy master,
He was later given the name Pacificus, for the way
He had perfectly clung to Christ and made his peace with Him.
    Countless folk, who were attracted to their father's miracles.   LMj IV 9
To an immense size grew the holy planting, the newly
Founded Order, this brightest shoot, under a father so great.
The flock committed to his charge the shepherd eagerly fed   LMj IV 10
And watched with care; at once, for those at home was he at hand,
And to those absent, miraculously, also present.
    Indeed, on one occasion when the brothers gathered, he absent
And very far away, the one bidden to address them
Being that brother and father, Anthony, then a doctor
Of renown, now a famed confessor of Christ, who the Church
Universal, by the life he led, his doctrine and wonders,
Jn 19:19Illumines, and taking as his theme: *"Jesus of Nazareth,*
King of the Jews," while he was preaching, a brother of tried
Virtue, Monaldus by name, who led such an unclouded life,
That it sparkled with salutary lessons of behavior,   1C 48
He, lifting up his eyes, observed standing there in the air   LMj IV 10
The father Francis, with his hands extended like a cross,

And giving the brothers his blessing. In that moment, infused
From on high came a spiritual sweetness with the wondrous
Exultation that filled the souls of the brothers that stood around.
It enlivened them, consoled them and stabilized them all.
That the holy man was present was something beyond doubt,
Bracing his followers by prayers and guiding them with care.
He who had once brought Ambrose to the funeral of Martin,
Was now at this time causing Francis to be present to them.

LMj IV 11   But the holy man, when his Order far and wide had spread,
Wanted the form of life, the previous pope had approved,
To receive now the confirmation of his successor.
By means of a vision, what steps to take he came to know.
For, bread in tiny particles he saw himself *gathering up*   Jn 6:12
From off the ground, little particles for him to distribute.
Lest they be lost he feared to give them out; then a voice came:
"Let a single host, Francis, be made out of all these crumbs,
And you are to present to those who wish to eat it."
When this was done, leprosy afflicted those that refused.
Alert again, he made no sense of what he had seen, but prayed
The more expectantly, till a voice from heaven told him
That these tiny little crumbs were the words of the Gospel;
That the host composed of the crumbs was the rule, that earlier
From gospel words was in a fashion quite diffuse produced,
And that would, in a form more condensed one day be confirmed;
Although the leprosy of guilt would stain its despisers.
With this advice and at the Lord's leading, taking up with him
Two of the brothers, he climbed a mountain, and there apart
Fasting, with bread and water the only solace he would
Accept, that his mind uncluttered might totally dwell on God,
He got it written, exactly as, while he was at prayer,
The Holy Spirit inwardly prompted him. Thereupon,
A few days having passed, the one who acted in his place
Lost it. Hereupon Francis, to the mountain again making his way,
Remade the rule, as though from God's mouth he had received it,
And in accord with his own intention, had it confirmed.
Like the old Law and the new, so was a new Rule later
On a mountain given, containing the sum of both Laws.
Francis, instructed from on high, decreed that everything
Be done according to *the pattern shown on the mountain.*   Ex 25:40

LMj XI 3   And as the spirit of prophecy was given to him,
Of hidden things, things far away, and those to happen still
What prescience he had, let some few facts now testify.
For when at Damietta, critical for the Christians

Was their conflict with the Saracens, and in that place
Present was Francis, fighting not with weapons but with prayers,
The army, desirous once for all to assail their foes,
Moved up to the strife, and battle lines were readied for combat.
Word came to Francis and, as the fatal outcome he foreknew,
He advised against war and announced what was to ensue;
How it would go horribly wrong and heavy losses yield.
They but laughed at the man, nor welcome did they give his words.
They marched in, battle began, they gave up, fled, were captured,
And there *perished by the sword* people in many thousands,
And for disdaining the holy man, late came their regrets.

Na 3:15; Mt 26:52

Visiting Celano to preach, and invited to a meal   LMj XI 4
By a knight earnestly entreating him, while he prayed before
Eating, on God's disclosing it, he knew his host was soon
To die; so he summoned him and admonished him to prepare
For his coming death, devoutly make confession of his sins,
And *set his house in order.* "Not here, my dear friend," he said,
"Are you this day to eat; elsewhere your table is prepared;
And for your kind deed in our regard, the Lord will you reward."
The holy man's word at once the man obeyed, and forthwith
Confessing to the saint's companion and setting the affairs
Of his house in order, while others had a mind to dine,
He was seized by sudden death, and by the merits of the guest
He had received, punishment eluded and won a crown;
Forewarned, he for good had come prepared and all the bad erased.
Kindness finds favor with God, and its fruit is a rich prize
The princely Rewarder permits not to be offered in vain;
Hardly is one that loves kindness cheated of God's kindness.

Is 38:1

There was the time that the holy man lay sick at Rieti,   LMj XI 5
When a prebendary[a] there had himself carried to him.   2C 47
He was a man by the name of Gideon, shifty, and who   LMj XI 5
For long lived a bad life, but was with a grave illness stricken.
To be signed with the sign of the cross he tearfully implored
The saint, while those around him were also pressing the plea.
Replied the holy man: "Since you have long lived a bad life
Without fear of the Lord, why should I sign you? However,
For those who are asking with you, I do you the favor
On this occasion. But you must know that should you now be cured
And return *to your vomit,* you will suffer still graver ills;
For an ungrateful man always deserves the worst misfortunes."

Prv 26:11; 2 Pt 2:22

---

a. The Latin word is *prebandarius* [prebendary], a word almost exactly translated in English to signify a person receiving part of the revenues of a cathedral paid as a clergyman's salary.

Therefore, the sign of the cross eventually made on him,
The man who was shriveled and languid arose on the spot,
Healed, in sound condition and, applauding: "I'm cured," said he.
And just like the sound dry twigs make if you were to break them,
So sounded his bones, once the sign of the cross had been made.
Not long afterwards the wretched man returning to his ways,
To vices and impurities exposed his body,
On a certain evening he had a meal in the dwelling
Of a certain canon. But it was while he slept there at night
That the roof of the house suddenly collapsed on everyone.
The others escaped with their lives, only that guilty one,
Surprised by wreck, died and paid with death an evil life's debts.
By the judgment of God, *worse* than the *first* state of this man   Mt 12:45
Was his *last* state of all. Thus *the faith word* of the saint   2 Tm 2:11
And the rigor of God's justice were shown in his relapse.
The thankless pardoned are more liable wrath to incur,
And crimes repeated are the greater offence to the Lord.

LMj XI 6   Noble was she and afire with zeal for saving her soul,
This lady that to Francis came and complained, that to her
Her husband was harsh and impeding her serving the Lord.
Upset over this, she had come to him her pain to unfold,
So that at the holy man's prayers God might deign to soften
His heart and turn it to good. Francis said to the lady:
"You may go and peace go with you, be confident and assured
That with all speed your spouse's encouragement will be yours.

    "You are to tell him on my behalf that the hour of goodwill
Is here and now, later comes the time of redress." Then blessed
By the holy man the woman, leaving, brought to her husband
The message. He at once, smitten with compunction of heart,
Gently replied: "My lady, your wish seems good that you and I
Pursue our saving." This he said, and carried out his word.
And for long were they living chastely when, united in heart,
They departed the same day, their lot being a happy end:
Thus a salutary deed portends and procures salvation.

LMj XI 7   While Francis was at one time in the city of Siena,
A man of religion, who was skilled in divinity,
Came seeking to know from him secrets that lay in the future.
The holy man disclosed all he sought, and at the same time
By whom and what kind of death would be inflicted on the man.
It was something else he said that confirmed what was to come:
A scruple the man had never told anyone of, Francis made known
To him, astounded as he was, and curing him checked it;

And the final outcome in fact confirmed the truth of his words.
    ^{70}Brother Riccerio was one who noticed that hidden from Francis

Addition
^{81}The power used was the same, though different the signs given.^{a}
    Many, throughout his acts, are the examples to be found   LMj XI 6

2 Kgs 2:9   Making clear that Elijah's double spirit was fully his,
    Letting him perform signs and come to know of future things
    And see into the minds of those present and those absent.   LMj XI 3
        ^{90}That was then; but oft and again in different signs

Addition
^{95}And whose special possession means owning nothing at all.
    And then with manifold virtue he shone, like a vessel   LMj V 4

Rv 21:19; Ez 28:13   Of gold that is *adorned with every kind of precious stone.*
    The spirit indeed of all the just ones enveloped him,
    So that in every virtue he became a man approved.
    Clearer will these statements be from even a few examples.

Gal 5:24   *The flesh with its passions crucifying* he so tortured
    As scarcely to allow his human nature to bear up.
    Living in a human world it was the common things he took,
    From the Gospel having taken doctrine for his way of life,
    Shunning that falsehood, that heresy that certain foods rejects.
    Nor is food in moral fault, but its abuse or lust for it;
    At home with his companions he abstained from dainty foods.
        ^{96}Although indulgence in meat was never his wish, once

Addition
^{111}Or else we are a race of perdition."
    Once in the night at prayer he three times Satan heard resound   LMj V 4
    The name "Francis"; "What do you want?" the holy man replied.
    Answered the demon: "A sinner there is none in all the world
    Who, if he is repentant, will not be spared, but to him who
    Living austerity extreme destroys himself, no pardon
    Will be given." The voice was that of the deceitful demon
    Intent on drawing back the holy man to tepidity.
    For a temptation of the flesh at once came upon him,

Jb 41:13   Instigated by the very one *whose breath sets coals afire.*
    As the holy man felt it coming, throwing off what he wore,
    Pitiless lashes he forcefully dealt himself with a cord.

---

a. The remaining verses, VL VII 82-89, are deleted and replaced by the following.

All ardor, moreover, going out from cell into garden
Where the snow would be thick, and into it naked he plunged.
And so, if his body froze as penalty externally,
Passion's flame was put out so perfectly internally,
That thenceforth nothing like it within him was he to endure.
If he is well fought, swiftly is a tempter defeated
And his combatant's brawn a foe cannot stand if impaired.

LMj V 5   When training others to engage in the wars of the flesh,
Like the carnal vices, so also the external senses
By which *death gains entry,* he was instructing them to restrain.   Jer 9:21
"He who does not shrink from talk with women or from their sight
Can come spotlessly clean away, unless very stout-hearted,"
He would say, "as likely as stay in a fire and not be burnt."

LMj V 6   Idle ways, he would say, as the deposit of vices,
Were to be avoided and the flesh to be tamed by toil.

LMj V 9   He practiced what he preached; let the flesh submit to spirit,
Spirit to Christ, obeying by waiting upon his beck.
Hence, fully submissive while he was to his Creator,
A marvel was the command he himself had over creatures,
And promptly the artifact obeyed its Maker's servant.
For when from all the tears he shed his eyesight had grown dim,
And the doctor urged him cauterized, the holy man obeyed,
Knowing it would be painful but salubrious as well.
His flesh before the red-hot iron shuddered, but to brace
His trembling body the man of the Lord admonished the fire
To take pity on him, and entreated the Lord to temper
Its burning heat so that he might be able to bear it.
Then over the glowing iron making the sign of the cross,
He thenceforth stood unflinching and, though cauterized from ear
As far as eyebrow, nothing of pain or of sore distress
Did he feel at all, so that, what a marvel to relate!
The fire became compliant, with no tortures to inflict.

LMj V 10   In its grip once again, a heavy attack of sickness
Compelled him to take to his bed, but so as to provide
For his servant a medicine, the clemency of Christ
Transformed water into wine, a draught of which, its flavor
Transmuting sweetly and to the warming effect of nature
Adding strength, all the disease's causes eliminated.
And when needing wine he looked for some and none was at hand,
He ordered water to be brought him which, when he blessed it,
At the sign of the cross became at once wine, cured his sickness,
And the saint's devotion enriched the poverty of the place.

On another occasion Francis lying ill had a wish,   <small>LMj V 11</small>
In the Lord, for the soothing of some sound that would cheer him
And that his spirit hard put by disease might find relief.
<small>2 Kgs 3:15</small>   For music changes our moods, as the minstrel moved Elisha:
At the sound of a harp a fool frolics; a decent man sings praise.
But the honest wish no mortal was found to satisfy,   <small>LMj V 11</small>
God fulfilled in his kindness through the service of an angel.
For at the time when it was night and he was still awake,
All at once there sounded, as of a harp's wondrous euphony,
A melody most rare, with so much of delight of feeling
Affecting him, that amid the pleasures of paradise
He thought, in ecstasy of soul, he was already present.
Whilst the swift herald of Christ the seeds of the divine word   <small>LMj V 12</small>
Was sowing far and wide, on a certain evening he arrived
At the River Po. As the dark night was now coming down,
There still was road to travel and with many perils fraught.
What should Francis do? Here was the river and there the swamps,
Nor did the dark night allow clear sight of the road ahead.
Said his companion to him: "Father, pray we do not perish
But that the perils we see may cease and not draw near us."
He prayed, and behold, a great light shone forth in that spot,
So that, although the night shrouded other places around,
They, by the rays of this miraculously brilliant light,
Could see not only the road but everything all around,
Till they reached their lodging singing the praise of the Lord.
For these reasons, consider well this great man's qualities:
Fire surrendered to him, water changed, and to his pleasure
An angel bowed, a heavenly light led him on his way;
To prove that to the service of God's servant came all things.
But the range of his humility what words can weave anew?   <small>LMj VI 1</small>
So much in his possession was the wholeness of this virtue,
It may be viewed as that in him which flourished most of all.
Shunning the heights of veneration and acclaim, at all times
Lesser in name and truth, man of lowest rank he wished to be.   <small>LMj VI 5</small>

Variation
[112]The praises and deference so very often shown him
Striving to render void, some one brother he would designate   <small>LMj VI 1</small>
Who, in contradiction of such praises lest perchance pride
Inflate his mind, was to say loud insulting things to him.
And the brother, despite his reluctance in discharging this,
Observing, however, his father's bidding and his wishes,

Spared him not at all as he sat among the distinguished,
But rather called him a mountain man and mercenary,
Reproaching him with being but a sluggard and a rustic.
Glad at all this was the holy man, blessing his curser,
120With honor for abuse, with praise for the insults,

Addition
125He puts to flight all that flatters human mentality.
As a great sinner did he think of himself in his heart,
Speak of himself with his lips, although most perfect he was,
Surpassing in worthiness, of the whole religious life
Model, "mirror," fountainhead, "and of virginal purity"
A shining snow-white blossom. This so well did he conceal
That even his confessor could hardly know it to the full,
Until he to whom all things are open revealed it to him.
Worthy was it, to be sure, and truly right and proper
That "flesh that was virginal" carry the sacred stigmata;
Thus was he great in the sight of God, though little in his own.

And because he was so humble, so sublime was the height
God raised him up to, here below and in the world above.
This was what was shown to a brother of proven virtue,
His companion at that time. He, when once intense in prayer,
Passing into ecstasy, had sight of many and varied
Thrones in heaven, of greater dignity one among them
With varied ornament, shone out, a thing of wonder; but he
Inquiring as to who would for it be chosen, heard this:
"This throne you see did once belong to one of those that fell
When the angelic band for their sinful lapse to ruin came;
But the throne that once was lost by him that swelled with pride
Is reserved for giving now to Francis who was humble."
The brother after this coming out once more of ecstasy,
Wishing to know what the man of the Lord thought of himself,
In conversing about God which both were doing intently
This he asked of him. The holy man replied: "I consider
Myself the greatest sinner of all." "This," asked the other,
"Can you possibly think or with all sober reason say?"
This was his reply: "Criminal none exists I reckon,
Who if God had done for him what he did for me, would not be
To Him more grateful for all that he had from Him received."
Confirmed was the brother hereby that what he saw bore the truth,
Noting that the holy man thought the lowest of himself,
And a humble man scaled the height whence the proud one fell.

LPr V
LMj VI 1

LPr V
LMj VI 6

Mt 20:16

As fervent imitator of Christ in His poverty, LMj VII 1
Her he did espouse with a love that was perpetual.
Among virtues she, he would say, was salvation's proper road
And like a queen to the others, for the very reason
1 Tm 6:15 That it was so vivid in *the King of kings* and likewise
In His Queen Mother. To keep back therefore nothing of his own
Was his wish in this world, to attain celestial riches,
The proper entitlement of those that were truly poor.
And since, as the prophet testifies, a beggar and pauper
Was Christ, the ideal model of virtue, so this man
His disciple made it his business to be both of these.
Nor was it solely to be poor, like any dispossessed
Or holding goods in common, but attaining poverty
At its apostolic peak, to be a beggar, go in want
With Christ was his wish; and the food he begged he used to call
Ps 78:25 *Angelic bread,* because it was bestowed at the prompting
Of angels, to provide for those that truly are in need.
To beg for the sake of Christ, he said, was no cause for shame.
"All things," he used to say, "are the alms the Lord gave mortals
Out of His tender pity, after the fall of humankind."

Satan attempted a snare to lay and play a trick on him. LMj VII 5
While through Apulia he was passing and nearing Bari,
There on the road appeared what is commonly called a "sling,"
A large purse, almost ready to burst, full as it was with coins.
His companion urged him to take it up and give it out
To the poor. Shrink from this did the holy man, saying that here
Lay a devil's trick; besides, nor to give away was it right
To purloin what was not their own; and away he went in haste.
But the brother, still deluded by a hollow kindness,
Kept pressing his advice and murmuring back in plaintive tones
How wrong to waste what could instead those in misery relieve.
At this point, the holy man to go back did agree, not to
Comply with his urger's wish, but to expose the foe's deceit.
And it was just then that a man was coming up and joined them.
First, therefore, saying a prayer, to the brother to lift the purse
He gave orders; the brother Satan's wiles foresaw and trembled.
He, however, lest he infringe the command, towards the purse
Was stretching his hand, when, next, there jumped a huge serpent
Out of the purse and the two suddenly vanished together.
So was found out by the servant of Christ the Devil's deceit.
Then said he to his companion: "Sordid money, my brother,
To the Lord's servants is the devil and a venomous snake."
Wis 12:13; Ps 55:23; Lk 5:11 He, having thoroughly *abandoned* all things, his own *caring* LMj VII 9

Committed to Him whose care of His own is forever.
Wherefore God's kindly providence catered not only for him,
But in fact minded those rendering his servant services.

LMj VII 11 For when he was ailing, a certain devoted physician
Treated him oftentimes, when he was close to Rieti
And abode in a hermitage where, dwelling with but a few,
He would more freely attend to godly meditations.
Having nothing, however, with which to repay the doctor,
He was so poor, divine goodness took care to repay him.
The doctor, out of all his earnings, had built himself a house,
Which when finished, from the upper part to the lowest
Split, and was threatening to collapse at any moment.
By handiwork unable to prevent its destruction,
Trusting fully in the holy man's merits, from companions
Of his he obtained of his hair that once been cut off
A few ribs, which one evening when he had inserted
In the fissure of the wall, on the following morning so
Joined did he discover it, so perfectly compacted,
That unable was he to retrieve what he therein had left,
Nor did there remain any signs of the break that was there.
Thus to the healer of the holy man's broken-down body
Payment was made by the buttressing of his broken-down home,
And God rewarded all that he had done for his servant.

LMj VII 12 One time, when crowds were sent off, returning to a hermitage,
Carried on the little ass of a poor man, went Francis,
Extremely weak that he was, already worn in body.
But as the man that led the ass ascended the mountain,
Overcome by the boiling heat and extreme exertion,
Began to feel the stress of an intensely burning thirst.
And now faltering, he cried, insistent, to the holy man:
"Look," said he, "I'm going to die, unless I soon get a drink."
The holy man at once alighting and upon the Lord
Calling with insistence, ceased not till water in abundance
Gushed out from a rock, delivering the thirsty man his drink.
Neither before nor after was a flow of water seen there,
Where, in that hour, God gave it at the prayers of the holy man,
For He was not letting suffer the one that did him service.

LMj VII 13 As to the way, however, the Lord provided for him,
Multiplying foods and, by marvels, granting things to enjoy,
The plain facts partially find utterance in their proper place.
Behold another Moses, at whose efficacious prayer   Ex 17: 1ff
A rock gave forth fresh water; here, too, another Elisha,   2 Kgs 4:1ff

By whom provisions gained increase: therefore in their merits
He resembled the Fathers of old, and also in their acts.
    The passionate burning of divine love had the effect   LMj X 2
Of moving his inner being so much, that often praying
Or meditating he was so totally absorbed within,
That his outer self was unaware of corporal events.
He passed through Borgo,[a] riding on an ass
Because of his feebleness; yet there he was, supernal
Things contemplating, his soul borne off to the celestial.
Converging on him out of devotion, people in droves
Touched in veneration and tugged him; though what they were doing
He neither mentally noticed nor physically felt.
After a long time, like one returning from some other place,
He would commence asking if they were approaching Borgo.
For raised aloft, he was unaware of events below him;
Very many times to him this was proven to have happened.
    And because to men of prayer worldly clatter is a hindrance,   LMj X 3
Just as holy quiet of much benefit proves itself,
To abandoned churches in the night and to lonesome places
He betook himself to pray. There with demons horrid battles
He endured, as they would hinder him, from the first moment
He gave himself to prayer, with various intimidation.
Assuredly, the more fiercely he was assailed by them,
The stronger and more fervid was his constancy in prayer.
To their confusion and their routing, with the Lord on his side,
At peace with himself he remained, inwardly and outwardly.   LMj X 5
The woods he filled with sighs, the area with tears bedewing
And cleaving to the relished embraces of his Beloved,
He would wholly dilate into spiritual ecstasies.
Praying at night, he could be seen away up in the air
Above the ground to stand, with his hands extended like a cross,
All about him a gleaming cloud, so that bearing witness
To his exalted and radiant soul should be the prodigious
Display itself of elevated body and of light.
    Assisi's presiding bishop, staunch friend of the holy man,   LMj X 5
Often used to come on a visit to him; and one time,
In a less than thoughtful way entering the praying man's cell,
When he put his head in to have a look at him praying,
Immediately was he driven back out by the Lord's power
And vehemently carried away backwards a good distance,

---

a. That is, San Sepolcro.

So that he grew stiff in his limbs and lost his power of speech.
He acknowledged his fault when the Lord gave him back his speech,
And learnt his lesson to show more respect to the holy man.
Once the abbot of Saint Justin, meeting the holy man,
Dismounted and eagerly commended himself to him.
On the abbot's departure Francis stayed in the spot to pray
As he had asked. While he was doing so, behold, far away
The abbot began to experience an unwonted warmth
Of soul and, inside himself, an overflow of sweetness,
So that he became all ecstatic and lost to himself,
Attending upon the Lord. Then once more coming to himself,
He realized it was due to the power of the man that prayed,
And to the brothers he was thereafter a devoted friend.

And then passionate was the zeal for souls that in Francis
Burned, nor did he consider himself to be the friend of Christ,
If it were that he cared not for the souls that He redeemed.
Hence his discussion whether to preach, his ardor for prayer,
His fervor to uplift, his efforts to recover the lost.
If ever he saw somebody stained with the filth of sin,
Stricken with heavy sorrow he almost wasted away.
Sometimes he would be upset by the bad example shown
By those that ought instead to be the builders of the Church.
Once whilst dreading this for his brothers anxiously he prayed,
This is the response from heaven he received back from the Lord:
"Why is it," said the Lord, "you are upset, poor little man?
Was it not over a religion of mine that I placed you,
Whilst its principal patron notwithstanding I remain?
I have by choice placed over it a man as simple as you,
Lest what through you I shall do report claim to be clever,
Natural talent or perception, and what ought to be
Ascribed to me, be credited instead to human counsels.
Those you commend to me," said He, "just as I have called them,
So also shall I feed, keep unharmed and cause to increase;
And no matter how much, though with oppression afflicted,
This poor little religious order of mine may be swayed,
Still it shall always, with me as its defender, remain safe."

See here a new David and Abraham, to whom the word
Of the Almighty promised house, revealed a posterity;
Francis at this, though, was not puffed up, but rather did he
Praise, honor and love Him who so many gifts on him bestowed.
¹²⁶**As he waits for the day of the Lord which reveals the secret.**

Marginal references:

LMj VIII 3
LMj IX 4

LMj VIII 1
LMj VIII 3

2 Sm 7:12-17;
Gn 22: 16-18

The Eighth Book
Multiplication of foodstuffs on board ship.
How he preached the faith of Christ to the Sultan.

Variation

[9]For themselves. As for him, fearing nothing at all, Christ giving   LMj IX 5
the lead,
With his companion, no sailors in sight, went on board ship.
But, lest they want in expenses, behold, there was this man—
And it is believed he was sent by the Lord—that turned up
Bearing food to suffice for them, and to a trustworthy man
Handing it, said to him: "Keep this by you, and to the poor
Brothers that are hiding in this ship deal out what is here,
Apportioning them as much as you shall see what they need."
[15]**The seafarers return, the anchor is weighed, ropes**

The Ninth Book
Creatures obey him, and the grace of healing.

Addition

[25]**Of winged creatures dares not ignore his orders**
That he had learnt they were always silent after his order;   LMj VIII 9
He grieved that they had so broken off for so long a time,
And as he bade them afresh to give their Lord their wonted praise
Their voices were loosed that instant as they had been before.
[26]**Then he makes his way to Greccio**

Addition

[42]**In servitude to Francis, rather than run away free.**
A taming effect on wild beasts even in their savage state   LMj VIII 11
Had Francis's power. Indeed when, playing havoc with animals
And humans, the hostile ferocity of wolves harassed
Greccio's inhabitants, it died down, checked through his prayers.
One wolf in particular through his agency, we are told,
Became a mild creature and with a village was reconciled.[a]
    Not only did brute beasts obey him present in person,
But had obeyed some persons at the mention of his name.
At Parma a swallow was disturbing a certain scholar,   LMj XII 5

---

a. This is the first reference to such a wolf. DBF XXIII expands on this and identifies the village as Gubbio, cf. infra 482-5, 601-4.

Causing him with its chatter extreme annoyance. He said,
With agitation, that this swallow must be one of those
That when Francis once had a mind to speak the word of God,
Impeded him until he calmed them down with a command.
Hence turning to the swallow, he said to it: "In the name
Of the Lord's servant Francis, be silent; and to come to me
I order you." It was silent all at once and, coming,
Into his hands entrusted itself. He was dumbfounded,
And left it go free again; however, from that moment on
The noise of its chattering never again did he hear.
    Raymond, a writer living in the city of Cahors,[a]
One day, close to the cell that he lodged in, was keeping
An attentive eye on a bird, that they call the thistle-finch.
In the name of Francis he commanded her to wait for him
To come to her, promising to do his captive no mischief.
This said, the bird stayed nor at his approach did it withdraw,
But let herself be taken, just as though hearing the name
Of the holy man she were in safe hands and feared no captor.
And at long last, as agreed upon released, she went her way.
The man, with proof in the bird episode of Francis's great power
With the Lord, becoming a Lesser Brother, to his Order's
Laws that he had adopted held fast perseveringly.
[43]**Thus it was that the holy man's remarkable mildness**

---

a. The addition of this new fact provides a clue concerning the author of these additions and variations by suggesting that he was a French brother from the area of Aquitaine. It is impossible to determine anything more.

A COLLECTION OF SAYINGS

OF THE COMPANIONS OF BLESSED FRANCIS

(LATE 13th – EARLY 14th CENTURY)

Introduction

Toward the latter half of the thirteenth century three clusters of Lesser Brothers began to form in Italy and France: in the Italian Provinces of the Marches and Tuscany, and the French Province of Provence.[1] They all shared the same ideal: to profess the *Rule* they inherited from Saint Francis to perfection, that is, "to the letter" and "without gloss." As the papal decrees, *Quo elongati,* September 28, 1230, of Gregory IX, *Ordinem vestrum,* November 14, 1245, of Innocent IV, and *Exiit qui seminat,* August 14, 1279, of Nicholas III continued to define the *Rule* and to influence the daily life of the Lesser Brothers, these pockets of "*Zelanti,*" the name they received because of the zeal for pure observance, began to marshal strength. In addition to having recourse to Francis's *Testament,* the final expression of his vision of Gospel life, they also cherished the reminiscences of the same mentors: the first companions of Saint Francis, many of whom they knew personally. Of these Leo, who died as late as 1278, became the most articulate and most frequently cited. His recollections were passed from one group to another and, with them, his interpretations of Francis's intentions.

Two collections of writings, in particular, seem to have been circulated in the late thirteenth century: the *Legenda Vetus* [An Old Legend], and the *Words of Blessed Conrad of Offida.* A third collection, the *Words of Saint Francis,* may also have been passed from one group to the other.[2] The influence of all three may be seen in the major compilations that emerge in the fourteenth century,[3] e.g. *The Assisi Compilation,*[4] two editions of *The Mirror of Perfection,*[5] and the *Deeds of Blessed Francis and His Companions.*[6] All three are alike in style and in subject matter. The repeated presence of the *Old Legend* and the *Words* of both Saint Francis and Brother Conrad suggests that they were shared among the *Zelanti* of the three Provinces of the Marches, Tuscany, and Provence.

An Old Legend

Paul Sabatier found the first of these collections, *An Old Legend,* in a manuscript in Avignon bearing the title *Fac secundum exemplar* which, he believed, was compiled by Fabianus of Hungary, a student friar in Avignon.[7] The manuscript contained a variety of documents, including an abbreviated version of *The Mirror of Perfection,* some stories that would later appear in *The Deeds of Blessed Francis and His Companions,* and seven others taken *de legenda veteri* [from an old legend]. John R.H. Moorman suggests that the title, *Fac secundum exemplar,* was taken from Exodus 25:40: "Make it according to the pattern shown to you on the mountain."[8] This being the case, the entire collection may well have been intended as meditative documents aimed at helping the Lesser Brothers in their observance of their life. Sophronius Clasen maintains that this "Avignon Compilation" can be dated to the 1330's,[9] while Jacques Cambell attempts to be more precise at dating it at 1343.[10] While she does not attempt to date this collection, Rosalind B. Brooke maintains that it is early and observes that it appears in other early manuscripts.[11]

Moreover, the compiler states that:

> . . . the General Minister had [these] read at table, with myself several times being the reader, while he was present for the benefit of himself and the brothers at Avignon to show that it was true, useful, authentic, and good.[12]

This statement caused others to view the seven stories differently. François Van Ortroy observed that they could be found in Angelo Clareno's *Exposition on the Rule* and speculated that they may well have been his creation.[13] Somewhat akin to Van Ortroy's judgment is that of John R.H. Moorman who maintains that the seven stories formed part of an earlier commentary on the *Rule* that was table reading for the friars at Avignon.[14] Raffaele Pazzelli distinguishes between the *Legenda antiqua* [Ancient Legend] and the *Legenda vetus* [Old Legend] and sees them as independent works.[15] In his study of the Avignon Compilation, Duncan Nimmo reflects on the difficulties of these statements and the puzzles they continue to present. Nevertheless, Nimmo concludes that the dissemination of these documents was quite extensive.[16]

The author of these seven incidents is unknown. The presence of Leo in two of the incidents, of Bernard in one, and of "a theologian from Germany," more than likely Caesar of Speyer, in another, suggests their influence. The points on which they touch are certainly the sensitive ones that occur repeatedly in later texts: the practice of poverty, the role of learning, the pursuit of primitive observance, and the place of Our Lady of the Portiuncula. There is also a foreboding of the future tribulations or trials that would afflict the Order. Nevertheless, the acrimony or intransigence of the later texts is missing, supporting the positions of Sabatier and Brooke that these were stories written at an early date, cherished, and distributed by those who were not pleased with the Order's direction.

The Words of Brother Conrad of Offida

The second collection comes from those *Zelanti* of the Province of the Marches, who gathered around Conrad of Offida (c. 1237-1306). Hugolino de Montegiorgio describes Conrad in *The Deeds of Saint Francis and His Companions* as "a remarkable zealot of the evangelical *Rule* of our blessed Father, Saint Francis . . . a man of such religious life and such merit before God, that both in life and in death the Lord Jesus Christ honored him in many ways." While many aspects of Conrad's life drew the *Zelanti* to him, his personal dealings with Brother Leo, Francis's close companion and one of *nos qui cum eo fuimus* [we who were with him], made him especially popular. So strong is the presence of Leo throughout these thirteen paragraphs that, as Moorman observes, they could be called "Words of Brother Leo." The phrase "Brother Conrad heard from Brother Leo . . ." or variations on it appears six times;[17] twice Leo himself is cited as a direct source.[18]

There is a strident, harsh, and disheartening tone to these passages. Francis is portrayed as inducing fear, proclaiming tribulation, always sad and living with great sorrow, and frequently confrontational. The Conrad/Leo description of the *Rule* extends the Moses imagery suggested by Bonaventure so that Francis enters the cave of Fonte Colombo to speak with God, "like Moses in the tent or on Mount Sinai, face to face." As the number of opponents to Francis's Gospel vision grows, so do his prophecies concerning the tribulations that would engulf the Order. Francis becomes quite clearly the "Prophet," gloomy, pessimistic, and thunderous.

The *Words of Brother Conrad* come in a manuscript, Codex 1/25, of the friary library of Saint Isidore's in Rome. It is dated between 1318 and 1350. As Nimmo notes: "Two appended notes of the fifteenth century connect it with Franciscan friaries at Perugia and Cibotolo in the Order's Province of Umbria, and at Città della Pieve in that of Tuscany."[19] Thus, Conrad's collection seems to have been circulated within a short period of time through those Italian Provinces, Rome, Umbria, and Tuscany. It can also be found in the Barcelona Compilation written in the second half of the fourteenth century.[20] There is no evidence of when these texts were originally written down. If they come directly from Leo by way of Conrad of Offida, they reveal an apocalyptic and acrimonious tone that is more characteristic of the early fourteenth century. They are certainly more harsh than the third collection of this packet, the *Words of Saint Francis,* that comes from Leo himself.

The Words of Saint Francis

The earliest manuscript of this collection comes, once again, from the friary library of Saint Isidore's in Rome, and contains this heading:

> Words of Saint Francis. A companion of Blessed Francis, Br. Leo, who was a man of true simplicity and holiness, wrote these words that state and reveal the intention and sense of his perfect *Rule* sincerely and faithfully.[21]

Because the seven statements reveal what Leo maintained was the "intention and sense" of the *Rule,* they repeatedly appear in the writing of the Spirituals. Six of them appear in the *Assisi Compilation;*[22] one appears in the Lemmens edition of *The Mirror of Perfection;*[23] and they are all scattered throughout that of Sabatier.[24] Ubertino da Casale quotes them in the fifth chapter of his *Tree of the Crucified Life of Jesus,* as does Angelo Clareno in his *Exposition on the Rule.*[25]

As Rosalind B. Brooke points out, these are words of conflict: conflict about the *Rule*, about poverty, about privileges. Two of Leo's stories involve conflicts between Francis and the ministers in which the ministers use Elias as their tool. Another describes a conflict between Francis and a group of wise and learned brothers who use Cardinal Hugolino. Since she finds no evidence of tension among the ministers, Hugolino, and Francis in Thomas of Celano's *Remembrance*, Brooke suggests that Leo may have written this collection after 1247, that is, after Thomas's work. It seems more probable that *The Words of Saint Francis* appeared after 1257, when John of Parma was asked to resign. And since Bonaventure incorporates some allusions to the *Words* into his description of the composition of the *Rule*, Brooke believes that it may have been written before the *Major Legend*.[26]

Notes

1. Cf. Livarius Oliger, "Spirituels," in *Dictionnaire de Théologie Catholique Contenant l'exposé des Doctrines de la Théologie Catholique Leurs Preuves et Leur Histoire,* tome XIV, 2nd part, ed. Alfred Vacant, Eugene Mangenot, Émile Amman (Paris: Librairie Letouzey et Ané, 1941), 2522-49.

2. Curiously the collection known as the *Intentio Regulae* [*Intention of the* Rule (hereafter IntR)] seems to have been unique unto itself. Rosalind B. Brooke maintains, as does Duncan Nimmo, that the five paragraphs—stories that contain clear teachings that claim to come from Francis himself—were circulated separately. Cf. *Scripta Leonis, Rufini et Angeli Sociorum S. Francisci [The Writings of Leo, Rufino and Angelo Companions of St. Francis],* ed. and trans by Rosalind B. Brooke (Oxford: Oxford at The Clarendon Press, 1970), 57-8; Duncan Nimmo, *Reform and Division in the Medieval Franciscan Order: From Saint Francis to the Foundation of the Capuchins.* Bibliotheca Seraphico-Capuccina 33 (Rome: Capuchin Historical Institute, 1987), 93.

3. A number of compilations have emerged and are named according to the manuscript in which they are found: the two Compilations of Barcelona, another of Dubrovnik, and that of Sant'Antonio in Rome. Cf. Jacques Cambell, "Glanes franciscaines: la première compilation de Barcelone," in *Ibero-Americano* 23 (1963): 65-91, 391-453; idem, "Glanes franciscaines: la seconde compilation de Barcelone," in *Ibero-Americano* 25 (1965): 223-98: Andrew G. Little, "Description du manuscript Canonic. Miscell. 525 de la Bibliothèque Bodlienne à Oxford," in *Opuscules de critique historique,* I (Paris: Librairie Fischbacher, 1903), 253-97; Livarius Oliger, "Descriptio codicis S. Antonii de Urbe unacum appendice textuum de S. Francisco," in AFH 12 (1919): 321-57.

4. Cf. FA:ED II 118-230. The *Assisi Compilation,* found in Codex 1046 of the Biblioteca Communale Augusta of Perugia, is composed of the *rotuli* [scrolls] containing the information sent to Crescentius of Iesi by the companions, IntR, the *Verba S. Francisci* [The Words of St. Francis (hereafter WSF)], the *Verba F. Conradi* [The Words of Brother Conrad of Offida (hereafter WBC)], and 2C. For the difficulties inherent to these texts, see FA:ED II 113-7.

5. Infra. The Lemmens edition of *A Mirror of Perfection* (hereafter 1MP), the more simple of the two, is made up of two *Admonitions,* selections from the scrolls or AC, and from 2C. The Sabatier edition of *A Mirror of Perfection* (hereafter 2MP), contains Francis's CtC, selections from the scrolls or AC, IntR, WSF, WBC, and the *Old Legend* (hereafter OL).

6. Infra. DBF resembles the 2MP in the materials it contains, AC, IntR, WBC, OL. But it contains a large amount of original material that, at times, seems the product of the compiler's imagination or literary license.

7. Paul Sabatier, "S. Francisci Legendae Veteris Fragmenta Quaedam ou De Quelques Chapitres de la Compilation Franciscaine connue sous le nom de Legenda Antiqua (circa 1322) qui paraissent provenir de la Legenda Vetus (circa 1246)," in *Opuscules de Critique Historique,* t. I, ed. Andrew G. Little, Pierre Mondonnet, Paul Sabatier (Paris: Librairie Fischbacher, 1902), 63-134, 393-5.

8. John R.H. Moorman, *The Sources for the Life of St. Francis of Assisi,* with introduction by Andrew G. Little (Manchester: Manchester University Press, 1940), 165.

9. Sophronius Clasen, *Legenda Antiqua S. Francisci. Untersuchung die nachbonaventurianischen Franziskusquellen. Legenda trium sociorum, Speculum perfectionis, Actus B. Francisci et sociorum eius und verwandtes Schriftum.* Studium et documenta franciscana, cura Fratrum Minorum in Austria, Belgio, Germania et Neerlandia edita, 5. (Leiden: E.J. Brill, 1967), 225, n. 2.

10. Jacques Cambell, "Une tentative de résoudre la Question franciscaine," *Miscellanea Franciscana* 69 (1969):187-206.

11. Cf. Brooke, *Scripta,* 43-50. In a comparison of Sabatier's *Legenda Vetus* with the manuscripts of Perugia, Upsala, St. Isidore's in Rome, and the Bodlean Library in Oxford, which she claims to be "the four earliest and best texts containing groups of stories," Brooke shows how all five collections had access to a common set of sources. In his examination of the document, Nimmo offers no attempt at dating the text beyond maintaining that it was part of that later thirteenth century packet of documents, the *Sayings.*

12. The General Minister to whom the text refers is Gerald Odonis who served from 1329-42.

13. François Van Ortroy, "Bulletin des publications hagiographiques," *Analecta Bollandiana* 21 (1902): 111-5.

14. Moorman, *Sources,* 166.

15. Raffaele Pazzelli, "La compilazione avignonese della 'Legenda Antiqua beati Francisci,' " *Analecta TOR* 25 (1994): 4-24.

16. Nimmo, *Reform,* 316-21.

17. Cf. WBC I 1; II 1; III 1; V 1; VI 2; XI 1.

18. Cf. WBC VII; X 1.

19. Cf. Nimmo, *Reform,* 313-4.

20. *Ibid.,* 332.

21. "Verba S. Francisci. Ista verba scripsit socius B. Francisci, videlicet Fr. Leo, qui fuit vir verae simplicitatis et sanctitatis, quae ipsius Regulae intentionem et sensum perfectae declarant et sincere et fideliter manifestant." Cf. Edith Pásztor, "Il manoscritto Isidoriano 1/73 e gli scritti leonini su S. Francesco," *Cultura e società nell'Italia medievale. Studi per Paolo Brezzi.* Studi Stoirici, 188-192. (Rome: 1988), 661-3.

22. AC 15, 16, 17, 18, 20, 21.

23. 1MP 44.

24. 2MP 1, 12, 13, 50, 52, 68, 79, 85.

25. Angelo Clareno, *Expositio super regulae Fratrum Minorum,* ed. Giovanni Bocalli with introduction by Felice Accrocca and translation by Marino Bigaroni (Sta. Maria degli Angeli, Assisi: Edizioni Porziuncola, 1995), 124-5, 236-7, 392-3, 434-7, 444-51, 622-3, 674-7.

26. Cf. Brooke, *Scripta,* 61-3.

Sayings of the Companions of Blessed Francis

An Old Legend
(*Legenda Vetus*)^a

I. On the future evil state of the brothers,
which Saint Francis predicted

¹Saint Francis predicted the following before the Lord of Ostia and many brothers, and often preached this to the people, as the companions who heard it, Brother Bernard, Brother Leo, and Brother Angelo, have testified. His brothers, by the working of evil spirits, would turn aside from the way of holy simplicity and highest poverty. They would receive money, legacies, and bequests. Abandoning poor little solitary places, they would build sumptuous places in towns and cities, which would not demonstrate poverty, but the luxury of the world of lords and princes. And, with great craftiness and human prudence, they would seek and receive from the Church and the Supreme Pontiffs privileges that would not only mitigate but even destroy the purity of their promised rule and life, revealed to them by Christ.

⁵Equipped with these, in their pride they will start quarrels and inflict harm not only on people of the world but also on the clergy and religious. They will dig the pit into which they will finally fall, and sow the seed from which many scandals will be reaped. And

---

a. This translation is based on Paul Sabatier, "S. Francisci legendae veteris fragmenta quaedam ou de quelques chapitres de la compilation franciscaine connue sous le nom de Legenda Antiqua (circa 1322) qui paraissent provenir de la Legenda Vetus (circa 1246)," in Andrew G. Little, Pierre Mandonnet, Paul Sabatier, *Opuscules de critique historique:* Tome I (Paris: Fischbacher, 1903), 87-109.

Christ will send them one worthy of their worth, not a shepherd but a destroyer, who will mete out retribution to them according to their conniving and striving, and will set in motion a great trial, as they deserve, so that once punished by God's just judgment they may return, humbled, to the state of their vocation. Thus they will be completely uprooted from the life-giving and salvific way of living that they promised in the Lord's presence to observe until the end. The truth of the preachers will be silent in practice or trodden underfoot, and thus the holiness of those professing it will be held in contempt. And those who fervently cling to piety will endure countless persecutions.

[9]At that time, he used to say, there will be such great insults and upheaval of demons and wicked humans against those walking in this way that, abandoning all, they will seek to reach deserted and solitary places and cross over to be among the unbelievers. Scattered, they will take back secular clothing, leading a pilgrim's wandering life, or hide in the homes of the faithful, amidst innumerable calumnies and insults, and will endure suffering and death. And, he would say, blessed is he who then will be able to find a faithful companion, since those persecuting them, driven by evil spirits, will say that it is a great service to God to wipe out such harmful people from the face of the earth.

II. The intention of Saint Francis about the observance of the *Rule*, where it says, "Wherever there are brothers who know and realize"

[1]When the brothers are certain and have learned from experience that in the places where they are staying they cannot observe the *Rule* according to a pure intention and true uprightness because of the bad habits practiced in the places, inevitably leading, for different reasons, to breaking the *Rule*, the brothers can and must have recourse to the ministers. As Brother Leo testifies, who was present, along with Brother Dominic,[a] when Saint Francis delivered the second Rule to the Lord Pope Honorius for confirmation at Christ's command, the Supreme Pontiff carefully examined everything contained in the *Rule*. He said to Blessed Francis: "Blessed is he who, strengthened by the grace of God, will observe this *Rule* happily and devotedly, for all the things written in it are holy and Catholic and perfect. However there are problems with these words: "they can and should have recourse to their ministers. Let the ministers,

---

a. This is a curious passage since there is no earlier record of the description of Francis presenting Pope Honorius III with the *Later Rule* and, therefore, no record of who might have accompanied him.

moreover, be bound by obedience to permit them, kindly and generously, their request. If they refuse to do this, the brothers themselves
have the permission and obedience to observe it literally, because all,
both ministers and subjects, must be subject to the *Rule*. These could
be the occasion of ruin and create the stain of division and scandal in
the religion for brothers not fully grounded in the love of virtue.
Therefore I want those words changed in such a way that every occasion of danger and division may be removed from the brothers and
the religion."

1 Pt 1:9

[7]Blessed Francis answered, "It was not I but Christ who put these
words in the *Rule*. He knows best what is useful and necessary for the
salvation of souls and of the brothers, and for the good state and preservation of the religion. All that will happen in the future to the religion and to the Church is clear and present to Him. I must not and
cannot change the words of Christ. It will happen that the ministers
and others in authority in the religion will cause many bitter tribulations for those who wish to observe the Rule faithfully and literally.
Therefore, since it is the will and obedience of Christ that this *Rule*
and life be understood literally, so it must be your will and obedience
that this be done and be written in the *Rule*."

[10]Then the Pope said to him, "I will do this in such a way that,
keeping the full sense of the words, I will modify the letter of the *Rule*
in this passage, in such a way that the ministers will understand they
are obliged to do what Christ wills and the *Rule* commands, and the
brothers will understand they have the freedom to observe the *Rule*
purely and simply. This will provide no occasion, to those who frequently look for one, to transgress the *Rule* under the pretext of
observing it." Therefore the pope changed the words of that clause,
as they now stand in the *Rule*.

III. An example of the will of Saint Francis mentioned above

[1]This is proved by the answer he gave at Saint Mary of the Angels
to that brother from Germany, a master of theology, who said to
Brother Francis with great reverence: "I promised firmly to observe
the Gospel and the *Rule* which Christ has spoken through you, until
the end, simply and faithfully, with the help of His grace. But one
favor I ask of you. If in my lifetime the brothers fall as far away from
the pure observance of the *Rule* as you predict through the Holy
Spirit, I ask by your obedience that I may withdraw from those who
do not observe it, alone or with some brothers who wish to observe it
purely."

[4]Hearing these things, Blessed Francis was overjoyed and, blessing him, said, "Know that what you asked is granted to you, by Christ and by me."

[5]And he *placed* his *right* hand *on his head,* saying to him: *"You are a priest forever according to the order of Melchisedek."* And Blessed Francis added that all the promises made to him by Christ would, in the end, be fulfilled in those who would strive to observe the Rule simply, to the letter, and without glosses and with joy.

Gn 48:18; Ps 110:4

IV. How Saint Francis predicted that a wind would overturn the house of his first-born offspring because of the brothers' love of learning and knowledge

[1]Saint Francis also predicted a very great trial of his brothers that was to come because of the love of learning, and that *a violent wind from the desert* would arise, and would *strike the four corners* and completely tear down *the house of his first-born* offspring, and *destroy all his children and daughters.* And, that he might avoid the danger of the ruin of souls, like another *Rechab* [a] he sent his own to lead a wandering life: not to build palaces; not to live in the midst of cities; not to plant the vineyards of various studies, nor drink the wine of secular knowledge and worldly philosophy but, enlivened by the warmth of the Holy Spirit, placed as a law for his sons the deeds of the most perfect life of Christ.

Jb 1:18-19

2 Sm 4:5-12

[4]But those wise ones, mentioned above, put up, as he said, the tents of those great harlots, and brought their sons inside, *living luxuriously* from the *pay of the harlots.* And the simplicity they promised will be considered laughable, corruptible, and despised in their eyes. They will become bold and presumptuous, and will glory in human praise, and will trust in the name of learning and activity or prudence, and at that time constant conversion of heart will be very bitter and intolerable.

Jer 5:7; Mi 1:7

V. To the same point, about an amazing apparition of an angel

[1]One day, while Blessed Francis was praying in the place of Saint Mary of the Angels, an angel appeared to him in an amazing form and appearance:[b] the *head* was *gold, arms and chest silver, stomach bronze,* feet of *iron,* and *clay;* the shoulders covered with vile and

2C 82

Dn 2:32-33

---

a. Some manuscripts read "Ahab." Cf. 1 Kgs 16; Jer 29:21.
b. This vision was described in different terms by Thomas of Celano (2C 82) who had described the angel's "form" as a lady, and by Ugolino of Montegiorgio (ABF 24) as a statue. Thomas of Eccleston narrates that, in the General Chapter of 1239, Pope Gregory IX preached about the "golden statue" prompting Brother Elias to make excuses for his actions.

rough sackcloth, and it showed it was rather ashamed of that sack-cloth covering.

[3]He was amazed at seeing this, and the angel said to him: "Why do you gawk and gaze? This form which you see signifies the beginning, development, and end which your religion will have, until the time it goes into labor, the time of the reform of the life of Christ and of the state of the Church. *The golden head* is you, with all your companions who are filled with the love of God and carry Christ and His death in your soul and body. But those who will come after you, having put aside prayer, will turn to *knowledge* which *inflates,* eagerness for lectures and a multitude of books under the pretext of their neighbor's edification and the *salvation of souls.* And because they prefer verbs to virtues, and science to sanctity,[c] they will remain cold within and devoid of charity, having changed gold into cold and heavy silver. They will pant for praises and honors, wishing, not to be better than others, but to appear so. Thus, to great loss, like bad merchants, they will exchange the silver of eloquence and learning for a hypocritical simulation in bronze, producing their works in order to get human praise, and always for a good profit. But their simulation and hypocrisy cannot be concealed for long; and they will lose their worth in the eyes of those who praised them, and when they sense this they will start to become angry and indignant against those they once tried so hard to please, eagerly seeking opportunities to persecute and afflict those who have stopped revering and complimenting them. In this way ringing bronze will be transformed into hard and harsh iron, and they will be fragile, and impatient like tile.

[10]"This cheap, rough and short sackcloth with which I cover my shoulders is the cheapness and austerity of poverty which the brothers promised the Lord they would wear proudly. But abandoning it, they will cling to every kind of relaxation concerning tunics, books, and other things. And they will rejoice so inanely before people in the name and reputation of poverty, but in deeds and behavior will be ashamed of it, and will persecute it among themselves and in others; therefore I show that I wear this habit with deep shame."

[12]And this is one of the reasons why it is said pointedly in the *Rule* that all the brothers should wear cheap clothing, so that the brothers who refuse to do this and prohibit doing this may have no excuse in their consciences.

Dn 2:38

1 Cor 8:1

1 Pt 1:9

2C 195; AC 47

---

c. The original has the word-play: *praeponent verba virtutibus et scientiam sanctitati* [literally: they prefer words to virtues and knowledge to holiness].

VI. THOSE GOING AMONG UNBELIEVERS FOR THE LOVE OF CHRIST

[margin: I 3; LR XVII 1]

[1]He believed that the highest obedience, in which flesh and blood had no part was **by divine inspiration going among the Saracens and non-believers,** either out of love of neighbor or the desire for martyrdom. He considered requesting this very pleasing to God, and

[margin: VI 4; LR XII 2]

that **the ministers should give them permission and not oppose them, if they see they are fit to be sent, for they will be bound to render an accounting to God.**

[margin: ER XVI 5-7]

[3]**The brothers who go can live among them** in a two-fold way. One way is not to engage in arguments or dispute in words, being subject to every human creature for God's sake and to acknowledge that they are Christians. The other way is to announce the word of God, when they see it pleases the Lord, in order that they may believe in God the Father, the Son, and the Holy Spirit, and be

[margin: ER XVI 10-11]

baptized and become Christians. And let the brothers remember that they have given themselves to our Lord Jesus Christ, and their bodies, for love of whom they must make themselves vulnerable to their enemies, both visible and invisible, because the Lord says, *"Whoever loses his life because of me will save it* in eternal life."

[margin: Lk 9:24; Mt 25:46]

VII. THE PLACE OF SAINT MARY OF THE ANGELS

[margin: AC 56]

[1]**Seeing that** God **willed** *to increase the number* of brothers, blessed Francis told them: "My dearest brothers and sons, I see that the Lord wants **you to increase.** Therefore, **it seems good and religious to me to receive** from the bishop and the canons of San Rufino, or from the abbot of the monastery of Saint Benedict, some small church where the brothers might say their hours and have next to it a house built where they can sleep and care for their needs. This place is not suitable and is very small for the brothers, since the Lord pleases to increase them, and especially because here we do not have a church where the brothers can say their hours. And, should one die, it would not be proper to bury him here or in a church of the secular clergy."

[margin: Acts 6:7]

[4]This *speech pleased the other* brothers.

[margin: Jos 22:33]

So he got up and **went to the bishop of Assisi. He made the same** speech before the **bishop** which he had made to the brothers. "Brother," the bishop replied, "I do not have any church that I can give you." Then he went to the canons of San Rufino and **said the** same thing. The canons replied as the bishop did. **Then he went to the monastery of Saint Benedict** under Assisi,[a] **and placed the same**

---

a. The Latin reads *sub Assisio* [under Assisi], possibly an allusion to the monastery's place under the jurisdiction of Assisi. It is unclear.

words before the abbot that he had spoken to the bishop and the canons, and also how the bishops and the canons had replied.

⁷The abbot, moved by piety, took counsel with his brothers about this. Since it was God's will, they granted blessed Francis and his brothers the church of Saint Mary of the Portiuncula, as the poorest little church they had. It was the poorest little one in the area of the city, which Blessed Francis desired. "Father, we have granted your request," he said. "But, if the Lord increases your congregation, we want this place to be the head of all your places." And this speech pleased blessed Francis and the other brothers.

⁹Blessed Francis was overjoyed at the place granted to the brothers, especially because of the name of this church of the Mother of Christ, and because it was such a poor little church, and because of the surname it had, for it was surnamed: "of the Portiuncula." This name foreshadowed that it would be the mother and head of the poor Lesser Brothers.[a] It was named "Portiuncula" after the neighborhood where that church was built, which from earliest times was referred to as "Portiuncula." Blessed Francis used to say: "This is why the Lord willed that no other church be granted to the brothers, and why the first brothers would never build any completely new church, and would not have any other but this one. For this church was a prophecy that has been fulfilled in the coming of the Lesser Brothers."

¹²And although it was already poor and almost in ruins, nevertheless, for a long time, the people of the city of Assisi and its entire neighborhood had held the church in great devotion and hold it in even greater devotion today. Soon after the brothers went to stay

Acts 6:7

there, almost daily the Lord *increased* their food,[b] and news of them and their fame flew throughout the whole valley of Spoleto. From old times, it was called Saint Mary of the Angels, and in the region was called Saint Mary of the Portiuncula. But after the brothers began to repair it, the men and women of that region used to say, "Let's go to Saint Mary of the Angels."

¹⁵Although the abbot and the monks had freely granted it to blessed Francis and his brothers without payment, every year he used to send a basket full of small fish called "lasche" as a sign of greater humility and poverty. They in turn, because of the humility of blessed Francis, who had done this of his own will, gave him and his

---

a. This statement is intended to contradict that of Pope Gregory IX who, in *Is qui ecclesiam*, March 5, 1230, proclaimed the newly built Basilica of Saint Francis in Assisi the *caput et mater* [mother and head] of the Order, cf. *Bullarium Franciscanum* I, 60 (hereafter BFr). Cf. 2MP 55, 298, 298 b.

b. The Latin, oddly, reads *victum* (food), rather than *numerum* (number).

brothers a jar filled with oil. We who were with blessed Francis *bear witness* that he spoke of that church with great conviction. He said the Lord had shown him there that it had a great prerogative, and it had been revealed to him in that place that, of all the churches of the world that she has, the blessed Virgin loved that church. Therefore, during his whole lifetime he always had the greatest reverence and devotion toward it. And so that the brothers would always keep remembrance of it in their hearts, near his death he wanted it written in his *Testament* that all the brothers do likewise. Jn 21:24

[19]About the time of his death, in the presence of the general minister and the other brothers, he said: "I want to leave and bequeath to the brothers the place of Saint Mary of the Portiuncula as a testament, that it may always be held in the greatest reverence and devotion by the brothers. Our old brothers did this: for although the place itself is holy, these preserved its holiness with constant prayer day and night and by constant silence. And if, at times, anyone spoke after the time established for silence, they discussed with the greatest devotion and decorum matters pertaining to the praise of God and the salvation of souls. If it happened, and it rarely did, that someone began *to utter* useless or *idle words,* immediately he was corrected by another. They used to mortify the flesh not only by *fasting,* but also by *many vigils,* and prayers, by *cold, nakedness,* and manual labor. In order not to remain idle, they very frequently went and helped poor people in their fields, and sometimes these people would give them some bread for the love of God. Mt 12:36 2 Cor 11: 27

[23]"By these and other virtues, they used to sanctify themselves and the place. And others who came after them did likewise for a long time. Therefore I want this place always to be under the jurisdiction of the general minister, that he may show greater concern and care in providing for it, especially in placing a good and holy family there. The clerics should be chosen from among the holiest and most upright brothers of the entire religion and who know how to say the office best. In this way, not only other people but also the brothers will gladly listen to them with great devotion. And some holy, discerning, and upright lay brothers should also be chosen, who may serve them.

[25b]"I also wish that none of the brothers or any other person enter this place except the general minister and the brothers who serve them. And they may not speak to anyone except the brothers who serve them and to the minister when he visits them.

[26b]"I likewise want the lay brothers who serve them to be bound not to relay to them news of the world that they may not hear what

is not useful to their souls. And that is the reason why I particularly want no one to enter that place, so that they may better preserve their purity and holiness. And in that place let no one speak useless and empty words, but let this entire place be preserved and held pure and holy in hymns and praises of the Lord.

²⁸"And when any of those brothers passes, another holy brother, no matter where he is staying, should be sent there by the general minister in the place of the one who died. For if at some time brothers stray in the places where they are staying from purity and holiness, I want this place to be a mirror and a good example for the entire religion, a candelabra *before the throne of God* and before the blessed Virgin. Thus may the Lord have mercy on the faults and failings of the brothers and always preserve and protect the religion, His little plant."

Rv 4:5; 7:15

The Words of Saint Francis[a]

A companion of blessed Francis, Brother Leo, who was truly a man of simplicity and holiness, wrote these words, which perfectly state and sincerely and faithfully manifest the intention and sense of his *Rule*.

AC 15 [1]Likewise blessed Francis often said these words to the brothers: "I have never been a thief, that is, in regard to alms, which are the inheritance of the poor. I always took less than I needed, so that other poor people would not be cheated of their share. To act otherwise would be theft."

AC 16 [2]When the brother ministers urged him to allow the brothers to have something at least in common, so that such a great number would have some resources, Saint Francis called upon Christ in prayer and consulted Him about this. Christ immediately responded that He would take away everything held individually or in common, saying that this is His family for whom He was always ready to provide, no matter how much it might grow, and He would always cherish it as long as it would put its hope in Him.

AC 17 [3]When blessed Francis was on a mountain with Brother Leo of Assisi and Brother Bonizo of Bologna to make the *Rule*,[b]—because the first, which he had written at Christ's instruction, was lost[c]—a great many ministers gathered around Brother Elias, who was the vicar of blessed Francis. "We heard that Brother Francis is making a new rule," they told him, "and we fear that he will make it so harsh that we will not be able to observe it. We want you to go to him and tell him that we refuse to be bound to that rule. Let him make it for himself and not for us." Brother Elias replied to them that he did not want to go because he feared the rebuke of Brother Francis. When they insisted that he go, he said that he refused to go without them; so they all went.

---

a. This translation is based on Pásztor, "Manoscritto Isidoriano 1/73," 661-3.

b. Little is known about Bonizo (Bonizzo) of Bologna. Arnaldo Fortini calls him "a gifted jurist of the University of Bologna," although he provides no source for that information, cf. Fortini, *Francis* 524. Rosalind B. Brooke is undoubtedly more accurate when she describes Bonizzo as simply "an obscure figure," cf. Brooke, *Scripta* 60.

c. There has been longstanding speculation and controversy about this loss and the reasons for it.

When Brother Elias, with those ministers, was near the place where blessed Francis was staying, he called him. Blessed Francis responded and, seeing those ministers, he said: "What do these brothers want?" "These are ministers," Brother Elias answered, "who heard that you are making a new rule. They fear that you are making it very harsh, and they say, and say publicly, that they refuse to be bound by it. Make it for yourself and not for them." Then blessed Francis turned his face to heaven and spoke to Christ in this way: "Lord! Didn't I tell you they wouldn't believe you?" The voice of Christ was then heard in the air, saying "Francis, nothing of yours is in the *Rule:* whatever is there is all mine. And I want the *Rule* observed in this way: to the letter, to the letter, to the letter, and without a gloss, without a gloss, without a gloss."[a] And He added: "I know how much human weakness is capable of, and how much I want to help them. Those who refuse to observe it should leave the Order." Then blessed Francis turned to the brothers and said: "Did you hear? Did you hear? Do you want me to have you told again?" Then the ministers, confused and blaming themselves, departed.

[4]When blessed Francis was at the general chapter called the "Chapter of Mats," held at Saint Mary of the Portiuncula, there were five thousand brothers present. Many wise and learned brothers told the Lord Cardinal, who later became Pope Gregory, who was present at the chapter, that he should persuade blessed Francis to follow the advice of those same wise brothers and allow himself to be guided by them for the time being. They cited the *Rule* of blessed Benedict, blessed Augustine, and blessed Bernard, which teach how to live in such order in such a way.[b] Then blessed Francis, on hearing the cardinal's advice about this, took him by the hand and led him to the brothers assembled in chapter, and spoke to the brothers in this way: "My brothers! My brothers! God has called me by the way of simplicity, and showed me the way of simplicity. I do not want you to mention to me any rule, whether of Saint Augustine, or of Saint Bernard, or of Saint Benedict.[c] And the Lord told me what He wanted: He wanted me to be a new fool in the world. God did not wish to lead us by any way other than this knowledge, but God will confound you by

AC 18

---

a. For background on the phrases *ad litteram* [to the letter] and *sine* glossa [without gloss], see FA:ED II 132 a.

b. For an alternate reading, see FA:ED II 132 b.

c. For a synthesis of the different paradigms of religious life expressed in these three traditions, i.e., the Benedictine, Cistercian, and Augustinian, see David Knowles, *From Pachomius to Ignatius: A Study of the Constitutional History of the Religious Orders* (Oxford: Oxford at The Clarendon Press, 1966), 1-41; Herbert Grundmann, *Religious Movements in the Middle Ages*, trans. Steven Rowan with introduction by Robert E. Lerner (Notre Dame, London: University of Notre Dame Press, 1995), 31-67.

your knowledge and wisdom. But I trust in the Lord's police that through them He will punish you, and you will return to your state, to your blame, like it or not." The cardinal was shocked, and said nothing, and all the brothers were afraid.

AC 21 ⁵One time the Lord Jesus Christ said to Brother Leo, the companion of blessed Francis: "I have a complaint about the brothers." "About what, Lord?" Brother Leo replied. And the Lord said: "About three things. They do not recognize My gifts which, as you know, I generously bestow on them daily, since they neither sow nor reap. All day long they are idle and complain. And they often provoke one another to anger, and do not return to love, and do not pardon the injury they receive."

⁶As an angel announced to him, Blessed Francis said that he had obtained from the Lord four things. Namely, the religion and the profession of the Lesser Brothers will last until the day of judgment. In addition, no one who deliberately persecutes the Order will live long. Furthermore, no evil person, intending to live an evil life in it, will be able to remain in it for long. Likewise, whosoever loves the Order wholeheartedly, however great a sinner, will obtain mercy in the end.

⁷Blessed Francis used to say that a good Lesser Brother is one who would possess the life and qualities of the following holy brothers: namely, the faith and love of poverty which Brother Bernard most perfectly had; the simplicity and purity of Brother Leo who was truly a man of most holy purity; the courtly bearing of Brother Angelo who was the first soldier to enter the Order and was endowed with every courtesy and kindness; the friendly manner and common sense of Brother Masseo, together with his attractive and gracious eloquence; the mind raised in contemplation which Brother Giles had even to the highest perfection; the virtuous and constant prayer of Brother Rufino who, whatever he was doing, even sleeping, always *prayed without ceasing* and whose mind was always intent on the Lord; the patience of Brother Juniper, who achieved the perfect state of patience because he always kept in mind the perfect truth of his low estate and the ardent desire to imitate Christ through the way of the cross; the bodily and spiritual strength of Brother John of Lauds, who at that time in his robust body surpassed everyone; the charity of Brother Roger whose life and conduct were spent in ardent love; the solicitude of Brother Lucidus who had the greatest care and concern and did not want to remain in any place for a month, and when he enjoyed staying some place, would immediately leave, saying: "*We do not have* a dwelling *here* on earth, but in heaven. Thanks be to God. Amen." 1 Thes 5:17

Heb 13:14

* * *

Another time,[a] some of the brothers told blessed Francis: "Father,   AC 20
don't you see that sometimes bishops do not permit us to preach,
allowing us to remain idle in an area for many days before we can
preach to the people? It would be better if you managed that the
brothers get a privilege from the Lord Pope: it would be the salvation
of souls."

He answered them with a stern rebuke, telling them: "You, Lesser
Brothers, you do not know the will of God, and will not allow me to
convert the whole world as God wills. For I want to convert the prelates first by humility and reverence. Then, when they see your holy
life and your reverence for them, they will ask you to preach and convert the people. These will attract the people to you far better than
the privileges you want, which would lead you to pride. And if you
are free of all avarice, and lead the people to give the churches their
due, they will ask you to hear the confessions of their people.
Although you should not be concerned about this, for if they are converted, they will easily find confessors.

"For my part, I want only this privilege from the Lord: not to have
any privilege from any human being, except to show reverence to all,
and, by the obedience of the holy *Rule*, to convert everyone more by
example than by word."

---

a. This concluding paragraph is not present in Manuscript 1/73 of the Saint Isidore's Library. Leonard
   Lemmens found it in Angelo Clareno's *Expositio Regulae Fratrum Minorum.* It is also found in 1MP
   44 (cf. infra 251-2, 251 a), and 2MP 50 (cf. infra 294, 294 b).

The Words of Brother Conrad[a]

[1]Blessed Conrad of Offida heard from blessed Brother Leo, companion of our blessed father Francis, that when he composed the *Rule* that we are still bound to observe, the holy father Francis was on the side of the mountain with two companions, namely Brother Leo and Brother Bonizo.

[2]These two were apart from Saint Francis, because he was down below in a cave, a stone's throw away. Whatever the Lord revealed to him in prayer, he reported to them. Brother Bonizo then dictated and Brother Leo wrote it down.

[3]So when Saint Francis went before the Lord Pope by whom the *Rule* was confirmed and sealed, Francis placed his hand upon it, swore and said that this was the will of God and no other. And he did this a second and third time.

[4]It is true that before he began the *Rule,* the Cardinal who was the protector of the Order said to Saint Francis: "Go, brother, and beg the Lord that He show you His will, because the Lord Pope and all the Cardinals love you and have placed great trust in you. Hence, whatever the Lord reveals to you will be approved and will be authoritative for you and your brothers." Saint Francis went off and did as the Cardinal had advised.

[6]Thus it happened that when the *Rule* was being dictated to them by our Lord Jesus Christ a great rumor resounded among the brothers throughout all of Italy that Saint Francis was drawing up another rule; thus each minister alerted another. So all of those in Italy gathered where the curia was and Brother Elias, who was then vicar, and they said to him: "We have heard that Brother Francis is making another rule, and we fear that it might be too strict. Because he is so hard on himself, he may demand some things that would be unbearable for us. So before it is done and confirmed, tell him." Brother Elias replied: "I have already undergone sharp rebukes; so if you want, you tell him. Not me." And because the holy father Francis had

AC 17// WSF 3

---

a. This translation is based on Andrew George Little, Pierre Mandonnet, and Paul Sabatier "Verba Fr. Conradi. Extrait de Ms. 1/25 de S. Isidore," in *Opuscules de Critique Historique*, tome I, (Paris: Librairie Fischbacher, 1903), 370-92.

this grace, that he was greatly feared and loved by everyone, a minister told Brother Elias the vicar he should go with him to Saint Francis.

¹⁰When they came near the place where Saint Francis was, but on the opposite side, not approaching him, for the place was a short distance, about two miles, from the city of Rieti, Brother Elias shouted: *"Sia lodate lo Signore* [Praised be the Lord]." At the sound of his voice blessed Francis came out, saw them, and said to Brother Elias: "Why have you come? Did I not command that no one come to me?" To which Brother Elias replied: "Well, all the ministers of Italy have gathered here because they were told that you wish to draw up another rule, and so they say you should make an observable rule, because if it isn't observable, they intend not to bind themselves to such a rule."

¹³Then Saint Francis cried out with a loud voice: "O Lord, You reply for me." And the Lord replied, in the hearing of all the ministers and Brother Elias, saying: "Francis, I am the one who is making this rule, not you. I do not want you to put in it anything of your own, and I want all the brothers to observe it to the letter." Then Saint Francis said: "Did you hear that, brothers?" So they all went back to their provinces.

¹⁵Blessed Francis re-entered the cave and spoke with God, like Moses in the tent or on Mount Sinai, face to face, and [God] said: "Francis, build me a wall between temporal affairs and your brothers." Thus blessed Francis put this in the *Rule:* **"Let the brothers not make anything their own, neither house, nor place, nor anything at all. As pilgrims and strangers in this world, serving the Lord in poverty . . ."** It is believed that the Lord ordered the whole *Rule.* But here I am speaking as he who wrote this, namely Leo. It is this *Rule,* dear [brothers], that we have professed, and in which we ought to advance, that is, to observe it without glosses. Thus did our holy father Saint Francis command, as he said in his most holy Testament: **"I strictly command all my cleric and lay brothers, through obedience, not to place any gloss upon the Rule or upon these words . . . but as the Lord has given me . . ."** The *Rule* was composed in the place called "Palumma," ^a near Rieti, and there the brothers dwell.

LR VI 1

Test 38

---

a. That is, *Fons Palumbae* [Fonte Columbo].

II. This is the prophecy that Brother Conrad said he had from Brother Leo, companion of Blessed Francis

[1]Blessed Conrad heard from Brother Leo, the companion of Saint Francis, that what had been done through blessed Francis was nothing compared to what was to happen in the future. So blessed Conrad asked him when that would be. He replied that it would be in the time of those great tribulations, but he did not say what it would be. Some have guessed that he would appear bodily in the world because of the questions and terrible tribulations that would arise.

III. A prophecy of Blessed Francis

[1]Once Brother Leo, companion of Saint Francis, sent a letter to Brother Conrad. In it were contained those terrible things that were to come upon the Order on account of sins. After some time he saw Brother Leo, and had it from his own mouth, as Brother Conrad himself tells it, that when blessed Francis came from prayer he always related something new.

2MP 71 [3]As *Moses* with God and God with him, so Saint Francis *spoke* with *the Lord,* and the Lord fully related to him future events, concerning not only the Order but also the whole Church until the end of the world. So one time he came from prayer seeming upset, and the brothers said to him: "What is it, father?" He replied: "While I was at prayer, I begged the Lord for peace for the Christian people, because it was revealed to me that many trials would come upon the Christian people. And so the Lord Jesus Christ was kind enough to appear to me and say: 'Francis, I am pleased that you beg for the peace of my people, but do this for me: that your brothers remain in the state in which I have placed them. And if in the whole world there remain no others, I promise you that for love of you and your brothers I will not allow another trial to come, except at the end of the world. But I inform you that the brothers will abandon me, and I will be forced to send them tribulations, though I will not do it as quickly as they deserve. Not for them will I delay, but for the world. The world has no second eye, and when it loses this one there will be no faith. But a time will come when I will call the demons and say to them: "Put scandal between the Lesser Brothers and the world, because I will not oppose you. And then those who want to be your brothers will have to wear your habit through the woods." ' " Ex 6:28

[9]Then blessed Francis replied: "Lord, how will the brothers be able to live?" The Lord said to him: "Francis, I will give them such strength and such flavor in plants, as the children of Israel had from the manna in the desert for forty years. Then it will be necessary that

the brothers return to their original state, willy-nilly, because there will be so many scandals and bad examples of the brothers that the good brothers will be ashamed to appear among people of the world. Then when the brothers go out for bread and say: 'Give us some bread for the love of God,' it will certainly be given them, but on their heads!"

IV. How Blessed Francis prophesied about the tribulations of the Order

[1]Another time when Saint Francis was at prayer he became intoxicated in spirit and placed his hand to his mouth and made as if he had a trumpet in his hand. And singing, like a trumpet, he said: "Many brothers, and few brothers!" Again he sang, saying: "The time will come when the brothers will go out for bread and it will certainly be given them: on their heads." He sang again saying: "Still a time will come when a brother will take off his habit or tunic on the road and will return to the world, and a person of the world will take it and go off with it to the desert."

V. Concerning the vision of Brother Leo

[1]One time holy Brother Conrad heard from Brother Leo, companion of Saint Francis, that Brother Leo once got up terrified by a dream to recite the hour of matins with blessed Francis. He told blessed Francis that he had had a dream that frightened him to no end. Saint Francis said: "What did you see?" He replied: "I thought I was standing next to a river that was churning and white. Many brothers were coming who had to cross it; they were carrying books and were drowned in the river. And I, while I wanted to cross, with this breviary, I would drown in the river. I threw it aside because otherwise I could not cross, and I crossed. [Indeed, I believe that breviary was cheap.]"[a] Then blessed Francis responded with sorrow and grief: "Brother Leo, those are the evil books that will destroy this Order. I hold that he is not a Lesser Brother who is not content to say the *Our Father*." I firmly believe this was to remove the desire and eagerness for books.

VI. Concerning a certain grace of Blessed Francis

[1]Another time blessed Francis said to Brother Leo: "Brother Leo, my son, there in paradise a certain glory is being kept for me which

---

a. In his commentary on this text, Paul Sabatier maintains that this is a copyist's written comment that eventually became part of the text. Cf. Sabatier, *Opuscules*, 378, n. 1.

no one else will have." It is believed that Francis said this after he had been assured of eternal life.

[2]The holy Conrad told how blessed Francis was always sad and lived with great sorrow, so much so that the Lord appeared to him to say: "Why are you so sad, Francis? Have I not forgiven all your sins?" Blessed Francis replied: "It is true, Lord, but you have not made me certain of eternal life." Christ gave no answer to this, so blessed Francis always remained downcast, and this is believed to have lasted several years. Because the Lord forgave blessed Francis every debt down to the last penny at the beginning of his conversion, he was assured of eternal life about the time the stigmata were impressed in his hands and feet and side. The remission of all his sins took place at Saint Mary of the Angels; the assurance of eternal life at San Damiano.

VII. A MIRACLE HE TOLD ABOUT BLESSED FRANCIS

[1]Brother Leo told this about himself, as if about another, saying in this way, that a certain companion of blessed Francis saw a miracle of his, in that going along the way with him, blessed Francis said to him: "Go back!" And he said this with vehement emotion. The brother was leaving him as quickly as he could, when he saw a piece of paper fall from the sky upon his head and swirl around his feet. The brother looked closely, caught the paper and picked it up. But what happened to the paper is unknown to this day.

VIII. A CERTAIN VISION OF BROTHER LEO

[1]Another time Brother Leo suffered a fever at night, and in the morning Francis called him and said: "Get up, brother, and come with me."

[2]Brother Leo got up and went with him without telling him that he had that night suffered a fever. He did this because he did not want to pass up the presence of blessed Francis. Then the Lord showed him this vision while walking down the road with our blessed father Francis. He saw the Lord ahead of blessed Francis, and the face of the Lord was looking at the face of blessed Francis.

[4]However, it is believed that whatever went on in the heart of blessed Francis appeared outwardly in the eyes of Brother Leo.

IX. How it was necessary in the beginning that the brothers be humbled

¹Brother Conrad told how, in the convent of Milan, a certain brother was received by blessed Francis in this way. Two brothers were staying where this man, who was a Doctor, was staying. When he saw our brothers he began to ask about their life, so they showed him the *Rule*, for it was the custom of the brothers of old to carry the *Rule* with them wherever they went.

³When he saw that the *Rule* was the expression of the Gospel, since he was a man taught by God and enlightened and correspondingly expert in learning, he recognized that the rule and life of the Lesser Brothers was the work of the Holy Spirit and was discovered and arranged as Christ revealed it to Saint Francis. And he said: "Brothers, I want to come to your life." The brothers said: "Sir, we have a father, Brother Francis, who accepts all those who wish to accept this way of life. So you must free yourself from the world and go to him in Assisi, at the place of Saint Mary of the Angels; and we will ask him to receive you."

⁶So he did everything he had heard from these brothers, and came to Assisi at the time set by the brothers, and there he found Saint Francis with the brother who had promised him assistance. Now he came with much baggage, well dressed, and on horseback. The brothers who recognized him told blessed Francis that some great learned man had come in order to accept the life of the brothers. He replied that they should bring him inside where he was with the brothers gathered. Then in the presence of that man he said: "Brothers, this one wants to come to our life, so I want to know what you think." And he began with that brother who had given him advice and said he would ask Saint Francis. Blessed Francis said: "Brother, what do you think of him? Should I accept him?" He replied: "Father, it does not seem to me that you should receive him." He questioned the other brothers similarly, and they all replied as the first one.

¹⁰Then blessed Francis said to the brothers: "Brothers, you have spoken well, for it does not seem to me that he is for us, and the majority of brothers is not with him. And if all of you had said that I should receive him, I would have received him." Then that brother who had been questioned first said to blessed Francis: "Father, you know what I think? I think this, that if he wants to do the cooking for the brothers, he should be accepted; otherwise not." Then blessed Francis asked the other brothers what they thought about what he had said. They all then said the same thing. And blessed Francis said the same. Then turning to that cleric he said: "Brother, did you hear

what the brothers say? What do you want to do?" The man stood there, stupefied and astonished at the brothers' words. Then he reckoned himself as knowing nothing. He replied: "I am prepared to do the cooking, and whatever else you want." Then blessed Francis received him and sent him to Rome to do the cooking for the brothers, and he did the cooking there for a month. Afterwards blessed Francis sent him another obedience, that he should carry out the office of guardian there and preach.

[15]Thus blessed Francis wanted the brothers to enter through the door of humility, and so both the wise and the uneducated should rise from strength to strength in humility, until the Lord inspired the prelates of the Order to exalt them with the grace of God and the virtue of humility, as long as they first have the grace of God and virtues, so they might teach others as much by right behavior as by teaching about the virtues and spiritual power, and produce a harvest of souls.

X. A PROPHECY OF BLESSED FRANCIS

[1]As Brother Leo writes, holy father Francis used to say in front of the lord of Ostia and many brothers and clerics and lay people, and also preached frequently to the people, that his brothers, at the instigation of evil spirits, would depart from the way of holy simplicity and highest poverty. They would accept money and bequests and all sorts of other legacies. They would abandon poor and solitary places and would build grand and sumptuous places in towns and cities. These would display not the status of the poor, but the status of the lords and princes of the world. And they would request and obtain letters and privileges from the Church and the Supreme Pontiffs with much cunning and human prudence and impudence. These would not only relax but destroy the purity of their promised rule and life revealed to them by Christ. Armed with these they would presume in their pride to dispute and inflict injury not only on worldly people, but upon other religious and clergy as well. And they would dig themselves a pit into which they would finally fall, and sow seeds from which they would reap many scandals. And Christ would send them one worthy of their worth, not a pastor but an exterminator, who would reward them according to their tricks and strivings. He would render them retribution and start war and bring upon a great trial as they deserved. Thus, they will be bound and ensnared in the lusts of their desires and will be punished by the just judgment of God. Then they will either return humbled to the state of their vocation, or they will be utterly torn from the life-giving and

salutary mode of life which they have sworn with a firm promise before the Lord to observe to the end.

[7]Blessed Francis also used to say: "Brothers who are led by an eagerness for learning will find their hands empty in the day of tribulation."

XI. A PROPHECY ABOUT OUR ORDER

[1]The holy Brother Conrad reported that he had had it from Brother Leo, who was the companion and confessor of Saint Francis, and he heard from his own mouth, that blessed Francis was once at prayer at Saint Mary of the Angels saying: "Lord, spare your people." Christ appeared to him and said: "I gladly grant you that, for it is of great value to me as well. But please do this for me, that your Order stay with me. But a time will come when they will depart from the way in which I put them. Then after that I will give power to the demons, and then if a son goes to his father's home for bread, he will give it to him like a stick on the head.

[4][“And there shall arise from your Order a Supreme Pontiff. In his time all these things will be fulfilled, and he will be blessed if he does well, but if not, he will die miserably.][a]

[5]"And if the brothers knew of the tribulations of those days, they would already begin to flee, and many shall flee to deserted places. But later they will come out and rebuild the Order in its original perfect state. But woe to those who congratulate themselves over only the appearance of a religious way of living, but grow sluggish in idleness, and fail to resist firmly the tribulations permitted to try the elect. For only those who have been tried will receive the crown of life, those who meantime are vexed by the wickedness of the condemned."

XII. THE ADVICE OF BLESSED FRANCIS FOR THE TIME OF THE ORDER'S TRIBULATION

[1]The advice of blessed Francis: namely, that in the time of tribulation, having taken on the *Rule,* his poor brothers would scarcely be able to hide among the faithful two by two. Some would betake themselves with tribulations to the lands of the non-believers and there find rest. Others would hide in the deserted places and be supported by some of the faithful. He himself, if he found himself in tribulation, would avoid it in order to persuade others to avoid it, lest

---

a. In manuscript 1/25 in the Library of Saint Isidore's Friary in Rome, this passage is written in the margin. In that of the friary of Ognisanti in Florence, it is incorporated into the text, cf. Sabatier, *Opuscules,* 385, n. 2.

they fail in the tribulation. And he would take on the habit and life of a pilgrim until the time of that dark tribulation should pass.

[3]Later the Lord would pour out the Holy Spirit upon many, and would call many to keep and reform the perfection of their life. And he described the sort of tribulation it would be, and predicted that only true lovers of God would escape it.

[4]Through the Holy Spirit he understood that the times of future tribulation were approaching. In those times, both temporally and spiritually, confusions and divisions would abound. The charity of many would grow cold, evil would overflow, and the power of demons would be more than usually unleashed, and the purity of his religion and of others would be disfigured. The prophesied departure and apostasy of both empires would be fulfilled, so that very few would obey the Supreme Pontiff and the Roman Church out of love of the truth. Further, one not canonically elected and corrupted with heretical depravity would be raised to the papacy at the moment of that tribulation. He would cleverly induce many to drink of his deadly errors. Then scandals would multiply and his religion would be divided, and many of the others would be shattered, because they did not oppose but agreed with the error. Opinions and splits among the people and religious clerics would be so great and numerous that, according to the word of the Gospel, *unless those days were shortened, if it* Mt 24:22, 24;
Mk 13:20, 22 *were possible, even the elect would be led into error,* if they were not sustained in such a whirlwind by the infinite mercy of the Lord.

LR I 2 [10]For this reason blessed Francis willed, according to what he received by revelation, these words of the *Rule:* **Brother Francis promises obedience and reverence to Lord Pope Honorius and to his successors canonically elected,** [11]he willed, I say, in what he adds, that is **canonically elected,** to show the necessary knowledge of discernment to that truly humble and poor, faithful and inseparable lover of Christ and his Church, according to the vow of gospel life promised. And in this way he willed to foretell the danger of scandal in the Church and to provide the remedy, namely that they should proceed cautiously and bind themselves more strongly and perfectly to their promised observance of the life and rule. When they see someone not canonically elected tyrannically usurp the papacy or hold on to it perversely when infected with heretical depravity, then, as he said, happy are those who persevere in what they have begun and freely promised the Lord to observe.

[14]For then truth will be covered over in silence by preachers or trampled and denied and held up to derision. But those of fervent spirit who will adhere to piety and truth out of charity will undergo endless persecutions as disobedient and schismatic. For then such

will be the insults and turmoil of demons and perverse men against those who walk simply and humbly that abandoned by all they will be forced to seek out deserted and solitary places, or cross to the non-believers, or scattered to lead a pilgrim's wandering life, having taken worldly clothing, or to hide out among some of the faithful, or to suffer punishment and death under ceaseless calumnies and accusations. And blessed, he said, will be he who in such a whirlwind is able to find a faithful companion. For those who persecute them, moved by evil spirits, will consider it a great service to kill such pestilential people and wipe them out from the earth.

[18]They do not understand that the demons turn all their force and fury to exterminate at its root all holiness of life and the truth of evangelical poverty and humility, which Christ had mercifully renewed through those two great heavenly lights, namely Dominic and Francis, and to test them, if allowed, right to their foundations. [19]When the impious act, they do not understand. For their eyes are blinded lest they see, and their back is ever bent so that, out of blindness, they may keep their intent yoked to evil. [20]Having provoked the Lord they fall from grace and incur eternal damnation unless, contrite, they are converted to Christ and see the ways to life and cease to persecute innocent and humble poor people out of hatred and oppression.

[21]The Lord shall be the refuge of the afflicted; he will save them and rescue them from sinners and free them because they hoped in him. For the Antichrist and his members wretchedly extol themselves against Christ and above Christ. [22]Then the poor and faithful servants of Christ, to be conformed to their head, will act confidently and will buy eternal life through death. They will not at all fear choosing to obey God rather than men and to die rather than assent to falsehood and faithlessness. [23]These, word for word, are the words of the companions of blessed Francis.

XIII. How Blessed Francis preached to the nuns

[1]The holy father, prompted by the frequent request of his vicar, that when he stayed at San Damiano, to present the word of God to his daughters, was finally overcome by his insistence and agreed. [2]When the Ladies had gathered as usual to hear the word of God, but no less to see their father, he raised his eyes to heaven where he always kept his heart, and began to pray to Christ. [3]Then he ordered that some ashes be brought to him; with them he made a circle on the floor around himself, and the rest he placed on his own head. When they saw their blessed father remain in silence within the

2C 207

circle of ashes, no little amazement arose in their hearts. [4]The saint suddenly arose, and to their astonishment, as his sermon recited *Have mercy on me, God.* When he had finished it, he quickly went outside.

Ps 51:1

[5]By virtue of this jest the ladies were filled with such contrition that they shed rivers of tears, and could scarcely restrain their hands from inflicting revenge on themselves. By his deed he taught them to consider themselves ashes, and that nothing should be allowed to come near their hearts that was not in accord with this consideration. This was his conduct with women, this visit so useful for them, coerced, however, and rare. This was his will for all his brothers whom he wished in this way for Christ, whom he served, so that they always be as cautious as feathered animals placed before snares.[a]

[7]Hence he once said: "I do not wish that anyone should offer to visit them of his own will, but I command that those who are unwilling and resist much should be appointed to serve them, only spiritual men who have been tested by a worthy and long-lasting conduct. Amen."

---

a. For an understanding of Francis's approach to women, at least as seen by Thomas of Celano, see FA:ED II 322 b.

THE TREE OF THE CRUCIFIED LIFE OF JESUS

Book Five

(Excerpts)

BY

UBERTINO DA CASALE

(1305)

Introduction

As Bernard of Besse was completing his trilogy on the history of the Franciscan movement and that anonymous friar was recasting Henri d'Avranches's *Versified Legend* in light of Bonaventure's *Major Legend,* Ubertino da Casale (1259-1330) was spending time with two friars whose influence on his life would be incalculable, John of Parma (c. 1208-1289) and Peter of John Olivi (1248-1298). After a decade or more of teaching in Florence where Ubertino was known for his critical views of the papacy, he was banished to LaVerna in 1305 and, in three months and seven days, wrote an inflammatory, devotional work, the *Arbor vitae crucifixae Jesu Christi* [Tree of the Crucified Life of Jesus]. This outpouring of his thought and frustration has been characterized as the "chief index to the Spiritual mind,"[1] exercising "an important and beneficial influence on such great masters of the fourteenth century as St. Bernardine [of Siena] (1380-1444)."[2] Ubertino's "index" is indeed "a mixture of fervent mystical rapture and bitter invective against all the enemies of the followers of the 'angelic state' destined to renew the Church."[3]

Born in Casale, a small village near Vercelli, Italy, Ubertino was a novice when Bonaventure died in 1274. He studied for nine years in the Couvent des Cordeliers in Paris, returned to Italy, and from 1287 until 1305 taught at Santa Croce, Florence. After his banishment to LaVerna ended in 1307, Ubertino was chosen to be chaplain to Cardinal Napoleone Orsini, whom Pope Celestine V (1294) had named Cardinal Protector of his Order of Poor Hermits, in effect, the first division of the Franciscan Order. Two years later, Ubertino became embroiled in controversies concerning the future of the Order. At first Pope John XXII (1316-1334) received Ubertino's advice with deference; within a year, however, the newly elected pope had him sent to the Benedictine Abbey of Gembloux and, in 1325, excommunicated him. The remaining facts of his life are not known.

From the opening paragraphs of *The Tree of the Crucified Life of Jesus* to its last, Ubertino cloaks himself in the mantle of mysticism. The very place of its composition, LaVerna, is reminiscent of Francis's own mystical experience of Christ Crucified and the seal of God's approval on his life, the stigmata. The title of the work, *Arbor vitae* [Tree of Life] evokes memories of Bonaventure's masterpiece of mystical theology, *Lignum vitae* [Tree of Life], focused entirely on the mysteries of Christ's life. Moreover, Ubertino writes in the Prologue that a certain holy woman from Città di Castello came to LaVerna to share with him revelations that would clarify his own thought. In addition to her counsel and encouragement, the unknown, mysterious woman prophesied that he would complete his work on September 28, 1304. Thus, in addition to the Apocalypse commentary of his mentor, Peter of John Olivi,[4] the writings of that *magnus Ioachita,* Hugh of Digne,[5] the declarations of the popes, and the stories of Leo and others, Ubertino was able to rely, he was convinced, on divine help. *The Tree of the Crucified Life of Jesus* emerges as "a devotional, even mystical work of striking power and vision," as Decima Douie characterizes it,[6] that marshals all the Spiritual arguments in defense of the primitive observance that was being subtly undermined.[7]

Faithful to Joachim of Fiore's apocalyptic view, in *The Tree of the Crucified Life of Jesus,* Ubertino describes history as divided into three ages,[8] each corresponding to one of the three Persons of the Trinity. The second age, pertaining to the Son of God, embraces the history of the Church and is the concern of *The Tree's* fifth book. Chapter One of Book Five enunciates seven periods in the Church's history: (1) the primitive foundation made by the Apostles, (2) its proven strength as seen in the martyrs, (3) its ability to define and defend the doctrines of the faith, (4) its profound anchoritic and austere life as seen in the desert tradition, (5) the well-being of monks and clergy with property, (6) the renewal of Gospel life and the victory over the sect of the Anti-Christ through voluntary poverty, and (7) the final period of contemplative participation in resurrected glory.

From the fifth period forward, when the clergy and monks begin to enjoy great wealth, Ubertino's narrative becomes profoundly pessimistic. The sixth period is ushered in by Francis, the Angel of the Sixth Seal whose mission is the reform of the Church by a thorough renewal of the life of the Gospel. While Francis is chosen to initiate this mission, the task of seeing it to completion is left to his followers who are bound to remain faithful to his way of life. Its energies enervated by opulence and ease, the Church is now devoured by the three concupiscenses symbolized by the horrible beasts created on the sixth day. And in this sorry state, two antichrists appear, one mystic, the other blatant, like the two high priests Annas and Caiaphas. In Ubertino's view these were Boniface VIII (1294-1303) and his successor, Benedict XI (1303-4), both of whom had allied themselves with the carnal Church, Babylon the Whore. Together they stand condemned by Francis and his *faithful* disciples of the most exalted poverty, the Spirituals.

According to Ubertino's testimony, the Fifth Book of *The Tree* was entirely "inspired" by the Holy Spirit. "It happened," he writes, "that at the first words of *Jesu futura previdens,* [the beginning of the ninth chapter of Book Four], I was forcefully seized by the Spirit of Jesus and impelled to describe His sufferings . . ." When this Fifth Book is read in light of the struggles of the Lesser Brothers during these early years of the tumultuous fourteenth century, the storm clouds are visible on the horizon. It is as if Ubertino had gathered in his text the tinder of the intensifying controversies dividing the Brothers and, with its publication, ignited an unquenchable fire.

One of the more practical results of Ubertino's *Tree* was the signal it gave the Brothers to scour their residence for the scrolls containing the reminiscences of Brother Leo and his companions. Thomas of Celano clearly had access to them in the preparation of *The Remembrance of the Desire of a Soul;* for his *Legends,* Bonaventure may have as well. At this critical period of struggling with the nature of Francis's vision, Ubertino expressed what others sensed: the unedited scrolls were of the utmost importance. Yet one has to wonder if, after *The Tree of the Crucified Life of Jesus,* it was possible to recapture the simplicity of that mid-thirteenth century vision of Francis's companions. For in its Fifth Book there are new images of Francis of Assisi with emphases adjusted to a new purpose.[9]

In the first place, Ubertino articulates, as does the *Sacred Exchange,* a theology of virtue in which poverty is seen as "the perfection and queen of all virtues." Ubertino, however, goes further in teaching that poverty "forms all those who yield to her wishes to the likeness of Jesus." Thus he describes Francis as completely united to Jesus through the practice of poverty: "Francis, emulator of the likeness of Jesus from the outset of his conversion, applied his every effort to seek out holy poverty and to follow her totally, ever eager to observe the likeness of Christ."[10] In doing so, Ubertino adds an important new nuance to the vocabulary of the following of Christ, moving from imitation to assimilation and beyond to conformity, a distinction he is careful to articulate:

> . . . he was not like the Son in a likeness of equality, such as Lucifer strove for (Is 44:14)—*I will make myself like the Most High.* His was rather a likeness of conformity; that is a likeness of learner to tutor, of recipient to adviser, of subject to commander, of imitator to exemplar. This properly occurs when our will is in conformity with the divine will, in the willer's motive, in the manner of willing, and in the end intended.[11]

Ubertino, in other words, sees the goal of poverty as bringing its practitioners into conformity with Christ. Cloaked in a subterfuge of biblical allusions and entwined in a sense of ecclesial mission, the pursuit of poverty becomes uppermost in Ubertino's mind.

From this perspective, Ubertino describes Francis as the "principal reformer" of the fifth age and, in the sixth age, establishing "a reformation of the life of Christ." The vocabulary of renewal and reform, already present in Thomas of Celano's *Life of Saint Francis,* is expressed more forcibly and, because of his perfect likeness to and conformity with Christ, Francis is portrayed as initiating a "new beginning of the Church." Ubertino clearly follows the apocalyptic thought of his mentor, Peter of John Olivi who also wrote of the renewal brought about by Francis. But the language of *The Tree* is the more provocative and inflammatory vocabulary later used by the Protestant reformers in separating from the Church of Rome.

The image of Francis as the apocalyptic angel of the sixth seal had appeared in Bonaventure's *Major Legend,*[12] but Ubertino, recalling a conversation with Peter of John Olivi, maintains that Bonaventure was convinced that "John the Evangelist actually had Francis, his form of life, and his Order in mind." From his Joachimist perspective, however, Ubertino furthers Bonaventure's thought by proposing that "he (John) beheld the fraternity of [Francis's] sons, who were perfect imitators of Christ, in all the verses he was writing about the sixth opening in the Apocalypse." The mission of the fraternity, in other words, is charged with the same mission as that of the angel of the sixth seal.

From his biblical perspective, moreover, Ubertino compares Francis in new ways to Jehoash, the young king who repaired the temple (2Kgs 12:1-12), the grain of mustard seed (Mt 13:32), Paul, the least of the saints (Eph 3:8-9), and, more extensively, Benjamin (Gn 42-46). Ubertino also places the Old Testament figures of Henoch and Elijah together and sees them prefiguring Dominic and Francis. But it is the image of Benjamin, more than the others, that provides insight into Ubertino's biblical images:

> Benjamin, in his birth, killed his mother; Francis, born in the midst of the fifth age, in the fullness of his birth through his reformed *Rule* killed its self-indulgence. Benjamin, in his sojourn, dwelt with his father in the land of Canaan, and (Gn 44:30) *his father's life depended upon his life*; Francis fully observed always, by the will of the eternal Father in heaven, a life of fervent Christ-like love, and what pleased the will of the Father was his adornment and repose. Benjamin was received by his brother Joseph, who revealed his news to his brothers at his arrival. Now it is said there that he made Benjamin's portion exceed by five portions that of the other brothers, and he gave him five fine robes, and afterwards he could not restrain himself when he said to the brothers in Benjamin's presence, (Gn 45:4) *"I am your brother Joseph, whom you sold."* Then the cup of the wise Joseph was secretly placed in Benjamin's sack, and he had him brought back first as a thief.[13]

This is a much different image of the biblical patriarch. Unlike the earlier medieval tradition, Ubertino does not highlight Benjamin as the contemplative but as the purifier, the herald of Joseph, and, eventually, the one betrayed.

The Tree of the Crucified Life of Jesus is a pivotal text among all the portraits of Francis, one whose importance cannot be underestimated. In the Fifth Book, Ubertino cleverly builds on his interpretation of history by placing the Founder, Francis, in the role of a prophet with a mission to save the world and the Church in a time of crisis. While this may be justified, Ubertino's re-casting of Francis as a "new Christ," a reformer of the Church, and as one rejected by his own, furthered the divisions already infecting the Lesser Brothers. When it is read with an awareness that the lost scrolls of what Francis's companions had sent to Crescentius had not yet been discovered,[14] the *Tree's* influence on the *Assisi Compilation,* the Sabatier edition of the *Mirror of Perfection,* and Angelo Clareno's *Chronicle of the Seven Tribulations* is evident. References to *The Tree* appear in Dante's Eleventh Canto in the *Divine Comedy's* "Paradise."[15]

And, as Charles T. Davis notes, "Its diffusion was very extensive, and manuscripts of it are scattered over Italy, Spain, Portugal, France, Germany, Belgium, and England."[16] Mystics and reformers alike revered its author, as they did his work. At the dawn of the tempestuous fourteenth century, Ubertino's *Tree of the Crucified Life of Jesus* became the spark and the touchstone of a new genre of portraits of Francis, the prophet.

Notes

1.Thaddeus MacVicar, *The Franciscan Spirituals and the Capuchin Reform,* ed. Charles McCarron (St. Bonaventure, NY: Franciscan Institute Publications, 1986), 20.

2. John V. Fleming, *An Introduction to the Franciscan Literature of the Middle Ages,* (Chicago: Franciscan Herald Press, 1977), 232.

3. Lazaro Iriarte, *Franciscan History: The Three Orders of St. Francis of Assisi,* trans. by Patricia Ross with Appendix, "The Historical Context of the Franciscan Movement" by Lawrence C. Landini (Chicago: Franciscan Herald Press, 1982), 54.

4. Cf. David Burr, *Olivi's Peaceable Kingdom: A Reading of the Apocalypse Commentary* (Philadelphia: University of Pennsylvania Press, 1993).

5. The term given to Hugh of Digne by Salimbene de Adam, who maintained that "he was a great Joachite, and he had all the books, in elaborate versions, that Abbot Joachim [of Fiore] wrote." Cf. *The Chonicles of Salimbene of Adam* trans. Joseph L. Baird, Giuseppe Baglivi, and John Robert Kane (Binghamton, NY: Medieval & Renaissance Texts and Studies, 1986), 228.

6. Decima L. Douie, *The Nature and the Effect of the Heresy of the Fraticelli* (Manchester: University of Manchester Press, 1932; reprint, New York, University of Manchester Press, 1978), 260.

7. Further background on Ubertino's work can be found in Marino Damiata, *Pietà e Storia nell'Arbor Vitae di Ubertino da Casale* (Florence, Edizioni "Studi Francescani," 1988).

8. Following the example of his mentor, Peter of John Olivi, Ubertino uses the word *status* to describe the three "ages" of world history and the seven "periods" of church history. He also uses *status* to refer to the calling of the Lesser Brothers. Thus *status* is used in a variety of senses, all of which are difficult to translate consistently. Cf. David Burr, *Olivi's Peaceable Kingdom: A Reading of the Apocalypse Commentary* (Philadelphia: University of Pennsylvania Press, 1993).

9. A thorough study can be found in Lorenzo DiFonzo, "L'Immagine di San Francesco negli Scritti degli Spirituali," in *Francesco d'Assisi nella Storia Secoli XII-XV,* ed. Servus Gieben (Roma: Istituto Storico dei Cappuccini, 1983), 63-122.

10. Infra 160.

11. Infra 185-6.

12. Cf. LMj Prol 1 in FA:ED II 527.

13. Infra 158.

14. Cf. FA:ED II 113.

15. Infra 881, 881 b.

16. Charles T. Davis, "Introduction," in Ubertino da Casale, *Arbor Vitae Crucifixae Jesu,* with an introduction and bibliography by Charles T. Davis (Torino: Bottega d'Erasmo, 1961), iii. Unfortunately, at the present moment, a critical edition of this work has not yet been undertaken.

The Tree of the Crucified Life of Jesus

Book Five

Chapter Three[a]

JESUS WHO BRINGS FORTH FRANCIS

[421b1]At the close of the fifth *status*[b] of the Church's pilgrimage,[c] the self-indulgent were teeming like oxen,[d] the avaricious crawling like reptiles, the arrogant as fierce as beasts, bringing an all-out defiling influence upon her life and causing her to be gnawed by a decep-

---

a. *Arbor vitae crucifixae Jesu*, Book V, Chapter 3: *Iesus Franciscum generans*. This translation is based on the reproduction of an edition produced in Venice, 1485. Cf. Ubertinus de Casali, *Arbor Vitae Crucifixae Jesu*, with an introduction and bibliography by Charles T. David, Monumenta Politica et Philosophica Rariora, Series I, Numerus 4 (Torino, Bottega d'Erasmo, 1961). The unnumbered folios are paginated as 421-434 and correspondingly throughout. For a general description of themes in the *Arbor*, see Marino Damiata, *Pietá e Storia nell Arbor Vitae di Ubertino da Casale* (Florence: Edizioni "Studi Francescani," 1988). The complete work, still awaiting a critical edition, comprises some 500 pages or 250 folios in the 1485 edition, with scattered references to Francis throughout, with the highest concentration in Book Five, selections from which are translated here. The numbering of the text, provided to facilitate the reader, is based on this 1485 edition.

b. Ubertino frequently uses the Latin *status*, a word with a variety of meanings. The editors have chosen not to translate it.

c. Ubertino writes of seven *status* or *tempi* in the history of the Church. The words, *status* and *tempus*, employed interchangeably by the author, are translated as "stage" i.e., degree of progress, or as "age." Chapter One of Book Five enunciates seven stages in the Church's history: (1) the primitive foundation made by the Apostles, (2) its proven strength as seen in the martyrs, (3) by its ability to define and defend the doctrines of the faith, (4) its profound life of anchoritic and austere life as seen in the desert tradition, (5) the well-being of monks and clergy with property, (6) the renewal of Gospel life and of the victory over the sect of the Anti-Christ through voluntary poverty, (7) the final period of contemplative participation in resurrected glory.

d. This image may well have been inspired by Canto XI of Dante's *Il Paradiso*, cf. infra 881 b.

tive, ungodly, and heretical horde.[a] It was out of jealous love for His Bride that Jesus was angry at her maliciousness, for great numbers of her children had gone the way of adulterers.

[7]Nevertheless, His anger did not diminish His mercy, and to the Church of the fifth age He directed a final call. Within her He raised up men of the loftiest integrity to root out greed and drive away indulgence. These men hated duplicity and stood up for the truth; they lit the fires of charity and restored the meaning of honor. They surpassed others in a remarkable imitation of Christ Himself,[b] and by the example of their life showed up a Church that was blemished. The word they preached stirred the people to penance, while the subject of their discourses confounded the distortions of heresy, and their praying was the shield that appeased the divine anger.

[18]Among these, the ones that shone brightest were Francis and Dominic,[c] whose prototypes were Elijah and Henoch. The one was touched by the purifying coal of the Seraph and aflame with a heaven-sent ardor, so that he seemed to set the whole world alight. The other, like the Cherub with protecting wings outstretched, bright with the light of wisdom, prolific through his preaching, had a most radiant effect on a darkened world. Those are the features they initially transmitted to their sons; although the resplendence and ardor of both these individuals must be linked to an extraordinary outpouring of the Spirit.

[26]The evil of the fifth age as a whole, however, lay in a perverse and widespread vainglory; the kind that is fed by greed and temporal affluence. Therefore, the man who thoroughly ruled out temporal possessions for himself and his *status* may be regarded as the principal reformer of that age. And since in him the Church's sixth *status* begins, and the "life of Christ" was to take shape anew in him,[d] we may say he is prefigured by that first man God *created* by His own   Gn 1:26

---

a. In the second chapter of this Fifth Book, Ubertino writes: ". . . It is sufficient to recall that the Church of that time had been reduced to such a state of humiliation that Jesus did not intervene by means of a new offspring possessing the spirit of poverty, so that the Church would have to undergo a judgment of death, as the calamities of heresy oppressing the Church's surface clearly demonstrates." Cf. Ubertino, *Arbor* V II 421.

b. For an overview of the development of the theology of imitation of Christ, see Edouard Cothenet, Etienne Ledeur, Pierre Adnés, Aimé Solignac, Bernard Spaapen, "Imitation du Christ," *Dictionnaire de Spiritualité Ascetique et Mystique* (Paris: Beauchesne, 1971), 1536-1601, 2355-2368; English translation, *Imitating Christ*, trans. Simone Inkey and Lucy Tinsley, with preface by John L. Boyle (St. Meinrad, IN: Abbey Press, 1974).

c. The close bond between Francis and Dominic emerges in AC and 2C 148-149, cf. FA:ED II 342-4. For the Dominican perspective, see FA:ED II 782-805.

d. Ubertino had already anticipated, in the first chapter of Book Five, the role of Francis: "Thus we can add to what we have called the Gospel *status*, the renewal in the Church by means of the least among the lesser, Francis, or to say it in a better way, by means of Jesus in Francis." Ubertino's view, in other words, is that Christ lives again in Francis and in him renews the Church, a theme to which the author repeatedly returns in this Fifth Book. (Cf. Ubertino, *Arbor* V 1, 409.)

deliberate counsel after the work of the five days *in the image of his own likeness,* that he might be master of all times.

[35]Take note that this does not mean that the saints of the sixth age are greater than the Apostles. For the latter, by reason of their unique following of Christ, must be excepted from comparison with all others. Yet from among these others Dominic takes his place in the spiritual reform, with his all-embracing, thorough, and complete spurning of earthly things. Each one of these saints fully and perfectly trampled mundane interests and commanded their descendants to do likewise. We have decided, however, to treat here and now of that man whose *status* is singled out for attack at present by those who are spoiling the evangelical life, just as from the outset it was under attack, only more forcefully, from crafty masters who reviled **the most exalted poverty.** So, let us turn our discussion directly on the man who, we can say, conspicuously represented the life of Christ, not only in the pattern of his behavior, but in the loftiness of his contemplation; not only by the extraordinary admiration he drew, but by that privilege that was his when marked with the wounds of the most holy passion of Jesus Christ.

LR VI 4

[Imitator of Christ]

[54]For if we are to talk of the way he lived, who is capable of telling in full how he sought to imitate the closest likeness to the life of Christ? His whole aim, in public and in private, was to reproduce in himself and in others those footprints of Christ which had been covered over and forgotten. And the unique privilege granted the blessed Francis was this: to be the first entitled to transmit to holy Church the life of Jesus, scrupulously in all its aspects, in a communal and durable state through his Order.

Eph 2:20

[422a4]In point of fact the holy *Apostles* were the peerless *foundations* upon which this life was laid, that is, after *the most important and principal cornerstone, Christ Jesus,* in whom the whole ecclesial edifice is built up, grows, and is completed. Nevertheless, as has been pointed out elsewhere, since the Synagogue was to be excluded for its sin of faithlessness and the Gentile world was not yet ready to take on such lofty standards, the Holy Spirit revealed to the Apostles that the actual *status* of Gospel perfection was not for passing on to all and sundry in those times. That is why they did not impose on the churches they governed the observance of that state of life which for themselves was prescribed by Christ and which they had adopted and observed to the full. For this was reserved for the third general *status* of the whole world's history,

when the Holy Spirit is manifested in a special manner, the time of the opening of the sixth seal, the sixth age of the Church, when she is to be presented with the life of Christ. Then is the life of Jesus returned to, as to the principle of perfection; it is as if a new circular journey were begun, a fresh beginning for the Church, as she returns to her first days.

²¹And that is why I told you earlier that this sixth age refers especially to the time of Christ. John speaks of this symbolically as the opening of the sixth seal *I saw another angel rising where the sun rises,* Rv 7:2 *carrying the seal of the living God.* Now, the abbot Joachim,[a] in his commentary on the *Apocalypse,* has this to say: "This angel is the one whom Christ looks upon as His like who is to come at the beginning of the third *status* of the world's history." Therefore, from the insight granted to Joachim, it is plain that at the beginning of the sixth *status* the world would be given an "angelic man" whom Christ regards as resembling Himself, since he is to appear as the one great restorer of the life of Christ.

³⁰I myself heard from a doctor of distinction belonging to this Order[b] that he was present when Brother Bonaventure, general minister at the time and himself a distinguished teacher, solemnly declared at a Paris Chapter that he was fully convinced that the blessed Francis was the angel of the sixth seal. He said that John the Evangelist actually had Francis, his form of life, and his Order in mind; that when he was writing, he saw Francis in spirit; that, in all the verses he was writing about the sixth opening in the Apocalypse, he beheld the fraternity of his sons, who were perfect imitators of Christ. Also at that Paris Chapter the same Brother Bonaventure stated, with a good deal of passion, as I heard from my source, unless my memory fails me, that he was fully satisfied no doubts could be entertained about all this, on account of significant and unequivocal revelations made to persons of serious caliber. I who write this am convinced, by the many testimonies of holy brothers of the past, that clear revelations were made to the blessed Francis and to many companions of his—whose apostolic life is beyond suspicion to the mind that is not dishonest, envious, or twisted—concerning the Order from its foundation, through its growth, dreadful decline and fall, to its glorious resurgence; rather like the sun's course, which in turn portrays the life of Christ. These things were revealed not to one

---

a. Joachim of Fiore, *In Apocalypsim et Psalmos,* (Venice, 1527; reprint: Frankfort: Minerva, 1961). For a succinct explanation of Joachim's understanding of the three stages of history, see Bernard McGinn, *The Growth of Mysticism. The Presence of God: A History of Western Mysticism* (New York: Crossroad, 1994), 337-41.

b. Most likely Peter of John Olivi (c.1248-1298).

person only but to many, and so explicitly that they recounted them with absolute assurance.

[Witness of John of Parma]

[52]Nor are we to omit the testimony of a holy man of God, one of the greatest men of perfection of our times, to judge by all visible proofs: I speak of that most holy brother, John of Parma.[a] He was General of this Order, a teacher of the highest renown, an excellent preacher; there were no bounds to his austerity, humility and charity, nor to his attaining contemplative heights and his pursuit of solitude. Distancing himself from all worldliness, he was devoured by a godly zeal over the debasement he saw in this institution and in the Church. Unflagging as he was in declaring the truth about this, he received the direst harassment and vilification, which he bore with the greatest patience. This did not deter him from passionately adducing the same realities before several popes and many cardinals. He most certainly deserves to be numbered, by those who sincerely love and imitate Jesus, among the seraphic heroes and with the celestial Church's great holy men.

[422b11]For the same man in fervor of spirit at an advanced age was bracing up his energies for activity, with the aid of grace, not nature; as though he were a disciple of John the Evangelist, he was willing to go and win back wayward Asia for Christ. He had obtained permission for this from the pope of the time, but while he was on his way and had reached Camerino, a town in the Marches, he was called to heavenly glory by Jesus, to whom he had been utterly devoted through observance of the Gospel and the *Rule* and *Testament* of the blessed father Francis. Of his glorification in heaven Jesus has given the world such numerous testimonies of this most humble one who glorified Him that I hardly remember reading of any saint with more numerous miracles for quite some time. For he raised several from the dead; from clear danger of death he snatched even more; he helped the blind, the mute, the deaf, the injured, the crippled, the withered, and those in need because of every kind of illness. These events were so numerous that, as little as he was approved by the carnal Church, which he opposed, so much the more does he seem to be gifted in the heavenly Church by the working of numerous miracles.

[29]Now this man used to maintain in no uncertain terms—which I myself with my unworthy ears have heard from his holy lips—that

---

a. For information concerning John of Parma (+1289), general minister from 1247-1257, see FA:ED II 18-20, 496.

the sixth seal begins with Francis and the Order he founded, and that the iniquity of the Church would be brought to a head by the shambles his life and *Rule* were in, due to his delinquent sons and those prelates who were wrong to indulge them. The Church I mean is the one that does not deserve to be called Jerusalem and Jesus' Bride, but Babylon and "Shameless Whore;" at whose judgment the "life of Christ" will be restored in all its brilliance, and at whose condemnation, in the sixth vision of the Apocalypse, the *Alleluia* is sung   Rv 19:1-8
with such solemnity by the holy ones.

[39]And yet I firmly believe that Jesus, who vindicates truth as His own, has displayed so many miracles when this holy man was invoked, that the frank declarations of the latter to an unspiritual Church, which were most abhorrent to Francis's degenerate sons, might be clearly authenticated for all who can see with faith, and receiving God's incontestable corroboration from heaven might be observed with firm faith and dedication.

[46]In fact, four years before his happy passing, I, who had always trembled at my transgressions of the observance of my promised state, heard a message expressed from his lips, while focusing on his angelic face. "My son," he said securely, "within four years God will tell you explicitly whom you should follow, and whose word of truth should be followed without hesitation." I was in Greccio where, on the Feast of Saint James, the eighth of the kalends of August, after the angelic man, leading an angelic life, heard the confession of my sins, I poured out my anxieties, because I did not know whom I should follow—for both the Church's prelates as well as those of the Order not only sustained this relaxation of life, but even imposed it. But he spoke in a manner opposed to them, and then, in tears and, I believe, kneeling at his holy feet in seclusion, he spoke those words to me.

[423a4]But four years later, I believe it was about the twentieth of March, he happily passed into heaven, continuing in that teaching, while I was living far off in many distractions and sorrows because of the imperfection of the *status,* pressed by the office of being a lector. On Pentecost, while I was tending to other matters, Brother Solomon, the minister of the Marches, suddenly appeared at our place with news of the death of John, a saint of God, and of the innumerable miracles with which he shone. Even though my mind had been preoccupied with other things, and I was not thinking at all about what I had heard from the holy man, immediately it was as if a lance pierced my heart. All that he had said brought back to my mind the Spirit of Christ's truth. It was as if I were seeing him before me speaking to my heart. "Look at him whom you should follow. For

God is not a witness to lying, because He confirms my teaching with such a large number of miracles."

Rv 17:3
Rv 17: 1
Rv 19: 11

[19]May these things be said as a memory and a testimony to that blessed saint, whom I do not doubt belongs to the angel of the sixth seal. I truly think he was symbolized as that angel who revealed to the admiring John the sacrament of the woman and the beast and *the condemnation of the great harlot* of Chapter Seventeen. But I believe that angel to be the one who had descended from heaven to whom Chapter Nineteen refers. For he descended from the life of heaven and from the throne of Jesus the King.

[26]And this man has individually a great power for observing the evangelical life in the midst of trials, and for bending the most stubborn necks of those who are more wicked. But the land of all the Church, that wished to produce new growth in Christ, has been enlightened by the glory of his life. These continually cry out in strength that the wicked Babylon has fallen from the true worship of God, and has revealed what was written in that Chapter of the Apocalypse. With all of his energy, he encouraged the chosen people to leave its midst.

[35]Therefore I heard that those holy imitators of Francis, indeed of the Lord Jesus Christ, who have suffered many persecutions because of their observance of the *Rule* and *Testament* of their father, cannot live the observance of the Gospel in the midst of Babylon. He counseled them to retreat to Asia until the pious Christ stoops to give reformers of the evangelical *status* to the Church, telling them beforehand that there they would be saved from the brunt of the storm.

[The Virtues of Austerity, Humility, and Obedience]

[42]So now, let us return to the perfection of Francis, whose identification with the angel of the sixth seal is borne out not only by external witnesses but by the excellence of his own life. He did indeed

Ps 84:8

come down from where the sun rises, as, ever rising *from strength to strength,* following the deeds of Christ as he grew in his humanity, he configured his holy way of living to the life of Christ. And this reached the high point of his carrying the seal of the living God; he lived to become worthy to have on his body the imprints of the wounds of the Crucified.

[50]Now, as to Christ's life itself, an attentive survey of the gospels will reveal its salient features, its most striking notes: the crucifixion, the profound humility, the extreme poverty, the fervor of charity shown by desiring our salvation in undergoing the torment of the cross, as well as by the sheer graciousness of His stooping to

compassionate sinners and the afflicted. Yet the crowning perfection of Christ's life lay in His interior cultivation and consummation of divine charity. In one continuous act, on His own behalf and that of all His members, He duly paid the service of worship to the divinity, to which in His own person He was united.

LMj V

423b1For the austerity in Francis's life, read his *Legend*.[a] There, despite its rather moderate treatment, you have enough about his amazing austerities to weigh in your mind. The fact is that the Blessed Jesus, virginal Son born of virginity, saw fit to transfuse purity into him, since complete cleanness cannot live in tainted flesh without a continuous crucifixion of self. That is why the most pious Jesus, in order to help us come to an austere crucifixion of our corrupt flesh for the preservation of purity, afflicted His own sacred flesh with many a cross as long as He lived. Francis, his true son and imitator, taking this to heart, disciplined himself so rigidly in regard to food, clothing, lodgings, sleep, and other similar bodily demands, that he scarcely took the minimum required to sustain nature. And although, after prolonged penance, his blameless body needed no chastising for any wrong, he continued to inflict hardships and burdens on it, keeping to harsher ways for the sake of others. So, he called his frail body an "ass," gave it endless hard work to do, provided it with coarse coverings and a bed of straw, and fed it with small amounts of inferior fare. In order to achieve full purity of heart he completely abstained from all familiarities which might inwardly defile him and give bad example to others. This meant that he recognized the face of hardly any woman. He further ordered every effort made to avoid, as a plague to purity, intimate dealings with women. It was because he was aware of spending his days in a valley of tears,[b] that he was habitually weeping.

LR XI 1

26All of this meant that he had become so candid in mind, so clean in heart, that he seemed to have attained the state of innocence at that time. For, as we read in his *Legend*, he had practically all creatures, even the inanimate, at his command; a level of grace, indeed, in which he surpassed natural innocence. There were instances of fire tempering its heat, water changing taste, the night sky shining like day, and a dry rock yielding a delicious spring. Thus did the elements put themselves at the service of the unspoiled Francis.

LMj V 8-12

33In deep humility and in eradicating all mundane glamor, he so perfectly imitated Christ that his wish was to place himself and his

---

a. A reference to Bonaventure's LMj V, cf. FA:ED II 560-8.
b. The Latin has *vale lacrymarum* [valley of tears], possibly a reference to the Marian Antiphon *Salve, Regina*.

Order at the feet of everybody. In order to be the least of all, he did not want to have any of the Church's authority, except her authority for observing the holy Gospel. He certainly wanted to promote the salvation of souls; but only through the virtue of humility, not with pompous power. And though it is very true that he had several Supreme Pontiffs at his beck and call—men who held him in the highest regard, sincerely convinced of his sanctity—even so, he would never ask for or accept any privilege that might diminish his being a humble subject. For he wished to be subject to all, and in this lowly subordination to be sacrificed for all in the charity of Christ.

ER VII 2; Test

⁴⁵Well did he know humility to be pliant: it is like something soft yielding to something resistant while, in effect, enclosing it inside its own softness; unlike inflexibility confronting inflexibility and bringing to naught both itself and its rival. For this reason Francis, in his holy *Testament,* forbids all the brothers, prelates, and subjects, to ask for any letter from the Apostolic See either to facilitate the work of preaching or to avoid persecution. The humble Francis used to say that when they meekly asked permission of bishops and priests, they were by their example edifying the very pastors of the Church. Then even if they refused permission, patience and humility will bring them to change their minds; meanwhile they themselves, by bearing the refusal patiently, will keep intact a virtuous and flawless way of acting. But if, on the strength of some privilege, the brothers presumptuously go against prelates' wishes, they are not behaving humbly and they only tempt prelates of lofty heart to oppose and malign them.

Test 25

⁴²⁴ᵃ⁶This results in a collision involving two tough courses of action, both of which cause scandal. And so, the word of truth is preached ineffectively, since no humility is shown by the one getting up to speak. If, on the other hand, prelates once or twice or even three times bar the brothers from preaching, and each time they react with humility and patience, then their conduct does the preaching to the people. Their holy example will soften the prelate's heart, who will not only give them permission but will look for them, so eager will he be to hear the preaching of such saintly brothers. The preaching of one such sermon will have a more uplifting effect than a thousand preached in a mood of contention and diminished humility. The truth of this was shown by Francis himself in the incident, mentioned in the *Legend,* with the bishop of Imola. Oh, how abundantly plain it is that Francis's approach was the more efficacious one! For there are so many around at the moment who are carried away with the "authority" they have and who brook no opposition; and yet one

LMj VI 8 // 2C

seldom is aware of any change of heart resulting from all their verbose sermons.

²¹To brothers who troubled him over their reluctance to be at this low level of submissiveness to everyone, he replied in deeply plaintive tones: "My brothers, my brothers, what you want of me is to give up overcoming the world. For Christ sent me to overcome the world by being really subject to everyone, so that by love I might draw souls to Him through the example of humility." And he went on: "My brothers, humble yourselves before others, and you will convert them all. Those who persecute you unjustly will turn to Christ, having seen your patience tried, and they will be anxious to kiss your footprints. But if I were to use the salvation of others as a pretext for wanting some prerogative, it would mean my forfeiting the humblest of positions which belongs to the condition I am in. And it is through this I advance in virtue, and the people advance in the mercy that saves them." 1 Jn 5:5

³⁴Things like this he told his brothers, as he wanted to rule out for them all affectation of ecclesiastical dignity and maintain them in their lowly existence. For this reason he called them *"lesser,"* so that they would not presume to become *"greater,"* and in no way did he wish them to aspire to the rank of prelacy. He once said to his patron, the lord bishop of Ostia: "If your lordship wants them to be fruitful in the Church, keep them in the state to which they were called and give them no permission whatever to rise to ecclesiastical prelacy." 1J VI 5; AC 49; 2C 148

⁴²As to how productive those are who have risen to ecclesiastical state from this and other Orders dedicated to poverty, those that know of it tell how grieved they are at their extravagance. For everybody knows well enough that their ascent to rank spelled their descent from virtue. Much of their behavior proves that what they sought in promotion was not so much an improvement of others' conduct as a life of relaxation for themselves. For, self-denying once, they have turned into gluttons; poor men once, they have become grasping and greedy; thought nothing of once, they have ended up proud and arrogant. They left the world when they joined their Orders, and as soon as they got rank, they returned to it. While they grease the palms of the mighty, they give no thought to the poor. They used to be the preachers, zealous for the salvation of souls; now they are among the worst offenders in neglecting souls. With every breath they collect temporalities for themselves and the benefit of their families. From the time they were infants in their Orders, poverty left them with nothing; now they seem bent on compensating themselves for that.

[424b1]Oh, what a true prophet Francis was! And what misfortunes this promotion business has brought on the Orders! For the intention of those striving seems to focus on this; in those that have some competence this ambition seems to boil up. So, they do the rounds of the curiae and make sure they lodge with dignitaries, on whom they fawn. Far from refusing favors, they procure them by all manner of contrivance, shrewdness, sham, and sophistry. They have reached the point where the saying is verified in them, "Like people, like priest"; indeed, like cleric, like ambitious and wandering religious. Is it any wonder that those who enter into this have no morally uplifting effect on people, but only cause them distress? All this is to say but little; words fail me to describe the malice of the times we live in.

[13]In contrast, the humble Francis, in order to keep himself on the lowest possible level and to confound the ambitions of the future, had no desire to be promoted to the priesthood. As he saw it, up to the manifestation of the Church's sixth *status,* the guidance of souls was not to be conducted through prelacy, if it were to be beneficial, but rather to be committed to the spirit of poverty. It is then that those who are like new apostles will be described as the pillars of the

Rv 3:12

future *status,* as Christ expressly promised the angel of Philadelphia, in which there is doubtless a figurative reference to this *status.* There-

Rv 3:8

fore it was said to him, that *"he has little power,"* that is to say, he has glorious humility. For the *status* of poverty first had to be tried in humility, so that afterward in a prelacy it might not be judged as a thing of high standing.[a]

[24]Because there are many who cloak their pride and, unsupported by privileges, cannot put up with clerical harassment, we can give a twofold reply based on sayings of the blessed Francis. One is that to men of perfection, which these are supposed to be, nothing should

Adm IX 3

be a source of bother except what would drive them to sin, to which, of course, no one is forced against his will. And if you speak of the many tribulations the clergy often inflict upon them and to which they are unequal, we must respond that such people simply should not embark on the way of perfection and, with their immaturity, wreck a state of perfection. Another rejoinder might be that these are the people who from the outset stood up to the clergy, while commandeering revenue—even though in a less obviously greedy way—by means of questing for alms and devotional stipends for Masses. For these reasons the clergy came down even harder on them. But if they had kept their humility and poverty intact,

---

a. Ubertino uses the word *status* in a variety of ways in this paragraph: the future status, a way of life, the state of poverty, or a position/state of prelacy.

harassment would have been sweetly borne; besides, they couldn't have had much to suffer, since they wouldn't have had anything to lose! Francis wanted them to flee to another place and do penance, if they were persecuted in one place instead of standing on privileges. He used to teach, according to the Gospel which we have promised to observe, that Jesus himself says: *If they persecute you in one town, take* Mt 10:23 *refuge in the next.* The most sacred *Testament* of the holy father Francis repeats this.

⁴⁶But how will this sound to those who, in the style of magnates build splendid residences, can scarcely be pulled away from where they grew up, even by order of those over them, and cannot tolerate holy brothers of other regions living in the same place? Those types have nothing in common with Francis; their portion, it is to be feared, must be in the devil's hands. But when they gladly hear that Francis and his state is the Church's reformation and the nourishment of the world, if he wanted others to be subject, how will they reform in pride? What we just said is true; for it is a fact that, apart from the blessed Jesus, his most humble Mother, and the college of the Apostles, never should the world have in it such a profound expression of lowliness as that of this *status* of poor lesser ones, nor indeed such a gross deformation of it as that of those who fall away. And because Francis crushed pride underfoot with his humility, he held off the proud demons with authority. Therefore he was showing that his *status* was blasting away pride from the world—something that will happen to these conceited corrupters of the *status*, much as they will dislike it.

^{425a5}For whoever, like Francis, keeps the humility of Jesus continually before his eyes and is delighted to resemble Him in meekness of heart, will subject himself to everyone and loathe issuing commands and prohibitions. The blessed Francis did commend humble obedience in the strongest terms, and observed it to the extent of always wanting to obey his brother companion. Still, he foresaw that there were sure to be those unprincipled enough to make the road of obedience a difficult one, issuing orders that contravened the poverty of the *Rule* while imposing absolute obedience on those under them. That is why he put in place a restraining clause to protect subjects, as well as those over them, when he told ministers not to be **commanding them anything that is against their souls and our** *Rule*, and subjects to obey in all things which they have promised the Lord to observe and are not against their souls and our *Rule*.

¹⁷This form of obedience, which the *Rule* contains, flows from the heart of him who said of himself, *I have come from heaven, not to do my* Jn 6:38 *own will, but to do the will of Him who sent me;* and to the Pharisees, who

Test 25-6

Test 26

LR X 1-2

Mt 15:6   were imposing their traditions on the disciples: *You have made God's word ineffective by means of your tradition.* For the obedience of Francis cannot contain a greater purity, integrity, or depth, since it obeys in all things and refuses to obey false traditions that destroy the *Rule*, for to obey them is to apostatize. Because it follows from the fact a prelate derives his authority from the *Rule*, that to command or obey something contrary to it is to apostatize from the *Rule*.[a]

²⁸But do we want to go on further with Francis's idea of obedience? He himself, after all, was in everything the least of all the lesser
2 Kgs 11:1-2   ones. Well might we compare him to the tiniest of infants, Joash,
Mt 13:32   who was rescued from the slaughter of Athalia; or to *the smallest of all the seeds,* the grain of mustard seed which grew into a great tree; or to
Eph 3:8   *the least of all the saints,* as Paul calls himself in Ephesians, entrusted
Eph 3:8-9   though he was with announcing hidden mysteries. *"To me, the least of all the saints, is given this grace, to preach among the Gentiles the unsearchable riches of Christ: and to enlighten all people, that they may see what is the dispensation of the mystery which has been hidden from eternity in God."*

Gn 42-46   ³⁷He might also be compared to Benjamin, the smallest of his brothers, who in many ways was a type of Francis: Benjamin, in his birth, killed his mother; Francis, born in the midst of the fifth age, in the fullness of his birth through his reformed *Rule*, killed its self-indulgence. Benjamin, in his sojourn, dwelt with his father in
Gn 44:30   the land of Canaan, and *his father's life depended upon his life;* Francis fully observed always, by the will of the eternal Father in heaven, a life of fervent Christ-like love, and what pleased the will of the Father was his adornment and repose. Benjamin was received by his brother Joseph, who revealed his news to his brothers at his arrival. Now it is said there that he made Benjamin's portion exceed by five portions that of the other brothers, and he gave him five fine robes, and afterwards he could not restrain himself when he said to the
Gn 45:4   brothers in Benjamin's presence, *"I am your brother Joseph, whom you sold."* Then the cup of the wise Joseph was secretly placed in Benjamin's sack, and he had him brought back first as a thief. All this can be found in Genesis forty-three and forty-four.

⁵³O Francis, true Benjamin! The first-born Joseph had you seated at the table of evangelical life with your other holy brothers. There your portion exceeds the others by the five portions of the sacred wounds, by which you receive five fine robes while those coming before you receive two. Now Christ first revealed Himself to the Jews,

---

a. This is the first articulation of an understanding of the authority of the *Rule* as superior to that of the ministers, giving special emphasis to the higher authority of the conscience.

His brothers according to the flesh; by your reformed *Rule* He leads the whole Church of the people of Israel to the evangelical life and the full news of Christ. But first the shame of theft precedes it: we see this now with our own eyes. Humble and despised, the cup of your brothers' evangelical wisdom and observance of the *Rule* and your most holy witness is contained, hidden, in the sack of the observance of poverty. In this cup Jesus, the true seer, sees the future in those little poor ones. And now, because of this cup which they carry, we see them treated like thieves, bound like enemies of Christ, whipped, excommunicated, and considered heretics, foreign to the blessing of Jesus.

[425b5]Like another Joseph, is Your heart not moved over your brother Benjamin? Why do You not retreat to the privacy of your chamber, that you might weep there out of compassion? Let the most merciful Jesus come out and fall upon your neck, so that the desire of both may be fulfilled. For the desire and the neck of both is one. He is Your brother, born of the same womb of Your most holy and poorest mother. Give the five robes of the glorious resurrection to Francis. Seeing them, he may dare to draw near to Your life, the gift of the Spirit of Your Father. Thus he may know that You truly live in the spirit of poverty and that, whether they wish or not, You rule over the darkness of the transgressors. For it is said of You truly in that passage, *"He is dead, and as if not dead,"* for he leaves behind him one who is like him, as it seems that in Francis You live again. So may this now become apparent, most merciful Jesus, in his offspring, that they may be reformed in the spirit of humility.

_{Sir 30:4}

[The Virtue of Poverty]

[26]We have already said that virginity, humility, and poverty were the outstanding signs of Christ Jesus and of His coming, and the first two have been somewhat examined. The third, poverty, has been constituted *the hidden treasure* by Jesus, Wisdom of the Father, for the acquiring of which everything must be sold. He himself led others by His example to observe it and decreed that evangelical perfection consists in poverty. For on this rock upon which the evangelical *house* is founded, no *floods* dashing into it can swamp it, no winds or downpours can shift it, no *gales* can knock it down. To this virtue Jesus has consigned the undisturbed possession in this life of *the kingdom of heaven;* whereas to the others He has merely promised its future possession. Because those who imitate true poverty in fervor of spirit must, of necessity, live off celestial fare. Because they give no thought to earthly wares and relish instead, during their present exile, the

_{Mt 13:44}

_{Mt 7:24-25}

_{Mt 5:8}

Mk 7:28 delicious crumbs that fall from *the table* of the angels, this is that most LR VI 4-6 exalted virtue of Christ Jesus on which His unique seal is imprinted on those who strive to observe it throughout the course of their perfection. For the one who shall espouse this virtue with fullness of faith, most fervent love and unsullied observance will be lacking in no perfection.[a] Not only is this poverty a virtue; it is the perfection and queen of all vir- LMj VII 1; ScEx 13, 16 tues. For she lays the very summits of all the virtues under her surveil- lance and above all, those who yield to her wishes she shapes to the likeness of Jesus, Son of God, by a renewal in which the perfecting of every state consists.

[52]Accordingly Francis, emulator of the likeness of Jesus from the outset of his conversion, applied his every effort to seek out holy Pov- erty and to follow her totally, ever eager to observe the likeness of Christ. He hesitated before no adversity, feared no menace, shrank from no toil, sought to avoid no physical discomfort, if only he could enjoy the embraces of Lady Poverty.

Sg 3:2 [426a][1]**This inquisitive explorer began his search** *in the streets and in* ScEx 5 *the squares* of the Church, questioning individuals from different states of life on how they loved Gospel poverty. The expression he used seemed obscure, almost uncouth to his listeners. None of them ever heard of it, recoiled from the very mention of it, and practically reviled him for questioning them. **"May the poverty you seek always be with you, your children and your seed after you." They said,** "We should be allowed to enjoy the good things of life in afflu- ence."

[8]When Francis heard this from those of a common state, he said, "I'll go to the supreme pontiffs, and speak with them. Surely they have long known the way of the Lord and the judgment of God. These commoners perhaps are unknowing and foolish, ignorant of the paths their own Lord Jesus trod." Yet those pontiffs responded more harshly. "What," they said, "is this new teaching we are hear- ing? Who could exist without temporal possessions? Are you better than our ancestors who gave us temporalities and occupied well-endowed churches? What is this poverty that tells us little? We do not know what you are talking about."

[18]Francis was amazed. Drunk with the spirit of poverty, he turned to the pursuit of prayer and began to invoke Jesus, the teacher of pov- erty:

---

a. In this section, until he comes to quote individual early brothers, Ubertino practically summarizes the *Sacred Exchange* (hereafter ScEx) and uses its language. He is, however, among those who have, incorrectly, interpreted *commercium* as "espousal" rather than "covenant."

[20]"O Lord Jesus show me the pathways of your beloved Poverty. I know that the Old *Testament* was a figure of the New, and that there you promised: *'Wherever the sole of your foot treads will be* Dt 11:24 *yours.'* To tread underfoot is to despise. Poverty treads on everything, and therefore she is queen of all things. But, my good Lord Jesus, pity me and Lady Poverty. For I, too, *languish with love for* Sg 5:8 *her* nor can I find rest without her. My Lord, you know it, you who loved me because of her. But even she sits in sorrow, rejected by all; *How like a widowed woman has she become,* she that Lam 1:1 was great among the nations, *abject and pitiful.* She, queen of all virtues, is now moaning on her dunghill because her friends have all betrayed her and become her enemies, and these are the very ones who for long have proved themselves adulterers and not spouses.

[33]"Look, Lord Jesus, how poverty is the great queen of the virtues, for the reason that You, leaving the angelic dwelling-places, came down to earth that You could espouse her in perpetual charity and in her, from her, and by her produce all the sons of perfection. And she clung to You with such fidelity that Your esteem for her began in Your own mother's womb, for You had, as is believed, the most diminutive of human bodies which, once it came forth from the womb, found its rest in the holy manger and stable. As long as You lived in the world, You so deprived yourself of everything as to lack even a place to lay Your head. Further, that faithful consort of Yours accompanied You loyally when You came to do battle for our redemption. And in the very conflict of the Passion, she stood by You as Your personal armor-bearer. And though the disciples abandoned You and denied Your name, she did not forsake You. Rather did she keep You, together with the whole company of her princes, close to those who remained faithful.

[48]"At that time Your own mother was alone in devoting herself to You and languishing with love for You as she joined in Your sufferings. Yet even for such a mother the cross was too high to reach and touch you. But Lady Poverty, destitute of everything, like Your dearest handmaid was embracing You more closely than ever before, her whole heart involved in Your torments. She was so deprived that she had leisure neither to smooth the cross nor put it together in rustic fashion, nor to manufacture as many nails as there would be wounds, nor yet to sharpen and refine them. All she could get ready were three, uneven and twisted ones to aid Your torments. Then, when You were dying of burning thirst, that faithful

spouse was there to assist You. For when You could not obtain
a little water, she made up a drink from what she could get
from shameful lackeys, which was so bitter that You could
only taste it rather than actually drink it. And so in the close
embrace of Your spouse You breathed Your last.

^{426b6}"Nor was this loyal spouse absent from Your burial.
For she would permit You to have nothing connected with
ointments and linen that was not lent by others. Nor yet was
Your most holy spouse missing from Your resurrection: for,
rising gloriously in her embraces, You left behind in the tomb
everything that had been lent for the occasion of Your burial.
You carried her with You to heaven, leaving to the worldly all
that belonged to the world. And You bequeathed to Lady Poverty the seal of the kingdom of heaven, for the signing of the
elect who wished to walk the path of perfection.

¹⁴"Oh, who is there who would not love this Lady Poverty
above all other things? I beg You that I be signed with the entitlement that is hers to give. I desire to be enriched with the treasure
she is. O most poor Jesus, I petition You, for the sake of Your
name, that this be the property my brothers and I will have for
ever, namely, never to be able to own anything under heaven.
And let this flesh of mine, as long as it lives, be sustained always,
though in utter frugality, by fare that comes from others."

²¹The Kindest One granted his petition by putting into his heart
and revealing to his mind an understanding of poverty's height and
gave him the desire to imitate it to the full. By a singular privilege—beyond all earlier saints—he wished him to transmit this to
his followers, so that it would be unique to his religion: never to be
able to have anything under heaven whatever as its own, but to live
by the strict use of the things of others.[a]   LR VI 6; Test

²⁷It was never Francis's wish to break his sacred association either   ScEx 36
with the Lady Poverty or Worldly Persecution, both of whom Christ
had as lawful wives.[b] On the contrary he wanted to love them both

---

a. The juridical concept of apostolic poverty as expounded in papal documents involving the total
denial of ownership and also the *ius utendi* [right of use]. All the Order retained was *simplex usus
facti* [simple use] of the lands, buildings, and goods owned by the papacy. For a thorough study of the
development of these concepts, see Malcolm Lambert, *Franciscan Poverty. The Doctrine of the
Absolute Poverty of Christ and the Apostles in the Franciscan Order, 1210-1323*, rev. ed (St.
Bonaventure, NY: Franciscan Institute Publications, 1998); David Burr, *Olivi and Franciscan
Poverty: The Origins of the* Usus Pauper *Controversy* (Philadelphia: University of Pennsylvania
Press, 1989).
b. Cf. ScEx 36: "the Lady Persecution, to whom God has given the kingdom of heaven just as he has
given it to me." Here Casale rightly interprets Francis's bond with poverty as that of humble servant
in an "alliance," rather than a "nuptial" union which is Christ's prerogative.

with an equal amount of charity, or rather with one and the same charity, since they are not really two but one. Therefore, in order completely to gain possession of the kingdom of heaven, which has been given to them both, he would have nothing to do with all those ways in which persecutors can be bypassed. It was because the rights of privilege stifle poverty and annul persecution, thus effectively divorcing a sacred marriage; for this reason, he wanted no papal document, no privilege.[a] All he wished for was that his poverty not be sullied. And now he grieves over being fraudulently despoiled of her by the conduct of his descendants. For this *status*[b] went *down from* *Jerusalem to Jericho and fell among robbers,* who did not *leave it half dead,* but completely dead! It now gives off a four-day-old stink, **since they shut it up in a tomb.** And having got what they wanted, they now boast about it in a wild frenzy. This disintegration the saint foresaw and fought to elude in no uncertain fashion his whole life long.

[45]His *Legend* speaks of what he found most offensive to look at, namely, anything in the brothers that was not completely consistent with poverty. He used to instruct the brothers to build, as poor people have to, little houses, which they were not to dwell in as if their own, but more *like pilgrims and strangers* in places belonging to others. By this he meant that if people wanted to evict them they were to offer no resistance, no right of their own or of another, no ownership, no clever ploy, or delaying tactic. They should simply get off other people's property and clear away, with complete trust in the Lord, in the conviction that they are now called, through the Holy Spirit, to go elsewhere, even if this means facing the fury of persecutors.

[56]And this is why poverty and earthly persecution are sisters and why the keys of the kingdom [427a1]of heaven are given them, not just in promise but to possess. For persecution is able to sweep away an entire world, while evangelical poverty has no power to defend what is mundane. The most prudent Creator made none of his creatures without its proper place; and since Poverty and Persecution had in this world no place they could call their own, he gave them heavenly mansions. Certainly *the unspiritual person cannot take in* these thoughts, nor do they make any sense to Lady Poverty's defiler, or to him whose dealings with her are a forced service and who craftily churns up his caricature of "poor use."[c] Yet those that have the spirit

ScEx 28

LMj VII 1-2

VI 2; Test 24

Lk 10:30

Jn 11:39

1 Pt 2:11

1 Cor 2:14

---

a. The Latin reads *idcirco nullam voluit bullam, nullum privilegium* [for this reason, he wanted no papal document, no privilege].

b. Once again the word *status*.

c. Cf. *infra* 146 c.

of Christ, who taught and lived poverty, have ears for these things and gladly observe them.

[427a12]The father's *Legend* says he ordered houses already built to be torn down or the brothers removed from them, if he noticed anything that contravened the poverty of the Gospel by reason of appropriation or expense. He said this was his Order's foundation, and the structure of the religion rested on it; it was strengthened by its strength, it was ruined in its ruin.   LMj VII 2

[18]That having been said, what sorrowful things actually followed! For if the most holy father's words are true—of course they are, for to cast doubt on them would make heretics of the sons who keep his *Rule*—we must conclude with sadness that we are looking at a religion in no sound state, in fact keeled over. There is not a single place from which poverty has not been brutally stripped. It is one thing the eyes of the world see plainly; it is commonly noticed that the most sumptuous and spectacular "palaces," those conspicuous for worldliness, are those built by so-called poor men.

These are the words and meanings of a certain holy doctor who professed this holy poverty and was its vigorous champion.[a] He inserted them in a treatise he composed about the exchange of poverty[b] where he himself was groaning over the evil things he saw. However, he couldn't have seen anything to compare with our situation. For it is as if a huge millstone were thrown into the sea and with great speed made its way to the bottom. Between that doctor's days and our own, the sheer weight of attachment to transient things has pulled so many of this Order down to the depths, that they no longer see it wrong to send poverty packing; they are more likely to regard being passionate about poverty as criminal and traitorous. Anyone who opens his mouth about the patent excesses in this field, especially if he criticizes the transgressors themselves, is branded as a public enemy. And I say this: if someone speaks of that poverty, which the perfection of profession indicates, all such things are removed.

[42]This, then, is what that holy man says, as he introduces the Lady Poverty's lament over her fall:

1 Jn 2:19   [44]"**There arose among us** *some who were not [of our com-*   ScEx 38
Dt 13:13   *pany], certain children of Belial,* speaking vanities, doing wicked
Rv 2:9; 3:9   things. *They called themselves* poor *when they were not,* and they
                   spurned and maligned me whom the glorious men about

---

a. Cf. FA:ED I 523-28 for background information about the identity of the author of ScEx.

b. The text has *de commertio paupertatis* [the exchange of poverty]. Cf. FA:ED I 527, n 1.

whom I have already spoken had loved with their whole heart. *They followed the path of Balaam of Bosor who loved the reward of wickedness, men corrupt in mind, deprived of truth, supposing their quest to be one of piety.* They were men who took up the habit of holy religion but did not *put on the new man* and only covered over the old. They detracted from their elders and sniped in secret about the life and conduct of those who founded their holy way of life. They call them undiscerning, *merciless, and cruel.* They accuse me, whom they had accepted, of being lazy, unkempt,[a] **crude, depraved, feeble,** and lifeless."

2 Pt 2:15;
Nm 22:28-33
1 Tm 6:5

Eph 4:24

Jer 50:42

[427b1]And much else does that holy doctor say by way of arousing lament over the breakdown of poverty which he could see developing.

[3]But we, at this point, do not need the words of others; we have acknowledged facts that not only provoke lovers of poverty to lament but, as bad example, cause general scandal to secular people. Moreover, the rich and powerful have reason to laugh at the type of excesses perpetrated by men who would like the name of being "poor."

[8]However, let us return to the saint's poverty. He was accustomed to call her at one time a spouse, at another a sister, at yet another a mother, at still another a lady, at another again a queen. And because he loved poverty with such generous faith, God, who provides for the poor, supplied Francis with sufficiency in his destitution. It was often a miracle that saw he did not go without food or drink or a house, when it was only too evident that there was no money, no facility, no natural resource to provide anything.

[15]What Francis's intention was in the observance of poverty he shared with Brother Riccerio of the Marches, a holy and noble man and dearly loved by the blessed father because of his search for poverty.[b] He responded when the holy father was lying in the house of the bishop of Assisi, weakened by the illness from which he eventually died. I place what he said in its Latin form, as that holy father who was the blessed Francis's constant companion, Brother Leo, wrote them with his own hand:

---

a. The *Arbor* has *insipidam* (dull, spiritless), a MS variant. A better reading is *hispidam* (unkempt, etc.).

b. Riccerio of Muccia is variously named elsewhere as Riccieri, Rizzerio, Rinieri.

[23]Brother Riccerio asked about the observance of the *Rule* on the point of poverty: "Tell me, Father, what is your thought today on the matter, and what do you believe it will be until the day of your death? So that I may be sure of your intention and of your first and last wish, so that we cleric brothers who have many books, may keep them although we will say that they belong to the religion?" Blessed Francis told him: "I tell you, brother, that it has been and is my first and last intention and will, if the brothers would only heed it, that no brother should have anything except a tunic as the *Rule* allows us, together with a cord and underwear." That is the saint's reply.

[35]Afterward the saintly Brother Leo tells how the blessed Francis told that he had received in a revelation that: "The religion of the Lesser Brothers is *a little flock,* which the Son of God in this very last hour, has asked of His Father, saying, 'Father, I want you to make and give me a new and humble people in this very last hour, who would be unlike all others who preceded them by their humility and poverty, and be content to have me alone.' And the Father said to His beloved Son, 'My Son, Your request has been fulfilled.' "

[45]And blessed Francis added: "Isn't it great that the Lord wanted to have a little people among all those who preceded them who would be content to have Him alone, the Most High and most glorious?"

[48]Therefore blessed Francis told that he had accepted in a revelation that: "He willed that they be called Lesser Brothers, because they are the people whom the Son of God asked of the Father. They are the ones whom the Son of God speaks in the Gospel: *"Do not be afraid, little flock, for it has pleased your Father to give you the kingdom;"* and again: *"What you did for one of these, the least of my brothers, you did it for me."* For, although the Lord may be understood to be speaking to all the spiritually poor, He was nevertheless predicting the religion of the Lesser Brothers that was to come in His Church."[a]

[428a1]Afterward the saintly Brother Leo moved to the question: If any brother wanted to ask why blessed Francis in his own time did not make the brothers observe such a strict

Margin references: AC 101; Lk 12:32; Lk 12:32; Mt 25:40

---

a. Ubertino continues quoting the entire *Intentio Regulae*, cf. FA:ED II 204 b. Only occasionally does he intervene to remind the reader of his source by some such phrase as, "Likewise the saintly Brother Leo tells us . . .", or to join different passages.

poverty as he told Brother Riccerio, and did not order it to be observed, we who were with him would respond to this as we heard from his mouth. Because he told the brothers this and many other things, and also had written down in the *Rule* what he requested from the Lord with relentless prayer and meditation for the good of the religion, affirming that it was completely the Lord's will.

[10]Afterwards when he showed them, they seemed *harsh and unbearable,* for they did not know what was going to happen to the religion after his death. And because he feared scandal for himself and for the brothers, he did not argue with them, and excused himself before God.

Mt 23:4

[15]The same one also says this, that one time a certain minister was asking Blessed Francis his understanding of the chapter on poverty. Blessed Francis answered him : "I want to understand it in this way, that the brothers should have nothing except a tunic with a cord and underwear, as contained in the *Rule,* and those compelled by necessity may have shoes." And the minister said to him: "What shall I do, for I have so many books worth more than fifty pounds?" He said this because he wanted to hold on to them with a clear conscience, most especially because he had a qualm of conscience about keeping so many books when he knew blessed Francis strictly interpreted the chapter on poverty.

AC 102

[27]"Brother," blessed Francis said to him, "I cannot and must not go against my own conscience and the perfection of the holy Gospel which we have professed." Hearing this, the minister became sad. Seeing how disturbed he was, blessed Francis said to him with intensity of spirit, intending this for all the brothers: "You, Lesser Brothers, want to be seen as and called observers of the holy Gospel, but in your deeds you want to have money bags."

[35]Although the ministers knew that, according to the *Rule* of the brothers they were bound to observe the holy Gospel, they nevertheless had that chapter of the *Rule* removed where it says "Take nothing for your journey, etc." believing, despite it, that they were not obliged to observance of the perfection of holy Gospel.

[40]Knowing this through the light of the Holy Spirit, blessed Francis said in the presence of some brothers: "The brother ministers think they can deceive God and me." Then he said: "Indeed, that all the brothers may know that

they are bound to observe the perfection of the holy Gospel, I want it written at the beginning and at the end of the *Rule* that the brothers are bound to observe the Holy Gospel of our Lord Jesus Christ. And that the brothers may always be without an excuse before God, I want to show with these deeds and always observe, with God's help, what God has placed in my mouth for the welfare and usefulness of my soul and those of my brothers. Because of this I have announced and do announce this to them and I want to show this to them by my deeds and, with the Lord's help, to observe this *in perpetuum.*" Therefore, he observed the holy Gospel to the letter from the day he began until the day of his death.

[54]Brother Leo likewise said that blessed Francis did not want his brothers to be desirous of learning and books, but wanted and preached to the brothers to be eager to have and imitate pure and holy simplicity, holy prayer, and Lady Poverty, on which the holy and first brother had built. And he believed this to be the more secure path for the soul's well-being.

[428b1]Not that he despised and disdained holy knowledge. On the contrary, he revered with great feeling all those who were wise in the religion, and all the wise, as he himself says in his *Testament:* "We must honor holy theologians and those who minister the divine words and respect them as those who minister to us spirit and life."

[7]But, foreseeing the future, he knew through the Holy Spirit and even repeated it many times to the brothers that "Many brothers, under the pretext of edifying others, would abandon their vocation, that is, pure and holy simplicity, holy prayer, and our Lady Poverty. And it will happen that, because they will afterwards believe themselves to be imbued with devotion and enflamed with the love of God because of an understanding of the Scriptures, they will occasionally remain inwardly cold and almost empty. And so they will be unable to return to their first vocation, especially since they have wasted the time for living according to their calling.

[17]"For there are many who, day and night, place all their energy and care in knowledge, losing their holy vocation and devout prayer. And when they have preached to others or to the people, and see and learn that some have been

edified or converted to penance, they become puffed up or congratulate themselves for someone else's gain. For those whom they think they have edified or converted to penance by their words, the Lord edified and converted by the prayers of holy brothers, although they are ignorant of it. This is the will of God so that they do not take notice of it and become proud.

27"These are my brothers of the round table, who hide in deserted and remote places, to devote themselves more diligently to prayer and meditation, weeping over their sins and those of others, whose holiness is known to God, and is sometimes ignored by the brothers and people."

31Later the saintly Brother Leo said the same thing, that he instructed all the brothers, the ministers as well as preachers, about work, telling them because of the office of ministry or of their zeal for preaching, that they should not abandon holy prayer, go for alms, and work with hands like the other brothers, for good example, and for the benefit of their souls as well as others. Therefore, that faithful zealot of Christ, while he was in good health, fulfilled what he taught his brothers.

40After these words the saintly Brother Leo said that twice, in two places with wonderful differences that I omit, he did not give permission to a novice possessing a psalter, even though he told him that the general minister wanted to grant it. But that devoted one did not want to have it unless with the permission of the saint who had already ceased the responsibility of governing the Order because of the relaxation that had begun to arise.

47On the second occasion, he said to that novice: "I was likewise tempted to have books. But, in order to know God's will about this, I took the book, where the Lord's Gospels are written, and prayed to deign to show it to me at the first opening of the book. After my prayer was ended, on the first opening of the holy Gospel this verse of the holy Gospel came to me: *To you it is given to know the mystery of the* Mk 4:11 *kingdom of God, but to the others all things are treated in parables.* They are many who willingly climb to the heights of knowledge; that person be blessed who renounces it for the love of God."

57Many months later, when blessed Francis was at the church of Saint Mary of the Portiuncula, at a cell behind the

AC 103

AC 104

AC 105

house on the road, that brother spoke to him again about the psalter. And blessed Francis said: "Go then, and do as your minister tells you." When he heard this, that brother began to go back by the same road he had come.

[429a5]Blessed Francis remained on the road, and began to think over what he had said to that brother. Suddenly he yelled after him: "Wait for me, brother, wait!" He went up to him and said: "Come back with me and show me the place where I told you to do with the psalter what your minister tells you." When they returned to the spot where he had said this, blessed Francis bent over in front of the brother and, kneeling, said to him: *"Mea culpa,* brother, *mea culpa.* Whoever wishes to be a lesser brother must have nothing but the tunics, a cord, and short trousers the *Rule* allows him; and for those forced by necessity or illness, shoes." Whenever brothers came to him to ask advice about such things, he would give them the same answer.

[17]The same Brother Leo narrated another time that while blessed Francis was staying sick in the palace of that bishop, one of his companions there said to him: "Father, excuse me, because what I want to say to you, many have already thought. You know how formerly through the grace of God, the whole religion flourished in the purity of perfection, that is, how all the brothers fervently and zealously observed holy poverty in all things, in small and poor dwellings, in small and poor furnishings, in small and poor books, and in poor clothing. And as in these things, as well as in other exterior things, they were of one will, concerned about observing everything that had to do with our profession and calling and good example. In this way they were of one mind in the love of God and neighbor.

[30]"But now for a little while, this purity and perfection have begun to change into something different, though the brothers make lots of excuses saying that because of large numbers, this cannot be observed by the brothers. In fact many brothers believe that the people are more edified by these ways than by those mentioned, and, it seems to them, more fitting to live and behave according to these ways. Therefore they consider worthless the way of simplicity and poverty, which were the beginning and foundation of our religion. Thinking this over, we believe that they displease

AC 106

you, but we really wonder why, if they displease you, you tolerate them and do not correct them."

[41]"May the Lord forgive you," blessed Francis said to him, "for wanting to be against me and opposed to me and involve me in these things that do not pertain to my office." And he said: "As long as I held office for the brothers, and they remained faithful to their calling and profession, and, although I was ill from the beginning of my conversion to Christ, with a little of my care, I satisfied them by my example and preaching. But afterwards I realized that the Lord multiplied the number of the brothers daily and that through tepidity and lack of spirit they began to turn away from the straight and sure way on which they used to walk and take, as you said, a broad way, without paying attention to their profession and calling and good example, or would not give up the journey that had already begun despite my preaching and my example. I entrusted the religion to the Lord and to the ministers. When I renounced and gave up among the brothers, I excused myself before the brothers at the general chapter saying that, because of my illness I could not take care of them and care for them. And yet, if the brothers had walked and were still walking according to my will, for their consolation I would not want them to have any other minister except me until the day of my death. As long as a faithful and good subject knows and observes the will of his prelate, then the prelate has to have little concern about him. Rather, I would be so happy at the goodness of the brothers and be so consoled, both on their account and my own, that even if I were lying sick in bed, it would not be considered a burden to me to satisfy them."

[429b9]He said: "My office, that is, a prelacy over the brothers, is spiritual, because I must overcome vices and correct them. Therefore, if I cannot overcome and correct them by preaching and example, I do not want to become an executioner who beats and scourges, like a power of this world. I trust in the Lord; invisible enemies, the Lord's police, who punish in this world and in the next those who transgress the commandments of God, will take revenge on them, having corrected men of this world, and thus they will return to their profession and calling.

[19]"Nevertheless, until the day of my death, I will not cease teaching the brothers by example and action to walk

by the path which the Lord showed me, and which I showed and explained to them. Thus, they will have no excuse before the Lord, and I will not be bound to render any further account about them or about myself before the Lord."

[24]Thus he had it written in his *Testament* that all houses of the brothers should be built of mud and wood, as a sign of holy poverty and humility, and the churches constructed for the brothers must be small. In fact, he wanted reform on this matter, that is, houses constructed of wood and mud, and in every other good example to begin in the place of Saint Mary of the Portiuncula. This was the first place where, after they settled there, the Lord began to multiply the brothers, and should be an external reminder to the other brothers who are in religion and those who will come to it.

[34]But some told him it did not seem good to them that the houses of the brothers had to be constructed of mud and wood because in many places and provinces wood is more expensive than stone. But blessed Francis did not wish to argue with them because he was very sick and close to death, and, he lived only a short time afterwards.

[40]This is the reason he wrote in his *Testament:* "Let the brothers be careful not to receive in any way churches or dwellings or any other things built for them, unless they are according to the poverty we have promised in the *Rule,* as pilgrims and strangers let them always be guests there." Test 24

[44]We who were with him when he wrote the *Rule* and almost all his other writings bear witness that he had many things written in the *Rule* and in his other writings, to which certain brothers, especially prelates, were opposed. So it happened that on points where the brothers were opposed to blessed Francis during his life, now, after his death, they would be very useful to the whole religion. Because he greatly feared scandal, he gave in, although unwillingly, to the wishes of the brothers. But he often repeated this saying: "Woe to those brothers who are opposed to what I know to be the will of God for the greatest good of the religion, even if I unwillingly give in to their wishes."

[56]He often said to his companions: "Here lies my pain and grief: those things which I received from God by His mercy with great effort of prayer and meditation for the

, present and future good of the religion, and which are, as He assures me, in accordance with His will, some of the brothers on the authority and support of their knowledge nullify and oppose me saying: 'These things must be kept and observed; but not those!' "

430a5But, as was said, because he feared scandal so much that he permitted many things to happen and gave in to their will in many things that were not according to his will. Up to this point these are the words of the holy Leo.

8From these passages it is very clear what a perfect zealot of the highest poverty he was, [a poverty] which must be called truly evangelical. They also make it obvious that ever since then the root of evil started sprouting until it is now grown and has produced the worst possible fruit. What a pain to his paternal heart it would be if, with his bodily eyes, he could see just how bad our times are! Yet he did see them in spirit, and was saddened. It was the cause, as the foregoing makes evident, of his giving up the office of governing the brothers; he was not able to prevent the course of future disaster. However, to the extent that Jesus will give us, we will speak of how this fitted into divine Providence.

[The Virtues of Charity, Piety, and Zeal for Souls]

18How Francis proved himself *the bridegroom's friend,* by striving to conform himself to Jesus through the fervor of his charity and desire for the salvation of those to whom he was brother, is evinced by the fact that from the beginning of his conversion to the end he blazed continually like a fire with an ardent love for Jesus. Fanned by the breath of the Holy Spirit, he kept the furnace of his heart ever ignited, so that once he heard the love of God mentioned he was as excited, moved, and animated as the beloved spouse, calling out continuously, *Sustain me with flowers, refresh me with apples; for I am sick with love.* All things created were a means by which he fired this love of his. 29Through looking on things of beauty he would contemplate the Beautiful; in frail creatures he could recognize the infirmities which Jesus in His goodness bore for our salvation. He made a ladder of every thing, by which he could reach the One he loved. Altogether special, however, was the love for Christ crucified which had such a recurrent transforming effect that he bore, not only in mental attitude but in bodily appearance, the likeness of the crucified Jesus. Our achievement of eternal happiness in the higher world was a passion that devoured him inwardly; he did not regard himself as

Jn 3:29

Sg 2:5

Mt 8:17; Is 53:4

LMj IX 1; 2C 165

Christ's friend unless he were all the time cherishing the souls He redeemed. Hence his exertions in prayer, his preaching labors, the lengths to which he went to give good example.

[39]The *Legend* has much to say on the fervor of this love, emphasizing that remarkable sign of his eternal election to the seraphic state, something he would speak about when he had *perfectly put on Christ*. When he was still in secular attire, he could hardly hear mention of the Lord's love without being transformed emotionally. To give, in exchange for a temporal alms, the wealth this love contains he called a noble extravagance, while those who did not value the rich offer of divine love he regarded as most foolish; for through the peerless love of Jesus it won for us an eternal kingdom and loved us so overflowingly, in the peerless love of Jesus, as to be the Love that must be greatly loved, so that we can say with the confidence of the Apostle, *"On account of Jesus and his love I count everything as loss and count them as refuse, in order that I may gain Christ."*

[52]It is in love alone that the worship of God is complete and perfect, and the whole meaning of the human nature of Christ Jesus was a perfect worshipping of God. He was worshipping, thanking, praising in the fullest possible sense, for Himself and for the sake of all creation; acknowledging the Source of all good and, through and in this worship, supplying for the deficiencies of all creation. Elsewhere this has been spoken about. We speak of His human conception as of the Holy Spirit. Accordingly, at the time He inaugurated His preaching, in order to show that this perfect worship of God by means of the fullest infusion of the Holy Spirit was fulfilled in Him as man, He said of Himself: *"The Spirit of the Lord is on me, for he has anointed me . . ."*

[430b5]In this perfect worshipping of God, Francis strove to imitate Jesus, being the zealous follower of His perfection. He was ever immolating himself over the fire of his soul; by rigorous fasting and other austerities he was offering up his body, a holocaust in the outer court, a burning of incense in the inner temple. His desire to undergo martyrdom, to be like Christ crucified, was so intense that three times he took on the hard undertaking of crossing to the non-believers; his aim was to be able to offer a rich sacrifice of himself by shedding his blood in honor of the name of Jesus.—Since prayer together with contemplation, in which true worship of God resides, will be spoken of separately, I shall here skip the subject.—But as things turned out, mere human hands were not to shed Francis's blood; instead, Jesus with His most holy hand mentally and corporally martyred and wounded Him with the pains and wounds of His most holy

Gal 3:27; Rom 13:14

Phil 3:8

Lk 4:18

LMj IX, XIII

LMj IX 1-3

LMj IX 5

LMj XIII

cross, so that the words of Hebrews might be applied to Him: *"Like the* Heb 7:3
Son of God, He remains a priest forever."

²²Insofar as it was possible and allowing for due proportion in certain areas, it was the entire life of the blessed Jesus, his most holy model, that Francis strove to imitate: Jesus' life spent as the price of the redemption of sinners, his daily exemplary conduct, his mirror-like contemplation, the mystery of his doctrinal instruction, his stooping to remedy the maladies of the frail.

LMj VIII 1, 11 ²⁹*Piety,* which according to the Apostle *gives power to all things*ᵃ was 1 Tm 4:8 so deep-rooted in Francis that he was moved by the deepest piety not merely toward those that shared his own nature but with everything LMj VIII 1 created. And spiritually it linked him with the souls Christ Jesus redeemed with His precious blood. Whenever he came to know they were defiled with any stain of sin, he would be overcome by such pity and tenderness and would shed so many tears, that he seemed like a LMj VIII 6-11 mother who was for ever giving birth to them in Christ. Even the ani- Gal 4:19 mals were closely drawn to him as though they sensed his kindly attitude towards them; hence he miraculously tamed wild beasts, domesticated creatures of the forest, taught things to the mild ones, and had brute beasts, that were by nature intractable to fallen man, bow down and obey him. Numerous miracles are written about in his *Legend* concerning wolves, pheasants, hares, fish, birds in abundance, and lambs and sheep. Is it any wonder, therefore, if this piety of his heart was carried farther in regard to Jesus' members, if it stirred him with such tender affection for the world of beasts? Nor is it a wonder that brutal hearts were converted by his most holy preaching. The saint's words taught them the lesson, his actions showed them the example; the glint of charity, brightly visible in his face, cast the javelin; gestures of kindly compassion brought them healing balm. And with one miracle after another, the whole world staged his testimonial.

LMj XII 1-2 ⁵¹It should not surprise us that it was God's inspiration and not his own boldness that impelled him to take on the mission of preaching. So full was his supply of virtues, so illumined was he by the splendor of divine truth, that two passions conflicted with each other within his heart: intimacy with the Bridegroom and salvation of his neighbor. There was, on the one hand, that strong desire to fly away and attend to that intimacy; on the other hand, there was the cry of the sheep in need of genuine fodder urgently requiring him to stoop to them in piety. It was his humility that addressed Jesus: *"I* Ex 4:10 *am slow and hesitant of speech, even since you have spoken to your servant.*

---

a. See FA:ED II 586 a, c.

The love to imitate You is what drives me to stoop down to my neighbor. Wretchedness draws me back, as I feel unworthy. But as I have placed myself fully under Your will, I await the word of Your command, since Your command has power to make up all deficiencies."

[431a7]It had been revealed to the holy man of God Sylvester and to the most holy consecrated virgin Clare, that God was pleased that Francis should go forth and be a preacher of good tidings. So eagerly and briskly did he set off, in accordance with the divine will, that it was as though *the hand of God were upon him* and he had been *clothed with the power from on high.* It was also as though the wisdom of Jesus were showing how Francis's preaching was providing people with wings—till then they were like plodding animals—that they might know and long for the things of the world above. The first push of his preaching was directed to a multitude of souls. But even at this stage there were indications that the Spirit of truth in him was moving swiftly to future things. [18]For through the Spirit of prophecy, to many he predicted many future happenings, and his preaching was not meant to convince *by persuasive language,* devised *by human wisdom,* but to demonstrate *the convincing power of the Spirit.* So unremitting was his devotion to souls, that after he had been marked by the Seraph's fiery coal and bore the wounds of the Crucified on his hands, and was unable to walk because of the protruding nail wounds on his feet, he had that body, which belonged to death, carried around to the cities and towns; so that, speaking as one crucified, he could inspire everybody to bear the cross of Christ.

[26]Most exemplary though was the temperance which he practiced in conforming to everybody else in the kind of food he ate, though when on his own he would get back to doing with little. He would leave the agitated atmosphere of crowds, to find out-of-the-way places suitable for lamentation. There he would water with tears of devotion what he had sown in preaching. And there, by thinking over his weaknesses he would wipe away any that had clung to him, by means of many an ecstatic contemplation and with the heat of a many-splendored charity. Hence, when his energy was restored through comforting intimacy with Jesus, he would return to the crowds in such fervor of spirit, that every word he said seemed armed with celestial bolts of lightning. [37]People of all ages and both sexes hastened to set their eyes on this new man the world was gifted with, and hear him. In dread of his power, demons fled the region. A host of the heavenly army attended in jubilation such magnificent praises of their Creator. The worst of sinners were converted; the still imperfect made headway; the perfect were fortified and filled with gladness.

Margin notes:
LMj XII 2

1 Kgs 18:46; 2 Kgs 3:15; Lk 1:66; Lk 24:49

LMj XI 3; XII 6

1 Cor 2:4

LMj XIV 1

1C 36

The Lord was working with him *and confirming the word by the* many miraculous *signs that accompanied it.* Mk 16:20

[44]Francis would not forget to retreat to a place of solitude at frequent intervals; engaged though he might be with crowds, by day or by night he would try to leave them, to give himself to contemplation on his own. He was continually recommending to his brothers this form of leading the life of preaching. Hence he wanted their places to be close to where people lived, so that they could kindly comply with their needs. Not so close, though, as to have no leisure, through over-involvement, no rest for attending to contemplation and prayer. What he wanted was to be near people while maintaining a certain distance; the places ought to be located alongside people and yet beyond where they actually lived, in quiet areas suitable for solitude.

[56]In this he was imitating his good Master Jesus, who showed His preachers of the evangelical life how to be at the disposal of others while maintaining the rightful demands of holy solitude. We read that for three reasons Jesus left the crowds. Once, for instance, the purpose was quiet refreshment, as in the sixth chapter of Mark when He said to His disciples: *"Come away to some lonely place all by yourselves* Mk 6:31 *and rest for a while."* But sometimes it was for prayer, as in the sixth chapter of Luke: *"Now it happened in those days that he went onto the* Lk 6:12 *mountain to pray; and he spent the whole night in prayer."* "He is forming us," comments Ambrose, "in the precepts of virtue through His own example." Again, it was to escape from human applause, as in the sixth chapter of John when they were going to take Him by force and Jn 6:15 make Him king, after the miracle of the loaves, and He fled back to the hills alone. Similarly, when He wished to give His teaching on perfection, in the fifth chapter of Matthew: *"Seeing the crowds, he went* Mt 5:1 *onto the mountain."* By thus taking His seat, not in the city or in a public square, but in the solitude of a mountain, He was teaching us to do nothing out of ostentation and to move away from commotion, especially when the time comes to talk about vices.

[The Order's Decline]

[431b17]Dear reader, you will be familiar with what David says in his prophecies: *Foreign children limped off to the side of the paths.* Now, one Ps 18:45-46 with a limp, even if he does it badly, can still walk on a path. So, those that are walking neither properly nor badly along the path of the *Rule* are not "foreign children;" they are *a tribe of rebels and scorpions* in Ez 2:6 respect of their own rule! They should more properly be called lions on the loose, or likened to that notorious wild beast that wreaked

such incredible universal havoc. For there is not a scrap of the life of Francis or of the *Rule* they professed that has not been broken, trodden on, and devoured by them.

[25]There is so much emotion in me, as I write these things, that my heart seems to be breaking asunder and I can scarcely keep my hand from tearing things up or my voice from crying out in anger! I can feel the pulse of interior happenings, but what I see is a link between rule and life, between father and sons, which is about as harmonious as that between black and white, between lamb and wolf, between good and bad, between those that convert souls and those that callously ruin them. For there are those who not only have no intention of observing what they promised but—and this has often been said and is often bemoaned—they harass those who do want to observe it. If you have eyes in your head, you can see they are not content with wandering around the market places; no, they must build their place right in the middle of them. Admittedly, they are not all in market places; but this is not because they don't want to, but because they can't always manage to locate them there. Wherever they are they find themselves a market place; by this I mean a multitude of people; they will crawl on hands and knees to draw teeming crowds to their places. Nor does it bother them if thereby they undermine the interests of some other *status,* gathering,[a] or person.

[43]It is all too clear that this proceeds from a conceited mentality, making the applause of the world and prestige their sole interest. If they say what they do is for the benefit of souls they can be told it is foolish to profit others at the cost of frittering away their own salvation and profession. Francis, surely, if I may say so, had more devotion to souls in his toenails than these ever had or pretended to have in all the disorder of the exercise they have undertaken. But would you like to see how false their claim to zeal for souls is, when their interest lies in temporalities, money, and mundane patronage? Take the poor or those not in a position to give them anything: they are not usually friends of such folk, nor do they hope to get burial fees and money offerings from them. Or again, they cannot bear to have in their vicinity another religious house which would care for souls, side by side with themselves. So, what they are after is not the care of souls; their aim is inspired by human greed.

[432a1]In order to conceal their mistakes they may make statements in abundance that are fox-like in cunning and craft but have no validity in spirit and truth. Anybody who knows, on the one hand,

---

a. Again *status,* in this instance referring to a religious order, as *collegio* [gathering] refers to a religious community.

the life they lead, and on the other, the *Rule* and most holy *Testament* and other utterances the blessed Francis made on a revelation of God, cannot but see that these transgress the life they professed and offer an insult to their father. However, I am not maintaining, here or anywhere else, that it is necessary for salvation that the entire Order observe the holy *Testament* and other works of perfection which the blessed Francis said pertained to gospel perfection. But what I am saying, unequivocally, is that to oppose the father's holy *Testament* and to have no mind to abide by his admonitions is to fall short of Gospel observance[a] and is, in effect, a sign of major backsliding. It is from here their decline from perfection began, until it ended in the mess they are in now. Admittedly, to keep the *Rule* in accordance with the *Declarations* and broader interpretations, which they have procured from several Roman Pontiffs, is sufficient for salvation.[b] But it is no way to observe that highest perfection which the blessed Francis said he received from Christ, and which he himself observed, and wanted for his brothers. It is, however, an "alternative way" and one that can indeed be called "evangelical perfection," as the Supreme Pontiffs themselves have said in their writings.

[23]But why waste time saying more?—when the fact is that, by the divine judgment, the more they sought solutions from these *Declarations,* so much the more did they end in a mess! Indeed, from the day Nicholas III gave the last *Declaration*—which appeared to be a possible exposition of the *Rule,* adapted to the kind of observance he saw in his time—it is as if the Order had a millstone hung round its belly and then, with all its later relaxations, has thrown itself headlong into the depths of the sea! I have experienced this, I who have stood in the ranks of the Order these many years. Even though he checked many obvious excesses, thinking to cure them, such was the degree of laxity that the medicine became lethal. He did prohibit some things in the strictest manner, so that people everywhere would shy off complaining about excesses the brothers were lax about, now here, now there. People today, if they compare facts to what is in writing, cannot but be aware that the brothers come out as transgressors of the very expositions, declarations, and broader interpretations they obtained for themselves.

[41]One is bewildered as to why an exposition is asked for regarding a piece of writing whose meaning is obvious; for there is no difficulty

---

a. Again the word *status* which is translated in this instance as observance.

b. A reference to the papal declarations of Gregory IX, *Quo elongati* in 1230, cf. FA:ED I 570-5; of Innocent IV, *Ordinem vestrum* in 1245, cf. FA:ED II 774-9; of Nicholas III, *Exiit qui seminat* in 1279; cf. infra 737-64. and of Martin IV, *Exultantes in Domino* in 1283. Cf. infra 764-7.

about the *Rule's* meaning. Instead, the difficulty is about bringing their life into harmony with that writing. Brothers were consistently willing to let their conduct plummet while at the same time seeking to harmonize their lives with a writing that dealt with the loftiest perfection. A solution to this harmonization they thought they would obtain through the authority of the Supreme Pontiff. But such a miracle would not be within even God's powers! For it would be beyond the possible, a fiasco and a deception, claiming two contradictory things to be true at the same time. Now, anybody of clear thinking who knows anything about the science of language, if he knows at first hand how these brothers live and if he reads the *Rule,* will certainly recognize two direct opposites, like being and non-being. They make a great case for their transgression, those who argue that evangelical perfection has not yet been given to the Roman Church. This is false, of course, since in Francis it has been given. It was corrupted, however, by some of his bad successors. There is no reason why it should be given anew; it should rather be revitalized through the infinite power and goodness of God.

Ps 106:35-37

⁴³²ᵇ¹It can be said with some truth of the situation that *they mingled with the nations and learned to act as they did. They worshipped the idols of the nations and these became a snare to entrap them.* And, what is sadder, *they even offered their own sons and their daughters in sacrifice to demons.* Almost universally their spiritual offices have been turned into agencies for simoniacal gain and fawning for favors—hence, sacrificed to demons. What else does the market place mean, where today's religious mostly build their places?

⁸Not so was it with Francis, whom Jesus, who is perfection, fashioned in the image of His own life, in the likeness of the way He Himself lived, in the perfect observance of the Gospel, that brought honor to him and salvation to his people; and did it in the most perfect manner human frailty could sustain and the measure of his grace

Gn 4:25

required. Truly could Jesus say in him, *"The Lord has appointed for me another child instead of Abel.* For in place of the apostolic choir, which was sacrificed in martyrdom and originally founded on the Synagogue, Jesus has raised up Francis and his *status* throughout the Roman world. Thus is it manifest how Francis resembled the blessed Jesus in the eminent level [of His way of life].

[The Prayer of Francis]

¹⁸The account of his life gives some clear evidence of how prominent the contemplative life was in Francis and how he loved his companions to give themselves to prayer. It was because Francis, ever

LMj X 1

growing in likeness to Jesus, realized that while he was at home *in the body he was exiled from the Lord,* that he had become, through the charity of Christ Jesus, altogether unaffected by external things and earthly desires. This made him strive, by means of unremitting prayer, to keep his spirit ever in the presence of God. Prayer was a solace to this contemplative who, going the rounds of the mansions above, had already become a fellow citizen of the angels, gazing upon

2 Cor 5:6

LMj X 1

their secrets. With burning desire he was seeking his Beloved, from whom the only partition separating him was his flesh. Prayer was likewise a safeguard to this man of action who, rather than rely on his own efforts in everything he undertook, would ask in persevering prayer to be guided by the blessed Jesus. By every possible means he would urge his brothers to be earnest in prayer.

LMj X 1

^{34}He was so constant himself in giving time to prayer that, whether walking, sitting down, working or resting, indoors or outside, he seemed to be always praying. It was as though he had dedicated to holy prayer, not only heart and body, but every piece of his activity and time. Many a time he was held in ecstatic contemplation to the extent that, caught up above himself and perceiving something beyond human experience, he was completely unaware of

LMj X 3

what was going on around him. He would seek out places of solitude and make his way to abandoned churches at night to pray, because the effect of solitude is to focus the human spirit on interior things, and intimate union with the Bridegroom is achieved far away from the gazing multitude. Although in solitude he was to undergo dreadful attacks from demons, that physically fought him hand to hand as they tried to impede his concentration on prayer, victory was his and, getting the better of them, he was on his own again and in a state of peace.

LMj X 4

^{50}In solitude he would fill the groves with sighs. There were times when brothers discovered him and could hear him interceding aloud that sinners might obtain God's clemency, and bemoaning the Lord's passion at the top of his voice, as though it were happening in front of him. At night he was seen praying with hands stretched out in the form of a cross, his entire body raised up from the ground and surrounded by a little shining cloud. The extraordinary brilliance around his body was there to testify to the marvelous illumination within his soul. In that solitude the secrets of divine wisdom were opened up to him, and it was there he learned what he wrote in the *Rule* and placed in the most holy *Testament,* and what he commanded

LMj XI 12

the brothers to observe. For it is also most patently true that an unwearied dedication to prayer and a habitual exercise of the virtues had led the man of God to such serenity of soul that, although he had no expert knowledge of the sacred writings acquired from scholarship, his mind could probe the depths of Scripture with remarkable discernment, and in the brilliant rays of a light not of this world. In solitude, too, he obtained from God a vivid spirit of prophecy, by which in his own time he predicted many future happenings which came to pass exactly as he had said they would, and of which many corroborations are given in the *Legend*.

^{433a14}It was also while in solitude he received the most vivid and lucid revelation concerning the progression of the Order and the path Christ wished the brothers themselves to take, that is, the path the saint himself unfolded to them by word and demonstrated by example. Nonetheless, he was shown simultaneously the disastrous path the brothers would in fact take; something he tried in every way to impede while he lived, and banned in his most holy *Testament* when lying on his deathbed, about to cross the threshold to Jesus in glory. To no avail, however, as far as the deviant were concerned, for their conceited, foolhardy prudence of the flesh and dogged rancor had prevailed. It was otherwise with his true sons, even though few of these survive, who in the light of all he said and of his most holy *Testament* carry on in the footprints of Jesus Christ, even while enduring much harassment from the unspiritual sons.

²⁸Yes, that most holy father, like another *Abraham, had two sons, one by the slave girl and one by the freewoman. The son of the slave girl came to be born in the way of the flesh,* and it is all too evident that his steps for the most part have been guided by the prudence of human nature. *But the son of the freewoman came to be born through a promise;* sure that Christ did not lie to his servant Francis, and sure that the same faithful servant, Francis, lied not in what he wrote in the *Rule* and the most holy *Testament*. Those who are like this son, therefore, are sure of their way through the depths of that same *Rule* and through the observance of what is written in it, and do not at all suspect it contains anything impossible or unobservable. However, just as at that time, the child born in the way of the flesh *persecuted the son born through the Spirit,* so now. It is as true now as of old that there is an *Ishmael* abroad, and he is a bowman shooting arrows at the sons who are true to the *Rule,* arrows in the shape of oppressions, censures, preposterous decrees, harsh pronouncements. But what is it that Scripture says? *"Drive away that slave girl and her son; the slave girl's son is not to share the inheritance with the son of the freewoman."* For to Abraham it was said: *"Isaac is the one through whom your name will be carried on. But the slave girl's son I shall also make into a great nation, for he too is your child."*

LMj XI 3-14

Gal 4:22-3

Gal 4:29-30

Gn 16:22

Gn 21:10-13

[47] We are asking, with great groaning of heart, for the expulsion of this slave girl's son, an illegitimate one as far as the *Rule's* observance is concerned. Not that we are asking that he be deprived of his paternal inheritance, should he be minded to walk the road of the *Rule,* but that he give up his deviant way of acting, his assuming a name under false pretenses, and his persecuting the legitimate heir.

[52] In fact the most holy father foresaw in the light of contemplation that all this would happen, and predicted it precisely. This is to be found expressly also in the sayings and writings of the holy man Brother Leo, his companion.[a] I myself have heard them from a man of proven virtue and saintliness, one of the father's true sons, revered and known far and wide, Brother Conrad of Offida. For fifty years or so he has walked the road of the *Rule* and most holy *Testament,* without murmur in the midst of *a stubborn and rebellious generation,* regarding himself as rich if he had **a tunic, cord and short trousers.** And yet it is an established fact that he has undergone innumerable persecutions and inquisitions at the hands of those who are no true sons, as if he were a heretic. All for observing the *Rule,* and also despite the fact that people who lament the misfortunes that have come to pass revere him as a father . . .

Ps 78:8

Test 16-7

[433b12] I have often heard this holy man Brother Conrad say that he himself heard of the things we have been speaking about, and many others of even greater moment, from the holy man Brother Leo, and also from the holy fathers, Brother Masseo and Brother Cesolo,[b] and from several other associates of the holy man, who himself waits, not without tears and a certain compassionate longing, for them to be over and done with.

[Brother Giles of Assisi]

[17] I have also heard from a great number of brothers, who lived in close acquaintance with Brother Giles, one of the saintliest of our fathers, many of the opinions of our antecedents and of things predicted by many of the early brothers and by that same holy father, which appeared incredible until they actually came true. Now, as that holy man, dear to God, Brother Masseo, knight of Perugia, recently gone to heaven, often told me with tears, the holy man Giles used to wail aloud at the way the *Rule* was being destroyed before his

---

a. Ubertino does not limit his references to the memoirs of Leo, but refers to the records of other brothers, such as Conrad of Offida (who entered the Order in 1250 and died in 1306).

b. Masseo of Marignano (+ 1280). Cesolo: a brother by this name cannot be identified among the "fathers" of the Order; the text here may be corrupt, and it is supposed that another name, such as "Angelo," should be read. Angelo Tancredi of Rieti, one of the first of Francis's companions, sometime called "Agnolo," e.g., in *The Little Flowers of Saint Francis,* 26 (hereafter LFl).

eyes; so much so that those who were ignorant of the way of the Spirit thought he was insane. Nor could Giles bear it any longer, were it not that on numerous occasions Christ Jesus assured him the ruinous action would end, the most holy *Rule* would be restored and the whole Church renewed.

[29]But who is able to give an adequate account of the saintliness of that holy man Giles? He was the fourth Lesser Brother, the third of the father's true sons. He started out by throwing himself vigorously into the active life. He was a real Martha. He was to be seen as one whose hands were full continually, with so many virtues to be practiced, active ministries to be engaged in, like manual labor, looking after lepers, and other humble tasks. He stayed at this until the day he was caught up in contemplation under the influence of Jesus' love, when he appeared to be more at home in the heavenly city than in the earthly one, though still living in the flesh. Many who witnessed it told me, that as soon as the glory of Paradise was mentioned, he went into ecstasy at the pleasure of it.

[41]Here was a man who, when he saw aspiring lectors or those ambitious to do studies, would, mockingly, make a trumpet of his two fists. This study and science of theirs, he would elucidate, was all for celebrity and worldly flourish, like the hollow sound of a trumpet!

[45]Here was a man who, as he witnessed the wanton pride conceited sons were taking in the miracles of their holy father, said he had procured from the Lord the favor that no ostentatious building be erected to honor his miracles. Moreover, those who led useless lives, he said, had no cause to boast of having the holiest forefathers, unwilling as they are to follow the path they trod. Because of the evident sanctity of that most blessed holy father Giles, the signs of which were openly witnessed everywhere, many brothers were expecting the same, if not even greater, things from him as they were experiencing from the blessed father Francis. Giles, through the activity of the Spirit, was not unaware of this; and that is why, I am told, he responded to it in the way I have just cited. He further said that nothing offensive to the *Rule* was to be built to honor any good he did, such as an extravagant edifice to acknowledge miracles, which, after all, they obtain from the Lord; they were to spare no effort to refrain from anything that would redound to the detriment of the saints. Nevertheless, due to the undoubted devotion he had to his holy father, the blessed Francis, he supported the idea of building a noteworthy church over the spot where the Saint's body lay, if only to impress upon people insensitive to the spiritual how eminently holy he was. But from all other buildings he shrank in horror.

^{434a6}It is not possible to give a brief description of the virtues, contemplative life, and almost continuous ecstasy, which this holy father Giles persevered in and practiced to the end of his life; the life of holiness he led would require a special volume to itself, and that a big one.

¹⁰The third way in which the evangelical man Francis resembled the blessed Jesus was in the prophetic wonders he wrought. Hence fittingly can that line of Ecclesiasticus be cited in his regard: *He made him like the saints in glory.* To be like the saints in glory, in this life, is to be renowned for miracles; by this the blessed Francis resembled Jesus in a very special way. Let us turn to what has been written down.

Sir 45:2

LMj V 10

LMj XII 6

¹⁵Like Jesus he changed water into wine, multiplied loaves of bread. From a boat—which had miraculously stayed still, surrounded by waves—after he had brought it to land, he taught the crowds on the shore who had come to listen. Every creature was seen to obey his command, as though in him primordial innocence had been restored. Not to mention everything, he restored sight to the blind, cured the deaf, the lame, the paralyzed, those going through all kinds of infirmities, cleansed lepers, drove out demons, rescued captives, helped the shipwrecked, and resuscitated very many dead persons. In all this, surely, since the days of the primitive Church, his like has not been found, nor a renown like his, for so many miracles in life and in death.

Mj Mir VII, VIII

²⁷The fourth resemblance to Jesus lay in his possessing privileged authorization. Most fittingly can that verse of the third chapter of Daniel be cited in his regard: *the form of the fourth is like the son of God.* He was fourth among the chief Levites: Stephen, Lawrence, Vincent, and Francis. He was also fourth among the founding fathers of Orders: Benedict, Augustine, Dominic, and Francis, as far as the Latins are concerned; for among the Greeks, it was the renowned Basil who first composed a *Rule,* and his appears to come closest to the perfection of the Gospel.

Dn 3:42

³⁵This, then, is Francis the standard-bearer, holding

> the seal of authority,
> the standard of activity,
> and the signet of charity.

More will be said about these later.

Is 44:14

[39]What emerges is that he was not like the Son in a resemblance of equality, such as Lucifer strove for —*I will make myself like the Most High*. His was rather a likeness of conformity; the kind that develops between learner and tutor, recipient and adviser, subject and commander, imitator and exemplar. This properly occurs when our will is in conformity with the divine will, in the willer's motive, in the manner of willing, and in the end intended. So that what is willed is goodness, what motivates is charity, what dictates the method is generosity, and the end is the delight of God at seeing His will accomplished in all things. Yet beyond these resemblances, there was in Francis that extraordinary likeness which was sealed upon his body. This being quite incommunicable, it is permissible to ask in wonder,

Ps 89:7

"Who among the sons of God is like God?" This man was, however, in an exceptional fashion a son of God and of the blessed Jesus.

He was
subject to Him to do Him honor;
attentive to imitate Him;
pleasing to recognize Him
prompt to obey,
configured to witness,
and to go forth to win and transform a whole world,
furnished with a seal to inflame it,
and to bring those willing to follow
the perfect likeness of the Crucified.

Lk 7:32

[434b1]But alas! *To what shall I compare the men of this generation,* who have strayed from the path of their father? *They are like children sitting in the market place and calling to one another.* They are like children, out to enjoy themselves; sitting in the market place, just lazing about; and calling to one another, a troublesome lot! And what are they talking

Lk 24:14

about? Not indeed about what happened at Christ's passion, as were those who were walking to Emmaus! No, nor about their own pretensions and worldly gossip; for they are full of bustle. The little ones, who must live among them, have to go through all this bustle which has issued from their avidity, their acquisition of property, their extinction of charity, their profusion of conceit; they feel like small boats tossed about in a stormy sea by the tempestuous corruption of this institution on the part of those I have been talking about. Four ill winds are these of the worst type, that do battle over this wide and rough sea.

Mt 14:25; Mk 6:48

Now that *the fourth watch of the night* is already with us and it will soon be dawn, would that Jesus came to us, with our father Francis, and

Mk 4:39; Lk 8:24

helped us to *subdue these waves* of wrongdoing!

Chapter Four

JESUS THE WINGED SERAPH[a]

[18]The holy man Francis, beloved of God, had already, in his holy way of living, portrayed the life of Jesus the Redeemer, which the world had consigned to oblivion, and had set it out in his evangelical *Rule,* as we shall show further on, so that it should be truly evident to all the world that what he was illustrating, both in the *Rule* and in the life he led, was the life of Jesus the Savior himself. Jesus in his exceeding goodness and mercy knew what the evangelical *Rule* of Francis and the perfect transformation he had brought about would have to endure from a future generation's persecutions, unfortunate expositions, and infringements. He would leave no one in doubt that the perpetrators were the progeny of a dead system, being opponents of a crucified Jesus. Within a short time after the *Rule's* institution, He would furnish with the seal of His high priesthood both the life of Francis and the established *Rule,* through a miracle unheard of in previous ages, by imprinting on the flesh of the blessed Francis the likeness of the wounds of His own most sacred passion. Christ's standard-bearer was Francis as he carried these on his sacred body for two years. Defying nature, he lived on with his side opened; blood flowed from it; a memorial of the blood of the living God, shed for us. Breathtaking are these signs; they call for maximum veneration of the Saint and love of the exceedingly good Jesus. They make for an unshakable confidence in those contemplating the following of Jesus.

They are reminders of God;
they are evidence of the sanctity of the man;
they are indications of what we are to be.
For by this sublime imprinting,
Jesus, in His exceeding goodness, demonstrated:

---

a. *Arbor* V, chap. 4: 434-443: a long meditation on the most marvelous of the signs of Francis's assimilation to Christ, spiritually and physically, namely, the privilege of the stigmata. In this chapter Casale, while keeping his eye on LMj XIII and its epilogue on the Miracles I, gives himself free rein as mystical theologian.

187

His benevolent approval of Francis,
His divine providence in sustaining him,
His justice in upholding him,
His power by imprinting upon him
what was beyond the limits of nature.

⁴⁶As the sign of His benevolence, He impressed marked traits of His own likeness on him who was not only His most faithful friend, but a most beloved son to Him, His other self! What He fixed upon his flesh were five of the most beautiful pearls, representative of the celestial treasure, five stones of the smoothest, like those used to defeat Goliath, five of the freshest roses with which to adorn his nuptial bed. So might He be addressing the words of the prophet Haggai to the person of Francis who, in soul and body, was beloved spouse to Him: *"I shall make you like a seal. For I have chosen you." "I shall make you,"* says Jesus; as if to say He were doing it Himself and not through another; just as He had taken flesh in His own Person, not in another's, and while living in flesh, susceptible of suffering, set the pattern of evangelical perfection. Thus He Himself shaped Francis into the seal of His pleasing perfection. He said, *"like a seal,"* because of the defects of analogy, because in all other ways he is so close to Christ Jesus. But adoption by grace cannot equal generation by nature; nor can personal union equal conformity of will. But He says, *"I have chosen you,"* because, by grace alone, I made you the angel of the sixth seal, which I have chosen from all the sons of grace for this purpose: for I choose *"the weak to confound the strong."*

^{435a7}Second, these signs from Jesus on the flesh of Francis demonstrated the wisdom of Providence, which a wise king said, *"no forgetfulness shall take away,"* and signed him with the sign of His greatest appearance. He sculpted the renewal of His passion in the heart of Francis, by the constant transformation of His cross, and the virtuous perfection of His cross which he wrote down in the holy *Rule*. He wished it to be stained by no spot. For this reason, a perpetual memorial, He stamped the signs of His passion on the flesh of Francis, so that human negligence, seeking reasons to flee the footprints of Christ, may not say, "We did not see the signs, so this is no prophecy." Jesus says of Francis that to whomever is his legitimate son, careful of imitating him, as in Exodus thirteen *"This will be as a sign on your hand,"* in your full observance of the *Rule* you have promised. The sign on the flesh of Francis will be evidence that cannot be doubted that through him My life is recalled. It continues, *"like a memorial hanging before your eyes,"* as something hanging before the eyes cannot be consigned to forgetfulness. So that the memory of the most holy

1 Sm 17:40; Mt 13:44-5

Hg 2:23

Hg 2:23

Hg 2:23; Rv 6:12

1 Cor 1:27

Dt 31:21

Ex 13:9

Ex 13:9

father may not fall away from the minds of his sons, and that the outpouring of the blood of Jesus not perish in forgetfulness, in the new wounds of Francis it grows warm again.

[28]Third, those happy signs of the wounds signified one preserving righteousness. A house is signed evangelically with a painted cross, so that it may be recognized as being under papal protection. Because of this pontiffs place signs on churches so that their consecration is visible. So Jesus, the Supreme Pontiff, placed a sign and consecrated the most holy temple of the soul and body of Francis and the *Rule* he instituted, taking it under His protection. Thus, *henceforth let no one dare trouble him, for he bears the marks of the Lord Jesus in his body.* This is clearly evident to the brothers, that the *Rule* is provided with such great protection, and *"whoever shall follow this rule, peace on them, and mercy, and upon the Israel of God."* Therefore the Tau of divine protection was first signed on Francis. But it is also his office to sign with the Tau, on the foreheads of the men who are grieving and mourning over the *Rule* as it is tread upon and transgressed, putting a sign on them so that they may not perish in the massacre of imminent distress, when the wrath of God will attack the *Rule's transgressors.*

[46]Fourth, in the sacred wounds of the saint, Jesus signified the power He impressed, striking terror into opponents and love into sons. For these are *the letters sealed with the ring of King Ahasuerus, which no one may dare contradict.* However much they may not wish to imitate him, that much does the power of Jesus imprint love and strength in the legitimate sons. Thus they may not doubt that, just as the strength of Jesus maintained the natural life of Francis in that wounded body by supernatural power, so, despite the natural defects of our flesh, the strength of Jesus protects them in the literal observance of the most holy *Rule's* rigor, upon which the vigor of the blood of the Crucified so openly flowed. Surely no one must doubt that his whole life is guided by Christ: whether in tribulation or in consolation; in illness or in health. Whoever shall wish to observe his promise to observe this most holy *Rule* must know that He will not permit anything to happen to the one who observes it except what is health-giving and useful. This is the sign about which Jesus could say to Francis, using that passage in the third chapter of Exodus, *"I will be with you and you will have this sign that I sent you, that when you have brought forth my people from Egypt you will sacrifice to the Lord on the holy mountain."* This is the sign that Jesus promised, to rouse the people, the sign of the *scarlet cord hanging in the window* of Francis's body, by which the harlot Rahab was protected from the destruction of Jericho. Therefore, let *the elephants* see *the blood of grapes and mulberries* in

Gal 6:17

Gal 6:16

Est 3:12; 8:8

Ex 3:12

Jos 2:18

1 Mc 6:34

the red wounds of their father; and let them *be roused to battle* against those attacking the observance of the holy *Rule,* never doubting that they will have a heavenly victory under the sign of His power through the imprinted marks of Jesus.

435b18See, therefore, in the sacred marks, with which the *Rule* is sealed, Jesus in His exceeding goodness embracing with benevolence observers of the holy *Rule,* enlightening them with wisdom as His legitimate sons, keeping them with equity as His counselors and secretaries, His preachers and messengers with a world mission. See Him empowering them to be members of His own household and workers in His vineyard. And besides, see Him supporting their temporal needs with sufficiency, their spiritual needs, however, with plenty. For they must have the spiritual vigor to seek first the kingdom of God and His justice; nor need they doubt Jesus' promise that *all* other *things will be given them as well,* and most fully, a pledge of which He gave them [in the seals] of His most sacred passion on the body of their father.[a]

Mt 6:33

[A Prayer of Love]

436b48When Jesus appeared to Francis, his face afire and scintillating with his divinity and humanity, he poured out upon his heart and body a vigorously flaming fire. So much so, that his *heart turned to wax, melting* inside him; for divine love has the power to melt, as has been said, and the power to shape, like wax flowing onto the mold of a seal. Thus did Francis dissolve mentally and bodily into the engraving of the wounds of his Beloved in the vision, and the lover was transformed into the Loved One. Fire has resilience, and while consuming earthly material, always reaches for the highest objects; characteristically it thrusts upwards. And so, the fire of divine love consuming the heart of Francis and, enkindling his flesh by burning a pattern into it, lifted him up to its own heights. Fulfilled in him then was what he used to pray would befall him:

Ps 22:15

I beg you, Lord, let the glowing and honey-sweet force of Your love draw my mind away from all things that are un-

---

a. Mt 6:33. There are two errors in the *Arbor* text: *mala* should read, *alia* ("other things"); in the clause following, *signa* and *a maculis* make no sense in the context, and should, probably, be joined to form one word, *signaculis* ([in the] "seals") as translated above.

A lengthy allegorical interpretation of the stigmata and the six wings of the Seraph now takes place, cf. 435b-441b. The following section, 436b 48-437a11, provides the background and text of a prayer attributed to Francis.

der heaven, that I may die for love of the love of You, who thought it a worthy thing to die for love of the love of me.[a]

[437b7]Therefore, those sons who have been fashioned in the likeness of their father, by the fire of his seraphic vision, must understand that their fashioning has to take place in their soul and be carried out by the glowing crucifixion of Jesus. So they will be living their lives like "little Christs," smaller figures of Jesus, as it were, perceiving themselves in their mortal flesh transformed into Christ.[b]

[The Angel of the Sixth Seal]

[441b44]Let us return to the seraphic Francis, who received such authentication from the seraphic apparition of Jesus that we must regard him as *"the angel of the sixth age."* For what John writes to the angel of Philadelphia, in the third chapter of the Apocalypse, befits him and his descendants. Now, Philadelphia is interpreted as "preserving steady attachment to the Lord." Oh, how accurately this holy Order and its most holy father match this Philadelphia and its angel! For here is preserved the heritage of the life of Christ and a complete attachment to His cross. All that is said to the angel is most fittingly applied to Francis, although there is no time to expound everything. However, let us take his triumphant victory. It is said: *He who conquers, I will make him a pillar in the temple of my God; never shall he go out of it, and I will write on him the name of my God, and the name of the city of my God, the new Jerusalem which comes down from my God out of heaven, and my own new name.*

[442a2]When Jesus, here and elsewhere, speaks of *"my God,"* or says something similar, he is doing so on behalf of His humanity only, in which He is subject to the Father, to His own divine Person, and to the Holy Spirit, as to His God of whom He is the purest worshipper. It is in view of the prize given for the victory He speaks of, that He has in mind Francis as the one who proves victorious, for he is the celebrated victor of whom it is sung that "he overcomes the world and sin, having already conquered himself."[c] The text, therefore, refers to two things about that prize: the first is the victor, likened to a

Rv 6:12

Rv 3:12

---

a. This prayer has been included in past collections of Saint Francis's writings. Its authenticity is no longer accepted, however, as it is a proven earlier medieval composition of patristic inspiration. Cf. Kajetan Esser, *Opuscula Sancti Patris Francisci Assisiensi*, (Grottaferrata, Rome: Editiones Collegii S. Bonaventurae Ad Aquas Claras, 1978), 39.

b. The lengthy allegorical interpretation of the stigmata and the six wings of the Seraph continues. Cf. 437a12-441b44.

c. Possibly a reference to the Sequence in honor of Saint Francis, *Sanctitatis Nova Signa* XVII; cf.FA:ED I 357.

pillar, gaining access to the temple; the second is what is written on that pillar . . .[a]

[The Mystical Temple of God]

Rv 3:12

442a18The seraphic soul thus enters into God, after the manner of a pillar firm and straight that is brought in as one of the roof's supports. Commonly it would be either round or quadrilateral, and is enclosed in the circular space around the inside of the temple. If, however, *temple* was understood as a material church, then pillars would support and adorn the temple and stand in the middle of it. Francis, and any of his sons, too, stand in this manner in the holy Order and in the Church of God; just as they stand in their proper manner in the celestial court, where higher ranks are supportive of the lower, and their humble simplicity and simple spirituality relate to the lower, less united, more dispersed ranks, as the center to a circle's circumference, or spirit to body. And the character of the temple shows this, in occupying a greater amount of space than a pillar. As the foundation of the Church on the first Apostles was in faith, so in these [later apostles] is the Church built up and her final perfect state of high contemplation underpinned. For this reason is it said in

Rv 3:12

Francis's regard: *Never shall he go out of it.* Neither apostasy nor any earthly preoccupation would draw him away from this temple which embraces the love of poverty most high, something he would never want to go out of by any means.

38Now, regarding what the text says is inscribed on him, know that in a soul like his, three things are written. The first is the most lucid vision and delightful contemplation of the three Persons of the Divinity and of the beatific glory they enjoy together. This is indi-

Rv 3:12

cated by: *I will write on him the name of my God.* For this is how the glory of God enters the soul and makes it supremely happy; it is rejoicing over the happiness of God. The second inscription is a perfect affinity with all in God's City and the company of the saints, whether on life's journey or hereafter . . . Now this city is said to come down from God out of heaven; for the full gladness of the saints springs from the immensity of God, signified by heaven, although this be inferior to God, who is infinite. In another sense, it comes down from heaven through humility, not only with respect to God, but even with respect to its special place in heaven, from which it comes down, regarding itself as unworthy.

---

a. Inspired by the biblical text, the author now interprets the temple as the immense sanctity of God. The frail soul is led into this sanctity and is fitted for contemplation and the fullness of divine worship by the strengths or virtues given it.

⁵⁷As it is here that the sixth *status* reform occurs, the new Jerusalem signifies this stage's peaceful contemplation of God and its renovation of the world through a thorough disdain for worldly things; hence it is called new, a fresh gift given by God. And this City's name can especially be said to be inscribed on Francis and on men like him, since with them all the renewal is inaugurated, established and sustained.

⁴⁴²ᵇ⁵The third inscription is the contemplation of Christ in His humanity and as Redeemer and Mediator. This is indicated by *and my own new name;* called *new,* because of the unique existence of His humanity in a divine Person, and also because in Him and through Him consists the complete renewal of the elect. And notice how his name is mentioned lastly: this is to show the complete circuit of contemplation, descending from God into the City of the saints and returning in Christ Jesus, to rest in Him in an embrace of delight. Thus is completed a glorious circle, starting out from God, moving through the saints, into the God-Man, the Holy of holies. Rv 3:12

¹⁷Observe now how to the sixth *status* is given an extraordinarily clear knowledge of God and of his entire City, and an extraordinary opening into and knowledge of the work of our redemption and of Christ Jesus. But it is upon this blessed man, Francis, that the name of God the Father is written, because he is being made the spiritual father of a worldwide religious Order. The name of the new Jerusalem is also inscribed on him, his soul being made worthy, by the sweetness of love, to be called Christ's spouse and gracious mother, bringing forth Jesus as offspring. Christ Jesus' new name is inscribed on him, when the figure of the Crucified is carved, not only into his soul, but on his body. Thus, of all Christ's members, among whom he holds primacy, he, by antonamasia, is called "anointed." Of such it is said, *Do not touch those I have anointed.* Ps 105:15; 1 Chr 16:22

³¹Observe also the orderly manner in which our text treats of the endowments given the holy father on this sacred mountain.ᵃ The first is a complete conquest of the world and of himself. The second is a foundational initiation into a contemplation that is joyous, deep, and stable. The third is the promised expansion of flawless descendants. The fourth is that splendid engraving of the wounds and name of Christ crucified. The first is referred to by *He who conquers:* he Rv 3:12 fully overcame himself and the world, as he fasted and prayed in this bleak and lonely place. The second is indicated by, *I will make him a* Rv 3:12 *pillar . . . the name of my God:* Francis was placed upon the firmest of

---

a. Ubertino employs the demonstrative pronoun, "this," here and a few lines further on, "this bleak and lonely place," consciously referring to Mount La Verna, where he is writing.

rocks, as a new pillar in the temple of God—even bodily and quite literally, here on this sacred mountain. And in that sublime apparition of Christ he was wonderfully enlightened with a knowledge of God and was confirmed for ever in the state of unifying grace and poverty. For this reason, we read, he felt happy at the gracious way Christ, in the form of the Seraph, looked upon him. He himself added that the One who appeared to him told him things which he would never reveal to anyone as long as he lived. To be sure, these concerned great things of a prophetic nature which are not for full hearing by human ears.

Rv 3:12 The third of the endowments is referred to in *and the name of the city,* etc. It was then he was promised that his Order would endure to the end of the world, and then also was revealed to him the death and resurrection of his *Rule.* And one astonishing thing came to my own ears, which with no brashness I aver, but in all seriousness shall recount for those sincerely interested. What I heard from the holy man Brother Conrad, and from several others who are trustworthy, was that the blessed Francis, after his glorification in heaven, revealed to the holy brother Leo—and to some others as well, they say—that in the apparition Christ foretold to him the tribulations his foundation and the Church would face, the rejection and corruption of his *Rule,* and how greatly upset the minds of spiritual men, and of those who came after them, would be at this universal assault on the *Rule.* And that therefore, for their comforting and enlightenment He, Jesus, out of his extreme goodness, would raise him up again, in a glorified body, and cause him to appear visibly to those aforesaid children of his.

443a11The outcome of this is something that may be awaited with devotion, so long as it is not avowed with indiscretion. However, this is where devotion is strongly supported by reasoned argument. For Francis was so remarkably like Christ Jesus in respect of His passion, that he might also, more than others, resemble Him in an anticipated resurrection. Above all, His being raised would strengthen the fidelity and sincerity required for the gospel life, which He wished to renew in Francis. That gospel life suffered under an unregenerate Church, as shall be shown further on, in the same ways that the Person of Christ suffered under the Synagogue; and therefore it would revive if Francis were raised again.[a]

---

a. While other sources mention the predictions concerning the future of the Order, none of them speaks of the resurrection of Francis. This chapter concludes with reflections on Francis as the angel of the sixth seal. Cf. 443a21-b23.

Chapter Five

JESUS ESTABLISHED THE FORM

^{443b27}Jesus, the perfection of our whole created world, established in His own life, and in that of His Mother most amiable, the gospel life in all its fullness, as though *upon the holy mountains* and on unshakable foundation. While the virgin born of that virgin with her most holy motherhood in extreme poverty, in the most profound humility He was humbled, obedient to the law and to His eternal Father, even to the hard offering of the cross in a perfect act of virtue and an enduring contemplation of the divine. In an inseparable bond they lived, loving their enemies, laying down and offering their entire life in death for the salvation of their enemies alone. For He had no friend except the one whom He met out of love for His enemy.

Hence the *Rule* of gospel living is founded in Christ Jesus and in His most holy mother and, by analogy, Christ passed this on, His own perfection, to the Apostles with the command that they observe it. For these reasons, it is not alone an evangelical *Rule,* having been established in and by Christ, but also an apostolic *Rule,* for it was laid down for the Apostles by Christ Jesus, and they kept it till their deaths. It was not passed on by them to the Church, however, as we have pointed out already, and it was unknown in the Church when the blessed Jesus began to renew it in Francis. That this was so can be clearly seen in what the *Legend's* Third Chapter tells us of Francis's petitioning the lord Pope to confirm his gospel life. To some of the cardinals it seemed novel, something arduous and beyond human powers. Which, of course, is nonsense; this would be to revile the Gospel of Jesus Christ. It is, therefore, obvious that Jesus made Francis the foundation of the evangelic and apostolic *Rule* in the Church, as far as its restoration was concerned.

^{443a1}That this might be what He imposed more widely is clear from the first motive, from the development in between, and from the conformity to the end, and by an observing deed and by explaining his intention.

⁴For his motive was listening to the Gospel of the sending out of the apostles; when it was said that they were sent to preach, He gave

Ps 87:1

LMj III 9-10

LMj III 1

195

Mt 10:9,10;
Lk 9:3; 10:4
the disciples an evangelical way of living, that is that they should not have *gold or silver, a wallet or purse, or two tunics, walking stick, or shoes.* For, with the unending fervor of his heart, Francis placed all his eagerness into fulfilling all that he had heard, and he transformed his uprightness into an apostolic rule. And, in the Gospel, Christ did not impose on the apostles anything except what he said to everyone, that they should take up the cross. Therefore Francis formed his habit according to the teaching of the Crucified in the form of a cross, that a crucified mind might fight under a crucified tunic.

[17]The *Rule* developed further when, inspired by the Holy Spirit, Francis opened the book of the Gospel. He opened it three times and came upon: perfect expropriation and the perfect abnegation of self, crucifixion of the life of the flesh, and the perfect following of Jesus. The holy man said: **"This is our life and rule, and that of all who wish to join our company."** The same Chapter Three of the *Legend* contains a further development, supporting our purpose. It tells how Francis, **Christ's** holy **servant, wrote for himself and his brothers a form of life in simple words, in which he placed observance of the holy Gospel as its unshakable foundation. He inserted a few other things which seemed necessary for a uniform way of life.** And it tells that he asked the Pope to confirm for him the full observance of the Gospel as the *Rule*. LMj III 3

LMj III 8

[31]The *Legend* shows fearful objections, based on the arduous novelty of such a state, and lack of earlier experience in the Church with temporalities. In the same place it shows the enlightened intervention of the **venerable man, the Lord John of Saint Paul, Bishop of Sabina,** when he said, **"when this poor man asks to be allowed to lead the Gospel life"** etc. The *Legend* also shows the contents of that form [of life] as it was then composed. I read that text and had it in my hand when I wrote these things: it contains a multitude of Gospel counsels, and it was twice or three times as long, though it had no more in content than this sacred *Rule* which we now have, which was written afterward through the Holy Spirit, witnessed by divine testimony given from heaven, and confirmed with papal protection. The final, confirmed form of that same *Rule* has a reduced number of words, witnessed by heaven and confirmed by the Pope. LMj III 9

[46]To the first point, Chapter Four of the *Legend* says: after the great growth of the Order, and shortly before he received the sacred stigmata, Francis was **warned by a revelation** from God. In a vision he saw **crumbs of bread,** which he made into **a host.** And some received worthily, and some refused and were struck with **leprosy.** Francis **did not understand,** and **while he kept vigil in prayer, he heard a voice from heaven** saying: **"Francis, the crumbs of last night are the** LMj IV 11

words of the Gospel; the host is the *Rule* and the leprosy is wickedness." O how sadly we see this vision proven true! But about this leprosy enough has been said above and will be said further on, if ever
we can say enough about it.

⁵⁶This vision occurred on a mountain near Rieti called Fonte
Colombo.ᵃ Under the guidance of the Holy Spirit and with two holy
and virtuous men, Brother Rufino and Brother Leo, he went up
there; and the name of the place does agree with the emanation of
the Holy Spirit. That is because the *Rule,* which launches the third *status* of the world, attributed to the Holy Spirit, came from "the fountain of the Holy Spirit." Fasting on bread and water, he had the *Rule*
written according to what the Holy Spirit revealed to him. This *Rule*
his vicar then lost, after the saint went up on the mountain and had
given it to him to keep.

⁴⁴⁴ᵇ⁹But the holy man went back to the place of solitude, and fasting and praying and weeping, he restored it, the very likeness of the
former one. Both the first and the second he wrote down taking the
words as if from the mouth of God with the breath of the Holy Spirit.

¹³This is the one, confirmed by the Supreme Pontiff, which today
is wholly coming apart. In its opening lines it has as its unshakable
foundation: **The rule and life of the Lesser Brothers is this: to
observe the Holy Gospel of Our Lord Jesus Christ.** At the end, as it
was confirmed for Saint Francis, it concludes: **". . . so that we may
observe poverty, humility, and the holy gospel** of God, **as we have
firmly promised."** So it is clear that the blessed Francis intended to
oblige himself and his whole Order to those same things to which he
could understand that Christ obliged His apostles.

²²And, to cover the fourth and fifth points rapidly, this observance
Francis and his first companions, perfect men, always did in fact
observe. Whenever the occasion to speak about these things arose,
he said vigorously that he understood and had understood the life in
this way. This is contained expressly in the words of the holy Brother
Leo written above. Anyone who doubts this is struggling to find a difficulty in something plain, a curve in something straight, ambiguity
in something clear.

²⁹Be rid of the idea there is any danger in such a promise, for
Jesus, who blows away all our dangers, counseled and commanded
nothing dangerous. Profession of the Holy Gospel and its observance
is not understood in a way different from what we find given to and
imposed on the apostles by Christ, that is, counsels to be observed as
counsels, precepts as precepts. The transgression of whatever was

LR I 1

LR XII 4

---

a. In Latin, *fons columbae* [fountain of the dove].

imposed on the apostles as precept is mortal [sin], and nothing else. On this point there can be different opinions; therefore the wise Jesus and the Holy Spirit made it clear by laying down spotless purity, extreme poverty, complete obedience, and a perfect denial of oneself, under firm and stable vow, as the foundation of all Gospel perfection. Everything else, in which the word "precept" or its equivalent does not appear is contained under the counsels, whether written in the *Rule* or in the Gospel. Both the sovereign pontiffs and the doctors say this well: Those who profess the Gospel *Rule* do not oblige themselves to any other counsel under vow binding under mortal [sin], unless that bond is expressed in the *Rule*.

[48]But even I do not recall any counsel of perfection imposed under precept on the apostles beyond those contained in the *Rule*. That opinion is certainly quite blind and irreverent which says that, by professing to observe any rule or the Holy Gospel, we bind ourselves under pain of mortal sin to those things that are there as counsels as much as to those which are there under the term of precept. But Christ did not intend counsels to be other than counsels, nor did the apostles observe then in any other way, for Christ gave the apostles the counsel to avoid every venial sin. Any wise person would give the same counsel.

[The Scrolls]

[445a1]We have an excellent case in the fifth chapter of Matthew, where Christ says: *"Be perfect as your heavenly Father is perfect."* The apostles could keep this, by appropriate analogy, more in desire than in fact. As James says in Chapter Three: *"We all offend in many things."* Nor does John use different language: *"If we say we have no sin we make God a liar."* And the Apostle writes to the Galatians that Peter *was deserving of blame.* About this passage, Augustine expressly states that he sinned venially. It is certain here that a counsel was neglected. Yet it is foolish either to impute mortal sin to the apostle, or to conclude that they were not held to observe the Holy Gospel. Therefore, neither here nor anywhere else in the whole book do I intend to say anything against the papal statement, but in its favor, for he excommunicates the errors mentioned above.

[15]As to the testimony from heaven which this *Rule* received from the Lord Jesus Christ, give ear, reader, and inscribe what follows deep inside your heart. In fact it comes from the holy Brother Conrad mentioned above, who heard it directly from the holy Bother Leo,

Mt 5:48

Jas 3:2

1 Jn 1:8

Gal 2:11

who was present at the time and did the writing down of the *Rule*. This was done on certain scrolls,[a] in his own handwriting, and these he sent to the Monastery of Saint Clare for safekeeping as a record for the future. After all, it was on these he had written many things he had heard from the lips of the father and many things he had seen him do. Their contents cover important matter about amazing things the saint accomplished, about the future debasement of the *Rule* and its subsequent revival, facts of great note about its institution and restoration on the part of God, and about the way in which the blessed Francis intended it to be observed, the very same way he himself used to say he had received it from Christ.

[31]Those things Brother Bonaventure omitted on purpose, not wanting to include them in his *Legend* for the eyes of all. His main reason was that there were some facts which openly showed there were aberrations from the *Rule* even earlier on, and he had no wish to prematurely disgrace the brothers before outsiders. It is obvious, however, that it would have been much better to write about them; because then the disasters that later occurred might not perhaps have been so bad. Of the greatest significance is what follows next; it was preserved since those earlier days. But I was very sad to hear that those scrolls have been pulled apart and, possibly, some missing; I was quite saddened over some of them. This account, however, is the one the holy brother Leo gave and the one he wrote, when he was fasting with the blessed Francis on the mountain they had gone to for the writing of the *Rule*.[b]

[Confrontation]

[42]The spirit of the devil, who from the outset raised obstacles against this most holy *Rule,* prompted a crowd of ministers and others who had the name of being men of discernment, to convene at Rieti for reasons of human timidity. These approached Brother Elias and told him to be their representative and go up to see the holy man and address him in the words that are written here below. And when he had said that he did not dare to go to him, because he was afraid of being stricken with a severe curse by the saint, all the more because he had never done anything with so much spirit as he now exhibited

---

a. *Rotuli* [little wheels] or rolls of paper—there is no evidence that they were of parchment. The few facts about these famous rolls, or scrolls, provided by Ubertino are to be noted with great attention, as their disappearance remains a mystery, as do their contents at first hand, although much, if not all, of what was in them has filtered through into other Franciscan literature.

b. Cf. LMj IV 11. Some details are not found elsewhere, other than in Ubertino: the decision of Elias to call out to Francis three times, from a spot behind the Saint's cell, and to go to him, should he not reply after the third call.

in getting the *Rule* written down, after long discussions they finally agreed that he should go together with them.

[53]But because he was always timid about blame from the saint, by God's providence he would not go up the mountain with those brothers, but going together with them through a deep valley, high up above which the saint's cell was visible, he arrived below the cell itself, having decided in his state of fear and reverence to call the saint three times by name, and if he did not answer to go back again.

[445b2]But at his first shout Francis, wondering what it was, came out of his cell to the precipice of the rock, and seeing such a multitude of the brothers standing with Elias in the valley, asked in surprise what he wanted. Elias, on behalf of them all, responded at the top of his voice: "These brothers are the ministers and discreets of Italy,[a] and they know how rigorous of spirit you are. They hear you are writing a new *Rule* and are making known to you, with respect to themselves and others, that they do not want you to write anything that is binding on them, unless you show it to them." When the holy man heard this he sent a loud wail up to heaven, and said: "Lord of all power, do you hear what at this moment these are saying?!" Then Jesus who is all goodness, sympathizing with the Saint's difficulties and wishing to give full assurance to a future generation, cried from heaven, so loudly and clearly that his words were heard and understood throughout the valley and the mountain: "Francis, *I am Jesus* and I am speaking to you from heaven. The *Rule* is my doing, and you have put nothing of your own in it. I am willing to give the help which I recognize is needed, as I recognize human frailty too. And taking these into consideration, I know that the *Rule* can very well be kept, and therefore I want it to be observed exactly as it is written, without any gloss. Those who are not happy with it, let them be gone, for I have no wish to make any changes in it."

Acts 9:5

[23]On hearing the thunder of Christ's voice, the holy man exulted in spirit and said to the brothers who were standing down in the valley: "My brothers, you have just heard the blessed Jesus; do you want me to have him repeat his words to you? You can now see clearly that it is our divine Jesus Christ's *Rule,* not mine, and that it was He who put into it whatever it contains." A trembling came upon the brothers, who beat their breasts and with bowed heads asked for pardon;

---

a. The term *discretus* [discreet, discerning] was used to describe both a local friary council or a delegate to a general or provincial council. In this instance, it is used to refer to those brothers chosen by their Italian confreres to represent them at the chapter approving the *Later Rule*. Cf. *Works of Saint Bonaventure: Writings Concerning the Franciscan Order*, edited with introduction by Dominic Monti (St. Bonaventure, NY: Franciscan Institute Publications, 1994), 59, n. 6.

and when they had received a blessing they went back to their own places.

It is the holy brother Leo who testifies to this; he was there for it all and heard the Lord Jesus Christ speaking.

[32]So, is there anyone left who is still unconvinced? If not, then let us no longer harden our hearts to the *Rule's* observance. Through those he spoke to from heaven Jesus was speaking to all, and bearing witness to a *Rule* that is holy and apostolic. He signified that it was apostolic by dividing it into twelve chapters, as if they were twelve apostolic foundation stones and twelve gates leading into the gospel life. It is like *the new Jerusalem that comes down from God out of heaven, on whose gates are written the names of the twelve Apostles of the Lamb.* And doubtless *a river of life, rising from the throne of God and of the Lamb, flows down the middle of its street;* for the Holy Spirit's influence is poured out generously upon it in a broad stream of charity, and it is only through that charity that a Gospel *Rule* can be resolutely adopted, fruitfully professed, and observed as sacrosanct.[a]

Rv 21:10-14

Rv 22:1-2

---

a. In 445b-447b the text proceeds to support Hugh of Digne, designating him a "saintly brother," who wrote a Commentary on the *Rule* in the mid-1240s or probably in 1253. Cf. Hugh of Digne, *Hugh of Digne's* Rule *Commentary, Spicilegium Bonaventurianum XIV,* ed. David Flood, (Grottaferrata, Rome: Collegium S. Bonaventura Ad Claras Aquas, 1979). The Declaration *Quo elongati* (1230) of Gregory IX which had decided the non-obligatory character of *The Testament,* from a strictly legal standpoint, had thereby opened the way for expositions of the *Rule,* private or official, on the part of the Order. Hugh, however, strongly dissociated himself from "expositors" and "glossators," claiming to be the *Rule's* "defender" in searching for its meaning in the "letter," rather than in the "mind of the one who put it together"—which he regards as a subterfuge. Since Ubertino concurs with this, and quotes Hugh's words, the latter must mean the presumed "intention" of the *Rule's* author rather than that testified to in eye-witness accounts.

Chapter Seven

JESUS DESPISED ANEW[a]

^{449a15}Christ Jesus is the eternal wisdom of the Father. He wanted His Spirit of Life renewed in the Church to lead in the exalted saint, the confessor Francis, through His paths. Along those same paths, that pious Jesus deigned to walk during the course of His life.

⁴⁵And because Francis was a man of ardor and filled with the Spirit of God that he could discern in his opponents the coming breakdown of the perfection revealed to him by Christ Jesus, he began to resist them courageously; he publicly said their human prudence was destructive and, with a holy and energetic indignation, set himself to demolish their works of defiance in their early stages. Hence, even in the *Legend* it is written how he ordered to be torn down residences that had been built, or else the brothers to be taken out of them. Many breathtaking things like this he did to confound the slyness of those who assailed his spirit. All this, Brother Bonaventure in his *Legend* only touches upon lightly, because he did not wish to make known to his readers how the disasters of our earlier times began. Although God in His providence permitted it so, and Bonaventure himself acted out of human prudence, still it was the cause of many getting no vision of the saint's fervent action against those baneful first steps; it was all covered up.

_{LMj VII 2}

[Brother Elias]

^{449b3}I shall recount one incident, which I heard once from a most reliable reporter, in which the saint reacted against excess and novelty in some people. It involves Brother Elias, who in his *desires* was forever *like the flesh in opposition to the spirit* of the Saint, albeit under the pretext of good sense. He had made himself a habit which, in length, width, size of sleeves, and capuche, and costly material, departed altogether from the shape and cheap quality which the saint had prescribed. He summoned him to where there was a good number of brothers and

_{Gal 5:17}

---

a. Ubertino traces the Order's decline from poverty and simplicity, and Francis's conflict with those who, under the pretext of pastoral need, began to build on a large scale, amass books, and acquire the patronage of the rich and powerful. After again criticizing Bonaventure for his cautious treatment of historical facts, he details the following incident in which Brother Elias is hauled over the coals by Francis; simultaneously amusing and daunting, it is not in other sources and it illustrates an aspect of Francis's character.

202

asked him if he could borrow the habit he was wearing. Then he put it on over his own, and wearing its girdle high up he went through the motions of arranging the pleats of the tunic and adjusting the capuche on his head, and making all the physical gestures he knew in his heart a generation of his sons would go in for. Then he began to walk up and down, head in the air, chest out, in a haughty, full-blown posture and, with a bellowing voice and in pompous yet flat tones, to salute the brothers, who were wide-eyed at what they were seeing, with, "Good people, the Lord give you peace!"

[20]When he ended, he was animated and showed his anger by disdainfully pulling off the habit and throwing it far away from him. Then he addressed Elias, with the others listening: "The Order's bastards go about just like that!" A while later, when he was in his own cheap, short, and close-fitting habit and looking, as the other first brothers did, like a man *crucified to the world,* he assumed a gentle and kindly expression, and all his physical gestures now evinced a tender charity and a profound humility. He began to move among those selfsame brothers and give them the greeting of the Lord's peace in such a friendly manner that this good friendliness seemed to be reflected in their faces. Then he said to Elias and the rest of the brothers: "This is the way the legitimate sons of mine ought to behave." Having done this, he sat down among them and set about encouraging them in compelling words to preserve their poverty and lower-class existence, and alerting them to the flood of back-sliding that would spring up at a future time.

[48]When he had a moment, an angry Elias confronted the holy father about his lack of discernment saying that those famous men who had sustained the Order were confused.

[51]The holy father, with the authority of the Spirit resting upon him, responded in a loud voice: "Elias, Elias, your disdainful pomposity, prudence of the flesh, and that of your own kind, have reduced my Order to nothing and have enervated all the truth of the spirit of the Gospel. But it is amazing that this God, Who knows your kind and Who wants me to leave the Order in your hands. I believe that God gave such a shepherd; He knows what kind of sheep there will be in the future."[a]

Gal 6:14

Test 23

---

a. The text continues with a lengthy rebuke of Elias, culminating in an abbreviated narration of the intervention of Cardinal Hugolino at a Chapter and, in order to express the vision of Francis, the *Letter to the Entire Order* or, as Hugolino describes it, "The letter that he sent to general chapter at the end of his life." Cf. FA:ED I 116-20. The entire text is presented except for the prayer with which it concludes. This is followed by an analysis of the causes of the Order's decadence in which Ubertino finds many parallels in the biblical story of Israel, and engages in a protracted interpretation, inspired by the works of Joachim of Fiore, of the "star fallen from heaven" and the devastation of locusts in the Book of Revelation.

A MIRROR OF THE PERFECTION,

RULE, PROFESSION, LIFE,

AND TRUE CALLING

OF A LESSER BROTHER

(THE LEMMENS EDITION, 1901)

AND

A MIRROR OF THE PERFECTION

OF THE *STATUS* OF A LESSER BROTHER

(1318)

(THE SABATIER EDITION, 1928)

Introduction

Ubertino da Casale's *Tree of the Crucified Life of Jesus* may have been the signal needed in 1305 for the Lesser Brothers to search their hermitages and residences for the scrolls in which he maintained the material sent by Leo and his companions could be found.[1] By 1311 Ubertino joyfully announced that some of the original *rotuli*—in Leo's handwriting—had been found, and another copy was preserved "in the cupboard of the brothers in Assisi." What exactly had Ubertino found? Did the first piece of the *rotuli* contain the *Intention of the Rule* and the *Words of Saint Francis?* Was the second what is now known as *The Assisi Compilation?* Whatever the answers to these questions, within a short period of time, two works incorporated the texts of the *rotuli* into what have become important reflections on the philosophy of the Spirituals: the *Mirror of the Perfection of the* Status *of a Lesser Brother* and the *Mirror of the Perfection,* Rule, *Profession, Life, and True Calling of a Lesser Brother.*

In modern times Paul Sabatier was the first to publish an edition of the *Mirror of Perfection* in 1897, and entitled his discovery: *Speculum perfectionis seu S. Francisci Assisiensis legenda antiquitissima, auctore frate Leone* [The Mirror of Perfection or The Most Ancient Legend of Saint Francis of Assisi, by the author, Brother Leo].[2] Convinced that the portraits of both Thomas of Celano and Bonaventure were inaccurate, Sabatier bolstered his position by maintaining that this was "the *legenda antiquitissima* [most ancient legend]," that it was written by Leo, and that the date of its composition, May 11, 1228, made it more authentic than the *Life of Saint Francis* by Thomas of Celano.

Sabatier's critics arose en masse to refute his position, most especially Michele Faloci Pulignani and Édouard D'Alençon.[3] Working totally independent of Sabatier, Leonard Lemmens discovered and published a shorter and different version of the *Mirror* in 1901.[4] Although based on only one manuscript, the manuscript 1/73 of the friary library of Saint Isidore in Rome, Lemmens identified his text as an earlier redaction of the Sabatier text.[5]

Meanwhile Sabatier continued to defend his work and, in doing so, to fuel the fires of what had become known as "the Franciscan Question," that is, "the search for the link between the various documents that take us back to the original documents, and those that are dependent on them."[6] As he studied forty-five manuscripts, eleven of which enabled him to examine the text critically, Sabatier recognized the mistake of a copyist in writing MCCXXVIII and not MCCCXVIII, the date written in the majority of the manuscripts. Shortly after his death, Sabatier's second edition was published, a thorough study of the manuscripts and a revised dating of the text, i.e., 1318.[7]

The "mirror" tradition initially was based on Saint Augustine's varied use of the image especially for the Scriptures which, according to him, offered examples or mirrors of holy living. This expanded in the twelfth century to include any literature that presents an exemplar of virtue. With Bernard of Clairvaux (1090-1153), the notion of mirror took a moral twist: any exemplar should not only inspire but also purify. In this same moral tradition, Hugh of St. Victor (+1141), identified the purpose of his *Explanation of the Rule of St. Augustine:* "This little book may well be called a mirror. In it we are able to see the state of our soul . . . whether it be holy or sinful . . . Those that aim at holiness constantly look into the sacred writings to examine their lives, to scrutinize their deeds."[8] He continues that if his readers "find anything reprehensible, inordinate, or out of keeping with their state, they must use at once every effort to amend and set it right, according to the light they have received."[9] These statement can easily be seen as providing the context for reading the fourteenth century compilations bearing the title "Mirror of Perfection."

These two texts have this twofold function: "to show us what we are and what we ought to be."[10] By its title, the Sabatier edition, *A Mirror of the Perfection of the* Status *of the Lesser Brother,* follows more explicitly Hugh of St. Victor's notions of purification and perfection of one's way of life. In the Sabatier *Mirror,* Francis is especially presented as the light that is to purify and amend the life of the Lesser Brothers who were living during the early part of the fourteenth century. The Lemmens edition, on the other hand, as its title—*A Mirror of the Perfection, Rule, Profession, Life and True Calling of the Lesser Brother*—suggests that "what we are and what we ought to be" is identified by the *Rule* and profession of the Lesser Brothers.

Both texts are compilations relying heavily on the *rotuli* or scrolls,[11] edited in such a way, however, to invite readers to scrutinize and amend their lives according to the examples of Francis. The shorter text, the Lemmens edition, accomplishes this by selecting and presenting earlier written examples of Francis from the *rotuli* in a simple and straightforward manner. The longer text, the Sabatier edition, draws from the same source, but, with the addition of many and sometimes sharp editorial comments, it is longer and more developed. It also has clear agenda and leaves little to the discretion of the reader as to how the scrutiny or amendment of life is to be realized in the state or *status* of the Lesser Brother.

Both editions offer the brothers of the early fourteenth century a sourcebook for Francis as the perfect imitator of Christ. In this context, earlier images of St. Francis are embellished as new images emerge. The notion, however, that Francis is an icon that must always be held before his followers to learn about themselves and their need to change and reform, is not new. Thomas of Celano, not only by his arrangement of material from the *rotuli* in The Second Book of his *The Remembrance of the Desire of a Soul,* but even as early as 1228/29 in *The Life of Saint Francis,* makes it clear: "If people intend to put their hand to difficult things, and strive to seek the higher gifts of a more excellent way, let them look into the mirror of his life, and learn all perfection."[12]

The Lemmens Edition

The Lemmens edition, the *Mirror of the Perfection, Rule, Profession, Life and True Calling of a Lesser Brother,* has enjoyed different titles. Because Leonard Lemmens believed the manuscript he found in St. Isidore's Library to be an earlier recension of the long edition published by Paul Sabatier, it was called the *Redactio Prior* [Earlier Redaction]. Others saw it as simply an abbreviated form of the Sabatier edition, entitling it the Minor [Shorter or Lesser] edition. Still others prefer to identify it through naming its modern editor, Lemmens, an identification that seems most preferable to the editors of *Francis of Assisi: Early Documents.* In this way, the editors believe that it stands on its own as a text independent of that published by Sabatier.

The Lemmens edition is basically made up of texts placed in forty-five paragraphs and taken, it would seem, from a source available to the editors of both *Mirrors.* This might have been the *rotuli* or scrolls or Manuscript 1046 of Perugia's Biblioteca Augusta, what is now known as the *Assisi Compilation;*[13] it may also have been taken from the other compilations that were in existence at the time. With the exception of its last number, *Admonitions* XI and XXI, all of the Lemmens edition is found in that of Sabatier, although ordered differently. It, however, contains none of the editorial comments that give the Sabatier edition such a distinctive flavor.

There is no logic to the way in which these forty-five paragraphs are presented. They move, for example, from three introductory paragraphs on begging to two paragraphs describing Francis's behavior at the approach of his death and another on the salutation of peace he wished his brothers to make. The manuscript's *incipit* provides no key to its order beyond introducing the stories about and writings of the saint that provide insight into his vision of holiness: "In the name of the Lord begins the mirror of the perfection, *Rule,* profession, life, and calling of a true Lesser Brother according to the will of Christ and the intention of blessed Francis." Quite simply, this compilation forms a scattering of insights into how its original editor understood Gospel perfection according to the mind of Francis.

While Sabatier claimed that Leo was the author of the manuscript he had discovered, Lemmens made no such claim and was content to let the manuscript's *incipit* speak for itself:

> It was composed from what was recounted in the writings of Brother Leo, a companion of blessed Francis, and of his other companions, which are not in the common Legend. In this mirror the perfection of the life of blessed Francis in some way also shines.

The text, in other words, was edited by someone dependent on that material written by Leo and the companions but omitted from the "common Legend," i.e., the *Major Legend* of Saint Bonaventure. Furthermore, in light of the *incipit,* Lemmens maintains that it was a supplement to Bonaventure's portrait and, therefore, written after the decree of the 1277 General Chapter of Padua.[14]

At the time of its publication, the Lemmens text undoubtedly caused a stir. It provided yet another insight into the tradition of Leo and his companions that had been lost. In 1922 Ferdinand Delorme's discovery of Manuscript 1046 of the Biblioteca Augusta in Perugia shed light on the Lemmens text and prompted scholars to intensify their discussions of the "Franciscan Question." Now it offers another collection of the "Leonine" tradition and yet another perspective as to how they were used to address the issues of the time.

The Sabatier Edition

From his first publication of the *Mirror of Perfection* in 1898 until shortly before his death, Paul Sabatier spent considerable energy examining forty-five manuscripts of this controversial text in order to publish a definitive edition. In 1923, Sabatier presented his findings to the British Society of Franciscan Studies and within two years sent the results to his publisher. By this time, however, illness was taking its toll and only after his death on March 4, 1928, was his work finally published.[15]

Sabatier's text of the *Mirror* contains one hundred and twenty-four chapters which the French scholar initially believed had come from the hand of Brother Leo. In 1907 Alphonse Fierens was among the first to contest Sabatier's conclusions about its origins,[16] but it was only after Ferdinand Delorme had discovered the Perugia Manuscript 1046 that it became clear that the *Mirror* was composed of materials taken from what is now known as the *Assisi Compilation,* the Words of Saint Francis, the works of Thomas of Celano and Conrad of Offida, and, in one instance, of Francis himself. One hundred and fifteen chapters of Sabatier's edition come from the same source as the *Assisi Compilation;* four come directly from Thomas of Celano's *The Remembrance of the Desire of a Soul,* and one from his *Life of Saint Francis;* and two from *The Words of Saint Francis.*[17] Only one paragraph, 84, is completely original: the poem in honor of the Portiuncula.

Nevertheless, an early study by Benvenuto A. Terracini of the Sabatier edition concluded that the compiler of the fourteenth century text was more concerned about the stylistic or exegetical nuances of his work than by polemical issues.[18] Although Terracini was only able to compare Sabatier's edition with Thomas's *Remembrance,* which some scholars of the time thought was its source, he discovered differences in syntax and tense, and observed that obscure ellipses of the earlier *Remembrance* text were clarified by repetitions and a generous supply of pronouns, adjectives, and additional verbs. Terracini also pointed out that the Sabatier edition was laced with what appeared to be glosses or editorial comments. Thus the editor of the Sabatier text takes many editorial liberties. Sometimes these introduce and interpret sections of the narrative, add additional information, emphasize certain details, and add rhetorical embellishment, but many of the editorial additions are directed toward literal and strict interpretation of the *Rule*. Contrary to the interpretation of Pope Nicholas III in *Exiit Qui Seminat* (1279), for example, the brothers who pursue knowledge and wisdom are described as guilty of idleness and offending the *Rule*.

Is it possible to determine the author of the Sabatier *Mirror?* The Frenchman tenaciously advocated that it was Leo, as the title of his initial publication indicates: *Speculum perfectionis seu S. Francisci Assisiensis legenda antiquitissima, auctore frate Leone* [The Mirror of Perfection or The Most Ancient Legend of Saint Francis of Assisi, by the author, Brother Leo]. Unfortunately Sabatier downplayed the incipit found in all the manuscripts:

> This work has been compiled in the form of a legend based on what the companions of blessed Francis had formerly written or caused to be written.[19]

As Théophile Desbonnets observes: "This remark embarrassed Paul Sabatier very much, for it ruined a great deal of his thesis and contradicted the date 1227 which he attributed to the *Speculum*."[20] Thus Sabatier's text offers yet another compilation. In this instance, however, the addition of *The Words of Brother Conrad of Offida* clearly suggest that the original editor was a Spiritual, probably from the Italian Province of the Marches, who was intent on righting the wrongs brought about by erroneous interpretations of the *Rule*.

A casual reading of the one hundred and twenty-four chapters, however, reveals a change in emphasis. Once again the stories are arranged differently, this time in twelve chapters. They are introduced by a re-telling of the confrontation of the ministers with Elias as their spokesman and Francis. The divine character and authority of the *Rule* is dramatically established by the voice of Christ that is now heard telling the troubled saint: "Francis, nothing of yours is in the *Rule:* whatever is there is mine. And I want the Rule observed in this way: to the letter, to the letter, to the letter, and without gloss, without gloss, without gloss." The contentious ministers, rebuked by Francis, are described as confused and now terrified. The text then weaves the now familiar stories in twelve different panels devoted initially to the fundamental virtues of the *Rule:* poverty, charity, humility and obedience. With the fourth chapter, however, the focus shifts. Francis, "the perfect zealot of the observance of the holy Gospel," is portrayed as burning "with great zeal for the common observance of the *Rule*" and, in the following chapter, for the perfection of his brothers. With the sixth chapter, the stories continue to exemplify Francis's virtues of love, compassion, prayer, joy, resistance to temptation, and prophecy, and eventually focus on God's unique care for him especially at the time of his death. In light of the pivotal fifth and sixth chapters, however, the frequently added superlatives, editorial comments, and interpolations seem to be written with one aim: to prod the reader to reflect on his own pursuit of the *Rule's* perfection.

Notes

1. Cf. supra.

2. *Speculum perfectionis seu S. Francisci Assisiensis legenda antiquissima auctore fratre Leone,* Collection de études et documents pour l'histoire religieuse et litteraire du Moyen Âges 1, ed. Paul Sabatier (Paris: Fischbacher, 1898). For further information on Sabatier's role in the advancement of Franciscan studies in the twentieth century, see C.J.T. Talar, "Saint of Authority and the Saint of the Spirit: Paul Sabatier's *Vie de S. François d'Assise,"* GR 10 (1996): 207-22.

3. Michele Faloci Pulignani, "Risposta alla Lettera di Paolo Sabatier," *Miscellanea Franciscana* 7 (1898): 35-51; "Nuove ricerche sulla data della compilazione dello Speculum perfectionis," *Miscellanea Franciscana* 7 (1898): 182-7; "Lo Speculum perfectionis e la sua data ," *Miscellanea Franciscana* 8 (1901): 43-4.Édouard D'Alençon, "Le Speculum Perfectionis Étude critique," *Annales Franciscaines* 22-3 (1897-8): 504-9; 558-573; "Studio critico sullo Speculum perfectionis," Miscellanea Franciscana 7 (1898): 51-7.

4. Leonard Lemmens, *Documenta Antiqua Franciscana* (Ad Claras Aquas, Quaracchi: 1901). See also Mario Bigaroni, *Speculum Perfectionis, Minus,* introduction by Raoul Manselli (Sta Maria degli Angeli, Assisi: Edizioni Porziuncula, 1985), 1731-1825.

5. Cf. Raoul Manselli, "Introduction," Bigaroni, *Speculum,* vii-xix.

6. This is the definition proposed by Théophile Desbonnets and used by Luigi Pellegrini in his article "A Century Reading the Sources for the Life of Francis of Assisi," in GR 7 (1993): 323-46.

7. *Le Speculum Perfectionis ou Memoires de Frère Leon.* 2 vols ed. Paul Sabatier (Manchester: Manchester University Press, 1928-31); *Fontes Franciscani* a cura di Enrico Menesto e Stefano Brufani e di Giuseppe Cermascoli, Emore Paoli, Luigi Pellegrini, Stanislao da Campagnola, Apparati di Giovanni M. Boccali (Sta Maria degli Angeli, Assisi: Edizioni Porziuncula:1995), 1829-2053. Five of the eleven manuscripts, the "Portiuncula Collection," shared many of the same traits, most importantly: they were written by non-professional copyists and all came from friaries of strict observance. The remaining six manuscripts formed the "Northern Collection." They too shared many of the same traits; in this instance, they were obviously the result of well-trained copyists and, significantly, came from non-Franciscan residences. Curiously, Sabatier noted, only one manuscript of the Portiuncula Collection, from the friary of Ognissanti in Florence, bore the date 1318; while only two of Northern Collection supported his original discovery of 1228. As he pursued his research, the French scholar concluded that the tradition of the Ognissanti manuscript was more accurate, for he recognized the mistake of a copyist in writing MCCXXVIII and not MCCCXVIII, the date written in the majority of the manuscripts.

8. Hugh of St. Victor, *Explanation of the Rule of Saint Augustine,* trans. Aloysius Smith (London and Edinburgh: Sands and Company, 1911), 119-20.

9. Hugh of St. Victor, *Explanation,* 120.

10. Rita Mary Bradley, "Background of the Title *Speculum* in Medieval Literature," *Speculum* 29 (1954): 111. This article offers a survey of the use of "mirror" in medieval literature.

11. Cf. FA:ED II 111-230.

12. Cf. 1C 90; FA:ED I 260.

13. AC 96-103=1MP 1-7; AC 4-14=1MP 8-19; AC 117-120=1MP 20-23; AC 50-65=1MP 24-33 and AC107-115=1MP 35-43. Only 1MP 34, 44, and 45 are not presented within the same block of text as found in the AC.

14. Cf. *Documenta Antiqua Franciscana,* Pars II, ed. Leonardus Lemmens, (Ad Claras Aquas, Quaracchi: Collegium S. Bonaventurae, 1901), 20-1.

15. Sabatier, *Speculum.*

16. Alphonse Fierens, "Les origines du *Speculum Perfectionis," Rapport sur les travaux du séminaire historique de l'Université de Louvain* (Louvain, n.p., 1907).

17. Cf. Daniele Solvi, "Lo 'Speculum Perfectionis' et le sue Fonti" in *Archivum Franciscanum Historicum* 88 (1995): 377-472 (hereafter AFH). See also Sophronius Clasen, *Legenda Antiqua S. Franscisci. Untersuchung uber die nachbonaverturianischen Franziskusquellen, Legenda trium Sociorum, Speculum Perfectionis, Actus B. Francisci et sociorum eius und verwandtes Schriftum.* Studia et Documenta Franciscana 5 (Leiden: E.J. Brill, 1967).

18. Benvenuto A. Terracini, "Il 'cursus' e la questione dello Speculum Perfectionis," *Studi Medievali* 4 (1912-3): 65-109.

19. *Istud opus compilatum est per modum legendae ex quibusdam antiquis quae in diversis locis scripserunt et scribi fecerunt socii beati Francisci.* Cf. Sabatier, *Speculum,* xxiii.

20. Cf. Théophile Desbonnets, "Introduction," *St. Francis of Assisi Writings and Early Biographies: English Omnibus of the Sources for the Life of St. Francis,* 3rd ed. edited by Marion A. Habig, translations by Raphael Brown, Benan Fahey, Placid Hermann, Paul Oligny, Nesta de Robeck, Leo Sherley-Price, with a Research Bibliography by Raphael Brown (Chicago: Franciscan Herald Press, 1973), 1109.

A Mirror of the Perfection, *Rule,* Profession, Life and True Calling of a Lesser Brother
(The Lemmens Edition)

In the name of the Lord begins the Mirror of the perfection,[a] *Rule,* profession, life, and calling of a true Lesser Brother according to the will of Christ and the intention of blessed Francis. It was composed from what was recounted in the writings of Brother Leo, a companion of blessed Francis, and of his other companions, which are not in the common Legend. In this mirror the perfection of the life of blessed Francis in some way also shines.

[1][b]

Blessed Francis held that to beg for alms for the love of the Lord God was of the greatest nobility, dignity, and courtesy before God and before **this** world, because everything that the heavenly Father has created for a human's use, after the sin, He has given freely, as alms, both to the worthy and the unworthy out of the love of His beloved Son.

Therefore, blessed Francis would say that a servant of God must beg alms for the love of God with greater freedom and joy than someone, who, out of courtesy and generosity, wants to buy something, and goes around saying: "Whoever will give me a penny, I will give him a hundred silver pieces, no, a thousand times more." Because a servant of God offers the love **of the Lord** which a person merits

↓AC 96 //2MP

---

a. This translation is based on the edition originally published by Leonard Lemmens, *Documenta Antiqua Franciscana,* pars II (Ad Claras Aquas, Quaracchi: Collegium S. Bonaventurae, 1901), 23-84; and reprinted in *Fontes Franciscani,* ed. Enrico Menestò, Stefano Brufani, Giuseppe Cremascoli, Emore Paoli, Luigi Pellegrini, Stanislao da Campagnola (S.Maria degli Angeli-Assisi: Edizioni Porziuncola, 1995), 1745-1825. Since the basis of this text is AC, only those words or phrases added by its anonymous editor are bolded.

b. Neither the Lemmens edition of 1901 nor its reprinted edition in the *Fontes Franciscani* provides chapter titles. In this instance, the editors of this translation have chosen to follow that precedent. Cross references to the earlier passages of AC, FA:ED II 118-230, will be indicated in the inner margins as ↓AC. Since Thomas of Celano used the material sent by the Three Companions, i.e., "we who were with him," in 2C, it is useful to recognize the repetition of many of the same pericopes throughout these later texts. To indicate these parallel texts, the editors have chosen to indicate their presence as //2C. In addition to cross references to earlier texts, the editors have indicated references to the Sabatier edition of the *Mirror of Perfection.* Since, at this point of scholarship, it is difficult to date this text, the cross references suggest that it is a parallel text.

when he gives alms; in comparison to which all things in this world and even those in heaven are nothing.

Therefore, before the brothers became numerous—and even after they grew in number—when blessed Francis went through the world **to preach,** and some noble and wealthy person invited him to eat and lodge with him, since as yet there were no places of residence for the brothers in many cities and towns, he would always go begging for alms at mealtime. He did this, even though he knew that his host had abundantly prepared everything he needed for the love of **the Lord,** to give a good example to the brothers and because of the nobility and dignity of Lady Poverty. Sometimes he would say to his host: "I do not want to renounce my royal dignity, my vocation, and my profession, and that of my brothers, that is, to go begging alms. Even if I were to bring no more than three alms, I always want to exercise my responsibility."

And so, he used to go **freely** begging alms,[a] and the one who invited him would unwillingly sometimes go with him. The alms that Francis acquired, he would accept and place them as relics out of his devotion.

He who writes has seen this many times, and bears witness to it.

[2]

AC 97 //2C 73
//2MP 23

Moreover, one time, when he was visiting the Lord Bishop of Ostia, who later was pope, he went out for alms at mealtime, secretly as it were, because of the lord bishop. And when he returned, the lord bishop was sitting at table and eating, particularly since he had invited to dinner some knights who were his relatives. Blessed Francis put his alms on the bishop's table and came to the table next to the bishop, because the lord bishop always wanted blessed Francis, whenever he was with him, to sit next to him at mealtime. The lord bishop was somewhat embarrassed that blessed Francis went begging alms, but said nothing to him particularly because of those at table.

After blessed Francis had eaten a little, he took some of his alms and sent a little on behalf of the Lord God to each one of the knights and chaplains of the lord bishop. They all accepted them with great devotion. Some ate them, others kept them out of his devotion. Moreover, because of devotion for Saint Francis, they even took off **their** emblems when they accepted the alms. From then on, the lord

---

a. For an explanation of the translation of this passage, see FA:ED II 199 a.

bishop was greatly amazed at their devotion, especially since those alms did not consist of wheat bread.

After the meal, the lord bishop got up and went to his room, taking blessed Francis with him. Lifting up his arms, he embraced blessed Francis with utmost joy and told him: "Why, my simple little brother,[a] did you shame me in my own house, which is also the home of your brothers, by going out as you did for alms?"

"On the contrary, Lord Bishop," blessed Francis answered, "I paid you an honor. Because when a subject exercises and fulfills his duty and the obedience of his lord, he does honor both to the lord and to his prelate."

Then he said: "I must be a model and example of your poor. Especially because I know that in the life and religion of the brothers there are and will be Lesser Brothers, in name and in deed, humble in all things, obedient and of service to their brothers. They are and will be such because of the love of the Lord God and by the anointing of the Holy Spirit, who teaches and will teach them in all things. There also are and will be those among them who, held back by shame and because of bad habit, are and will be scorned by humbling themselves, by demeaning themselves by begging alms, and by doing this kind of servile work. Therefore, I must teach by deed all those who are or who will be in religion, that they might be without excuse in the eyes of God in this age and in the future.

"While I am with you, who are our Lord and Pope, and with other great and wealthy people in the eyes of the world, who for the love of the Lord God and with great kindness, not only receive me into their houses, but even compel me to do so, I do not want to be ashamed to go for alms. Indeed I want to have and hold it as a sign of great nobility, as the highest dignity and an honor to that most exalted King, who though He was Lord of all, willed for our sake to become the servant of all, and, although he was rich and glorious in majesty, came as one poor and despised in our humanity. So I want all who are and will be brothers to know that I hold it a greater consolation for both soul and body when I sit at a poor little table of the brothers and see before me the meager alms they begged from door to door for the love of God, than when I sit at your table and that of other lords, set abundantly with all kinds of food, even though they are offered to me with great devotion. For the bread offered as alms is holy bread which the praise and love of God have hallowed, because when a brother goes out begging, he must first say: "Praised and blessed be

---

a. For the translation of this passage, see FA:ED II 200 a.

the Lord God!" Afterwards he must say: "Give us alms for the love of the Lord God."

The lord bishop was greatly edified by the holy father's words of instruction.[a] He said to him: "My son, do what seems good in your eyes, for the Lord is with you and you with Him."

For the will of blessed Francis, as he often said, was that no brother should procrastinate in going for alms, so that he not be ashamed to go later on. Indeed, the greater and nobler a brother had been in the world, so much the more, **therefore,** was he pleased and happy when he went for alms and did servile work of this sort because of good example. Thus it was in the early days.

[3]

At the religion's beginning, when the brothers were staying at Rivo Torto, there was a brother among them who prayed little, did not work, and did not want to go for alms because he was ashamed; but he would eat heartily. Giving the matter some thought, blessed Francis knew through the Holy Spirit that the man was carnal. He therefore told him: "Go on your way, Brother Fly, because you want to feed on the labor of your brothers, but wish to be idle in the work of God, like Brother Drone that does not want to gather or work, yet eats the work and gain of the good bees."

So he went his way. And because he lived according to the flesh, he did not ask for mercy.

[4]

When blessed Francis lay gravely ill in the palace of the bishop of Assisi, to comfort his soul and ward off discouragement in his severe and serious infirmities, he often asked his companions during the day to sing the Praises of the Lord which he had composed a long time before in his illness. He likewise had the Praises sung during the night for the edification of their guards, who kept watch at night outside the palace because of him.

When Brother Elias reflected that blessed Francis was so comforting himself and rejoicing in the Lord in such illness, one day he said to him: "Dearest Father, I am greatly consoled and edified by all the joy which you show for yourself and your companions in such affliction and infirmity. Although the people of this city venerate you as a saint in life and in death, nevertheless, because they firmly believe

---

a. For the translation of this passage, see FA:ED II 201 a.

(margin note beside [3]:) ↓AC 97 //2C 75 //2MP 24

(margin note beside [4]:) AC 99 //2MP 121

that you are near death due to your serious and incurable sickness, upon hearing praises of this sort being sung, they can think and say to themselves: 'How can he show such joy when he is so near death? He should be thinking about death.' "

"Do you remember," blessed Francis said to him, "when you saw the vision at Foligno and told me that it told you that I would live for only two years? Before you saw that vision, through the grace of the Holy Spirit, who suggests every good in the heart, and places it on the lips of his faithful, I often considered day and night my end. But from the time you saw that vision, each day I have been even more zealous reflecting on the day of my death.

He continued with great intensity of spirit: "Allow me to rejoice in the Lord, Brother, and to sing His praises in my infirmities, because, by the grace of the Holy Spirit, I am so closely united and joined with my Lord, that, through His mercy, I can well rejoice in the Most High Himself."

[5]

Another time during those days, a doctor from Arezzo, named Good John, who was known and familiar to blessed Francis, came to visit him in the bishop's palace. Blessed Francis asked about his sickness saying: "How does my illness of dropsy seem to you, Brother John?"

For blessed Francis did not want to address anyone called "Good" by their name, out of reverence for the Lord, who said: *No one is good but God alone.* Likewise, he did not want to call anyone "father" or "master," nor write them in letters, out of reverence for the Lord, who said: *Call no one on earth your father nor be called masters,* etc.

The doctor said to him: "Brother, by the grace of the Lord, it will be well with you." For he did not want to tell him that he would die in a little while.

Again blessed Francis said to him: "Tell me the truth. How does it look to you? Do not be afraid, for, by the grace of God, I am not a coward who fears death. With the Lord's help, by His mercy and grace, I am so united and joined with my Lord that I am equally as happy to die as I am to live."

The doctor then told him frankly: "According to our assessment, your illness is incurable and you will die either at the end of this month or on the fourth day before the Nones of October.[a] Blessed Francis, while he was lying on his bed sick, with the greatest

Margin notes:
↓AC 100 //2MP

Lk 18:19

Mt 23:9-10

---

a. For an understanding of the "fourth day before the Nones of October," see FA: ED I 258 c.

devotion and reverence for the Lord stretched out his arms and hands with great joy of mind and body and said to his body and soul: "Welcome, my Sister Death!"

[6]ᵃ

101 //2MP 26

Test 23

The Lord also revealed to blessed Francis the greeting that they should use, as he **himself** had written in his *Testament:* **"The Lord revealed a greeting to me that we should say** *'May the Lord give you peace.'* **"**

Nm 6:26

At the beginning of the religion, when blessed Francis would go with a brother who was one of the first twelve brothers, that brother would greet men and women along the way as well as those in their field, saying: *"May the Lord give* **you** *or you peace."*ᵇ

2 Thes 3:16

And because people had never before heard such a greeting from any religious, they were greatly amazed. Indeed, some would say almost indignantly: "What does this greeting of yours mean?" As a result that brother began to be quite embarrassed. Then he said to blessed Francis "Let me use another greeting."

Blessed Francis told him: "Let them talk, for *they do not grasp what is of God.* But do not be embarrassed, for one day the nobles and princes of this world will show respect to you and the other brothers because of a greeting of this sort."

1 Cor 2:14

[7]ᶜ

103 //2MP 73

Blessed Francis instructed **all** the brothers, the ministers as well as preachers, about work, telling them that, because of a prelacy and an office and of zeal for preaching, that they should not abandon holy and devout prayer, going for alms, and working with hands like the other brothers, for good example and for the benefit of their souls as well as others.

He said: "The brothers who are subjects are very edified when their ministers and preachers devote themselves freely to prayer; and

---

a. The following paragraph contains one of the collection, the *Intentio Regulae* [Intention of the Rule], cf. FA:ED II 204 b. In this instance, the passage found in AC 101 has been greatly abbreviated so that the proclamation of peace is accentuated.

b. The Latin text, *Dominus det tibi vel vobis pacem,* curiously offers a singular and a plural form of the second person pronoun.

c. The following paragraph contains another of the collection of *Intentio Regulae* [Intention of the Rule], cf. FA:ED II 204 b. In this instance, the passage found in AC 103 has also been greatly abbreviated so that the fundamental values of prayer, begging for alms, and manual labor are accentuated. However, this saying is bolstered by the addition of a phrase underscoring the exemplary role of the prelates and *majores* [greater ones] in fostering the humility of subjects.

the subjects are inclined to humility, when they see the prelates and the greater ones co-operating in their enterprises and labors."

Therefore, that faithful disciple **and imitator** of Christ,[a] while he was in good health, practiced what he taught the brothers.

[8]

One day when blessed Francis lay sick in the palace of the bishop of Assisi, one of the brothers, a spiritual and holy man, smiling and playfully, said to him: "You will sell all your sackcloth to the Lord for a good price! Many canopies and silk coverings will hang over this body of yours now clothed in sackcloth." At the time blessed Francis, on account of his illness, wore a fur cap covered with sackcloth as well as a tunic of sackcloth. With great fervor of spirit and joy blessed Francis—not himself, but the Holy Spirit through him—answered: "You're right because that's how it will be."

↓AC 4 //2MP 1〔

[9]

While he was staying in that palace, blessed Francis, realizing that he was getting sicker by the day, had himself carried on a litter to the church of Saint Mary of the Portiuncula, since he could not ride horseback because of his **great** illness. When those who were carrying him passed along the road **near** the hospital, he asked them to place the litter on the ground. Since he could hardly see because of the serious and prolonged eye-disease, he had the litter turned so that he would face the city of Assisi. Raising himself up slightly on the litter, he blessed the city of Assisi. " Lord," he said, "just as I believe that at an earlier time this city was the abode of wicked and evil men, with a bad reputation throughout all this region; so now I realize that, because of Your abundant mercy and in Your own time, You have shown *an abundance of Your mercies* to it. Now it has become the abode of those who acknowledge You, *give glory to Your name*, offer the fragrance of good life, doctrine, and good reputation to the whole Christian people. I ask You, therefore, Lord Jesus Christ, *Father of mercies*, not to consider our ingratitude. May it always be mindful of the abundant mercies which You have shown to it, that it always be an abode for those who acknowledge You, and glorify *Your name blessed and glorious throughout the ages.* Amen."

After saying these things, he was carried to Saint Mary of the Portiuncula.

↓AC 5 //2MP 12〔

Neh 13:22; Ps 51:3
Ps 115:1
2 Cor 1:3
Dn 3:26; Rom 1:25; 2 Cor 11:31

---

a. Cf. For an understanding of this phrase, cf. FA:ED II 256 a.

[10]

↓AC 6

AC 7 //2MP 123

From the time of his conversion till the day of his death, blessed Francis, whether healthy or sick, was always concerned to know and follow the will of the Lord. One day a brother said to blessed Francis: "Father, your life and manner of living were and are a light and a mirror[a] not only for your brothers but also for the entire Church of God, and your death will be the same. Although for the brothers and many others your death will mean great grief and sorrow, for you it will rather be a great consolation and infinite joy. You will pass from great toil to the greatest rest, from many sorrows and temptations to infinite happiness, from your great poverty, which you always loved and carried from the beginning of your conversion till the day of your death, to the greatest, true and infinite riches, from death in time to life in eternity. There *you will* forever *behold face to face* the Lord your *God* whom you have contemplated in this world with so much desire and love."

1 Cor 13:12; Gn 32:30

After saying these things he said to him openly: "Father, you should know the truth: **if** the Lord **does not** send his own remedy from heaven to your body, your sickness is incurable and, as the doctors already said, you do not have long to live. I told you this to comfort your spirit, that you may always rejoice, inside and out; especially so that your brothers and others who come to visit you, may find you rejoicing in the Lord, since they know and believe that you will die soon. Thus, as they see this and, after your death, others hear about it, your death, like your life and manner of living, may be held in remembrance by all."

Although racked with sickness, blessed Francis, praised God with great fervor of spirit and joy of body and soul, and told him: "If I am to die soon, call Brother Angelo and Brother Leo that they may sing to me about Sister Death."[b]

CtC 1-11

Those brothers came to him, and with many tears, sang the *Canticle of Brother Sun* and the other creatures of the Lord, which he had composed in his illness for the praise of the Lord and the consolation of his own soul and that of others. Before the last stanza he added one about Sister Death:

CtC 12-13

"Praised be You, My Lord, through our Sister Bodily Death
    from whom no one living can escape.
    Woe to those who die in mortal sin.

---

a. Aside from the title of and introduction to this work, this word, *speculum* [mirror], appears only twice more, 1MP 27, 42.

b. For information concerning Brother Angelo, see FA:ED II 67 a; and concerning Brother Leo, FA:ED II 66 d.

Blessed are those whom death will find in Your most holy will,
for the second death shall do them no harm."

[11]

One day blessed Francis called his companions to himself: "You   ↓AC 8 //2MP 11
know how faithful and devoted Lady Jacoba dei Settesoli was and is
to me and to our religion.[a] Therefore I believe she would consider it a
great favor and consolation if you notified her about my condition.
Above all, tell her to send us some cloth for a tunic of religious cloth
the color of ashes, like the cloth made by Cistercian monks in the
region beyond the Alps.[b] Have her also send some of that confection
which she often made for me when I was in the City.[c] This confection, made of almonds, sugar or honey, and other things, the
Romans **speak of as** *mostacciolo*."

That spiritual woman was a **holy** widow, devoted to God. She
belonged to one of the more noble and wealthy families of the entire
City."[d] Through the merits and words of blessed Francis she had
obtained such grace from God that she seemed like another Magdalene, always full of tears and devotion for love of God.

After the letter was written, as dictated by the holy father, while
one brother was looking for another one to deliver the letter, there
was a knock at the door. When one of the brothers opened the gate,
he saw Lady Jacoba who had hurried from the City to visit blessed
Francis. With great joy the brother immediately went to tell blessed
Francis that Lady Jacoba had come to visit him with her son and
many other people. "What shall we do, Father," he said, "shall we
allow her to enter and come in here?" He said this because blessed
Francis a long time ago had ordered that in that place no women
enter that cloister out of respect and devotion for that place. Blessed
Francis answered him: "This command need not be observed in the
case of this lady whose faith and devotion made her come here from
so far away." And in this way, she came in to see blessed Francis, crying many tears in his presence.

They marveled: she brought with her shroud-cloth, that is,
gray-colored cloth, for a tunic, and all the other things that were
written in the letter. This made the brothers greatly marvel at the
holiness of blessed Francis.

---

a. For information concerning Lady Jacoba de Settelsoli, see FA:ED II 122 b.
b. Cf. FA:ED II 122 a.
c. Cf. FA:ED II 49 a.
d. FA:ED II: 49 a.

"While I was praying," Lady Jacoba told the brothers, "a voice within me said, 'Go, visit your father, blessed Francis, without delay, and hurry, because if you delay long you will not find him alive. Moreover, take such-and-such cloth for his tunic, as well as the ingredients for making that particular confection. Also take with you a great quantity of wax **for his lamps** and some incense, **as blessed Francis had written in the letter.'** " But the Lord Himself willed to inspire that lady as a reward and consolation for her soul. In this way we would more easily recognize the great holiness of that saint, that poor man, whom the heavenly Father wished to honor so greatly in the days he was dying. He inspired the Kings *to travel with gifts* to honor the child, His beloved Son, in the days of His birth and His poverty. So too He willed to inspire this noble lady in a faraway region to travel with gifts to honor and venerate the glorious and holy body of His servant the saint, who loved and followed the poverty of His beloved Son with so much fervor and love in life and in death.

One day **she** made that confection the holy father wanted to eat. He ate only a little of it, however, since he was near death, and daily his body was becoming weaker on account of his illness.

She also had many candles made which would burn around his holy body after his death. From the cloth she had brought for his tunic, the brothers made him the tunic in which he was buried. He ordered the brothers to sew pieces of sackcloth on the outside of it as a sign and example of most holy humility and poverty. It happened, as it pleased **the Lord,** that during the same week that Lady Jacoba arrived, blessed Francis passed to the Lord.

[12]

From the beginning of his conversion blessed Francis, *with God's help,* like *a wise man,* established himself and *his house,* that is, the religion, *upon a* firm *rock,* the greatest humility and poverty of the Son of God, calling it the religion of "Lesser Brothers."

On the greatest humility: thus at the beginning of the religion, after the brothers grew in number, he wanted the brothers to stay in hospitals of lepers to serve them. At that time whenever nobles and commoners came to the religion, they were told, among other things, that they had to serve the lepers and stay in their houses.

On the greatest poverty: as stated in the *Rule:* let the brothers remain *as strangers and pilgrims* in the houses in which they stay. Let them not seek **to have anything under heaven,** except holy poverty, by which, **in this world,** they are nourished by **God** with bodily food and virtue, and, in the next, will attain a heavenly inheritance.

Margin notes:
Mt 2:1-2
↓AC 9 //2MP 44
Mk 16:20
Mt 7:24
LR VI 2
LR VI 6
1 Pt 2:11

He established himself on the greatest poverty and humility, because, although he was a great prelate in the church of God, he wanted and chose to be lowly not only in the church of God, but **also** among his brothers.

[13]

One day he was preaching to the people of Terni in the piazza in front of the bishop's residence. The bishop of that city, a discerning and spiritual man, attended that sermon. When the sermon was over, the bishop stood up and, among other words of God that he spoke to them, he said: "From the beginning, when the Lord planted and *built His church,* He always **brightened** it with holy men who would improve it by word and example. Now, *in this final hour,* God has beautified his Church with this little poor man, lowly and unlettered," pointing all the while to blessed Francis. "And because of this," he continued, "you should love and honor the Lord and avoid sin *for He has not done thus for every nation.*"

After the sermon, blessed Francis came down from the place where he was preaching, and together the Lord Bishop and blessed Francis entered the bishop's church. Blessed Francis bowed down before the Lord Bishop and *fell down at his feet,* saying to him: "I tell **you** the truth, my Lord Bishop: no person in this world has yet honored me as much as you have today. Other people say: 'That man is a saint!' They attribute glory and holiness to the creature, not to the Creator. You, however, like a discerning man, *have separated what is precious from what is vile.*"

Often when blessed Francis was honored and people said, "This man is a saint," he would respond to such expressions by saying: "I am still not sure, **since** I might have sons and daughters." And he would say: "If at any moment the Lord wanted to take back the treasure He has loaned to me, what would I have left except just body and soul, which even non-believers have? I must believe, rather, that if the Lord had granted a thief and even a non-believer as many gifts as He has given me, they would be more faithful to the Lord than I."

He continued: "As in a painting of the Lord and the Blessed Virgin on wood, it is God and the Blessed Virgin who are honored; God and the Blessed Virgin are held in memory. The wood and the paint attribute nothing to themselves because they are merely wood and paint. In the same way, a servant of God is a painting, that is, a creature of God, in whom God is honored because of His goodness. Like wood or paint, he must not attribute anything to himself, but give all *honor and glory to God.* He should not attribute anything to himself

Mt 16:18
1 Jn 2:18

Ps 147:20

Mk 5:22; Acts 10:25

Jer 15:19

1 Tm 1:17

↓AC 10 //2C 14
//2MP 45

↓AC 10 //2C 133

while he is alive except shame and trouble, because, while he is alive, the flesh is always opposed to God's gifts."

[14]

AC 39//2C 143
//2MP 39
Blessed Francis wanted to be humble among his brothers, **in order to pursue and** preserve greater humility. A few years after his conversion he resigned the office of prelate before all the brothers during a chapter held at Saint Mary of the Portiuncula. "From now on," he said, "I am dead to you. But here is Brother Peter di Catanio: let us all, you and I, obey him."

↓AC 11
Then all the brothers began to cry loudly and weep profusely, but blessed Francis bowed down before Brother Peter and promised him
ER Prol 4
obedience and reverence. From that time on, until his death, he remained a subject, like one of the other brothers.

[15]

AC 11//2MP 46
He wished to be subject to the general minister and the provincials,[a] so that in whatever province he stayed or preached, he obeyed the minister of that province. What is more, a long time before his death, for the sake of greater perfection and humility, he said to the general minister: "I want you to put one of my companions in your place regarding me, so that I may obey him as I would obey you. For the sake of good example and the virtue of obedience, in life and in death I always want you to be with me."

↓AC 11//2C 151
From that time until his death, he always had one of his companions as a guardian whom he obeyed in place of the general minister.[b] One time he said to his companions: "Among other favors, the Most High has given me this grace: I would obey a novice who entered our religion today, if he were appointed my guardian, just as readily as I would obey him who is the first and the eldest in the life and religion of the brothers. A subject should not consider his prelate, a human being, but God, for love of Whom he is subject to him." He likewise said: "There is no prelate in the whole world who would be as feared by his subjects and brothers as the Lord would make me feared by my brothers, if I wished. But the Most High gave me this grace: that I want to be content with all, as one who is lesser in the religion."

---

a. The Latin here is *provincialibus* [provincials], the first time the word is found in the form of a noun in this literature. Throughout the earlier tradition, those entrusted with the care of their brothers in provinces are identified through their ministry in those areas, i.e., provincial ministers.

b. For an understanding of the title *guardianus* [guardian], see FA:ED I 98 a.

We who were with him witnessed this often with our own eyes. Frequently, when some of the brothers did not provide for his needs, or said something to him that would ordinarily offend a person, he would immediately go to prayer. On returning, he did not want to remember it by saying "Brother so-and-so did not provide for me," or "He said such-and-such to me."

[16]

Moreover, one time during his sickness, for the sake of greater perfection and poverty, he resigned as the general minister for all his companions, saying: "I do not wish to have a special companion; but for the love of the Lord God, brothers can go with me from place to place and provide for me as the Lord inspires them." And he added: "I have seen a blind man who had no guide for his journey except one little dog." Thus, the closer he approached death, the more careful in complete perfection he became in considering how he might live and die in complete humility and poverty.

↓AC 40//2C 144
//2MP 40

↓AC 11//2MP 4

[17]

The day Lady Jacoba prepared that confection for blessed Francis, the father remembered Bernard. "Brother Bernard likes this confection," he said to his companions. Calling one of his companions, he told him "Go, tell Brother Bernard to come to me immediately." The brother went at once and brought him to blessed Francis. Sitting next to the bed where blessed Francis was lying, Brother Bernard said: "Father! I beg you, bless me and show me your love. I believe that, if you show me your love with fatherly affection, God Himself and the other brothers of the religion will love me more."

↓AC 12//2MP

Blessed Francis was not able to see him, since for many days he had lost his sight. *Extending his right hand, he placed it on the head* of Brother Giles, the third of the first brothers, who at that moment was sitting next to Brother Bernard. He thought he was placing it on the head of Brother Bernard. Feeling the head of Brother Giles, like a person going blind, he immediately recognized him by the Holy Spirit, and said, "This is not the head of my Brother Bernard."[a]

Gn 48:14

Brother Bernard immediately drew **himself** closer to him. Blessed Francis, placing his hand on his head, blessed him. "Write what I tell you," he then said to one of his companions. "Brother Bernard was the first brother *the Lord gave me.* He began first and most perfectly

Dt 9:11

---

a. For the significance of the blessing of Bernard, see FA:ED II 126 b.

fulfilled the perfection of the holy Gospel, distributing *all his goods to* Mt 19:21; 25:14
the poor. Because of this and his many other prerogatives, I am bound
to love him more than any other brother in the whole religion. As
much as I am able, it is my will and command that whoever becomes
general minister should love and honor him as he would me. Let the
other provincial ministers and the brothers of the whole religion
hold him in my place."[a] Because of this, Brother Bernard was greatly
consoled as were the other brothers who saw this.

//2C 48   Another time, considering the outstanding perfection of Brother
Bernard, blessed Francis prophesied about him in the presence of
some of the brothers: "I tell you, some of the greatest and most cunning devils have been sent to test Brother Bernard. They will send
him *many trials and temptations.* The merciful Lord, however, will Acts 14:22; 20:19
deliver him toward the end of his life from all troubles and temptations, internal and external. And He will place his spirit and body in
such peace, quiet, and consolation that all the brothers who see or
hear of this will be greatly astonished, and consider it a great miracle.
In peace, quiet, and consolation of both body and soul he will pass
from this world to the Lord."

The brothers who heard this from blessed Francis were greatly
astonished, since everything he predicted about him through the
Holy Spirit came true, to the letter, point by point. **For** in his last illness Brother Bernard was in such great peace and quiet of spirit that
he did not want to lie down. And if he lay down, he lay in a sitting
position so that not even the lightest mist of humors would reach his
head, inducing fantasies or dreams, rather than thoughts of God.
And if this happened, he would immediately get up and strike himself, saying "What was that? Why was I thinking that way?" For
relief, he gladly used to smell rose water, but as he drew closer to
death, he refused to do even this, for the sake of constant meditation
on God. He would say to anyone offering it: "Don't distract me."

In order to die more freely, peacefully, and quietly, he had **by now**
let go of the care for his body, putting himself in the hands of one of
the brothers who was a doctor and who was taking care of him. "I do
not wish to be concerned about eating or drinking," he would say,
"but I entrust myself to you. If you give me something, I'll take it. If
you don't, then I won't."

He requested that holy anointing be given him, and when the
brothers came prepared and began to do the anointing, suddenly
the vessel containing the holy oil broke apart. The Brother
Peregrino from the Marches, a spiritual and holy man who was

---

a. See FA:ED II 127 a.

Mk 14:3 then his companion, said laughing under his breath: "Look, *the alabaster jar of oil is* now *broken,* now abundant graces will descend and be sprinkled about." And during the anointing Brother Bernard could not restrain himself, but cried abundant tears, he who was previously so withdrawn. Then he had the brothers gathered Mt 17:14 and threw himself to the ground *on his knees* and confessed his guilt for all his offenses, saying: "I have not been a lesser brother except in temptations; in these the Lord supported me."

And he begged the brothers to pray devoutly for him; "But especially this prayer: that when you have me in mind, you think of yourselves." On Friday a basket of cherries was brought, and he said to the brothers who were with him and to the brother doctor: "Give me some cherries, and permit me to eat them, for I shall eat no more. I also ask you to eat with me and do the Passover with me." While he ate he could not restrain his tears. The brothers, Gn 42:8 therefore, began to say: "This saint *was* truly *not recognized!"* The brothers wept and joyfully regarded him as one of the Lord's saints.

When he began to grow weaker, he wanted to have a priest brother with him at all times, until the hour of his death. Whenever any thought entered his mind for which his conscience reproached him, he immediately confessed it and then said his penance.

After his death, his flesh became white and soft and he seemed to be smiling, so that he appeared more handsome after death than before.[a] Whoever gazed on him experienced more delight in seeing him this way than when he was alive, because he looked like a saint who was smiling.

[18]

During the week in which blessed Francis died, Lady Clare was ↓AC 13 //2MP seriously ill. She was the first plant of the Order of Sisters, the abbess of the Poor Sisters of the monastery of San Damiano in Assisi, who emulated Saint Francis in observing always the poverty of the Son of God.[b] She feared that she would die before blessed Francis. She wept 2 Sm 17:8 *in bitterness of spirit* and could not be comforted, because she would not be able before her death to see her only father after God, that is, blessed Francis, her comforter both internally and externally, and, in God's grace, her first founder granted her by that glorious Lord before her conversion and in her holy manner of living."

---

a. For a similar description of Francis after his death, see 1C 112, FA:ED I 280.
b. For the nature of this illness, see FA:ED II 128 a.

She sent word of this to blessed Francis through one of the brothers. Blessed Francis heard this and was moved to piety, since he loved her and her sisters with fatherly affection because of their holy manner of living, and especially because, a few years after he began to have brothers, she was converted to the Lord through his advice, *working with the Lord.* Her conversion not only greatly edified the religion of the brothers, but also the entire Church of God.

Mk 16:20

Blessed Francis **truly** considered what **Lady Clare** desired, that is, to see him, could not be done then **because** they were both seriously ill. To console her, he wrote his blessing in a letter and also absolved her from any failings, if she had any, regarding his commands and wishes or the commands and wishes of the Son of God. Moreover, so that she would put aside all her grief and be consoled in the Lord, he, or rather the Spirit of God speaking through him, spoke to the brother **Lady Clare** had sent. "Go and take this letter to the Lady, and tell her to put aside all her grief and sorrow over not being able to see me now. Let her be assured that before her death, both she and her sisters will see me and will receive the greatest consolation from me."[a]

Soon afterwards blessed Francis passed away during the night. In the morning, all the people of the city of Assisi, men and women, with all the clergy, took the holy body from the place where he had died. With hymns and praises, all carrying tree-branches, they carried him to San Damiano at the Lord's will, in order to fulfill that word which the Lord had spoken through His saint to console His daughters and servants.

The iron grille was removed from the window through which the servants of Christ usually receive communion and sometimes hear the word of God. The brothers lifted his holy body from the stretcher and, raising him in their arms, they held him in front of the window for over an hour. By then Lady Clare and her sisters had received **great** consolation from him, although with many tears and afflicted with great grief, because, after God, he was their one consolation in this world.[b]

[19]

↓AC 14//3C 32
//2MP 113

Saturday evening before nightfall, after vespers, when blessed Francis passed to the Lord, many birds called larks flew low above

---

a. See FA:ED II 129 a.

b. As noted in AC 13, there are significant differences between this account of the body of Francis being brought to San Damiano and that of Thomas's *Life of Saint Francis*, cf. 1C 116-117.

the roof of the house where blessed Francis lay, wheeling in a circle and singing.

We, who were with blessed Francis, have written about this. We bear witness that we often heard him say: "If I ever speak to the emperor, I will beg him, for the love of God and by my entreaties, to enact a written law forbidding anyone to catch our sister larks or do them any harm. Likewise, all mayors of cities and lords of castles and villages should be bound to oblige people each year on the Nativity of the Lord to scatter wheat and other grain along the roads outside towns and villages, so that all the birds, but especially our sister larks, may have something to eat on such a solemn feast. Also, out of reverence for the Son of God, whom His Virgin Mother on that night *laid in a manger,* everyone should have to give Brother Ox and Brother Ass a generous portion of fodder on that night. Likewise, on the Nativity of the Lord, all the poor should be fed their fill by the rich."

For blessed Francis held the Nativity of the Lord in greater reverence than any other of the Lord's solemnities. For, although the Lord may have accomplished our salvation in his other solemnities, nevertheless, once He was born to us, as blessed Francis would say, it was certain that we would be saved. On that day, he wanted every Christian to rejoice in the Lord, and, for love of Him *who gave Himself to us,* wished everyone to be cheerfully generous not only to the poor but also to the animals and birds.

Concerning larks, blessed Francis used to say, "Our Sister Lark has a capuche like a religious, and is a humble bird, who gladly goes along the road looking for some grain. Even if she finds it in the animals' manure, she pecks it out and eats it. While flying, she praises the Lord, like good religious looking down on earthly things, *whose movement is always in heaven.* Moreover, her clothes, that is, her feathers, resemble earth, giving an example to religious not to wear clothes that are colorful and refined, but dull, like earth." And because blessed Francis considered all these things in sister larks, he loved them very much and was glad to see them.

[20]

When blessed Francis was invited at the request of the Lord Cardinal Leo to remain awhile with him in the City, especially because it was winter, he consented. On the first night, the devils beat him. Calling his companions he said to them: "Why did the devils beat me? Why *has* the Lord *given them power* to harm me?"

And he began to say: "The devils are the police of our Lord. Just as the *podestà* sends his police to punish a wrong-doer, in the same way,

//2C 200//2MP

Lk 2:7

Ti 2:14

Phil 3:20

↓AC 117 //2C 1⟩

//2MP 67

Rv 9:3

//2C 120

the Lord *punishes and corrects those whom He loves* through the demons, Heb 12:6, 7; Prv 3:12
who are His police and act as His ministers in this office.

"Even a perfect religious very often sins in ignorance. Consequently if he does not realize his sin, he is punished by the devil so
that he may see and carefully reflect internally and externally
because of that punishment how he may have offended. For in this
life the Lord leaves nothing unpunished in those whom He loves tenderly. *By the mercy* and grace *of God,* I do not know if I have offended Rom 12:1
Him in any way which I have not corrected by confession and satisfaction. Indeed the Lord in His mercy granted me this gift. He makes
me understand through prayer any way in which I please or displease Him.

"It seems to me that it could be that the Lord punished me
through His police because, although the Lord Cardinal gladly does
this mercy to me and my body needs to accept, and I can accept it
from him confidently, nevertheless, my brothers, who go through
the world suffering hunger and many hardships, and other brothers
who stay in poor little **places** and hermitages, may have an occasion
for grumbling against me when they hear that I am staying with the
Lord Cardinal: 'We are enduring so many hardships while he is having his comforts.' I am bound always to give them good example;
because I was given to them, especially for this. For the brothers are
more edified when I stay in poor little places rather than in other
places. When they hear and know that I am **carrying** the same trials,
they endure theirs with greater patience."

Blessed Francis was always sickly. Even in the world he was by
nature a frail and weak man, and each day grew more sickly until the
day of his death, he nevertheless considered that he should show a
good example to the brothers and always take away from them any
occasion for complaining about him, so the brothers could not say:
"He has all he needs, but we don't."

Whether he was healthy or sick, until the day of his death, he
wanted to endure so much need, that if any of the brothers who
knew this, as we did, we who were with him for some time until the
day of his death, and if they brought this back to mind, they would
not be able to restrain their tears; and when they suffer some need or
troubles, they would bear them with greater patience.

And coming to the cardinal, **he told him** all that had happened
and **what** he said to his companion. And he added: "People have
great faith in me and think that I am a holy man, and **this night** the
devils **expelled me** from the cell." **He said this about the tower
which was within the city wall where he wanted to stay as in a
remote cell.**

Thus, blessed Francis **with the cardinal's** permission returned to
the hermitage of Saint Francis at Fonte Colombo near Rieti.[a]

[21]

Blessed Francis said: "If the brothers knew how many trials the   ↓AC 118 //2M
demons cause me, there would not be one of them who would not
have great piety and compassion for me." As a result, as he often said
to his companions, he was unable by himself to satisfy the brothers
or sometimes to show them the friendliness which the brothers
desired.

After he left the world, blessed Francis did not want to sleep on a   ↓AC 119//2C €
mattress nor have a feather pillow for his head, when he was sick or   //2MP 98
for any other reason. **Although once, when he was sick with an
eye-affliction and** the brothers forced him against his will, **for his
head** he used a pillow filled with feathers that he had received from
Lord John of Greccio, whom the saint loved with great affection.
Jn 13:27   **Because** *the devil entered into* that pillow, the saint was unable to sleep
during that night or to stand erect for prayer. After the saint recog-
nized this, he threw it away, and said to his companion, "The devil is
Rom 12:1   very cunning and subtle. Because *by the mercy* and grace *of God* he cannot harm me in my soul, he wanted to disturb the need of the body by
preventing me from sleeping and standing up to pray, in order to stifle the devotion and joy of my heart so that I will complain about my
sickness."

[22]

For many years blessed Francis suffered from serious illness of his   ↓AC 119//2MP
stomach, spleen, and liver, as well as from a disease of the eyes.[b] Yet,
he was so devout and prayed with so much reverence, that during
times of prayer, he refused to lean against a wall or partition, but
always stood **erect,** without a capuche over his head, and sometimes
on his knees, especially when he spent the greater part of the day and
night in prayer.

When he went through the world on foot **preaching,** he always   ↓AC 119//2C 9
would stop walking in order to say his Hours. If he was riding on
horseback, because he was always sick **and getting sicker,** he would
get down to say his Hours.

---

a. Cf. FA:ED II 196 a, for the curious reference to "the hermitage 'of Saint Francis' at Fonte Colombo."
b. Concerning Francis's eye disease, cf. FA:ED II 185 a.

↓AC 120
One time, when he was returning from the City, it rained the whole day as he was leaving the City. Since he was very sick, he was riding on horseback, but he got off his horse to say his Hours, standing on the roadside despite the rain which completely soaked him.

//2C 96
He said: "If the body wants to eat its food in peace and quiet, and both it and the body eventually will become food for worms, in what peace and quiet should the soul receive its food, which is God Himself!"

And he used to say: "The devil is delighted when he can extinguish or prevent devotion and joy in the heart of a servant of God which spring from clean prayer and other good works. For if the devil can have something of his own in a servant of God, he will in a short time make a single hair into a beam, always making it bigger, unless the servant of God is wise, removing and destroying it as quickly as possible by means of contrition, confession, and works of satisfaction"

[23]

C 120//2MP 97
Blessed Francis used to say that if Brother Body could not have its needs fulfilled whether healthy or sick, because of want or poverty, and after requesting them decently and humbly for the love of God from his brother or his prelate they are not given to him, then let him patiently bear this for the love of God and it will be credited to him as martyrdom. And because he did what is his to do, making his needs known, he would be excused from sin, even if the body only on this account would become very sick, **that is from vigils, prayers, and other good works.**

//2MP 95
Blessed Francis had this as his highest and main goal: he was always careful to have and preserve in himself spiritual joy internally and externally, even though from the beginning of his conversion until the day of his death he **would** greatly afflict his body. He used to say that if a servant of God strives to have and preserve joy internally and externally which proceeds from purity of heart, the devils can do him no harm. They would say: "Since the servant of God has joy both in tribulation and in prosperity, we do not know where to find an entrance to enter him and do him harm."

And he also used to say: "If I feel tempted and depressed and I look at the joy of my companion, because of that joy I turn away from the temptation and depression and toward inner **and outer** joy."

[24]

Blessed Francis **used to say:** "My brothers, I say that each of you must consider his own constitution, because, although one of you may be sustained with less food than another, I nevertheless **want** one who needs more food **not** to try **imitating** him in this. Rather, considering his constitution, he should provide his body with what it needs. Just as we must beware of overindulgence in eating, which harms body and soul, so we must beware of excessive abstinence even more, because the Lord *desires mercy and not sacrifice.*"

And he said: "Let each one provide his body with what it needs as our poverty allows. This is what I wish and command you."

For the first brothers and those who came after them for a long time mortified their bodies excessively, not only by abstinence in food and drink, but also *in vigils, cold,* and manual *labor.* Next to their skins those who could get them wore iron rings and breastplates and the roughest hair shirts, which they were better able to get. Considering that the brothers could get sick because of this, and in a short time some were already ailing, the holy father therefore commanded in one of the chapters that no brother wear anything next to the skin except the tunic.

We who were with him bear witness to this fact about him: from the time he began to have brothers, and also during his whole lifetime, he was discerning with the brothers, provided that in the matter of food and other things, they did not deviate at any time from the norm of the poverty and decency of our religion, which the early brothers observed. Nevertheless, even before he had brothers, from the beginning of his conversion and during his whole lifetime, he was severe with his own body, even though from the time of his youth he was a man of a frail and weak constitution, and when he was in the world he could not live without comforts.

One time, perceiving that the brothers had exceeded the norm of poverty and decency in food and in things, he said in a sermon he gave, speaking to a few brothers, who stood for all the brothers: "Don't the brothers think that my body needs special food? But because I must be the model and example for all the brothers, I want to use and be content with poor food and things, not fine ones."

[25]

In the first days, because the brothers were few in number, **they went alone for alms.** And when they returned, each one showed blessed Francis the alms he had collected, one saying to the other, "I collected more alms than you!"

Hos 6:6

2 Cor 11:27

↓AC 50 //2MP 2

↓AC 50//2C 21
//2MP 27

//1C 40

↓AC 51 //2MP 1

And blessed Francis rejoiced, seeing them so happy and cheerful. From then on each of them more willingly asked permission to go for alms.

1C 52//2MP 19   At that time, when Blessed Francis was with his brothers whom he had then, he was of such purity that, **from that time,** that hour when the Lord revealed to him that he and his brothers should live

ER Prol 1   according to the form of the holy Gospel, he desired and strove to observe it to the letter during his whole lifetime.

Therefore he told the brother who did the cooking for the brothers, that when he wanted the brothers to eat beans, he should not put them in warm water in the evening for the next day, as people usually do. This was so the brothers would observe the words of the holy Gospel: *"Do not be concerned about tomorrow."* So that brother used to   Mt 6:34 put them in water to soften after the brothers said matins.

Because of this, for a long time many brothers observed this in a great many places where they stayed on their own, especially in cities. They did not want to collect or receive more alms than were enough for them for one day.

[26]

AC 53//2MP 28   One time when blessed Francis was at **Rivo Torto,**[a] a certain spiritual brother, an elder in religion, was staying there. He was very weak **and getting sicker, toward whom the father** *was moved to piety.*   Lk 7:13 The brothers back then, sick and healthy, with **enthusiasm** and patience took poverty for abundance. They did not take medicines in their illnesses, but more willingly did what was contrary to the body. Blessed Francis said to himself: "If that brother would eat some grapes early in the morning, I believe it would help him."

//2C 176   One day, therefore, he secretly got up early in the morning, and called that brother and took him into the vineyard which is near that **place.** He chose a vine that had grapes that were good and ready for eating. Sitting down with that brother next to the vine, he began **to chew on** some grapes so that the brother would not be ashamed to eat alone, and while they were eating them, that brother praised the Lord God. As long as he lived, he always recalled among the brothers, with great devotion and flowing tears, the mercy the holy father had done to him.

---

a. For information on the Rivo Torto, see FA:ED I 220 a.

[27]

The abbot of Saint Benedict of Monte Subasio granted blessed   ↓AC 56
Francis and his brothers the Church of Saint Mary of the Portiuncula
as the poorest little church they had. **And he wanted that,** if the Lord
increased **the brothers,** it be the head of the whole religion. And
blessed Francis granted this.

And he was overjoyed at the place granted to the brothers, **and**   //2C 18// 2MP
because **it was called in this way,** and because it was such a poor little church **in the district of Assisi,** and because of the surname it
had, for it was surnamed: "of the Portiuncula," **in contrast to what it
had previously been called.** This name foreshadowed that it was to
be the mother and head of the poor Lesser Brothers. Blessed Francis
used to say: "This is why the Lord willed that no other church be
granted to the brothers, and why the first brothers would not build
any completely new church, and would not have any other but this
one. For this church was a prophecy that has been fulfilled in the
coming of the Lesser Brothers." And although it was poor and almost
in ruins already for a long time, the people of the city of Assisi and its
neighborhood had always held it in great devotion.

Although the abbot and the monks had freely granted that
church to blessed Francis and his brothers without any payment or
annual tax, blessed Francis, a good and experienced teacher who
Mt 7:24; Lk 6:48   wished to *build his house on solid rock,* that is, his congregation on great
poverty, every year he used to send the abbot a basket full of small
fish called *"lasche."*[a] He did this as a sign of greater humility and poverty, so that the brothers would not have any place of their own, and
would not remain in any place that was not owned by others, and
thus they in no way had the power to sell it or give it away. Each year,
when the brothers brought the little fish to the monks, they in turn,
because of the humility of blessed Francis, who had done this of his
own will, gave him and his brothers a jar filled with oil.

We who were with blessed Francis bear witness that he spoke of
that church with great conviction, because of the great preference
that the Lord indicated there and revealed to him in that place,
namely that among all the other churches of this world the blessed
Virgin loves that church. About the time of his death, **he left that
church to the brothers** in a **testament that it might be held in the
greatest devotion and reverence by the brothers.**[b]

---

a. Lasche or lasca, is the common name given to several species of fish in the Cyprinidae family.
   According to Petru M. Banarescu, lasche were a very tasty fish that could be served in a variety of
   ways. Cf. Petru M. Banarescu, *Freshwater Fish of Europe,* vol. 5/1 (Kempten/Allgau, AULA-Verlag,
   1999), 288. The word lasca is found in the Italian proverb: *Ogni lasca ha la sua lisca* [Every fish has
   its bone].
b. Cf. FA:ED II 157 a.

And he wanted it to be under **the ordinance of the general,** who would place a holy family there, cleric brothers and lay brothers who would serve them, and he wanted the place to be kept especially pure and holy in hymns and praises of the Lord. And he used to say: "If the brothers and their places, where they stay, some day stray from the purity and holiness and decency befitting them, I want this place to be a mirror and a good example for the entire religion, a candelabra *before the throne of God* and before the blessed Virgin. Thus may the Lord have mercy on the faults and failings of the brothers and always preserve and protect this religion, His little plant."

But the brothers who once dwelt there served the father's will. They used to mortify the flesh not only *by fasting,* but *by* their *many vigils, by cold, nakedness,* and *manual labor.* For, in order not to remain idle, they very frequently went and helped poor people in their fields, and sometimes these people would give them some bread for the love of God. In this way, they preserved the holiness **of the place** and with constant prayer day and night and by constant silence. And if, at times, they spoke after the time established for silence, they discussed with the greatest devotion and decorum matters pertaining to the praise of God and the salvation of souls. If it happened, and it rarely did, that someone began to utter useless or idle words, immediately he was corrected by another. And by these and other virtues, they used to sanctify themselves and the place.

[28]

Francis returned when the general began to have a small house built at the ancient site of Saint Mary of the Portiuncula for the brothers who were suffering great need because of those arriving unexpectedly for whom they would, as it should be, give way. Hearing the work on the house, he called the minister telling him: "Brother, this place is the model and example for the entire religion. And it is my will that the brothers of this place endure trouble and need for the love of God, so that the brothers of the whole religion who come here will take back to their places a good example of poverty, rather than have these brothers receive satisfaction and consolation. Otherwise, the other brothers of the religion will take up this example of building in their places. They will say: 'At Saint Mary of the Portiuncula, which is the first place of the brothers, such and such buildings are built, so we can certainly build in our own places.' "

[29]

One of the brothers, a spiritual man, to whom blessed Francis was ↓AC 57 // 2M very close, was staying in a hermitage. Considering that if blessed Francis came there at some time he would not have a suitable place to stay, he had a little cell built in a remote place near the place of the brothers, where blessed Francis could pray when he came. After a few days, it happened that blessed Francis came. When the brother led him to see it, blessed Francis said to him: "This little cell seems too beautiful to me. If you want me to stay in it for a few days, have it covered inside and out with ferns and tree-branches."

That little cell was not made of stonework but of wood, but because the wood was planed, made with hatchet and axe, it seemed too beautiful to blessed Francis. The brother immediately had it changed as blessed Francis had requested.

For the more the houses and cells of the brothers were poor and religious, the more willingly he would see them and sometimes be received as a guest there.

And so, through **God's** example, he did not want to have a house or cell in this world, nor did he have one built for himself. Moreover, if he ever happened to say to the brothers: "Prepare this cell this way," he would refuse afterwards to stay in it, because of that saying

Lk 12:22; Mt 6:31, 34 of the holy Gospel: *"Do not be concerned."*

[30]

Once when he was in Siena for treatment of the disease of his ↓AC 58//2MP eyes, he was staying in a cell, where after his death a chapel was built out of reverence for him. Lord Bonaventure, who had donated to the brothers the land where the brothers' place had been built, said to him: "What do you think of this place?" Blessed Francis answered him: "Do you want me to tell you how the places of the brothers should be built?" "I wish you would, Father," he answered.

And he told him: "When the brothers go to any city where they do not have a place, and they find someone who wants to give them enough land to build a place, have a garden, and whatever is necessary for them, they must first consider how much land is enough for them, always considering the holy poverty we have promised, and the good example we are bound to offer to others."

The holy father said this because he did not want the brothers for any reason to go beyond the norm of poverty either in houses or churches, in gardens or in other things they used. And he did not want them to possess the right of ownership to these places, but always to stay in them *as pilgrims and strangers*. For this reason, he did not want the brothers to have to be assigned to places in large groups, because it seemed to him that it was difficult for poverty **to be preserved.** From the beginning of his conversion until the end, at his death, this was his will: that holy poverty be observed to its fullest.

Test 24 1 Pt 2:11

Afterwards they should go to the bishop of that city and say to him: "Lord, for the love of the Lord God and the salvation of his soul, such-and-such a person wants to give us enough land so that we can build a place there. Therefore, we have recourse to you first, because you are the father and lord of the souls *of the entire flock* entrusted to you, as well as our souls and those of the other brothers who will stay in this place. Therefore, with the blessing of the Lord God and yours, we would like to build on it."

Acts 20:28

The saint would say this, because **he always wanted the brothers to honor and revere prelates:** "For this reason let them be called Lesser Brothers because, in name as well as example and deed, they should be **humbler** than all others of this world." And he used to say: "From the beginning of my conversion, when I separated myself from the world and father in the flesh, the Lord *put* His *word in the mouth* of the bishop of Assisi so he could counsel me well in the service of Christ and comfort me. Therefore, as well as the greater excellence that I consider in prelates **and in clerics,** not only in bishops, but in poor priests as well, I want to love them, revere them and regard them as my lords.

Ex 4:45; Is 51:16

"After receiving the bishop's blessing, let them go and have a big ditch dug around the land which they received for building the place, and as a sign of holy poverty and humility; let them place a hedge there, instead of a wall. Afterwards they may have poor little houses built, of mud and wood, and some little cells where the brothers can sometimes pray and where, for their own greater decency and also to avoid idle words, they can work.

"They may also have **small** churches made: however, the brothers must not have large churches made, in order to preach to the people there or for any other reason, for it is greater humility and better example when the brothers go to other churches to preach, so that they may observe holy poverty, and their humility and decency.

"And if prelates and clerics, religious or secular, should sometimes visit their places, their poor house, little cells, and churches in that place will preach to them and edify them."

And he said: "The brothers often have large buildings made, breaking with our holy poverty, resulting in **grumbling** and bad example to their neighbor. Afterwards, they abandon those places and buildings for the sake of better or healthier places, prompting those who gave alms there, as well as others who see or hear about this to be scandalized and greatly upset. It is, therefore, better that the brothers have small and poor places built, observing their profession, and giving their neighbor good example, rather than making things contrary to their profession and offering bad example to others. For, if it should ever happen that the brothers leave their little places and poor buildings for the sake of a more decent place, that would be very bad example and scandal."

During those days and in the same cell where blessed Francis spoke about these things to Lord Bonaventure, one night, vomiting blood **he came close to death. Therefore, fearing that he was dying, his brothers said to him:** "Father, bless us and the other brothers in the Order, and leave us some remembrance **to which we may have recourse after your death.**" ↓AC 59//2MP 8

Brother Francis had Brother Benedict of Piratro, who celebrated for **him,**[a] **called,** since, although he was sick, he always wanted, gladly and devoutly, to hear Mass whenever he was able. And when he had come, blessed Francis told him: "Write that I bless all my brothers, those who are and who will be in the religion until the end of the world."

And blessed Francis told him: "Since I cannot speak much because of my **illness,** I am showing my will to my brothers briefly in these three words: as a sign of remembrance of my blessing and my testament, may they always love each other; may they always love and observe our Lady Holy Poverty; and, may they always remain faithful and subject to the prelates and all the clerics of holy Mother Church."[b]

[31]

At one time while blessed Francis was staying at Saint Mary of the Portiuncula, **he** used to go through the villages and churches in the area around the city of Assisi, proclaiming and preaching to the people that they should do penance. And he would carry a broom to sweep the churches. ↓AC 60 // 2MP 9

---

a. See FA:ED II 162 a.
b. See FA:ED II 162 b.

For blessed Francis was very sad when he entered some church and saw that it was not clean. Therefore, after preaching to the people, at the end of the sermon he would always have all the priests who were present assembled in some remote place so he could not be overheard by secular people. He would preach to them about the salvation of souls and, in particular, that they should exercise care and concern in keeping churches clean, as well as altars and everything that pertained to the celebration of the divine mysteries.

AC 61//2C 190
//2MP 57
When blessed Francis was sweeping a church in a village one day, talk about this spread immediately through that village, especially because people enjoyed seeing and hearing him.

A man named John heard it, a man of amazing simplicity, who was *plowing in a field* of his near the church, and he immediately went to him. Finding him sweeping the church, he said to him: "Brother, give me the broom because I want to help you." Taking the broom from him, he swept the rest. 1 Kgs 19:19

When they sat down, he said to blessed Francis: "Brother, it's a long time now that I've wanted to serve God, especially after I heard talk about you and your brothers, but I did not know how to come to you. Now that it pleased God that I see you, I want to do whatever pleases you."

Considering his fervor, blessed Francis rejoiced in the Lord, especially because he then had few brothers, and because it seemed to him that, on account of his pure simplicity, he would make a good religious. So he said to him: "Brother, if you wish to belong to our company, you must expropriate yourself of all your things that you can get without scandal, and give them to the poor according to the counsel of the holy Gospel, because my brothers who were able to do so have done this."

As soon as he heard this, he immediately went into the field where he had left the oxen, and, untying them, brought one of them back to blessed Francis. "Brother," he said to him, "I have served my father and everyone in my household for many years. Although my portion of the inheritance is small, I want to take this ox as my share and give it to the poor, as you think best according to God."

But when his parents and brothers, who were still small, saw that he wanted to leave them, they and the entire household began to cry so bitterly that blessed Francis was moved to piety, **and he** said to them: "Prepare and serve a meal so we can all eat together, and don't cry, because I will make you happy." So they prepared it at once, and all of them ate with great joy.

After the meal **the saint** said to them: "This son of yours wants to serve God, and you should be glad and not sad about this. This will be

Mt 19:21
counted an honor and advantage to your souls and bodies, not only according to God but also according to the world, because God will be honored by your own flesh and blood, and all our brothers will be your sons and brothers. And, because he is a creature of God and wishes to serve his Creator, and to serve Him is to reign, I cannot and should not return him to you. But in order that you **may have** some consolation from all this, I want him to expropriate himself of this ox by giving it to you, although, according to the counsel of the holy Gospel, it ought *to be given* to other *poor people."* They were all consoled by the words of blessed Francis, and they rejoiced especially that the ox was returned to them, since they were poor.

Because blessed Francis greatly loved and was always pleased by pure and holy simplicity in himself and in others, he immediately dressed him in the clothing of the religion and took him as his companion. He was a man of such simplicity, that he believed he was bound to do everything blessed Francis would do.

Dt 32:40
So, whenever blessed Francis was in some other place to pray, he wanted to observe him so that he could imitate all his gestures. If blessed Francis knelt, or joined *his hands toward heaven,* or spat, or coughed, he would do the same. With great joy, blessed Francis began to reprove him for these kinds of simplicity. But he answered: "Brother, I promised to do everything you do. Therefore I want to do everything you do."

And blessed Francis marveled and **delighted,** seeing him in such purity and simplicity. For he began to be perfect in all virtues and good habits, so that blessed Francis and the other brothers greatly marveled at his perfection **in which** he died. After his death, therefore, Saint Francis, telling the brothers about his **conversion,** would call him "Saint John."

[32]

↓AC 64//2MP 5
Brother James the Simple, to whom the saint had entrusted a leper with many severe sores, was like a doctor **cleaning,** changing, and treating their wounds, for in those days the brothers stayed in the houses or hospitals of lepers. He led the leper with severe sores to Saint Mary of the Portiuncula.[a] As if reproving him, blessed Francis said: "You should not take our Christian brothers about in this way since it is not right for you or for them." Blessed Francis used to call lepers "Christian brothers."

---

a. These first two sentences are a greatly compressed section of AC 64. In doing so, the focus of the story is greatly sharpened, that is, the example of Brother James in caring for lepers.

Although he was pleased that he helped and served them, the holy father said this because he did not want him to take those with severe sores outside the hospital because people **abhorred** them.

After he said these things, blessed Francis immediately reproached himself, and he told his fault to Brother Peter of Catanio, who was then there, especially because blessed Francis believed that in reproving Brother James he had shamed the leper. And because of this he told his fault, to make amends to God and to the leper. Blessed Francis said to Brother Peter: "I tell you to confirm for me the penance I have chosen to do for this, and do not oppose me in any way."

Brother Peter told him: "Brother, do as you please."

Brother Peter so venerated and feared blessed Francis, and was so obedient to him, that he would not presume to change his obedience.

Blessed Francis said: "Let this be my penance: I will eat together with my Christian brother from the same dish."[a]

While blessed Francis was sitting at the table with the leper and other brothers, a bowl was placed between the two of them. The leper was completely covered with sores and ulcerated, and especially the fingers with which he was eating were deformed and bloody, so that whenever he put them in the bowl, blood dripped into it.

Brother Peter and the other brothers saw this, grew very sad, but did not dare say anything out of fear of the holy father.

The one who wrote this, saw it and bore witness to it.

[33][b]

↓AC 65//C 122
//2MP 59, 60

When blessed Francis remained alone one night to pray in the Church of Saint Peter of Bovaria, near the leper hospital of Trebio,[c] he felt a diabolical illusion. He got up and signing himself said: "On behalf of Almighty God, I tell you, demons, you may do in my body whatever God told you."

And Brother Peter, his companion, saw in the church that throne that had been Lucifer's, so that the response to him was that it was reserved for blessed Francis.

---

a. FA:ED II 167 a.

b. This is also a radically abbreviated version of AC 65. The editor reduces the story from twenty-three sentences to three.

c. The manuscript has Trebio, that is, the present village of Trevi between Foligno and Spoleto, Cf. infra Map Six.

↓AC 22//2C 21(
//2MP 88

[34]

One night blessed Francis was so afflicted with the pains of his illness that he could barely rest or sleep that night. In the morning, when his pain eased a bit, he had all the brothers **present** called, and when they were seated around him, he considered them and regarded them as representatives of all the brothers.

Gn 48:17

Beginning with one brother, he blessed them, *placing his right hand on the head* of each one, and he blessed all **the brothers** who were in

Jn 1:15; Dn 7:18

the religion and *all who were to come until the end of the world.* He seemed to feel sorry for himself because he was not able to see his sons and brothers before his death.

Mt 26:26

Afterwards he ordered loaves of *bread* to be brought to him and *he blessed* them. Unable to break them because of his illness, he had them *broken* into many little pieces by one of the brothers. *Taking* them, he offered each of the brothers a little piece, telling them *to eat* all of it. Just as the Lord desired to eat with the apostles on the Thursday before His death, it seemed to those brothers that, in a similar way, blessed Francis, before his death, wanted to bless them and, in them, all the other brothers, and that they should eat that blessed bread as if in some way they were eating with the rest of their brothers.

//2C 217

And we can consider this obvious because, while it was a day other than Thursday, he told the brothers that he believed it was Thursday. One of the brothers kept a piece of that bread, and after the death of blessed Francis some people who tasted it were immediately freed from their illnesses.

Blessed Francis said to his companions, when they did not immediately obey him: "My Brothers, you should not make me say everything."[a]

[35]

When blessed Francis ordained that, in the place of Saint Mary, for any idle word, one *Our Father,* praising God at the beginning and end of this prayer, should be said, **he wanted** the accused brother, should he, after being corrected, offer an excuse, refusing to say the *Our Father,* be bound to say two *Our Father's.* **He is bound to say** the *Praises,* as mentioned, loud enough and clear enough for the brothers

↓AC 107//2C 160
//2MP 82

---

a. The Latin reads: *Dicebat beatus Franciscus ad socios, quando sibi statim non obediebatur: "Fratres mei, non deberetis michi rem facere dicere totiens."* In addition to containing a number of grammatical errors, e.g. shifts from the plural to the singular, the sentence does not make sense in the context. A possible explanation of the text may be found in AC 68: *Dixit ad socios suos beatus Franciscus: "Modice fidei, nolite me facere amplius dicere"* [Blessed Francis told his companions: "Oh you of little faith! Don't make me tell you again!"]

staying there to understand and hear, and while he is saying them, the brothers must be quiet. **And doing otherwise,** he would be bound to say one *Our Father* in the same way with the *Praises of God* for the soul of the brother who spoke.

He also ordained that when any brother enters a cell, a house or any place and finds a brother or brothers there or anywhere, he should always earnestly praise and bless God. It was the custom of the most holy father always to say those *Praises,* and it was his fervent wish and desire. And **he wanted** the other brothers to be similarly careful and **attentive** in saying them.

[36]

C 108//2MP 65

Blessed Francis had such reverence and devotion to the Body of Christ, that he wanted it written in the *Rule* that the brothers in the regions where they stay have care and concern, and should preach to **the people, and admonish the** clerics and priests to place the Body of Christ in a good and fitting place; that, if they did not do so, the brothers were to do it.

//2C 201

Moreover, at that time, he wanted to send some brothers with pyxes through every region and wherever they found the Body of Christ placed illicitly, they were to place It honorably in them. **Likewise** he wanted to send others with beautiful wafer irons for making hosts **at all times.**

[37]

AC 108//2MP 65

When blessed Francis **sent brothers through the regions to preach penance, he said to them:** "Go, in the name of the Lord, *two by two* along the way, decently, in the greatest silence from dawn until after terce, praying to the Lord *in your hearts.* And let no idle or useless words *be mentioned among you.* Although you are traveling, nevertheless, let your behavior be as decent as if you were staying in a hermitage or a cell because wherever we are or wherever we travel, we have a cell with us. Brother Body is our cell, and the soul is the hermit who remains inside the cell to pray to God and meditate. So if the soul does not remain in quiet and solitude in its cell, a cell made by hands does little good to a religious."

Lk 10:1

Col 3:16

Eph 5:3

//2C 108

One day when blessed Francis was preaching, he said to them: "I speak to you as to those in demons' chains. You bound and sold yourselves like animals in the market because of your wretched state, **because** you exposed yourselves to the will of those who destroyed and destroy themselves, and want to destroy the whole city."

At the time of **that** chapter in which the brothers were sent for the first time to regions **beyond the mountains**, when the chapter had ended, blessed Francis said: "Dearest brothers, I must be a model and example to all the brothers. If therefore I sent my brothers into far distant countries where they will endure toil, shame, hunger, and many other types of needs, it seems to me just that I also go to a **remote** region, especially so that the brothers may be able to bear their trials more patiently when they hear that I am also undergoing the same thing."

And after prayer, as was his custom in all activities, he said: "In the name of the Lord and His Mother and all the saints, I choose the region of France, especially because among Catholics of the holy Church, they show great reverence to the Body of Christ, which pleases me very much. Because of this, I will gladly live among them."

And, among the other companions, he took Brother Sylvester, the priest, a man of God, of great faith and admirable simplicity and purity, whom the holy father venerated as a saint.

When he reached Florence, he found there the Lord Cardinal Hugo, the Bishop of Ostia who afterwards was pope. He rejoiced over the saint and learning **where he wanted to go did not want him to do so. Thereupon the holy father** said to him: "Lord, it is a great shame to me, if I remain in these regions when I send my brothers to **remote** parts." The Lord Bishop, however, said to him as if rebuking him: "Why did you send your brothers so far away to die of hunger and to so many other trials?"

Rv 19:10

In great fervor of spirit and in *the spirit of prophecy,* blessed Francis answered him: "Lord, do you think or believe that the Lord sent the brothers only for these regions? But I tell you in truth that the Lord chose and sent the brothers for the benefit and salvation of the souls of all people in the whole world and they should be received not only in the land of believers, but also in that of non-believers. As long as they observe what they promised the Lord, the Lord will minister to them in the land of non-believers as well as in the countries of believers.

The Lord Bishop marveled at his words and admitted that he spoke the truth. But the Lord Bishop did not allow him to go to France. Instead blessed Francis sent Brother Pacifico there with other brothers, and he returned to the Spoleto Valley.

[38]

C 109//2C 145
//2MP 64

Once when the time for the chapter of the brothers **was at hand,** to be held at Saint Mary of the Portiuncula, blessed Francis said to his companion: "It seems to me that I am not a Lesser Brother unless I have the attitude I will tell you." And he said: "The brothers come to me with devotion and veneration, invite me to the chapter and, touched by their devotion, I go. And they ask me to preach to them as *the Holy Spirit instructs me.*

Lk 12:12

"After the sermon, suppose that they speak against me: *'We do not* Lk 19:14 *want you to rule over us.* You are not eloquent. We are very ashamed to have such a simple and contemptible prelate over us. From now on do not presume to call yourself our prelate.' And so, with insults, they throw me out.

"It seems to me that I am not a Lesser Brother unless I am just as happy when they insult me, as when they honor me, if in both cases the benefit to them is equal. If I am happy about their benefit and devotion when they praise and honor me, which can be a danger to the soul, it is even more fitting that I should rejoice and be happy at my benefit and the salvation of my soul when they revile me as they throw me out in shame, which is profit for the soul **and for salvation."**

[39]

AC 111//2MP 16

One day, when **blessed Francis** was returning from prayer, he said with great joy to his companion: "I must be the form and example of all the brothers; so, although it is necessary for my body to have a tunic with patches, nevertheless I must take into consideration my brothers who have the same need, but perhaps do not and cannot have this. Therefore, I must stay down with them to suffer those same necessities they suffer so that in seeing this, they may be able to bear them more patiently."

We who were with him could not say how many and how great were the necessities that he denied his body in food and clothing, to give good example to the brothers and so that they would endure their necessities in greater patience. At all times, especially after the brothers began to multiply and he resigned the office of prelate, blessed Francis had as his highest and principal goal to teach the brothers more by actions than by words, what they ought to do and what they ought to avoid.

[40]

↓AC 112//2C1
//2MP 81

Noticing and hearing at one time that some brothers were giving a bad example in religion and that the brothers were turning aside from the highest summit of their profession, *moved inwardly with sorrow,* one time he said to the Lord in prayer: "Lord I give back to you the family You gave me."

Gn 6:6

And the Lord *said* to him *in spirit:* "Tell me, why are you so upset when one of the brothers leaves religion and when others do not *walk the way I showed* you? Also tell me: Who planted the religion of the brothers? Who makes a man convert and to do penance in it? Who gives the strength to persevere in it? Is it not I?"

Acts 11:12

1 Kgs 8:36

And it was *said* to him *in spirit:* "I did not choose you as a learned or eloquent man to be over my family, but I chose you, a simple man, so that you and the others may know that *I will watch over* my flock. But *I have placed you as a sign* to them, so that the works that I work in you, they should see in you, emulate, and do them. Those *who walk* in my *way have and will* then *have more abundantly;* while those who refuse to walk in my way, that *which they seem to have will be taken away from them.*

Acts 11:12

Jer 1:12; Hg 2:23

Ps 128:1

Jn 10:10

Mt 13:12; 25:29

"Therefore, I tell you, don't be so sad; do what you do, work as you work, for I have planted the religion of the brothers *in everlasting love.* Know that I love it so much that if any brother, *returning to his vomit,* dies outside religion I will replace him with another in religion who will have his crown in his place, and supposing that *he has not been born,* I will have him born. And so that you know that I love the life and religion of the brothers, suppose that in the whole life and religion of the brothers only three brothers remained: **I would not destroy** it."

Jer 31:3

2 Pt 2:22; Prv 26:11

Mt 26:24

These words comforted the mind of blessed Francis **very much,** for he was immensely saddened when **he heard** anything about bad example regarding the brothers.

Although he could not totally restrain himself from becoming sad **about this,** after being comforted by the Lord in this way, he remembered this and spoke to his companions about it.

Therefore blessed Francis often used to say to the brothers in chapters and also in his words of instruction: *"I have sworn and declared* to observe the *Rule* of the brothers and all the brothers also pledged the same. For this reason, after I resigned office among the brothers from now on, because of illnesses and for the greater good of my soul and those of all the brothers, I am bound in regard to the brothers only to show good example.

Ps 118:106

"**I received** that from the Lord and know in truth that even if my illness had excused me, the greatest help I can render to the religion of the brothers is to spend time in prayer to the Lord for it everyday, that He govern, preserve, protect, and defend it. I have pledged myself to this, to the Lord and to the brothers, that if any one of the brothers perishes because of my bad example, I be held *to render an account* to the Lord."

Mt 12:36

And even though from time to time a brother would tell him that he should occasionally put himself forward in the affairs of the religion, he used to reply with words like these: "The brothers have their *Rule,* and furthermore have sworn to it. And so they have no excuse. After it pleased the Lord to decide that I would be their prelate, I also swore to it in their presence and I want to observe it to the end. So, since the brothers already know what they should do and what to avoid, the only thing left for me to do is to teach them by actions, because this is why I have been given to them during my life and after my death."

[41]

↓AC 113//2C 84
//2MP 17

One day when blessed Francis met a poor man, he said to his companion: "This man's poverty brings great shame on us; it passes judgment on our poverty."

"How so, brother?" his companion replied. "I am greatly ashamed," he answered, "when I find someone poorer than myself. I chose holy poverty as my Lady, my delight, and my riches of spirit and body. And the whole world has heard this news, that I professed poverty before God and people. Therefore I ought to be ashamed when I come upon someone poorer than myself."

[42]

↓AC 114//2C 85
//2MP 37

One time a little, poor, and sickly man came **to blessed Francis. Feeling compassion for him,** he began to speak to his companion about his nakedness and illness.

"It is true, brother," his companion said to him, "that he is poor, but perhaps there is no one in the whole province who desires riches more." Blessed Francis rebuked **him** for not speaking well, and he admitted his fault.

Blessed Francis told him: "Do you want to do the penance I will tell you?" "Willingly" he replied. "Go, *strip off your tunic,*" he said, "and *go naked* before that poor man, throw yourself at his feet, and tell him how you sinned against **him,** how you slandered him, and ask him to pray for you that God may forgive you."

Bar 5:1

So he went and did everything blessed Francis **told** him. When he finished, he got up, put on his tunic, and returned to blessed Francis. And blessed Francis said to him: "Do you want me to tell you how you sinned against him, and even against Christ?"

And he said: "Whenever you see a poor person you ought to consider Him in whose name he comes, that is, Christ, who came to take on our poverty and weakness. This man's poverty and weakness is a mirror for us in which we should see and consider lovingly the poverty and weakness of our Lord Jesus Christ which *He bore in* His *body* for **the redemption** of the human race."

Is 53:4; 1 Cor 6:20; Gal 6:28

[43]

↓AC 115//2MP

At one time robbers who were in those woods above Borgo San Sepolcro used to come sometimes to the hermitage of the brothers to ask the brothers for bread.[a] Some of the brothers of that place said: "It is not right to give them alms because they are robbers and they do very evil things to people." Others, taking into consideration that they begged humbly and were compelled by great necessity, used to give them alms sometimes, always admonishing them to be converted to penance.

Meanwhile blessed Francis arrived at the place. The brothers asked whether they should give them bread, or not. "If you do as I tell you," blessed Francis told them, *"I trust in the Lord* that you will win their souls. Go get some good bread and good wine and take it to them in the woods where you know they are staying, and cry out: 'Come, Brother robbers, come to us, because we are brothers and we **brought** you some good bread and good wine.' They will immediately come to you. Then you spread out **a table cloth** on the ground, placing the bread and wine on it, and, while they are eating, humbly and joyfully wait on them. After the meal, speak to them some words of the Lord. Finally, for the love of the Lord ask them for this first: make them promise you that they will not strike anyone or injure anyone's person. Do not ask for everything all at once, or they will not listen to you. Because of the humility and charity you show them, they will at once make you this promise. The next day, get up and, because of the promise they made to you, besides eggs and cheese, bring them the bread and wine, and take these to them, and wait on them until **they have eaten.** After the meal, say to them: *'Why do you stay here all day long,* dying of hunger, suffering many evil

Ps 11:1

Mt 20:6

---

a. That is, the hermitage of Monte Casale. For historical background, cf. Teobaldo Ricci, *Sulle Orme di Francesco in Toscana: Pellegrinaggio La Verna, Montecasale, Le Celle di Cortona* (Padua: Edizioni Messaggero Padova, 2000), 50-53.

things and in your actions doing many evil things for which **you have lost** your souls unless you are converted? It is better to serve the Lord, who will both supply your bodily needs in this world and save your souls in the end.' Then the Lord in His mercy will inspire them to convert and they will be converted because of the humility and charity you show them."

So the brothers got up and did everything as blessed Francis told them. And by the mercy of God and His grace which descended on them, those men listened and observed to the letter point by point all the requests which the brothers asked of them. Further, because of the friendliness and charity the brothers showed them, they began carrying wood on their shoulders to the hermitage. By the mercy of God, through the charity and friendliness that the brothers showed them, some entered religion, others embraced penance, promising in the hands of the brothers no longer to commit these evil deeds, but to live *by the work of their hands.*

Ps 128:2

The brothers and others who heard or knew about this, were quite amazed, as they reflected on the holiness of blessed Francis, how he had predicted the conversion of those who were of means, perfidious, and wicked human beings, and how quickly they converted to the Lord.

[44]ᵃ

AC 20//2MP 50

One time or other some of the brothers told blessed Francis: "Father, don't you see that sometimes bishops do not permit us to preach, allowing us to remain idle in an area for many days before we can preach to the people? It would be better if you managed that the brothers get a privilege from the Lord Pope: it would be the salvation of souls."

He answered them: "You, Lesser Brothers, you do not know the will of God, and will not allow me to convert the whole world as God wills. For I want to convert the prelates first by humility and reverence. Then, when they see your holy life and your reverence for them, they will ask you to preach and convert the people. These will attract the people to you far better than the privileges you want, which would lead you to pride. And if you are free of all avarice, and lead the people to give the churches their due, they will ask you to hear the confessions of their people. Although you should not be concerned about this, for if they are converted, they will easily find confessors.

---

a. This is the only use of the collection, *Verba Sancti Francisci* [The Sayings of Saint Francis], as found in AC 20, cf. FA:ED II 130 a. Only the fifth and last of these saying is quoted and is done so with only one insignificant addition, *aliquando* [one time or other].

"For my part, I want only this privilege from the Lord: not to have any privilege from any human being, except to show reverence to all, and, by the obedience of the holy *Rule,* to convert everyone more by example than by word."

[45]

Blessed Francis used to say: "Nothing should displease a servant of God except sin. And no matter how another person may sin, if a servant of God becomes disturbed and angry because of this and not because of charity, he is storing up guilt for himself.

"That servant of God who does not become angry or disturbed at anyone lives correctly without anything of his own. And blessed is the one for whom nothing remains except for him *to return to Caesar what is Caesar's and to God what is God's.*

"Blessed is the servant who, when he speaks, does not disclose everything about himself under the guise of some reward and is not *quick to speak,* but who is wisely cautious about what he says and how he responds.

"Woe to that religious who does not hold in his heart the good things the Lord reveals to him and does not reveal them by his behavior, but, under the guise of a reward, wishes instead to reveal them with his words. *He receives his reward* and his listeners carry away little fruit."

Adm XI

Mt 22:21; Lk 20:25

Adm XXI

Prv 29:20

Mt 6:2, 16

The Beginning of A Mirror of Perfection
of the *Status*[a] of a Lesser Brother[b]
(The Sabatier Edition)

[Introduction][c]

[1]After the second rule which blessed Francis wrote had been
lost, *he went up* a *mountain* with Brother Leo of Assisi and Brother
Bonizo of Bologna to make **another** rule,[d] which he had written at
Christ's instruction.

A group of many ministers **came to Brother Elias, who** was the
vicar of the blessed Francis. "We heard that Brother Francis is making a new rule," they told him, "and we fear that he will make it so
harsh that we will not be able to observe it. We want you to go to him
and tell him that we refuse to be bound to that rule. Let him make it
for himself and not for us."

Brother Elias replied to them that he did not want to go because
he feared the rebuke of **blessed** Francis. When they insisted that he
go, he said that he refused to go without them; so they all went
together.

---

a. The Latin word here is *status*, a word that appears fourteen times in this text but with different
   meanings (2MP 1, 43, 64, 68–2x, 64, 71, 76, 80, 85, 105, 112, 124). Cf. supra, 145, note 8.

b. This translation is based on the edition originally prepared by Paul Sabatier: *Speculum (lLe)
   Perfectionis ou Mémoires de frère Léon sur la seconde partie de la vie de Saint François d'Assise*, ed.
   Paul Sabatier, Andrew George Little, I, (Mancester: British Society of Franciscan Studies 13, 1928),
   1–350; and reprinted in *Fontes Franciscani*, ed. Enrico Menestò, Stefano Brufani, Giuseppe
   Cremascoli, Emore Paoli, Luigi Pellegrini, Stanislao da Campagnola (S. Maria degli Angeli-Assisi:
   Edizioni Porziuncola, 1995), 1849-2053. Since the basis of this text is AC, only those words or
   phrases added by its anonymous editor are bolded.

c. Unlike the Sabatier and *Fontes* editions, this first number is simply called the introduction, in order
   to avoid giving the remaining twelve chapters a confusing double set of numbers. In this way, it is
   also clear that this opening pericope describing the controversial loss and rewriting of the *Regula
   bullata* [Later Rule] serves as an introduction to the following twelve chapters that focus on its ideals
   and the controversies surrounding it.
       In this instance, the editors of this translation have chosen to follow that precedent. Cross
   references to the earlier passages of AC, FA:ED II 118-230, will be indicated in the inner margins as
   AC. Since Thomas of Celano used the material sent by the Three Companions, i.e., "we who were
   with him," in 2C, it is useful to recognize the repetition of many of the same pericopes throughout
   these later texts. To indicate these parallel texts, as well as similar passages in the Lemmens edition,
   supra 214-52, the authors have chosen to indicate their presence as //2C.

d. Information about Bonizzo of Bologna can be found in FA:ED II 131b. Parallel descriptions of the
   composition of LR can be found in LMj IV 11, FA:ED II 557-8.

When Brother Elias and the ministers were near the place where blessed Francis was staying, Brother Elias called him. Blessed Francis responded, and seeing the ministers, he said: "What do these brothers want?" "These are ministers," Brother Elias answered, "who heard that you are making a new rule. They fear that you are making it very harsh, and they say and say publicly, they refuse to be bound by it. Make it for yourself and not for them."

Then blessed Francis turned his face toward heaven and spoke to Christ in this way: "Lord! Didn't I tell you, they wouldn't believe me?" The voice of Christ **was then heard** in the air, saying "Francis, nothing of yours is in the *Rule:* whatever is there is mine. And I want the *Rule* observed in this way: to the letter, to the letter, to the letter, and without a gloss, without a gloss, without a gloss."[a] And He added: "I know how much human weakness is capable of, and how much I want to help them. Therefore, those who refuse to observe it, should leave the Order." Then blessed Francis turned to the brothers and said: "Did you hear? Did you hear? Do you want me to have you told again?" Confused **and terrified,** the ministers departed blaming themselves.[b]

a. For further information on the phrases *ad litteram* [to the letter] *sine glossa* [without gloss], see FA:ED II 132a.

b. This first number is also a direct quotation of WSF, cf. supra FA:ED II 130a. These *Sayings* are quoted again in 2MP 12, 13, 50, 68.

Chapter One
PERFECT POVERTY

2
IN THE FIRST PLACE
HOW BLESSED FRANCIS MADE KNOWN HIS WILL AND INTENTION
WHICH HE MAINTAINED FROM THE BEGINNING TO THE END
CONCERNING THE OBSERVANCE OF POVERTY

↓AC 101 Brother Riccerio of the Marches, noble **by birth** and more noble by holiness, was loved by **blessed** Francis with great affection.[a] One day he came to visit blessed Francis in the palace **of the bishop of Assisi.** Among other points he discussed **with him** the state of the religion and observance of the *Rule,* he asked him **specifically:** "Tell me, father, when you first began to have brothers, what was your intention? And what is it **now,** and what do you believe it will be until the day of your death? Because I want to be sure of your intention and of your first and last wish, so that we, cleric brothers who have many books, may keep them, although we will say that they belong to the religion."

Blessed Francis told him: "I tell you, brother, that it has been and is my first and last intention and will, if the brothers would only heed it, that no brother should have anything except a tunic as the *Rule* allows us, together with a cord and underwear."

If any brother wanted to ask why blessed Francis in his own time did not make the brothers observe such a strict poverty as he told Brother Riccerio, and did not order it to be observed, we who were with him[b] would respond to this as we heard from his mouth. Because he told the brothers this and many other things, and also had written down in the *Rule* what he requested from the Lord with relentless prayer and meditation for the good of the religion, affirming that it was completely **according to** the Lord's will.

Afterwards when he showed **this to the brothers,** they seemed *harsh and unbearable,* for they did not know what was going to happen to the religion after his death. And because he **greatly** feared scandal for himself and for the brothers, he did not want to argue with them; Mt 23:4

---

a. This (2MP 2) and the following paragraphs, 2MP 3, 4, 11, 72, 73 contain sections from the collection, the *Intentio Regulae* [Intention of the Rule]. Cf. FA:ED II 204 b.

b. At this point, the editor introduces the phrase *nos qui cum eo fuimus* [we who were with him], a passage that regularly appears in the AC as a means of identifying its authors, i.e., Francis's companions. Cf. FA:ED II 115.

Ex 4:15

Is 55:11

Acts 9:31

but he complied with their wish, although not willingly, and excused himself before the Lord. But, that *the word of the Lord,* which He put *in his mouth* for the good of the brothers, *would not return to* the Lord empty, he wanted to fulfill it in himself, so that he might then obtain a reward from the Lord. **And, at last,** he found peace in this and his *spirit was comforted.*

3

HOW HE ANSWERED A MINISTER WHO WISHED
TO HAVE BOOKS WITH HIS PERMISSION,
AND HOW THE MINISTERS, WITHOUT HIS KNOWLEDGE,
HAD REMOVED FROM THE *RULE*
THE CHAPTER CONTAINING THE GOSPEL PROHIBITIONS

Lk 9:1-6

At the time when he returned from overseas,[a] a minister spoke ↓AC102 with him about the chapter on poverty. He wanted to know his will and understanding, especially since at the time a chapter had been written in the *Rule* from prohibitions of the holy Gospel: *Take nothing with you on the journey,* etc.

LR II 14-5

And blessed Francis answered him: "I understand it in this way, that the brothers should have nothing except a tunic with a cord and underwear, as contained in the *Rule,* and those compelled by necessity, may wear shoes." And the minister said to him: "What shall I do, for I have so many books worth more than fifty pounds?"

He said this because he wanted to hold on to them with a clear conscience, especially because he had **a disturbed conscience** since he had so many books, and knew how strictly blessed Francis interpreted the chapter on poverty.

Mt 23:5-7

Blessed Francis said **to him, "I do not wish,** I cannot and must not go against my own conscience and the perfection of the holy Gospel which we have professed."[b] Hearing this, the minister became sad. Seeing **him** disturbed, blessed Francis said to him with **great** intensity of spirit, intending this for all the brothers: "You, Lesser Brothers, want *to be seen* as *and called* observers of the holy Gospel, but in your deeds you want to have money bags."

Although the ministers knew that, according to the *Rule* of the brothers they were bound to observe the holy Gospel, they **nonetheless** had that chapter of the *Rule* where it says "Take nothing for your

---

a. Concerning Francis's journeys, cf. FA:ED I 229-233.

b. The word *perfectio* [perfection], while coming into this text through IntR, cf. AC 101-106; FA:ED II 204b, becomes a frequently used concept in the 2MP, appearing 63 times.

journey, etc." removed, believing, **because of this,** that they were not obliged to observance of the perfection of the Gospel.

Knowing this through the light of the Holy Spirit, blessed Francis said in the presence of some brothers: "The brother ministers think they can deceive God and me." Then he said:" Indeed, that all the brothers may know that they are bound to observe the perfection of the holy Gospel, I want it written at the beginning and at the end of the *Rule* that the brothers are **strictly** bound to observe the holy Gospel of our Lord Jesus Christ. And that the brothers may always *be without an excuse* before God, **since I proclaim and still proclaim,** I want to show with these deeds and always observe, with God's help, what God *has placed in my mouth* for my and their welfare."

Therefore, he observed the **entire** holy Gospel to the letter from the day he began to have brothers until the day of his death.

Rom 1:20

Ex 4:15; Is 51:16

4

THE NOVICE WHO WISHED TO OWN A PSALTER WITH HIS PERMISSION

↓AC103

Another time, there was once a brother novice who could read the psalter, **although** not very well, and **he obtained** permission from the general minister to have it. **But because** he had heard that blessed Francis did not want his brothers to be desirous of learning and books, **he was not content to have it without the permission of blessed Francis.**

When blessed Francis came to the place where that novice was living, therefore, the novice said to him: "Father, it would be a great consolation for me to have a psalter. But, although the general minister has given me permission to have it, I still want to have it with your knowledge."

Blessed Francis **answered him:** "The Emperor Charles, Roland, and Oliver, and all the paladins and valiant knights who were mighty in battle, pursuing unbelievers with great toil and fatigue even to death, had a memorable victory for themselves, and, finally, died in battle fighting as holy martyrs for the faith in Christ.[a] And **now** there are many who want to receive honor and praise by only relating what they did. **Thus there are many among us who** want to receive honor and **praise** by recounting and preaching about them. As if he were saying: **We must not care about books and learning,**

---

a. In order to understand this reference to the Emperor Charles, Roland, and Oliver, et al., it is helpful to read the legend of the French epic hero Roland. *The Song of Roland* portrayed the virtues of the Christian knight, especially those of valor and wisdom, and found its apex in an embrace of fidelity. See Franco Cardini, "The Warrior and Knight," in *The Medieval World: The History of European Society,* ed. Jacques LeGoff, trans. Lydia G. Cochrane (London: ParkgateBooks Ltd, 1987), 75-111.

1 Cor 8:1
but about virtuous deeds, because *Knowledge puffs up, but charity builds."*

↓AC 104
After a few days, when blessed Francis was sitting near a fire, warming himself, the same **novice** spoke to him again about a psalter. And blessed Francis told him: "After you have a psalter, you will desire and want to have a breviary; after you have a breviary, you will sit in a chair of authority like a great prelate,[a] **and you will tell** your brother: 'Bring me the breviary.' "

Saying this with great intensity of spirit, **blessed Francis took** some ashes in his hand, put them on his head rubbing them around his head as though he were washing **his head. He said:** "I, a breviary! I, a breviary!" He spoke this way many times, passing his hand over his head. The brother was stunned and ashamed.

Afterwards blessed Francis said to him: "Brother, I was likewise tempted to have books. But, in order to know God's will about this, I took the book, where the Lord's Gospels are written, and prayed to the Lord to deign to show it to me at the first opening of the book. After my prayer was ended, on the first opening of the book this verse
Lk 8:10
of the holy Gospel came to me: *To you it is given to know the mystery of the kingdom of God, but to the others all things are treated in parables."* And he said: "There are many who willingly climb to the heights of knowledge; that person be blessed who renounces it for the love of God."

↓AC 105
After many months, when blessed Francis was **at the place** of Saint Mary of the Portiuncula, at a cell behind the house on the road, **that brother** spoke to him **again** about the psalter. Blessed Francis said **to him:** "Go and do **this** as your minister tells you." When he heard this, that brother began to go back by the same road he had come.

Blessed Francis remained on the road, and began to think over what he said to that brother. Suddenly he yelled after him: "Wait for me, brother, wait!" He went up to him and said: "Come back with me and show me the place where I told you to do with the psalter what your minister tells you."

When they returned to that spot, blessed Francis **knelt** in front of the brother and said to him: *"Mea culpa,* brother, *mea culpa.* Whoever wishes to be a lesser brother must have nothing but the tunics, a cord, and short trousers the *Rule* allows him; and for those forced by **manifest** necessity or illness, shoes."

---

a. The Latin text reads *in cathedra* [in a chair of authority]. The nuance refers to the *cathedra,* a word signifying a position of authority such as a royal throne, a bishop's see, or a teacher's platform. Cf. infra, 2MP 48 where a corpse is *exaltetur in cathedra* [raised on a throne].

Whenever brothers came to him to ask advice about such things, he would give them the same answer. For this reason he used to say: "A person is only as learned as his actions show; and a religious is only as good a preacher as his actions show;" for *a good tree is known only by its fruit."*

Mt 12:33; Lk 6:44

5
OBSERVING POVERTY IN BOOKS, BEDS, BUILDINGS, AND FURNISHINGS[a]

The most blessed father used to teach **the brothers** that in books *the testimony of the Lord,* not value, should be sought, edification rather than elegance. He wanted few books kept **and** *in common,* and these should be available to the brothers who needed them.

Beds and coverings abounded in such plentiful poverty, that if a brother had a ragged sheet over some straw, he considered it a bridal couch.

Moreover, he taught his brothers to make poor little dwellings out of wood, and not stone, and **he wanted them built and constructed** according to a crude sketch.

And he not only hated pretense in houses; he also abhorred having many or fine furnishings in them. He disliked anything, in tables or dishes, which seemed worldly, **so that everything would shout of poverty, would sing** of exile and pilgrimage.

Ps 19:8

Acts 2:44; 4:32

AC 25//2C 62

AC 26//2C 63

AC 23//2C 56

AC 24//2C 60

6
HOW HE COMPELLED ALL THE BROTHERS TO LEAVE A HOUSE
WHICH WAS CALLED A HOUSE "OF THE BROTHERS"

2C 58

Passing through Bologna he heard that a house of the brothers had recently been built there. **As soon as he heard that it was called** "the house of the brothers," he turned back **and left the city.** He **firmly** commanded that **all** the brothers leave it quickly and **not to live there anymore.**

Accordingly all of them vacated the house. Not even the sick brothers could stay **there,** but were evicted together with the others, until the Lord Hugo, the bishop of Ostia and the papal legate in Lombardy, announced publicly that the house belonged to him.

---

a. Marginal references to 2C indicate passages that are either (a) quoted verbatim in the AC, (b) reflect a similar narrative in the AC but are not textually identical, or (c) are texts re-worked independently of the AC.

Jn 21:24

A brother who was sick, and was thrown out of that house, *writes this and bears witness to it.*

7

HOW HE WANTED TO DEMOLISH A HOUSE
THE PEOPLE OF ASSISI HAD BUILT AT SAINT MARY OF THE PORTIUNCULA

↓AC 56//2C 57

As a **general** chapter **was approaching,** which in those days was held annually at Saint Mary of the Portiuncula, the people of Assisi Acts 2:47 considered that the brothers were *daily increasing* in number **and that each year they gathered there.** Yet they had nothing but a poor and small dwelling, with a roof of straw and walls of branches and mud. After they summoned a general meeting, within a few days, with haste and **the greatest** fervor, they built there a large house **constructed** of stone and cement without the consent of blessed Francis while he was away.

When blessed Francis returned from a certain province, and came **to that place** for the chapter, he was **very** amazed at the house that they had constructed. **He feared** that, upon seeing this house, the **other** brothers would build or have built great houses **in the places where they now stayed or where they would stay in the future.** And especially because he wanted this place always to be a model and example for all **the other** places **of the Order,**[a] before the chapter ended, he climbed on the roof of that house, and ordered the brothers to climb up with him. And, **together** with **these** brothers, he began to throw the tiles covering that house to the ground intending to destroy **it to its very foundation.**

Some knights of Assisi, who were there to protect that place against **the large number of** outsiders who came to see the brothers' chapter, saw that blessed Francis and the other brothers intended to destroy that house. They immediately went to him and said: "Brother, this house belongs to the Commune of Assisi and we are its representatives. **We forbid** you to destroy our house." **When he heard this,** blessed Francis said: "If the house belongs to you, I do not want to touch it." He and the other brothers immediately came down.

That is why **from that time** the people of the city of Assisi decreed that the *podestà* **of the city,** whoever he is, **would be bound** to make

---

a. When adding phrases to the AC, the editor consistently uses the word *ordo* [order] in contrast to the earlier, more frequently used term, *religio* [religion]. Thus in the early fourteenth century, Order became the more common way of referring to Franciscan religious life. For explanations of the words *religio* and *ordo*, cf. FA:ED II 34 a.

repairs. **And every year for the longest time, this statute was observed.**

8
HOW HE REPROVED HIS VICAR FOR HAVING A SMALL HOUSE BUILT
AT THE PORTIUNCULA FOR THE RECITATION OF THE OFFICE

↓AC 56

Another time **blessed Francis's vicar began to build** a small house where the brothers would be able to rest and say their hours. Because a large number of brothers would gather in that place, the brothers had no place where **they could say the Office. For all the brothers of the Order flocked there, and no one was received into the Order except there.**

When this house **was almost completed,** behold blessed Francis returned to that place, and **staying in a cell,** heard the noise **of the laborers. He called** his companion and asked **what those brothers were doing?** His companion told him the whole story.

Immediately he had **his vicar** called, and said to him: "Brother, this place is a model and example for the entire religion. **And therefore,** I want the brothers of this place **first of all** to bear trials and **inconveniences** for the love of the Lord God, so that **the other brothers** who come here will bring back to their places a good example of poverty, rather than their experiences of consolation, and the other brothers will take this as an example of building to their places. They will say: 'If at Saint Mary of the Portiuncula, which is the first place **of the Order,** such and such buildings are built, **we too** can build well in our own places.' "

9
HOW HE DID NOT WISH TO STAY IN A COMFORTABLE CELL
OR IN ONE WHICH WAS CALLED HIS OWN

57//2C 59//1MP 29

One of the brothers, a **deeply** spiritual man, to whom blessed Francis was very close, was staying in a hermitage. He had a cell built, a little distance away in which blessed Francis would be able to stay for prayer **whenever he came there.**

When blessed Francis arrived at that place, that brother took him to the cell. Blessed Francis told him: "This cell is too beautiful!" **For it was constructed of wood, rough hewn with axe and hatchet.** "If you want me to stay **there,** have a cell made of ferns and tree branches inside and out." **For the more the houses and cells were**

poor, the more willingly he was to stay there. When the brothers had done this, blessed Francis stayed there for a few days.

2C 59

One day, when he had come out of that cell, a certain brother went to see it, and afterwards came to the place where blessed Francis was. Upon seeing him blessed Francis said to him "Where are you coming from, brother?" He told him: "I am coming from your cell." "Because you said this is mine," blessed Francis said, "someone else will stay there from now on: I will not."

Mt 8:20; Lk 9:58

We who were with him often heard him repeat the passage: *Foxes have dens and the birds of the air have nests; but the Son of Man has nowhere to lay his head.*

Mt 4:2

And again he said: "When the Lord stayed in the desert where he prayed and *fasted for forty days and forty nights,* He did not have a cell or a house built there, but He sought shelter under the rocks of the mountain."

And so, after his example, he did not want to have a house or cell called his own, nor did he ever have one built. Moreover, if it ever happened that he would accidentally say to the brothers: "Go, prepare that cell," he would refuse afterwards to stay in it, because of

Lk 12:22; Mt 6:31, 34

that passage of the holy Gospel: *Do not be anxious.*

Shortly before his death, he had it written in his *Testament* that all the cells and houses of the brothers ought to be only of mud and wood, the better to safeguard poverty and humility.[a]

10
The Manner of Selecting Sites in the City
and Building There According to the Intention of Blessed Francis

↓AC 58//1MP 30

Once when he was in Siena for the treatment of the disease of his eyes, the Lord Bonaventure, who had donated to the brothers the land on which the brothers' place had been built, said to him: "Father, what do you think about this place?" Blessed Francis answered him: "Do you want me to tell you how the places of the brothers should be built?" "I wish you would, Father," he answered.

And blessed Francis told him: "When the brothers go to any city, where they do not have a place, let them find someone there who wants to give them enough land to build a place, have a garden, and whatever is necessary for them. They must, first of all, consider how

---

a. While *The Testament* 24 (hereafter Test) does speak of the poverty of buildings, there is no directive as specific as this. For a discussion of this passage, cf. Raoul Manselli, "From the Testament to the Testaments of St. Francis," GR 2 (1988): 91-99.

much land is enough for them, always considering the holy poverty and the good example we are bound to give to others."

He said this because he did not want the brothers **in any way** to go beyond the norm of poverty either in houses, in churches, in gardens or in other things they used. And he did not want them to possess the right of ownership to these places, but to stay in them as *strangers and* 1 Pt 2:11
pilgrims. For this reason, he did not want the brothers to be assigned to places together in a **large** number, because it seemed difficult to him that poverty be fully **observed in a large crowd.**[a]

From the beginning of his conversion until the end, this was **his intention:** that poverty be observed **in all things** to its fullest.

"After the brothers have considered the land necessary for a place, they should go the bishop of that city and say to him: 'Lord, for the love of the Lord God and the salvation of his soul, such a person wants to give us enough land so that we can build a place there. Therefore, we have recourse to you, first of all, because you are the father and lord of the souls of the entire flock entrusted to you, as well as our souls and those of **all** the brothers who will stay in this place. Therefore, with the blessing of the Lord God and yours, we would like to build there.' "

The saint said this because the harvest of souls that the brothers wanted to make was better achieved by peace with the clerics, winning them and the people rather than by scandalizing them, even though they might win the people.

"The Lord," he used to say, "has called us to help His faith and the prelates and clerics of holy Church. And, **therefore,** we are always bound to love, honor, and revere them as much as we can. For this reason let them be called Lesser Brothers, because, in name as well as in example and in deed, they should be humbler than all other people of this world. From the beginning of my conversion, the Lord *put* Ex 4:15; Is 51:16
His *word in the mouth* of the bishop of Assisi that he might counsel me well in the service of Christ and comfort me. On account of this, as well as many other excellent qualities that I consider in prelates, not only in bishops, but in poor priests as well, I want to love them, revere them, and regard them as my lords.

---

a. 2MP changes the text of AC 58 from *paupertatem servari* to *paupertatem observari*, which may both be translated as "observed." While seemingly insignificant, this subtle change highlights an important polemic of this text, that is, to *ob-servare* [to keep before one's eye] the *Rule* and, most importantly, poverty. *Observare* [to observe] occurs 33 times in 2MP; *paupertas* [poverty] occurs 65 times, one of the most frequently used words in 2MP. An attentiveness to the words *observantia* [observance] and *observare* [to observe] throughout this text reveals their importance as a central theme. See *Legenda seu Compilatio Perusina, Speculum Perfectionis.* Corpus des Sources Franciscaines IV, ed. Jean-François Godet and George Mailleux (Louvain-la-Leuve: Publications du CETEDOC, 1978), 259-60.

"After receiving the bishop's blessing, let them go and have a big ditch dug around the land which they received for the building of a place. As a sign of holy poverty and humility, let them place a hedge, instead of a wall. Afterwards they may have poor huts made of mud and wood, and some little cells where the brothers can sometimes pray and work for greater benefit and also **to avoid idleness.**

"Let them also have **small** churches made. The brothers, however, must not have large churches built in order to preach to the people or for any other reason, for there is greater humility and better example when they go to other churches to preach.

"And if prelates and clerics, religious or secular,[a] **should** sometimes **visit** their places, their poor house, cells, and **little** churches, those living in that place will preach to them and, therefore, edify them **more than any words.**"

He said: "The brothers often have large buildings made, breaking with our holy poverty, **resulting in complaints,** disgrace, and bad example to their neighbor. And when they abandon **or destroy** those places and buildings for better or healthier places, **motivated by greed or covetousness, and build others that are large or imposing in order to have a better and more hallowed place, or to attract a greater influx of people,** they cause those who gave alms for that place, as well as others who see or hear about this to be scandalized and greatly upset. It is, therefore, better that the brothers have small and poor places built, observing their profession, and giving their neighbor good example, rather than making things contrary to their profession and offering bad example to others. For, if **the brothers** leave their poor little places for the sake of a more decent place, there would be less scandal."

11
HOW THE BROTHERS, ESPECIALLY THE PRELATES AND SCHOLARS, OPPOSED BLESSED FRANCIS'S DESIRE TO BUILD POOR PLACES AND DWELLINGS

When blessed Francis decreed that the churches of the brothers should be small and that their houses should be built **only** of mud and wood, as a sign of holy poverty and humility, he wanted this to begin in the place of Saint Mary of the Portiuncula. Thus this would be a **perpetual** reminder to **all** the brothers, **now and in the future,**   ↓AC 106

---

a. The Latin word is *saeculares* [seculars], a word that is used a total of eleven times in 2MP, generally in a "worldly," that is, negative sense; this is in contrast with earlier texts, e.g., all those of Thomas of Celano in which the word appears only eight times. While meaning "of or pertaining to the world," it is more commonly used to refer to those living 'in the world' and not in monastic seclusion, cf. *The Compact Edition of The Oxford English Dictionary* (Oxford: Oxford University Press, 1971), 365.

since this was the first and principal place in the whole Order. **Some brothers opposed him in this matter** and told him that in **some** provinces wood is more expensive than stone. **Thus** it did not seem good to them that houses be **built** of wood and mud. **But** blessed Francis did not wish to argue with them because he was very sick and close to death.

Test 24   This is the reason he had written in his *Testament:* "Let the brothers be careful not to receive in any way churches or dwellings or any other things built for them, unless they are according to poverty . . . as pilgrims and strangers let them always be guests there."

We who were with him when he wrote the *Rule* and almost all his other writings bear witness that he had many things written in the *Rule* and in his other writings, to which **many** brothers, especially prelates **and the wise ones among us,** were opposed. **Nowadays these things would be very** useful **and necessary** for the whole religion. Because he greatly feared scandal, he gave in, although unwillingly, to the wishes of the brothers. But he often repeated this saying: "Woe to those brothers who are opposed to what I **firmly** know to be the will of God for the greatest good **and necessity** of the **whole** religion, even if I unwillingly give in to their wishes."

He often said **to us,** his companions: "Here lies my pain and grief: those things which I received from God by His mercy with great effort of prayer and meditation for the present and future good of the religion, and which are, as He assures me, in accordance with His will, some of the brothers relying on the authority of their knowledge and **false** providence nullify and oppose me saying: 'These things must be kept and observed; but not those!' "

12
HOW HE CONSIDERED IT A THEFT
TO ACQUIRE ALMS OR USE THEM BEYOND ONE'S NEED

↓AC15   Blessed Francis often said these words to **his** brothers: "I have never been a thief, that is, in regard to alms, **acquiring or using them beyond necessity.** I always took less than I needed, so that other poor people would not be cheated of their **portion.** To act otherwise would be theft."

13
HOW CHRIST TOLD HIM HE DID NOT WISH THE BROTHERS
TO POSSESS ANYTHING IN COMMON OR INDIVIDUALLY

When the brother ministers urged him to allow **the brothers**   ↓AC 16
something at least in common, so that such a great number would
have some resources, **blessed** Francis called upon Christ in prayer
and consulted Him about this. Christ immediately responded **to
him,** saying: **"I will take away** everything held individually or in
common. **I will** always **be** ready to provide for this family, no matter
Ps 91:14; Ps 22:5   how much it might grow, and **I will always cherish** it as long as *it
will put its hope in me."*[a]

14
HIS ABHORRENCE OF MONEY
AND HOW HE PUNISHED A BROTHER WHO TOUCHED MONEY

Francis, a true friend of God **and imitator of Christ,**[b] perfectly   ↓AC 27//2C 65
despised all worldly things. He detested money above all. He encour-
aged **his brothers in word and example** to flee from it as from the
devil himself. He gave his **brothers** this observation: money and
manure are equally worthy of love.
Gn 39:11   Now *it happened one day* that a layman came to pray in the church
of Saint Mary of the Portiuncula and placed some money by the cross
as an offering. When he left, one of the brothers simply picked it up
with his hand and threw it on the windowsill. **When this was
reported to blessed Francis,** and he, seeing he had been caught,
immediately ran to ask forgiveness, threw himself to the ground,
and offered himself to be whipped.

The saint rebuked him and reprimanded him severely for touching coins. He ordered him to pick up the money from the windowsill
with his own mouth, take it outside the fence of that place, and with
his mouth to put it on the donkey's manure pile. While that brother
was gladly carrying out this command, **all who saw or heard** were
filled with **great** fear. **From then on, they valued money as much as**
manure, holding it in as great a contempt **as ass's dung.** They were
encouraged to despise it by new examples every day.

---

a. This is the first passage that portrays Christ as speaking directly to Francis concerning the direction
   of the brothers.
b. As noted in 2C 18, the term "imitation of Christ" is rare in early Franciscan literature, cf. FA:ED II
   256a. The phrase occurs once again in LMj XI 2 (FA:ED II 613). Its use in this text, cf. 2MP 73, 85,
   88, reflects the influence of Ubertino da Casale's *Tree of the Crucified Life of Jesus*, Book V (hereafter
   TL), in which the theme is repeatedly expressed. Cf. FA:ED II 256 a.

15

AVOIDING LUXURIOUS AND ABUNDANT CLOTHING
AND ON BEING PATIENT IN NEED

AC 28//2C 69

Clothed with virtue **from on high,** this man was warmed **inwardly** more by divine fire than **outwardly** by what covered his body.

AC 29//2C 69

He detested those in the Order who dressed in three layers of clothing or who wore soft clothes without necessity. As for "necessity" not based on reason but on pleasure, he declared that it was a sign of a *spirit* that was *extinguished.* "When the spirit is lukewarm," he said, "and gradually growing cold as it moves from grace, *flesh and blood* inevitably *seek their own interests.* When the soul **lacks spiritual** delight, what is left except for the flesh to look for some? Then the base instinct covers itself with the excuse of necessity, and the mind of the flesh forms the conscience."

AC 30//2C 69

And he added: "If one of my brothers encounters a real necessity and **immediately** rushes to satisfy it, *what reward will he get?* He found an occasion for merit, but clearly showed that he did not like it. Not bearing patiently with need is the same as *returning to Egypt."*

Finally, on no account did he want the brothers to have more than two tunics, although he allowed these to be mended with patches on them.[a]

He used to say that fine fabrics should be shunned, and those who acted to the contrary he rebuked publicly with biting words. To confound them by his example, he sewed **coarse** sackcloth on his own rough tunic and at his death he **ordered** that the tunic for his funeral be covered in cheap sackcloth. But he allowed brothers pressed by illness or other necessity to wear a soft tunic next to the skin, as long as rough and cheap clothing was kept on the outside. For, **with great sorrow** he said: "A time will come when strictness will be relaxed, and tepidity will hold such sway, that sons of a poor father will not be the least ashamed to wear even velvet cloth, just changing the color.[b]

Lk 24:49

1 Thes 5:19

Gal 1:16; Mt 16:17

Phil 2:21

Gn 29:15

Nm 14:2-4

---

a. In addition to echoing the words of Francis, *The Earlier Rule* II 14 (hereafter ER), LR II 16, Test 16, this prescription is repeated in Nicholas III, *Exiit qui seminat* (1279), article 14, infra 756-7; and Clement V, *Exivi de paradiso* (1312), article 5, infra 774-5.

b. For the interpretation of *scarulaticus* [velvet], cf. FA:ED II 138 b.

16
HOW HE DID NOT WANT TO SATISFY HIS BODY WITH THINGS
THAT HE THOUGHT OTHER BROTHERS WERE LACKING

One time blessed Francis was staying at the hermitage of
Sant'Eleuterio in the district of Rieti. Since he was wearing only one
tunic, **as was his custom,** one day because of the extreme cold, he
patched his tunic and that of his companion with scraps of cloth on
the inside, so that his body began to be comforted a little.

A short while afterwards, when he was returning from prayer, he
said with great joy to his companion: "I must be the form and example of all the brothers; so, although it is necessary for my body to have
a tunic with patches, nevertheless I must take into consideration my
other brothers who have the same need, but perhaps do not and cannot have this. Therefore, **in this** I must stay down with them and I
must suffer those same necessities they suffer so that in seeing this
in me, they may be able to bear them more patiently."

We who were with him cannot **express in words or in writing**
how many and how great were the necessities that he denied his
body to give good example to the brothers and so that they would
endure their necessities in greater patience. For after the brothers
began to multiply, his highest and principal goal was to teach the
brothers, more by actions than by words, what they ought to do and
what they ought to avoid.

17
HOW HE WAS ASHAMED TO SEE ANYONE POORER THAN HIMSELF

Once when he met a poor man, noticing his dire poverty, he said
to his companion: "This man's poverty brings great shame on us; it
passes judgment on our poverty. **For** I am **most** ashamed when I find
someone poorer than myself. I chose holy poverty as my Lady, my
delight, and my riches of spirit and body. And the whole world has
heard this news, that I professed poverty before God and people."

18
HOW HE MOTIVATED AND TAUGHT THE FIRST BROTHERS
WHO WERE ASHAMED TO GO BEGGING

When Francis began to have brothers, he was so happy about
their conversion and that the Lord had given him good company,
that he loved and revered them so much that he did not tell them to

go for alms, especially because it seemed to him that they would be ashamed to go. Rather, sparing them shame, he himself would go for alms alone every day.

He was gravely worn out **by this,** especially since in the world he had been a refined man, and of a weak constitution; and he had become **more debilitated** because of the excessive fasting and suffering he endured.

//2C 74 He considered that he could not bear so much labor **alone,** and that they were called to this, even though they would be ashamed **to do this, because** they did not fully understand; but neither had they been discerning enough to tell him: "We **also** want to go for alms." So he talked to them. "My dearest brothers and sons, don't be ashamed to go for alms, because *for our sake, the Lord* **made Himself** 2 Cor 8:9

LR VI 3 **poor** in this world. Therefore, because of His example, we have chosen the way of the most genuine poverty. This is our inheritance, which the Lord Jesus Christ acquired and bequeathed to us and to all who want to live in **most** holy poverty according to His example. I tell you the truth: many of the noblest and wisest of this world will come to this congregation and they will consider it a great honor **and grace** to go for alms. Therefore, go for alms confidently with joyful hearts with the blessing of the Lord God. And you ought to go begging more willingly and with more joyful hearts than someone who is offering a hundred silver pieces in exchange for a single penny, since you are offering the love of God to those from whom you seek alms. Say to them: 'Give alms to us for the love of the Lord God: compared to this, heaven and earth are nothing!' "

Because **the brothers** were still few in number so that he could not send *them out two by two,* so he sent each one separately through Lk 10:1 the towns and villages. When they returned **with the alms they received,** each one showed blessed Francis the alms he had collected, one saying to the other, "I collected more alms than you!"

This gave blessed Francis reason to rejoice, seeing them so happy and cheerful. From then on each of them more willingly asked permission to go for alms.

19
HOW HE DID NOT WANT THE BROTHERS TO BE
FARSIGHTED AND CONCERNED ABOUT THE MORROW

↓AC 52 At that time, as Blessed Francis was with his brothers whom he had then, **he lived with them in** such purity that **they** observed the holy gospel **in all things and throughout all things** to the letter,

namely from the very day the Lord revealed to him that he and his   Test 14
brothers should live according to the form of the holy Gospel.

For this reason he told the brother who did the cooking for the
brothers, that when he wanted the brothers to eat beans, he should
not put them in warm water in the evening for the next day, as people usually do. This was so the brothers would observe the words of
the holy Gospel: "*Do not be concerned about tomorrow.*" So that brother   Mt 6:34
delayed setting them in water to soften until after the brothers said
matins on the very day they were to be eaten.

Because of this, for a long time many brothers observed this in a
great many places, especially in cities. They did not want to collect or
receive more alms than were necessary for them for one day.

20

HOW BY WORD AND EXAMPLE HE REPROVED THE BROTHERS
WHO PREPARED A SUMPTUOUS TABLE ON CHRISTMAS
BECAUSE A MINISTER WAS PRESENT[a]

When a minister of the brothers came to blessed Francis in the   ↓AC 74//2C 61
place of the brothers in Rieti, in order to celebrate the feast of Christmas with him, the brothers on Christmas day prepared the table
elaborately and attentively. To honor the minister and the feast,
they covered it with lovely white tablecloths and glasses.

Blessed Francis came down from the cell to eat, and when he saw
the table set on a dais and finely prepared, he immediately went
secretly and took the hat of a poor man who had arrived there that
very day, and the staff he carried in his hand. Summoning one of his
companions in a whisper, he went outside the door of the place,
unnoticed by the brothers of the house. His companion remained
inside near the door.

Meanwhile the brothers came to the table, for blessed Francis
had ordered that whenever he did not come at once to eat at mealtime, the brothers were not to wait for him.

After standing outside for a while, blessed Francis knocked on
the door and his companion immediately opened it for him. When
he entered the door of the house where the brothers were eating,
with his hat on his back and with staff in hand, like a poor pilgrim he
cried out: "For the love of the Lord God, give alms to this poor, sick
pilgrim."

---

a. While AC 74 describes this event as taking place on Christmas, 2C 61 places it on Easter. The editor
   of 2MP maintains the AC tradition.

That minister and the other brothers recognized him at once. The minister told him: "Brother, we are also poor, and because we are so many, we need the alms **we have.** But, for the love of that Lord you invoked, come into the house, and we will give you some of the alms which the Lord has given us."

When he came in and stood in front of the brothers' table, the minister gave him the bowl from which he was eating and some bread. Taking it, he **humbly** sat down on the floor beside the fire, facing the brothers who were seated at the table. Sighing he said to the brothers: "When I saw the table finely and elaborately prepared, I considered that this was not a table of poor religious, who go door-to-door **for alms** each day. **Dearest brothers,** more than other religious, we should follow the example of poverty and humility **of Christ,** because we have been called to this and have professed this before God and people. So, now it seems to me I'm seated like a **lesser** brother. **The feasts of the Lord and of other saints are more honored by the want and poverty by which the saints won heaven, than by the luxury and excess which cause a soul to become estranged from heaven."**

The brothers were ashamed at this, considering that blessed Francis was speaking the **pure** truth. Some of them began to weep loudly, considering how he was seated on the ground, wishing to correct **and teach** them in such a holy and simple way.

He **admonished** the brothers that they have a humble and decent table so as to edify secular people. And if a poor person **should visit,** or be invited by the brothers, he should sit with them **as an equal,** and not have the poor person sit on the ground with the brothers sitting on high.

21

HOW AT THE TIME OF A CHAPTER
THE LORD OF OSTIA WEPT AND WAS EDIFIED
BY THE POVERTY OF THE BROTHERS

↓AC 74//2C 63   When the Lord of Ostia, **who later became** Pope Gregory, came **to the chapter** of the brothers at Saint Mary of the Portiuncula, with many knights and clerics, he entered the house to see the brothers' dormitory. And when he saw that the brothers lay on the ground, with nothing underneath except a little straw, no pillows, and some poor coverings, torn and threadbare, he began to weep **bitterly** before them all. "Look where the brothers sleep," he said. "But we, wretched creatures, enjoy such a surplus. What will become of us?"

Both he and the others were greatly edified. He did not see a table there because the brothers ate on the ground. As long as **blessed Francis** lived, **all** the brothers there sat on the ground to eat.

22

HOW SOME KNIGHTS ON THE ADVICE OF BLESSED FRANCIS
OBTAINED WHAT THEY NEEDED FROM DOOR-TO-DOOR

When blessed Francis was in the place of Begnara, north of Nocera, his feet began swelling **severely** because of dropsy, **and** he became **seriously** ill **there.** When the people of Assisi heard of this, they quickly sent some knights of Assisi to that place to bring him back to Assisi, fearing that he would die there and others would claim his most precious remains.

↓AC 96//2C 77

While they were bringing **him** back, they stopped to eat in a small town belonging to the Commune of Assisi. Blessed Francis rested in the house of a **poor** man who **willingly and joyfully** received **him.** The knights, however, went about the town, attempting to buy things for their needs, but did not find anything. And they returned to blessed Francis, saying to him **as a consolation:** "Brothers, you must give us some of your alms, because we can find nothing to buy."

Blessed Francis, with great intensity of spirit, told them: "You didn't find anything because you *placed your trust* in flies, that is, in coins, and not *in God.* But go back to the houses where you went looking for things to buy, and do not be ashamed, and ask them for alms for the love **of the Lord** God. The Holy Spirit will inspire them and **they will give to you** abundantly."

Mt 27:43

So they went and begged alms, as **blessed Francis** told them to do. **And those from whom they asked alms gave them joyfully** and generously whatever they had. **Realizing a miracle** had happened to them, *they returned* to blessed Francis *praising* the Lord **with great joy.**

Lk 24:52-53

For blessed Francis held that to beg for alms for the love of the Lord God was of very great nobility, dignity, and courtesy before God and before the world. He held this because everything that the heavenly Father has created for a human's use, after the sin, He has given freely as alms, both to the worthy and the unworthy on account of the love of His beloved Son.

//1MP 1

He used to say that a servant of God must beg alms for the love of God **more willingly and more joyfully** than someone, who, out of courtesy and generosity, would go about saying: "Whoever will give me **only one** penny, I will give him **a thousand** pieces **of gold.**"[a] For a servant of God offers the love of God to those from whom he begs alms, in comparison to which, all things **on earth** and in heaven are nothing.

Therefore, before the brothers became numerous—and even after they grew in number—when **he** would go through the world preaching, if he were invited by someone, **however** noble and wealthy, to eat and lodge with him, he would **always** go begging for alms at mealtimes. He did this **before he went to his host's house,** to give good example to the brothers and **because of the dignity of Lady Poverty. Many times** he would say to his host: "I do not want to renounce my royal dignity, my heritage, my vocation, and my profession and that of **my** brothers, namely, to go begging alms **door-to-door.**"

And **sometimes** the one who invited him would go with him and would take the alms which blessed Francis acquired, and, out of his devotion, save them as relics.

The one *who wrote these things* has seen **this** many times and *bears witness to it.*

Jn 21:24

23

HOW HE WENT BEGGING FOR ALMS BEFORE
HE SAT DOWN AT THE CARDINAL'S TABLE

//2C 73//1MP 2

Moreover, one time, when **blessed Francis** was visiting the Lord Bishop of Ostia, who later was Pope **Gregory,** he secretly went **from door-to-door** for alms at mealtime. When he returned, the Lord **of Ostia** was at table together with **many** knights **and nobles.** When blessed Francis **approached,** he put the alms **which he had collected** on the table and sat down next **to the cardinal,** because he always wanted blessed Francis to sit next to him at table. **The cardinal** was somewhat embarrassed that blessed Francis went begging alms **and laid them on the table,** but said nothing to him **at that moment** because of those at table.

After blessed Francis had eaten a little, he took some of his alms and distributed a little on behalf of the Lord God to each one of the knights and chaplains of the lord **cardinal.** They all accepted them with **great respect and** great devotion, **pushing back their hoods**

---

a. The editor of the 2MP changes the text of AC 96 from "a hundred pieces of silver" to "a thousand pieces of gold," thus dramatically making his point of contrast.

and removing their head-covering. Some ate them, others kept them out of his devotion. The Lord **of Ostia** was overjoyed at their devotion, especially since those alms did not consist of wheat bread.

After the meal, the lord bishop got up and went to his room, taking blessed Francis with him. Lifting up his arms, he embraced blessed Francis with utmost joy and told him: "Why, my simple little brother,[a] did you shame me **today coming** to my house, which is also the house of your brothers, by going out for alms?"

"On the contrary, Lord Bishop," blessed Francis answered, "I paid you **the greatest** honor. Because when a subject **does** his duty and **fulfills** the obedience of his lord, he does to his lord honor. I must be a model and example of your poor," he said, "especially because I know that in **this** religion of the brothers there are, and will be **brothers,** Lesser Brothers, in name and in deed. For the love of the Lord God and by the anointing of the Holy Spirit, who *will teach them in all things,* they will be humble in all things, obedient, and of service to their brothers. There also are and will be those among them who, held back by shame and because of bad habit, are and will be scorned by humbling themselves, by demeaning themselves by begging alms, and by doing **other** servile work of this kind. Therefore, I must teach by deed those who are or who will be in religion, *that they might be without excuse* in the eyes of God in this age and in the future.

"While I am with you, who are our Apostolic Lord, and with **other** great and wealthy people of **this** world, who for the love of the Lord God and with great kindness, not only receive me into **your** houses, but even **compel** me to do so, I do not want to be ashamed to go for alms. Indeed I want to have and hold this as a sign of the **greatest** nobility, royal dignity and an honor of Him Who, although He was Lord of all, chose for us to be a servant, and, *although He was rich* and glorious in majesty, came in our **humility,** poor and despised.[b]

"So I want all who are and will be brothers to know that I hold it a greater consolation for both soul and body when I sit at a poor little table of the brothers and see before me the meager alms they begged from door to door for the love of the Lord God, than when I sit at your table and that of other lords, abundantly set **with a variety of dishes.** For the bread offered as alms is holy bread which the praise and love of God have hallowed, because when a brother goes out begging, he

1 Jn 2:27; Jn 14: 26

Rom 1:20

2 Cor 8:9

---

a. For the translation of *frater mi simpliçione* [my simple little brother], see FA:ED II 200 a.

b. The editor of the 2MP changes AC 97 from *humanitate* [humanity] to *humilitate* [humility]. A change suggesting the editor's preoccupation with the virtue of humility. *Humilitas* [humility] occurs fifty-five times in 2MP, *humilis* [humble] twenty-three, and *humiliter* [humbly] twenty-eight. Thus, the development of this virtue is one of the most important themes of this text; it is second only to the pursuit of poverty.

must first say: *'Praised and blessed be the Lord God!'* Afterwards he must say: 'Give us alms for the love of the Lord God.' "

Ps 113:1-2; Lk 24:53

The cardinal was greatly edified by **blessed Francis's** words of instruction.[a] He said to him: "My son, *do what seems good in your eyes, for the Lord is with you* and you with Him."

1 Sm 14:36

2 Sm 7:3

For the will of blessed Francis, as he often said, was that no brother should procrastinate in going for alms, **both because of its great merit and** so that he would not be ashamed to go later on. Indeed, the greater and nobler a brother had been in the world, so much the more pleased and happy was he when he went for alms and did **other** servile work **that the brothers were at that time accustomed to do.**[b]

24
A BROTHER WHO NEITHER PRAYED NOR WORKED BUT ATE WELL

*//2C 75//1MP 3

At the religion's beginning, when the brothers were staying at Rivo Torto, **near Assisi,** there was a brother among them who prayed little, did not work, and did not want to go for alms; but he ate heartily. Giving the matter some thought, blessed Francis knew through the Holy Spirit that the man was carnal. He told him: "Go on your way, Brother Fly, because you want to feed on the labor of your brothers, but wish to be idle in the work of God, like **a lazy and sterile bee,** that does not gather or work, yet eats the work and gain of the good bees."

So he went his way. And because he lived according to the flesh, he neither asked for mercy **nor found it.**

25
HOW HE WENT OUT FERVENTLY TO A POOR MAN
WHO WAS PASSING BY WITH ALMS PRAISING GOD

↓AC 98

Another time while blessed Francis was at Saint Mary of the Portiuncula, a **very** spiritual poor man was coming back **along the road** from Assisi with a bag of alms. **As he drew near the church of Saint Mary,** *praising God* **as he went his way,** in a loud voice with **great** joy, blessed Francis heard him.

Ps 150:1

---

a. For the translation of *in collatione verborum suorum* [conference], cf. FA:ED II 201 a.

b. The addition of "other" to the phrase "servile work" suggests that begging alms was seen as a form of servile work. It is also worthy of note that the editor hearkens back to this early practice of the fraternity in contrast to what seems to have become the custom of the day.

Immediately, **with the greatest fervor and delight,** he ran up to him **on the road** and, with great joy, kissed his shoulder on which he was carrying the bag with the alms. Taking the bag from his shoulder and putting it on his own shoulder, he carried it to the home of the brothers. He said to the brothers: "This is how I want a brother of mine to go for alms and to return happy and joyful **praising God.**"

26

HOW IT WAS REVEALED TO HIM BY THE LORD
THAT THE BROTHERS ARE TO BE CALLED LESSER
AND SHOULD ANNOUNCE PEACE AND SALVATION

Another time, **blessed Francis** said: "The religion and life of the Lesser Brothers is *a little flock,* which the Son of God *in* this *very last hour* has asked of His heavenly Father, saying: 'Father, I want you to make and give me a new and humble people in this very last hour, who would be unlike all others who preceded them by their humility and poverty, and be content to have me alone.' And the Father said to His beloved Son: '**My** Son, Your request has been fulfilled.' " _{↓AC 101}

Lk 12:32; 1 Jn 2:18

This is why blessed Francis would say: "Therefore, the Lord willed **and revealed to him** that they be called Lesser Brothers, because they are the **poor and humble** people whom the Son of God asked of the Father. They are the ones of whom the Son of God speaks in the Gospel: *Do not be afraid, little flock, for it has pleased your Father to give you the kingdom;* and again: *What you did for one of these, the least of my brothers, you did it for me.* For, although the Lord may be understood to be speaking of all the spiritually poor, he was nevertheless predicting the religion of the Lesser Brothers that was to come in His Church." //1MP 6

Lk 12:32

Mt 25:40

Therefore, as it was revealed to blessed Francis that it was to be called the Religion of the Lesser Brothers, he had it so written in the first rule, when he brought it before the Lord Pope Innocent III, **who** approved and granted it, and later announced it to all **in a consistory.**[a] Likewise, the Lord also revealed to him the greeting that the brothers should use, as he had written in his Testament: "The Lord revealed a greeting to me that we should say *'May the Lord give you peace.'* " Test 23

Nm 6:26

At the beginning of the religion, when **he** would go with a brother who was one of the first twelve brothers, that brother would greet men and women along the way as well as those in their field, saying: "May the Lord give you peace."

---

a. While *consistorio* [consistory] is a change from *consilio* [council] in AC 101, the same nuance can be found in L3C 53, cf. FA:ED II 98 a.

And because people had never before heard such a greeting from any religious, they were greatly amazed. Indeed, some would say almost indignantly: "What does this greeting **of yours** mean?" As a result **of this** that brother began to be embarrassed. Then he said to blessed Francis "Let me use another greeting."

Blessed Francis told him: "Let them talk, for *they do not know the*   1 Cor 2:14
ways of God. But do not be embarrassed, for one day the nobles and princes of this world will show respect to you and the other brothers because of this greeting. Isn't it great that the Lord wanted to have **one, new, and** little people, **singular**[a] **and unique in life and in word** from all those who preceded them, who would be content to have Him alone, the Most High and most glorious?"

---

a. Unlike Thomas of Celano's use of *singularis* [singular], in this instance the editor of the *Mirror of Perfection* uses the word in a positive sense. Elsewhere, he uses it in the more negative sense of Thomas of Celano, 2MP 26, 40-2x, 76, 82-2x, 83, 95, 96, 108, 113, 116, 118- 2x. Cf. FA:ED II 253 a.

Chapter Two
CHARITY, COMPASSION, AND SELF-EMPTYING FOR A NEIGHBOR

27
IN THE FIRST PLACE
HIS SELF-EMPTYING TOWARD A BROTHER DYING OF HUNGER
BY EATING WITH HIM
AND HOW HE THEN ADMONISHED HIS BROTHERS TO USE DISCERNMENT
IN DOING PENANCE

One time, when blessed Francis began to have brothers, he was staying with them at Rivo Torto **near Assisi.** One night around midnight, when **all the brothers** were asleep, one of the brothers cried out, saying: "I'm dying! I'm dying!" Startled and frightened, all the brothers woke up.

↓AC 50//2C 22

Getting up, blessed Francis said: "Brothers, get up and light a lamp." After the lamp was lit, **he** said: "Who was it who said, 'I'm dying?' "

"I'm the one," the brother answered.

"What's the matter, brother?" **he** said to him. "Why are you dying?"

"I'm dying of hunger," he answered.

So that that brother would not be ashamed to eat alone, blessed Francis, a man of great charity and discernment, immediately had the table set and ate with him. **At his request,** all **the other** brothers ate as well. This brother, as well as **all** the others, were newly converted to the Lord and afflicted their bodies excessively.

After the meal, blessed Francis said to the other brothers: "My brothers, I say that each of you must consider his own constitution, because, although one of you may be sustained with less food than another, I still do not want one who needs more food to try imitating him in this. Rather, considering his constitution, he should provide his body with what it needs **that it may suffice to serve the spirit.** Just as we must beware of overindulgence in eating, which harms body and soul, so we must beware of excessive abstinence even more, because the Lord desires *mercy and not sacrifice.*"

//1MP 24

Hos 6:6;
Mt 9:13; 12:7

And he said: "Dearest brothers, great necessity and charity compelled me to do what I did, namely, that out of love for our brother we ate together with him, so he wouldn't be embarrassed to eat alone. But I tell you in the future I do not wish to act this way because it

278

wouldn't be religious or decent. Let each one provide his body with what it needs as our poverty will allow. This is what I wish and command you."

The first brothers and those who came after them for a long time mortified their bodies excessively, not only by abstinence in food and drink, but also in *vigils, cold,* **coarse clothing,** and manual *labor.* Next to their skins they wore iron rings, and the roughest hair shirts. Considering that the brothers could get sick because of this, and in a short time some were already ailing, he commanded in one of the chapters that no brother wear anything next to the skin except the tunic.

2 Cor 11:27

We who were with him bear witness to this fact about him: although during his whole lifetime, he was discerning **and moderate** with the brothers, provided that in the matter of food and other things, they at **no** time deviated from the norm of the poverty and the decency of our religion; **nevertheless, the most holy father,** from the beginning of his conversion **until the end of his life,** was severe with his own body, even though he was a man of a frail and weak constitution, and when he was in the world he could not live without comforts.

One time, perceiving that the brothers had exceeded the norm of poverty and decency in food and in **all** things, he said in a sermon he gave, speaking to a few brothers, who stood for all the brothers: "Don't the brothers think that my body needs special food? But because I must be the model and example for all the brothers, I want to use and be content with meager and poor food and **all other** things **in accordance with poverty, shunning everything that is expensive and** delicate."

28

HOW HE EMPTIED HIMSELF BEFORE A SICK BROTHER
BY EATING GRAPES WITH HIM

»AC 53//2C 176
//1MP 26

Another time when blessed Francis was at that same place, a certain spiritual brother, an elder in religion, was there. He was very sick and weak. Considering him, blessed Francis was moved to piety toward him. The brothers back then, sick and healthy, with **great** cheerfulness took poverty for abundance. They did not use **nor ask for** medicines in their illnesses, but **rather** willingly **chose** what was contrary to the body. Blessed Francis said to himself: "If that brother would eat some ripe grapes early in the morning, I believe it would help him."

And he did what he had been thinking. One day he secretly got up early in the morning, and called that brother and took him into the vineyard which was close **by the place.** He chose **one** vine with good grapes to eat. Sitting down with that brother next to the vine, he began to eat some grapes so that the brother would not be ashamed to eat alone, and while they were eating them, that brother **was cured and together they** praised the Lord God. As long as he lived, he **very often** recalled among the brothers, with great devotion and flowing tears, the mercy **and piety** the holy father **had shown** to him.

29

HOW HE STRIPPED HIMSELF AND HIS COMPANION
TO CLOTHE A POOR OLD WOMAN

In Celano at winter time **when blessed** Francis was wearing a piece of folded cloth as a cloak, which a friend of the brothers had lent him, an old woman came up to him *begging for alms.* He **immediately** unfastened the cloth from his neck, and, although it belonged to someone else, he gave it to the poor old woman, saying: "Go and make yourself a tunic; you really need it."

The old woman laughed; she was stunned—I don't know if it was out of fear or joy—and took the piece of cloth from his hands. She ran off quickly, so that delay might not bring the danger of having to give it back, and cut **the cloth** with scissors. But when she saw that the cut cloth would not be enough for a tunic, she returned **to the holy father,** knowing his earlier kindness, and showed him that the material **was not enough cloth for a tunic.** The saint turned his eyes on his companion, who **wore** the same cloth on his back. "Do you hear what this poor woman says?" he said. "For the love of God, let us **endure** the cold: give **this** poor woman the cloth so she can finish her tunic." And **immediately** the companion offered his as he had done; and **so** both were left naked, so the **poor** woman could be clothed.

30

HOW HE CONSIDERED IT A THEFT NOT TO GIVE A CLOAK
TO SOMEONE WHO HAD A GREATER NEED

Once, when he was coming back from Siena, he met a poor man, and said to his companion: "We must give back to this poor man the mantle that is his. *We accepted* it *on loan* until we should happen to find someone poorer than we are." The companion, seeing the need of his

Acts 3:2

Lk 6:34; Prv 22:7

↓AC 31; 2C

↓AC 32//2C

pious father, stubbornly objected that he should not provide for someone else by neglecting himself. But he said to him: "I do not want to *be a thief;* we will be accused of theft if we do not give this to someone in greater need." **Thus the pious father handed over the** mantle **to the poor man.**

Jn 12:6

31
HOW HE GAVE A NEW CLOAK TO A POOR PERSON WITH A CERTAIN CONDITION

↓AC 33//2C 88

At "Le Celle" of Cortona,[a] blessed Francis was wearing a new mantle that the brothers had gone to some trouble to find for him. A poor man came to the place weeping for his dead wife and his poor little family that was left desolate. The saint **compassionately** said to him: "I'm giving you this cloak, but on the condition that you do not hand it over to anyone unless **he buys it and pays you** well." **Upon hearing this,** the brothers came running **to the poor man** to take the mantle away. But the poor man, taking courage from the father's look, clutched it with both hands and defended it as his own. **Finally** the brothers had to redeem the mantle, **paying** the price **owed the poor man.**

32
HOW A POOR MAN FORGAVE THE HURTS
AND CEASED TO HATE HIS MASTER
BECAUSE OF THE ALMS OF BLESSED FRANCIS

↓AC 34//2C 89

At Colle[b] in the county of Perugia, **blessed** Francis met a poor man whom he had known before in the world. He asked him: "Brother, how are you doing?" The man malevolently began to heap curses on his lord. "Thanks to my lord, *may the Almighty Lord curse* him, I'm very bad off **because he stripped me of all my possessions!"**

Rv 1:8; Gn 5:29

When blessed Francis **saw that the man** persisted in mortal hatred, **he felt pity for his soul.** He said to him: "Brother, forgive your lord for the love of God, so you may *set your soul free,* and it may be that *he will return* to you what *he has taken.* **Otherwise** you will lose not only your property but also your soul." He replied: "I can't entirely forgive him unless he first gives back **to me** what he took." **Then** blessed Francis said to him: "Here, I'll give you this cloak, and beg you to forgive your

Est 4:13; Ex 22:12

---

a. For background on "Le Celle" of Cortona, see FA:ED II 139 b.
b. See FA:ED II 140 b.

lord for the love of the Lord God." **Immediately his heart** sweetened, and, moved by this kindness, he forgave **his lord's** wrongs.

33
HOW HE SENT A CLOAK TO A POOR WOMAN
WHO, LIKE HIMSELF, SUFFERED FROM AN EYE ILLNESS

A poor woman from Machilone came to Rieti **because of** an illness of her eyes. When the doctor came to visit blessed Francis, he said to him: "Brother, a woman with eye trouble came to see me. But, she is so poor that I have to pay her expenses."

When blessed Francis heard this, moved **immediately** by piety for her, he called one **of the brothers,** who was his guardian, and said to him: "Brother Guardian, we have to give back what belongs to someone else." "And, what is that, brother?" he said. "That mantle," he replied, "which *we accepted on loan* from that poor and sick woman. We must give it back to her." "Do what you think best, brother," the guardian answered.

With joy, blessed Francis **then** called a spiritual man, who was close to him, and said: "Take this mantle and a dozen loaves of bread with you, and go to that poor woman suffering **from eye disease** whom the doctor, who is taking care of her, will point out to you. Say to her: 'The poor man to whom you lent this mantle thanks you for the loan of the mantle. *Take what belongs to you.*' "

He went then and told **the woman** everything as blessed Francis had told him. Thinking he was joking, she replied with fear and embarrassment: *"Leave me in peace! I don't know what you are talking about!"* He placed the mantle and the dozen loaves of bread in her hands. When the woman reflected that he had spoken the truth, she accepted everything with fear and **reverence, rejoicing and praising the Lord.** Then, fearful that he would take it back, she secretly got up during night and joyfully returned to her home.

Moreover, blessed Francis **arranged with** his guardian that he should give her food every day for as long as she stayed there.

We who were with blessed Francis bear witness that, sick or well, he displayed such charity and piety, not only to his brothers, but also toward **other** poor persons, whether healthy or sick. Thus, he deprived himself of the necessities of his body that the brothers procured for him with great **labor** and solicitude. At first coaxing us not to worry, with great inner and outer joy, **he would give away to the poor** things he had denied his own body, even though they were extremely necessary for him.

↓AC 89//2C 92

Lk 6:34; Prv 22:7

Mt 20:14

1 Sm 20:13; Mt 26:70

And that is why the general minister and his guardian ordered him not to give his tunic to any brother without their permission. Because the brothers, out of the devotion they had for him, would occasionally ask him for his tunic, and he would immediately give it to them. He would at times cut his habit in half, giving one part to him and keeping the other for himself, **because** he wore only one tunic.

34
HOW HE GAVE HIS TUNIC TO BROTHERS
SEEKING IT FOR THE LOVE OF GOD

AC 90//2C 181

Once when he was traveling through a certain region preaching, two brothers from France happened to meet him. From this they enjoyed great consolation. **Finally,** for the love of God they asked **him** for his tunic. As soon as he heard "the love of God," he immediately took off his tunic **and gave it to them,** remaining naked for almost an hour.

When asked for his cord or tunic or anything else for the love of God, he never refused anyone. Furthermore, he would be greatly displeased, and would **frequently** reprimand the brothers when he heard them invoking the love of God **needlessly.** For he would say: "The love of God is so very exalted **and so precious** that it should be mentioned with great reverence rarely and only in dire necessity." Then one **of the brothers** took off his tunic and gave it to him.

Similarly he endured great need and hardship when he gave away his tunic or a part of it to someone, because he could not quickly find or have another one made. This was true especially since he always wished to wear a poor tunic patched **at times** inside and out. Because he rarely, if ever, wanted to have or wear a tunic made from new cloth, but would acquire one worn by a brother for **some** time. Sometimes he would accept one part of his tunic from one brother and another **part** from another. But, because of his many illnesses and chills **of the stomach and spleen,** he would occasionally patch it on the inside with new cloth.

He held and observed this kind of poverty in his clothing until the year when he returned to the Lord. For a few days before his death, because he was suffering from dropsy and almost completely dehydrated and weakened by many of the other sicknesses he had, the brothers made several tunics for him, so that they could change his tunic night and day as was necessary.

35

How he wanted to give a piece of cloth secretly to a poor man

↓AC 91

Another time a poor man came **to the place where blessed Francis was staying,** and, for the love of God, asked for a piece **of cloth** from the brothers. **On hearing this,** blessed Francis told one of the brothers: "**Look** around the house and, if **you can,** find a piece of cloth and to give it **to the poor man.**" And going around the whole house, (Sir 29:9) that brother told him that he did not find any. So that *the poor man* would not go away *empty-handed,* blessed Francis went out secretly, so that his guardian would not forbid him. He took a knife, and sitting in a hidden place, he began to cut away a piece of his tunic, which was sewed on the inside of the tunic, wanting to give it to the poor man secretly. But the guardian becoming aware of this went to him and forbade him to give it away, especially since the weather was then very cold, and he was extremely sick and cold.

Blessed Francis **therefore** told him: "If you do not want me to give him **this piece of cloth,** you must, **by all means,** make sure that some piece is given to the poor brother." And so, at the prompting of blessed Francis, the brothers gave the poor man some cloth from their own clothes.

When he traveled through the country preaching, he went on foot or, after he became ill, astride a donkey, because **otherwise** he did not want to ride on a horse unless compelled by the greatest necessity. And such was the case shortly before his death. **If any** brother lent him a mantle, he did not want to accept it unless, in some way, he could give it to **any** poor person he might meet or who might approach him, if his spirit convinced **him** that the person was in **more** evident need.

36

How he told brother Giles before he was received into the order to give his cloak to a poor person

↓AC 92

At the beginning of the religion, when he was staying at Rivo Torto with only two brothers whom he had at that time, the third brother, **a man named Giles,**[a] came **to him** from the world to receive his life. When he had stayed **there** for a few days, still wearing his secular clothes, a poor man happened to come to the place **asking** alms of blessed Francis. **Turning to Giles,** blessed Francis said to him: "Give the poor brother your mantle." Immediately, with great

a. Cf. FA:ED I 204 b; II 47 a, b.

joy, he took it off his back and gave it to **the poor man.** It then seemed to him that, at that moment, the Lord immediately had infused new grace into his heart because he had given the poor man his mantle with joy. **So he was received by blessed Francis and constantly progressed in virtue to a very great state of perfection.**

37

THE PENANCE HE IMPOSED ON A BROTHER
WHO JUDGED A POOR MAN HARSHLY

C 114//2C 85
//1MP 42

When blessed Francis went **to a place** of the brothers[c] near Rocca di Brizio to preach, it happened that on the very day that he was to preach, a poor sick man came to him. Feeling **great** compassion, he began to speak to his companion about the man's poverty and illness. "It is true, brother," his companion said to him, "that he **seems** poor enough, but perhaps there is no one in the whole province who desires riches more."

Immediately blessed Francis rebuked him **severely** and he admitted his fault. Blessed Francis told him: "Are you willing to do the penance I will tell you **for this?**" "Willingly!" he replied. "Go, *strip off your tunic,*" he said, "throw yourself naked at the feet **of the poor man,** tell him how you sinned against him, how you slandered him, and ask him to pray for you." Mt 15:30

So he went and did everything blessed Francis had told him. When he finished, he got up, put on his tunic, and returned to blessed Francis. And blessed Francis said to him: "Do you want **to know** how you sinned against him, and even against Christ?"

And he said: "Whenever you see a poor person you ought to consider Him in whose name he comes, that is, Christ, who came to take on our poverty and weakness. **For** this man's poverty and weakness is a mirror for us[b] in which we should see and consider with piety the poverty and weakness of our Lord Jesus Christ which He endured in His body for **our** salvation."

---

c. The editor changes the identification of the hermitage near Rocca di Brizio to simply "a place." That *eremitorio* [hermitage] appears in AC twenty-six times and in 2MP twelve suggests that 2MP is not as bound to the eremitical tradition as the earlier text upon which it relies.

b. With the exception of the title, this is the first use of the word *speculum* [mirror]. The word appears in the title and conclusion (2MP 1, 124) and only 4 times in the text to refer to Christ (2MP 37), to the Blessed Virgin Mary (2MP 55), to Francis (2MP 123) and, in a generic way, to the Friar Preachers (2MP 43). For background on the rich medieval use of the word, see FA:ED I 260 a; FA:ED II 257 c.

38

HOW HE HAD A NEW TESTAMENT GIVEN TO A POOR WOMAN,
THE MOTHER OF TWO OF THE BROTHERS

Another time while he was staying at Saint Mary of the ↓AC 93//2C
Portiuncula, a poor old woman who had two sons in religion, came to
that place seeking some alms of blessed Francis.

Blessed Francis **immediately** said to Brother Peter of Catanio,
who was the general minister at the time: "Have we anything to give
our mother?" For he used to say that the mother of any brother was
his own and that of all the brothers. Brother Peter told him: "We do
not have anything in the house that we can give her, especially since
she wants such alms as would **nourish** her body. In the church we
only have one New Testament for reading the lessons at matins." At
that time, the brothers did not have breviaries and not many psal-
ters.

Blessed Francis responded: "Give our mother the New Testament,
so she can sell it for her needs. I firmly believe that the Lord and the
Blessed Virgin will be pleased **more** by giving it to her than if you
read in it." And so he gave it to her. For it can be said and written
Jb 31:18   about **him** what **was read** about Job: *Mercy grew up with me and it came
out with me from my mother's womb.*

For us, who were with him, it would **be very difficult** to write **or**
recount not only what we learned from others about his charity and
piety toward **the brothers and the other** poor, but also what we saw
1 Jn 1:1   *with our own eyes.*

Chapter Three

THE PERFECTION OF HOLY HUMILITY AND OBEDIENCE
IN HIM AND IN HIS BROTHERS

39

IN THE FIRST PLACE,
HOW HE RESIGNED THE OFFICE OF GENERAL MINISTER
AND APPOINTED BROTHER PETER OF CATANIO THE GENERAL MINISTER

AC 39//2C 143
//1MP 14

In order to preserve the virtue of holy humility, a few years after his conversion, at a chapter,[a] he resigned the office of prelate before all the brothers, saying: "From now on, I am dead to you. But here you have Brother Peter of Catanio; let us all, you and I, obey him." And **prostrating himself on the ground** before him, he promised him obedience and reverence.

ER Prol 4

Therefore all the brothers were weeping, and sorrow drew **uncontrolled** deep groans from them, as they saw themselves orphaned of such a father. As blessed Francis got up, he joined his hands and, *lifting his eyes to heaven,* said: "Lord, I give back to You the family which until now You have entrusted to me. Now, sweetest Lord, because of my infirmities, which You know, I can no longer take care of them and I entrust them to the ministers. If any brother should perish because of their negligence, or bad example, or even harsh correction, let them be bound *to render an account* for it before You, Lord, *on the day of judgment."*

Is 51:6

Mt 12:36

From that time on, he remained subject until his death, behaving more humbly **in all things** than any of the others.

40

HOW HE CONSIGNED HIS OWN COMPANIONS
NOT WANTING TO HAVE A SPECIAL COMPANION

AC 40//2C 144
//1MP 16

Another time he consigned all his companions to his vicar, saying: "I don't want to seem singular because of this privilege of freedom **to have a special companion;** any brothers can go with me from place to place as the Lord inspires them." And he added: "Why, I have seen a blind man who had no guide for his journey except one little dog,

LR II 7

---

a. This was the Pentecost Chapter held at the Portiuncula in September 1220, shortly after Francis's return from the East. Thus, "a few years after his conversion" cannot be taken literally.

287

and I do not want to seem better than him." This indeed was **always** his glory: he gave up any appearance of being singular or important,

2 Cor 12:9 so that *the power of Christ might dwell in him.*

41
HOW HE RENOUNCED THE OFFICE OF PRELACY
BECAUSE OF BAD PRELATES

Once a brother asked him why he had renounced the care of all ↓AC 44//2C 18 the brothers and turned them over into the hands of others as if they did not belong to him. He replied: "**My** son, I love the brothers as I 1 Pt 2:21 can, but if they would *follow my footsteps* I would surely love them more, and would not make myself a stranger to them. For there are some among the prelates who draw them in a different direction, placing before them the examples of the ancients and paying little attention to my warnings. But what they are doing **and the way in which** they are **now** acting will **appear more clearly** in the end.

A short time later, when he was suffering a serious illness, he raised himself up in bed in an angry spirit **and cried out:** "Who are Jn 10:28 these people? *They have snatched out of my hands* my religion and **my** brothers. If I go to the general chapter, I'll show them what is my will."

42
HOW HE HUMBLY OBTAINED MEAT FOR THE SICK
AND ENCOURAGED THEM TO BE HUMBLE AND PATIENT

Blessed Francis was not embarrassed to go through the city's pub- ↓AC 45//2C 17 lic **places** to find some meat for a sick brother. However, he also advised the sick to be patient when things were lacking and not stir up a scandal if everything was not **fully** to their satisfaction.

Because of this he had these words written in the **first** *Rule:*[a] "I beg ER X 4 all my sick brothers that in their illness they do not become angry or upset at the Lord or the brothers. They should not anxiously seek medicines, nor desire too eagerly to free the flesh that is soon to die 1 Thes 5:18 and is an enemy of the soul. *Let them give thanks for all things* and let them desire to be, however, as God wills them to be. Those whom **the** Acts 13:48 **Lord** *has destined to eternal life,* He teaches with the rod of punishment

---

a. The editor corrects AC 45 by identifying the specific rule, that is the *Earlier Rule*, in which the following passage is found.

and sickness, as he himself has said: *'Those whom I love I correct and* Rv 3:19
chastise.' "

43

THE HUMBLE REPLY GIVEN BY BLESSED FRANCIS AND BLESSED DOMINIC
WHEN THEY WERE BOTH ASKED BY THE CARDINAL
WHETHER THEY WANT THEIR BROTHERS TO BE PRELATES IN THE CHURCH

9//2C 14//BPr V

Those **two** bright lights of the world, namely, **blessed** Francis and **blessed** Dominic,[a] were once **together** in the City **of Rome** with the Lord of Ostia, who later became Supreme Pontiff. As they took turns pouring out honey-sweet words about the Lord, **the Lord of Ostia** finally said to them: "In the early Church the Church's shepherds **and prelates** were poor, and men of charity, not on fire with greed. Why don't we make bishops and prelates of your brothers who excel **all others** in teaching and example?"

There arose **a humble and devout** disagreement between the saints about answering, neither wishing to go first, but rather each deferring to the other. Each urged the other to reply. At last humility conquered Francis **as he did not speak first,** but it also conquered Dominic, since in speaking first, he humbly obeyed Francis. Blessed Dominic therefore answered: "My lord, my brothers are already raised to a good level, if they will only realize it, and as much as possible I would **never** allow them to obtain any other mirror of dignity." As this brief response ended, Blessed Francis bowed **to the lord** and said: "My lord, my brothers are called 'lesser' precisely so they will not presume to *become 'greater.'* They have been called this to teach them to stay down to earth, and to **imitate** *the footprints of Christ's* humility, **so that, through this,** they may be exalted *in the sight of the saints.* If you want them *to bear fruit in the Church of God,* keep them in the status in which they were called and hold them to it, **and those who would climb to lofty positions, bring them abruptly down to earth. Do not** allow them to rise to **any** prelacy!" These were the replies **of the saints.** Mt 20:26
1 Pt 2:21
Wis 3:13
Jn 15:2, 8; Phil 3:6

2C 150

When they finished their replies, the Lord of Ostia was greatly edified by the words of both, and gave unbounded *thanks to God.* And as they **both** left that place **together,** blessed Dominic asked Saint Francis to be kind enough to give him the cord he had tied around him. Francis **refused** out of humility what the other requested out of charity. At last the happy devotion of the petitioner won out and, Acts 27:35

---

a. See FA:ED II 148 a.

after blessed Dominic accepted blessed Francis's cord out of a passionate love, he girded himself with it underneath his inner tunic,
and from that time on he wore it devoutly. Finally one placed his
hands in those of the other, and one most sweetly commended himself to the other in a shared commitment. And so blessed Dominic
said to Saint Francis: "Brother Francis, I wish your religion and
mine might become one, so we could share the same form of life in
the Church."

Acts 15:39   At last, when they had *parted from each other,* blessed Dominic said
Lk 4:25   to the many bystanders: "*In truth I tell you,* the other religious should
imitate this holy man Francis, as his holiness is so perfect."[a]

44
HOW HE WANTED ALL THE BROTHERS TO SERVE LEPERS
AS A FOUNDATION FOR HUMILITY

From the beginning of his conversion blessed Francis, with the   ↓AC 9//1MP
Mt 7:24   Lord's help, *like a wise* builder, established himself *upon solid rock,* that
is the greatest humility and poverty of the Son of God, calling his
religion "Lesser Brothers" because of great humility.

At the beginning of the religion, he wanted the brothers to stay in
hospitals of lepers to serve them, laying the foundation of holy
humility in this way. Whenever nobles and commoners came to the
Order, they were told, among other things, that they had to serve the
lepers humbly and stay in their houses, as it was prescribed in the
first rule.

They did not desire to have anything under heaven, except holy   LR VI 6
poverty, by which, in this world, they are nourished by the Lord with
bodily and spiritual food, and, in the next, will attain a heavenly
inheritance.

He laid the foundation both for himself and for others on the
greatest humility and poverty, because, although he was a great prelate in the church of God, he wanted and chose to be lowly not only in
the church, but also among his brothers. In his opinion and desire,
this lowliness was to be the most sublime exaltation in the sight of
God and of the people.

---

a. The editor of 2MP changes twice the more dynamic notion of *sequi* [follow] to *imitari* [imitate] "to
imitate the footprints of Christ" and "to imitate this holy man Francis." Cf. supra 2MP 14; ~~TL V~~.

45

HOW HE WISHED TO ATTRIBUTE GLORY AND HONOR TO GOD ALONE FOR ALL HIS GOOD WORDS AND DEEDS

When he had preached to the people of Terni **in the city** piazza, the bishop of that city, a discerning and spiritual man, **immediately** stood up at the end of the sermon and said **to the people:** "From the beginning, when the Lord planted and built His church, He always beautified it with holy men who would improve it by word and example. Now, *in this final hour,* God has beautified his Church with **Francis,** this little poor man, lowly and unlettered. And because of this," he continued, "you should love and honor the Lord and avoid sin *for He has not dealt thus with any other nation.*"

When he had finished speaking, the bishop came down from the place where he had preached, and entered the bishop's church. Then blessed Francis **approached him,** bowed down before him and, *prostrating* himself *at his feet,* said to him: "I tell you the truth, my Lord Bishop: no person in this world has yet honored me as much as you have today. Other people say: 'That man is a saint!' They attribute glory and holiness **to me,** not to the Creator. You, however, like a discerning man, *have separated what is precious from what is vile.*"

When blessed Francis **was praised** and called a saint, he would respond to such expressions by saying: "I'm still not sure that I won't have sons and daughters. If at any moment the Lord wanted to take back the treasure **He has entrusted** to me, what would be left except just body and soul, which even non-believers have? I must believe, rather, that if the Lord had granted a thief and even a non-believer as many gifts as He has given me, **they would be** more faithful to the Lord **than I.**

"For, as in a painting of the Lord and the Blessed Virgin on wood, it is **the Lord** and the Blessed Virgin who are honored, while the wood and the paint attribute nothing to themselves. In the same way, a servant of God is a painting **of God,** in whom God is honored because of His goodness. But he must not attribute anything to himself, **because, in comparison with God, he is less than wood and paint. Indeed, he is nothing at all. Therefore,** *honor and glory* should be given to God alone, and while he lives **amid the miseries of the world** he should attribute to himself **only** shame and trouble."

AC 10//2C 141
//1MP 13

AC 10//2C 133
//1MP 13

1 Jn 2:18

Ps 147:20

Acts 10:25

Jer 15:19

1 Tm 1:17; Rv 5:13

46

HOW UNTIL HIS DEATH HE WISHED
TO HAVE ONE OF HIS COMPANIONS AS HIS GUARDIAN
AND LIVE IN SUBJECTION

Wishing to persevere in perfect humility and subjection until his death, for a long time before his death he said to the general minister: "I ask you to put one of my companions in your place regarding me, so that I may obey him as I would obey you. For obedience is so beneficial that I always want you to be with me in life and death." ↓AC 11//2C 14 //1MP 15

From that time until his death, he always had one of his companions as a guardian whom he obeyed in place of the general minister.[a] One time he said to his companions: "Among other favors, **the Lord** has given me this grace: I would promptly obey a novice who entered our religion today, if he were appointed my guardian, just as readily as I would obey him who is the first and the eldest in our life and religion. A subject should not consider his prelate, a human being, but God, for love of Whom he is subject to him." He then said: "There is no prelate in the whole world who would be as feared by his subjects and brothers as the Lord would make me feared by my brothers, if I wished. But **the Lord** gave me this grace: that I want to be content with all, as one who is lesser in the religion."[b] 2C 151

We who were with him witnessed this often with our own eyes. Frequently, when some of the brothers did not provide for his needs, or said something to him that would ordinarily offend a person, he would immediately go to prayer. On returning, he did not want to remember anything, **and he never** said "Brother so-and-so did not provide for me," or "He said such-and-such to me."

Persevering in this way, the closer he approached death, the more careful he became in considering how he might live and die in complete humility and poverty **and in the perfection of every virtue.** //1MP 16

47

THE PERFECT MANNER OF OBEYING WHICH HE TAUGHT

The most holy father used to say to his brothers: "Dear brothers, do what you are commanded the first time you are told, and do not wait for it to be repeated. Do not pretend that something is 2C 51

---

a. For an explanation of the word *guardianus* [guardian], see FA:ED I 98 a.

b. AC 11 uses the term *Altissimus* [the Most High] which is now changed to *Dominus* [the Lord]. While this may be a subtle reference to Francis's *Testament* in which he repeatedly writes of the gifts that *the Lord* had given him (Test 1, 2, 4, 6, 14), nevertheless this is a curious change of language referring to God.

impossible; for even if what I command is beyond your strength, obedience will find the strength."[a]

48
HOW HE COMPARED PERFECT OBEDIENCE TO A CORPSE

2C 152

Another time, while he was sitting with his companions, he let out a sigh: "There is hardly a single religious in the whole world who obeys his prelate **well!**"

Immediately his companions said to him: "Tell us, Father, what is the perfect and highest obedience?" In reply he described someone truly **and perfectly** obedient using an analogy of a dead body.[b] "Take a lifeless corpse and place **it** wherever you want. You will see that it does not resist being moved, does not complain about place, or protest if dismissed. **Lift it up** onto a royal throne,[c] it will look down, not up; dress it in purple, it will look twice as pale. This one is truly obedient **who** does not argue about why he is moved, does not care where he is placed; so that he does not threaten when changed. **Promoted** to an office, he keeps his usual humility. The more he is honored, the more unworthy he considers himself."

Purely and simply he called commands, not requests, holy obedience.[d] But he believed that the highest form of obedience, in which *flesh and blood* has no part, was the only one by which one goes among the unbelievers under divine inspiration, either for the good of one's neighbor or out of a desire for martyrdom. He considered this request most *acceptable to God.*

XV 3; LR XII 1

Mt 16:17

Phil 4:18

49
HOW PERILOUS IT IS TO COMMAND TOO QUICKLY THROUGH OBEDIENCE OR NOT TO OBEY A PRECEPT OF OBEDIENCE

↓AC 1//2C 153

The blessed father used to consider that only rarely should something be commanded under obedience, for the weapon of last resort should not be the first one used. As he said, "The hand should

---

a. This paragraph is taken directly from the last section of 2C 51 and is not found in AC. Thus the 2MP editor seems to be deliberately emphasizing the demand of immediate, unquestioning obedience. This is a different expression of obedience than what is described in the earlier tradition.

b. The Latin word is *figura* which may be translated as figure, symbol, or image. The editors have chosen to translate the word as analogy since it seems a more accurate English translation.

c. The Latin is *in cathedra* [in a royal throne]. Cf. supra 258 a.

d. In this direct quotation from 2C 152, the editor excludes "the requests and permissions" that Thomas affirms as a good together with "holy obedience." In this instance, he maintains his more narrow interpretation of the Gospel ideals.

not reach quickly for the sword." **However he also used to say that** he who does not hurry to obey what is commanded under obedience **without a pressing reason for delay** neither *fears God nor respects man.* Nothing could be truer. For, what is a command in a rash leader, but a sword in the hands of a madman?

Lk 18:4

And what could be more hopeless than a religious who **neglects and** despises obedience?

50
HOW HE ANSWERED THE BROTHERS
URGING HIM TO SEEK THE PRIVILEGE OF PREACHING FREELY

Some of the brothers told blessed Francis: "Father, don't you see that sometimes bishops do not permit us to preach, **making** us remain idle in an area for many days before we can **proclaim the word of God?** It would be better if you managed that the brothers get a privilege from the Lord Pope **about this:** it would be the salvation of souls."[a]

↓AC 20//1MP

He answered them with a stern rebuke, telling them: "You, Lesser Brothers, you do not know the will of God, and will not allow me to convert the whole world as God wills. For I want to convert the prelates first by **holy** humility and reverence. Then, when they see your holy life and your **humble** reverence for them, they will ask you to preach and convert the people. These will attract the people to **preaching** far better than your privileges, which would lead you to your pride. And if you are free *of all avarice,* and lead the people to give the churches their due, they will ask you to hear the confessions of their people. Although you should not be concerned about this, for if they are converted, they will easily find confessors.

Lk 12:15

"For my part, I want only this privilege from the Lord: **never** to have any privilege from any human being, except to show reverence to all, and, by the obedience of the holy *Rule,* to convert everyone more by example than by word."[b]

---

a. In 1281, Pope Martin IV issued a papal decree, *Ad fructus uberes,* giving the brothers full permission to preach and hear confessions without the permission of a diocesan ordinary and local clergy. Cf. *Bullarium Franciscanum,* vol. III (hereafter BFr), ed. Johannes H. Sbaraglia (Rome, 1759-68), 480.

b. According to Lemmens' edition, this is the last of the WSF, cf. Leonard Lemmens, *Scripta Fratris Leonis, Socii S.P. Francisci.* Documenta Antiqua Franciscana I (Ad Claras Aquas, Quaracchi: Collegium S. Bonaventurae, 1901), 105, supra.

51

How the brothers at that time forgave one another
when one offended the other

AC 41//2C 155 He used to affirm that the Lesser Brothers *had been sent from* the Lord in these *last times* to show forth examples of light to those wrapped in the darkness of sins. He would say that *he was filled with the sweetest fragrance* and *anointed* with strength from *precious ointment whenever he heard of the great deeds* of holy brothers **dispersed** throughout the world.

Jn 1:6
Jude 18
Ex 29:18
Mt 26:7
Acts 2:11

It happened that a brother **once** threw out an insulting word at another brother in the presence of a nobleman of the island of Cyprus. But, when he saw that **his** brother was rather **upset** on account of this, he **immediately** took some donkey manure, and put it into his mouth to chew **with his teeth,** saying: "Let the tongue that *poured out the poison* of anger on my brother now chew manure!"

Prv 23:32

At seeing this, that man was thunder-stuck, and went away **greatly** edified; from that time on, he put himself and **all** he had at the disposal of the brothers.

All the brothers observed this custom without fail: if any of them spoke a **hurtful or** upsetting word to another, he would **immediately** fall to the ground, **humbly beg forgiveness,** and kiss the feet of the one he had offended. **The** holy **father** rejoiced over such behavior, when he heard the examples of holiness that his sons themselves produced, and he would heap *blessings worthy of full acceptance* on those brothers, who, *by word or deed,* led sinners to the love of Christ. Zeal for souls, which filled him completely, made him want his sons to resemble him as a true likeness.

1 Tm 1:15
Col 3:17

52

How Christ complained to brother Leo,
the companion of Blessed Francis,
about the brothers' ingratitude and pride[a]

↓AC 21 One time the Lord Jesus Christ said to Brother Leo,[b] the companion of blessed Francis: **"Brother Leo,** I have a complaint about the brothers." "About what, Lord?" Brother Leo replied. And the Lord said: "About three things. They do not recognize My gifts which, as

---

a. According to Edith Pásztor, this text reflects one of the *Verba Sancti Francisci* [Sayings of Saint Francis] as found in a manuscript of the library of St. Isidore's Friary, Rome. Cf. Edith Pásztor, "Il manoscritto Isidoriano 1/73 e gli scritti leonini su S. Francesco," *Cultura e società nell'Italia medievale. Studi per Paolo Brezzi.* Studi Stoirici, 188-192. (Rome: n.p., 1988), 661-3.

b. Cf. FA:ED II 66 d.

Lk 12:24; Mt 20:6

you know, I generously **and abundantly** bestow on them daily, since they *neither sow nor reap. All day long they are idle* and complain. And they often provoke one another to anger, and do not return to love, and do not pardon the injury they receive."

53

HOW HE HUMBLY AND SINCERELY ANSWERED A QUESTION
OF A DOCTOR OF THE ORDER OF PREACHERS
CONCERNING A PASSAGE OF SCRIPTURE

While he was staying in Siena, someone from the Order of Preachers **came to him;** he was a **humble and very** spiritual man and a Doctor of Sacred Theology.

As he and blessed Francis discussed the words of the Lord together for some time, this teacher asked **him** about the words of Ezekiel: *If you do not warn the wicked man about his wickedness, I will hold you responsible for his* soul. He said: "I'm acquainted with many people, good father, who live in mortal sin, as I'm aware. But I don't always warn them about their wickedness. Will I then be held responsible for their souls?"

Blessed Francis **humbly** said that he was an unlettered man, and it would be better for him to be taught by the other rather than to answer a question about Scripture. But that humble teacher replied: "Brother, it's true I have heard these words explained by some wise men; still, I'd be glad to hear how you understand it." So blessed Francis said to him: "If that passage is supposed to be understood **in a general way,** then I understand it to mean that a servant of God should be burning with life and holiness so brightly, that by the light of example and the tongue of his **holy** manner of living, he will rebuke all the wicked. In that way, I say, the brightness of his life and the fragrance of his reputation will *proclaim their wickedness* to all of them."

The doctor went away greatly edified, and said to the companions of blessed Francis: "My brothers, the theology of this man, held aloft by purity and contemplation, is a soaring eagle, while our learning *crawls on its belly on the ground.*"

Ez 3:18-20; 33:7-9

Ez 3:19

Gn 3:14

↓AC 35//2C 10

↓AC 36//2C 10

54

THE HUMILITY AND PEACE THEY MUST HAVE WITH CLERICS

Rom 12:18

Although blessed Francis wanted his sons *to keep peace with all,* and to behave as little ones toward everyone, he taught them to be

↓AC 19//2C 14

particularly humble toward clerics by his word and showed them by his example.

He used to say: "We have been sent to help clerics for the *salvation of souls* so that we may make up whatever may be lacking in them.[a] Each *shall receive a reward,* not *on account of* authority, but because *of the work* done. Know then, brothers, that the profit of souls is what pleases God the most, and this is more easily obtained through peace with the clergy than fighting with them. If they should stand in the way of the people's salvation, *revenge is* for God, *and he will repay* them *in due time.* So, be subject to prelates so that as much as *possible on your part* no **evil** jealousy arises. *If you are children of peace,* you will win over both clergy and people for the Lord, and **this is** *more acceptable* **to God** than only winning the people while scandalizing the clergy. Cover up their **flaws,** make up for their many defects, and *when you have done* this, be even more humble."

1 Pt 1:9

1 Cor 3:8

Dt 32:35

Rom 12:18

Lk 10:6

1 Pt 2:5

Lk 17:10

55

HOW HE HUMBLY OBTAINED THE CHURCH OF SAINT MARY OF THE ANGELS
FROM THE ABBOT OF SAINT BENEDICT IN ASSISI,
AND HOW HE WANTED THE BROTHERS TO DWELL THERE ALWAYS
AND TO LIVE THERE HUMBLY

↓AC 56

Seeing that the Lord willed *to increase the number* of brothers, blessed Francis told them: "My dearest brothers and sons, I see that the Lord wants us to increase. Therefore, it seems good and religious to me to obtain from the bishop, or the canons of San Rufino, or from the abbot of the monastery of Saint Benedict, some church where the brothers can say their hours and only have next to it a small and poor little house built of mud and branches where they can sleep and **work.** This place is not suitable **and not adequate** for the brothers, since the Lord **wants** to increase them, and especially because here we do not have a church where the brothers can say their hours. And, should any **brother** die, it would not be proper to bury him here or in a church of the secular clergy." This *speech pleased all the* brothers.

Acts 6:7

Jos 22:33

So **he** went to the bishop of Assisi. He made the same speech to **him.** "Brother," the bishop answered him, "I do not have any church that I can give you." The canons **said the same thing. Then** he went **to the abbey** of Saint Benedict on Mount Subasio, and placed the same words before them. The abbot, **guided by grace and the divine** will, took counsel **with** his **monks** about this. They granted blessed

---

a. For an echo of Canon 10 of the IV Lateran Council, see FA:ED II 133 b.

Francis and his brothers the church of Saint Mary of the Portiuncula, as it was **favorable for a lesser one** and the poorest little church they had.[a]

"Brother, we have granted your request," the abbot told blessed Francis. "But, if the Lord increases your congregation, we want this place to be the head of all your places." And this speech pleased blessed Francis and his brothers.

Blessed Francis was **especially** overjoyed at the place granted to the brothers, especially because of the name of this church of the Mother of Christ, and because it was such a **small and** poor little church, and because it was surnamed: "of the Portiuncula." This name foreshadowed that it was to be the mother and head of the poor Lesser Brothers.[b] It was called "Portiuncula" after the neighborhood which from earliest times was called "Portiuncula."

Blessed Francis used to say: "This is why the Lord willed that no other church be granted to the brothers, and why the first brothers would not build any completely new church, and would not have any other but this one. For this church was a prophecy that has been fulfilled in the coming of the Lesser Brothers." And although it was already poor and almost in ruins, **nevertheless, for a long time,** the people of the city of Assisi and its **entire** neighborhood had held the church in the **greatest** devotion even till today, **and it increases even daily.**

Acts 6:7 As soon as the brothers went to stay there, almost daily the Lord *increased* their *number;* and **the fragrance of** their fame spread throughout the whole valley of Spoleto, **and extended marvelously throughout many parts of the world.** From old times, **it was called** Saint Mary of the Angels, **because, as is claimed, songs of angels were very often heard there.**[c]

Mt 7:24 Although the abbot and the monks had freely granted it to blessed Francis and his brothers, blessed Francis, a good and experienced teacher who wished to *build* his *house on* solid *rock,* that is, his **religion** on the **greatest** poverty, every year used to send **the abbot and the monks** a basket **or container** full of small fish called lasche.[d] He did this as a sign of greater humility and poverty, so that the brothers would not have any place of their own, and would not remain in any

---

a. The Latin text reads *pro minori* [favorable for a lesser one], a phrase added by the editor of 2MP.
b. Cf. supra, OL VII 12. This statement is intended to contradict that of Pope Gregory IX who, in *Is qui ecclesiam*, March 5, 1230, proclaimed the newly built Basilica of Saint Francis in Assisi the *caput et mater* [mother and head] of the Order, cf. BFr I, 60.
c. This is the first mention of angelic choirs singing at the Portiuncula. It is expanded in a poetic manner in 2MP 84.
d. Cf. supra 236 a.

place that was not owned by others, and thus they in no way had the power to sell it or give it away. Each year, when the brothers brought the little fish to the monks, they in turn, because of the humility of blessed Francis, who had done this of his own will, gave him and his brothers **one** jar filled with oil.

We who were with blessed Francis *bear witness* that he spoke of that church with great conviction. He said—because of the many prerogatives the Lord revealed there—it had been revealed to him in that place that, of all the churches **of the world** that she loved, the blessed Virgin **loved** that church **most affectionately.** Therefore, **from that moment,** he **always** had the greatest reverence and devotion toward it. And so that the brothers would always keep its remembrance in their hearts, at his death he wanted it written in his *Testament* that **all** the brothers do likewise.

Jn 21:24

About the time of his death, in the presence of the general minister and the other brothers, he said:

"I want to leave and bequeath to the brothers the place of Saint Mary of the Portiuncula as a testament, that it may always be held in the greatest reverence and devotion by the brothers. Our old brothers did this: for although the place itself is holy, **beloved and chosen by Christ and the glorious Virgin,** they preserved its holiness with constant prayer day and night and by constant silence. And if, at times, they spoke after the time established for silence, they discussed with the greatest devotion and decorum matters pertaining to the praise of God and the salvation of souls. If it happened, and it rarely did, that someone began *to utter* useless or *idle words,* immediately he was corrected by another **brother.** They used to mortify the flesh not only by *fasting,* but also by *many vigils,* by *cold, nakedness,* and manual labor. In order not to remain idle, they very frequently went and helped poor people in their fields, and sometimes these people would give them some bread for the love of God.

Mt 12:36

2 Cor 11: 27

"By these and other virtues, they used to sanctify the place **and preserve themselves in holiness.** Afterwards, however, a great number of brothers **and seculars** would come to that place more than was usual, and especially because the brothers are colder in prayer and other **virtuous** works than in the past, they are more careless about exchanging idle and useless words and even worldly news. **This** place is not held in such great reverence and devotion **as much as it was** and as I would wish."

When blessed Francis had said these words, he immediately concluded, saying with great enthusiasm: "Therefore, I want **this place** always to be under the **immediate** jurisdiction of the general minister **and servant,** that he may show greater concern and care in providing for it, especially in placing a good and holy family there. The clerics should be chosen from among the **best,** holiest, and most upright brothers of the entire religion and who know how to say the office best. In this way, not only **seculars,** but also the brothers, will gladly **see and** listen to them with great devotion. And some holy, discerning, **humble,** and upright lay brothers should also be chosen, who may serve them.

"I also wish that none of the brothers or any other person enter that place except the general minister and the brothers who serve **them.** And they may not speak to anyone except the brothers who serve them and to the minister when he visits them.

"I likewise want the lay brothers who serve them to be **bound never to speak to them either idle words** or news of the world, **or anything whatsoever** that is not useful **to their souls.** And that is the reason why I particularly want no one else to enter that place, so that they may better preserve their purity and holiness. **Let nothing at all be done or said there that is not edifying,** but let **this** entire **place** be held pure and holy in hymns and praises of the Lord.

Rv 4:5; 7:15

"And when any of these brothers passes **to the Lord,** I want another holy brother, no matter where he is staying, **be sent there by the general minister** to replace **him. For even if some day other brothers** stray from purity and holiness, I want this place **to be blessed and to remain always** a mirror and a good example for the entire religion, a candelabra **always burning and shining** *before the throne of God* and before the blessed Virgin. Thus may the Lord have mercy on the faults and failings of **all** the brothers and always preserve and protect **this** religion, His little plant."

56
THE HUMBLE REVERENCE WHICH HE SHOWED
REGARDING CHURCHES BY SWEEPING AND CLEANING THEM

At one time while blessed Francis was staying at Saint Mary of the Portiuncula, and there were still only a few brothers, blessed Francis sometimes used to go through the villages and churches in the area around the city of Assisi, proclaiming and preaching to the people that they should do penance. And he would carry a broom to sweep the **dirty** churches.

↓AC 60//1MP 31

For blessed Francis was very sad when he entered some church and saw that it was not clean, **as he wished.** Therefore, after preaching to the people, at the end of the sermon he would always have all the priests who were present assembled in some remote place so he could not be overheard by secular people. He would preach to them about the salvation of souls and, in particular, that they be careful to keep churches clean, as well as altars and everything that pertains to the celebration of the divine mysteries.

57

THE PEASANT WHO FOUND HIM HUMBLY SWEEPING A CHURCH,
AND AFTER HIS CONVERSION,
HOW HE ENTERED THE ORDER AND BECAME A HOLY BROTHER

One day blessed Francis went to a church in **one of the villages** of the city of Assisi and began to sweep **and clean it with humility.** Immediately talk about this spread through that **entire** village, especially because those people were happy to see him and **even happier** to hear him.

A man named John heard it, **a peasant** of amazing simplicity, who was plowing in a field of his near the church, and he immediately went to him. Finding him **humbly and devoutly** sweeping the church, he said to him: "Brother, give me the broom because I want to help you." Taking the broom from **his hands,** he swept the rest.

When they sat down **together,** he said to blessed Francis: "Brother, it's a long time now that I've wanted to serve God, especially after I heard talk about you and your brothers, but I did not know how to come to you. Now that it pleased God that I see you, I want to do whatever pleases you."

Considering his fervor, blessed Francis rejoiced in the Lord, especially because he then had few brothers, and because it seemed to him that, on account of his pure simplicity, he would make a good religious. So he said to him: "Brother, if you wish to belong to our life and company, you must expropriate yourself of all your things that you can get without scandal, and *give* them *to the poor* according to the counsel of the holy Gospel, because **all** my brothers who were able to do so have done this."

As soon as he heard this, he immediately went into the field where he had left the oxen, and, untying them, brought one of them back to blessed Francis. "Brother," he said to him, "I have served my father and everyone in my household for many years. Although my portion of the inheritance is small, I want to take this ox as my share and give it to the poor, as you think best."

But when his parents and brothers, who were still small, saw that he wanted to leave them, they and the entire household began to cry

AC 61//2C 190
//1MP 31

R II 4; LR II 5

Mt 19:21; Lk 18:22

so bitterly and wail so loudly **while beating their breasts** that blessed Francis was moved to piety, because the family was large and penniless. Blessed Francis said to them: "Prepare and serve a meal **for all of us** so we can all eat together, and don't cry, because I will make you **very** happy." So they prepared it at once, and all of them ate **together** with great joy.

After the meal blessed Francis said to them: "This son of yours wants to serve God, and you should be **very** glad and not sad about this. This will be counted a **great** honor and advantage to your souls and bodies, not only according to God but also according to the world, because God will be honored by your own flesh and blood, and all our brothers will be your sons and brothers. And, because he is a creature of God and wishes to serve his Creator, and to serve Him is to reign, I cannot and should not return him to you. But in order that you receive and keep some consolation from all this, I want him to expropriate himself of this ox by giving it to you, although, according to the counsel of the holy Gospel, *it ought to be given to* other *poor* people."

Mt 19:21

They were all consoled by the words of blessed Francis, and they rejoiced especially that the ox was returned to them, since they were **very** poor. Because blessed Francis greatly loved and was always pleased by pure and holy simplicity in himself and in others, he immediately dressed him in the clothing of the religion and **humbly** took him as his companion. He was a man of such simplicity that he believed he was bound to do everything blessed Francis would do.

So, whenever blessed Francis was in some church or in some other place to pray, he wanted to watch and observe him so that he could **fully** imitate all his **actions and** gestures. If blessed Francis knelt, or *raised* his hands toward heaven, or spat, coughed, **or sighed,** he would do the same. **When he became aware of this,** blessed Francis began to reprove him with great joy for this kind of simplicity. But he answered: "Brother, I promised to do everything you do, **and it is right that I imitate you in every thing."**

Dt 32:40

And blessed Francis marveled and rejoiced **over this,** seeing him in such purity and simplicity. For he began to be perfect in all virtues and good habits, so that blessed Francis and the other brothers greatly marveled at his perfection. A short time afterwards he died in the holy **pursuit of virtues.** Therefore, with joy **of mind and body,** blessed Francis used to tell the brothers about his manner of living and would call him not "Brother John," but "Saint John."

58

HOW HE PUNISHED HIMSELF BY EATING OUT OF THE SAME DISH WITH A LEPER BECAUSE HE HAD HUMILIATED HIM

1C 64//1MP 32

When blessed Francis had returned to Saint Mary of the Portiuncula, he found there Brother James the Simple with a leper covered with **many** sores. **Blessed Francis** had entrusted this leper to him, and all the other lepers who had severe sores. For, **then,** the brothers stayed in the leper hospitals. That Brother James was like the doctor for those with severe sores, and he gladly touched, changed, and treated their wounds.

As if reproving Brother James, blessed Francis told him: "You should not take our Christian brothers about in this way since it is not right for you or for them."

Although he was pleased that Brother James helped and served them, the holy father said this because he did not want him to take those with severe sores outside the hospital because people were **very** revolted by them. This was especially because Brother James was very simple, and he often went with them **from the hospital** to the church of Saint Mary, **as though he were walking with brothers.** Blessed Francis used to call lepers "Christian brothers."

After he said these things, blessed Francis immediately reproached himself, **believing** that in reproving Brother James, he had shamed the leper. **And, therefore, wishing to make** amends to God and to the leper, he told his fault to Brother Peter of Catanio, who was then the general minister. He said, "I tell you to confirm for me the penance I have chosen to do for this **fault,** and do not oppose me **in any way."**

Brother Peter responded: "Brother, do as you please." Brother Peter so venerated and feared him, that he would not presume **to contradict him,** although he **frequently** suffered on this account.

Blessed Francis said: "Let this be my penance: I will eat together with my Christian brother from the same dish."

While blessed Francis was sitting at the table with the leper and other brothers, a bowl was placed between **blessed Francis and the leper.** The leper was **repulsive and** completely covered with sores and ulcerated, and especially the fingers with which **he took morsels of food from the dish** were deformed and bloody, so that whenever he put them in the bowl, blood and **pus from his fingers** dripped into it.

Brother Peter and the other brothers saw this and grew very sad, but they did not dare say anything out of fear **and reverence** for the holy father.

The writer witnessed these things himself, and gave testimony concerning them.   Jn 19:35; 21:24

59
HOW HE PUT THE DEVILS TO FLIGHT WITH HUMBLE WORDS

At one time blessed Francis **went to the church of Saint Peter of** ↓AC 65//2C 12
Bovara near the castle of Trevi in the valley of Spoleto with Brother
Pacifico, who in the world had been known as "King of Verses," a
nobleman and courtly master of singers.[a]

The church there was deserted. Blessed Francis said to Brother
Pacifico: "Go back to the hospital **of the lepers** because I would like
to remain here alone tonight. Come back to me at dawn tomorrow."

So blessed Francis remained there by himself. After he said
compline and other prayers, he wanted to rest and sleep, but could
not do so, and his soul grew afraid, **his body began to tremble** and to
feel diabolical suggestions. He immediately got up, went outside **the
church,** signed himself, and said: "On behalf of Almighty God, I tell
you, demons, do whatever the Lord Jesus Christ has permitted you,
to harm my body. I am prepared to endure anything, because the
Lk 18:3   greatest enemy I have is my body. Therefore, *you will be avenging me on
my opponent* and **worst** enemy."

And immediately those suggestions stopped **completely** and,
1 Sm 3:9   when he returned *to the place* where he had been lying, he slept
peacefully.

60
THE VISION BROTHER PACIFICO SAW
IN WHICH HE HEARD THAT THE THRONE OF LUCIFER
IS RESERVED FOR THE HUMBLE FRANCIS

When morning came Brother Pacifico returned to him. Blessed ↓AC 65//2C 123
Francis was **at that moment** standing in prayer in front of the altar.
Brother Pacifico waited for him outside the choir, in front of the crucifix, praying to the Lord at the same time. As he began to pray,
2 Cor 12:2-4   Brother Pacifico was taken up **and seized into heaven,** *whether in the
body or out of the body, God knows.* And he saw many thrones in heaven,
one of them higher than the others, glorious, **and more** resplendent
Rv 21:19   **than all the others,** *adorned with every precious stone.* As he admired its
Acts 9:4   beauty, he began to wonder whose it might be. All at once *he heard a
voice telling him:* "This was Lucifer's throne and **humble** Francis will
sit on it in his place."

As he came back to himself, blessed Francis came out to him. **That
brother** immediately prostrated himself **extending his arms** in the

---

a. For background information on Brother Pacifico, see FA:ED II 167 b.

form of a cross at the feet of blessed Francis. Looking at blessed Francis as if he were already in heaven **sitting on that throne,** he said to him: "Father, do me a favor. Ask the Lord to be merciful **and to forgive my sins.**" Extending his hand, blessed Francis lifted him up, and he **immediately** realized that the brother had seen something in prayer. He appeared almost totally changed, and spoke to blessed Francis not as if he were living in the flesh, but as if he were already reigning in heaven.

Afterwards, inasmuch as he did not want to speak to blessed Francis about the vision, he began to talk about other matters **and, among things,** asked him: "What do you think of yourself, Brother?"

Blessed Francis responded **and said to him:** "It seems to me that I am a greater sinner than anyone in this world." And immediately Brother Pacifico was told this in his **soul:** "From this you can know that *the vision* you saw *was* true. For as Lucifer was cast down from that throne because of his pride, so blessed Francis will merit to be exalted and to sit on it because of his humility."

Dn 8:26

61
HOW HE HAD HIMSELF LED NAKED BEFORE THE PEOPLE
WITH A ROPE TIED AROUND HIS NECK

↓AC 80//1C 52

One time when he had recovered somewhat from a very serious illness, after some consideration, it seemed to him that he had received some little delicacies during that illness, although he ate only a little. Although he had **not yet** recovered from a quartan fever, he got up one day and had the people **of the city** of Assisi called to the piazza for a sermon. When he had finished preaching, he ordered **the people** that no one leave until he had returned **to them.**

Entering the **cathedral** church of San Rufino with **many** brothers and with Brother Peter of Catanio, **who had been a canon of that church** and the first general minister chosen **by blessed Francis,** he spoke to Brother Peter. **He ordered him under obedience** to do whatever he told him **without** contradicting him. Brother Peter answered him: "Brother, in what concerns you and me, I cannot, and should not want anything else except what pleases you."

Taking off his tunic, blessed Francis ordered him **to drag him** naked with a rope tied around his neck in front of the people to the place where he had preached to them. He ordered another brother to take a bowl full of ashes and to go up to the place where he had preached and, **when he would be dragged to that place,** to throw **those** ashes in his face. But, moved by **great** piety and compassion towards him, the brother did not obey him. Brother Peter, **however, taking the rope, fastened it around his neck and** dragged him **behind himself** as he was ordered to do. He wept bitterly as did the other brothers with him, **shedding tears of the greatest compassion and grief.**

When he had been led naked before the people to the place where he had preached, he said: "You believe me to be a holy man, as **all** others do who, following my example, leave the world, and enter the religion and life of the brothers. But I confess to God and to you that during my illness I ate meat and broth flavored with meat."

Almost all the people began to weep out of piety and compassion for him, especially since it was wintertime and was **bitterly** cold and he had not yet recovered from the quartan fever. And striking their breasts, they accused themselves saying: "This holy man," they said, "whose life we know **to be holy,** accuses himself with such shame over a just and manifest necessity. Yet because of excessive abstinence and the severity with which he treats his body from the moment of his conversion to Christ, we see him living in flesh that is almost dead. What shall we do, wretches that we are, we who all our life have lived, and **continue** to live, according to *the desires of the flesh?*"

Eph 2:3

62

HOW HE WANTED EVERYONE TO KNOW WHAT COMFORT HIS BODY RECEIVED

Likewise, at another time, **when** he was staying in **a certain** hermitage for the Lent of Saint Martin,[a] **he ate some food cooked with lard,** because oil did not agree with him during his illnesses. When the forty days had ended and he was preaching to a large crowd of people, in the opening words of his sermon he told them: "You came to me with great devotion, believing me to be a holy man. But I confess to God and to you that during this Lent, I have eaten food flavored with lard."

↓AC 81//2C 13

Indeed, it happened **almost always** that when he ate **with seculars,** or when the brothers prepared a special dish for him because of his illnesses, he immediately told this to the brothers or lay people who did not know about it, whether inside the house or outside. He would publicly say: "I ate such and such foods." He did not wish to conceal from people what was known to God.

---

a. Concerning "the Fast of Saint Martin," see FA:ED II 182 b.

In the same way, if his soul were tempted to vainglory, pride, or any vice, no matter where he was, or in whose presence, whether they be religious or lay, he would at once confess it to them openly, without concealing anything. That is why he told his companions one day: "I want to live in hermitages and other places where I stay, **as if all** the people see me. If they **think** I am a holy man and I **were not** to lead a life becoming a holy man, I would be a hypocrite."

When it was bitterly cold, one of the companions, who was his guardian, wanted to sew a **small** piece of fox fur **underneath his tunic** because of the illness of his spleen and stomach. Blessed Francis answered him: "If you want me to wear fur under the tunic, allow me to sew a piece of the fur on the outside of it that everyone may know that I have a piece of **fox** fur underneath." And this is what he had done; and, although it was **very** necessary, he wore it for only a short time.

63
HOW HE IMMEDIATELY ACCUSED HIMSELF OF VAINGLORY WHICH HE RECEIVED IN GIVING ALMS

_{AC 82//2C 132}

When he was going through the city of Assisi, a poor old woman asked him for alms for the love of God and he immediately gave her the mantle he had on his back. And, **without delay,** he confessed to **those who were following him** that he felt vainglory.

We who were with him have seen and heard many other examples **of his great humility** similar to these **that** we cannot **relate in spoken or written words.**

Blessed Francis's highest and principal concern was that he should not be a hypocrite before God. Although he **frequently** needed special food for his body because of his infirmity, nevertheless, he thought that he must always offer good example to the brothers and to others. **In this way,** lest he give **someone reason** to complain, he **patiently** endured **every privation.**

64
HOW HE DESCRIBED IN HIMSELF THE *STATUS* OF PERFECT HUMILITY

_{AC 109//2C 145
//1MP 38}

When the time for the chapter was approaching, blessed Francis said to his companion: "It seems to me that I am not a Lesser Brother unless I have the *status* I will tell you."[a] And he said: "The brothers

---

a. Cf. supra 145, n. 8.

come to me with great devotion and **reverence,** invite me to the
chapter and, touched by their devotion, I go to the chapter with
them. After they assemble, they ask me to proclaim the word of God

Lk 12:12 **and preach** among them. And I rise and preach to them *as the Spirit
instructs me.*

Lk 19:14   "After the sermon, suppose that they **all shout** against me: *'We do
not want you to rule over us.* You are not **as** eloquent **as you should be**
and you are too simple **and illiterate.** We are very ashamed to have
such a simple and contemptible prelate over us. From now on do not
presume to call yourself our prelate.' And so, **with abuse and contempt,** they throw me out.

"It seems to me that I am not a Lesser Brother unless I am just as
happy when they insult me and throw me out in shame, refusing
that I be their prelate, as when they honor and revere me, if in both
cases the benefit to them is equal. If I am happy about their benefit
and devotion when they praise and honor me, which can be a danger
to the soul; it is even more fitting that I should rejoice and be happy
at my benefit and the salvation of my soul when they revile me as
they throw me out in shame, which is **certain** profit for the soul."

65

HOW HE HUMBLY WANTED TO GO TO DISTANT LANDS
JUST AS HE HAD SENT OTHER BROTHERS.
HOW HE TAUGHT THE BROTHERS TO GO
THROUGHOUT THE WORLD HUMBLY AND DEVOUTLY

When the chapter that sent **many** brothers to regions overseas   ↓AC 108//1MP
had ended, blessed Francis stayed back with a few brothers. He said
to them: "Dearest brothers, I must be the model and example to all
the brothers. Therefore, if I sent my brothers into far distant countries to endure toil, shame, hunger **and thirst,** and many other types
of need, it is just and **dictated by holy humility** that I also go to some
far distant region. The brothers may be able to bear their **hardships**
more patiently when they hear that I am also undergoing the same
thing.

"Therefore go and ask the Lord that He may allow me to choose
that region which will be more **to His** praise, the salvation of souls,
and the good example to our religion."

When **he wanted to go to some** region, it was the custom of our
most holy father first to pray to the Lord and to send his brothers to
pray, so that the Lord might direct his heart to go wherever **it would
be more pleasing** to God.

The brothers, therefore, went off to pray and when their prayer was finished they returned to him. **At once, filled with joy,** he said **to them:** "In the name of our Lord Jesus Christ, of his glorious Virgin Mother and of all the saints, I choose the region of France, in which there is a Catholic people, especially because among the other Catholics, they show great reverence to the Body of Christ, which pleases me very much. Because of this, I will **most** gladly live among them."

201///1MP 36   Now blessed Francis had such reverence and devotion to the Body of Christ, that he wanted it written in the *Rule* that the brothers, in the regions where they stay, exercise **great** care and solicitude about this, admonishing clerics and priests to reserve the Body of Christ in a good and fitting place. And, if they **neglect** to do so, the brothers should do it.

For he wanted it put into the *Rule* that wherever the brothers should find the names of the Lord or those words through which the Body of the Lord is made present not well and honorably kept, they should collect them and store them decently, thus honoring the Lord in his words. And although he did not write these things in the *Rule,* because it did not seem good to the ministers that the brothers have these as a command, nevertheless in his *Testament* and in some of his other writings he wanted to leave for the brothers his will in these matters.

Moreover, at one time, he wanted to send throughout every region **some** brothers **who would carry many beautiful and decorated** pyxes. And wherever they would find the Body **of the Lord carelessly lying around,** they were to place it fittingly in them. He also wanted to send throughout every region other brothers with good and beautiful wafer irons for making **fine and pure** hosts.

//1MP 37   When blessed Francis had chosen from those brothers the ones he wished to take with him, he said to them: "Go, in the name of the Lord, *two by two* along the way, **humbly and** decently, in **strict** silence from dawn until after terce, praying to the Lord *in your hearts.* And let no idle or useless words *be mentioned among you.* Although you are traveling, nevertheless, let your behavior be **as humble and as** decent as if you were staying in a hermitage or a cell because wherever we are or wherever we travel, we **always** have a cell with us. Brother Body is our cell, and the soul is the hermit who remains inside the cell to pray to God and meditate **on Him.** So if the soul does not remain in quiet in its cell, a cell made by hands does little good to a religious."

When blessed Francis reached Florence, he found there Lord Hugo, the bishop of Ostia, who later became Pope **Gregory.** When he heard from blessed Francis that he wanted to go to France, he

Mk 6:7; Lk 10:1

Col 3:16

Eph 5:3

prohibited him from going, telling him: "Brother, I do not want you to go beyond the mountains, because there are many prelates who would willingly block the religion's interests in the Roman Curia. The other cardinals and I, who love your religion, can protect and help it more willingly if you stay within the confines of this region."

But blessed Francis said to him: "Lord, it is a great shame to me, if I remain in these regions when I send my **other** brothers to remote

Rv 1:9

and far away regions, **and** *do not participate in the hardships* **they will endure for the Lord."** The Lord Bishop, however, said to him as if rebuking him: "Why did you send your brothers so far away to die of

Rv 19:10

hunger and to so many other trials?" In great fervor and in *the spirit of prophecy,* blessed Francis answered him: "Lord, do you think that the Lord sent the brothers only for these regions? But I tell you in truth that the Lord chose and sent the brothers for the benefit and salvation of the souls of all people in this world. They should be received not only in the land of believers, but also in that of non-believers, **and they will win over many souls."**

The Lord Bishop **of Ostia** marveled at his words and admitted that he spoke the truth. But he did not allow him to go to France. Instead blessed Francis sent Brother Pacifico there with many other brothers. He himself, however, returned to the Spoleto Valley.

66
HOW HE TAUGHT SOME BROTHERS TO WIN OVER THE SOULS OF THIEVES BY HUMILITY AND CHARITY

From time to time robbers used to come for bread to the hermit-

↓AC 115//1M

age of the brothers above Borgo San Sepolcro.[a] They used to hide in the forest and rob travelers. Some of the brothers claimed that it was not good to give them alms. Others, **out of compassion,** used to give them alms, admonishing them to penance.

Meanwhile blessed Francis came to that place. The brothers asked him whether **it was good to** give them **alms.** "If you do as I tell you,"

Ps 11:1

blessed Francis told them, *"I trust in the Lord* that you will win their souls. Go, **therefore,** get some good bread and good wine, take it to them in the woods where they are **staying,** and cry out: 'Come, Brother robbers, come to us, because we are brothers, and we are bringing you some good bread and good wine!' They will immediately come to you. Then spread out a table cloth on the ground, placing the bread and wine on it, and, while they are eating, humbly **and**

---

a. That is, the hermitage of Monte Casale.

joyfully wait on them. After the meal, speak to them about the word of the Lord. **Finally,** for the love of God, ask them for this first request: make them promise you that they will not strike anyone or injure anyone's person. Do not ask for everything all at once, or they will not listen to you. Because of your humility and charity, they will at once make you this promise. On another day, because of the promise they made to you, besides eggs and cheese, bring them the bread and wine, and wait on them while they eat. After the meal, say to them: *'Why do you stay here all day long,* dying of hunger, **and putting**   Mt 20:6
up with so many hardships? When you do so many evil things, in will and in deed, you will lose your souls unless you convert **to the Lord.** It is better to serve the Lord, who will both supply your bodily needs in this world and save your souls in the end.' Then the Lord will inspire them to convert because of the humility and charity you have shown them."

So the brothers did everything as blessed Francis told them. And by the mercy and grace of God, **the robbers** listened and observed to the letter point by point everything the brothers asked **humbly** of them. Further, because of the friendliness and **humility** the brothers showed them, they **humbly** began **to serve the brothers** carrying wood on their shoulders to the hermitage. **Finally,** some **of them** entered religion. Others, confessing their sins, did penance **for their offences,** promising in the hands of the brothers to live *by the work of*   Ps 128:2; Eph 4:28
their hands **and never to do such things again.**

67

↓AC 117   Blessed Francis once went to Rome to visit the Lord of Ostia. **After he stayed** with him a few days, he went to the Lord Cardinal Leo, who was **very fond of blessed Francis.**[a] He asked him to spend a few days with him, especially because it was winter and **bitterly** unfit for travel **because of** the cold, wind, and rain.

The cardinal also told him **that he would be fed together with the other beggars who each day used to eat** in **his** house. He said this because he knew that blessed Francis always wanted to be received wherever he lodged as a poor person, although the Lord Pope and the cardinals **welcomed him with great devotion and reverence, and**

---

a. For information on Leo Brancaleone, Cardinal Deacon of Santa Lucia, and Cardinal Priest of the Roman Basilica of Santa Croce in Gerusalemme, cf. FA:ED II 224.

venerated him as a saint. And he added: "I will give you a good remote house where you can pray and eat as you wish."

Then Brother Angelo Tancredi, **who was** one of the first twelve brothers **and was also staying with the cardinal,** said to blessed Francis: "Brother, near here there is a very spacious and **remote** tower where you can stay as if you were in a hermitage."

On seeing it, blessed Francis liked it, and returning to the lord cardinal said to him: "Lord, perhaps I will stay with you a few days." The lord cardinal was **very** pleased.

So Brother Angelo went and prepared **a place in the tower for** blessed Francis and his companion. **And since** blessed Francis did not wish to come down from there as long as he was staying with the cardinal **and did not want anyone to come to him,** Brother Angelo **promised and arranged** to bring food to blessed Francis and his companion each day.

Blessed Francis went there with his companion. But when he wanted to sleep there on the first night, demons came and beat him most severely. He called his companion and told him: "Brother, the demons have beaten me **severely** so I want you to stay next to me because I am afraid to stay here alone." His companion stayed by him that night for blessed Francis trembled all over like a man suffering a fever. Both of them remained awake that whole night. During that time, blessed Francis **said to** his companion: **"Why** did the devils beat me? Why *has the Lord given them the power* to harm me?"

//1MP 20

Rv 9:3; 13:5, 7;
2 Cor 12:7

And he said: "The devils are the police of our Lord. Just as the *podestà* sends his police to punish **one who sins,** in the same way, the Lord *punishes and corrects whomever He loves* through the demons, who are His police and act as His ministers in this office.

Prv 3:12; Heb 12:5

"Even a perfect religious very often sins in ignorance. Consequently if he does not realize his sin, he is punished by the devil so that he may see and carefully reflect internally and externally how he may have offended. For in this life the Lord leaves nothing unpunished in those whom He loves tenderly. *By the mercy* and grace *of God,* I do not know if I have offended Him in any way which I have not corrected by confession and satisfaction. Indeed the Lord in His mercy granted me this gift. In prayer I **received clear** knowledge of any way in which I please or displease Him.

Rom 12:1

"But it could be that He punished me **now** through His police because, although the Lord Cardinal gladly does this mercy to me and my body needs to accept **this rest,** nevertheless, my brothers, who go through the world suffering hunger and many hardships, and other brothers who stay in poor little houses and hermitages,

may have an occasion for grumbling against me when they hear that
I am staying with the lord cardinal. 'We are enduring so many hardships while he is having his comforts!' I am bound always to give
them good example, for this is why I have been given to them. For
the brothers are more edified when I stay in poor little places among
them rather than in other places. When they hear that I am **also
enduring** the same trials, they **carry** theirs **more patiently."**

It **was our father's paramount and constant concern to give**
good example **to everyone** and to the other brothers and to take
away from them any occasion for complaining about him. **That is
why,** whether in sickness or in health, **he suffered so much and so
severely,** that if any of the brothers knew this, as did we who were
with him until the day of his death, **as often as they read these
things** or recalled them to mind, they would not be able to restrain
their tears. They would **endure all** their hardships and privations
with greater patience **and joy.**

Very early in the morning, blessed Francis came down from the
tower, and went to the Lord Cardinal, telling him all that had happened to him **and what he** and his companion **had endured.** And he
added: "People think that I am a holy man, and as you see the devils
have driven me from the cell."

The Lord Cardinal was very happy with him and, since he knew
and venerated him as a saint, **he did not want to contradict him**
after he was unwilling to remain there.

Thus, blessed Francis **took leave of him and** returned to the hermitage at Fonte Colombo near Rieti.[a]

68

HOW HE REBUKED THE BROTHERS WHO WANT
THE WAY OF THEIR WISDOM AND LEARNING
AND NOT THE WAY OF HUMILITY
AND HOW HE PREDICTED THE REFORM AND RETURN OF THE ORDER
TO ITS ORIGINAL *STATUS*

↓AC 18   When blessed Francis was at Saint Mary of the Portiuncula for the
general chapter known as the Chapter of Mats **because the only
dwellings there were made of rush-mats,** there were five thousand
brothers present. Many wise and learned brothers **went to** the Lord
of Ostia, who was there and told him: **"Lord,** we **want you** to persuade **Brother** Francis to follow the advice of the wise brothers and

---

a. Cf. FA:ED II 196 a.

allow himself to be guided by them." They cited the *Rule* of blessed Benedict, blessed Augustine, and blessed Bernard, which teach how to live in such order in such a way.[a]

The cardinal **related everything to blessed Francis, giving him some advice as well.** Then blessed Francis took **him** by the hand, **saying nothing,** and led him to the brothers assembled in chapter, and spoke to the brothers **in the fervor and power of the Holy Spirit:** "My brothers! My brothers! God has called me by the way of simplicity **and humility,** and has **truly** shown me **this** way **for me for those who want to trust and imitate me.** Therefore I do not want you to mention to me any *Rule,* whether of Saint Augustine, or of Saint Bernard, or of Saint Benedict, **or any other way or form of life except the one that the Lord in His mercy has shown and given to me.**[b] And the Lord told me what He wanted: He wanted me to be a new fool in **this** world. God did not wish to lead us by any way other than this knowledge, but God will confound you by your knowledge and wisdom. But I trust in the Lord's police that through them **God** will punish you, and you will return to your *status,* **with** your blame, like it or not."

The cardinal was **greatly** shocked, and said nothing, and all the brothers were **greatly** afraid.

69

HOW HE FORESAW AND PREDICTED THAT LEARNING
WOULD BE AN OCCASION OF RUIN FOR THE ORDER
AND HOW HE FORBADE ONE OF HIS COMPANIONS
TO PURSUE THE STUDY OF PREACHING

1 Cor 8:1

1 Cor 7:20, 24

Hos 9:7

Ps 37:39

2 Chr 15:4; Prv 1:27

↓AC 47//2C 195

It grieved blessed **Francis** when brothers sought *learning* **which inflates** while neglecting virtue, **especially** if they did not *remain in* that *calling in which they were* first *called.* He said: "Those brothers of mine who are led by curiosity for knowledge will find themselves empty-handed *on the day of reckoning.* I would prefer that they grow strong in virtue, so that when *the time of tribulation* arrives they may have the Lord with them *in their distress.* For *a tribulation is approaching,* when books, useful for nothing, shall be thrown into cupboards and closets!"

---

a. The text may also be rendered: "which teach living in such and such a way, with order"; or "which teach living in this way, and in such an orderly manner"; or even, "which teach how to live in such and such a way, like an Order."

b. Cf. FA:ED II 133 a.

He did not say these things out of dislike for the **reading of Holy** Scripture, but to draw all of them back from excessive concern for learning. **Rather he wanted them** to be good through charity rather than be dilettantes through curious **learning.**

Besides, he could smell in the air that a time was coming, and not too far away, when he knew *learning* **which inflates** would be an occasion of ruin. **For this reason,** he appeared after his death in a vision to one of the companions who was once **avidly** tending toward preaching, and **he rebuked and** forbade him to do so. He commanded him **to pursue** the way **of humility and** simplicity.

1 Cor 8:1

70

HOW THOSE WHO WILL ENTER THE ORDER
IN A TIME OF FUTURE TROUBLE WILL BE BLESSED,
AND THOSE WHO WILL BE TESTED WILL BE BETTER
THAN THOSE WHO PRECEDED THEM

↓AC 2//2C 157

Blessed Francis also said: *"A time will come* when the religion loved by God will have such a bad reputation because of bad examples **of evil brothers,** that it will be embarrassing to go out in public. Whoever comes to receive **the habit** of the Order, at that time will be led only by the working of the Holy Spirit; *flesh and blood* will put no blot on them; they will be truly *blessed by the Lord.* Although they will not do works of merit, for the love that makes saints work fervently will have grown cold, still they will undergo temptations; and whoever passes the tests of that time will be better than those who came before.

Ez 7:12

Mt 16:17

Ps 115:15

"But woe to those who congratulate themselves over the appearance **and the show** of a religious way of living, to **those found** idle **trusting in their knowledge and wisdom, that is,** not engaged in **virtuous deeds, in the way of the cross and of penance,**[a] **in the pure observance of the Gospel which they are bound to observe purely and simply by their profession!**[b] For these men do not firmly resist the temptations that **the Lord** permits to test the chosen! But *those*

Jas 1:12

---

a. This is the first text of this literature to use the phrase *via crucis* [the way of the cross], one that will become popular in the later tradition. In contrast to the earlier texts, 2MP accentuates twice the "pure observance" of the Gospel (2MP 70, 80). The concept also appears in relation to simplicity (2MP 72), obedience (2MP 57), and the Portiuncula (2MP 55). In this sense, it is similar to the call of the AC to live the *Rule sine glossa* [without gloss] and *ad litteram* [to the letter]. Cf. FA:ED II 132 a. The phrase occurs again in 2MP 76 in a reference to "our profession," and 2MP 87 in regard to imitation of Christ.

b. In *Exiit qui seminat*, art. 16, Pope Nicholas III explicitly states that the passage on idleness in LR V 2 does not apply to those engaged in study, divine services, and ministry. It is quite the contrary, because "spiritual labor outweighs manual labor." Cf. infra 757-8.

who are tested **and proven** will receive the crown of life, to which the malice of reprobates all the while spurs them."

71

HOW HE ANSWERED HIS COMPANION
WHY HE DID NOT CORRECT THE ABUSES
THAT OCCURRED IN THE ORDER AT HIS TIME

One of blessed Francis's companions **once** said to him: "Father, excuse me, because what I want to say to you, many have already thought. You know," he said "how formerly through the grace of God, the whole religion flourished in the purity of perfection, that is, how all the brothers fervently and zealously observed holy poverty in all things, in small and poor dwellings, in small and poor furnishings, in small and poor books, and in clothing. And as in these things, as well as in **all** other exterior things, they were of one will **and fervor,** concerned about observing everything that had to do with our profession and calling, and **eager to give** good example **to everyone.** In this way they were of one mind in the love of God and neighbor, **and were truly apostolic and evangelical men.**

"But, for some time now, this purity and perfection have **very much** begun to change into something different, although many use the great number of brothers as an excuse, **claiming that on this account these things** cannot be observed by the brothers. In fact many brothers **have become so blind** that they think people are more edified **and moved to devotion** by these ways than by **the former ones.** And it seems to them more fitting to live and behave according to these ways. Therefore they **despise and** consider worthless the way of **holy** simplicity and poverty, which were the beginning and foundation of our religion. Thinking this over, we **firmly** believe that they displease you. But we are **greatly amazed. Why,** if they displease you, do **you** tolerate them and do not correct **them?"**

"May the Lord forgive you," blessed Francis **responded** to him, "for wanting to be against me and opposed to me and involve me in these things that do not pertain to my office. As long as I held the office **of prelate** for the brothers, and they remained faithful to their calling and profession, and, although I was **always** ill from the beginning of my conversion, I satisfied them with a little of my care, by my example and preaching. But afterwards I realized that the Lord *multiplied the number* of the brothers, and that, due to tepidity and lack of spirit, they began to turn away from the straight and sure way which they **had been accustomed** to walk. They would take *the*

↓AC 106

Acts 6:7

Mt 7:13

broader *road that leads* to death, without paying attention to their profession and calling and good example. They refused to give up this perilous and fatal way that they had begun despite my preaching, my admonitions, and my example that I consistently gave them. Therefore I entrusted the prelacy and governance of the religion to the Lord and to the ministers.

"However, although I renounced the office of prelacy among the brothers, I excused myself before the brothers at the general chapter saying that, because of my illness I could not take care of them and care for them. And yet, if the brothers would have been willing to walk according to my will, I would not want them to have any other minister except me to help and comfort them until the day of my death. As long as a faithful and good subject knows and observes the will of his prelate, then the prelate has to have little concern about him. Rather, I would be so happy at the goodness of the brothers, both on their account and my own. Thus, even if I were lying sick in bed, it would not be considered a burden to me to satisfy them, because my office of prelacy is only spiritual, namely to overcome vices, and spiritually correct and cure them. Inasmuch as I cannot overcome and correct them by preaching, admonitions, and example, I do not want to become an executioner who punishes and scourges, like the powers of this world. For *I trust in the Lord.* Invisible enemies, the Lord's police, who punish in this world and in the next those who transgress the commandments of God and the vows of their profession, will take revenge on them, having corrected men of this world, and thus they will return to their profession and calling. *Ps 11:1*

"Nevertheless, until the day of my death, I will not cease teaching the brothers at least by example and good deeds *to walk by the path* which the Lord *showed* me, and which I have already taught and showed them by word and example. Thus, *they will have no excuse* before the Lord, and I will not be bound to render any further account about them or about myself before the Lord." *1 Kgs 8:36* *Rom 1:20*

[Interpolation][a]

Brother Leo, the companion and confessor of Saint Francis,   WBC III
wrote to Brother Conrad of Offida[b] the following account, claiming
that he had it from the mouth of blessed Francis. This same
Brother Conrad related this at San Damiano near Assisi.

Saint Francis was standing in prayer behind the pulpit in the
church of Saint Mary of the Angels, with his hands raised on high,
and he was crying out to Christ to have mercy on the people in the
great calamity that was to come. And the Lord said: "Francis, if you
want Me to have mercy on the Christian people, do this for Me. Let
your Order remain in that state in which it was founded, because
there is nothing else left in the world for Me. And I promise you
that, for love of you and your Order, I will not permit any calamity
to come upon the world.

"But, I tell you, that they must withdraw from the way on which
I have set them. And they will provoke me to such great anger that
I will rise up against them, and I will summon the demons and give
them all the power that they wanted. And they will place such
scandal between them and the world that no one will be able to
wear your habit except in the woods. And when the world loses the
faith of your Order, light will no longer remain, because I have set
Mt 5:14   them as *the light of the world."*

And Saint Francis said: "How will my brothers who dwell in the
woods survive?"

Christ answered: "I will feed them as I fed the children of Israel
Dt 8:16; Jn 6:31   *with manna in the desert,* because they will be as good as they were, and
then they will return to the original state in which it was founded
and began."

---

a. The following paragraphs or interpolation can be found in some manuscripts without a number and a
   title. In other manuscripts, these paragraphs are seen as part of the general structure of the 2MP, are
   numbered accordingly, and are given appropriate titles. The paragraphs are taken from the *Verba
   Conradi* [The Sayings of Conrad of Offida]. Cf. Paul Sabatier, "Verba Fratris Conradi. Extrait du Ms.
   1/25 de S. Isidore," *Opuscules de critique historique* I (Paris, 1903): 370-392; Daniele Solvi, "Lo
   'Speculum Perfectionis' e Le Sue Fonti," AFH 88 (1995): 394-5, especially 395 n. 57.
b. Conrad of Offida (c. 1237-1306) entered the Order in 1251, lived in the hermitages of Le Marche of
   Ancona, Fermo, and La Verna, and personally knew Leo, Francis's companion, Ubertino of Casale,
   and Peter of John Olivi. Favoring the Poor Hermits of Celestine V, he was accused of favoring a split
   in the Order, but remained in the Order, and became a favorite of the Spirituals.

72
HOW SOULS ARE CONVERTED BY THE PRAYERS AND TEARS
OF HUMBLE AND SIMPLE BROTHERS,
WHICH SEEM TO BE CONVERTED BY LEARNING AND PREACHING OF OTHERS

_{↓AC 103} **The most holy father** did not want his brothers to be desirous of learning and books, but wanted and preached to **them** to be eager **to lay the foundation** on holy humility and to imitate the pure simplicity, holy prayer, and Lady Poverty on which the holy and first brothers had built. And **he used to say that this was the only** secure path for their well-being, **because Christ, Whom we are to follow, has shown us that this is the only way and taught us so both by word and example.**[a]

Foreseeing the future, **the blessed father** knew through the Holy Spirit and even repeated it many times to the brothers, that many brothers, under the pretext of edifying others, would abandon their vocation, that is, **holy humility,** pure simplicity, prayer, **devotion,** and our Lady Poverty. And **it will come to the point** that, because **they will think** themselves to be more imbued **and filled** with devotion and enflamed by love **and enlightened by knowledge** of God because of their understanding of the Scriptures. As a result, they will occasionally remain inwardly cold and empty. And so, they will be unable to return to their first vocation, since they have wasted the time for living according to their calling **in vain and false study.** And I fear that even *what they seemed to possess* will be *taken away* from them, because **they completely neglected what had been given them, namely to maintain and imitate** their vocation.[b] _{Mt 25:29}

He used to say: "There are many **brothers** who, day and night, place all their energy and **all their** care **in acquiring** knowledge, losing their holy vocation and **straying from the path of humility and holy** prayer. And when they have preached to the people,[c] and see or learn that some have been edified or converted to penance, they become puffed up or congratulate themselves for someone else's gain, **as though it were their own. But they will have preached**

---

a. While citing AC 103, it is interesting to note that the editor of 2MP omits the following passage: "Not that he despised or disdained holy knowledge. On the contrary, he revered with great feeling those who were knowledgeable in religion, and for all knowledgeable persons, as he himself says in his *Testament:* 'We must honor all theologians and those who minister the divine words and respect them as those who minister to us spirit and life.'" By this omission, the editor of the 2MP hardens his opposition to study, a position not supported in the earlier tradition. Cf. FA:ED II 207.

b. The Latin reads: *vocationem suam tenere et imitari* [to maintain and imitate their vocation], which is a different expression than that of AC 103 which speaks of *vivendi secundum vocationem suam* [living according to their vocation], a more dynamic consideration.

c. The Latin, *Et cum aliquibus vel populo praedicaverint* [when they have preached to others and to the people], is cryptic. It probably refers to preaching to one another, that is, to the brothers themselves, and, in another instance, to the people.

rather to their own condemnation and judgment, and have really achieved nothing except as instruments to those through whom the Lord has effected this result. The Lord actually edified and converted those who they thought they had edified and converted to penance by their learning and preaching. And the Lord did it because of the prayers and tears of holy, poor, humble, and simple brothers, although they are ignorant of this. For this is the will of God, that they do not know this, lest it be an occasion of pride for them.

"These brothers of mine are knights of the round table,[a] who hide in deserted and remote places to devote themselves more fervently to prayer and meditation, to weep over their sins and the sins of others. While living simple and humble ways of life, their holiness is known to God alone, and frequently unknown to the brothers and to other people. When the souls of these men are presented to the Lord by the angels, the Lord will then reveal to them the fruit and *reward of their labors,* namely, the many souls saved through their examples, prayers, and tears. And He will say: 'My beloved sons, behold all and such souls have been saved by your prayers, tears and examples; *because you were faithful in little things, I will set you over many.'* Others have preached and labored with their words of wisdom and learning, and I have worked out the fruit of salvation by your merits. Receive, then, the reward of your labors and the fruit of your merits, which is the eternal kingdom that you have vehemently seized by humility, your prayers and tears.

"And carrying their sheaves with them, namely, the fruit and merit of holy humility and their simplicity, they will *enter into the joy of the Lord,* rejoicing and exulting.

"But those who did not care for anything except to know and to show the way of salvation to others, and have done nothing on their own behalf, will stand naked and empty-handed *before the judgment seat of Christ,* bearing only the sheaves of confusion, shame and sorrow.

"Then the truth of holy humility and simplicity, of holy prayer and poverty, which is our vocation, will be exalted, glorified, and proclaimed. Those *inflated* with the wind *of learning* this truth betrayed by their lives and by the empty words of their wisdom, saying that truth is falsehood and, like blind people, cruelly persecuting

Wis 10:17

Mt 25:21

Mt 25:21

2 Cor 5:10

1 Cor 8:1

---

a. Cf. FA:ED II 208 b. By 1170, the legends of Arthur, Lancelot, Tristan, and other knights of the Round Table were known to European troubadours. Cf. J.B. Hall, "A Process of Adaptation: The Spanish Versions of the Romance of Tristan," in *The Legend of Arthur in the Middle Ages,* ed. P.B. Grout, R.A. Lodge, C.E. Pickford, E.K.C. Varty (Cambridge: Boydell and Brewer, 1983), 76-85, 235-7.

those who walked in the truth. Then the error and falsehood of their opinions according to which they walked, which they preached as truth, and by which they have thrust many people into *the pit of blind-ness,* will end in grief, confusion and shame. And they with their murky opinions will be cast *into exterior darkness* with the spirits of darkness."

Mt 15:14

Mt 25:30

Frequently blessed Francis, therefore, used to speak about this passage: *The barren one has given birth to many children and the mother of many languishes.* "The barren one is the good, simple, humble, poor and looked down upon, the miserable and contemptible religious who by holy prayers and virtues continually edifies others and *brings* them *to birth with* sorrowful *groans.*"

1 Sm 2:5

Rom 8:22, 26

He used to say this passage very often to the ministers and the other brothers, especially in a general chapter.[a]

73
HOW HE WISHED AND TAUGHT THAT PRELATES AND PREACHERS
OUGHT TO OCCUPY THEMSELVES
IN PRAYER AND WORKS OF HUMILITY

The faithful servant and perfect imitator of Christ, Francis, sensing himself most powerfully transformed into Christ through the virtue of holy humility, desired that humility in his brothers before all other virtues. And that they would love, desire, acquire, and preserve it unceasingly, he would more passionately stimulate them by word and example, and would especially admonish and incite the ministers and preachers to exercise works of humility.

↓AC 103//1MP 7

For he used to say that, because of the office of prelacy or of zeal for preaching, they should not abandon holy and devout prayer, going for alms, *working* at times *with their hands,* and performing other humble tasks like the other brothers, for good example and for the benefit of their souls, as well as others.

1 Thes 4:11

He said: "The brothers who are subjects will be very edified when their ministers and preachers devote themselves freely to prayer, and give themselves to humble and lowly tasks. Otherwise they cannot admonish the other brothers about these things without confusion, prejudice, and blame. For we must, after Christ's exam-ple, first *act and* then *teach,* or act and teach simultaneously."

Acts 1:1

---

a. The source of this extended insertion to AC 103 is unknown.

74
HOW, HUMBLING HIMSELF, HE TAUGHT THE BROTHERS TO RECOGNIZE
WHEN HE WAS A SERVANT OF GOD AND WHEN HE WAS NOT

Blessed Francis called together many of the brothers and said to them: *"I prayed to the Lord* that he might deign to show me when *I am his servant* and when I am not, for I **desire** to be nothing else except to be his servant. And now the gracious Lord himself in his mercy is giving me this answer: 'Know that you are in truth my servant when you think, speak, and do things that are holy.' And so I have called you brothers **and disclosed this to you so that I can be** filled with shame before you **whenever you see me lacking in all or in some of these things."**

2 Cor 12:8; Ps 119:125

↓AC 3//2C 159

75
HOW HE EXPRESSLY WANTED ALL THE BROTHERS
TO WORK OCCASIONALLY WITH THEIR HANDS

He used to say that *the lukewarm* who do not apply themselves constantly **and humbly** to some work, would quickly be *vomited out of the Lord's mouth.* No idler could appear in his presence without **immediately** feeling the sharp bite of his criticism. This exemplar of every perfection worked **humbly** with his hands, not allowing the great gift of time to go to waste. And so he would often say: "I want all my brothers to work and **humbly** keep busy **in good works,** and those who **do not know how to work** should learn, so that we may be less of a burden to people, and that in idleness the heart and tongue may not stray." **He would say that** profit or payment for work should not be left to the whim of the worker, but is to be entrusted to the guardian or the family.

Rv 3:16

↓AC 48//2C 161

ER VII; LR V

Test 20-21

Chapter Four
HIS ZEAL FOR PROFESSION OF THE *RULE*
AND FOR THE ENTIRE RELIGION

76
FIRST, HOW HE PRAISED THE OBSERVANCE OF THE *RULE*
AND WANTED THE BROTHERS TO KNOW IT, DISCUSS IT, AND DIE WITH IT

AC 46//2C 208 Blessed Francis, the perfect zealot of the observance of the holy Gospel, burned with great zeal for the common profession of our *Rule,* which is nothing else than the perfect observance of the Gospel. He endowed those who are and were true zealots about it with a special blessing. He used to tell his imitators that our profession was the *Book of Life, the hope of salvation,* the pledge of glory, the marrow of the Gospel, the way of the cross, the state of perfection, the key of Paradise, the pact of an *eternal covenant.* He wanted all to have it, all to know it. In their conversations he wanted the brothers to speak of it often and to let it speak more often to the inner man, as *encouragement in weariness* and as a reminder of a sworn oath. He taught them to keep it always before their eyes as an encouragement and reminder of the life they should lead, and of the obligation of regular observance. What is more, he wanted and taught the brothers that they should die with it.

Rv 3:5; 21:27; 1 Thes 5:8

Heb 13:20

Wis 8:9

77
A HOLY LAY BROTHER MARTYRED HOLDING THE *RULE* IN HIS HANDS

AC 46//2C 208 This teaching and holy instruction of the most blessed father was not forgotten by a certain lay brother who we believe was admitted into the choir of martyrs. When he was among non-believers because of a desire for martyrdom and taken by the Saracens, he held the *Rule* with great fervor in both hands, and kneeling humbly, said to his companion: "I confess myself guilty before *the eyes of the* divine Majesty and before you of everything I ever did against this holy *Rule!*" The stroke of the sword followed this short confession, and with his martyrdom he ended his life with the crown of a martyr. This brother had entered the Order so young that he could hardly bear the *Rule's* fasting, yet even as a boy he wore a harness next to his skin.

Is 3:8

Oh happy child, who began happily to end even happier!

78
How he wanted the Order always to be under the protection and discipline of the Church

Blessed Francis used to say: "I will go and **recommend the religion of the Lesser Brothers** to the holy Roman Church. The evil-minded will be **terrorized and restrained** by the rod of power. The *sons of God* will enjoy *complete freedom,* which will help to increase eternal salvation everywhere. From now on, let the children acknowledge their mother's sweet favor, and always follow her holy footprints with special devotion.

"**For** with her protection, *nothing evil* will happen to the Order, and no *son of Belial* will trample the *vineyard of the Lord* unpunished. She, that holy **mother,** will emulate the glory of our poverty and **will in no way allow** the praises of humility from being obscured by clouds of pride. She will *preserve* intact among us the *bonds of charity and peace,* striking dissidents with harsh punishments. In her sight the sacred observance of the purity of the Gospel will constantly flourish and she will not allow the *sweet fragrance* **of a good reputation** and holy **manner of living to be destroyed** even *for an hour."*

2C 24

Mt 5:9; Col 2:19; Gal 4:31

Jer 5:12; Ti 2:8

1 Sm 25:17; Is 5:7

Col 3:14; Eph 4:3

2 Cor 2:15

2 Cor 7:8

79
The four privileges which the Lord gave to the Order and declared to Blessed Francis

As an angel **announced to him,** Blessed Francis said that he had obtained **from the Lord** four things. Namely, **the religion and** the profession of the Lesser **Brothers** will last until the day of judgment. **In addition,** no one who deliberately persecutes the Order will live long. **Furthermore,** no evil person, intending to live an evil life in **it,** will be able to remain in it for long. **Likewise, whosoever** loves the Order wholeheartedly, **however great** a sinner, will obtain mercy **in the end.**

WSF 6

80
The qualities he considered necessary for a general minister and his associates

So great was his zeal to preserve perfection in the religion, and so important did he consider the perfect observance of the *Rule,* that he often considered who might be suitable to govern the whole religion after his death and, with God's help, to preserve its

LAC 42//2C 18

perfection. However, he was not able to find anyone suitable. Consequently, near the end of his life, a brother said to him: "Father, you will pass on to the Lord, and this family of your followers will remain *in this vale of tears*. Point out to us someone in the Order, if you know one, on whom your spirit may rest, and on whom the burden of the general ministry may worthily be laid." Blessed Francis, drawing a sigh with every word, replied: "My son, I find no one adequate to be the leader of such a large and varied army, or the shepherd of such a far-reaching flock. But I would like to paint one for you to show clearly what kind of person the leader and shepherd of this family should be.

Ps 84:7

2C 185

"This person," he said, "must be of very dignified life, of great discernment, and of praiseworthy reputation. He must be without personal favorites, lest by loving some more than others, he create scandal for all. He must be a committed friend of prayer, who can distribute some hours for his soul and others for his flock. Early in the morning, he must put first the most holy sacrifice of the Mass and then, with prolonged devotion, lovingly commend himself and his flock to divine protection.

"After prayer, he must make himself centrally available for all to pick at him, and he should respond to all and provide for all with charity, patience, and meekness. He should not play favorites, so that he does not care less for the simple and illiterate than for the learned and educated. Even if he should be allowed the gift of learning, he should all the more bear in his behavior the image of piety, simplicity, patience, and humility, and nourish these virtues in himself and others, constantly exercising them in patience and inspiring others to do so more by example than by words. He should loathe money, which is the principal corrupter of our profession and perfection. As the head and exemplar for all to imitate, he must never engage in the abuse of using any money pouch.

↓AC 43//2C 185

"For his needs," he said, "a habit and a little book should be enough for him and, for the others' needs he should have a pen, an inkwell, paper, and a seal. He should not be a book collector, or too intent on reading, so that he does not take away from his duties what he spends on his studies. Let him be someone who piously comforts the afflicted, and *the final* remedy *of the distressed,* so that the sickness of despair does not overcome the sick because he did not offer healing remedies. In order to bend rebels to meekness, let him lower himself and let go of some of his rights *that he may gain a soul for Christ*. As for runaways from the Order, let him open the heart of piety to them and never deny them mercy, for they are like *lost sheep;* and he

Ps 32:7

Phil 3:8; Mt 16:26

Lk 15:4

knows how overpowering those temptations can be which can push
someone to such a fall. Were God to permit him to be tested the
same way, perhaps he would fall into an even deeper pit.

"I want all to honor him with devotion and reverence as the vicar   2C 186
of Christ, and to be provided for in everything with all kindness
according to his needs by everyone as fitting for our state of life.
However, he must not enjoy honors, nor delight in approval more
than insults, so that honors do not change his conduct except for
the better. If he should need more substantial and better food, he
should not eat it in secret but in a public place, so that others may be
freed from embarrassment at having to provide for themselves in
their sickness and infirmity.

"It especially pertains to him to discern what is hidden in consciences and to draw out the truth from its hidden veins. Let him initially consider all accusations as suspect, until, after diligent
inquiry, the truth begins to appear. Let him not listen to gossip and
consider the accusations of garrulous people especially suspect,
and let him not believe them too easily. In order to maintain his
honor, let him be a person who in no way betrays or relaxes the vir-
ile form of justice and equity. Let him take care never to destroy a
soul by excessive severity, so that torpor not be aroused by undue
lenience, and dissolution of discipline be undermined by lax
indulgence. In this way he will be feared by all and loved by those
who fear him. Let him always consider and feel the office of prelacy
as a burden to him rather than as an honor.

"I would like him to have companions endowed with honesty,
firmly opposed to sinful pleasures, resolute in difficulties, kind
and compassionate to offenders, having the same affection for all.
Let him not receive any remuneration for his work, except for his
bodily needs. Let him seek nothing but the glory of God, the good
of the Order, merit for his own soul, and for the salvation of all the
brothers. Let him be friendly toward all and receive everyone who
comes to him with holy cheerfulness, demonstrating in themselves
purely and simply the form and example of the observance of the
Gospel according to the profession of the *Rule.*

"There," he concluded, "the general minister of this religion
should be like this and such is the kind of companions he should
have."

81
How the Lord spoke to him when he was profoundly distressed by brothers who deviated from perfection

Because of the boundless zeal that he had at all times for the perfection of the religion, he was naturally grieved when he would hear or see any imperfection in it. He began to realize that some brothers were giving a bad example in religion and that the brothers were already beginning to turn aside from the highest summit of their profession. One time, moved *inwardly with* very great *sorrow of heart,* he said to the Lord in prayer: "Lord I give back to you the family You gave me."

And the Lord **immediately** said to him: "Tell me, **simple and unlettered little man,** why are you so upset when one of the brothers leaves religion and when others do not *walk the way I showed you?* Also tell me: Who planted this religion of the brothers? Who makes a man convert and do penance? Who gives the strength to persevere in it? Is it not I? I did not choose you as a learned or eloquent man to be over my family. **I do not want you nor those I gave you who intend to be true brothers and true observers of the** *Rule* **that I gave you to walk the way of learning and eloquence. But I chose you, a** *simple* **and unlettered** man, so that you and the others may know that I will watch over my flock. But *I have placed you as a sign* to them, so that the works that I work in you, they should see in you, emulate, and do them. **For** those who walk in the way **I showed you,** have me and have me more abundantly. Those who **want** to walk in **another** way, that *which they seem to have will be taken away from them.* Therefore, I tell you, **from now on** don't be so sad; do what you do, work as you work, for I have planted the religion of the brothers *in everlasting love.* Know that I love it so much that if any brother, *returning to his vomit,* dies outside religion I will replace him with another in religion who will have his crown in his place, and supposing that he has not been born, I will have him born. And so that you know that I love the life and religion of the brothers, suppose that in the whole religion of the brothers only three brothers remained, **it would still be my religion and** I would never abandon it."

And when he heard these things, his soul was **wonderfully** comforted.

And, although **on account of the great zeal that he always had for the perfection of the religion,** he could not totally restrain himself from becoming **extremely** sad when he heard of **any imperfections of the brothers from which** bad example or scandal could

AC 112//2C 158 //1MP 40

Gn 6:6

1 Kgs 8:36

Acts 4:13

Hg 2:24

Mt 25:29

Jer 31:3

Prv 26:11; 2 Pt 2:22

Ps 119:106

arise. Nevertheless, after **he was** comforted by the Lord **in this way,** he remembered that [passage] of the psalm: *"I have sworn and deter-mined to keep* **the justice** of the Lord and to observe the *Rule* **that the Lord Himself gave to me and to those who desire to imitate me.** All **these** brothers **have also** bound themselves **to this as I have. And therefore,** after I resigned the office among the brothers because of my illnesses and **other reasonable causes,** I am not bound **at all except to pray for the religion and** to show good example. For **I have** this from the Lord and know in truth that if my illness had not excused me, the greater help I can render to the religion is to spend time everyday in prayer to the Lord for it, that He govern, preserve, and protect it. **For** I have bound myself to the Lord and to the broth-ers in this, that if any one of the brothers perishes because of my bad

Mt 12:36

example, I want to be held to *render an account* to the Lord **for him."**

He used to say these words to himself to quiet his heart and more often, in addresses and in chapters, he explained them to the brothers. And even though, if from time to time a brother would tell him that he should occasionally put himself forward in **the gover-nance of the Order,** he used to reply: "The brothers have their *Rule* and have sworn **to observe it.** And so that they have no excuse **on my account** after it pleased the Lord to decide that I would be their prel-ate, I also swore to it in their presence to observe it **as well.** So, since the brothers already know what they should do and what to avoid, the only thing left for me to do is to teach them by actions, because this is why I have been given to them during my life and after my death."

82

THE SINGULAR ZEAL HE HAD FOR SAINT MARY OF THE PORTIUNCULA
AND THE PRESCRIPTIONS HE MADE AGAINST IDLE TALK THERE

As long as he lived, more than for other places in the Order, he always had singular zeal and extraordinary attentiveness to pre-serve every perfection of life and manner of living in the holy place of Saint Mary of the Angels, as the head and mother of the entire religion. He intended and wanted this place more than all places to be the form and example of humility, poverty, and of all gospel per-fection. He wanted all the brothers living there always to be, more than the other brothers, solicitous and cautious in all things to be done and to be avoided in view of the perfect observance of the *Rule.*

AC 107//2C 160
//1MP 35

One time, **in order to avoid** idleness, **which is** *the root of all evil,* 1 Tm 6:10
especially in a religious, he ordered the brothers **to join him daily,**
immediately after a meal, in some kind of work. **Thus they would**
not lose, totally or partially, the good **they earned** during the time of
prayer by useless and idle words **to which people are especially**
prone after a meal. And he also ordered it to be **firmly** observed that
if any brother, while walking or working in the company of other
brothers at something, utters **some** useless or idle word, he must say
one *Our Father,* praising God at the beginning and end of this prayer.
If **perhaps** he is the first to notice it and accuses himself of what he
did, let him say the *Our Father* for his own soul together with *The*
Praises **of the Lord** as was said. But if another brother rebuked him
first, he is bound to say **this** in the way mentioned for the soul of the
brother who corrected him.

If after being corrected, he offers an excuse **and does not want** to
say the *Our Father,* he is bound to say two *Our Father's,* as above, for
the soul of the brother who corrected him. Further, if it is judged as
true, **either on his own testimony** or on that of another, **that he** has
spoken an idle word, he shall say the *Praises of God,* as mentioned, at
the beginning and end of that prayer loud enough and clear enough
for **all** the brothers staying there to understand and hear. And while
he is saying them, the brothers must be quiet and listen. If **any**
brother hearing another saying idle words keeps silent about this
without correcting him, he shall be bound to say one *Our Father* in
the same way with the *Praises of God,* for the soul of the brother who
spoke.

When any brother enters a cell, a house or **any other** place and
finds a brother or brothers there, he should **immediately and**
devoutly praise and bless **the Lord.** The most holy father was always
solicitous to say those *Praises of the Lord,* with a fervent wish and
desire **he taught and encouraged** the other brothers to be similarly
careful and devout in saying **these** *Praises.*

83

HOW HE ADMONISHED THE BROTHERS NEVER TO ABANDON THAT PLACE

1C 106

Although blessed Francis knew *the kingdom of heaven* Mt 5:3
was established in every corner of the earth,
and believed that divine grace **could be given**
to *God's chosen ones* in every place, Rom 8:33
he nevertheless knew from his own experience
that the place of Saint Mary of the Portiuncula

was especially full of grace
and was filled with visits of **heavenly** spirits.
So he often told the brothers:
"See to it my sons, that you **never** abandon this place.
If you are thrown out of one door,
go back **through** another,

Ez 42:13

for *this* is truly a *holy place,*
and the dwelling place of **Christ and His Virgin Mother.**
Here
the Most High increased our numbers,

1 Chr 16:19

when we were only a few;
here
He *enlightened the* **souls** of His poor ones
with the light of His wisdom;
here
He kindled our wills with the fire of his love;
here
all who pray wholeheartedly will receive what they ask
while offenders will be severely punished.
Therefore, my sons, hold **this** place,

Eph 2:22

truly *the dwelling place of God.*
with all reverence
and as **most** worthy of all honor,
particularly dear to Him and to His mother.
In this place

Ps 42:5

in cries of joy and praise

Jer 29:13

with your whole heart
here praise God **the Father**
and **His Son, the Lord Jesus Christ,**
in the unity of the Holy Spirit."

84

THE PREROGATIVES GRANTED BY THE LORD AT THE PLACE OF SAINT MARY OF THE ANGELS[a]

Holy of holies,
that truly place of places,
worthily held worthy
of the greatest of graces.

---

a. The author of this poem, unique to 2MP, is unknown. In *De conformitate vitae beati Francisci ad Vitam Domini Iesu,* Liber II xvi, Bartholomew of Pisa attributes it to *quidam frater versificator* [a "versifying" brother], AF V, 331. Luke Wadding maintains the same position, cf. *Annales* II 160.

Blessed nickname,
more blessed name,
chosen with such a surname
as an omen of its fame.

An angelic power
habitually hymns do shower
here to dazzle the light,
here to dispel the night.

After laying in ruins was all,
Francis undid its downfall,
one plus a pair
that father repaired.

This the father chose
when in sack his members clothed;
here the body he opposed
and to his mind did dispose.

In this temple's confines
the wondrous life of the father shines;
thus was born the Lessers's Order
and here a crowd of men was quartered.

The bride of God, Clare,
here first shed her hair,
the world's pomp refused,
and her Christ pursued.

Thus a sacred mother
to ladies and to brothers
gives forth a brilliant birth
for whom she brings Christ on earth.

Here has been narrowly cast
an aging world's broad path
while virtue has been extended
in a people befriended.

A rule was kindled,
holy poverty enkindled,

glory was appalled,
in its midst the cross recalled.

If anywhere preoccupied
and at any time sorely tried,
here was Francis soothed
and his mind renewed.

Here was touted
the truth that might be doubted,
moreover it was given
whatever the father himself had bidden.

Chapter Five
HIS ZEAL FOR THE PERFECTION OF THE BROTHERS

85
FIRST, HOW HE DESCRIBED THE PERFECT BROTHER

The most Blessed Father, having in a certain way transformed the brothers into saints by the ardor of his love and the fervent zeal which he had for their perfection, often used to ponder within himself about the qualities and virtues which should abound in a good Lesser Brother.

WSF 7 And,[a] he used to say that a good Lesser Brother is one who would possess the life and qualities of the following holy brothers: namely, the faith and love of poverty which Brother Bernard most perfectly had; the simplicity and purity of Brother Leo who was truly a man of most holy purity; the courtly bearing of Brother Angelo who was the first soldier to enter the Order and was endowed with every courtesy and kindness; the friendly manner and common sense of Brother Masseo, together with his attractive and gracious eloquence; the mind raised in contemplation which Brother Giles had even to the highest perfection; the virtuous and constant prayer of Brother Rufino who, whatever he was doing, even sleeping, always *prayed without ceasing* and whose mind was always intent on the Lord; the patience of Brother Juniper, who achieved the perfect state of patience because he always kept in mind the perfect truth of his low estate and the ardent desire to imitate Christ through the way of the cross; the bodily and spiritual strength of Brother John of Lauds, who at that time in his robust body surpassed everyone; the charity of Brother Roger whose life and conduct were spent in ardent love; the solicitude of Brother Lucidus who had the greatest care and concern and did not want to remain in any place for a month, and when he enjoyed staying some place, would immediately leave, saying: *"We do not have a dwelling here on earth, but in heaven."* 1 Thes 5:17 Heb 13:14

---

a. According to Edith Pásztor, this text also reflects one of the *Verba Sancti Francisci* [Sayings of Saint Francis] as found in a manuscript of the library of St. Isidore's Friary, Rome. Cf. Edith Pásztor, "Il manoscritto Isidoriano 1/73 e gli scritti leonini su S. Francesco," *Cultura e società nell'Italia medievale. Studi per Paolo Brezzi.* Studi Stoirici, 188-192. (Rome: n.p., 1988), 661-3.

86
HOW HE DESCRIBED IMPURITY OF THE EYES
TO INCITE THE BROTHERS TO THE PRACTICE OF CHASTITY

Among the other virtues he loved and wanted to be in his brothers, after the foundation of holy humility, he particularly loved a
beauty and purity of character. Therefore, since he wanted to teach
his brothers to have chaste eyes, he used to pierce eyes that are
impure with this parable. "A powerful and pious king sent two messengers to his queen, one after the other. The first returned and simply reported her words verbatim, and he said nothing about the
queen. Truly *the eyes of the wise man* stayed *in his head* and did not dart
about the queen. The other returned and, after reporting a few
words, launched into a long story about the queen's beauty. 'Truly,
my lord,' he said, 'I saw a lovely woman; happy is he who enjoys her!'
And the king said, 'You evil servant, you cast your shameless eyes on
my wife? It is clear that you would like to buy what you inspected so
carefully!' He then called back the first messenger and asked: 'What
did you think of the queen?' And he answered: 'I thought very highly
of her, for she listened gladly and patiently, and then replied wisely.'
'And don't you think she's beautiful?' the king asked. 'My lord,' he
said, 'this is for you to see and discern; my job was simply to deliver
messages.'

"And the king then pronounced his sentence: 'You have chaste
eyes, even more you are chaste in body. Stay in my chamber and
enjoy my delights. Let that unchaste man leave my house, so he
does not defile my marriage bed.' "

Therefore he used to say: "Who would not fear to look at the bride
of Christ?"

(margin: ↓AC 37//2C 113)
(margin: Eccl 2:14)
(margin: 2C 114)

87
THE THREE RECOMMENDATIONS HE LEFT FOR THE BROTHERS
TO PRESERVE THEIR PERFECTION

One evening he wanted to vomit because of the disease of his
stomach.[a] Because of the excessive exertion he put on himself, he
vomited up blood all night until morning.

When his companions saw him already almost dying from the
great weakness and affliction, they said to him with the greatest
sorrow and flowing tears:

(margin: ↓AC 59//1MP 30)

---

a. AC 59 is far more descriptive in its treatment of Francis's condition. For information on the nature of
   this illness, see FA:ED II 161 a.

"Father, what shall we do **without you? To whom shall you leave
us, your** *orphaned children?* You have always been a father and a   Jn 14:18
mother to us. You have conceived us and *brought us forth in Christ.* You   Gal 4:19
have been our leader and shepherd, teacher and corrector, teaching
and correcting us more by your example than by your words.

"**Where shall we go,** *sheep without a shepherd,* orphaned children   Jdt 11:19; Mt 9:36
without a father, simple and unlettered men without a guide? Where
shall we go to look for you, **O** *glory* of poverty, *praise* of simplicity, and   Jdt 15:9-10
honor of our lowliness?

"**Who will show us, blind as we are, the way of truth? Where
shall we find a mouth to speak to us and a tongue that offers us
counsel? Where will your burning spirit be found, directing us on
the way of the cross and training us for evangelical perfection?
Where will you be,** *light of our eyes,* that we may hurry to you and seek   Tb 10:4
you, counselor of our souls? Lo and behold, Father, you are dying.
See how you are leaving us abandoned, grieving and full of despair.

"**Alas,** *a day of weeping* and bitterness approaches, a day of desola-   Is 22:5
tion and grief, *a bitter day* that we always dreaded to see while we   Zep 1:14-15
were together with you, a day that we had not even been able to
imagine!

"**And no wonder! Since your life has been a constant light for us
and your words have been like burning torches, always enlightening us along the way of the cross to evangelical perfection and to
the love and imitation of the sweet crucified One.**

"**Therefore, Father, at least** bless us and the rest of your brothers,
your sons whom you have begotten in Christ. Leave us some
remembrance of your will that your brothers may always keep it in
their memory and **be able** to say: 'Our father left these words to his
sons and brothers at his death.' "

The most pious father, turning his paternal eyes to his sons,
then told them: "Call Brother Benedict of Piratro for me."[a] He was a
brother priest, discerning and holy. He sometimes celebrated for
blessed Francis **where he was lying ill, because** he always wanted to
hear Mass whenever he could, **no matter how sick he was.** And
when he had come, he told him: "Write that I bless all my brothers,
those who are and who will be in the religion until the end of the
world. And, since I cannot speak much because of weakness and the
pain of my illness, I am showing my will **and intention** to all my
brothers **present and future.** As a sign of my remembrance, blessing,
and testament, may they always *love one another* as **I have loved** and   Jn 13:34; 15:12

---

a. Concerning Benedict, cf. FA:ED II 162 a.

love them; may they always love and observe our Lady Poverty; and may they always remain faithful and subject to the prelates and all the clerics of holy Mother Church."

At the close of chapters, it was always **customary for our father** to bless and absolve all the brothers present and the others who were to come to this religion. **In the fervor of his charity,** he **frequently** did **this outside** of chapter.

He used to warn the brothers to fear and beware of bad example, **and** he cursed all those who by bad example caused people to blaspheme the religion and life of the brothers **since** the good and holy brothers were ashamed **of this** and **many were** distressed.

88

THE LOVE HE SHOWED THE BROTHERS WHILE NEAR DEATH,
GIVING EACH OF THEM A MORSEL OF BREAD AS CHRIST DID

One night blessed Francis was so afflicted with the pains of his illness that he could barely rest or sleep that night. In the morning, when his pain eased a bit, he had all the brothers staying in that place called to him, and when they were seated around him, he considered them and regarded them as representatives of all the brothers.

Placing his right hand on the head of each one, he blessed all who were **present and absent** in the religion and all who were to come to **the Order** *until the end of the world.*[a] He seemed to feel sorry for himself because he was not able to see **all** his sons and brothers before his death.

Desiring to imitate his Lord and Master in death as he had so perfectly done in his life, he ordered *loaves of bread* to be brought to him. *And he blessed* them and had them broken into many little pieces because he was unable to do so because **he was extremely weak.** Taking them, he offered each of the brothers a little piece, telling them to eat all of it. Just as the Lord *desired to eat* with the apostles **as a sign of His love** on the Thursday before His death, **in the same way His perfect imitator,** blessed Francis, **wanted to show the same sign of love to his brothers.**

And it is clear he wished to do this in imitation of Christ, because he later asked if the day were a Thursday.

And since it was another day, he said he thought it was Thursday.

Gn 48:17

Dn 7:18

Mt 26:26

Lk 22:15

↓AC 22//1MP

//2C 217

---

a. In contrast with the earlier account of this final blessing, no brother in particular is mentioned, i.e., neither Bernard of Quintavalle nor Elias. Cf. FA:ED II 126 b.

One of the brothers kept a piece of that bread, and after the death of blessed Francis many sick people who tasted it were immediately freed from their illnesses.

89
HOW HE FEARED THAT THE BROTHERS WOULD BE PERTURBED
BECAUSE OF HIS ILLNESS

↓AC 86   **When** he was not able **to rest because** of the pains of his illness, **he saw the brothers were greatly distressed and worn out on account of him. Since he loved the brothers more than his own body, he began to fear that the brothers, worn out by their efforts on his behalf, might commit some small offense of impatience against God because of him.**

This is why he once told his companions with piety and compassion: "My dearest brothers and sons, do not grow weary because of your care for me in my illness. The Lord, on my behalf, His little servant, will return to you, in this world and the next, all the fruit of the good work that you are unable to do because of your care for me in my illness. In fact, you will obtain an even greater profit than **if you had labored for yourselves. For,** whoever assists **me, helps the whole religion and the life of the brothers.** You should even tell me: 'We're paying your expenses, but the Lord, on your behalf, will be our debtor.' "

The holy father spoke in this way because, **motivated by great zeal for the perfection of their souls,** he wanted to help them and lift them up in their faint-heartedness. **He was apprehensive that,** stressed because of their work, they would say: "We can't pray and we can't put up with all this work." And thus they would become weary and **impatient,** and thus lose the **great** fruit of their **meager** labor.

90
HOW HE ADMONISHED THE SISTERS OF SAINT CLARE

↓AC 85

CtExh   Blessed Francis, after he composed the *Praises of the Lord* for his creatures, also composed some holy words with chant for the greater consolation **and edification** of the Poor Ladies, realizing how much his illness troubled them.

And since he was unable to visit them personally, **he sent** those words **to them** by his companions. **In these words,** he wanted to reveal his will to them, how they should **live and conduct themselves**

humbly and be united in charity. **He saw** their conversion and **holy** manner of living were not only a glory for the religion of the brothers, but also the **greatest** edification for the entire Church of God.

He was always moved to piety **and compassion** for them, knowing that, from the beginning of their conversion, they had led a strict and poor life.

With these words, then, he begged **them** that, as the Lord had gathered them from many different parts into one for holy charity, holy poverty, and holy obedience, so in these they should live and die. And he **admonished them** particularly to provide for their bodies with discernment from the alms which the Lord would give them, with cheerfulness and thanksgiving. And he especially asked them to remain patient: the healthy, in the labors which they endure for their sick sisters; and the sick, in the illnesses and the needs they suffer.[a]

CtExh 1-2, 4

---

a. Cf. Octavian Schmucki, "Rediscovery of the *Canticle of Exhortation 'Audite'* of St. Francis for the Poor Ladies of San Damiano," GR (1989): 115-26.

Chapter Six

CONTINUAL INTENSITY OF LOVE
AND COMPASSION FOR THE SUFFERING OF CHRIST

91
FIRST, HOW HE WAS NOT CONCERNED ABOUT HIS OWN INFIRMITIES
BECAUSE OF THE LOVE OF THE PASSION OF CHRIST

↓AC 77   **Such was blessed Francis's fervent** love and compassion for the suffering **and passion of Christ that each day** he afflicted himself **because of that passion so severely,** both inwardly and outwardly, that he did not pay attention to his own **infirmities.** Thus, for a long time and even until the day of his death, blessed Francis suffered ailments of the liver, spleen, and stomach. From the time **he returned from** overseas, he **constantly** had very severe **pain** in his eyes. Yet he refused any treatment for their cure.

↓AC 83   **The Lord** of Ostia, seeing how **he** was always severe with his body, and especially because he was rapidly losing his eyesight because he refused to have himself treated, admonished him with great kindness and compassion. He told him: "Brother, you do not do well in not allowing yourself to be helped with your eye-disease, for your health and your life are of great value **to the brothers, the seculars, and the whole Church.** If you have compassion for your sick brothers, and have always been and still are **pious and** merciful to them, you must not be cruel to yourself in such need. I therefore order you to allow yourself be helped and treated."

↓AC 77   **For that most holy father took** what was bitter to his body as sweet, **because** he **continually** drew **great** sweetness from the humility and footprints of the Son of God.

92
HOW HE WAS FOUND LOUDLY LAMENTING THE PASSION OF CHRIST

↓AC 78//2C 11   Once, **a short time** after his conversion, he was walking alone one day along the road not too far from the church of Saint Mary of the Portiuncula, crying loudly and wailing as he went. A spiritual man met him, **and fearing** that he was suffering from **some** painful illness, he asked him: "Brother, what's wrong?" And he answered: "I should go through the whole world this way, without any shame,

339

crying and bewailing the Passion of my Lord." At this, the man began to weep and cry aloud together with him.

We knew **this man** and learned this from him. He also displayed great comfort and compassion **to blessed Francis and to us, his companions.**

93

HOW EXTERNAL SOLACE SOMETIMES TURNED
TO TEARS AND COMPASSION OF CHRIST

Intoxicated by love and compassion for Christ, blessed Francis sometimes did this: a sweet melody of the spirit bubbling up inside him would **frequently** become on the outside a French tune; the *thread of a divine whisper* which *his ears heard secretly* would break out in a French song. ↓AC 38//2C 12

Jb 4:12

Other times, picking up a stick from the ground and putting it over his left arm, **he would draw another stick across it with his right hand like** a bow on a viola **or some other instrument.** Performing all the right movements, he would sing in French about **the Lord Jesus.**

All of this dancing often ended in tears, and the cry of joy dissolved into compassion for Christ's suffering. Then he would sigh without stopping and sob without ceasing. Forgetful **of what he was holding** in his hands, he was caught up to heaven.

Chapter Seven
HIS ZEAL FOR PRAYER AND THE DIVINE OFFICE
AND FOR PRESERVING SPIRITUAL JOY
IN HIMSELF AND IN OTHERS

94
FIRST, PRAYER AND THE DIVINE OFFICE

AC 119//1MP 22

Although **he had been afflicted** with illness for many years, he was, nevertheless, especially devout and reverent toward prayer **and the divine office. Thus, when** he was praying or reciting the canonical hours, he **never** leaned against a wall or partition, but always stood erect, **with** his head **uncovered,** and sometimes on his knees, especially when he spent the greater part of the day and night in prayer.

2C 96

When he went through the world on foot, he always would stop walking **when he wanted** to say his hours. If he was riding on horseback, **because of** his infirmity, he would **always** get down to say **the office.**

↓AC 120

One time, it was raining **very** heavily, and he was riding horseback **because of** his illness **and pressing need. Since** he was **already** completely soaked, **when he wanted** to say the hours he got off his horse; and **he said the office,** standing in this way on the roadside with the rain **continually** pouring down **on him, with such fervor of devotion and reverence,** and as if he had been in a church or in a cell. **And** he said **to his companion:** "If, in peace and quiet, the body wants to eat its food **which, with** the body, will eventually become food for worms, in what peace and quiet, **and with what reverence and devotion,** should the soul receive its food, which is God Himself!"

95
HOW HE ALWAYS LOVED INTERNAL AND EXTERNAL SPIRITUAL JOY
IN HIMSELF AND IN OTHERS

↓AC 120//BPr VI
//1MP 23

Blessed Francis **always** had this as his highest and main goal: **constantly** to have in himself spiritual joy, internally and externally, **outside the times of prayer and the divine office. This is also what** he especially liked in his brothers, and he would, moreover, frequently rebuke them because of their acedia and sadness.[a]

He used to say: "If a servant of God always strives to have and preserve internally and externally the **spiritual** joy that proceeds from purity of heart **and is acquired through the devotion of prayer,** the devils could do him no harm. They would say: 'Since the servant of God has joy both in tribulation and in prosperity, **we are not able** to find an entrance to enter him and do him harm. **The devils would be** delighted when they can extinguish or prevent devotion and joy in the heart of a servant of God which spring from clean prayer and other **virtuous deeds.**

"For if the devil can have something of his own in a servant of God, he will in a short time make a single hair into a beam, always making it bigger, unless the servant of God is wise **and careful,** removing and destroying it as quickly as possible by means of **the power of holy prayer,** contrition, confession, and works of satisfaction.

"Therefore, **my brothers, because spiritual joy springs from integrity of heart and the purity of constant prayer, it must be your primary concern to acquire and preserve these two virtues, to possess internal, as well as external joy. I so fervently desire and love to see this both in myself and in you, for the edification of the neighbor and the defeat of the enemy. It is the fate of the devil and** his minions to be sad, and it is our lot to *rejoice always* and *be glad in the Lord.*"

Phil 4:4

96
HOW HE REBUKED A BROTHER WHO HAD A GLOOMY FACE

Blessed Francis used to say: "Since I know that the devils envy me because of the gifts that the Lord **has given me, I know and see inasmuch as** they cannot harm me through myself, they try to hurt me through my companions. If they cannot do harm either through me or through my companions, they withdraw in great confusion. Indeed whenever I feel tempted and depressed and I look at the joy of my companion, because of that joy I **immediately** turn away from temptation and acedia toward inner **and outer** joy."

↓AC 120

That is why the father rebuked severely those who showed their sadness outwardly. One day he reproved one of his companions who looked sad and long-faced. He told him: "Why do you outwardly

---

a. Cf. FA:ED II 329 a.

show your sadness and sorrow over your offenses? **This sadness** is a matter between you and God. Pray to Him, that by His mercy He may spare you and grant your soul *the joy of salvation* of which it was deprived by the guilt of sin. Try to be joyful always around me and others, because it is not fitting that a servant of God appear before his brother or others with a sad and **gloomy face."**

Ps 51:14

It should not be understood or believed, however, that our father, a lover of total maturity and integrity, would have wanted this joy to be shown through laughter or even empty words, when, through this, it is not spiritual joy that is shown but vanity and foolishness. In fact, he abhorred laughter and an idle word to an exceptional degree in a servant of God, since he not only wanted him not to laugh, but not even to give the slightest occasion for others to laugh. Therefore, in one of his *Admonitions,* he quite clearly expressed what the joy of a servant of God must be: **Blessed is that religious who has no pleasure and delight except in the most holy words and deeds of the Lord and, with these, leads people to God with gladness and joy. Woe to that religious who delights in idle and empty words and leads people to laughter with them.**

Adm XX 1-2

By a joyful face he understood the fervor and solicitude, the disposition and readiness of a mind and body to willingly undertake *every good work;* because through this kind of fervor and disposition others are at times more motivated than through the good deed itself. In fact, if an act, however good it might be, does not seem to be done willingly and fervently, it brings forth tedium rather than motivating good.

Ti 3:1

That is why he did not want to see a gloomy face, which more often shows laziness, a closed mind, and a body listless for *every good work.* Most of all, he always loved, both in himself and in others, a seriousness and maturity in expression and in all the body's members and senses, and, as much as he could, he led others to this by word and example. For he knew by experience that this kind of seriousness and modest behavior is like a wall and a very strong shield against the arrows of the devil, and that a soul without the protection of this wall and shield is like a naked soldier among the most powerful and armed enemies incessantly rabid and intent on its death.

Ti 3:1

97
How he taught the brothers how to satisfy their bodily needs so that prayer would not be neglected

The most holy father, realizing and understanding that the body was created for the soul and that bodily needs are to be fulfilled because of spiritual ones, used to say: "In eating, sleeping, and fulfilling other bodily needs, a servant of God must satisfy his body with discernment. In this way Brother Body cannot grumble, saying: 'Because you do not satisfy **my needs,** I cannot stand up straight and persevere in prayer, or rejoice in tribulations, or do other good works.'

↓AC 120

"On the other hand, if a servant of God, with discernment, has satisfied his body well enough, but Brother Body wants to be lazy, negligent, and sleepy in prayer, vigils and other good works, then he should punish it like any wicked and lazy beast of burden, because it wants to eat but refuses to work **and** carry its weight.

"If, however, because of want or poverty, Brother Body, whether healthy or sick, cannot have its needs fulfilled, after he has requested them decently and humbly for the love of God from his brother or his prelate and they are not given to him, then let him patiently bear this for the love of God **Who also** *suffered want and found not one to comfort* him. If he bears this need with patience, the Lord will credit it to him as martyrdom. And because he did what is his to do, making his needs known **humbly,** he would be excused from sin, even if the body on this account became **more gravely** ill."

//1MP 23

Ps 69:21

Chapter Eight
THE TEMPTATIONS THE LORD ALLOWED HIM

98
FIRST, HOW THE DEVIL GOT INSIDE THE PILLOW UNDER HIS HEAD

AC 119//2C 64

At one time blessed Francis was staying in the hermitage of Greccio. He remained in prayer day and night in the last cell, behind the large cell. One night, during the first sleep, he called his companion who was sleeping near him. And the companion, getting up, went to **the entrance of the cell** where blessed Francis **was staying. The saint** said to him: "Brother, I couldn't sleep this whole night, or remain upright and pray; my head and my knees are **violently** shaking as if I had eaten bread made from rye grass."[a] His companion talked with him, trying to console him. Blessed Francis said: "I **truly** believe there's a devil in this pillow I have for my head."

After he left the world, he wanted **neither a feather** mattress nor a feather pillow. **Nevertheless** the brothers forced him to **have a feather pillow** against his will, because of his eye disease. He **therefore** threw it at his companion who picked it up in his right hand and **placed** it on his left shoulder. **When** he left **the entrance of the cell,** he suddenly lost the power of speech, could not throw the pillow, nor move his arms. There he stood, bereft of his senses. He stood like this **for some time** until, through **the grace** of God, blessed Francis called him. Immediately he returned to himself, letting the pillow **fall** behind **his back.**

He returned to blessed Francis and told him everything that happened to him.

The saint said to him, "Last night as I was saying compline, I sensed the devil had come into my cell. **I see from this that** the devil is very cunning. **Inasmuch as** he could not harm **my** soul, he wanted to disturb the need of the body by preventing me from sleeping and

---

a. The concern for eating rye bread was rooted in fear of contracting ergot poisoning or "Saint Anthony Fire,"caused by a fungus on rye flour kept too long over the winter. Cf. *Merck Manual of Diagnosis and Therapy*, ed. D.N. Holvey (Rahway, NJ: Merck, 1972), 714-6. Since it was not understood and, at times, seen as a diabolical tool, Saint Anthony of the Desert was invoked for relief or for cures of this illness. Barbara W. Tuchman notes: "Life expectancy was short [in the fourteenth century] owing to overwork, overexposure, and the afflictions of dysentery, turberculosis, pneumonia, astha, tooth decay, and the terrible rash called Saint Anthony Fire, which by constriction of the blood vessels (not then understood) could consume a limb as by 'some hidden fire' and sever it from the body." Cf. *A Distant Mirror: The Calamitous 14th Century* (New York: Ballantime Books, 1978), 174.

standing up to pray, in order to stifle the devotion and joy of my heart so that, **through this,** I would complain about **my** sickness."

99
THE GRAVE TEMPTATION HE ENDURED FOR TWO YEARS

When he was staying in the place of Saint Mary, a very serious temptation of the spirit afflicted him for the benefit of his soul. He was **so** tormented, **in mind and in** body, that he **frequently** withdrew **from the company** of the brothers, because **he was unable** to be his usual cheerful self. **Nevertheless,** he inflicted upon himself not only abstinence from food **and drink,** but also from talking. He prayed **more earnestly** and poured out his tears more abundantly, so that the Lord would be kind enough to send him **sufficient help** for this great trial.

↓AC 63

He was troubled **in this way** for more than two years. One day while he was praying in the church of Saint Mary, he happened to hear in spirit that saying of the holy Gospel: *"If you have faith like a mustard seed, and you tell* that *mountain to move* from its place *and move* to another place, it will happen."* Saint Francis **immediately** replied: **"Lord,** what is that mountain?" He was told: "That mountain is your temptation." "In that case, Lord," said blessed Francis, *"be it done to me* as you have said." Immediately he was **completely** freed in such a way that it seemed to him that he never had that temptation.

2C 115

Mt 17:19

Lk 1:38

Likewise, at the time he received **on his body** the stigmata of the Lord on the **holy mountain** of La Verna, **he suffered so many temptations and afflictions from the devil that he was unable to appear his former joyful self. He said to his companion:** "If the brothers knew how many trials **and how great are the afflictions** the demons cause me, there would not be one of them who would not **be moved** to piety and compassion for me."

↓AC 118//1MP

100
THE TEMPTATION INFLICTED ON HIM BY MICE
AND HOW THE LORD COMFORTED HIM,
ASSURING HIM OF HIS KINGDOM

Two years before his death, while he was staying at San Damiano in a little cell made of mats, he suffered **intensely** from the disease of his eyes. For more than fifty days, he was unable to bear daylight **nor even** the light of a fire.[a]

↓AC 83

---

a. Cf. FA:ED II 185 a.

In order to increase both his afflictions and his merit, many mice, **with divine permission,** overran his cell where he was lying, which was made of mats in one part of the house. Day and night, as they were running around him and even over him, they prevented him **from praying or taking some rest.** They even disturbed him greatly at the time of prayer. They also climbed up on his table when he was eating **and disturbed him very much,** so much so that his companions, and he himself, **clearly perceived** it as a temptation of the devil.

One night as blessed Francis was reflecting on all the **afflictions that tormented him,** he was moved by piety for himself. "Lord, " he said to himself, *"make haste to help me* in my illnesses, so that I may be able to bear them patiently."

And **immediately** he was told in spirit: "Tell me, brother, what if, in exchange for your illnesses and troubles, someone were to give you a treasure? And it would be so great and precious that, even if the whole earth were changed to pure *gold,* all *stones* to *precious stones,* and all water to balsam, you would still hold all these things as nothing, compared to **this** great treasure which was given you. Wouldn't you greatly rejoice?"

"Lord," blessed Francis answered, "this treasure would indeed be great, very precious, greatly lovable, and desirable."

And he heard it again saying to him: "Then, brother, be glad and rejoice in your illnesses and troubles, **and,** as of now, you are as secure as if you were already in my kingdom."

The next morning on rising, he said to his companions: "If the emperor were to give a whole kingdom to one of his servants, shouldn't **that servant** greatly rejoice? But, what if **he were to give him** the whole empire, wouldn't he rejoice even more?" And he said to them: "I must rejoice greatly in my illnesses and troubles and be consoled in the Lord, *giving thanks always to God the Father,* to His only Son, *our Lord Jesus Christ,* and to the Holy Spirit for such a great grace bestowed on me **by the Lord, because** He has given me, His unworthy little servant still living in the flesh, the promise of **His** kingdom.

"Therefore for His praise, for our consolation and for the edification of our neighbor, I want to write a new *Praise of the Lord* for His creatures, which we use every day, and without which we cannot live. Through them the human race greatly offends the Creator, and we are **continually** ungrateful for such great graces **and good gifts, not praising** because we do not praise, as we should, our **Lord** the Creator and the Giver of all good."

Ps 71:12

Wis 7:9

Rv 10:8

Eph 5:20

Sitting down, he began to meditate **a short while,** and then he said: "Most High, all-powerful, good Lord." He composed a melody for these words and taught it to his companions so they could recite **and sing** it. For his spirit was then in such sweetness and consolation, that he wanted to send for Brother Pacifico, who in the world was called "The King of Verses," and was a very courtly master of singers. **He wanted** to give him a few good and spiritual brothers who, **together with him,** would go through the world preaching and **singing the** *Praises of the Lord.* C1C

He said that he wanted **that** one **among them** who **best** knew how to preach, to preach first to the people and, after the sermon, **all** were to sing **together** the *Praises of the Lord* as minstrels of the Lord. After the praises, he wanted the preacher to tell the people: "We are minstrels of the Lord, and this is what we want as payment: that you live in true penance." 2C 213

And he said: "What are the servants of God if not His minstrels, who must **lift** people's hearts and **move** them up to spiritual joy?" And he said this especially to the Lesser Brothers, who have been given to the people **of God** for their salvation.

Chapter Nine
THE SPIRIT OF PROPHECY

101
FIRST, HOW HE FORETOLD THAT PEACE WOULD BE RESTORED
BETWEEN THE BISHOP AND THE *PODESTÀ* OF ASSISI
BY THE PRAISE OF THE CREATURES THAT HE HAD COMPOSED
AND HOW HE ORDERED HIS COMPANIONS TO SING IT TO THEM

↓AC 84

After blessed Francis had composed *The Praises* **of the Creatures,** which he called *The Canticle of Brother Sun,* a serious misunderstanding arose between the bishop and the *podestà* of the city of Assisi. **Thus** the bishop excommunicated the *podestà,* and the *podestà* issued an order that no one was to sell **anything** or buy **anything** from the bishop, or to draw up **any** legal document with him.

Although blessed Francis was very ill **when he heard about this,** he was moved by piety for them, especially since there was no one intervening **to make** peace between them. He said to his companions: "It is a great shame for **us,** servants of God, that the bishop and the *podestà* hate one another in this way, and that there is no one intervening for peace and harmony between them."

And so, for that reason, he **immediately composed** one verse for the *Praises,* **and he dictated:**

CtC 10-11

Praised be You, my Lord, through those
who give pardon for Your love
and bear infirmity and tribulation.
Blessed are those who endure in peace
for by You, Most High, they shall be crowned.

Afterwards he called one of his companions and told him: "Go to the *podestà* and, on my behalf, tell him to go to the bishop's residence together with the city's magistrates and bring with him as many others as he can."

And when **the brother** had gone, he said to two of his other companions: "Go and sing the *Canticle of Brother Sun* before the bishop, the *podestà,* and the others who are **with them. And** *I trust in the Lord* that He will **immediately** humble their hearts and they will return to their earlier friendship and love."

Ps 11:1

Therefore, when they had all gathered in the piazza inside the cloister of the bishop's residence, the two brothers rose and one of them said: "In his illness, blessed Francis wrote the *Praises of the Lord* for His creatures, for the praise of His Lord and for the edification of his neighbor. He asks you, then, to listen to them with great devotion." And so, they began to sing and to recite them. And immediately the *podestà* stood up and, folding his arms and hands with the greatest devotion, he listened to them intently, even with many tears, as if to the Gospel of the Lord. For he had a great faith and devotion toward blessed Francis.

When the *Praises of the Lord* were ended, the *podestà* said to everyone: "I tell you the truth, not only do I forgive the lord bishop, whom I want and must have as my lord, but I would even forgive one who

Mt 15:30

killed my brother or my son." And speaking in this way, *he cast himself at the feet* of the bishop and told him: "Look, I am ready to make amends to you for everything, as it pleases you, for the love of our Lord Jesus Christ and of his servant, blessed Francis."

Taking him by the hands, the bishop stood up and said to him: "Because of my office humility is expected of me, but because I am naturally prone to anger, you must forgive me." And so, with great kindness and love they embraced and kissed each other.

The brothers were dumbfounded and overjoyed, seeing that what blessed Francis had foretold about harmony between them had been fulfilled, to the letter. All the others who were present took this for a great miracle, crediting it to the merits of blessed Francis, that the Lord had so swiftly visited them, and that without recalling anything that had been said, they returned to such harmony from such dissension and scandal.

Therefore we who were with blessed Francis bear witness that always whenever he would predict "such and such a thing is or will be this way," it always happened to the letter. We have seen so many and such marvelous things that would be too long to write down or recount.

102

HOW HE FORETOLD THE FATE OF A BROTHER
WHO DID NOT WANT TO GO TO CONFESSION
UNDER THE PRETEXT OF OBSERVING SILENCE

There was a brother outwardly of a decent and holy way of living, who day and night seemed concerned with prayer. He observed constant silence so that when he went to confession to a brother priest, he confessed only with signs, not with words. He appeared so devout and fervent in the love of God, that sometimes when sitting with the

↓AC 116//2C 2

brothers, although he **marvelously** did not speak, he rejoiced internally and externally on hearing some good words so that he **often** moved to devotion the **other** brothers who saw him.

After he had been living this way for several years, it happened that blessed Francis came to that place where **he was staying.** When he heard the brothers tell him about this brother's way of life, he said: *"Know for a truth* that this is diabolical temptation and deception, because he does not want to confess."

In the meantime the minister general came there to visit blessed Francis and began to praise this brother in front of blessed Francis. "Believe me, brother," blessed Francis told him, "this brother is led and deceived by an evil spirit."

The general minister **said:** "I find it amazing and almost unbelievable that this can be about a man who **possesses** so many signs and works of holiness."

"Test him then," blessed Francis replied. "Tell him to go to confession twice or even once a week. If he does not listen to you, *you will know what I told you is true."*

Therefore, the general minister told that brother: "Brother, I want you to confess twice or at least once a week."

He, **however,** put a finger on his lips and shook his head, showing by signs that he would in no way do this **because of his love for silence.** The minister, however, fearing that he would scandalize him, let him go. *Not many days afterward,* **that brother** left the **Order** of his own will, and returned to the world wearing secular clothing.

One day while two companions of blessed Francis were walking along some road, they met him. He was walking alone like a very poor pilgrim. Feeling compassion for him, they said: "You wretch, where is your holy and upright life? You used to love the solitary life so much that you did not want to show yourself to your brothers nor speak to them. And now you go wandering through the world like a man who *does not know God."*

He began to speak to them, often swearing on his faith like secular people.

"Wretched man," the brothers told him, "why do you swear on your faith like secular people, you who abstained not only from idle words, but from even good ones."

They left him. And a **little** later, he died.

And we were greatly amazed, **seeing how in this way it was true to the letter,** as blessed Francis had predicted **about him,** at a time when **that wretch** was considered a saint by the brothers.

103
THAT MAN WHO WEPT IN FRONT OF BLESSED FRANCIS
TO BE ADMITTED TO THE ORDER

At a time when no one was received into **the Order** without the permission of blessed Francis, the son of a nobleman from Lucca, together with **many** others who wished to enter **the Order,** came to see blessed Francis. At the time he was sick and was staying at the palace of the bishop of Assisi. When the brothers presented **all of** them to blessed Francis, the son of the nobleman bowed before **him** and began to cry aloud, begging to be received.

Looking at him, Blessed Francis said: "O wretched and fleshly man! *Why are you lying to the Holy Spirit* and to me? You **wail** in the flesh and not in the spirit!"

After he said these things, his relatives suddenly arrived outside the palace on horseback, wanting to seize him and take him **away. Hearing** the clatter of horses, he looked out the window and saw his relatives. He immediately got up, and went down to them. He returned to the world with them, just as blessed Francis had **fore-seen.**

↓AC 70//2C 4

Acts 5:3

104
A PRIEST'S VINEYARD THAT WAS DESPOILED OF GRAPES
BECAUSE OF BLESSED FRANCIS

Because of the disease of his eyes, blessed Francis was staying with a **little,** poor priest in the church of San Fabiano near the city **of Rieti.** The Lord Pope Honorius, **together with his whole court,** was also staying in the city **at that time. Many of** the cardinals and other great clerics, because of the devotion they had for **him,** used to visit **blessed Francis** almost every day.

That church had a small vineyard next to the house where blessed Francis was staying. There was a door **in that** house through which nearly all those who visited him passed. Since the grapes were ripe **then,** and the place was **very** pleasant, the entire vineyard was ruined **and almost stripped of its grapes.**

The priest began to be offended and upset, saying: "Even though it's small, I **nevertheless** got enough wine from **the vineyard,** that I had enough wine to take care of my needs! **And this year I lost it!"**

When blessed Francis heard of this he had him called and said to him: "**My lord,** do not be disturbed any longer. We can't do anything about it **now.** *trust in the Lord,* because for me, His little servant, He

↓AC 67

But Ps 11:1

can restore your loss **completely.** Tell me, how many measures **of wine** did you get when your vineyard was at its best?"

"Thirteen measures, father," the priest responded.

"Do not be sad over this any more," blessed Francis told him, "and do not say anything offensive to anyone because of **this.** Trust the Lord and my words, and if you get less than twenty measures of wine, I will make it up to you."

From then on, the priest calmed down and kept quiet. And, by divine dispensation, he obtained **at the time of vintage** twenty mea-sures **of wine from that vineyard** and no less. Those who heard about it, as well as the priest himself, were amazed, **realizing that even** if it had been full of grapes, **it would be** impossible **for it to produce** twenty measures **of wine.**

We who were with him bear witness **about this and about every-thing he foretold,** that it always happened **exactly according to his word.**

105

HOW THE KNIGHTS OF PERUGIA INTERFERED WITH HIS PREACHING

↓AC 75//2C 37

When blessed Francis was preaching in the piazza at Perugia to a large crowd gathered there, all of a sudden some knights of Perugia began racing their horses around the piazza, jousting with their weapons, and thus disturbing the preaching. Although **those who were there protested, they still did not stop.** Blessed Francis turned to them **therefore,** and, with a fiery spirit, said: "Listen and under-stand what the Lord is telling you through me, His **little** servant, and don't say, 'This one is from Assisi!' " He said this because **there was and is** a long-standing enmity between the people of Perugia and those of Assisi.[a]

"The Lord has exalted you above all your neighbors," he said.   Ps 26:5 "Because of this, you must acknowledge your Creator all the more, and humble yourselves not only before God but also before your neighbors. But *your heart is puffed-up by arrogance* and you attack your   Dt 17:20; Ez 28:2, 5 neighbors and have killed many of them. Because of this I tell you, unless you quickly turn to **God** and compensate those whom you have injured, the Lord, who *leaves nothing unavenged,* to your greater   Jb 24:12

---

a. Civil strife erupted in Perugia in 1214 and flared up again in 1217. In this instance, however, Assisi took advantage of Perugia's internal weakness in order to claim the road from Assisi to Perugia by occupying the castle of Postignano. In 1222, another outbreak of civil strife divided Perugia and, once again, Assisi took advantage by moving against the commune of Bettona. Thus Francis would be looked down upon by the knights of Perugia, hostile to Assisians. Cf. Arnaldo Fortini, *Francis of Assisi*, translated by Helen Moak (New York: Crossroad, 1981), 569-574.

punishment and disgrace, will cause you to rise up against each other. You will be torn apart by sedition and civil war, suffering by far a greater calamity than your neighbors could ever inflict on you."

As a matter of fact, when he preached blessed Francis was never silent about people's vices, but rebuked all publicly and boldly. The Lord had given him such grace, that everyone who saw or heard him, no matter of what rank or condition, feared and revered him because he had such an abundance of grace from God. As a result, no matter how much he reprimanded them, they were always edified by his words and they would either turn to the Lord or would repent inwardly.

A few days later, by divine consent, a scandal broke out between the knights and the people. The people drove the knights out of the city. The knights, supported by the Church, destroyed many of their fields, vineyards and trees, doing as much harm to them as they could. The people likewise destroyed all the property of the knights. And so, according to the word of Saint Francis, the people and the knights were punished.

106
HOW HE FORESAW A BROTHER'S SECRET TEMPTATION AND AFFLICTION

There was a certain brother, a very spiritual man, who was close to blessed Francis, and who for many days suffered the most severe suggestions of the devil, so that he was almost cast into the depths of despair. He was tormented daily so much that he was ashamed to confess so frequently. And, because of this, he afflicted himself with fasting, with vigils, with tears, and with beatings. [↓AC 55//2C 124]

It happened by divine guidance that blessed Francis came to that place. One day that brother was walking with blessed Francis who, through the Holy Spirit, knew his difficulties and temptation. As he withdrew a short distance from the other brother who was walking with him, he walked with the one being tempted. And he said to him: "My dearest brother, from now on I want you not to be bound to confess these suggestions of the devil. Don't be afraid, because they have not harmed your soul. But, I give you my permission just to say seven *Our Father's* as often as you are troubled by these."

And that brother was exceedingly overjoyed at what he said to him, that he was not bound to confess those things, since he was very worried about this. Nevertheless, he was greatly amazed that blessed Francis knew about this since only the priests to whom he had confessed knew.

And, through the grace of God and the merits of blessed Francis, he was immediately freed from that great trial. From then on, he lived in the greatest serenity and peace. And because the saint was hoping for this, he therefore excused him confidently from confession.

107

PREDICTIONS HE MADE CONCERNING BROTHER BERNARD AND HOW THESE WERE ALL FULFILLED

C 12//1MP 17   Around the time of his death, a certain savory confection had been prepared for him,[a] and he remembered Bernard, who was the first brother he had. "Brother Bernard likes this confection," he said to his companions. He immediately had him called to himself.

When he arrived he sat next to the bed where the saint was lying, Brother Bernard said: "Father! I beg you, bless me and show me your love. I believe that, if you show me your fatherly affection, God Himself and all the brothers will love me more."

Blessed Francis was not able to see him, because many days earlier he had lost his sight. *Extending his right* hand, he placed it on the head of Brother Giles, the third brother. He thought he was placing it on the head of Brother Bernard who was sitting next to him and, immediately becoming aware of this through the Holy Spirit, he said, "This is not the head of my Brother Bernard."[b]   Gn 48:14

Brother Bernard then immediately drew closer to him. Blessed Francis, placing his hand on his head, blessed him. "Write what I tell you," he then said to one of his companions. "Brother Bernard was the first brother the Lord gave me. He began first and most perfectly fulfilled the perfection of the holy Gospel, distributing *all his goods to*   Mt 19:21; 25:4 *the poor.* Because of this and his many other prerogatives, I am bound to love him more than any other brother in the whole Order. As much as I am able, it is my will and command that whoever becomes general minister should love and honor him as he would me. Let the other provincial ministers and all the brothers of the whole religion hold him in my place."[c] Because of this, Brother Bernard and the other brothers were greatly consoled.

---

a. The editor omits any mention of Lady Jacoba as the one preparing this "savory confection," as found in AC 12.

b. Cf. FA:ED II 126b.

c. In his critical edition of the works of Saint Francis, *Die Opuscula des hl. Franziskus von Assisi: Textkritsche Edition.* Spicilegium Bonaventurianum, 13, (Grottaferrata, Rome: Collegium S. Bonaventurae Ad Claras Aquas, 1976), 176. Kajetan Esser placed this passage among the "Dictates."

Considering the **outstanding** perfection of Brother Bernard, blessed Francis prophesied about him in the presence of some of the brothers: "I tell you, some of the greatest and most cunning devils have been sent to test Brother Bernard. They will send him many trials and temptations. The merciful Lord, however, will deliver him toward the end of his life from all troubles and temptations. And He will place his spirit and body in such peace and consolation that all the brothers who see this will be **greatly** astonished, and consider it a great miracle. In **this** quiet and consolation of both body and soul **he will go** to the Lord."

2C 48

Afterwards, all these things were fulfilled to the letter **in Brother Bernard, not without all the brothers' greatest admiration.** All the brothers who heard about these things from blessed Francis were astonished. In his last illness Brother Bernard was in such great peace and **consolation** of spirit that he did not want to lie down. And if he lay down, he lay in a sitting position so that not even the lightest mist would reach his head, **which could disturb his meditations** on God **through** dreams or **other** fantasies. And if this **would** occasionally **occur,** he would immediately get up and strike himself, saying "What was that? Why was I thinking that way?" **He did not want to take any medicine, but** would say to anyone offering it: "Don't distract me."

In order to die more freely, peacefully, and quietly, he expropriated himself of care for his body, putting himself in the hands of one of the brothers who was a doctor telling him. "I do not wish to be concerned about eating or drinking," he would say, "but I entrust myself to you. If you give me something, I'll take it. If you don't, **I will not ask for it."**

When he began to grow weaker, he wanted to have a priest brother with him at all times, until the hour of his death. Whenever any thought entered his mind for which his conscience **reproved** him, he immediately confessed it.

After his death, he became white and his flesh soft, and he seemed to be almost smiling. Thus he was more handsome **dead than alive,** and **everyone** delighted more at seeing him dead in this way than alive; **for** the saint **truly** seemed **to be smiling.**

108
HOW SHORTLY BEFORE HIS DEATH, HE NOTIFIED BLESSED CLARE
THAT SHE WOULD SEE HIM
AND HOW THIS WAS FULFILLED AFTER HIS DEATH

C 13//1MP 18

During that week in which blessed Francis died, Lady Clare, the first plant of the Poor Sisters of San Damiano in Assisi, the **outstanding** emulator of blessed Francis in observing **gospel perfection,**[f] feared she would die before him, **for they were both very ill at the time.** She wept bitterly and could not be comforted, because **she thought** she would not be able to see before her death her only father after God, that is, blessed Francis, her comforter **and teacher,** and her first founder in God's grace.

She sent word of this to blessed Francis through one of the brothers. Hearing this, **the saint** was moved to piety **for her,** because he loved her **singularly** with fatherly affection. Realizing, however, that what **she wanted, that is, to see him,** could not be done, he wrote his blessing in a letter **to console her and her sisters** and also absolved her from any failings **against his admonitions and against** the commands **and counsel** of the Son of God. Moreover, so that she would put aside all her grief, he was guided by the **Holy** Spirit to say to the brother she had sent, "Go **and tell** Lady Clare to put aside all her grief and sorrow over not being able to see me now. Let her be assured that before her death, both she and her sisters will see me and, because of me, **they will be greatly consoled."**

Soon afterwards blessed Francis passed away during the night. In the morning, all the people of the city of Assisi, with all the clergy, **came and** took **his** holy body from the place where he had died. With hymns and praises, carrying tree branches, they carried him in this way to San Damiano at the Lord's will, *in order to fulfill that word* which the Lord **had spoken** through **blessed Francis** to console His daughters and servants.

1 Kgs 2:27; Jn 18:9

The iron grille was removed through which the servants of Christ usually receive communion and hear the word of God. The brothers lifted his holy body from the **bier** and, raising him in their arms, they held him in front of the window for **a long time.** By then Lady Clare and her sisters had received the greatest consolation from him, although they wept profusely and were afflicted with great grief,

---

f. 2MP 108 changes AC 13 from *in conservando semper paupertatem filii Dei* [in observing always the poverty of the Son of God] to *in conservanda perfectione evangelica* [gospel perfection]. At first the change seems insignificant; however it suggests that the profound Christological dimension of Clare's following of Gospel poverty—as that of Francis—is diminished.

seeing themselves deprived of the consolation and counsel of such a father.

109
HOW HE FORETOLD THAT HIS REMAINS WOULD BE HONORED AFTER HIS DEATH

One day when blessed Francis lay sick in the **residence** of the bishop of Assisi,[a] **a spiritual brother,** smiling and playfully, said to him: "You will sell all your sackcloth to the Lord for a good price! Many canopies and silk coverings will hang over this **little** body of yours that is now clothed in sackcloth." At the time he wore a cap covered with sackcloth as well as a tunic of sackcloth. With great fervor of spirit and joy blessed Francis—not himself, but *the Holy Spirit through him*—answered: "You're right because that's how it will be **for the praise and glory of my Lord.**"

↓AC 4//1MP

Acts 1:16; 28:25

---

a. FA:ED II 119 b.

Chapter Ten
DIVINE PROVIDENCE FOR HIM IN EXTERNALS

110
FIRST, HOW THE LORD PROVIDED FOR THE BROTHERS
SITTING AT A POORLY PREPARED TABLE
WITH A DOCTOR

↓AC 68//2C 44   When blessed Francis was in the hermitage of the brothers at Fonte Colombo near Rieti because of the disease of his eyes, one day the eye doctor^c visited **him. After staying there** for some **time** and **by now** ready to leave, blessed Francis said to one of his companions: "Go and give the doctor the best **to eat.**" "Father," his companion answered, "we're ashamed to say that, because we're so poor **now** we'd be ashamed to invite him to eat." Blessed Francis told his companions: *"O you of little faith!* Don't make me tell you again!"   Mt 14:31

The doctor said to blessed Francis and his companions: "Brother, it is because the brothers are so poor that I am happy to eat with them." **For** the doctor was **very** rich and, although blessed Francis and his companions had often invited him, he **never wanted** to eat there.

The brothers went and set the table. With embarrassment, they placed the little bread and wine they had as well as the few greens they had prepared for themselves.

When they had sat down at the **little poor** table and **were beginning to eat,** there was a knock on the door of the **place.** One of the brothers **rose,** went, and opened the door. And there was a woman with a large basket filled with beautiful bread, fish, crab-cakes, honey, and freshly picked grapes, which had been sent to brother Francis by a lady of a town about seven miles away.

When they all saw this, the brothers and the doctor were greatly amazed **and greatly overjoyed.** Realizing the holiness of blessed Francis, **and attributing the whole incident to his merits,** the doctor told them, "My brothers, neither you nor we sufficiently recognize the holiness of this **man.**"

---

c. Cf. FA:ED II 171 a.

111
THE FISH HE CRAVED IN HIS ILLNESS

Another time, **when he was very sick** in the palace **of the bishop**   ↓AC 71
of Assisi, the brothers begged him to eat. He answered: "I don't have
the wish to eat; but if I had a bit of that fish **called** *squalo,* perhaps I
would eat some."

After he said this, someone **came** carrying a basket in which there
were three large and well prepared *squali*[a] and crab-cakes **that** the
holy father gladly ate. These were sent to him by Brother Gerardo,
the minister at Rieti.

Marveling **at divine providence,** the brothers praised the Lord
who **had provided these things** for his servant, because it was winter and such things were impossible **to obtain in Assisi.**

112
THE FOOD AND BREAD HE CRAVED AT HIS DEATH

When he was at the place of Saint Mary of the Angels, sick with   ↓AC 8//BPr VII
2 Kgs 13:4   **his final** *illness that brought about his death,* one day he called his com-   //1MP 11
panions **and said:** "You know **how** faithful and devoted Lady Jacoba
dei Settesoli **was and** is to me and to our religion. **And therefore** I
believe she would consider it a great favor and consolation if you
notified her about my condition. Above all, tell her to send **me** some
cloth for a tunic, the cloth the color of ashes. **With this cloth** have her
also send some of that confection which she often made for me in the
City." This confection, made of almonds, sugar or honey, and other
things, the Romans call *mostacciolo.*

That **very** spiritual **lady** was a widow. She belonged to one of the
more noble and wealthy families **in all of Rome.**[b] Through the merits
and words of blessed Francis she had obtained such grace from God
that she seemed like another Magdalene, always full of tears and
devotion, moved by the love **and sweetness of Christ.**

They wrote a letter then, as dictated by **the saint.** While one
brother **went looking** for another brother to deliver the letter **to the
lady,** there was **suddenly** a knock **at the gate of the place.**

When one of the brothers opened the gate, he saw Lady Jacoba
who had come in **great** haste to visit blessed Francis. **When he**

---

a. A *squalo* may be any small shark of the genus *Squalus,* often the Picked Dogfish, *Squalis acanthius,*
   found today in the Mediterranean Sea. Cf. Giorgio Bibi, *Atlante dei Pesci delle Coste Italiane:
   Leptocardi-Ciclostomi-Selaci.* (Rome: Mondo Sommerso Editrice, 1967).
b. Background information on Jacoba (or Giacoma) dei Settesoli can be found in FA:ED II 122 b.

recognized her, one of the brothers quickly went to blessed Francis, and with great joy told him how Lady Jacoba came from Rome to visit him with her son and many other people. "What shall we do, Father?" he said. "Shall we allow her to enter and come in here?" He said this because Saint Francis had ordered that in that place no women enter that cloister out of great respect and devotion. Blessed Francis answered him: "This command need not be observed in the case of this lady whose faith and devotion made her come here from so far away." This Lady thus came in to see blessed Francis, crying many tears in his presence.

It was certainly amazing: she brought with her shroud-cloth, that is, a gray-colored cloth, for a tunic, and all the other things that were requested in the letter, as if she had received the letter.

"My brothers, while I was praying," Lady Jacoba told the brothers, "a voice within me said, 'Go, visit your father, blessed Francis, without delay, and hurry, because if you delay long you will not find him alive. Moreover, bring with you such-and-such cloth for his tunic, as well as the ingredients for making that particular confection. Take with you also a great quantity of wax for the lamps and also incense.' " All these things, except the incense, were mentioned in the letter that was to be sent. Thus, He Who inspired the Kings to travel with gifts to honor the child, His Son, in the days of His birth, in the same way inspired this noble and holy lady to travel with gifts to honor His most beloved servant in the days of his death, or, rather, of his true birth.

That lady, therefore, made that confection the holy father longed to eat. He ate only a little of it, because he was continually becoming weaker as he was near death.

She also had many candles made which would burn around his most holy body after his death. From the cloth she had brought, the brothers made him the tunic in which he was buried. He himself ordered the brothers to sew pieces of sackcloth on the outside of it as a sign and example of most holy humility and Lady Poverty. And during the same week that Lady Jacoba arrived, our most holy father passed to the Lord.

Chapter Eleven
His love for creatures
and creatures' love for him

113
First, the love he had especially for birds
which are called hooded larks
because they symbolize a good religious

Completely absorbed in the love of God, blessed Francis perfectly discerned the goodness of God not only in his own soul, already adorned in the perfection of every virtue, but also in any creature whatever. Because of this, by a singular and profound love, he was moved toward creatures, especially to those in which something of God or something pertaining to religion was symbolized.

Of all the birds, he particularly loved a little bird called the lark, commonly called the cowled lark.[a] Concerning these, he used to say: "Sister Lark has a capuche like religious, and is a humble bird, because she gladly goes along the road looking for some grain. Even if she finds it in manure, she pecks it out and eats it. While flying, she praises the Lord very sweetly, like good religious looking down on earthly things, whose *way of life is* always *in heaven* and intention is always for the praise of God. Her clothes, that is, her feathers, resemble the earth and give an example to religious not to wear colorful and refined clothing, but those of a cheaper price and color, just as the earth is of little worth compared to the other elements."

And because he considered these things in them, he was very glad to see them. Therefore it pleased the Lord that these little birds should show some signs of affection for him at the hour of his death. For on the Saturday evening after vespers, before the night on which he passed to the Lord, a great flock of these birds called larks came over the roof of the house where he lay, and flying low and

↓AC 14

Phil 3:20

---

a. Several different larks, members of the genus *Alaudidae*, are found today on the Italian peninsula. All may be described as melodious; none is especially "hooded" or "cowled." If this reference is to a lark, the European Skylark may be intended. Other hooded birds are either not found in Italy or do not produce a melodious song. A lark-like bird that produces a melodious song, carries a distinct cap or hood, and is found in large numbers in Italy is the Blackcap warbler, *Sylvia atricapilla*, and may be the bird described in this passage. Cf. Augusto Toschi, *Avifauna Italiana*, vol. III, (Florence: Olimpia, 1986), 1095-1100.

wheeling in a circle **around the roof** and singing **sweetly, they seemed to praise the Lord.**

114
How he wanted to persuade the emperor to enact a special law that on Christmas day people provide generously for birds, cattle, asses, and the poor

↓AC 14//2C 200
//1MP 19

We, who were with blessed Francis, and who wrote these things about him, bear witness that we often heard **him** say: "If I ever speak to the emperor, I will beg **and persuade him,** for the love of God and **of me,** to enact a **special law** forbidding anyone to catch **or kill** our sister larks or do **them** any harm. Likewise, all mayors of cities and lords of castles and villages should be bound to oblige people **each** year on **the day of** the Nativity of the Lord to scatter wheat and other grain along the roads outside towns **and villages,** so that our sister larks and other birds may have something to eat on such a solemn feast.

"Also, out of reverence for the Son of God whom **the most blessed** Virgin **Mary** on that night *laid in a manger* between an ox and ass, I would add that **whoever has an ox and an ass be bound** on that night **to provide them** a generous portion of **the best** fodder. Likewise, **on that day,** all the poor should be fed **good food** by the rich." Lk 2:7

For blessed Francis held the Nativity of the Lord in greater reverence than any other of the Lord's solemnities, **saying: "After the** Lord *was born to us,* it was certain that we would be saved." On that day, he wanted every Christian to rejoice in the Lord, and, for love of Him *Who* gave *Himself to us,* wished everyone **to provide** generously **not only** to the poor but also to the animals and birds. Is 9:5; Lk 2:11 Ti 2:14

115
The love and obedience of fire toward him when he was cauterized

Ordered by obedience by the Lord of Ostia and by Brother Elias, the general minister, he came to the hermitage of Fonte Colombo near Rieti to undergo a cure for his eyes. One day a doctor came to see him.

↓AC 86

Considering the condition of his disease, he told blessed Francis that he wanted to cauterize from the jaw to the eyebrow of the weaker eye.[a] Blessed Francis, however, did not wish the treatment to

---

a. Cf. FA:ED II 189 a.

begin until Brother Elias arrived, since he had expressed a desire to be there when the doctor would begin the procedure for that cure. And feeling disturbed and upset to experience so much solicitude about himself, he consequently wanted the general minister to oversee everything.

He therefore waited for him, and he did not come because, on account of many engagements he had, he could not come. And so blessed Francis finally permitted the doctor to do what he wanted. When the iron had been placed in the fire to make the cautery, wanting to comfort his spirit so it would not become afraid, blessed Francis spoke in this way to the fire: "My Brother Fire, noble and useful among all the creatures the Most High created, be courtly to me in this hour. For a long time I have loved you and I still love you for the love of that Lord who created you. I pray our Creator who made us, to temper your heat now, so that I may bear it." And as he finished the prayer, he made the sign of the cross over the fire.

Then we who were with him, overcome out of piety and compassion for him, all ran away, and he remained alone with the doctor. However, when the cauterization was finished, we returned to him. "You, faint-hearted, *of little faith,*" he said to us, "why did you run away? I tell you the truth: I did not feel any pain or even heat from the fire. In fact, if it's not well cooked, cook it some more!"

Mt 8:26

The doctor was greatly amazed and said: "My brothers, I tell you, and I speak from experience: I doubt that any very strong man with a healthy body could bear such a severe burn, much less this man, who is weak and sick. But he did not flinch nor show the slightest sign of pain."

It was necessary to cauterize all the veins, extending from the ear to the eyebrow, but it did not help him at all. Similarly, another doctor pierced both his ears with a red hot iron, but it did not help him at all.

It is not surprising that fire and other creatures obeyed and showed him reverence because, as we who were with him very often saw, how much he loved them, and how much delight he took in them. His spirit was moved to so much piety and compassion toward them that he did not want to see when someone did not treat them decently. He used to speak with them with joy, inside and out, as if they were rational creatures, on which occasions he was frequently rapt in God.

116
HOW HE DID NOT WANT TO EXTINGUISH A FIRE,
OR ALLOW IT TO BE EXTINGUISHED,
THAT WAS BURNING HIS BREECHES

Among all the lesser and inanimate creatures, he loved fire with singular affection because of its beauty and usefulness. That is why he never wanted to impede its function.

↓AC 86

Once when **he was sitting** close to a fire, without being aware of it, his linen pants **or breeches** next **to the knee** caught fire. Although he felt the heat of the fire, **he did not want to extinguish it.** His companion, **however, seeing** that the fire was burning his pants, ran **to him,** wanting to put out the fire. Blessed Francis **prohibited** him saying: "No, dearest brother, do not hurt Brother Fire." And **thus, in no way did he want** him to extinguish it.

So the brother **quickly** ran to the brother who was his guardian, and brought him to blessed Francis. **At once, contrary to the will of blessed Francis,** he began to extinguish **the fire. Because of this, however urgent the need, he never wanted** to extinguish a fire, a lamp, or a candle, moved as he was with such piety for it.

He also did not want a brother to throw fire or smoldering wood **from one place to another,** as is usually done, but wanted him simply to place it on the ground, out of reverence for Him who created it.

117
HOW HE DID NOT WANT TO USE A PELT
BECAUSE HE DID NOT ALLOW IT TO BE BURNED BY FIRE

↓AC 87

While he was keeping a lent on Mount La Verna, his companion **built** a fire at mealtime one day in the cell where he ate. Once the fire was lit, he went for blessed Francis **to another cell** where he usually prayed, **carrying with him a missal in order** to read to him the Gospel of the day. Whenever **he** was unable to hear Mass, he always wanted to hear the Gospel that **was read** on that day, before he would eat.

When blessed Francis **came to eat in the cell** where the fire was lit, the flames **had already reached the roof of the cell** and were burning it. His companion tried his best to extinguish **the fire** but could not do it by himself. But blessed Francis did not want to help him: he took the hide that he used to cover himself at night, and went into the forest **with it.**

The brothers of the place, **who** stayed some distance from **this** cell, seeing that the cell **was burning, immediately** came and extinguished **the fire.** Afterwards, blessed Francis returned to eat. After the meal, he said to his companion: "From now on, I don't want this hide over me since, because of my avarice, I did not want Brother Fire to consume it."

118
THE EXCEPTIONAL LOVE HE HAD FOR WATER, STONES, WOOD AND FLOWERS

Next to fire he had a singular love for water through which holy penance and tribulation is symbolized and by which the filth of the soul is washed clean and because of which the first cleansing of the soul takes place through the waters of Baptism.

Because of this, when he washed his hands, he chose a place where **the water that fell to the ground** would not be trampled underfoot. Whenever he had to walk over rocks, he would walk with **great** fear and reverence out of love for Him who is called "the rock."

↓AC 88//2C 16

2 Sm 22:2;
Ps 18:3; 31:4; 94:22
Ps 61:3

Whenever he recited the verse of the psalm, *"You have set me high upon the rock,"* he would say, out of great reverence and devotion: "You have set me high at the foot of the rock."

He also told the brother who cut **and prepared** the wood for the fire **never** to cut down the whole tree, but to cut **the tree in such a way** that one part **always** remained **intact out of love for Him Who willed to accomplish our salvation on the wood of the cross.**

In the same way he used to tell the brother who took care of the garden not to cultivate all the ground in the garden for vegetables, but to leave a piece of ground that would produce wild plants. Thus, in their season, they would produce "Brother Flowers" **out of love of Him Who is called** *"the flower of the field" and "the lily of the valley."*

Sg 2:1

Moreover, he used to tell the brother gardener that he should **always** make a beautiful flower bed in some part of the garden, planting and cultivating every variety of fragrant plants and those producing beautiful flowers. Thus, in their time they would invite all who saw **those herbs and those** flowers to the praise of God. For every creature says and exclaims: "God made me for you, O mortal!"

We who were with him saw him rejoice so much, inwardly and outwardly, in all creatures, **that** touching and looking at them, his spirit seemed no longer on earth but in heaven. And because of the many consolations he had and continued to have in creatures, shortly before his death, he composed the *Praises of the Lord* in His creatures to move the hearts of his listeners to the praise of God, and so that in His creatures the Lord might be praised by everyone.

119
How he praised the sun and fire over other creatures

↓AC 83

More than all creatures lacking reason, he most affectionately loved the sun and fire. For he used to say: "At dawn, when the sun rises, everyone should praise God, who created it **for our use**, because through it **our** eyes are lighted by day. And in the evening, when it becomes night, everyone should praise God for another creature, Brother Fire through **whom** the eyes are lighted at night. For we are all almost blind, and the Lord lights up our eyes through these two **brothers of ours. And, therefore,** we should always give **special** praise to the glorious Creator for these and for His other creatures which we use every day."

He **always** did this until the day of his death. Indeed, when his illness grew more serious, he himself began to **sing** the *Praises of the Lord* that he **had composed about creatures,** and afterwards had his companions sing it, so that in reflecting on the praise of the Lord, he could forget the sharpness **of his** pains and illnesses.

And because he considered and said that the sun is more beautiful than other creatures, and could more easily be compared to God, especially since, in Scripture, the Lord Himself is called *the sun of justice;* he therefore called those *Praises* he composed for creatures when the Lord had assured him of His kingdom the *"Canticle of Brother Sun."*

Mal 3:20

120
This is the praise of creatures he composed when the Lord assured him of His kingdom

CtC 1-14

Most High, all-powerful, good Lord,
> yours are *the praises, the glory,* and *the honor,* and all *blessing.*

Rv 4:9, 11

To You alone, Most High, do they belong,
> and no human is worthy to mention Your name.

Praised be You, my *Lord,* with all *Your creatures,*
> especially Sir Brother Sun,
> who is the day and through whom You give us light.

Tb 8:7

And he is beautiful and radiant with great splendor;
> and bears a likeness of You, Most High One.

Praised be You, my Lord, through Sister *Moon* and the *stars,*
> in heaven You formed them clear and precious and beautiful.

Ps 148:3

Praised be You, my Lord, through Brother Wind,
    and through the air, cloudy and serene, and every kind of weather,
    through whom You give sustenance to Your creatures.

Ps 148:4, 5 *Praised* be You, my Lord, through Sister *Water,*
    who is very useful and humble and precious and chaste.

Dn 3:66 *Praised* be You, my Lord, through Brother *Fire,*
Ps 78:14   through whom *You light the night,*
    and he is beautiful and playful and robust and strong.

Dn 3:74 *Praised* be You, my Lord, through our Sister Mother *Earth,*
    who sustains and governs us,
Ps 104:13-14   and who produces various *fruit* with colored flowers and *herbs.*

Praised be You, my Lord, through those
    who give pardon for Your love,
    and bear infirmity and tribulation.
    Blessed are those who endure in peace
    for by You, Most High, shall they be crowned.

Praised be You, my Lord, through our Sister Bodily Death,
    from whom no one living can escape.
    Woe to those who die in mortal sin.
    Blessed are those whom death will find in Your most holy will,
Rv 2:11; 20:6   for the *second death* shall do them no harm.

Dn 3:85 *Praise* and bless my *Lord* and give Him thanks
    and serve Him with great humility.

Chapter Twelve
His death:
THE JOY HE SHOWED WHEN HE KNEW FOR CERTAIN
THAT HIS DEATH WAS AT HAND

121
FIRST, HOW HE ANSWERED BROTHER ELIAS
WHO REPROVED HIM FOR SHOWING SO MUCH JOY

AC 99//1MP 4

When blessed Francis lay ill in the palace of the bishop of Assisi and *the hand of the Lord* seemed to be *weighing down* on him more than ever before, the people of Assisi, fearing that should the saint die during the night, the brothers would secretly take his holy body away and **carry** it **to** another city, placed a vigilant guard each night around the palace's walls. 1 Sm 5:6

For the consolation of his spirit, **that most holy father** often had his companions sing the *Praises of the Lord* during the day, lest he lose heart **because of the severity of his pains which tormented him unceasingly.** He likewise had the *Praises* sung during the night for the edification **and solace** of those **seculars** who kept watch outside the palace because of him.

Brother Elias, seeing how blessed Francis was so comforting himself and rejoicing in the Lord in such **illness,** said to him: "Dearest brother, I am **greatly** consoled and edified by all the joy which you show for yourself and your companions in such infirmity. Although the people of this city venerate you as a saint, nevertheless, because they firmly believe that you are near death due to your incurable sickness, upon hearing praises of this sort being sung **day and night,** they can say to themselves: 'How can he show such joy when he is so near death? He should be thinking about death.'"

"Do you remember," blessed Francis said to him, "when you saw the vision at Foligno and told me that it told you that I would live for only two years? Before you saw that vision, through the grace of **God,** who suggests every good in the heart, and places it on the lips of his faithful, I often considered day and night my end. But from the time you saw that vision, each day I have been even more zealous reflecting on the day of my death."

He **immediately** continued with great intensity of spirit: "Allow me *to rejoice in the Lord,* Brother, and to sing His praises *in my infirmities,* because, by the grace of the Holy Spirit, I am so closely united 2 Cor 12:9

369

and joined with my Lord, that, through His mercy, I can well rejoice in the Most High Himself."

122
HOW HE PERSUADED A DOCTOR TO TELL HIM HOW LONG HE HAD TO LIVE

During those days, a doctor from the city of Arezzo, named Good John, who was **very** familiar to blessed Francis, came to visit him in the bishop's palace. Blessed Francis asked **him** saying: "How does my illness of dropsy seem to you, Brother John?" **He did not want to call him by his** proper name **because he never** addressed anyone called "Good," out of reverence for the Lord, who said: *No one is good but God alone.* Likewise, he did not want to call anyone "father" or "master," nor write them in letters, out of reverence for the Lord, who said: *Call no one on earth your father nor be called masters,* etc.

The doctor said **to him:** "Brother, by the grace of the Lord, it will be well with you."

Again blessed Francis said to him: "Tell me the truth. How does it look to you? Do not be afraid, for, by the grace of God, I am not a coward who fears death. **For,** with the grace **and help of the Holy Spirit,** I am so united and joined with my Lord that I am equally as happy to die as I am to live."

The doctor then told him frankly: "According to our assessment, your illness is incurable and **I believe that** you will die either at the end of September or on the fourth day before the Nones of October.[a] **Then** Blessed Francis, lying on his bed sick, with the greatest devotion and reverence **stretched out his hands** to the Lord and, with great joy **of mind and body,** said: "Welcome, my Sister Death!"

123
HOW, AS SOON AS HE HEARD THAT DEATH WAS IMMINENT,
HE HAD THE PRAISES THAT HE COMPOSED, SUNG

After this a brother said **to him:** "Father, your life and manner of living **have been** and are a light and a mirror not only for your brothers but also for the entire Church, and your death will be the same. Although for the brothers and **many** others your death will be **reason for** great grief and sorrow, for you it will rather be a consolation and an infinite joy. You will pass from great toil to the greatest rest, from many sorrows and temptations **to eternal peace,** from the **earthly**

Lk 18:19

Mt 23:9-10

↓AC 100//1MP

↓AC 7

---

a. For an understanding of the "fourth day before the Nones of October," see FA:ED I 258 c.

poverty, that you always loved and **perfectly served,** to true and infinite riches, from **this** death in time to **everlasting** life. There you will forever *behold face to face* the Lord your *God* whom you have **loved** in this world with so much desire and love."

Gn 32:30

After saying these things he said to him openly: "Father, you should know the truth: unless the Lord sends his own remedy from heaven to your body, your sickness is incurable and, as the doctors already said, you do not have long to live. I told you this to comfort your spirit, that *you may always rejoice in the Lord,* inside and out; so that your brothers and others who visit you, may find you *always* rejoicing in the Lord, and that, after your death, for seeing this and for others hearing about it, your death may be, like your life and manner of living, a **perpetual** remembrance **as it was and always will be."**

Phil 4:4

Phil 4:4

Then blessed Francis, **although in greater pain than usual, seemed to put on a great joy of soul on hearing that Sister Death was imminent.** He praised God with great fervor of spirit, **telling them:** "If **it pleases my Lord that** I am to die soon, call Brother Angelo and Brother Leo that they may sing to me about Sister Death."

When these two brothers came to him, **filled with grief and sorrow** and with many tears, they sang the *Canticle of Brother Sun* and the other creatures of the Lord, which the Saint himself had composed. **And then,** before the last stanza **of this canticle** he added some verses about Sister Death:

CtC 1-11

CtC 12-13

"Praised be You, My Lord, through our Sister Bodily Death
   from whom no one living can escape.
   Woe to those who die in mortal sin.
   Blessed are those whom death will find in Your most holy will,
      for the second death shall do them no harm."

124

HOW HE BLESSED THE CITY OF ASSISI
WHEN HE WAS BEING TAKEN TO SAINT MARY TO DIE THERE

While he was still staying in that palace, the most holy father was already assured of his imminent death, both by the Holy Spirit and the prognosis of the doctors. He felt himself growing steadily worse and his physical strength waning. He had himself carried on a litter to Saint Mary of the Portiuncula, **so that there the life of his body would come to an end where he had begun to experience the light and life of his soul.**

↓AC 5

When those who were carrying **him arrived at the hospital halfway between Assisi and Saint Mary,** he asked **those carrying the** litter to place it on the ground. Since he could hardly see because of

↓AC 5//1MP 9

the serious and prolonged eye disease, he had the litter turned so that he would face the city of Assisi.

Raising himself up slightly on the litter, he blessed **this** city. "Lord," he said, "just as, at an earlier time, **this** ancient city was, I believe, the place and abode of wicked and evil men, now I realize

Ps 51:3

that, because of Your *abundant mercy* and in Your own time, You have **singularly** shown *an abundance of Your mercies* **to it. Solely on account of your goodness, you have chosen it for Yourself so** that it may become the place and abode of those who, **in truth,** acknowledge

Ps 29:2

You, *give glory to Your name,* **exude** the fragrance of a **holy** life, of the **truest** doctrine, of a good reputation, and of **evangelical perfection** to the whole Christian people. I ask you, therefore, Lord Jesus Christ, Father of mercies, not to consider our ingratitude. Be mindful of Your **most** abundant **piety** which You have shown to it, that it always be an abode for those who **truly acknowledge** You, and glorify Your

2 Cor 11:31;
Rom 1:25; Phil 4:20

name *blessed* and most glorious *forever and ever. Amen."*

After saying these things, he was carried to Saint Mary **where, having completed the fortieth year of his life, the twentieth year of perfect penance, in the year of the Lord one thousand, two hundred and twenty-six, on the fourth day before the Nones of Octo-**

Mt 22:37

ber, he passed to the Lord Jesus Christ Whom he loved *with his whole heart, with his whole mind, with his whole soul,* and with all his strength, with a most burning desire, and with the fullness of affection, following Him most perfectly, hastening swiftly after Him, and, at last, attaining Him most gloriously, Who lives and reigns with the Father and the Holy Spirit forever and ever. Amen.

Here ends the Mirror of Perfection of the *status*[a] of a Lesser Brother, in which is mirrored most sufficiently the perfection of his vocation and profession.

> All praise and glory to God the Father,
> and to the Son and to the Holy Spirit.
> Alleluia! Alleluia! Alleluia!
> Let honor and gratitude be given
> to the Most Blessed Virgin Mary.
> Alleluia! Alleluia! Alleluia!
> Let grandeur and exaltation be given
> her most blessed servant, Francis.
> Alleluia!
> Amen

---

a. Cf. supra 145, n. 8.

THE BOOK OF CHRONICLES

OR

OF THE TRIBULATIONS
OF THE ORDER OF LESSER ONES
(PROLOGUE AND THE FIRST TRIBULATION)

BY

ANGELO CLARENO

(1323–1325-6)

Introduction

The Book of Chronicles or of the Tribulations of the Order of Lesser Ones is as controversial as is its author, Angelo Clareno (+1337). It is a work of the heroic and of the heinous, of fact and of fiction, of ideals and of politics. While attempting to chronicle the history of the first century of the history of the "Lesser Ones" through the lens of the sufferings inflicted on them, it has the sense of a personal apologia written by a man tormented by the contradictions of his life. Scornful of the academic, his writings reveal a scholar facilely quoting even the more obscure patristic authors. Disdainful and skeptical of authority, even to the point of being branded a schismatic, his life reveals the obeisance of an individual torn by the riptides of the history that continued to engulf him.

Historians estimate the author's birth at Fossombrone in the Marche of Ancona at about 1255.[1] He was given the name Pietro. He entered the Order of Lesser Brothers in 1270, sided with the *zelanti* clustering in Le Marche, and was sentenced in 1279 to seclusion and privation. When liberated in 1290 by Raimondo Gaufridi, the newly elected General Minister, Pietro was sent with three other *zelanti* to Armenia but the Lesser Brothers there greeted them with hostility and forced them to return. In 1294 they did so; Modaldo, Provincial Vicar of Le Marche, treated them viciously, forcing them to have recourse to the General Minister, Raimondo.[2] At his prompting, Pietro joined a group led by Pietro of Marcerata and had recourse, sometime during the six months of his papacy, July to December, 1294, to Pope Celestine V. The sympathetic pope permitted them to leave the Order and to establish themselves as the "Poor Hermits" or the "Celestines."[3] They promised direct obedience to the pope, to wear a monastic habit, and to observe the *Rule* and *Testament* as Francis had wanted. At this point, Pietro of Marcerata took the name *Liberatus* [Freed], Pietro took that of *Angelus* [Angel], *(Clarenus* [Shining] was added later).

Upon the resignation of Celestine V, the euphoria of the new group was dissipated. On Christmas Eve, 1294, Boniface VIII was elected pope and within a few days stripped the Poor Hermits of papal protection. According to Angelo's account, Liberato, Angelo and their companions withdrew to a remote place in Greece, the island of Thessaly, to serve the Lord "without people's annoyance and scandal."[4] It was during these years that Angelo became proficient in Greek and, in addition to steeping himself in the Greek Fathers, he translated many of them into Latin.

In 1305, the group returned to Italy. Six years later, Angelo moved to Avignon to the court of Clement V (1305-14) whose *Dudum ad apostolatus,*

375

April 14, 1310, was favorable to the Spirituals. Angelo took up residence with Cardinal Giacomo Colonna who employed his talents during the Council of Vienne (1311-2). He stayed with Colonna until the Cardinal's death in 1318, cultivating friends among the papal staff during that time in hope of reacquiring papal protection for the Poor Hermits, now called "Clareni." Whether due to another Spiritual Franciscan, Pietro Rainalducci who, from 1328 to 1330, was an anti-pope living in Rome, or to the influence of the General Minister, Michael of Cesena (1316-28), Clement's successor, John XXII (1316-34), refused to grant Angelo's request. Disgruntled, Angelo left Avignon and sought refuge among the Benedictine Celestines at Subiaco. They reluctantly provided a haven from which he began to pour out his writings on Franciscan life, among them *The Book of Chronicles or of the Tribulations of the Order of Lesser Ones* which he wrote between 1321-2.[5] On June 15, 1337, Angelo Clareno died at Santa Maria d'Aspro in Basilicata, Italy, where he had fled in 1334 to avoid the threat of inquisitorial proceedings initiated by John XXII.

The Book of Chronicles or of the Tribulations of the Order of Lesser Ones

Like Peter of John Olivi and Ubertino da Casale, Angelo describes the history of the Order in apocalyptic terms.[6] The same vocabulary of the *status* of history frequently appears, but, in addition to these, Angelo describes seven periods that unfold after the appearance of Francis, each with its own unique tribulation.[7]

After a lengthy prologue that places Francis's *Rule* in a rich biblical setting, Angelo divided the *Book of Chronicles* into seven sections, each describing a tribulation of the Order. The first of these begins with Francis's absence (in 1220-1) and describes the rejection of Francis's *Rule* by those brothers who did not think it possible to observe it. Although this first "tribulation" echoes many allusions to the earlier portraits of Thomas of Celano and Bonaventure and, at times, incorporates material from the *Assisi Compilation,* Angelo adds significantly to these. He does so by inserting biblical references and allusions that cleverly corroborate his retelling of these incidents. The second tribulation begins after Francis's death in 1226 and describes the generalate of Elias (1232-9) in terms of seduction, tyranny, and persecution. Victims of Elias's abuse of power are clearly Caesar of Speyer, Bernard of Quintavalle, Simone "of the Countess," and the relics of Saint Anthony of Padua.

The generalate of Crescentius of Iesi (1244-1247) is the occasion for the third tribulation in which Angelo sees ambition for and achievement of learning and honors stifling the humility and poverty cherished by Francis. Only the subsequent generalate of John of Parma (1247-1257) offered an antidote, but even that was quickly and effectively abandoned during the fourth tribulation, the generalate of Bonaventure (1257-1274). Angelo reserves his bitterest attack for Bonaventure, interpreting his persecution and imprisonment of John of Parma as evidence of the enduring ruin brought upon the Order by the theologian of Paris. He offers four reasons for Bonaventure's treatment of

John: his statements that Francis's *Rule* and *Testament* were inseparable, his adherence to the Trinitarian and apocalyptic teachings of Joachim of Fiore, the sermons of two of his unnamed companions, and the plan of God, at least, according to Angelo, as Francis announced it to Giles, Giacomo of Auxerre, Giacomo of Massa, Ugo, Buonromeo, and others.

After Bonaventure's death, the tribulations continued during the brief but equally cruel generalate of Jerome of Ascoli (1274-1279), later Pope Nicholas IV. Angelo's involvement in this fifth period is obvious from his lengthy, detailed descriptions of the condemnation of the *zelanti* of Le Marche in 1275, the persecution and death of Peter Jean Olivi during the generalate of Bonagrazia of San Giovanni in Persiceto (1279-1283), the abrupt end of the papacy of the sympathetic Pope Celestine V in 1294, Olivi's death in Narbonne in 1298, and, finally, the later persecution of the brothers of the Provinces of Provence and Le Marche. The papal doctor, Arnald of Vallanova (+1311), Popes Boniface VIII (+1303), Clement V (+ 1314), and most especially John XXII (+1334) are the principal villains of the sixth tribulation that, for a period of time, co-exists with the fifth. Angelo places his final reflections in the context of the final tribulation at the end of time. This seventh tribulation provides the rationale for the trials Angelo sees as inevitable as he points to the sufferings of Christ to which all Christians are called and to the habit of Francis that is made in the form of a cross.

Revisionist History

Historians continue to wrestle with the reliability of Angelo's account of Franciscan history. He does seem to be factual; however, he is very selective. In the sixth tribulation, for example, he writes that a further book would be required were he to describe completely all the arguments between Ubertino and the general minister, Bonagratia of Bergamo. Thus he paints a picture which is of his own making. Furthermore, Angelo provides a great deal of information concerning John of Parma, Peter of John Olivi, and Ubertino of Casale, but tells us little about St. Bonaventure.[8] Finally, Angelo's perspective is that of the Spirituals. As one of its leading figures, he struggled for a rigorist interpretation of the *Rule* of Saint Francis and from this point of view, the *Book of Chronicles* is an apologia. In his attempt to tell the stories of the heroes and villains of his life, Angelo offers a revisionist interpretation of history, seeing events in terms of seven periods of tribulation.

In this light, Angelo's portrait of Francis takes on significance.[9] The opening sentence of *The Book of Chronicles* expresses the characteristics of Francis dearest to Angelo: "the poor and humble man of God." While this image of the saint appears frequently throughout the Prologue and first tribulation, Angelo frequently qualifies it by noting Francis's likeness to Christ Crucified, at times writing of him as *christiformis* or *cruciformis*. Angelo's intense identification of Francis with Christ leads to his understanding of the call to sharing Christ's suffering. "Christ especially loved him," Angelo states, "and was kind and familiar with him, cleansing, illuminating, and forming him; drawing him after Himself to follow the footprints of His perfection, appearing to him crucified." From this perspective, the unfolding of the first tribulation, that endured by Francis himself, is understandable. "[Christ] so transformed him into Himself," Angelo writes, "that from then on he lived not for himself but, fully crucified, for Christ."

This intimacy with Christ also brought Francis special graces: apparitions, revelations, privileged conversations. Angelo never tires of accentuating the origin in these revelatory experiences of not only Francis's *Rule* but also his *Testament.* "Ground yourself," Christ tells Francis, "your rule and life on the poverty and nakedness of My cross . . ." In paragraphs that are among the most uplifting in Franciscan literature, Angelo describes the inspiration of Francis's vision and life—and that of his followers—in Christ alone, and, for this reason, he re-iterates the saint's command that no glosses should be placed on his *Rule* and, he adds, the *Testament.*

The Prologue to *The Book of Chronicles* does not continue very long in this lofty presentation; it soon turns pessimistic as Angelo describes the increasing diminishment and decline of the Order. He places these prophecies on the lips of Francis and brings them to a conclusion by repeating the vision that, according to the *Old Legend,* the saint received from an angel of the statue described in the Book of Daniel.[10] According to the vision, the golden head of the statue represents Francis and his companions "who have carried Christ and His death in their hearts . . ." After them, however, the statue diminishes in the value of its composition and each element represents another degradation in the Order. Francis's followers, Angelo states, "prefer verbs to virtues, and science to sanctity." Those who remain faithful to Francis's *Rule* and especially his *Testament,* Angelo maintains, are called to suffer, to undergo the trials and tribulations of Christ crucified.

Thus Angelo lays the groundwork for his revisionist understanding of the history of the Order and, in particular, of the heritage of Francis. Unlike the prophetic figure of the angel of the sixth seal proposed by Bonaventure, Angelo Clareno sees the saint—and his faithful followers—as totally identified with the sufferings of Christ.

The growing tensions among the Lesser Brothers converged with the turmoil in the Avignon papacy and both washed over Angelo Clareno whose personal struggle drove him ever more deeply into despondency. Such were the influences that shaped *The Book of Chronicles or of the Tribulations of the Order of Minors.* Brilliantly written, *The Book* is nonetheless a disturbing, almost convoluted interpretation of history, a history that encompasses much of the material contained in the three volumes of *Francis of Assisi: Early Documents.* Its influences on that history and on subsequent portraits of Francis, directly and indirectly, are enormous. In addition to being a principal source for the history of the Spirituals,[11] *The Book* was used by Hugolino of Montegiorgio in *The Deeds of Blessed Francis and His Companions,* and its popular Italian translation, *The Little Flowers.* More than twenty chapters of the later compilation, the *Life of the Poor and Humble Servant of God, Francis,* are taken verbatim from Angelo's *Book.* Moreover, much of the prejudice that developed against Bonaventure's

Major Legend seems to have been formed by Angelo's personal animosity to the Seraphic Doctor. Tragic figure that he is, Angelo Clareno continues to be a shadow figure in the contemporary understanding of Francis. His *Book of Chronicles or of the Tribulations of the Order of Minors* is one of its landmarks.

Notes

1. For biographical material, cf. Gian Luca Potestà, "Gli studi su Angelo Clareno. Dal ritrovamento della raccolata epistolare alle recenti edizioni," *Rivista di Storia e Letteratura Religiosa* 25 (1989): 111-43; Felice Accrocca, "Angelo Clareno, testimone di Francesco. Testi sulla Vita del Santo e dei primi Frati contenuti nell 'Expositio Regulae Fratrum Minorum' e sconosciuti alle primitive fonti francescane," AFH 89 (1996): 615-27; idem, "I 'Miracula beati Angeli' (ms. Magliabecchi XXXIX, 75) e gli ultimi anni del Clareno in Basilicata," AFH 89 (1996): 615-27;

2. Angelo recounts all these events in the fifth persecution or tribulation, cf. *Liber Chronicarum sive Tribulationum Ordinis Minorum di Frate Angelo Clareno.* Publicazioni della Biblioteca Francescana Chiese Nuova-Assisi. Edited by Giovanni Boccali, with introduction by Felice Accrocca and Italian translation by Marino Bigaroni (Santa Maria degli Angeli: Edizioni Porziuncola, 1998), 379-403.

3. Cf. Felice Accrocca, "Pauperes Eremite Domini Celestini," AFH 84 (1991): 273-8.

4. Cf. Clareno, *Liber Chronicarum,* 403.

5. Cf. Clareno, *Liber Chronicarum,* 20-1. Other works include: *Ad Alvarum Pelagium Apologia pro vita sua,* ed. V. Doucet, AFH 39 (1946): 63-200; idem, *Expositio super regulam Fratrum Minorum,* ed. Giovanni Boccali, with introduction by Felice Accrocca and Italian translation by Marino Bigaroni (Sta. Maria degli Angeli, Assisi: Edizioni Porziuncola, 1995).

6. Cf. supra 142.

7. The editors have published only the Prologue and First Tribulation of The Book of Chronicles, that is, those sections that touch directly on Angelo's portrait of Saint Francis. Other insights into his knowledge of Francis, those coming from his *Exposition on the Rule of the Lesser Brothers,* are published in Related Documents, cf. infra 818-22.

8. In talking about Bonaventure the only event that he considers significant is the trial conducted against John of Parma.

9. Cf. Lorenzo DiFonzo, "L'Immagine di San Francesco negli Scritti degli Spirituali," *Francesco D'Assisi nella Storia Secoli XII-XV,* Attti del Primo Convegno di Studi per L'VIII Centenario della Nascita di S. Francesco (1182-1982), ed. Servus Gieben (Roma: Istituto Storico dei Cappuccini, 1983): 100-20.

10. Cf. infra 17-9; supra 393-5.

11. Cf. Duncan Nimmo, *Reform and Division in the Medieval Franciscan Order: From Saint Francis to the Foundation of the Capuchins.* Bibliotheca Seraphico-Capuccina 33 (Rome, Capuchin Historical Institute, 1987).

[Prologue]^a

[Prologue]ᵃ

[Prologue][a]

[Prologue][a]

Ps 82:4

[1]The life of Francis, *poor and humble* man of God, founder of the three Orders, has been written by four estimable persons, brothers brilliant in learning and holiness, namely John[b] and Thomas of Celano,[c] Brother Bonaventure, minister general after blessed Francis,[d] and a man of marvelous simplicity and holiness, Brother Leo, the companion of Saint Francis.[e]

[4]Anyone who reads and diligently examines these four descriptions or histories will be able to know in part from the matters told in them the vocation, way of life, holiness, innocence, life, and first and last intention of that seraphic man;[f] and how Christ especially loved him and was kind and familiar with him, cleansing, illuminating, and forming him; drawing him after Himself to follow the footprints of His perfection, appearing to him crucified. He so transformed him into Himself, that from then on he lived not for himself but, fully crucified, for Christ.

[8]To him Christ was substance, impulse, sense, light, and life;[g] he was imprinted by fire in his memory, intellect, and passion; he was united and secretly conformed to the cross deep within his marrow. And all that he was, all that he desired, thought, spoke, and did, he received from Christ, and he vigilantly, humbly, and blessedly arranged and perseveringly fulfilled all according to Him and on account of Him.

BPr VII 1

---

a. This translation is based on Angelo Clareno, *Liber Chronicarum sive Tribulationum Ordinis Minorum*, ed. Giovanni Boccali, introduction by Felice Accrocca, with Italian translation by Marino Bigaroni (Sta. Maria degli Angeli, Assisi: Edizioni Porziuncola, 1998). The bracketed titles are based on this edition.

b. For the difficulty in determining the identity of this "John of Celano," see infra 832-3.

c. FA:ED I 180-308; 319-26; FA:ED II 239-393; 399-468.

d. FA:ED II 525-683; 684-730.

e. A reference to Leo's involvement in the composition of the L3C and AC, FA:ED II 66-110; 118-230.

f. This passage, "the first and last intention of the seraphic man," is repeated three times in this Prologue and may be seen as a leitmotif of the entire work. Cf. HTrb Prol 13, 144, 577; VI 87.

g. In her study of the images of Christ found in the Spirituals, Edith Pásztor focuses on these opening paragraphs of Clareno's text as underscoring, in the form of a dialogue, the Christocentric basis of Francis's inspiration. Cf. Edith Pásztor, "L'Immagine di Christo negli Spirituali," in *Chi Erano Gli Spirituali: Atti del III Convegno Internazionale, Assisi, 16-18 Ottobre 1975* (Assisi: Società Internazionale di Studi Francescani, 1976): 109-124.

380

[Christ Instructs Francis]

^{12}*Jesus Christ* found him *faithful,* obedient, grateful, simple, upright, humble, *in accord with* His *heart;* and revealed to him the first and last perfection of His evangelical life and that of His mother, His apostles, and the evangelists. He *opened* his *ears* and *trained* him *with a powerful hand* in the incorruptible and perfect works of heaven, and *placed* Himself *in* his *heart,* his mouth, and his arms.   Rv 1:5

1 Sm 2:35

Is 50:4; Is 8:11

Sg 8:6

^{16}Christ said to him: *"Take from* my *hand the scroll,* the law of grace and humility, of poverty, piety, charity, and peace; the form of life which I kept with my disciples, a life-giving rule for a spotless life and fullness of grace, the sure acquisition of glory for the soul directing in action and in thought the possession and ascent to heavenly and divine things. This I created substantially in the saints from the beginning and showed it to be the form of perfection.[a]   Ez 3:3; Rv 10:10

^{20}"Naked, being born of the Virgin in a way words cannot describe, I was *wrapped in the swaddling clothes* of poverty, and *lay in the manger* of humility, because I did not want to have a *place in the inn,* so that, in a mystery, I might show poverty to be the sure way to the kingdom of heaven, and I might confirm in words and deeds the humble lovers and observers *of poverty* to be *heirs* and kings of that same *kingdom,* ordained by my Father from eternity.   Lk 2:7,12

Lk 2:7

Jas 2:5

LR VI 4

^{24}"A powerful angel, *in spirit and power* the prophet Elias, herald of my advent and incarnation, John the Baptist, I sent *before me to prepare* my *ways* and to *make straight the paths,* to preach penance and, in deeds and in word, *to give knowledge of salvation for the remission of sins.* Thus, through him, *all might believe* in me, and for believing, loving, and observing the perfection of my poor, *meek,* and *humble* way of living and most divine life, all *wishing to come after me* might have a pious and most sure director, guide, and patron from this point until the end of the world.   Lk 1:17

Lk 1:76

Is 40:3; Mk 1:23

Lk 1:77

Jn 1:7

Mt 16:24; Lk 9:23

^{28}"For this reason, giving to those choosing *to come after me* escape from the shadows of error and the damnation of eternal confusion and death, and *entry to the kingdom of God, reborn of water and the Holy Spirit,* as soon as I was baptized by him I was *led into the desert by the* Holy *Spirit.* In *fasting, vigils,* and prayer I consecrated by example the period of *forty days,* teaching through this that the lifetime of the baptized ought to be consecrated fully and perfectly to divine worship; and so those following me, by my power might conquer *the prince* of death, *ruler* of the world of *this darkness,* and *dead* to the world and all   Eph 3:1; Mt 16:24; Lk 9:23

2 Pt 1:11; Jn 3:5

Mk 4:1

2 Cor 6:5; 11:27

Mt 4:2

Eph 6:12

Rom 6:10; 1 Cor 1:27

---

a. The following eight paragraphs, lines 20-57, form a synthesis of Christ's life as the *forma* [form, pattern, model] of that of Francis and his followers.

Col 3:1-2
things *which are of the world,* they might *live for God* alone, *seeking and minding things that are above, not those on earth.*

Mt 4:17; Jer 2:23
Ps 16:11; Acts 2:28
Lk 9:3; 10:4
Mt 8:20
34*"I preached penance* and *the kingdom of heaven,* like *a swift runner,* covered with one tunic and a cheap cloak, opening up *the ways of life* to my disciples, going along together with them without *money, sandals, bag, or purse.* Lacking a roof, I who made the heavens *had no place to lay* my *head,* so that I might show to those imitating me that the world

1 Jn 1:15; Phil 3:8
and all things *which are of the world* must be *accounted as loss and dung* and despised.

Lk 6:12;
Lk 13:10; 19:47; 21:37
38*"I spent the night* awake *in prayer before God, by day teaching in the synagogues and the temple* hatred of the world, desire, greed, hypocrisy, and of lies, pride, and malice. And so that they might recognize Me as the Messiah promised to our forefathers, God made human,

Mt 8:16; 11:5
Emmanuel, and might accept Me for salvation, *curing* by My power all illnesses and infirmities, I cast out *demons, cleansed lepers,* raised *the dead,* and forgave sins.

Jn 15:19
41*"I made those whom I chose from the world* otherworldly, Brother, by both My word and the example of My poor, humble, heavenly life.

Jn 18:9; Lk 22:28;
Jn 17: 17,19
Jn 17:16
I did not lose any of them, but they *remained with Me in My trials,* and I *sanctified them.* Leaving *the world,* I commended them to the Father,

ER XXII 42-55
1LtF 1:14-19;
2LtF 10:13-18

Jn 17:10; Jn 17:14
because they *were Mine* and *not of the world.* By My example they were

Rom 10:18; Ps 19:5
to be supernaturally victorious, and to preach *through the whole earth*

Mt 10:22; Lk 21:17
to Jews and *Gentiles hatred* and contempt of the world *on account of My*

1 Pt 5:10
name, and profess faith in Me and the *eternal glory* and honor of My

Jn 18:36
kingdom, which *is not of this world.*

Mk 16:20; Lk 22:20
47*"I confirmed* My *preaching in My blood* through death on the cross,

Heb 13:12; Jn 19:18;
Lk 23:39
naked, *outside the gate hanging in the midst of thieves,* abandoned to insults and the most bitter sufferings, boundless and innumerable,

Mt 27:6; 1 Cor 6:20
so that, *redeemed by the price of* My *blood* and the power of My death, I might raise up those corrupted by pride, vanity, and carnality, those rightly condemned to a double death; so that I might make them most ardent lovers of My pains and death and cross, overcoming

Jn 10:15; 15:13
themselves, the world, and the devil. Just as I *laid down My life* for the

Phil 2:11
salvation of humankind to the honor and *glory of the Father,* so they,

Jn 13: 37-38;
Rom 16:27; Heb 2:7,9
redeemed through Me, might *lay down their life,* to the *glory and honor* of My name, holding fast to the means of My death and the cross, by

Jn 16:33; 14:30
which *the world,* with *the prince* of death, *is conquered,* grace is possessed in the present, and glory in the future.

Phil 3:10
54*"I conformed* them *to My death, sharing* My pains and *suffering,* so

Rv 20:12
that they might understand the beginning of the *opening of the book of life* and, in it, the inscription and message of My infinite love, the door leading into the *brilliance* of My *wisdom,* and the key opening the

Rv 7:12
secret splendors of My works, words, precepts, counsels, sacraments

and promises, and the sure revelation of the blessings of my glory, by which *the children of light* and My grace are separated from the children of darkness and sin, and the citizens of the kingdom from the citizens of Babylon and Hell."

Jn 12:36; 1 Thes 5:5

TL V 3:37

[58]This Benjamin, Francis, along with Paul, *the least of the saints,* learned and received all the things which he wrote in the *Rule* and the *Testament* and in his letters and admonitions, neither *from men* nor through a man, but *by revelation of Jesus Christ* appearing to him, seraphically dwelling in him, and speaking to him in the form of the cross.[a] These things he preached blatantly in very clear, brief words, and perfectly fulfilled them in faithful deeds.

Eph 3:8

Gal 1:12

[61]He was so ignited by *the fire of the Holy Spirit* when Christ Jesus appeared to him as if nailed to the cross, that after the example of Christ Jesus the redeemer, who *hung* on the cross naked *in the midst of thieves* and died, he firmly proposed that, naked and separated from the world, unrecognized by all men, as we read about Mary Magdalene and many other saints, he would serve Christ even unto death, or he would offer himself to any harsh tortures and martyrdom to preach the faith and witness to Christ Jesus among the Saracens or other unbelievers. Turned toward Christ, he begged with devout prayers and burning desires, to be enlightened about his direction and reassured by Him from whom *every* good thing and *every gift* is freely given to all and without whom nothing pleasing to God can be accomplished.

Lk 3:16; Mt 3:11

Lk 23:39; Jn 19:18

XVI 3; LR XII 1

Jas 1:17

[68]Appearing to him,[b] Christ Jesus, our Savior, said: "Francis: *follow Me,* and hold to the footprints of the poverty and humility of My life. To be conformed and united to Me in the senses, intellect, and action is the goal of My every promise and fulfillment of grace and glory. For if you cling to Me *with your whole heart, your whole soul, your whole mind, and your whole strength,* so that your every thought is in Me and about Me, all your words are from Me, for Me, and with Me, and all your works are done always on account of Me and for the *honor and glory* of My name, *you will be My servant* and *I will be with you,* and *I will speak through your mouth,* and *whoever* hears you, *hears Me,* and *whoever receives* you, *receives Me,* and *whoever blesses you,* will be *blessed* and *whoever curses you, will be cursed.*

Mt 9:9; Mk 2:14;
Lk 9:59; Jn 21:19

Dt 6:5; Lk 10:27

XIII 8; 2LtF 18;
PrOF 5

1 Tm 1:17;
Rv 4:11; 5:12

Is 41: 9-10;
Ex 4:12,15

Lk 10:16

Mt 10:40;
Gn 12:3; 27:29

[80]"You and all *your* brothers *whom I will give* you are to live in My likeness living, *as strangers and pilgrims,* dead to the world. Ground yourself, your rule and life on the poverty and nakedness of My cross,

Is 8: 18

1 Pt 2:11

---

a. Clareno boldly asserts that everything contained in the writings of Francis came through revelation, a conviction he later places on Christ's lips, cf. infra 390, 395.

b. This vision does not appear in any earlier source and seems to be a vehicle used by the author to underscore the central role of Christ in Francis's vision.

because My substance of all communicable riches of grace and glory is grounded and based on poverty, and the infinite blessed enjoyment of all My goods is possessed in striving toward My humility. For the depth of humility is immense, and in those who truly love and possess poverty and humility is the look of My happiness and the resting-place and dwelling of My favor.

Is 61:3

[85]"Therefore the congregation of your brotherhood will be called the religion of lesser ones, so that from the name they might understand that above all they are to be truly humble of heart; since humility is the *cloak of* My *honor* and praise, and anyone passing from this life with this habit will find the gates of My kingdom open.

1 Jn 2:18
Mt 11:29

[88]"I asked My Father to grant Me in this *last hour* a little poor people, *humble, and meek,* and mild, who would be like Me in all things, in poverty and humility, and who would be content to have only Me; I would come to rest and remain in this people, just as My Father rests and remains in Me: and this people would rest and *remain in Me* just *as* I remain *in the Father* and rest in His Spirit. My Father gave you to Me, along with those who *with their whole heart* and with *unfeigned faith* and *perfect charity* cling to Me through you; and I will guide and nourish them, and *they shall be sons to Me,* and *I shall be a father to them. Whoever receives you, receives Me;* and *whoever persecutes you, persecutes and despises Me:* and My judgment will come upon your despisers and persecutors; but My *blessing* will remain upon those receiving and *blessing* you.

AC 101; 2MP

Jn 15:4, 5
Jn 14:10; 17:21
Lk 10:27; 1 Tm 1:5
1 Jn 4:17-18
2 Sm 7:14
Mt 10:40;
Lk 10:16; Jn 15:10
Gn 12:3

[98]"Let My Gospel be your *Rule,* and My life be your life, My cross your repose, My charity your life, My death your hope and resurrection. Let the *reproaches, blasphemies,* and mockery against Me be your honors, blessings, and commendations; let your life, joy, and glory be to endure death and torments for Me; let your portion and riches be to wish to have nothing under heaven; let your distinction, consolation, and triumph be to be humbled beneath all and to rejoice to be afflicted and vilified on account of My name.

Heb 11:26; Mt 27:39

LR VI 6-7

[104]"The places in which the brothers will live *as strangers and pilgrims* to worship and praise Me, shall be vile, poor little buildings, made of mud and wattle, set apart from the vanities and tumult of the world, and lacking ownership and rights. With the obedience, permission, and good pleasure of bishops and clerics they shall accept the buildings *as strangers and pilgrims,* staying in them only as long as the owners of the places wish it and it pleases the bishops, always prepared to leave there willingly and thankfully when their hosts ask them to leave. They shall be like Me and conformed to Me when they spend time in worshiping Me, living in these places as strangers, preaching My name in deed and conduct; and *as strangers*

1 Pt 2:11

Test 24; AC 58
1MP 30; 2MP

1 Pt 2:11

1 Pt 2:11

and pilgrims they shall leave very willingly when asked, showing perfectly by such a glad and humble gesture that they hold onto nothing there and did not wish to hold onto anything."

¹¹⁰Therefore in his *Testament,* which he made near his death,[a] he says: "After the Lord gave me brothers and companions, no one showed me what I ought to do, but the Most High Himself revealed to me that I ought to live according to the pattern of the Holy Gospel. And I had this written down simply and in a few words, and the Lord Pope confirmed it for me."

¹¹⁴And for the pure and Catholic observance of this life, in the end he made his *Testament,* in which he showed that he received the beginning, development, and end of his conversion through revelation from Jesus Christ. The **faith** and obedience of the **Roman Church** and of all the **priests** ordained by the same Church, though sinners, are to be venerated, so much so that, **if he had as much** *wisdom as Solomon,* he **would not preach in their parishes against their will** and obedience. Enlightened by Christ he taught them **to respect, love, and honor** the ministers of the sacraments of the Church **as their lords,** and above all that these sacraments and **divine words** and all masters and doctors of sacred theology must be **venerated and honored** because, he said, through this we share in *spirit and life* through their ministry. They should perform **the Office according to the** custom of the Roman Church. The brothers should be **content with one tunic patched inside and out** for the sake of the true observance of poverty, and **not wish to have more,** but be sincerely **subject to all,** showing the lesser state of humility in their way of life and work, **working with** their **hands for the sake of example** and love of virtue, **to avoid idleness,** and to provide for the needs of their bodies and of those of their brothers in an evangelical way; showing that it is great humility, ineffable dignity, and participation at the table of the King of glory Himself **to have recourse to the table of the Lord and seek alms from door to door when they are not paid for their work.**

¹²⁷Blessed Francis had learned from Christ that it is a great dignity and incomparable honor according to God and man for the evangelical poor to seek alms for the love of the Lord God, because *all things* created both *in heaven and on earth* cannot be compared to the love of God, for all things which the heavenly Father created for human use out of love for His beloved Son, after sin, have been given, free, as alms, to the worthy and the unworthy. Therefore, what is

Test 14-16

Test 1-19

Test 6-8

Test 13

Test 30

Test 16-17

Test 20-21

Test 22-23

C 77; LMj VII 10;
AC 96; 1MP 1;
2MP 22

1 Kgs 5:9

Jn 6:64

Eph 1:10

---

a. The following paragraphs, lines 111-26, present a synthesis of Test 1-26 which Angelo clearly underscores as an expression of his "first and last intention."

2 Cor 8:9

Ps 78:25

1 Cor 11:23

1 Pt 2:11

2 Cor 8:2

Mt 8:23

LR VI 1-6

Test 25-26

Test 34-35

Test 38-39

asked and given for the love of the Lord God and the love of Christ Jesus His Son, *who became poor for us* so that by His poverty He would make *us rich* in present grace and sanctify us as blessed in future glory, can be called *the bread of angels* rather than *the food* of the body.

[133]Thus, according to what *he received from* Christ, Francis says in his *Rule:* "Let the brothers not make anything their own, neither house, nor place, nor anything at all; but *as pilgrims and strangers* in this world, serving the Lord in poverty and humility, let them go seeking alms with confidence; and they should not be ashamed because, for us, the Lord made Himself poor in this world. This is that sublime height of *the highest poverty* which has made you, my most beloved brothers, heirs and kings of the Kingdom of Heaven, poor in temporal things, exalted in virtue. Let this be your portion, which leads into the land of the living. Giving yourselves totally to this, most beloved brothers, never seek anything else under heaven for the name of our Lord Jesus Christ."

[140]In order to preserve purely and completely the perfection of the highest evangelical poverty revealed to him by Christ, Francis, in the strength and certitude of the spirit of Christ, **strictly** orders: "**Wherever they may be, they are not to dare to ask any letter from the Roman Curia, either personally or through an intermediary, whether for a church or a place, or under the pretext of preaching or the persecution of their bodies; but wherever they have not been received let** the brothers *flee into another* country to do penance with the blessing of God."

[144]He adds at the end that his *Testament* is not another *Rule,* but an exhortation or remembrance of both his first and last intention, revealed to him by Christ, a testament which he made for his blessed brothers, that they might observe the *Rule* they promised the Lord in a more Catholic way, because the Catholic, faithful, and pure observance of the *Rule,* which he received from Christ, was contained in the literal understanding of the *Testament* and *Rule.*

[147]Therefore he strictly commanded by obedience that they were not to place glosses on the *Rule* and *Testament,* saying: "They should be understood in this way." But **as the Lord granted him to speak and write the Rule and Testament simply and purely, they were to understand them simply and purely without gloss, and observe them with a holy activity until the end.**

[152]Therefore anyone who possesses the truth of the faith and charity of Christ knows how many absurd and inappropriate things are said by those who attempt to void or nullify Saint Francis, his *Rule* and *Testament,* things against Christ, the apostles, their disciples, the

evangelists, anchorites, cenobites, heads of churches, founders of all the orders of perfection and, in fact, even against the Roman Church itself.

¹⁵⁶Christ was familiar with Francis, like a father with his most beloved son. He informed him of the good pleasure of His will; and showed him what was useful, fit, and helpful at the moment, and for coming, foreseen tribulation. He showed through him and in him the preparations for the final perfect state of contemplation in the heaven of the Church. But *his own did not accept him.*

Jn 1:11

[Francis Instructs His Companions]

¹⁶⁰His companions—namely Bernard of Quintavalle,^a Giles,^b Angelo,^c Masseo,^d and Leo^e—related that Saint Francis once said in secret to these five:

"Brothers, although I may be the most vile man and least worthy creature of God, nevertheless, that you may grow in reverence and faith in your vocation and the promise of the life and *Rule* revealed to me by the Lord, know that Christ reveals His presence to me with great kindness and familiarity, especially whenever I cry out to Him for the benefit of the religion. He so fully and clearly agrees to all the things that I ask for that—as the Lord Himself once told me—He gave to very few, to the rarest of saints, such an abundance of His presence. By His kindness and grace alone He called me and revealed Himself to me, and He taught me that I should seek confirmation of His spotless life from the Church and the Lord Pope. And Christ swayed the Lord Pope and his brothers the Lord Cardinals, and they understood that I had been sent to them by the Lord Jesus Christ Himself, and the Lord Pope granted me everything that I asked.

¹⁷¹"Happy are they who faithfully and devoutly strive to live according to their vocation, and observe purely and simply until the end the things which they promised the Lord, for *theirs is the Kingdom of Heaven* with unique glory. And woe to those who attempt to nullify out of their knowledge those things which He deigned to reveal to me to the glory of His grace, for the present and future benefit of the whole religion, and for *the salvation of the souls* of all the brothers. Because such people deprive themselves of grace, and drag others

Mt 5:3,10

1 Pt 1:9

---

a. Cf. FA:ED I 203 d.
b. Cf. FA:ED I 204 b
c. Cf. FA:ED II 67 a.
d. Cf. FA:ED II 67 d.
e. Cf. FA:ED II 66 d.

away from salvation, they deserve the most bitter punishments of Gehenna."

[177]Christ did not wish to hide from him the good things and the bad, defects and progress, slips and falls, what trials and tribulations, what struggles, and what revelations would follow and happen to the religion until the end.

[178]Now, after that remarkable vision and its effect on the heart of each—when, *absent in body,* Francis was present to his brothers *in a fiery chariot* and their consciences were laid bare to each other, as the holy man Brother John of Celano[a] wrote in his legend—on returning to the brothers he first comforted them regarding the heavenly vision shown them, then foretold in detail what was to happen in the religion after them.

[186]"Do not be discouraged, brothers, because you are few and simple. Shortly many shall come to this life and religion, not only simple men, but also the *wise* and *noble,* rich and poor, laymen and clerics; and not only Italians, but also French, Spanish, Scots, Irish, Germans, Slavs, Hungarians, and those from other nations. *Behold, the sound of* their *feet* is in my ears.

[186]"Therefore be grateful to God and strive with all your might to make firm before Him *your vocation and election in* both *works* and holy feelings, because God placed us—unlettered, *contemptible,* and abject—as founders of this humble, poor, and first and last final state in this *last hour.* It follows that it is fitting that we be even more humble, and with *fear and trembling work out* our *salvation* and *bear worthy fruit of penance* before God, Who by His good will alone called us to the heavenly following of His life.

[190]"Since *many will be called and few chosen* even in this religion, especially *in the last days,* when the times *of tribulation* approach, you should understand the truth of future happenings. The Most High will fill us now, at the beginning of the religion, with gifts and graces, with *the sweetness of* His *blessing* and the fruits of charity. Like guests at His table, *He will feed* us *the bread of life and understanding* and *give us to drink* spiritual joy and happiness, and content us with the ineffable taste of peace and wisdom.

[195]"But *an enemy* will try *to sow weeds* in the religion, and many will enter the religion who will begin to *live not for Christ but for themselves,* and will follow *the prudence of the flesh* more than *obedience to the faith* and the *Rule,* granting much to the flesh and little to the spirit, acquiescing to the fragility of nature, and closing the ears of the heart to

---

a. If, according to Edouard d'Alençon, the text of John of Celano is taken from the text assumed into the Liturgical Office of the Friars Preacher, this passage is clearly missing. Cf. infra 832-6.

Margin references:

1 Cor 5:3; Col 2:5; 2 Kgs 2:11 — 1C 47; LJS 29; LMj IV 4; LM

1 Cor 1:26 — 1C 27; LJS 18; BPr 1:12-13

1 Kgs 14:6; 2 Kgs 6:32; Acts 5:9

2 Pt 1:10

1 Cor 1:28

1 Jn 2:18

2 Cor 7:15; Phil 2:12; Mt 3:8; Lk 3:8

Mt 20:16; 22:14

Dn 12:13; Mt 24:29

Ps 21:4

Sir 15:3

Mt 13:25,28

Rom 6:11; 2 Cor 5:15

Rom 8:6; 1:5

grace. They shall neglect to do *violence* to themselves that they may *seize the kingdom* of God. Because of this the religion will diminish and decline from perfection, and the fervor of perfect charity will begin to grow tepid. There shall also be some who innocently and faithfully follow after us in sorrow and weariness, and they shall be afflicted and oppressed by those who differ from them.

²⁰¹"Then, *after that tribulation* of evils and sufferings, the situation will decline toward what is worse and even more bitter. Evil spirits shall attack the religion, and many shall rise against it: those living carnal, animal lives in the religion shall be multiplied, and they shall be entangled and caught in the delights and the cares of life.[a]

²⁰⁴"They shall shamelessly throw themselves into lawsuits in order to acquire money, bequests, and legacies. They shall withdraw from love of holy poverty and humility. In hatred they shall persecute and punish those in the religion who resist them. Because of this their words and deeds, internally and externally, shall be very bitter. Internally, they shall move away from poverty, humility, and prayer; they shall give themselves ambitiously to learning and lecturing, and they shall prefer words to virtues, learning to holiness, pride and arrogance to humility. Accusing those who oppose them, they shall call it piety to shame and oppress them by deceit, and will preach that it is justice to wage war upon them. They shall disturb clerics and fall away from reverence for them, contradicting the humility they promised. The laity shall be scandalized by their greed for things, and they shall give an example of frivolity and vanity in their changing places, and in sumptuous and ornate buildings. They will *bite and devour each other.* They will pant for ecclesiastical honors, competing among themselves to be and to appear superior. But they shall despise as crazy brothers who try to cling to humility and labor to rise up to Heaven through a pure observance of their promises. They will revile such brothers as useless and good for nothing, but they will admire and extol those intent on seeking *high* offices, and praise their prudence.

²²⁰"Therefore, after these things, their conduct and life will be very bitter and completely unbearable to everyone, and they shall shame and persecute and defame each other. The stench of their conduct will be impossible to hide. Then the religion beloved by God will be so defamed by bad example that the good brothers will be ashamed to go out in public. Then every wicked man will turn the

Mt 11:12

OL 1; WBC 12

Mt 24:29; Mk 13:24

Gal 5:15

Rom 12:16

2C 157; 2MP 70

---

a. Cf. Angelo Clareno, *Expositio super regulam Fratrum Minorum,* ed. Giovanni Boccali, with an introduction by Felice Accrocca, and Italian translation by Marino Bigaroni (Sta. Maria degli Angeli, Assisi: Edizioni Porziuncola, 1995), I 285-6; IV 41.

stench of his own malice back at the brothers, and will start to excuse and minimize his crimes by comparing his deed to those of the brothers, saying: 'The brothers do things that are even worse.' Only a few, with many tribulations and much opposition, will turn themselves wholeheartedly to Christ and the observance of their vocation. The novices who shall then enter the religion, lacking the example and direction of their superiors, will be stunned by the things they will see and their life-giving desires and works of grace will dry up, and they shall *look back*. But some of them shall cry out to Christ in prayer and, lacking the guidance of masters, they shall *be filled* with outstanding gifts of grace and *blessings* from the Lord and shall be led to the summit of highest perfection. In the end what will become of them is what usually happens with fishermen: they *cast their net into the sea*, and catch a great multitude of bad *fish* and a few good ones. Hauling *it to shore* they pick out the few *good ones* and place them in their *containers*, but they toss out *the bad ones* and leave them on the shore to be devoured by birds."

²³⁶This is already happening to this religion *in* these *last days*.

[Confirmation of the Rule]

²³⁷*After a few days*, when their number had now come to twelve, Christ appeared to him again and said: "Write down the life which I have revealed to you and present it to My Vicar. Request in My name that it be confirmed for you, your companions, and all who wish to accept it. Those who shall receive it humbly and reverently, and observe it simply and faithfully, will share in the spirit of life and be clothed in the light of My splendor. Those who despise it shall be wrapped up in darkness and shadows, and they shall be worse off than other men for they will have fallen from a higher state and calling."

²⁴³What he requested seemed very difficult, almost impossible, for the weakness and tepidity of the men of his day, so the Supreme Pontiff urged him to accept some order or rule that was already approved. But he insisted that he had been sent by Christ to request this life, not another, and remained firm in his petition. Then Lord John of Saint Paul, Bishop of Sabina, and Lord Hugo, Bishop of Ostia, moved by the spirit of God, stood by Saint Francis, and in the presence of the Supreme Pontiff and the cardinals offered many reasonable and very effective arguments for the things he was asking.

²⁴⁷Meanwhile, *that night*, the Supreme Pontiff *saw in a dream* a man identical in every way to Saint Francis, supporting on his shoulders the Lateran church, which was leaning so far that it would fall,

Lk 9:62

Ps 21:4

Mt 13:47

Mt 13:48

Dn 12:13

1 Sm 18:27

Acts 23:11; Gn 28:12

1C 32; AP 31; L
AC 56; 2MP 55
1C 32-33; L3C 4
2C 16-17; LMj I
LMn II 4

LMj III 9; TL V

L3C 51; 2C 17;
LMj III 10; LMr

and kept it upright by his strength.[a] And the next day Saint Francis, instructed by the spirit of Christ, presented before the pope a parable about a poor and beautiful woman who conceived and bore sons resembling the king; and she raised them in the desert. Some time later, passing through the area again, the king recognized them as his offspring, placed them at his table, and made them heirs and kings of his kingdom.

[251]The Supreme Pontiff understood that what he was asking came from *Christ* and *not from man,* and giving thanks to God, granted his requests, and by his authority made them preachers of the Gospel, and promised in the future that if they asked for something he would do it generously and graciously.

Gal 1:1,12

[Angelic Prophecies]

[254]After the *Rule* was confirmed and they were returning, meal time had passed, and they were weak and exhausted from the labor of their journey, and far away from the homes of any people. Suddenly a handsome youth joined them on the road, and offered them his bread which he brought with him, and he discussed many things with them about the perfection of the evangelical life of Christ. With the power of his words he inflamed them with a great burning of charity, and their minds were overcome with astonishment at the wonder of his words. He immediately disappeared in an amazing way, and left them enkindled with the life-giving love of Christ.

1C 34; LJS 22; LMj IV 1

[259]They all realized at the same moment that it had been an angel of God who offered them the bread. Restored both in spirit and in body, they *gave* great *thanks to God* for His *gift* and kindness. *In fervor of spirit they knelt* together, lifting their feelings and hearts to Him, and they promised and swore not to shrink from the promise of holy poverty under the pressure of any need or tribulation. They had understood by God's providence and the angelic words that God has greater care for their bodies and souls than a mother has for her child, in fact, even more than He has for heaven and earth; and that *it is impossible for God* not to provide His servants with what is useful and needed for the body; not to hear the prayers of the poor, and not to fulfill the holy desires which He alone inspires. For He Himself said: *"I will not desert you, nor forsake you,"* and *"Do not be afraid, little flock, because it has pleased* my *Father to grant you the kingdom; how much more the necessities* of life."

Rom 1:8; 2 Cor 9:15; Acts 18:25; Eph 3:14

Mt 19:26; Lk 1:37

LR VI 8

Heb 13:5; Dt 31:6; Jos 1:5; Lk 12:32
Lk 11:8,13

---

a. The same dream is recounted in the third *Life of Saint Dominic* by Constantius Medici written around 1244-5. Cf. FA:ED II 97 a.

²⁶⁸Saint Francis himself used to say that the almighty power of God is made known and shines forth in the faith and endurance of the saints, because *we have been saved* by faith, and all the works of God are done in faith. *Without faith it is impossible to please God;* as it is written, *one who doubts* divine providence is like *the waves of the sea, moved and tossed about by the wind.* For *that man should not suppose that he will receive anything from God,* because someone like that *is devious in spirit and erratic in all his ways.*

²⁷²*All things are possible to one who believes,* and all things, however bitter, are sweet and light to one who loves. The apostles, martyrs, and the Fathers, naked and withdrawn from the world, serving God

in faith and charity *lived* for Christ and *not for themselves.* Having before their eyes the examples of Christ like a cloud of witnesses of

eternal refreshment, *"they went about in the skins of sheep and goats, needy, afflicted, tormented: the world was not worthy of them."* How many

torments all the saints *suffered* so that they might safely reach the kingdom with the palm of martyrdom! They *shared in the sufferings of Christ* and were abandoned to temptations, *infirmities, wants,* and *the persecutions* of demons and humans; to be tested and proven in the

crucible of tribulations, *as in fire,* and through endurance to be numbered among the saints, *reigning with Christ in the kingdom of heaven.* We are given great and immeasurable gifts of the spirit and benefits from the Lord at the very time when, for the moment, we are afflicted and tempted, so that, once our endurance has been proven, we may reach Christ with the palm of martyrdom.

²⁷⁹When we are living just and holy lives and when, because of our observance of obedience, poverty, and chastity, we incur need, sick-

ness, and death, we should rejoice, looking at Him who, *for the sake of the joy that lay before Him, endured the cross, despising the shame.* In the same way they rejoice who win victory over opponents: they find it all the more valuable the longer they sought and longed for it. Every one

of the saints *puts on* the elegance and beauty of *incorruptible* and eternal glory, placed in the line moving toward the undying good at the mo-

ment when each of them completely dies to *vices and passions* in ex-

change for imitation and profession of the life of Christ, desiring *to be freed from the body,* and through tortures and torments to pass over to

Him, who *endured suffering* and *death on the cross* for us, who *were enemies* of God and *slaves of sin* and most *deserving of* eternal *death.*

²⁸⁷Christ Jesus worked in His servant Francis in the same way as in the early saints, and many rushed toward the fragrance of his life and that of his companions, and were drawn by the power of the Spirit of Christ to love heavenly things and put them into practice.

²⁸⁹Fervent in the spirit of Christ they preached the Gospel in deed and in word. The hearts of those who saw them were transformed, and to confirm their life and preaching Christ daily worked

innumerable signs and miracles through Francis. Caught up in the spirit of God, they condemned the world with its passions; and, according to the counsel of Christ, *selling all they had* and giving it *to the poor,* they were joined in heart and habit to the poor of Christ.

II 4; LR II 5
Mt 19:21; Lk 18:22

²⁹³*The number* of brothers quickly *multiplied,* and were organized under ministers and custodians in the various provinces of the Christian people. But it is certainly no small undertaking to take on the discipleship of the life of Christ and to pursue the things demanded by so great a profession, because to begin something good is for *many,* but *perseverance until the end* is for *the few* and the perfect. To *mortify* the senses; to silence the tongue and heart according to the counsel of the Gospel; in a Christ-like way to offer continually both *body* and soul *to God;* to intend and accomplish both internal and external works *according to the pleasure of God's will;* and to endure in these things until the end is a gift from God, but it is not pursued and preserved without great *anguish* and—I might say—*sweating blood,* sharing in pains like those of the cross.

Acts 6:7
Mt 22:14; 24:13; Col 3:5; Rom 12:1
Rom 12:2
Lk 22:44

²⁹⁹Our weakness is great and we all fall easily into things of sensuality; and the *prudence of the flesh,* under the cloak of discernment, like the force of a violent wind, drives us strongly toward those things—iron chains and a cell of bronze—consenting to the first and following the second. For there will be no one *in the lot of the saints* who follows those things.

Rom 8:6
Col 1:12

³⁰²Through this *the first man* conceived the beginning of ruin and became involved in both the worst evils of self-love and self-satisfaction. Under the appearance of discernment the brothers began *to open their eyes* and to take their example from other religious ways of life. Some of the more learned ones among them suggested to the simpler ones that this would be safe and useful. Without considering their fault of presumption, infidelity, and disobedience, and dragging others after themselves by word and deed, they had a taste for things contrary to Christ, to the founder, and to the *Rule* they professed. These things reached the ears of their father and he, punishing those who did such things with harsh rebukes, turned to Christ, praying that they be set right.

1 Cor 15:45
Gn 3:5, 7

³⁰⁷While he was praying *an angel of the Lord appeared* to him in an amazing form and appearance:[a] the *head* was *gold, arms and chest silver, stomach bronze,* legs of *iron,* feet of earth and *clay;* the shoulders covered with vile and rough sackcloth. The angel showed Saint Francis that he was rather ashamed of that sackcloth covering.

2C 82; OL 5
Mt 1:20
Dn 2:32-33

---

a. This vision was described in different terms by Thomas of Celano (2C 82) who had described Angelo's "form" as a lady, and by Ugolino of Montegiorgio (DBF XXIV) as a statue. Thomas of Eccleston narrates that, in the General Chapter of 1239, Pope Gregory IX preached about the "golden statue" prompting Brother Elias to make excuses for his actions, cf. ChrTE 13. Angelo also uses the story in his *Expositio* II 175-93. It also appears in Chr XXIVG 231.

[310]He was amazed at seeing this.

The angel said to him: "Why do you gawk and gaze? This form, in which I was sent to appear to you, signifies the beginning, development, and end which your religion will have, until the time it goes into labor, the time of the reform of the life of Christ and the state of the Church.

Dn 2:38

[313]"*The golden head* is you, with all your companions who have carried Christ and His death written in your heart, have loved to cling to His footprints with your whole heart, and have wished for all time to have nothing under heaven on account of His love. But just as the *descent* of *the seed of Abraham* was *promised* not in *Ishmael* but in Isaac, so the descent of your name will not be in *sons* of flesh, but in *sons* of spirit, in deed and in truth.

Gn 17:23; 1 Chr 1:28; Gal 3:16
Gal 4:30

[316]"For they shall abandon the state of the golden life of humility and poverty, *having nothing,* wishing nothing, and seeking and loving Christ alone. Having put aside prayer and devotion, they will turn to *knowledge* which *inflates,* eagerness for lectures and the accumulation of a multitude of books under the pretext of their neighbor's edification and the *salvation of souls.* And because they prefer verbs to virtues, and science to sanctity,[a] they will remain cold within and devoid of charity, having changed gold into cold and porous silver.

2 Cor 6:10

1 Cor 8:1

1 Pt 1:9

AC 47; 2C 19; 2MP 69

[319]"Since they shall speak much but do little,[b] they will start to trample on the solidity of the humble life and the substance of their foundation, namely the truth of poverty; taking on distracting cares and concerns they will change silver into bronze, and they will not be concerned about returning to the earlier good things, namely to the fervor of heavenly desires. They will put on a simulation of humble and religious manners of great holiness, but inwardly they will be clothed in hypocrisy, panting for praises and honors. They will wish, not to be more outstanding and holier than others, but to be considered and to appear so. Thus they will sink to worse things and, to their own great loss, like bad merchants, will exchange the silver of eloquence and the product of learning for a hypocritical simulation in bronze, producing their works in order to get human praise.

[325]"But their simulation and hypocrisy cannot be concealed for long; and when it is laid bare, they will sense that they are losing their worth in the eyes of those who praised them, day to day becoming filthier, and because of this they will start to become angry and indignant and will persecute those they once tried so hard to please,

---

a. The original has the word-play: *praeponent verba virtutibus et scientiam sanctitati* [they prefer words to virtues and knowledge to holiness].

b. Cf. *Dicta beati Aegidii Assiensis* (Ad Claras Aquas, Quaracchi: Collegium S. Bonaventurae, 1905), 91; AF III (1897) 86: 13-17. Giles is quoted as exclaiming: "*Bo! Bo! Molto dico, poco fo!*"

seeking opportunities to afflict those who have stopped revering and complimenting them. In this way they shall change red and ringing bronze into hard and harsh iron. Changed into an iron nature, they will be ready and bold, not just to take revenge but also quick to do evil for insults received, but fragile, petty, and impatient beyond measure when it comes to bearing any insults.

[330]"Like the *iron mixed* with *tile* you see *in* my *feet,* so in the end the brothers will be, like iron, quick and cruel in inflicting evils and, like *tile,* impatient and fragile in bearing them. And so those brothers who at the beginning were clothed in the purest gold of the charity of Christ, *in the last days,* when the religion you founded will go into labor, will be considered like clay pots.

Dn 2:41, 43

Dn 12:13

[332]"This sackcloth I am wearing, and of which I show that I am ashamed, is the cheapness and austerity of poverty which the brothers promised the Lord they would wear proudly and joyfully. But they have abandoned their earlier charity: it was this that united them to God, and made them think that holding to the submissiveness of poverty and humility in all things was the first payment of heavenly honor, and the pledge of eternal glory. So they will refuse to bear the labors and shortages of poverty inwardly; and outwardly they will bear it only in appearance and in words, and even then with shame."

[335]After this the angel left him and, filled with grief, he began to lament anxiously in the presence of the Lord about all that he had seen and heard. Christ appeared to him and said: "Why are you so troubled and sad, Francis? I was the one who called you out of the world, ignorant, weak, and simple, so that in you I might show forth my wisdom and strength. Anything good that you have begun or done in the Church and in the religion will be credited to my name. I am the one who created humanity, assumed it, redeemed, repaired, and reconciled it freely. I direct, protect, and preserve those whom I have chosen and *call to penance.* And *without me* no one *can* will or *accomplish* the good. *I called you* from the world when you were in sin. I enlightened you and taught you *to take* the *easy yoke* of my way of life *upon you* and carry it humbly. I will guard and preserve all that I founded and planted through you. I will raise up whatever falls, and will repair whatever is destroyed, and I will substitute others for those who have fallen. If they are not yet born, I will cause them to be born. And even if your religion should be reduced in numbers to three, it will still remain, by my favor, unshaken until the end of time.

AC 112; 2C 158;
VIII 3; 1MP 40;
2MP 81

Test 1

Lk 5:32; Jn 15:5

Is 42:6

Mt 11:29, 30

[348]"*The Word of God did not fail* because the Jews *did not accept* me but rather *persecuted me* and killed my disciples, *the remnant* of my chosen

Rom 9:6; Jn 1:11

Jn 15:20;
Rom 9:27; 11:5

Mal 1:11

1 Jn 2:18

one *have been saved* and *will be saved;* and *my name* has been *made great among the nations.* In a similar way, in this *last hour,* the chief effect and fruit of my promise and intention, which I decided to produce through you, cannot be hindered or destroyed by any opposition, whether human or satanic."

Rom 1:20; 2:1

Mk 16:20

[351]His spirit was consoled by the words of Christ. And in order that the brothers might *have no excuse* in the sight of God, he fulfilled in himself what he preached to the brothers, and *confirmed* by the example of his deeds what he taught in *words.* For he inspired them to observe perfectly the *Rule* revealed to him by the Lord.[a] Before their eyes Christ multiplied virtues and signs so that He might increase in them fidelity and love for this way and for His life and *Rule* which they professed, and that He might unite them in hatred of anything contrary to it.

1 Cor 2:9

[356]While [Francis] was at the Speco of Sant'Urbano,[b] Christ Jesus sent him a glorious angel. The angel revealed to him the privileges or unique favors granted by God in heaven to those who love and observe the *Rule* purely to the very end. The angel encouraged him to announce to the brothers the unique glory *which* Christ *has prepared* in heaven for those who carry out the life and *Rule* faithfully and devoutly: blissful exaltation to the kingdom without any delay in the pains of Purgatory; the gleaming bright mansions for the disciples of Christ; defense during the exile of this pilgrimage; unique protection from the snares of the demons and from falling into mortal sin; joy-

Rom 8:11

ful and Christ-like *dwelling of* Christ and His *Spirit* in the souls and bodies of those who observe the *Rule* purely and faithfully; and for those dying within the religion in the habit of humility and poverty, the forgiveness of all sins of commission and omission because of the sign and the reality, if they were found in it at the last, when they mercifully accepted the end. To those who have devotion for those who observe the *Rule* and for our religion, and to those who receive them devotedly and assist them kindly: an increase of the gifts of grace; protection from enemies; freedom from sins. If they listen to the brothers and persevere in their early love and reverence for them until the end, they will receive at the end mercy and the rest of eternal peace.

1C 61; LJS 40; 3
LMj V 10; LMn

---

a. Once again Angelo repeats his conviction that Christ Himself revealed the *Rule* to Francis, cf. HTrb I 371, 457; IV 87. The same sentiment is expressed in *Apologia* 137, n 98; and Letter 14, in *Angeli Clareni Opera,* I, *Epistole,* ed. Lidya von Auw (Roma, n.p., 1980), 74.

b. The tradition of the Speco di Sant Urbano, outside of Narni, maintains that Francis came there on his way from Rome and the approval of the *propositum vitae* by Innocent III. Thomas of Celano records a miracle here, see 1C 61; 3C 17. See Edward Hutton, "Over the Somma to Narni," in *Assisi and Umbria Revisited* (London: Hales & Carter, 1953), 99-105.

365To those, on the other hand, who persecute, attack, and hate those brothers and their religion and this way of life, there will come, in the present, deprivation of grace; darkness of mind; entanglement in sin; bitterness of heart; and ungodliness; and, if they do not repent and regain their senses before death, the curse of Christ and eternal damnation will come upon them.[a]

367Instructed by Christ and his heavenly messenger, *in the power of the Holy Spirit* Francis announced to the brothers the incomparable dignity, hidden glory, and sublimity of the imitation of the poor and humble life of Christ. With signs and extraordinary deeds, and with *living and effective words,* the upright of heart among them were inflamed to a pure observance of the life they had undertaken, and were strengthened in their reverence for the *Rule* they professed.

365To those he knew to be perfect in love of Christ he revealed the secrets of his heart and what he had received directly from Christ. He told them that love and full, faithful observance of the poverty and humility of Christ were the foundation, the substance, and the root of the evangelical life and *Rule* revealed to him by Christ. Jesus, the Son of God, consecrated it: born of a poor little mother in a cave, *lying in a manger,* and *wrapped in swaddling clothes because* he had *no place in the inn;* he was circumcised and offered to God; *fleeing into Egypt* and on His return from there, *dwelling in Nazareth;* begging for *three days,* fasting, preaching; dying, buried in another's tomb, *rising from the dead.* He declared that this was the root of obedience; the mother of renunciation; the death of self-satisfaction, greed, and avarice; the obedience and activity of faith; the expression of hope; the proof of humility; giving birth to *the peace of God which surpasses all understanding.*

375He said to the brothers: "Christ has assured me that the religion, when the foundation of poverty is removed, will become a cheap and miserable ruin. For this religion has been consecrated in a special way to the reverent service of charity and of the cross, in order to preserve humble poverty and the bonds of the commands of Christ. It has been chosen to receive spiritually and *give birth* to Christ Jesus *in the inn* of the Church *in the last days,* like another *Virgin Mary* in the Spirit. It is to promise, love and preserve this 'having nothing' on earth. Loving and preserving this, the brothers will bear Christ Jesus and His Spirit reverently and humbly. *Persevering to the end,* they will leave this life safe and sure of the kingdom of heaven."

Rom 15:13, 19

Heb 4:12

Lk 2:7

Mt 2:13, 23

Lk 2:46

Lk 24:46

Phil 4:7

Lk 2:7

Dn 12:13; Lk 1:27

Mt 10:22; 24:13

---

a. Similar promises are related in 2MP 79 and in Chr TE XIII in which Brother Leo told Brother Peter, Provincial Minister of England, that Francis had revealed these promises to Brother Rufino, cf. *Thirteenth Century Chronicles,* 161-2.

[381] Because of this he wanted them all to have the *Rule*, all to know it and, what is more, they were to die with it. Mindful of this admonition, that holy lesser brother who always carried a breastplate next to his flesh, in the end was sentenced to death by the Saracens for preaching and constantly confessing the faith. Taking the *Rule* which he always carried with him, he raised his *eyes* and his hands with the *Rule to heaven, saying: "Into your hands, Lord Jesus Christ, I commend my spirit.* And if, human as I am, I have in any way sinned against this *Rule,* may You, lover of all, graciously forgive me." After these words he was beheaded and passed to Christ with the palm of martyrdom.

[388] Blessed Francis called this *Rule the tree of life,* the fruit of wisdom, the fountain of paradise, the ark of salvation, *the ladder ascending* into *heaven, the pact of the eternal covenant, the Gospel of the kingdom,* and the *brief word* which *the Lord made* on earth with His disciples. He taught the brothers that through the *Rule* they would *find* true *rest for* their *souls* and bodies, and experience the blessed *sweetness* of the *easy* and light *burden and yoke* of Christ, the weight that bears them up to heaven.

[391] In this way he had already organized and fully formed the brothers, assuring and strengthening them to the best of his ability by holy words and example to revere and observe purely and faithfully the life they professed. Then, on fire with the seraphic love which carried him into Christ, and to put words into action, he longed to offer himself *to God* as *a living sacrifice* through the fire of martyrdom. Three times he started out on journeys to the lands of unbelievers. But in order to test more fully the fire of his fervor, twice he was prevented by divine intervention.

[395] The third time, however, by Christ's design, he was led to the Sultan of Babylon after suffering many insults, chains, beatings, and hardships. Standing in the presence of the Sultan, he was entirely aglow with the fire of the Holy Spirit. He preached to him Christ Jesus and the faith of the Gospel with such force, such lively and moving words, that the Sultan and the bystanders were amazed. By the power of the words which Christ spoke through him the Sultan, moved to gentleness, willingly listened to his words against the decree of his own wicked law, and insistently invited him to arrange to stay in his land. He ordered that Francis and all his brothers were to be able have access to the Sepulcher freely, without paying tribute.[a]

---

a. That this permission was given is difficult to deny. That it was acted upon prompts a number of questions. Cf. infra 400 b.

[The First Tribulation or Persecution of the Order of Blessed Francis]

¹Meanwhile, with the shepherd away, the *ravenous wolf* tries *to seize and scatter* the flock, and *the gate is opened* to him by the very brothers who, more than others, were expected to oppose his attack and take precautions against his ambush. Those especially who were in authority and seemed wiser and more intelligent than the rest turned to pleasing their own way of thinking.[a] They covered tepidity and infidelity under the appearance of discretion; and preached through cunning words and deeds a manner of life different from that given to them, the one their shepherd had received from heaven, supporting their views with passages from the Scriptures and the example of other religious. They did not understand that by human *prudence,* which is called *death* by the Apostle, they were *digging* the pit of the abyss for themselves, forging the calf of idolatry, and retreating from the height of perfection they had promised.

²They judged it foolish, dangerous, and impossible to imitate and follow Christ simply and obediently, although He was the one who had spoken to them and had revealed the pattern of their life in Francis and through Francis. The sons *of Israel,* after *coming out from Egypt* and crossing *the Red Sea,* became unbelieving, and sure of their own self-sufficiency. They gave no thought to the wonders they had experienced, seen, and heard while God was acting and *speaking* to them through *Moses.* In much the same way, these leaders, having left the world, given up their own will, taking on the evangelical life of the Cross, persuaded themselves and others that it was not useful

a. According to ChrJG 11: "Blessed Francis . . . left behind two vicars, Brother Matthew of Narni and Brother Gregory of Naples. Matthew he put at St. Mary of the Portiuncula, so that remaining there he could receive those who were to be received into the Order; but Gregory he appointed to travel about Italy to strengthen the brothers. And because according to the first *Rule* the brothers fasted on Wednesdays and Fridays and, with the permission of Blessed Francis, also on Monday and Saturdays, and ate meat on other days when eating meat was lawful, these vicars celebrated a chapter along with certain older brothers of Italy, in which they ordained that the brothers were not to eat meat that had been procured for them on days on which meat was permitted, but only such meat as might be offered them by the faithful of their own accord. And in addition, they ordained that they were to fast on Mondays and on two other days, and that on Mondays and Saturdays they were not to procure for themselves milk products, but were to abstain from these, unless perhaps they were offered to them by the devoted faithful." *Thirteenth Century Chronicles,* 26-7. For background information, see Rosalind B. Brooke, *Early Franciscan Government: Elias to Bonaventure* (Cambridge: Cambridge at the University Press, 1959), 76-105.

Mt 7:15; Jn 10:12

Jn 10:3

Rom 8:6; Mk 12:1

Ps 114:1

Ex 13:18

Dt 1:1

humbly and obediently to follow Christ, who spoke and worked in Francis, the man sent to them by heaven. They therefore judged it necessary and just to drag behind them those who walked in simplicity and fidelity: they considered it praiseworthy.

[During Francis's Absence]

[13]The presumption and boldness of these men increased after Saint Francis went on pilgrimage overseas to visit the holy places, preach the faith of Christ to the unbelievers, and gain the crown of martyrdom, as has been said. In many provinces they treated cruelly and harshly the brothers who resisted their efforts and opposed their decrees and who followed instead the footprints and teachings of their father with all their hearts. They not only inflicted unjust penances on them, but expelled them from their company and community as people lacking good sense.

Acts 18:25

3 Jn 9

[16]A great many brothers, especially the *fervent in spirit,* considered disobedient, *were not received* by them; and others, giving way to their fury, were scattered and wandered here and there. They deplored the absence of their holy shepherd and guide, and *with* many *tears* and constant prayers begged the Lord for his return.

2 Mc 11:6; Acts 20:31

Ps 53:3

[18]*God* was *looking down* from on high on their invocations and pleas and was moved by their afflictions. He therefore appeared to Francis after that sermon to the sultan and his princes.[a] "Francis," he said, "go back. The flock of your poor *brothers* which you *gathered* in my name has been *dispersed.* It has taken the wrong way and needs your leadership so that, being united and strengthened, it may grow. They have already begun to turn from the way of perfection which you handed on to them and are not remaining in the love and practice of charity, humility and holy poverty, and the innocence of simplicity in which you planted and established them."

Ex 4:18, 19; Is 56:8

[23]After this apparition, and after visiting the Lord's Sepulcher,[b] he hastened back to the land of the Christians. *His flock,* which he had

Ez 34:12

---

a. The ChrJG 12-3 offers a different version of this "revelation." According to Jordan, "A certain lay brother became very angry over these constitutions, inasmuch as these vicars had presumed to add something to the *Rule* of the holy father and, taking with him these constitutions, he set out to cross the sea without the permission of the vicars . . . At this same time, there was beyond the sea a certain prophetess who predicted many things that came true, wherefore she was called the tongue that speaks the truth. She said: 'Return, return, because on account of the absence of Brother Francis, the Order is disturbed, torn asunder, and scattered. . .' "

b. This is the first mention of a journey to Jerusalem. That in itself is surprising since it would have been significant not only for Francis but for his companions. Moreover, the decree of Honorius III, *Cum carissimi in Christo,* July 24, 1217, under pain of excommunication prohibited pilgrims' visiting Holy Places under control of Muslims, to avoid paying tolls to them. There are, therefore, a number of discrepancies that make Angelo's statement questionable.

left united, he found *dispersed* as the Lord had said. Seeking it out with great effort and tears, he gathered it together.

²⁵When the afflicted brothers heard of his return, they went to him with haste, great desire, and immense joy of heart. *Giving thanks to God, they threw themselves at his feet* and honored the very footprints of the shepherd they had missed for so long. He encouraged the timid, consoled the sorrowing, rebuked the restless, and reprimanded the fault of those who dispersed them; and he brought together in charity those who were scattered and those who scattered them. He inspired and inflamed both groups by his exhortations and admonitions to bear happily all hardships small or great and even death for the sake of Christ and observance of the *Rule*. Lk 17:16; Mt 17:14

²⁹*All were filled with wonder at the words of grace which came from his mouth;* and they were amazed on considering the perfection of his life, his outstanding practice of virtue, and the countless signs and wonders God accomplished every day through him. Those who put the prudence of their own ideas before his warnings and exhortations could not openly resist or reasonably argue against his words. Lk 4:22

³²They all remained silent therefore and seemed to follow and obey him with reverence. Some obeyed with *pure heart* and *good conscience* and *unfeigned faith;* others obeyed out of human prudence and the demands of their vow, but not willingly. The latter, fearing any note of disgrace in the eyes of men, especially of prelates, decided among themselves that when the time came, they would rule themselves and others by their own judgment and maintain with their followers an honorable reputation for holiness and integrity, meanwhile, through their prudence, moving back and away from the intention and desire of the founder. For they feared him and humbled themselves before him, showing externally great friendliness and devotion to him in word and deed. In this way, under the mantle of his holiness, they covered up their intended plans. 1 Tm 1:5

³⁹For they knew that the Father of Christians, the Lord Supreme Pontiff, and his brothers, the lord cardinals, revered and loved him particularly, and out of regard for his holiness granted him generous favors and venerated him with sincere affection. They also knew that love, reverence, and faithful and obedient attachment to him merited the good will and confidential access to those same people; and acting otherwise would gain their displeasure and exclusion from their friendship.

[43]Those ministers and custodians, as well as Brother Elias himself and his followers, to whom they gave incentives for disbelief, disrespect, and disobedience toward the founder, tried to approach the Lord Cardinal[a] who, out of devotion, liked to be present at the General Chapter which was then held every year at Saint Mary of the Portiuncula, or "of the Angels." They cautiously suggested to him that Saint Francis, because of his great purity and innocence, was not concerned about discussing with the brothers and deciding matters that were necessary and appropriate for the religion. By himself he was not strong enough to satisfy or provide adequately for such a great multitude of brothers, especially since he was uneducated, compared to the many wise brothers, of great perfection in holiness, upright conduct, and learning who were under his governance. They would be able to direct him and help him with many things, as he was sick and physically weak. "You should exhort him, so that it will not seem that these words are coming from us: he should make decisions about the business of the religion with his brothers who are better prepared for such things. He should take advantage of their advice and assistance, for a firmer and more secure governance of the whole religion."

AC 18; 44; 2M

[51]Their words pleased the Lord Cardinal and seemed reasonable and quite necessary. Since the Lord Cardinal used to confer with Francis frequently on spiritual matters, on one such occasion, the Cardinal in a friendly conversational tone congratulated him, saying: "You ought to be very happy and give great thanks to God, Brother Francis. God has expanded the religion and has given you many wise and holy brothers who should be capable of directing and governing not only the religion but even the whole Church. You must therefore be very grateful to God for this, and you should ask their advice and make use of the prudence and discernment of such great men for the good governance, preservation, and stability of the whole religion."

2C 148; LMj VI
AC 49; 2MP 43

[58]Through the Spirit of God Saint Francis understood both the weight of the cardinal's words and the source from which they sprang. He said to him: "Come, my Lord, and I will speak to the brothers in your presence."

---

a. Cardinal Rainerio Capocci, rather than Cardinal Hugolino, who was in Lombardy at the time. Rainerio Capocci (+1252) was Cardinal Deacon of Sta. Maria in Cosmedin, Bishop of Viterbo and Rector of the Ducato in Spoleto. According to Chr JG 16, he was present at the Chapter of 1221. Also, cf. FA:ED I 295 c.

SF 3; TL V 7;
2MP 68

[60]In his presence then, Blessed Francis said to the brothers: "Christ called me, an unlearned and simple man,[a] to follow the foolishness of His cross. He said to me: 'I want you to be a new fool in the world and in word and deed to preach the foolishness of my cross; to look to me, both you and all your brothers, and to be joined to me, without any examples from the *Rules* of Augustine or Benedict or Bernard.' But you! You wish to follow your own ideas and your learning and drag me along: in the end your learning will put you to shame."[b]

VSF 3; AC 18;
L V 7; 2MP 68

[68]And turning to the Lord Cardinal he said: "These wise brothers of mine, whom you praise, think that with their human prudence they can deceive God, you, and me as they deceive and mislead themselves. They invalidate and trample under foot what Christ is saying and has said to them through me for the *salvation of their souls* and the good of the whole religion. I do not say and have never said anything of myself, but only what I have received from Him, with conviction of spirit, through His grace and goodness alone. But they, to the great peril of their souls, prefer their own mind to *the mind of Christ* and their own will to the will of God. They govern themselves badly and they govern the others who believe them badly as well. They do not build: they try to overturn and destroy what Christ out of sheer goodness and charity has determined to plant and to build in me and in them for the sure *salvation of* our *souls* and the building up of the whole Church."[c]

[76]The force and power of his words *changed the mind* of the Lord Cardinal, and he recognized that what he was saying was absolutely true.

[77]He called together the brothers who had persuaded him to present their proposals to Saint Francis. He said to them: *"Brothers, listen to me. Watch yourselves. Do not deceive yourselves.* Do not be ungrateful for the gift of God. God really is in this man, and Christ and His Spirit speak in him. *Whoever hears him* does not *hear* a man, but God. *Whoever rejects him rejects God, not man.* Humble your hearts and obey him if you wish *to please God.* If you offend him, thinking and acting contrary to his commands and counsels, you will deprive yourselves of

1 Pt 1:9

1 Cor 2:16

1 Pt 1:9

Ex 14:5; 1 Sm 10:9

Acts 15:13

Lk 21:34; Acts 5:35;
Col 2:4, 8

Lk 10:16

1 Thes 2:4; Heb 11:6

---

a. The Latin phrase is *idiotam et simplicem* [unlearned and simple]. In Test 19, Francis uses *idiotae* to describe himself and his first companions, and, in *A Letter to the Entire Order* 39 (hereafter LtOrd), to describe himself. It can also be found as a derogatory remark on those refusing Francis hospitality in *True and Perfect Joy* 11 (hereafter TPJ).

b. While this passage can be found in 2MP 68, its presence in TL V as well as in this text suggests that it was used frequently by the Spirituals and was part of that collection of sayings that was passed from one group to another to support their position.

c. These words to Cardinal Rainierio Capocci seem to be an expression of literary license in which Angelo builds on earlier sources. The same may be written of the lengthy discourse that follows, lines 77-136, in which the reader may wonder if this is the teaching of Francis or, more likely, of Angelo.

Heb 4:12; Dt 8:3

Heb 4:12

Ps 7:10; Rv 2:23;
1 Cor 2:10

the fruit of salvation and of your vocation. You will lessen the state of your religion. You will darken your hearts, wrapped in darkness in your many offenses and faults. *The living word of God comes from* his *mouth* and, as the Apostle says, it is *more penetrating than a two-edged sword.* He is not ignorant of the cunning of Satan. No, he *reaches even* the secret *intentions and thoughts,* satanic and human. He cannot be deceived by human tricks because he has in him the Spirit of God who searches *minds and hearts* and *even the depths of God."*

[89]Before leaving, the Lord Cardinal preached the word of God to all there, both the brothers who had gathered in a great multitude for the chapter, to the devout persons there, and the people of the city of Assisi. He was a wise man and led a good and upright life. After wisely, eloquently, and effectively preaching for the edification of souls and the correction of conduct, at the end of his sermon he turned to complimenting, commending, and praising the brothers. He extolled their life and perfection with repeated praise, in an effort to attract and inflame all the people present to reverence and respect for the brothers and their holy religion.

[95]When the sermon was finished, Francis knelt before the Lord Cardinal and asked both for his blessing and his permission to say a few words to the brothers and the people in his presence. Having received the blessing, he spoke to all of them: "Out of the great good will and charity he shows to everyone, especially toward my brothers and religion, our revered Father the Lord Cardinal has been greatly deceived. He supposes and believes that there is great holiness in us, unique virtue, and love of perfection. But it would not be right for us to provide the occasion for falsehood and lies. Both you and he would be deceived if you believed in that perfection and excellence that he preached to you about us: it would be an occasion of harm and great danger, both to you and to us. We are ungrateful to God for our vocation; we do not have the works and accomplishments of real poor and humble men, or real lesser Brothers, and we are not striving to have them as we promised. I have only one wish: that the Lord Cardinal and all of you may know the works, words, and desires which Lesser Brothers ought to have and demonstrate, so that you are not deceived about them, and they may not deceive and mislead themselves and you as well.

[Future Failings]

[107]"You will see that the Lesser Brothers do not persuade the novices whom they receive to *give all* they have *to the poor* according to form of the Gospel as they promised, but rather suggest to them that

Lk 18:22

they save something for books, for the church, or some reason or other, for themselves, or for the needs of the brothers. You will see brothers acquiring material goods beyond their daily bodily needs. You will see them begging money or coins for themselves and their places or for building churches, and accepting legacies and inheritances from you for whatever reason or pretense. Then you will know they are deceived and misled, because the Lesser Brothers have been sent by Christ to demonstrate His poverty and humility more by their deeds than by words.

¹¹³"You will see them abandon poor little places, worthless and small, located far from the world, and exchange them and buy beautiful and luxurious places inside villages and towns, under the pretext that these are for preaching and for your benefit. You will see them dismiss holy prayer and devotion to apply themselves to study and the acquisition of books, the gaining of burial rights,^a wishing for and getting abundantly the use of all things. To get and hold onto

Test 25-26 all these things they will seek privileges from the Roman Curia and bring lawsuits based on the rights of such privileges. At that time, open your eyes and watch yourselves. Do not follow them or listen to them. Such men will be Lesser Brothers in name only. By word and deed they attack and destroy, in themselves and others, the poverty and humility which they promised to the Lord. Through them much evil will happen in the religion and in the Church.

¹²⁴"I tell you these things before they happen so that both you and they may be on guard against the snares of demons and the wickedness of evil men and may avoid future evils. For *times* of many tribulations and *deceptions are approaching.* The first sign of all these things, which will soon appear, is that the brothers will turn from love and observance of the life and Gospel of Christ. For neither learning nor wisdom nor eloquence will draw the world to Christ, but only a pure and holy way of living and perfect observance of the commands and counsels of Christ." Lk 21:8

¹³⁰Then the Lord Cardinal said to him: "Brother Francis! Why have you nullified my sermon? Why are you predicting such great imperfections about your brothers, in your religion?" Saint Francis said to him: "I have honored your preaching by telling the truth about me and my brothers with restraint. I have also spared myself

---

a. In addition to the acquisition of books, the struggle to gain burial rights became a preoccupation of Angelo. The concept returns six different times in HTrb: III 4; IV 26; V 183, 194, 213, 297. It also appears in his *Exposition on the Rule,* II 24. Salimbene de Adam writes that this was one of the accusations hurled at the brothers by the secular clergy, undoubtedly because of economic reasons. Cf. *Chronicle of Salimbene de Adam,* trans. Joseph L. Baird, Giuseppe Baglivi, and John Robert Kane (Binghamton, NY: Medieval & Renaissance Texts & Studies, 1986), 404.

and them, by setting the word of truth as an obstacle against ruin and wishing, on this occasion, to contrast your public praise with a healthy and necessary admonition to my brothers who are not yet fully formed in humility."

[137]Those words that Saint Francis proclaimed to the brothers, words given to him by Christ, seemed generally *heavy* and unbearable to those who were *wise according to the flesh.* And the ministers had that chapter of the first rule removed, the one about the prohibitions of the Holy Gospel, as Brother Leo writes.

[139]Although Saint Francis was fervently proclaiming to the brothers what the Lord revealed to him, and perfectly demonstrated in himself by the example of his deeds the things that he preached, the brothers closed their ears to his holy words and turned their eyes away from his deeds. Rather they wanted to draw him to their own way against his will, instead of submitting to his health-giving divine counsels and commands, and being conformed in a healthy way to the examples of perfection in his deeds.

[143]For when he had returned from regions overseas,[a] a minister was speaking with him, as Brother Leo reports, about the chapter on poverty, to understand fully the will of Blessed Francis and his understanding of it. Blessed Francis said to him: "I understand the chapter on poverty just as the words of the Holy Gospel and the *Rule* sound literally. The brothers may have nothing and ought to have nothing except a garment with a cord, trousers, and shoes, if forced by necessity."

[149]And the minister said to him: "What am I to do, father? I have so many *books* worth *fifty* pounds." He said this because he wished to keep them as well as his conscience, since he was keeping all those books with remorse of conscience, as he knew that Francis understood literally the chapter on poverty strictly in that way.

[153]Blessed Francis said to him: "Brother, I cannot and must not act against my conscience and the profession of the Holy Gospel we have promised because of your books." On hearing this, the minister became sad. Blessed Francis, seeing that he was upset, spoke to him in great fervor of spirit as standing for all his brothers: "You, Lesser Brothers, wish to seem and to be called observers of the Holy Gospel, but in fact you want *to hold the purse.*"

[158]I myself saw a brother who heard him preaching at Bologna—those who saw this reported it—when he entered the town he wanted to head toward the place of his brothers. There he saw a

---

a. This passage is an almost exact quote from IntR 5, cf. FA:ED II 204 b. It is a passage that Angelo also repeats in his *Exposition on the Rule,* I 166-8.

house had been built that exceeded the limits of poverty. He turned back and went instead to the house of the Preachers, and they received him with great joy.

[161]There was a Brother Preacher of extraordinary holiness and learning who listened devoutly and humbly to the words of Saint Francis. He knew why Saint Francis refused to stay with his own brothers, and felt compassion for the brothers' desolation. He tried to persuade him to go to them and pardon them if they had offended him in any way. Blessed Francis said to him: "It would not be kind indulgence to them for me to approve by my action such a notorious transgression against the poverty they promised, and an offense to God if I were to accept their hospitality while they remain in sin."

[165]Seeing that he could not convince Blessed Francis to do this, he said: "For the sake of your other brothers, so that they not incur dishonor from the way you turned back, let us go to these brothers: you will rebuke them with charity for their offense, and so you will fulfill your duty. If *because of conscience* you do not wish to remain in such a house, we will come back. In this way the reputation of the brothers will be preserved and they will make amends for their offense." Blessed Francis agreed to follow the brother's advice. He found the brothers ready to accept whatever penance he wished to impose on them and he pardoned them.

1 Cor 10:27, 28

[172]But then he learned of the firm, or rather stubborn attitude of one of his brothers, Brother Pietro Stacia by name, who had been a doctor of law in the world. Through the Spirit he knew that the brother's conscience, his ways of acting, and his teachings were all contrary to the purity of the *Rule,* so he cursed him. He had been a great man in the world and was much loved by the ministers because of his learning. The brothers therefore, near the end of Saint Francis' life, asked him to pardon and to bestow the favor of his blessing on such a great man he had cursed, but he answered: "My sons, I cannot bless anyone whom the Lord has cursed, and he is cursed."

[177]What more can be said? After a short time, that brother grew ill and was close to death. Shaking, with a terrifying voice, he began to scream at the brothers standing by him: "I am damned! Here are the demons! They are carrying me away, cursed, to the torments of the eternal curse and damnation."

[180]All present, after experiencing this frightening and sorrowful spectacle of a horrible and fearful judgment learned from it that anyone whom Blessed Francis cursed was eternally cursed beforehand by God. Whether he blessed or cursed anyone, he was moved not by any human emotion or opinion. Rather, having been made

Christ-like, he revealed the secrets of divine judgments and the divine will, and perceived in the Word the future as if it were the past.

[184]As Brother Thomas of Celano writes of him, when he once heard of the boundless excesses of some brothers and of the bad example they gave to lay people, he was overcome by grief and turned himself completely to Christ. Then some others arrived unexpectedly and told him about the holy way of living of some other brothers, the edification of lay people, and their conversion to the state of penance. The lover of the good and of the *salvation of souls* rejoiced on hearing this. Enlightened by a heavenly revelation he understood the rightness of divine justice which embraces and blesses good people and rejects and curses the evil.

[188]In great force and strength of spirit, he cursed those who apostatized from the profession of the life they promised and defamed the religion by their perverse deeds. He blessed the ones who kept their promises and edified their neighbors by the example of a holy life and caused the religion to spread the fragrance of a *good reputation*. All who heard him realized that a blessing or a curse pronounced by Saint Francis on earth came from God and was ratified in heaven.

[191]The brothers who were really wise, and truly loved Christ, realized that his words and deeds came from Christ and His Spirit. *Those who welcomed* him and *listened* to him, *welcomed* and *listened to* Christ speaking in him. The upright and pure of heart listened to him and followed him without hesitation.

[194]But those who love themselves, *inflated* with human *knowledge,* who *seek their own interests rather than those of Jesus* Christ, *trembled with fear where there was no fear.* They *did not accept him,* because *they did not call upon* God. How could they believe? They desired and grasped at human *glory* since they were *not seeking the glory which comes from God* alone. For *God scatters the bones of those* who seek *to please men.* They will be *put to shame* because *God has rejected them.*

[199]"For anyone who prefers learning to holiness," Saint Francis said to the brothers, "will never prosper. Whoever loves human praise is a slave to lies. But God who *is truth* will destroy those who cultivate lies."

[202]**Knowing the future through the Holy Spirit,** he would say: "With **the pretext** of preaching and **edifying others, the brothers shall abandon their vocation, that is, pure and holy simplicity, prayer,** humility, **and our Lady Poverty. It will happen that, because they believe themselves inflamed with the devotion and love of God, they will remain cold, empty** of charity. **And so they will be unable to return to their vocation, as they have wasted the**

AC 41; 2C 155
LMj VIII 3; 2M

1 Pt 1:9

Phil 4:8

Mt 10:40;
Lk 9:48; 10:16

1 Cor 8:1

Phil 2:21;
Ps 14:4; 53:6
Jn 1:11; Ps 14:5

Jn 5:44

Ps 53:6; Gal 1:10;
Eph 6:6
Ps 53:6

Jn 14:6

AC 103; 2MP 7

time for living according to their calling; and it is to be **feared that what they seemed** *to have* **will be** *taken away from them* and they will find their hands empty on the day of tribulation. The people they think they converted to the Lord through their preaching were actually converted to the Lord by the prayers of the holy brothers in deserted places who weep over their own sins and those of others. *It has been given* by Christ to true Lesser Brothers *to know the mystery of the kingdom of God, but to the rest* to know *only in parables.* There are so many who willingly climb up toward knowledge that anyone who renders himself sterile of it for the love of God will be blessed."

Lk 8:18; Mk 4:25

Lk 8:10

²¹²Some brothers came from France and reported to him that the brothers had recently received an important man, a master of sacred theology in Paris.[a] Both the people and the clergy were greatly edified by this. Blessed Francis listened, then sighed and responded: "I am afraid, my sons, that in the end such masters will destroy my plant. The true masters are those who show their way of life to their neighbors through good works with gentle wisdom. **A person** has only as much **learning as his actions show;** and is wise only as much as he loves God and neighbor; **and a religious is only as good a preacher as** much as he humbly and faithfully does the good that he understands."

²²⁰A holy brother, a master of theology, came from Germany at that time to see Saint Francis, to be sure about his understanding and intention regarding the *Rule.*[b] As he learned and listened to his intention about life according to the *Rule,* his spirit became as tranquil and consoled as if Christ Jesus Himself, not a man, had spoken.

²²⁴After the interview the brother knelt humbly before Saint Francis and said: "I now promise again, into your hands, to observe, faithfully and purely, this evangelical life and *Rule* according to the pure and faithful intention which the Holy Spirit has spoken clearly through your mouth, until the end of my life, as much as Christ's grace will allow me. But one favor I ask of you. If in my lifetime it happens that the brothers fall away from the pure observance of the *Rule* as you foretell through the Spirit, so much that, because of their opposition, I cannot observe it freely among them, I ask by your obedience that I may withdraw to observe the *Rule* perfectly, alone or with some brothers who also wish to observe it purely."

---

a. The identity of this person is unknown, as is the source of the story.
b. From Angelo's narration of the difficulties that faced Caesar of Speyer, cf. infra HTrb II 29, 93-104, this theologian from Germany may well have been Caesar himself. For further insights, cf. FA:ED I 526-7. Angelo repeats this same story in his *Exposition on the Rule*, X 76-81.

Gn 48:18; Ps 110:4

[231]Hearing these things, Blessed Francis was overjoyed, and blessed him, *placing* his *right* hand *on his head,* saying: *"You are a priest forever according to the order of Melchisedek.* Know that what you asked is granted, by Christ and by me." [He showed in this way that all the promises made to him by Christ about his religion would, in the end, be fulfilled in those who would strive to observe the *Rule* simply, to the letter, and without glosses.][a]

Mt 11:30

[237]Those who bear the *easy yoke* of Christ's life and *Rule* with bitterness are sons of the flesh, always twisting the holy and pious understanding of the *Rule* toward their own fleshly way of thinking. They

Gal 4:29

are like Ishmael, *born according to the flesh,* who was hostile to Isaac who was born *according* to the promise *of the* Holy *Spirit* and lived a spiritual and holy life. So it will be in this life and religion: the sons of the flesh will persecute the sons of the spirit. But God, who divided

Dt 5:15

the sons of Israel from the Egyptians *with a strong hand and an outstretched arm,* will separate the true sons of the *Rule* from the sons of

Rom 8:6

the prudence of the flesh. He will abandon the latter in the shadows of error and the coldness of greed and self-love. The former He will lead

2 Cor 4:6

into the light of *divine brilliance* and the cross-like perfection of seraphic charity, and make them conformed *to the body of His brilliance* by the power with which *He subjects all things to himself.*

[The Beginning of Division]

[246]There was in the time of Saint Francis apparent unity outwardly among the brothers regarding the habit, living together, and obedience. But there was a hidden schism and great diversity in regard to the purity of the *Rule,* observing and loving it, and obedience and sincere following of the intention of the founder. Lacking

2 Cor 13:11;
Phil 2:2; 3:16
Rom 15:5; Phil 4:2

among them were the following: *to be of one mind;* to have the same charity; *to have the same mind* among all; to do *nothing out of rivalry* or

Phil 2:21

for *empty glory, each* considering *others superior; not seeking their own interest* but, with the founder, *those of Christ,* for the consolation of others, what is useful to them, and serves mutual edification.

Ps 57:7

[252]Brother Elias, having given himself to the subtleties of philosophy, secretly drew after himself a gang of rebels in a spirit of greed and vanity. *He opened up and dug a pit* for himself and, deceived, *he fell* into it and died.[b] He failed to recognize the stratagems, tricks, and inventions of Satan, and so, unaware, he prepared the ways for

---

a. While this sentence seems to be an insertion into a later manuscript, it can be found almost exactly in OL III 5, as well as in Angelo's *Exposition on the Rule* X 81.

b. For information on Brother Elias, his "giving himself to the subtleties of philosophy," character, and death, cf. HTrb II.

them, improved the route, and made their paths straight, opposing, in the founder, Christ Himself.

[256]Christ Himself kindly revealed this to a holy and venerable priest, the rector of a parish in Massa Trabaria, named Don Bartolo, whom Saint Francis designated to act in his place in all things and for all things because of his outstanding holiness. He was a very discerning man, a consoler of the sorrowful, full of mercy, piety, and charity. The brothers approached him confidently as the kindest of fathers and the instructor of their souls. He used to receive brothers into the religion and reconciled those who had been expelled and had left. With divine and clear reasoning and living example he demonstrated to them that the counsels of human wisdom that disagree with the way of perfection and the intention of the founder were more than useless: they were infected with *deadly poison.*

Jas 3:8

[262]This man, pleasing to God, at Christ's command, *in ecstasy of mind* while praying, was led to the lower reaches of hell. There he saw Lucifer in his place of punishments, surrounded by the chief spirits of the lower regions. The *prince of darkness* posed an angry question to them as he asked for advice. "We have received unpleasant and troubling news from the desert of the world, through men we hold in our power. Some men have appeared unexpectedly in the world. They despise and trample under foot the world *with the flesh* and its *vices.* They threaten the rights and the places of our domain. Unless we offer them some resistance, they will inflict *damage and great loss* on us. So think carefully what we should do to oppose them. You can hear more fully about their circumstances from those who have just come from there."

Ps 31:23;
Acts 10:10; 11:5

Eph 6:12

Gal 5:24

Acts 27:10

[270]At Lucifer's command they began to report, describing the life and perfection of these men. One huge demon stood up. He and some of the evil spirits under him were engaged in an extraordinary struggle with Saint Francis and his religion. He said: "Even though, as our prince said, many are rising against us recently in various ways, there is one man in particular, a man of lowly condition, unschooled and simple, who has a small society of others like himself. He is the one who has risen up against us *in* such *strength of spirit,* that it seems not a man but *Jesus of Nazareth* in person battling against us in him. No trick of ours, however subtle, no deception, however strong, can deceive or overthrow him or his followers. No matter how many traps we lay, left and right, we cannot capture or overcome him. What is even more painful, any of our faithful followers who go near become our adversaries and deadly enemies. Yet we cannot capture even one of their members."

Is 11:15

Mk 1:24; Lk 4:34

[279]There was a period of silence among them. Then the individual captains began to propose wicked plans as to how victory over their adversaries might be won quickly. The details I omit for the sake of brevity.

[281]They discussed various vices in many different ways, and proposed examples of how they gained unexpected victories over very great and—as they thought—unassailable saints. Then another demon, Lucifer's second in command, spoke after all the rest: "You have described numerous sly and workable plans; yet no one, believe me, has thought of the one way to win an overwhelming victory over them."

[286]All the demons were interested in hearing his plan and proposal, so he went on: "We cannot defeat these men unless we turn all our commitment, effort, cunning and activity, to the following. We must inspire those who are proud, boasting, curious, deceitful and dishonest, greedy, envious, presumptuous and false, whom we know are ours. By every means we must suggest to them and foster in them the desire to do penance and join them to serve the Lord. Once we have our faction among them, we will seek to increase it every day. By it we will upset them, infect their religion; we will undermine their vows, their words, habits and works. We will make their reputation rot so badly that they, because of the deadly stench, all who approach them will smell the odor of death, and will not smell the enlivening fragrance that leads to life."

[294]That plan of subversion pleased Lucifer and all his princes. From then on their policy was to pursue that last proposal with all their strength. God permitted, by His secret and hidden judgment, that the demons move men in tune with their aims and in sympathy with their spite to enter that religion, whose basic principles they hated as most opposed to theirs.

[298]At the beginning when Francis alone received the brothers, the demons were unable to carry out their evil plans for trickery, because he, enlightened like the cherubim by the Holy Spirit, *had eyes front and back, inside* and out. But then the number of ministers increased throughout the world, who lacked even a modicum of the spiritual perfection essential to forestall the hidden plots of the demons. And the spirit of every one of the ministers was carried away by the desire to increase the number of brothers, under the pretext of the *salvation of souls* and the expansion of the religion.[a] They *multiplied the people* but

Rv 4:6, 8

1 Pt 1:9

Is 9:3

---

a. Angelo touches on two issues, vocations and formation. In his *Exposition on the Rule*, Angelo points to the way in which some of the brothers went "recruiting" followers, cf. *Exposition on the Rule* II 8. Now he directs his remarks at those with "a modicum of spiritual perfection" who want "to increase the number of brothers," and writes of them in a most pejorative way.

did not increase the joy, as they mixed many perverse men among the innocent. These arrogant ministers, relying on their own prudence, wanted to rule, not to be ruled; to make a rule, for themselves and others, based on their own opinion and will, rather than observe the *Rule* humbly, mortifying their own will.

[Reunification of Office]

[305]Consequently for the founder, and for the brothers who walked in simplicity, *labor, sorrow, and affliction of spirit* increased. For the tepid, danger grew; for the dissatisfied, glee; and for the malicious, confidence in evil-doing.[a]

Ps 10:7; Eccl 1:17

[306]These evils grew so much even before the death of Saint Francis that he, who was the dwelling place of the Holy Spirit, was unable to remedy them by his words, his example, or signs and miracles of healing. Instead he chose, after praying, as the better role for himself, to spend time with God and renounce his office among the brothers.

151; AC 11, 39; MP 14; 2MP 39

[308]When he had done this,[b] one of his companions said to him: "Father, excuse me, because all I want to say to you, many have already thought. You know," he said, "how formerly through the grace of God, the whole religion flourished and remained in the state of purity and perfection, that is, how all the brothers fervently and zealously observed humility and poverty in all things, in small and poor dwellings, in small and poor books, and in cheap and poor clothing. And in these things, as well as in other exterior things, they were of one will, concerned about observing carefully everything that had to do with our calling and profession and good example. In this way they were of one mind in the love of God and neighbor. But now for a little while, this purity and perfection have begun to change into something different. In fact, many brothers believe they are being edified more by these ways than by those things mentioned; and it seems to them more fitting to live and behave according to these ways. Therefore they consider worthless the way of simplicity and poverty, which were the beginning and foundation of our religion . Thinking this over, we believe that they displease you, but we really wonder why, if they displease you, you tolerate them and do not correct them."

LC 106; 2MP 71

[319]"May the Lord forgive you," Blessed Francis said to him, "for wanting to be against me and opposed to me and involve me in

---

a. Again, Angelo points to the results of poor formation, cf. *Exposition on the Rule* II 6-7.

b. The following paragraphs, lines 308-340, present another lengthy citation from IntR.

these things that do not pertain to my office." And he said: "As long as I held office for the brothers, and they remained faithful to their calling and profession, and, although I was ill from the beginning of my conversion to Christ, with a little of my care, I satisfied them by my example and preaching. But afterwards I realized that the Lord *multiplied the number* of the brothers daily, and that through tepidity and lack of spirit they began to turn away from the straight and sure *way on which* they used *to walk* and take, as you said, a broad way, without paying attention to their calling and profession and good example, or would not give up the journey that had already begun despite my preaching and my examples, I entrusted the religion to the Lord and to the ministers.

328"When I renounced and gave up office among the brothers at the general chapter, I excused myself saying that, because of my illness, I could not take care of them and care for them. And yet, if the brothers had walked and were still walking according to God's will and my will, for their consolation I would not want them to have any other minister except me until the day of my death. As long as a faithful and good subject knows and observes the will of his prelate, then the prelate needs to have little concern about him. Rather, I would be so happy at the goodness of the brothers and be so consoled, both on their account and my own, that even if I were lying sick in bed, it would not be considered a burden to me to satisfy them."

333He said: "My office is spiritual, to overcome vices and correct them. Therefore, if I cannot overcome and correct them by preaching and example, the *Rule* must teach them. I do not want to become an executioner who beats and scourges, like a power of this world. *I trust in the Lord.* Invisible enemies, the Lord's police, who punish in this world and the next those who transgress the commandments of the Lord God, will take revenge on them, having them corrected by men of this world, to their disgrace and shame, and thus will return to their profession and calling. Nevertheless, until the day of my death I will not cease teaching the brothers by example and action *to walk by the path* which the Lord *showed* me, and which I showed and explained to them. Thus *they will have no excuse* before the Lord, and I will not be bound *to render* any further *account* about them or about myself before the Lord."

341For we who were with him when he wrote the *Rule* and almost all his other writings, bear witness that he wrote many things in the *Rule* and in his other sayings to which certain brothers were opposed during his life, which now, after his death, would be very useful to the whole religion.

Acts 6:7

1 Kgs 8:36

Ps 11:2

1 Kgs 8:36

Rom 1:20

Mt 12:36; Lk 16:2

Jn 21:24; 3 Jn 12

2C 120; AC 18, 1
1MP 20; 2MP 67

AC 106; 2MP 1

[344]He often said to his companions: "Here lies my pain and grief: those things which I received from the Lord by His mercy with great effort of prayer and meditation for the present and future good of the religion, and which are, as He assures me, by His will, some of the brothers, out of the subtlety and prudence of their knowledge, nullify and oppose me saying: 'These things must be kept and observed; but not those!' "

[349]The brothers pierced his soul and exasperated him, preferring things contrary to God and His saint. They bitterly tried him with their tricks, their innovations, and their refusal to obey, to the point that at their general chapter he renounced the office of minister imposed on him by Christ and His Vicar; and according to their wishes and merits, as *Samuel* once gave *Saul* to the sons of Israel, he allowed them to have Elias the alchemist[a], just what they deserved.

1 Sm 9:22

[353]After that he turned himself so completely to prayer that, absorbed in God, he really seemed to be **a person of another age.**

36, 82; LJS 44;
Mj IV 5; L3C 54

[354]Brothers who thought and taught things contrary to him were annoyed by the uprightness and purity of his words and the fervent zeal he showed in his discourses against the evils already widespread in the religion. They would not allow novices and other devout people free access to him, hindering them as much as they could in various, crafty ways, because he clearly and openly foretold things that would happen to the religion until the end, unmasking the evils of the present as if he already saw them in the past.

[359]With his prophetic eye he perceived therefore the evils that had already taken root in the religion as well as those that were to come until the end. With *fasting and prayer,* and *unutterable groans,* he unceasingly begged Christ Jesus, who can do all things, beyond our understanding and imagining, to apply a remedy that was fitting and needed.

Mt 17:20; Mk 9:28;
Rom 8:26

[361]Therefore Saint Francis cried out to God unceasingly with humble prayers and fiery affection for the preservation of his religion, pleasing to God, for the sure salvation of all the brothers past and future. The Most High heard the prayers of His servant, and the Lord said to him: "Francis, go and withdraw *in a desert* place *for forty days.* You will set your rule in order according to My word, which I will speak to you. I will give you what you ask, remedies that are

Mk 1:13

---

a. Alchemy, an early form of chemistry, with philosophical and magical associations, flourished in the 13th and 14th centuries. Examples of friars—Preachers and Lessers—who wrote alchemist treatises are Thomas Aquinas, Albert the Great, Roger Bacon, Ramon Lull, et al. Rosalind B. Brooke claims that certain alchemist treatises and *sonetti* bear the name of Elias, but "it has been much disputed whether in fact he wrote them." Cf. Brooke, *Government*, 153, n. 3. Salimbene is quite clear that Elias was an alchemist and cultivated friendships with those who shared his leanings. Cf. Salimbene, *Chronicle*, 152.

short, clear, and sure, which you will include in it. By these, the transgressors will be stricken in consciences, and will be without excuse before Me and My Church. Those who are pure and faithful lovers and observers of the *Rule* will have a reliable witness to its pure and faithful observance, and about your intention, and will not be able to doubt that your intention is *in accord with the good pleasure* of My will."

Eph 1:9

³⁶⁸These things happened before he gave up the office of minister, wishing to spend time with himself and God, and, as mentioned above, entrusted the religion to the ministers.

[The Composition of The Rule]

³⁶⁹He withdrew, therefore, according to the revelation the Lord gave him, and enclosed himself in the hermitage of Fonte Colombo, in the little cell which was in the jagged rock below the place. Only two brothers, Leo of Assisi and Bonizio of Bologna,ᵃ whom he chose as companions, dared to go near him. There he wrote down the *Rule* as Christ revealed it to him. He put in it nothing of his own but wrote only what Christ Jesus revealed to him from heaven.

LMj IV 11; AC 2MP 1

³⁷²Brother Elias and his followers and some ministers were in *an uproar* and turmoil while this *Moses,* Francis, spent time with God. They did not dare oppose him openly, so they furtively or secretly took the *Rule* from that man of God Brother Leo, to whom it had been given by the saint for safekeeping. They hid it, thinking in this way to prevent Saint Francis's plan, based on the word of Christ sent to him from heaven, to present it and have it approved by the Supreme Pontiff. *Having their understanding darkened,* those who carried this out did not want to hear of the seriousness of their presumptuous wickedness in doing such a thing, and to admit that in preferring their own wills to divine inspirations and commands they committed *a sin of divination;* and by *refusing* obedience *the crime of idolatry, not submitting* to the teachings of the saint and instructor whom God gave them.

WSF 4; WBC II

LMj IV 11

Ex 32:17

Eph 4:18

1 Sm 15:23

³⁷⁸The *holy man* understood that the grave offense of the brothers came from the envy of demons. Inspired by Christ,ᵇ whose goodness

2 Kgs 4:9

---

a. Otherwise unknown, "Bonizio" may be a misreading of an abbreviation in a text consulted by Angelo. The text may have read "Riccerio, Riziero or Rizerio of Bologna." This brother, from the noble Baschi family of Bologna, was a law student when he joined the brothers. He is pictured in 1C 49 as being close to Francis and is associated with the drafting and the observance of the *Rule,* cf. LJS 31; AC 101; 2C 44 a; 2MP 2. Ubertino da Casale states it was Br. Rufino who accompanied Francis and Leo to Fonte Colombo, cf. TL V 5:56. Cf. FA:ED II 66 d, 131 b.

b. The image of the "inspired" Francis is a favorite of Angelo. It appears in HTrb Prol 265; I 222, 266, 282, 376; III 22; in his *Exposition on the Rule* Prol 32; I 7, 11, 89, 170, 177, 286, etc; and in his *Apologia* 98.

is not overcome by human malice, he returned to the same place a second time and devoutly consecrated another Lent to God. There, with Christ as his teacher, in the same words and expressions, he rewrote the *Rule* maliciously stolen by the sin of his own. Like another *Moses* he prepared a second one, set down and *written by the finger of* the living *God.*

³⁸²While he was occupied above with God, with heavenly and burning desires asking Christ to restore the *Rule* stolen from him, the devil urged and incited the ministers of different provinces. They came together as if driven by *the North wind* to meet with Brother Elias. Boldly they went up to Saint Francis intending to complain and protest. Though they had not succeeded by the theft of the *Rule* in having it revoked, nor deflected him from his purpose, they might impede, slow up, and trouble him by their objections.

³⁸⁶*They stood at a distance* and shouted, to show that they wished to observe his command that no one should presume to go to him before the end of that Lent. In their shouting they demonstrated that they had a necessary and urgent need, because of which they had gathered so they might come to look for him.

³⁸⁸With the usual signal, Saint Francis called Brother Leo and ordered him to find out who those brothers were who were shouting, and the reason they had come. Brother Leo answered him: "Father, the ministers have come with Brother Elias to confer with you on some necessary business." Saint Francis said to him: "Let them say what they wish and I will listen, but they are not to come to me."

³⁹¹They stood facing him below the cell in a place where their voices could be heard clearly. Brother Elias, speaking for all of them, said to him: "Brother Francis, these brothers heard in their provinces that for the fuller observance of the life promised, you have decided to change or add things in the *Rule.* They consider that they and the brothers under them are weaker than you. The Lord has given you such fervor of spirit to strengthen you that everything pleasing to God, however hard and difficult, seems to you sweet and easy. The brothers have come as much for their brothers as for themselves, to tell you and remind you that what they have already promised to observe is more than enough for their weakness. Their weakness demands concessions and dispensations for what they have already promised more than obligations to more perfect things, no matter how worthy, which are beyond their strength."

³⁹⁷Saint Francis listened to them and remained silent. Touched *inwardly with sorrow of heart,* he made no answer to their requests. Then he went back immediately into his little cell and turned to his usual refuge of prayer. With *hands spread out* to *heaven,* he cried out to

Ex 31:18; Dt 9:10

Zec 6:8

Lk 17:12

Gn 6:6

1 Kgs 8:22, 54

Mt 19:27
Christ with all his heart, saying: *"Behold,* Lord Jesus Christ, *I have followed you,* never contradicting You. What you commanded me to do, I have done obediently. I am not the kind of person who can do anything pleasing or acceptable to You without Your help, and nothing useful or health-giving to them. You ordered me to compose and to write what I am writing and have written for Your glory and for their salvation, according to Your will and teaching. Answer them for me, and show that these words are Yours, not mine."

Mk 1:11; Lk 3:22

Lk 9:35; Is 41: 8; 44:2

Lk 10:16

Is 37:7; Ez 37:6

[403]When Francis had finished saying these things with a trusting heart to Christ, *a voice sounded* in the air, in the person of Christ, in a marvelous way, above the place where Saint Francis was praying. It said: *"This is My servant* Francis, *whom I have chosen,* and I have placed My spirit in him, and have commanded him to do what he has done, and to write the *Rule* which he is writing. Both the life and the *Rule* which he is writing is Mine, and is from Me, not from him. *Whoever hears* him *hears Me; whoever rejects* him *rejects Me.* To those I will call to observe this life and *Rule I will give the spirit* and the strength to observe it. And I want this *Rule* to be observed to the letter, to the letter."[a]

[410]Hearing these things in wonder and amazement, they returned, each to his own province, and stopped what they had begun in opposing Saint Francis.

[412]And when the *Rule* was completed, Saint Francis, according to the command given to him by Christ, with his companion Brother Leo, went to the Lord Honorius, then the Supreme Pontiff, who especially loved blessed Francis and revered him with a particular affection because certain experience taught him that the Spirit of Christ rested fully on him.

[415]The Supreme Pontiff rejoiced at the arrival of Francis, the poor man of Christ. Like a good father he received and blessed him lovingly and kindly with a smiling face and a happy spirit. He listened carefully to all the things Francis, on behalf of Christ, proposed and asked. He took the *Rule* that Francis had written, studied it, and considered it carefully. Then with the approval of his brother cardinals, after the example of his predecessor of happy memory, Pope Innocent, he approved and confirmed the *Rule* which he had carefully reviewed and assiduously examined.[b]

[420]But—as witnessed by Brother Leo who was present then—when the Supreme Pontiff had carefully and attentively examined everything contained in the *Rule,* he said to blessed Francis:

---

a. Cf. FA:ED II 132 a.

b. The confirmation was given in the papal decree *Solet annuere,* on November 29, 1223, FA:ED I 99.

"Blessed is he who, strengthened by the grace of God, will serve this *Rule* and life until the end: for all the things written in it are pious and perfect. However, there are problems with those words in the tenth chapter, namely: '**Wherever the brothers may be who know and feel they cannot observe the *Rule* literally, they can and should have recourse to their ministers. Let the ministers, moreover,** be bound by obedience to grant them, kindly and generously, the permission requested. If they refuse to do this, the brothers themselves have the permission and obedience to observe it literally, because all the brothers, both ministers and subjects, must be subject to the *Rule*.'[a] These could be the occasion of ruin and division in the religion for those not fully grounded in the understanding of the truth and love of virtue. Therefore I want the words in this chapter changed, so that every occasion of danger and division in the religion and among the brothers may be avoided."

⁴³⁰Blessed Francis answered him: "It was not I but Christ who put these words in the *Rule;* He knows best what is useful and necessary for the *salvation of souls* and for the good standing and preservation of the religion. All that will happen in the future to the religion and to the Church is clear and present to Him. Therefore I must not and cannot change these words, because it will happen that the ministers and others in authority in the religion will cause many bitter tribulations for those who wish to observe the *Rule* literally, according to Christ's holy will. Therefore, since it is the will and obedience of Christ that this *Rule* and life, which are His, be observed literally, so it must be your will and obedience that this be done and be written in the *Rule*."

⁴³⁶Then the Supreme Pontiff said to him: "Brother Francis, I will do this in such a way that, keeping the full sense of the words, I will change the letter of the *Rule* in this passage, in such a way that the ministers will understand they are obliged to do what Christ's will and the *Rule* commands, and the brothers will understand they have the freedom to observe the *Rule*. This will provide no occasion, to those who frequently look for one, to transgress the *Rule* under the pretext of observing it."

⁴⁴¹Therefore the Supreme Pontiff changed the words of that clause, saying: "**Wherever the brothers may be who know and feel they cannot observe the *Rule* spiritually, they can and must have**

LR X 4-6

LR X 4-6

1 Pt 1:9

---

a. A briefer version of this redaction of Chapter X of the LR can be found in OL 2. Angelo also quotes and comments on this redaction in his *Exposition on the Rule* X 64-74 and appears a favorite, as seen in light of the situation of the theologian from Germany, cf. supra HTrb I 224-34, that of Bernard, cf. infra II 131-3, of a group that fled to Greece, cf, V 402-3, 449-56, and of those from Narbonne and Britany, cf. VI 288-90.

recourse to their ministers. Let the ministers, moreover, receive them charitably and kindly and have such familiarity with them that these same brothers may speak and deal with them as masters with their servants, for so it must be that the ministers are the servants of all the brothers."

[The Testament]

[445]But so that he might remove every scruple of doubt from the hearts of all the brothers, Blessed Francis toward the end of his life clearly declared in his *Testament* the truth of his intention, as he had it in the *Rule,* just as he had received it from Christ. He **strictly commanded** all his cleric and lay brothers, **through obedience, not to place any gloss upon the** *Rule* **or the** *Testament,* **saying: "They should be understood in this way,"** but as the Lord gave him to **write the** *Rule* and *Testament* **purely and simply, they should understand them purely and simply and observe them purely and simply** until the end, blessing all **who observe** them **in this way** and firmly blocking the way toward **asking letters** or privileges **from the Roman Curia, either personally or through an intermediary,** against the pure and literal observance of the *Rule* handed over to him by Christ.[a]

Test 38-40

Test 25

[452]The commands and words of the saint himself, therefore, make it clear that he received the *Rule* and *Testament* by revelation from Christ, and that the correct, true, pure, faithful, and spiritual understanding and observance of the *Rule* is the literal observance. The other "declarations" are pious concessions made by pious doctors for those who are ill, useful and necessary dispensations for the *salvation of souls* of those who are unable or unwilling to be obliged to that difficult and perfect observance of the *Rule* which the founder taught and fulfilled and received from Christ directly.

1 Pt 1:9

[457]But a reform of the *Rule* revealed to Saint Francis, to be carried out after the mystery marked by his cross, will be the pure, simple, and literal observance of the *Rule* and *Testament,* as the Holy Spirit fills those whom He chooses and calls to preach the life of Christ in word and deed like seraphim, cherubim, and thrones. Like the seraphim, confident that He dwells in them, they will carry Christ in body and soul in the form of the cross. As a sign of this, Francis appeared as nailed, first in soul and afterwards in the flesh,

---

a. While seemingly quoting the *Testament* as the expression of Francis's will, it is important to note how Angelo adds phrases to the text that (a) give equal weight to the *Rule* and *Testament,* (b) specify not simply letters but also privileges, and (c) point clearly to whatever is "against the pure and literal observance of the *Rule* handed over to him by Christ."

prefiguring an opposing reality in adversities. Like the cherubim, because the uncreated intelligence, begotten of the Father from eternity, he will penetrate, enlighten, and confirm the understanding of the humble lesser brothers through feeling and virtue. He will make them wise in the light, communicating to them what is figured in the seventh "F,"[a] when he, like another *Elijah* appeared to six brothers in *a fiery chariot,* and their consciences were laid bare, one to the other. Like the thrones, the strength of the all-powerful Father, the brightness of the faith and its living action will help them mightily. Their prayers will be answered, their vows fulfilled, their threats and curses feared, and their blessings will be loved and revered.

[466]Without Christ Jesus dwelling in them like the seraphim, enlightening them like cherubim, and resting and sitting in them like the thrones, the chosen ones would not be strong enough to sustain the burden of the last tribulation. In it *the power of the dragon,* set loose in the man of perdition, will be lifted up and extolled to such an extent that *seated in the temple of God, he will display himself, above all that is called "God" or is worshipped as such.*

[470]For just as the life of Christ, His preaching, passion, death, wounds, burial, resurrection, ascension, and all the rest of His deeds and teachings, present, past, and future, singly and all together, humanly and divinely, begin and complete, grant and announce, seal and open, so too the dignity and majesty of His grace and glory are revealed and appear in the saints, and the secrets of His counsel are communicated in an orderly plan, so that all things which are of Christ may shine forth in each of Christ's members and each may glow more gloriously in all by effect and virtue.

[475]Christ Jesus *is the truth*—Eternal Wisdom, uncreated, begotten and creating all things, containing all things, and completing all things—and communicates himself wholly in *many* and *varied ways,* human and divine, *to each one* and to all *as He wills according to the capacity* of each, for the completion of His mystical body, *renewing signs and working wonders* through His Spirit for His glorification. He wished to give to all in Francis a unique *memorial* of Himself and *His wonders:* therefore, after He had given through Francis the *Rule* and teaching of His life, He clothed him with the sign of His flesh and cross, so that the newest members would realize that they ought to be conformed to their head.

[481]And just as *the depth of the riches of the wisdom and knowledge of God* and His *inscrutable* judgments, which are sealed, are closed and openly revealed by the Father through the Holy Spirit in Christ; just

---

a. "F[rancis]" ?

as the kindly operation of God's mercy through Christ and predestined election are completed and manifested in the saints; just as the
righteousness of justice and the equity of judgment are affirmed and
shown in the wicked and perverse: so now in this *last hour* Christ
placed *the sign* of the Cross *in the heaven* of the Church, and willed it *to
appear* in Francis, so that those *who look at him put on Christ* and follow
him and *flee in front of the* plundering *sword* of the hellish man, and are
not *caught in the trap* of his errors, nor cling to falsehood through the
work of lies, and thus fall away from the truth.

489For by extolling himself *Lucifer* fell *from heaven:* and *Adam,*
deceived by *woman,* fell into lying; and *the sons* of Seth, depraved by
the daughters of men, perished in the flood. And so the sons of Noah,
growing arrogant against God, clothed themselves in *confusion and
relapsed into* idolatry. From *Abraham,* the father of our faith, came
Ishmael, the first *born according to the flesh, persecuting Isaac, the son of the
promise,* who was *cast out* by the spirit so that he should not *be an heir.*[a]
Esau persecuted *Jacob* and imitated *Cain,* the killer of innocent Abel.
The jealous sons of Jacob *sold* Joseph, beloved of God and their
father, and they deceived Israel, who *could* still *see,* by lies in word and
deed. Only two of *the six hundred thousand* had faith in God; the rest
were prevented from *entering the promised land. Saul* persecuted *David*
and, except for Hezechiah and Josiah, *all* the kings *sinned* and *killed
the prophets sent* to them from heaven; and, last, they killed the precursor, *holy* from *the womb,* cutting off his *head.* And the priests,
scribes, and Pharisees, lifted up on the cross the Messiah, God and
Lord of the prophets, *outside the gate, in the midst of thieves,* adding to all
their crimes *blasphemy against the Spirit* of Christ and the persecution
and death of His holy disciples, because of which *the wrath of God
comes upon them until the end.*

503Finally, as someone says, **how was it** *far from* Francis *to glory
except in the cross of the Lord? Who can express it? Who can understand?* It
was given to him alone to experience it. For this reason perhaps it had
to appear in the flesh, since it *could not be explained in words.* This alone
intimates to human ears what is not yet entirely clear: why that *sacrament appeared* in the saint, as what is revealed by him to him, and
draws understanding from the future: at the end **it will be true and
worthy of faith, to which nature,** *law,* **and** *grace* **will be witnesses; for
the sign cries out** the signified; **let silence speak where** *words fall
short.*

Margin references: 1 Jn 2:18; Rv 12:1; Nm 12:8; Rom 13:14; Gal 3:27; Is 21:15; Is 24:18; 8:14; Is 14:12; Gn 3:12; Gn 6:2; Gn 11:8, 9; Gn 16:15; Gal 4:23, 29; Gal 4:28, 29; Gal 4:30; Gn 27:41; Gn 4:8; Gn 37:28, 32; Ex 12:37; Nm 14:30; 1 Sm 18:9-12; Sir 49:4; Mt 23:31, 17; Lk 1:15; 6:27; Heb 13:12; Lk 23:33; Jn 19:18; Mt 12:31; 1 Thes 2:16; Gal 6:14; Mt 19:21; Mt 13:11; Eccl 1:8; 1 Tm 3:16; Jn 1:17; Sir 43:29. Side: TL 5:3; 2C 203.

---

a. It is helpful to recall the image of Ishmael presented by Ubertino, cf. TL V 3: "It is as true now as of old that there is an (Gn 16:22) Ishmael abroad, and he is a bowman shooting arrows at the sons who are true to the *Rule,* arrows in the shape of oppressions, censures, preposterous decrees, harsh pronouncements."

-95; LMj Prol 2

[511]For now that all these things have happened, there is the beginning of clarity about those secrets, revealed through the seraph to Francis himself, and closed within the signs of the wounds. Christ Jesus, true God and man, *the beginning and the end* of created nature, law, grace, and glory, circumscribed and enclosed in the cross the immensity of His omnipotence, the infinity of His wisdom, the bounty of His mercy, and the ineffable goodness of His charity. He destroyed death by death and enlightened life and incorruptibility through the Gospel; and Francis, professing it, was made, in word and action, its herald in the Church by Christ.

Rv 1:8; 22:13

[515]Christ crucified, rising from the dead, and giving the apostles the Holy Spirit, from the death of *the letter* poured forth *the Spirit* of life. The synagogue, clinging to the letter, remained dead and buried as in a shadowy tomb, full of the infernal stench and worms of the demons.[a] And just as Eve, by the transgression of a command, lost the innocence and dignity of created nature, grace, and immortality and incurred the death of body and soul, so too the synagogue, because of the death of Christ, remained stripped of the gifts and goods promised through Scripture and given through grace, and became the prey of eternal death, of hell, and of demons.

2 Cor 3:6

[520]Rising from the dead, Christ gave this revelation, received from the Father through death, to His servants the apostles; and they understood and preached that their mother the synagogue was dead. And they knew that they had received, through the death of the flesh, the life of the life-giving Christ; and being made saints among the saints by the power of sanctification through His Spirit, they preached life-giving faith against deadly and death-dealing unbelief.

[523]And their tongue was made the key of heaven, opening the ways of life to God's worthy and faithful ones, demonstrating by signs, words, and deeds the destruction of the world and the demise and eternal perdition of those who love it. They *separated the precious from the vile,* truth from lies, goodness from malice, and they were made the mouth of God and the chariot of His omnipotence against the world and *the prince of the world.*

Jer 15:19

Jn 12:31; 14:30

[526]They preached the Gospel to the crucifiers of Christ, those who despised His humility. Through the presumption of pride and arrogance, they presented themselves as zealous for the law of God and the honor of the synagogue, bragging that they had the *key of knowledge* and divine authority. The apostles tried, through the love of heavenly things and the acknowledgment and imitation of Christ, to draw them away from infidelity and disobedience to God, which they incurred through the sin of envy against Christ, and from the enmity of God, which they incurred under the pretext of preserving

Lk 11:52

---

a. The parallel is a powerful indictment of those who cling to the law and not the spirit.

divine worship and the fleshly state of the synagogue, through greedy avarice, to restore them to His friendship and submission.

Ps 58:5; Am 1:5 They, like *asps, stopped* their *ears,* but God *broke* them and *dispersed*
Mal 1:11 them and *made* His *name great among the nations.*

[533]Those who were his brothers in name only denied and opposed by their words and deeds the evangelical life and perfection, which was solemnly introduced and renewed by Christ in the Church through Francis in opposition to the cunning of demons and the errors and fallacies of the precursors of Antichrist. They induced clergy and laity to persecute, hate, and deny that life; those who truly loved and observed it they separated, punishing them by the Church's authority as disobedient and contumacious, and having them killed. Then the sign of his wounds will cry out and proclaim the malice of the persecutors signified in the wounds and silence, and speaking, will declare that innocence and perfection truly exists in those who will endure persecution.

[539]For faith, as it is sure knowledge of God, not having demonstrable first principles, since it is one of those things above the mind and understanding, is an existing substance, and works beyond nature in those who are truly faithful. Those dependent upon the reasonings of human philosophy will attempt, with the devil agitat-
Eph 3:17 ing them, to overturn and revoke those who are *grounded, rooted* in it, demonstrating by sophistry that they live contrary to Scripture and the example and teachings of the early fathers; and that they act foolishly, rashly and irrationally, presuming to live and observe things impossible for human nature, out of harmony with common custom and tradition of the early fathers, derived from the saints and by the saints up to the present time. Accordingly, Christians will con-
Jn 16:2 sider that they *are doing a service to God* when they kill those Christians striving for true perfection with all their might.

[546]For this reason, the one who wrote the first legend says that **it**   2C 203
will be true and worthy of faith, to which nature, law, and grace will be witnesses, since the innocence of Abel, the meekness and humility of Moses, and the kindness and charity of Christ will bear witness for these latest poor men, humble in mind and heart. They are truly blessed, much like the saints before them, who once served the Lord under the law of nature, the law of Moses, and the law of the grace,[a] and they will suffer in the end of the time of the Church of the nations.
Rv 12:9; 20:2 [550]At last *the ancient serpent,* who by his own pride was cast down from his high state, seduced the first man, attacked Moses, tempted Christ, and had Him crucified, at the beginning of the fullness of the

---

a. A theme Angelo repeats, cf. I 509, 512; V 325; VI 191.

end will be let loose to tempt the Church of the nations. In his release wickedness will overflow, or abound, and *charity will grow cold,* so that the humility, faith, poverty, purity, and charity of Christ will be considered pride, perfidy, heresy, sterility, and foolishness.

⁵⁵⁵For Brother Pacificus, who *in ecstasy of mind saw* and heard that *the seat of Lucifer* was reserved for the humble Francis. And Brother Salvo^a saw that Francis was chosen by God from all the saints to have a particular battle with Lucifer. And another brother saw that Lucifer had entered into the religion of the Lesser Brothers, and assumed the habit, so that he could vanquish Francis more easily.

⁵⁵⁸These visions and all the ones like them, if they bear some truth, indicate principally what Christ says in the Gospel, that *the first will be last and the last will be first;* and that *many are called but few are chosen;* and that *a man's enemies*—Christ's in clothing but not in fact—are *those of his own household;* and that *the sons of Abraham* and the circumcision denied Christ; and that the successors of Christ and the humble man Peter would be embarrassed concerning poverty and humility with the time *of desolation approaching;* and that the Lesser Brothers in appearance and name will attack and persecute the Brothers who are Lesser in fact and deed, and will hate them in a fanatical and insane way, and boldly follow a leader of foolishness, error, and disbelief, the enemy of Francis, the most humble and poorest man, namely, Lucifer, and, having drawn the *sons of* his *flesh* away from him, in irreverence, incredulity, and disobedience they will have *provoked* and *exasperated him* as long as he lived.

⁵⁶⁷This was, therefore, the first conflict of incredulity and irreverence and disobedience against Francis, the founder under Christ, and his true and heartfelt followers, against which Christ, in Francis and his companions, stood and went out conquering, so that he might vanquish through true poverty and humility, and rule triumphantly in peace and charity.

⁵⁷⁰So be it. Amen.^b

⁵⁷¹Near the time of the passing of the humble, poor servant of God Francis, he had all the brothers of the place called to him, and spoke consoling words to them about his death. With fatherly affection and powerful words he exhorted them to observance of the life and *Rule* they had promised, to divine mutual love, and to reverence and obedience to the holy mother Roman Church and all clerics. With the most powerful and reliable words he inflamed them to possess poverty, humility, peace, and mutual love, leaving and bequeathing

---

a. The source of this story concerning Brother Salvo is unknown, as is further information about its subject.
b. In one manuscript: "The second tribulation or persecution of the Order of Minors begins here."

these as inheritance rights; and to ardent following of the footprints of Jesus Christ and contempt and hatred of the world.

[576]As they were sitting around him he ordered a brief testament written, in which he wrote down all the truth of his first and last intention, revealed to him by Christ, purely and clearly, both for those present as well as for those absent and those to come to the religion until the end of the age. And he ordered with all possible strictness that it be faithfully and reverently observed and preserved under the protection of the Most High heavenly Father and His blessed Son Jesus Christ and His blessing. He blessed all the brothers, present and absent in the power and name of Jesus Christ Crucified, *his arms crossed, extending* over them in the form of a cross, his *hands* marked with the *wounds of Jesus* Christ.

[580]He also had Brother Bernard of Quintavalle, the first brother, called to him. *Placing* his *right hand on the head* of this brother in front of all the brothers, he blessed him with particular, heartfelt affection. After the blessing, Blessed Francis ordered one of his companions: "Write what I tell you: the first brother the Lord gave me was Brother Bernard, and he first began and perfectly fulfilled the perfection of the Holy Gospel, distributing *all* he had *to the poor*. Because of this, and many other prerogatives given to him by God, I am held to love him more that any other brother of the whole religion. Therefore, it is my will and my command, as much as I am able, that the general minister of the religion, whoever he may be, should love him and honor him as myself, and also all the Provincial ministers and the brothers of the whole religion should hold him in my place."

[587]And Saint Francis also prophesied about Brother Bernard that toward the end of his life he would be supplied with many graces and gifts from Christ Jesus, and would pass from this life to Christ, in assurance and *filled* with the anointing *of the Holy Spirit* in admirable peace and rest of body and soul, as clearly appeared later to all the brothers who were present at his passing. Then, as the brothers observed his confidence in Christ at death, and his overwhelming devotion to his last breath, they *could not* restrain *themselves* from crying, but out of gladness and wonder said: "This man was truly an unrecognized saint!"

[592]After his death *they looked upon him* as a saint of God, spreading gladness and joy with a marvelous fragrance and singular beauty which he did not have before when he was living. And they were delighted by his appearance, because a certain power came forth from him, cheering those standing by and looking at him, and it filled them with both sweetness and spiritual consolation.

Gn 48:14
Gal 6:17
Gn 48:17, 18
Lk 18:22
Acts 4:8; 13:9
Gn 45:1
Jn 1:42; Acts 3:4
AC 12; 1MP 1; 2MP 107

THE DEEDS OF BLESSED FRANCIS

AND HIS COMPANIONS

BY

UGOLINO BONISCAMBI OF MONTEGIORGIO

(1328-1337)

AND

THE LITTLE FLOWERS OF SAINT FRANCIS

(A TRANSLATION AND RE-EDITING OF

THE DEEDS OF SAINT FRANCIS

AND HIS COMPANIONS

BY AN ANONYMOUS)

(After 1337)

Introduction

The Deeds of Blessed Francis and His Companions

The Deeds of Blessed Francis and His Companions—and its Italian translation, *The Little Flowers of Saint Francis*—may well be the written response to Jerome of Ascoli's request in 1276 for information concerning the saint and his first followers. Subsequently, *The Little Flowers* became for many a first and perhaps major source of information concerning Francis of Assisi. Although written more than a century after the saint's death, it remains one of the most enduring classics of spiritual literature as well as one of the most problematic.

Two dates provide a framework within which *The Deeds* was written. A catalog of manuscripts found in the library of Assisi's Sacro Convento in 1381 identifies manuscript 102 as *The Book of the Deeds of Blessed Francis and His Companions*.[1] At the other end of the spectrum, *The Deeds* tell of the death of John of LaVerna which, according to Giacomo Sabatelli, took place in 1322.[2] With this information, it is clear that *The Deeds* was written within this time span. The scope can be narrowed by the repeated references to the work in the *Avignon Compilation* that is dated 1343,[3] a reference to the closing of the friary of Soffiano which occurred in 1327, and a reference to the friary on the Island of Trasimeno established in 1328.[4] From these indications, recent scholarship maintains that *The Deeds* was written in its present form between 1328 and 1337.[5]

The Book of the Deeds of Blessed Francis and His Companions consists of four sections. The first thirty-one chapters are taken up with the origins of the primitive fraternity centered on Francis himself. These are followed by sixteen chapters that look in a more focused way on the primary players in its history, especially in Umbria, while the next eleven concentrate on those in the Marches. The final nine chapters treat a variety of different stories that, for the most part, concern the practice of poverty among those in both Umbria and the Marches. *The Deeds,* in other words, is not simply a collection of information about Francis and his first companions. It does not consider those who went on mission to England and Germany, nor is it concerned with the first Brothers who went to France or Spain. Its primary concerns are limited to the histories of just two Italian Provinces, Umbria and the Marches. As such, *The Deeds* provides background information on the emerging attitudes of the *zelanti* in what were becoming hothouses nurturing the Spiritual faction of the Lesser Brothers.

Unlike earlier texts, the location of this text's composition is important for two reasons: for a better understanding of the work itself, and for insights into its author. It is obvious that *The Deeds* was written in the Province of the

Marches. One has only to read this poetic description: "The Province of the Marches of Ancona was like a beautiful starry sky, with outstanding stars, that is, with holy Lesser Brothers who high and low before God and neighbor shone with radiant virtues, and (Sir 45:1) *whose memory* is truly *held in* divine *blessing.*"[6] Granted many of the stories told in *The Deeds* take place in the Province of Umbria, it does not receive the praise and adulation devoted to the Province of the Marches. Within that Province, the Custody of Ancona garners special attention. Offida, Fermo, Mogliano, Massa Fermana, Penna S. Giovanni, Falerone, and Brunforte: all of these towns—all of which are found in what was then the Lesser Brothers' Custody of Ancona—are mentioned in the text. Finally, since the friary of Soffiano figures strongly in a number of incidents and had ties with that of San Liberato inhabited by the followers of Angelo Clareno, Soffiano is possibly the precise locale in which the author of *The Deeds* gathered and transcribed his materials.

Twice *The Deeds of Blessed Francis and His Companions* makes a reference to its author, Ugolino of Monte Santa Maria.[7] On another occasion, however, Ugolino is mentioned as the witness of an episode described by another,[8] and, on twelve occasions direct or indirect allusions leave the question of authorship in question.[9] Scholars have generally assumed that more than one person had a hand in the composition of *The Deeds,* although that of Ugolino Boniscambi of Monte Santa Maria is recognized as primary.

Little is known about Ugolino Boniscambi. The date of his birth in Monte Santa Maria—now known as Montegiorgio—a small town in the Province of the Marches, is unknown.[10] Since he mentions hearing John of LaVerna, who died in 1274, Ubertino must have entered the Order before that time. A document in the archives of Amandola places Ugolino in Gabbiano in 1319 as an official witness to a peace treaty between the towns of Amandola and Massa Fermana;[11] another document of 1331 describes his presence in Naples before the general minister, Girard Oddone or Ot, accusing the former provincial minister of Penne, Andrea of Gagliano, of the heresy of "Michaelism," the belief that Christ and the apostles possessed no earthly goods.[12] In 1342 Ugolino was chosen as fiduciary of the will of a priest, Conrad of Falerone. Like the day of his birth, that of his death is unknown.

An examination of the text indicates that Ugolino clearly had access to Bonaventure's *Major Legend,* possibly some version of the scrolls of the companions, and the writings of Angelo Clareno. It also reveals his talent for remembering and narrating stories, especially those originating in his own Province of the Marches. These two characteristics, however, present problems in dealing with the historicity of the sixty-eight chapters of Ugolino's *Deeds.* Although thirty-one chapters tell stories found in earlier texts and, therefore, are historically reliable, ten others present details in incidents that are otherwise historically reliable. These details are changed to be more faithful to Sacred Scripture, as in the case of Francis's prophetic vision of the Order's future;[13] to sustain a thesis, as in the case of Bernard's perfect obedience;[14] to give greater prominence to some deed;[15] to demonstrate Francis's affection for creatures;[16] or, quite simply, to reinforce details.[17] It is easy to get the impression that Ugolino is, therefore, telling his stories in a somewhat flamboyant way to catechize his confreres. Thus his text is not simply a retelling of history in a popular way. Ugolino uses history to underscore values that he senses are neglected.

Four, possibly five, other incidents contain questionable details. In the opening paragraph of *The Deeds,* for example, John of Capella appears as another Judas, Francis's follower who hanged himself. Ugolino seems to be relying on information supplied by Angelo Clareno; but Angelo himself is contradictory in his description of John.[18] Angelo Clareno seems also to be the only source of information concerning Angelo of Borgo, the petulant Guardian of Monte Casale. Although the incident of his scolding the robbers is narrated in the *Assisi Compilation*[19] and later in the Sabatier edition of the *Mirror of Perfection,*[20] no description is provided of his entrance into the Order or of Francis giving him the name, Angelo. Ugolino is the only author to end his account of Lady Jacoba's devotion to Francis by telling that she "ended her days" in Assisi and "arranged to be buried in the Church of Saint Francis." The *Considerations on the Holy Stigmata* corrects the story's details and adds that Lady Jacoba was indeed buried in the Church of Saint Francis as she wished.[21] Ugolino's descriptions of Brother Masseo's stay at Cibotella also present conflicting details that, for historical accuracy, demand clarification since they echo similar incidents found in the *Anonymous of Perugia* or the *Chronicle of the Twenty-Four Generals.* Finally, Ugolino's narratives of Bernard of Quintavalle and Sylvester raise questions: Bernard's problematical dealings with Francis, as well as his and Sylvester's eremitical sojourns on Monte Subasio. While these details are not monumental in themselves, they tend to prompt a historian to look more carefully at the veracity of this text and to question those whose vision of life is largely based on it.

Other details, however, are clearly mistaken. The discovery of the Gospel texts by Francis and Bernard was during a Mass not in the Bishops' church in Assisi, but in San Nicolò.[22] Ugolino's descriptions of two conversions in the court of the Sultan, events that would be significant, never appear in any earlier text,[23] nor do Francis's vision of Saints Peter and Paul, and the kiss and embrace they give him.[24] When narrating events in the lives of Francis's followers, Ugolino not only exaggerates but invents stories that have no foundation in reality. In describing Francis's visits to the Poor Ladies of San Damiano, for example, Thomas of Celano states that his companions were shocked that the saint visited them rarely and that Elias had to insist that he speak to them.[25] Ugolino, on the contrary, maintains that Francis went frequently to encourage them.[26] The visit of the King of France, Saint Louis, to Brother Giles also has no historical foundation since the king's *Process of* his *Canonization* states explicitly that he never set foot in Italy.[27] In light of earlier texts, Ugolino's narration of the blessing of Giles, not Elias, certainly seems a fabrication.[28] But that change underscores the omission of Elias as a witness of Francis's stigmata,[29] and the addition of the tale of Elias's refusal to be disturbed by an angel.[30]

Regardless of its defects, both chronologically and historically, *The Deeds of Blessed Francis and His Companions* and, more importantly, its Italian translation, *The Little Flowers,* have had an enormous impact of the shaping of the Franciscan tradition of spirituality. Part of the success of both works lies in Ugolino's ability to capture the spirit of Francis and his followers in vivid, colorful detail and the translator's genius in an Italian that is timeless. The saint emerges through stories that wonderfully capture his love for all creatures, even those that are the smallest and least attractive such as the birds of Bevagna, the doves of Siena, and the feared wolf of Gubbio. At the same time, the founder is portrayed as tough and, at times, unrelenting as he punishes disobedience, withstands the skillful attacks of the devil, and puts the Sultan to the test by walking through fire. As *The Deeds* unfold, Francis of Assisi appears as a man of unrelenting prayer, of humility incarnate, an untiring, passionate apostle of the Gospel, a loving brother not only of his followers, but of all humans, and of all creatures.

The Deeds is, however, a text of the fourteenth century, one in harmony with Thomas à Kempis's *Imitation of Christ* and so many writings of the *Devotio Moderna.* Its hallmark is undoubtedly a devotional attachment to the person of Francis and, in its light, *The Deeds* promote a moralistic spirituality that emphasizes the austerity, *fuga mundi* [flight from the world], and self-denigration that characterizes much of the spiritual literature of the period. Thus the saint and founder becomes a prophet of the disturbing currents of the fourteenth century and in his joyful simplicity an antidote for the pessimism that permeated it. For many, however, this fourteenth century vision originating in the Marches of Ancona is the only Francis of Assisi they have known.

The Little Flowers of Saint Francis

The Little Flowers of Saint Francis, undoubtedly one of the most popular classics of Christian spirituality, is an Italian translation of the Latin text of *The Deeds of Blessed Francis and His Brothers* by Ugolino Boniscambi of Montegiorio.[31] Attempts have been made to identify the translator. He remains anonymous. Noting differences between these texts, scholars of the past argued about the precise nature of the text: was it a translation or an original work?[32] They also turned their attention to questions of its date and the location of its origin, that is, Tuscany or the Marches of Ancona.[33] Contemporary scholars generally accept the linguistic arguments that maintain that *The Little Flowers* is a translation, and they, therefore, look for linguistic or stylistic nuances that might shed light on historical issues.[34]

The earliest manuscript of *The Little Flowers* is dated 1396.[35] This fact led some scholars to maintain that *The Little Flowers* was written in the last decade of the fourteenth century.[36] In his thorough study of the manuscripts and texts of both works, Jacques Cambell proved that *The Little Flowers* was for the most part a translation of *The Deeds. The Considerations of the Sacred Stigmata,* the second part of a later edition of *The Little Flowers,* was a re-editing of certain sections undertaken at a later date since it shows the influence of

Bartholomew of Pisa's *Book of Conformities* that was begun in 1385. At the present state of research, it is difficult to be more precise.

Every translation, however, is an interpretation. In any language, words take on a variety of meanings and shades of nuance that make their precise translation difficult. *The Little Flowers* is no exception. Even a superficial comparison of *The Deeds* and *The Little Flowers* reveals how the translator divided chapters differently, undoubtedly to make reading them more manageable. At the same time, he inverted the order of certain chapters and, within chapters, changed the order of paragraphs and sentences. The result is that the geographic divisions of *The Deeds* are re-arranged so that, in *The Little Flowers,* the first forty-one chapters focus on Francis and his first followers, while the last ten describe the Lesser Brothers of the Marches. At a later date, chapters nine, eighteen, thirty-six, thirty-eight, and thirty-nine were rearranged to form four of the five *Considerations on the Sacred Stigmata.*

One significant addition to the text is the formula found at the end of almost every chapter: "To the praise of Jesus Christ and the little poor man Francis." The additional focus on Francis, the Poverello, the little poor man, is not found at the end of each chapter of *The Deeds.* In addition to underscoring the close bond between Jesus and Francis, *The Little Flowers* goes out of its way to broaden popular devotion to the saint. This may also be seen in the translator's penchant for writing of *il glorioso messere san Francesco* [the glorious Sir Saint Francis]. Thus the translator interprets *The Deeds* by bringing into sharper focus the unique identification of Francis with Christ and, by doing so, moves closer and closer to the vision of Bartholomew of Pisa's massive *Book* of *Conformities.*[37]

Notes

1. Leto Alessandri, *Inventario dell'antica Biblioteca del S. Convento* (Assisi: n.p., 1906), 82.

2. Ugolino de Montegiorgio, DBF: "How glorious is our Father Francis in the sight of God is apparent in his chosen sons whom the Holy Spirit brought together into the Order, so that truly the glory of such a great Father are his wise sons. Among these holy Brother John of Fermo, also known as 'of La Verna,' shone forth in a special way, and as a wonderful star he glittered in the sky of the Order with the brilliance of grace." Cf. Giacomo Sabbatelli, *Vita del Beato Giovanni della Verna* (LaVerna, n.p., 1965), 132.

3. Cf. Andrew G. Little, "Description du manuscript Canonic. Miscell. 525 de la Bibliothèque Bodléienne, à Oxford," and Paul Sabatier "Description du Speculum Vitae beati Francisci et Sociorum ejus," in Andrew G. Little, Pierre Mandonnet, Paul Sabatier, *Opuscules de Critique Historique,* t. I (Paris: Librairie Fischbacher, 1903), 294, 335.

4. Cf. infra 448 b.

5. *Actus Beati Francisci et Sociorum Eius: Nuova Edizione Postuma di Jacques Cambell,* Marino Bigaroni and Giovanni Boccali (Santa Maria degli Angeli-Assisi: Tipografia Porziuncola, 1988).

6. DBF XLVII, infra,

7. Ibid., 58: "And Brother John himself related all this to me, Ugolino." Ibid, 55 "And I, Brother Ugolino of Monte Santa Maria stayed there for three years and observed this miracle as a fact, well-known both to lay persons and to the brothers of that custody."

8. Ibid 9: "Brother James de Massa received this account from the mouth of Brother Leo, and Brother Ugolino of Monte Santa Maria had it from the mouth of this Brother James, and I, the writer, had it from the mouth of Brother Ugolino."

9. In the chapters devoted to John of LaVerna (+1322), Ugolino is not expressly mentioned, although the stories are written in a very personal form and the first person singular appears nine times, i.e, ibid., 9, 16, 49, 53, 55, 56, 57, 58, 64.

10. A detailed life of Ugolino Boniscami of Montegiorgio can be found in the Introduction to *I Fioretti di san Francesco*. Con una introduzione storico-critica del Giacinto Pagnani. (Rome: Fides, 1959), 28-30.

11. Cf. P. Ferranti, *Memorie Storiche della città di Amandola* III, (Ascoli Piceno, n.p., 1891), 165-6.

12. BFr VI, 609a. For information concerning Michaelism, see Nimmo, *Reform,* 241-3.

13. Compare Francis's prophetic vision of the Order in DBF 25, OL 5, 2C 82; the list of Francis's first twelve followers.

14. Compare DBF 3 and 1C 30 where Bernard, not Francis, accompanies Giles.

15. Compare DBF 34 and AC 80 (FA:ED II 181-2) in which Francis makes Peter Catanio drag him naked around Assisi with no reference to a similar act of Rufino.

16. Compare DBF 23, the wolf of Gubbio, with AC 74, 2C 35-6, and the *Passion of San Verecondo* (FA:ED II 175-8, 269-70).

17. Compare DBF 8 and 1C 52; DBF 5 and AC 11; DBF 42 and the *Legend of St. Clare* 29 and her *Process of Canonization* VII 9; DBF 43 and *Vita Innocentii IV* in L.A. Muratori, *Rerum Italicarum Scriptores,* volume III, part 1 (Bologna, n.p., 1932), 235-7; DBF 49 with the *Legenda Assidua* 9.

18. Cf. DBF 1. In his *Exposition on the Rule,* Angelo places John of Capella in the twelfth place among Francis's first disciples, cf. Angelo Clareno, *Expositio Regulae Fratrum Minorum,* ed. Livarius Oliger (Ad Claras Aquas, Quarachi: Collegium S. Bonaventurae, 1912), 4-5. In a letter of 1334, he places him in the seventh place and makes no mention of his suicide.

19. Cf. AC 115 (FA:ED II 221-2).

20. 2MP 66, supra 310-1.

21. An anonymous author wrote *The Consideration of the Holy Stigmata* between 1370 and 1385. Toward the end of the Fourth Consideration, "How, After the Imprinting of the Holy Stigmata, St. Francis Left Laverna and Returned to St. Mary of the Angels," the author supplies previously unknown information about Lady Jacoba of Settesoli. Cf. *St. Francis of Assisi Writings and Early Biographies: English Omnibus of the Sources for the Life of St. Francis,* translations by Raphael Brown, Benen Fahy, Placid Hermann, Paul Oligny, Nesta de Robeck, Leo Sherley-Price, with a Research Bibliography by Raphael Brown. Edited by Marion A. Habig. (Chicago: Franciscan Herald Press, 1972), 1464.

22. Compare DBF I (infra 437-8) with AP 10 (FA:ED II 378) and L3C 28 (FA:ED II 85).

23. Cf. DBF XXVII.

24. Cf. DBF XIII.

25. Cf. 2C 205.

26. DBF XLIII.

27. Cf. DBF XLVI. "Processus canonizationis S. Ludovici," *Analecta Franciscana, sive Chronica aliaque varia documenta ad historiam Fratrum Minorum spectantia edita a Patribus Collegii S. Bonaventurae,* vol. VII (Ad Claras Aquas, Quaracchi: Collegium S. Bonaventura, 1951), XVII-XXIII.

28. Compare DBF V with AC 12 and 1C 108.

29. Compare DBF XXXIV with 1C 95 and LMj XIII 8.

30. Cf. DBF III.

31. In order to express the flavor of the Italian translation, the editors have chosen not to Anglicize proper names and, when possible, to maintain "Italianisms."

32. As early as the eighteenth century, Giovanni G. Sbaraglia (1687-1764) argued that Giovanni Marignolli (+1359) was the author of *I Fioretti,* cf. *Supplementum et castigatio ad Scriptores Trium Ordinum S. Francisci a Waddingo aliisque descriptores,* Part I (Rome, A. Nardecchis, 1906-36), 385. In 1883, Luigi Tassi argued that Ugolino Brunforte of Sarnano was the author, an argument that was later advanced by Luigi Marconi, cf. Luigi Tassi, *Disquisizione istorica intorno all'autore dei Fioretti di S. Francesco* (Fabriano: Tipografia Gentile, 1883), 7ff; Luigi Marconi, "Attorno agli autori dei 'Fioretti,' " *Studii Francescani* 23 (1926): 355-365.

33. Armando Quaglia proposed that *I Fioretti* was composed originally by Ugolino of Montegiorgio and later served as the basis of a Latin translation undertaken by an anonymous friar of the Marches of Ancona, cf. Armando Quaglia, *Studi su I Fioretti di S. Francesco* (Ancona: Falconara M., 1977), 56-61, 65; Idem, "Origine volgare e marchigiana dei 'Fioretti' di San Francesco," *Studii Francescani* 78(1981): 149-58.

34. Gianna Tosi, for example, maintains that *"The Little Flowers* are most faithful to the Latin text, even follow it in its tiniest details never introducing even less, a new tale . . ." Cf. Gianna Tossi, *La Lingua dei Fioretti di S. Francesco* (Messina-Milano: G. Principato, 1938), 184.

35. Cf. *I Fioretti di san Francesco.* With a Historical-Critical Introduction by Giacinto Pagnani (Rome: Editrice Fides, 1959), 21.

36. Benvenuto Bughetti argued from a linguistic perspective that *I Fioretti* was written by an anonymous Tuscan friar. Cf.Benvenuto Bughetti, "Alcune idee fontamentali sui 'Fioretti di San Francesco,'" AFH 19(1926): 324-7.

37. For an evaluation of *The Little Flowers* in fourteenth-century Christian spirituality, see the Introduction to *I Fioretti di San Francesco.* L'Anima del Mondo 14. Edited with introduction by Felice Accrocca (Asti: Edizioni Piemme, 1997), 5-27.

The Deeds of Blessed Francis and His Companions

HERE BEGIN SOME DEEDS OF SAINT FRANCIS AND HIS COMPANIONS[a]

To the praise and glory of our Lord Jesus Christ and of our most holy Father Francis. Here are written down some notable things about blessed Francis and his companions, and some of their admirable deeds which have been passed over in his legends and which are very devout and useful.

I

THE PERFECT EXPROPRIATION OF HOLY BROTHER BERNARD AT THE PREACHING OF OUR MOST HOLY FATHER FRANCIS

[LMj III 7]

[1]One must first of all know that our blessed Father Francis was conformed to Christ in all his deeds.[b] For just as the blessed Christ in the beginning of his preaching took to Himself *twelve apostles who left all things,* so also did Francis have twelve chosen companions who chose highest poverty. And just as one of the twelve apostles *hanged himself with a rope,* so did one of the twelve companions, John de Capella, hang himself with a rope.[c] And just as those holy apostles were admirable to the whole world and were filled with the Holy Spirit, so too these most holy companions of Saint Francis were men of such holiness that the world had not had such men since the time of the apostles. For one of them *had been caught up to the third heaven:* this was Brother Giles. An angel *touched the lips* of one *with a burning coal* as Isaiah had been: this was Brother Philip the Tall. One *spoke* with God as friend *with friend* as that most pure man, Brother

[Mt 10:2; 19:27]

[Mt 27:5]

[LMj III 4]

[1C 25; BPr I 3]

[2 Cor 12:2]

[Is 6:6, 7]

[Ex 33:11]

---

a. This translation is based on *Actus Beati Francisci et Sociorum Eius: Nuova Edizione Postuma di Jacques Cambell*, Marino Bigaroni and Giovanni Boccali (Santa Maria degli Angeli-Assisi: Tipografia Porziuncola, 1988). The number of each paragraph follows that of the Cambell, Bigaroni, Boccali edition.

b. The author uses the Latin word *conformare* [to conform] to summarize Francis's life, a word used sporadically in earlier Franciscan literature (1C 76, 83, 99; 2C 99, 128, 190; 3C 13, 14; LJS 9; L3C 6, 73; AC 61; LMj V 1; X 4; XIII 1; 2MP 57). While in some of these references, the word indicates conformity to Francis, in most instances it refers to conformity to Christ.

c. Cf. FA:ED II 41 b, 88 a. The first reference to John de Capella as a tragic Judas figure is in BPr, cf. supra FA:ED III. It is repeated in ChrXXIVG, p. 4 in which John is identified as one of Francis's first companions, "who was the first in the Order to devise some kind of hat or biretta to be worn over the cowl;" and "who as another Judas, became leprous in the Order. Inflamed with madness, he left the Order. And so, abandoned by God into the hands of demons, he hung himself."

Hb 1:8

Sylvester, did.[a] One *soared*, like *an eagle*, to the light of divine wisdom: this was the most humble Brother Bernard, who made clear the most profound passages of Scripture. One of these was sanctified by the Lord and canonized in heaven while he was still alive on earth, as if sanctified in the womb: this was Brother Rufino, a nobleman of Assisi, a man most faithful to Christ. And so all of these companions were illustrious because of a special prerogative as will be shown below.

1C 24; AP 11; 2C 15; LMj III

[10]**The first-born** of these, both by precedence, by time, and by privilege of holiness, was Brother Bernard of Assisi who was converted in the following manner.[b] Saint Francis was still wearing secular clothing, and yet was already completely looked down upon and despaired of by worldly hope, because once he was so completely unsightly and dirty that many thought that he was crazy. He was nevertheless *seasoned by* divine *salt*, and grounded and confirmed in tranquility by the Holy Spirit, even though for a long time he was pelted with stones and mud and endured countless insults both from his own people and outsiders as he went through Assisi. He passed through all this with the greatest patience, and as if *deaf* and *mute* with a happy countenance.

Col 4:6

Ps 38:14

[13]Lord Bernard of Assisi, who was one of the most noble, wealthy, and wise men of the city, to whose advice everyone consented, began to consider wisely Saint Francis's profound contempt of the world and his great constancy and patience in tolerating insults, since for almost two years, tested and despised by all, he seemed to become ever more steadfast. He said to himself: "In no way can this Francis have great grace from God."

[15]Inspired by God, he invited Francis to eat with him in the evening. Francis assented to this request and ate with him that very evening. But Lord Bernard had in mind the wish to probe the holiness of Saint Francis and therefore invited Francis to sleep in his home that night. When Saint Francis humbly agreed to this, Lord Bernard had a bed prepared in his own room, where a lamp was continually burning at night. However, as soon as Saint Francis entered the room, in order to conceal the divine grace he possessed, he immediately threw himself on the bed, indicating that he wanted to go to sleep. But Lord Bernard intended to watch him secretly during the night, so he used this precaution: after he lay on his bed quietly for a little while, he feigned a deep sleep by snoring very loudly.

---

a. Concerning Brother Sylvester, see FA:ED II 39 a. While Bonaventure writes of Sylvester's intimacy with the Lord, cf. LMj XII 2, this is the first text to describe him in terms of another Moses speaking with God "as friend with friend."

b. Whereas various elements in this account come from earlier texts, this account is entirely new and provides details not found in earlier texts.

²⁰When Saint Francis, that faithful mask of God's secrets, felt that Lord Bernard was sleeping deeply, he rose from his bed in the deep silence of the night. Turning his face towards heaven and raising his hands and eyes to God, totally intent and fervently inflamed, he prayed most devoutly, saying: "My God and all!" With many tears he groaned these words to God. He kept on saying them with such devout exactness that until morning he said nothing else but: "My God and all!" Saint Francis used to repeat these words because he regarded with admiration the height of divine majesty that graciously chose to come down to a perishing world and through Saint Francis himself, a little, poor man, determined to provide a healing remedy. Enlightened by the prophetic spirit, he foresaw the great things God would do through him and his Order, and instructed by that spirit, he considered his own insufficiency and the insignificance of his strength. He was invoking the Lord, so that what he was unable to do, God could accomplish, without whom human frailty can do nothing. That is why he kept saying, "My God and all!"

²⁶Now Lord Bernard saw all this by the light of the lamp there, carefully noted those words and, by attentive observation, weighed the devotion of the saint. Touched by the Holy Spirit in the secret recesses of his heart, in the morning he immediately called to Francis and said: "Brother Francis, I have decided to leave the world entirely and follow you in whatever you command." When Saint Francis heard this, he rejoiced in spirit and said with great joy: "Lord Bernard, that task is so difficult that the advice of our Lord Jesus Christ is needed that he may graciously show us His good pleasure about how we must carry it out. Therefore, let us go together to the bishop's residence where there is a good priest and let us have Mass said. Then after hearing Mass, we will pray there until terce. In our prayer let us ask our Lord Jesus Christ kindly to show us, in opening the Missal three times, the way that is pleasing to him which we must choose." Bernard said: "What you say pleases me."

³¹So they went to the bishop's residence,ª heard Mass and prolonged their prayer until terce. Then, at the request of Saint Francis and Lord Bernard, the priest took the Missal and, preparing himself with the sign of the Cross, opened it in the name of our Lord Jesus

---

a. AP 10 states simply: "They went to one of the city's churches"; while L3C 28 is more explicit: "they went to the church of San Nicolò next to the piazza of the city of Assisi." The "bishop's palace" refers to the Church of Santa Maria Maggiore, next to the bishop's residence. According to legend, it was built in the fourth century over the ruins of the ancient Roman Temple of Janus and was Assisi's cathedral until 1035 when the title of cathedral was transferred to the Church of San Rufino. Nevertheless, the bishop's residence remained next to Santa Maria Maggiore. Cf. Maurizio Della Porta, E. Genovesi, and Elvio Lunghi, *Guide to Assisi History and Art* (Assisi: Editrice Minerva, 1992), 160-2.

Mt 19:21

Lk 9:3

Lk 9:23; Mt 16:24

Christ. At this first opening came: *"If you seek perfection, go, sell* all *that you have,* and *give to the poor."* At the second opening: "Take nothing for the journey." And in the third opening: *"Whoever wishes to be my follower must deny his very self, take up his cross each day, and follow me."* After they saw these, Saint Francis said: "Lord Bernard, what we have here is the Lord's advice. Go and carry out what you heard. Blessed be our Lord Jesus Christ, who was kind enough to show us his evangelical way."

³⁶Lord Bernard immediately took all his goods, which were of very great value, and he joyfully gave them all to the poor. With his lap full of money, he liberally and generously distributed it to widows, orphans, pilgrims and servants of God, with Saint Francis accompanying and faithfully helping him in all those things. But Lord Sylvester, when he saw all of this being dispersed, was led by greed and said to Saint Francis: "You did not pay in full for some stones you bought from me for repairing churches." Saint Francis, astonished at his greed, did not want to argue with him. But as a true observer of the Gospel, *giving to all who ask,* he put his hand into Lord Bernard's purse, and put a handful of money into Lord Sylvester's lap and said that if he wanted even more, he would give him more. But, he left contented.

Lk 6:30

⁴¹Later, after Lord Sylvester returned home and was thinking that evening about what he had done that day, he regretted his greed and recalled Lord Bernard's fervor and Saint Francis's holiness. For a first, then a second, and a third night he had a vision of a golden cross issuing from the mouth of Francis. Its top touched the heavens and its arms, extended on each side, seemed to reach to the ends of the earth. Because of this, touched by the Lord, he took all his goods and gave them to the poor. Afterwards he became a Lesser Brother of such holiness and grace that he used *to speak* with God as friend *with friend,* as Saint Francis often experienced, as will be evident below.

Ex 33:11

⁴⁴After Lord Bernard dispersed everything for the Lord, having become entirely a gospel poor man, he gained such grace from God that he was often caught up to God. Saint Francis declared that he was worthy of all reverence and used to say that he had founded the Order because, by distributing everything to the poor, he was the first to inaugurate evangelical poverty. He kept nothing at all for himself, but offered himself naked to the arms of the Crucified Who is *the Lord blessed for ever.*

Rom 9:5; 11:31

II

THE HUMILITY AND OBEDIENCE OF SAINT FRANCIS AND BROTHER BERNARD[a]

[LMj V 8] [1]Blessed Francis, that most devout servant of the Crucified Christ, became almost entirely blind. Because of the rigor of his penance and continuous weeping, he could see very little.

[2]Once he left the place where he was and went to the place where Brother Bernard was staying, so that they could talk to each other about divine things. Bernard was standing in the woods totally withdrawn and joined to the Lord in divine contemplation. Then Saint Francis went into the woods and called to Brother Bernard: "Come and talk to this blind man." Since Brother Bernard was a man of great contemplation and his spirit at that time was clinging to God, he did not answer Saint Francis nor did he go to him. Brother Bernard had a unique gift of speaking about God, as Saint Francis had already experienced many times, and that is why he wanted to speak with him. Therefore, after a short interval, he called him a second and a third time, repeating the same words: "Come and talk to this blind man." Brother Bernard paid no attention either time; he neither came nor spoke to Saint Francis. Then Saint Francis left, feeling a little abandoned, surprised, and almost complaining to himself because even though being called three times Brother Bernard had refused to move.

[7]Saint Francis was thinking about this as he was leaving and, as he walked along the road, he said to his companion: "Wait for me a moment!" Then, while giving himself to prayer in a solitary place, an answer suddenly came to him from God: "You poor little man, why are you disturbed? Should a man leave God for some creature? When you called Brother Bernard, he was joined to me, and therefore could not come to you nor answer. You should not be surprised if he could not speak to you, for he was so far beyond himself that he did not hear a word you said." As soon as he heard this, Saint Francis hurried back to accuse himself humbly before Brother Bernard for his earlier thoughts. But Brother Bernard, a truly holy man, immediately came toward Saint Francis and threw himself at his feet. The humility of Saint Francis and the love and reverence of Brother Bernard *met each* [Ps 85:11] *other.* After recounting the divine reproof he had received, Saint Francis ordered Brother Bernard under obedience to do whatever he would order. However, Brother Bernard feared that Saint Francis would impose something excessive upon himself as he usually did. Therefore, wishing to submit with a pious obedience, he said:

---

a. There is a parallel between this chapter and ChrXXIVG 41-3.

"Father, I am prepared to carry out your obedience as long as you also promise me obedience in what I will say." Saint Francis said: "I agree." Brother Bernard then said: "Tell me what you wish me to do, Father." Then Saint Francis said: "I order you under holy obedience to punish me for my boldness and audacity of heart. I will lie on the ground. You will then press the heel of one of your feet on my throat and the other on my mouth. With your feet thus placed on my throat and mouth, you will walk over me three times from one side to the other. And while you are walking over me, you will insult me, saying: 'Lie down, you peasant son of Pietro di Bernardone.'[a] You will inflict me with many other greater insults, such as: 'Where did you get such pride, you worthless creature?' "

[16]Brother Bernard heard this, but found it hard to do. Nevertheless, because of obedience, he carried it out as courteously as he could. When he was finished, Saint Francis said to him: "Now, Brother Bernard, command me to do what you wish because I promised obedience to you." Brother Bernard said; "I command you under holy obedience that, whenever we are together, you correct me and rebuke me sharply for my failings." When Francis heard this, he was very surprised, because Brother Bernard was so holy that Saint Francis held him in great reverence. From that time on Saint Francis avoided staying with him for any length of time so that he might not happen to disturb such a holy and godly soul by some correction because of that obedience. But when he wanted to see Brother Bernard or hear him speak about God, he would quickly leave him after a short time. This was wonderful to see: how in the venerable father and in the first born son, Brother Bernard, the obedience and the love, the patience and the humility of both *met each other* and vied with each other in a real contest.

Ps 85:11

To the praise and glory of our Lord Jesus Christ.
Amen.

III

An Angel Crosses a River with Brother Bernard[b]

[1]In the beginning of the Order, when there were few brothers,   1C 30
and places had not yet been taken, Saint Francis went to visit
Santiago, taking some companions with him, one of whom was

---

a. Ugolino repeats this identification of Francis as "the son of Pietro di Bernardone" in three other passages, cf. DBF 33:5, 28; 34:6.

b. There is a parallel between this chapter and ChrXXIVG 39-40.

Brother Bernard.[a] As they were going along together in a certain town they came upon a sick man. Having compassion on him, Saint Francis said to Brother Bernard: "Son, I want you to remain here and serve this sick man." Brother Bernard immediately knelt down and bowed his head, reverently accepting the obedience of the holy father. Then leaving Brother Bernard with the sick man, Saint Francis went on to Santiago with the other companions.[b] While they were staying and praying in Santiago, it was revealed to him by the Lord in that church that he would take places throughout the world, because his Order was to expand into a great multitude.[c] From that time on because of the divine command he began to take places all around.

[5]As Saint Francis was returning by the same road as before, he found Brother Bernard and the sick man, who was now perfectly healthy.[d] Therefore, Saint Francis allowed Brother Bernard to go to Santiago during the following year. In the meantime Saint Francis returned to the Valley of Spoleto.

And while he and Brother Masseo and Brother Elias and some others were staying in a deserted place, Saint Francis one day went into the woods to pray. His companions, who held him in great reverence, were concerned about disturbing his prayer in any way because of the wonderful things God did for him in prayer.

[8]It happened that a very handsome young man came to the door, his clothes tied tightly for he was travelling on foot. He knocked rapidly and for a long time, which was not the custom. Brother Masseo came to the door, opened it, and said to that young man: "Son, I don't believe that you've ever come to the door of the brothers before, because you don't know how to knock with moderation." The other responded: "How should it be done?" Brother Masseo said: "Knock three times, slowly one knock after another. Then wait until the brother can finish one *Our Father* and comes to you. If he does not come within this interval, then knock again." But the young man replied: "I'm in a great hurry. That's why I knocked that way. I have a long journey to make. I came here to speak to Saint Francis, but he is now in contemplation in the woods, so I don't want to disturb him.

---

a. This is Santiago de Compostela, the shrine to Saint James the Apostle, in northwestern Spain. This contradicts 1C 30 where Bernard is accompanied by Giles, cf. FA:ED I 207.

b. While Thomas of Celano explicitly states that Francis did reach Spain, cf. 1C 56, there is no indication that he visited Santiago de Compostela. Cf. FA:ED I 230.

c. Both Thomas of Celano (1C 26-7) and Bonaventure (LMj III 6) tell of this prophecy about the growth of the Order when Francis has only six followers.

d. In *The Treatise on the Miracles* by Thomas of Celano 34 (hereafter 3C), Thomas indicates that Bernard was walking with Francis during his return from Spain. The text is ambiguous in determining if they were together in Spain or met elsewhere. Moreover, there is no mention of the sick man entrusted to Bernard.

But go and send Brother Elias to me. I've heard that he is very wise,[a] and I want to ask him just one question."

[13]But when Brother Masseo told Brother Elias to go to him, he got annoyed and, growing proud and angry, he refused to go. Brother Masseo did not know what to do, because if he said that he was not able to come, he would be lying; if he said that he was upset, he feared that would give bad example. In the meanwhile, since he was delayed coming back, the young man knocked again as he did before. Then the brother arrived at the door and said to the young man: "You did not observe my rule, my instruction about knocking." But that young man was an angel of God and anticipated Brother Masseo's answer. He said: "Brother Elias doesn't want to see me. Go to Brother Francis and tell him that I came to speak to him, but that I do not wish to disturb him. Tell him to send Brother Elias to me."

[17]Then Brother Masseo went to Brother Francis, who was standing in the woods praying with his face raised to heaven, and told him about the youth's message and Brother Elias's response. Then Saint Francis said, without changing his position or lowering his gaze from heaven: "Go, and tell Brother Elias under obedience to go to him immediately." So Brother Elias went to the door so upset that he flung the door open with a loud crash and said to the young man: "What do you want?" That young man replied: "Careful, dear man, you seem to be upset and anger prevents the mind from seeing the truth." Then Brother Elias said: "Say what you want!" The young man replied: "I ask you, are those who observe the holy Gospel allowed *to eat* of everything *that is set before* them, as Christ taught? And is anyone allowed to impose on observers of the holy Gospel some things contrary to the freedom of the Gospel?" Brother Elias, out of pride, answered: "I know this well, but I won't tell you. Go away, mind your own business!" The young man responded: "I'd know how to answer that question better than you." Indignant, Brother Elias slammed the door shut and went away. But as he thought to himself about that question, he hesitated and did not know how to untangle it. When he was the vicar of the Order, he had presumed to legislate beyond the Gospel and the *Rule,* and had already crafted a regulation that no brother in the Order should eat meat. So, that question was aimed entirely at him. Since he did not know how to explain himself, and considering the young man's modesty, and that he had even said that he knew how to entangle

Lk 10:8 *(margin)*

ER III 17; LR *(margin)*

---

a. Elias's reputation as *valde sapiens* [very wise] is also described by Clare, cf. *Second Letter to Agnes of Prague* 15-6; Letter of 1244 of Frederick II to Henry I, King of Cyprus, in *Collection d'Études et de Documents sur l'histoire religieuse et littéraire du Moyen âge* 3 (Paris, 1901) 146, n. 1.

that question better than himself, Brother Elias returned to the door and opened it to ask the young man to untangle it for him. But when he opened the door, no one was there, and even though he looked here and there, the young man was not to be found. This young man was an angel of God, and, for this reason, did not wait, and went away, because a proud heart was not worthy to converse with an angel.

[27]After this occurred and it had all been revealed to him, Saint Francis came back from the woods and rebuked Brother Elias shouting: "You are a proud man, Brother Elias! You do wrong! You turn away holy angels who come to visit and teach us. I tell you that I very greatly fear that your pride will make you end up outside this Order." And that is what happened to him later, just as Saint Francis had foretold through the spirit of prophecy.

HTrb II

On the same day and at the same hour when that angel left that brother mentioned above, that angel appeared in the same form to Brother Bernard who was returning from Santiago and was standing by the side of a large river that he could not cross. The angel greeted Brother Bernard in his native dialect: *The Lord give you peace,* good brother."[a] Brother Bernard was surprised at his beauty, at the way he knew his tongue, at his greeting of peace, and his smiling face; so he asked him: *"Where do you come from, good young man?"* The young man replied: "I come from such and such a place, where Saint Francis is staying. I went to speak with him, but I could not because he was in the woods contemplating the things of God. With him in that place were Brother Masseo, Brother Giles, and Brother Elias. Brother Masseo taught me how to knock at your door. But Brother Elias would not bother to listen to me about a question I asked him; later he was sorry and *wished to see me and hear me* but could not." After saying this, the angel said to Brother Bernard: "Dear Brother, why are you waiting to cross the river?" He answered: "Because I'm afraid of that dangerous depth of the water I see." Then the angel said: "Let's cross together; don't be afraid!" Taking hold of Brother Bernard's hand, in the blink of an eye the angel put him down safely on the other side of the river. Realizing that this was an angel of the Lord, Brother Bernard said with great devotion, reverence and joy: "O blessed angel of God, will you *tell me* your *name?"* He replied: "Why are you *asking my name* which is 'wonderful'?" Having said this, he

Test 27; 1C 23;
1C 26; LMj III 2

Nm 6:26

Tb 5:5

Lk 10:24

Gn 32:29

---

a. The greeting is given in its Latin form, *Dominus det tibi pacem.* Bernard's *idiomate proprio* [native dialect] was Umbrian-Italian which is translated in the *Fioretti* [Little Flowers] as *"Iddio ti dia pace, o buono frate!"*

disappeared and left Brother Bernard so greatly consoled that he walked all the rest of the way home in joy.

[38]Brother Bernard noted the day and the hour when the angel appeared to him. Then after he reached the place where Saint Francis was staying with his companions, he told them everything in detail. From this they realized clearly that that same angel had appeared to them at the same hour on the same day.

To the praise of our Lord Jesus Christ, Who is blessed forever.
Amen.

IV
BROTHER BERNARD GOES TO BOLOGNA[a]

[1]From the Cross and to the Cross, God had called both our blessed Father Francis and his companions. Therefore he and his blessed first companions were rightly seen as men of the Crucified, which they really were. Carrying the cross in habit and in all their deeds, preferring the insults of Christ to the empty and deceitful compliments of the world, they were happy when insulted and, for this reason, were saddened when honored. They went through the world *as pilgrims and strangers* carrying with them nothing but Christ. As a result, because they were living branches of the true vine, wherever they went, they produced the greatest fruit of souls.

[4]Once it happened at the beginning of the Order that Saint Francis sent Brother Bernard to Bologna to produce fruit for God there according to the grace given to him by the Lord. So, equipping himself with the cross of Christ, and with the virtue of obedience as his companion, Brother Bernard went to Bologna.

[5]When children saw him clothed in an odd, disreputable habit, they began to shower him with insults. But Brother Bernard, a real saint, endured these not just patiently, but quite happily. As a true disciple of Christ who became *the scorn of men, despised by the people,* he deliberately positioned himself in the city where people could more easily make fun of him. While he was sitting there, many gathered around him, both children and adults. Some pulled his capuche back and forth, some threw dirt at him, and others threw stones; some climbed on him, rocking him violently back and forth. Through all these insults, Brother Bernard remained patient and cheerful and at no time did he ever resist or complain. And there is something even

1 Pt 2:11

LR VI 3

Ps 22:7

---

a. There is a parallel between this chapter and ChrXXIVG 36-8.

greater: he deliberately kept returning to that piazza over several days to be insulted in the same way. No matter how many insults he suffered from these people, his smiling face always showed his spirit unperturbed. And because it is patience that takes a work and approves it as perfect, a wise judge waited and carefully watched a consistent virtue thoroughly undisturbed over so many days. He said to himself: "It's impossible for that not to be a holy man!" Approaching Brother Bernard, he asked: "Who are you? Why did you come here?" Brother Bernard put his hand into his breast pocket and brought out the evangelical *Rule* of Saint Francis which he carried in his heart and showed by his deeds. When the judge had read the very high standard of this *Rule,* being an intelligent man, he was completely dumbstruck. Then turning to his companions, he said with the greatest admiration: "This state of life is higher than any I've ever heard of, and, for that reason, this man and his companions are some of the holiest men in this world. So whoever heaps insults on them commits a grave sin. He should be singled out for the highest honors, not insults since he is truly a friend of the Most High." Then he said to Brother Bernard: "Dear Brother, if someone were to offer you a place that suits you, where you could better serve God and you were willing to accept it, I would most willingly give it to you for the salvation of my soul." Brother Bernard responded: "My very dear sir, I believe that our Lord Jesus Christ has inspired you to do this."

[18]Then the judge took Brother Bernard to his home and there received him with great love and joy. He later showed him the place he had promised and at his own expense he fully and devoutly took care of everything. This judge became the defender and special father of Brother Bernard and his companions. Because of his holy life among them Brother Bernard began to be honored so much by the people that whoever was able to touch, hear, or see him considered himself blessed.

[20]But Brother Bernard, like the truly humble disciple of Christ that he was, feared that the honor shown him might at the same time impede his tranquility and salvation. So he left and returned to Saint Francis. "A place to live has been accepted in Bologna. Therefore, Father, send brothers who will live there. I am not gaining anything there anymore. In fact, due to the great honor shown to me there, I fear that I will lose more than I gain." Saint Francis listened one after another to all the things which had been done through Brother Bernard, and rejoicing and exulting in spirit he began to praise the Most High who for the salvation of the people was thus spreading out these poor little disciples of the Cross. From that time on he selected some of his companions and sent them into

Lombardy, and with the devotion of the faithful increasing, he accepted very many places all around for living quarters.

To the praise of our Lord Jesus Christ, Who is blessed forever. Amen.

V

THE GRACE-FILLED DEATH OF BROTHER BERNARD[a]

[1]Brother Bernard possessed such sanctity that as long as Francis was living, he venerated him with great affection, showed his regard for him by frequent conversations and in Bernard's absence extolled him with great praise. It happened that one day while Francis was praying, it was revealed to him that Brother Bernard with the permission of God was being attacked by many very fierce devils. While Saint Francis with a compassionate heart was pondering over these things concerning such a beloved son, he tearfully prayed for many days and asked our Lord Jesus Christ to give him victory over so many assaults. And during this prayer while Francis was ever alert, troubled, and attentive, he received an answer from God: "Brother, never fear. All the temptations by which Brother Bernard is being assailed were given to him for the purpose of improvement and a crown, and at the end of all these attacks on him he will joyously carry off the palm of victory. Brother Bernard is one of those who will

Mt 2:10   eat at the same table with God in his kingdom." Saint Francis *greatly rejoiced* at this response and gave very great thanks to our Lord Jesus Christ. From that time on he did not have any fear or worry about Brother Bernard, but he always loved him with a greater joy and moved to a fuller affection for him. Saint Francis demonstrated this affection both in life and in death.

[8]When Saint Francis was on the point of death, like the patriarch Jacob, with his sons standing around him and devoutly weeping for

Gn 49:3   the departure of such a loving Father, he said: "Where is *my*
Gn 27:4   *first-born?* Come here, my son, that *my soul may bless you* before *I die."* Then Brother Bernard whispered to Brother Elias who was then vicar of the Order: "Father, go to his right hand so that he may bless you." After Brother Elias placed himself on the right side and Saint Francis, blind because of his tears, placed his right hand on Elias's head, he said: "This is not the head of my first-born, Brother Bernard." Then Brother Bernard approached his right side. Saint Francis with

---

a. There is a parallel between this chapter and ChrXXIVG 39-40.

his arms crossed placed his left *hand on the head* of Brother Elias and his *right on the head* of Brother Bernard. Then he said: *"May the Father of our Lord Jesus Christ bless you in heaven with every spiritual blessing in Christ.* Just as you were chosen first in this Order to give the example of the Gospel and to imitate Christ in evangelical poverty, because not only did you freely give away your possessions and disperse them entirely for love of Christ, but you also gave yourself as *a sacrifice* to God *in the odor of sweetness,* therefore, may you be blessed by our Lord Jesus Christ and by me his poor little servant with everlasting blessings, whether you are coming or going, awake or sleeping, living or dying. *May he who blesses you be filled with blessings, and whoever curses* you will not be immune. Be the master of your brothers, and may all of them be subject to your authority. And whomever you wish to receive into this Order, let them be received, and whomever you wish to expel, let them be expelled. Let no brother have authority over you, and may you be freely able to go or to stay wherever you will."

[17]After the death of Saint Francis when the blessed son was approaching death,[a] many of the brothers came from different localities because they loved him with the affection due a father. Among them was that very holy and God-like man, Brother Giles, who, after he saw Brother Bernard, said with great joy: *"Sursum corda!* Brother Bernard, *sursum corda!"* Brother Bernard whispered to a brother to prepare a place suitable for contemplation where Brother Giles could contemplate the things of heaven.

[20]When Brother Bernard reached the last hour before dying, he had himself raised and he said to the attending brothers: "My most dear brothers, I do not want to speak many words, but you ought to consider that I was once in the condition that you are now, and that you will be in the condition that I am now. I have found in my soul that not for a thousand worlds equal to this one would I wish not to serve our Lord Jesus Christ. And I accuse myself before my God and Savior the Lord Jesus Christ and before you for every offence that I committed. I ask you, my most dear brothers, *to love one another."*

[22]After these words and other salutary exhortations, he lay back on his bed. His countenance became exceedingly brilliant and joyful to the astonishment of all who were standing around. And with that joy his soul, happy with the victory which was promised to him earlier, passed over to the joys of the blessed.

To the praise and glory of God.

---

a. That is, Brother Bernard.

Gn 48:14

Eph 1:3

Lv 2:9

Gn 27:29

Jn 13:34

VI
THE LENTEN FAST OF SAINT FRANCIS

[1]Because Francis, that very real servant of Christ, was in some things another Christ given to the world, God the Father made this fortunate man conformed in many things to Christ, his Son, as was apparent in his venerable band of holy companions, in the wonderful mystery of the stigmata of the Cross, and the holy fast of forty continuous days.

[3]At one time when Francis was near the Lake of Perugia, he was at Mardi Gras a guest of a man devoted to him. He asked his host to take him for the love of God to an island on the lake where no one lived and to do so during the night before Ash Wednesday so that no one would know about it.[a] The host did this very eagerly because of the great devotion he had for Francis. He prepared his little boat at night and transported him on Ash Wednesday to the island. Saint Francis brought nothing for food except two small loaves of bread.

[6]After he reached the island he asked his ferryman to tell no one and to come back for him on Holy Thursday. Since there was no shelter there where he could rest, he crawled into a dense thicket where thorn bushes had formed an enclosure, and he stayed there immobile for the whole forty days, neither eating or drinking.

[9]His host came looking for him, as they had agreed, on Holy Thursday and he found that, except for part of one, the two little loaves of bread had not been touched. It is believed that Saint Francis ate part of one loaf so that with a little bread he would expel the poison of vainglory and thus the glory of a forty day fast be reserved for
Mt 4:2   the blessed Christ. Yet he did fast *forty days and forty nights* after the example of Christ.

[11]In that place where Saint Francis did such remarkable penance, many miracles were performed through his merits. Therefore, people began to build and live on this island, and in a short period of time a large village and a house for the brothers were established there.[b] The people of this village still show great reverence for that place where Saint Francis kept the Lenten fast.

---

a. Luke Wadding places this Lent at 1211, cf. *Annales Minorum* I, a. 1211, 12; also N. Cavanna, "L'Umbria Serafica," *Miscellanea Franciscana* 2 (1887): 30.

b. According to Agostino da Stroncone, the date of this foundation on the Isola Maggiore in Lago Trasimeno (cf. Map Eight) was 1328, cf. *Umbria Serafica*, Biblioteca Communale, cod. CC.VII, 269; N. Cacanna, *L'Umbria Francescana Illustrata* (Perugia: 1910), 205, 212, n. 26.

To the glory of God.
To the praise of our Lord Jesus Christ, Who is blessed forever.
Amen.

VII
SAINT FRANCIS TEACHES BROTHER LEO THAT PERFECT JOY IS IN THE CROSS[a]

[1]On one day in winter Saint Francis was going from Perugia to
Saint Mary of the Angels. Brother Leo was with him and they were
suffering very acutely from the cold. Saint Francis called to Brother
Leo who was walking a short distance in front of him. "Brother Leo,"
he said, "although in every area the Lesser Brothers give great example of sanctity, honesty, and edification, nevertheless write, that is,
diligently note that perfect joy does not consist in this." Then after he
walked a little farther, he called to him again: "O Brother Leo, even if
a Lesser Brother should give sight *to the blind,* straighten crooked
limbs, cast out demons, give hearing *to the deaf,* movement to the halt,
speech to the dumb, and, what is more, life *to one dead* for four days,
write that this is not perfect joy." And calling again he said: "O
Brother Leo, if a Lesser Brother knew *the languages* of all peoples, *all
knowledge,* and all Scriptures, so that he *could prophesy* and reveal not
only the future but also the consciences of others, write that this is
not perfect joy." And while they were walking he called again: "O
Brother Leo, little lamb of God, even if a Lesser Brother *spoke with the
tongue of an angel,* and knew the courses of the stars and the powers of
herbs, and knew the locations of the earth's treasure, if he knew the
worth and properties of bird and *fish,* of animals, men, roots, trees,
stones, and waters, write down and diligently note that perfect joy is
not there." And after a little while he cried out again: "O Brother Leo,
even if a Lesser Brother knew how to preach so well that he could
convert all infidels to the faith, write that this is not perfect joy."

[2]This type of talking went on for about two miles. Brother Leo,
however, was in admiration about all this and said: "Father, I ask
you in God's name to tell me where will I find perfect joy?" Francis
answered: "When we arrive at Saint Mary of the Angels so drenched
by the rain and frozen by the cold, spattered with mud and suffering

Mt 11:4

1 Cor 13:2

1 Cor 13:2

1 Kgs 5:13

a. Following the example of Luke Wadding, Kajetan Esser placed this teaching of Francis among the
Dictates of the Saint, cf. Luke Wadding, *B.P. Francisci Assisiatis Opuscula. Nunc primum collecta
tribus tomis distincta, notis et commentariis asceticis illustrata.* (Antwerp: 1623); Kajetan Esser, *Die
Opuscula des Hl. Franziskus von Assisi: Neue textkritische Edition* (Grottaferrata, Rome: Editiones
Follegii S. Bonaventurae ad Claras Aquas, 1976). Esser, however, did not publish this version, but
that found in the Codex Florentino C.9.2879 as published by B. Bughetti in "Analecta de S.
Francisco Assisiensi saeculo XIV ante medium collecta (e Cod. Florentino C.9.2879)," AFH 20
(1927): 107, number 50 See FA:ED I 166-7.

from hunger, and we knock on the door of the place and the porter comes and angrily says: 'Who are you?' And we say: 'We are two of your brothers'; and he says in return: 'You are, in fact, coarse fellows who go about the world stealing alms from the poor, and he will not let us enter but keeps us standing in snow and water, in cold and hunger until it is night, and then if we patiently endure such insults and rebuffs without being disturbed or murmuring, and humbly and charitably feel that even this porter knows us for what we are and that God loosened his tongue against us, O Brother Leo, write that this is perfect joy. And if we persevere in knocking, and the porter, disturbed at our importunity, comes out and attacks us with very hard blows and says: 'Leave here, you worthless idlers, and go to an inn! Who do you think you are? You certainly are not going to eat here!' And if we bear these things patiently and with love accept the insults wholeheartedly, O Brother Leo, write that this is perfect joy. And if thoroughly suffering from great hunger and painful cold as night comes on we continue to knock and call out and tearfully cry out for admittance, and the aroused porter says: 'These men are very impudent and bold, and I will quiet them!' Then coming out with a knotty club and grabbing us by the capuche, he throws us to the ground in mud and snow, and so beats us with the club that we are filled with wounds on all sides. And if we endure so many evils, so many insults and blows with joy, thinking that we ought to bear and endure most patiently these pains of the blessed Christ, O Brother Leo, among all the gifts of the Holy Spirit, which Christ gives to his friends is to conquer oneself and willingly endure abuse for Christ and for the love of God. For in all the wonderful things mentioned above we cannot glory, because they are not ours but God's: *Name something you have that you have not received. If, then, you have received it, why are you boasting as if it were your own?* But we can *boast in the cross* of tribulation and affliction, because that is our own. Therefore, the Apostle says: '*May I never boast of anything but the Cross of our Lord,*' to whom be praise forever.

Gal 6:14

Gal 6:14

Amen."

VIII
GOD SPEAKS TO SAINT FRANCIS THROUGH BROTHER LEO[a]

[1]In the beginning of the Order our holy Father Francis was staying in a little place with Brother Leo and they did not have the books to recite the Office. One night when they arose for matins,

---

a. There is a parallel between this chapter and ChrXXIVG 69-70.

Saint Francis said to his companion: "Dear brother, we do not have a breviary so we can say matins, but in order to spend the time in praising God, say what I tell you and do not change a word. I will say this: 'O Brother Francis, you have committed so many sins in the world that you deserve hell.' And you Brother Leo will respond: 'It is true that you deserve hell'" The pure-minded Brother Leo answered with the simplicity of the dove: "Willingly, Father. Begin in the name of the Lord." Then Saint Francis began: "O Brother Francis, you have committed so many sins in this world that you deserve hell." Brother Leo answered: "God will work such good through you that you will go to paradise." Saint Francis said: "Do not say that, Brother Leo. When I say: 'O Brother Francis, you have performed so many evil deeds against God that you deserve to be cursed,' you will answer: 'You deserve to be listed among the damned.'" Brother Leo answered: "Certainly, Father."

⁷With many tears and sighs and beating his breast Saint Francis said in a loud voice: "O Lord, O God of heaven and earth, I have done so many evil things against you that I deserve to be thoroughly cursed." Brother Leo responded: "O Brother Francis, God will make you such that you will be singularly blessed among the blessed." Saint Francis, amazed that Leo answered to the contrary, said: "Brother Leo, why do you not answer as I instruct you? I command you under holy obedience to answer according to the words I tell you. I will say: 'O Brother Francis, you miserable little man, do you think that God will have mercy on you even though you have committed so many sins against *the Father of mercies and the God of all consolation* that   2 Cor 1:3
you are not worthy to find mercy? And you, Brother Little Lamb, will respond: 'In no way are you worthy to find mercy.'" Brother Leo answered: "God the Father, whose mercy is infinitely greater than your sin, will grant you great grace and mercy, and add many more graces besides."

¹³Saint Francis, mildly irritated and patiently disturbed, said: "Brother, why have you dared to act contrary to obedience and answered so many times contrary to what I proposed?" Then Brother Leo humbly and reverently replied: "God knows, my dear Father, that I always intended to say just what you ordered, but God made me speak according to His will and not according to my intention." Saint Francis was amazed at this and said: "I ask you, my dear brother, that this time when I accuse myself as before, you say that I am not worthy of mercy." And with many tears he kept on proposing this for Brother Leo to say. Brother Leo responded: "Tell me again, Father, for this time I will answer as you wish." Saint Francis, shouting out with many tears, said: "O Brother Francis, you great sinner, O

Brother Francis, you miserable little man, you know that God will not show you mercy!" Brother Leo replied: "Yes, Father, God will show you mercy; in fact, you will receive great glory from God your Savior, and he will exalt and glorify you for all eternity, because *everyone who humbles himself shall be exalted.* I am not able to speak differently because God is speaking through my mouth." In this contest of humility they remained awake until dawn in tears of compassion and in divine consolation.

Lk 14:11

To the praise of our Lord Jesus Christ.

IX
THE FINDING OF MOUNT LA VERNA

[1]Francis, that most faithful servant and friend of Jesus Christ, through himself and others honored his Creator and Savior with all his strength. Therefore, our most gracious and kind Savior Jesus in turn honored him, for *whoever glorifies me, I will glorify him,* says the Lord. For that reason wherever Saint Francis went, he was held in such veneration by people that it was as if the whole world ran together towards such an amazing man. Whenever he approached a place, a town or a village, a person considered himself fortunate if he would touch or see him.

Mt 10:32

[4]At one time before he received the stigmata of our Savior, it happened that he left the Valley of Spoleto and went to Romagna. When on his journey he came to the town of Montefeltro,[a] a celebration for a new knighting was being held there with great solemnity.[b] When our holy Father learned about this from the inhabitants, he said to Brother Leo, his companion: "Let us go to these people, because with the help of God we will make some progress among them." In the celebration there were many noblemen gathered from various regions. Among them was a lord named Orlando from Tuscany. He was very rich and noble, and because of the wonderful things he had heard about Saint Francis, he conceived a great devotion for him and wished to see and listen to him.

---

a. For the background of Montefeltro, known today as San Leo, in Romagna, see Fortini, *Francis,* 547 a.

b. Military Orders of the time were associations of knights and other persons who followed a monastic rule established by a pope or church council. The most famous of these were the orders of the Templars, Hospitallers, and the Teutonic Knights. Cf. Malcolm Barber, *The New Knighthood: Fighting for the Faith, Caring for the Sick* (Aldershot & Brookfield, 1994). For information about the ceremony of knighting, see: Maurice Keen, *Chivalry* (New Haven and London: Yale University Press, 1984), 64-82; Andrea Hopkins, *Knights* (New York: Quarto Publishing, 1990), 39-43.

[7]When Saint Francis entered the town, he climbed a wall in order to be more easily heard by the throng and he preached there to the multitude. In the local idiom this is the theme he set forth:

Tanto è il bene ch'io aspetto,
    ch'ogni pena m'è diletto.

The sense of this is: Such is the good which I await, that every pain delights me. On these words the Holy Spirit poured forth divine declarations through the mouth of Saint Francis by referring to the pains of the martyrs, the martyrdoms of the apostles, the severe penances of the confessors, and the many tribulations of holy men and women. He did this so devoutly that the people stood there in rapt attention as if listening to an angel. Among these people was Orlando who rejoiced in the desired presence of Saint Francis and was inwardly touched by his wonderful sermon. He proposed for the salvation of his soul to discuss a transaction with our holy Father.

[11]Therefore, when the preaching was finished, he said to Saint Francis: "Father, I would like to speak to you about the salvation of my soul." However, Saint Francis, totally *grounded with the salt* of discernment, said to him: "My lord, go this morning and honor your friends since they invited you to the celebration, and after your meal we will talk as much as you wish," Orlando agreed to this and after his dinner he fully set forth before Saint Francis the matter of the salvation of his soul. At the end he said: "Brother Francis, I have a very abandoned and solitary mountain in Tuscany which is called Mount La Verna. It is very suitable for those who wish to live a solitary life. If this mountain pleases you and your companions, I would very willingly give it to you for the salvation of my soul."[a]

Col 4:6

[15]Saint Francis was thoroughly inclined and desirous of finding a solitary place where he could more completely give himself to divine contemplation, so that when he heard this offer, he first gave praise to God who through his faithful people provides for his little sheep, and then he gave thanks to Lord Orlando, and said: "My lord, when you return to your region, I will send you two of my companions. You show them this mountain and, if it seems suitable, I most willingly accept your charitable offer." Orlando lived in a castle near Mount La Verna.

[17]After the celebration was finished and Orlando returned to his home, Saint Francis sent him two of his associates who looked for him, but because that area was unknown to them it was with great

---

a. This is confirmed by a legal document made by the sons of Count Orlando, signed in Chiusi on June 9, 1274. Cf. infra 801-3.

difficulty that they found Orlando's castle. When they found him, he most willingly and charitably received them as though they were angels of God. With about fifty men, heavily armed for fear of wild animals, they were led to Mount La Verna. Looking for a place where they could prepare a home to live in, they finally found there a small piece of level ground where in the name of the Lord they decided to stay. Those laymen who came with the brothers built a hut of branches which they had cut from the trees with their broad swords. After they accepted the place there, they went for Saint Francis and told him that the place was very remote and suitable for divine contemplation.

²³When he heard this, Saint Francis gave praise to God. He then took Brother Leo, Brother Masseo and Brother Angelo, a former knight, and together they went to La Verna. When he was climbing the mountain with his blessed companions and was resting for a little while at the foot of an oak tree, a great number of different kinds of birds flew to blessed Francis with joy and song and a sportive flapping of their wings. Some of the birds settled on his head, some on his shoulders, some on his knees and some on his hands. Seeing this remarkable and unusual thing, blessed Francis said to his companions: "I believe, my very dear brothers, that our Lord Jesus Christ is pleased that we have accepted a place on this solitary mountain where our sisters, the birds, show such pleasure at our coming." Then rising totally joyful in spirit, he made his way to the place where there was yet nothing but the very poor little hut made from the branches of trees. And when he saw a solitary place where, separated from the others, he could pray, he made a poor little cell on the side of the mountain, and ordered that none of his companions should come to him, nor should they allow anyone else to come except Brother Leo, because he intended to keep a forty days' fast there in honor of Saint Michael.ᵃ He told Brother Leo not to come to him more than once a day with bread and water; and once at night at the time for matins; and at that time to approach him saying nothing but

Ps 51:17 *"Lord, open my lips."* And if then Francis answered from within: *"And my mouth shall declare your praise,"* they would recite matins together. But if there was no immediate response, Brother Leo should leave. He ordered this because sometimes he was in such an ecstasy of spirit and so absorbed in God that he was not able to speak through-

---

a. Thus, in 1224, Francis would have fasted from Thursday, August 16, to Saturday, September 29.

out the day or night.[a] Brother Leo most attentively observed this precept.

[32]Nevertheless, Brother Leo silently took notice as much as he could of what the holy man was doing. Sometimes he found him outside his cell, elevated in the air to such a height that he could touch his feet. And then weeping he would embrace and kiss Francis's feet, and say: *"O God, be merciful to me a sinner,* and through the merits of this most holy man let me find mercy." Once he found Francis elevated to a very high altitude above the ground in the middle of a grove of beech trees. Once he found him elevated to such a height into the air that he could hardly see him. And then Brother Leo would go down on his knees and stretch out on the ground in the place from which his holy Father in prayer was caught up into the heights. Brother Leo, while praying and as before recommending himself to God through the merits of his holy Father, experienced the greatest visitations of divine grace. Because of these things which Brother Leo had often noticed about the saint, he had such devotion towards him, that very often night and day he examined Francis's hidden zeal with a pious shrewdness. Lk 18:13

[37]It happened that during the forty days' fast Brother Leo went once very early in the morning just as Saint Francis required. And as soon as he entered and said: *"O Lord, open my lips"* as had been asked by the saint, and the saint did not respond, he saw by the light of the moon which entered through the doorway that the saint was not in his cell. Thinking that he was praying, he looked here and there through the woods. Then he heard Francis speaking. Going closer to hear what the saint was saying, by the light of the moon he saw the saint kneeling with his face raised towards heaven and his arms extended towards God and saying these words. "Who are you, my most dear God, and who *am I, a worm* and your little servant?" He kept repeating this and said nothing else. While Brother Leo watched, he saw one most beautiful *flame of fire,* very brilliant and delightful to the eyes, descending from the height of the heavens to the top of the head of Saint Francis. A voice came from this flame and spoke with Saint Francis, and Saint Francis replied to the one speaking. Ps 51:17 Ps 22:7 Ex 3:2

[43]Brother Leo was afraid and, retreating, he hid himself, lest he impede the holy man in secrets so holy that he did not understand

---

a. This description of Francis's time in prayer on LaVerna adds to the tradition. In 1C 83, Thomas of Celano writes that Francis was *contemplatione suspensus* [suspended in contemplation]. In LMj XIII 3, Bonaventure writes that Francis *seraphicis desideriorum ardoribus sursum ageretur in Deum* [with the seraphic ardor of desires, he was being borne aloft into God]. Now Ugolino writes that Francis was *absoprtus in Deum* [absorbed into God].

what the words meant. Yet he saw Saint Francis extend his hand three times towards the flame. When the flame withdrew, Brother Leo began to withdraw completely lest the saint notice his presence. But Saint Francis hearing the sound of his feet stepping on twigs, said: "I command you, whoever you are, in virtue of our Lord Jesus Christ to stand still. Don't move from the spot." Because of the saint's oath Brother Leo immediately stopped and said: "It is I, Father." Afterwards Brother Leo said that at that moment he was so terrified that if the earth had opened up before him, he would have willingly hidden there. For he feared that, if he offended the saint, he would lose his gracious companionship. Such was his love for the saint and the confidence he had in him, that he believed that he could in no way live without him. Because of this, whenever anyone would speak about the saint, Brother Leo would say: "Beloved, all the saints are great, but Saint Francis is also among the great saints because of the miracles which God works through him." When the saint recognized Brother Leo's voice, he said: "Brother Little Lamb, why have you come to this place? I told you many times not to come looking for me, didn't I? Under obedience I ask you to tell me whether you saw anything." Leo answered: "Father, I heard you speaking, talking and with much wonder frequently praying: 'Who are you, my most dear God, and who am I, a worm and your little ser-

Ex 3:2

vant.' And then I saw *a flame of fire* descending from heaven and speaking with you. And I saw you replying to the voice many times and extending your hand to it three times, but what you said, I do not know."

^{52}Brother Leo knelt and with great reverence asked the saint: "I ask you, Father, to explain for me the words which I heard and tell me what I did not hear." Saint Francis had a great love for Brother Leo because of his purity and his gentleness, and he said: "O Brother Little Lamb of Jesus Christ, two lights were opened for me in what you saw and heard: one, a knowledge of the Creator, and the other a knowledge of myself. When I said: 'Who are you, Lord my God, and who am I,' then I was in the light of contemplation in which I saw the abyss of infinite divine Goodness and the tearful depths of my own vileness. Therefore, I kept on saying: 'Who are you, O Lord, supremely wise and supremely good and supremely merciful, that you visit me who am utterly vile, an abominable and despised little

Ex 3:1, 2

worm.' The flame was God who was speaking to me as he spoke *to Moses in a flame.* And among other things which God then said, he asked me to give him three things. I replied: 'I am totally yours, O Lord, and I have nothing except a tunic and a cord and trousers, and ER II 13; LR II 8
these are likewise yours. Therefore, what can I offer to the greatness

of your dominion? Heaven and earth, fire and water and everything that is in them are yours, O Lord. For who owns anything but you? Therefore, when we offer you anything, we are returning to you what is already yours. What, therefore, shall I be able to offer you, O Lord God, king of heaven and earth and of all creation?' And then God said to me: 'Put your hand into your pocket and offer to me whatever you find there.' When I did this, I found a gold coin, larger, shinier and more beautiful than I had ever seen in this world, and this I offered to God. Again God said: 'Offer me something again as before.' But I said to God: 'Lord, I don't have anything, nor do I love, nor do I want anything but you. For love of you I despise gold and everything else. If anything else is found in my pocket, you put it there, and I return it to you as the possessor of all things.' And this I did three times. After the third offering was made, I knelt down and praised God who gave me what I could offer. Immediately I was given to understand that the threefold offering was figuratively golden obedience, the most exalted poverty and the most beautiful chastity which God through his grace gave me to observe so perfectly that my conscience does not reprove me in any way. And just as when I put my hand into my pocket, I offered and returned those coins to God himself who put them there, so God gave me the power in my soul always to praise and magnify him with heart and mouth for all the things which his most holy goodness has given me. These were the words you heard and the extension of arms which you saw. But beware, Brother Little Lamb, of coming and watching me again. Return to your cell with the blessing of God. Be solicitous of taking care of me. For in a few days on this mountain God will perform an astonishing miracle which the whole world will admire. For he will do something new which he has never done before to any creature in this world."[a]

[68]Then Brother Leo withdrew very consoled.

LMj XIII 3; 3C 4
During that very same forty days' fast and on that same mountain around the feast of the Exaltation of the Holy Cross,[b] Christ appeared under the form of a winged Seraph as though crucified and impressed both the nails and the stigmata on the hands and feet and side of Saint Francis just as it says in his *Legend*. The vision appeared at night with such splendor that it illuminated the mountains and

---

a. The source of this account is the *Instrumentum de stigmatibus b. Francisci*, a document written in October, 1282, and kept at the Friary of Santa Croce, in Firenze, Italy. Cf. AF III 644-5. In Ugolino's narration, however, it is greatly expanded.

b. Although he had access to the *Instrumentum* which states clearly that the stigmata were given on the Feast of the Exaltation of the Holy Cross (AF III 643), Ugolino adopts the phrase of Bonaventure *circa festum* [about the feast].

Lk 2:8 valleys all around more than if the brilliance of the sun had appeared there.[a] All *the shepherds* who were awake and *keeping watch with the sheep* in this region were witnesses to this. Why these sacred stigmata had been impressed on Saint Francis has not become entirely clear. But as Francis himself said to his companions, this great mystery is being put off for the future.

[71]Brother James de Massa received this account from the mouth of Brother Leo, and Brother Ugolino of Monte Santa Maria had it from the mouth of this Brother James, and I, the writer, had it from the mouth of Brother Ugolino. All these were men worthy of trust in all things.

To the praise of our Lord Jesus Christ.
Amen.

X

BROTHER MASSEO INVESTIGATES THE HUMILITY OF SAINT FRANCIS

[1]At one time Saint Francis was staying at Saint Mary of the Portiuncula with Brother Masseo who possessed in abundance the grace of God's word, and great discretion. For this he was greatly loved by the saint. One day Saint Francis was returning from the woods where he was praying, and had already reached the exit from the woods. Brother Masseo met him and wanted to see how humble he was. He said to Saint Francis: "Why you? Why you? Why you?"
Jn 12:19 Saint Francis replied: "What does Brother Masseo mean?" *"The whole world* seems to be coming *after* you, and everyone is seeking to see you, to hear you, and to obey you: you are not a handsome man; you are not a man of great knowledge or wisdom; you are not of noble birth! Why does the whole world come to you?" Hearing this, Saint Francis became joyful in spirit. He raised his countenance to heaven and stood for a long period of time with his mind directed toward God. Then returning to himself, he dropped to his knees, praising and giving thanks to God with great spiritual fervor. Then turning to Brother Masseo he said: "You want to know why me? You want to know why me? You want to know, and well you should, why me; why the whole world comes after me? I know this from those most holy eyes of God Who everywhere sees the good and the bad. Those blessed and most holy eyes have not seen among the bad a greater sinner than me or one more unqualified and more vile. And

---

a. This passage is reminiscent of the antiphons written for the celebration of the feast of the Stigmata established in 1337. Cf. infra 661-4.

therefore, to perform this miraculous deed which he intends to perform, he did not find in the world a more vile creature, so he chose me: because *God chose those whom the world considers absurd to shame the wise; he singled out the weak of this world to shame the strong. He chose the world's lowborn and despised, those who count for nothing,* to reduce to nothing those who were something, in order to show that the sublimity of virtue comes from God and not from a creature and *so that all flesh can do no boasting before God,* but *let him who would boast, boast in the Lord,* so that *glory and honor be given for all eternity to God alone.*

1 Cor 1:27-29

1 Cor 1:29

1 Tm 1:17

¹⁰At this humble response which he gave with such fervor, Brother Masseo was amazed and he truly knew that his holy father as a true and humble disciple of Christ was founded in true humility.

Amen.

XI

SAINT FRANCIS KNEW THE SECRETS OF BROTHER MASSEO'S HEART[a]

DBF X 1

¹Saint Francis once started out on a journey with Brother Masseo. He took him for a companion very willingly because of his gift of words, outstanding discernment, and the help provided him when in rapture, satisfying the rushing crowds and hiding the saint so they would not bother him.[b] One day as they started out together, Brother Masseo walked a short distance ahead of Saint Francis on the road. But when they arrived at a three-way crossroads where he could head either toward Siena, Florence or Arezzo, Brother Masseo said: "Father, which way should we take?" The saint replied: "Let's take the way that God wills." Brother Masseo replied: "How will we be able to know the Lord's will?" The saint answered: "By a sign that I'll show you. So, by merit of holy obedience I command that right in the crossroads where your feet are standing, you twirl around in a circle, as children do, and don't stop twirling until I tell you."

⁶As a truly obedient man Brother Masseo twirled around for so long at that stop that he fell down several times from dizziness in the head which twirling induces. But since the saint did not tell him to stop and he wished to obey faithfully, he got up each time and continued spinning around. After Brother Masseo was twirling rapidly, Saint Francis said: "Stand still. Don't move!" And he stopped suddenly. Saint Francis said: "What direction are you facing?" Brother

---

a. There is a parallel between this chapter and ChrXXIVG 116-7.

b. Ugolino builds on his earlier description of Brother Masseo as a man gifted with words and of outstanding discernment. Now he is described as providing help for Francis while he was in rapture.

Masseo replied: "Towards Siena." Then Saint Francis said: "That's the way God wants us to go." And as they went their way Brother Masseo was really wondering about all this: that Francis made him act like a child and had him twirling around in front of lay people passing by. But out of reverence he did not dare to say anything to the holy Father. As they neared Siena and the people of the city heard of the saint's arrival, they came out to meet him and carried both Francis and his companion, dangling in such a way that their feet never touched the ground, all the way to the bishop's residence.

[11]At that very moment some people of Siena were fighting one another and two people had already been killed. Blessed Francis got up and preached in such a divine and holy way that he led them all back to peace and great harmony. Because of this admirable and amazing deed the Bishop invited Saint Francis and received him with great thanks and honor. But the next day, in the morning, Saint Francis, who was truly humble and sought only the glory of God in his deeds, got up early and with his companion left without saying goodbye to the bishop.

[14]Because of this Brother Masseo was walking the road, muttering to himself: "What is this good man doing? He made me twirl around like a child, and he didn't say a single good word to the bishop who showed him such honor, or even thank him." And it seemed to him that all these things showed a lack of discernment. Finally, at God's pleasure he turned back to his heart and corrected himself very severely: "Brother Masseo, you're really being proud! You're judging God's works! You're worthy of hell, rebelling against God with your proud discernment. On this journey such holy deeds were done through Brother Francis that even if an angel of God had done them, they wouldn't have been any more amazing. So even if he tells you to throw rocks, you should obey! For everything he accomplished on this journey succeeded by a divine plan, and that's clear from the final result, which was excellent. If he had not led those who were fighting back to peace, not only would the sword have destroyed the bodies of many—and that had already begun—but, even worse, the pit of hell would have consumed the souls of many people; the devil would see to that. So, you're a complete fool and a proud one to grumble about things which clearly come from the will of God."

[20]These are the things Brother Masseo was saying to himself as he walked along at a little distance in front of Saint Francis. But Saint Francis was enlightened by the divine Spirit and to whom everything is uncovered and open, and called out behind Brother Masseo, exposing those secret thoughts of his heart: "Hold on to the things

you're now thinking, because they are good and useful for you and inspired by the Lord. As for that earlier grumbling you were doing, it's blind and evil and proud, planted in your mind by the devil." Brother Masseo was amazed at hearing this, and he clearly realized that Francis knew what was hidden in his heart; and, even more, understood with certainty that the Spirit of divine wisdom guided the holy Father in all his actions.

To the praise of our Lord and the glory of Jesus Christ.
Amen.
Thanks be to God.

XII
SAINT FRANCIS TESTS BROTHER MASSEO[a]

[1]Blessed Francis wished to humble Brother Masseo so that the many gifts granted by the Most High might increase from virtue to virtue. The holy Father was staying in a solitary place with those truly holy first companions, among them brother Masseo.[b] Saint Francis said to all of them gathered together: "O Brother Masseo, all these companions of yours have the grace of praying and contemplating, but you have the gift of the word of God to people's satisfaction. Therefore, I want you take care of the door, the alms and the kitchen so that these companions of yours can spend time in prayer and contemplation. When the brothers are eating you will eat outside the entrance door, so that before visitors knock at the door, you can satisfy them with some good words, so that no one will have to go outside except you. Do this by merit of saving obedience."

[2]Brother Masseo immediately bowed his head, pulled back his capuche and humbly obeyed, and for several days took care of the door, the alms and the kitchen. His companions, however, like most people enlightened by God, began to feel a great conflict deep in their hearts, since Brother Masseo was a man of great perfection and prayer as much as they were, and even more; yet the whole burden of that place had been placed on him. For this reason they asked the holy Father to distribute those duties among them, because their consciences could never bear that this brother was subjected to so many burdens. Besides, they would keep feeling unprepared in

---

a. There is a parallel between this chapter and ChrXXIVG 115-6.
b. Masseo does not appear in any earlier list of Francis's first twelve followers. Arnald of Sarrant later accepts this piece of information and includes Masseo among the twelve, cf. *infra* 691.

prayer, and confused in conscience unless Brother Masseo was relieved of those burdens.

[10]On hearing this Blessed Francis acquiesced to their charitable advice. Calling Brother Masseo, he said: "Brother Masseo, these companions of yours want part of the duties I imposed on you, and therefore I want these duties to be distributed." Brother Masseo patiently and humbly, replied: "Father, whatever you impose on me, all or part, I consider it all done by God."

[12]And then Saint Francis, seeing their charity and Brother Masseo's humility, preached wonderfully on most holy humility, encouraged them that the greater the gifts conferred on us by the Most High, the humbler anyone should be, because without humility no virtue is acceptable to God. After saying this, he distributed the duties with charity and blessed them all with the gladness of the Holy Spirit.

To the praise of our Lord Jesus Christ.
Amen.

XIII

SAINT FRANCIS LIFTS BROTHER MASSEO INTO THE AIR WITH HIS BREATH
AND SAINTS PETER AND PAUL APPEAR TO SAINT FRANCIS
IN THE CHURCH OF SAINT PETER IN ROME[a]

Lk 10:1

[1]Just as the Savior *sent* His disciples *two by two into every city and place where he was about to go,* in order to conform himself to Christ in all things, this remarkable servant and true disciple of Christ, Saint Francis, after he had some companions and their number came to twelve, sent them two by two into the world to preach.[b] So that he might himself show the others an example of true obedience, by the

Acts 1:1

example of the blessed Christ, he first began *to do* before he *taught.* Therefore, at one time when he was assigning the other companions to different parts of the world, choosing Brother Masseo for a companion, he set out toward the Province of France.

AC 108

[4]As they were traveling together, they arrived at some homes of the faithful, from whom, according to what the *Rule* says, they should beg for the needs of the body. Saint Francis went through one neighborhood and Brother Masseo through another. Because Saint Francis was unremarkable and small, and therefore looked down

LR VI 2

---

a. There is a parallel between this chapter and ChrXXIVG 117-8.

b. Ugolino is mistaken in stating that Francis sent the brothers on mission when their number had reached twelve. In 1C 29, Thomas states that he did so when their number reached eight.

upon by everyone as unimportant because the foolish human eye judges only what is outside, not the inside, that holy man collected leftovers of cheap bread and some small scraps. But Brother Masseo, who was a big and handsome man, received more and better-looking ones.

[8]When they both met in a place outside town to eat the food together, they found a spring with a handsome, broad stone placed at its edge. Delighted with this, they placed on the stone the pieces of bread they had gotten. When Saint Francis saw that Brother Masseo's scraps of bread were better looking and more than his, he rejoiced in spirit because of his desire for poverty, and he said: "O Brother Masseo, we're not worthy of such a great treasure." Then gradually raising his voice, he repeated this three times. Brother Masseo replied: "Dear Father, how can you call this a treasure when so much is lacking: no tablecloth, no knife, no dish, no bowl, no house, no table, no servant and no maid?" Saint Francis replied: "I consider this a great treasure because there is nothing here that was prepared by human industry. Rather whatever is here has been served by divine providence, as it clearly appears in the bread we got, in such a fine stone and in such a clear spring. Therefore, I want us to ask God to make us love with our whole hearts the treasure of holy poverty, so noble that it has God as its administrator."[a]

[14]With divine praises they joyfully took their food and drink from the crusts of bread and the spring, then they got up to head toward France. And when they arrived at a church, Saint Francis said to his companion: "Let's go in here to hear the Mass of the Lord." But since there was no priest, Saint Francis hid himself behind the altar of that church to pray. And there he received such overwhelming fervor from a divine visitation, which totally inflamed his soul with longing for poverty, it seemed he released from his face and his open mouth something like flames of love. Then, with his mouth burning this way, he came out toward his companion and kept saying wildly: "Ah! Ah! Ah! Brother Masseo, give me yourself!"—he did this three times—and Brother Masseo, stunned at such wild fervor, when Saint Francis said for the third time: "Give me yourself!" immediately threw himself fully into the arms of the holy Father. Then, his mouth wide open in the fervor of the Holy Spirit, in the loud echoing noise of "ah! ah! ah!," Saint Francis lifted Brother Masseo into the air with his own breath, and tossed him in front of himself to the length of one long spear. As Brother Masseo experienced this, he was completely astonished by such amazing fervor of the holy father. Later he

---

a. This passage contains echoes of ScEx cf. FA:ED I 529-54.

told the companions that, as Saint Francis tossed him, he felt all over such sweetness and consolation of the Holy Spirit that he could not remember ever in his life having such great consolation.

[20]After this Saint Francis said: "Dear brother, let's go to Saint Peter and to Saint Paul, and let's ask them to teach us and help us to possess the indescribable treasure of most holy poverty." And Saint Francis continued, telling Brother Masseo: "My most dear, most beloved brother, the *treasure* of blessed poverty is so worthy and so divine that we are not worthy to possess it *in* our most vile *vessels,* since it is that heavenly virtue by which all earthly and transitory things are trampled under foot, by which all obstacles are moved out of the way, so that the human spirit may freely be joined to the eternal Lord. It is she who makes the soul, while still on earth, dwell with the angels in heaven. It is she who accompanied Christ on the Cross, was hidden with Christ in the tomb, and with Christ rose and ascended into heaven, because she grants to souls who love her, even in this life, lightness to fly above the heavens. And she holds the weapons of true humility and charity. Therefore, let us ask those most holy apostles of Jesus Christ, who were lovers of this evangelical pearl, to obtain this grace for us from our Lord Jesus Christ, so that he, who was the observer and teacher of holy poverty, may in his most holy mercy grant us to be worthy of being true observers and humble disciples of that most precious, loving and angelic poverty."

[27]When they arrived in Rome, they entered the Church of the most Blessed Peter, Prince of the Apostles. After they entered, Saint Francis went to one corner of the Church and Brother Masseo to another to beg God and His holy apostles that they train and help them to possess the treasure of holy poverty. They begged for this with great devotion and with many tears. And as they persisted humbly in their prayer, suddenly blessed Peter and blessed Paul appeared in great brightness to Blessed Francis, kissing him, embracing him, and saying: "Brother Francis, because you ask this and desire what Christ himself and his Holy Apostles observed, we on his behalf inform you that your desire has been fulfilled. The Lord Jesus Christ sent us to you to announce to you that *your* prayer *has been heard,* and that the treasure of most holy poverty has been granted most perfectly to you and to your followers. And we tell you on behalf of Christ that whoever by your example perfectly follows this desire will be assured of the kingdom of blessedness, and you and all your followers will be blessed by the Lord."

[32]When they had said these things, they departed, leaving him inwardly consoled. Saint Francis then rose up from prayer, met his companion, and asked him whether he had received anything from

2 Cor 4:7

Lk 1:13

the Lord. Brother Masseo answered that he had received nothing. Saint Francis then told Brother Masseo how Blessed Peter and Blessed Paul appeared to him and revealed those words of consolation mentioned above. Both of them were filled with such great joy and happiness over this that they forgot about going to France, as they had originally planned. Instead, they hurried back to the valley of Spoleto where this heavenly and angelic way was to begin.

To the praise of Our Lord Jesus Christ.
Amen.

XIV

WHILE FRANCIS SPEAKS ABOUT GOD WITH HIS COMPANIONS CHRIST APPEARS IN THEIR MIDST

[1]When he wished to speak about God and the salvation of the soul, our most holy Father Francis cast all his thinking on the blessed Christ and set all his striving and desire, his way of praying and speaking and acting according to Christ's good pleasure for himself and his companions. One time, he and his holy and apostolic companions were meeting in a certain place at the beginning of his conversion when they were still few. The kind father, sitting among such blessed sons, in a fervor of spirit ordered one of them in the name of the Lord to open his mouth and say about God whatever the Holy Spirit brought to him. But as he began obediently without any delay, the Holy Spirit burst out with amazing words, and the holy Father told this first one to be silent, and ordered another in the name of the Lord's instruction to open his mouth. This brother obeyed, by the grace of God proclaiming the mighty works of God, when Saint Francis imposed silence on this second one as with the first. He then ordered a third son to break out in praise of the Lord Jesus Christ. Following the example of those before him, this third one, complying in humble obedience, brought to light such wonderful, hidden depths of the divine secrets that no one doubted that the Holy Spirit was speaking through him and the others.

[6]As these vessels, simple saints, one by one poured out the fragrant balm of divine grace, speaking honeyed words about divine things at the command of the holy Father, suddenly our Lord Jesus Christ appeared in their midst in the form of a very handsome young man, blessing all with such sweetness of grace that both the holy Father and all the others were enraptured. They lay as if dead, sensing absolutely nothing of this world. As they returned to themselves,

Wis 10:21
the holy Father said: "My dearest brothers, give thanks to the Lord Jesus Christ, because he was pleased to scatter heavenly treasures through the mouths of the simple: He who opens *the mouths of infants and mutes,* makes the *tongues* of the simple most wise and *eloquent.*"

To the praise of our Lord Jesus Christ, Who is blessed forever.
Amen.

XV

Saint Francis and his companions together with Saint Clare are enraptured in the place of the Portiuncula

¹While Clare, the blessed spouse of Christ, was still living, Francis, the servant of the Most High God, when he stayed in Assisi, frequently visited her with his words of sacred encouragement.[a] Several times she asked blessed Francis to give her this consolation: that they eat a meal together once. Saint Francis, however, always refused to do this. So the companions of the holy Father, pondering Saint Clare's desire, said to blessed Francis: "Father, it seems to us that such rigidity is not in accordance with divine charity, that you do not heed blessed Clare, such a sacred virgin, beloved by God; especially since it was at your preaching that she left the pomp of the world. So can't she eat some food even once with you? But were she asking a greater favor of you, you would have to grant it to your little plant!" Blessed Francis responded: "You think I should heed this desire of hers?" The companions said: "Yes, Father; *she is worthy* of this consolation, which you should give her." Saint Francis answered: "Since this pleases you, then it seems that way to me. But, for her to be consoled more fully, I wish this to happen at Saint Mary of the Angels. She has stayed enclosed at San Damiano for a long time, so she'll be rather happy to see the place of Saint Mary again, where she was tonsured and became the spouse of the Lord Jesus Christ. There in the name of the Lord we will eat together."

Lk 7:4

⁸So the day was set for her to come out with a companion and, with the companions of the holy father escorting her, Blessed Clare come to Saint Mary of the Angels. After humble and reverent adoration of the most blessed Mother of God, and, out of devotion, a tour all around the place, it was time to eat. The humble and divine Francis, as he often used to do, had the table prepared on the bare ground.

---

a. This statement contradicts that of 2C 207 in which Francis's vicar pestered him "with repeated requests that he should present the word of God to his daughters, and he finally gave in to his insistence."

He and blessed Clare sat down, and one of the companions of Saint Francis with the companion of Saint Clare, and all his other companions took their places on the ground at that table. For the first course Saint Francis began to speak about God in such a sweet, holy, exalted and divine way that Saint Francis himself, Saint Clare, her companion, and all the others who were at that poor little table, were enraptured by the abundance of the grace of the Most High which came over them.

[12]While they were sitting there enraptured in this way with their eyes and hands raised to heaven, it seemed to the people of Assisi, Bettona and the area all around that Saint Mary of the Angels and the whole place and the woods, which then were still next to the place, were all burning, and that one huge fire was consuming everything: the church, the place and the woods. So to save the place, the people of Assisi came running very fast, firmly believing that everything was being destroyed by the fire. But, when they reached the place, they saw that everything was unharmed and completely intact. Entering the house they found blessed Francis with blessed Clare and all those companions caught up to the Lord, all sitting at that very humble table, *clothed in power from on high.* Then they knew   Lk 24:49
with certainty that it was a divine fire which, because of the devotion of such holy men and holy women, inflamed that place with the abundant consolations of divine love. They departed from there greatly edified and consoled.

[16]Blessed Francis and Blessed Clare and the others, restored by such abundant divine consolation, had little or no interest in other food. Then, having consumed such blessed food, Blessed Clare returned to San Damiano. Her sisters were very glad to see her, because they feared that Saint Francis wanted to send her to direct another monastery, as he had already sent her sister, Saint Agnes, to be the Abbess at Florence—at that time Saint Francis used to send those who directed outlying monasteries—and he once said to Saint Clare: "If it becomes necessary, be ready to go wherever I send you." As a daughter of true obedience, she said: "Father, I am ready to obey, wherever you send me." Because of this the sisters were glad to have her back, and Blessed Saint Clare from then on remained very consoled.[a]

---

a. For the veracity of this story, see Lazaro Iriarte, "Clare of Assisi: Her Place in Female Hagiography," *GR* 3 (1989):199, where the author places the story in the context of mythologizing. Also Margaret Carney, "Francis and Clare: A Critical Examination of the Sources," *GR* 3 (1989): 335-7, where the author examines the story as either "embellishment" or "parable."

To the praise of our Lord Jesus Christ.
Amen.

XVI

GOD REVEALS TO SAINT CLARE AND BROTHER SYLVESTER THAT SAINT FRANCIS MUST PREACH[a]

[1]In the beginning of his conversion, at a time when Saint Francis had already gathered several followers, he found himself struggling with a great doubt: should he spend his time in constant prayer, should he sometimes go out preaching. He very much wanted to know what would best please the Lord Jesus Christ. And holy humility would not allow Saint Francis to decide this in advance for himself; he turned to the safe haven of others, so that by their prayers he might discover God's good pleasure. So he called Brother Masseo, and said to him: "My dear brother, go to Clare, and tell her for me that she, along with one of her spiritual companions should beg God on bended knee to show me whether I should sometimes preach, or constantly spend time in prayer. Go also to Brother Sylvester who is staying on Mount Subasio[b] and tell him the same thing." This was that same Lord Sylvester who saw a gold cross coming from the mouth of Francis as high as the heavens and as wide as the ends of the earth. He was a man of such great holiness and grace that whatever he asked was immediately granted. The Holy Spirit had made him uniquely worthy of conversation with God, and for this reason Saint Francis held him in great devotion and had great faith in him. This saintly Brother Sylvester was staying by himself in that place.

LMj XII 2

2C 109; LMj III

[6]As he had been ordered by Saint Francis, Brother Masseo first brought the message to Blessed Clare, and then to Brother Sylvester. Brother Sylvester immediately went to pray, and when he prayed, he immediately received an answer from God. He quickly came out to Brother Masseo and said: "God says this: 'You tell Brother Francis I did not call him only for himself, but so that he might produce a harvest of souls and that through him many might be won.' " After this, Brother Masseo went back to Saint Clare to find out what she had received from the Lord. She said that both she and her companion

---

a. This story is an embellishment of LMj XII 2.

b. A reference to Sylvester's stay in the hermitage of the Carceri. See Marcella Gatti, "A Historical Look at the Carceri in the Pre-Franciscan and Early Franciscan Period," in *Franciscan Solitude*, ed. André Cirino and Josef Raischl (St. Bonaventure, NY: Franciscan Institute Publications, 1995), 128-38.

got an answer from the Lord similar in every way to Brother Sylvester's answer.

¹⁰So Brother Masseo returned to Saint Francis. The saint received him with charity, washing his feet and preparing a meal. When the food had been eaten, he called Brother Masseo into the woods, and, baring his head, crossing his hands and kneeling he asked: "What does our Lord Jesus Christ wish me to do?" Brother Masseo answered that the blessed Christ's answer to Brother Sylvester and to Sister Clare and her companion was the same: "He wants you to go out preaching, because God did not call you only for yourself, but also for the salvation of others." Then *the hand of the Lord came over* Saint Francis. In a fervor of spirit he rose up completely on fire with the power of the Most High, and said: "In the name of the Lord, let's go!"

¹⁴He took Brother Masseo and Brother Angelo as his companions, both holy men. He went like a thunderbolt driven in spirit, paying no attention to road or path, until they came to a town called Cannara. There he preached with such fervor, and by a miracle swallows kept silent at his command, so all the people of Cannara, men and women, wanted to leave the town and follow him. However, Saint Francis said to them: "Don't be hasty! I will arrange what you should do for your salvation." From that time on he thought about making a Third Order for the salvation of everyone everywhere.

¹⁷He sent them away greatly consoled and ready for penance, then he left from there and went from Cannara and Bevagna. As he passed through that territory with his companions along the road he saw some trees in which perched such a great flock of different kinds of birds that a similar gathering had never before been seen in those parts. And in the field near those trees there was another great flock of different birds. As Saint Francis looked with amazement at this huge flock, the Spirit of God came over him and he said to the companions: "Wait for me here on the road. I will go and preach to my sisters, the little birds." He went into the field toward the birds resting on the ground. As soon as he began to preach, all the birds in the trees came down to him and together with the others in the field remained motionless, even though Saint Francis touched many of them with his tunic as he walked among them. None of them moved at all, as that holy man, Brother James of Massa reported. He heard all of this from the very mouth of Brother Masseo who was one of the holy father's companions when that miracle happened. Saint Francis said to the birds: "Birds, my sisters, you owe God a great deal. You ought to praise Him always and everywhere for the freedom you have to fly everywhere, for the double and triple garment you have,

for your ornate and colorful clothing, for the food prepared without your labor, for the song given to you by your Creator, for your numbers multiplied by the blessing of God, for your seed preserved by God in Noah's Ark, and for the element of air reserved for you. *You neither sow nor reap, yet God feeds you.* He gives you the rivers and springs for drink; the mountains and hills, the rocks and crags as refuges; the high trees for nests; and even though you do not know how to sew or weave, he gives you and your children the clothing you need. Therefore, your Creator who gave you all these benefits, loves you very much. You be careful, my little birds, don't be ungrateful, but try to praise God always." At these words of the most holy father all those birds began to open their beaks, spread their wings, stretch their necks, and reverently bend their heads to the ground, showing with their singing and movements that the words which the holy father spoke greatly delighted them. And Saint Francis too, as he saw this, exulted in spirit, amazed, and marveled over such a large flock of birds of such beautiful variety, over their affection and unanimous friendliness. For this he praised the Creator wonderfully in them, and sweetly invited them to praise of the Creator.

[29]When he finished his preaching and his exhortation to praise God, he made the sign of the Cross over all those birds and as he gave them leave to go, admonished them to praise God. Then all the birds together flew upwards and in the air sang together a great and marvelous song. As their song concluded, they divided themselves into the form of a cross, after the pattern of the Cross made by the holy father, and set out in four directions. With wonderful singing each group flew on high, headed to one of the four parts of the world: one towards the east, one to the west, the third one to the south and the fourth to the north. Thus they demonstrated that just as it had been preached to them by the most holy future standard-bearer of the Holy Cross,[a] so they divided themselves into the form of a cross, and singing, they flew in a cross-formation to the four parts of the world. They were indicating that the preaching of the Cross, renewed by the most holy father, was about to be carried throughout the whole world by his brothers who, like the birds, possess nothing on earth as their own, and entrust themselves only to the providence of God. For this reason such people are called "eagles" by Christ when He said: *"Wherever the body is, there the eagles gather."* The holy ones who hope in the Lord *will take wing like eagles,* will fly to the Lord, *and will not faint in eternity.*

Lk 12:24

Mt 24:28

Is 40:31

---

a. This is similar to Thomas of Celano's depiction of Francis as *Christi signifer* [Christ's standard bearer], cf. 3C 149, 173.

To the praise and glory of Our Lord Jesus Christ.
Amen.

XVII
Saint Francis declined the title "Master"

[1]Francis, the humble imitator of Christ, realized that the title "Master" befitted only Christ *through whom all* works are done. He used to say that he was very willing to know how to do them all, but was unwilling to be a master or be decorated with the title "Master." Using such a title would make him seem to go against the word of Christ in the Gospel, forbidding anyone *to be called "master."* So it was better to be humble because of his poor little knowledge than to do and presume to act contrary to the humble teachings of the glorious Master. The title "Master" suits no one but the blessed Christ, whose works are perfect. And therefore He Himself commanded that no one on earth should presume to be called "master," because there is one, single, true master, without faults, in heaven: the blessed Christ, who is God and man, light and life, the maker of the world, praiseworthy and glorious forever.

Amen.

Jn 1:3; 1 Cor 8:6

Mt. 23:10

XVIII
The death of Saint Francis is revealed to Lady Jacoba of Settesoli and eternal salvation is revealed to Blessed Francis

[1]A few days before his death when blessed Francis was lying ill in the palace of the bishop of Assisi, out of devotion he frequently sang certain praises of God with some of his companions. And when because of illness he was not able to sing, he often made his companions sing. The people of Assisi meanwhile, fearing that such a valuable treasure might be taken out of Assisi, had that palace closely guarded night and day by many armed men.

[3]When the holy man had been lying ill there for several days, one of his companions said to him: "Father, you know that the people of this city have great faith in you and consider you a holy man. Therefore, they might think that if there is holiness in you, as everyone says, you should be thinking about death while you are so seriously ill, and weep rather than sing. Now this singing of praises which we're doing here is being heard by many people, because on your account the palace is being guarded by a great multitude of armed

men and they might be getting bad example. So, I think that we'd do well to leave here and all return to Saint Mary of the Angels because it's not good for us to stay here among lay people." Saint Francis replied to the one who told him this: "Dear brother, you know that already two years ago, while we were staying in Foligno, the Lord revealed to you the end of my life. Moreover, he has revealed to me that in a few days, that is, in this illness, that end would come. And in this revelation God assured me of the remission of all my sins and the blessedness of paradise.[a] Until that revelation I wept over my death and my sins. But after that revelation was made to me, I am filled with such joy that I can't weep anymore; I'm living in joy all the time.

Ps 13:6
That's why I sing and *I will* keep *singing* to God *Who has given me the gifts* of grace and assured me of the gifts of the glory of paradise. But I do agree that we should leave this place. But prepare yourself to carry me, because I'm so weak I can't walk."

¹⁰Carrying him in their arms, those brothers together with a large escort set out for Saint Mary of the Angels. But when they reached the hospital that is on the way there,[b] Saint Francis asked if he was there yet: his eyes were clouded over from penance and his earlier weeping and he was not able to see clearly.

¹²When he learned that he was at the hospital, he had himself put down on the ground and said: "Turn me toward Assisi." Standing in the road with his face turned toward Assisi, he blessed it with many blessings: "May you be blessed by God, because through you many souls will be saved; in you many servants of the Most High will dwell; and from you many will be chosen for the eternal kingdom." After he said these words, he had himself carried as before.

¹⁴When he reached Saint Mary and was set down in the infirmary, he called one of his companions and said to him: "Dear brother, God has revealed to me that in this illness I will die on such-and-such a day, and you know that Lady Jacoba of Settesoli, who is devoted and very dear to our Order, will be inconsolably grieved if she were to learn of my death and were not present.[c] So that she is not upset, let's notify her that if she wishes to see me alive, she should come to Assisi immediately." The brother answered: "You're right, Father, because with the great devotion she has for you, it would not be right at all if she were not present at your death."

AC 8; 3C 37-9

---

a. Thomas of Celano places this revelation, i.e., the forgiveness of Francis's sins, at an early point in his life, during his return from Rome after the approval of the *propositum vitae*, cf. 1C 25. The revelation of the blessedness of heaven is described in AC 83 and 2C 213, at San Damiano, not Foligno.

b. Fortini maintains that this was the leper hospital, San Salvatore delle Parenti, along the Strada Francesca, cf. Fortini, *Francis*, 604-5.

c. Background information on Lady Jacoba of Settesoli may be found in FA:ED II 122 b.

Blessed Francis then said: "Bring me paper and a pen, and write to her what I tell you." And the brother started writing:

> To Lady Jacoba, servant of the Most High, from Brother Francis, Christ's poor little one, greetings and fellowship with the Holy Spirit in the Lord Jesus Christ! You should know, my very dear one, that the blessed Christ by His grace has revealed to me that the end of my life is near. So, if you want to find me alive, come quickly to Saint Mary of the Angels as soon as you read this letter. For if you do not come before such-and-such a day, you will not be able to find me alive. Bring with you a piece of hair-shirt in which you may wrap my body, and wax for the burial. I ask you also to bring me some of those things to eat which you used to give me when I was sick in Rome.[a]

[20]While this was being written, it was revealed to Saint Francis in the Holy Spirit that Lady Jacoba was on her way to him, bringing with her all the things he mentioned. So he suddenly said to the brother who was writing: "Don't write any more. It's not necessary. Put the letter away." They all wondered why he did not allow the letter to be finished. A short time later Lady Jacoba rang at the door.[b] When the porter went to the door, he found Lady Jacoba the most noble Roman lady, who had come to Saint Francis with her two sons, the senators, and a very large escort of knights.[c] She brought with her all those things which Saint Francis wrote in the letter. God had revealed to Lady Jacoba while she was in Rome praying both that the death of Saint Francis was near and also those things he requested in the letter. Moreover, she brought such a large supply of wax that it abundantly supplied everything not only for the burial but also during the Masses and over the body of the saint for many days.

[25]When that Lady went inside to Saint Francis, who was still alive, the sight of each other gave them both the greatest consolation. Falling at his feet, stamped with divine markings, she received there such consolation, grace and abundance of tears, that just as the Magdalene washed *the feet* of the Lord *with tears* her faithful lips were pressing kisses all over *the feet* of one like another Christ, as she was   Lk 7:44-45

---

a. Cf. FA:ED II 418 b.

b. According to *A Book of Exemplary Stories*, the description of Lady Jacoba's arrival comes from Brother Leo, cf. "Liber exemplorum Fratrum Minorum Saeculi XII," ed. Livarius Oliger, *Antonianum* 2 (1927): 67.

c. Cf. FA:ED II 419 b. In his *Nova Vita di San Francesco*, Arnaldo Fortini identifies the other son as Graziano, cf. Arnaldo Fortini, *Nova Vita di San Francesco*, II (Assisi: Edizioni Assisi, 1958-60), 453-4.

devoutly crying and embracing them in such a way that the brothers were not able to tear her away from the feet of the saint. Finally, when she was taken aside and asked how she had come so well-prepared, she responded that when she was praying in Rome during the night, she heard a voice from heaven saying: "If you wish to find Brother Francis alive, go to Assisi right now, without delay, and take with you those things which you used to give him when he was sick, and also whatever will be needed for the burial."

[30]Lady Jacoba stayed until Saint Francis passed away, and she showed his body amazing honor. Some time later she came to Assisi out of devotion for Saint Francis, and ended her days there in holy penance and virtuous living, and arranged that she be buried in the Church of Saint Francis.[a]

Amen.

XIX
CHRIST AND THE BLESSED VIRGIN,
SAINTS JOHN THE BAPTIST AND THE EVANGELIST
WITH A MULTITUDE OF ANGELS SPEAK WITH BLESSED FRANCIS

[1]While Saint Francis was living, a boy marked by dove-like purity and angelic innocence was received into the Order, and was staying in a small place where the brothers, lacking everything, slept in a field for a bed. Saint Francis came to this small place. In the evening after compline was said, he appeared to go to bed before the others, so that afterward—as he often used to do—he might get up at night when the others were asleep. The boy, however, had put it into his heart to examine carefully where the saint went or what he did at night when he got up. To make sure that sleep would not cheat him, he put himself to bed next to Saint Francis and tied his little cord to the saint's cord, so that he would be able to tell when the saint got up, but in such a way that Saint Francis would not notice the cords had been tied.

[5]Saint Francis got up when all the others were sound asleep. Feeling his cord caught, he untied it from the boy's cord so cautiously that the boy felt nothing. He went to pray alone on a hill near the place where there were beautiful woods. But the boy woke up;

---

a. According to Wadding, *Annales*, 1239 XIV, Lady Jacoba died in 1239. Sabatier believes that she lived in Assisi until her death on October 18, 1273, and bases his opinion on a record that a Domina Iacoba de Roma received a legacy of 20 *soldi* in a will of that date. At first her body was interred in the Lower Church of the Basilica of Saint Francis in Assisi, but in 1933 was re-interred in the crypt in an urn opposite the tomb of the saint. Cf. Fortini, *Francis*, 616 e.

discovering that the saint's cord was untied from his little cord, he got up immediately to look for the holy Father as he had planned. When he found the gate leading to the woods open, realizing the saint had gone out that way, he immediately went into the woods after him and made his way to the top of the hill where Saint Francis had stopped to pray. When the boy stopped for a little while, he began to hear in the distance many voices speaking. Going closer so that he might more clearly hear what was being said, he suddenly saw a wonderful light surrounding Blessed Francis on all sides, and in that light he saw Christ and the Blessed glorious Mary and blessed John the Baptist and the Evangelist and a very great multitude of angels speaking with Blessed Francis. On seeing and hearing all this, the boy, trembling, was taken in ecstasy and fell as if dead on the path by which the saint was about to return.

[10]When this wondrous and sacred conversation was finished, Saint Francis started back to the place. As he was returning, it was still night, and with his feet he found the boy lying as if dead on the path. The holy Father, moved by compassion, lifted him up in his loving arms and, like a good shepherd, he carried his own little sheep back to bed. Later, learning from the boy that he had seen that vision, he ordered him to tell no one as long as the saint lived. The boy obeyed the order and, in the grace of God and the devotion of Saint Francis, he ended well as an important man in the Order. After the death of Saint Francis, he himself revealed this to the brothers.

To the praise and glory of our Lord Jesus Christ.
Amen.

XX

THE DIVINE PROVISION MADE FOR THE GENERAL CHAPTER
AT SAINT MARY OF THE ANGELS
AND SAINT DOMINIC CAME TO THAT CHAPTER WITH SEVEN OF HIS BROTHERS

[1]More than five thousand brothers gathered for a General Chapter which Francis, the most faithful servant of Christ celebrated on the plain of Saint Mary of the Angels.[a] Saint Dominic, the head of the Order of Preachers, and seven brothers of his Order were also present. Moreover, the Lord Cardinal was there, a man very devoted to

AP 43, 2C 63

---

a. The Chapter of Mats, cf. LMj IV 10; ChrJG 16; ChrTE 6. According to AP 43, 2C 63, Cardinal Ugolino was present; according to Peter of John Olivi, Dominic was also present and, after seeing the poverty of Francis and his brothers, renounced all property for his Order of Friars Preacher. Cf. Peter of John Olivi, *Super Lucam* I, in *S. Bernardini Senensis Opera Omnia*, vol. IX (Ad Claras Aquas, Quaracchi: Collegium S. Bonaventurae, 1965), 38, num. XXI, 13-21.

blessed Francis and his brothers and whom Saint Francis predicted   1C 100
would become Pope, and that is what happened. Since the Court of
Ostia of the Lord Pope was then at Perugia, the Cardinal made a point
of coming to Assisi. He came every day to see and hear Saint Francis
and the brothers, and every time he sang Mass, he also preached a
sermon to them.

³And when the cardinal came to visit that sacred assembly, he   2C 63
would see them in the field in troops of sixty, of a hundred and of
three hundred sitting there in conversation about God, in prayer and
tears, and in the works of charity, in such silence that there was no
Sg 6:4   noise or din there. Marveling at such a multitude like *an orderly line of
troops,* he said with tears and great devotion: "These are truly the
troops of God!" For no one among them dared to tell tall tales or
jokes, but wherever they gathered, they either prayed or wept or
spoke about the salvation of the soul. There in the field they had separate shelters by troop, made of reeds all around and on top. For this
reason, this was called the Field of Reeds. Their beds were the bare
ground or a little straw. For their pillows they used stones or pieces of
wood. Because of this everyone had such devotion for them that
many from the nearby court flocked there: counts and barons, dukes
and knights, even cardinals in person with bishops and clerics,
nobles and commoners; all came to see such a holy and humble gathering that the world had never seen one like it. They came also to see
that very holy man Francis, their head, who had snatched such a
beautiful prey from the world and was directing such a devout flock
to the blessed pasture of Christ.

⁹After all had gathered, Francis, that holy shepherd and venerable
leader, rose up and in the fervor of the Holy Spirit proclaimed the
word of life to that blessed flock in a loud voice like a trumpet, which
divine anointing poured into him. This is the theme he announced:
"Great things have we promised; greater things are promised us;   2C 191
let us observe the former, and yearn for the latter; pleasure is short,
punishment is eternal; suffering is slight, glory infinite."[a] He
preached very devoutly on this theme, exhorting all to obedience to
Holy Mother Church, to the gentleness of brotherly charity, to prayer
for all the holy people of God, to patience in adversity, to purity and
angelic chastity, to peace and harmony with God and people, to
humility and meekness with everyone, to contempt of the world and
a fervent zeal for evangelical poverty; to concern and vigilance for
Ps 55:23   prayer and divine praises, to the *casting of all care* and concern of soul

---

a. According to ChrJG 16 Francis preached on Ps 144:1, *Blessed be the Lord my God, Who trains my
hands for battle.*

and body on the Good Shepherd, the Nourisher of souls and bodies, our blessed Lord Jesus Christ. "And to observe this better, I command all of you brothers assembled here by virtue of saving obedience, not one of you is to have any care or concern about anything to eat or drink or for the body, but to be intent only on prayer and the praise of God, *casting all care* on Christ, since he has a special care for you." They all did this, hurrying lightheartedly to prayer.

Ps 55:23

¹⁶Saint Dominic, who was present for all this, wondered about the command which Saint Francis had given, and considered him as acting without discernment since he had commanded that no one in such a great multitude should be concerned about things necessary for the body. He figured that in such a great multitude difficulties would have to arise.

¹⁷But the Lord Jesus wished to show that he would take special care of such dear sheep, his poor. With sudden inspiration the hand of the Lord came over the people of Perugia, Spoleto, Foligno, Spello, Assisi and all the surrounding towns. They came with *donkeys,* mules and horses and carts loaded *with bread and wine,* beans and cheese, and all the good things which they thought those blessed poor men needed. They also brought tablecloths, platters and dishes, and whatever utensils were needed. Those who could serve them more devoutly and more attentively considered themselves blessed, eagerly providing all the necessities of that blessed multitude. You could see knights and nobles devoutly serving that gathering of holy men. You could see there devout clerics and laymen hurrying back and forth like servants. You could see there lively young men, serving with such reverence that they seemed to be serving not poor brothers but apostles of the Lord Jesus Christ.

1 Sm 25:18

²²When Saint Dominic saw all this and realized that divine providence was truly there, he humbly censured himself for his judgment of lack of discernment. Kneeling before Blessed Francis, he humbly confessed his fault, and said: "God is truly taking care of these poor little holy men and I did not know it. Therefore, from now on I promise to observe holy evangelical poverty, and on behalf of God I curse all the brothers of my Order who presume to keep anything of their own in the Order."

²⁴Saint Dominic then left greatly edified by the faith of Saint Francis and by the obedience and poverty of such a large and orderly assembly, by the divine providence and by the abundant supply of everything. For as a truly holy and wise man, he recognized in all his

words the most faithful God. For just as He makes the earth grow plants and lilies, and just as He feeds even the birds of the air, so He provides everything necessary for his devoted poor.[a]

²⁶During that Chapter Saint Francis was told that many of the brothers were wearing chain-mail and iron bands next to their skin, which caused some to become sick, others to die, and many to be prevented from praying. Therefore, as a very discerning father, he commanded them all under saving obedience, that whoever had chain-mail and iron bands to put them down in his sight. Five hundred pieces of chain-mail were found, and iron bands for arms and waists in such numbers that they made a huge pile, which he made them leave there. After this the holy Father instructed and consoled them all. He taught them how to leave behind this present worthless world; then, when all were consoled with the blessing of God and spiritual joy he sent them back into the various provinces of the world.

To the praise of our Lord Jesus Christ.
Amen.

XXI

GOD SPEAKS TO SAINT FRANCIS AND SAINT FRANCIS MAKES THE WINE
INCREASE
IN A VINEYARD WHERE THERE ARE NO GRAPES

¹When Saint Francis was suffering from a grave eye affliction, Lord Hugolino, Cardinal Protector of the Order, who loved him deeply, sent for him to come to Rieti where there were some excellent eye doctors. After he received the letter from the Lord Cardinal, Blessed Francis went first to San Damiano, where Saint Clare was staying, the most devout spouse of Christ. For he had resolved that, before he left, he would give consolation to Saint Clare, and then leave for Rieti.

³So, Saint Francis went to San Damiano, and the next night his eyes became so weak that he was unable to see any light. Therefore Blessed Clare made a little cell of for him where Saint Francis could stay somewhat removed. And he stayed there for fifty days with such pain in his eyes and with such demon-instigated annoyance from

AC 83

---

a. ChrJG 16: ". . . though there was such a great number of brothers there, the people supplied all things so cheerfully that after seven days of the chapter the brothers had to close the door and receive nothing further, and on top of it they had to remain there two days longer so that they might use up what had been offered and accepted."

multitudes of mice that he was unable to rest by night or day. Then Saint Francis, recognizing the Lord's chastisement began to give thanks to God, to praise him with his whole heart and voice, and from the depths of his heart cried out that he deserved these infirmities and trials, and much greater ones. With this he begged the Lord: "Lord Jesus Christ, good shepherd, Who put Your most worthy mercy in hard trials for us who are unworthy, give grace and strength to me, your little sheep, so that I do not leave You during any trial or pain."

[7]After he said this, *a voice* came to him *from heaven:* "Francis, tell me: if all the earth were gold, all the sea and rivers and springs were fragrant balsam, and all the mountains, hills and stones were gemstones; and if you found another treasure worth more than all these, as much as gold is worth more than earth, as fragrant balsam is more noble than water, precious stones more than mountains and rocks, and this more valuable expensive treasure were given to you instead of this infirmity of yours, you would rejoice greatly, wouldn't you?" Saint Francis answered: *"Lord, I am not worthy* of such a precious treasure." And then the Lord said to him: "Rejoice now, Brother Francis, because this is the treasure of eternal life, which I have reserved for you. From this moment I invest you with it. This infirmity and affliction is the pledge of that blessed treasure."

[10]Then Saint Francis, turning very happy, called his companion and said: "Let's go to the Lord Cardinal." First consoling Blessed Clare with honey-sweet and divine words, and bidding her a humble farewell as he usually did, he set off on the journey toward Rieti.

[11]But when he neared Rieti, such a multitude of the people was flocking toward him that he refused on that account to enter the city rather he took refuge in a church two miles outside Rieti.[a] The citizens, however, on learning that he was staying at that church, came hurrying to him with such a great multitude that, since it was vintage time, the whole vineyard of the priest of that church was demolished and even worse, the grapes devoured. The priest, seeing the damage, was very sad and regretted that he allowed Saint Francis to enter that church. Saint Francis, knowing this through the Holy Spirit, had the lord priest called and said: "Dearest Father, how many barrels of wine does this vineyard give you when it has its best crop?" He answered: "Twelve." Saint Francis said: "I beg you, Father, bear with me patiently, let me stay in this church of yours because of the

Jn 12:28

Mt 8:8

AC 85

---

a. Arduino Terzi maintains that this is the Church of San Fabiano, which today is that of S. Maria della Foresta, cf. *Memorie francescane nella Valle Reatina* (Rome: Tipografia "Artistica" A. Nardini, 1957), 275-96.

quiet which I always find here. And out of love for God and for me, allow the little poor ones, everyone, to take your grapes. On behalf of Our Blessed Lord Jesus Christ I promise you that this year you will harvest twenty barrels of wine." Saint Francis did this because of the great salvation of souls which the Lord was accomplishing there. For he saw many of those who came inebriated with divine love and, forgetful of the world, turned toward desire for heaven. For this reason, he judged that it was better that a material vineyard be demolished than that *the vineyard of the Lord of hosts* become fruitless for making heavenly wine.

Is 5:7

[18]The priest trusted the promises of the saint, and gladly left the vineyard as food for the people arriving. It was quite amazing: the vineyard was completely demolished, everything devoured by visitors; only small bunches remained. However, when harvest-time came, the priest still trusted the promise of the saint. He collected those few bunches of grapes and placed them in the winepress as usual. True to the promise of Saint Francis, he obtained twenty barrels of the best wine. By this miracle it was clearly shown that just as by the merits of Saint Francis the vineyard stripped of grapes produced wine more abundantly, so by the teaching of Saint Francis the Christian people out of fruitlessness of sin overflowed with the rich fruit of penance.

To the praise of our Lord Jesus Christ, Who is blessed forever.
Amen.

XXII
A YOUNG BROTHER IS TEMPTED BUT IS FREED THROUGH A WONDERFUL VISION

[1]A young man, very noble and refined, came to the Order of Saint Francis. He was clothed in the habit of the brothers, but after a few days, at the instigation of the devil, he began to feel such an aversion for the habit he wore that it seemed to him a worthless sack. He despised the sleeves and hated the capuche, and thought that the length of the tunic and its roughness were an unbearable burden. And so it happened that his annoyance with the religion increased and he decided to throw away the habit entirely and go back to the vomit of the world. However his master, the one in charge of him from the beginning, had taught him to kneel with great reverence, uncover his head and with folded hands, bow whenever he passed in front of the convent altar, on which the most holy Body of Christ was reserved. This young man always observed this carefully.

⁵It happened that the night he decided to throw off the habit and return to the world, he had to pass in front of the altar. By force of habit, he knelt in the usual way. Immediately he was taken up in spirit, and a marvelous vision was shown to him. For he saw an almost infinite multitude passing in procession before him. All in this blessed procession walked two by two and were clothed in robes decorated with gems. Their faces, their hands and whatever of their bodies could be seen shone more brightly than the sun. They moved along singing solemnly and very sweetly with the chant and hymns of angels. Among those passing were two more noble than the others, surrounded by such brilliance that they brought wonder and astonishment to those who saw them. Toward the end of that procession he saw one decorated with such glory that he seemed like a new knight being specially honored by everyone.

¹⁰When the young man saw all this, he was left wondering and did not know what it all meant. He did not dare to question those who passed by, nor could he, since he was speechless from overwhelming sweetness. But when the procession had passed by, and he could still see those who were last, he regained his courage. He ran to them and asked: "My dear friends, I beg you, please tell me who these people are, these admirable people who make up this venerable procession?" They turned their very brilliant faces toward him and said: "We are all Lesser Brothers who have just come from the glory of paradise." He asked another question: "Who are those two who shine more brightly than the others?" They responded: "Those two, brighter than the others, are Saint Francis and Saint Anthony. And the one at the end, being honored so greatly, is a holy man who just died. Because he fought bravely against temptations and persevered to the end in his holy purpose, we are leading him with glory and triumph to the glory of the eternal kingdom, escorted not only by saints but also by the rejoicing. These splendid robes we wear were given to us because of the rough tunics we patiently wore in the religion. The glorious brightness you see was given to us by God because of the humble penance we did, and because of the holy poverty and obedience and spotless chastity we have observed to the end with a cheerful heart. Therefore, son, do not let the wearing sackcloth of the religion, which is so profitable, be a burden to you. Because if you manfully stay in the sackcloth of Blessed Francis, for love of our Lord Jesus Christ, by spurning *the world,* mortifying *the flesh* and by fighting against the devil, you will shine with us in similar clothing and light."

¹⁶After this, the youth returned to himself, comforted by this vision, and he cast off the whole temptation. He acknowledged his

1 Jn 2:16

fault before the guardian and the brothers, and from that time he longed for harsh penance and clothing as if luxuries. And thus changed for the better, he ended in a holy life.

To the praise of our Lord Jesus Christ.
Amen.

XXIII
BLESSED FRANCIS LEADS A WOLF TO BECOME VERY TAME

[1]A remarkable, noble event, worthy of remembrance, happened in the city of Gubbio while our most holy Father Saint Francis was still living. There was a wolf in the vicinity of the city of Gubbio, terrifying in physical size and ferocious with rabid hunger.[a] This wolf not only destroyed other animals but even devoured men and women, keeping all the citizens in such danger and terror that when they went outside the town, they went armed and guarded as if they had to advance toward deadly battles. Yet, even armed, they were not able to escape the deadly teeth or the savage fury of that wolf when they accidentally met. As a result, everyone was filled with such terror that hardly anyone dared to go outside the city gate.

[4]But God wished to make known to the citizens the holiness of blessed Francis. When Saint Francis was staying there, having compassion for them, Saint Francis decided to go out to meet that wolf. On learning this, the citizens said to him: "Be careful, Brother Francis, don't go outside the gate, because the wolf, which has already devoured many people, will certainly kill you." But Saint Francis put his hope in the Lord Jesus Christ who rules the spirits of all flesh. Without the protection of a shield or helmet, but protecting himself with the sign of the holy Cross, he went out the gate with a companion, casting all his confidence on the Lord who makes those who believe in him *tread* unharmed *on the basilisk and the asp,* and trample not only the wolf, but even *the lion and dragon.* And so Francis, that most faithful soldier of Christ, steadily began taking the path that made others hesitate, not wearing chain-mail or a sword, not carrying a bow or weapons of war, but protected by the shield of holy faith and the sign of the Cross. And while many were looking on from places where they had climbed in order to see, suddenly that

Ps 91:13

---

a. Wolves appear in earlier stories, AC 74, 2C 35-6, and the *Passion of San Verecondo,* cf. FA:ED II 175-8, 269-70, 807. A thirteenth manuscript of Sarnano, E.70, concerning Francis's charity contains both the story of the wolf of Gubbio and the following story of the doves of Siena, leading Marino Bigaroni and Giovanni Boccali to accept the authenticity of these stories. Cf. Biagroni, Boccali, ed., *Actus,* 58 n. 201, n. 285.

terrifying wolf, jaws wide open, rushed at Saint Francis. Saint Francis confronted the wolf with the sign of the Cross, restrained it by the power of God away from himself and from his companion, stopped it in its tracks and closed those savage gaping jaws. Finally he called the wolf to himself: "Come here, Brother Wolf. On behalf of Christ I order you not to harm me or anyone else." Surprising to say, at the sign of the Cross, the wolf closed those terrifying jaws! And as soon as that command was given, the wolf immediately bowed its head, lying down at the saint's feet, and already like a lamb, not a wolf. And as the wolf lay there, Saint Francis said: "Brother Wolf, you've done great damage in this area, and you've committed horrible crimes, mercilessly destroying God's creatures. You've destroyed not only irrational animals, but have dared something more detestable, killing and devouring *humans made to the image of God*. Therefore, you   Gn 1:26, 27 deserve to be sentenced to a horrible death like a robber or vile murderer. Everyone is crying out the complaint against you, and this whole city is your enemy. But, Brother Wolf, I want to make peace between you and them, so that they no longer will be harmed by you, and they will dismiss all your past offenses, and both men and dogs will no longer pursue you."

¹⁴The wolf gestured with its body, tail and ears, and bowed its head, showing that it fully accepted what the saint said. Saint Francis then spoke again: "Brother Wolf, since you want to make this pact, I promise you that as long as you live I will have your needs constantly provided for by the people of this city, so that you will never again suffer hunger, because I know that, whatever evil you do, you do because of the frenzy of hunger. But, my Brother Wolf, for me to obtain this favor for you, I want you to promise me that you will never harm any animal or person or dare to harm anything. Will you promise me that?" The wolf gave a clear sign by bowing its head that it promised to do what the saint demanded. Saint Francis then said: "Brother Wolf, I want you to give me a pledge so that I may confidently believe what you promise." When Saint Francis extended his hand to receive this pledge, the wolf raised its right paw, and gently placed it on the hand of Saint Francis, giving its pledge with the only sign it could. Then Saint Francis said: "Brother Wolf, *I command you*   Acts 16:18 *in the name of Jesus Christ,* come with me now, don't hesitate, so we can make this pact in the name of the Lord."

²¹The wolf obeyed and, like the meekest lamb, immediately went with Saint Francis. The people of the city who saw this were completely astonished; and the news immediately spread through the whole town, so that everyone, old and young, both men and women, commoners and nobles, converged together on the town square,

where Saint Francis was standing with the wolf. With this multitude of people gathered, Saint Francis got up and preached a marvelous sermon to them, saying among other things that such disasters are permitted because of sin, and that the consuming flames of Gehenna, which hold the damned for all eternity, are more dangerous than the frenzy of a wolf which *can kill* only *the body;* and how much one should fear being sunk in the pit of hell, when one small animal held such a multitude in such great fear and danger. "My very dear friends, return to the Lord and do worthy penance, and the Lord will free you now from the wolf, and in the future from the pit of consuming fire."

Mt 10:28

²⁷Then he said to them: "My dear friends, listen! Brother Wolf, who stands here before you, promised me to make peace with you, and he made a pledge of this promise: he promised never to hurt you in any way, if you promise to give him what he needs every day. And for this wolf I give my word that he will faithfully observe this pact."

²⁹Then everyone gathered with a great shout promised to feed the wolf consistently. In front of them all Saint Francis said to the wolf: "And you, Brother Wolf, do you promise to keep this pact, namely, that you will not harm any animal or person?" The wolf, kneeling with head bowed, clearly showed to all by the gestures of its body, the wagging of its tail and ears that it would fulfill the pact as promised. Saint Francis said: "Brother Wolf, I want you to give me your pledge on this, just as you gave me your pledge when I was outside the gate. So here before all these people give me a pledge that you will observe these things, and will not abandon me when I have given my word for you." Then the wolf lifted its right paw and, in front of everyone standing there, gave its pledge on the hand of Saint Francis, who had given his word.

³³And everyone's great amazement turned into rejoicing, as much out of devotion for the saint as for the novelty of the miracle and, even more, for the peace between people and the wolf. They all shouted to the heavens, *praising and blessing the Lord* Jesus Christ who sent them Saint Francis, through whose merits He freed them from the jaws of the terrible beast and brought them back from such a horrible scourge to peace and quiet.

Lk 24:53

³⁵From that day they kept the pact arranged by Saint Francis: the people with the wolf and the wolf with the people. The wolf lived for two years and was courteously fed, going from door to door, harming no one and not being harmed by anyone. And this is remarkable: no dog ever barked at the wolf. Finally, Brother Wolf grew old and died. The citizens grieved greatly at his absence, because the peaceful and

kindly patience of the wolf roaming through the city recalled to their memory the remarkable sanctity and virtue of Saint Francis.

Thanks be to God.
Amen.

XXIV
SAINT FRANCIS ASKS A YOUNG MAN WHO HAD CAUGHT MANY DOVES
TO GIVE THEM TO HIM
AND HE MADE NESTS FOR THEM

[1]A boy in the city of Siena at the time of Blessed Francis caught a great number of doves in a snare and was carrying them away alive to be sold.[a] Now Saint Francis, who was always full of pity, had an amazing compassion toward gentle animals, saw these doves and moved by compassion said: "O good young man, I beg you, hand them over to me, so that such innocent birds, which Scripture compares to chaste, humble and faithful souls, may not fall into the hands of cruel killers." The boy, inspired by God, immediately handed all those simple doves over to Blessed Francis. After the kind father Francis took them into his lap, he began to speak to them sweetly: "O, my sister doves, simple, chaste and innocent, why did you allow yourselves to be captured? I want to snatch you from death and make nests for you so that you can be fruitful, and fulfill the Creator's command that you multiply." And Blessed Francis went off and made nests for all those doves.

[6]The doves took to the nests prepared by Saint Francis, and bred and raised their young in the presence of the brothers. They showed such familiarity toward Saint Francis and the other brothers that they seemed like chickens that had always been raised by the brothers. They never left the brothers until Saint Francis, with a blessing, gave them permission. The saint said to the boy who gave him the doves: "Son, you will soon be a Lesser Brother and serve our gracious Lord Jesus Christ." It happened just as the saint predicted. He later became a Lesser Brother, and lived a praiseworthy and exemplary life until his death. So Saint Francis not only provided relief in this present life for those doves, but also provided for that young man the joys of eternal life.

---

a. A similar story, although concerning a pheasant, is found in 2C 170 (FA:ED II 356-7).

To the praise of our Lord Jesus Christ, Who is blessed forever.
Amen.

XXV

A STATUE LIKE THE STATUE OF NEBUCHADNEZZAR, BUT DRESSED IN A SACKCLOTH, SPEAKS TO BLESSED FRANCIS AND TELLS HIM ABOUT THE FOUR STAGES OF HIS ORDER

[1]Once when Saint Francis was devoutly praying to the Most High in the place of Saint Mary of the Angels, suddenly there appeared before his bodily eyes a most amazing vision. There appeared before him an immense statue similar to the statue which King Nebuchadnezzar had seen in dream.[a] It had *a head of gold* and a very beautiful face. *Its chest and arms* were *of silver,* its *belly and thighs bronze,* its *legs* were of *iron,* its *feet* were *partly of iron* and *partly clay,* and its dress was of sackcloth, and this sackcloth seemed to embarrass it greatly. Blessed Francis, gazing at the statue, was thoroughly amazed by its almost indescribable beauty, its extraordinary size, and the embarrassment it seemed to have about the cheap sackcloth which it was wearing. And while he was looking in wonder at its very beautiful and lovely face, that very statue spoke to Saint Francis: "Why are you surprised? God has sent me as an example to you, so that in me you may learn what will happen to your Order.

[5]"The golden head you see on me with its lovely face: this the beginning of your Order, placed on the heights of evangelical perfection. And just as this element is more precious than other metals, the face more handsome than the rest, and the head's position more outstanding than the other members, so the beginning of your Order will be more precious because of its solid golden charity, more beautiful because of its angelic integrity and more outstanding because of its evangelical poverty which the whole world will admire. And *the Queen of Sheba,* that is, holy Mother Church, will marvel and her heart will expand, when she sees in those first chosen ones of your Order such beauty of Christ's holiness and such high evangelical poverty and brilliance of spiritual wisdom reflecting as if in angelic mirrors. Blessed will they be who, conforming themselves to Christ, shall strive to imitate the virtues and behavior of those first precious

margin notes: 2C 82; OL 5; HTrb Prol

Dn 2:32

1 Kgs 10:1,4,7

---

a. This vision was described in different terms by Thomas of Celano (2C 82) who describes Ugolino's "statue" as a beautiful lady. *The Old Legend* found among the *Sayings of the Companions* I 5 contains basically the same vision; in this instance, Ugolino's statue is an angel. It appears again in HTrb, but as simply a "form" cf. HTrb Prol 307. Thomas of Eccleston narrates that, in the General Chapter of 1239, Pope Gregory IX preached about the "golden statue" prompting Brother Elias to make excuses for his actions. Cf. ChrTE 13.

stones, those golden heads, clinging more to their heavenly beauty than to the deceit of worldly glitter.

¹⁰"The chest and arms of silver will be the second stage of the Order, which will be as inferior to the first stage as silver is inferior to gold. And just as silver has great value, brightness and melodious sound, so in that second stage there will be those of value in the divine Scriptures, brilliant in the light of sanctity and melodious in sounding the word of God. They will be eminent, as some of them will be lifted to the offices of pope[a] and cardinal,[b] and many of them, of bishop. And since human strength is represented by the chest and arms, so God at that time will raise up in this Order two men, silvery in learning and shining in virtue, who both by their knowledge and their virtue will defend this religion, and also the universal Church, from many attacks of demons and from various assaults of wicked men. But even though that will be a remarkable generation, it will not reach that most perfect stage of those who came first, but will be to it what silver is to gold.

¹⁴"After this there will be a third stage in the Order, like the bronze belly and bronze thighs. Just as bronze is considered less valuable than silver, so those of the third stage will be less than those of the first and second stages. And although, like bronze, they will be spread in great quantity throughout the whole wide world, they will be those *whose god is their belly* and *the glory* of the religion will *confound those who delight* only *in things of earth*. Because of their learning, they will have tongues with a wonderful sound, like brass, but because they will worship the belly and thighs—sad to say—the Lord will consider them, as the Apostle says, *like noisy brass, a clanging cymbal,* for they will boom heavenly words to others and will generate spiritual sons as if *from the thighs;* and after showing *the fountain of life* to others, they themselves will hug the ground on a dry belly.

¹⁸"After these there will come a fourth stage which will be fearful and terrifying. This is now shown to you in the iron legs. For just as *iron breaks* up and separates bronze, silver and gold, so this stage will have the hardness and crookedness of iron. Because of the coldness and the terrible rust and the iron-hard ways of that perilous time, everything will be handed over to oblivion which had been built up

Phil 3:19

1 Cor 13:1

Ex 1:5; Ps 36:10

Dn 2:40

---

a. A reference to Jerome of Ascoli, provincial minister in 1272, and, at the death of Bonaventure, general minister. Because of his diplomatic skills, Pope Nicholas III made him a Cardinal in 1278; in 1288 he was elected Pope and took the name Nicholas IV. He died on April 4, 1292.

b. In addition to Bonaventure and Jerome, other cardinals were Bentivenga da Todi (1278), Matteo d'Acquasparta (1288), James Tommasi Gaetani (1295), Gentile da Montefiore (1300), Giovanni da Morrovalle (1302). Cf. Umberto Betti, *I cardinali dell'Ordine dei Frati Minori* (Rome: Edizioni Francescane, 1963); Remigio Ritzler, "Cardinali e Papi O.F.M. Conv," *Miscellanea Franciscana* 71(1971): 10-32.

in the Church of Christ good: the golden charity of the first ones, the silvery truth of the second ones, and the bronze or resounding gift of speech of the third ones. Nevertheless, just as the legs hold up the body, so they, by some rusty strength of hypocrisy, will hold up the body of the Order. And both the belly and these iron legs will be hidden under clothes, because they will hide under the habit of the religion: in fact they will wear a pious habit, but *on the inside they will be ravenous wolves.* And such as these, rusty and hard as iron, serving only the belly, are indeed hidden from the world but visible to the Lord, because they will reduce to nothing those precious goods by the hammer of their crooked life. Therefore, these like the hardest iron will be pounded by the fire of tribulations and the hammers of dreadful trials. They will be beaten not only by demons but also by worldly rulers with fire and hot coals so that the powerful will suffer powerful torments. And because they sinned by irreverent hardness, they will suffer hard torments from the irreverent. But because of these trials they will grow so impatient that, just as iron resists all metals, so they will obstinately resist not only secular powers but spiritual ones as well, thinking that, like iron, they can crush all things. For this they will greatly displease God.

Mt 7:15; Acts 20:29

²⁶"The fifth stage will be partly of iron as regards those hypocrites just mentioned and partly of dirt as regards those who will totally immerse themselves in worldly affairs. Just as you have seen in the feet that brick, baked from clay, and iron appear together, though they cannot be fused in any way, so it will be in the last stage of this Order. An abominable division will occur between the ambitious hypocrites and those made of brick, baked from the clay of temporal things and the concupiscence of the flesh; like iron with brick, they will be able to join together because of their great differences. They will despise not only the Gospel and the *Rule,* but also with their brick and iron feet, that is, with crooked and unclean longings, they will trample underfoot all the discipline of this holy Order. And just as brick and iron divide from each other, so many of these brothers will be separated from each other both inside and out: inside, by living in conflict; and outside, by clinging to factions and secular rulers. Therefore, they will be so displeasing to everyone that they will hardly be able to enter towns or stay there and, even worse, will hardly be able to wear the habit openly. Many of them will be punished and ruined by horrible torments of worldly people, because every house and floor place will shun such abominable feet. All this will happen to them because they withdrew from the golden head. But blessed will they be who in those dangerous days return to the admonitions of that precious head, because the Lord *proved them as*

Wis 3:6

gold in a furnace and *as* rich *holocausts* will crown them and receive them forever.

34"This sackcloth which seems to embarrass me is holy poverty, the beauty and mirror of the whole Order, the unique safeguard, crown and foundation of every kind of holiness. When all virtuous striving is gone, as mentioned above, degenerate sons will be embarrassed by most holy poverty; shedding their cheap garments, they will choose costly ones and procure vain capes through anxious care and simony. But happy and blessed will be those *who will have perse-* Mt 24:13 *vered to the end* in those things which they promised the Lord."

36bAfter these things were said, the statue disappeared. Saint Francis thoroughly amazed by all this, like a good shepherd, with many tears entrusted his sheep, present and future, to God.

Thanks be to God.
Amen.

XXVI

SAINT MARY OF THE ANGELS IS BESIEGED BY DEMONS
BUT NOT ONE CAN ENTER

1When our holy father Francis was giving himself to prayer in the place of the Portiuncula, he saw the whole place surrounded and besieged by demons as if by a huge army; but not one of them was able to enter the place because the brothers remained in such holiness that there was no one to offer them an entrance.

3In the meantime a brother who was staying there was violently disturbed by anger and impatience, contriving accusations and revenge against a brother companion. In this way the gate of virtue was abandoned and the door of wickedness opened, offering a way for the devil to enter. As Saint Francis watched, one of those demons quickly entered the place and attacked that brother, as victor to victim. However, the kind father and shepherd, who kept very faithful watch out of care for his flock, realized that a wolf had entered to devour one of his little sheep, and knowing through the Spirit that a sheep had been placed in great danger, had that brother summoned to him at a run. As the brother obediently came running to the concerned shepherd, the blessed father ordered him to disclose immediately the fabricated poison he was storing in his heart against his neighbor and because of which he had been *given over into the hands* of Mt 26:45 the enemy. Terrified, he uncovered the wound, admitted his fault and humbly asked for pardon with a penance. After he did this, he was absolved from his fault and a penance was imposed on him. Then, suddenly, before the holy father's eyes, the devil fled. The sheep, however, snatched from the jaws of the ferocious beast, gave thanks to his holy, protecting shepherd, to God and to blessed Francis, and returned to the holy assembly of the flock, having learned from then on to avoid such deadly danger; he ended in good holiness.

To the praise and glory of our Lord Jesus Christ.
Amen.

XXVII

HOW THE SULTAN OF BABYLON WAS CONVERTED TO THE FAITH AND BAPTIZED
BY BROTHERS SENT BY SAINT FRANCIS

[1]Our most holy father Francis, urged on by his zeal for the faith and by a fervent desire for martyrdom, crossed overseas with twelve of his most holy brothers,[a] intending to direct their course straight to the Sultan.[b]

[2]After he arrived in the territory of the pagans where those who guarded the roads were so cruel that no Christian passing there could escape death, they did indeed avoid death by God's plan. However, they were captured, mistreated in many ways, very harshly bound, and led to the Sultan. In the Sultan's presence, instructed by the Holy Spirit, Saint Francis preached with such divine power about the holy Catholic faith that he offered himself for proof by fire.[c] Observing this, the Sultan conceived a great devotion for him both because of the constancy of his faith, his contempt of the world—even though very poor, he did not want to accept anything from him—and also because of his fervent desire for martyrdom. From that moment the Sultan gladly listened to him, and asked that he come to him frequently. Moreover, the Sultan liberally allowed Saint Francis and his companions to preach freely anywhere they wished. He then gave them a particular sign: seeing it, no one would harm them.

[8]With this generous permission Saint Francis sent his chosen companions, two by two, here and there into various regions of the pagans, among which he with his companion chose one. When he

1C 57; LMj IX

---

a. There is a question of the number of companions. No other source speaks of twelve. Bonaventure writes of only Illuminato (LMj IX 8); Jordan of Giano writes of Peter of Catanio, cf. ChrJG 11, but later implies that Elias and Caesar of Speyer may also have been with him, ChrJG 14.

b. For information on the Sultan, Malik al-Kamil (1180-1238), cf. FA:ED I 231 c, and infra 492.

c. Bonaventure is the only author to write of Francis's offer to walk into the fire together with the Sultan's priests as a proof of the true faith, cf. LMj IX 8 (FA:ED II 602-3).

arrived at an inn where it was necessary for him to stay in order to rest, he found there a woman with a beautiful face but a very filthy mind who solicited Saint Francis for a vile act. Saint Francis answered: "I accept your offer." "So, let's go and get a bed ready," she replied. Saint Francis said: "Come with me and I'll show you the most beautiful bed." He led her to the huge fire which had then been lit in that house. In fervor of spirit he stripped and placed himself naked on that red-hot hearth as if on a bed. And calling her he said: "Undress! Hurry! Enjoy this splendid, flowery, wonderful bed. You have to be here, if you wish to obey me." That fire did no harm to Saint Francis. He lay smiling on that hot, burning hearth as if on flowers. The woman, dumbstruck on seeing something so amazing, was converted to our Lord Jesus Christ not only from the manure of sin but also from the darkness of unbelief, and she became a person of such admirable holiness and grace that, helped by the merits of the holy Father she won many souls for the Lord in that region.

[15]Saint Francis, however, seeing that he was unable to produce fruit there, by God's revelation decided to regather his companions and return to the lands of the faithful.[a] Returning to the Sultan he explained his decision to return. The Sultan said: "Brother Francis, I would willingly be converted to the faith of Christ, but I am afraid to do it now, because these men, if they heard of it, would immediately kill me and you with your companions. Since you can yet accomplish much and I have to put some great affairs in order for the salvation of my soul, I would not willingly bring about an unexpected death for you and me. But tell me how I may be saved. I am prepared to obey you in all things." Saint Francis said to him: "Lord, I am indeed leaving you now; but after I return to my country, at God's call I shall pass on to heaven. But after my death, by God's design I will send two of my brothers, from whom you will receive baptism and you will be saved, just as the Lord Jesus Christ has revealed to me. In the meantime, free yourself from all your present affairs so that, when the grace of God comes, it will find you prepared in faith and devotion." The Sultan joyfully agreed and faithfully obeyed. Then Saint Francis bid him farewell and returned to the lands of the faithful with that venerable assembly of holy companions.

[20]Some years later this Sultan fell ill. Awaiting the promise of the saint, who had already passed to blessed life, he posted lookouts at port entrances so that, when two brothers in the habit of Saint

---

a. The information we have concerning this decision is confusing. Jordan of Giano presents a different motivation from that of Ugolino, i.e., the difficulties of the brothers in Italy, cf. ChrJG 11-13. Jordan alone mentions that Peter of Catanio, Elias, and Caesar of Speyer returned with him to Italy, cf. ChrJG 14.

Francis appeared, the guards would quickly bring them to him. At that very time, blessed Francis appeared to two of his brothers and ordered them to go without delay to the Sultan and carefully see to his salvation as he had promised him. The brothers devoutly fulfilled this command. Crossing the sea, they were led to the Sultan by those lookouts. When he saw them, the Sultan was *filled with great joy,* and said: *"Now I truly know that the Lord sent* his servants. Just as Saint Francis promised, by the Lord's revelation, he has kindly sent these brothers to me for my salvation." From these brothers the Sultan received instruction in the faith and holy baptism. Reborn in this illness, his soul was saved through the merits of the holy father and he passed to eternal happiness in the Lord.[a]

Mt 2:10

Acts 12:11

To the praise and glory of the Lord.
Amen.

XXVIII
THE BLASPHEMOUS LEPER HEALED BY SAINT FRANCIS IN SOUL AND BODY

[1]While he was still living in this miserable and mournful world our blessed father Francis, illuminated by the Holy Spirit, always strove with all his strength to imitate the footprints of our Lord Jesus Christ. Therefore, just as Christ himself deigned to become a pilgrim, so blessed Francis showed himself and his Order to be pilgrims. Even in the *Rule* he had it written that all his brothers should serve the Lord in this world *as pilgrims and strangers.* Moreover, just as Christ came not only to serve lepers, cleansing and healing them in body, but also to die for them, cleansing and sanctifying them in soul, so blessed Francis, wishing to be conformed to Christ, served the lepers with deep feeling, bringing them food, washing their decaying limbs, cleaning their clothes, and beyond this, hurrying fervently to kiss them. He also ordered the brothers of his Order in the various places of the world, for the love of Christ who for us willed to be *considered as a leper,* should devotedly serve lepers wherever they might be. The brothers as true sons of holy obedience willingly did this.

1 Pt 2:11

Is 53:4

LR VI 3

1C 17, 103

1C 39

[6]It happened that in a particular place where they were serving lepers, there was one leper so malignant, impatient, and unruly, that no one doubted that he was being driven by an evil spirit, for the Spirit of God moves the soul to everything wholesome, and the evil

---

a. Malik al-Kamil died on March 8, 1238, at age sixty, leaving a legacy of tolerance for Christianity, cf. René Grousset, *Histoire des Croisades et du royaume franc de Jérusalem,* vol. III (Paris: Plon, 1934-6), 370.

spirit to everything wicked. Now that leper not only hurled terrible curses at those who were serving him and fired insults at them, but, even worse, wounded them with all kinds of beatings and blows. Moreover, what was dreadful and evil, the leper blasphemed the blessed Christ, His most blessed Mother, and other saints. Although the brothers patiently tried their best to store up merit from those insults and blows, nevertheless their consciences could not stand the blasphemies lest they seem to be participating in such crimes. Therefore, they decided to abandon this leper so that they should not become supporters of a blasphemer of God and a vessel of the devil.

¹¹But they did not want to do what they had decided unless they first explained all this thoroughly to Saint Francis, who was staying in another place. After listening to them, Saint Francis made his way to that leper and on entering, said to him: *"May God give you peace, dearest brother."* The leper responded: "What kind of peace do I have? God, in fact, took all peace from me, because I'm all rotten." Saint Francis said: "Dear brother, be patient, because the evils inflicted on our bodies here provide the salvation for the soul, if they are endured with serenity." The leper replied: "How can I patiently bear it, when my pain lasts night and day? For not only am I being consumed and tortured by my illness, but I am being terribly afflicted by the brothers you gave me as servants. None of them serves me as he should."

¹⁵Through the Holy Spirit, Saint Francis knew that the man was being disturbed by an evil spirit, so he went and pleaded devoutly with the Lord for him. After his prayer, he returned to the sick man and said: "Dear bother, I want to take care of you since you're not content with the others." The leper replied: "I like that. But what more can you do than the others?" Saint Francis said: "I'll do whatever you want." "I want you to wash me," the leper said. "I stink all over so much that I can't stand myself."

¹⁷Saint Francis immediately had some water heated with many sweet-smelling herbs. Undressing the leper, Saint Francis began to wash him with his holy hands, while another brother poured the water. As his body was being washed on the outside, on the inside his soul was being cleansed. When the leper started being healed, he suddenly began to weep bitterly out of deep remorse. And just as the leper's body was washed with water and cleansed from leprosy, so his conscience was baptized with tears and cleansed from all malice. When he was completely washed and healed externally, he was perfectly anointed and healed internally, and then burst into tears with such remorse that he wept and cried out in a very voice, saying he was worthy of hell because of the insults he heaped on the brothers, for the blows and beating he gave them, and for his impatience and

Test 23; 1C 23

Nm 6:26

his blasphemies against God. For about fifteen days this amazing wailing continued, breaking out from the depths of his heart as he constantly begged for the mercy of God and nothing else. With these tears and remorse he confessed all his sins to a priest.

²³Blessed Francis, seeing such an evident miracle, gave thanks to God and then went away from there to a remote area, for if this miracle became known to the people, everyone would come running to him. This was something that the saint avoided by every possible

Mt 24:45

means. For, as a *faithful and prudent servant,* he strove to return honor and glory to God and among people to reserve shame and dishonor for himself.

²⁵After his miraculous healing and the remorse it provoked, the leper became ill and, after a few days, provided with the sacraments of the Church, he came to his end in the Lord. Saint Francis was praying in a remote place in the woods when the deceased leper appeared

Wis 7:29

to him, shining *more brightly than the sun* and uplifted in the air, and said: "Do you recognize me?" Saint Francis asked: "Who are you?" He answered: "I am the leper the blessed Christ cured because of your merits. Today I'm going to the blessed kingdom, for which I give thanks to God and to you. Blessed be your soul and your body; blessed be your words and deeds, because through you many souls in the world are being saved and will be saved. Know that there is not a single day when the holy angels and all the saints, men and women, do not give great thanks to God for the holy fruit that is being produced by you and your Order throughout the world. For this reason be comforted, give thanks to God and remain with the blessing of God." Having said this, he went on to the Lord, and Saint Francis remained very consoled.

To the praise of our Lord Jesus Christ.
Amen.

XXIX
THROUGH BLESSED FRANCIS ROBBERS ARE CONVERTED, ENTER THE ORDER, AND LIVE VERY HOLY LIVES

¹Our blessed Father Francis, wishing to lead everyone to salvation, traveled around the world through various regions; and wherever he was traveling, since he was led by the divine Spirit, he kept building a new family for the Lord. He was like a chosen vessel of the Lord, pouring out the balm of grace. He went into Slavonia, the March of Treviso, the March of Ancona, Apulia, Saracen lands, and

many other regions, multiplying the servants of our Lord Jesus Christ everywhere.

[3] As he was passing through Monte Casale, a town in the district of Borgo San Sepolcro,[a] he received there a young noble man from Borgo. He came to Saint Francis and said to him: "Father, I would gladly become your brother." Saint Francis replied: "My son, you are young, refined, and noble. You might not be able to endure our poverty and austerity." But he said: "Father, aren't you human beings like me? You are like me and you endure it, so I'm able to endure it, too, with God's help!" This answer pleased Saint Francis very much. He immediately received him, blessed him, and named him Brother Angelo. He conducted himself so graciously that a little later Saint Francis made him guardian in the place of Monte Casale.[b]

[7] In those days there were three famous robbers who committed many crimes all around. One day these robbers came to that place and asked Brother Angelo, the guardian, to provide them with food. But the guardian rebuked them with a sharp reproof, saying: "You thieves! Savage murderers! You're not ashamed to steal what others work for, and now you're even bold enough to try devouring alms given to the servants of God! You don't deserve to have the ground hold you up! You respect no one and you despise the God who created you. So go, mind your own business and never come back here again!" They were very upset and left, deeply offended. But that same day Saint Francis returned to that place from begging with a companion, carrying a sack of bread and a small jug of wine. When Brother Angelo told him how he had driven away those men, Saint Francis rebuked him severely, saying that he had acted wickedly, because sinners are brought back more easily by sweet kindness than by cruel rebukes. "For even Christ, our master, whose Gospel we promised to observe, said: *'It is not the healthy who need a doctor but the sick,'* and *'I have not come to call the Just, but sinners,'* and therefore *he frequently ate with sinners.* Therefore, since you acted against charity and contrary to the example of the blessed Christ, I command you under obedience. Go immediately, take this sack of bread and jug of wine which I received, and search carefully throughout the mountains and valleys until you find those robbers. Then on my behalf you will present all this bread and wine to them. Then you will get down

Mt 9:12,13

Mt 9:11

C 115; 2MP 66

---

a. Cf. Teobaldo Ricci, *Sulle Orme di Francesco in Toscana* (Padua: Edizioni Messagero Padova, 1999), 50-5.

b. Little is known about this Angelo da Borgo San Sepolcro beyond this paragraph. James Oddi writes that he died in 1228, cf. James Oddi, *La Franceschina: Testo volgare umbro del secolo XV, scritto dal P. James Oddi di Perugia, edito per la prima volta nella sua integrita*, tom. I, ed. Nicola Cavanna (Florence, Olschki, 1931) 117. Boccali and Bigaroni suggest that his surname is Tarlati and that his death occurred in 1228, cf. Boccali, Bigaroni, *Actus*, 334-5, n. 365.

on your knees in front of them and humbly confess your fault of being cruel to them. Then ask them on my behalf not to do evil anymore, but to fear God and not to offend their neighbors. And if they do this, I promise to provide them constantly with the things necessary for their bodies. And when you have humbly told them these things, return here."

[16]In the meantime Saint Francis prayed to the Lord for them, that He soften their hearts to do penance. So it happened that when the robbers ate the alms sent by Saint Francis, they began to discuss with each other saying: "What miserable and unhappy men we are! The hard pains of hell are waiting for us. We go on robbing our neighbors and wounding people, even killing them, but we're not moved by fear of God or remorse of conscience over such horrible crimes. And here comes this holy brother to us, humbly accusing himself in front of us over some very just words he blurted out because of our wickedness. And besides this, with the bread and wine he brought us a gift of charity and relayed the very generous promise of the holy father to provide for our needs. They really are holy men of God who deserve the heavenly homeland. We are sons of eternal perdition, daily amassing avenging flames for our abominable crimes! I don't know; with the crimes we've committed can we find mercy from God?" One of them said these or similar words and the other two said: "What do we have to do?" But the first one said: "Let's go to Saint Francis. If he gives us hope that we can find mercy from God for our great sins, whatever he says, we'll do, to free our souls from the pit of hell."

[23]All three together agreed with this suggestion, so they went quickly to Saint Francis and said: "Father, because of our many evil crimes, we don't believe we can find the mercy of God. But if you believe God will accept us into His mercy, then here we are, ready to do penance with you." Saint Francis received them kindly and charitably, and by encouraging them with many examples he assured them of finding the mercy of God. Moreover, he bound himself to obtain mercy for them from the Lord Jesus Christ. And he taught them that the immeasurable greatness of God's mercy would far exceed all our sins, even if they were infinite, and that, as the Gospel and Saint Paul the Apostle testify, Christ came into this world to redeem sinners.

[27]Because of this healthy encouragement, the three robbers renounced the world and were received by the holy father, binding themselves to him in habit and in spirit.[a] Two of them lived only a

---

a. There is no other evidence of these three robbers having entered the Order, suggesting that this is a literary invention of the author.

short time after this praiseworthy change, departing from this world at the call of the Lord. The third, the survivor, meditating on the many great sins that he had committed, subjected himself to such penance that except for the common Lents which he made as the others did, for fifteen continuous years he ate only bread and water three times a week. He was content with only one little tunic; he always walked barefooted and never went to sleep after matins. During this fifteen-year period Saint Francis passed from this world to the heavenly Father.

³⁰After this brother had held to this strict penance for many years without ceasing, one night after matins such a temptation to sleep suddenly overcame him that no convincing argument could make him resist sleep nor keep vigil, as he usually did. Since he was not able to resist nor able to pray, he gave in to the temptation and went to his bed to sleep. As soon as his head touched the bed, he was led in spirit *to a very high mountain,* where there was a very deep ravine, broken boulders here and there and different rocks jutting out unevenly. The one who was guiding him pushed the brother from the top of the ravine. Falling headlong over the stones, and crashing against rock after rock, when he came to the bottom of the ravine all his limbs seemed torn and his bones broken.

Mt 4:8

³³While he was lying there badly battered, his guide called to him to get up, because he still had a long journey to make. The brother replied: "You're a hard man with no discernment. You see me bruised all over to the point of death, but you still tell me to get up." The guide came over and touched him, and his bruised limbs were immediately and perfectly healed. Then he showed the brother a great plain full of sharp stones, thorns and thistles, swamps and sink-holes, over which he had to walk barefoot to reach the end of the plain where there was a red-hot furnace which he saw from a distance and which he had to enter. After he passed over that plain with great difficulty, the angel said to him: "Get into the furnace: you have to." The brother replied: "You're a hard guide. You see me so painfully hurt by this torturous plain that I need complete rest, and you say: 'Get into the furnace.' " As he looked around the furnace, he suddenly saw demons standing on all sides with pitchforks. As he hesitated to go into the furnace with their forks they quickly pushed him in.

³⁸As he entered that fire, he met one of his godparents, who was burning all over. He cried out, "O godfather, you unlucky man! How did you come to be here?" And the other said, "Go on a little further into this fire and you'll find my wife, your godmother, who will tell you the cause of my damnation." So he went on a little further

through the fire and suddenly his godmother appeared, burning, sunk completely enclosed in a measure for grain. He said to her, "O godmother, unlucky and miserable woman! How did you fall into such torture?" She answered, "Because my husband and I, at the time of the great famine, which blessed Francis foretold, were selling grain and we falsified the measure: that's why I'm burning, stuck tightly in this measure." At these words, the angel pushed him out of the fire and said: "Get ready to travel. You still have to pass through a great danger." The brother said: "You're the hardest guide! You have no compassion. You see that I am almost completely burned, and you say: 'Keep going to horrible danger!' " But the angel touched him and he was perfectly healed.

2C 52

[40b]Then the angel led him to a bridge which could not be crossed without great danger because it was very narrow and extremely slippery.[a] Under the bridge flowed a frightening river full of serpents, dragons, scorpions, toads, and a dreadful stench. The angel said: "Cross this bridge. It's very fitting that you cross it." But the brother replied: "How will I be able to cross without falling into such a dangerous river?" The angel replied: "Follow me and place your foot where you see me place mine, and you'll cross safely." Following the angel and placing his foot where the angel did, he safely reached the middle of the bridge.

[44]When he was in the middle of the bridge, the angel flew away up to a high place to a most amazing hut on the heights, and he noted well how the angel flew to it. He remained on the bridge without a guide, and the frightful animals of the river were now raising their heads to devour him if he fell. He stood there in such terror that he had no idea what to do, for he could not go forward or backward. Placed in such distress and danger, he bent over and hugged onto the bridge. Realizing that God was his only refuge, he began to invoke the Lord Jesus Christ from the bottom of his heart, that in His most holy and kind mercy He might be kind enough to help him. After his prayer, it seemed to him that he was sprouting wings. Happy about this, he waited until the wings grew, hoping to fly away from the river to the place where the angel had flown.

[48]But he had been in too much of a hurry to fly and because the wings were not fully grown his flying failed, he fell onto the bridge and all his feathers fell off too. Terrified he again hugged the bridge and tearfully begged for Christ's mercy. Again it seemed to him that he was sprouting wings, but as before he rushed to fly before the

---

a. This incident is similar to DBF III in which an angel transports Brother Bernard of Quintavalle across a swollen river. Cf. supra 440-4.

wings were full-grown; he fell again onto the bridge and the wings fell off as before. Realizing that it was because of his haste that he could not fly, *he said in his heart:* "If I sprout wings a third time, I will wait until I won't fail in flying." And it seemed to him that from the first to the second and third time the wings sprouted, he waited for more than one hundred and fifty years. When it seemed to him that the wings had fully grown this third time, he raised himself powerfully into the air and flew to the hut where the angel had flown. When he arrived at the door of that remarkable dwelling, the porter said to him: "Who are you who are coming here?" The brother replied: "I am a Lesser Brother." "Wait," he said, "until I get Saint Francis to see if he recognizes you."

⁵⁴While the porter went for Saint Francis, the brother began to inspect the walls of this wonderful city, and those walls were so amazingly clear that he clearly saw everything that was happening inside, and the marvelous choirs of saints inside. While he was looking, he suddenly saw Saint Francis and holy Brother Bernard and Brother Giles, and behind Saint Francis such a great multitude of men and women saints of God following in his footsteps that they seemed innumerable. When Saint Francis reached him, he said to the porter: "Let him enter. He is one of my brothers." Then Saint Francis led him inside, pointing out many wonderful things to him. As soon as he entered, he experienced such consolation and sweetness that he forgot all the distress which he experienced before as if it never happened at all. Then Saint Francis said: "Son, you must return to the world and remain there for seven days. During this time make all possible preparations, because after seven days I will come for you and you will come with me to this wonderful place of the blessed."

⁵⁹Saint Francis was wrapped in a mantle decorated with very beautiful stars. His five stigmata were like five brightly glittering stars, which gleamed with such light that the whole city seemed to be illuminated by their rays. Brother Bernard had *on his head the most beautiful crown of stars.* Brother Giles was completely surrounded by a marvelous light. And he recognized many other holy Lesser Brothers there in glory with Saint Francis, brothers he had never seen before.

⁶¹This brother was given permission, though reluctant, to return to the world. As he returned, the brothers were striking prime. No more time had passed than from after matins to the dawn of that same night, although it seemed many years to him.

⁶²This brother revealed in full the vision and the limit of seven days to his Guardian, and immediately he began to be ill with fever. On the seventh day Saint Francis came with a glorious company of

Ps 10:6, 11

Rv 12:1

saints and led his soul, purged in that vision with the angel-guide, to the joys of the blessed.

To the praise of our Lord Jesus Christ.
Amen.

XXX

SAINT FRANCIS, WHILE PREACHING AT BOLOGNA,
CONVERTS TWO NOBLES FROM THE MARCHES OF ANCONA,
BROTHER PELLEGRINO AND BROTHER RICCERIO

[1]Once when Saint Francis was traveling through the world, he came to the city of Bologna. When the people learned of his arrival, they all came running to him, so that he could hardly move along the ground. They all wanted to see this new flower of the world and angel of the Lord. As a result he could reach the city square only with the greatest pains. With the great crowd of people gathered there, men, women, and many scholars,[a] Saint Francis arose in their midst and with the Holy Spirit dictating, he preached such marvelous and amazing things that he seemed not a man but an angel. For those heavenly words of his seemed like *sharp arrows of a warrior* coming from the bow of divine wisdom, which so powerfully penetrated the hearts of them all that he turned the huge multitude of men and women from a state of sin to tears of repentance.[b]

Ps 120:4

[5]Among those who were there were students from the more noble families of the Marches of Ancona, that is Pellegrino of the house of Falerone and Riccerio of Muccia. These among others, touched deeply by the holy words of the holy Father, came to blessed Francis and said that they wished to leave the world entirely and take the habit of his brothers. Saint Francis, considering their fervor, knew by the Holy Spirit that they were sent by God; and he also knew the way of living each would take on himself. So he received them happily, and said: "You, Pellegrino, hold to the way of humility; and you, Riccerio, serve your brothers." And so it was.

---

a. By the time of Francis, Bologna had become well-known for its university. Established in the 11th century, its school of law attracted scholars which, by the 13th century, had divided into two colleges, the *Ius Canonicum* and the *Ius Civile sive Caesarerum.* The 13th century also saw the development of the *Collegium artistarum et medicorum* for the imparting of education in the mathematical, liberal, and mechanical arts. Cf. Hastings Rashdall, *The Universities of Europe in the Middle Ages,* ed. Frederick M. Powicke and Alfred B. Emden (Oxford: Oxford University Press, 1936).

b. Francis's sermon left a strong impression on the Croatian Thomas of Split (+1268) who, writing between 1250-65, graphically described the event. Cf. FA:ED II 807-8.

⁹For Brother Pellegrino never wished to be a cleric, and he remained lay, though he was well-educated, an expert in Canon law. Because of his humility he arrived at the greatest perfection of virtue, particularly at the grace of compunction and love of our Lord Jesus Christ. Burning with the love of Christ and inflamed by desire for martyrdom he went to Jerusalem to visit the most sacred places of the Savior, carrying with him the Book of the Gospels.

¹²As he viewed the holy places where God and humans had walked, and touched them with his feet and observed them with his eyes, he bowed over to pray to God. He embraced those most holy places with the arms of faith, kissed them with the lips of love, and watered them all with tears of devotion, so that he moved all who saw him to the greatest devotion. However, as arranged by divine plans, he returned to Italy and, as a true Pellegrino,ᵃ a pilgrim of the world and citizen of the heavenly kingdom, he very rarely visited his noble relatives. But he encouraged them to despise the world, and by speaking to them seriously urged them to love God, and then he would leave them promptly and quickly, saying that Christ Jesus, who makes the soul noble, is not found *among relatives and acquain-*   _{Lk 2:44}
tances.

¹⁵Brother Bernard, the first-born of his most holy Father Francis, had this one remarkable thing to say about this Brother Pellegrino: that Brother Pellegrino was one of the most perfect brothers of this world. He was indeed a true pilgrim: for the love of Christ which always burned in his heart did not permit him to find rest in any created thing, nor to fix his affection on anything passing, but always to push on toward his homeland, to long for his homeland and to rise from virtue to virtue until the lover is transformed into the beloved. Finally, filled with virtue, he passed to Christ whom he loved with all his heart, and, with many miracles before and after his death, he rested in peace.

To the praise of our Lord Jesus Christ.
Amen.

XXXI
SAINT FRANCIS FREES BROTHER RICCERIO FROM A VERY GREAT TEMPTATION

¹Brother Riccerio, companion of that same Brother Pellegrino on earth and now a fellow citizen with him in heaven, while he lived

---

a. A play on his name, Pellegrino, which, in Italian, means "pilgrim."

walked along the active way, serving both God and neighbor most faithfully, and he became very friendly with and dear to Saint Francis. So he learned many things from Saint Francis, and with the saint as his teacher, he understood the truth about many doubtful things, knew the will of the Lord about business to be done and according to the prophecy of the holy Father he served the brothers. He was made Minister in the March of Ancona; and because of the zeal for God which always burned in his heart, he directed the Province with the greatest peace and discernment, following the example of Christ who first wished to do, rather than teach.

⁴After some time, the divine plan allowed him to have a grave temptation for the good of his soul, that he might be tested and refined like *precious gold.* Filled with anxiety and worry because of this great temptation, he afflicted himself with abstinence and disciplines and tears and prayers; but he was not able to free himself from the temptation. Many times he was led to the greatest despair, for because of the enormity of the temptation he believed that he was abandoned by God. Left in utter desolation and desperation he thought to himself: "*I will arise and go to my Father* Francis. If he shows me friendship, I believe that God will be well-disposed towards me; if he doesn't, it will be a sign that I'm abandoned by God." Quickly setting out, he went to Saint Francis. Saint Francis, however, lay very gravely ill in the palace of the Bishop of Assisi. And while he was thinking about the Lord, that brother's temptation was revealed to him, and his arrival, and his purpose. Immediately calling his companions, Brother Masseo and Brother Leo, he said: "Go quickly to meet my son, Brother Riccerio. On my behalf embrace him and greet him. Tell him that among all the brothers in the world I have a particular love for him." As true sons of obedience, they immediately left to meet Brother Riccerio. Finding him, they embraced him, just as Saint Francis had said, and they repeated the Father's loving words, which filled his soul with such consolation that he almost melted with happiness. This can hardly be expressed in words: how much joy he showed, how he jumped for joy, and how much praise and thanks he returned to God because God *had prospered his journey.* Oh good Jesus, you never abandon *those who hope in You,* but always *give aid with the temptation that we may be able to bear it*!

¹²What more can we say! He arrived at the place where the angelic and most divine man Francis was lying, who, though Francis was seriously ill, got up and went to meet him, embracing him, saying: "My son, Brother Riccerio, among all the brothers who are in the whole world I love you." And making the sign of the Cross on his forehead and kissing him on the same place most lovingly, he said:

Bar 3:30

Lk 15:18

Ps 68:20

Ps 17:7; 1 Cor 10:13

"My dearest son, this temptation was given to you for your great benefit, but if you don't want that benefit anymore, you won't." Remarkable to say, all that diabolical temptation left him at once as if he had never experienced it in his whole life, and he remained greatly consoled in God.

To the praise of our Lord Jesus Christ.
Amen.

XXXII
BROTHER BERNARD'S GIFT OF CONTEMPLATION[a]

[1] How much grace the Most High Father showed toward the evangelical poor who voluntarily left all things for Christ, is apparent in that same Brother Bernard whose mind, after he took on the habit of the holy Father, was very frequently rapt into God.[b]

[2] It happened one time that he was present to hear Mass in a church, and his whole mind was suspended in things divine. He was so absorbed in God that, when the Body of Christ was being elevated he noticed nothing, nor did he kneel when the others knelt, nor did he pull back his capuche. His eyes remained unblinking and he stayed in this condition completely senseless from morning until after nones. Returning to himself after nones, he came out calling in a surprised voice: "Oh brothers! Oh brothers! Oh brothers! No one in this country is so great and so noble that if he were promised a palace full of gold, it wouldn't be easy for him to carry a sack filled with the most vile manure in order to merit so noble a treasure."

[5] Brother Bernard was lifted up in mind to this heavenly treasure reserved for the lovers of God. For fifteen years he often went about with his mind and his face turned toward heaven. Because of the elevation of his intellect to the supercelestial lights and the great absorption of his affections to divine charisms, never during these fifteen years did he satisfy his bodily hunger at table. He ate a little of everything that was placed before him, and he said that we cannot say we are abstaining from food that we do not even taste, because true abstinence consists in struggling against the things that taste good. He had also reached such clarity of understanding that even great clerics came to him, and he untangled obscure questions in any

---

a. There is a parallel between this chapter and ChrXXIVG 43-4. Whereas the previous thirty-one chapters consider more generally stories of Francis and his companions, the next fifteen chapters 32-47, with the exception of Chapters 44-46, present incidents concerning Francis's followers in the Province of Umbria.

b. See similar descriptions of Bernard in DBF II.

passage of the Bible he was asked to explain. Because his mind was entirely released from earthly things, he flew like a swallow to the heights, and sometimes for twenty days, sometimes for thirty, he would fly alone among mountain peaks, contemplating only heavenly things. For this reason holy Brother Giles used to say that God did not give to everyone this gift, which had been given to Brother Bernard of Quintavalle, that like a swallow he could feed himself while flying.[a] Because of this outstanding gift given to him by the Lord, Saint Francis often and gladly conversed with him for whole days and nights. Sometimes both together were found rapt into the Lord for the whole night in the woods where they met to speak about the Lord Jesus Christ, who is blessed forever.

Amen

XXXIII
THE TEMPTATION OF BROTHER RUFINO AND HOW CHRIST APPEARED TO HIM[b]

[1]At one time while blessed Francis was still alive, Brother Rufino, one of the more noble men of Assisi and a companion of blessed Francis, was being seriously harassed in soul by the devil about predestination.[c] The ancient enemy suggested to him that he was not among those predestined to life and that he was wasting whatever he was doing in service to the religion. Because of this harassment which went on in his mind for many days, he was overcome with sadness and melancholy and he was ashamed to tell Saint Francis about his struggle. But he never gave up his usual prayers.

2 Cor 2:3[3]But the ancient enemy, wishing to add *sorrow upon sorrow* for him, which deeply wounds servants of God, also added an external struggle to the internal one. The devil appeared to him under the appearance of the Crucified and said: "Oh Brother Rufino, why do you afflict yourself with prayers and penance, since you are not among

---

a. ChrXXIVG 44 adds: "Bernard gained such a clarity of intellect from the light of contemplation that important clerics came hurrying to him with difficult questions in theology. Once when he had not experienced divine consolation for eight days, he was extremely distressed and, remaining secluded, he fervently prayed to God for relief. Suddenly in the air there appeared to him a hand holding a violin. Another made one downward draw of the bow and the music of that violin filled him with such consolation that he believed that he would have expired if the hand had made an upward thrust of the bow."

b. There is a parallel between this chapter and ChrXXIVG 50-2.

c. This is the first of five chapters dedicated to Brother Rufino, a first cousin of Saint Clare and one of Francis's first followers. Together with Angelo and Leo, "*nos qui cum eo fuimus* [we who were with him]," Rufino is closely identified with L3C and AC. While Angelo died in 1258, both Rufino and Leo lived until 1278. All three are buried near Francis's tomb in the Basilica of Saint Francis in Assisi.

those predestined to life? You should believe me about this because *I* Jn 13:18
know the ones I have chosen. Don't believe the son of Pietro Bernardone,
if he tells you otherwise. Don't even ask him about this subject
because he and others don't know this, but I who am the Son of God
surely know. Therefore, believe me, it's certain: you are among the
number of the damned. And Brother Francis himself, your father is
damned; and whoever follows him is being deceived."

[7]Brother Rufino was so blinded by the prince of darkness that he
already lost confidence and love for Saint Francis, and he did not
bother to tell him about this. But the Holy Spirit revealed to the holy
Father what Brother Rufino did not tell him. Therefore, the kind
Father, seeing in spirit his brother's great danger, sent Brother
Masseo for him, that at all costs he must come to him. Now Brother
Rufino and Brother Francis were staying in the place on Mount
Subasio near Assisi.[a] Brother Rufino replied to Brother Masseo:
"What do I have to do with Brother Francis?"

[10]Then Brother Masseo, a man completely filled with the wisdom
of God, clearly recognized a trick of the wicked enemy and said: "Oh
Brother Rufino, don't you know that Saint Francis is like an angel of
God? He has enlightened so many souls in the world and through
him we too have received so many gifts of divine grace. Therefore, I
demand that you go to him at all costs, because I clearly see that
you're deceived by the devil." Brother Rufino immediately went to
Saint Francis.

[12]And when Saint Francis saw him from a distance, he began to
call out: "Oh, Brother Rufino, you bad little man, did you believe
him?" And then Saint Francis described in detail the temptation he
had, inside and out. The holy father then explained to him that it was
the devil, not Christ who suggested these things; therefore, in no
way should he give in to these suggestions: "But when he tells you:
'You are damned,' you answer firmly: *'Apri la bocca mo te caco!'* Let this
be a sign to you that he is the devil: as soon as you can say these
words, he will run away. You should have recognized by now that he
was the devil because your heart had become hardened to all good,
which is precisely his work." But the blessed Christ never hardens
the heart of a faithful person; in fact, he says: *I will take away your* Ez 11:19
hearts of stone and give you a heart of flesh. While Saint Francis in this way
was describing thoroughly the course of the temptation which had
harassed him both inside and out, Brother Rufino began to sob. And
adoring the saint and humbly acknowledging his fault in hiding this
from Saint Francis, and fully comforted in the Lord by the advice of

---

a. More than likely this was the hermitage of the Carceri, cf. supra 468 b.

the holy Father, he was changed completely for the better. Saint Francis said to him: "Go, my son, and make your confession. Do not neglect your usual dedication to prayer, and know for certain that this temptation will be of great usefulness and consolation to you, as you will experience very soon."

[18]Brother Rufino returned to his cell in the woods to pray. While he was standing there, praying with many tears, the ancient enemy arrived impersonating Christ and said: "Brother Rufino, didn't I tell you not to believe the son of Pietro Bernardone? And that because you're damned, you shouldn't wear yourself out with prayers and tears? What good is it to you, if you afflict yourself while you're alive, and when you die, you're damned?" Brother Rufino immediately replied: *"Apri la bocca mo te caco."*

[20]Then the devil, outraged, left in such a great storm and falling of rocks on Mount Subasio that for a long time a great mass of rocks kept sliding, and that frightening rock-slide is still visible.[a] And even in the valley the rocks of the mountain gave off a great number of sparks as they collided with each other. Startled by this terrifying roar of rocks, Saint Francis and his companions came outside the place to see this strange event. Then Brother Rufino definitely recognized that the enemy had deceived him. So he then went to Saint Francis a second time and prostrating himself on the ground, he again acknowledged his fault. Then, comforted by Saint Francis, he returned to complete peace.

[23]Afterwards when Brother Rufino was praying there and shedding many tears, the blessed Christ suddenly appeared to him and melted his whole soul with divine love: "You did well, my son, to believe Brother Francis, because the one who made you sad was the devil. I am Christ, your Master; and in order to convince you of this completely, let this be a sign to you: while you are in this world, you will never be sad again." Christ blessed Brother Rufino and sent him off in such happiness, sweetness of spirit and with such an uplifted mind that he was absorbed in God day and night. From that time on, he was confirmed in such grace and blessing and assurance of eternal salvation that he was completely renewed, another man. He was confirmed in such uplifting of mind and perseverance in prayer that he would have stayed constantly within a small circle night and day, contemplating the things of God if no one stopped him.[b] Therefore,

---

a. In his *Nova Vita di San Francesco*, Arnaldo Fortini writes of the Carceri's *buco del diavolo* [the devil's pit], cf. Fortini, *Nova Vita* III, 150.

b. 2MP 85 maintains that Francis described some attributes of the perfect Lesser Brother in terms of "the virtuous and constant prayer of Brother Rufino who, whatever he was doing, even sleeping, always prayed without ceasing and whose mind was always intent on the Lord."

Saint Francis used to say this about him: while still living, Brother Rufino had been canonized in heaven by the Lord Jesus Christ; and that he had no hesitation about calling him—in his absence—"Saint Rufino," while he was still living on earth.

To the praise of our Lord Jesus Christ.
Amen.

XXXIV
THE ADMIRABLE AND HUMBLE OBEDIENCE OF BROTHER RUFINO[a]

[1]Because of his constant dedication to contemplation Brother Rufino was so absorbed into God that, rendered almost senseless, as it were, he very rarely spoke. Moreover, he was not gifted with the grace of disseminating the word for he did not have the courage or ability to speak. However, one day Saint Francis ordered Brother Rufino to go to Assisi and preach to the people whatever the Most High would inspire him. But Brother Rufino replied: "Reverend Father, spare me. Don't send me to do this because, as you well know, I don't have a gift for words, and I'm also simple, unlettered and ignorant."[b] Saint Francis said: "Because you did not obey me immediately, I therefore command you under obedience that you go to Assisi naked except for your trousers, and enter some church and, naked as you are, you will preach to the people."

[5]As a truly obedient man, he immediately went to Assisi naked, and after making his reverence in a certain church he got up to preach. Children and adults began to laugh, and say: "Look, these men are doing so much penance that they're going crazy!" In the meantime, however, Saint Francis, considering the prompt obedience of Brother Rufino and his own harsh command, began to rebuke himself very harshly, saying: "You! Son of Pietro Bernardone, vile little man, since when do you command Brother Rufino, one of the most noble citizens of Assisi, to go naked to preach to the people? By God! I'll make you feel yourself what you command someone else!" Saying this, in fervor of spirit he stripped off his tunic and went into Assisi naked, taking with him Brother Leo who, with great discernment, carried his tunic and that of Brother Rufino.

[8]When the Assisians saw him naked, they ridiculed him as a fool, thinking that both he and Brother Rufino had gone insane from

---

a. There is a parallel between this chapter and ChrXXIVG 47-8.
b. Rufino speaks of himself in the same terms as Francis, cf. *A Letter to the Entire Order* 3, 47, cf. FA:ED I 116, 120, 126 (hereafter LtOrd).

penance. Blessed Francis found Brother Rufino who had just begun
to preach. He was saying devoutly: "Oh, my dear people, flee the
world; abandon sin; return what is not yours, if you wish to avoid
hell; keep the commandments by loving God and neighbor, if you
wish to reach heaven, and *do penance for the kingdom of God is at hand."*
And then Saint Francis, naked, got up into the pulpit and preached
such wonderful things about contempt of the world, holy penance,
voluntary poverty, the desire for the kingdom of heaven, about the
nakedness, insults, and most holy Passion of Jesus Christ crucified,
that all the men and women who had gathered in a great crowd,
began to weep loudly. And with incredible devotion and remorse,
they called to high heaven for the mercy of the Most High so that
almost all were transformed into a new astonished state of mind.

[Mt 3:2]

¹²In Assisi there was such wailing by the people who were present
that never was such grief heard in that city over the Passion of our
Lord Jesus Christ. Now that the people were edified and Christ's
sheep were consoled and the name of our Lord Jesus Christ was
blessed in loud voices, Saint Francis had Brother Rufino get dressed
again and he also got dressed. And dressed again in their tunics, they
glorified and praised God because they had won a victory over themselves, had edified the Lord's sheep, and pointed out how the world
should be scorned. Then they returned to the place of the
Portiuncula. Those people considered themselves blessed who were
able *to touch the hem of their garments.*

[Lk 8:44]

To the praise of our Lord Jesus Christ.
Amen.

XXXV
BROTHER RUFINO FREES A DEMONIAC[a]

¹Because of his heart's great attention to God and his angelic
peace of mind, that same Brother Rufino, whenever he was called by
someone, responded with such seriousness, such sweetness, and
with such a hesitant voice to the one calling him that he seemed to be
returning from another world. When he once was called by a companion to go for bread, he responded in a truly godlike manner:
"Fra-a-a-te mi-mi-o, mu-u-u-ultu voluntiere." That is: "Ve-e-e-rrry
gla-a-a-add-ly, m-m-m-my b-b-b-brother."[b]

---

a. There is a parallel between this chapter and ChrXXIVG 48.
b. This opening paragraph is missing in the parallel chapter of ChrXXIVG 48.

³While he was begging for bread in Assisi, a demoniac, strongly bound and escorted by many people, was being led to Saint Francis to be freed from the devil. When he saw Brother Rufino from a distance, he immediately began to cry out and rage so furiously that he broke all his bonds and escaped from the hands of them all. The people were astonished by this strange event and they swore him to tell them why he was being tortured more than usual. He replied: "Because that poor little Brother, that obedient, humble, holy Brother Rufino, who is coming with his sack, burns and tortures me with his holy virtues and humble prayers, and therefore I cannot remain in this man any more." Saying this, the demon suddenly left. When Brother Rufino heard about this, because those people and even the healed man showed great reverence toward him, he gave praise to the Lord Jesus Christ, and exhorted them in all things to glorify our God and Savior, the Lord Jesus Christ.

Amen.

XXXVI
BROTHER RUFINO SEES AND TOUCHES THE WOUND IN SAINT FRANCIS'S SIDE[a]

¹Our blessed Father Francis so diligently concealed from the eyes of all those most holy wounds which Christ, the Son of God, had miraculously impressed in his hands and feet and side that, while the saint was living, hardly anyone was able to see them plainly. From that time on, he went about with his feet covered, and only the tips of his fingers were visible to his companions, for he hid his hands in his sleeves, remembering what was said to the holy Tobias by the angel: *It is good to keep the secret of a king.*

Tb 12:7

³While he was still living, Saint Francis particularly hid the wound in his side at all times so that, except for Brother Rufino who managed to see it by a pious strategy, no one else was able to see it. By three-part evidence Brother Rufino assured himself and others about the most holy wound in the side. First, he sometimes had to wash the holy father's knee-breeches, and he found they were often stained with blood on the right side, and from this he concluded that it was blood which flowed from the wound in the right side. Saint Francis rebuked Brother Rufino when he noticed him spreading out those knee-breeches to look for that mark.

a. There is a parallel between this chapter and ChrXXIVG 52-3.

[6]Second, Brother Rufino, to be more certain about this, once while he was rubbing holy father stuck his finger into that wound. Saint Francis, very distressed, let out a loud yell and said: "Oh, may God forgive you, Brother Rufino! Why did you do this?"

[7]Third, this same Brother, wishing to see this venerable wound with his bodily eyes, said to Saint Francis with a certain charitable caution: "I ask you, Father, to give me a very great consolation: you give me your tunic and in fatherly charity you take mine." Brother Rufino was doing this so that when Saint Francis undressed, he could see with his own eyes the wound in his side which he had once touched with his hand. And so it was done. Saint Francis, giving in to charity for Brother Rufino, took off his tunic and accepted that of Brother Rufino, and since he was wearing only one tunic, while undressing he could not cover himself in such a way that Brother Rufino could not look at that wound.[a] Thus by these three pieces of evidence that wound of the saint was fully confirmed.

To the praise and glory of our Lord Jesus Christ.
Amen.

XXXVII
BROTHER RUFINO IS ONE OF THREE CHOSEN SOULS[b]

Jn 10:14

Jn 10:11

[1]Just as our blessed Lord Jesus Christ says in the Gospel: *I know my sheep, and my sheep know me,* so our blessed Father Francis, as a *good shepherd,* knew by the Lord's inspiration all the merits and virtues of his companions. Moreover, he knew their shortcomings and vices and therefore knew how to provide appropriate remedies for them all: by humiliating the proud; by exalting the humble; by censuring vices and extolling virtues, just as anyone can see in the remarkable revelations which he had concerning that original family of his.

[3]I might recall one of many examples: once Saint Francis was staying in a little place with his companions and he spent his time with them speaking of divine matters. Brother Rufino, a man certainly outstanding in his holiness, was not with them at the time of that divine discussion, because he had not yet come out of the woods where he had gone to pray. While Saint Francis continued his holy exhortations and conversations about God with them, Brother

---

a. Thomas of Celano states three times that Rufino saw and touched Francis's wounds, 1C 95, 2C 138, 3C 4. Others also saw the wounds: Elias (1C 95, 2C 138) and witnesses who testified sometime between 1237 and 1250, cf. FA:ED II 770-1.

b. There is a parallel between this chapter and ChrXXIVG 46.

Rufino, a noble citizen of Assisi but a more noble servant of God, a most pure virgin, raised up by the more noble prerogative of divine contemplation, and adorned before God and man with the flowers of a fragrant way of living, came out of the woods where he had been staying to meditate on heavenly things, and was passing a short distance from Saint Francis. When the saint saw him from a distance, he turned toward his companions and said: "Tell me, dear brothers, who is the holiest soul that God now has in this world?" They humbly replied that they thought that Saint Francis himself had been raised to this privilege. But he answered: "Dear brothers, of myself I am a more vile and unworthy man than any God has in the world. But do you see this Brother Rufino now coming out of the woods? The Lord revealed to me that his soul is one of the three holiest souls which God now has in this world. And I tell you firmly that I have no hesitation about calling him 'Saint Rufino' while he's still living in the body since his soul is confirmed in grace, and sanctified and canonized in heaven by the Lord Jesus Christ."

[10]Saint Francis said these words in the absence of that brother. In this he showed that the holy father himself as *a good shepherd* knew which virtues his sheep were lacking. He showed this with Brother Elias, when he rebuked him for pride; and with Brother John de Capella when he predicted that, because of his malice, he would hang himself; and with that brother whose throat was held by the devil when he corrected him for disobedience; and with those brothers coming from Terra di Lavoro when he rebuked one of them for plaguing his companion along the road. Moreover, he knew the graces in which his sheep abounded as is apparent in Brother Bernard and in that Brother Rufino, and in many others about whom God revealed great deeds to Saint Francis, the good shepherd.

Jn 10:11

To the praise and glory of our Lord Jesus Christ.
Amen.

XXXVIII
SAINT FRANCIS APPEARS TO BROTHER LEO[a]

[1]Francis, lover of glorious innocence which adorns the body and leads the soul to grace and glory, frequently took Brother Leo as his companion and both day and night admitted Leo to his secrets, because he discerned in Brother Leo great purity and dove-like

---

a. There is a parallel between this chapter and ChrXXIVG 68, 70-1.

innocence. Therefore, among all the companions of the holy father, that same Brother Leo was the one who knew more about his secrets and marvels.

³He frequently saw him lifted up into the air, as will be told below.ᵃ He frequently heard him speaking with Christ, with the Blessed Virgin and the angels. Moreover, he saw a fiery light descending from the heavens upon Saint Francis, and he heard a voice from that light speaking with him.

⁵One day when they were traveling together, he saw a very beautiful cross moving along facing the holy father, and Christ hanging on it. He also saw that this marvelous cross would stop when Saint Francis did, and when he walked, it walked too; and wherever Saint Francis turned, the cross went forward, facing him. That cross was so brilliant that it illuminated not only the saint's face but also made the air all around beautiful and bright. And Brother Leo saw all these things in clear light.

⁸Saint Francis gave wonderful consolation to Brother Leo not only when the saint was alive, but even after his death he appeared to him frequently. Once when Brother Leo was keeping vigil in prayer, Saint Francis appeared to him and said: "Oh, Brother Leo, do you remember this? When I was in the world that I predicted a great famine would come over the whole world, and I said that I knew a certain little poor man for love of whom God would relent; and while this little poor man was living, the plague of famine would not be sent?" Brother Leo responded: "I remember well, most holy Father." Then Saint Francis said: "I was that creature, that little poor man, for love of whom God did not send famine on people, but out of humility I did not wish to reveal this. Know for certain now, Brother Leo, that now that I have left this world, a terrible world-wide famine will come upon earth, and many people will die from hunger."

¹²And so it happened. About six months after these words, such a great famine raged everywhere that people would eat not only the roots of plants but also the bark of trees, and because of this a very great number of people died from hunger. From what has been said, the innocence of Brother Leo, Saint Francis's friendship with God, and his infallible prophecy are evident.ᵇ

To the praise and glory of our Lord Jesus Christ.
Amen.

---

a. The author will describe this again in Chapter XXXIX 5-7.
b. Cf. FA:ED II 282 b.

XXXIX
BROTHER LEO SEES SAINT FRANCIS LIFTED ABOVE THE EARTH[a]

[1]When Saint Francis began to experience new, divine charisms in that blessed soul of his, he was not only frequently lifted into the air mentally but also lifted up from the earth bodily. God's wonderful plan for him was being carried out in these elevations. The more he felt the growing gifts of divine grace, the higher he was elevated from the earth, as many of his companions saw with the eyes of faith, particularly Brother Leo. Saint Francis quite frequently allowed him, because of his dove-like, even angelic innocence, to participate in his hidden dedication to prayer. Therefore, Brother Leo himself often deserved to see the holy father lifted into the air higher or lower according to the degree of heavenly feelings through which, growing from virtue to virtue, he was being carried up into God.

DBF VIII 4

[5]That same Brother Leo once saw Saint Francis lifted so high above the earth that he could touch the saint's feet. Another time he deserved to see the same most holy Father lifted to the tops of the trees; and once he was taken up to such a height that he was hardly able to see him. When he was able to touch the feet of blessed Francis, he would embrace them and kiss them with tears of devotion, saying: *"God, be merciful to me, a sinner,* and through the merits of this most holy man, make me find Your mercy." When Brother Leo saw him lifted so high that he could not touch him, he would prostrate himself below Saint Francis and say a prayer similar to the former. These elevations of the holy Father were in the place of La Verna and in many other places.

DBF IX 32,34

Lk 18:3

DBF IX 33,35

[8]Saint Francis allowed only Brother Leo to touch his stigmata, while Leo was changing the bandages which he applied between those marvelous nails and the rest of the flesh in order to hold the blood and ease the pain. He changed them every day of the week except Thursday evening, and all day Friday, when he wanted no remedy to be applied, in order that for the love of Christ, on the day of the Crucifixion, truly crucified by the pains of the cross, he might hang with Christ. Sometimes Saint Francis would deliberately place his hands, marked with such venerable stigmata, on Brother Leo's heart. Brother Leo would feel such devotion in his heart from that touch that he would almost faint, untouched by frequent sobs in a healing numbness.

---

a. There is a parallel between this chapter and ChrXXIVG 65-6.

To the praise and glory of our Lord Jesus Christ.
Amen.

XL

HOW THE LORD JESUS CHRIST SPOKE TO BROTHER MASSEO[a]

[1]Those holy companions of our father Francis, poor in things but rich in God, did not try to become wealthy in gold or silver, but deliberately attempted to become rich in holy virtues by which one arrives at true, eternal riches. It so happened that one day Brother Masseo,[b] one of the chosen companions of Saint Francis, and other companions were speaking about God, one of them said that there was a certain friend of God, who possessed great grace of both the active and contemplative life. And with these he also had a profound depth of humility which made him consider himself the greatest of sinners. This humility strengthened and sanctified him, and made him constantly grow in these gifts and, what is better still, never permitted him to fall away from God.

[4]As Brother Masseo listened to these remarkable things and realized that this was the treasure of life and eternal salvation, he was inflamed to such love, wanting to have this virtue of humility, so worthy of the embrace of God, that with great fervor he raised his face to heaven and most firmly bound himself by vow never to wish to be happy in this world until he felt that this outstanding humility was present in his soul. After making this vow and holy plan, he con-
Rom 8:26 stantly stayed enclosed in a cell, and constantly offered himself *with indescribable groans.* For it seemed to him that he was someone thoroughly worthy of hell, unless he reached that most holy humility, by which this friend of God he had heard about considered himself, who was full of virtues, lower than everyone; even considering himself thoroughly worthy of hell.

[8]While Brother Masseo remained so sad for many days, sacrificing himself with hunger, thirst, and many tears, one day he happened to go into the woods. Walking through them, he kept on letting out moans and cries and tearful sighs because of this ardent desire, and he begged God to give him this virtue. Because the Lord
Lk 4:18 *heals the contrite of heart* and listens to the cries of the humble, a voice came from heaven and called out twice: "Brother Masseo! Brother Masseo!" Recognizing through the Holy Spirit that it was the blessed

---

a. There is a parallel between this chapter and ChrXXIVG 119.
b. Masseo first appears in these sources in the letter introducing L3C in which he is mentioned as one of the witnesses of Francis's holiness. Cf. L3C 1; also FA:ED II 67 d.

Christ, he replied: "My Lord! My Lord!" The Lord asked him: "What would you give? What would you give to possess this grace?" Brother Masseo replied: "The eyes of my head, my Lord." The Lord said to him: "I want you to have the eyes and the grace too." Brother Masseo remained in such great grace of that humility that he desired, and in such light from God that he was constantly joyful. Often when he was praying, he would make a joyful sound on an even pitch in a soft voice like a dove. "Oo-oo-oo." With a cheerful, smiling face he spent time in contemplation, and above all this he became most humble and considered himself the least of everyone.

[12]Brother James of Falerone of holy memory asked him why he did not change notes in his joyful sound. He responded with great cheerfulness: "Because when all good is found in one thing, the tune should not be changed."

Thanks be to God!

XLI
SAINT CLARE IS CARRIED TO THE CHURCH OF SAINT FRANCIS ON CHRISTMAS EVE

[1]When the most devoted bride of Christ, Clare in fact and Clare in name,[a] was seriously weakened by bodily illness and was staying at San Damiano, she was not able to go to the church with the others to carry out the canonical hours. The solemnity of the Nativity of our blessed Lord Jesus Christ arrived when the Sisters usually participated in matins and devoutly received Communion at the Mass of the Nativity.[b] But blessed Clare remained alone in the place, seriously ill, while the others went to the solemnities. She felt great desolation because she could not take part in such devout solemnities.

[4]But the Lord Jesus Christ, not wishing his most faithful spouse to feel such desolation, made her participate personally in spirit both at matins and the Mass and the whole festive solemnity in the Church of Saint Francis; so that she clearly heard the chant of the brothers and instruments all the way to the end of Mass. And what is more, she received Holy Communion and remained fully consoled.

---

a. The Latin is: *Clara re et Clara nomine*, a play on the word *Clara*, clear or brilliant. The phrase is taken from the Magnificat antiphon of First Vespers for the Feast of St. Clare.
b. The source of this incident is Sister Balvina da Cocorano who related it when interviewed about Clare's holiness. Cf. Acts *of the Process of Canonization* VII 9, in *Clare of Assisi: Early Documents*, 2nd ed., ed. and trans. Regis J. Armstrong (St. Bonaventure, NY: Franciscan Institute Publications, 1993), 162-3.

⁶When the Office in San Damiano was finished the Sisters returned to Saint Clare, and said: "O dearest Lady Clare, what great consolation we had on this Nativity of the Lord, our Savior! If only you could have been with us!" She replied: "I thank my Lord, the blessed Jesus Christ, my dearest daughters and sisters, because like you I was consoled at all the solemnities of this night and at greater and more devout solemnities than you. For by the work of my Lord Jesus Christ and the intercession of my most blessed Father Francis, I was present in the church of my father Francis, and with my bodily and spiritual ears, I heard all the singing and the instruments, and moreover I received Communion there. Therefore, rejoice at the great gift given to me, and with your whole heart praise the blessed Christ Jesus, because I lay here ill and—I do not know how—whether *in the body or outside the body,* I was present, as I said, for the whole solemnity at Saint Francis.

2 Cor 12:2,3

To the praise and glory of our Lord Jesus Christ.
Amen.

XLII
SAINT CLARE MIRACULOUSLY STAMPS THE CROSS ON LOAVES OF BREAD^a

¹Saint Clare, the most devoted disciple of the cross and precious little plant of Blessed Francis, was a woman of such holiness that not only bishops and cardinals but even the Supreme Pontiff affectionately desired to see and hear her, and often personally visited her.^b One time the pope came to the monastery of Saint Clare in order to hear from her, the sanctuary of the Holy Spirit, heavenly and divine words. Both of them for a long time discussed the salvation of the soul and the praise of God. In the meantime, Saint Clare had loaves of bread for the Sisters arranged on all the tables, wishing the loaves of bread be kept to be blessed by the Vicar of Christ.

⁴When their holy conversation was finished, Saint Clare genuflected with great reverence, and asked the Supreme Pontiff to bless the bread placed on the tables. The Pope, however, replied: "Faithful Sister Clare, I want you to bless this bread, and make over it the cross of the blessed Christ to whom you have offered yourself entirely as a rich sacrifice." But she replied: "Most holy Father, spare me, because

---

a. There is a parallel between this chapter and ChrXXIVG 182-3.

b. Innocent IV was in Assisi in April, May, and from June to October 6, 1253. Niccolò da Clavi's *Vita Innocentii IV* records two visits of the pope to San Damiano, cf. F. Pagnotti, "Niccolò da Clavi e la sua vita di Innocenzo IV," *Archivo della Società Romana di storia patria,* XXI (1898): 4-120.

for this I should be thoroughly censured, if in the presence of the Vicar of Christ, I, a vile little woman, would presume to give such a blessing." The Pope responded: "So that this will not be considered presumption, but even be to your credit, I command you by holy obedience to make the sign of the cross over these loaves of bread, and that you bless them in the name of the Lord."

[7] As a true *daughter of obedience,* she blessed those loaves very devoutly, making over them the sign of the cross. This is remarkable: immediately there appeared on all the loaves of bread a most beautiful sign of the cross. Many of these loaves were eaten with great devotion, and many were kept for the future because of the miracle. The Pope, looking with great wonder at the powerful cross made by the spouse of Christ, first gave thanks to God and afterwards consoled blessed Clare with his blessing.[a]

1 Pt 1:14

[9] Living in this same monastery were Sister Ortulana, Saint Clare's mother and Sister Agnes, her sister,[b] together with many other holy nuns and spouses of Christ, all filled with the Holy Spirit. It was to them that Saint Francis sent many sick people, now to one, now to another of them, so that they would make the sign of the cross over the sick. By virtue of the cross of Christ which they cherished with their whole heart, as many as they blessed with this sign received a healthy remedy.

To the praise and glory of our Lord Jesus Christ,
Who is blessed forever.
Amen.

Rom 1:25

XLIII

THE MIRACULOUS REVELATION MADE IN THE HEARTS
OF THE HOLY BROTHER GILES
AND SAINT LOUIS, KING OF FRANCE[c]

[1] Saint Louis, King of France, decided to make a pilgrimage to shrines for seven years. He had heard the truthful rumors of Brother Giles's amazing holiness, and in his heart decided by all means to visit him. Therefore, on his pilgrimage he turned toward Perugia

---

a. None of the sources for the life of Saint Clare mentions this event which is surprising since the visit of the pope is described explicitly by Sister Filippa in the *Acts of the Process of Canonization* III 24, cf. Armstrong, *Clare,* 151.

b. Concerning Ortulana, see Armstrong, *Clare,* 137b; concerning Agnes, Clare's sister, ibid., 140 a.

c. There is a parallel between this chapter and ChrXXIVG 90-1.

where he heard Brother Giles was staying.[a] Arriving like a poor, unknown pilgrim, at the Brothers' door escorted by few companions, he urgently asked for Brother Giles, without revealing to the porter anything about his identity. The porter went and told Brother Giles that a pilgrim was asking for him at the door. In spirit Brother Giles immediately knew that this was the king of France. As if intoxicated he left his cell and ran quickly to the door. There they both rushed together in amazing embraces and fell to their knees in devout kisses, as if they had known each other before and were the oldest of friends. After showing these signs of charitable love, neither said a word to the other, and observing complete silence they departed from each other.

[6]As the king was leaving, one of his companions was asked by the brothers who that man was who rushed into such affectionate embraces with Brother Giles. He replied that it was Louis, King of France, who in his travels on pilgrimage wished to see Brother Giles. Having said this, he and the king's companions hurried off.

[7]The brothers were grieved that Brother Giles had not offered some good word to the king and complained over and over: "O Brother Giles, why didn't you say something to such a great king who came from France to see you and to hear some good word from you?" Brother Giles replied: "Dearest brothers, don't be surprised if we didn't say anything to each other, because as soon as we embraced, the light of divine wisdom revealed his heart to me, and my heart to him. And in that eternal mirror, whatever he thought about saying to me, or I wanted to tell him, we heard with soft consolation without the noise of lips or tongue, and better than if we had spoken with our lips. If we had wished to describe by using the sounds of the voice things which we felt inside, that very speaking would have caused desolation rather than consolation to both of us because of the insufficiencies of human language, which can describe divine secrets only by dim metaphor. Therefore, you should know that the king departed wonderfully consoled."

To the praise and glory of our Lord Jesus Christ,
Who is blessed forever.
Amen.

Rom 1:25

---

a. Louis IX, king of Francis from 1226 to 1270, traveled outside of France between 1248-1254 when he embarked on a crusade to win back the Holy Land. While his travels are known, there is no record of any trip that he might have made to Perugia. Cf. Margaret Wade Labarge, *Saint Louis: Louis IX, The Most Christian King of France* (Boston: Little Brown, 1968).

XLIV
SAINT ANTHONY PREACHES IN ONE LANGUAGE AND IS UNDERSTOOD
BY PEOPLE OF DIFFERENT LANGUAGES[a]

[1]Saint Anthony of Padua, that admirable vessel of the Holy Spirit,
was one of the chosen disciples of Blessed Francis. While he was
preaching before the pope and cardinals in a Council where there
were Greeks and Latins, French, Germans, Slavs, English, and many
others of diverse tongues and languages, Saint Francis called him his
bishop.[b] Filled with the breath of the Holy Spirit, inflamed by the
tongue of an apostle, and pouring out the honey-sweet word of God,
he held them suspended in great admiration and devotion because
all those of such diverse languages gathered at the council heard him
sharply and clearly and understood him distinctly. It seemed that
the ancient miracle of the apostles had been renewed as they said in
amazement: *"Is he not a Spaniard?[c] How do we all hear him in our own
native language,* Greeks and Latins, French and Germans, Slavs and
English, Lombards and foreigners?"

[4]The pope, amazed at the profound things set before them from
the Holy Scriptures by Saint Anthony, said: "He is truly 'the ark of
the covenant' and 'the repository of Holy Scripture.' "[d]

[5]Such were the knights that Saint Francis, our leader, had, capable of feeding not only the flock of Christ but even the Vicar of Christ
and his venerable college with the rich food of the Holy Spirit, supplying them with heavenly weapons against the snares of the enemy.

To the praise of our Lord Jesus Christ.
Amen.

XLV
SAINT ANTHONY PREACHES TO THE FISH[e]

[1]The blessed Lord Jesus Christ, wishing to show the great holiness
of his most faithful servant, Anthony, and how devoutly his preaching and sound teaching should be heeded, rebuked the foolishness of

Marginal references: LtAnt; Acts 2:4; Acts 2:7, 8

---

a. There is a parallel between this chapter and ChrXXIVG 121-2.
b. According to Wadding, this took place in 1227 at Easter time during the reign of Pope Gregory IX
   (1227-1241), who assumed the papal insignia on Easter in the presence of those who came to gain
   the Easter indulgence. Cf. Wadding, *Annales,* ad 1227, no. 15.
c. A reference to his birth c. 1195 in the Iberian Peninsula, i.e., in Lisbon, Portugal. Since he is buried
   in Padua, where he died in 1231, he is popularly referred to as "of Padua."
d. These are phrases quoted from the papal proclamation of Anthony's canonization, *Cum dicat
   Dominus,* May 30, 1232. Cf. Wadding *Annales* II ad 1232, 320-2.
e. There is a parallel between this chapter and ChrXXIVG 122-3.

the faithless, the foolish, and the heretics by using irrational animals, that is, by using fish, just as the ass rebuked the foolishness of
Balaam.

Nm 22:21-33

²For when blessed Anthony was in Rimini, where a great number
of heretics lived, wishing to bring them back to the way of truth and
to the light of the true faith, he preached to them for many days from
the Catholic Scriptures. But they had become like stone in their stub-
bornness, and they not only would not agree to his holy words, but
even refused to listen.

⁴Inspired by the Lord, Saint Anthony went one day to the mouth
of the river near the sea, and standing on the bank near both river
and sea, he began as if for a sermon by calling the fish on behalf of
the Lord, saying: "Listen to the Word of God, you fish of the sea and
the river, because the faithless heretics refuse to listen." And suddenly, such a multitude of small and large fish immediately came to
Saint Anthony that nothing like it had ever been seen in that place,
and all held their heads a little above the water.

⁶You would have seen large fish there side by side with small
ones, and the small ones resting peacefully under the fins of the large
ones. You would have seen all different kinds of fish, each hurrying
to those like themselves, and lining up facing the saint like a painted
field marvelously decorated in a variety of colors. You would have
seen there schools of large fish like an *orderly line of troops,* taking their
places to hear the sermon. You would have seen there medium-sized
fish take the middle places and, as if instructed by the Lord, they
stayed in those places without any splashing. You would have seen
all around there a very great multitude of small fish, rushing like pilgrims to an indulgence, trying to draw closer to the holy Father as if
under a tutor. So for this sermon, by heavenly arrangement, there
were first the smaller fish; second the medium-sized ones; and third,
where the water was deeper, the very large fish: all awaiting Saint
Anthony.

Sg 6:4,10

¹⁰When all the fish were arranged in this way, Saint Anthony
began to preach solemnly: "My brother fish, you have a great obligation to give thanks in your own way to your Creator, who has given
you such a noble element for your home. You have fresh or salt
waters according to your need. He has given you many shelters that
you may avoid the discomfort of storms. Moreover, he has given you
an element that is transparent and clear, ways to travel, and food to
eat so you may live. Your kind Creator also prepares necessary food
for you even in the depths of the abyss. At the creation of the world
you had from the Lord a command to multiply with His blessing. In
the Flood, when other animals perished, you were preserved without

harm. Adorned with fins and filled with strength, you can go anywhere you please. By the command of the Lord it was given to you to preserve Jonah, the prophet, and after the third day to place him unharmed on the shore. You offered the coin for the Lord Jesus Christ when, as a poor man, he did not have anything to pay the tax. You were specially chosen as the food of the Eternal King, our blessed Lord Jesus Christ before the Resurrection and after the Resurrection. Because of all this you, who more than other animals have already received so many special gifts, are most obliged to praise and bless the Lord."

[15]At these words and similar exhortations some fish made sounds; some opened their mouths; and all bowed their heads, praising the Most High by what signs they could. Gladdened in spirit by the reverence of the fish Saint Anthony cried out in a loud voice, saying: "Blessed be the Eternal God, because God is more honored by fish in the sea than by men in heresy, and unreasoning beasts pay more attention than unbelieving humans!"

[17]The more blessed Anthony preached, the more the number of fish increased, and none of them left the place it had taken. The people of the city and even the heretics came running at the word of this miracle. They saw this unusual and amazing event, with irrational creatures listening to Saint Anthony; and all of them, stricken to the heart, sat at the feet of Saint Anthony begging him to preach to them.

[19]Then *opening his mouth* Saint Anthony preached so wonderfully   Mt 5:2
about the Catholic faith that he converted all the heretics who were there; and believers strengthened in the faith remained there with joy and a blessing. The fish also, given leave by the saint, left for other areas, happy and joyful with amazing tricks and approving nods.

[21]For many days after this Saint Anthony preached at Rimini and produced great fruit in the conversion of heretics and in the devotion of the clergy.

To the praise and glory of our Lord Jesus Christ.
Amen.

XLVI

BROTHER CONRAD OF OFFIDA CONVERTS A YOUTH
AND FREES HIM FROM PURGATORY AFTER DEATH[a]

[1]The holy Brother Conrad of Offida was a remarkable zealot of the
evangelical Rule of our blessed Father, Saint Francis.[b] He was a man
of such religious life and such merit before God, that both in life and
in death the Lord Jesus Christ honored him in many ways.

[2]For while he was still living and had come to Offida as a guest,
the brothers asked him for the love of God to talk to a very young
brother, who was acting so childishly and improperly that he disturbed both the young and the old of that family, and he cared little
or nothing about the canonical Hours or other religious disciplines.

[4]Brother Conrad, pitying this young man and the other brothers
who were troubled in many ways because of him, gave in to their
pleas and called the young man aside. With heartfelt charity he

Ez 1:3

spoke to the youth such divine, effective words that *the hand of the*

1 Sm 10:6

Lord came down over that young man immediately. *He was changed into
another man,* from a boy into an elder. He became so obedient and
kind, so diligent and devoted, so peaceable and respectful, and so
dedicated to every virtuous work, that just as before the whole family
was upset by him, so afterwards everyone rejoiced at the complete
conversion he had made to virtue, and all showed affection to him as
if to an angel.

[7]A few days after this conversion, he fell ill and passed from this
world, which caused much grief among the brothers. When Brother
Conrad, who had converted him, was at prayer before the altar of
that same convent, the soul of that brother appeared and devoutly
greeted Brother Conrad as a father. Brother Conrad said: "Who are
you?" The answer was: "I am the soul of that young man who just
died." Brother Conrad said: "How are you, my dear son?" He replied:
"Dear father, by the grace of God and your teaching, I am well
because I am not damned; however, because of some faults of mine
which were not fully purged because of the short time I had, I am
suffering the great pains of purgatory. I ask you, Father, that just as
in your kindness you helped me when I was alive, so now please help
me in my sufferings by saying some *Our Fathers,* for me, because your
prayers are very acceptable to God."

[11]Brother Conrad gladly agreed, and he said one *Our Father*
together with an *Eternal rest.* After he finished the prayers, the soul

---

a. There is a parallel between this chapter and ChrXXIVG 423-4.
b. For background on Conrad of Offida, supra 318, infra 694-5.

said: "O holy Father, what great profit I received from that! I ask you to say them again for me." After he prayed a second time, the soul said: "Holy Father, while you are praying, I am totally relieved, so I ask you not to stop praying." Brother Conrad, realizing that this soul was being helped by his prayers, said one hundred *Our Fathers* for him.

[13]When he finished praying, the soul said: "On the part of our Lord Jesus Christ, I thank you. Out of His love may He give you an eternal reward, because due to your prayer I have been liberated from all punishment and I am now going to the glory of paradise."

After he said this he passed on to the Lord. In order to bring joy to the brothers, Brother Conrad related everything that had gone before during the night, and as a result he and the others were consoled very much.

To the praise and glory of our Lord Jesus Christ.

Amen.

XLVII

A GREAT TYRANT SEES A BROTHER ELEVATED THREE TIMES, IS CONVERTED, AND BECOMES A LESSER BROTHER[a]

[1]The following was a most evident sign that the Order of blessed Francis was founded by God, because as soon as it began to increase in number, it spread almost to the ends of the earth. Therefore, Saint Francis, striving to conform himself in all things to Christ, sent his brothers two by two to preach throughout every region. And the Lord did such wonders through them that it was as if *through all the earth their voice resounded, and to the ends of the world, their message.*   Ps 19:5

[4]It happened once that two of these new disciples of their blessed Father traveled to an unknown land and came to a castle filled with very evil men.[b] In this castle there was a great tyrant who was very cruel and irreligious, and was a kind of head and leader of all those very evil men and thieves. He was, however, noble by birth, though very evil and ignoble in behavior. When in their simplicity these two brothers arrived *like sheep among wolves* at the castle in the evening,   Lk 10:3

---

a. There is a parallel between this chapter and ChrXXIVG 34-5. However it is significantly embellished in this version.

b. The incident seems to have a foundation in a similar account found in Salimbene's *Chronicle* in which the two brothers in question are identified as Berthold of Regensburg (+1272) and an anonymous lay brother, cf. *The Chronicle of Salimbene of Adam*, trans. Joseph L. Baird, Giuseppe Baglivi, and John Robert Kane (Binghamton, NY: Medieval & Renaissance Texts & Studies, 1986), 568-9.

suffering from hunger and cold and exhaustion, they asked that tyrant through a messenger that for the love of the Lord Jesus Christ the master of the castle receive them as guests for the night. The tyrant, inspired by God, graciously received them, and he showed them great compassion and courtliness. He had a large fire set for them, and a meal fit for nobles.[a]

[8]When the brothers and all the others took their places, one of the brothers who was a priest and had a special gift for speaking about God, noticed that none of those at table was speaking about God or discussing the salvation of souls. They were speaking only about the robbing and killing and many other evil deeds which they had done here and there, and they rejoiced in the very evil things and in the ungodliness which they had done everywhere. Therefore, when they had finished feeding the body, that brother, wishing to feed their host and the others with heavenly food, said to that lord: "My lord, you have shown us great courtliness and charity, and therefore we would be very ungrateful if we did not attempt to repay you with some good words about God. So we ask that you gather your whole household so that, for the gifts for the body we received from you, we may repay you with gifts for the spirit." The tyrant agreed to their requests and had everyone gather in front of the brothers.

[12]The brother began to speak about the glory of paradise;[b] how there is eternal joy there, the company of the angels, the security of the blessed; there is also infinite glory there, an abundance of heavenly treasures, everlasting life, indescribable light, undisturbed peace, incorruptible health, the presence of God, everything good and nothing evil. But because of their sins and wretchedness people lose all these many good things and get hell instead: where there is sorrow and everlasting sadness, the company of demons, serpents and dragons; where there is infinite misery and life without life, palpable darkness and the presence of Lucifer; where there is trouble and anger, eternal fire and ice, worms and madness, hunger and thirst; where there is death without death, groans, and tears, *gnashing of teeth* and eternal torment; where there is all evil and the absence of all good. "All of you, as I have observed, are running fast to all this evil, for among you there is no evidence of any good deed or any good word. Therefore, I advise you and warn you, dear friends, that for the

Mt 8:12

---

a. Salimbene provides a different account: ". . . he was captured by some assassins, the followers of a certain bandit, and carried off to a castle, where he was kept that night without food and treated very harshly." Cf. *ibid.*

b. Once again Salimbene presents a different version in which the lay brother appeals to the famous preacher, Berthold: "If you ever preached well of the pains of hell and the glories of paradise, you have need to do so now." At which point, Berthold "preached the word of salvation so splendidly to that audience that they were all moved to the most bitter tears." *Ibid.*

vile things of the world and the pleasures of the flesh, which *all pass*   Wis 5:9
like *shadows,* do not lose those highest good things of heaven which
will last forever, and do not keep rushing to such great and bitter torments."

¹⁷After the brother said these things by the power of the Holy
Spirit, the lord of the castle was deeply moved, and feeling remorse
in his heart, he threw himself at the brother's feet. Then he and all
his men began to weep very bitterly, and he asked and begged the
brother to show him the way of salvation. With many tears and deep
remorse he made his confession to the brother, who told him that to
redeem his sins he would have to make pilgrimages to sanctuaries,
mortify himself with fasting, keep prayerful vigils, and apply himself
to abundant almsgiving and other works of piety. But the lord
replied: "Dear Father, I've never been outside this region. I don't
know how to say the *Our Father* or other prayers, so you should give
me another penance." That holy brother responded: "Dear sir, I will
stand as guarantee for you, and out of God's charity I will intercede
with the Lord Jesus Christ for your sins, that your soul may not perish. But now at present, I don't want you to do any other penance
except that this evening, with your own hands, you bring me some
straw on which my companion and I can sleep."

²²The lord happily brought some straw and he carefully prepared
the bed in a room where a light was burning. Noting that this brother
had spoken such holy and powerful words, he believed that he was a
holy man, he decided in his heart to investigate diligently what the
brother would do that night. He saw the brother that evening settle
down in bed. But when the brother thought that everyone was sleeping soundly, he got up in the silence of nighttime and, for the guarantee he gave, stretched out his hands to the Lord praying for him
that the Lord would grant pardon for all his sins.

²⁵And while he was praying the brother was suddenly lifted up
into the air to the top of the palace, and there in the air he wept and
lamented, and pleaded for pardon of that lord's sins. Hardly ever was
a man seen to weep so sincerely over the death of dear relatives or
friends as this brother wept for the sins of this man. During that
night the brother was lifted three times into the air, always lamenting pitiably and weeping compassionately. The lord secretly watched
all this; he heard and saw the brother's charitable lament and his
compassionate sobbing. So as soon as it was morning the lord threw
himself at the brother's feet, and with tears of remorse asked him to
lead him onto the path of salvation, since he was firmly determined
to do whatever the brother ordered.

Lk 19:8
²⁸Therefore, on the advice of the holy brother, he sold everything he had, and *restored* what had to be returned, and distributed all the rest *to the poor* according to the holy Gospel; and offering himself to God, he entered the Order of Lesser Brothers, and with laudable perseverance observing his promise he completed a holy life.ᵃ His other old partners in crime and accomplices, with heartfelt remorse, changed their lives for the better. Thus the holy simplicity of those brothers bore fruit not by preaching about literary authorities or Aristotle, but about the pains of hell and the glory of paradise in brief words, as it says in the Holy *Rule*.ᵇ

LR IX 3

Thanks be to God!
Amen.

XLVIII
THE WONDERFUL DEEDS OF SOME BROTHER
OF THE PROVINCE OF THE MARCHES
AND HOW THE BLESSED VIRGIN APPEARED
TO BROTHER CONRAD IN THE WOODS AT FORANO

¹The Province of the Marches of Ancona was like a beautiful starry sky, with outstanding stars, that is, with holy Lesser Brothers who high and low before God and neighbor shone with radiant virtues, and *whose memory* is truly *held in* divine *blessing*.ᶜ

Sir 45:1

²Among them there were some like the greater stars more brilliant than others,ᵈ such as Brother Lucido the Elder, who was truly *shining* in holiness *and burning* with divine charity. His renowned gift of speech, taught by the Holy Spirit, produced admirable fruit.ᵉ

Jn 5:35

---

a. Salimbene ends the story differently by narrating that the now converted tyrant entered the city, was recognized, captured, and hanged by the people. *Ibid*, 569.

b. This passage echoes one of Angelo Clareno's HTrb III 20: "and after they have left prayer, they prefer the painstaking and sterile wisdom of Aristotle, more eagerly yearn to hear natural and dialectic masters, and ardently strive to have and multiply scholars of these sciences." Cf. Angelo Clareno, *Liber Chronicarum sive Tribulationum Ordinis Minorum*, ed. Giovanni Boccali, intro. Felice Accroca, Italian trans., Marino Bigaroni (Sta. Maria degli Angeli, Assisi: Edizioni Porziuncola, 1998), 336-8.

c. This opening paragraph serves as an introduction to the third part of DBF, that is, Chapters XLVIII-LIX, which deal with incidents involving the Lesser Brothers of the Italian Province of the Marches. According to Giralomo Gulubovich, *Biblioteca Bio-bibliografica della Terra Santa* 2 (Ad Claras Aquas, Quaracchi: Collegium S. Bonaventurae, 1906), 216, it was one of the first eleven provinces established in 1217.

d. There is a parallel between these paragraphs, 2-6, and ChrXXIVG 409-10.

e. Lucido is praised in 2MP 85: "the solicitude of Brother Lucido who had the greatest care and concern and did not want to remain in any place for a month, and when he enjoyed staying some place, would immediately leave, saying: 'We do not have a dwelling here on earth, but in heaven.' " He is also mentioned in HTrb III 75 as having lived with Bernard, and HTrb IV 158 with James of Massa, Juniper, and Giles.

³There was also Brother Bentivoglia of San Severino, whom Brother Masseo, of that same town, saw lifted to a great height into the air when he was praying in the woods.ᵃ Because of this miracle, Brother Masseo gave up his parish and became a Lesser Brother, a man of such holy life that he performed many miracles; and he now rests at Morro. While Brother Bentivoglia was staying alone at Ponte della Trave and taking care of a leper, he was forced by obedience to leave and, not wishing to abandon the leper, he lifted him onto his shoulders and went with his burden from that place at Trave to Monte San Vicino where there was another place; a distance of fifteen miles, from the break of dawn until sunrise. If he had been an eagle, he could hardly have flown that route with such a weight in such a short time. All who heard about this divine miracle were extraordinarily astonished.

⁶Brother Pietro of Monticulo was lifted into the air in the sight of Brother Servadeo of Urbino, who was then his Guardian in the old place at Ancona.ᵇ He was lifted up to the feet of the crucifix, located up high, perhaps five or six cubits or so from the floor of the church.

⁷He fasted during the Lent of Saint Michael the Archangel and on the last day of the fast, he confined himself to the church.ᶜ A brother, just a boy, had concealed himself on purpose behind the altar, and heard him speaking with the most holy Archangel Michael and the archangel with him. And the words which they said were these. The archangel said: "Brother Pietro, you have labored faithfully and very often afflicted yourself for me. I have come to console you: ask for any grace you wish. I will ask this grace from the Lord for you." Brother Pietro replied: "Most holy prince of the heavenly army and most faithful zealot of the honor of God, most kindly protector of souls, I ask this grace of you that you beg for me the remission of all sinners." Michael most holy responded: "Ask for another grace, for I will obtain this one for you very easily." But Brother Pietro would not ask for another. The Archangel concluded, saying: "Because of the confidence and devotion you have toward me, I will procure for you the grace you ask and many others besides." When this conversation, which lasted a great part of the night, was ended, the angel left him deeply consoled.

---

a. Bentivoglio Boni (+1262) was a noble of San Severino in the Italian Province of Macerata who was drawn to the Order by Paolo of Spoleto. Cf. *Bibliotheca Sanctorum* 2 (1962), 1250.

b. Pietro of Monticulo or Monticello (+1289) is considered among the saints and blessed of the Franciscan Order. His feast is celebrated on March 14.

c. There is a parallel between this paragraph, 7, and ChrXXIVG 410.

[Lk 2:28]

[Ps 45:3]

[Acts 4:32]

¹²Also at the time of this truly holy Brother Pietro, there was Brother Conrad of Offida already mentioned.^a When they were staying together in the family at the place of Forano in the Custody of Ancona, Brother Conrad went into the woods to meditate on the things of God. Brother Pietro followed him secretly to see what would happen to him. Brother Conrad began to pray very devoutly and tearfully to the most Blessed Virgin that she would obtain this grace for him from her Son: that he would be able to experience some of that sweetness which the holy Simeon felt on the day of the Purification when he held Christ, the blessed Savior, *in his arms.*

¹⁴That most merciful Lady heard his plea and suddenly there was the Queen of glory with her blessed Son in such a bright light, which not only put the darkness to flight, but also outshone every other light. Approaching Brother Conrad she placed in his arms that child *more beautiful than the sons of men.* Brother Conrad received Him most devoutly, pressed his lips to His, and embraced Him breast to breast, and he melted completely in these embraces and kisses of charity. Brother Pietro, however, saw all this in the clear light and from it also experienced wonderful consolation. He remained hidden in the woods. The Blessed Virgin Mary departed with her Son, and Brother Pietro hurriedly retraced his steps to the place. When Brother Conrad returned, all merry and rejoicing, he was called by Brother Pietro: "O heavenly brother, you've had great consolation today!" Brother Conrad said: "What do you mean, Brother Pietro? What do you know about what I have?" Brother Pietro replied: "I know very well that the most Blessed Virgin and her blessed Son visited you." Hearing this, Brother Conrad, because he was truly humble, wanted it to be a secret and asked him not to tell anyone. For there was such love between these two that they seemed to have *one heart and one soul.*

¹⁹Praying in the place at Sirolo, this same Brother Conrad freed a girl possessed by a demon and then immediately fled from the place so that the mother of the freed girl would not find him, and a crowd of people would gather. Brother Conrad had been praying that whole night and appeared to the mother of the girl, and by appearing had freed the girl.

To the praise and glory of our Lord Jesus Christ.
Amen.

---

a. There is a parallel between these paragraphs, 12-14, and ChrXXIVG 422-3.

XLIX
CHRIST APPEARS TO BROTHER JOHN OF LA VERNA,
WHO BECOMES ENRAPTURED WHILE EMBRACING HIM

[1]How glorious is our Father Francis in the sight of God is apparent in his chosen sons whom the Holy Spirit brought together into the Order, so that truly the glory of such a great Father is his wise sons.

[2]Among whom holy Brother John of Fermo,[a] also know as "of La Verna," shone forth in a special way, and as a wonderful star he glittered in the sky of the Order with the brilliance of grace. While he was still of a young age, in his wisdom he acted with the heart of an old man, and with his whole heart he desired the way of penance which guards the purity of mind and body. Therefore, while still a child, he wore chain mail and an iron band next to his flesh, and he carried the cross of abstinence daily. For before he took the habit of the brothers of Saint Francis he was staying at San Pietro at Fermo with the canons.[b] They were living splendidly, while he bound himself to abstinence with remarkable rigor, and amid evil doings he practiced the martyrdom of abstinence. But since he often endured obstacles from his companions who were opposed to his angelic zeal, to the extent that they stripped him of his chain-mail and impeded his abstinence, he was inspired by God to leave the world and those who loved it and offer the flower of his angelic youth to the arms of the Crucified.

[8]Therefore, still a boy, he put on the habit of the Lesser Brothers and was assigned to a Master for training in spiritual things.[c] At times when he was listening to the words of God from the Master, *his heart, melting* like *wax,* was so filled internally with gentle grace that externally he was forced to run, sometimes through the garden, sometimes through the church, sometimes through the woods, here and there as the inner flame forced him.

Ps 22:15

[10]With the passage of time the grace of God raised this angelic man to different states, and made his actions orderly. Sometimes divine grace would carry him off to the splendors of the cherubim;

---

a. There is a parallel between these paragraphs, 2-28, and ChrXXIVG 439-440. John of Fermo or LaVerna (1259-1322) spent much of his life in the hermitages of the Marches of Ancona and Fermo. He eventually moved to LaVerna where, after forty years, he died in about 1290. He was beatified in 1880.

b. The church of S. Pietro at Fermo had been entrusted to the care of the Augustinian Canons Regular since 1251, cf. *Italia pontificia, sive, Reprtorium privilegiorum et litterarum a Romanis pontificibus ante annum MCLXXXXVIII.* Vol. IV, ed. Paul Fridolin Kehr (Berlin: Weidmannos, 1906), 140. According to Luke Wadding, the Lesser Brothers came to Fermo in 1240, cf. Wadding, *Annales* III, 42.

c. According to his biographer, Giovanni de Settimo Pisano, *Vita del B. Giovanni della Verna*, ed. G. Melani (La Verna: 1962), John entered the Order when he was thirteen years old, that is, in 1272.

sometimes to the fire of the seraphim, and sometimes to the joy of the angels.[a] And what is more, it sometimes raised him as an intimate friend to divine kisses and repeated embraces of Christ's love, which he not only tasted inwardly but also showed outwardly.

[12]Therefore, it happened one time when he was inflamed for a space of three years with the fire of Christ's love, he received wonderful consolations and in such ardor he was frequently rapt in God. But because God takes special care of His sons, now consoling them with prosperity, now trying them with adversity, that fiery ray and state was taken from Brother John while he was staying in a certain place, and he remained without love and light and in the greatest sadness.

[14]When his soul was not feeling the presence of his beloved, he became anxious and went through the woods grieving and anxious, searching for his friend who had hidden himself on purpose for a short while. But in no way and in no place was he able to find as he used to those most sweet embraces and the sweet and blessed kisses of the blessed Jesus Christ. He endured this tribulation for many days, lamenting, sighing and weeping. One day when he was walking through the woods in which he himself had made a path for walking, he sat down afflicted and desolate, leaning against a beech tree and raised his tearful face to heaven.

Ps 147:3

Rom 8:26

[16]Suddenly He *who heals the contrite of heart and binds up their wounds,* the blessed Lord Jesus, appeared on the path, saying nothing. When Brother John recognized him, he immediately threw himself at the Lord's feet, and *with indescribable groans* entreated and begged the Lord to help him:

> Because without you, most sweet Savior, I remain in darkness and grief; without you, most meek Lamb, I remain in distress and terror; without you, Son of the Most High God, I remain confused and ashamed! For without you, I am deprived of all good. For without you I am blinded by darkness. Because you, "O Jesus, are the true light of our minds."[b] Without you I am lost and damned, because you are the life of souls and the life of the vines. Without you I am sterile and dry, because you are the fountain of graces. Without you I am totally desolate because you are "Jesus,

---

a. A reference to Gregory the Great, *Homilia 34a in Evangelia*, II, 7, 8 (*Patrologia Latina* 76: 1249, 1250 [hereafter PL]).

b. A reference to the Hymn of Lauds for the Feast of St. Anthony of Padua, cf. Eliseo Bruning, *Cantuale Romano-Seraphicum*, 3rd ed. (Paris: Desclee & Co., 1951), 190.

our redemption, our love, and our desire,"[a] the unfailing
bread and wine that give joy to the choirs of angels and to
the hearts of all the saints. O most gracious Master and
most kind Shepherd enlighten me, because I am your poor
little sheep, even though unworthy.

[22]Because a deferred desire begets a greater love, the blessed
Christ, still retreating along the path, said nothing at all. Brother
John, seeing that Christ was retreating and was not listening to him,
rose to his feet again, and with holy boldness he ran like *a needy poor* Ps 70:6
man to Christ. Humbly falling at Christ's feet, he begged him with
devout tears: "O most sweet Jesus, *have mercy on me, for I am afflicted!* Ps 31:10
In the abundance of your mercy and *in the truth of your salvation, hear me,* Ps 69:14
and *give me back the joy of your salvation.* Because *the earth is filled with* Ps 51:14;
your mercy, you know how violently I am being afflicted! I beg you to Ps 33:5; 119:64
bring aid quickly to my darkened soul."

[25]Again the Savior retreated, saying nothing to Brother John, nor
offering any consolation. It seemed that He wanted to leave as He
went along the path, doing what a mother does with her child in
order to stir up the child's desire by depriving the baby of her milk as
the baby is seeking milk. Then when the baby cries, the mother
kisses and embraces him, then offers her milk indulgently, with
greater sweetness. So Brother John for the third time followed the
blessed Jesus Christ, crying very much like a suckling child after its
mother, a little boy after his father and a humble disciple after a merciful Master.

[28]After Brother John reached him, the blessed Christ turned His
beloved face to him and stretched out his venerable hands, like a
priest when he turns toward the people. Then Brother John saw
wonderful rays of light coming from the most sacred breast of Christ,
which illuminated not only the woods outside, but also his body and
soul inside, filling them with divine brilliance. Then Brother John
was taught how he should maintain a humble and reverent attitude
with Christ. He immediately threw himself at Christ's feet. Then the
blessed Christ mercifully showed him those most holy feet, where
Brother John poured out so many tears, that he seemed to be another
Magdalene, asking Christ not to regard his sins, but through His
most holy Passion and the shedding of His glorious Blood to revive
his soul to the grace of divine love: "For this is Your commandment
that *we love You with our whole heart* and *with all* our *strength,* which no Lk 10:27; Dt 6:4,5

---

a. A reference to the Hymn of the Vespers of the Ascension, cf. *Analecta Hymnica,* vol. II, ed. Clemens
   Blume, Guido Maria Dreves (Leipzig, 1903), n. 49.

one is able to do without your help; therefore, help me, most loving Jesus Christ, to love you with all my strength."

[33]While Brother John was earnestly praying, lying at the feet of Jesus most sweet, he received so much grace that he was totally renewed, and like Magdalene, consoled and at peace.[a] Then Brother John, feeling that gift of grace, began to thank the Lord and humbly kiss His feet, and standing up, to look at his Savior as he was thanking Him. The blessed Christ opened his arms and offered Brother John his most holy hands to be kissed. As Christ opened his hands Brother John arose and went to the breast of the Lord Jesus. He embraced Jesus and blessed Jesus embraced him.

[36]While Brother John was kissing the most holy breast of Christ, he sensed such a divine fragrance that, if all the fragrances of the world were gathered into one, it would be considered a putrid stench compared to this divine fragrance. And over and above this, those rays were issuing from the Savior's breast, illuminating his mind inwardly and, outwardly, everything around them. And in this embrace, fragrance, and illumination, Brother John was enraptured in the blessed breast of Jesus Christ, totally consoled and wonderfully illuminated. From that time on, since he had drunk at the sacred fountain of the Lord's breast, he was filled with the gift of wisdom and the grace of God's word, and he often poured forth marvelous words beyond description. And because there flowed *from His side streams of living waters* which he had drunk from the depths of the breast of our Lord Jesus Christ, he changed the minds of his listeners and produced wonderful fruit.

Jn 7:38

[41]Moreover, that fragrance and brilliance which he had experienced there, remained in his soul for many months. And, what is more, on the path in the woods where the Lord's feet had passed and in a wide area all around he experienced that same brilliance and fragrance for a long time. When Brother John returned to himself after this rapture, the blessed Christ disappeared and he afterwards remained always consoled and enlightened.

[43]And at that time he did not find the humanity of Christ, as I heard from the one who heard it from the mouth of Brother John himself. Rather he found his soul buried in the abyss of the divinity, and this is approved by many well-known witnesses. He used to utter such exalted and profoundly illuminating words before the Roman Curia, before kings, barons, Masters and Doctors that all were wonderfully astonished. Although Brother John was a man with little education, nevertheless he gave extraordinary explanations about the

---

a. There is a parallel between these paragraphs, 33-43, and ChrXXIVG 442-3.

most subtle questions concerning the Trinity and other mysteries of Scriptures.

[46]As we have seen above, Brother John was received first with tears at the feet of Christ, then with thanks into the hands of Christ and finally at his blessed breast with rays and rapture. These are great mysteries which cannot be explained in a few words. But if anyone wishes to know this, read Bernard on the *Canticle of Canticles,* who puts these stages there according to their order: namely, the beginners at the feet, those making progress at the hands, and the perfect at the kiss and embrace.[a] By the fact that the blessed Christ without saying a word gave such grace to Brother John, He taught us that, as the Best Shepherd, He tried to nourish the souls more by internal sensing of God than by external sounds in the ears of the flesh; because the kingdom of God is not found in external things but in internal things, as the psalmist says: *All his glory is from within.*

Ps 45:14

To the praise and glory of our Lord Jesus Christ.

Amen.

L

A DIVINE ANSWER IS GIVEN TO BROTHER JOHN
WHILE PRAYING FOR ANOTHER BROTHER,
AND ALSO BLESSED LAWRENCE APPEARED TO HIM[b]

[1]Brother John was asked by Brother James of Falerone to ask God about a certain scruple of conscience which worried him very much. It was about certain things which pertained to the priestly office. Brother John had an answer from the Lord before the feast of Saint Lawrence, as he himself said. He said that the Lord told him: *"He is a priest according to the order* of God." But as his conscience still troubled him, he asked Brother John again to ask the Lord about this.

Ps 110:4

[3]Therefore, when on the night of the vigil of Saint Lawrence[c] Brother John was faithfully keeping vigil and praying to the Lord that through the merits of Saint Lawrence He might reassure him about Brother James's scruple, blessed Lawrence dressed in white robes like a Levite appeared to him in his prayerful vigil, and said: "I am Lawrence the Levite. He for whom you are praying is a priest

---

a. Bernard of Clairvaux, Sermons 2-4, in *Song of Songs I:* The Works of Bernard of Clairvaux, vol. 2, trans. Kilian Walsh, introd. M. Corneille Halflants (Kalamazoo, MI: Cistercian Publications, Inc., 1981), 8-24.

b. There is a parallel between this chapter and ChrXXIVG 440-1.

c. From the evening of August 9th to the morning of the 10th.

according to the order of God." And from then on he was reassured and very greatly consoled regarding the doubt which he had.

When the brothers were singing the *Salve Regina* in the evening, Saint Lawrence again appeared to Brother John in the form of a young man dressed in a red dalmatic and carrying an iron grill. He said: "This grill has done me a favor in heaven, and the pain from the burning coals gave me the fullness of God's sweetness."[a] Then he added: "If you wish to have the glory and sweetness of God, patiently endure the suffering and bitterness of the world."

Blessed Lawrence remained visible to him until that antiphon ended. Afterwards the brothers went to rest, but he remained in the choir with Saint Lawrence. Then after assuring and consoling him, Saint Lawrence disappeared, and left him in such divine love and sweetness that for the whole night of that feast he did not sleep, but passed the night in wonderful consolation.

When this same Brother John was once celebrating Mass with the greatest devotion and after the host had been consecrated, the appearance of bread totally disappeared before his eyes, and in a blink of an eye Christ appeared there, with a very beautiful beard and clothed in a red robe. Christ gave him such sweet consolation that, if he had not remained aware of himself, he would have been rapt into ecstasy. In that vision he was assured that because of that Mass God was reconciled with the whole world and especially with those commended to Him.

To the praise of Christ.
Amen.

LI

WHILE CELEBRATING MASS FOR THE DEAD,
BROTHER JOHN SEES SOULS FREED FROM PURGATORY[b]

[1]When Brother John was celebrating Mass on the commemoration of all the dead,[c] he offered this most high Sacrament, whose efficacy the souls of the dead desire above all, with such emotions of love and tender compassion that he was totally dissolved in this sweetness of piety and honey-sweet brotherly love.

---

a. A reference to the legendary account of his passion in which Lawrence was roasted on a gridiron and said "*Assum est; versa, et manduca* [It is well done! Turn it over and eat]!"

b. There is a parallel between this chapter and ChrXXIVG 441.

c. All Souls Day, November 2nd, traditionally attributed to Saint Odilo (+1048), the fifth abbot of Cluny, because of his decree that all Cluniac monasteries should follow the example of the monks of Cluny in offering special prayers for the dead on the day following the feast of All Saints, November 1.

²Therefore, when in this Mass he devoutly raised on high the most holy Body of Christ, offering It to God the Father praying that, for the love of Him who hung upon the Cross, He mercifully free the souls, created and redeemed by Him, from their prison, he saw an almost infinite number of souls leave purgatory, like a multitude of sparks from a lighted furnace. He saw them soaring toward their heavenly homeland because of the merits of Christ who for the salvation of the human race hung upon the Cross, and is offered daily in that most sacred host for the living and the dead: who is God and blessed man, light and life, redeemer and justification, and eternal sanctification, *Who is blessed forever.*

Rom 1:25

Amen.

LII

BROTHER JOHN SEES BLESSED FRANCIS WITH MANY HOLY BROTHERS AND BROTHER JAMES SPEAKS TO HIM AFTER DEATH[a]

¹At the time when Brother James of Falerone, a holy man, was ill in the place at Mogliano of the Custody of Fermo in the Province of the Marches, Brother John of La Verna prayed to the Lord God for Brother James, who was gravely ill, in mental prayer and with heartfelt desire because he loved Brother James as a father.

²While he was attentively praying, he fell into ecstasy and with great clarity he saw in the air above his cell, which was in the woods, a host of angels and saints. There was such light there that the whole surrounding area glowed.

³Among the angels and saints he saw the sick brother for whom he was praying, standing there, very handsome and resplendent in white robes. He also saw there our blessed Father Francis marked with the sacred Stigmata and shining with a marvelous glory. He saw and recognized holy Brother Lucido and Brother Matteo the Elder of Monte Rubbiano, and many other brothers whom he had never seen in this life, who together with many saints shone with similar glory. And while he was watching all this, it was revealed to him that the sick brother was certainly saved and that in this sickness he would pass over to God: but that he would not immediately go to heaven because he had to be purged for a little while.

⁶Brother John who saw all this rejoiced so much in the salvation and glory of that brother that in sweetness of spirit he would

---

a. There is a parallel between this chapter and ChrXXIVG 441-2.

frequently call out to Brother James, saying within the recess of his heart: "Brother James, my Brother James; my most faithful servant of Christ; Brother James, my sweet father; Brother James, companion of the angels; Brother James, member of the blessed." Assured about the death of Brother James, and joyful about the salvation of his soul, he left the place at Massa where he had this vision, and went to that of Mogliano, where he found the sick man so weighed down with illness that he could hardly speak. Brother John announced to him that he was about to die, and that like a lion, rejoicing and assured, he would be passing into life.

⁹Brother James, now certain about his salvation, was overjoyed both in mind and expression and received Brother John with a beautiful smile and joyful face, because he had brought such happy news to him, and because he loved Brother John like a son. And commending himself intimately to Brother James, he indicated to him that he was already being freed from his body. Brother John asked him please to speak to him after death. Brother James promised to do this, if the kind Savior would permit it.

¹¹After these things were said and the hour of departure approached, Brother James began to say devoutly: "Oh, *in peace;* Oh, *in Him;* Oh, *I will sleep;* Oh, *I will rest!*" As he said his, he passed to the Lord with a joyful and cheerful expression.

Ps 4:9

¹²Brother John returned to Massa and awaited Brother James's promise on the day when he had said that he would speak to him. While he was waiting Christ appeared to him with great brightness and with a magnificent escort of angels and saints.

¹³Brother John remembered Brother James and commended him to Christ. After this, on the following day, when Brother John was staying in the woods at Massa, Brother James, totally glorious and happy, appeared to him escorted by angels. Brother John said to him: "Oh Father, why didn't you come to talk to me on the day you promised?" He replied: "Because I was in need of some purging; but at the same moment when Christ appeared to you, I appeared to the lay brother James of Massa, a living saint, who was serving at Mass where at the time of the elevation he saw that the sacred host turned into a living, very handsome boy. Then I said to this brother: 'Today I'm going with that Boy to the kingdom of heaven, because no one can go there except through Him.' And you, Brother John, when you commended me to Christ, your prayer was heard, and at the same time I was speaking to Brother James, I was set free."

¹⁷And when he finished speaking, he went to the Lord. Brother John remained greatly consoled. And Brother James of Falerone passed on the vigil of Saint James the Apostle, whose feast is kept in

the month of July, and he rests at Monte Mogliano where he performed many miracles.

To the praise of Christ.

Amen.

LIII
BROTHER JOHN POSSESSES THE SPIRIT OF REVELATION

[1]Certain people had dreadful and hidden sins which no one could know except through divine revelation. Some of these had died, and some were still living. Through divine revelation Brother John disclosed their hidden sins to those who were still alive.

[2]As a result of this, they were converted to penance. One of them said that the sin which Brother John disclosed was committed before Brother John was born to the world. The one to whom this happened told me. And they declared that the things Brother John had said about them were true.

[4]It was revealed to him that some of them who had died perished in both a temporal and eternal death, and some, in only a temporal death; and this was demonstrated to him with certitude. And I saw a trustworthy brother who knew those people.

To the praise of our Lord Jesus Christ.

Amen.

LIV
A BROTHER SEES HIS BROTHER'S SOUL BEING CARRIED BY ANGELS

[1]After the death of our blessed father Francis there were two brothers who were Brothers in the Order, Brother Pacifico and Brother Humilis, men of wonderful holiness and perfection. When one of them died at Soffiano, the other was staying in a place far away. While he was praying in a solitary, deserted place the hand of the Lord came over him and, rapt in ecstasy, he saw his brother's soul rise into heaven without any delay.

[2]After many years had passed, the brother who was still living was assigned to the family at Soffiano where his brother was buried. Then, at the request of the lords of Brunforte, the place at Soffiano was exchanged for another place, and the brothers also transferred there the remains of the holy brothers.[a] When they came to the tomb

---

a. According to G. Pagnani, the lord of Brunforte, a castle near Valaiano in the Province of the Marche, was Rinaldo (+1282), the father of the provincial minister of the Marche from 1344 to 1348. This Ugolino may well have been the source of this story, cf. G. Pagnani, *I viaggi di S. Francesco d'Assisi nelle Marche* (Milano, n.p., 1262), 61. Soffiano was abandoned in 1327 when the brothers moved to Sarnano.

of that brother's brother, with the greatest devotion he took his brother's bones, washed them with the finest wine, wrapped them in a white cloth, and would not stop kissing them with great devotion and many tears.

[4]The brothers were surprised by this and rather displeased because although he was known for great sanctity, he seemed to be weeping out of sensual affection in a worldly way; and, besides, they insisted that the bones of the other brothers deserved just as much honor. But he satisfied them when he said: "My dearest brothers, don't say: 'Blessed God! I'm drawn by affection for the flesh,' when I do for my brother's bones what I didn't do for others. I acted in this way because when my brother passed to the Lord I was praying in a place far from him, and I saw his soul ascend directly into heaven. So these bones are holy and are to be in the Paradise of God. It is for this reason that I do the things you see."

[6]The brothers, realizing his devout intention, were greatly edified and praised God, who does great wonders in His saints.

To the praise and glory of our Lord Jesus Christ.
Amen.

LV
BROTHER SIMON AND HIS MIRACULOUS LIFE[a]

[1]In the beginning of our Order while Saint Francis was still living there came to the Order a young man who was called Brother Simon. The Most High *provided* him with such graces *of blessing* and *sweetness,* and brought him to such an elevation of mind and contemplation that during his whole life he was a mirror of holiness. As I heard from those who had lived with him, he was very rarely seen outside his cell; but when he was with the brothers he always occupied himself in speaking about God.

Ps 21:4

[3]He never studied grammar but always lived in the woods; yet he would speak so profoundly and sublimely about God and the love of the blessed Christ that his words seemed supernatural. One evening when he went into the woods with Brother John of Massa to talk about God,[b] he spoke so sweetly about divine love that, as recounted by him who was with him, they spent the whole night this way, yet it seemed to them that they stayed only a short time.

---

a. There is a parallel between this chapter and ChrXXIVG 159-61.

b. James of Massa is undoubtedly the source of knowledge of Simon of Assisi. According to HTrb III 74, Simon was one of those brothers who escaped to the Marche between 1244-7, where he would have met James who, in turn, would have told Ugolino about him.

⁵Brother Simon enjoyed such sweetness of the Holy Spirit that, when he had an inkling of divine illuminations and visitations and of love, he would put himself to bed, as if he wanted to go to sleep, because the tranquil sweetness of the Holy Spirit required repose not only of the mind but also of the body. So he was often rapt into God during such visitations and was rendered completely insensible to exterior things.

⁷It happened one time that, while he was drawn to heavenly things, entirely inflamed interiorly and anointed by divine charisms and entirely insensible to external things, one brother, wishing to prove by experiment whether he truly was the way he seemed, placed a burning coal on his naked foot. Yet Brother Simon did not feel the coal at all and, even more than this, he suffered no harm even though that coal stayed on his foot until it had completely burned out.

⁹When he was at table with the brothers, before taking food for the body, he always offered his companions spiritual food. Once when he was speaking about God, a very vain youth of San Severino was converted to the Lord. In the world he was noble, refined, and lusty. But even though Brother Simon gave the young man the habit of the religion, he kept those clothes he had removed. This young man stayed with him to be formed by him. But our adversary, the devil, who strives to prevent everything good, *like a roaring lion* pounced on the young man, and with his evil breath made the coals glow, making such burning urges arise in the flesh that he gave up hope of being able to resist the temptation. So he went to Brother Simon and said: "Give me back the clothes I wore in the world, because I am not able to endure this temptation anymore." But Brother Simon had compassion for him and said: "Son, sit with me a little while." And as Brother Simon dripped the dew of divine words into the young man's ears immediately the whole temptation would be removed. And this happened several times, his asking for the clothes and the removal of the temptation. One night the violence of temptation urged him more than usual and he went to Brother Simon and said: "You must absolutely give back my clothes: there is no way I can stay any longer." But the kind father, feeling great compassion for him, said: "Son, come and sit with me a little while." The young man, in great anguish, sat down next to Brother Simon and lay his head on Brother Simon's breast. Then *raising his eyes to heaven* Brother Simon, feeling great compassion for him, prayed for the young man with great devotion and compassion. He was rapt into God and his prayer was also heard. While Brother Simon was returning from that rapture, the young man was totally freed from his

1 Pt 5:8

Lk 6:20; Jn 17:1

temptation as if he had never felt it, and the harmful ardor was turned into the ardor of the Holy Spirit; and his whole self burned for God because, as he was leaning against a burning coal, namely Brother Simon, he was wholly rekindled in the Lord. So later on when a criminal had been captured and was to have both his eyes torn out, this young man in fervor of spirit boldly approached the ruler in full council and with many tears and prayers begged him to grant him this grace: to take one of his eyes and leave one to the other man. When they saw the piety of the young man and his burning charity, they pardoned both of them. I observed this young man as an eyewitness.

[17]That same Brother Simon one day was staying in the woods, feeling great sweetness from the Lord, but some birds, called *gaulle,* were preventing this by their loud noise and cries. He ordered them in the name of the Lord Jesus Christ never to come there again. Amazing to say, for the next fifty years and more at that place of Brunforte in the Custody of Fremo, those birds were never seen or heard in the whole area around the place and everywhere in the distance. And I, Brother Ugolino of Monte Santa Maria stayed there for three years and observed this miracle as a fact, well-known both to lay persons and to the brothers of that custody.

To the praise of our Lord Jesus Christ.
Amen.

LVI

How Brother John of La Verna was rapt in an abyss of divinity[a]

[1]After Brother John denied himself all the pleasures of this world, he was solicitous in finding his consolation in God alone. As a result, when the principal solemnities of our Lord Jesus Christ occurred, he by the grace of God enjoyed new consolations and marvelous revelations.

[2]Therefore, it happened that the Nativity of our Savior was approaching, when he was sure that he could expect consolation from the humanity of the blessed Christ, the Holy Spirit, who knows how to dispense his gifts according to time and place, as he wishes, *not* paying attention to the proposal *of the one wishing* or *of the one running, but* to the wisdom of the Lord *of mercy,* did not give Brother John the consolation he expected from the humanity of Christ, but showed him rather such a most fervent love from the goodness of

Rom 9:16

---

a. There is a parallel between this chapter and ChrXXIVG 444-5.

God that it seemed to him that his soul was snatched from his body. For his body was inflamed a hundred times more than if he were in a furnace, and because of this ardor his spirit became uneasy and panted and was ardently brought to such a state that he would cry out in a loud voice. Due to an exceeding fire of love and a violent impulse of his spirit, he could not restrain himself from crying out.

⁶At the time when he experienced such great ardor of love, the hope of salvation became very strong in him and he did not believe that, if he had died at that moment, he would be passing through Purgatory. Such love as this, although not constant, lasted for half a year. The ardor, however, lasted for more than a year, so that for an hour he seemed to be breathing out his spirit.

⁸After this time he had visitations and innumerable consolations, just as I myself have seen many times with the eyes of faith and many others have frequently evaluated with care. For due to the excess of love and ardor he could not conceal these visitations: in fact, he was enraptured many times in my presence. On one particular night he was raised to such wonderful illumination that he saw all created things, celestial and terrestrial, in their Creator with all things disposed according to their rank: how, for instance, the choirs of blessed spirits are below God, and so too, the earthly paradise and the humanity of Christ. There were also the lower choirs which were similarly arranged, and he saw and felt how all things represent the Creator.

¹¹Afterward God raised him above every creature so that his soul was absorbed and assumed into the abyss of divinity and illumination, and was buried in the sea of the eternity and infinity of God, to such a degree that he experienced nothing created, nothing formed, nothing finite, nothing imaginable which the human heart could conceive or human tongue could relate. That soul of his was absorbed in that abyss of divinity and in that sea or type of illumination like a drop of wine absorbed in the depths of the sea. And just as the drop of wine finds nothing in itself but sea, so that soul saw nothing but God in everything, above everything, within everything and outside everything, and therefore he saw the three Persons in one God, and one God in three Persons. He discerned that eternal love which, as far as his humanity is concerned, prompted the Son of God to become incarnate in obedience to the Father, and he arrived at ineffable light by way of the incarnation and passion of the Son of God by meditating, by carrying the Cross, and by weeping over the Passion. For there is no other way by which souls can enter into God except through Christ who is *the way, the truth, and the life.*   Jn 14:6

[17]In the same vision he also saw whatever was done through Christ from the fall of the first man until the entrance of Christ into eternal life, who is the head and leader of all the elect who have existed from the beginning of the world, who are living now and will live in the future until the end, just as it was announced by the holy prophets.

To the praise and glory of our Lord Jesus Christ.
Amen.

LVII
Brother John sees the glorious Christ in the Host[a]

[1]Something wonderful and worthy of widespread remembrance happened to this same Brother John, as those who were present have related it.

[2]Brother John was staying in the place at Mogliano in the custody of Fermo of the Province of the Marches. On the first day after the octave of Saint Lawrence, that is, within the octave of the Assumption of the Blessed Virgin Mary,[b] he got up before the hour of matins. And with a great anointing of grace which the Lord gave him, he said matins with the brothers. After saying matins, he went into the garden, because he was feeling such an abundance of immense sweetness and delight which he had from the great grace of tasting in his mind the words of the Lord: *This is my Body,* that he let out loud cries and said in his heart: *This is my Body.*

Mt 26:26

[5]At these words he was illuminated by the Holy Spirit and the eyes of his mind were opened. He saw the blessed Christ with the blessed Virgin Mary and a multitude of angels and saints, and he understood this saying of the Apostle: *We all though many are one body in Christ and individually members one of another;* and that other one: *Thus you will be able to grasp fully, with all the saints the breadth and length and height and depth and to know the love of Christ which surpasses all knowledge;* because all is in that most high Sacrament which is brought about when *This is my Body* is said. When dawn came, so moved by that grace, he entered the church with anxious fervor of spirit, thinking no one could hear him, although there was a brother in the choir who heard this. Still feeling anxious because of the

Rom 12:5
Eph 3:18
Eph 3:19
Mt 26:26

---

a. There is a parallel between this chapter and ChrXXIVG 443-4.
b. That is, August 18.

immensity of the grace, he could not contain himself and let out a loud cry.

[10]As he approached the altar to celebrate the Mass which he had to sing, the grace expanded and that love increased; and he was given an ineffable feeling of God, which he could not in any way express in words. And fearing that this feeling and wonderful fervor would grow which would force him to stop the Mass, he did not know what to do, whether he should proceed or wait.

[12]Yet because he had once experienced a similar thing, and the Lord had so tempered it that he did not have to stop the Mass because of it, he was confident that he could proceed. Nevertheless, what he feared would happen did happen, because such divine fusions are not under human control.

[14]Therefore, when he came to the Preface of the Blessed Virgin, that illumination and gracious sweetness increased so much that, as he came to "on the day before," he was hardly able to endure such sweetness and delight. Then, as he came to *This is my Body,* he kept groaning: "This is," "this is," over and over and could proceed no further. He was feeling the presence of God and a multitude of angels and saints, and he almost fainted because of the immensity of the things he felt in his soul. So the guardian of the place hurried to the aid of the anxious brother and stood next to him, a brother with a lighted candle behind him. The rest of the brothers watched fearfully, together with many other men and women, with whom were some of the greater ones of the province.

Mt 26:26

[18]But Brother John, as outside himself from blessed and sweet joy, was standing there and not proceeding to finish the most holy consecration, because he was feeling the Lord Jesus Christ, who would not enter the host, or rather, the host would not be transubstantiated into Him, until he would add *my Body* to *This is.* And as the paradise of the mystical Body of Christ was shown to him, he was not able to bear such great majesty of the blessed Head, that is, Christ, and he cried: *my Body*! Immediately the appearance of bread vanished and the Lord Jesus Christ appeared to him, the blessed Son of God, incarnate and glorified, showing him that humility which made Him become incarnate, and makes him come daily into the hands of the priest. Such humility held Brother John in sweetness and wonder and indescribable delight that he was not able to complete the words of consecration. For the humility and regard of God our Savior for us is so amazing, as Brother John himself said, the heart cannot bear it nor was he able to control his words to describe it, and for this reason he was not able to continue.

Mt 26:26

Mt 26:26

Mt 26:26 ²³For this reason, after *This is my Body,* powerfully shaken, he fell backwards, but as soon as he said this, the guardian, who was standing beside him, held him so he would not fall to the ground. The brothers and the other men and women who were in the church came running, and he was carried, as if dead, to the sacristy. His body had become cold like the body of a dead man. The fingers of his hands were so tightly contracted that they could hardly be straightened or moved. He lay there, as if dead, from morning until late terce: it was during summer.

²⁵I was present for this, and I very much wanted to know what the Savior's mercy had done to him. Almost as soon as he returned to himself, I went to him and asked him for the love of God to be kind enough to tell me about it.

²⁶Since he had great trust in me, he told me in detail everything by the grace of God. Moreover, he said that before and while he was consecrating, his heart was melted like thoroughly dissolved wax; and his flesh seemed to have no bones so that he could hardly lift either his arms or hands to make the sign of the Cross over the host. He added that before he became a priest, he was shown that he would faint in this way during the Mass. But because he had read many Masses, and what had been predicted to him had not happened, he thought that he had been deceived about this. But about fifty days before the Assumption of the Blessed Virgin, he had been shown again that this would happen to him around the Assumption, but he had forgotten about this promise.

To the praise and glory of our Lord Jesus Christ.
Amen.

LVIII
BROTHER JOHN OF PENNA AND HIS ANGELIC CONVERSATION^a

¹When Brother John of Penna, one of the greatest lights of the Province of the Marches,^b was still a little boy in the world, a very handsome boy called to him one night and said: "Oh, John, go to Santo Stefano, for one of my brothers is going to preach there. Pay

---

a. There is a parallel between this chapter and ChrXXIVG 332-4.

b. Penna is Penna San Giovanni in the Province of Marcerata and was at the heart of the Custody of Fermo, therefore, in the Province of Le Marche. According to ChrJG 5, John was one of the first brothers sent to Germany who suffered abuse because of their ignorance of the language; he was later sent to Paris in 1231 to accompany the English brother, John of Reading, to Saxony where he had been nominated provincial minister, cf. ChrJG 60. He died in 1274/5.

attention to his words and believe his teaching, for I have sent him. But you have a long road to travel and then you will come to me."

[3]He immediately got up and felt a marvelous change in his soul. Going to the indicated place, he found a great multitude of men and women who had come from various regions to hear the word of the Lord. And the one who was to preach was called Brother Philip.[a] And he rose up and preached *not in learned words of human wisdom but in the power of the Spirit* of Christ, proclaiming the Kingdom of God. Now this Brother Philip was almost one of the first brothers who came to the March of Ancona; and few places had yet been taken in the Marches. When the sermon was ended, Brother John went to Brother Philip and said: "Father, if you will, please receive me into the Order. I will do penance willingly and serve the blessed Lord Jesus Christ." That brother, holy and enlightened man, seeing that the young man had marvelous innocence and a ready will, said to him: "On such and such a day come to me in the city of Recanati and I will have you received." A chapter was to be celebrated there at that time.[b]

[6]Since the young man was very pure, he said to himself: "This will be the long road that I have to take, as it was revealed to me, and then I will go to heaven." He went, therefore, was immediately received into the Order, and believed that he was going to God. However, in the chapter the Minister said: "Whoever for the merit of holy obedience wishes to go to the Province of Provence,[c] I will send him." When Brother John heard this, he wanted to go there, thinking to himself that perhaps this was the long road which he had to take but he was ashamed to tell anyone. Trusting in Brother Philip who had him received, he went to him and said: "Father, I beg you to get me this grace, that I may go to the Province of Provence to stay."

[9]The brothers of that time longed to go into foreign Provinces, that they might be *pilgrims and strangers* in this world, and *citizens with the saints in the household of God* in heaven. Brother Philip, recognizing his pure and holy intention, acquired permission for him to go to that province. Brother John believed that, after this journey was completed, he would go to heaven. He stayed in that province for twenty-five years and lived an exemplary life of the greatest

Margin references:
1 Cor 2:4, 13

LR VI 3 | 1 Pt 2:11; Eph 2:19

---

a. This is Philip the Tall.

b. The Provincial Chapter of Recanati in the Province of Le Marche.

c. According to Livarius Oliger, in addition to the Province of Le Marche, that of Provence was also a center for the Spirituals, possibly because of the presence of Hugh of Digne (+ c 1255). Hugh's *Exposition on the Rule* contained many of the seeds nurtured by Peter of John Olivi (+1298) and his followers, Ubertino da Casale, et al. Cf. Livarius Oliger, "Spirituels," in *Dictionnaire de Theologie Catholique* (Paris: Libraire Letouzey et Ané, 1941): 2532-8.

holiness, and every day he looked forward to the fulfillment of the promise made to him. And although he increased in every good behavior to the height of sanctity, and in that whole province was dear and beloved to both the brothers and the laity, yet he did not see his desire being fulfilled.

Ps 120:5-6

[13]One day while he was praying and weeping before the Lord because his *stay,* as it seemed to him, *was being* excessively *prolonged,* the blessed Christ suddenly appeared to him. At the sight his soul was melted. Christ said to him: "My son, ask of me what you wish." He answered: "My Lord, I don't know what to say. I want nothing but you; but I do ask you this: that you pardon me and forgive all my sins, and that you give me the grace to see you again when I will have the greatest need." Then the Lord said to him: *Your prayer has been heard.* Then Christ slipped away from his sight; and he remained totally comforted in the Lord.

Acts 10:31

[16]Finally, the brothers of the Marches, hearing his reputation, arranged with the General that he return to the Marches. When he saw the obedience, he said to himself: "This is the long journey, and when it is completed, I will go to God."

[17]After he returned to the province, he was not recognized by any of his relatives. He waited day after day for the mercy of God, and that the promise would be fulfilled. But the journey was prolonged further. After his return he stayed a good thirty years in the Marches, and during this time he had the office of guardian.[a] The Lord worked many miracles through him,[b] and among many other gifts he had the spirit of prophecy.

[18]Once when he was away from the place, one of his novices was tempted by the demon to apostasize from the Order. He made this agreement with the tempter: that, as soon as Brother John returned, he would leave immediately. When Brother John returned, he immediately called that novice to him: "Listen to me, son. First, I want you to go to confession." And as he went, Brother John said: "Listen to me, son, first." Then he recounted the whole temptation to him, and he said: "Because you waited for me and refused to leave without my blessing, God will give you this grace: that you will never leave this Order, but with the blessing of the Lord you will die in this Order." Then that novice was confirmed in his good will and became a holy brother. And Brother John himself related all this to me, Ugolino.[c]

---

a. He died in 1274/5.

b. Cf. BPr I 27, FA:ED supra.

c. That Ugolino heard this from John of Penna himself indicates that he had entered the Order before John's death in 1274/5.

²²Brother John was always tranquil of soul and quiet, and he rarely spoke. He was a man of great devotion and prayer; and, in particular, he never returned to his cell after matins. On a certain night after matins when he was praying, the angel of the Lord appeared to him and said: "Brother John, that journey of yours for which you have been waiting now for a long time is finished. Therefore, I announce to you on God's behalf that you may ask for any grace you wish, and that, moreover, *you may choose* for yourself either *one* natural day in Purgatory or *seven* days of affliction in this world."

2 Sm 24:12, 13

²⁵He chose the seven days of affliction and suddenly became ill with many different infirmities. He was tortured by fevers, by pains, by gout, by the cramps of intestinal distress, and by many other weaknesses. But worse than all these, an evil spirit stood facing him, holding a written list of all his faults and defects, and said to him: "Because of all these evil things which you thought and said and did, you are damned." The sick brother forgot all the good things he had done, nor did he remember he was and had been in the Order. He thought only that he was damned, just as the evil spirit was telling him. Therefore, when he was asked by anyone how he was, he replied: "Bad, because I'm damned."

²⁹On hearing this, the brothers sent for Brother Matteo the Elder of Monte Rubbiano, who was a very holy man who deeply loved Brother John. He arrived on the seventh day of these tribulations, greeted him and said: "My dearest brother, how are you?" He replied: "Bad, because I'm damned." Brother Matteo said: "Don't you remember that you frequently made your confession to me, and I absolved you fully? Don't you remember that you have served God for many years in the Order? Don't you remember that divine mercy exceeds all the sins of the world, and that Christ our blessed Savior paid an infinite price for us? You should have complete confidence that you will be saved, not damned."

³²And then, because the end of the seven days of purgation had arrived, the temptation left him, and in its place came blessing; and with great joy he said: "Brother Matteo, you are tired and it's time to rest, so I beg you, go and rest." As Brother John remained alone with an attendant, suddenly Christ appeared to him with great brilliance and a sweet fragrance, just as he had promised to appear again at the opportune time. And that brother, with hands joined and giving thanks, was united to his Head as an eternally chosen member, whom he had always loved and always desired, the Lord Jesus

Christ. Rejoicing and consoled in this way he passed to the Lord, and rests in the place at Penne San Giovanni.

To the praise of Our Lord Jesus Christ.

Amen.

LIX

THE BLESSED VIRGIN APPEARS TO A SICK BROTHER
IN THE PLACE AT SOFFIANO[a]

[1]In the March of Ancona, in a deserted place called Soffiano, there was of old a lesser brother, whose name I do not remember, a man of such holiness and grace that he seemed to be completely divine, and he was often rapt into God. Here, once when he was absorbed and lifted into God, as he had a remarkable gift of contemplation, birds of different kinds came and, in a very friendly way, settled on his head and shoulders, on his hands and arms, and there they sang wonderful songs.

Here, when he returned from his contemplation, he came with such joy of spirit that he seemed a man, or even an angel of another age, because then his face shone so wonderfully from the divine companionship of conversation that he provoked wonder and astonishment in those who saw him. Here, always staying alone, he would very rarely speak, and when someone asked him a question, he responded as if he were an angel of the Lord; and his words were always flavored with divine salt. Here, neither by night nor by day, did he cease praying and contemplating the things of God, nor did he rest his unconquered spirit from meditating on the eternal light, that is, Christ. Therefore, the brothers revered him with tender affection as another Moses. And in this laudable dedication he finished the course of his virtuous and heavenly life and, ardently persevering in God, he came to this end.

[6]And while he was so sick unto death that he could not eat anything and asked for no bodily medicine, but trusted in the blessed Jesus Christ alone, that is, the life-giving bread *that came down from heaven* and restores all things merely by a word, he merited by divine mercy to be wonderfully consoled by the most Blessed Virgin Mary.

Jn 6:33

[7]One day, as he was lying there alone, preparing himself for death with all his strength, the glorious Lady, the most blessed Mother of

---

a. There is a parallel between this chapter and ChrXXIVG 411-2. Concerning Soffiano, cf. 537 a.

Christ suddenly appeared to him with a great multitude of angels and holy virgins, and approached his sick-bed in a wonderful light. When he saw her, he was consoled and delighted in mind and body, and he asked the Queen of Mercy to beg her Son that by His Mother's merits He would lead him forth from the dark prison of the flesh. And while he asked for this with many tears, the Blessed Virgin replied, calling him by name and saying: *"Do not fear, son, your prayer has been heard.* For I have seen your tears, and I have come to you so you may be comforted a little before you depart." Tb 4:21; Acts 10:31

⁹Three holy virgins came with the Blessed Virgin, carrying in their hands three little containers of an elixir with such a wonderful fragrance and sweetness that it can hardly be described in words. The Blessed Virgin took one of the containers and as soon as she opened it, it filled everything with its fragrance. Taking a spoon in her glorious hands, she offered the sick man a dose of the first heavenly elixir. When he tasted it, he felt such grace and sweetness that he thought that his soul could not stay in his body, and he said to the Blessed Virgin: "No more, sweet Mother and blessed Lady! No more, O blessed Doctor and Savior of the human race! No more, because I cannot bear any more of such sweetness!"

¹²But the most kindly Mother and gracious Consoler encouraged the sick man, repeatedly offering him some of that elixir until the whole first container was empty. And after that first container or bottle was empty, the Blessed Virgin took the second. When the sick man saw it, he said: "O blessed Mother of God, if *my soul* almost *melted* completely at the fragrance and sweetness of the first elixir, how will I be able to endure the second? I beg you, blessed beyond all saints and angels, not to give me any more!" The blessed Virgin and Mother answered him: "Just taste a little of this, son." Sg 5:6

¹⁴And taking it, she gave him a little from the second one, saying: "Now you've taken as much as you need. Be strong, son, because I am coming quickly to lead you to the kingdom of my Son, for which you have always longed and which you have always desired." And taking leave of him, she slipped from his sight. He remained in such sweetness of spirit because of that mixture brought from the heavenly apothecary and administered by the hands of the most blessed Virgin Mary, that he was completely illuminated internally and the eyes of his mind were opened in such tranquility of the divine light that he clearly saw *in the book of* eternal *life* all who were to be saved until the day of judgment. And he was so filled to satisfaction by the sweetness of that elixir—for it was not earthly but heavenly medicine—that for many days he remained strong without any bodily food. And on the last day of his life, as he was talking and rejoicing Phil 4:3; Rv 13:8

with the brothers, in great joy of mind and rejoicing of body, he passed over to the Lord.

To the praise and glory of Our Lord Jesus Christ.
Amen.

LX
THE VISION OF BROTHER LEO REVEALED TO SAINT FRANCIS[a]

[1]At a time when Saint Francis was seriously ill, Brother Leo was serving him with great diligence and devotion. Once when Brother Leo was staying near Saint Francis and was praying, he was taken into ecstasy and led to a great, wide river with a strong current.

[2]As he was watching those crossing over, he saw some brothers carrying burdens enter the river. These were immediately overwhelmed by the strong current of the river and the devouring depth swallowed them. Some went a third of the way across, and then perished; some, half way; and some, all the way to the end; but because of the burdens and loads which they carried, all were drowned by the river in different ways according to their different kinds of baggage, and without any relief they all most cruelly perished. Brother Leo, seeing such danger, felt compassion for them. But then some brothers appeared without any burdens or baggage of any kind, in whom only most holy poverty was shining. Entering the river they crossed without any harm.

[5]Saint Francis, knowing by the Holy Spirit that Brother Leo had seen some vision, called to him after Brother Leo had returned to himself, and said: "Tell me what you saw." Then he related in detail all that he had seen. Saint Francis said to him: "What you saw is true: for the river is this world. The brothers swallowed by the river are those who do not follow evangelical profession and voluntary poverty. Those who crossed the river without danger are the brothers who have the Spirit of God, who neither possess nor seek anything earthly, anything of the flesh, but *having food and clothing they are content with these.* Following Christ naked on the Cross, they daily embrace the burden of His Cross and the yoke of His obedience which are light and sweet. Therefore, they pass from temporal things to eternal things easily and without danger."

1 Tm 6:8

ER IX 2

---

a. There is a parallel between this chapter and ChrXXIVG 69.

To the praise of our Lord Jesus Christ.
Amen.

LXI
BLESSED FRANCIS CONVERTS A NOBLEMAN

[1]The venerable father and admirable Saint Francis once came to the home of a powerful nobleman as a guest. He and his companion were received with so much devotion and generous courtesy that it seemed that nobleman was receiving angels as guests. Because of this courtesy Saint Francis nourished great devotion toward that man.

[2]That lord received Saint Francis as he entered the house with a friendly embrace and a kiss of peace. After he entered, the man washed his feet and dried them and kissed them humbly. He furnished a big fire and prepared the table with an abundance of every good thing, and while they ate, he waited on them with a joyful expression on his face. After the food was eaten, the lord said to Saint Francis and his companion: "Father, I give you myself and everything I have; whenever you need tunics or mantles, buy them and I will repay you. And be aware that I am prepared to provide for all your needs, because the blessed God has given me an overflowing abundance of everything necessary; and so for love of Him I gladly spend it on the poor and needy."

[4]For this reason Saint Francis, seeing how abundantly he provided things and hearing how abundantly he offered things, conceived such love for him in his heart that, as the man left, he said to his companion: "This man really would be good for our company! He is so grateful to God, so friendly to his neighbor, so generous to the poor, and so eager and courteous toward his guests. For courtesy, dear brother, is one of the qualities of God, who courteously bestows His sun and His rain and all things on the just and the unjust. Well-ordered courtesy is the sister of charity, the extinguisher of hatred and the conserver of love. And since I recognize so much divine virtue in this good man, I would gladly have him as a companion. So I want us to come back to him one day. Perhaps God will touch his heart so that he wants to join us in serving the Most High. Let us ask the Lord God to put this desire in his heart and that he be given the grace to put it into effect!"

[7]In an amazing way, after a few days passed, the Lord granted Blessed Francis his *heart's desire* and did *not* cheat *him of the wish of his lips.* After first praying, after some days Saint Francis said to his

Ps 21:3

companion: "Dear brother, let's go to that courteous lord, because I trust in the Lord that with courtesy this man will give himself as a companion." They set out on their journey and neared the house of that man.

⁸Blessed Francis, however, before going to him, said to his companion: "Wait for me, brother, because I first want to ask God to make our journey fruitful: that Christ, by the power of his most holy passion, may kindly grant us, little and weak as we are, the noble prey we are planning to take from the world." Saint Francis then gave himself to prayer in a place where he could be clearly seen by that courteous lord. By Christ's permission, as that lord was looking here and there he saw Saint Francis at prayer, standing devoutly in front of Christ, and the blessed Christ standing in front of Francis graciously and in great brilliance. And while standing in this light, Saint Francis was lifted up from the earth both in mind and in body.

Ez 1:3

¹⁰As that lord saw all this clearly, suddenly *the* saving *hand of the Lord came over him:* in body he left his palace; in spirit he despised the world; in fervor of spirit he ran to Blessed Francis. When he reached him, he found him standing on the ground and praying with great devotion. So that nobleman immediately gave himself to prayer in the same way. He prayed insistently that he would kindly receive him to do penance and to remain with him.

¹¹As Saint Francis saw and heard that what he himself desired was the very thing that man was asking; and he realized that this amazing *change* had been made *by the right hand of the Lord.* Getting up in joy of spirit, he rushed to hug and kiss him with devotion, returning thanks and praise to the Most High who had added such a knight to his army. And in the midst of this the man said: "Father, what do you command me to do? At your order I give everything to the poor, freeing myself of earthly things. Now here I am, ready to run with you after Christ!" And so it happened: by the merits and prayers of Saint Francis, he left all things and became a Lesser Brother of such perfect life and good behavior that through meritorious penance he finished with a praiseworthy ending.

Ps 77:11; 118:16

To the praise of our Lord Jesus Christ.
Amen.

LXII
IT IS REVEALED TO SAINT FRANCIS
THAT BROTHER ELIAS WAS TO APOSTASIZE FROM THE ORDER[a]

[1]While Brother Francis and Brother Elias were members of the family in a certain little place, it was revealed to Saint Francis that Brother Elias was damned and was to apostasize from the Order and die outside the Order. For this reason Saint Francis conceived such dislike for him that he refused to speak with him or stay with him. And if Brother Elias happened to come toward him, he would head in the opposite direction. Brother Elias noticed that Saint Francis had conceived some dislike for him, so one day he joined Saint Francis and, restraining him from fleeing with courteous force, he asked him insistently to be pleased to state the reason for which he kept fleeing his company and conversation. Saint Francis said to him: "Because it was revealed to me by the Lord that you're damned!" Brother Elias responded: "Reverend Father, I beg you for the love of Jesus Christ that you do not throw me away because of this but, like a good shepherd, after the example of Christ, seek out your sheep which is perishing; and pour out for me your holy prayers to the Lord that, if it is possible, He revoke my sentence of damnation. For it is written that God can change a sentence if a man makes amends for the crime. I have such faith in your prayers that, even if I were lying in hell, I would trust that you were praying for me and would feel some relief. So I beg you again that you commend me, a sinner, to the Lord, that He may kindly receive me to His mercy." And Brother Elias said this with great devotion and many tears.

[6]And Saint Francis, moved by fatherly piety and heartfelt compassion, committed himself to pray for him. And as he poured out prayers for him, he knew that he had been heard by the Lord in regard to revoking the sentence, that is, that he would not be damned at the end, though he certainly would apostasize from the Order and finish his life outside the Order.

[7]And so it happened. When Frederick, King of Sicily, rebelled against the Church and the pope excommunicated him for that reason, along with all those who gave him help or advice, Brother Elias, who was considered one of the wisest men of the world, was called by that king. And by going to him, he became a rebel to the Church and an apostate from the Order. Because of this he was excommunicated by the pope and deprived of the habit of his religion.[b]

---

a. There is a parallel between this chapter and ChrXXIVG 250-1.

b. Cf. ChrTE VI, in *Thirteenth Century Chronicles*, trans. Placid Hermann, introduction and notes by Marie-Therese Laureilhe (Chicago: Franciscan Herald Press, 1961), 122.

[8]While he remained excommunicated he became gravely ill. When his own brother heard about this—he was a lay brother who remained in the Order, a man of good life, upright and praiseworthy behavior—he went to visit him. Among other things he said to him: "Dearest brother, I am deeply saddened that you're excommunicated and will die without the habit outside the Order. If you can see a way that I can free you from such great danger, I'll gladly assume the task for you." Brother Elias said to him: "My dearest brother, I see no other way than that you go to the pope, and beg him for the love of Christ and blessed Francis, His sign-bearer, at whose advice I left the world, to absolve me from the excommunication and return to me the habit of the religion." His brother replied: "I'll gladly work for your salvation if I can get this favor."

[10]He went from the Kingdom of Sicily to the pope and humbly asked, for the love of Christ and Saint Francis, the favor mentioned above. And it happened that, by divine permission and with the help of Saint Francis's prayers, the Lord Pope granted to that brother that, if he found Brother Elias alive, he should absolve him, on his behalf, from the excommunication and return the habit to him.[a]

[11]That brother, leaving the curia, rushed toward the Kingdom of Sicily to absolve Brother Elias, as said above. By work of divine strength and the prayer of Saint Francis, that Brother found him alive, though he had left Brother Elias struggling and almost at the end. Receiving the papal absolution, and with his habit returned, he passed to the Lord. And it is believed that this favor gained for him at the end happened by the merits of Saint Francis, in whose prayers Brother Elias had rejoiced.

To the praise of our Lord Jesus Christ.
Amen.

a. According to a manuscript in the Sacro Convento of Assisi, the process of absolving Elias took place between May 2-6, 1253. Cf. Edward Lempp, *Frère Élie de Cortone: Etude Biographique* (Paris: Libraire Fischbacher, 1901), 179-87; Giulia Barone, "Brother Elias Revisited," GR 13 (1999): 1-18.

LXIII
BROTHER PIETRO AND BROTHER CONRAD
AND HOW THEY WERE TWO SHINING STARS[a]

[1]The venerable priest of God, Brother Pietro of Monticulo,[b] and Brother Conrad of Offida,[c] whose life was admirable in the sight of God and people: these two, like two shining stars of the Province of the Marches, were heavenly men and earthly angels. They were staying together in the Custody of Ancona, perhaps in the place at Forano, which pleased them very much because of the great love which attached them to each other in the bond of the Holy Spirit, so that they seemed to share one soul. They bound each other to an agreement that whatever consolation the mercy of God should grant to one of them should be revealed to the other in the charity of God.

[2]After agreeing to this pact, one day Brother Pietro was devoutly meditating on the passion of Christ, and how His most blessed Mother and John, His most beloved disciple, remained co-crucified with Him, and how our Blessed Father Francis stood crucified before the Crucified. And he had a devout curiosity to know which of them grieved more: the Mother who gave birth to Him; the beloved disciple, who slept on His breast; or the most devoted Francis, who was crucified with the Crucified.

2C 10

[3]While he remained in this holy and devout meditation with many tears, suddenly the Blessed Virgin Mary, Mother of God, appeared to him, and Blessed John the Evangelist and our blessed Father Francis, dressed in the brilliant robes of blessed glory, though Blessed Francis was dressed in a robe that seemed brighter than that of blessed John. As they stood before Brother Pietro, who was shaking with fear, Blessed John comforted him, saying: "Do not fear, dearest brother in the Lord, because we have come to console you and to solve your doubt. You should know that, even though His Mother and I grieved more than everyone over the Passion of Christ, after us Blessed Francis grieved more than everyone, and for this reason you see him in such great glory."

[6]Brother Pietro replied: "Most holy apostle of Christ, why does the robe of Blessed Francis seem more glorious than your robe?" Blessed John answered: "Because, while he was in the world, for the love of Christ he wore clothes more vile than I did." On saying this, John offered Brother Pietro a glorious robe that he was carrying in his hands, saying, "Take this robe, because I brought it to give it to you."

[8]And when Brother Pietro put on this robe, Brother Pietro started running, out of surprise and wonder—he was seeing this while

---

a. There is a parallel between this chapter and ChrXXIVG 410-1.

b. Cf. 527 b.

c. Cf. supra 318, infra 694-5.

awake, not while sleeping—and began to shout: "Brother Conrad!
Dear Brother Conrad! Hurry! Run and see something wonderful!"
During these words the holy vision slipped away. And after this, holy
Conrad arrived, to whom he told all of this in detail. And they were
both consoled by this, and returned thanks to God.

To the praise and glory of our Lord Jesus Christ.
Amen.

LXIV

HOW GOD OPENED TO BROTHER JAMES OF MASSA THE DOOR OF HIS SECRETS[a]

[1]Brother Giles of Assisi and Brother Marco of Montino knew of no
one in the world and believed there was no one greater than Brother
James of Massa for whom God opened the door to His secrets.[b]
Brother Juniper and Brother Lucido felt the same way. I made the
effort to see him, at the direction of Brother John, the companion of
Brother Giles.[c] When for the purpose of edification I was questioning
Brother John about something, Brother John said to me: "If you
wish to be instructed in things spiritual, hurry to talk to Brother
James of Massa, because Brother Giles desired to be illuminated by
him, and could not add anything to or subtract anything from his
talks . . ." And that his mind had passed over to hidden things, and
words are the words of the Holy Spirit, and that there is no man on
earth whom I desire so much to see.[d]

[4]Around the beginning of the ministry of Brother John of Parma,
this same Brother James was once enraptured and remained insensible for three days, so much so that the brothers began to wonder if
he were dead.[e] He was given the knowledge and understanding of
the Scriptures, and divinely given knowledge of the future.

[5]I asked him: "If what I heard about you is true, do not hide it
from me. For I heard that at the time when you lay as if dead for three
days, God showed you, among other things, the things which will
happen in the religion." For Brother Matteo, who was then the Minister of the Province of the Marches, called Brother James to him
after this rapture and under obedience ordered him to make known
to him what he had seen. Brother Matteo was a man of remarkable

---

a. There is a parallel between this chapter and ChrXXIVG 283-5.

b. In his HTrb IV 157, Angelo Clareno writes of James in these very words: *frater Jacobus de Massa, cui Deus aperuit ostium secretorum suorum* [Brother James of Massa to whom God opened the door of His secrets].

c. That is John of Perugia (+c. 1270), cf. FA:ED II 32.

d. The narrator moves unwittingly from the third to the first person here.

e. If this event took place "around the beginning of the ministry of Brother John of Parma," the date would have to be about 1247/8, a date which would seem to make James of Massa a young man.

meekness, holiness, and simplicity; and he frequently said in his talks with the brothers: "I know a brother to whom God manifested everything which is going to happen in the religion, and wonders if the hidden things which, if they were told, I do not say they could be understood, but they could even hardly be believed."

[8]Brother James, among other things he revealed to me, said something really astonishing, namely, that after the many things that were shown to him about the *status* of the Church Militant,[a] he saw a beautiful and very tall tree whose root was gold with branches of silver and leaves of gilded silver.[b] The fruit of the tree were men, all Lesser Brothers. The number of the principal branches was divided according to the number of the provinces, and each branch had as much fruit as there were brothers in that province. And he knew the number of brothers in the whole Order, and in each of the provinces, their names, their faces, their ages, their qualities, their offices, their ranks, their dignities, their sins, and their graces. And he saw Brother John of Parma standing on the highest branch in the middle of the tree. At the tips of the branches surrounding the middle branch stood the Ministers of the individual provinces.

[12]And after this he saw Christ sitting on a very large, dazzling white throne. He was sending Saint Francis out with two angels and there was given to him a full chalice filled with *the spirit of life.* And he was told: "Go and visit your brothers and have them drink of the chalice of *the spirit of life,* because the spirit of Satan will rise up and attack them, and many of them will fall and they will not try to rise."

[13]Saint Francis came to administer the spirit of life to his brothers according to what was commanded him. And beginning with Brother John he gave him the chalice full *of the spirit of life;* and he took the chalice from the hand of Saint Francis and quickly and devoutly drank it all. And when he finished drinking he was made as luminous as the sun; and after him Saint Francis gave the chalice *of the spirit of life* to all in turn. There were very few who received it with due reverence and drank it all.

[15]Those few who devoutly drank it all were all clothed in the brilliance of the sun; those, however, who poured it all out were turned into darkness. They became dark and deformed and terrifying, and like demons they were frightening to look at. Some drank a part, and the other part they poured out, and so according to what each one drank or poured out *of the spirit of life* given to him in the chalice by

Gn 6,17; 37:14;
Rv 11:11

Gn 6:17; 37:14;
Rv 11:11

Gn 6:17; 37:14;
Rv 11:11

Gn 6:17; 37:14;
Rv 11:11

Gn 6:17; 37:14;
Rv 11:11

---

a. The use of *status* in this passage suggests the influence of Ubertino da Casale and, more strongly, Angelo Clareno, cf. supra 145, n. 8, 146 c.

b. For the significance of the symbol of the tree, cf. supra 141.

Saint Francis, by the same measure each was clothed in darkness or light.

[17]Brother John was shining with light more than all who were on the tree.[a] He was entirely turned toward contemplating the abyss of the true light; and he realized that a great, strong whirlwind was about to rise up against the tree.[b] Leaving the very great height of the branch on which he was standing, and leaving the other branches behind, he hid himself on the more solid place of the tree's trunk. And while he was directing his attention to himself, Brother Bonaventure, who had ascended to the place from which Brother John had descended and had drunk part and poured out part of the chalice given to him,[c] was given sharp iron fingernails like sharp-edged razors for cutting hair.[d] Brother Bonaventure, moving from his place, wanted to make an attack on Brother John. But Brother John, seeing this, shouted to the Lord, and at the shout of Brother John Christ called Saint Francis, and gave him a very sharp stone called a flint, and ordered him: "Go, and cut on the living stone Brother Bonaventure's nails, with which he wants to tear Brother John to pieces, so that he cannot hurt him." Saint Francis went and cut Brother Bonaventure's iron nails, and Brother John stayed in his place shining like the sun.[e]

[23]After this a raging storm arose and rushed upon the tree and the brothers began to fall from it. The first to fall from the tree were those who poured out all of *the spirit of life*. But Brother John and those who had drunk all of *the spirit of life* were transported by divine power to the realm of life, light, and splendor. Those falling who were darkened were carried off by the ministers of darkness to places of darkness and misery.

[25]He who saw this vision understood in detail all that he was seeing, so he clearly distinguished and firmly remembered the names,

Gn 6:17; 37:14; Rv 11:11
Gn 6:17; 37:14; Rv 11:11

---

a. The image of John of Parma sitting on the tree of the Order is prominent in HTrb IV 174.

b. In HTrb IV, Angelo Clareno presents four reasons for the persecution of John of Parma, that is, the unfolding of the Fourth Tribulation of the Order: abuses against the *Rule*, Joachimism, sermons written by certain brothers that were Joachimistic, and, more spiritually, the plan of God. Thus, John, a champion of the Spirituals, is presented in this most positive light to contrast the "darkness" of Bonaventure.

c. Ugolino's portrait of Bonaventure is strongly influenced by Angelo Clareno. Angelo's HTrb III concludes with the statement that after he had become general minister, "the fourth tribulation began," on February 2, 1257 when at the Chapter of Rome John of Parma resigned and nominated Bonaventure of Bagnoreggio to take his place. What follows is suspect because of its prejudicial sources.

d. Jacques Cambell discovered earlier texts in which Francis himself had the "fingernails like sharp edged razors" in order to defend his brothers' souls. Cf. Jacques Cambell, "Glanes franciscaines Deux Manuscrits de la Compilation Venitienee," *Franziskanische Studien* 49 (1967), 341.

e. John of Parma went to Greccio where he stayed until 1289 prior to his death. He died in Camerino on March 19, 1289, and is buried there in the church of San Francesco. He was beatified in 1781.

the persons, the regions, the ages, and the offices of both sides, that is, of light and of darkness. That whirlwind and savage storm, justly permitted, lasted until the tree, torn up by the roots, crashed to the ground, broken and splintered by the whirlwind, and the storm vanished, dispersed to the four winds.

[27]When this whirlwind and storm ended, a golden shoot sprang up from that golden root; it was entirely golden and produced golden leaves and fruits and flowers. It is better to keep silent than to speak about the spreading, the depth, the height, the fragrance, the beauty, and strength of this tree.

[28]However, I do not want to omit this one thing which the one who contemplated this true vision said and which sounded remarkable to my ears. He said, "The manner of reforming will not be like the manner of founding, but entirely unlike it: for the working of the Spirit of Christ will choose uneducated youths without a leader, simple, overlooked, and despised people; and without example or teacher, in fact, contrary to the teaching and customs of the teachers, and will select them with holy fear and the most pure love of Christ. And after he will have multiplied such as these in various places, then he will send them a shepherd and leader who is completely divine, completely holy, innocent, and conformed to Christ.

To the praise and glory of our Lord Jesus Christ.
Amen.

Appendix

LXV
THE MIRACLE OF THE STIGMATA OF SAINT FRANCIS, WHAT HAPPENED IN A CONVENT OF THE FRIARS PREACHER[a]

[1]How worthy were those wonderful stigmata of Saint Francis is apparent from a certain venerable miracle which was evidently brought to view in a certain convent of the Friars Preacher. In that convent there was a Friar Preacher who in his heart so disliked blessed Francis that he could neither look at a picture, nor listen to a word, nor believe in his heart that Francis had been marked with the sacred stigmata. Therefore, when this brother was staying in a convent beyond the Alps, in the refectory of which was a picture of Saint Francis with the sacred stigmata, he was incited by his lack of belief

---

a. For another, more abbreviated version of this story, cf. infra 662.

and his ill will and secretly went and scratched the sacred stigmata off the picture of our holy Father so that they were in no way visible.

[4]On the following day, when this same brother was seated at table, he looked at the image of Saint Francis, and he saw the stigmata there in the places were he had erased them. They seemed to be new and like the first marks. He angrily thought that he had not scratched them off well enough in the first place. Watching for a time when no one was present, because he who does evil hates the light, he went and a second time scraped off the stigmata of the saint in such a way, however, that the base paint was not destroyed. On the third day, when the same brother was seated at table, he looked at the image of Saint Francis. And again he saw those sacred stigmata, more beautiful and new than they had ever appeared before. Then this brother, blinded by wickedness and led on by unfaithfulness, added a third sin to the second. He said to himself: "By God, I will blot out that stigmata in such a manner that it will never be seen again!" And as he did before, he watched for the time when the eyes of men would not see him; and, forgetting that the eyes of God make all things bare and open them to view, he took a knife and in a furious attack gouged out the signs of the stigmata from the picture by digging into the color and the base.

[9]As soon as he finished his gouging, blood began to flow, and with the blood violently spurting forth, it began to stain with blood the brother's hands, face and tunic. Terrified, he fell down as though he were dead. Like a stream that blood flowed down the wall from that sacred stigmata which were gouged by that miserable man. In the meantime the brothers of that convent came upon him lying on the ground as if devoid of life, and remembering his malice they were filled with sorrow. Seeing, moreover, that the blood continued to flow, they stopped up those holes with cotton and bandages, but they could not stem the flow of blood. Therefore, fearing that the laity would see it and as a result they would have to endure scandal and scorn, they devoutly thought that they should have recourse to Saint Francis. The Prior together with all in the convent took off their habits in front of the image of Saint Francis, and applied the discipline to their backs, and in tearful prayer they asked Saint Francis to forgive the offense of their brother and to graciously stem the flow of blood.

[14]Due to their humility their prayer was immediately heard. The blood flowed no more and the stigmata of the saint remained in all its beauty to be venerated by all. From that time on the brother became most devoted to Saint Francis. And, as the brothers at La Verna have testified, this same brother out of devotion made a visit

to La Verna. He brought some of the bloody cotton with him and gave it to the brothers.

[16]Out of devotion and with great tearful reverence he also visited Saint Mary of the Angels and all the places associated with Saint Francis. In fact, wherever he was able to find anything that was associated with the deeds and effects of Saint Francis, he would burst into such devout tears that he made even others weep.

[18]He also spoke about these miracles before many Lesser Brothers at La Verna and Assisi, but only in the absence of his associates, lest perhaps he bring opprobrium on his own Order. By the merits of Saint Francis this brother became so friendly with Francis's brothers that, just as he was not able to see them sometimes, so later strengthened by the love of God, he venerated them with the affection of brotherly love.

To the praise of our Lord Jesus Christ.
Amen.

LXVI
THE MIRACULOUS WORD SPOKEN BY BROTHER GILES OF PERUGIA[a]

[1]When the saintly Brother Giles was staying at Perugia, Lady Jacoba of Settesoli, a noble woman and very devoted to the Lesser Brothers, came to see him. Later Brother Guardian[b] of the Order of Lesser Brothers, a very spiritual man, came to listen to some good advice from him. In the presence of many other brothers, Brother Giles said this in the vernacular language: "Because of what a man can do, he arrives at what he does not wish to do."

[3]To make Brother Giles speak further, the Brother Guardian said: "I am surprised, Brother Giles, that man because of what he can do, arrives at what he does not wish to do, since man of himself can do nothing. I can prove this by many arguments: first, because 'to be able' to do something presupposes 'to be' something. Therefore, the operation of something depends on its essence, just as fire warms because it is hot. But man of himself is nothing. For this reason the Apostle says: *If anyone thinks that he amounts to something, when in fact he is nothing, he is only deceiving himself.* Therefore, if man is nothing, he
Gal 6:3

a. There is a parallel between this chapter and ChrXXIVG 102-4.

b. There is a discrepancy in the manuscript tradition here. Some manuscripts have the word *Geraldinus;* others have *Guardianus.* Cf. *Actus Beati Francisci et Sociorum Ejus: Nuova Edizione Postuma di Jacques Cambell con Testo dei Fioretti a Fronte,* ed. Marino Bigaroni and Giovanni Boccali (Sta. Maria degli Angeli, Assisi: Edizioni Porziuncola, 1988), 579, n. 776.

can do nothing. Secondly, I prove in this way that a man can do nothing: for if a man can do anything, he does it only because of his soul, or only because of his body, or because of both combined. It is certain that he can do nothing by reason of his soul only, because the soul without the body cannot gain merit or lose merit. He can do nothing by reason of the body only, because the body without the soul is deprived of life and form, and therefore it cannot act because every act is form. A man can do nothing by reason of both joined together because, if he could so something, it would be by reason of the soul which is its form. But, as has been said, if the soul outside the body Wis 9:15 can do nothing, much less can it when joined to the body, for *the corruptible body burdens the soul.* Now I set this example before you, Brother Giles. If an ass is not able to walk without a load, much less can he do it with a load. Therefore, by this example it seems that the soul is less able to operate when joined to the body than when free from it; but the freed soul can do nothing; therefore, neither can it when joined to the body."

¹⁰He made many more arguments, about a dozen more than the above, opposing Brother Giles in order to make him talk. All who were present were in admiration at these arguments.

¹¹Brother Giles replied: "Brother Guardian, your reasoning was faulty. Admit that you are wrong about all this." Smiling, the Brother Guardian confessed that he was at fault. But Brother Giles, seeing that the Brother Guardian was not sincere, said: "That admission means nothing, Brother Guardian, and when such a confession of fault means nothing, nothing remains for man to recover."

¹²Then Brother Giles spoke again: "Do you know how to sing, Brother Guardian? Sing with me!" Brother Giles took from his sleeve a lute made from a millet reed such as boys make, and beginning at the first chord he refuted and proved false all the twelve arguments in rhythmic words by using all the chords of the lute. Beginning with the first argument, he said: "I do not speak about the essence of man before creation, Brother Guardian, because it is true that because there was nothing then, he could do nothing. But I speak about the essence of man after the creation, to whom God gave free will by which he is able to gain merit by consenting to the good, and lose merit by not consenting to it. Therefore, you spoke badly and proposed a fallacy to me, Brother Guardian, because the Apostle Paul does not speak there about the absence of substance nor about the 1 Cor 13:3 absence of potency, but of no merit, as he said in another place: *If I do not have charity, I am nothing.* For this reason I have not been speaking of a soul freed, or of a dead body, but about a living man who by co-operating with grace can do good, if he wills; and by rejecting

grace, he does evil, which is nothing else but turning away from good. But you allege that the corruptible body burdens the soul. Yet Scripture does not say because of this that it takes free will from the soul, so that it could do neither good nor evil; but he wishes to say that the affections and intellect are impeded, and that even the memory of the soul is occupied with temporal things. Therefore, in the same place of Scripture we find: *The earthen shelter weighs down the* Wis 9:15 *mind that has many concerns,* because they do not allow the soul to think freely and to seek *what pertains to higher realms where Christ is* Col 3:1 *seated at God's right hand,* to the extent that the force of the soul's powers is impeded in various ways because of many kinds of occupations and also because of the powers of the earthly body; and therefore, Brother Guardian, you spoke incorrectly."

[19]He similarly refuted all the other arguments, so that the Brother Guardian again acknowledged that he was wrong, but this time from his heart, and that a creature could do something. Then Brother Giles said: "Your confession of fault is now worth something." And again he said: "Do you wish me to show you more clearly that a creature is capable of something?"

[20]Ascending to a certain area, he cried out in a terrifying voice: "O damned man lying in hell!" Then he in the person of the damned one responded in a mournful voice and in a way that terrified everyone: "Oh! Woe is me! Alas! Alas!" Brother Giles said: "Tell us why you went to hell." And he replied: "Because the evil I was able to avoid, I did not avoid, and the good which I was able to do, I rejected." And questioning him, he went on to say: "What would you do, if time were given you to repent, O damned rascal?" Brother Giles answered for him: "I would throw the earth little by little behind me in order that I might avoid eternal punishment. There would be an end to that, while my punishment is eternal."

[23]Turning to Brother Guardian he said: "Do you hear, Brother Guardian, that a creature can do anything?" Then Brother Giles said: "Tell me whether a drop of water falling into the sea imposes its name on the sea, or the sea on the drop of water?" He answered that both the substance and the name "drop" is brought into and absorbed by the name "sea."

[24]After saying this, Brother Giles was enraptured in the presence of all who were there. He understood that human nature, in contrast to divine nature, like the drop, was absorbed in the great—yes, in the infinite—sea of divinity in the Incarnation of our Lord Jesus Christ, *who is blessed forever.* Rom 1:25

Amen.

LXVII
BROTHER GILES SAYING VIRGIN BEFORE THE BIRTH, VIRGIN IN THE BIRTH, AND VIRGIN AFTER THE BIRTH CAUSES THREE LILIES TO APPEAR[a]

[1]At one time during Brother Giles's lifetime there was a great Master of the Order of Preachers who for many years endured the greatest doubt about the virginity of the Mother of Jesus Christ. For it seemed to him that it was impossible for her to be both mother and virgin. Yet, as truly a man full of faith, he grieved over such a doubt as this, and he wished that some inspired man would free him from it. Hearing that Brother Giles was an illustrious man, he went to him.

[3]The holy Brother Giles, knowing in spirit that he was coming, what his purpose was, and the battle he was enduring, went out to meet him. Before he reached the Friar Preacher, he struck the ground with his staff which he carried in his hand, and said: "O Friar Preacher, a virgin before the birth." And immediately a very beautiful lily sprang up where Giles struck the ground with his staff. Striking the ground a second time, he said: "O Friar Preacher, a virgin during the birth!" And another lily sprang up. Striking the ground a third time, he said: "O Friar Preacher, a virgin after the birth!" And immediately a third lily sprang up. After this, Giles fled.

[6]That Friar Preacher was entirely freed from the temptation, and from then on he always had a great devotion towards the holy Brother Giles.

To the praise and glory of our Lord Jesus Christ,
Who is blessed forever.
Amen.

Rom 1:25

LXVIII
THE WONDERFUL ADVICE BROTHER GILES GAVE BROTHER JAMES OF MASSA[b]

[1]Brother James of Massa was a holy and very devout lay brother who lived at the time of Saint Clare and of many of the companions of Saint Francis. Since he possessed the gift of ecstasy and wishing to get Brother Giles's advice, he asked Giles to counsel him on how he should conduct himself while enjoying this gift. Brother Giles responded: "Neither add nor subtract; and flee from crowds as much as you can." Brother James said: "What are you saying? Explain it to me, Reverend Father." Brother Giles replied: "When the mind is

---

a. There is a parallel between this chapter and ChrXXIVG 90.
b. There is a parallel between this chapter and ChrXXIVG 91-2.

ready to be introduced to that most glorious light of divine Goodness, it neither should presume to add anything, nor take anything away through negligence, and it should love solitude as much as possible, because the gift should be guarded."

> To the praise and glory of our Lord Jesus Christ,
> *Who is blessed forever.*   Rom 1:25
> Amen.

The Little Flowers of Saint Francis

IN THE NAME OF OUR LORD JESUS CHRIST CRUCIFIED
AND OF HIS VIRGIN MOTHER MARY.
IN THIS BOOK ARE CONTAINED CERTAIN LITTLE FLOWERS,
MIRACLES AND DEVOUT EXAMPLES
OF THE GLORIOUS LITTLE POOR MAN OF CHRIST
SIR SAINT FRANCIS
AND SOME OF HIS HOLY COMPANIONS.
TO THE GLORY OF JESUS CHRIST.
AMEN.

Chapter 1
THE FIRST TWELVE COMPANIONS OF SAINT FRANCIS[a]

We must first consider how the glorious Sir Saint Francis was conformed to the blessed Christ in all the acts of his life; as Christ at the beginning of His preaching chose *twelve apostles* to despise *all* worldly *things,* and to follow Him in poverty and in the other virtues; in the same way Saint Francis chose at the beginning of the foundation of the Order twelve companions who possessed highest poverty. And just as one of the twelve Apostles, the one called Judas Iscariot, became an apostate from the apostolate, betraying Christ, and *hanging himself* by the neck, so one of the twelve companions of Saint Francis, who was named Brother John of Cappella, became an apostate and finally hung himself by the neck. And to the chosen this is a great example and cause for humility and fear, considering that no one is certain of persevering to the end in the grace of God. And as those holy Apostles were admirable to the whole world for their holiness and humility, and full of the Holy Spirit, so these holy companions of Saint Francis were men of such holiness, that from the time of the Apostles the world did not have such admirable and holy men. For one of them was *caught up to the third heaven* like Saint Paul, and this was Brother Giles. One of them, that is Brother Philip the Tall,

DBF 1:1-9

Mt 10:2; 19:27

Mt 27:5

2 Cor 12:2

---

a. Since this is basically a translation and reediting of Ugolino Boniscambi of Montegiorgio's *The Deeds of Saint Francis and His Companions,* cross references, notes, and other critical apparatus have been omitted. Readers are advised to consult the corresponding chapters or paragraphs in BDF. This translation is based on: "*I Fioretti di San Francesco,*" *riveduti su un nuovo Codice da P.B. Bughetti* (Quaracchi: Collegio San Bonaventura, 1926), as found in *Fonti Francescane* (Assisi: Movimento Francescano, 1977), 1441-1624.

was *touched* on *the lips* by the Angel with the *fiery coal* like Isaiah the Is 6:6-7
prophet. One of them, and that was Brother Sylvester, *spoke* with God Ex 33:11
as one *friend* with another, as Moses did. One through subtlety of
intelligence *soared* to the light of divine wisdom like *an eagle,* that is, Hb 1:8
John the Evangelist, and this was the very humble Brother Bernard,
who explained the depths of Holy Scripture. One of them was sanctified by God and canonized in heaven while still living in the world,
and that was Brother Rufino, a gentleman of Assisi.[a] Thus all were
marked by a singular sign of holiness, as described in what follows.

Chapter 2
BROTHER BERNARD OF QUINTAVALLE,
THE FIRST COMPANION OF FRANCIS

DBF I 10-46 The first companion of Saint Francis was Brother Bernard of
Assisi, who was converted in this way. Saint Francis was still in secular clothing, though he had already despised the world, and was
going about all despised and mortified by penance, so that many
considered him a fool, and he was scorned as a madman and driven
away with rocks and mud by relatives and strangers, and he
remained patient as if deaf and mute to every injury and insult. Sir
Bernard of Assisi, who was one of the noblest and richest and wisest
people of the city, wisely began to consider Saint Francis: his great
scorn for the world; his great patience in injuries. Even after being so
despised and scorned by everyone for two years, he always seemed
even more constant and patient. He began to think and say to himself: "It cannot be that this Francis does not have great grace from
God." And he invited him for the evening for supper and lodging;
and Saint Francis accepted and dined with him in the evening and
lodged there.

Then Sir Bernard decided in his heart to examine his holiness. He
had a bed prepared in his own chamber, in which a lamp always
burned at night. And Saint Francis, to conceal his holiness, as soon
as he entered the chamber jumped into bed and gave the appearance
of sleeping. And Sir Bernard also, after a little while, lay down and
began to snore loudly, as if he were sleeping very deeply. Then Saint
Francis, truly believing that Sir Bernard was sleeping, during the
first time of sleep, got up from the bed and set himself to praying, lifting his eyes and his hands to heaven, and with great devotion and
fervor said: "My God, My God." Saying this, and sobbing, he

---

a. The original reads *Ascesi*, an ancient name for Assisi, used also by Dante Alighieri in the *Divine
Comedy*, cf. infra 883 f.

remained like this until early morning, constantly repeating: "My God, My God," and nothing else. And Saint Francis said this while contemplating and admiring the excellence of the Divine Majesty, which had kindly come down to the perishing world, and through Francis, His little poor man, had prepared to offer a healing remedy for his own soul and that of others. Enlightened by the Holy Spirit, or through the spirit of prophecy, foreseeing the great things that God would do through him and his Order, and considering his own incapacity and small virtue, he was calling and praying to God that, by His mercy and omnipotence, without which human frailty can do nothing, he should supply, help, and fulfill that which he could not do by himself. As Sir Bernard saw by the light of the lamp the very devout acts of Saint Francis, and considering devoutly the words he said, he was touched and inspired by the Holy Spirit to change his life.

Thus, when morning came, he called Saint Francis and said this: "Brother Francis, I am fully prepared in my heart to abandon the world and to follow you in what you will command me." Hearing this, Saint Francis rejoiced in spirit and said: "Sir Bernard, what you say is such a great and difficult thing that our Lord Jesus Christ must be asked for counsel. Pray to Him that He be pleased to show us His will about this, and to instruct us how we may put this into action. So let us go together to the bishop's residence, where there is a good priest, and we will have him say Mass and then we will stay in prayer until terce, praying to God that after three openings of the missal he may show us the way that pleases Him that we choose." Sir Bernard replied that this pleased him very much, so they got up and went to the bishop's residence. And after they heard Mass and had stayed in prayer until terce, the priest, at the request of Saint Francis, took the missal and, after making the sign of the most holy Cross, opened it three times in the name of our Lord Jesus Christ. And at the first opening there occurred that word that Christ said in the Gospel to

Mt 19:21

the young man who asked about the way of perfection: *"If you wish to be perfect, go and sell what you have, and give to the poor, and follow me."* At the second opening there occurred that word that Christ said to the

Lk 9:3

Apostles when He sent them to preach: *"Do not carry anything on the way, neither a staff, nor wallet, nor shoes, nor money."* Through this He wanted to instruct them that they should place all their hope in God for something to live on, and have as their whole intention to preach the holy Gospel. At the third opening of the missal there occurred

Mt 16:24

that word that Christ said: *"Whoever wishes to come after me, let him renounce himself, take up his cross and follow me."* Then Saint Francis said to Sir Bernard: "Here is the counsel that Christ gives to us: go, therefore, and do entirely what you have heard; and blessed be our Lord Jesus Christ, who has deigned to show us His evangelical life." Hearing this, Sir Bernard went off and sold what he had—and he was very rich, and with great joy distributed everything to the poor, to widows, to orphans, to prisons, to monasteries and hospitals. And in everything Saint Francis faithfully and carefully helped him.

And one, whose name was Sir Sylvester, seeing that Saint Francis gave so much money to the poor and made others give, grasped by greed said to Saint Francis: "You didn't pay me in full for those stones you bought from me to repair the church, but now that you have so much money, pay me." Then Saint Francis, amazed at his greed, and not wishing to argue with him, as a true observer of the holy Gospel, reached his hands in Sir Bernard's lap and, with his hands full of money, put it in the lap of Sir Sylvester, saying that if he wanted more, he would give him more. Sir Sylvester, happy with that money, went away and returned home. In the evening, thinking over what he had done that day, he reproached himself for his greed, considering the fervor of Sir Bernard and the holiness of Saint Francis. The following night and the next two nights he had from God this vision: from the mouth of Saint Francis came forth a cross of gold; its top touched the sky, and its arms reached from the East all the way to the West. Because of this vision he gave what he had for God, and became a Lesser Brother, and remained in the Order in such holiness and grace that he *spoke* with God as one *friend* with another, as Saint Francis found out more than once, as will be told more fully below. _{Ex 33:11}

Sir Bernard similarly had such grace from God that he was often rapt away to God in contemplation, and Saint Francis said of him that he was worthy of every reverence and that he had founded the Order, because he was the first who had abandoned the world, keeping nothing for himself, but giving everything to the poor of Christ, starting evangelical poverty, offering himself naked into the arms of the Crucified.

May He be *blessed* by us *forever*. _{Rom 9:5; 2 Cor 11:31}
Amen.

Chapter 3

BECAUSE OF AN EVIL THOUGHT THAT SAINT FRANCIS HAD
AGAINST BROTHER BERNARD HE COMMANDED THE SAME
BROTHER BERNARD TO WALK THREE TIMES OVER HIS
NECK AND MOUTH WITH HIS FEET

Sir Saint Francis, the most devout servant of the Crucified, had   DBF II
become almost blind and saw little because of severe penance and
constant weeping. One time among others he left the place where he
was and went to a place where Brother Bernard was, to speak with
him about divine things. On reaching the place, he found that he was
in prayer in the woods, completely lifted up and joined with God. So
Saint Francis went into the woods and called him: "Come," he said,
"and talk to this blind man." And Brother Bernard did not reply at
all, since he was a man of great contemplation and had his mind suspended and lifted up to God. But he had a singular grace in speaking
of God, as Francis had experienced more than once; and it was for
this reason that he desired to speak with him. After a pause, he called
him a second and third time in the same way. And each time Brother
Bernard did not hear and did not reply and did not come to him. So
Saint Francis left, a little discouraged, surprised, and unhappy
within himself that Brother Bernard, called three times, did not
come to him.

Leaving with this thought, Saint Francis, when he had gone a little way, said to his companion: "Wait here for me." And he went
away to a solitary place and, throwing himself down in prayer,
prayed to God to reveal to him why Brother Bernard did not reply to
him. And while he was there, a voice from God came to him that said
this: "O poor little man, what are you upset about? Should a person
leave God for a creature? When you called him, Brother Bernard was
joined to me. And therefore he could not come to you, nor respond to
you. So do not be surprised if he could not answer you. He was so
much outside himself that he did not hear anything you said." As
Saint Francis received this answer from God he immediately
returned to Brother Bernard in a great hurry, to accuse himself humbly of the thought that he had against him.

And seeing him coming, Brother Bernard went to him and threw
himself at his feet. And then Saint Francis made him get up and told
him with great humility about the thought and the irritation he had
against him, and how God had answered him about that. And he
concluded in this way: "I command you by holy obedience that you
do what I will command you." Brother Bernard, fearing that Saint
Francis might command something excessive, as he usually did,

wanted to avoid that obedience fairly, so answered in this way: "I'm prepared to do your obedience, if you promise then to do what I will command you." And Saint Francis promised. Brother Bernard said: "Now, father, tell me what you want me to do." Then Saint Francis said: "I command you by holy obedience that, to punish my presumption and the anger of my heart, I will now throw myself flat on the ground, and you put one foot on my neck and the other on my mouth, and in this way you walk over me three times from one side to the other, saying things to shame and insult me, and say specifically: 'Lie there, vile son of Pietro Bernardone! Where do you get such pride, when you're such a vile creature?'" Hearing this, Brother Bernard, though it was hard for him to do, even for holy obedience, fulfilled what Saint Francis had commanded him as courteously as he could. And having done this, Saint Francis said: "Now you command me what you want me to do, because I promised you obedience." Brother Bernard said: "I command you by holy obedience that every time that we're together you rebuke and correct me severely for my shortcomings." Saint Francis was greatly surprised by this, since Brother Bernard was a man of such holiness that he held him in great reverence and did not consider him subject to rebuke for anything at all. But from that time on Saint Francis took care not to stay with him much, because of that obedience, so he would not have to give any word of correction to one he knew was so holy. But when he wanted to see him, or hear him speak of God, as soon as possible he would move away from him and depart. And it was a great cause of devotion to see the great charity, reverence, and humility of Saint Francis, the father, and how he behaved and spoke with Brother Bernard, his firstborn son.

To the praise and glory of Jesus Christ
and the little poor man Francis.
Amen.

Chapter 4
THE ANGEL OF GOD PROPOSED A QUESTION TO BROTHER ELIAS,
GUARDIAN OF A PLACE IN THE VALLEY OF SPOLETO,
AND WHEN BROTHER ELIAS ANSWERED HIM PROUDLY,
HE LEFT AND WENT ON THE WAY OF SAINT JAMES,
WHERE HE FOUND BROTHER BERNARD, AND TOLD HIM THIS STORY

DBF III   At the beginning and foundation of the Order, when the brothers were few and places had not yet been taken, Saint Francis in his

devotion went to Santiago in Galicia, and took with him some brothers, among whom was Brother Bernard. And as they were going
together along the road, in a certain village he came upon a sick little
poor man. Having compassion for him, he said to Brother Bernard:
"Son, I want you to remain here to serve this sick man." And Brother
Bernard, humbly kneeling and bowing his head, accepted the holy
father's obedience and remained in that place. And Saint Francis
with the other companions went to Santiago. When they arrived
there, remaining in prayer during the night in the Church of Saint
James, God revealed to Saint Francis that he must take many places
throughout the world since his Order was to expand and grow into a
great multitude of brothers. And because of this revelation Saint
Francis began to take places in those regions. As Saint Francis was
returning by the way he took earlier, he again found Brother Bernard; and the sick man, with whom he had left him, was perfectly
healed. So Saint Francis allowed Brother Bernard to go to Santiago
the following year.

   And thus Saint Francis returned to the Valley of Spoleto. And he
stayed in a deserted place, he and Brother Masseo and Brother Elias,
and some others, all of whom were very careful not to annoy or distract Saint Francis from prayer. They did this because of the very
great reverence they had for him, and because they knew that God
revealed great things to him in his prayers. It happened one day that,
while Saint Francis was at prayer in the woods, a handsome young
man dressed for travelling came to the door of the place and knocked
so fast and loud and long that the brothers were very surprised at
such an odd way of knocking. Brother Masseo went and opened the
door and said to that young man: "Where do you come from, son? It
seems that you've never been here before if you knocked in such an
odd way." And the young man replied: "And how should I knock?"
Brother Masseo said: "Knock three times, one after the other, slowly,
then wait long enough for the brother to say the 'Our Father' and
come to you." The young man replied: "I'm in a hurry. That's why I
knocked so loudly. I've got a long journey to make and I've come here
to talk to Brother Francis. But he's in the woods now in contemplation, so I don't want to disturb him. But go, send Brother Elias to me.
I want to ask him a question, because I understand he's very wise."
Brother Masseo went and told Brother Elias to go to that young man.
Brother Elias was provoked, and did not want to go. So Brother
Masseo did not know what to do or what to reply to him, except to
say, lying, that Brother Elias could not come; he said he was upset
and did not want to come, since he was afraid of giving him bad
example. In the meantime, as Brother Masseo took a long time to

return, the young man knocked again as he had the first time. And shortly Brother Masseo returned to the door and said to the young man: "You didn't observe my instructions about knocking." The young man answered: "Brother Elias doesn't want to come to me, so go tell Brother Francis that I've come to talk to him, but since I don't want to disturb his prayer, tell him to send Brother Elias to me." So Brother Masseo went to Saint Francis, who was praying in the woods, with his face lifted up to heaven, and told him the whole message of the young man and the response of Brother Elias. And that young man was the Angel of God in human form.

Then Saint Francis, without moving from the place or lowering his face, said to Brother Masseo: "Go tell Brother Elias by holy obedience to go to that young man." On hearing the obedience of Saint Francis, Brother Elias went to the door very upset and opened it with great force and noise and said to the young man: "What do you want?" The young man replied: "Be careful, Brother. Don't get upset, as you seem to be, because anger impedes the spirit and doesn't allow the truth to be discerned." Brother Elias replied: "Tell me what you want from me." The young man replied: "I ask you if it's lawful for those who observe the holy Gospel *to eat what is set before them,* as Lk 10:7-8 Christ told His disciples? And I also ask you if it's lawful for any man to put forward something contrary to evangelical freedom?" Brother Elias replied proudly: "I know this well, but I don't want to answer you. Go mind your own business." The young man replied: "I'd know how to answer this question better than you." Then Brother Elias, upset and furious, closed the door and went away. Then he began to think about that question and to have doubts within himself, and he could not resolve them. He was the Vicar of the Order and had ordered and made a constitution beyond the Gospel and beyond the Rule of Saint Francis, that no brother of the Order should eat meat. So that question was directed expressly against him. Not knowing how to express himself, and considering the modesty of the young man, and that he had said that he would have known how to answer that question better than he could, he went back to the door and opened it to ask the young man about that question. But he had already left, since the pride of Brother Elias was unworthy to speak with the Angel. At this Brother Francis, to whom God had revealed everything, came back from the woods, and rebuked Brother Elias severely in a loud voice: "Proud Brother Elias! You do wrong: you drive away from us the holy angels who come to teach us. I tell you, I fear your pride will make you end up outside this Order." And so it happened with him, as Saint Francis foretold, because he died outside the Order.

The same day, at the same hour when that Angel departed, he appeared in that same form to Brother Bernard, who was returning from Saint James and was on the bank of a great river. He greeted

him in his own language, saying: *"Iddio ti dia pace, o buono frate."* And good Brother Bernard was very surprised, considering the beauty of the young man and the speech of his homeland; and with a peaceful

greeting and a happy expression asked him: *"Where do you come from, good young man?"* The Angel replied: "I come from that place where Saint Francis is staying, and I went to talk with him and could not, because he was in the woods contemplating divine things, and I didn't want to disturb him. And in that place dwell Brother Masseo and Brother Giles and Brother Elias. And Brother Masseo taught me how to knock on the door as the brothers do. But Brother Elias didn't want to answer the question I posed to him; then he regretted it and

wished to hear me and see me and couldn't." After these words the Angel said to Brother Bernard: "Why don't you cross over there?" Brother Bernard replied: "I'm afraid of the danger of the deep water I see." The Angel said: "Let's cross together; don't doubt." And taking his hand, in the blink of an eye he placed him on the other side of the river. Then Brother Bernard understood that he was the Angel of God, and with great reverence and joy said out loud: "O Blessed

Angel of God, tell me your name." The Angel replied: "Why do you ask my name, which is 'wonderful'?" And having said this, the Angel disappeared and left Brother Bernard much consoled, so much so that he continued along that whole journey in joy. And he considered the day and the hour that the Angel appeared to him, and, reaching the place where Saint Francis was staying with the companions mentioned above, he recounted everything to them in detail. And they understood with certainty that that same Angel, on that same day and at that hour, had appeared to them and to him. And they gave thanks to God.

To the praise of Jesus Christ
and the little poor man Francis.
Amen.

Chapter 5
HOW THE HOLY BROTHER BERNARD OF ASSISI
WAS SENT BY SAINT FRANCIS TO BOLOGNA
AND TOOK A PLACE THERE

DBF IV Saint Francis and his companions were called by God and chosen to carry in their hearts and preach with their works and words the Cross of Christ. They appeared to be, and were, crucified men, both in their habit and in their austere life, in their deeds and their works. Therefore they desired to endure shame and scorn for love of Christ rather than honors of the world or reverence or empty praise. Instead they rejoiced over insults and were saddened by honors. In this way they went through the world *as pilgrims and strangers,* not carrying with them anything besides Christ crucified. And because they were of the true vine, that is, Christ, they produced great and good fruit: the souls they won for God.

1 Pt 2:11

It happened, at the beginning of the Religion, that Saint Francis sent Brother Bernard to Bologna and there, according to the grace God gave him, he should produce fruit for God. Brother Bernard, making the sign of the most holy Cross, departed out of holy obedience, and arrived at Bologna. When the children saw him in an odd and rough habit, they made many jokes at him and insults, the way people do with someone crazy. Brother Bernard patiently and joyfully bore it all for love of Christ. In fact, so that he could be insulted more easily, he deliberately placed himself in the city's piazza. As he was sitting there many children and adults gathered around him, and they pulled his capuche, one backwards, one forward; some threw stones, and others, dirt; and they pushed him here and there. Brother Bernard, always with the same manner, and with the same patience, and with a happy expression, did not complain and did not move. What is more, he returned to that same place, just to endure similar things. Because patience is a work of perfection and a proof of virtue, a wise doctor of law, seeing and considering such constancy and virtue in Brother Bernard, who could not be disturbed by any annoyance or insult after so many days, said to himself: "It's impossible that he's not a holy man." Drawing near to him he asked him: "Who are you and why have you come here?" And Brother Bernard answered by putting his hand to his chest and taking out the Rule of Saint Francis, and gave it to him to read. On reading it, considering its most high state of perfection, with great surprise and wonder the man turned to his companions and said: "Truly this is the highest state of religion that I ever heard of; so this one and his companions are some of the holiest men in this world. And whoever insults them commits the greatest of sins. He should instead be honored most highly, since he's a friend of God." And he said to Brother Bernard: "If you want to take a place in which you can serve God fittingly, I'll gladly give it to you for the good of my soul." Brother Bernard replied: "Sir, I believe that our Lord Jesus Christ inspired you to do this. Therefore I gladly accept your offer, for the honor of Christ." Then, with great joy and charity that judge took Brother Bernard to his house. And then he gave him the place he promised, and he prepared it all and finished it at his own expense. From that moment on he became the father and special defender of Brother Bernard and his companions.

And Brother Bernard began to be greatly honored by the people because of his holy way of living, so much so, that whoever could touch or see him considered himself blessed. But he, as a true disciple of Christ and of the humble Francis, fearing that the honor of the world might be an obstacle to the peace and health of his soul, left one day and returned to Saint Francis and said to him: "Father, the place in the city of Bologna has been taken. Send some brothers there to keep it and stay there, because I wasn't making any profit there. Rather, because of the excessive honor given me there, I fear I'd lose more there than I'd gain." Then, on hearing in detail everything that God had accomplished through Brother Bernard, Saint Francis thanked God, who in this way began to spread the poor little disciples of the Cross, and he then sent some of his companions to Bologna and into Lombardy, and they took many places in various areas.

To the praise of Jesus Christ
and the little poor man Francis.
Amen.

Chapter 6
HOW SAINT FRANCIS BLESSED HOLY BROTHER BERNARD
AND LEFT HIM AS HIS VICAR WHEN ABOUT TO PASS FROM THIS WORLD

Brother Bernard was a man of such great holiness that Saint   _{DBF V} Francis held him in great reverence and often praised him. One day, as Saint Francis was devoutly in prayer, it was revealed to him by God that Brother Bernard, by divine permission, would have to endure many and diverse and fierce battles with demons. Because of this Saint Francis, having great compassion for the same Brother Bernard, whom he loved as his dear son, prayed tearfully for many days, praying to God for him and commending him to Jesus Christ, that he should give him victory over the demon. And while Saint Francis was praying devoutly in this way God one day replied to him: "Francis, do not be afraid, because all the temptations by which Brother Bernard is to be attacked are permitted by God as an exercise of virtue for him and a crown of merit, and he will finally have the victory over all his enemies, because he is one of the guests of the banquet of the Kingdom of heaven." At this reply, Saint Francis had *great joy* and thanked God. And from that moment on he always bore greater love and reverence toward him.

Mt 2:10

And he clearly showed this toward him not only during his life but also at his death. For when Saint Francis was approaching death like that holy patriarch Jacob, with his devoted sons standing around him, grieving and tearful at the departure of such a lovable father, he asked: "Where is *my firstborn?* Come to me, dear son, so *my soul may bless you* before *I die."* Then Brother Bernard said secretly to Brother Elias, who was Vicar of the Order: "Father, go to the right hand of the Saint, so he may bless you." Brother Elias placed himself at his right hand and Saint Francis, who had lost his sight from so many tears, put his right hand on the head of Brother Elias and said: "This is not the head of the firstborn, Brother Bernard." Then Brother Bernard went to him, at his left hand, and Saint Francis crossed his arms like a cross, and then *placed his right hand on the head* of Brother Bernard, and *the left on the head* of Brother Elias, and said: "Brother Bernard, *may the Father of our Lord Jesus Christ bless you with every spiritual and heavenly blessing in Christ,* since you are the firstborn chosen in this holy Order to give an evangelical example, following Christ in evangelical poverty. For you not only gave away what was yours and distributed it entirely and freely to the poor for love of Christ, but you also offered your own self to God in this Order as *a fragrant sacrifice.* Therefore may you be blessed by our Lord Jesus Christ and by me, His poor little servant, with eternal blessings, whether moving or staying, waking or sleeping, living or dying. And *may whoever blesses you be filled with blessings: whoever curses you* will not remain unpunished. May you *be the* first *among your brothers,* and let all the brothers obey your command. You have permission to receive into this Order anyone you wish, and no brother is to have lordship over you, and let it be permitted for you to go and stay wherever you please."

Gn 49:3; Gn 27:4

Gn 48:14

Eph 1:3

Lv 2:9

Gn 27:29

And after the death of Saint Francis the brothers loved and revered Brother Bernard as a venerable father And as he approached death, many brothers from diverse regions of the world came to him. Among them came that hierarchic and divine Brother Giles. When he saw Brother Bernard, he said with great joy: *"Sursum corda,*

Brother Bernard, *sursum corda!"* And the holy Brother Bernard secretly told a brother to prepare for Brother Giles a place suitable for contemplation, and so it was done. As Brother Bernard was at the last hour of death, he had himself raised, and spoke to the brothers in front of him, saying: "Dearest brothers, I don't want to say many words to you, but you must consider that the state of the religion that I have had, you have; and what I have now, you will also have. And I know this in my soul: even for a thousand worlds equal to this one I would not wish to have served another lord besides our Lord Jesus Christ. And for every offense I have done, I accuse myself and declare myself at fault, to my Savior Jesus Christ and to you." And after these words and other good instructions, he lay down again on the bed, and his face became radiant and happy beyond measure, and all the brothers marveled greatly at this. And in that joy his most holy soul, crowned with glory, passed from the present life to the blessed life of the Angels.

To the praise of Jesus Christ
and the little poor man Francis.
Amen.

Chapter 7
HOW SAINT FRANCIS MADE A LENT
ON AN ISLAND IN THE LAKE OF PERUGIA
WHERE HE FASTED FORTY DAYS AND FORTY NIGHTS
AND ATE NOTHING BUT HALF A LOAF OF BREAD

The true servant of Christ, Saint Francis, was in certain things like another Christ given to the world for the people's salvation. So God the Father willed to make him in many of his actions conformed and similar to His Son, Jesus Christ. This is shown to us in the venerable company of the twelve companions and in the wondrous mystery of the sacred Stigmata and in the unbroken fast of the holy Lent which he made in the following way.

Once Saint Francis was alongside the Lake of Perugia on the day of Carnival, at the house of a man devoted to him, where he was lodged for the night. He was inspired by God to go to make that Lent on an island in the lake. So Saint Francis asked this devout man that, for love of Christ, he carry him with his little boat to an island of the lake where no one lived, and that he do this on the night of the Day of the Ashes, so that no one would notice. And this man, out of love—from the great devotion he had for Saint Francis—promptly

DBF VI

fulfilled his request and carried him to that island. And Saint Francis took nothing with him except two small loaves of bread. Arriving at the island, as his friend was departing to return home, Saint Francis asked him kindly not to reveal to anyone that he was there, and that he should not come for him until Holy Thursday. And so that man departed, and Saint Francis remained alone.

Since there was no dwelling in which he could take shelter, he went into some very thick brush that was formed like a little den or a little hut by many bushes and saplings. And in this place he put himself in prayer and contemplation of heavenly things. And there he stayed the whole of Lent without eating or drinking, except for half of one of those little loaves, as his devoted friend found on Holy Thursday when he returned for him; for of the two loaves he found one whole one and a half; the other half, it is supposed, Saint Francis ate, out of reverence for the fast of the blessed Christ, who fasted for *forty days and forty nights* without taking any material food. And thus, with that half of a loaf he drove away from himself vainglory, and after the example of Christ he fasted forty days and forty nights.

Later in that place where Saint Francis had done such marvelous abstinence, God did many miracles through his merits. For this reason the people began to build houses and live there, and in a short time a good, large village was built there, and there was a place of the brothers there, called the Place of the Island, and the men and women of that village still have great reverence and devotion for that place where Saint Francis made that Lent.

To the praise of Jesus Christ
and the little poor man Francis.
Amen.

Chapter 8
HOW SAINT FRANCIS, WALKING ALONG THE ROAD WITH BROTHER LEO, EXPLAINED TO HIM THOSE THINGS THAT ARE PERFECT JOY

As Saint Francis was once going with Brother Leo from Perugia to Saint Mary of the Angels in wintertime, and the very great cold stung him sharply, he called Brother Leo, who was walking in front and said this to him: "Brother Leo, if it should happen that the Lesser Brothers in every land should give great example of holiness and give good edification, nonetheless write and note carefully that perfect joy is not in that." And walking along further Saint Francis called

Mt 11:4 him a second time: "O Brother Leo, even if a Lesser Brother gives sight to *the blind,* straightens the crippled, drives out the attacks of demons, restores hearing *to the deaf* and walking to the lame, speech to the mute and, what is even a greater thing, raises those *dead* for four days, write that perfect joy is not in that." And walking on a little, Saint Francis cried out loudly, "O Brother Leo, if a Lesser Brother

1 Cor 13:2 knew all *languages,* all the sciences and all the Scriptures, if he knew how to *prophesy* and reveal, not only future things, but also the secrets of consciences and people, write that perfect joy is not in that." Walking on a bit further Saint Francis cried out even louder, "O Brother Leo, little lamb of God, even though a Lesser Brother may

1 Cor 13:2 *speak with the tongue of an angel,* and know the courses of the stars and the powers of herbs, and all the treasures of the earth were revealed

1 Kgs 5:13 to him, and he knew the virtues of birds, *fish* and all animals and stones and waters, write that perfect joy is not in that." And walking along a bit, Saint Francis cried out loudly, "O Brother Leo, even if a Lesser Brother knew how to preach so well that he converts all the unbelievers to the faith of Christ, write that perfect joy is not in that."

This way of talking had lasted for a good two miles, when Brother Leo with great amazement asked him and said, "Father, I ask you, for the sake of God, to tell me where perfect joy is." And Saint Francis replied to him, "When we come to Saint Mary of the Angels, soaked with rain like this and frozen from the cold and covered with mud and suffering from hunger, and we knock at the door of the place, and the porter comes out angrily and says, 'Who are you?' and we say, 'We are two of your brothers,' and he says, 'You're not telling the truth: you two are scoundrels who go around tricking people and stealing the alms of the poor. Go away,' and he doesn't open for us, and makes us stay outside in the snow and water, cold and hungry until nighttime, then we patiently endure such insults and cruelty and abuses without becoming upset or complaining about him, and think humbly that that porter in fact recognizes us, that it is God who makes him speak against us: O Brother Leo, write that here is perfect joy. And if we even continue knocking and he comes out upset, and drives us away with curses and blows, like aggravating vagrants, saying 'Get out of here, you dirty little thieves, go to the hospital, because you're not going to eat here or stay here;' if we endure this patiently and with happiness and good love, O Brother Leo, write that here is perfect joy. And if, driven by hunger and cold and night, we knock even more and call out and beg for the love of God with loud crying that he open the door for us and let us at least come inside, and he becomes angrier and says, 'These are aggravating vagrants, I'll pay them well for what they're worth,' and comes outside with a knobby stick and grabs us by the capuche and throws us on the ground and rolls us in the snow and beats us from head to toe with that stick; if we endure these things patiently and with happiness, thinking of the sufferings of the blessed Christ, which we must endure for His love, O Brother Leo, write that here and in this is perfect joy. But hear the conclusion, Brother Leo. Above all the graces and gifts of the Holy Spirit, which Christ grants to His friends, is that of conquering our own selves and gladly, for the love of Christ, to endure sufferings, injuries and insults and difficulties, because we cannot glory in all the other gifts of God, since they are not ours but God's, as the Apostle says, *'What do you have that you do not have from God, and if you have had it from Him, why do you boast of it, as if you had it from yourself?'* But in the cross of trouble and affliction we can glory, as the Apostle says, *'I do not want to glory except in the cross of our Lord Jesus Christ.'* "

1 Cor 4:7

Gal 6:14

To the praise of Jesus Christ
and of the little poor man Francis.
Amen.

Chapter 9
HOW SAINT FRANCIS TAUGHT BROTHER LEO TO RESPOND
BUT HE COULD ONLY SAY THE OPPOSITE OF WHAT FRANCIS WANTED

DBF VIII

Once at the beginning of the Order Saint Francis was with Brother Leo in a place where they did not have books for saying the Divine Office. When the time for Matins came, Saint Francis said to Brother Leo: "Dearest Brother, we do not have a breviary with which we can say Matins; but so that we may spend the time in praising God, I'll speak and you'll respond as I teach you. And be careful that you don't change the words into something different from what I teach you. I'll say this: 'O, Brother Francis, you have done so many evil things and so many sins in the world that you are worthy of hell.' And you, Brother Leo, will respond: 'That's true: you deserve the lowest place in hell.' " And Brother Leo with dove-like simplicity responded: "Of course, Father, begin, in the name of God." Then Saint Francis began to say, "O Brother Francis, you have done so many evil things and so many sins in the world that you are worthy of hell." And Brother Leo responded, "God will do so many good things for you that you will go to Paradise." Saint Francis said, "Don't say that, Brother Leo! When I say, 'Brother Francis, you have done so many evil things against God that you deserve to be cursed by God,' you will respond like this: 'Truly, you deserve to be put among the cursed.' " And Brother Leo responded, "Of course, Father." Then Saint Francis, with many tears and groans and beating his breast said in a loud voice, "O my Lord of heaven and earth, I have committed so many iniquities and sins against you, that I thoroughly deserve to be cursed by You." And Brother Leo responded, "O Brother Francis, God will do so much for you that you will be singularly blessed among the blessed." And Saint Francis, surprised that Brother Leo responded the opposite of what he had told him, rebuked him in this way: "Why don't you respond the way I teach you? I command you by holy obedience to respond as I teach you. I will say this: 'O evil little Brother Francis, do you think God will have

2 Cor 1:3

mercy on you? You have committed so many sins against *the Father of mercy and God of every consolation,* that you don't deserve to find mercy.' And you, Brother Leo, little lamb, will respond: 'You in no way deserve to find mercy.' " But when Saint Francis said, "O evil little Brother Francis," etc., Brother Leo responded: "God the Father, whose mercy is infinitely more than your sin, will have great mercy on you, and on top of this He will add many graces." At this response, Saint Francis, sweetly angered and patiently upset, said to Brother Leo, "And why have you got the presumption to act contrary to obedience? You've already responded several times the opposite of what I've ordered you!" Brother Leo responded very humbly and reverently, "God knows, my Father: each time I tried in my heart to respond as you commanded me, but God makes me speak as it pleases Him, not as it pleases me." Saint Francis was surprised by this, and said to Brother Leo. "I beg you most dearly that you respond this time as I've told you." Brother Leo responded, "In the name of God, say it, and this time for sure I will respond as you want." And Saint Francis said tearfully, "O evil little Brother Francis, do you think that God has mercy on you?" Brother Leo responded, "More than that, you will receive great grace from God and He will exalt you

Lk 14:11

and glorify you forever, since *whoever humbles himself will be exalted.* And I cannot say anything else, since God speaks through my mouth." And so, in this humble contest, with many tears and much spiritual consolation, they kept vigil until daybreak.

To the praise of Jesus Christ
and the poor little man Francis.
Amen.

Chapter 10
HOW BROTHER MASSEO, AS IF JOKING,
TOLD SAINT FRANCIS THAT THE WHOLE WORLD
WAS FOLLOWING AFTER HIM;
AND HE REPLIED:
THAT WAS FOR THE WORLD'S CONFUSION AND BY THE GRACE OF GOD
BECAUSE I AM THE MOST VILE MAN IN THE WORLD

DBF X   Once Saint Francis was staying in the place of the Portiuncula with Brother Masseo of Marignano, a man of great holiness, discernment and grace in speaking of God, for which Saint Francis loved him very much. One day Saint Francis was returning from the woods and from prayer, and when he was at the edge of the woods, that same Brother Masseo, wanting to test how humble he was, went up to him and, as if joking, said, "Why after you, why after you, why after you?" Saint Francis responded, "What do you mean? Brother Masseo said, "I'm saying why does *the whole world* come after you, and everyone seems to desire to see you and hear you? You aren't a handsome man in body, you aren't someone of great learning, you're not noble; so why does the whole world come after you?" Hearing this, Saint Francis was overjoyed in spirit and, turning his face to heaven, stood for a long time with his mind lifted up into God. Then returning to himself, he knelt down and gave praise and thanks to God. Then with great fervor of spirit he turned to Brother Masseo and said, "Do you want to know why after me? You want to know why after me? You want to know why the whole world comes after me? I have this from those eyes of the Most High God, which gaze in every place on the good and the guilty. Since those most holy eyes have not seen among sinners anyone more vile, nor more incompetent, nor a greater sinner than me; to perform that marvelous work, which he intends to do, He has not found a more vile creature on the earth, and therefore He has chosen me to confound the nobility and the greatness and the strength and beauty and wisdom of the world, so that it may be known that every virtue and every good is from Him, and not from the creature, and no person may boast in His sight. But *whoever boasts must boast in the Lord,* to whom is every honor and glory forever." Brother Masseo was shocked at such a humble response, said with such fervor, and knew certainly that Saint Francis was truly grounded in humility.

Jn 12:19

1 Cor 1:31

To the praise of Christ
and the little poor man Francis.
Amen.

Chapter 11
How Saint Francis made Brother Masseo
turn round and round many times,
and then he went to Siena

One day Saint Francis was travelling with Brother Masseo, and the same Brother Masseo was walking a little bit ahead. When he reached a three-way crossroads, by which they could go to Florence, to Siena or Arezzo, Brother Masseo said, "Father, which road should we take?" Saint Francis answered, "The one that God wills." Brother Masseo said, "And how will we know the will of God?" Saint Francis answered, "By the sign that I will show you. I command you by virtue of holy obedience that in this crossroads, in the place where you have your feet placed, you turn round and round, as children do, and don't stop turning yourself if I don't tell you to." So Brother Masseo started to twirl around, and he turned so much that, because of dizziness in his head, which is normal with such turning, he fell down on the ground several times. But since Saint Francis did not tell him to stop and he wanted to obey faithfully, he kept getting up. Finally, while he was spinning quickly, Saint Francis said, "Stop! Don't move!" And he stopped, and Saint Francis asked him, "Where is your face pointing?" Brother Masseo answered, "Toward Siena." Saint Francis said, "That is the way that God wants us to go."

Travelling along that road, Brother Masseo was greatly amazed at what Saint Francis had made him do, like a child, in front of lay people who were passing by. But out of reverence he did not dare to say anything to the holy father.

As they neared Siena, the people of the city heard of the coming of the saint, and went out to meet him. Out of devotion they carried him and his companion to the bishop's palace, and his feet did not touch the ground at all. At that time many men of Siena were fighting each other, and two of them had already died. Arriving there, Saint Francis preached to them in such a devout and holy way, that he returned them all to peace and great humility and harmony with each other. Because of this, when the Bishop of Siena heard of the holy deed that Saint Francis had done, he invited him home, and received him with great honor that day, and also for the night. And the next morning Saint Francis, truly humble, who sought only the glory of God in his deeds, got up early with his companions, and left without the Bishop's knowledge.

Along the road Brother Masseo grumbled within himself about this, saying "What's this that this good man has done? He made me twirl around like a child, and to the bishop, who did him so much

DBF XI

honor, he didn't even say a kind word or thank him." And it seemed to Brother Masseo that Saint Francis had acted in this way without discernment. But then, by divine inspiration, returning to himself and reproving himself, he said within his heart, "Brother Masseo, you are too proud, you judge the works of God, and you're worthy of hell for your indiscreet pride. Yesterday Brother Francis did such holy deeds that if they had been done by an Angel of God they would not have been more marvelous. So if he should command you to throw stones, you would have to do it and obey him, since what he has done on this road came from divine operation, as demonstrated by the good end that followed. If he had not brought peace to those who were fighting, not only would many bodies be dead from the sword, as had already begun to happen, but even more than that, the devil would have carried many souls off to hell. But you're very stupid and proud, grumbling about what clearly comes from the will of God."

And all these things that Brother Masseo was saying in his heart, while walking ahead, were revealed by God to Saint Francis. So Saint Francis drew up to him and said, "Hold onto those things that you're thinking now, because they are good and useful and inspired by God. But that first grumbling you were doing was blind and vain and proud and it was put into your mind by the demon." Then Brother Masseo clearly saw that Saint Francis knew the secrets of his heart, and understood surely that the spirit of divine Wisdom guided the holy faith in all his actions.

To the praise of Jesus Christ
and the little poor man, Francis.
Amen.

Chapter 12
HOW SAINT FRANCIS PUT BROTHER MASSEO IN CHARGE OF THE DOOR,
ALMS AND COOKING;
THEN AT THE REQUEST OF THE BROTHERS HE REMOVED HIM

DBF XII

Saint Francis wanted to make Brother Masseo humble, so that he would not lift himself up in vainglory because of the many gifts and graces God gave him, but by virtue of humility with these to grow from virtue to virtue. One time when he was staying in a solitary place with those truly holy first companions of his, among whom was the same Brother Masseo, he said one day to Brother Masseo, in front of all the companions: "O Brother Masseo, all these companions of yours have the grace of contemplation and prayer; but you have the gift of preaching the word of God to content the people. So I want you to have charge of the door and alms and cooking, so that these brothers may pursue contemplation. And when the other brothers eat, you will eat outside the door of the place, so that those who come to the place, before they start knocking, can be satisfied by some good words of God from you, so there will be no need then for anyone besides you to go outside. And do this in merit of holy obedience." Brother Masseo pulled back his capuche and bowed his head and humbly accepted and carried out this obedience for many days, taking charge of the door, alms and cooking.

The companions, as men enlightened by God, began to feel great remorse in their hearts over this, considering that Brother Masseo was a man of great perfection like them and even more, and the whole burden of the place was placed on him and not on them. For this reason all of them, moved by one will, went to ask the holy father that he be pleased to distribute those duties among them, since their consciences could not bear that Brother Masseo carry so many burdens. Hearing this, Saint Francis accepted their advice and agreed with their will. He called Brother Masseo and said to him, "Brother Masseo, your companions want to do part of the jobs I gave to you, so I want these jobs to be divided." Brother Masseo said, with great humility and patience, "Father, whatever you assign me, all or part, I'll consider it all God's doing." Then Saint Francis, seeing the humility of Brother Masseo and the charity of the others, preached to them a wonderful and great sermon about most holy humility, teaching them that the greater the gifts and graces God gives us, the more we must be humble, because without humility no virtue is acceptable to God. When he finished preaching he distributed the jobs with very great charity.

To the praise of Jesus Christ
and the little poor man Francis.
Amen.

Chapter 13
HOW SAINT FRANCIS AND BROTHER MASSEO
PUT THE BREAD THEY RECEIVED
ON TOP OF A ROCK NEXT TO A SPRING,
AND SAINT Francis PRAISED POVERTY MUCH.
THEN HE PRAYED GOD AND SAINT PETER AND SAINT PAUL TO GIVE HIM LOVE
FOR HOLY POVERTY,
AND HOW SAINT PETER AND SAINT PAUL APPEARED TO HIM

DBF XIII The wonderful servant and follower of Christ, that is, Sir Saint Francis, in order to conform himself perfectly to Christ in everything, who, according to what the Gospel says, *sent* His disciples *two by two* Lk 10:1 to all those *cities and places* where they had *to go,* after the example of Christ, sent them two by two through the world to preach. And to give an example of true obedience to them, he *began* first *to do* what Acts 1:1 he *taught.* Thus, having assigned the other parts of the world to the companions, he took the road toward the region of France, taking Brother Masseo as companion. And one day coming to a village quite hungry, they went begging bread for the love of God, according to the *Rule.* And Saint Francis went through one neighborhood and Brother Masseo through another. But since Saint Francis was such a worthless-looking man and small of body, and for that reason was considered a lowly little poor man by those who did not know him, he only got a few mouthfuls and some little pieces of dry bread. But Brother Masseo, since he was a big man and handsome of body, was given good, large portions, and plenty of them, and whole loaves of bread.

Having received these, they met together in a place outside the town to eat, where there was a beautiful spring, with a good big rock next to it, upon which each placed all the alms he had received. And when Saint Francis saw that Brother Masseo's pieces of bread were greater in number, in beauty, and in size than his own, he expressed great joy and said, "O Brother Masseo, we don't deserve such a great treasure." And as he was repeating these words several times, Brother Masseo replied, "Father, how can you call this a treasure, where there is such poverty and lack of essentials? Here there is no table-cloth, no knife, no dishes, no bowls, no house, no table, no waiter, no maid." Saint Francis said, "And this is what I consider the great treasure, where there is not a single thing prepared by human skill; but what there is here is prepared by divine providence, as you can see clearly in the bread we received, in such a beautiful table of rock, and such a clear spring. But I want God to make us love wholeheartedly the treasure of holy poverty, so noble as to have God for a servant." And having said these words and made a prayer and taken bodily nourishment with these pieces of bread and that water, they got up to walk to France.

And on reaching a church, Saint Francis said to his companion, "Let's go into this church to pray." And Saint Francis went behind the altar and placed himself in prayer, and in that prayer he received from a divine visitation such overflowing fervor, so inflaming his heart with love of holy poverty that, by the color of his face and the movements of his mouth, he seemed to be spewing out flames of love. And, thus inflamed, coming to his companion, he said to him, "Ah! Ah! Ah! Brother Masseo! Give me your very self." And he said this three times, and the third time Saint Francis, with his breath, lifted Brother Masseo into the air and threw him forward the space of a long spear. Brother Masseo was greatly surprised by this: he later told the companions that as he was lifted and tossed this way by Saint Francis, he felt such sweetness of spirit and consolation of the Holy Spirit that he had never felt anything like it in his life. And having done this, Saint Francis said, "My dear companion, let's go to Saint Peter and Saint Paul, and pray to them to teach and help us to possess the immeasurable treasure of most holy poverty, since she is such a worthy *treasure* and so divine that we are not worthy to possess her *in* our worthless *vessels:* she is that heavenly virtue by which all earthly and passing things are trodden underfoot and every obstacle is removed from the soul's path, so that it can freely join with the eternal God. This is the virtue that makes the soul, even while on earth, live in heaven with the Angels. She is the one who accompanied Christ onto the cross; with Christ she was buried; with Christ she rose up to heaven; and even in this life she grants to souls who fall in love with her, the ability to fly into heaven, since she holds the weapons of true humility and charity. So let us pray to the most holy Apostles of Christ, who were perfect lovers of this evangelical pearl, that they gain for us this grace from our Lord Jesus Christ: that by His most holy mercy he grant us to be considered worthy to be true lovers, observers and humble disciples of most precious, most beloved and evangelical poverty."

And while talking this way they reached Rome and entered the church of Saint Peter; and Saint Francis placed himself in prayer in one corner of the church, and Brother Masseo in another. And as Saint Francis remained in prayer for a long time with devotion and many tears, the most holy Apostles Peter and Paul appeared to him with great splendor and said, "Since you request and desire to observe what Christ and the holy Apostles observed, our Lord Jesus Christ sends us to you to announce that your prayer *has been heard:* God most perfectly grants to you and your followers the treasure of

2 Cor 4:7

Lk 1:13

most holy poverty. And further, on His behalf, we tell you that whoever by your example will perfectly follow this desire is assured of the blessedness of eternal life. And you and all your followers will be blessed by God." After saying these words they disappeared, leaving Saint Francis filled with consolation. He rose from prayer and went to his companion, and asked him if God had revealed anything to him, and he answered, "No." Then Saint Francis told him how the holy Apostles had appeared to him and what they had revealed to him. Each was full of joy because of this and they decided to return to the valley of Spoleto, giving up their journey to France.

To the praise of Jesus Christ
and the little poor man Francis.
Amen.

Chapter 14
HOW, AS SAINT FRANCIS WAS WITH HIS BROTHERS TO SPEAK OF GOD,
GOD APPEARED IN THEIR MIDST

DBF XIV   At the beginning of the religion, Saint Francis had gathered in a place with his brothers to speak of Christ. In fervor of spirit he commanded one of them in the name of God to open his mouth and speak of God as the Holy Spirit inspired him. As the brother fulfilled the command, speaking wonderfully of God, Saint Francis imposed silence on him, and commanded a similar thing of another brother. As he obeyed and spoke subtly of God, Saint Francis similarly imposed silence on him; and commanded the third one to speak of God. He similarly began to speak so profoundly of the secret things of God that Saint Francis knew for certain that he, like the other two, spoke by the Holy Spirit. And this was shown by an example and a clear sign, since while they were speaking, the blessed Christ appeared in their midst in the appearance and form of a very handsome young man, who blessed them all, filling them with such grace and sweetness that all were rapt out of themselves, lying as if dead, feeling nothing of this world. Then, as they returned to themselves, Saint Francis said to them, "My dearest brothers, give thanks to God who has willed to reveal the treasures of divine wisdom through the mouths of the simple, since God is the one who opens *the mouth of the mute,* and makes *the tongues* of the simple speak very *wisely."*   Wis 10:21

To the praise of Jesus Christ
and the little poor man Francis.
Amen.

Chapter 15
HOW SAINT CLARE ATE WITH SAINT FRANCIS
AND HIS BROTHER COMPANIONS
IN SAINT MARY OF THE ANGELS

While Saint Francis was staying in Assisi he visited Saint Clare DBF XV
many times, giving her holy instructions. She greatly desired to eat
once with him and she asked him for this many times, but he never
wanted to grant this consolation. So his companions, seeing the
desire of Saint Clare, said to Saint Francis: "Father, it does not seem
to us that this rigidity is in accord with divine charity, that you do not
grant to Sister Clare such a small thing as eating with you, as she is
such a holy virgin, beloved of God; especially considering that she
abandoned the riches and vanities of the world because of your
preaching. Truly, even if she were to ask you a greater favor than this
you should do it for your spiritual plant." Then Saint Francis replied,
"It seems to you that I should grant her request?" The companions
responded, "Yes, Father, it is only right that you grant her this favor
and consolation." Then Saint Francis said, "Since it seems this way
to you, it also seems that way to me. But so that she may be even
more consoled, I want this meal to be held at Saint Mary of the
Angels, since she has been enclosed for a long time in San Damiano,
and it will do her good to see the place of Saint Mary, where she was
tonsured and became the spouse of Jesus Christ; and there we will
eat together in the name of God."

When the appointed day arrived, Saint Clare with a companion
came out from the monastery, was accompanied by companions of
Saint Francis, and came to Saint Mary of the Angels. After she
devoutly greeted the Virgin Mary in front of her altar, where she had
been tonsured and veiled, they took her around to see the place until
it was time to eat. And in the meantime Saint Francis had the table
prepared on the bare ground, as he usually did. When it was time to
eat they sat down together: Saint Clare with Saint Francis; one of the
companions of Saint Francis with the companion of Saint Clare;
then all the other companions gathered humbly at the table. And as a
first course Saint Francis began to speak of God so sweetly, so deeply,
and so wonderfully that the abundance of divine grace descended
upon them, and all were rapt into God.

And while they were enraptured this way, their eyes and hands lifted up to heaven, the people of Assisi and Bettona and those of the surrounding area saw Saint Mary of the Angels burning brightly, along with the whole place and the forest, which was next to the place. It seemed that a great fire was consuming the church, the place and the forest together. For this reason the Assisians in a great hurry ran down there to put out the fire, believing that everything really was burning. But on arriving at the place, not finding anything burning, they went inside and found Saint Francis with Saint Clare and all their companions sitting around that humble table, rapt into God through contemplation. From this they clearly understood that that was divine, not material fire, which God had made appear miraculously, to demonstrate and signify the fire of divine love, burning in the souls of these holy brothers and holy nuns. Then they departed with great consolation in their hearts and with holy edification.

Then, after a long time, Saint Francis and Saint Clare together with the others returned to themselves; and feeling themselves well comforted by spiritual food, they had little concern for bodily food. And thus finishing that blessed meal, Saint Clare, well accompanied, returned to San Damiano. On seeing her the sisters were very glad, because they feared that Saint Francis might have sent her to govern some other monastery, as he had already sent Sister Agnes, her holy sister, as abbess to govern the monastery of Monticelli in Florence. Saint Francis had once said to Saint Clare, "Prepare yourself, in case I have to send you someplace"; and she, as a daughter of holy obedience had responded, "Father, I'm always prepared to go wherever you send me." So the sisters rejoiced greatly when they had her back; and Saint Clare from then on remained greatly comforted.

To the praise of Jesus Christ
and the little poor man Francis.
Amen.

Chapter 16
HOW SAINT FRANCIS, COUNSELED BY SAINT CLARE
AND HOLY BROTHER SYLVESTER TO PREACH AND CONVERT MANY PEOPLE,
FORMED THE THIRD ORDER, PREACHED TO THE BIRDS,
AND MADE THE SWALLOWS REMAIN SILENT

DBF XVI   The humble servant of Christ, Saint Francis, a short time after his conversion, having already gathered and received many companions into the Order, was greatly preoccupied and in serious doubt about what he ought to do: whether to dedicate himself solely to prayer, or sometimes to preach; and he greatly desired to know the will of God about this. Since the holy humility in him did not allow him to rely on himself or his own prayers, he decided to seek the divine will with the prayers of others. So he called Brother Masseo and said to him: "Go to Sister Clare and tell her for me that she, with some of her more spiritual companions, should devoutly pray to God that He be pleased to show me what is better: to dedicate myself to preaching or only to prayer. Then go to Brother Sylvester and tell him the same." Now in the world this man had been Sir Sylvester, the one who had seen coming out of the mouth of Saint Francis a golden cross as tall as the sky and as wide as the ends of the earth. And this Brother Sylvester was a man of so much devotion and holiness that whatever he asked and begged of God was granted, and he often spoke with God; and therefore Saint Francis had great devotion toward him.

Brother Masseo went and, following the command of Saint Francis, delivered the message first to Saint Clare, then to Brother Sylvester. And he, as soon as he received the message, knelt down in prayer, and as he prayed he received God's answer. He turned to Brother Masseo and said, "God says this: tell Brother Francis that God did not call him to this state only for himself, but to bear fruit, the fruit of souls, that through him many may be saved." On receiving this response, Brother Masseo returned to Saint Clare to learn what she had received from God. And she replied that she and the other companions had received from God the same response that Brother Sylvester had received.

At that Brother Masseo returned to Saint Francis, and Saint Francis received him with the greatest charity, washing his feet and preparing him something to eat. After the meal, Saint Francis called Brother Masseo into the forest and there knelt down in front of him and pulled back his capuche, making a cross with his arms, and asked him, "What does my Lord Jesus Christ command me to do?" Brother Masseo replied, "Christ answered both Brother Sylvester and Sister Clare with the sisters, and revealed that it is His will that you go through the world to preach, because He has not chosen you only for yourself, but rather for the salvation of others." Then Saint Francis, having heard this answer and knowing Christ's will by it, got up with great fervor and said, "Let's go, in the name of God." And he took as companions Brother Masseo and Brother Angelo, both holy men.

And setting out with an eager spirit, without considering road or path, they came to a village called Cannara. And Saint Francis began to preach, and he first commanded the swallows to keep silent until he had finished preaching. And the swallows obeyed him. And he preached there with such fervor that in their devotion all the men and women of that town wanted to follow him and abandon the town. But Saint Francis did not allow them, saying, "Don't be in a hurry, and don't leave: I'll arrange what you must do for the salvation of your souls." And then he got the idea of starting the Third Order for the universal salvation of all. And thus he left them much consoled and well disposed towards penance, and he then departed and came to a place between Cannara and Bevagna. And as he was going along further in that same fervor he raised his eyes, and along the road he saw some trees in which there was an almost infinite multitude of birds. Saint Francis marvelled at this and said to his companions: "You wait for me here on the road, and I'll go and preach to my sisters the birds." He entered the field and he began to preach to the birds that were on the ground. And quickly the birds that were in the trees all came down to him and together remained still while Saint Francis finished preaching, and did not leave until he gave them his blessing. And, according to what Brother Masseo later told Brother James of Massa, as Saint Francis went among them, touching them with his tunic, not one of them moved. The substance of Saint Francis's sermon was this: "My sister birds, you owe much to God your Creator and you ought to praise Him always and everywhere because He has given you the freedom to fly everywhere, and has given you two and three layers of clothing. He preserved the seed of you all in the Ark of Noah so that your kind would not disappear. And you are also indebted to Him for the element of air that He assigned to you. Furthermore you *neither sow nor reap,* and God *feeds you,* and gives you the rivers and springs for your drink; and He gives you the mountains and valleys as your refuge, the high trees to make your nests; and since you do not know how to spin or sew, He clothes you, you and your little ones. Therefore, your Creator loves you very much, since He gives you so many benefits. So beware, my sisters, of the sin of ingratitude and always strive to praise God." As Saint Francis was saying these words all those birds began to open their beaks, stretch their necks, open their wings, and reverently bend their heads to the ground, and with singing and movements showed that the holy father gave them great delight. And Saint Francis together with them was filled with joy and delight, and marveled greatly at such a multitude of birds and their beautiful variety, their attention and friendly manner. Therefore, he devoutly praised the Creator in them. Finally ending his sermon, Saint Francis made the sign of the Cross and gave them permission to leave. Then all

Gn 7:3

Lk 12:24

those birds rose into the air with marvelous songs. Then, following the Cross Saint Francis made over them, they divided themselves into four groups: one group flew toward the east, one toward the west, one toward the south and one toward the north. And each group went singing marvelous songs. Thus they signified that just as Saint Francis, the banner-bearer of the Cross of Christ, had preached to them, and made the sign of the Cross over them, according to which they divided themselves into the four parts of the world, so, in the same way, the preaching of the Cross of Christ, renewed by Saint Francis, was to be carried through the whole world by himself and his brothers who, like the birds, possess nothing of their own in this world, and entrust their life only to the providence of God.

To the praise of Jesus Christ
and the little poor man Francis.
Amen.

Chapter 17
How, while Saint Francis was praying at night, a young brother, a boy, saw Christ and the Virgin Mary and many other saints talk with him

A boy who was very pure and innocent was received into the Order while Saint Francis was living; and he was staying in a small place where the brothers, out of necessity, slept outside on the ground. Saint Francis once came to this place and in the evening after saying compline, he went off to sleep as he usually did, so he could get up at night to pray when the other brothers were asleep. The boy had in mind to spy attentively on Saint Francis's movements in order to find out about his holiness and especially to know what the saint did at night when he arose. To make sure that sleep would not overcome him, he lay down to sleep at Saint Francis's side and tied his cord to that of Saint Francis, so he would feel when the saint arose. And Saint Francis did not feel any of this. That night, during the first time of sleep, when all the other brothers were sleeping, Saint Francis got up and found his cord tied that way. He gently untied it so that the boy did not feel it, and Saint Francis went alone into the woods near the place, entering a little cell there and set himself to pray. The boy awoke after a while and found the cord untied and Saint Francis gone, so he got up to look for him. When he found the gate to the woods open, he thought that Saint Francis had gone out there, so he entered the woods. Reaching the place where Saint

DBF XIX

Francis was praying, he began to hear a great sound of voices. Going closer so that he might see and understand what he heard, he saw a wonderful light surrounding Saint Francis on all sides, and in it he saw Christ and the Virgin Mary and Saint John the Baptist and the Evangelist and a great multitude of angels speaking with Saint Francis. When the boy saw and heard this, he fell to the ground as if dead. Then, when the mystery of that holy apparition ended, Saint Francis was returning to the place. And his foot bumped into the boy lying almost dead on the path. Out of compassion, he lifted him up, took him in his arms and carried him back, as a good shepherd does with his little sheep.

Learning from him later about how he saw the vision, he ordered him never to tell anyone, that is, while he lived. The boy, growing in the grace of God and devotion to Saint Francis, was an important man in the Order, and, after the death of Saint Francis, he revealed that vision to the brothers.

To the glory of Jesus Christ
and the little poor man Francis.
Amen.

Chapter 18
THE MARVELOUS GENERAL CHAPTER THAT SAINT FRANCIS
HELD AT SAINT MARY OF THE ANGELS
WHERE THERE WERE MORE THAN FIVE THOUSAND BROTHERS

DBF XX   The faithful servant of Christ, Saint Francis, once held a General Chapter at Saint Mary of the Angels, and at that chapter five thousand brothers gathered. Saint Dominic came there, the head and foundation of the Order of Brother Preachers, as he was then going from Burgundy to Rome. Hearing of the gathering of the General Chapter that Saint Francis was holding on the plain of Saint Mary of the Angels, he went to see it with seven brothers of his Order. Also at that Chapter there was a cardinal very devoted to Saint Francis whom he had prophesied would become pope, and that is what happened. That cardinal had come especially to Assisi from Perugia, where the Court was staying. He came every day to see Saint Francis and his brothers, and he sometimes sang Mass and sometimes preached a sermon to the brothers in the Chapter. And that Cardinal experienced great delight and devotion when he came to visit that holy gathering. He saw the brothers sitting on that plain around Saint Mary of the Angels, group by group, forty here, there a hundred, further on eighty together, all busy in speaking of God, in prayer, in works of charity. And they remained in such silence with such modesty that no sound or loud noise could be heard. Marveling over such a crowd gathered as one in such order, he said with tears and great devotion: "This is truly the camp and the army of the knights of God!" In that great multitude no one was heard telling stories or lies, but wherever a group of brothers gathered, they either prayed or said the Office, or wept over their own sins or those of their benefactors or spoke about the salvation of souls. There in that field there were huts of mats and reeds, separated into groups for the brothers of different Provinces. For this reason, that Chapter was called the Chapter of Mats or of Reeds. Their beds were the bare ground and some had a little straw; their pillows were stones or pieces of wood. For this reason there was such devotion toward them among those who heard or saw them, and such was their reputation for holiness that many came from the pope's Court, which was then at Perugia; and from other areas of the Spoleto Valley came many counts, barons, knights and noblemen, common people, cardinals, bishops, abbots and many other clerics, to see such a holy and great and humble gathering of so many holy men together, the likes of which the world had never seen. They came particularly to see the head and most holy father of that holy people, who had robbed the world of such beautiful prey and gathered such a lovely and devout flock to follow the footprints of the true shepherd, Jesus Christ.

After the whole General Chapter was gathered, the holy father of all and general minister, Saint Francis, in fervor of spirit proclaimed the word of God in a loud voice, preaching what the Holy Spirit gave him to say. And he offered these words as the theme of the sermon: "My sons, we have promised great things to God; greater things are promised to us by God if we observe what we have promised Him: let us await confidently those promised to us. Brief is the delight of the world; but the punishment that follows is eternal. The suffering of this life is small, but the glory of the other life is infinite." He preached most devoutly on these words, comforting and encouraging all the brothers to obedience and reverence for Holy Mother Church, to brotherly love; to pray to God for all the people, to have patience in the hardships of the world and temperance in prosperity, to keep purity and angelic chastity, to have harmony and peace with God, the people and their own conscience, to love and observance of most holy poverty. Then he said to them, "By virtue of holy obedience, I command all you gathered here: have no care or anxiety about what to eat or drink or other things necessary for the body, but to concentrate only on praying and praising God; and leave all care for your body to Him, since He has a special care for you." They all received this command with joyful hearts and glad faces. And when Saint Francis finished the sermon, they all hurried to prayer.

Saint Dominic, who was present for all these things, was greatly surprised by the command of Saint Francis, and considered it lacking in discernment, being unable to imagine how such a great multitude could be governed without any care or concern for the things necessary for the body. But the principal shepherd, the blessed Christ, wishing to show His care for His sheep, and love for His poor ones, immediately inspired the people of Perugia, Spoleto and Foligno, Spello and Assisi and the surrounding areas, to bring food and drink to that holy gathering. There quickly came from those places men with *donkeys,* horses, and carts loaded *with bread and wine,* beans and cheese, and other good things to eat, according to what was needed by the poor of Christ. Moreover, they brought table-cloths, pots, dishes, cups and other utensils that could be used by such a multitude. People considered themselves blessed if they could bring more things, or could serve more attentively, so that even the knights, barons and other noblemen who came to see them, served them with great humility and devotion. For this reason Saint Dominic, on seeing these things, truly understood that Divine Providence was at work among them, and humbly recognized that he had falsely judged Saint Francis as lacking discernment in his command. Kneeling before Saint Francis, he humbly confessed his fault, and added: "God truly takes special care of these holy little poor men and I did not know it. From now on I promise to observe holy and evangelical poverty, and on behalf of God I curse all the brothers of my Order who presume to have something of their own in the Order." Thus Saint Dominic was very edified by the faith of the most holy Saint Francis and by the obedience and poverty of such a large and orderly assembly, by Divine Providence and by the overflowing abundance of every good thing.

During that same Chapter Saint Francis was told that many brothers were wearing harnesses and iron rings next to their skin, which caused many to become sick and then to die, and many to be impeded in their prayers. Therefore, Saint Francis as a most discerning father, commanded under holy obedience that whoever had a harness or iron rings to bring them and put them in front of him. And so they did. And there were counted as many as five hundred iron harnesses and even more iron rings for arms and waists, so many that they made a huge pile, and Saint Francis made them leave them all there.

1 Sm 25:18

When the Chapter ended, Saint Francis consoled them all well and taught them how to escape this wicked world without sin. With the blessing of God and his own, he sent them, now all consoled with spiritual joy, back to their provinces.

To the praise of Jesus Christ
and the little poor man Francis.
Amen.

Chapter 19
HOW GRAPES WERE TAKEN AND TRAMPLED IN THE VINEYARD OF THE
PRIEST OF RIETI, IN WHOSE HOUSE SAINT FRANCIS WAS PRAYING,
BECAUSE OF THE MANY PEOPLE THAT CAME TO HIM
AND THEN MIRACULOUSLY IT GAVE MORE WINE THAN EVER,
AS SAINT FRANCIS HAD PROMISED. AND HOW GOD
REVEALED TO SAINT FRANCIS THAT
HE WOULD RECEIVE PARADISE AT HIS DEPARTURE

Once when Saint Francis had a serious eye disease, Sir Hugolino, DBF XXI
Cardinal Protector of the Order, because of the great tenderness he
had for him, wrote to tell him to go to Rieti where there were excellent eye doctors. Saint Francis, after he received the letter of the Cardinal, went first to San Damiano, where Saint Clare was, the most
devout spouse of Christ, to give her some consolation and then to the
Cardinal. While he was there, that night his eyes became so much
worse that he was unable to see any light. So, since he could not
depart, Saint Clare made him a little cell of reeds, where he could rest
more easily. But Saint Francis, because of the pain of the illness and
because of the many mice that troubled him greatly, could not rest at
all by night or by day. Bearing that pain and disturbance for several
days, he began to think and understood this as a punishment from
God for his sins, and he began to give thanks to God with his whole
heart and voice, and cried out in a loud voice and said, "Lord, my
God, I am worthy of this and of much worse. O Lord Jesus Christ,
good shepherd, who have shown your mercy to us sinners in different bodily pains and sufferings, give grace and strength to me, your
little lamb, that I may not turn away from you because of any illness
Jn 12:28   or tribulation or suffering." After he made this prayer, *a voice* came to
him *from heaven,* saying: "Francis, answer me: if the whole world
were gold, and all the seas and springs and rivers were balsam, and
all the mountains, hills and stones were precious stones; and if you
found another treasure more noble than all these things, as much as
gold is more noble than earth, balsam more than water, precious

stones more than mountains and rocks, and that more noble treasure were given to you for this illness, wouldn't you be happy and
quite joyful?" Saint Francis answered, *"Lord, I am not worthy* of such a
precious treasure." And the voice of God said to him: "Rejoice, Francis, because that is the treasure of eternal life, which I have kept for
you, and from now on I invest you with it. This illness and affliction
is the pledge of that blessed treasure." Then Saint Francis called his
companion with the greatest joy over such a glorious promise, and
said: "Let us go to the Cardinal." And first consoling Saint Clare with
holy words, and humbly taking leave of her, he started his journey
toward Rieti.

Mt 8:8

When he drew near there, such a multitude of people came out to
meet him that he did not want to enter the city, so he turned aside to
a church about two miles away from the city. The citizens, knowing
that he was at that church, rushed around it in such numbers to see
him, that the vineyard of the church was completely ruined and the
grapes were all taken. The priest grieved deeply over this in his heart
and he regretted that he had received Saint Francis in his church.
God revealed the priest's thought to Saint Francis, who had the
priest called to him and said to him, "Dearest father, how many loads
of wine does this vineyard give you in a year when it yields best?" The
priest replied that it yielded twelve loads. Saint Francis said: "I beg
you, Father, to endure patiently my staying here for a few days
because I find great rest here. And for the love of God and of me, a little poor man, allow everyone to take grapes from this vineyard of
yours. On behalf of my Lord Jesus Christ I promise you that this year
it will produce for you twenty loads." Saint Francis did this while
staying there because of the great harvest of souls which he saw happening to the people who came there, many of whom went away inebriated with divine love and abandoned the world. The priest trusted
the promise of Saint Francis, and freely left the vineyard to those
who were coming to him. An amazing thing: the vineyard was totally
demolished and devoured, so that barely a few small clusters of
grapes remained. But when harvest-time came, the priest collected
those little clusters and put them in the press and pressed them. And
according to the promise of Saint Francis, he obtained twenty loads
of the best wine. By this miracle it was clearly shown that just as by
the merits of Saint Francis the vineyard stripped of its grapes
abounded in wine, so the Christian people, fruitless in virtue because
of sin, through the merits and teaching of Saint Francis abounded
many times over in the good fruit of penance.

To the praise of Jesus Christ
and the little poor man, Francis.
Amen.

Chapter 20
A VERY BEAUTIFUL VISION
SEEN BY A YOUNG BROTHER, WHO HAD SUCH DISGUST FOR THE TUNIC
THAT HE WAS READY TO GIVE UP THE HABIT
AND LEAVE THE ORDER

A young man, very noble and refined, came to the Order of Saint   DBF XXII
Francis. After a few days, at the instigation of the demon, he began to
feel such disgust for the habit which he was wearing that it seemed
to him that he was wearing a filthy rag. He loathed the sleeves and
hated the capuche; and he thought its length and roughness were an
unbearable burden. His distaste for the Religion also increased and
he finally decided to give up the habit and return to the world.

He had already taken up the custom, as his master had taught
him, that whenever he passed in front of the altar of the convent, in
which the Body of Christ was reserved, to kneel with great reverence,
pull back his capuche, and to bow with his arms crossed. It happened
that on the night when he was to depart and leave the Order he had
to pass in front of the altar of the friary. As he passed, according to his
custom, he knelt down and made his reverence. Immediately he was
caught up in spirit, and a marvelous vision was shown to him by God.
For he saw in front of him, an almost infinite multitude as in a procession, two by two, clothed in very beautiful robes of precious cloth.
Their faces and hands shone like the sun, and they walked along
with the singing and music of angels. Among those saints there were
two more nobly dressed and adorned than all the others, and they
were surrounded by such brightness that they caused great wonder
to those who saw them. Almost at the end of the procession he saw
one adorned with such glory that he seemed like a new knight, more
honored than the others. When the young man saw this, he was
amazed and did not know what that procession meant. He did not
dare to ask about it, and he remained dumbstruck with sweetness.
Nevertheless, when the whole procession had passed by, he decided
to dare and ran toward the ones at the end and, with great fear, asked
them: "Dear friends, I beg you, please tell me who are these marvelous people forming this venerable procession?" They replied: "Son,
realize that we are all Lesser Brothers who have now come from the
glory of paradise." Then he asked: "Who are those two who shine

more brightly than the others?" They responded: "Those are Saint Francis and Saint Anthony, and that last one you saw so greatly honored is a holy brother who just died. Because he fought valiantly against temptations and persevered to the end, we are leading him with triumph to the glory of Paradise. These robes of beautiful cloth which we wear were given to us by God in exchange for the harsh tunics which we patiently wore in the Religion. The glorious brightness which you see in us was given to us by God for the humility and patience, holy poverty and obedience and chastity which we observed to the end. Therefore, dear son, do not let the wearing of such a fruitful thing as the tunic of the Religion be hard for you, because if, with the tunic of Saint Francis, for the love of Christ you despise *the world* and mortify *the flesh* and fight courageously against the demon, you will have, together with us, a similar robe and the brightness of glory." When these words ended, the youth returned to himself and, comforted by this vision, he drove away from himself every temptation. He acknowledged his fault before the Guardian and the brothers, and from then on he longed for the harshness of penance and of clothing, and he finished his life within the Order in great holiness.

1 Jn 2:16

To the praise of Jesus Christ
and the little poor man Francis.
Amen.

Chapter 21
THE VERY HOLY MIRACLE THAT SAINT FRANCIS WORKED
WHEN HE CONVERTED THE VERY FIERCE WOLF OF GUBBIO

DBF XXIII

At the time that Saint Francis was staying in the city of Gubbio, in the district of Gubbio there appeared a very big wolf, fearsome and ferocious, which devoured not only animals but even human beings, so that all the citizens were in great fear, because many times he came near the city. All would go armed when they went out of the city as if they were going to combat, yet with all this, those who were alone and encountered him could not defend themselves from him. And out of fear of this wolf it came to the point that no one dared to leave that town.

For this reason Saint Francis had compassion on the people of the town, and decided to go out to this wolf, even though all the citizens advised against it. Making the sign of the most holy cross, he went out of the town, he and his companions, placing all his confidence in

God. As the others hesitated to go any further, Saint Francis took the road toward the place where the wolf was. Then that wolf, seeing many citizens who had come to see this miracle, ran toward Saint Francis with his mouth open. Drawing close to him, Saint Francis made the sign of the most holy cross on him and called him to himself and said this: "Come here, Brother Wolf. I command you on behalf of Christ that you do no harm to me or to anyone." An amazing thing to say! Immediately, when Saint Francis had made the sign of the cross, the fearsome wolf closed his mouth and stopped running; and once the command was given, it came meekly as a lamb, and threw itself to lie at the feet of Saint Francis. And Saint Francis spoke to him thus: "Brother Wolf, you do much harm in this area, and you have done great misdeeds, destroying and killing the creatures of God without His permission. And not only have you killed and devoured beasts, but you have dared to kill *people, made in the image of God.* For this reason you are worthy of the gallows as a thief and the worst of murderers. And all the people cry out and complain against you, and all this town is your enemy. But I, Brother Wolf, want to make peace between you and these people, so that you do not offend them any more, and they may pardon you every past offense, and so neither the people nor the dogs will persecute you any more. And after these words were said, the wolf showed that he accepted what Saint Francis said and wanted to observe it, by movement of his body and tail and ears and by bowing his head. Then Saint Francis said, "Brother Wolf, since it pleases you to make this pact of peace and keep it, I promise that I will have food given to you constantly, as long as you live, by the people of this town, so that you will no longer suffer hunger, since I know very well that you did all this harm because of hunger. But in order for me to obtain this grace for you, I want you, Brother Wolf, to promise me that you will never harm any human person nor any animal. Do you promise me this?" And the wolf, bowing his head, made a clear sign that he promised it. And Saint Francis said this: "Brother Wolf, I want you to guarantee this promise, so that I can truly trust it." Saint Francis reached out his hand to receive his guarantee, the wolf lifted his right paw in front of him, and tamely placed it on top of the hand of Saint Francis, giving the only sign of a guarantee that he was able to make.

Then Saint Francis said, "Brother Wolf, *I command you in the name of Jesus Christ:* come with me now without any hesitation, and we will go to seal this peace-pact in the name of God." And the obedient wolf went with him like a tame lamb; and the citizens, seeing this, were greatly amazed. Immediately this news was known throughout the whole city; and because of it all the people, men and women, great

Gn 1:26-27

Acts 16:18

and small, young and old, poured into the piazza to see the wolf with Saint Francis. And once all the people were fully assembled Saint Francis got up and preached to them, saying, among other things, that God allows such things and pestilences because of sins; and the flame of hell, which lasts forever for the damned, is much more dangerous than the fierceness of the wolf, which *can* only *kill the body.* Mt 10:28 "How much should the mouth of hell be feared when the mouth of a little animal holds such a great multitude in fear! Dear people, return to God, therefore, and do fitting penance for your sins, and God will free you from the wolf in the present, and from hell's fire in the future." When he finished the sermon, Saint Francis said, "Listen, my brothers! Brother Wolf, who is here before you, has promised me, and given me his guarantee, to make peace with you, and never to offend you in anything, if you promise him to give him every day the things he needs. And I make myself trustee for him that he will firmly observe the peace-pact." Then all the people with one voice promised to feed him regularly. And Saint Francis, in front of them all, said to the wolf: "And you, Brother Wolf, do you promise to observe the peace-pact with these people, that you will not harm the people, the animals, nor any creature?" And the wolf knelt down and bowed his head and with gentle movements of his body and tail and ears showed, as much as possible, that he wished to observe every part of the pact with them. Saint Francis said: "Brother Wolf, as you gave me a guarantee of this promise outside the gate, I also want you to give me in front of all the people a guarantee of your promise, that you will not deceive me in my promise and the guarantee that I gave for you." Then the wolf, lifting his right paw, placed it in the hand of Saint Francis. Because of this action, and the others mentioned above, there was such rejoicing and wonder among all the people, both for the devotion of the Saint and for the novelty of the miracle and for the peace of the wolf, that they all began to cry out to heaven, *praising and blessing* God who sent Saint Francis to them who, Lk 24:53 through his merits, had freed them from the jaws of the cruel beast.

Afterwards that same wolf lived in Gubbio for two years, and he tamely entered the houses, going from door to door, without doing harm to anyone and without any being done to him; and he was kindly fed by the people, and as he went this way through the town and the houses, no dog barked at him. Finally after two years Brother Wolf died of old age, at which the citizens grieved very much, because when they saw him going through the city so tamely, they better recalled the virtue and holiness of Saint Francis.

To the praise of Jesus Christ
and the little poor man Francis.
Amen.

Chapter 22
HOW SAINT FRANCIS TAMED THE WILD DOVES

A young man one day caught many doves and was carrying them DBF XXIV
off to sell. Saint Francis met him and, always having singular kindness for meek animals, looking at those doves with a look of pity, said
to the young man: "O good young man, I beg you to give them to me,
so that such innocent birds, which are compared in Scripture to
chaste, humble and faithful souls, may not fall into the hands of
cruel people who will kill them." The young man, inspired by God,
gave them all to Saint Francis, and he, taking them to his breast,
began to speak sweetly to them: "O my sister doves, simple, chaste
and innocent, why did you let yourselves be caught? Now, you see, I
want to rescue you from death and make nests for you so that you
can bear fruit and multiply according to our Creator's command."

And Saint Francis went and made nests for them all. And they
used them, and began to lay eggs and raise their young among the
brothers. They stayed and behaved tamely with Saint Francis and
the other brothers as if they were chickens that the brothers had
always fed. And they never departed unless Saint Francis with his
blessing gave them permission to leave.

Saint Francis said to the boy who gave him the doves: "Son, you
will yet become a brother in this Order and you will graciously serve
Jesus Christ." And so it happened: that young man became a
brother, and lived in the Order with great holiness.

To the praise of Jesus Christ
and the little poor man Francis.
Amen.

Chapter 23
HOW SAINT FRANCIS FREED A BROTHER
WHO WAS IN SIN AND WITH THE DEMON

One time when Saint Francis was in prayer in the place of the DBF XXVI
Portiuncula, by divine revelation, he saw the whole place surrounded and besieged by demons as though by a huge army; but
none of them was able to enter the place because the brothers there

were of such holiness that there was no place for them to enter. But they persevered, and one day one of those brothers was offended by another, and thought in his heart how he could accuse him and get revenge against him. Hence, while he remained in these bad thoughts, the demon, finding the entrance open, entered the place, and settled on the neck of that brother. The merciful and caring shepherd, who always kept watch over his flocks, saw that the wolf had entered to devour this little sheep of his, had the brother called to him at once, and commanded him to disclose immediately the poison of hatred he conceived against his neighbor, because of which he was *in the* enemy's *hands*. Terrified, seeing that the holy father knew, he disclosed all the poison and rancor, recognized his fault and humbly asked for a penance with mercy. When this was done, and he was absolved from his sin and had received a penance, the demon immediately left in front of Saint Francis, and the brother, freed from the hands of the cruel beast by the goodness of the good shepherd, gave thanks to God, and returned, corrected and instructed, to the flock of the holy shepherd, and lived from then on in great holiness.

Mt 26:45

> To the praise of Jesus Christ
> and the little poor man Francis.
> Amen.

Chapter 24
HOW SAINT FRANCIS CONVERTED TO THE FAITH
THE SULTAN OF BABYLON AND THE PROSTITUTE
WHO INVITED HIM TO SIN

DBF XXVII

Saint Francis, urged by zeal for the faith of Christ and desire for martyrdom, once went overseas with twelve of his most holy companions, headed toward the Sultan of the land of Babylon. They reached the territory of the Saracens, where some very cruel men guarded the roads so that no Christian who passed there could escape without being killed. But, as it pleased God, they were not killed but were captured, beaten and bound, and led before the Sultan. And once in his presence Saint Francis, instructed by the Holy Spirit, preached in a divine way about the faith of Christ, and that for this faith they were willing to go into the fire. As a result, the Sultan began to have great devotion for him both because of the constancy of his faith and the contempt of the world that he saw in him, since he did not want to receive any gift from him, though he was very poor, and because of the fervent longing for martyrdom he saw in him. From that moment on the Sultan listened to him willingly, and he asked that he come back to him often, granting freely to him and his companions that they could preach anywhere they pleased. He then gave them a sign, because of which they would not be harmed by anyone.

Having received this liberal permission Saint Francis sent those chosen companions, two by two, into various territories of the Saracens to preach the faith of Christ. He, along with one of them chose one area, and on arriving there they entered an inn to rest. There was a woman there with a very beautiful body but a filthy soul, and this cursed woman invited Saint Francis to sin. Saint Francis said to her: "I accept, let's go to bed," and she led him into a room. And Saint Francis said, "Come with me, and I will take you to a very beautiful bed." He led her to a huge fire which had been lit in that house, and in fervor of spirit he stripped himself naked and threw himself beside the fire on a spot that was red-hot and invited her to strip and come to lie with him on that beautiful feather bed. Saint Francis remained there a long time, not burning or even turning red, and that woman was dumbstruck by such a miracle, and was stricken to the heart. Not only did she repent of her sin and her evil intention, but also was converted perfectly to the faith of Christ, and became a person of such holiness that through her many souls in that area were saved.

Saint Francis, finally seeing that he could gain no more fruit in that region, by divine revelation decided to return, with all his companions, among believers. Gathering them all together, he returned to the Sultan and took his leave from him. The Sultan then said to him: "Brother Francis, I would willingly convert to the faith of Christ, but I am afraid to do it now, because if these people learn of it, they would immediately kill you and me and all your companions. Since you can do much good and I have to finish some things of great importance, I do not want to bring about now your death and mine. But teach me how I may be saved: I am prepared to do what you command." Saint Francis then said: "My Lord, I am now leaving you, but after I return to my country and have gone to heaven, by the grace of God, after my death, as God pleases, I will send you two of my brothers, from whom you will receive the holy baptism of Christ and you will be saved, just as my Lord Jesus Christ has revealed to me. In the meantime, free yourself from every hindrance so that when the grace of God comes to you, you will be prepared for faith and devotion." This he both promised to do and did.

Having done this, Saint Francis returned with that venerable company of his holy companions. After some years Saint Francis returned his soul to God through bodily death. And the Sultan fell ill, and waiting for the promise of Saint Francis, he had guards placed at certain passes, commanding that if two brothers in the habit of Saint Francis appeared there, they should be brought to him immediately. At that time Saint Francis appeared to two brothers and ordered them to go without delay to the Sultan and obtain his salvation just as he promised him. The brothers set out without delay and, having crossed the sea, they were taken to the Sultan by those guards. When he saw them, the Sultan was *filled with the greatest joy,* and he said: *"Now I truly know that* God *has sent* His servants to me for my salvation, according to the promise that Saint Francis made to me by divine revelation." From these brothers he received instruction in the faith of Christ and holy baptism. And thus reborn in Christ, he died in that illness, and his soul was saved through the merits and prayers of Saint Francis.

To the praise of Jesus Christ
and the little poor man Francis.
Amen.

Chapter 25

HOW SAINT FRANCIS CURED A MAN WITH LEPROSY OF SOUL AND BODY AND WHAT THE SOUL SAID TO HIM WHILE GOING TO HEAVEN

Sir Saint Francis, the true disciple of Christ, while living in this miserable life, always strove with all his strength to follow Christ, the perfect teacher. Therefore, it often happened by divine action, that those whose bodies he healed were healed in soul by God at the same time, as we read of Christ. Not only did he willingly serve the lepers himself, but besides this he set down that the brothers of his Order, while staying or travelling through the world, should serve the lepers for love of Christ, who wished for our sake to be *considered a leper.* It once happened that at a place where Saint Francis was staying at that time the brothers were serving sick lepers in a hospital. One of the lepers there was so impatient, so unbearable and obstinate that everyone believed as certain that he was possessed by the demon, and so he was. He so rudely insulted anyone who served him with words and blows and, what is worse, he hurled such angry blasphemies against the blessed Christ and his most holy mother the Virgin Mary, that no one at all could be found who could or would serve him. Although the brothers strove to bear patiently the insults and harm to themselves, in order to increase the merit of patience, nevertheless their consciences could not bear those against Christ and His

Mt 2:10

Acts 12:11

DBF XXVIII

Mt 9:1-8

Is 53:3-4

Mother, so they decided to abandon that leper entirely. But they did not want to do this until they explained this in detail to Saint Francis, who was then staying in a place near there.

After they explained this, Saint Francis went to that perverse leper and, coming up to him, greeted him, saying: "My dear brother, *may* God *give you peace."* The leper responded: "What peace can I have from God? He has taken from me peace and every good thing, and has made me all decayed and stinking!" Saint Francis said: "My son, be patient, because the illnesses of the body are given to us by God in this world for salvation of the soul, so they have great value, when they are borne patiently." The sick man replied: "How can I patiently bear the constant pain that torments me night and day? And I am suffering not only from my illness, but the brothers you gave me to serve me make me worse, and don't serve me as they should." Then by revelation Saint Francis knew that this leper was possessed by an evil spirit, so he went and placed himself in prayer, and prayed to God devoutly for him.

After his prayer, he returned to him and said: "My son, I want to serve you myself, since you are not content with the others." The sick man said: "I like that. But what more can you do than the others?" Saint Francis answered: "I'll do whatever you want." The leper said: "I want you to wash me all over. I stink so bad I can't stand myself." Then Saint Francis quickly had some water heated with many fragrant herbs. He undressed the man, and began to wash him with his holy hands, while another brother poured the water. By a divine miracle, where Saint Francis touched him with his holy hands the leprosy went away, and there remained only perfectly healed flesh. And as the flesh began to heal, the soul also began to heal. When the leper saw himself being cured, he began to feel great compunction and repentance for his sins, and began to weep very bitterly. So while externally the body was being cleansed of leprosy by washing with water, so internally his soul was being cleansed of sin by contrition and tears.

Completely healed in both body and soul, he humbly accused himself of his fault and said, weeping out loud, "Woe to me! I'm worthy of hell for the injuries and insults I said and did to the brothers, for my impatience and blasphemies against God." For fifteen days he persevered in bitter weeping for his sins and asking mercy from God, and made a full confession to the priest. Saint Francis, seeing such an evident miracle, which God had performed through his hands, thanked God and then left from there, going to a faraway country, because through humility he wished to flee all glory, and in all his actions he sought only the honor and glory of God, not his own.

Nm 6:26

Then, as it pleased God, that leper who had been cured in body and soul, after fifteen days of penance, became ill with another illness. Armed with the sacraments of the Church, he died a holy death. And his soul, going to Paradise, appeared in the air to Saint Francis, who was praying in the woods, and said to him: "Do you recognize me?" "Who are you?" Saint Francis said. "I am the leper the blessed Christ cured through your merits, and today I am going to eternal life, and I give thanks to God and to you. Blessed be your soul and your body; and blessed be your holy words and actions, because through you many souls will be saved in the world. Know that there is never a day when the holy angels and the other saints do not thank God for the holy fruit that you and your Order produce in different parts of the world; and be comforted and thank God, and remain with His blessing." Having said these words, he went to heaven, and Saint Francis remained greatly consoled.

To the praise of Jesus Christ
and the little poor man Francis.
Amen.

Chapter 26
How Saint Francis converted
three murderous robbers and
they became brothers; and the very noble
vision seen by one of them who was
a very holy brother

DBF XXIX   One time when Saint Francis was going through the area of Borgo San Sepolcro, he passed through a village named Monte Casale, and a young man came to him. He was noble and refined, and said to him: "Father, I would very much like to be one of your brothers." Saint Francis responded: "My son, you are young, refined and noble: perhaps you couldn't bear our poverty and hardship." But he said: "Father, aren't all of you human, like me? If you can endure it, so can I, with the grace of Christ." This answer pleased Saint Francis very much and so, blessing him, he immediately received him into the Order, and gave him the name Brother Angelo. And this young man behaved so graciously that shortly afterward Saint Francis made him Guardian in that place of Monte Casale.

At that time three famous robbers frequented that area, and they committed many evil deeds in the area. One day they came to that place of the brothers and asked Brother Angelo, the Guardian, to give them something to eat. But the Guardian answered them in this way, rebuking them sharply: "You! Robbers and cruel murderers! You aren't ashamed to steal the hard work of others and now you're bold and shameless enough to try to devour the alms sent to the servants of God! You aren't worth the ground to hold you up! You have no respect for people or the God who created you. Go! Mind your own business, and never show yourselves here again!" At this they left, disturbed and deeply offended.

Then Saint Francis returned from outside with a sack of bread and a small jug of wine that he and his companion had obtained. When the Guardian related how he had driven away those men, Saint Francis rebuked him severely, saying that he had acted cruelly: "They would be brought back to God more easily by sweetness than by cruel rebukes. Therefore our teacher Jesus Christ whose Gospel we have promised to observe, says that *it is not the healthy who need a doctor, but the sick,* and that He did *not come to call the just but to call sinners* to repentance, and for that reason *He* often *ate with them.* Therefore, since you have acted against charity and against the holy Gospel of Christ, I command you under holy obedience: immediately take this sack of bread and jug of wine that I obtained and go after them diligently through mountains and valleys until you find them. Then on my behalf present all this bread and wine to them. Then kneel down before them and humbly tell them your fault of being cruel. Then ask them on my behalf not to do evil anymore, but to fear God and not to offend their neighbors. And if they do this, I promise to provide for them in their need and constantly give them food and drink. And when you have told them these things, return here humbly." And while that Guardian went to carry out the command, Saint Francis placed himself in prayer and asked God to soften the hearts of those robbers and convert them to penance.

The obedient Guardian reached them and presented the bread and wine to them, and did and said what Saint Francis had commanded him. And, as it pleased God, as those robbers were eating the alms of Saint Francis, they began to say together: "Woe to us, miserable wretches! We can expect the hard pains of hell, and we go on not only robbing our neighbors and beating and wounding them, but we even kill them. Yet we have no remorse of conscience nor fear of God over so many evil deeds and such horrible things as we do. And here comes this holy brother to us, who has very humbly told us his fault for saying a few words which he said to us rightly because of our wickedness, and moreover, he has brought us bread and wine and the generous promise of the holy father. These really are holy brothers of God who deserve the paradise of God, and we are sons of

Mt 9: 12-13

Mt 9:11

eternal perdition, who deserve the pains of hell; and daily we increase our perdition, and we don't know if we'll be able to return to the mercy of God from the sins we have done up to now." As one of them was saying these and similar words the other two said: "What you're saying is really true, but what do we have to do?" The first one said: "Let's go to Saint Francis and if he gives us hope that we can turn from our sins to the mercy of God, we'll do what he commands us, and we can free our souls from the pains of hell."

This suggestion pleased the others, and so all three agreed and went quickly to Saint Francis and said to him: "Father, because of the many horrible sins we have done, we do not believe we can return to the mercy of God. But if you have any hope that God will receive us into His mercy, we're prepared to do what you tell us and to do penance with you." Then Saint Francis, receiving them charitably and kindly, encouraging them with many examples and assuring them of the mercy of God, promised them as certain that he would obtain this from God for them, showing them that the mercy of God is infinite: "And if we had infinite sins, the divine mercy is still greater than our sins, according to the Gospel; and the Apostle Saint Paul said, 'The blessed *Christ came into this world to redeem sinners.'*" _{1 Tm 1:15} Through these words and similar teachings, those three robbers renounced the demon and his works and Saint Francis received them into the Order, and they began to do great penance. And two of them lived only briefly after their conversion and went to Paradise. But the third survived and, thinking over his sins, gave himself to doing such penance that continually for fifteen years, except for the common Lents which he made with the other brothers, at other times he always fasted three days a week on bread and water, always going barefoot and wearing only one tunic; and he never slept after Matins.

During this time Saint Francis passed from this miserable life. And that brother, having continued such penance for many years, one night after Matins was overcome with such a temptation to sleep that he could in no way resist sleep and keep awake as he usually did. Finally, unable to resist sleep or to pray, he went to bed to sleep. As soon as he put down his head, he was caught up and led in spirit to the top of *a very high mountain,* where there was a very deep ravine, _{Mt 4:8} with broken boulders here and there and jagged rock formations coming out of the boulders, so that it was a frightening sight to look into that ravine. And the angel who was leading this brother pushed him and threw him down into that ravine. Falling headlong and striking rock after rock, and boulder after boulder, he finally came to the bottom of this ravine, all his limbs broken and torn, as it seemed to him. While he was lying there on the ground in bad shape, the one leading him said: "Get up, you must still make a long journey." The brother replied: "You seem to me a very undiscerning and cruel man. You see me about to die from the fall that has smashed me in this way, and you tell me 'Get up!'? " The angel came up to him and touched him, mending all his limbs perfectly and healing him. Then he showed him a huge plain of sharp and cutting stones, thorns and thistles, and told him that he had to run across that whole plain, going barefoot, until he reached the end, where he saw a burning furnace which he had to enter.

After the brother crossed that whole plain with great anguish and pain, the angel said to him: "Go into this furnace, for that is what you must do." The brother replied: "Oh, you are a cruel guide; you see me nearly dead from this terrible plain, and now for a rest you tell me to go into this burning furnace. And as he looked he saw around the furnace many demons with iron pitchforks in hand, and with these, since he hesitated to go in, they suddenly pushed him in. Once inside the furnace, he looked around and saw someone who had been his godfather and he was burning all over. And he asked him: "Poor Godfather, how did you come to be here?" And the other replied: "Go on a little further and you'll find my wife, your godmother and she'll tell you the reason for our damnation." As the brother went on further, that godmother appeared, all burning, enclosed in a measure for grain all made of fire, and he asked her: "Poor, pitiful Godmother, why did you come to such a cruel torment?" And she replied: "Because at the time of the great famine, which Saint Francis predicted in advance, my husband and I used false measures for the grain and meal we sold, therefore I am burning, tight in this measure."

At these words, the angel who was leading the brother pushed him out of the furnace and then said to him: "Prepare yourself to make a horrible journey, which you must undergo." The brother, grieving, said : "Oh, you're a hard guide, and you have no compassion for me. You see that I'm almost totally burned in this furnace, and you still want to take me on a dangerous and horrible journey!" Then the angel touched him and made him whole and strong. Then he led him to a bridge, which he could not cross without great danger because it was very thin and narrow and very slippery and without side-supports. Under it flowed a frightening river full of serpents and dragons and scorpions, and it gave off a great stench. The angel said to him: "Cross this bridge: you must absolutely cross it." But the brother replied: "How will I be able to cross it without falling into that dangerous river?" The angel said: "Follow me and put your foot where you see me put mine, and so you will cross safely." The brother, following the angel as he had told him, reached the middle of the bridge. And once he was in the middle of the bridge, the angel flew away and, leaving him, went up to a very high mountain quite far from the bridge. He noted carefully the place where the angel had flown, but remaining without a guide and looking down, he saw those terrifying animals raising their heads out of the water and their mouths open, ready to devour him if he fell. He stood there in such terror that he did not at all know what to do or say, for he could not turn back nor go forward.

Seeing himself in such distress and having no other refuge than in God alone, he bent over and embraced the bridge, and with all his heart and with tears he entrusted himself to God, that He should aid him by His most holy mercy. Having made this prayer, it seemed to him that he was starting to sprout wings, and because of this with great joy he waited for them to grow so that he could fly beyond the bridge to where the angel had flown. But after a little while, because of the great desire that he had to cross that bridge, he tried to fly; and since the wings on him had not yet grown, he fell onto the bridge and the feathers fell from him. So once again he embraced the bridge and entrusted himself to God as before. Having made this prayer, again it seemed to him that he was sprouting wings, and, as before, he did not wait for them to grow perfectly; and so, trying to fly ahead of time, he once again fell on the bridge, and the feathers fell from him. Because of this, seeing that he fell on account of the haste he had about flying too soon, he began to say to himself: "Surely if I sprout wings a third time, I will wait until they are big enough for me to fly without falling again." And as he had these thoughts it seemed to him that he was sprouting wings for a third time; and he waited a long time, until they were really big; and it seemed to him that for the first and second and third time the wings sprouted he had been waiting a good one hundred and fifty years. In the end this third time, with all his effort he lifted himself in flight, and he flew all the way to the place where the angel had flown.

When he arrived at the door of the palace where the angel was, the porter asked him: "Who are you who've come here?" The brother replied: "I am a Lesser Brother." The porter said: "Wait, because I want to bring Saint Francis here to see if he knows you." As he went to get Saint Francis, the brother began to look at the marvelous walls of this palace, and those walls appeared so shining and clear that he clearly saw the choirs of saints and what was done there. While he was standing there, he was dumbfounded by what he saw: Saint Francis was coming with Brother Bernard and Brother Giles, and behind Saint Francis such a multitude of men and women saints who had followed his life that it seemed innumerable. As Saint Francis reached him, he said to the porter: "Let him enter because he is one of my brothers."

And as soon as he entered there he felt so much consolation and so much sweetness that he forgot all the troubles he had, as if they had never existed. Then Saint Francis led him inside, pointing out many wonderful things to him, and then said to him: "My son, you must return to the world and remain there for seven days, in which you must carefully prepare yourself, because after seven days I will come for you, and then you will come with me to this place of the blessed." And Saint Francis was covered with a wonderful mantle, decorated with the most beautiful stars; and his five stigmata were like five beautiful stars of such brightness that they lit up the whole palace with their rays. And Brother Bernard had *on his head a crown of* the most beautiful *stars,* and Brother Giles was adorned by a marvelous light. And he met many other holy brothers among them, whom he had not seen in the world. Then, given permission by Saint Francis, he returned, although unwillingly, to the world.

Rv 12:1

As he awoke and returned to himself, the brothers were ringing for Prime, so he had not been in that state except from matins to Prime, although it seemed to him to have been there many years. As he recounted this vision in detail to his Guardian, within seven days he began to have a fever, and on the eighth day Saint Francis came for him, according to his promise, with a great multitude of glorious saints and brought his soul to the kingdom of the blessed, to eternal life.

To the praise of Jesus Christ
and of the little poor man Francis.
Amen.

Chapter 27
HOW AT BOLOGNA SAINT FRANCIS CONVERTED TWO STUDENTS AND THEY BECAME BROTHERS; AND THEN HE LIFTED A GREAT TEMPTATION FROM ONE OF THEM

Once as Saint Francis arrived at the city of Bologna all the people of the city ran to see him; and it was such a great crowd that the people could reach the piazza only with great difficulty. As the whole piazza was filled with men, women and students, Saint Francis got up in the middle of the place, up high, and began to preach what the

DBF XXX-I

Holy Spirit moved him to say. He preached so wonderfully that it seemed an angel was preaching, not a man; and his heavenly words seemed like *sharp arrows,* which so penetrated the hearts of those who heard him that during the sermon a great multitude of men and women were converted to penance.

Ps 120:4

Among these were two noble students from the March of Ancona, one named Pellegrino and the other Rinieri. These two, their hearts touched by divine inspiration, came to Saint Francis, saying that they wholeheartedly wished to leave the world and be among his brothers. Then Saint Francis, knowing by revelation that they had been sent by God and that they were to lead holy lives in the Order, and considering their great fervor, received them joyfully, saying to them: "You, Pellegrino, hold to the way of humility in the Order; and you, Rinieri, serve the brothers." And so it was: for Brother Pellegrino never wished to be a cleric brother but a lay brother, even though he was very educated and a great canonist. Because of his humility he arrived at the greatest perfection of virtue, so that Brother Bernard, the first-born of Saint Francis, said of him that he was one of the most perfect brothers in this world. Finally, this Brother Pellegrino, full of virtue, passed from this life to the blessed life, with many miracles before his death and afterward. And Brother Rinieri devotedly and faithfully served the brothers, living in great holiness and humility; and he became very friendly with Saint Francis, and Saint Francis revealed many secrets to him. He was made Minister of the March of Ancona, and governed it for a long time with the greatest peace and discernment.

After some time, God allowed a very great temptation in his soul. Troubled and anguished by it, he afflicted himself severely with fasts, with disciplines and with tears and prayers, day and night; but he could not drive out that temptation. Many times he was in great desperation, for because of it he believed that he was abandoned by God. In this desperation he decided to go to Saint Francis, thinking like this: "If Saint Francis looks kindly on me, and shows me friendship, as he usually does, I believe that God will still have pity on me; but if he doesn't, it will be a sign that I'll be abandoned by God." He set out therefore, and went to Saint Francis.

Saint Francis at that time was gravely ill, staying in the palace of the Bishop of Assisi. And God revealed to him everything about Brother Rinieri's temptation and desperation, his decision and his arrival. Saint Francis immediately called Brother Leo and Brother Masseo, and said to them: "Go quickly to meet my very dear son, Rinieri, and embrace him for me, and greet him and tell him that among all the brothers who are in the world I particularly love him."

They went and found Brother Rinieri on the road and embraced him, saying what Saint Francis had ordered them. Such consolation and sweetness came into his soul that he was nearly beside himself; and thanking God with all his heart, he went on and reached the place where Saint Francis was lying ill. And even though Saint Francis was gravely ill, he got up and went to meet him, embraced him, and said to him: "My dearest son, Brother Rinieri, among all the brothers who are in the world I particularly love you." After saying this, he made the sign of the most holy Cross on his forehead and kissed him there, and then said to him: "My dearest son, God permitted this temptation for you to gain great merit, but if you don't want to gain any more, you won't." An amazing thing happened: as soon as Saint Francis had said these words, all the temptation left him at once as if he had never experienced it in his whole life, and he remained utterly consoled.

To the praise of Jesus Christ
and the little poor man Francis.
Amen.

Chapter 28
OF A RAPTURE THAT CAME TO BROTHER BERNARD THAT
LEFT HIM OUT OF HIS SENSES FROM MORNING UNTIL NONE

The great grace that God showed many times to the evangelical poor who abandoned the world for love of Christ was shown in Brother Bernard of Quintavalle who, after he had taken the habit of Saint Francis, was very frequently rapt in God through contemplation of heavenly things. Among other times, once he was in church to hear Mass, and while his whole spirit was suspended in God, he became so absorbed and rapt in contemplation that, when the Body of Christ was being elevated he noticed nothing, nor did he kneel, nor did he pull back his capuche as the others did who were there. But without blinking his eyes, with a fixed stare, he remained out of his senses from morning until None. Returning to himself after None, he went through the place crying out in admiration: "Oh brothers! Oh brothers! Oh brothers! There is no one in this region so great or so noble for whom, if he were promised a very beautiful palace full of gold, it would not be easy to carry a sack full of manure in order to gain so noble a treasure."

Brother Bernard was so lifted up in spirit to this heavenly treasure, promised to lovers of God, that continually for fifteen years he

DBF XXXII

always went about with his spirit and his face lifted toward heaven. And during that time he never relieved his hunger at table, though he ate a little of what was placed before him, because he said that we do not practice perfect abstinence from things if we do not taste them; true abstinence is refraining from things that taste good to the mouth. And with this he had come to such clarity and light of intelligence that even great clerics came to him for solutions to the most difficult questions and obscure passages of Scripture; and he enlightened them on every difficulty.

Because his spirit was entirely set free and removed from earthly things, like the swallows he flew very high through contemplation, and sometimes for twenty days, sometimes for thirty days, he remained alone on the peaks of high mountains, contemplating heavenly things. For this reason Brother Giles used to say about him that others had not received this gift, which had been given to Brother Bernard of Quintavalle, that is, like a swallow, finding food for himself while flying. And because of this outstanding grace that he had from God, Saint Francis often and willingly talked with him by day and by night, so that sometimes they were found together rapt in God the whole night long in the woods where both of them met to speak with God.

To the praise of Jesus Christ
and the little poor man Francis.
Amen.

Chapter 29
HOW THE DEMON IN THE FORM OF THE CRUCIFIED
APPEARED SEVERAL TIMES TO BROTHER RUFINO, TELLING HIM
THAT HE WAS LOSING THE GOOD THAT HE WAS DOING
BECAUSE HE WAS NOT ONE OF THOSE CHOSEN FOR ETERNAL LIFE.
SAINT FRANCIS KNEW THIS BY GOD'S REVELATION,
AND MADE BROTHER RUFINO RECOGNIZE THE ERROR
THAT HE HAD BELIEVED

DBF XXXIII

Brother Rufino, one of the most noble men of Assisi, companion of Saint Francis, a man of great holiness, was once severely attacked and tempted in soul by the demon of predestination, because of which he was all melancholy and sad. For the demon even put into his heart the idea that he was damned, and was not among those predestined to eternal life, and that he was wasting whatever he was doing in the Order. And this temptation continued day after day, but he did not reveal it to Saint Francis; nevertheless he did not give up

2 Cor 2:3 his usual prayers and fasting; so the enemy began to add *sorrow* to *sorrow;* and besides the battle inside, also attacked him with false apparitions.

Thus one time the demon appeared to him in the form of the Crucified and said to him: "Oh Brother Rufino, why do you afflict yourself with penance and prayer, since you are not among those Jn 13:18 predestined to eternal life? Believe me, because *I know whom I have chosen* and predestined; and don't believe the son of Pietro Bernardone if he should say the opposite; and don't ask him about this matter because neither he nor others know it, but only I who am the Son of God. Therefore believe me: you are certainly among the number of the damned. And the son of Pietro Bernardone, your father, and also his father are damned, and whoever follows him is being deceived." And after these words were spoken Brother Rufino began to be so darkened by the prince of darkness that he had already lost all the faith and love he had for Saint Francis, and he did not bother to tell him anything about this.

But the Holy Spirit revealed to the holy father what Brother Rufino did not say. Therefore Saint Francis, seeing in spirit the great danger to this brother, sent Brother Masseo to get him, but Brother Rufino replied to him, grumbling: "What do I have to do with Brother Francis?" Then Brother Masseo, completely filled with divine wisdom, and recognizing the deceit of the demon, said: "Oh Brother Rufino, don't you know? Saint Francis is like an angel of God, who has illuminated so many souls in the world; and we have received from him the grace of God. So I want you absolutely to come with me to see him, because I clearly see that you are deceived by the demon." When this was said, Brother Rufino got up and went to Saint Francis.

And when Saint Francis saw him coming at a distance, he began to call out: "Oh, Brother Rufino, bad little man, whom did you believe?" And as Brother Rufino reached him, Saint Francis told him in detail the temptation he had had from the demon, inside and out, clearly showing him that the one who had appeared to him was the demon, and not Christ; and that, in no way should he consent to these suggestions, "But the next time the demon tells you, 'You are damned,' you tell him: 'Open your mouth and I'll shit in it.' This will be a sign for you that he is the devil and not Christ, that once you give this reply, he will flee immediately. You still should have recognized that he was the devil because by this he hardened your heart to all good: that is his special work. But the blessed Christ never hardens the heart of a faithful person; in fact, He softens it, as He says Ez 36:26 through the mouth of the prophet: '*I will take away your hearts of stone*

and give you hearts of flesh.' " Then Brother Rufino, seeing that Brother
Francis told him in detail the whole course of his temptation, was
stricken by his words, and began to weep heavily and adore Saint
Francis and humbly acknowledged his fault in hiding the temptation from him. And thus he remained completely consoled and comforted by the admonitions of the holy father, and completely
changed for the better. Finally Saint Francis said to him: "Go, my
son, and make your confession, and don't give up dedication to your
usual prayer, and know for certain that this temptation will be of
great profit and consolation for you, as you will soon discover."

Brother Rufino returned to his cell in the woods, and as he
remained in prayer with many tears, the enemy came impersonating
Christ in outward appearance and said to him: "Oh, Brother Rufino,
didn't I tell you not to believe the son of Pietro Bernardone? And not
to wear yourself out in tears and prayers, because you're damned?
What use is it to you to afflict yourself while you're alive, and then
when you die, you'll be damned?" Brother Rufino immediately
replied: "Open your mouth and I'll shit in it." The demon, indignant,
left immediately with such a great storm and shaking of rocks on
Mount Subasio up above there that for a long time rocks kept tum-
bling down. The crashing they made in colliding with each other was
so great that they sent horrible sparks of fire throughout the valley.
At this terrifying sound they made Saint Francis with the companions come outside the place in order to see what new thing this might
be; and people can still see that great pile of rocks. Then Brother
Rufino clearly recognized that the one who had tricked him was the
demon. He then went back to Saint Francis and once again threw
himself to the ground and acknowledged his fault. Saint Francis
comforted him with sweet words and sent him back, all consoled, to
the cell.

There, as he remained very devoutly in prayer, the blessed Christ
appeared to him and warmed his whole soul with divine love, and
said: "You did well, my son; you believed Brother Francis, because
the one who made you sad was the demon. But I am Christ, your
Master; and to make you quite certain I give you this sign: as long as
you live, you will not feel any sadness or melancholy." Having said
this, Christ departed, leaving him in such joy and sweetness of spirit
and elevation of soul that he was absorbed and rapt in God day and
night.

From then on, he was so confirmed in grace and in the assurance
of his salvation that he was completely changed into another man,
and he would have stayed contemplating the things of God day and
night, if others had let him. Therefore, Saint Francis used to say that

Brother Rufino was canonized by Christ in this life, and that he would not hesitate, except in front of him, to call him Saint Rufino, though he was still living on earth.

To the praise of Jesus Christ
and the little poor man Francis.
Amen.

Chapter 30
ABOUT THE BEAUTIFUL SERMON THAT SAINT FRANCIS AND BROTHER RUFINO GAVE IN ASSISI, WHEN THEY PREACHED NAKED

The same Brother Rufino was so absorbed in God through con- DBF XXXIV stant contemplation that he became as if unaware and mute. He very rarely spoke and, besides, he did not have the grace, the urge, or ability to preach. Nevertheless, Saint Francis once ordered him to go to Assisi and preach to the people whatever God should inspire him. At this Brother Rufino responded: "Reverend Father, I beg you to excuse me and not send me because, as you know, I do not have the grace of preaching, and I'm simple and uneducated." Then Saint Francis said: "Because you did not obey promptly, I command you under holy obedience that in just your breeches, naked as you were born, get to Assisi, and go into a church naked as you are, and preach to the people." At this command, the same Brother Rufino stripped himself and went to Assisi, and went into a church. After making his reverence to the altar, he climbed into the pulpit and began to preach. Children and adults began to laugh at such a thing, and they were saying: "Look, these men are doing so much penance that they're going crazy, out of their minds!"

In the meantime, as Saint Francis reflected on the prompt obedience of Brother Rufino, who was one of the great gentlemen of Assisi, and on the harsh command that he had given him, he began to rebuke himself, saying: "Where did you get such presumption, son of Pietro Bernardone, you vile little man, to command Brother Rufino, one of the great gentlemen of Assisi, to go preach naked to the people like a madman? By God, you'll experience yourself what you command of others!" In fervor of spirit he quickly stripped himself naked in the same way and went to Assisi, taking Brother Leo with him, who carried his habit and that of Brother Rufino. When the Assisians saw Saint Francis in that same state, they mocked him, thinking that he and Brother Rufino had gone crazy from too much penance. Saint Francis went into the church where Brother Rufino was preaching in these words: "My dear people, flee from the world and abandon sin; give back what belongs to others, if you want to avoid hell; observe the commandments of God, loving God and your neighbor, if you want to go to heaven; *do penance,* if you want to possess *the kingdom* of heaven." And then Saint Francis climbed into the pulpit naked and began to preach so wonderfully about despising the world, holy penance, voluntary poverty, the desire for the heavenly kingdom, about the nakedness and shame of the Passion of our Lord Jesus Christ, that all who were at the sermon, men and women in great numbers, began to weep loudly, with amazing devotion and compunction of heart; and not only there, but through all of Assisi there was such weeping that day over the Passion of our Lord Jesus Christ that there was never anything like it.

Mt 3:2

With the people edified in this way and consoled by the action of Saint Francis and Brother Rufino, Saint Francis reclothed Brother Rufino and himself, and thus reclothed, they returned to the place of the Portiuncula, praising and glorifying God who had given them grace to conquer themselves by despising themselves, and to edify Christ's sheep with good example, and showed how the world should be despised. And on that day the people's devotion toward them increased so much that those who were able *to touch the hem of* their habit considered themselves blessed.

Lk 8:44

To the praise of Jesus Christ
and the little poor man Francis.
Amen.

Chapter 31
HOW SAINT FRANCIS KNEW IN DETAIL THE SECRETS OF CONSCIENCE OF ALL HIS BROTHERS

DBF XXXVII

Just as our Lord Jesus Christ says in the Gospel: *"I know my sheep, and my sheep know me . . ."* so the blessed Father Saint Francis, as a good shepherd, knew by divine inspiration all the merits and virtues of his companions and also knew their failings; therefore he knew how to provide the best remedies for them all, that is: humbling the proud; exalting the humble; reviling vices and praising virtues, just as we read in the amazing revelations he had about his earliest family.

Jn 10:14

Among these we find that once Saint Francis was in a certain place with that same family conversing about God, and Brother Rufino was not with them for that conversation, but was in the woods in contemplation. As that conversation about God continued, Brother Rufino came out of the woods and passed by, a short distance from them. Then Saint Francis, seeing him, turned to the companions and questioned them, saying: "Tell me, which is the holiest soul that God has in this world?" And they replied that they thought that it was his. And Saint Francis said to them: "My dear brothers, of myself I'm the most vile man that God has in this world. But do you see this Brother Rufino who's now coming out of the woods? God has revealed to me that his soul is one of the three holiest souls in the world. And I tell you confidently that I wouldn't hesitate to call him Saint Rufino during his lifetime, since his soul is confirmed in grace, and sanctified and canonized in heaven by our Lord Jesus Christ." And Saint Francis would never say these words in the presence of that same Brother Rufino.

In a similar way, how Saint Francis knew the faults of his brothers can be clearly seen regarding Brother Elias, whom he often rebuked for his pride; and regarding Brother John de Capella, about whom he predicted that he would hang himself by the neck; and regarding that brother whom the devil held tightly by the throat when he was being corrected for his disobedience; and regarding many other brothers whose secret faults and whose virtues he knew clearly by Christ's revelation.

To the praise of Jesus Christ
and the little poor man Francis.
Amen.

Chapter 32
HOW BROTHER MASSEO RECEIVED FROM CHRIST
THE VIRTUE OF HOLY HUMILITY

The first companions of Saint Francis strove with all their strength to be poor in earthly things and rich in virtues, by which one arrives at true riches, heavenly and eternal.   DBF XL

It happened that one day when they were gathered together to speak about God, one of them gave this example: "There was someone who was a great friend of God, and he had great grace in active life and contemplative life; and with this he had such excessive humility that he thought himself the greatest of sinners. This humility sanctified him and confirmed him in grace, and made him grow constantly in virtues and the gifts of God, and never allowed him to fall into sin." As Brother Masseo heard such wonderful things about humility and realized that this was a treasure of eternal life, he began to be so inflamed with love and desire for this virtue of humility that, raising his face to heaven in great fervor, he made a vow and a very firm promise never to be happy in this world until he felt this virtue perfectly in his soul. And from then on he remained almost constantly enclosed in a cell, mortifying himself with fasting, vigils, prayers and loud weeping before God, to receive from Him this virtue, without which he believed himself worthy of hell, and with which that friend of God was so gifted, as he had heard.

As Brother Masseo remained many days with this desire, he happened one day to go into the woods and, in fervor of spirit, walked through the woods pouring out tears, sighs and cries, asking God for this divine virtue with fervent desire. And since God willingly hears the prayers of the humble and contrite, as Brother Masseo remained in this state a voice came from heaven and called him twice: "Brother Masseo! Brother Masseo!" Knowing in spirit that it was the voice of Christ, he replied: "My Lord!" And Christ said to him: "And what do you want to give to have this grace you ask?" Brother Masseo responded: "Lord, I want to give the eyes in my head." And Christ said to him: "And I want you to have the grace and the eyes too." At these words the voice disappeared; and Brother Masseo remained full of such grace of that desired virtue of humility and of the light of God that from then on he was always jubilant. Often when he was praying, he would constantly make a formless cry of joy with a soft voice like a dove: "Ooo, Ooo, Ooo;" and would remain in contemplation with a happy face and cheerful heart. And with this, having become very humble, he considered himself the least of all the people of the world.

When asked by Brother James of Fallerone why he did not change the tune in his cry of joy he responded with great joy that when in one thing all good is found, there is no need to change the tune.

To the praise of Jesus Christ
and the little poor man Francis.
Amen.

Chapter 33

How Saint Clare, at the Pope's Command, Blessed the Bread
That Was on the Table;
And on Every Loaf There Appeared
The Sign of the Cross

Saint Clare, a most devoted disciple of the Cross and noble plant
of Sir Saint Francis, was of such holiness that not only the bishops
and cardinals but even the pope desired with great affection to see
her and listen to her, and often visited her personally.

DBF XLII

One time among others the Holy Father went to her at the monastery to hear her speak of heavenly and divine things; and as they
were speaking together about various things, Saint Clare had the
tables prepared and bread placed on them, so that the Holy Father
might bless it. So, when their spiritual conversation was finished,
Saint Clare knelt down with great reverence, and asked him to be
kind enough to bless the bread placed on the table. The Holy Father
replied: "My most faithful Sister Clare, I want you to bless this bread,
and make over it the sign of the most holy Cross, to which you have
given your whole self." And Saint Clare said: "Most Holy Father, forgive me, because I would be worthy of the greatest rebuke if in front
of the Vicar of Christ I, who am a vile little woman, should presume
to give such a blessing." And the pope replied: "So that this may not
be attributed to presumption but to the merit of obedience, I command you under holy obedience to make the sign of the most holy
Cross over this bread and bless it in the name of God." Then Saint
Clare, as a true *daughter of obedience,* very devoutly blessed that bread
with the sign of the most holy Cross of Christ. An amazing thing happened! Immediately the sign of the Cross appeared, beautifully cut
into each loaf. And then some of these loaves were eaten and others
were kept because of the miracle. And the Holy Father, having seen
the miracle, took some of that bread and, giving thanks to God,
departed, leaving Saint Clare with his blessing.

1 Pt 1:14

At that time living in that monastery were Sister Ortulana,
mother of Saint Clare, and Sister Agnes, her sister, both together,
with Saint Clare, filled with virtues and with the Holy Spirit, and
many other holy nuns. To them Saint Francis sent many sick people;
and with their prayers and the sign of the most holy Cross they
returned them all to health.

To the praise of Jesus Christ
and the little poor man Francis.
Amen.

Chapter 34
HOW SAINT LOUIS THE KING OF FRANCE
WENT IN PERSON TO PERUGIA DRESSED AS A PILGRIM
TO VISIT THE HOLY BROTHER GILES

DBF XLIII

Saint Louis, the King of France, went on pilgrimage to visit the shrines throughout the world. Hearing about the great reputation for holiness of Brother Giles, who was one of the first companions of Saint Francis, he decided in his heart and firmly determined to visit him personally. For this reason he went to Perugia where Brother Giles was staying.

Arriving at the door of the place of the brothers like a poor, unknown pilgrim, with few companions, he asked urgently for Brother Giles, not telling the porter anything about who was asking for him. So the porter went to Brother Giles and said that there was a pilgrim at the door who was asking for him; and God inspired him and revealed to him in spirit that it was the King of France. So with great fervor he immediately came out of the cell and ran to the door, and without any further questions, though they had never seen each other, they both knelt down with great devotion, embraced each other and kissed each other with such familiarity as if they had shared a great friendship for a long time. But during this whole time neither of them said anything to the other but remained in silence, embracing with those signs of charitable love. Having stayed this way for a long time without saying a word to each other, they parted from each other; and Saint Louis resumed his journey, and Brother Giles returned to the cell.

As the King was leaving, a brother asked one of his companions who that man was, who had been embracing Brother Giles, and he replied that it was Louis, King of France, who had come in order to see Brother Giles. When he told this to the other brothers they were very upset that Brother Giles had not spoken a word to him, and they said to him bitterly: "O Brother Giles, why were you so rude? Here is a king who came from France to see you and to hear some good word from you, and you didn't say anything to him?" Brother Giles replied: "O dear brothers, don't be surprised at this: he couldn't say a word to me, nor I to him, because as soon as we embraced, the light of divine wisdom revealed and manifested his heart to me, and mine to him; and so, by divine action, as we looked into each other's hearts: whatever I wanted to say to him, or he to me, we already knew much better than if we had spoken with our mouths, and with greater consolation. And if we had wanted to express out loud what we felt in our hearts, that would have been more a cause of

desolation than consolation because of the defects of human language, which cannot express clearly the secret mysteries of God. But
you should know for certain that the King departed wonderfully
consoled."

To the praise of Jesus Christ
and the little poor man Francis.
Amen.

Chapter 35
HOW SAINT CLARE WHILE SHE WAS ILL
WAS MIRACULOUSLY CARRIED
TO THE CHURCH OF SAINT FRANCIS ON THE NIGHT
OF THE FEAST OF CHRISTMAS
AND HEARD THE OFFICE THERE

Once Saint Clare was seriously ill, so that she could not go to say   DBF XLI
the Office in church with the other nuns. When the solemnity of the
Nativity of Christ arrived, all the others went to matins, and she
remained in bed, unhappy that she could not go together with the
others to have that spiritual consolation. But Jesus Christ, her
spouse, not wishing to leave her this way without consolation, had
her miraculously carried to the Church of Saint Francis to be present
for the whole Office of matins and the night Mass, and besides this,
to receive Holy Communion, and then had her carried back to her
bed.

When the Office in San Damiano was finished and the nuns
returned to Saint Clare, they said to her: "O Sister Clare, our Mother,
what great consolation we've had on this Holy Nativity! If only it
pleased God that you could have been with us!" And Saint Clare
replied: "My sisters and dearest daughters, I give thanks and praise
to Our Blessed Lord Jesus Christ, because I have been present at all
the solemnities of this holy night, and at greater ones than you have
been, with much consolation to my soul, for by the intercession of
my father Saint Francis and by the grace of Our Lord Jesus Christ,
with the ears of my body and spirit I heard the whole Office and the
music of the organ there and in that very place I received Holy Communion. Therefore, rejoice and thank God for such grace shown to
me."

To the praise of Jesus Christ
and the little poor man Francis.
Amen.

Chapter 36
How Saint Francis described to Brother Leo
A beautiful vision he had seen

DBF LX One time when Saint Francis was seriously ill and Brother Leo was taking care of him, that same Brother Leo was near Saint Francis and was praying, and he was rapt in ecstasy and led in spirit to a very great river, wide and turbulent. As he was watching those crossing over, he saw some brothers with heavy loads entering that river. They were immediately overwhelmed by the force of the river and drowned. Several others went a third of the way across the river, and some as far as the middle of the river, and some as far as the shore; but all of them, because of the force of the river and the loads they carried with them, finally fell in and drowned. Brother Leo, seeing this, felt great compassion for them; and suddenly, as he stood there, a great multitude of brothers arrived, without any loads or burdened by anything at all, and in whom shone holy poverty. They entered the river and crossed it without any harm at all. Having seen this, Brother Leo returned to himself.

Then Saint Francis, sensing in spirit that Brother Leo had seen a vision, called him to himself, and asked him what he had seen. And the same Brother Leo told him the whole vision in detail, and Saint Francis said: "What you saw is true. The great river is this world; the brothers who drowned in the river are those who do not follow their evangelical profession especially in regard to the highest poverty. Those who crossed without danger are those brothers who neither seek nor possess anything earthly or anything of the flesh, but *are content having* only basic *food and clothing,* following Christ naked on the Cross and willingly and happily carrying the burden and the gentle yoke of Christ and of holy obedience; and therefore they cross easily from temporal life to eternal life." 1 Tm 6:8

To the praise of Jesus Christ
and the little poor man Francis.
Amen.

Chapter 37
How the Blessed Jesus Christ, at the prayer of Saint Francis,
made a rich and noble knight convert and become a brother,
a man who had rendered great honor and service to Saint Francis

DBF LXI Saint Francis, the servant of Christ, late one evening reached the house of a great and powerful gentleman, who received him as a

guest, him and a companion, like angels of God, with the greatest
courtesy and devotion. For this reason Saint Francis had great love
for him, considering how on entering the house he had embraced
him and kissed him in a friendly way, and then had washed his feet
and dried them and kissed them humbly, and lit a great fire and prepared the table with many good kinds of food, and while he was eating the man kept serving him constantly with a happy expression.
So, when Saint Francis and the companion had eaten, this gentleman said: "Look, my father. I offer you myself and my things; whenever you have need of a tunic or mantle or anything at all, buy it and I
will pay; and you see that I'm prepared to provide for all your needs
since, by the grace of God, I can do so because I have an abundance of
temporal goods, but for the love of God, who gave them to me, I
gladly give them to His poor."

Saint Francis, seeing such courtesy and loving kindness in him
and the generous offer, conceived such love for him that as he left
with his companion he said: "Truly this gentleman would be good
for our religion and company, he is so thankful and grateful to God
and so loving and courteous to his neighbor and to the poor. Dear
Brother, know that courtesy is one of the qualities of God, who gives
His sun and his rain to the just and unjust out of courtesy; and courtesy is the sister of charity, extinguishing hatred and preserving love.
And since I have recognized such divine virtue in this good man, I'd
gladly have him as a companion; so I want us to return to him one
day, if God should perhaps touch his heart to make him want to join
us in the service of God; and in the meantime we'll pray to God that
He put this desire in his heart and gives him the grace to put it into
practice." Something amazing happened: a few days later, after
Saint Francis had made his prayer, God put that desire in the heart of
this gentleman; and Saint Francis said to the companion: "My
brother, let's go to that courteous man, because I have firm hope in
God that he who shows courtesy in temporal things will give his very
self and will be our companion." And off they went.

On reaching his house, Saint Francis said to the companion:
"Wait for me a bit, because I first want to pray to God that He make
our journey fruitful, that Christ, by virtue of His most holy passion,
be pleased to give us poor and weak men this noble prey that we're
planning to take from the world." Having said this, he placed himself
in prayer in a place where that courteous man could see him. And it
pleased God, as that man was looking here and there he saw Saint
Francis devoutly at prayer before Christ, who had appeared to him
during that prayer and was in front of him; and as the man stood
there, he saw Saint Francis lifted up bodily from the earth. Because

Mt 5:45

of this he was so touched by God and inspired to leave the world, that he suddenly came out from his palace and in fervor of spirit ran toward Saint Francis and coming up to him, as he was still in prayer, knelt down at his feet and with great urgency and devotion begged him to be pleased to receive him to do penance together with him. Then Saint Francis, seeing that his prayer had been heard by God, and that what he desired was what that gentleman was asking with great urgency, he got up in fervor and joy of spirit and embraced and kissed the man, devoutly thanking God, who had added to his company such a knight. And that gentleman said to Saint Francis: "What do you command me to do, my father? See, I am prepared at your command to give what I possess to the poor and with you to follow Christ, letting go of every temporal thing."

And he did just that, following the advice of Saint Francis: he distributed what he had to the poor and entered the Order, and he lived in great penance and holiness of life and worthy behavior.

To the praise of Jesus Christ
and the little poor man Francis.
Amen.

Chapter 38
HOW SAINT FRANCIS KNEW IN SPIRIT
THAT BROTHER ELIAS WAS DAMNED AND WOULD DIE OUTSIDE THE ORDER;
AND WHY, AT THE PRAYER OF BROTHER ELIAS,
HE PRAYED TO CHRIST FOR HIM AND WAS HEARD

DBF LXII   Once while Saint Francis and Brother Elias were staying together with a family at a certain place it was revealed to Saint Francis by God that Brother Elias was damned and would be an apostate from the Order and finally die outside the Order. For this reason Saint Francis conceived such dislike for him that he would not talk or stay with him. And if Brother Elias at times walked toward him, he would change direction and walk the other way so as not to meet him. Brother Elias began to be aware of this and to understand that Saint Francis was displeased with him. So, wanting to know the reason for this, one day he drew alongside Saint Francis to speak with him; and as Saint Francis turned to avoid him, Brother Elias politely but firmly held him and began to ask him carefully that he please indicate to him the reason why he was avoiding his company in this way or even speaking with him. And Saint Francis answered him: "The reason is this: because it has been revealed to me by God that because of your sins you will be an apostate from the Order and will die outside the Order, and God also revealed to me that you are damned." When Brother Elias heard this, he said: "My revered Father, I beg you, for the love of Christ, that because of this you do not avoid me nor drive

Lk 15:4-7

me away from you, but like a good shepherd, following the example of Christ, that you find and pick up the sheep that will perish if you do not help him; and pray to God for me that, if it is possible, He revoke the sentence of my damnation, because we find it written that God can change the sentence if the sinner turns from his sin; and I have such faith in your prayers that, if I were in the middle of hell and you prayed to God for me, I would feel some relief. Therefore, once again I beg you that you recommend me, a sinner, to God, who came to save sinners, that He may receive me into His mercy." And Brother Elias said this with great devotion and tears; because of which Saint Francis, like a merciful father, promised him that he would pray to God for him, and so he did.

As he was praying to God very devoutly for him he understood by revelation that God had granted his prayer in regard to the sentence of damnation for Brother Elias, that at the end his soul would not be damned, but that he certainly would leave the Order and would die outside the Order. And so it happened: because, when Frederick, King of Sicily, rebelled against the Church and was excommunicated by the pope, along with anyone who gave him help or advice, the same Brother Elias, who was considered one of the wisest men of the world, at the request of the same King Frederick, joined him and became a rebel against the Church and an apostate from the Order; for which he was excommunicated by the pope and deprived of the habit of Saint Francis.

While he was still excommunicated, he became seriously ill; and hearing of the illness, a brother of his who was a lay brother, and who had remained in the Order and was a man of good and worthy life, went to visit him, and among other things said to him: "My dearest brother, it hurts me greatly that you are excommunicated, and outside your Order, and will die like this; but if you can see a way or manner by which I can save you from this danger, I would willing undertake any hardship for you." Brother Elias answered: "My brother, I see no other way except if you go to the pope and beg him, for the love of God and of Saint Francis his servant, because of whose teachings I abandoned the world, to absolve me from his excommunication and restore to me the habit of the Religion." His brother said that he would gladly wear himself out for the sake of his salvation; and on leaving him, he went to the feet of the holy pope, begging him humbly to pardon his brother for the love of Christ and of Saint

Francis his servant. And, as it pleased God, the pope granted this: he was to return and, if he found Brother Elias alive, he should absolve him on his behalf from the excommunication and restore the habit to him. So the brother departed happy over this and returned to Brother Elias in a great hurry; and finding him alive, but almost at the point of death, he absolved him from the excommunication and, as he was putting the habit on him, Brother Elias passed from this life, and his soul was saved by the merits of Saint Francis and by his prayer, in which Brother Elias had such great faith.

To the praise of Jesus Christ
and the little poor man Francis.
Amen.

Chapter 39
ABOUT THE WONDERFUL SERMON GIVEN BY SAINT ANTHONY OF PADUA, LESSER BROTHER, IN CONSISTORY

DBF XLIV

Sir Saint Anthony of Padua, that wonderful vessel of the Holy Spirit and one of the chosen disciples and companions of Saint Francis, whom Saint Francis called his bishop, was preaching one time before the pope and the cardinals in a consistory, and in that consistory there were men of different nations, Greek, Latin, French, German, Slavs, English and many others of diverse languages of the world. Inflamed by the Holy Spirit, he proclaimed the word of God so effectively, so devoutly, so subtly, so sweetly, so clearly, and so understandably that all those who were in the Consistory, though of different languages, understood clearly his every word, as if he had spoken in the language of each of them; and all were amazed, and it seemed that the ancient miracle of the Apostles at the time of Pentecost had been renewed, as they had spoken in every language by virtue of the Holy Spirit. Acts 2:4-13

Together they said to each other in amazement: "The one who is preaching, *is he not* from Spain? Then how do *we* all *hear* in his words *the language of* our own countries?" The pope also, reflecting and marveling at the profundity of his words, said: "He is truly the Ark of the Covenant and the Library of Holy Scripture." Acts 2:7, 8

Acts 9:15

To the praise of Jesus Christ
and the little poor man Francis.
Amen.

Chapter 40
OF THE MIRACLE THAT GOD PERFORMED WHEN SAINT ANTHONY
AT RIMINI PREACHED TO THE FISH OF THE SEA

The blessed Christ, wishing to show the great holiness of his most   DBF XLV
faithful servant, Sir Saint Anthony, and how devoutly his preaching
and holy teaching should be heeded, refuted the foolishness of unbelieving heretics by using irrational animals, one time among others,
by using fish, just as in ancient times in the Old Testament He had
Nm 22:22-35   refuted the foolishness of Balaam by the mouth of the ass. For once
when Saint Anthony was in Rimini, where there was a great number
of heretics, and wishing that they return to the light of the true faith
and the way of truth, he preached to them for many days and discussed the faith of Christ and the Holy Scriptures. But as they not
only did not agree with his holy speeches, but actually became hardened and obstinate, and did not want to hear him, by divine inspiration Saint Anthony went one day to the mouth of the river close by
the sea, and standing on the bank between the river and the sea, he
began, as if preaching, calling the fish on behalf of God: "Listen to
the Word of God, you fish of the sea and the river, because the unbelieving heretics refuse to listen." And as soon as he said this, immediately such a multitude of large fish came to him at the bank that such
a great multitude had never been seen there. They all held their
heads above the water, all turned to face Saint Anthony, and all in
great peace and meekness and order: in front of the bank and closer
in were the little fish, and behind them the medium fish, and then
behind them, where the water was deepest, the biggest fish.

When all the fish were arranged and lined up in this way, Saint
Anthony began to preach solemnly and said: "My brother fish, you
have a great obligation, according to your ability, to give thanks to
your Creator, who has given you such a noble element for your home.
You have fresh or salt water, as you like. And he has given you many
shelters to avoid storms. Moreover, He has given you an element that
Gn 1:20-22   is clear and transparent, and food to eat by which you can live. God,
your courteous and kind Creator, when He created you, gave you a
commandment to increase and multiply, and He gave you His bless-
Gn 6-7   ing. Then when there was the Flood over everything, and all the
other animals died, God preserved only you without harm. Further-
Jn 2:1-11   more, He has given you fins so you can go anywhere you please. By
the command of God you were allowed to preserve Jonah the
prophet, and after the third day to spit him onto the land, safe and
Mt 17:23-26   sound. You presented the tax-coin to our Lord Jesus Christ when, as
Mt 15:32-37;   a little poor man, he did not have any way to pay. You were the food
Lk 24:41-43;
Jn 21:1-14

of the Eternal King Jesus Christ before the Resurrection and after it, by a singular mystery. Because of all these things you are greatly bound to praise and bless God, Who has given you so many and such great gifts, more than to other creatures." At these and similar words the fish began to open their mouths and bowed their heads, and with these and other signs of reverence, according to what was possible to them, they praised God. Then Saint Anthony, seeing the great reverence of the fish toward God the Creator, rejoicing in spirit, cried out in a loud voice: "Blessed be the Eternal God, because aquatic fish honor God more than heretic humans, and unreasoning animals hear His word better than unbelieving people!" And the more Saint Anthony preached, the more the number of fish increased, and not one left the place which it had taken.

The people of the city began to run toward this miracle, and among them were even those same heretics who, on seeing such an amazing and clear miracle, stricken to the heart, threw themselves at the feet of Saint Anthony to hear his sermon. And then Saint Anthony began to preach about the Catholic faith, and he preached about it so nobly that he converted all those heretics and they returned to the true faith of Christ; and all the faithful were filled with joy, comforted and strengthened in the faith. Having done this, Saint Anthony dismissed the fish with God's blessing, and all of them departed with amazing gestures of joy, and the people too. And then Saint Anthony stayed for many days in Rimini, preaching and producing great spiritual fruit of souls.

To the praise of Jesus Christ
and the little poor man Francis.
Amen.

Chapter 41
HOW THE VENERABLE BROTHER SIMON
FREED FROM A GREAT TEMPTATION A BROTHER
WHO FOR THIS REASON WANTED TO LEAVE THE ORDER

DBF LV   Near the beginning of the Order, while Saint Francis was alive, a young man of Assisi came to the Order, and he was called Brother Simon, and God adorned him and gifted him with so much grace and so much contemplation and elevation of spirit that his whole life was a mirror of holiness, as I heard from those who were with him for a long time. He rarely was seen outside the cell and, if he was with the brothers sometimes, he always spoke of God. He had never learned grammar and nevertheless he spoke of God and the love of Christ so deeply and highly that his words seemed supernatural. Therefore, one evening when he had gone into the woods with Brother James of Massa to speak of God, and speaking very sweetly of divine love, they remained all night in that conversation; and in the morning it seemed to them only a very brief time had passed, as the same Brother James recounted to me. And that same Brother Simon received divine illuminations and loving visitations from God with such gentleness and sweetness of spirit that often, when he felt them coming, he would lie down on the bed, because the serene gentleness of the Holy Spirit required not only repose of his soul, but even of his body. And in those divine visitations he was very often rapt into God and became completely unaware of bodily things. Therefore once when he was thus rapt in God and unaware of the world, and he burned inwardly with divine love and felt nothing outwardly with the bodily senses, a brother who wanted to test this, to see if he was as he seemed, went and took a burning coal and put it on his naked foot. And Brother Simon felt nothing, and it made no mark on his foot, even though it stayed there for such a long time that it put itself out. That same Brother Simon, when he sat at table, before taking bodily food, took for himself and distributed spiritual food by speaking of God.

Once through his devout speaking a young man from San Severino was converted, one who was a very vain and worldly young man in society, noble in blood and very delicate in body. And Brother Simon, when receiving the young man into the Order, kept his secular clothes with him, as the young man stayed with Brother Simon to be informed about the Rule's observance. Because of this the demon, striving to prevent every good thing, put into him such a strong impulse and such a burning temptation of the flesh that the young man could not resist it by any means. For this reason he went to Brother Simon and said to him: "Give me back the clothes that I wore in the world, because I can't resist the temptation of the flesh any longer." And Brother Simon, having great compassion for him, said to him: "Son, sit down here with me for a little while." And he began to speak to him of God, in such a way that the whole temptation left him; and then after a while, as the temptation returned, and he kept asking for his clothes, Brother Simon would drive it away by speaking of God.

Having done this several times, finally one night that temptation attacked him more strongly than usual, and he could not resist it for anything in the world. He went to Brother Simon demanding absolutely to have his secular clothes, because he could by no means stay there any more. Then Brother Simon, as he usually did, had him sit down beside him and, as he was speaking to him of God, the young man leaned his head onto Brother Simon's breast out of melancholy and sadness. Then Brother Simon, because of the great compassion he had toward him, *raised his eyes to heaven* and, praying to God devoutly for him, was enraptured and heard by God; then he returned to himself, and the young man felt himself completed freed from that temptation, as if he had never felt it.

Rather, the heat of the temptation changed into the heat of the Holy Spirit, because he was near burning coal, that is, near Brother Simon, and he became all inflamed with love of God and neighbor, so much that when a criminal was once captured, both of whose eyes were to be torn out, he, out of compassion, went hotly to the Rector in front of the whole Council, and with many tears and devout pleas asked that one of his eyes be torn out, and another from the criminal, so the man would not be deprived of both. But the Rector and the Council, seeing the great fervor of charity of this brother, gave a pardon to the one and the other.

When the same Brother Simon was in the woods one day at prayer and feeling great consolation in his soul, a flock of crows began to annoy him with their cries, so he commanded them in the name of Jesus Christ to depart and not return there again. And those birds departed at that moment, and from then on they were never heard nor seen, neither there nor in the whole surrounding area. And this miracle was known throughout the whole custody of Fermo, in which that place was located.

To the praise of Jesus Christ
and the little poor man Francis.
Amen.

Chapter 42
ABOUT THE BEAUTIFUL MIRACLES GOD WORKED
THROUGH THE HOLY BROTHERS, BROTHER BENTIVOGLIA,
BROTHER PETER OF MONTICELLO AND BROTHER CONRAD OF OFFIDA;
AND HOW BROTHER BENTIVOGLIA CARRIED A LEPER FIFTEEN MILES
IN A VERY SHORT TIME;
AND SAINT MICHAEL SPOKE TO ANOTHER;
AND THE VIRGIN MARY CAME TO ANOTHER AND PUT HER SON IN HIS ARMS

The Province of the March of Ancona in olden days was adorned with holy and exemplary brothers as the sky is with stars, and they, like the lights of heaven, have illuminated and adorned the Order of

Lk 6:20; Jn 17:1

DBF XLVIII

Jn 5:35

Saint Francis and the world with their example and teaching. Among others the first were Brother Lucido the Elder, who was truly lucid, *shining* in his holiness and *burning* with divine love; and his glorious tongue, guided by the Holy Spirit, produced wonderful fruit in preaching.

Another was Brother Bentivoglia of San Severino, whom Brother Masseo of San Severino saw lifted up in the air for a long time while he was praying in the woods. Because of this miracle, the devout Brother Masseo, who was then a parish priest, gave up his parish and became a Lesser Brother; and he was a man of such holiness that he performed many miracles in life and after death, and his body now rests at Marro. That same Brother Bentivoglia was staying alone at Trave Bonanti to care for and serve a leper; and being commanded by the Prelate to depart from there and go to another place, which was fifteen miles away, and not wishing to abandon that leper, with great fervor of charity he took him and put him on his shoulders and carried him from dawn until sunrise the whole way, fifteen miles, to that other place where he had been sent, called Monte Sancino. If he had been an eagle, he could not have flown on that journey in such a short time. And there was great amazement and wonder at this miracle in that whole town.

Another was Brother Peter of Monticello, whom Brother Servadeo of Urbino, who was at that time Guardian in the old place at Ancona, saw lifted up bodily from the ground five or six arm-lengths, to the feet of the crucifix of the church, in front of which he was praying. And this Brother Peter was fasting once for the Lent of Saint Michael the Archangel with great devotion, and on the last day of that Lent, as he stayed in the church at prayer, he was heard by a young brother, who had hidden himself under the high altar to see some act of his holiness, and he heard him speak with Saint Michael the Archangel, and these were the words they said. Saint Michael said: "Brother Peter, you have labored faithfully for me and have afflicted your body in many ways. I have come to console you, so you may ask me for any grace you wish, and I will ask God for this grace for you." Brother Peter replied: "O most holy Prince of the heavenly army and most faithful zealot of divine love, and merciful protector of souls, I ask you for this grace, that you beg God for me the pardon of all my sins." Saint Michael responded: "Ask for another grace, for I will obtain this one for you very easily." But Brother Peter would not ask for anything else, so the Archangel concluded: "Because of the confidence and devotion you have toward me, I will procure for you this grace which you ask and many others." When they ended their conversation, which lasted a long time, the Archangel Saint Michael departed, leaving him greatly comforted.

In the time of this holy Brother Peter, there was the holy Brother Conrad of Offida, who together with him was in the family at the place of Forano in the custody of Ancona. That same Brother Conrad one day went into the woods to contemplate about God, and Brother Peter followed him secretly to see what would happen to him. And Brother Conrad began to put himself at prayer, praying very devoutly to the Virgin Mary that with great mercy she would acquire for him this grace from her blessed Son: that he could feel a little of that sweetness which Saint Simeon felt the day of the Purification when he held *in his arms* the blessed Savior Jesus. When this prayer was finished, the merciful Virgin Mary granted it; the Queen of heaven appeared with her blessed Son in her arms, with a very bright light. Drawing near Brother Conrad she placed in his arms that blessed Son, and he took Him, embracing Him most devoutly, kissing Him, and hugging Him to his breast, and he was completely consumed and dissolved in divine love and unspeakable consolation. And in a similar way Brother Peter, who saw everything from his hiding place, felt in his soul the greatest sweetness and consolation. And as the Virgin Mary departed from Brother Conrad, Brother Peter hurried to return to the place so he would not be seen by him. But when Brother Conrad returned, all happy and glad, Brother Peter said: "O heavenly brother, you've had a great consolation today!" Brother Conrad said to him: "What do you mean, Brother Peter? What do you know about what I received?" Brother Peter said: "I know, I know very well: the Virgin Mary with her blessed Son visited you." Then Brother Conrad asked him not to tell anyone, because he was a truly humble man and hoped to keep the graces of God secret. And there was such love between these two from that time on that it seemed in all things there was *one heart and one soul* between them.

And one time the same Brother Conrad, in the place at Sirolo, by means of his prayers freed a woman possessed by a demon, praying for her all night long and appearing to her mother; and in the morning he fled so as not to be found and honored by the people.

> To the praise of Jesus Christ
> and the little poor man Francis.
> Amen.

Lk 2:28

Acts 4:32

Chapter 43
HOW BROTHER CONRAD OF OFFIDA CONVERTED A YOUNG BROTHER
WHO BOTHERED THE OTHER BROTHERS.
AND HOW THAT SAME YOUNG BROTHER, WHEN HE WAS DYING
APPEARED TO THE SAME BROTHER CONRAD,
BEGGING HIM TO PRAY FOR HIM; AND HOW HE FREED HIM
FROM THE GREAT PAINS OF PURGATORY

The same Brother Conrad of Offida was an admirable zealot of   DBF XLVI
evangelical poverty and of the Rule of Saint Francis, and was of such
religious life and such merit before God that the blessed Christ honored him with many miracles in life and in death.

Among these, one time he had come as a guest to the place at
Offida, and the brothers asked him for the love of God and charity to
admonish a young brother who was in that place, who was acting
childishly, and was so rowdy and dissolute that he disturbed both
the old and the young of that family, and he cared little or nothing
about the Divine Office and other observances of the Rule. So
Brother Conrad, because of compassion for that young man and the
pleading of the brothers, one day called the young man to one side.
With fervent charity he spoke such effective and devout words of
instruction to the young man that by the work of divine grace he
became, as a boy, an old man in his way of living, so obedient and
kind and concerned and devout, and also so peaceable, so ready to
serve, and so zealous for everything virtuous, that just as before the
whole family was upset by him, now they were all content with him
and consoled, and they loved him deeply.

As it pleased God, it happened that a few days after his conversion, that same young man died, which made those same brothers
grieve. And a few days after his death, his soul appeared to Brother
Conrad, who was praying devoutly in front of the altar of that same
friary; and devoutly greeted him as a father. Brother Conrad asked
him: "Who are you?" And the answer was: "I am the soul of that
young brother who died in these days." And Brother Conrad said:
"How are you, my dearest son?" He replied: "Dearest Father, by the
grace of God and your teaching, I am well because I am not damned;
but because of some sins of mine I did not have time to purge adequately, I am bearing the great pains of Purgatory. But I beg you,
Father, that just as in your mercy you helped me when I was alive, so
now please help me in my sufferings by saying some Our Fathers for
me, because your prayers are very acceptable in the sight of God."
Then Brother Conrad, kindly assenting to his prayers, said one Our
Father with the *"Requiem aeternam,"* and that soul said: "O dearest

Father, what great good and refreshment I feel! Now I ask you to say that again." And Brother Conrad said it another time, and after he did, the soul said: "Holy Father, when you pray for me, I feel completely relieved, so I ask you not to stop praying for me." Then Brother Conrad, seeing that this soul was being helped by his prayers, said one hundred Our Fathers for him. When he finished, that soul said: "On behalf of God, I thank you, dearest Father, for the charity you have had toward me, because through your prayer I am freed from all punishment and I am now going to the heavenly kingdom." After saying this that soul departed. Then Brother Conrad, to give joy and comfort to the brothers, related that whole vision to them in detail.

To the praise of Jesus Christ
and the little poor man Francis.
Amen.

Chapter 44
HOW THE MOTHER OF CHRIST AND SAINT JOHN THE EVANGELIST
AND SAINT FRANCIS APPEARED TO BROTHER CONRAD AND TOLD HIM
WHICH OF THEM BORE THE GREATEST SORROW
OVER THE PASSION OF CHRIST

DBF LXIII

At the time when Brother Conrad and Brother Peter, two shining stars in the Province of the March and both heavenly men, were staying together in at the place of Forano, in the custody of Ancona, there was such love and charity between them that it seemed there was one and the same heart and soul between the two of them; they bound each other to this pact: that every consolation which the mercy of God gave to them, they should both reveal to each other in charity.

Having sealed this pact, it happened one day that while Brother Peter was in prayer, thinking devoutly about the Passion of Christ, and how the most Blessed Mother of Christ and the most beloved John the Evangelist and Saint Francis were painted at the foot of the cross, crucified with Christ through suffering of spirit, a desire came to him, to know which of those three had experienced the greatest suffering over the Passion of Christ: the Mother who had given Him birth; or the disciple who had slept on His breast; or Saint Francis who was crucified with Christ. And while he was in this devout thought, there appeared to him the Virgin Mary with Saint John the Evangelist and Saint Francis, clothed in the most noble clothing of blessed glory; but Saint Francis appeared dressed in clothing more beautiful than Saint John's. As Brother Peter was completely startled by this vision, Saint John comforted him and said to him: "Do not fear, dearest Brother, because we have come to console you and clear up your doubt for you. So you should know that the Mother of Christ and I more than any creature suffered over the Passion of Christ; but after us Saint Francis felt greater suffering than any other; and therefore you see him in such glory." And Brother Peter asked him: "Most Holy Apostle of Christ, why does the clothing of Saint Francis appear more beautiful than yours?" Saint John replied: "The reason is this: because when he was in the world he wore more vile clothing than mine." After saying these words, Saint John gave to Brother Peter a glorious robe that he held in his hand and said to him: "Take this robe, which I have brought to give to you." And as Saint John wanted to dress him in that robe, Brother Peter fell to the ground, startled, and began to cry out: "Brother Conrad, Brother Conrad, quick, help me, come and see amazing things!" And at these words, that holy vision disappeared. When Brother Conrad arrived, he told him everything in detail, and they gave thanks to God.

To the praise of Jesus Christ
and the little poor man Francis.
Amen.

Chapter 45
ABOUT THE CONVERSION AND THE LIFE AND MIRACLES AND DEATH
OF THE HOLY BROTHER JOHN OF PENNA

When Brother John of Penna was still a schoolboy in the Province of the March, a very beautiful boy called to him one night and said: "John, go to Santo Stefano, where one of my brothers is preaching. Pay attention to his words and have confidence in his teaching, for I have sent him there. Afterwards you have to take a long journey and then you will come to me." On hearing this, he immediately got up and felt a great change in his soul. Going to Santo Stefano, he found a great crowd of men and women who were there to hear the sermon. And the one who was to preach was a brother named Brother Philip, who was one of the first brothers to come to the March of Ancona, when there were still only a few places that had been taken in the March. This Brother Philip climbed up to preach, and he preached very devoutly, not in words of human wisdom, but with the power of the Holy Spirit of Christ, proclaiming the kingdom of

DBF XLIX

eternal life. When the sermon was ended, that boy went to the same Brother Philip and said: "Father, if you will, please receive me into the Order, I'll willingly do penance and serve our Lord Jesus Christ." Brother Philip, seeing and recognizing in this boy wonderful innocence and a will ready to serve God, said to him: "Come to me on such and such a day at Recanati and I will have you received." In that place a Provincial Chapter was to be held. At this the boy, who was very pure, thought to himself that this was the great journey that he had to take, as had been revealed to him, and then he would go off to Paradise; and that is what he thought he would do as soon as he was received into the Order. So he went and was received, but he saw that what he had thought did not happen then. But in the Chapter the Minister said that if anyone wished to go to the Province of Provence for the merit of holy obedience he would give him permission. And Brother John got a great desire to go there, thinking that this was the great journey which he had to make before he went to Paradise. But he was ashamed to say so, so finally confiding in that same Brother Philip who had him received into the Order, he asked him kindly to obtain for him the grace of going to the Province of Provence. Brother Philip, recognizing his purity and his holy intention, obtained permission for him to go; and Brother John, with great joy, prepared to go, firmly convinced that, once that journey was completed, he would go to Paradise. But, as it pleased God, he stayed in the province mentioned for twenty-five years, in great expectation and desire, living in great goodness and holiness and good example, constantly growing in virtue and in the grace of God and of the people, deeply loved by both the brothers and the laity.

One day while Brother John was devoutly at prayer, weeping and lamenting that his desire had not been fulfilled and that his pilgrimage in this life was becoming too prolonged, the blessed Christ appeared to him, and on seeing Him his soul completely dissolved, and Christ said to him: "My son, Brother John, ask me for what you want." And he answered: "My Lord, I don't know what to ask of You except Yourself, because I desire nothing else; but I do ask You this one thing, that You forgive me all my sins, and that You give me the grace to see You again when I have the greatest need." Christ said: "Your prayer has been heard." And after saying this, He departed, and Brother John remained completely consoled.

Finally, when the brothers of the March heard of his reputation for holiness, they so insisted with the General that he sent him the obedience to return to the March; and he received it happily, setting off on the road, thinking that once he finished that journey he would go to heaven, according to the promise of Christ. But when he had returned to the Province of the March, he lived in it for thirty years, and was not recognized by any of his relatives, and every day he awaited the mercy of God, that He would fulfill the promise. And during this time he carried out several times the office of Guardian with great discernment, and through him God worked many miracles.

And, among the other gifts he had from God, he had the spirit of prophecy. Thus one time while he was away from the place, one of his novices was attacked by the demon and so strongly tempted that, consenting to the temptation, he decided within himself to leave the Order as soon as Brother John returned. Brother John, knowing through the spirit of prophecy about the temptation and the decision, returned home immediately and called that novice to him, and told him that he wanted him to go to confession. But before he made his confession Brother John told him in detail all about his temptation, as God had revealed it to him, and concluded: "Son, because you waited for me and didn't want to leave without my blessing, God grants you this grace: you will never leave this Order, but you will die in the Order, with divine grace." Then that novice was confirmed in his good will and, remaining in the Order, became a holy brother. And he recounted all these things to me, Brother Ugolino.

That same Brother John was a man with a joyful and tranquil spirit, and he rarely spoke. He was a man of great prayer and devotion, and in particular he never returned to the cell after matins, but stayed in church praying until day. One night after matins when he was praying, an angel of the Lord appeared to him and said: "Brother John, that journey of yours, for which you have been awaiting for a long time, is finished. Therefore, I announce to you on God's behalf that you may ask for any grace you wish, and I also announce to you that you may choose whichever you want: either one day in Purgatory or seven days of punishment in this world." Brother John chose the seven days of punishment in this world, and suddenly became ill with various illnesses. He got a high fever, gout in the hands and feet, pain in his side and many other pains. But what hurt him most was a demon who stood before him, holding in his hand a big chart, and written on it were all the sins he had ever done or thought, and he said: "Because of these sins which you did in thought, word and deed, you are damned to the depths of hell." And Brother John could not remember anything good he had ever done, nor that he was in the Order or had ever been in it, but thought that he was damned, as the demon told him. Therefore, when asked how he was, he replied: "Bad, because I'm damned." Seeing this, the brothers sent for an old brother named Brother Matteo of Monte Rubbiano, who was a holy man and a great friend of this Brother John. Brother Matteo came to him on the seventh day of his tribulation, greeted him and asked him how he was. He replied that he was bad, because he was damned. Then Brother Matteo said: "Don't you remember that you frequently made your confession to me, and I absolved you fully from all your sins? Don't you even remember that you've constantly served God for many years in this holy Order? Furthermore, don't you remember that the mercy of God exceeds all the sins of the world, and that the blessed Christ our Savior paid an infinite price to redeem us? You should have good hope because you surely are saved." And as this was said, because the time of his purgation was finished, the temptation left and consolation arrived.

And with great joy Brother John said to Brother Matteo: "Since you are tired and the hour is late, I beg you to go and rest." Brother Matteo did not want to leave him but finally, after he insisted, left him and went to rest. And Brother John remained alone with the brother who was serving him. But then the blessed Christ came to him with great splendor and a most sweet fragrance, just as he had promised to appear to him again when he had the greatest need. And He healed him completely of all his illnesses. Then Brother John, with hands joined and giving thanks to God, with a fine ending completed his great journey in this present miserable life, and entrusted his soul into the hands of Christ and returned it to God, passing from this mortal life to eternal life with the blessed Christ, whom he had desired and waited to see for such a long time. And that Brother John rests in the place of Penna di San Giovanni.

To the praise of Jesus Christ
and the little poor man Francis.
Amen.

Chapter 46
HOW BROTHER PACIFICO, WHILE AT PRAYER,
SAW THE SOUL OF HIS BROTHER, BROTHER UMILE,
GO TO HEAVEN

DBF LIV

In that same Province of the March, after the death of Saint Francis, there were two brothers in the Order: one was named Brother Umile and the other was named Brother Pacifico; and they were men of the greatest holiness and perfection. The former, that is, Brother Umile, was in the place at Soffiano, and he died there; and the latter was in the family at another place at some distance. As it pleased

God, one day Brother Pacifico, while praying in a solitary place, was rapt in ecstasy and saw the soul of his brother Umile ascending straight into heaven, without hesitation or obstacle, as it departed from the body.

It happened that many years later, this Brother Pacifico who remained, was assigned to the family in that place at Soffiano where his brother had died. At that time, at the request of the lords of Brunforte, the brothers moved from that place to another, and among other things they transferred the remains of the holy brothers who had died at that place. On coming to the tomb of Brother Umile, his brother, Brother Pacifico, took his bones and washed them with good wine and then wrapped them in a white napkin and, crying, kissed them with great reverence and devotion. The other brothers were surprised at this and did not take it as good example from him, because although he was a man of great holiness, it seemed that he was weeping over his brother because of sensual and worldly love, and that he showed more devotion toward his remains than toward those of the other brothers, who were no less holy than Brother Umile and deserved just as much reverence.

Brother Pacifico, knowing the sinister imagination of the brothers, humbly satisfied them by saying: "My dearest brothers, don't be surprised if I did for my brother's bones what I didn't do for others; but, blessed be God, it was not fleshly love that prompted me to do this, as you believe. I did this because when my brother passed from this life, I was praying in a deserted place far from him, and I saw his soul ascend straight to heaven, so I'm certain that his bones are holy and will be in Paradise. And if God had granted me such certainty about the other brothers, I would have shown that same reverence for their bones." Because of this the brothers, seeing his holy and devout intention, were much edified by him and praised God, who does such marvelous things for his holy brothers.

To the praise of Jesus Christ
and the little poor man Francis.
Amen.

Chapter 47
About that holy brother to whom
the Mother of Christ appeared when he was ill,
bringing him three bottles of elixir

DBF LIX

In that place of Soffiano, mentioned above, there was of old a Lesser Brother of such holiness and grace that he seemed wholly divine and was often rapt in God. Once while he was lifted up and completely absorbed in God, since he had particularly the grace of contemplation, birds of different kinds came to him and tamely settled on his shoulders, on his head and on his arms, and sang in wonderful way. This man was a great solitary, and rarely spoke, but whenever he was asked something, he responded so graciously and wisely that he seemed more angel than man, and he was a person of great prayer and contemplation, and the brothers held him in great reverence.

As this brother was finishing the course of his virtuous life, according to divine plan he became sick to the point of death, so that he could not eat anything, and he did not want to accept any human medicine, since all his confidence was in the heavenly doctor, the blessed Jesus Christ and in his blessed Mother, by whom, through divine clemency, he merited to be mercifully visited and treated. Thus once while he was in bed, preparing himself for death with all his heart and devotion, the glorious Virgin Mary, Mother of Christ, appeared to him with a great multitude of angels and holy virgins, in great splendor, and drew near to his bed. On seeing her he received great consolation and delight in body and soul, and began to ask her humbly to beseech her beloved Son, that through His merits he free him from the prison of miserable flesh. As he persevered in this prayer with many tears, the Virgin Mary replied, calling him by name: *"Have no* doubts, *son, your prayer has been heard,* and I have come to comfort you a little before you depart from this life." Tb 4:21; Acts 10:31

Beside the Virgin Mary were three holy virgins, carrying in their hands three bottles with an elixir of inexpressible fragrance and sweetness. Then the glorious Virgin took one of those bottles and opened it, and the whole house was filled with the fragrance. She took a spoonful of that elixir and gave it to the sick man, and as soon as he tasted it, he felt such comfort and sweetness that it seemed his soul could not stay in his body, so he began to say: "No more, O most holy and blessed Virgin Mary, blessed doctor and lady savior of the human race: no more, because I can't bear so much sweetness." But the merciful and kind Mother kept offering that elixir to the sick man and made him take it until the whole bottle was empty. Once the first bottle was empty, the Blessed Virgin took the second, and put the spoon in it to give him some, but he complained sweetly, saying: "O most blessed Mother of God, if my soul almost entirely melted away at the fragrance and sweetness of the first elixir, how can I bear the second? I beg you, O blessed above all the saints and all the angels, not to give me any more." The glorious lady replied: "My son, taste just a little from this second bottle." After she gave him a little, she said to him: "You've had enough for today. Be comforted, my son, because I will soon return for you and lead you into the kingdom of my Son, which you have always desired and sought." Having said this, bidding him farewell, she departed; and he remained so consoled and comforted by the sweetness of that mixture that he lived for several days, feeling full and strong, without any bodily food. And after some days, while joyfully speaking with the brothers, with great gladness and jubilation he passed from this miserable life.

To the praise of Jesus Christ
and the little poor man Francis.
Amen.

Chapter 48

HOW BROTHER JAMES OF MASSA SAW IN A VISION
ALL THE LESSER BROTHERS OF THE WORLD
IN THE VISION OF A TREE
AND KNEW THE VIRTUES AND THE MERITS
AND THE VICES OF EACH ONE

Brother James of Massa, to whom God opened the door of His secrets and gave perfect knowledge and understanding of Holy Scripture and future events, was a man of such holiness that Brother Giles of Assisi and Brother Marco of Montino and Brother Juniper and Brother Lucido said that they knew no one in the world greater before God than this Brother James.

I had a great desire to see him, because while I was asking Brother John, companion of that same Brother Giles, to explain to me certain things of the spirit, he said to me: "If you want to be well instructed in the spiritual life, try to talk to Brother James of Massa, because Brother Giles desired to be enlightened by him, and nothing can be added or subtracted from his words, since his spirit has passed through heavenly secrets, and his words are the words of the Holy Spirit, and there is no man on earth whom I so desire to see." This Brother James, at the beginning of the ministry of Brother John of

DBF LXIV

Parma, was once rapt into God while praying and remained rapt in
this ecstasy for three days, suspended from any bodily feeling, and
he remained there so unaware that the brothers began to wonder if
he was dead. And in this rapture God revealed to him what must
happen concerning our religion, and when I heard this, my desire to
hear him and speak with him increased.

And when it pleased God that I have the chance to talk with him, I
asked him: "If what I heard said about you is true, I ask you not to
hide it from me. I heard that when you remained as if dead for three
days, God revealed to you, among other things, what is to happen in
this Religion of ours, and this was said by Brother Matteo, Minister
of the March, to whom you revealed it under obedience." Then
Brother James, with great humility, admitted to him that what
Brother Matteo said was true.

What he said, that is Brother Matteo, Minister of the March, was
this: "I know this from Brother James, to whom God revealed everything that is to happen in our Religion, because Brother James of
Massa confided in me and told me the following. After God revealed
many things to him about the status of the Church Militant, he saw
in a vision a beautiful and very large tree: its root was of gold; its fruit
was men, and they were all Lesser Brothers. Its main branches were
divided according to the number of the provinces of the Order, and
each branch had as many brothers as there were in the province designated for that branch. And so he knew the number of all the brothers of the Order and of each province, and also their names, their
ages, their conditions, their important duties, their dignities, and the
graces of all, their merits and their faults. And he saw Brother John
of Parma at the tip of the middle branch of this tree, and on the tips of
the branches around this middle branch were the ministers of all the
provinces. And after this he saw Christ sitting on a very large, dazzling white throne, and Christ called Saint Francis and gave him a
chalice full of *the spirit of life* and ordered him: "Go and visit your   Rv 11:11
brothers and give them to drink of this chalice of the spirit of life,
because the spirit of Satan will rise up against them and strike them,
and many of them will fall and will not rise up again." And Christ
gave Saint Francis two angels to accompany him.

And so Saint Francis came to offer the chalice of life to his brothers and began to offer it to Brother John, who took it and quickly and
devoutly drank it all, and immediately became all shining like the
sun. And after him Saint Francis offered it to all the others, and there
were few of them who would take it and drink it all with proper reverence and devotion. Those who took it devoutly and drank it all
quickly became as bright as the sun; and those who poured it out and

did not take it with devotion became black and dark and deformed and horrible to see. Those who drank some and poured out some, became part shining and part shadowy, more or less according to the amount they drank or poured out. But Brother John was resplendent beyond all the others, he who had most fully drunk the chalice of life, and so he contemplated most deeply that abyss of the infinite divine light, and in this he understood the adversity and the storm which was to arise against that tree, breaking and displacing its branches. Because of this that same Brother John left the top of the branch on which he was standing and, descending below all the branches he hid himself at the foot of the tree's trunk and stayed there, very pensive. And Brother Bonaventure, who had taken some from the chalice and had poured out some, went up onto that branch to the place from which Brother John had come down. And while he was standing in that place, his fingernails became fingernails of iron, sharp and cutting like razors; and at this he moved from the place to which he had climbed, and with force and fury tried to throw himself against that same Brother John to harm him. But Brother John, seeing this, cried out loudly and entrusted himself to Christ, who was sitting on the throne: and Christ, at his cry, called Saint Francis and gave him a sharp flint, and said to him: "Go with this flint and cut Brother Bonaventure's fingernails, with which he wants to scratch Brother John, so that he cannot harm him." Then Saint Francis went and did what Christ had commanded. When this was done, a windstorm arose and struck the tree so hard that the brothers fell from it to the ground, and the first to fall from it were those who poured out the whole chalice of the spirit of life, and they were carried off by the demons to dark and painful places. But that same Brother John, together with those who had drunk the whole chalice were transported by the angels to a place of life and eternal light and blessed splendor. And the aforesaid Brother James, who saw this vision, knew and discerned specifically and distinctly all that he was seeing, regarding the names, the conditions and the status of each with clarity. And that storm lasted long enough that the tree fell and was carried away by the wind. And then, as soon as the storm ended, from this tree's root, which was gold, another tree sprang up, all of gold, which produced golden leaves and fruit. About this tree, its growth, its depth, beauty and fragrance and virtues, at the present time it is better to keep silent than to speak.

To the praise of Jesus Christ
and the little poor man Francis.
Amen.

Chapter 49
HOW CHRIST APPEARED TO BROTHER JOHN OF LA VERNA

DBF XLIX

Among the other wise and holy brothers and sons of Saint Francis, those whom Solomon says are the *glory of a father,* there was in our times in the same Province of the March Brother John of Fermo who, because of the long time he stayed in the holy place of La Verna, and there passed from this life, was also called Brother John of La Verna, because he was a man of outstanding life and great holiness. This Brother John, while still a boy in the world, desired with all his heart the way of penance which keeps the body and the soul clean. Therefore, as a very little boy, he began to wear a harness of mail and an iron band next to his flesh and to practice great abstinence. And particularly while he was staying with the canons of San Peter of Fermo, who lived in splendor, he fled bodily delights and afflicted his body with very strict abstinence. But since his companions were quite opposed to this, stripping him of his harness and impeding his abstinence in various ways, he was inspired by God and decided to leave the world and those who love it, and to offer himself completely to the arms of the Crucified, with the habit of the crucified Saint Francis. And he did just that.

Prv 10:1

Therefore, still a boy, he was received into the Order and was entrusted to the care of the master of novices, and he became so spiritual and devout that sometimes, as he listened to that same master speaking of God, his *heart* would *melt* like *wax* near a fire; and he was so warmed by divine love that, unable to stay put and endure so much sweetness, he would get up and run as if drunk: sometimes through the garden, sometimes through the woods, sometimes through the church, as the flame and force of the spirit drove him. With the passage of time divine grace made this angelic man grow from virtue to virtue in heavenly gifts and divine elevations and raptures, to such a degree that at times his spirit would be lifted to the splendors of the cherubim; at other times to the ardor of the seraphim; sometimes to the joy of the Blessed; at other times to loving and effusive embraces of Christ, not only through inner, spiritual sensations, but even through visible, outward signs and bodily sensations. And once in particular, the flame of divine love ignited his heart in an extraordinary way, and it remained in this flame for a good three years, during which time he received wonderful consolations and divine visitations and frequently was rapt in God. And this was on the holy mountain of La Verna.

Ps 22:15

But because God takes special care of His sons, He gives them different things at different times: consolation at this time, tribulation at another; now prosperity, then adversity; because He knows they need to keep themselves in humility, or rather to inflame more fully their desire for heavenly things. So it pleased the divine goodness, after three years, to take away from the same Brother John that ray and flame of divine love, and to deprive him of any spiritual consolation: so he remained without light and without love of God and completely desolate and afflicted and sorrowful. Because of this he wandered here and there through the woods in this anguish, calling out with cries and tears and sighs for the beloved Spouse of his soul, who had hidden Himself and departed from him; and without His presence his soul found neither rest nor repose. But he could not find the sweet Jesus in any place or in any way, nor could he return to those sweet spiritual sensations of the love of Christ as he had been accustomed. And he endured this tribulation for many days, in which he persevered in constant weeping and sighing and begging God in His mercy to return to him the beloved Spouse of his soul.

Finally, when it pleased God to have tested his patience sufficiently and ignited his desire, one day when Brother John was walking through the same woods, afflicted and troubled as he was, he was tired and sat down next to a beech tree; and he stayed there with his face all wet with tears looking toward heaven. Suddenly Jesus Christ appeared near him on the path by which Brother John had come, but He did not say anything. Brother John saw Him, and recognizing clearly that He was Christ, immediately threw himself at His feet, and with uncontrolled weeping humbly begged Him: "Help me, my Lord, because without You, my most sweet Savior, I remain in darkness and grief; and without You, meekest Lamb, I am in anguish and pain and fear; without You, Son of the Most High God, I am in confusion and shame; without You, I am deprived of all good and blinded, because You are Jesus Christ, the true light of souls; without You I am lost and damned, because You are the life of souls and the life of lives; without You I am sterile and dried up, because You are the fountain of every gift and every grace; without You I am completely desolate, because You are Jesus, our redemption, love and desire, the bread that restores and the wine that gladdens the choirs of Angels and the hearts of all the Saints. Enlighten me, O most gracious Master and most kind Shepherd, because, though unworthy, I am your little sheep."

But since the desire of holy men that God delays in granting inflames them to greater love and merit, the blessed Christ departed without granting it and without saying anything to him, and went away by that same path. Then Brother John jumped up and ran after Him and once again threw himself at His feet, and with holy insistence held Him back and with devout tears begged him, saying: "O most sweet Jesus Christ, *have mercy on me* in my tribulation. Hear me, through *the abundance of Your mercy and the truth of Your salvation,* and *give me the joy of Your* face and Your merciful glance, because *the* whole *earth is filled with Your mercy."* And Christ departed again and said nothing to him, nor did He give him any consolation; and acted like a mother to a child when she wants him to desire the breast, and makes him come after her crying, so that he will then take it more willingly.

So Brother John with even greater fervor and desire followed Christ, and when he reached Him, the blessed Christ turned to him and looked at him with a happy and kind expression and, opening His most holy and merciful arms, embraced him most sweetly; and as those arms were opened Brother John saw shining rays of light coming from the most sacred breast of the Savior, which illuminated all the woods and his whole self, body and soul.

Then Brother John knelt down at Christ's feet; and the blessed Jesus, as He did to the Magdalene, kindly offered him His foot to kiss; and Brother John, taking it with the greatest reverence, bathed it with so many tears that he truly seemed to be another Magdalene, and said devoutly: "I beg you, my Lord, not to look on my sins, but through Your most holy Passion and the shedding of Your most holy Blood, revive my soul in the grace of Your love; for this is Your commandment, that *we love You* with *our whole heart* and affection, a commandment which no one can fulfill without Your help. Help me, therefore, most loving Son of God, that I may love You with all my heart and with all my strength."

And while Brother John was saying these things at the feet of Christ, his prayer was granted and he received back from Christ that first grace, that is, the flame of divine love, and he felt himself totally renewed and consoled; and realizing that the gift of divine grace had returned within himself, he began to thank the blessed Christ and to kiss His feet devoutly. And then as he was straightening up to look Christ in the face, Jesus reached out and offered him His most holy hands to kiss, and when Brother John had kissed them, he got closer to touch the breast of Jesus and embraced Him and kissed Him, and similarly Christ embraced and kissed him. And in this embracing and kissing, Brother John smelled a fragrance so divine that if all the fragrant spices and every fragrant thing of the world had been gathered together they would have seemed like a stench compared with that fragrance; and in this Brother John was enraptured and consoled and enlightened, and that fragrance remained in his soul for many months.

Ps 31:10

Ps 69:14

Ps 51:14;
Ps 33:5; 119:64

Lk 7:37-51;
Jn 12:3-8; 20:11-18

Lk 10:27; Dt 6:5

And from then on, from his mouth, which had drunk from the fountain of divine wisdom in the Lord's sacred breast, there came forth wonderful, heavenly words that produced great fruit in the souls of his listeners. And on the path in the woods, on which the blessed feet of Christ had stood, and in a wide area around there, when he walked there long afterward Brother John always smelled that fragrance and saw that brightness.

As Brother John returned to himself after that rapture, and the bodily presence of Christ disappeared, he remained so enlightened in his soul, in the abyss of His divinity that, though he was not educated through human study, nevertheless he marvelously resolved and explained the most subtle questions of the divine Trinity and the deep mysteries of Holy Scripture. And later he often spoke before popes and cardinals and kings and barons and masters and doctors, and he left all of them in great surprise because of the high words and deep statements that he said.

To the praise of Jesus Christ
and the little poor man Francis.
Amen.

Chapter 50
HOW BROTHER JOHN OF LA VERNA, WHILE SAYING MASS
ON THE DAY OF THE DEAD, SAW MANY SOULS FREED FROM PURGATORY

Once, while the same Brother John was saying Mass the day after All Saints for all the souls of the dead, as the Church required, he offered that most high Sacrament (which because of its efficacy, the souls of the dead desire above all the other good things which above all can be done for them) with such charity and feelings of compassion that he seemed as if completely melted by the sweetness of pity and fraternal charity. Therefore, in that Mass as he devoutly raised the Body of Christ and offered it to God the Father, he prayed that for love of His blessed Son Jesus Christ, who was hung on the Cross to redeem souls, He should be pleased to free from the sufferings of Purgatory the souls of the dead, created and redeemed by Him. Then he immediately saw an almost infinite number of souls leave Purgatory, like innumerable sparks of fire from a lighted furnace, and he saw them rise into heaven through the merits of the Passion of Christ, Who is offered daily for the living and the dead in that most sacred host, worthy of adoration forever.

DBF LI

To the praise of Jesus Christ
and the little poor man Francis.
Amen.

Chapter 51
ABOUT THE HOLY BROTHER JAMES OF FALLERONE
AND HOW, AFTER HE DIED, HE APPEARED TO BROTHER JOHN OF LA VERNA

DBF LII　　At the time when Brother James of Fallerone, a man of great holiness, was seriously ill in the place at Mogliano, in the Custody of Fermo, Brother John of La Verna, who was then staying in the place at Massa, hearing of his illness, because he loved him as his dear father, began praying for him, asking God devoutly in mental prayer to restore the health of his body, if that were best for his soul. And while he was praying devoutly, he was rapt into ecstasy and he saw in the air above his cell, which was in the woods, a great army of angels and saints, with such splendor that the whole area around him was illuminated. And among these angels he saw this sick brother for whom he was praying, standing in bright and shining white clothing. He also saw among them the blessed Father Saint Francis adorned with the sacred Stigmata of Christ and great glory. He also saw there and recognized the holy Brother Lucido and Brother Matteo the Elder of Monte Rubbiano, and other brothers whom he had never seen or known in this life. And as Brother John was looking with great delight at that blessed troop of saints, it was revealed to him with certainty the salvation of the soul of that sick brother, and that he would die from that illness, but not immediately, and that he would go to Paradise, though it was better for him to purify himself a little in Purgatory. The same Brother John had great joy at that revelation, over the salvation of the soul, which felt nothing of the death of the body, and with great sweetness of spirit he called out to him within himself: "Brother Giacomo, my sweet father! Brother Giacomo, my sweet brother! Brother Giacomo, most faithful servant and friend of God! Brother Giacomo, companion of the angels and member of the blessed!" And in this certainty and joy he returned to himself, and he immediately departed from the place and went to visit the same Brother Giacomo at Mogliano.

And finding him so gravely ill that he could hardly speak, he announced to him the death of the body and the salvation and glory of the soul, according to the certainty he had received by divine revelation. Brother James received him with happiness in his spirit and on his face, with great joy and a cheerful laugh, thanking him for the good news he brought to him, and commending himself to him with devotion. Then Brother John fondly asked him to return and speak to him after death about his condition; and Brother James promised him this, if it pleased God. After these things were said and the hour of his passing neared, Brother James began to say devoutly this verse of the Psalm: *"In pace in idipsum dormiam et requiescam,"* that is, "In peace in eternal life I will fall asleep and rest;" and after saying this verse, with a cheerful, joyous expression he passed from this life.

Ps 4:9

And after he was buried, Brother John returned to the place at Massa and waited for Brother James's promise, that he would return to him on the day he said. But on that day, while he was praying, Christ appeared to him with a great company of angels and saints, and Brother James was not among them; so Brother John, much surprised, devoutly commended him to Christ. Then, on the following day, when Brother John was praying in the woods at Massa, Brother James, all glorious and happy, appeared to him accompanied by the angels, and Brother John said to him: "Oh dearest Father, why didn't you return to me on the day you promised?" Brother James replied: "Because I needed some purification, but at the same hour that Christ appeared to you, and commended me to Him, Christ heard you and freed me from every punishment. And then I appeared to Brother James of Massa, a holy lay brother, who was serving Mass, and he saw the sacred host, when the priest raised it, changed and turned into a living and very handsome boy, and I said to him: 'Today I'm going with that boy to the kingdom of eternal life, to which no one can go without Him.' After saying these words Brother James disappeared and went to heaven with that whole blessed company of angels; and Brother John remained, greatly consoled.

That same Brother James of Fallerone died on the vigil of Saint James the Apostle in the month of July, in that same place at Mogliano, where after his death divine goodness, through his merits, performed many miracles.

To the praise of Jesus Christ
and the little poor man Francis.
Amen.

Chapter 52
ABOUT THE VISION OF BROTHER JOHN OF LA VERNA
IN WHICH HE KNEW THE WHOLE ORDER OF THE HOLY TRINITY

DBF LVI   The same Brother John of La Verna, since he had perfectly denied every worldly and temporal delight and consolation, and had placed all his delight and all his hope in God, was granted by the divine goodness wonderful consolations and revelations, especially on the solemnities of Christ. Therefore, one time when the solemnity of the Nativity of Christ was approaching, he confidently awaited consolation from God in the sweet humanity of Jesus. And the Holy Spirit put into his spirit such great and abundant love and fervor of Christ's charity, by which He had humbled Himself to take our humanity, that it really seemed to him that his soul was snatched from his body and was burning like a furnace. Unable to bear that burning, he suffered and melted completely and cried out in a loud voice, because through the force of the Holy Spirit and the great heat of love, he could not restrain himself from crying out. In that same moment of boundless heat there came with it such a strong and certain hope of salvation that he would not believe for anything in the world that if he died then he would have to pass through Purgatory. And this love lasted for a good six months: he did not have that excessive heat constantly; rather it came to him at certain hours of the day.

And during this time he later received wonderful visitations and consolations from God; and he was enraptured many times, as seen by that brother who first wrote these things. Among other times, one night he was so raised and rapt in God that he saw in Him, the Creator, all created things, heavenly and earthly, and all their perfection and ranks and distinct orders. And he then knew clearly how each created thing appeared to its Creator, and how God is above and inside and outside and beside all created things. Then he knew one God in three Persons, and three Persons in one God, and the infinite charity that made the Son become incarnate by obedience to the Father. And finally in that vision he knew that there was no other way by which the soul may go to God and have eternal life except through the blessed Christ, Who is *the way, the truth and the life* of the   Jn 14:6
soul.

To the glory of Jesus Christ
and the little poor man Francis.
Amen.

Chapter 53
HOW, WHILE SAYING MASS, BROTHER JOHN OF LA VERNA
FELL DOWN AS IF DEAD

To that same Brother John the following wonderful event DBF LVII occurred in the aforesaid place at Mogliano, according to what is recounted by the brothers who were present there. On the first night after the octave of Saint Lawrence, and within the octave of the Assumption of the Lady, after he had said matins in church with the other brothers, the anointing of divine grace came over him, and he went into the garden to contemplate the Passion of Christ and to prepare with all his devotion to celebrate the Mass, which it was his turn to sing that morning. And while contemplating the words for the consecration of the body of Christ, that is, *Hoc est corpus meum,* and Mt 26:26 considering the infinite charity of Christ, by which He willed not only to purchase us with His precious blood, but also to leave His most worthy body and blood as the food of souls, the love of the sweet Jesus began to grow within him with so much fervor and sweetness that his soul could no longer endure so much sweetness, so he cried out loudly, as if drunk in spirit, repeating to himself, *Hoc est corpus meum,* and in saying these words he seemed to see the blessed Christ with the Virgin Mary and a multitude of angels. And in saying this he was enlightened by the Holy Spirit about all the deep and high mysteries of that most high Sacrament.

When dawn came, he entered the Church with that fervor of spirit and that anticipation and that phrase, thinking he was not seen or heard by anyone; but in the choir there was a brother in prayer, who heard and saw everything. And in that fervor being unable to contain himself because of the abundance of divine grace, he cried out in a loud voice; and he stayed this way so long that it was time to say Mass, so he went to the altar to vest and began Mass. And as he went on, the further he proceeded, the more the love of Christ and that fervor of devotion grew, and with it he was given an inexpressible feeling of God, one that he himself did not and could not express in words. Since he was afraid that that fervor and feeling of God was growing so much that it would be better to stop the Mass, he was in great perplexity and did not know which way to turn: whether to go on with the Mass or to stop and wait. But, since something similar had happened to him another time, and the Lord had so tempered that fervor that he did not have to stop the Mass, he was confident that he could do the same this time, and with great fear he started to proceed with the Mass; and when he got to the Preface of the Lady, divine grace and gracious gentleness of the love of God began to grown so much in him that, as he came to *Qui pridie quam,* he could hardly bear such gentleness and sweetness. Finally reaching the act of consecration, after saying half of the words over the host, that is, *Hoc est enim,* there was no way he could go further, and he just kept repeating those same words, that is, *Hoc est enim.* And the reason he could not go further was that he felt and saw the presence of Christ with a multitude of angels, whose glory he could not bear; and he saw that Christ did not enter the host, or rather that the host did not transubstantiate into the body of Christ if he did not say the other half of the words, that is, *corpus meum.* At this, as he stood there in this anxiety without going further, the Guardian and the other brothers and also many lay people who were in church to hear Mass came up to the altar and were amazed to see and consider the actions of Brother John, and many of them were crying from devotion. Finally, after a long time, that is, when God pleased, Brother John said *corpus meum* in a loud voice; and immediately the form of the bread disappeared, and in the host appeared the blessed Jesus Christ incarnate and glorified, and He showed him the humility and charity that made Him become incarnate from the Virgin Mary and that made Him come daily into the hands of the priest when he consecrates the host. Because of this he was lifted higher into the sweetness of contemplation. So, after elevating the host and consecrated chalice, he was rapt out of himself; and with his soul suspended from bodily feeling, his body fell backward and, if he had not been held by the Guardian, who was behind him, he would have fallen flat on the ground. At this the brothers and the lay people who were in church, men and women, ran to him, and he was carried into the sacristy as if dead, since his body was cold like a dead body, and his fingers were so contracted that they could hardly be straightened or moved. He lay like this, half-dead or rather enraptured until terce, and it was summer.

Since I, who was present there, desired very much to know what God had done to him, as soon as he returned to himself, I went to him and asked him for the love of God to tell me everything. Since he trusted me very much, he told me everything in detail; and among other things he told me that when he looked at the body and blood of Jesus Christ and even before, his heart was liquid like melted wax; and it seemed his flesh had no bones, so much so that he could hardly lift his arms or his hands to make the sign of the Cross over the host or over the chalice. He also told me that before he became a priest, it was revealed to him by God that he would faint during the Mass, but because he had already said many Masses, and this had not happened to him, he thought that the revelation had not been from God. Nevertheless, five years earlier on the Assumption of the Lady, on which the aforesaid event happened to him, it was again revealed to him by God that this would happen to him around that same feast of the Assumption, but then he did not remember that revelation.

To the praise of Jesus Christ and the little poor man Francis.
Amen.

LITURGICAL TEXTS

FOR THE FEAST OF THE STIGMATA

OF SAINT FRANCIS

(1337–1340)

)

Introduction

Beyond the identity of their author, little is known of the origins of the antiphons and responsories written for the liturgical celebration of the Feast of the Stigmata of Saint Francis. The very origins of the feast are shrouded in mystery. The decrees of Popes Gregory IX, Innocent IV, Alexander IV, Nicholas III and Nicholas IV are certainly indicative of the controversies that surrounded Francis's stigmata, which Thomas of Celano called "a prerogative of love."[1] The rivalries between the secular clergy and the religious, between the followers of Francis and those of Dominic, and between the developing factions among the Lesser Brothers themselves: these all fueled fires that would not make the environment conducive for establishing such a unique liturgical celebration.[2]

In his description of Giraldus Odonis or Giral Ot, General Minister of the Lesser Brothers from 1329 to 1342, Arnald of Sarant mentions the institution of the feast of the Stigmata at the Chapter of Cahors in 1337.[3] The first official indication of the feast, however, is an item of legislation coming from the Chapter of Assisi in 1340:

> It was also ordered that the Office of the Sacred Stigmata, composed by the reverend Father General, should be kept and carried out in the whole Order, and the readings should be read from the *Legend* of Brother Bonaventure, in the Chapter "On the Sacred Stigmata," and the Office should be that of a double on September 17.[4]

There is nothing written about the circumstances surrounding the establishment of the liturgical celebration. In both instances, however, nothing is mentioned about ecclesiastical approval of the feast.[5]

By this time, literary descriptions of Francis's stigmata were widely diffused among the Lesser Brothers, the Friars Preacher, and other religious. Iconographic representations were also becoming more common as churches and chapels built in Francis's honor grew more numerous.[6] In his *Treatise on the Miracles,* Thomas of Celano tells of a miracle in which the bleeding wounds that had been omitted by the painter, imprinted themselves on the image of the saint.[7] A story that appears in a 1343 manuscript of the *Avignon Compilation,*[8] however, may assist in understanding the environment of the first half of the fourteenth century in which the Feast of the Stigmata was established:

At the time of the Lord Pope Benedict XII [1334-42], it happened that near Avignon, in a city where the brothers had a cloister, one day, while all the brothers were in choir at the Divine Office, two brothers of another religion arrived and walked around. Then one of them saw painted on the wall the image of Saint Francis with the sacred stigmata. He said to his companion: "Those Lesser [Brothers] want to make their saint resemble Christ." And he took out his knife and said, "I want to gouge out those stigmata from this image, so he won't look similar to Christ." And having said this he carried out his work. And when he had gouged out those five stigmata they started to drip blood profusely.

On seeing this, he said to his companion, "Oh! What should I do?" The companion said, "You've committed a real mortal sin! I advise you, run quickly to a confessor and confess." And so he did. After confession he returned to the image, but the blood did not cease flowing. Seeing this that wretch was very upset and returned to the confessor and told him this. The confessor advised him to run to the Pope and tell him all this and get his advice about what to do.

And, as fast as he could, he carried out the order, went to the Pope and revealed all this to him. When the Pope heard this, he asked him if the thing were really like this. And the man confirmed with an oath that it was so. Then the Pope said, "In any case, I want to see this wonder." And when he came there, he saw blood flowing profusely from the sacred stigmata of that image. Then the lord Pope, greatly astonished, knelt down before the image. Reaching his hands out toward heaven, he said: "Saint Francis, forgive the harm of that wretched sinner, for I promise you that I want to institute the celebration of the feast of your stigmata, and I particularly want to order your brothers that throughout the whole Order they are to celebrate the feast of your stigmata solemnly." As soon as the lord Pope made the vow, the blood stopped flowing. Then the Pope imposed a penance on that wretched sinner.

And thus he instituted the feast of the sacred stigmata, and from then on no one dared to disparage those sacred stigmata. And whoever further presumed to do this is to be judged a heretic. Let us therefore beg Saint Francis that because of his sacred stigmata he pray to the Lord for us, that after this life he would lead us to the eternal homeland. Amen.

A similar story appears in *The Deeds of Blessed Francis and His Companions*, but it contains some important nuances. While the *Avignon Compilation* describes "two brothers of another religion" arriving at a convent of the Lesser Brothers in Avignon, *The Deeds* tell of a Friar Preacher in "a certain convent of the Friars Preacher" in an unknown locale.[9] In other words, *The Deeds* aims at being more conciliatory, undoubtedly addressing the growing tension between the Friars Preacher and the Lesser Brothers characterizing the early fourteenth century. More dramatic, however, is *Avignon Compilation's* description of the recourse of the culprit brother to Pope Benedict XII (1334-42), an event that is omitted in *The Deeds* and more understandable in the Avignon setting.

Only in the sixteenth century do the ecclesiastical origins of the feast arise. In his recounting of the events of 1304 in the *Annales Minorum*, Luke Wadding had stated that the Dominican Pope, Benedict XI (1303-4), permitted the Lesser Brothers to celebrate a feast in honor of the Stigmata of Saint Francis on September 17.[10] Wadding provides no proof for this, nor is there any in *Le Registre de Benôit XI*, the *Bullarium Romanum*, or the *Bullarium Franciscanum*. Since he was pope for less than nine months, that is from October 22, 1303, to July 7, 1304, Wadding's assertion seems doubtful. The Irish scholar corrected himself in writing the history of the Chapter of Assisi and recording the chapter's decree.[11] While scholars have debated the authenticity of these dates, it seems reasonable to assume that the Chapter of Cahors may have established the feast, and the Chapter of Assisi mandated the use of the liturgical texts. Nonetheless, this liturgical celebration was a privilege afforded the Lesser Brothers; there is no indication of it in the universal church. Contemporary studies add little light to the subject. *The Roman Calendar: Text and Commentary*, for example, maintains that the Feast of the Stigmata of Saint Francis was "placed in the Roman calendar in 1585, suppressed in 1602 and restored in 1615 . . ."[12]

Notes

1. 1C 90.
2. Cf. André Vauchez, "The Stigmata of Saint Francis and Its Medieval Detractors," GR 13(1999): 61-89.
3. Arnald of Sarrant, ChrXXIV 528: *"In eodem autem capitulo [Caturci] fuit institutum, ut fieret festum de sacris beati Francisci stigmatibus per Ordinem universum* [In that same Chapter—of Cahors—it was decided that the Feast of the Sacred Stigmata of Blessed Francis would be celebrated throughout the entire Order."
4. Cf. Ferdinand M. Delorme, "Actus et Constitutiones Capituli Generalis Assisiensis (1340)," AFH 6 (1913): 255; also Ferdinand Doelle, "De institutione festi SS. Stigmatum e Cod. Wratislaviensi narratio," AFH 3 (1910): 169.
5. How widespread was this celebration is unknown. A fourteenth-century manuscript of a Franciscan missal in the Bodelian Library, Oxford, England, contains no reference to the existence of such a feast. Cf. Veronica Condon, *Ms. Douce 313* (Victoria, Australia: Spectrum Publications, 1979), 6-7.
6. Of the approximately 200 surviving paintings of Francis from Italy before ca.1320, at least eight show Francis without stigmata. As far as can be determined, none is of Franciscan provenance. Several come from Benedictine commissions and at least one is Dominican. The latest of these images dates from ca.1300 and was perhaps from the cathedral of Florence; it is currently in the Detroit Institute of Fine Arts. For these paintings, see William R. Cook, *Images of St. Francis of Assisi in Painting, Stone and Glass from the Earliest Images to c.1320 in Italy: A Catalogue*, (Florence: Casa Editrice Leo S. Olschki, 1999). Those images without the stigmata are #4, 40, 59, 103, 108, 128, 134, 193. Those of secure Benedictine provenance are #40 (Bominaco, Abruzzi), #103

(Montelabate, Umbria), #193 (Subiaco, Lazio). The Dominican image is now in the Yale University Museum of Art in New Haven, CT.

7. Cf. 3C 8, FA:ED II 405.

8. Ferdinand Doelle, "De institutione festi SS. Stigmatum e Cod. Wratislaviensi narratio," AFH 3 (1910): 169.

9. DBF 65, cf. infra 559-561.

10. Writing of his election Wadding states: *Illud vero praecipuum indulsit, ut de sancti Francisci Stigmatobus officium fieret ecclesiasticum sub ritu duplici, et anniversaria colerentur solemnitate* [He granted that unique request that there be an ecclesiastical Office celebrated for the Stigmata of Saint Francis and its anniversaries celebrated with solemnity]. Luke Wadding, *Annales Minorum* ad an. 1304, n. 14 (VI, 39).

11. Luke Wadding, *Annales Minorum*, ad an. 1337, n. 4 (VII, 204).

12. United States Catholic Conference, *The Roman Calendar: Text and Commentary* (Washington, D.C: Publications Office United States Catholic Conference, 1976), 92. Cf. Omer Englebert, *Saint Francis of Assisi: A Biography*, trans. Eve Marie Cooper, 2nd ed. (Chicago: Franciscan Herald Press, 1965), 311-2. *Proper Offices of Franciscan Saints and Blesseds in the Liturgy of the Hours*, trans. and edited by Friars of the Franciscan Liturgical Projects (New York: Catholic Book Publishing Co., 1975), 286.

The Divine Office of the Feast of the Stigmata[a]
"The Stigmata of Saint Francis"[b]

First Vespers

I. Antiphons:

LMj XIV 1

1. Francis sated with drink
   of the thirsty cross of Jesus,
   wounded with the wounds of Jesus
   merits the honor of the Leader.

1C 112

2. The King of Mercy
   did marvelous wonders
   in the flesh of Francis
   preceded by the splendor of uprightness.

3. Through Christ's true insignia,
   which he bore
   Francis will be famed throughout the world.
   in eternal memory.

4. Upon the humble Francis
   God looked most mercifully
   and made him someone noble
   by these signs especially.

Off XXI 21

5. Francis is blessed
   by all born in this world
   for he is made in truth
   like to Christ in these wounds.

At the Magnificat:

Francis, the kinship of Jesus
whom you especially loved

---

a. Guidao Maria Dreves, S.J., ed., *Analecta Hymnica Medii Aevi XVII: Hymnodia hibernica. Liturgische Reimofficien aus Spanischen Brevieren, Carmina Compostellana die Lider des s. g. Codex Calixtinus* (Leipzig: Reisland, 1894), 100-102.

b. Franciscan manuscript breviary, (15th-16th century), Cod. Parisin. 1064. There are also four hymns for the office: at First Vespers, "Franciscus amat unice"; at Nocturns, "Franciscus mundi prospera"; at Lauds, "Francisci in visceribus"; at Second Vespers, "Ad Francisci fama prisci." Cf. Dreves, 102, note.

honors you by exalted grace
above all,
and mercifully crowns you
while you, with every effort,
direct all your heart on Him.

Matins

Invitatory [Antiphon]

In the praise of Francis
May Jesus be magnified
by the privilege of wounds
of which he was considered worthy.

First Nocturn:

1.   The passion of Jesus   1C 113
which was in the will of Francis,
is proved beyond doubt
by the truth of the wounds.

2.   Let no one now discourse   3C 5; LMj Mir I
against the stigmata of Francis,
for these are gifts of Christ:
Rome has now declared this.

3.   Jesus, the glory of Francis,
greatly exalted him,
with the holy insignia of the stigmata
which He granted to him.

Responsories:

1. R/ Francis, angelic man,   1C 112
strives to revere the angels
and in a heavenly way wishes
to afflict the flesh;
Now the noted servant of Christ
wishes to rejoice in Christ.

    V/ To him the whole world was bitter   1C 115
to him only Jesus was sweet,
and Him he strove to contemplate.

1C 92   2. R/   Francis, as he meditated
            the single deeds of Jesus,
            examined His Passion
            with careful attention,
            The Cross was his heart's food,
            in which he delighted.

        V/   His Cross the rule of life,
             His Cross the heart's small cell,
             in the Cross he boasted.

1C 55-7   3. R/   Francis strove to conform himself
            to the deeds of Jesus,
            and for Him, overseas,
            exposed himself to death ;
            and the merciful Jesus decided
            to make him like Himself.

        V/   His Cross frequently shining forth,
             To him the Crucified appeared,
             wishing to sign him beforehand.

Second Nocturn:

Antiphons:

1.   Jesus made wondrous
     Francis His servant
     above all the throng of saints
     when He stigmatized him.

2.   Francis in the morning stood
     before Jesus on Mount La Verna,
     Jesus gave to him
     gifts for eternal praise.

3.   Francis wondrously makes
     the name of Jesus shine out
     as the sign of Jesus nobly
     appears in the flesh of Francis.

Responsories:

1. R/   While Francis bursts
with Seraphic flames
and for the sufferings of Jesus
bravely sighs,
Jesus appears with hands extended,
as if on the Cross.

      V/   Covered with Seraphic wings,   1C 114
beautiful and shining,
he is without any spot.

2. R/   Francis is filled with joy   LMj XIII 3
at the presence of the
crucified redeemer,
because of his tears of sorrow
he receives the burning flames
of the highest love of Jesus.

      V/   From the inflowing of the Seraph
and the brightness in its limbs
is the honor of Francis.

3. R/   Once that same vision disappeared,   1C 94
Francis remained and there, pictured on his flesh,
were those glorious five marks.
That wondrous godly picture
is truly made, not false.

      V/   The feet, the hands, the side   1C 95
shine like a wondrous lily,
and the suffering flesh gleams.

Third Nocturn:

Antiphons:

1.   The flesh of Francis then shone   1C 112-3
to our great astonishment;
at Jesus' gift it gleams
clearly through the stigmata.

2. Jesus, You changed the
weeping of Francis sweetly,
when You tore the sack of flesh
in that five-fold way.

3. The heart of Francis is pierced
with loving arrows,
the piercing showing forth
in his flesh with beautiful wounds.

Responsories:

LJS 62

1. R/ Francis, while he tried to hide
the sacred stigmata,
wishes them to be evident
to those who are his throughout
the regions of the world:
through these the height
of Francis's teachings can shine forth.

V. The sparks of love truly glisten,
the inscriptions of the life of Francis
shine forth.

6,7; LMj Mir 5,6

2. R/ By the insignia of Francis
the storm subsides,
animals are cured,
the doctor is amazed
as those burdened by every illness
are restored to health.

V. By sight, by touch, by evident events
wondrously accomplished,
this truth shines forth.

Lauds:

Antiphons:

1. The image of Christ Jesus
which he truly showed forth
graciously fit the holiness
of Francis.

2.   The wondrous wounds of Francis
     Christ made, not him,
     the One who perfected the heart of Francis
     with His love.

3.   Francis often kept vigil
     to contemplate Jesus,
     while contemplating
     glowing red with that
     sign that must be revered.

4.   Francis rejoiced in God
     in the furnace of love,
     Jesus made Him like Himself
     in a true likeness.

5.   Francis fluent in devout praises
     of the Redeemer
     shines with His stigmata,
     made by the force of love.

Benedictus Antiphon

Francis, Father of the poor,   LMj XIV 4
the glory of obedience,
prophet of things most high,
is marked with the likeness of the
Cross and wounds of Christ,
a tested athlete of the Cross.

Second Vespers:

Magnificat Antiphon

Francis, standard-bearer of Christ
by merciful handiwork,
cross-bearer, give to Jesus, whom you loved,
the prayers of the cross,
through that outstanding martyrdom
of which you were held worthy.

THE KINSHIP OF SAINT FRANCIS

BY

ARNALD OF SARRANT

(1365)

Introduction

The Kinship of Saint Francis, the final work of this third volume, is generally unknown. Dedicated to identifying nine "conformities" between the lives of Saint Francis and Christ, it is the work that paved the way for the massive *The Conformity of the Life of the Blessed Francis to the Life of the Lord Jesus* by Bartholomew of Pisa.[1] Thus The *Kinship* marks the end of one period in the history of Franciscan hagiography and introduces another.

The existence of only two known manuscripts of *The Kinship* suggests that neglect has continually plagued it. The oldest, Codex 558 of the library of the Sacro Convento in Assisi, comes from the fifteenth century;[2] the other, the Latin Manuscript 12707 of the Bibliotheque National of Paris, bears the date August 18, 1508.[3] While the Assisi manuscript is badly mutilated, presents many gaps, and is, at times, difficult to read, its Parisian counterpart is better preserved, better written and, notwithstanding lacunae, more complete. Ferdinand Delorme, who is responsible for bringing the text to modern awareness, entitled it *De cognatione S. Francisci* [The Kinship of Saint Francis]; in doing so, Delorme was following the indication of the Assisi manuscript. Forty years later, Marian Michalczyk, studying the Parisian manuscript, entitled the work *De conformitate B. Francisci ad Christum* [The Conformity of Blessed Francis to Christ], arguing that only the first part of the prologue of the work dealt with Francis's natural and religious family, while the bulk of the work described the author's intent: the saint's conformity to Christ.

A note at the beginning of the Paris manuscript of the work identifies its author:

> These are some excerpts and items worthy of note taken from a compilation that was made, I believe, by Brother Arnald of Sarrant, the former provincial minister of Aquitaine and a grand master of sacred theology, on the life and deeds of our blessed father Francis and his companions not contained in his *Legend,* as they were written down and brought to light.[4]

When describing the French Province of Aquitaine and, in particular, its Custody of Toulouse, Bartholomew of Pisa (+1401) wrote of Arnald:

> In the Province of Aquitaine, there is a place called Sarano that claimed Master Arnald of Sarano, who was Minister of Aquitaine for a long while. He was a man of praiseworthy life

and talent, who transcribed everything he could find about blessed Francis.[5]

Although there is no precise record of the dates, it seems that Arnald served his brothers as Provincial Minister between the years 1361 and 1383; yet there is little recorded about his ministry among them.[6] In the *Annales,* Luke Wadding notes that Arnald was sent by Pope Gregory XI to Spain between 1373 and 1375.[7] Aside from this information, nothing is known about Arnald. *The Chronicle of the Twenty-Four General Ministers*—from Saint Francis to Leonard di Giffoni (1373-1378)—is generally recognized as his work,[8] and, according to the Parisian manuscript, so too is *The Kinship of Saint Francis.*

Two clues suggest when Arnald wrote the *Kinship.* The first is a reference to Francesco, one of two great-grand-nephews of the saint who became Lesser Brothers. According to Arnald, Francesco lived *ad mortalitatem,* an expression indicating that he was a victim of the Black Plague of 1349. The second reference is to the saint's great-grand-niece, Francesca, whom Arnald states *vivit et est adhuc juvencula anno Domini 1365* [is living and still a young girl in the year of the Lord, 1365]. The parameters are quite unmistakable: the text was written after 1349 and clearly after 1365.

At the outset Arnald is clear in articulating his purpose in writing this work. In no way does he intend it to replace the "principal legend" of Bonaventure for which he has great respect. Its author, Arnald maintains, is an "outstanding teacher"; it was written in a "marvelous style"; and it is "sufficient" for providing an overview of the life of Francis. As he articulates it, Arnald's purpose is to gather together in a more easily followed manner "those things that touch on the same material in other different legends, that are scattered in the scrolls and sayings of the companions, things that the lord Bonaventure omitted totally or partially because everything could not come to his awareness." Since both manuscripts are badly preserved and filled with large gaps, it is impossible to determine how successfully Arnald achieved his purpose. The last five chapters of his work contain only fragments. Should other manuscripts of the *Kinship* ever be found, it will be especially interesting to discover how Arnald portrays Francis's evangelization of the peoples, a theme that is largely overlooked in the fourteenth century documents.

Nothing in the text reveals the circumstances prompting the composition of the text, although there are two statements that may provide an understanding of the historical environment in which it was presented to the friars. In the first place, Arnald's text clearly places him in the apocalyptic line of the followers of Joachim of Fiore, Peter of John Olivi and Ubertino. "At last, in the sixth age, almost on the sixth day, came a human being, Francis, made in God's image and likeness." Once again Francis is understandably portrayed as a prophet appearing in eschatological terms. *The Kinship* reveals Arnald's awareness of the Black Plague (1347-1350) that had just reached its worst phase, the enervating problems of the papacy that remained at Avignon (1308-78), and the increasing tensions among the Lesser Brothers. To underscore Francis's role in this apocalyptic milieu, Arnald introduces the theme that characterizes his work: "He appeared conformed to that one, true sun of justice in everything, that he would be clearly visible to his followers." By doing so, Arnald hearkens back to the theme of conformity that appears as early as Thomas of Celano's *Life of Saint Francis*.[9] At the hand of Arnald, however, it begins to take the sweeping dimensions we see introduced in *The Kinship,* as he now presents the nine ways in which he understands Francis conforming to the "true sun of justice," Jesus:

> He appeared uniquely conformed to Christ in calling his friends, in establishing their way of behaving, in contemplating the sublime, in revealing mysteries, in instructing peoples and transforming their members, in storing up merit, in gathering reward, in performing wonders.[10]

Curiously Arnald limits himself to only nine conformities; Bartholomew of Pisa later develops forty. Such a restriction, however, suggests that Arnald may have deliberately provided nine chapters as part of a novena or celebration of an extended octave.

The result of Arnald's efforts is a careful weaving together of earlier texts. The chapters that have survived in complete form reveal Arnald's thorough knowledge of these texts and, like the *Assisi Compilation,* the *Tree of the Crucified Life of Jesus,* and the Sabatier edition of *The Mirror of Perfection,* raises questions about the availability of these sources after the decree of 1266 mandating their deletion. At the same time, these chapters present yet another approach to the compiling and editing of those texts circulated among the friars more zealous for the pure observance of Francis's *Rule.* In this instance, the compiler seems to be more balanced, even conciliatory in his approach.

In addition to the gaps in the manuscripts, other problems plague the text. Arnald's first conformity, for example, the calling of his friends, begins with a description of Francis's family, the first such list in this literature. It begins with the saint's parents and continues for four generations. Not only is it difficult to ascertain Arnald's reason for beginning with such a list of Francis's family; beyond an understandable word-of-mouth, it is difficult to know his source.[11] The list of Francis's first religious family, his twelve followers, presents its own set of problems, problems of historicity and of interpretation. While earlier texts provide fragmentary information concerning Francis's first followers, there is a lack of consistency about their identity. A thorough list of the first eleven does not appear until the early fourteenth century, a list to which Angelo Clareno had access.[12] In this light, Arnald's list raises a number of questions prompting the reader to wonder if he allowed his interpretations to influence his historical accuracy. Furthermore, his use of Jerome's interpretation of biblical names, while quite accepted in Arnald's time, seems quite contrived.

Arnald's second chapter raises further questions about interpretation. He is obviously selective about his choice of texts from the *Assisi Compilation* and, for the most part, quotes it consistently. When it is read within the context of the Lesser Brothers' turbulent history in the fourteenth century, Arnald appears to be side-stepping many of the more acrimonious, divisive passages assumed into the more expansive of the *two Mirror* texts, i.e., the Sabatier edition. Moreover, as he attempts to defend the honor of Caesar of Speyer and justify the actions of those who followed his example, he introduces the word "community" into the vocabulary of these texts. The implications of the paragraph seemed to have so jarred the one transcribing it that he adds an interpretive comment: "This statement is an addition or an interpretation on that permission [given above], as I believe, of Brother Arnald of Sarrant of happy memory, formerly the Provincial Minister of the Province of Aquitaine and a Master of Theology."

The most vexing questions about *The Kinship* center on what is missing. That which is available provides additional insights into the struggles of the Lesser Brothers and their attempts to resolve them not only by having recourse to the life of Francis, but also by marshalling the sources of his life to satisfy their needs. While Bonaventure's *Major Legend* may have articulated nine primary virtues of Francis's—and his followers'—life, Arnald's treatise presented an alternative perspective in which Christ's life became the form to which Francis—and his followers—were called to conform. Arnald's work seems to have had little impact beyond providing possible inspiration for Bartholomew of Pisa.

Writing of the sixtieth General Chapter, Marianus of Florence wrote:

> The sixtieth General Chapter was celebrated in Assisi in the year of the Lord 1390 by the General, Brother Henry.[13] At that Chapter Bartholomew of Pisa presented a book concerning the conformities of Blessed Francis which he had recently produced. This Brother Bartholomew was a teacher of sacred theology, a devout man in all ways, and an exemplary zealot of his perfection and profession, who freed many people possessed by the devil and performed other miracles.[14]

Bartholomew had begun writing his own description of the conformities fourteen years earlier, that is in 1385. Although it was initially received with great enthusiasm and continued to be regarded with great esteem, by the sixteenth century it was ridiculed and scorned. Erasmus Alber wrote a scathing criticism of the work entitled *Alconranus Franciscanus* [The Franciscan Qur'an] and, in the aftermath of the Reformation, Bartholomew's work has been neglected. In its shadow, however, Arnald's work has also been lost. One can only hope that future research will uncover lost and neglected manuscripts so that the fullness of Arnald's contribution may one day be savored.

Notes

1. Bartholomew of Pisa, *De conformitate vitae beati Francisci ad vitam domini Jesu,* AF IV-V (Ad Claras Aquas, Quaracchi: Collegium S. Bonaventurae, 1906), 537.

2. Cf. Ferdinand Delorme, "Pages inédites sur S. François écrites vers 1365 par Arnaud de Sarrant, Min. prov. D'Aquitaine," *Miscellaneas Franciscana* 42 (1942): 104-32.

3. Cf. Marian Michalczyk, "Une Compilation Parisienne des sources primitives franciscaines" (Paris, Nationale, ms. Latin 12707), AFH 74 (1981): 3-32, 401-55; 76 (1983): 3-97.

4. Michalczyk, *Parisienne,* 23.

5. Bartholomew, *De Conformitatibus* XI, 537. Michalczyk notes that the place of Arnald's origin is also debated. While the Parisian manuscript has Sarranno, Wadding has Serrano, cf. Wadding, *Annales Minorum seu Trium Ordinum a. S. Francisco Institutorem,* (Ad Claras Aquas, Quaracchi: Collegium S. Bonaventurae, 1931), ad an. 1373, nn. 25-6. In his *Chronicle,* Nicholas Glassberger has Serano, cf. "Cronica," AF II 212, n.3. And Bartholomew of Pisa has Sarnano. This confusion prompted Johannes H. Sbaralea to distinguish two different Arnald's: one from Serano, the second from Serrano, cf. Johannes H. Sbaralea, *Supplementum et castigatio ad Scriptores trium Ordinum S. Francisci a Wadding aliisve descriptos,* vol. I (Roma: n.p., 1908): 103. The editors have decided to follow the judgments of Othon de Pavie who determined that Arnald's place of origin was Saran, a locality in Gers and of Ferdinand Delorme who called it Sarrant. Cf. Michalczyk, *Compilation,* 24.

6. Othon De Pavie, *L'Aquitaine séraphique,* t. I 245, 248; t. II 103.

7. Luke Wadding, *Annales* ad an. 1376, 8: "The complexion of religious life has been greatly tarnished in Castile due to the tumult of the wars between Pedro, the former king, and the nobles of the kingdom, and between Pedro and his brother, Enrique. The brothers had been expelled from many convents and were wandering about without definite residences. Irregular customs and abnormalities were introduced into the communities of religious because of the very liberal lifestyle of Pedro and of many of the aristocrats and patrons who invited the superiors of the Order into their territory. Therefore, the Pontiff thought it was his duty to fight against these evils. From France he sent Br. Arnald of Serranno, Master of Theology and Minister of the Province of Aquitaine, together with his companions from Spain, Br. Didacus of Palencia from the friary at Toledo and John Gonsalvo of Opta from Cuenca, both of whom were lectors. And later he sent John of Ubeda. The Pope exempted these three from all obedience to religious superiors except to Arnald. The Pope did this by the letter: *Cum nos cupientes* which was sent from Villeneuve in the diocese of Avignon on the 29th of August 1373."

8. Arnald of Sarrant, *Chronicle of the Twenty-Four Generals of the Order of Lesser Brothers,* translated by Canisius Conners, notes and introduction by Conrad L. Harkins (publication pending).

9. *Conformare* and its different forms are found in 1C 46, 76, 83, 99; 2C 99, 128, 190; 3C 13, 14. It is also found in LJS 7, 23, 66; LMj Prol 1V 1; X 4; XIII 1.

10. Cf. infra 679.

11. Cf. Arnaldo Fortini, *Nova vita di S. Francesco* II (Assisi, n.p., 1959), 100ff. Fortini was able to confirm the accuracy of Arnald's list through a document of 1344 that speaks of Francesco, son of Petruccio, and of Giovanni, son of Bernardo, but not of Francesca and Giovanna.

12. Cf. Codex Florentino, c. 9, 2878. Cf. Benvenutus Bughetti, "Analecta de S. Francisco Assisiensi Saeculo XIV ante Medium Collecta (E Cod. Florentino c. 9. 2878)," AFH 20 (1927): 89.

13. The Chapter was actually celebrated in 1399, not 1390 as Marianus reported.

14. Marianus of Florence, *Compendium Chronicarum Ordinis Fratrum Minorum* (Ad Claras Aquas, Quaracchi: Collegium S. Bonaventurae, 1911).

The Kinship of Saint Francis

These[a] are some excerpts and items worthy of note taken from a compilation that was made, I believe, by Brother Arnald of Sarrant, the former provincial minister of Aquitaine and a grand master of sacred theology, on the life and deeds of our blessed father Francis and his companions not contained in his *Legend,* as they were written down and brought to light.

Sir 50:6   Resplendent as the dawn and *the morning star,*

Sir 50:7   or even *the rising sun,*

setting the world on fire,

enlightening and making it fruitful,

the most perfect man Francis,

the shepherd and leader of the Lesser Brothers,

arose in the city of Assisi.

[He was]

like the sun warming that world

nearly covered by a winter of cold, darkness and sterility,

giving it light with the brilliant rays of word and deed,

dazzling it with truth,

inflaming it with charity,

renewing it with abundant fruit of merits

Gn 1:11   and enriching it with *a variety of fruit-bearing trees*

in the three Orders established by him,

producing marvelous virtue

both renewing and making the earth attractive

with a variety of embellishments.[b]

At that time, then, those two great lights, Francis and Clare, like the greater and the lesser light, shone among different stars in the

---

a. This translation is based on the two existing manuscripts of this text: (a) that found in the library of the Sacro Convento in Assisi, Cod. 558; and (b) that found in the Bibliotheque Nationale in Paris, Cod. Lat., 12707. Studies and transcriptions of both manuscripts can be found in Ferdinand Delorme, "Pages inédites sur S. François: Ecrites ver 1365 par Arnaud de Sarrant, Min. Prov. D'Aquitaine," *Miscellanea Franciscana 42* (1942): 103-31; Marian Michalczyk, "Une Compilation Parisienne des Sources Primitives Franciscaines, Paris, Nationale, Ms. La. 12707," AFH 74 (1981): 3-32, 401-55; 76 (1983): 3-97.

b. As noted in FA:ED II 68 a, this prologue is also found in a manuscript of the L3C, codex Vaticanus 7339.

firmament of the Church. At last, in the sixth age, almost on the sixth day, came a human being, Francis, made in God's image and likeness. He appeared conformed to that one, true sun of justice in everything, that he would be clearly visible to his followers. He appeared uniquely conformed to Christ in calling his friends, in establishing their way of behaving, in contemplating the sublime, in revealing mysteries, in instructing peoples and transforming their members, in storing up merit, in gathering reward, in performing wonders.

And so this work will be carried out in nine chapters. This will not proceed according to the course and "order of time" of the holy father, as the outstanding teacher, Brother Bonaventure, did with a more marvelous style, because that principal legend of the father is sufficient for this. Only those things that touch on the same material in other different legends, that are scattered in the scrolls and sayings of the companions, things that the lord Bonaventure omitted totally or partially because everything could not come to his awareness: these have been gathered together that they might be more easily found in the same chapter.

[Chapter I]

[THE CHOICE OF FRIENDS]^a

In the first place, then, the most perfect man Francis appeared conformed to our Lord Jesus Christ in the choice of his friends.

³Christ had some prophets who predicted many things about his coming, holiness, preaching, death, and glory; had a precursor who would incline people's hearts to devotion and reverence for him, so that they would believe in him. And He had twelve Apostles, one of

Mt 27:5

whom *went and hanged himself with a halter*. He had, among others, four evangelists, and had four principal doctors expounding his teaching against heretics and exercising ecclesiastical office; and He had martyrs, confessors and virgins. Francis likewise is seen to have had such people as is clearly evident in what is written below.

^{3b}Therefore, Francis son of Pietro Bernardone, son of Bernardone of Assisi, had a brother called Angelo and a mother named Pica. His brother, Angelo, fathered Giovanni and Picardo; Giovanni fathered Siccolo, who fathered Giovanni, Angelo, Petruccio, Bernardo, and Francesco, and their sisters Francesca and Chiara.^b Angelo and Francesco,^c great grand-nephews of Francis, were Lesser Brothers and lived during the time of the Lord Pope John XXII. Brother Francesco, moreover, lived until the plague.^d Petruccio fathered a daughter called Francesca who, in the year of the Lord 1365, was still a young girl. Bernardo also had another daughter, Giovanna, who is also still alive.

^{3c}Before the approval of *The Rule*, Saint Francis, a most eminently pure virgin, fathered in Christ eleven sons who were the first Lesser Brothers with whom he presented himself before the Lord Pope Innocent III for the confirmation of the Gospel Rule. These were:

---

a. The numbering of these paragraphs is based on the text published by Marian Michalczyk, cf. Supra 678 a.

b. In the archives of the Sacro Convento, Arnaldo Fortini found a document, Str. X 29, stating that Chiara was a Poor Clare of the Monastery of Sant' Angelo in Panzo and listed among its abbesses. Cf. Arnaldo Fortini, *Nova Vita di San Francesco* (Assisi: Edizioni Assisi, 1959), 100.

c. Fortini also found in the same archives, Str. IX 29, a reference to Francesco as living at the Sacro Convento and, later, as guardian of San Damiano, cf. Fortini, *Nova Vita*, 100.

d. The Latin *ad mortalitatem* [until the plague] is an expression found in fourteenth century literature referring to the plague of 1349.

Brothers Bernard of Quintavalle, the first, and Peter Catanio, the second; the third was the most holy Brother Giles; the fourth Brother Sabbatino; the fifth, Brother Morico the Short; the sixth, Brother John of Capella; the seventh, Brother Philip the Tall; the eighth, brother John of San Costanzo; the ninth, Brother Barbaro; the tenth, Brother Bernardo Vigilante or de Vida; the eleventh, Brother Angelo Tancredi, who was the first knight of the Order.[a]

Now after the approval *he fathered* in Christ's Gospel so many *sons*   Gn 5:4
and daughters, that his seed, spread throughout the whole world,
seems *beyond number, like the sand of the seashore.* So much for his kin-   Jb 6:3
ship and genealogy.

[4]In the first place, therefore, the following should be seen concerning those who predicted in the way of the prophets many future things about blessed Francis.

[4a]For Abbot Joachim, many years before the birth of Francis, predicted many things about his coming, order, and habit and painted his portrait in the Church of Saint Mark in Venice with the habit and cord, his bare feet and his sacred stigmata, maintaining that he was a most holy man, and should be honored by everyone.[b]

[4b]Many years before the birth of Francis, there was another abbot in the regions over seas who foretold in speaking and writing, among other things, his coming and his Order. "Oh that, in the future, I would see Gospel men going about without purse, money, and shoes in the manner of the Apostles preaching throughout the world!" When that was circulated in the monastery and the monks wished wholeheartedly to see such men, as once before the holy Fathers had wished to see Christ, by chance, after the foundation of the Order, two Lesser Brothers came to that monastery. As the monks questioned them with admiration and were told by them about their life and profession, those monks immediately welcomed them with joy and the greatest respect, bowing before them, and kissing their feet

---

a. While differing from other lists of Francis's first followers, this list coincides with one found in an early XIVth century manuscript, Codex Florentino, c. 9, 2878. Cf. Benvenutus Bughetti, "Analecta de S. Francisco Assisiensi Saeculo XIV ante Medium Collecta (E Cod. Florentino c. 9. 2878)," AFH 20 (1927): 89.

b. Majorie Reeves maintains that the first time this "prophecy" appears is the anonymous *Brevis Historia Fratrum Praedicatorum* dated 1367, cf. Majorie Reeves, *Prophecy in The Later Middle Ages: A Study in Joachimism,* (Oxford: Oxford at The Clarendon Press, 1969), 73, 96-106. Further information can be found in Otto Demus, *The Mosaics of San Marco in Venice,* Volume I: The Eleventh and Twelfth Centuries, with a contribution by Rudolph M. Kloos (Chicago & London: The University of Chicago Press, 1984), 256-9.

as if they were receiving the Apostles of Christ because of that earlier prophecy.[a]

[4c]Another of Christ's confessors, Saint Dominic, also revealed more clearly in an earlier divine oracle the reform to be accomplished by him and Saint Francis when he recognized him in Rome without anyone pointing him out.[b]

[4d]Lady Pica also, the mother of Saint Francis, foretold the wonderful renovation of his life, as will be shown more clearly in chapter seven in the treatise *De Liberalitate.*[c]

L3C 1; 2C 3

[4e]Even Lord Innocent the Third foretold that he would be a support of the Church that was falling into ruin because of an earlier vision he had that the Lateran Basilica was near ruin and understood that it was being supported by some little poor and looked down upon person.

2C 17; LMj II

[4f]Brother Elias, the holy Father's companion, informed by heaven, clearly foretold the time of his death two years before the saint's passing.

1C 109

[4g]And Brother Pacifico in a vision foresaw him, while he was praying, being raised to the throne of Lucifer and preached this to others.

AC 65; 2C 12
LMj VI 6

Saint Francis was also seen to have a precursor, as Christ once had. For there was **a certain simple** and devout **man of Assisi, whom, it is believed, God** had forewarned before blessed Francis's conversion. **Whenever he met him, he would take off his cloak and spread the garment under his feet,** as if to show that God had sent him in advance, to prepare the paths of the most holy Francis. Doing this, therefore, he would publicly show that **Francis was worthy of every respect, since he was destined to do great things in the near future and would be magnificently honored by the entire body of the faithful.**

L3C 1; LMj I

[A portrait of Jesus Christ
is placed here][d]

[A portrait of Saint Francis
is placed here]

---

a. Relying on a statement of Bartholi della Rossa, Marianus of Florence states that this unnamed abbot came "from 'Montagna Nera' about seven miles from the famous city of Antioch (modern Hatay in Turkey), where there was a famous abbey of monks of St. Basil." Cf. *Fratris Francisci Bartholi de Assisio Tractatus de indulgentia S. Mariae de Portiuncula. Nunc primum integre edidit Paul Sabatier. Accedunt varia documenta inter quae duo Sancti Francisci Assisiensis opuscula hucusque inedita, et dissertatio de operibus Fr. Mariani de Florentia quae a pluribus saeculis delituerant nunc autem feliciter inventa,* ed. Paul Sabatier, (Paris: Fischbacher, 1900), CXXX, 145.

b. Cf. FA:ED II 787.

c. Unfortunately, this chapter is missing.

d. The Assisi manuscript contains rubrics for placing these two portraits; the Paris manuscript has no such indications, prompting Michalczyk to place subtitles into his transcription of the text. As will be seen, the editors have chosen both methods.

[5]Christ chose twelve disciples whom he called Apostles. Of these, eleven were most perfect. One, however, was a traitor who, in the end, hanged himself. In a similar way, Francis chose twelve out of all brothers of his time. Of these, eleven were holy and shone with miracles. One, however, *hanged himself with a halter*. That the likeness   Mt 27:5
might appear stronger, we will compare each of Christ's Apostles with each of Francis's companions. But first a hidden likeness between the Son of God and Francis must be made clear.

[6]The Son of God had two names that immediately were able to show the Apostles that it was useful to follow Him. For he was both the Christ, that is, anointed with the fullness of grace, and He was Jesus, the Savior. Therefore He could give them a fitting reward for their labor, that is, grace because He was Christ, and glory because   ; 2C 3; LMj I 1
He was Jesus. In the same way, Francis had two similar names. For at his birth when his father was away in France, his mother called him John. But when his father returned from France, because of his return from that country, he called him Francis.

Francis and the Son of God, therefore, have similar names meaning about the same things. John is interpreted as he "in whom there is grace,"[a] Christ means "anointed with the anointing of grace."[b] Francis, then, was "John" because of fullness of grace and, consequently, "Christ," that is, anointed with grace, and Christ could be called "John," because of the anointing of grace. But Jesus means "Savior."[c] Francis is spoken of as *the keeper* of his brothers, of his fel-   Gn 4:9
low citizens." Francis was, therefore, the keeper of his brothers and keeper of those who are *fellow citizens of the Saints* and members *of the*   Eph 2:19
household of God, and, consequently, Jesus was "savior" and the Son of God was "Francis," that is, the guardian of the brothers, because he was Savior.

[Saint Andrew]   [Bernard of Quintavalle]

[6a]Andrew was the first of the Apostles whom we read came to   Jn 1:40
Christ and some speak of him as the first Christian. Afterwards,   Mt 4:20
Andrew led Peter to Jesus and together, *after they* both *left* everything,
they followed him. In the same way, Brother Bernard of Quintavalle   1C 24; 2C 15
was the first to come to blessed Francis. Afterwards he took Brother

---

a. Cf. Jerome, *Liber Nominum* PL XXIII 1216. *Joannes, in quo est gratia . . .*

b. In this instance, the author follows the teaching of Peter Lombard's *Collectanea in Epistolam ad Romanos I:* "*Christus autem unctus est non oleo visibili sed invisibili, id est oleo gratiae spiritualis* [Christ was anointed, however, not with a visible but with an invisible oil, that is with the oil of spiritual grace]." Cf. PL CIXC 1304.

c. Cf. PL XXIII 1286.

Peter Catanio with him and, together, after they left everything at the command of Saint Francis and gave it to the poor, they followed him.

Surely blessed Brother Bernard can be called "Andrew." Andrew is spoken of as *ana,* which is "on high" and *tropos,* "conversion," as if he was "converted on high."[a] For Brother Bernard almost always had his mind above, turned to God, for, as it is written in his life, **"his mind was totally freed from the things of earth and like a swallow winging its way on high." Alone, sometimes for twenty days, sometimes for thirty, he wended his way to the mountaintops by contemplating only heavenly things. "Because of this, Brother Giles used to say that there was not given to everyone what was given to Brother Bernard so that he would feed himself by wending his way like a swallow."**

DBF XXXII

Or Brother Bernard was Andrew, which means "the one responding,"[b] because, as we find in his life, "he arrived at such clarity of understanding in contemplation that even great clerics would run to him." For "he unraveled the obscurities of questions" most clearly, responding clearly when asked "about each passage of the Bible," as Andrew very lucidly explained our faith in the presence of the Aegean mysteries.[c]

Acts 30:9-10

[Saint Peter]   [Brother Peter Catanio]

[6b]Brother Peter Catanio was not only like Saint Peter the Apostle in name and in life, but also in authority. For as Christ made Peter his vicar on earth and placed him as prince of the Church, so blessed Francis made Brother Peter Catanio his vicar and placed him as head of his religion, so that he might seem more lowly.

2C 67, 143, 15
AC 80; 2C 143

As Peter and Andrew were crucified as Christ was, so Brothers Bernard and Peter were the first to receive from blessed Francis the habit of the cross. See this wonderful mystery! Francis left his father, Pietro Bernardone, for Christ, and God gave him two better than his father. And that he received them from God in recompense for his father, it was clearly demonstrated by their names. In place of Pietro Bernadone, he had Peter and Bernard together. And from these it

AP 14

---

a. Jerome, "Liber Interpretationis Hebraicorum Nominum," *Corpus Christianorum, Series Latina* LXXII (Turnholti: Typographi Brepolis Editores Pontificii, 1959): 142 (hereafter CCSL).

b. Ibid.

c. A reference to a belief held at that time that Andrew was crucified by order of the Roman Governor, Aegeas or Aegeatas, cf. *Epistola de Martyrio Sancti Andreas, Patres Greci* II: 1218-48; *Liber Miraculorum S. Andreae Apostoli,* PL LXXI: 1261-64.

appears that all the deeds of Francis were filled with and hidden in a variety of mysteries.

[Saint James the Greater]   [Brother Giles]

[6c]The third companion of blessed Francis was the holy Brother Giles, like another James of Zebedee since they were greatly similar in name and in life, in traveling and in contemplation. For James is spoken of as *supplantans festinantem* [tripping up someone in a hurry] that is, having the world underfoot.[a] But *Egidio* [Giles] means: from *e*, that is *sine* [without], and *geos* [earth], and *dius*, that is *divinus* [divine], as if "divine without earth." Giles, then, was "divine without earth," because he tripped someone in a hurry, that is the world, because he was divine without earth. James tripped the hurrying world so perfectly, because he was "divine without earth."

James is also spoken of as *"of Zebedee,"* since *Zebedee* is either "flowing between" or "donated."[b] Giles can be spoken of as *"egens dives* [a needy rich man],"* either name meaning rich and poor, because he tripped the world and earthly things by evangelical poverty, and as *"fluens* [flowing],"* because of the overflow of divine grace. He, that is, Giles, is spoken of as in need of earthly things, rich in heavenly gifts. For unless James had been flowing with the greatest graces and gifts, pilgrims would not thus be running to him from all over the world.[c] In an ancient legend of Saint Francis, we read about Brother Giles, however, that many knew from experience that, in matters of their soul, he whom they devoutly invoked, helped them.[d] During his life, then, he was overflowing with so many heavenly gifts that people from many far away places ran to see and hear him. Even Saint Louis, the King of France, came to him from Paris, as did

Mt 10:3; 4:21

DBF XLIII

---

a. James is seen as a form of *ya 'aqobh* [Jacob] which Jerome translated as *supplantator* [one who takes by the heel], *supplanter*, [one who trips]. Cf. PL XXIII 184; CCSL LXXII 136.

b. Cf. Jerome, *Liber Nominum*, PL XXIII 1212.

c. A reference to the shrine to Saint James, Santiago de Compostella, cf. FA:ED I 207 b.

d. This may be a reference to "Catologus sanctorum fratrum minorum," in *Fragmenta Franciscana* III (Rome: Typis Sallustiana, 1903), 8, a text that is dated 1335. Giles's reputation for holiness was later described by Arnald of Sarrant in his *Chronicle of the Twenty Four Generals*, "Brother Giles, The Most Holy and Contemplative Man," "When Giles died, the citizens of Perugia, seeking stone to build his tomb, found a marble sepulchre on which the history of Jonah had been inscribed. They then knew that this was the evident sign of his sanctity which was foretold by him," ChrXXIVG. All future references to this work will indicate the passages printed on the appropriate page of AF III, in this instance ChrXXIVG 14.

Lady Jacoba da Settesoli from Rome, as did many others,[a] as his *Legend* describes more completely.

DBF XXII

Mt 10:3; Lk 6:14

By his call Saint James was the third apostle and is always placed third in the Gospel in which the Apostles are listed. In a similar way, Brother Giles was the third brother called after Francis, that is, after Bernard and Peter, just as James, leaving what was his, followed Christ after Andrew and Peter.

AP 14

Mt 17:6; Mk 9:5; Lk 9:32

As James visited Spain by his preaching and, later, Jerusalem and the Holy Land, so Brother Giles, in encouraging people to penance, traveled first to Spain to visit James to whom he was conformed and, later, to the Holy Land.[b] While ascending the mountain James saw with his own eyes Christ transfigured and fell as if dead from fright. In the same way, among all the companions of Saint Francis, Brother Giles, having the grace of rapture, once saw Christ with his bodily eyes. And, out of amazement and his heart's sweetness, which his human frailty was hardly able to endure, he seemed to have died, as his *Legend* narrates.[c]

["Saint" John the Evangelist]   [Brother Leo]

Jn 20:2; 21:7, 20

[6d]Francis's fourth companion was Brother Leo, his confessor, who was very much like blessed John the Evangelist. Blessed John was very pure, simple, and thoroughly gentle, so that Christ loved him more than the others. In the same way, Brother Leo was very innocent, simple, and gentle, so that Francis called him "the little lamb" and loved him most dearly.[d] As Christ was closer to John and revealed His secrets to him more than to the others, so Saint Francis was much closer to Brother Leo and revealed to him more than to the others mysteries of his heart, even things God had revealed to him.

2MP 85

DBF VII, VIII

---

a. According to Arnald of Sarrant's ChrXXIVG 104, one of these visitors was Pope Gregory IX: "When Pope Gregory IX came to Perugia and heard about the mighty deeds of Br. Giles, he sent someone to summon him. As soon as Giles entered the palace with his companion, he experienced a certain spiritual sweetness which was accustomed to precede his ecstasies. Fearing, therefore, that he would go into ecstasy in front of the Pope, Giles was disinclined to enter into his presence. Instead he sent his companion to ask to be excused because he could not come to the Pope at that time. His companion did this and, when the Pope asked the reason, the brother answered: 'Most holy Father, Brother Giles is below but I believe that, fearing that he would be enraptured before you, he dreads to come.' Then the Pope with a greater desire to see Giles ordered him to enter. As soon as Giles began to speak to the Pope, he went into ecstasy and stood immobile with his eyes raised to heaven. The Pope was astonished and, now seeing in person the things that he had heard about Giles, he said: 'If you leave this life before me, I will not look for any other reason for adding your name to the catalogue of the Saints.' "

b. Cf. ChrXXIVG 76ff.

c. Cf. ChrXXIVG 96.

d. ChrXXIVG 65: "Blessed Francis loved him because of his dove-like simplicity, and he frequently called him the 'Little Lamb of God.' "

DBF IX

As John saw Christ transfigured on the mountain, so, on LaVerna, Brother Leo frequently saw Saint Francis lifted from the earth speaking with God and the angels in the midst of the greatest brilliance. He was also with him when he received Christ's stigmata, just as John was the only one of the Apostles at the foot of the cross when Christ was pierced by a lance. As John wrote Christ's Gospel, so Brother Leo wrote a life of Saint Francis, as will be shown below.[a] As John saw many future events, as is obvious in the *Apocalypse,* so Brother Leo had a number of figurative visions about the future that Saint Francis occasionally would explain more clearly to him, as will be clear below. John, speaking about Christ, says of him: *And the one who saw*   Jn 19:35 *bears witness.* In a similar way, Leo, speaking of Saint Francis, frequently says in the legend he wrote: "We who were with him until his death bear witness . . ."[b]

4, 50, 56, 57, 82, 84, 86, 89, 106, 111, 117

As John saw in the *Apocalypse* Christ conquering the evils of Asia's   Rv 19:11–20:15 rulers and subjects, so once Brother Leo saw Christ Who spoke to him about conquering the lazy, lukewarm, ungrateful, and quarrelsome brothers.[c]

AC 21

Among the Apostles, John lived the longest; Brother Leo likewise passed away extremely old.

[Saint Thomas]   [Brother Rufino]

[6e]The fifth companion of Saint Francis was the ecstatic man, Brother Rufino, who was very much like the Apostle Thomas. Thomas means "the twin,"[d] because of his twofold love of God and neighbor. Rufino, however, is named like *ruphus* [red] because of the color of golden love.[e] Thus the name of both men indicates that they were filled with love. Or Thomas is spoken of as *totus means* [traveling totally] into God, while Rufino is like *ruens in finem* [hastening to the end], that is, to God. As Saint Thomas was doubtful about Christ's   Jn 20: 25-29 resurrection, so was Brother Rufino about Francis's glorification. For

---

a. A reference to Leo's participation in the composition of L3C and the AC, cf. FA:ED II 61-5, 113-7; and infra 697.

b. Cf. Raoul Manselli, *Nos Qui Cum Eo Fuimus: Contributo alla questione francescana* (Rome: Biblioteca Seraphico-cappuccina, 1980), 44-57.

c. ChrXXIVG 72: "At another time Jesus Christ appeared to Br. Leo, saying: 'I am disturbed about the brothers of your Order.' When the trembling Leo asked the reason, Christ answered: 'Because as you know they do not acknowledge either spiritual benefits or the temporal benefits which are so necessary to the body, and which, since they neither sow nor do they reap, I confer on them every day. Furthermore, they frequently murmur and give themselves over to idleness; they provoke themselves to anger and do not quickly return to love by forgiving injuries as they ought.' "

d. Cf. Jerome, *Lexicon Graecum Nominum Hebraicoum,* PL XXIII 887; CCSL LXXII 138.

e. Cf. ChrXXIVG 46.

the devil once appeared to him in the form of the Crucified and told him that Saint Francis was among the foreknown and condemned, and that he should not believe him. He was so blinded that he lost the love and faith he had in Francis, until Saint Francis called him, revealing that delusion to him and recalled him to his original state.

DBF XXXI

Jn 20:27

As Thomas saw the wound of Christ's hands and placed his fingers in the wound of His side, so Brother Rufino did exactly the same in the wounds of Saint Francis. For he wanted to rub Saint Francis, and then he placed his finger in the wound. Saint Thomas was frequently standing with his eyes raised and fixed on heaven, so that he was dining on such sweetness. Likewise, Brother Rufino "reached such an elevation of his mind and perseverance in prayer that he would stand continually in a small circle contemplating night and day divine things unless he was prevented by others." Just as Christ once appeared to Saint Thomas and strengthened him, so He appeared to Brother Rufino and "made his soul melt with divine love."

1C 95; 3C 4; DB

DBF XXXI

Acts 31

["Saint" James the Lesser]   [Brother Sylvester]

[6f]The sixth companion of Saint Francis was Brother Sylvester who was very similar to blessed James Alpheus, like Alpha, first in name, since James means *supplantator* [tripping one], and Alpheus means *fugitivus* [fugitive].[a] Sylvester is spoken of as *silvas terens* [eroding trees], *supplantare* [to trip] the world, that is, to place under foot, and *silvas terens,* I believe, shows in both men a contempt of worldly things. Because he was *Alpheus,* that is, a fugitive, and Sylvester was *silvas terens* [eroding trees], solitude is evidently present in both. For blessed James was exceptionally solitary and always spending time in prayer; therefore, because of his abundant prayers and genuflections he had calluses on his knees like those on his heels.[b] In the same way, Sylvester was almost always in prayer and frequently stayed in lonely places, especially on Monte Subasio where there was a cell of blessed Francis.[c]

---

a. Cf. Jerome, *Liber Nominum*, PL XXIII 1264.

b. The description comes from a passage in Eusebius Caesarea telling of the prayer of James for the welfare of his people. Cf. Eusebius Caesarea, *Historia ecclesiastica* II 23, Patrologia Graeca XX 198 (hereafter PG).

c. For an understanding of the Latin word *carcer* [cell], see FA:ED II 286 c.

Blessed James was the first of the Apostles to celebrate Mass. Sylvester, likewise, was "the first priest to enter the Order."[a]

James was also called a *brother of the Lord* because of his extraordinary holiness and his resemblance to Christ. Brother Sylvester was so holy that he spoke with Christ *face to face* as if he were a brother of the Lord. For God would always reveal to him what he asked to be revealed to him. Aware of this, whenever Saint Francis wanted to know the Lord's will, he would send to Brother Sylvester and it would immediately be revealed to him.[b]

Gal 1:19

Ex 33:11

II 2; DBF XVI

[Saint Philip]   [Philip the Tall]

[6g]The seventh companion of Saint Francis was Brother Philip the Tall who was very much like the apostle Philip not only in name, but also in deed and in activity. Philip has been interpreted as *os lampadis* [the mouth of a lamp].[c] For when the blessed apostle Philip was told by the Lord Jesus about the mysteries of the Trinity he would pour out sweet words to the people, symbolized by the oil, words that were also very clear, as in Syria he extinguished the heresy of the Ebionites through his preaching. In a similar way, Brother Philip the Tall was the sweetest preacher of all of Francis's companions, as the Life of Saint Clare describes him: "Brother Philip," it says, "was present, one who used to pour forth the Lord's fervent and honey-flowing words."[d]

Or he is called Philip from *philos,* that is "love," and *iper,* that is "above," as if he were a lover of things from above.[e] In every way, he was a lover of those who were above. Because of this the Apostle Philip said to Christ: *Lord, show us the Father and that is enough for us.* Brother Philip *was touched by an angel on the lips with a burning coal,* as Isaiah once was, and it set him on fire, and he resounded with fiery words.

Jn 14:8
Is 6:7

Philip is said to have had two virgin daughters through whom the Lord converted many persons to God. Likewise Brother Philip in

---

a. ChrXXIVG 7: "At the sound of his preaching and of that of the other friars, many men were moved to penance and were received into the Order. Among them was Sylvester, the first priest to enter the Order."

b. Cf. LMj XII 1-2; BPr I n.8 - footnote; ChrXXIVG, p. 7: "Here he attained such dignity of soul that, as Br. Bernard of Besse says in the legend of Saint Francis which he compiled, Sylvester spoke with God as if it were face to face. Therefore, when St. Francis wished to know the will of God in doubtful matters, he asked Sylvester to speak to God for him."

c. Cf. Jerome, *Liber Nominum,* PL XXIII 1206.

d. This quotation is from an unknown *Legend of Saint Clare.* For information concerning Philip's role as chaplain to the Poor Ladies of San Damiano, see the *Process of Canonization* X 8 and the *Legend of St. Clare* 37.

e. Cf. Jerome, *Liber Nominum,* PL XXIII 1206.

some way had two virgin daughters, that is Saint Clare and her sister Agnes, through whom innumerable virgins of the Order of Saint Clare and other persons were converted to God. For he was appointed visitator, governor, and corrector, the father of the poor ladies, that is, of Saint Clare and her sisters, and was the first visitator of that Order.[a]

[Saint Matthew]   [Brother Angelo]

[6h]The eighth companion was Brother Angelo Tancredi who was very much like blessed Matthew the Evangelist. Among the Evangelists, blessed Matthew is portrayed as an angel, that is, as a winged man.[b] This companion of Francis, who is like him, is called "angel," just as Saint Matthew can be called "angel." Matthew means *donum festinationis* [a gift of haste] because of his hasty conversion.[c] Tancredi, however, the surname of Brother Angelo, means *statim credens* [immediately believing]. Saint Matthew could be called "Angelo" because of his image, and "Tancredi" by reason of his quick conversion, because he immediately believed in Christ Who was calling him. Brother Angelo could also be called "Matthew" because he also had the gift of haste in his conversion.

And he can be called a levite, which means *appositus* [added] or *assumptus* [assumed],[d] because, when there were only eleven brothers in the Order, he was added that the number of the twelve apostles might be complete. He was also taken in the state of perfection as a true levite for divine worship.

Before his call, Matthew was very worldly and taken up with secular affairs, as was Brother Angelo. Earlier he was a knight and was extremely worldly. As Matthew wrote Christ's Gospel, Angelo wrote Saint Francis's life.[e] As Matthew is portrayed by a human being, so Brother Angelo, of all the companions of Saint Francis, was humane and courteous, and because of this Saint Francis greatly commended him.

2MP 85

---

a. For a listing of the first Visitators of the Poor Ladies of San Damiano, see "Documenta Originis Clarissarum," ed. Livarius Oliger, AFH 15 (1922): 75, 81.

b. According to Rv 4:7, the symbol of Matthew is not an angel, but a man. Cf. *Lexicon der christlichen Ikonographie*, ed. Herder, (1968), 696-713.

c. Cf. Jerome, *Lexicon*, PL XXIII 886, 1214; CCSL LXXII 137.

d. Cf. Jerome, *Lexicon*, PL XXIII 1352; CCSL LXXII 68.

e. As with Leo, this is a reference to Angelo's involvement in writing the L3C and AC, FA:ED II 61-5, 113-7.

[Saint Bartholomew] [Brother Masseo]

[6i]The ninth companion of Saint Francis was Brother Masseo of Marignano who was very much like to blessed Bartholomew both in name and in life. For Bartholomew means *filius suspendentis me* [son of the one suspending me].[a] In this the austerity of his repentance can be noticed, as if he said: "I afflict my body so much that I can be called son, that is, like the one suspending me *and reduce* my spirit *to service.*" Brother Masseo was left-handed as if the son of one who suspended him, because of all the companions of Saint Francis he afflicted his body to obtain the highest humility, as his life will show below.

1 Cor 9:27

Bartholomew also means *filius suspendentis aquas* [son of the one suspending the waters][b] because the waters of the graces of his devotion and tears were falling down and rising up through God and thus they lifted him from the things of earth to those of heaven. In his prayer he genuflected hundreds of times throughout the night. Therefore, he could also have Brother Masseo's surname, that is, Marignani, or *in mari nans* [swimming in the sea], because he was not drowned in tribulations but was swimming as in the sea, being held up and lifted on waters. For the waters of Brother Masseo's devotion were lifted into God as if suspended, for he was an exceptionally contemplative person and, in his mind, hanging onto God.

DBF XL

Just as Blessed Bartholomew was always happy and joyful in spirit, so it was written of Brother Masseo that he was always "spending time in contemplation with a happy expression."

[Saint Simon] [Brother Pacifico]

[6k]The tenth companion of Saint Francis was Brother Pacifico, who is very similar to the Apostle Saint Simon in name and in life. Simon means *obediens* [obeying] or from *syn*, that is *simul* [both together], and from *monos* [one], as if "both together as one," and this through the bond or union of peace.[c] Simon, therefore, appears to sound the same as Pacifico. Who is more peaceful and obedient but one who is both together as one, that is, one who is united with all? Brother Pacifico could be said to be Simon the obedient one and both together as one, for Saint Francis called him Pacifico because of

---

a. Cf. CCSL LXXII 144.

b. Cf. Jerome, *Lexicon*, PL XXIII 883.

c. Cf. Jerome, *Liber Nominum*, PL 23 1221, 1249.

his obedience, simplicity, and gentleness by which he did not offend anyone.

As Saint Simon was also known as "zealot," that is, burning with zeal for God, so Brother Pacifico bore a zeal and a most burning love for Saint Francis. Afterwards he saw in a vision that he would be lifted to a most high throne, speaking with him as if he were already glorified in heaven. Saint Simon was living amid luxury, jests, and songs, and was immediately converted to Christ: for it is probable from the Gospel that the blessed apostle Simon was converted at the wedding to which Christ was invited. For he was from that village, Cana of Galilee, and so he was called a "Cananean" and was a rela-

Jn 2:2

tive of the groom and of Christ. *His disciples* were invited with Christ, "not those who were then his disciples," according to the Gloss, "but those who would be in the future."[a] After the miracle he performed

Jn 2:11

there, *his disciples believed in Him,* that is, Simon, Jude, son of James, and Joseph the Just, who were his brothers and were from that village, as well as relatives of the groom, that is, John the Evangelist. In a similar way, Brother Pacifico had previously enjoyed luxury and songs, for he was "a diligent creator of songs" in that he was

2C 106

"crowned such by the Emperor" and called "King of Verses." From that state, he was converted immediately to Francis.

Simon was also crucified and many marveled that an old man could endure the suffering of the cross. Likewise Brother Pacifico

2C 106; LMj LMn II 9

once saw Saint Francis as if crucified on two crossed swords, while preaching in a monastery. He was suddenly converted to God, and said to Saint Francis after his sermon: "Brother, what you say in word, you should do in deed." Francis asked him why he said that, and he replied, "Give me your tunic." And the saint immediately gave it to him, and he put it on, saying: "Now I want to serve God in this habit." And thus, in that same habit, made in the form of the cross, he was co-crucified with Francis. This amazed many, that a man who spent so many years concerned about luxuries and singing now bore the suffering of the cross.

[Saint Thaddeus]   [Brother Elias]

[61]The eleventh companion of Saint Francis was Brother Elias who is very much like the Apostle Thaddeus in name and in life. For Thaddeus is spoken of as *tuus Deus* [your God], or from *theos [Deus]* he

---

a. This is a comment of Saint Augustine in the context of the disciples who "were" with Jesus and who prefigured those who would be. Cf. St. Augustine, *De consensu evangelistarum* II 17, n. 38, PL 34, 1096.

is called "God God."[a] Elias means "My God"[b] and therefore Elias and Thaddeus seem to mean the same thing. Thaddeus was similar in one thing to Judas the Traitor, because he was also called Judas, but only in name, not because of a betrayal, or his life. Brother Elias was somewhat similar to Brother John of Capella who left the Order. For Brother Elias was accused by the pope of following the schismatic emperor Frederick, excommunicated,[c] and deprived of the habit. But when he excused himself with many tears and sought forgiveness, he was absolved and his habit was restored.[d]

[Judas]   [Brother John of Capella]

[6m]The twelfth companion of blessed Francis was the unhappy Brother John of Capella, who was at first John, that is, "one in grace,"[e] as was Judas, who was initially holy, but then became like his surname "capella," that is, *caput pellens* [spurning the head]. For as Judas spurned his head Christ, so did he spurn blessed Francis. He became a leper in the Order, almost insane, angry at God and at the Order. He stripped off the habit and hanged himself from a tree, so that Francis would also be conformed to Christ in having such a perverse disciple.[f] Whoever sees this happen to such a chosen companion should *watch out if he is standing, lest he fall* more severely.

Mt 26:20-5; Jn 13:21-6
Mk 14:17-21;
Lk 22:21-3;

BPr I 5

1 Cor 10:12

[Saint Mathias]   [Brother William of England]

[6n]As, after Christ's death, Mathias, by divine lot, was taken by the Apostles for apostleship in place of Judas, so, by lot of divine miracles, the English brother, William may be seen to be numbered among Francis's companions in place of the miserable John of Capella. For in that testimony about the Portiuncula indulgence made by Michele Bernardi, among the many companions of blessed Francis from whom he heard that the Portiuncula indulgence was

Acts 1:26

---

a. Cf. Jerome, *Liber Nominum*, PL XXIII 1319-20.

b. Cf. Jerome, *Liber Nominum*, PL XXIII 1211.

c. Cf. ChrTE VI, in *Thirteenth Century Chronicles*, trans. Placid Hermann, introduction and notes by Marie-Therese Laureilhe (Chicago: Franciscan Herald Press, 1961), 122.

d. According to a manuscript in the Sacro Convento of Assisi, the process of absolving Elias took place between May 2-6, 1253. Cf. Edward Lempp, *Frère Élie de Cortone: Etude Biographique* (Paris: Libraire Fischbacher, 1901), 179-87; Giulia Barone, "Brother Elias Revisited," GR 13 (1999): 1-18.

e. Cf. Jerome, *Liber Nominum*, PL XXIII 1322.

f. Cf. ChrXXIVG 4, 19-22.

true, he names in the last place Brother William.[a] We read that he alone was interred in Assisi among blessed Francis's companions, who are eight in number and, with him, nine.[b]

In the place of Mathias, by lot, he shone with so many miracles, that some, because of him, were not being attracted to Saint Francis. Because of this, Brother Elias, who was then the general, went to the grave of Brother William and ordered him under obedience not to overshadow the fame of Saint Francis. From then on, he performed no miracles.[c]

[Saint Paul]	[Saint Anthony]

[60]Just as, after the death of Christ, Paul was taken to be an apostle, so too, in a certain way, was Christ's blessed confessor, Anthony. For they both agree in name, for Paul is called *os tube* [the mouth of the trumpet], while Anthony is called *alte tonans* [high sounding].[d] As the former was the greatest preacher among the apostles, so was the latter among all the brother-companions of that time and after him. As Paul spoke of himself as preaching *Christ Jesus crucified,* so Anthony was preaching on the inscription on the cross when blessed Francis at Arles showed him worthy of that office. As Paul spread his teaching widely, so did Saint Anthony: as he in many ways by word and example enlightened Spain, overseas regions, Bologna, and all of Italy, Provence, Burgundy, and Aquitaine.[e]

1 Cor 1:23 · 1C 46; LMj II; LMn IV 4

[Saint Barnabas]	[Brother Conrad]

[6p]But another of Francis's disciples shining among all of them with Saint Anthony like another Barnabas was Brother Conrad of Offida of renowned holiness.[f] He can well be called precisely Barnabas, which is interpreted *filius consolationis* [son of consolation].[g] For once, while praying to the blessed Virgin that she would obtain for him the ability to feel something of that consolation that Simeon felt

DBF XLVIII

---

a. Cf. Related Documents, infra 810.
b. Cf. ChrXXIVG 252.
c. Cf. ChrXXIVG 217.
d. Cf. Jerome, *Liber Nominum,* PL XXIII, 903. The interpretation of Anthony as "high sounding" comes from the anonymous author of the *Vita prima Sancti Antonii "Assidua,"* V:14, cf. *Life of St. Anthony "Assidua,"* by a *Contemporary Franciscan,* trans., Bernard Przewozny, introduction by Vergilio Gamboso (Padua: Edizioni Messaggero, 1984), 8.
e. The author of this work, Arnald of Sarrant, belonged to the Lesser Brothers' Province of Aquitaine.
f. Cf. infra, 318.
g. Cf. Jerome, *Lexicon,* PL XXIII 899.

when he held in his arms the Lord Jesus Christ, the blessed Virgin appeared to him and placed in his arms the one *beautiful beyond the sons of men.* Brother Conrad, "kissing him on the lips and drawing Him close to his breast," received indescribable consolation. Ps 45:3

Barnabas is also called *filius prophete* [a prophetic son].[a] In the same way, Brother Conrad was Saint Francis's special son, a wonderful prophet who frequently made public the prophecies that he spoke concerning the future condition of the Order.[b]

[6q]It would be too long to narrate all of the individual disciples of Francis: how many were martyrs, how many shone with different miracles. Experience amply shows how many trials that religion "endured" because of the examples of evil brothers, as, of old, holy mother Church is seen at times being shaken under tyrants and heretics, how many schisms there were under that rule, and how many sects.

[7]The blessed father Francis also had, on earth, a mother without a father; in heaven, a father without a mother, and in this, conformed in some way to Jesus Christ.

2C 3 For we do not read that he left his mother who was holy and devout, but like *a new man* at the beginning of his conversion he completely left his father, and, by the breath of the divine Spirit, abdicated his own fatherhood. For standing before the bishop, as he returned everything he had from his father and despising what by law he could legitimately have, he said to his father: "Until now I have called you my father on earth; now I can say: *Our Father Who art in heaven.*" Eph 4:24; Col 3:10

L3C 6; 2C 12; LMj II 4 Mt 6:9

AP 9; L3C 23 And as Christ had on earth only His presumed father, Joseph, in a similar way blessed Francis adopted as a father an elderly poor man by the name of Albert, who would bless him as his first father was cursing him, and whom he would nourish as a father from the alms he had begged.

[7b]As we read that Christ was carried by Simeon *in his arms* and that he also prophesied many things about Christ, thus, on the same day Francis was born, a pilgrim made his way to the door of his family's house seeking alms. When he accepted the alms from a maid's hand, the pilgrim said: "I must see the child born here today." At this the maid was horrified, sending him off as a fool, but the pilgrim Lk 2:28ff

---

a. Cf. Jerome, *Liber nominum,* PL XXIII 1272.

b. Cf. *"Verba S. Conradi:* Extrait du Ms 1/25 de S. Isidore," in *Opuscules de Critique Historique,* Tom I, ed. Andrew G. Little, Pierre Mandonnet, Paul Sabatier, (Paris: Librairie Fischbacher, 1903), 370-92.

asserted he would not leave until he had seen the boy. When the maid told Lady Pica, the mother of blessed Francis, she ordered her to show him the child as the pilgrim had said. When she had done this, the pilgrim *took him in his arms,* and said joyfully and devoutly to the maid: "Today two children were born in this neighborhood, one of whom, this one, will be among the better of the world, the other among the worst."[a] This is clear to all about Francis; many bear witness about the other.[b]

Lk 2:28

[8a]Just as Christ had many hermits and anchorites, so Francis established many hermitages in which he wanted some to live the life of Martha, and others that of Mary. Therefore he wrote statutes for those hermitages: Let those who wish to stay in hermitages in a religious way be three brothers or, at the most, four; let two of these be "the mother" and have two "sons" or at least one. Let the two who are "mothers" keep the life of Martha and the two "sons" the life of Mary and let them have one enclosure in which each one may have his cell in which he may pray and sleep. And let them always recite compline of the day immediately after sunset and strive to maintain silence, recite their hours, rise for matins, and seek first the kingdom of God and His justice. And let them recite prime at the proper hour and, after terce, they may end their silence, speak with and go to their mothers. And when it pleases them, they can beg alms from them as poor little ones out of love of the Lord God. And afterward let them recite sext, none and, at the proper hour, vespers. And they may not permit anyone to enter or eat in the enclosure where they dwell. Let those brothers who are the "mothers" strive to stay far from everyone and, because of obedience to their minister, protect their "sons" from everyone so that no one can speak with them. And those "sons" may not talk with anyone except with their "mothers"

RH

Lk 10:38-42

---

a. According to the *Chronicle* of Albert of Strade (+1261), the Empress Constance gave birth to a son, later Emperor Frederick II, while staying with her cousin Conrad di Urslingen. Cf. Arnaldo Fortini, *Francis of Assisi,* trans. Helen Moak (New York: Crossroad, 1981), 108-9, esp. note ee.

b. The *Liber exemplorum* contains a different version of this tale attributed to Brother Nicholas of Assisi: "My father's house," he narrates, "was next to that of blessed Francis. And so my mother told me that, as women are accustomed to do in childbirth, blessed Francis's mother was resting on her bed after his birth. Some neighboring women were about her. A pilgrim came to the door as though he were seeking alms. After he had received a piece of chicken that blessed Francis's mother sent out to him, he began insisting and saying that he wanted to see the child that had been born. When he was rebuked by the women who were there, he began to shout that he would not leave until he had first seen the child. The Lady Pica, the mother, said 'Bring him the infant that he might see it.' When he saw the complexion, etc., he spoke in this way: 'Today two infants were born in this neighborhood, this one and another. One of them, this one, will be among the best people in the world; the other among the worst.' " Cf. "Liber Exemplorum Fratrum Saeculi XIII (Excerpta e Cod. Ottob. Lat. 522)," ed. Livarius Oliger, *Antonianum* 2 (1927), 262-3. Cf. L3C 3, FA:ED II 69.

and with the minister and his custodian when it pleases them to visit with the Lord's blessing."[a]

[Saint John the Evangelist	Lord Brother Bonaventure	An Eagle
Saint Luke	Brother Julian	An ox
Saint Mark	Brother Leo	A Lion
Saint Matthew	Brother Thomas	An Angel]

[9]Just as in the beginning Christ called simple, unlettered, and ignorant men and through them attracted the world's rulers and learned, so did blessed Francis exactly. He chose the poor, simple, and unlettered in whom only the wisdom of God shone.

BPr Intro 1-3;
HTrb Prol 1

Blessed Francis also had four authors who wrote more authentically of his life, just as Christ had four evangelists.[b] For although many have written a life of Francis and his deeds, nevertheless four are more authentic, thoroughly holy men; just as many wrote a Gospel, yet only four Gospels are authentic and accepted by the Church without hesitation.

[9a]Brother Leo, who, like another Mark, is symbolized by a lion, wrote his life out of great zeal, roaring against violators of his *Rule*. In that life he explains in particular Francis's intention about the *Rule* and his zeal against those wanting to mitigate it.[c]

[9b]The second author of his life was the German Brother, Julian, who, like another Luke, can be symbolized as an ox, because he was totally dedicated to God, conspicuous for his learning and holiness, and thus can be said to be Luke as in *lucendo* [shining in merit].[d] He also composed the greater part of the "night office in lyrics and in chant."[e] This man in particular wrote of Francis's tears and the fervor that he had for people's conversion.

[9c]The third author was the thoroughly courteous, gracious, and humane Brother Thomas who can be symbolized, like Matthew, as a human being. Because of the Lord Pope Gregory IX's decree, he described Francis's affection for his own, and also his bodily afflictions.[f]

---

a. *Rule for Hermitages* 10 (hereafter RH). The last sentence of RH that concerns exchanging roles, is omitted. See FA:ED I 61-2.

b. The concept of four biographers began with Bernard of Besse who wrote of two from Italy, Thomas of Celano and John, and two from France, Bonaventure and Julian. Angelo furthered this by identifying Thomas, John, Bonaventure, and Leo, cf. BPr Intro 1-3; HTrb Prol 1.

c. A reference to the collection of Francis's statements concerning the *Rule*, IntR, cf. AC 101-106, FA:ED II 204-13. For background information, see FA:ED II 204 b.

d. Cf. FA:ED I 368-420.

e. Cf. FA:ED I 327-43.

f. Cf. FA:ED I 180-308.

[9d]The fourth author, like another John, the eagle, was Brother Bonaventure who was in learning extremely lofty like an eagle, and later became general minister like the king of the birds. This man described more clearly than the others the rapture and mental elevations of Francis and revealed that vision and apparition of the Seraph more clearly than the rest.[a]

The writings of these men are of greater authority; those of others should be considered apocryphal because the general together with the general chapter had approved the writings of these men.

Lord John the prothonotary wrote with great devotion his life that begins *Quasi stella matutina.*[b]   BPr 1

[10]Afterwards there were four principal teachers of Francis, describing his life and composing the Office said on his feast. The first of these was Pope Gregory IX who issued a declaration concerning the *Rule* and wrote that first hymn, *Proles de coelo prodiit,* and the prayer, that responsory, *De paupertatis horreo,* and that sequence *Caput draconis,*[c] and granted an indulgence to those saying them. In deed and in name, he was very much like Gregory I the Great, the first doctor who established the Roman Office, the first of ecclesiastical offices.

[10b]The second doctor, like Jerome, another cardinal-priest, was the Lord Thomas who composed those hymns *In celesti collegio* and *Decus morum.*[d]

[10c]The third was the Lord Cardinal Raynerius who composed the hymn, *Plaude turba,* which proceeds very allegorically and mystically in the style of Ambrose.[e]

[10d]The fourth was the anagogical doctor, very profound in learning, like another Augustine, Lord Bonaventure, who established the readings and another office,[f] though I would not say other responsories, because Brother Julian the German wrote those.[g]

---

a. Cf. FA:ED II 525-683.

b. Cf. infra 832-3.

c. FA:ED I 328, 336, 355. Salimbene de Adam clearly identifies Gregory IX as author of these works Cf. Salimbene de Adam, *The Chronicle of Salimbene de Adam,* trans. Joseph L. Baird, Giuseppe Baglivi, and John Robert Lane (Binghamton, NY: Medieval & Renaissance Texts and Studies, 1986), 384-5.

d. FA:ED I 331, 342. Salimbene also identifies Cardinal Thomas of Capua as the author of these works, but adds the responsory *Carnis spicam.* Cf. Salimbene, *Chronicles,* 385.

e. FA:ED I 338. The anonymous author of the *Chronicon Provinciae Argentinensis Ordinis Fratrum Minorum* identifies Cardinal Rainerius of Viterbo as the author of these works, cf. Livarius Oliger, "Documenta Hujusque Inedita Saeculi XIII," AFH 4 (1911), 673-4.

f. Bonaventure, *Minor Legend of Saint Francis* (hereafter LMn), FA:ED II 684-717.

g. Cf. supra 697.

[11]Or these doctors may be the four supreme pontiffs who primarily issued declarations on his *Rule,* that is, Gregory IX,[a] Innocent IV,[b] Nicholas III,[c] and Clement V.[d] Or were you to select from among the Brothers, you have four teachers who expounded very authentically on the *Rule:* in particular, Alexander of Hales and the others who expounded on it because of the decree of the minister.[e] And the fourth is Bonaventure who wrote that declaration *Innominato magistro.*[f]

[12]The blessed father Francis was also conformed to Christ in naming subjects and prelates. For Christ sometimes called the apostles "brothers," as we read in the last chapter of Matthew: *Go, announce to my brothers;* and, at another time, called them "the least:" *As long as you did it to one of the least of mine . . ."* In the same way, Francis, joining the two, called those practitioners of his *Rule* "lesser brothers."

Mt 28:19

Mt 25:40

3; LR I 1; 1C 38

ER VI 11

Because Christ also said *Whoever is the greater among you, let him be your minister* and whoever wanted to be first is to be the servant of all, [Francis] wanted the general to be called, and to be, "the minister and servant of all the brothers," and the others, who were practitioners, should also be called "ministers."[g]

Mt 20:26

As Christ even changed the names of his disciples, so too did [Francis] change the names of some of his disciples. He called Brother Leo "Pecorella [The Little Lamb]," another one "Mansueto [The Meek One]," another brother "John the Simple," another brother "Angelo," and another "Pacifico."[h]

[13]A certain holy woman asked the Lord to reveal to her to what extent He accepted the Order of Saint Francis. The Lord replied that, in that Order, there were men who were more pleasing to God than all those on earth, and there were others who were more displeasing to Him than all others.[i]

---

a. Gregory IX, *Quo elongati,* FA:ED I 570-5.

b. Innocent IV *Ordinem vestrum,* FA:ED II 774-9.

c. Nicholas III, *Exiit qui seminat,* infra 737-64.

d. Clement V, *Exiit de paradiso,* infra 767-83.

e. A reference to the *Exposition of the Four Masters,* cf. FA:ED II 15, 23.

f. Bonaventure, "A Letter in Response to An Unknown Master," in *Works of Saint Bonaventure: Writings Concerning The Franciscan Order,* introduction and translation by Dominic Monti (St. Bonaventure, NY: Franciscan Institute Publications, 1994), 39-56.

g. The Assisi manuscript has a textual variant in this phrase. Instead of *qui erant professores* [who were practitioners], it reads *qui erant precessores* [who were predecessors].

h. At this point the Paris manuscript adds the following three paragraphs.

i. The first comment was later quoted by Bartholomew of Pisa in his *Book of Conformities* , cf. AF IV 563.

[14]And He complained to her that His name was not sufficiently mentioned by or among the brothers. One of the older brothers said: "Three things have caused a great wound in my Order: change of place, the care of monasteries, and ambition for studies."[a]

[15]Always loving what was done in common, blessed Francis avoided in everything singularity, which reeks of every vice. "Singularity should always be avoided," he said, "since it is nothing other than **an abyss** and destruction."

2C 14

2C 28

---

a. This is a new statement, the source of which cannot be traced.

[Chapter II]

[THE ESTABLISHMENT OF RESPONSIBILTIES]

[16]In the second place, he was conformed to Christ in the establishment of responsibilities. For three levels of holy persons can be distinguished in Christ's family: the highest rank of the Apostles who shared Christ's life and most high Gospel poverty; the second rank of the holy women who chose that life, of whom the Virgin Mary was the first and the abbess; the third rank of men and women living in holiness and justice, yet not ascending to the height of poverty, but ministering to Christ and the Apostles from their resources. Similarly, the glorious Francis repaired that threefold ranking, almost totally destroyed in his day, in the three orders founded by him. He placed Brother Peter Catanio over the first, that is, the Order of Lesser Brothers, as Christ did Peter over the Apostles. Over the second order, that is, over the Minoresses, he placed Saint Clare, which harmonizes with the name of the Virgin because that woman was called Mary, meaning "enlightened," and in this does not sound very different from the name of Saint Clare, "brilliant." And as we do not read that Christ placed prelates other than the Apostles over those of the third rank, so Francis placed the Penitents under the correction of the Lesser Brothers, as we can find in their *Rule.*

In a vision a devout man, who was called Pietro Pettinario of Siena, saw that reform in the great church. He saw Christ Jesus with many saints walking on a path and many following Him, one going here, another there, covering his footprints with dust, and many were leaving from them. He then saw Francis coming from afar, searching here and there for Christ's footprints. Noticing they were covered with dust, he removed the dust with his clothes and, after finding Christ's footprint, used to place his foot there. Then finding another footprint, he would place his foot there, and was continuing that way until he came to Christ without any detour. And because today there are—and there were—some who want to hide Francis's footprints, that is his intention that he placed in *The Rule,* his companion Brother Leo wrote clearly of the intention which he had in this way:[a]

---

a. It is helpful to note that, once again, the order of these paragraphs of IntR is changed and certain sections dropped.

701

[Francis's Intention on Keeping Books and Other Things]

[17]Brother Riccerio of the Marches of Ancona, whom **blessed**   2MP 2//AC 101
Francis loved with great affection, came one day to visit the sick
blessed Francis in the palace of the bishop of Assisi. **Among other**
points he discussed with blessed Francis about the state of the
religion and the observance of the *Rule,* he said to blessed Francis:
"Tell me, Father, when you first began to have brothers, what was
your intention? And what is it now, and what do you believe it will
be until the day of your death? Because I want to be sure of your
intention and of your first and last wish, so that we, cleric brothers
who have many books, may keep them, although we will say that
they belong to the religion?"

Blessed Francis told him: "I tell you, Brother, that it has been
and is my first intention and will, if the brothers would only heed
it, that no brother should have anything except a tunic as the *Rule*   LR II 9
allows us, together with a cord and underwear."

[17a]Another time the holy man said: "Our religion and that **of the**   2MP 26//AC 101
Lk 12:32; 1 Jn 2:18 brothers is *a little flock,* which the Son of God *in* this *very last hour*
has asked of His heavenly Father, saying: 'Father, I want you to
make and give me a new and humble people in this very last hour,
who will be unlike all others by their humility and poverty, and be
content to have me alone.' And the Father said to His beloved Son:
'My Son, Your request has been fulfilled.' "

This is why blessed Francis would say: "Therefore, the Lord   2MP 26//1MP 6
willed and revealed to him that they be called Lesser Brothers,
because they are the poor and humble people whom the Son of
God asked of the Father. They are the ones of whom He said in the
Lk 12:32 Gospel: *'Do not be afraid, little flock, for it has pleased Your Father to give*
you the kingdom;' and again, *'What you did for one of the these,* the
lesser *of my brothers, you did it for me.'* For, although the Lord may be
understood to be speaking of all the spiritually poor, he was nevertheless predicting the religion of the Lesser Brothers that was to
come to His Church."

[17c]And blessed Francis added: "Isn't it great that the Lord   2MP 26; AC 101
wanted to have one, new, and little people among all those who
preceded them, who would be content to have Him alone, the
Most High and most glorious?"

[REVELATIONS OF WHAT HE WOULD ACHIEVE
AND THE BROTHERS WOULD NOT WANT TO ACHIEVE]

2MP 2//AC 101
//TL V 10

¹⁸If any brother wanted to ask why blessed Francis in his own time did not make the brothers observe a strict poverty as he told Brother Riccerio, and did not order it to be observed, we who were with him would respond to this as we heard from his own mouth. Because he told the brothers this and many other things, and also had written down in the *Rule* what he requested from the Lord with relentless prayer and meditation for the good of the religion, affirming that it was completely the Lord's will.

Afterwards, when he showed this to the brothers, they seemed *harsh and unbearable,* for they did not know what was going to happen to the religion after his death. And because he greatly feared scandal for himself and for the brothers, he did not want to argue with them; but he complied with their wish, although unwillingly, and excused himself before the Lord and before them. But, that *the word of the Lord,* which He put *in his mouth* for the good of the brothers, *would not return to* the Lord *empty,* he wanted to fulfill it in himself, so that he might obtain a reward from the Lord. And, at last, he found peace in this and his spirit was comforted.

2MP 11; AC 106

^{18b}And Brother Leo added: "We who were with him when he wrote the *Rule* and almost all his other writings bear witness that he had many things written in the *Rule* and in his other writings, to which certain brothers, especially prelates, were opposed. So it happened that on points where the brothers were opposed to blessed Francis during his life, now, after his death, they would be very useful to the whole religion. Because he greatly feared scandal, he gave in, although unwillingly, to the wishes of the brothers. But he often repeated this saying: 'Woe to those brothers who are opposed to what I know to be the will of God for the greatest good of the religion, even if I have unwillingly given in to their wishes.'

"He often said to his companions: 'Here lies my pain and grief: those things which I received from God by His mercy with great effort of prayer and meditation for the present and future good of the religion, and which are, as He assured me, in accordance with His will, some of the brothers relying on the skill of their prudence, oppose me saying: "These things must be kept; but not those!" ' "

Mt 23:4

Ex 4:15

Is 55:11

[FRANCIS'S RESPONSE TO A MINISTER WHO WANTED TO KEEP BOOKS]

Therefore once when he returned from overseas, a minister   2MP 3; AC 102
spoke with him about the chapter on poverty. He wanted to know
his will and understanding, especially since at the time a chapter
had been written in the *Rule* from prohibitions of the Holy Gospel:
Take nothing with you on the journey, etc.

Lk 9:1-6

And blessed Francis answered him: "I want to understand it in
this way, that the brothers should have nothing except tunics with
a cord and underwear, as contained in the *Rule,* and those compelled by necessity, may wear shoes." And the minister said to
him: "What shall I do, for I have so many books worth more than
fifty pounds?"

He said this because he wanted to hold on to them, especially
because he had a disturbed conscience since he had so many
books, and knew how strictly blessed Francis interpreted the
chapter on poverty.

Blessed Francis said to him: "I cannot and must not go against
my own conscience and the perfection of the holy Gospel which we
have professed." Hearing this, the minister became sad. Seeing
him disturbed, blessed Francis said to him with great intensity of
spirit, intending this for all the brothers: "You, Lesser Brothers,
Mt 3:4-5   want *to be seen* as *and called* observers of the Holy Gospel, but in your
deeds you want to have money bags."

Although the ministers knew that, according to the *Rule* of the
brothers they were bound to observe the holy Gospel, they none-
Lk 9:1-16   theless had that chapter of the *Rule* where it says "Take nothing for
your journey, etc." removed, believing, because of this, that they
were not obliged to observance of the perfection of the holy Gospel.

Knowing this through the light of the Holy Spirit, blessed Francis said in the presence of some brothers: "The brother ministers
think they can deceive God and me." Then he said: "Indeed, that
all the brothers may know that they are bound to observe the perfection of the entire Gospel, I want it written at the beginning and
at the end of the *Rule* that the brothers are bound to observe the
holy Gospel of our Lord Jesus Christ. And that the brothers may
Rom 1:20   always *be without an excuse* before God, I proclaim and still proclaim
that I want to show with these deeds and always observe, with
Ex 4:15; Is 51:16   God's help, what God *has placed in my mouth* for the my welfare and
their own." Therefore, he observed the entire holy Gospel to the
letter until the end of his life.

[HE WAS NOT EAGER THAT THE BROTHERS STUDY]

LR X 7

[20]Therefore, because the holy man feared that, by reason of learning, the brothers would want to have a number of books and, in this way, sidestep poverty, and he had already foreseen that, by reason of learning, the devotion and perfection of the brothers would be lost, he therefore did not care that the brothers be free for study. And aforementioned Brother Leo testified to this, expressing blessed Francis's intention on the passage of the *Rule:* **"Let those who are illiterate not be anxious to learn."**

2MP 72; AC 103

"Blessed Francis did not want," he said, **"his brothers to be desirous of learning and books, but he wanted** and desired that **they be eager to have the pure and holy simplicity, prayer, and holy obedience, and Lady Poverty on which the first and holy brothers had built.**[a] Not that they **despised knowledge. On the contrary, they revered all knowledgeable persons and theologians in the religion and, to a great degree, others . . ."**[b]

As he himself says in his Testament: **"We must honor all theologians and those who minister to us spirit and life."**

But, foreseeing the future, he knew through the Holy Spirit, as he also repeated many times to the brothers, that many brothers, under the pretext of edifying others, would abandon their vocation, that is, pure and holy simplicity, holy prayer, and our Lady Poverty. And it is happening[c] that, because, while they believe themselves to be more imbued and more inflamed with the love of God out of an understanding of Sacred Scripture, they will occasionally remain inwardly cold and empty. And they will be unable to return to their vocation. **"There are many who place all their energy and care in knowledge, losing their holy vocation and devout prayer. And when some have been edified because of their sermons or it might seem that they have been converted because of a sermon, they become proud and puffed up about the deed. For those whom they think they have edified or converted to penance by their words, the Lord edified and converted by the prayers of holy brothers, although they are ignorant of this, so that they do not boast. These brothers are, therefore, knights of the round table,**

---

a. It is difficult to determine how this paragraph ends since there are two different versions. AC 103 ends quite simply: "And he believed this to be the more secure path for the soul's well-being." 2MP 72 is more complicated: "And he used to say that this was the only secure path for their well-being, because Christ, Whom we are to follow, has shown us that this is the only way and taught us so both by word and example."

b. Once again, it is difficult to determine how this paragraph ends.

c. This may only be a mistaken reading of the manuscripts or a reflection on the course of events. AC 103 reads *accidet* [will happen]; the Paris manuscript has *accidit* [is happening or has happened].

the brothers who hide in deserted and remote places, to devote themselves more generously to prayer, weeping over their sins and those of others, whose holiness is known only to God, and is sometimes ignored by the brothers and by people. And when their souls will be presented to God by the angels, the Lord will then reveal to them the fruit of their labors, that is, the many souls saved by their prayers, saying to them: 'My sons, behold these souls have been saved by your prayer' and, *'since you were faithful in little things, I will set you over many.'* And he used to say about this passage: *'The barren one has given birth to many children,* as it is described in the *Legend.'* "[a]

 [20b] And elsewhere: "My brothers who are led by curiosity for knowledge will find themselves empty-handed on *the day of reckoning.* I would prefer that they work more for virtue, so that when *the time of tribulation* arrives they may have the Lord with them in their need. Because *a tribulation is approaching,"* he said, "when books, useful for nothing, shall be thrown into cupboards and closets."

Marginal references:
Mt 25:21
1 Sm 2:5
LMj VIII 2
Hos 9:7
2MP 69//AC 47
Ps 37:39
Ps 22:12; Prv 1:27

[The terrible punishment on the place of studies in Bologna][b]

[21] Once it happened that Brother John de Schiacia, minister of Bologna, who was a very educated man, established a place of studies in Bologna without permission from blessed Francis and while he was away. When blessed Francis heard this, he immediately went there and harshly chastised the minister, saying: "You want to destroy my Order! For I desire and want my brothers to pray more than to read." And so he had the place of study destroyed.

When he left Bologna, however, that minister again established the center of study. At this an upset blessed Francis cursed him with a harsh curse. After the saint's curse, he immediately became gravely ill. He then sent by way of two brothers a request to Blessed Francis asking him to take back that curse. Blessed Francis replied: "In heaven our Lord Jesus Christ confirmed that curse which I have given him. He is cursed by Him." The sick minister, therefore, laid thus on his bed. As he was lying there, a fiery drop of sulfur came down from on high on his body, and it bored completely through him

---

a. Arnald's reference is to LMj VIII. However, the same passage can be found in AC 103 and 2MP 72 indicating its continuity in the tradition.

b. The Latin here is *studium* [place of studies], a word still used in the official vocabulary of the Order of Friars Minor.

and the bed on which he was lying. And with a great stench he expired.

[THE NOVICE WHO WANTED A PSALTER]

AC 103

2MP 4

²²There was once a novice who could read the psalter, although not very well, and he sought permission from the minister. But he did not wish to have it unless he first had permission from blessed Francis, especially since he had heard that blessed Francis did not want his brothers to be desirous of learning and books.

²²ᵇOne day blessed Francis happened to come to the hermitage where that novice was staying. Then that novice said to blessed Francis: "Father, it would be a great consolation for me to have a psalter. And, although the general minister has given me permission to have it, I still want to have it with your knowledge." Blessed Francis answered him: "The Emperor Charles, Roland, and Oliver, and all the paladins and valiant knights who were mighty in battle, pursuing unbelievers with great toil and fatigue even to death, had a glorious and memorable victory for themselves, and, finally, died fighting as holy martyrs for the faith in Christ. And there are many who want to receive honor and praise by only relating what they did. Thus there are many among us who want to receive honor and praise by recounting and preaching about them." And after explaining and applying this to the proposal of that novice, he said: "The saints have done these deeds, and we want to receive honor and glory by recounting and preaching about them," as if to say, *"Knowledge puffs up, but charity builds."*

Adm VI 3

1 Cor 8:1

AC 104

Another time, when blessed Francis was sitting near a fire, warming himself, the same novice spoke to him again about a psalter. And blessed Francis told him: "After you have a psalter, you will desire and want to have a breviary; after you have a breviary, you will sit in a chair of authority like a teacher or a great prelate,ᵃ telling your brother: 'Bring me the breviary.'"

Speaking in this way with great intensity of spirit, blessed Francis took some ashes in his hand, put them on his head rubbing them around his head as though he were washing his head. He said: "A breviary, a breviary, a breviary!" The brother was stunned and ashamed.

---

a. The Latin text reads *in cathedra* [in a chair of authority]. The nuance refers to the *cathedra*, a word signifying a position of authority such as a royal throne, a bishop's see, or a teacher's platform. Cf. supra, 2MP 48 where a corpse is *exaltetur in cathedra* [raised on a throne].

Afterwards blessed Francis said to him: "Brother, I was like-wise tempted to have books. But, in order to know God's will about this, I took the book where the Lord's Gospels are written and prayed to the Lord to deign to show it to me at the first opening of the book. After my prayer was ended, on the first opening of the holy Gospel this verse of the holy Gospel came to me: *To you it is given to know the mystery of the kingdom of God, but to the others all things are treated in parables."*

Lk 8:10

And he said: "There are many who willingly climb to the heights of knowledge; that person be blessed who renounces it for the love of God."

After many months, when blessed Francis was at the church of Saint Mary of the Angels, at a cell behind the house on the road, that brother spoke to him for a third time about the psalter. Blessed Francis said to him: "Go and do this as your minister tells you." When he heard this, that brother began to go back by the same road he had come.

AC 105

Blessed Francis remained on the road, and began to think over what he had said to that brother. Suddenly he yelled after him: "Wait for me, Brother, wait!" He went up to him and said: "Come back with me and show me the place where I told you to do with the psalter what your minister tells you."

When they came to the spot where he had said this, blessed Francis knelt in front of the brother and said to him: *"Mea culpa,* brother, *mea culpa.* Whoever wishes to be a Lesser Brother must have nothing but one tunic, a cord, and short trousers the *Rule* allows him; and for those forced by manifest necessity or illness, shoes."

Whenever brothers came to him to ask advice about such things, he would give them the same answer. For this reason he used to say: "A person is only as learned as his actions show; and a religious is only as good a preacher as his actions show;" as if to say *a good tree is known* only *by its fruit."*

Mt 12:33; Lk 6:44

Ps 19:8

[22c]Therefore the most holy father used to say: "In books *the testimony of the Lord,* not value, should be sought, edification rather than abundance." He wanted a few kept and, in common, available to the mind and need of the brothers.

AC 25; 2C 62

[KEEPING BOOKS IN COMMON]

[23]When the brother ministers urged him to allow something at least in common, so that such a great number would have some re-

2MP 13; AC 16

sources, blessed **Francis called upon Christ in prayer and consulted Him about this. Christ immediately responded to him**, saying: "I will take away everything held individually or in common. I will always be ready to provide this for this family, no matter how much it might grow, and I will always cherish it as long as *it will put its hope in me.*"

Ps 91:14; 22:5

²³ᵇTherefore no one should be surprised that the Supreme Pontiffs, in commenting on that passage in the *Rule* "The brothers may not make anything their own . . ." said: This should be understood either individually or in common. For Gregory the Ninth, who said this first, was speaking according to blessed Francis's intention, which he knew well, since he was very close to him.ᵃ The intention of blessed Francis, then, was that the brothers possess nothing individually or in common, and that they only have in common use of a few books and other necessary things. And, therefore, he did not want that frequently spoken-of novice to have his own use of a psalter.

LR VI 1

[THE CHASTISEMENT OF THE BROTHERS BEFORE THE LORD OF OSTIA]

2MP 68; AC 18

²⁴**When blessed Francis was at Saint Mary of the Portiuncula for the general chapter known as the Chapter of Mats because the only dwellings there were made of rush-mats, there were five thousand brothers present. Many wise and learned brothers went to the Lord of Ostia,** who was at that time the Protector of the Order and had come then to the Chapter.

AP 43
L3C 61
AP 43

²⁴ᵇFor blessed Francis had petitioned him to be present in whatever year there was a General Chapter. **And he agreed and came each year;** as long as the Curia was in Perugia, he would come. **And all the brothers gathered at the chapter went** personally **to meet him. As** they were coming, he would dismount from his horse and go on foot with the brothers to the church because of the devotion he had for them. Afterward he would preach to them and celebrate Mass during which blessed Francis would chant the Gospel.

2MP 68; AC 18

²⁴ᶜDuring that chapter, many distinguished and learned brothers of the Order, therefore, came to the Protector, saying: "Would you please tell **Brother Francis to follow the advice of the wise brothers and allow himself to be guided by them?" They cited the** *Rule* **of blessed Benedict, blessed Augustine, and blessed Bernard, which teach how to live in such and such an Order in such a way.**ᵇ

---

a. Cf. Gregory IX, *Quo elongati* 6, FA:ED I 573.
b. The text may also be rendered: "which teach living in such and such a way, with order"; or "which teach living in this way, and in such an orderly manner"; or even, "which teach how to live in such and such a way, like an Order."

The cardinal related everything to blessed Francis, giving him some advice as well. Then blessed Francis took him by the hand, saying nothing, and led him to the brothers assembled in chapter, and spoke to the brothers in the fervor and power of the Holy Spirit: "My brothers! My brothers! God has called me by the way of simplicity and humility, and has truly shown me this way for me, but also for those who want to trust and follow me. Therefore I do not want you to mention to me any *Rule,* whether of Saint Augustine, or of Saint Bernard, or of Saint Benedict, or any other form of life except the one that the Lord in His mercy has shown and given to me.[a] And the Lord told me what He wanted: He wanted me to be a new fool in this world. God did not wish to lead us by any way other than this knowledge, but God will confound you by your knowledge and wisdom. But I trust in the Lord's police that through them God will punish you, and you will return to your state, with your blame, like it or not."

The cardinal was shocked, and said nothing, and all the brothers were afraid.

[HIS RENUNCIATION OF THE GOVERNMENT OF THE BROTHERS]

Another time, while blessed Francis remained sick in that palace of the Bishop of Assisi, one day one of the companions said to him: "Father, excuse me, because what I want to say to you, many have already thought. You know," he said, "how formerly through the grace of God, the whole religion flourished in the purity of perfection, that is, how all the brothers fervently and zealously observed holy poverty in all things, in small and poor dwellings, in small and poor furnishings, in small and poor books, and in clothing. And as in these things, as well as in all other exterior things, they were of one will, concerned about observing everything that had to do with our profession and calling, and eager to give good example to everyone. In this way they were of one mind in the love of God and neighbor, and were truly apostolic and evangelical men.

"But, for some time now, this purity and perfection have very much begun to change into something different, although many use the great number of brothers as an excuse, claiming that on

2MP 71; AC 1@
WSF 4

---

a. Cf. FA:ED II 133 a.

this account these things cannot be observed by the brothers. In fact many brothers have become so blind that they think people are more edified and moved to devotion by these ways than by the former ones. And it seems to them more fitting to live and behave according to these ways. Therefore they despise and consider worthless the way of holy simplicity and poverty, which were the beginning and foundation of our religion. Thinking this over, we firmly believe that they displease you. But we are greatly amazed. Why, if they displease you, do you tolerate them and do not correct them?"

"May the Lord forgive you," blessed Francis responded to him, "for wanting to be against me and opposed to me and involve me in these things that do not pertain to my office. As long as I held the office of prelate for the brothers, and they remained faithful to their calling and profession, and, although I was always ill from the beginning of my conversion, I satisfied them with a little of my care, by my example and preaching. But afterwards I realized that the Lord *multiplied the number* of the brothers, and that, due to tepidity and lack of spirit, they began to turn away from the straight and sure way which they had been accustomed to walk. They would take *the* broader *road that leads* to death, without paying attention to their profession and calling and good example. They refused to give up this perilous and fatal way that had begun despite my preaching, my admonitions, and my example that I consistently gave them. I entrusted the prelacy and governance of the religion to the Lord and to the ministers.

"However, although I renounced the office of prelacy among the brothers, I excused myself before the brothers at the general chapter saying that, because of my illness I could not take care of them and care for them. And yet, if the brothers would have been willing to walk according to my will, I would not want them to have any other minister except me to help and comfort them until the day of my death. As long as a faithful and good subject knows and observes the will of his prelate, then the prelate has to have little concern about him. Rather, I would be so happy at the goodness of the brothers, both on their account and my own. Thus, even if I were lying sick in bed, it would not be considered a burden to me to satisfy them, because my office of prelacy is only spiritual, namely to overcome vices, and spiritually correct and cure them. Inasmuch as I cannot overcome and correct them by preaching, admonitions, and example, I do not want to become an executioner who punishes and scourges, like the powers of this world.

Acts 6:7

Mt 7:13

Ps 11:2

For *I trust in the Lord*. Invisible enemies, the Lord's police, who punish in this world and in the next those who transgress the commandments of God and the vows of their profession, will take revenge on them, having corrected men of this world, and thus they will return to their profession and calling.

1 Kgs 8:36

"Nevertheless, until the day of my death, I will not cease teaching the brothers at least by example and good deeds *to walk by the path* which the Lord *showed* me, and which I have already taught

Rom 1:20

and showed them by word and example. Thus, *they will have no excuse* before the Lord, and I will not be bound to render any further account about them or about myself before the Lord."

[FUTURE TEMPTATION OF BROTHERS BECAUSE OF LEARNING]

[26]Saint Francis also predicted a very great trial of his brothers   OL IV

Jb 1:18-19

that was to come because of the love of learning, and that *a violent wind from the desert* would arise, and would *strike the four corners* and completely tear down *the house of his first-born* offspring, and *destroy all his children and daughters*. And, that he might avoid the danger of

2 Sm 4:5-12

the ruin of souls, like another *Rechab* [a] he sent his own to lead a wandering life: not to build palaces; not to live in the midst of cities; not to plant the vineyards of various studies, nor drink the wine of secular knowledge and worldly philosophy but, enlivened by the warmth of the Holy Spirit, placed as a law for his sons the deeds of the most perfect life of Christ.

[26b]Therefore he said: Let those not knowing letters not be eager   LR X 8

to learn, etc. For until simplicity—contemptible and looked down upon in the eyes of the learned—shall have been guaranteed, they will lay claim to audacity and presumption, and, in the name of scholarship, will be glorified in praise, and will trust in the effort of their own prudence."

[THE *RULE* dictated by CHRIST]

[27a]We must note that blessed Francis wrote a rule that was perhaps incorporated into those that followed. It began: "In the name of the Father . . ." The Lord Pope Innocent the Third confirmed this by word alone, without a seal. Afterwards he wrote that which the Lord

---

a. Some manuscripts read "Ahab," Cf. 1 Kgs 16; Jer 29:21.

Pope Honorius the Third confirmed with a seal. Before it received the seal, many things were being taken from that *Rule* by the ministers contrary to the intention of blessed Francis.

AC 17; WSF 3

[27b]After the second rule which blessed Francis wrote had been lost, *he went up* a *mountain* with Brother Leo of Assisi and Brother Bonizo of Bologna to make another rule,[a] which he had written at Christ's instruction.

Ex 24:18; Mt 5:1

A group of many ministers came to Brother Elias, who was the vicar of the blessed Francis. "We heard that Brother Francis is making a new rule," they told him, "and we fear that he will make it so harsh that we will not be able to observe it. We want you to go to him and tell him that we refuse to be bound by that rule. Let him make it for himself and not for us."

Brother Elias replied to them that he did not want to go because he feared the rebuke of blessed Francis. When they insisted that he go, he said that he refused to go without them; so they all went together.

When Brother Elias and the ministers were near the place where blessed Francis was staying, he called him. Blessed Francis responded, and seeing the ministers, he said: "What do these brothers want?" "These are ministers," Brother Elias answered, "who heard that you are making a new rule. They fear that you are making it very harsh, and they say—and say publicly—that they refuse to be bound by it. Make it for yourself and not for them."

Then blessed Francis turned his face toward heaven and spoke to Christ in this way: "Lord! Didn't I tell you, they wouldn't believe me?" The voice of Christ was then heard in the air, saying, "Francis, nothing of yours is in the *Rule:* whatever is there is mine. And I want the *Rule* observed in this way: to the letter, to the letter, to the letter, and without gloss, without gloss, without gloss."[b] And He added: "I know how much human weakness is capable of, and how much I want to help them. Therefore, those who refuse to observe it should leave the Order." Then blessed Francis turned to the brothers and said: "Did you hear? Did you hear? Do you want me to have you told again?" Confused and terrified, the ministers departed.[c]

---

a. Information about Bonizzo of Bologna can be found in FA:ED II 131 b. Parallel descriptions of the composition of the *Regula bullata* [Later Rule] can be found in LMj IV 11, FA:ED II 557-8.

b. For further information on the phrases *ad litteram* [to the letter] *sine glossa* [without gloss], see FA:ED II 132 a.

c. In addition to being a reference to AC 17, this first number is also a direct quotation of the *Verba S. Francisci* [The Sayings of Saint Francis], cf. FA:ED II 130 a. These *Sayings* are quoted again in 2MP 2, 12, 13, 50, 68, 79, 85.

[THE BROTHER WANTING TO OBSERVE THE *RULE* purely]

[28a]At Saint Mary of the Angels there was a brother from Germany, a master of theology, who spoke with Saint Francis with great reverence: "I promised firmly to observe the Gospel and the *Rule* which Christ has spoken through you, until the end, simply and faithfully, with the help of His grace. But one favor I ask of you. If in my lifetime the brothers fall as far away from the pure observance of the *Rule* as you predict through the Holy Spirit, I ask by your obedience that I may withdraw from those who do not observe it, alone or with some brothers who wish to observe it purely."

Hearing these things, Blessed Francis was overjoyed and, blessing him, said, "Know that what you asked is granted to you, by Christ and by me."

Gn 48:18; Ps 110:4   And he *placed* his *right* hand *on his head,* saying to him: *"You are a priest forever according to the order of Melchisedech."* And Blessed Francis added that all the promises made to him by Christ would, in the end, be fulfilled in those who would strive to observe the *Rule* simply, to the letter, and without glosses, and with joy.

[28b]And out of those some shamelessly decided to withdraw from the community of the Order of their own will; because of which, as they say, the brothers observe the *Rule* not according to the letter, but as it is commented upon and interpreted by the Roman Pontiffs. To say this is reckless, to follow it is insane. For blessed Francis never gave anyone permission to leave the community, except to someone who is prevented from observing the *Rule* to the letter. And then he first ordered such brothers to have recourse to the ministers. The Roman Pontiffs have interpreted the *Rule* according to the intention of blessed Francis. Pope Gregory the Ninth maintained this, he who, I believe, knew blessed Francis's intention better than anyone living at that time since he was closest to him and was an advisor on the composition of the *Rule,* and was an ardent advocate for its confirmation. Pope Nicholas the Third also stated that he knew the saint's intention through his companions and deviated from it minimally in his declaration. Therefore, it should not be doubted that the Order's community understands the *Rule* and wishes to observe it according to blessed Francis's intention without gloss. But I call this for now the Order's community, not this or that convent, or this or that Province; but the intention of the Order's community. I speak here of what I believe to be the declarations and statutes of the General Chapter.

This statement is an addition or an interpretaion on that permission [given above], as I believe, of Brother Arnald of Sarrant of happy memory, formerly the Provincial Minister of the Province of Aquitaine and a Master of Theology.

[HOW GOD PROVIDED FOR TWO STARVING BROTHERS]

²⁹There were two of our brothers who wanted to leave a place and, because of greater perfection, took nothing with them, not even bread or anything to eat. Walking for the greater part of a day, they were not able to find any bread. Hungry and almost fainting from weakness, they asked bread for the love of God from a priest they had found in some church. Since he had none, they left him, not knowing what to do. As they went, they met a young man who said to them: "Why are you standing still and why don't you have anything? Is it because you set out so sluggishly and almost tired?" They answered: "We looked for bread but could not find any, so we are almost fainting from hunger." The youth said to them: "Sit down. Look here are the two pieces of bread I have. Eat them!" Taking them with great joy, he ate whatever was his. For that bread was tempting and mouth-watering, because it had a very delicious aroma. After he had eaten, the young man said to them: "Swallow your pride. Why are you afraid? Why don't you *cast all your care on the Lord?* Doesn't it say in the Gospel: *'Take nothing with you for the journey'?* But you, straying from your father blessed Francis, have deleted that passage from the *Rule.* And therefore, because you do not hope in God, Who never abandons any poor animal, you do not find whatever you need to satisfy yourselves in time of need. But your Order has been split in three. For there are some who, once the soul is separated from the body, fly through Purgatory to heaven, brothers who are purified here through trials, and perfectly observe the *Rule.* There are others who observe it half-heartedly, and, in this world, blessed Francis serves them in the same way by not taking care of them. There are others whom he does not admit in any way." Hearing this, the brothers then spoke openly to one another: "Perhaps this young man is an angel!" And while they were saying this, he immediately disappeared.

³⁰He burned with great zeal for the common profession of our *Rule,* which is nothing else than the perfect observance of the Gospel. He endowed those who are and were true zealots about it with a special blessing. He used to tell his imitators that our profession was the *Book of Life, the hope of salvation, the pledge of glory,* the marrow of the Gospel, the way of the cross, the state of perfection, the key of Paradise, *the pact of an eternal covenant.* He wanted all to have

Ps 55: 23

Lk 9:3

2MP 76//2C 208

Rv 3:5; 13:8;
Rom 3:5; 21:27

Gn 16:13

it, all to know it. In their conversations he wanted the brothers to speak of it often and to let it speak more often to the inner man, as *encouragement in weariness* and as a reminder of a sworn oath. He taught them to keep it always before their eyes as a reminder of the life they should lead, and, what is more, he wanted and taught the brothers that they should die with it.

It is therefore obvious that blessed Francis gave the very same rule to his brothers, as Christ gave to his followers.

Wis 8:9

[Chapter III]

[THE APPARITIONS OF BLESSED FRANCIS]

[31]Blessed Francis appeared to be like Christ in the contemplation of things above. For we read that God the Father sometimes appeared and spoke to him in a cloud, the angels also spoke with him and ministered to him, and even holy men, as Moses and Elijah at the Transfiguration. In the same way, we read that Christ spoke with blessed Francis twenty or more times or appeared visibly to him, as angels and many saints did many times, as we can see more clearly from the examples written below.

MP 81; AC 112;
MP 40//2C 158

[31b]Because of the boundless zeal that he had at all times for the perfection of the religion, he was naturally grieved when he would hear or see any imperfection in it. He began to realize that some brothers were giving a bad example in religion and that the brothers were already beginning to turn aside from the highest summit of their profession. One time, moved *inwardly with* very great *sorrow of heart,* he said to the Lord in prayer: "Lord I give back to you the family You gave me."

And the Lord immediately said to him: "Tell me, simple and unlettered little man, why are you so upset when one of the brothers leaves religion and when others do not *walk the way I showed you?* Also tell me: Who planted this religion of the brothers? Who makes a man convert and do penance? Who gives the strength to persevere in it? Is it not I? I did not choose you as a learned or eloquent man to be over my family. I do not want you nor those I gave you who intend to be true brothers and true observers of the *Rule* that I gave you to walk the way of learning and eloquence. But I chose you, a *simple and unlettered* man, so that you and the others may know that I will watch over my flock. But I have placed *you as a sign* to them, so that the works that I work in you, they should see in you, emulate, and do them. For those who walk in the way I showed you, have me and have me more abundantly. Those who want to walk in another way, that *which they seem to have will be taken away from them.* Therefore, I tell you, from now on don't be so sad; do what you do, work as you work, for I have planted the religion of the brothers *in everlasting love.* Know that I love it so much

Gn 6:6

1 Kgs 8:36

Acts 4:13

Hg 2:24

Mt 25:29

Jer 31:3

717

Prv 26:11; 2 Pt 2:22 that if any brother, *returning to his vomit,* dies outside religion I will replace him with another in religion who will have his crown in his place, and supposing that he has not been born, I will have him born. And so that you know that I love the life and religion of the brothers, suppose that in the whole religion of the brothers only three brothers remained, it would still be my religion and I would never abandon it."

And when he heard these things, his soul was wonderfully comforted.

And, although on account of the great zeal that he always had for the perfection of the religion, he could not totally restrain himself from becoming extremely sad when he heard of any imperfections of the brothers from which bad example or scandal could arise. Nevertheless, after he was comforted by the Lord in this way, Ps 119:106 he remembered that [passage] of the psalm: *"I have sworn and determined to keep the justice* of the Lord and to observe the *Rule* that the Lord Himself gave to me and to those who desire to imitate me. All these brothers have also bound themselves to this as I have. And therefore, after I resigned the office among the brothers because of my illnesses and other reasonable causes, I am not bound at all except to pray for the religion and to show good example. For I have this from the Lord and know in truth that if my illness had not excused me, the greater help I can render to the religion is to spend time every day in prayer to the Lord for it, that He govern, preserve, and protect it. For I have bound myself to the Lord and to the brothers in this, that if any one of the brothers perishes because of Mt 12:36 my bad example, I want to be held to *render an account* to the Lord for him."

[THE TREASURE OF POVERTY GRANTED TO BLESSED FRANCIS THROUGH THE APOSTLES PETER AND PAUL]

[32]Saint Francis said to Brother Masseo: "Dear brother, let's go to   DBF XIII Saint Peter and to Saint Paul, and let's ask them to teach us and help us to possess the indescribable treasure of most holy poverty." And Saint Francis continued, telling Brother Masseo: "My 2 Cor 4:7 most dear, most beloved brother, the *treasure* of blessed poverty is so worthy and so divine that we are not worthy to possess it *in* our most vile *vessels,* since it is that heavenly virtue by which all earthly and transitory things are trampled under foot, by which all obstacles are moved out of the way, so that the human spirit may freely be joined to the eternal Lord. It is she who makes the soul, while

still on earth, dwell with the angels in heaven. It is she who accompanied Christ on the Cross, was hidden with Christ in the tomb, and with Christ rose and ascended into heaven, because she grants to souls who love her even in this life lightness to fly above the heavens. For she holds the weapons of true humility and charity. Therefore, let us ask those most holy apostles of Jesus Christ, who were lovers of this evangelical pearl, to obtain this grace for us from our Lord Jesus Christ, so that he, who was the observer and teacher of holy poverty, may in his most holy mercy grant us to be worthy of being true observers and humble disciples of that most precious, loving and angelic poverty."

When they arrived in Rome, they entered the Church of the most Blessed Peter, Prince of the Apostles. After they entered Saint Francis went to one corner of the Church and Brother Masseo to another corner to beg God and His holy apostles that they train and help them to possess the treasure of holy poverty. They begged for this with great devotion and with many tears. And as they persisted humbly in their prayer, suddenly blessed Peter and blessed Paul appeared in great brightness to blessed Francis, kissing him, embracing him, and saying: "Brother Francis, because you ask this and desire what Christ himself and his Holy Apostles observed, we on his behalf inform you that your desire has been fulfilled. The Lord Jesus Christ sent us to you to announce to you that *your* prayer *has been heard,* and that the treasure of most holy poverty has been granted most perfectly to you and to your followers. And we tell you on behalf of Christ that whoever by your example perfectly follows this desire will be assured of the kingdom of blessedness, and you and all your followers will be blessed by the Lord."

When they had said these things, they departed, leaving him inwardly consoled.

Lk 1:13

[Chapter IV]

[THE REVELATION OF THE HIDDEN THINGS OF GOD MADE BY BLESSED FRANCIS]

Blessed Francis also appeared to be like Christ in revealing hidden things. For as Christ revealed things hidden in the present and in the future and in souls, so expressly did Francis, as we evidently see in the examples written below, etc.

[33]When blessed Francis, our father, came before Lord Pope Innocent the Third for confirmation of the first rule, the Pope replied: "My son, your life is very hard and severe if you wish to found a congregation possessing nothing in this world. For where will you obtain the necessities of life?" Blessed Francis responded: "My Lord, I trust in my Lord Jesus Christ. Since He has promised to give us life and glory in heaven, He will not deprive us of our bodily necessities when we need them on earth." "What you say is true, son," the pope replied, "but human nature is weak and never remains in the same state. But, go and pray to the Lord with all your heart, so that He may show you what is better and more beneficial for your souls. Come back and tell me and I will then grant it."

AP 34

Francis withdrew to pray. With a pure heart, he prayed to the Lord that in His ineffable piety He would reveal this to him. While he was engaged in prayer, with his whole heart focused on the Lord, the word of the Lord came to his heart and spoke to him figuratively. "There was a little, poor woman in a desert, whose beauty fascinated a great king. He wanted to take her as his wife, because he thought that, from her, he would have handsome sons. After the marriage was celebrated and consummated, there were many sons born and raised. Their mother spoke to them in this way: 'My sons, do not be ashamed, for you are sons of the king. Therefore, go to his court and he will provide for all your needs.' When they went to see the king, he was struck by their good looks, and noticing a resemblance to himself in them, he asked them: 'Whose sons are you?' When they answered they were the sons of the little, poor woman living in the desert, the king embraced them with joy. 'Do not be afraid,' he said, 'for you are my sons. If strangers are fed at my table, how much more will you, who are my lawful sons.' He

L3C 50//2C 16

then ordered the woman to send to his court all of the children she had borne to be fed."

When these things had been shown to blessed Francis while he was praying, the man of God understood that the poor woman signified him.

After he completed his prayer, he presented himself to the supreme pontiff and narrated point-by-point the story that the Lord had revealed to him. "My lord," he said, "I am that little poor woman whom the loving Lord, in His mercy, has adorned, and through whom He has been pleased to give birth to legitimate sons. The King of kings had told me that He will nourish all the sons born to me, because, if He feeds strangers, He must provide for His own. For if God gives temporal goods to sinful men out of love for providing for His children, how much more will He give to Gospel men who deserve these things out of merit."

On hearing this, the pope was greatly amazed, especially since, before blessed Francis's arrival, he had seen in a vision the church of Saint John Lateran threatening to collapse, as we read in the Legend. Then the pope embraced him, and immediately blessed Francis bowed down and humbly and devoutly promised obedience and reverence to the Lord Pope.

AP 36

[A PROPHECY CONCERNING THE PERSECUTION OF THE ORDER]

[34]For as the Lord Jesus Christ also revealed the end to His disciples in love growing cold, so blessed Francis revealed the future tribulations of the Order to his companions. For Brother Leo and blessed Francis's other holy companions wrote them down:[a]

Mt 24:12

"Blessed Francis understood that the times of the future tribulation revealed by the Holy Spirit were drawing near, in which confusing events and crises would inundate the church and the love of many would grow cold and evildoing would abound. Then the power of demons would be let loose more than usual. The purity of his own religion and that of others would become polluted. This prophesied abandonment and apostasy by both ruling powers will be so extensive that very few will obey the supreme pontiff and the Roman Church out of love for the truth.

Mt 24:12

"Therefore he wished to give a remedy—even though they would have to walk cautiously, and strengthen themselves even more

---

a. The following paragraphs are taken from Angelo Clareno, *Expositio Regulae Fratrum Minorum*, ed. Livarius Oliger (Ad Claras Aquas, Quaracchi: Collegium S. Bonaventurae, 1912), 44-7.

bravely and faithfully in their promised observance, when they see a pope, not canonically elected, usurping power tyrannically or holding opinions infected with heretical perversity. For then truly blessed would be those who persevere in what they have begun.

"Saint Francis used to say and frequently preach in the presence of the Lord of Ostia and many brothers and even to the people, as Brothers Leo and Angelo are witnesses, that, through the working of evil spirits, his brothers would fall away from the holy way of simplicity and the highest poverty, and would receive money and wills and whatever else might be left to them. They would leave their little poor solitary places and, instead, build great and sumptuous places in fortresses and in cities, which would not reflect the state of poor men but rather that of the rulers and princes of this world. They would, with much cunning and human prudence, insolently seek and obtain privileges from the church and the supreme pontiffs, not only relaxing the *Rule* and life revealed to him by Christ which they had promised, but destroying its purity.

"In their arrogance, they would arm themselves with these privileges to dare to enter lawsuits and cause injuries, not only to lay people, but even to the religious and clergy. In this way, they would sow the seeds from which many scandals would spring. In doing these things, they would dig a pit into which they themselves would finally fall. For it would not be fitting for Christ to show himself a pastor, but an avenger. Thus He Who *rewards all people according to their ways and according to the fruit of their deeds,* and Who stirs up combat and powerful temptation, will see to it that they are caught up and trapped by the cupidity of their own desires, just as they have deserved. And so, they would be chastised by the just judgment of God. Humbled in this way, they would either return to the state of their vocation and be revivified, or be utterly removed from this life-giving and saving path, which they had sworn to serve in firm commitment until the end.

"The truth will be covered up by the silence of preachers or be denied and trodden under foot, and those who profess it will hold people of holy life up to scorn. Those who are fervent will adhere to piety, and will sustain countless persecutions.

"For then, as he used to say, there will be so many insults and agitation by demons and evil persons against those proceeding simply that, leaving everything, they would be driven to seek solitary places in the wilderness or go among non-believers, or else be forced to scatter. Assuming secular clothing, they would lead a wandering life or hide among some faithful people, or, suffering countless malicious charges and accusations, they would submit to punishments and

Jer 32:19

death. And blessed would that brother be, he said, who would be found still faithful amid such trials. For their persecutors, stirred up by evil spirits, will say that they *are offering* great *worship to God;* thus these evil people will kill them and cast them from the earth."

Jn 16:2

157; 2MP 70

^{34b}"*A time will come,*" blessed Francis used to say, "when the religion loved by God will have such a bad reputation because of bad examples that it will be embarrassing to go out in public. Whoever comes to enter the Order at that time will be led only by the working of the Holy Spirit; *flesh and blood* will put no blot on them; they will be truly *blessed by the Lord.* Although they will not do works of merit, for the *love* which makes saints work fervently *will have grown cold,* still they will undergo temptations; and whoever passes the tests of that time will be better than those who came before. But woe to them who congratulate themselves over the appearance of a religious way of living, those numbed by idleness, those who do not firmly resist the temptations which are permitted to test the chosen! Only those who are *tested will receive the crown of life,* those who, in the meantime, are disturbed by the malice of the wicked."

Ez 7:12

Mt 16:17

Ps 115:5

Jas 1:12

[A SYMBOL OF THE ORDER'S DECLINE]

XV; HTrb Prol

³⁵The entire decline of the Order also was revealed to blessed Francis through a marvelous symbol. There appeared before him an immense statue similar to the statue that King Nebuchadnezzar had seen in dream. It had *a head of gold* and a very beautiful face. *Its chest and arms* were *of silver,* its *belly and thighs bronze,* its *legs* were of *iron,* its *feet* were *partly of iron* and *partly clay,* and its dress was of sackcloth, and this sackcloth seemed to embarrass it greatly. Blessed Francis, gazing at the statue, was thoroughly amazed by its almost indescribable beauty, its extraordinary size, and the embarrassment it seemed to have about the cheap sackcloth which it was wearing. And while he was looking in wonder at its very beautiful and lovely face, that very statue spoke to Saint Francis: "Why are you surprised? God has sent me as an example to you, so that in me you may learn what will happen to your Order.

Dn 2:32

"The golden head you see on me with its lovely face: this is the beginning of your Order, placed on the heights of evangelical perfection. And just as this element is more precious than other metals, the face more handsome than the rest, and the head's position more outstanding than the other members, so the beginning of your Order will be more precious because of its solid golden charity, more beautiful because of its angelic integrity and more outstanding because of its evangelical poverty which the whole world will admire. And the Queen of Sheba, that is, holy Mother Church, will marvel and her heart will expand, when she sees in those first chosen ones of your Order such beauty of Christ's holiness and such high evangelical poverty and brilliance of spiritual wisdom reflecting as if in angelic mirrors. Blessed will they be who, conforming themselves to Christ, shall strive to imitate the virtues and behavior of those first precious stones, those golden heads, clinging more to their heavenly beauty than to the deceit of worldly glitter.

"The chest and arms of silver will be the second stage of the Order, which will be as inferior to the first stage as silver is inferior to gold. And just as silver has great value, brightness and melodious sound, so in that second stage there will be those of value in divine Scriptures, brilliant in the light of sanctity and melodious in sounding the word of God. They will be eminent, as some of them will be lifted to the offices of pope and cardinal, and many of them, of bishop. And since human strength is represented by the chest and arms, so God at that time will raise up in this Order two men, silvery in learning and shining in virtue, who both by their knowledge and their virtue will defend this religion, and also the universal Church, from many attacks of demons and from various assaults of wicked men. But even though that will be a remarkable generation, it will not reach that most perfect stage of those who came first, but will be to it what silver is to gold.

"After this there will be a third stage in the Order, like the bronze belly and bronze thighs. Just as bronze is considered less valuable than silver, so those of the third stage will be less than those of the first and second stages. And although, like bronze, they will be spread in great quantity throughout the whole wide world, they will be those *whose god is their belly* and *the glory* of the religion will *confound those who delight* only *in things of earth*. Because of their learning, they will have tongues with a wonderful sound, like brass, but because they will worship the belly and thighs—sad to say—the Lord will consider them, as the Apostle says, *like noisy brass, a clanging cymbal,* for they will boom heavenly words to others and will generate spiritual sons as if *from the thighs;* and after showing *the fountain of life* to others, they themselves will hug the ground on a dry belly.

"After this there will come a fourth stage which will be fearful and terrifying. This is now shown to you in the iron legs. For just as

Phil 3:19

1 Cor 13:1

Ex 1:5

Ps 36:10

iron breaks up and separates bronze, silver, and gold, so this stage will have the hardness and crookedness of iron. Because of the coldness and the terrible rust and the iron-hard ways of that perilous time, everything will be handed over to oblivion which had been built up in the Church of Christ good: the golden charity of the first ones, the silvery truth of the second ones, and the bronze or resounding gift of speech of the third ones. Nevertheless, just as the legs hold up the body, so they, by some rusty strength of hypocrisy, will hold up the body of the Order. And both the belly and these iron legs will be hidden under clothes, because they will hide under the habit of the religion: in fact they will wear a pious habit, but *on the inside they will be ravenous wolves.* And such as these, rusty and hard as iron, serving only the belly, are indeed hidden from the world but visible to the Lord, because they will reduce to nothing those precious goods by the hammer of their crooked life. Therefore, these like the hardest iron will be pounded by the fire of tribulations and the hammers of dreadful trials. They will be beaten not only by demons but also by worldly rulers with fire and hot coals so that the powerful will suffer powerful torments. And because they sinned by irreverent hardness, they will suffer hard torments from the irreverent. But because of these trials they will grow so impatient that, just as iron resists all metals, so they will obstinately resist not only secular powers but spiritual ones as well, thinking that, like iron, they can crush all things. For this they will greatly displease God.

"The fifth stage will be partly of iron as regards those hypocrites just mentioned and partly of dirt as regards those who will totally immerse themselves in worldly affairs. Just as you have seen in the feet that brick, baked from clay, and iron appear together, though they cannot be fused in any way, so it will be in the last stage of this Order. An abominable division will occur between the ambitious hypocrites and those made of brick, baked from the clay of temporal things and the concupiscence of the flesh; like iron with brick, they will not be able to join together because of their great differences. They will despise not only the Gospel and the *Rule,* but also with their brick and iron feet, that is, with crooked and unclean longings, they will trample underfoot all the discipline of this holy Order. And just as brick and iron divide from each other, so many of these brothers will be separated from each other both inside and out: inside, by living in conflict, and outside, by clinging to factions and secular rulers. Therefore, they will be so displeasing to everyone that they will hardly be able to enter towns or stay there and,

Dn 2:40

Mt 7:15; Acts 20:29

even worse, will hardly be able to wear the habit openly. Many of them will be punished and ruined by horrible torments of worldly people, because every house and floor place will shun such abominable feet. All this will happen to them because they withdrew from the golden head. But blessed will they be who in those dangerous days return to the admonitions of that precious head, Wis 3:6 because the Lord *proved them as gold in a furnace* and *as* rich *holocausts* will crown them and receive them forever.

"This sackcloth which seems to embarrass me, is holy poverty, the beauty and mirror of the whole Order, the unique safeguard, crown, and foundation of every kind of holiness. When all virtuous striving is gone, as mentioned above, degenerate sons will be embarrassed by most holy poverty; shedding their cheap garments, they will choose costly ones and procure vain capes through anxious care and simony. But happy and blessed will be Mt 24:13 those *who will have persevered to the end* in those things which they promised the Lord."

After these things were said, the statue disappeared. Saint Francis, thoroughly amazed by all this, like a good shepherd, with many tears entrusted his sheep, present and future, to God.

[Chapter V]

[THE CONVERSION AND INSTRUCTION OF THE PEOPLE][a]

[36]By now the blessed father Francis was similar to Christ in the conversion and instruction of the people. For as Christ preached to believers and non-believers and sent disciples to preach the Gospel throughout the world and subjected rulers and the learned to the humility of faith, so blessed Francis both by himself and by his brothers filled the whole world with the gospel teaching, and subjected those of every worldly and ecclesiastical rank to the humility of his Order.

---

a. The remaining chapters of this work in both the Assisi and Paris manuscripts are deficient. In his study of the Paris manuscript, Michalczyk found twenty-eight fragments taken from different sources, the writings of Francis of Assisi, Thomas of Celano, et al. Cf. Michalczyk, *Une Compilation* (1983), 44-53. While Michalczyk numbers the remaining chapters alphabetically, the editors have chosen to continue a number system. Thus 36=335 a.

[Chapter VI]

[THE TRANSFORMATION OF THE MEMBERS OF HIS BODY]

[37]Blessed Francis was even like Christ in the transformation of the members of his body. This can be seen by first describing the bodily conditions of Christ Himself and then those of Francis, for they were similar. But there is a unique likeness made in the impression of the sacred stigmata.

For we read in some annals which are in Rome that the Lord Jesus Christ, whom the Gentiles called "a prophet of truth," was of medium height, imposing, and handsome. He had a dignified countenance that those who saw could both love and fear, hair like ripe hazel-nut reaching to the ears, curls hanging to the shoulders, and parted in the middle in the Nazarean style. His forehead was smooth and serene with a face that was without a wrinkle or blemish, which a mild ruddy color made attractive. His nose was straight and there was nothing displeasing about his mouth. He had a full, youthful beard, the same color as his hair, not long but forked at the chin. He had a simple, mature glance from eyes of a varied blue: when rebuking it was terrifying, and in admonishing it was mild, loving, and pleasant while preserving dignity. Sometimes he cried, but he never laughed. His bearing was straight and upright, his hands and arms pleasant to look at. His speech was serious, reasonable, rare and modest. Therefore the prophet testified to him in a passage from Ps 45:3 psalm forty-four: *You are beautiful above the sons of men.*

Note that Francis's bodily conditions were almost like those of Christ. We read that blessed Francis was: **"very eloquent, with a** 1C 83 **cheerful appearance and a kind face; free of laziness and arrogance. He was of medium height, closer to short, his head was of medium size and round. His face was somewhat long and drawn, his forehead small and smooth, with medium eyes black and clear. His hair was dark; his eyebrows were straight, and his nose even and thin; his ears small and upright, and his temples smooth. His tongue was peaceful, fiery, and sharp; his voice was powerful, but pleasing, clear, and musical. His teeth were white, well set, and even; his lips were small and thin; his beard was black and sparse; his neck was slender, his shoulders straight; his arms were short,** his hands slight, his fingers long, and his nails tapered. He had thin legs, small feet, fine skin, and little flesh. His clothing was rough, his sleep was short, his hand was generous. Because he was very humble, he showed meekness to all people, and duly adapted himself to the behavior of all. Holier among the holy, among sinners he was like one of them." A strong likeness amply appears except for his coloring and hair, which are not very important, since coloring is easily changed by various circumstances.

[Chapter VII]

[THE ARRAY OF HIS MERITS]

³⁸Seventh, blessed Francis was like Christ principally in his array of merits, especially in humility and obedience, in poverty and indigence, in charity and friendship, in purity and continence, in infirmity and patience, in strictness and penance, in impartiality and justice, in piety and clemency, in devotion and joy, in discernment and wisdom, in employment and diligence.

In the first place, blessed Francis was like Christ in many ways with respect to meritorious deeds in humility. For as Christ, meek and humble of heart, did not seek His own glory, but that of the Father, He was seen to despise Himself by saying: *"If I glorify myself, my glory is nothing."* In a similar way, blessed Francis fled his own glory and despised himself in many ways, etc. He was seen to be conformed to Christ in many ways through the intensity of his most burning love. For Christ underwent many evils in the world out of the highest intensity of love so that *He would reconcile the world to the Father,* for which reason He said he had come *to send the fire* of love *on the earth.* So Francis, totally inflamed with burning charity bore such an enkindling of love to God and his neighbor that, for the honor of God, for the reparation of the entire world, he looked down on the prosperity of the world and continually underwent harshness of the flesh even unto death.

He was also conformed to Christ in another way, in the purity and virginity of his flesh. For Christ was not only a most pure virgin, but his flesh never rebelled against his spirit. He had many imitators, although not in the first degree of excellence; of the second, there were none, except His Mother. Still blessed Francis was a most pure virgin not only in his mind, but also in his flesh, as God revealed to Brother Leo, his confessor, as he wrote to the general minister. For, once, he saw blessed Francis in a vision standing upon a very high mountain, and he was asked: "Do you know what these things signify? That high mountain is virginity; on its summit Francis is standing." Lord Bonaventure therefore said that, although **he was brought up among wanton youths, with God's protection,** he did not pursue **the drives of the flesh.** That flesh arrived at such purity

Mt 11:39; Jn 8:50, 54

2 Cor 2:5, 19

LMj 11

through penance, vigils, fasting, cold, discipline, and continual mortification, that it hardly rebelled against the spirit,

Blessed Francis was also conformed to Christ in many ways in employment and diligence. For Christ continually did some work for your salvation, first *doing* and then *teaching* and encouraging his disciples *to stay awake and pray.* In a similar way, the blessed father Francis . . .   Acts 1:1; Mt 26:41

In many ways he was also like Christ in impartiality and patience. For as Christ courageously and most patiently suffered the abuse of humans, diabolical temptations, bodily afflictions, so did blessed Francis patiently endure trials of humans, as well as of demons and of infirmities.

[Chapter VIII]

[THE ACCUMULATION OF REWARDS]

[39]In the eighth place, in many ways he was conformed to Christ in his ascension and in accumulating rewards, even though with the greatest inequality of glory and rewards. For Christ ascended into heaven *in the sight* of the Apostles in *a* bright *cloud.* Thus, blessed Francis did something similar, for, after his death, six brothers saw him ascending in the form of the sun with indescribable brilliance.[a]

Acts 1:9

---

a. ChrXXIVG 253: "Brother Jacobo, who saw the soul of blessed Francis rise to heaven as a star upon a brilliant cloud, as well as six brothers who saw blessed Francis in the form of the sun, are buried in the Portiuncula."

[Chapter IX]

[THE PERFORMANCE OF MIRACLES]

⁴⁰Lastly, he was in many ways like Christ in performing miracles. For just as Christ had complete power *in heaven and on earth,* so we see Francis as receiving power from Christ over all creatures. For, as I speak of the first of the four elements and their arrangement, he had power over fire, because he frequently tempered its heat. Even the weather obeyed his pleasure, because its assaults, that is, storms and hail, frequently stopped at his command. Water also appeared to be completely subject to his power: for Christ changed water into wine, and even gave water the power to cleanse the soul by a touch of his most pure flesh. So too Francis, by the water used for washing his hands and feet, drove away animal diseases; frequently, at his command, a stone or a jar produced water in abundance, providing the desired health by divine power alone.^a

Mt 28:18

AC 94

3C 3, 15;
[I 12; XIII 6, 7

---

a. The Assisi manuscript ends with this statement: "I, Brother Antonio of Città della Pieve, have extracted and compiled this from the library of the Convent of Toulouse."

RELATED DOCUMENTS

(1261–1323)

Papal Documents

Constitution *Exiit Qui Seminat* of Pope Nicholas III (1279)

This apostolic constitution, intended by Pope Nicholas III as a response to developments in both the Church and the Order over the past quarter of a century, is the most famous of the papal clarifications of the *Later Rule*. At first glance, the body of this new bull resembles its predecessors, Gregory IX's *Quo elongati*[a] and Innocent IV's *Ordinem vestrum*.[b] It consists of a series of questions arising from passages in the *Rule* of 1223, to which the Pope gives a definitive interpretation. Many of these had been brought up in the two previous bulls, and although sometimes the Pope simply repeats the verdict of his predecessors, in most cases he gives a substantial elaboration of their position.

But reading the long preamble to this declaration alerts us to a much more polemical context. Whereas the two previous decrees were directed primarily to the brothers themselves, this one had the whole church for its audience. Through this declaration Nicholas intended, once and for all, to put an end to the attacks on the Franciscan way of life by disgruntled clergy and theologians. As the changing Order moved much more heavily into pastoral ministry between 1230 and 1250, complaints from the secular clergy became more vehement. The theological faculty of the University of Paris emerged as the flash point of this controversy in 1253, when the secular masters, led by William of St. Amour, questioned the biblical and canonical bases of the "novel" mendicant orders.[c] The Lesser Brothers thus became involved in a long and difficult public contest about their very legitimacy.[d]

Bonaventure's career was profoundly shaped by this controversy.[e] As the newly installed regent master of the Franciscan school of theology, he responded to William's attack in his *Disputed Questions on Evangelical Perfection*. He and other mendicants argued that they were not introducing "novelties," but returning to the very life led by Christ and His disciples. The new Pope, Alexander IV, who had been Cardinal protector of the Lesser Brothers for

---

a. FA:ED I 570-5.

b. FA:ED II 774-9.

c. Cf. Moorman, *A History of the Franciscan Order* (Oxford: Oxford at The Clarendon Press, 1968), 123-31, 177-8.

d. Roberto Lambertini, *Apologia e crescita dell'identità francescana, 1255-1279* (Rome, 1990) sees the importance of these years of conflict, culminating with *Exiit qui seminat*, for the establishment of the Order's institutional self-identity within church and society.

e. See Decima Douie, "St. Bonaventure's Part in the Conflict between Seculars and Mendicants in Paris," *S. Bonaventura 1274-1974*, ed. Jacques Guy Bougerol, vol. 2 (Grottaferrata, Roma: Collegio S. Bonaventura, 1974), 585-612.

many years, gave the brothers his unstinting support, as did his two successors, and the controversy died down for some time.

But following the death of Clement IV in 1268, a long vacancy in the Holy See ensued. This provided an opportunity for a new round of attacks by the secular masters, this time led by Gérard of Abbeville. In 1269 Bonaventure composed a vigorous response, the *Apologia pauperum* ("The Defense of the Poor"). A new Pope, Gregory X, was finally elected in 1271. The next year he called for a general council; one of the items on the agenda was the status of the mendicant orders in the church. Gregory eventually named Bonaventure a cardinal and a member of the preparatory commission for the assembly. Despite strong opposition against the friars, the Second Council of Lyons ended in July 1274 by endorsing the valuable work of the Franciscans and Dominicans.

This still-simmering secular-mendicant controversy provides the atmosphere in which this decree was composed. Its author, Pope Nicholas III, was the former Giovanni Gaetano Orsini; Bonaventure had specifically asked to have him named Cardinal Protector of the Order in 1261. This choice proved to be a wise one: Orsini was Bonaventure's close collaborator for the rest of his long generalate, and a strong defender of the Order. When he became Pope in 1278, Nicholas decided to take the initiative to support the brothers. Shortly after the chapter of Assisi in 1279, he met with the newly elected general minister, Bonagratia of San Giovanni in Persiceto; they agreed on the need for a new and definitive commentary on the Rule. To assist him, Nicholas named a special commission including the two Franciscan cardinals,[a] Bonagratia himself, several prominent provincial ministers, and a number of eminent Curial canonists,[b] who examined the issues for several months over the summer. The Pope, acting quickly on their recommendations, issued this decree in August of 1279.

In many ways the deceased Bonaventure is the virtual "ghost writer" of *Exiit Qui Seminat*.[c] The Papal committee basically took over the main arguments of Bonaventure's *Apologia pauperum*. These provide the grounds for the Pope's assertions that the Lesser Brothers are perfect imitators of the poverty of Christ. In the lengthy closing twenty-third article, Nicholas incorporates Bonaventure's teachings into the official collection of the church's doctrinal statements, prescribing penalties for theologians who dissented from them.

But in addition to its apologetic function, *Exiit* was also intended to respond to the vast changes which had taken place among the Franciscans

---

a. The members of the commission are named in the ChrXXIVG 369. Nicholas' predilection for the Franciscans is shown in the fact that he had very quickly named two of them cardinals: Bentivegna of Aquasparta (d. 1290), his confessor, whom he made Cardinal Bishop of Albano, and Jerome of Ascoli.

b. Among the latter was Benedetto Gaetani, the future Boniface VIII. Perhaps this is one reason why he was so harsh on those Spirituals who criticized the Papal declarations. Erroneously, sometimes Peter of John Olivi is stated to have been a member of this commission. He was not, but was one of several Franciscan theologians asked to contribute position papers to it.

c. Cf. V. Maggiani, "De relatione scriptorum quorundam S. Bonaventurae ad Bullam 'Exiit' Nicholae III," AFH 5 (1912): 3-21.

since the last Papal interpretation of the *Rule* that was issued thirty years previously. The lengthy and detailed prescriptions about the ways in which the brothers might licitly accept money donations, for example, vividly attest to the fact that the Lesser Brothers were now a major institution within the church, with an important role to play in its pastoral ministry and with corresponding organizational needs. The Pope felt he had to make these as easy as possible for the brothers to fill, but without betraying their distinctive way of life. Here again he followed the policy of Bonaventure, who as general minister maintained a middle path between the forces of liberalization and primitivism that were increasingly dividing his Order. Like him, Nicholas was convinced that the Lesser Brothers filled a providential role in God's history of salvation, but he also knew that their favored place in the Church was dependent on their living the "apostolic life" of poor Gospel preachers.[a]

The text of the bull[b] does not have articles; they were, however, quickly added by teachers and commentators.

Nicholas, Bishop, Servant of the servants of God, for an everlasting record.

[1]*The Sower went out to sow his seed,* that is, Jesus Christ, the Son of God, clad in the garb of human nature, came forth from the bosom of the Father into the world to spread the Word of the Gospel among all people: the good and the bad, the foolish and the sensible, the eager and the indolent. As the *husbandman* foreseen by the Prophet who was to *come into the land,* He made no distinction as He scattered the seed of Gospel teaching among everyone. Wishing *to draw all things to Himself,* He came to save all people; thus for the salvation of all humankind, He offered Himself as a sacrifice to God the Father as the price of its redemption.

Mt 13: 3

Jer 14:8

Jn 12:32

Although in God's abundant love the seed [of the Gospel] was scattered among all humankind, some of it fell along the wayside, that is, on hearts corrupted by the temptations of the demons; others fell on stony ground, that is on hearts never broken by the plowshare of faith; others fell among thorns, that is, on hearts torn by their anxiety for wealth. So we *read* that some seeds were trodden underfoot by base passions, others parched for lack of the moisture of grace, whereas others were smothered amid inordinate preoccupations. Some seed, however, was welcomed by the good soil of a meek and ready heart.

Mt 13:18-23

---

a. For the context within the Order, see Malcolm Lambert, *Franciscan Poverty,* rev. ed. (St. Bonaventure, NY: Franciscan Institute Publications, 1998), 109-56; David Burr, *Olivi and Franciscan Poverty* (Philadelphia: University of Pennsylvania Press, 1989), 1-37.

b. BFr, vol. 3, 404-416, no. 127. A superior edition is found in *Bullarii Franciscani Epitome,* ed. Conrado Eubel (Ad Claras Aquas, Quaracchi: Collegium S. Bonaventurae, 1908), 290-300.

²Such is the meek and willing religion of the Lesser Brothers, deeply rooted in poverty and humility by that loving confessor of Christ, Francis. Himself sprouting up from that authentic seed [of God's Word], by means of his *Rule* he spread that shoot to the sons he begot for himself and God by his ministry of Gospel observance.

Jas 1:21 These sons, in the words of Saint James, have *welcomed in meekness the eternal Word,* the Son of God, engrafted on humankind in the garden of the Virgin's womb and *endued with the power to save souls.* Such truly are those who profess that holy *Rule,* a rule founded on the teaching of the Gospel, confirmed by the example of Christ, and approved by the words and actions of His apostles, the founders of the Church Militant.[a]

Jas 1:27; Jas 1:17 *This* then *is religion pure and undefiled before God the Father. Coming down from the Father of lights,* it was passed on by His Son to the apostles in word and example, and finally, through the work of the Holy Spirit, it inspired blessed Francis and his followers.[b] It bears then, so to speak, the witness of the whole blessed Trinity. To cite Saint Paul,

Gal 6:17 it is something about which *no one ought henceforth to make trouble,* since Christ has sealed it with the brand marks of His passion, desiring to distinguish its author in a visible way with the signs of His own suffering.

Rv 12:9 ³Yet, even so the guile of the *ancient Enemy* has not relented
Mt 13:25 against the Lesser Brothers and their *Rule.* On the contrary, in his effort to sow weeds amidst the good seed and thus overcome it, he has here and there roused antagonists against them. Stirred up by jealousy, ill will, and misguided righteousness, these men, like dogs, have been snapping at the brothers and barking at their *Rule* as something illicit, impossible to observe, and dangerous. They overlook the fact that, as mentioned above, the said holy *Rule* is based on salutary precepts and counsels; that it has the support of apostolic practice, the endorsement of several Roman pontiffs, and even the formal approval of the Apostolic See. That it enjoys confirmation in
Ps 93:5 so many divine *testimonies* has become *exceedingly credible indeed* in so many holy men who have spent and completed their days while observing this *Rule,* some of whom have been enrolled in the canon of the saints by the said Apostolic See on account of their lives and miracles. Yes, as recently as our own day the *Rule* was commended by our predecessor Pope Gregory X of pious memory because of the

---

a. A clear statement that the Lesser Brothers are following the evangelical life *par excellence.*

b. Pope Nicholas III takes Francis at his word that "the Most High revealed to me that I should live according to the pattern of the Holy Gospel" and that "the Lord has given me to speak and write the *Rule,*" Test 14, 39, FA:ED I 124-7.

manifest benefit deriving from it to the universal Church, as made clear in the general Council of Lyons.[a]

We are no less aware, indeed it makes us the more deeply thoughtful—as it should make all who profess the Catholic faith ponder even more carefully—that God Himself is watching over the Order and its members. With His saving help He has so preserved them from the rancor raging up against them that the tempest has neither dashed them down nor dismayed the courage of the members of the Order. On the contrary, they go on growing in their religious vigor and making progress in the observance of their rule of life.

[4]Nevertheless, it is our desire that this Order flourish in distinct and undimmed clarity, with all annoying handicaps whatsoever removed from its path. The brothers of the Order themselves, assembled in a general chapter,[b] have given occasion to this desire. Our beloved sons, the general minister and several of the provincial ministers who had gathered at the chapter, appeared in our presence on that occasion. We recognized their fervent determination to observe the *Rule* in its entirety with vigor of spirit. Thus we have decided to put a stop to the biting attacks of their critics, to resolve certain matters in the *Rule* that might appear doubtful, to treat with fuller clarity certain points previously explained by our predecessors, and to provide a clean conscience for the brothers in regards to certain other matters involving their *Rule*.

[5]As for ourselves, from our tender years we have bestowed our affection on the said Order.[c] As we grew in age, we held frequent discussions on the said *Rule* and the holy intentions of blessed Francis with certain companions of the Confessor who were acquainted with his life and ways. At length, as cardinal and, later on, when appointed by the Holy See to be the governor, protector and corrector of the Order, our responsibilities put us in direct touch with its affairs.

Now, installed in the Apostolic office, we can give our attention to the said Order supplied with full information, gleaned also from the

---

a. Lyons II, 1274. The criticism of the brothers did have some effect at the Council. Canon 23 suppressed most of the new mendicant orders, although it specifically exempted the Franciscans and Dominicans: "Of course, we do not allow the present constitution to apply to the Orders of Preachers and Lesser Brothers; their approval bears witness to their evident advantage to the universal church." *Decrees of the Ecumenical Councils* (hereafter DEC), vol. 1, ed. Norman Tanner (London, Washington D.C: Sheed & Ward, Georgetown University Press, 1990), 327.

b. The general chapter of Assisi in 1279.

c. Pope Nicholas III was the son of the Roman nobleman Matteo Rosso Orsini, a prominent early member of the Order of Penance, cf. Luke Wadding *Annales Minorum*, vol. 2 (Ad Claras Aquas, Quaracchi, Collegium S. Bonaventurae, 1931) 35-36.

long experience described above, both as regards the pious intention of the said Confessor and as regards whatever pertains to the *Rule* and its observance. We have, too, fully and considerately gone over everything our predecessors are known to have approved and clarified, whether on the *Rule* itself or whatever touches on it. In the present document, therefore, we have enacted, decreed, and endorsed a number of things in a precise manner, or have in a formal way approved, promulgated or conceded what has been previously endorsed, treating a number of points with greater detail and clarity, as more fully explained in the articles which follow.

Article 1: Observance of the Gospel

[1]First of all, we understand there is doubt in some minds as to whether the brothers of the said Order are bound in conscience to the counsels of the Gospels as well as its precepts. For at the beginning of their *Rule* it states: "The rule and life of the Lesser Brothers is this: to observe the holy Gospel of our Lord Jesus Christ by living in obedience, without anything of their own, and in chastity." Again, farther on in the said *Rule* there is the passage: "When the year of probation has come to an end, they may be received to obedience, promising always to observe this rule and life." And again, at the end of the rule there are the words: "so that . . . we may observe the poverty, humility, and the Holy Gospel of our Lord Jesus Christ, as we have firmly promised."

Now, our predecessor Pope Gregory IX of happy memory did indeed clarify this and certain other points of the *Rule*.[a] Due, however, to the carping attacks of certain antagonists of the brothers and their *Rule,* his explanation has proved to be unclear in certain particulars, incomplete in others, and inadequate to cover many other points contained in the *Rule*.

[2]It is our intention, therefore, to remove any such lack of clarity and adequacy by means of an explanation that shall interpret the points perfectly, and to excise whatever scruple of anxiety might exist from the minds of all by means of the certainty of a fuller exposition. We affirm, therefore, that when the beginning of the *Rule* states: " The rule and life of the Lesser Brothers is this: to observe the Holy Gospel of our Lord Jesus Christ by living in obedience, without anything of their own, and in chastity," this is not intended to be an absolute statement, but one with some degree of qualification, or restriction

LR I 1

LR II 11

LR I 1, 2; XII

LR I 1

---

a. In Gregory IX, *Quo elongati* 4, see FA:ED I 571-2.

and specification. For subsequently the *Rule* goes into great detail on the latter three points [obedience, poverty, and chastity], whether in terms of precept or prohibition, or in terms of advice, warning, admonition, or similar expressions which are reducible to one or the other of two modalities [precept or prohibition].

Thus it is quite evident that the seemingly absolute statement in the profession formula, "promising always to observe this rule and life," and the one in the concluding sentence "that we may observe the Holy Gospel of our Lord Jesus Christ, as we have firmly promised," must be understood as the *Rule* intends, that is, in the qualified, restricted, and specified sense of its opening verse. Thus, following what we said above, the phrase "observing the Gospel" is qualified, restricted, and specified by the *Rule* itself to mean only the three Gospel counsels.

For it is not likely that the Saint would, without a clear-cut reason, want a statement initially made by him with a certain qualification, restriction, and specification, to lack in its later repetitions; however tersely he might have made them, the same qualification, restriction, and specification he attached to the earlier statement. The procedure of both courts of law likewise bears out that quite frequently initial material also refers to intermediate and concluding material, intermediate material to initial and concluding, and concluding material to one or to both of the other portions.

[3]For if it be granted that the declaration: "I promise to observe the Holy Gospel," is to be understood absolutely, then a person making such a profession would be intending to obligate himself to the observance of all the evangelical counsels. But such an obligation would imperil the salvation of his soul, for he could hardly or never observe all of these counsels literally. And even if a person had such an intention, it is evident that making a profession in that form, i.e., "I promise to observe the Holy Gospel," would not have to be stretched any further in its meaning than that one should observe the Gospel in the manner it was handed down by Christ. So the person making much a profession would be promising to observe the [Gospel] precepts as precepts, and the counsels as counsels.

The blessed Francis himself plainly indicates in his own words that this was his intent by the very way he develops the *Rule*. For he enjoins certain Gospel counsels simply as counsels, using words of admonition, exhortation and advice; whereas he enjoins other counsels using words of prohibition or command. It is clear, therefore, that it was not the author's intention that by professing this *Rule* the brothers would be bound to all the counsels in the Gospel as well as to its precepts, but only to those counsels which he set down in that *Rule* in the form of a precept or a prohibition or their equivalent.

Wherefore, to put the consciences of the brothers of the said Order fully at ease, we declare that in consequence of professing this *Rule* the brothers are bound in conscience to observe only those evangelical counsels expressed in the same *Rule* by precept, prohibition, or equivalent words.

[4]As for the rest of the counsels found in the Gospel, the brothers' state of life requires that they be held to them more strictly than other Christians because they have embraced a state of perfection. For through a profession such as theirs, they have offered themselves to the Lord as *a sacrifice of the heart* by their utter disregard of all earthly things.

Ps 51:19

[5]But as for all the other things contained in the said *Rule,* be they command or counsel or whatever else, the vow the brothers make at their profession binds them to observe these things only in the way in which the *Rule* expresses them. In other words, they are obliged in conscience to observe those things the *Rule* imposes on them in obligatory terms. As far as observing those points which are expressed [in the *Rule*] by way of admonition, exhortation, or similar terms, the brothers should certainly strive to carry them out as things that are good and right for those who have chosen to follow more closely the narrow way of Christ, in imitation of such a father.

Article 2: Renunciation of Ownership

[1]Furthermore, the said *Rule* states explicitly that "let the brothers not make anything their own, neither house, nor place, nor anything at all." Our predecessor Gregory IX and several others[a] have also declared that this point must be observed both individually and in common. But this total renunciation of property has been vilified by the senseless cunning of certain individuals and their venomous disparaging remarks.

LR VI 1

Now, lest the said brothers have the clear grasp of their ideal distorted by the unreasonable talk of such people, we affirm that such renunciation of the ownership of all things, both individually and in common, for God's sake, is holy and meritorious. Christ himself, in demonstrating the path of perfection, taught it in word and confirmed it by example. The first founders of the Church Militant drew

---

a. Gregory IX *Quo elongati* 6, in FA:ED I 573; Innocent IV, *Ordinem vestrum* 6, in FA:ED II 777.

it from that font and channeled it through the streams of their teaching and manner of life to those desirous of a life of perfection.[a]

[2]Nor let anyone think that this value is disproved by the fact that Christ is said at times to have had a purse.[b] For Christ did everything perfectly: He so practiced the path of perfection in all He did, that on occasion He stooped to the imperfections of the weak. While extolling the path of perfection, He did not on the other hand condemn the weaker course of the imperfect.[c]

Thus Christ assumed the role of the weak by keeping a purse, and in certain other ways He took upon himself the weaknesses of human nature, as the Gospel narrative bears witness, stooping to our frailty not only in body but in spirit as well. For He assumed human nature in such a way that, always being perfect in what He did, He lowered Himself to our human state while remaining ever on the exalted plane of His divine nature. And so He was moved in the condescension of His total love for us to perform certain actions conformable to our imperfect nature without thereby deviating from the straight course of absolute perfection.

So, Christ did indeed perform and teach the works of perfection, but He also performed acts proper to our weakness, as is clear from His taking flight at times, and having a purse. Both courses, however, He carried off perfectly, so as to commend himself as the way of salvation for perfect and imperfect alike, just as He had come to save both and as He wished eventually to die for both.

[3]Nor let anybody at this point make the erroneous objection that people who renounce the ownership of all things for the love of God are in this way putting their life in jeopardy, like suicides or persons that tempt God. For in their way of life, the brothers do not commit themselves to God's providence in a manner that scorns the course of human provision; on the contrary they seek sustenance either from alms freely offered, or from what they humbly beg, or from what

---

a. The Latin text reads: *"Dicemus, quod abdicatio proprietatis huiusmodi omnium rerum tam in speciale quam etiam in communi propter Deum meritoria est et sancta, quam et Christus vitam perfectionis ostendens verbo docuit et exemplo firmavit."* This is exactly Bonaventure's thesis in the *Apologia pauperum,* VII 2-5 in S. Bonaventurae, *Opera Omnia,* Vol. VIII, ed. Patres Collegii S. Bonaventurae (Ad Claras Aquas, Quaracchi: Collegium S. Bonaventurae, 1898), English translation by José de Vinck, *Defense of the Mendicants* (Paterson, NJ: St. Anthony Guild Press, 1966), 126-9. Here Bonaventure distinguishes the perfection of renouncing individual ownership, as seen in the early Jerusalem community, and the higher perfection of the renunciation of property both by individuals and in common, as seen in the earthly life of Jesus and his disciples. Franciscan poverty is thus on a higher plane than that of other religious. Cf. Lambert, *Franciscan Poverty,* 133-136.

b. The classic text used by opponents of the Franciscan ideal of the common renunciation of property was John 13:29: "Some felt that, because Judas held the common purse, Jesus was telling him, 'Buy what we need.' "

c. The argument here is simply a compressed version of Bonaventure's *Apologia Pauperum:* that Christ performed some actions as an example to the perfect, and others out of condescension to the imperfect, cf. *Apologia Pauperum* I 6; VII 35-40 (VIII 236-7; 284-6), *Defense* 10-13, 158-163.

they gain in return for their labor, which threefold means of livelihood is expressly provided for in the *Rule*.

Surely, if, as our Savior has promised, the faith of the Church shall
never fail, it follows also that Christians will never stop practicing the
works of mercy. But such an assurance would seem to remove from
Christ's poor all grounds for every kind of misgiving. And
even—which is not to be presumed in the least!—were all such
means to fail, the said brothers, like anybody else, would still in the
pinch of extreme need have open to them the so-called right of existence, that is to provide for their natural sustenance, a path conceded
to every person in the grip of dire necessity, since such a condition is
exempt from any law.

Article 3: The Use of Things

[1]No one should think, however, that such renunciation of every
form of proprietorship likewise implies renunciation of the use of
things. For in temporal concerns it is of prime importance to distinguish between ownership, possession, usufruct, the right of use, and
simple use of fact.[a] Now, while mortal life can exist without the
capacities mentioned first, the last named is indispensable to it, so
that a profession which were to exclude the use of things necessary
for subsistence would be altogether null. On the other hand, it is
totally fitting that a profession freely pledging itself to the pursuit of
the poor Christ in such poverty should abdicate the ownership of
everything and content itself with the necessary use of the things
conceded to it.

But it does not follow that, because the profession [of the *Rule*]
clearly renounces the right of use along with the ownership of everything, therefore also the mere use of things in fact stands renounced.
For we insist this use which is styled not use by right, but use in fact
only, is a mere factual use, and confers no right at all on the users in
making such use. Rather, with the exception of money as discussed
below, both according to the *Rule* and in truth a moderate use is
allowed the brothers as regards the things necessary either to sustain
their life or to discharge the duties of their station in life. Thus the
brothers can lawfully make use of such things to the extent of the

---

a. The Latin text reads: *"Nam cum in rebus temporalibis sit considerare praecipuum, proprietatem,
possessionem, usum fructum, ius utendi, et simplicem facti usum."* Again, this argument is based on
Bonaventure's legal analysis of the various possible ways a person may be said to "have" temporal
goods. Bonaventure gives four categories, the commission has added a fifth: the "right of use." The
"simple use of fact" is simply permission to use certain things, revocable at the will of the donor, who
still retains ownership. *Apologia*, XI 4-5 (VIII 311-2); *Defense*, 240-1.

donor's permission and the conditions contained in the present detailed analysis.

²Nor is there any difficulty found here in a provision fittingly established by civil authority in human affairs, to the effect that the use or usufruct [of a thing] cannot be severed permanently from dominion.ª That provision has been established merely to safeguard temporal advantage and keep proprietary right from becoming useless to the proprietor through permanent forfeiture of its use. But retaining the ownership of such things while turning over their use to the poor is not unprofitable to the owner, since it is meritorious for eternity in giving seasonable help to the poor in their profession; indeed it is rated so much the more profitable to the owner as it exchanges temporal for eternal goods.

³It was certainly not the purpose of the Confessor of Christ in writing the *Rule* [to renounce the use of anything that is necessary]. On the contrary, he set down the opposite in the *Rule* and observed it in the way he lived, for he availed himself of temporal things as needed, and he makes clear in several passages of the *Rule* that such use is lawful to the brothers.

LR III 1 ⁴For he says in the *Rule* that "the cleric [brothers] shall recite the Divine Office . . . for which reason they may have breviaries," thus plainly indicating that his brothers were to have the use of breviaries and books helpful in [celebrating] the Divine Office. In a further
LR IV 2 chapter it is said that "the ministers and custodians alone shall take special care through their spiritual friends to provide for the needs of the sick and the clothing of the others according to places, seasons, and cold climates, as they judge necessary." Elsewhere too, exhorting the brothers to avoid idleness by being occupied with suitable
LR V 3 work, he says that "in payment for their work they may receive whatever is necessary for the bodily support of themselves and their
LR VI 2 brothers." In still another chapter the words are found that "let them go out seeking alms with confidence." Again we have the passage of
LR IX 3 the *Rule* that "when they preach let their language be well considered and chaste, for the benefit and edification of the people, announcing to them vices and virtues, punishment and glory." But it stands to reason that such things presuppose knowledge, and knowledge requires study; the pursuit of study, however, cannot readily be pursued without using books.

⁵All of these examples show clearly, from the *Rule* itself, that the use of things necessary for food, clothing, divine worship, and the

---

a. Again, following Bonaventure, the Pope is forced to confront a maxim of civil law, that use could not be totally separated from dominion. *Apologia*, XI 7-11 (VIII 312-4); *Defense*, 242-248.

pursuit of knowledge, is allowed to the brothers. From the above analysis it is thus clear to anyone who thinks in a rational fashion that, by demanding renunciation of ownership, the *Rule* is not only observable as possible and permissible, but also as meritorious and perfect. In fact, [by demanding renunciation of ownership in common] it is even more meritorious, as pointed out above, because those who profess it are so much the more removed from temporal concerns for the love of God.

Article 4: The Church's Ownership of Things Allowed the Brothers

[1]As said above, the brothers can acquire nothing for themselves or for their Order either individually or in common. Yet, when something is offered, granted, or donated to the brothers for the love of God, it is presumed, unless otherwise specified, to be the likely intention of the person so offering, granting, or donating the thing to make a complete offering, grant, or donation of it, abdicating any right thereto and desiring to transfer the right to some one else for the love of God. There is, however, no one to whom in God's place the ownership of such a thing can be more fittingly transferred than to the Holy See or the person of the Roman Pontiff, the Vicar of Christ. Although he is the father of all the faithful, in a special way he is father of the Lesser Brothers.[a]

Now, the ownership of such things should not be left in doubt. And so, just as respectively, a son acquires for his father, a bondsman for his master, and a monk for his monastery whatever is offered, granted, or donated to him: we of our Apostolic authority take over for ourselves and for the Roman Church the property rights and ownership of all the utensils, books, and other movables present and future which, or the use of which—simple use of fact, of course—the Order or the brothers may lawfully have, just as our predecessor Pope Innocent IV of happy memory is known to have done.[b] And with this Constitution, to be perpetual in its effect, we decree that the said right pertains wholly and without reserve to us and to the said Church.

[2]Moreover, places bought with various alms, or offered or granted to the brothers under whatever formality, we do likewise with the same authority take over as the right, property and domain of ourselves and the said Church from the persons possessing said places *in*

---

a. Cf. *Apologia* XI 7-8 (VIII 312-3); *Defense*, 242-4.
b. Innocent IV *Ordinem vestrum* 6, cf. FA:ED II 777.

toto or sharing them in part, provided said possessors in whole or in part have not in such offering or cession reserved anything thereof to themselves. The brothers, however, are cautioned in any such transactions not to use terms that are incompatible with their state of life.

[3]On the other hand, if the brothers at the pleasure of the benefactor are dwelling in places or houses still to be granted or offered by an individual or a group to the brothers as their place of abode, the brothers may live there only for the duration of the benefactor's pleasure. Should the benefactor change his mind and signify as much to the brothers, let them without demur relinquish the said places, except the church, oratories meant for church purposes, and the cemetery. These latter we do in like manner and with like authority accept, both present and future, as the right and property of ourselves and the said Roman Church.

However, in regards to the ownership and the proprietary right of the said places themselves we are retaining nothing whatsoever for ourselves or the said Roman Church, unless they are accepted with the explicit consent of ourselves or the said Roman Church. Whenever the benefactor in extending his favor has reserved the ownership of such places to himself, such ownership shall not pass over into the right of the said oft-mentioned Church by reason of the brothers residing therein, but rather it shall remain fully and without reserve with the benefactor.

Article 5: Restrictions on Use

[1]Now, as stated above, the brothers may not have an unlimited use of things. Therefore, they are to accept neither utensils nor anything else allowed them for their [physical] needs and for discharging the duties of their state in life, to the point of any excess, wealth or abundance derogatory to poverty,[a] or to the extent of accumulating stores thereof, or with the purpose of conveying or selling them, whether under the pretext of providing for the future or under any other allegation. On the contrary, everything they have must reflect complete renunciation of ownership and necessity as to use.

---

a. Nicholas III warns the brothers that their renunciation of ownership implies a restricted use of things. They are to avoid any semblance of affluence. This is in line with Bonaventure's teaching in his encyclical letters, e.g., his letter of 1266: "The way we live ought to be in harmony with the high profession we have made. For it is truly a filthy, base lie for someone to claim to have voluntarily professed the highest poverty if he is not willing to put up with want, who at home enjoys the affluence of the rich and yet goes out to beg as poor people do." *Works of St. Bonaventure, Vol. 5: Writings concerning the Franciscan Order*, trans. Dominic Monti (St. Bonaventure, NY: Franciscan Institute Publications, 1994), 228. Olivi would later appeal to this article of *Exiit* as supporting his doctrine of "poor use."

^{2}It is for the ministers and custodians jointly and singly in their provinces and custodies to regulate these matters with discreet attention to personal and local demand, because making provision for such needs will vary in degree and manner with personal constitution, seasonal changes, local conditions, and other pertinent circumstances.

This, however, is to be done in a way that holy poverty should always shine in the brothers and their acts, as is found to be enjoined on them in their *Rule*.

Article 6: Money Alms for Past Needs

^{1}Again, in the said *Rule* there is a strict prohibition in the form of a precept "that the brothers not receive coins or money in any form, [LR IV 1] either personally nor through intermediaries." Now, the brothers desire to continue to observe that prohibition and feel obliged to comply with it as their duty. Lest, however, the brothers have the pure observance of this precept defiled in any particular, or have their consciences pricked by any barbs, we are taking up that article, thanks to the carping of its detractors, to give it deeper consideration than has been done by our predecessors, and to follow it up with clearer specifications.[a]

Therefore, we affirm first of all that the said brothers must refrain from contracting loans, since to contract a loan is a point forbidden them in view of their state in life. Still, when needs[b] arise and the brothers are unable to obtain sufficient alms at that moment to meet them, they may, without binding themselves with any formal tie, declare that they will labor faithfully to make the respective payment by means of alms or through other friends of the brothers.[c]

^{2}In such a case let the brothers see to it that the prospective donor makes the required payment in whole or in part as the Lord will inspire him, either personally or through an agent; the latter, if at all possible, should not be designated by the brothers but selected at the pleasure of the donor. Now it may happen, however, that the donor is unwilling or unable to name an agent, either because of impending departure, or because he knows no reliable persons to whom he

---

a. The next several articles (6-11) are an amplification of the role of "agents" permitted by *Quo elongati* 5 and *Ordinem vestrum* 4 to receive money alms, see FA:ED I 572-573; FA:ED II 776.

b. Pope Nicholas stipulates here and in the following articles that money alms may be requested only in the case of "necessities," as Gregory IX stipulated in *Quo elongati* 5, see FA:ED I 573, rather than for the more elastic "useful things," which Innocent IV had added in *Ordinem vestrum* 4, see FA:ED II 776. The Order in 1279 was still officially refusing to use this more liberal permission.

c. This repeats the prescriptions of the 1260 Constitutions of Narbonne, cf. Monti, *Writings*, 85.

cares to commit the charge, or because of some other circumstance or reason. In such cases we affirm and declare that it does not at all violate the pure spirit of the *Rule* or in any way defile its observance, if the brothers themselves acquaint the donor with some person or persons, or designate or even introduce some person or persons, to whom the execution of the said charge can be committed at the pleasure of the donor, and with his consent to the substitutions described below.

It is understood, however, that the ownership, proprietary right and possession of the said money remain with the donor to their full, unlimited, and undiminished extent, together with the unrestricted right to demand the money back at any time until it has been converted to the intended purpose. On their part, the brothers have no right whatsoever to the said money, nor to its control or disposal, nor to action or prosecution or any other such measure in or out of court against any such agent, whether designated by them or not, and whatever the agent's capacity may be, regardless of how he may conduct himself in discharging his particular trust.

The brothers may nonetheless intimate and specify or explain their needs to the agent and request him to make payment. They may go as far as to exhort and persuade the agent to comply faithfully with his trust and to consult the welfare of his soul in executing the trust committed to him. But in so doing, as said above, the brothers must refrain in every way from any control or disposal of the money and from any action or prosecution against the agent.

[3]Now it may happen that the agent, whether he was designated by the brothers or not, is unable to execute the aforesaid trust personally, due to absence, illness, unwillingness, the distance of the locality in which payment or compensation is to be made and to which he does not want to travel, or for some other reason. In such a case, if the brothers are unable or unwilling to have recourse to the original donor, they may with a clean conscience arrange with such an agent to substitute some other agent to execute the aforesaid trust, so long as they observe the same procedure we prescribed above in regard to the first agent.

It is evident—assuming ordinarily that the required compensation can readily be accomplished—that generally the service of two agents substituted thus successively will suffice to discharge the aforesaid trust. Now and again, however, due to the remoteness of the locality in which the compensation is to be made, or due to other conditions and circumstances, a situation may arise where the service of more such substitute agents may appear advisable. In such a case, according to the nature of the business at hand and observing the procedure prescribed above, the brothers shall be free to invite, designate, or introduce further agents to discharge the said service.

Article 7: Money Alms for Future Needs

[1]Now, besides meeting the needs of the brothers already demanding payment or compensation as described immediately above, it is advantageous, indeed imperative, that, under the aforesaid restrictions, seasonable provision should also be made for impending needs. This may be a matter of imminent needs that can be met within a short time, or of needs, comparatively few though they be, that require a length of time for provision, such as copying books, constructing churches or buildings for dwelling purposes, buying books or cloth at remote distances, and whatever other needs of the kind that may occur.

With this distinction clearly made, we declare that the brothers can safely and with a clean conscience proceed as follows:

In the case of an approaching or imminent need that can be met within a brief time (or also, occasionally, due to special circumstances, a less brief time than indicated just above), the same procedure may be followed in all intents and particulars, both as regards the donor and the designated or substituted agent, exactly as we have explained in the immediately preceding article describing payment for past needs.

[2]On the other hand, an impending need may arise of such a kind, as mentioned above, that by its very nature involves a length of time [to meet]. In such cases, either because the places to which one has to go to meet the particular need are so distant, or because of other circumstances involved in the nature of the need, it is probable that there might be frequent instances where the money designated to meet such a need would have to pass through a number of hands and persons. Consequently, to know who all those persons are would be virtually impossible for the original donor who designated money for this need, or his designated agent, or even a third agent substituted by the latter, should this occur.

In order, therefore, to preserve in every way the integrity of the *Rule* and of those who profess it: in addition to the two forms of procedure prescribed above, which are to be observed in cases of past needs and needs which can be met in a short time, or in an occasional longer term, we affirm and declare that if in that event a donor for such an alms or a person qualified to act for him is available, the brothers shall expressly tell him beforehand what they would like to

get, so that, no matter through how many hands or persons designated by him or by the brothers the money or alms may pass, the
entire procedure shall take place with his consent, will, and authority. The donor is to retain the unrestricted ownership of the money
with the unrestricted right to demand the money back at any time
until it has been converted to the purpose intended, just as was said
in the two cases above. If the donor agrees to the aforesaid, the brothers may safely use what is bought or acquired with such money, by
anybody whatsoever, in keeping with the manner above outlined.

LR IV 1   [3]To be totally clear about all the above instances, we declare in this
our detailed provision which is to remain in force forever: that if the
brothers observe the forms of procedure which we have prescribed
above regarding money to supply their past and impending needs,
they are not understood to be, nor may they be said to be "receiving
money either personally or through an intermediary" in violation of
their *Rule* or the pure spirit of their religious profession. For in light of
what has been explained above, it is manifestly clear that the said
brothers are keeping their distance not only from the acceptance,
ownership, proprietary right and use of such money, but even from
the mere handling of it and its very presence.

Article 8: Expending Money on the Death of the Donor

It may occur, however, that the donor of the money may die
before the money itself has been expended in lawful exchange for
something the brothers were to have or use. In such a case, if in making his gift the donor explained or signified that whatever happened
to him in life or in death, a deputy was to expend the money for the
necessary use of the brothers, then, whether the donor has left an
heir or not, the brothers may petition the said deputy to have the
money expended, notwithstanding the donor's death or the heir's
objections, just as they could have petitioned the owner and donor in
person.

Article 9: Surplus Money

Since we are concerned with tender and cordial affection for the
pure spirit of the said Order, we stipulate in addition that when
money is donated by someone for a specific need, the brothers may
request the donor to agree that if any of the money should remain
after meeting that specific need, any such surplus may be applied to
other things to meet the brothers' necessities. If the donor does not

agree to this request, whatever surplus remains must be restored to him. And the brothers must be on their guard and take careful precaution that they do not knowingly permit more to be set aside for them than the likely estimated cost of the necessary item for which the money is set aside.

Article 10: Standing Presumption in Favor of the Lawful Procedure

Now, in carrying out the procedures so solemnly explained above, mistakes can easily be made by the giver or the receiver. Therefore, we wish to provide more clearly and surely for the benefit of the donors and the simple nature of certain uneducated people on one side, and the pure ideal of the Order and the welfare of [the brothers'] souls on the other. And so it is our will with this present and permanently valid Constitution to make clear and bring to general attention the interpretation at which any right-thinking person readily arrives in this regard, namely: whenever money is sent or offered to the said brothers, it is always to be understood as to have been offered or sent in terms of the procedure that we have prescribed above, unless the person sending or offering it expressly signifies the contrary. For it is not likely that, without stipulating as much, anyone would want to set conditions to his alms which would cheat the giver of his merit or deprive the persons for whose needs he intends to provide with his gift, either of the benefit of the gift or the purity of their conscience.

Article 11: Testamentary Legacies

[1]Then too, occasionally things are bequeathed to the said brothers under various terms in last wills, and neither the *Rule* nor the declarations of our predecessors contain any specifications as to what should be done about such bequests. Lest there be any doubt in this matter in the future, and in order to make provision for the testators as well as to safeguard the consciences of the brothers, we affirm, ordain and declare that, if the testator in his bequest specifies terms that the brothers cannot accept due to their state in life, they must by all means decline any such legacy and not accept it—for example, if the testator left the brothers a vineyard or a tract of land for cultivation, or a house to be rented out, or if in such matters he used similar terms or wanted similar conditions observed.

[2]On the other hand, if in the bequest the testator specified a procedure permissible for the brothers [to accept], saying, for example,

"I bequeath money to be expended for the needs of the brothers; or I bequeath them a house, a piece of land, a vineyard, or the like, to be sold through some capable agent or agents, the proceeds to be applied toward buildings or other needs of the brothers;" or if he uses similar terms or methods in the bequest; then, so far as the brothers are concerned, due attention being paid to their needs and the afore-mentioned restrictions, we decree that they shall observe in all par-ticulars and for all intents what we have declared above concerning money alms granted to the brothers.

[3]In executing such legacies both the heirs and the executors are to act generously. And, should the occasion arise, prelates and laymen competent by law or custom to adjudicate such matters, are to act promptly, as their office demands, to carry out the pious wishes of the departed.

We ourselves intend to see to it by means which are permissible and conformable to the *Rule* of the brothers that both the pious pur-pose of the deceased be not circumvented and that the cupidity of heirs be chastised by legal measures, so that the brothers are not defrauded of seasonable assistance.

[4]If, however, anything is bequeathed to the brothers in general terms, without specification, we wish and command permanently through this present Constitution that in the case of such a legacy drawn up in a general fashion, everything shall be understood and observed in every particular and for all purposes as we have wished and specified above in regards to money or other alms indetermi-nately offered or sent to the brothers. This means that such a bequest is to be understood as left to the brothers in a way that is permissible for them to accept it; so that neither the testator be cheated of his merit nor said brothers of the benefit of the legacy.

Article 12: Exchanging Books and Movables

[1]It is recognized that the ownership of books and other movables used by the Order and the brothers pertains in a particular way to the Church whenever the ownership is not retained by anyone else. Now, sometimes it is convenient or advantageous that such books and movables be sold or exchanged.

Wherefore, desiring to provide for the convenience and the con-science of the brothers, we grant under the same authority[a] that the exchange of such things for other items which the brothers may use, may proceed with the authorization of the general or provincial

---

a. The propriety rights of the Holy See, cf. art. 4 supra 748-9.

ministers, acting jointly or singly, in their respective fields of ministry. We likewise give them permission to make regulations allocating
the use of such items.

²On the other hand, if articles of the kind are to be sold for a price,
since by their *Rule* the brothers are prohibited from accepting money
personally or through anyone else, we ordain and command that
such proceeds be accepted and expended on something the brothers
are permitted to use, through the services of a procurator deputized
by said Holy See or by the Cardinal charged by the same Holy See
with the government of said Order,[a] in keeping with the procedure
ordained above with regard to past and impending needs.

Article 13: Donating Things of Low Value

As to movable goods of low price and value, it shall be permissible
for the brothers, as herewith by us conceded, to make presents
thereof to other persons, both within and without the Order, for the
sake of piety or devotion or any other proper and reasonable purpose,
after previously obtaining the permission of their superiors, respect-
ing at all times the regulations made by the brothers in their general
or provincial chapters concerning this practice. Such regulations
should specify both the limit of the value of such items and the permission itself—that is, from whom and in what manner such permission should be obtained.

Article 14: The Number of Tunics

Since the *Rule* states that the brothers "may have one tunic with a
hood and another, if they wish, without a hood," it would appear to
have been the founder's intention that, in the absence of some
necessity, they are not to have the use of several tunics. We therefore
declare that the brothers may have the use of several tunics with the
permission of their ministers and custodians acting singly or jointly
in the limits of the ministry committed to them, with due consideration of the needs of the brothers and of other circumstances which
under God and the *Rule* are found to need attention.

LR II 14

Nor should the brothers be regarded as departing from their *Rule*
in doing so, since the *Rule* states expressly that "the ministers and
custodians alone may take special care . . . for the needs of the sick

LR IV 2

---

a. Nicholas III introduces here the office of a procurator who can dispose of the Holy See's property used by the brothers. This within just a few years opened the door to the general permissions of *Exultantes in Domino* of Martin IV, cf. infra 764-7.

and for the clothing of the others according to places, seasons, and cold climates, as they judge necessary."

Article 15: The Ministers and Their Delegates
for Needs of the Brothers

LR IV 2   As just mentioned, the *Rule* states that "for the needs of the sick and for clothing the others the ministers and custodians alone may take special care." The word "alone" may seem at first glance to restrict this care to the ministers and custodians in such a way that all others are excluded from it. We must, however, carefully consider the time when the *Rule* was composed, when the brothers were few in number by present comparison, so perhaps at that time the ministers and custodians seemed entirely adequate to make such provision. On the other hand, at the present time the circumstances are quite different due to the multiplied number of the brothers and the altered state of conditions.

Now, it is not likely that Saint Francis, the author of the *Rule*, intended to lay on the ministers and custodians such an impossible burden, or that he wanted the brothers to lack things necessary as a result of such an impossible condition.

We therefore herewith allow the ministers and custodians to exercise this care and solicitude through others. Such other brothers are to diligently apply that same care that is primarily incumbent on the ministers and custodians according to the *Rule*, whenever it has been committed to them by the latter.[a]

Article 16: The Manner of Working

LR V 1-2   [1]In addition, the *Rule* states: "let those brothers to whom the Lord has given the grace of working work faithfully and devotedly so that, while avoiding idleness, the enemy of the soul, they do not extinguish the Spirit of holy prayer and devotion."

Up to now certain people have abused that passage in malicious attempts to brand the said brothers for idle living and transgressing their *Rule*. To repress such evil-minded criticism, we declare that, if one considers how this text as well as the form and manner of the terms employed in it urge the brothers to pursue their occupation, it does not appear to have been the founder's intention that those engaged in study, in the divine services, and in the ministry should

---

a. This article is an expansion of Innocent IV, *Ordinem vestrum* 5, cf. FA:ED II 776-7.

be subjected, or, still more, restricted, to manual labor or activity. For the example of Christ and of many holy Fathers shows that such spiritual labor outweighs manual labor in the same way as the concerns of the soul take precedence over bodily concerns.[a]

[2]We do, on the contrary, declare that this passage refers to the other brothers who are not engaged in such spiritual activity, lest they lead an idle life if they do not busy themselves with legitimate services to the other brothers.[b] Of course, such brothers too might be so advanced and distinguished in the life of prayer and contemplation that it would be right not to withhold them from so good and pious an occupation.

[3]But regardless of the fact that certain brothers are not engaged in study and the sacred ministry, but are attached to the service of those brothers who are engaged in study or the divine services or the ministry, such brothers are entitled to their support along with those at whose service they are. That stands fairly approved by the law enacted in all justice by the valiant warrior David of old, to the effect that those going into battle and those remaining with the supplies should share and share alike.

1 Sm 30:21-25

Article 17: Preaching

[1]It is expressly stated in the *Rule* that "the brothers may not preach in the diocese of any bishop when he has opposed their doing so." Deferring to the *Rule* on this point while nevertheless preserving the plenitude of our Apostolic authority, we affirm that this passage must be observed to the letter just as the *Rule* sets it down, except insofar as for the good of the Christian people the Apostolic See has granted or ordained otherwise or shall in the future so grant or ordain.[c]

LR IX 1

[2]In the same chapter of the *Rule* it is immediately added: "let none of the brothers dare to preach in any way to the people unless he has been examined and approved by the general minister . . . and the office of preaching has been conferred upon him."

LR IX 2

Now, bearing in mind the past condition of the Order with its limited membership, and its present-day status with the multiplied

---

a. Cf. Bonaventure, *Apologia*, XII 12-17 (VIII 320-1) *Defense*, 265-270.

b. Nicholas's acceptance of the clericalization of the Order is evident here. He cannot envision the legitimacy of lay brothers in the Order unless they are "waiting on" the ordained brothers, who were now providing the principal work of the brothers in the church. Cf. Gregory IX, *Quoniam abundavit*, cf. FA:ED I 575-7; and the *Constitutions of Narbonne*, 1.2-4, cf. Monti, *Writings*, 76-77.

c. Usefulness to the apostolic work of the Church as determined by the Holy See now takes precedence over Francis's desire to remain subject to local bishops, Test 25-26, FA:ED I 126.

number of the brothers, and also mindful of the good of souls as is proper [to us], we hereby grant that not only the general minister may examine and approve the brothers for public preaching and grant them the license to preach—insofar as such licensing concerns the person's qualifications and the office of preaching, as contained in the *Rule*—but that the provincial ministers acting together with the definitors may also do so in their provincial chapters. That is said to be the practice observed even to this day, and to be contained among the privileges granted the brothers.[a]

The said ministers likewise have the power to revoke, suspend and restrict this license as and when it appears advisable to them.

Article 18: Admitting Brothers to the Order

[1]It is our fond desire for the glory of God to have the salvation of souls promoted and to have the said Order increase in merit and numbers because of the way it goes on inflaming the hearts of Christians toward the love of God. We therefore grant, and with this Constitution we confirm, the faculty not only of the general minister but also of the provincial ministers to receive persons fleeing the world into the brotherhood. The said general minister, however, may restrict this faculty of the provincial ministers, as he may find it advisable.

[2]The vicars of the provincial ministers, however, should understand that this faculty is denied them in their capacity as vicars, unless they have this faculty expressly committed to them by their ministers, for whom we hereby declare it lawful to commit this faculty to their vicars as well as to others. The said provincial ministers, however, shall take care not to give this commission rashly and randomly but upon due consideration of each instance, while strengthening those to whom they entrust this faculty with dependable directions, so that everything may proceed with discretion.

[3]Nor should everyone be admitted to the Order indiscriminately, but only such as, with education, fitness and other qualifications to recommend them, can be of benefit to the Order while being of advantage to themselves with a life of merit and to others with a good example.[b]

---

a. By Innocent IV, *Ordinem vestrum* 9, cf. FA:ED II 778.

b. This paraphrases the *Constitutions of Narbonne* 1.3, see Monti, *Writings*, 76.

Article 19: The Custodians at the General Chapter

[1]Moreover, the brothers of the aforesaid Order have been in doubt concerning the passage of the *Rule* which says that "when [the general minister] dies, let the election of his successor be made by the provincial ministers and custodians in the Chapter of Pentecost." The question is whether all the great number of custodians must convene for the general chapter, or whether it suffices, the better to transact everything with tranquility, to have only certain ones from each province attend, with a voice for the rest.

LR VIII 2

This is our reply: the custodians of the several provinces shall select one of their number to accompany their provincial minister to the chapter in their stead, commissioning him to vote and act in their place.

[2]Since this is also a procedure that the brothers themselves have established, we have found it deserving of approval. That, too, is the response which our predecessor Gregory IX is said to have given in like case.[a]

Article 20: Access to Monasteries of Nuns

[1]Finally, in the *Rule* there is the passage which states that the brothers "may not enter the monasteries of nuns, excepting those brothers to whom special permission has been granted by the Apostolic See." Now, the brothers have been maintaining that this is to be understood more specifically of the monasteries of the Poor Cloistered Nuns, since the said Holy See has special charge of them; furthermore, such an interpretation is believed to have been handed down in a statute enacted by the provincial ministers at a general chapter held in the lifetime of Saint Francis, at the time when the *Rule* was written. Nevertheless the brothers have asked to be reassured as to whether the passage must be understood in general of all monasteries, since the *Rule* makes no exception, or only of the monasteries of the aforesaid Nuns.

LR XI 1

[2]We reply therefore, that the prohibition holds for the monasteries of all nuns whatsoever. By the term "monastery," however, we mean the interior enclosure, the living quarters, and the workshops. Those brothers to whom the superiors have given such permission by reason of their maturity and suitability may go into the other areas to which lay people also have access in order to preach or beg alms, always excepting the monasteries of the aforesaid Cloistered Nuns.

---

a. Gregory IX, *Quo elongati* 10, cf. FA:ED I 574-5.

No one has any access to them without special permission from the Apostolic See, just as our predecessor Gregory IX is said to have replied in this case.[a]

Article 21: The Testament of Saint Francis

[1]Finally, the Confessor of Christ, Francis of holy memory, is said toward the end of his life to have commanded in an injunction called his *Testament* that the words of the *Rule* are not to be glossed and, to use his own words, no brother is to say: "they should be understood in this or that way." Furthermore, he added that the brothers are in no way "to ask any letters from the Roman Curia," as well as certain other directives that cannot be observed without great difficulty. For that reason the brothers were in doubt as to whether they were bound to observe this *Testament,* so they petitioned our predecessor, Gregory IX, to remove such uncertainty from their consciences.[b]

[2]It is said that Pope Gregory, considering the danger to their souls and the difficulties they might incur as a consequence, removed all anxiety from their hearts by declaring that the brothers are not bound to observe this injunction [the *Testament*]. For without the consent of the brothers, especially the ministers, Francis could not make obligatory a matter that touches everyone. Nor could he in any way whatsoever bind his successor because an equal has no authority over his equal.

Therefore, we see no reason to make any further decision regarding the point at issue.

Article 22: Other Papal Declarations Superceded

[1]In this regard, we understand that various letters have been issued by certain of our predecessors, the Roman pontiffs, clarifying the *Rule,* or concerning the *Rule* itself and what pertains to it. That fact, however, has not availed to quell the attacks of the aforementioned bitter critics of the *Rule* and the brothers. Then too, these letters do not make due provision for the state of the brothers in many particulars, while subsequent experience with many problems of more recent origin has indicated the necessity of further or different provision in these particulars.

Test 38

Test 25

---

a. The whole article is a verbatim repetition of Gregory IX, *Quo elongati* 11, cf. FA:ED I 575.

b. Nicholas' response to this question simply repeats Gregory's. Cf. *Quo elongati* 3, cf. FA:ED I 571.

²Lest, therefore, any discrepancy between such past [papal] letters and this present Constitution cause different interpretations,
confusing the minds of the brothers in their observance of the aforesaid points; and at the same time to make a fuller, cleaner, and surer
provision for the status of the brothers and their observance of their
Rule in all and sundry items contained in this present Constitution,
regardless of whether they or any part thereof be contained in others
of the above mentioned Apostolic letters: we do herewith decree that
this our Constitution or declaration and ordinance alone shall be
observed by the brothers, exactly and inviolably for all time.

Article 23: The Present Constitution Itself

¹It is clearly evident from what has been said above, as well as
from similar investigations made by us with mature deliberation,
that the *Rule* is permissible, holy, perfect, observable, and open to no
apparent danger. Therefore, from the fullness of our Apostolic
authority, we herewith endorse, formally approve, and give permanent force to it, as well as to everything we have herein enacted,
ordained, conceded, regulated, decided, clarified, and supplemented
concerning the said *Rule*. Furthermore, we command strictly in virtue of obedience that, like all other constitutions and decretal letters,
this Constitution shall be read in the schools.[a]

²Now, there may be some persons who, with an outward show of
obedience to the law, still may wish to pour out the venom of their
malice on the brothers and their *Rule* in the course of their lectures,
expositions and commentaries, thus vitiating with their subtle
devices the true sense of this Constitution by giving it alien and unfavorable interpretations. Such differences of opinion and the distor-
tion of the meaning of this Constitution may baffle many a pious
soul and keep many a heart from the resolution to enter the religious
life. The need of obviating the perversity of such detractors compels
us to block their path to such evasive actions and so to prescribe a
definite procedure for lectures on this Constitution.

Wherefore, under pain of excommunication and deprivation of
office and benefice, we strictly command that in lecturing on the
present Constitution it shall be expounded faithfully and literally
just as it is written, with no evasions being made by the lecturers or
expositors by citing similarities, contrasts, or divergent or opposite
opinions. No glosses shall be made on the said Constitution except

---

a. In other words, Pope Nicholas III is commanding that *Exiit* be added to the official church
documents which served as the texts in schools of canon law and theology.

perhaps by way of explaining a phrase, its meaning and construction, or the Constitution itself grammatically and to the letter. In no instance is the lecturer to vitiate or distort the sense of it toward any other meaning but that conveyed by the letter of the law.

[3]And lest the Holy See be obliged to take further action against such detractors, we strictly command each and all—of whatever prominence, condition, or position—not to offer opinions, write, argue, preach or speak unfavorably, in public or in private, against the said *Rule* or the state of life of the aforementioned brothers, or against anything by us herein enacted, ordained, conceded, regulated, decided, clarified, supplemented, endorsed, or even formally approved. Should any cause for doubt in these particulars arise in the mind of anyone, let the matter be referred to the supreme tribunal of the said Apostolic See, to have the intent rendered clear by its Apostolic authority, which in these matters has the sole competency to issue decrees and to clarify them once issued.

[4]As for those, however, who compose glosses on this Constitution in any way other than we have indicated; moreover, as for doctors or lectors who in their public teaching knowingly and deliberately vitiate the sense of this Constitution, or also issue commentaries, writings or pamphlets, or knowingly and deliberately give interpretations in their classes or sermons contrary to the above or any part or parts thereof: let such persons know that they are under sentence of excommunication, which we pronounce against them as of this moment and of which they can be absolved by no one but the Roman pontiff. This penalty is incurred regardless of any privileges or indults or Apostolic letters granted to whatever ranks, persons, orders or places, religious or secular, in general or in particular, under whatever form or statement of terms, nothing of which shall in any way whatever avail anyone in the aforesaid matters.

[5]Furthermore, it is our will that persons against whom this sentence of excommunication has been pronounced by us, as well as anyone else who may contravene the above regulation or any part thereof, shall be denounced to the notice of ourselves and of the aforementioned See, so that if the equitable measures we have devised do not deter them from their proscribed course, the severity of Apostolic chastisement shall so restrain them.

Article 24: Conclusion

It is forbidden, therefore, for anyone whomsoever to infringe upon what we have clarified, ordained, conceded, regulated, supplemented, endorsed, formally approved, and enacted in this document, or rashly dare to oppose it. If anyone presume to attempt this, let him know that he shall incur the anger of almighty God and of his holy Apostles Peter and Paul.

Given at Soriano,[a] on the fourteenth day of August, in the second year of our Pontificate (1279).

Bull *Exultantes in Domino* of Pope Martin IV (1283)

In many ways the constitution *Exiit* marked the end of an era in the history of the Lesser Brothers. In the last two decades of the century, assured of their important role in the Church and buoyed by their popularity, Franciscans embarked on a course of aggressive ministerial expansion.[b] Large and impressive churches were built to accommodate the throngs of worshippers and to display God's blessings on the Order.[c] To a great extent, this expansion was due to increased papal favor. Martin IV, who had been impressed by the work of the Order during his many years as papal legate in France, issued a bull in 1281 giving the brothers full permission to exercise their ministry of preaching and hearing confessions even without the permission of the bishop and local clergy.[d] This decree naturally reignited the old animosity of many clerics, leading to numerous confrontations with the brothers who naturally wanted to defend their rights.

This expansion also had an impact on the brothers' life-style. Larger facilities demanded greater and more reliable financial support. The elaborate mechanisms prescribed in *Exiit* stood in the way of more efficient operations. The brothers had no control over the activities of the "agents" who collected alms for them, even when the agents were uncooperative;[e] they could not take legal action to obtain alms bequeathed to them in wills;[f] and they had to have recourse to representatives of the Holy See, the owners of their belongings, to make major dispositions concerning them.[g] In an attempt to make life easier for the brothers, Martin IV issued this bull, *Exultantes in Domino,* in

---

a. A small town near Viterbo where Nicholas III had his summer residence.

b. On the period from 1279 to 1312, see Moorman, *History,* 181-204; Lambert, *Poverty,* 157-214; David Burr, *Olivi, passim;* and Duncan Nimmo, *Reform and Division in the Medieval Franciscan Order* (Rome: Capuchin Historical Institute, 1987): 51-134.

c. Among the many large construction projects were new churches in Siena (1289), Florence (1294), Pisa (1300), and London (1306).

d. Martin IV, *Ad fructus uberes,* BFr 3: 480.

e. Nicholas III, *Exiit,* 6.2. Cf. supra 750-1.

f. Nicholas III, *Exiit,* 6.2; 11.2. Cf. supra 750-1.

g. Nicholas III, *Exiit,* 12.2. Cf. supra 756.

1283.[a] This instituted a new office, the Papal procurator or syndic,[b] who was given complete freedom to collect needed funds, administer the property of the brothers in the name of the Holy See, and to defend their interests in court. This position, with its sweeping powers, gradually absorbed the functions of the old "spiritual friends" and "agents" prescribed in the *Rule* and the Papal declarations. What made this new office strikingly different from the old ones, however, is that the procurator was clearly the agent of the brothers themselves, rather than the benefactors. The brothers had complete control over the procurator: he was appointed by them and served at their pleasure, and he acted under their direct control. This certainly blurred the theoretical distinctions hammered out in *Exiit:* how could the Franciscans claim to have renounced all "dominion" and have simply a "right of use,"[c] when they controlled the activities of their financial managers? Did this not make the brothers' claim to absolute poverty a legal fiction? Such a fear had led an earlier generation of Lesser Brothers to renounce a similar Papal privilege;[d] this time, at the general chapter of 1285, the Order accepted the offer. In 1290, the Franciscan Pope, Nicholas IV, reissued this privilege in a more definitive form as an apostolic constitution.[e]

> To our beloved sons, the general and provincial ministers and the custodians of the entire Order of Lesser Brothers:
>
> [1]We exult in the Lord that the members of your holy Order are confirmed in God's favor by the eagerness of their devotion and activity; for they strive with all their might to follow in the footsteps and remain on the path of the One who, *coming down from the Father of lights* and *taking the form of a servant,* offered Himself as a pleasing sacrifice of praise. And so we have been led to consider some honorable means of assistance through which the pure observance of the Order might be maintained in its vigor: so that the brothers, who can go to court for no temporal thing, might be free from all cares and thus more freely and peacefully apply themselves to the divine services; and so that the pious intention of those people who, out of devotion to God, offer, give, concede, or who in their last will bequeath some goods to your Order or to brothers of your Order is not frustrated.

Jas 1:17

Phil 2:7

a. Nicholas IV, *Exultantes in Domino,* BFr 3:501, no. 40; text in Eubel, 301.

b. Actually the office was first created for the benefit of the basilica and convent of San Francesco in Assisi, which was directly papal property, in 1240 (BFr 1: 288). This privilege was extended to the whole Umbrian province in 1265 (BFr 3:24). *Exiit* (12.2) mentions the office of procurator, but offers no specifics as to their appointment. However, existing records indicate that prior to *Exultantes,* where such procurators existed, other than Umbria, they were appointed by local bishops acting in virtue of faculties given them by the Cardinal protector.

c. Nicholas III, *Exiit,* 3.1. Cf. supra 746-7.

d. *Quanto studiosus* of Innocent IV (1247); his liberalizing permissions were rejected by the chapter of 1251 and successive chapters, such as Narbonne (1260). Cf. FA:ED II 774 e.

e. Nicholas IV, *Religionis favor,* BFr 4:190.

For in our watchful care, we recognize that as often as necessity forces you or usefulness persuades, your Order is forced to have recourse to the Roman Church for your needs, as the right, ownership, and dominion of all moveable and immovable goods that your brothers can use belong to that Church. We therefore wish to kindly lessen the inconvenience or even difficulties that can mount up for the brothers when they attempt to carry out this stipulation. We also want to obviate the negligence of heirs and executors, so that the brothers, by some honorable means appropriate to your Order, are not defrauded of alms bequeathed to them in wills. And we hope that these things which are to be done for the prosperous state of your Order, by which you will be fortified with a greater authority in such situations, will be considered a more beneficial and useful situation for you.[a]

We therefore, through these present letters, concede to you the faculty to nominate at your discretion, in which we have full confidence in the Lord, special persons, who do not belong to your Order, for the needs of each place. These persons so named by you may exercise legitimate, general, and free administration of these goods. And by the fullness of our power and by authority of these present letters, we decree that such persons are our true and legitimate administrators, managers, syndics, and representatives. As such we invest them with full authority to receive such [bequeathed] goods themselves, the proceeds of such goods, and other alms in the name of the said Roman Church, for the purpose of converting these donated items to the advantage of the brothers, in ways that the *Rule* or the declaration on the *Rule*[b] allow, whenever and for the purpose that you, our son, as general minister, or each of you [ministers and custodians] in your individual provinces and custodies, may direct them, or as requested by brothers appointed by you in each place.

Furthermore, these persons shall enjoy the full, general, and free power of the Apostolic see to request, demand, receive and sell the said goods. They thus have the authority to take whatever action is necessary, both in and out of court—whether by purchase, exchange, agreement, pledge, remittance, challenge, compromise, or legal action through defending the brothers from unjust accusations, or taking an oath to tell the truth, or through whatever type of lawsuit may be required—to obtain either the mobile and immobile goods or their equivalent value or the alms that are bequeathed to the brothers in wills, with and against those who would take

---

a. The Pope seems to recognize there will be some opposition to this privilege among the brothers.
b. Nicholas III, *Exiit*, 11, cf. supra 754-5.

possession of these goods, or who would violently take them away, or who would by any means whatever contrary to the will of the brothers prevent these goods from being given to them. Such persons also have the general authority to take similar action for any reason on behalf of the places and things that belong to the said [Roman] Church and are conceded for the use of the brothers, as well as to defend the immunities, liberties, rights, and privileges of the same brothers.

We also concede to you by authority of these present letters the faculty of removing these persons and substituting others in their stead, or of nominating in the same fashion as many such persons as might be opportune. All such persons will enjoy the same full and free power in the same or similar matters [that we have described above].

It is forbidden, therefore, for anyone to tamper with this decree which we have confirmed, or rashly dare to oppose it. If anyone presume to attempt this, let him know that he shall incur the anger of almighty God and of His blessed apostles Peter and Paul.

Given at Orvieto, the eighteenth day of January, in the second year of our pontificate (1283).

Constitution *Exivi de Paradiso* of Pope Clement V (1312)

As the mainstream of the Order increasingly moved to a more liberal interpretation of the *Rule* toward the end of the thirteenth century, this provoked a strong reaction among those brothers who wished to remain faithful to what they saw as a simpler and more authentic way of their life. The Spiritual movement was born.[a] The Spirituals were convinced, first of all, that Francis's cherished poverty did not consist simply in the renunciation of ownership, but in actually living with a severely restricted use of material goods. They decried the growing academic and clerical professionalization of the Order, which was establishing a caste system in the brotherhood. They were opposed to Papal privileges, especially the institution of procurators, as they believed these had simply opened the door to flagrant abuses, which the superiors of the Order were either unable or unwilling to correct. With their slogan that the *Rule* must be observed "to the letter, without a gloss," they saw themselves as prophets calling the Order back to living as true Lesser Brothers. In return, the provincial ministers by and large viewed the Spirituals as self-righteous malcontents who were standing in the path of progress, criticizing other brothers who were providing essential pastoral services to the

---

a. For literature, see notes under *Exultantes in Domino*. Cf. supra 764-7. In addition, cf. Nimmo, *Reform*, 139-90.

contemporary church. Furthermore they were disobedient, refusing to abide by decisions legitimately made in chapter by the community. As a result, the Spirituals were harassed, even persecuted, by many superiors.

By the turn of the fourteenth century, the rhetoric had escalated on both sides. Some of the Spirituals in Italy had even renounced their obedience to the Pope, as they considered Boniface VIII to have been invalidly elected and an enemy of the Gospel way of life. The general minister, John of Murrovale, a personal friend of the Pope, was leading a severe repression of their movement. Protesting brothers were imprisoned. Luckily for the Spirituals, a number of factors began turning in their favor around 1307. The new Pope, Clement V, a Frenchman, was open to influence from some prominent advocates of the Spiritual cause: members of the royal houses of Aragon, Sicily, and Naples, as well as powerful cardinals who had been out of favor under Boniface VIII. In the summer of 1309, the Pope summoned representatives of the Order's central government ("the Community") and the leaders of the Spiritual cause to the Curia in Avignon. A Papal commission was set up to conduct a full investigation of the Order.

Both sides in this intramural Franciscan debate assembled dossiers of source material and composed treatises for the commission's consideration.[a] Leaders of the Spiritual "prosecution" of the Community were the former general minister, Raymond Geoffroi, and Ubertino of Casale; the Community's "defense" was mounted at first by the general minister, Gonsalvo of Valboa, and then by the brilliant polemicist Bonagratia of Bergamo. In 1311, a general council of the church opened in Vienne. One of its decrees severely cut back the lavish ministerial privileges extended to the brothers by Martin IV.[b] It was toward the end of this council, in May of 1312, that Clement V announced his verdict on the disputes wracking the Franciscan Order in his constitution *Exivi de paradiso*.[c]

Exivi was actually a finely wrought compromise document. Each side scored points, but neither won a clear-cut victory. On the one hand, the Papal commission had agreed with the Spiritual charge that there were some grave abuses in the Franciscan house; the bull attempted to correct these by a number of restrictions. On the other hand, the basic thesis of the Spirituals—that the Lesser Brothers were indeed bound to a "poor use" of material things—was accepted only in a very limited sense. On several points of disputed interpretation, *Exivi* left the practical judgment to the discretion of the superiors of the Order, whom the Spirituals considered lax. Perhaps most importantly, the decree did nothing to cut back on mitigating privileges,

---

a. It was precisely during this time that much of the alternate source material on the life of Francis, which had been stored in the archives of the Sacro Convento in Assisi, came to light.

b. See introduction to *Exultantes in Domino*, cf. supra 764-5. Vienne decreed that friars of the mendicant orders needed permission of the local clergy to preach other than in their own churches; that they had to be licensed by the bishop before they could hear the confessions of the laity; and that they could bury lay people in their churches only if they turned back to the appropriate pastor a portion of the burial fees.

c. Text in BFr 5:195; superior edition in *Seraphicae legislationis textus originales* (Ad Claras Aquas, Quaracchi: Collegium S. Bonaventurae, 1897), 229-260.

especially the bull *Exultantes* of Martin V, which was anathema to the Spirituals. In the short term, *Exivi* did little to heal the disputes in the Order, as circumstances never gave it a chance to be implemented.[a] In the long run, its
great service was to offer further clarifications as to the interpretation of the
Rule.

Clement, Bishop, Servant of the servants of God, for an everlasting record.

[1]*I came out of Paradise, I said, I will water my garden of plants.* Thus
speaks the heavenly Husbandman, who is truly *the source of wisdom,
the Word of God,* begotten of the Father from all eternity while abiding
in the Father. *In these last days,* made flesh in the womb of the Virgin
through the work of the Holy Spirit, as *man* He *went forth to the* arduous *work* of redeeming the human race, giving Himself to humanity
as the model of a heavenly life. But because so often people, overcome by the anxieties of this mortal life, turned their mental gaze
away from such a model, He, our true Solomon, laid out in the field of
the Church Militant, among other gardens, a certain garden of
delight, far from the stormy seas of the world, in which men could
devote themselves with greater peace and security to contemplate
and imitate a model such as this. It was into that garden that Christ
went when He entered this world, to refresh it with the fertile waters
of spiritual grace and doctrine.

Now this garden is the holy religion of the Lesser Brothers which,
securely hedged within the firm walls of regular observance, is content with God alone and is constantly adorned with fresh shoots, its
sons. Visiting this garden, the beloved Son of God gathers therein *the
myrrh and spices* of mortification and penance which by their marvelous fragrance diffuse to everyone the perfume of an attractive sanctity. This is the form and *Rule* of heavenly life sketched by that
celebrated confessor of Christ, Saint Francis, who taught his sons to
observe it by both word and example.

[2]The devoted professors and followers of that said holy *Rule,* as
both pupils and true sons of so great a father, have aspired and still
ardently aspire to observe in its pure and full extent the *Rule* to which
they are firmly pledged. Finding, however, that there were certain
points contained in the text of the *Rule* that might be doubtful in
meaning, they have in the past prudently taken recourse to the highest tribunal of Apostolic authority to have these doubts resolved.
Receiving assurance from that See, at whose feet they are to remain
ever subject according to their *Rule,* they were able to serve the Lord,

Sir 24:29

Sir 1:5

Heb 1:2

Ps 104:23

Ex 30:23

LR XII 4

---

a. See John XXII, *Ad Conditorem,* infra 783-9.

free from all doubt, in the fullness of charity. Several Roman pontiffs, our predecessors of happy memory, rightly heeded the pious and just entreaties of the brothers; they successively issued declarations on doubtful points, promulgating certain interpretations and making some concessions, as they thought good for the consciences of the brothers and the purity of their religious observance.

But because there are delicate consciences that very often fear sin where it does not exist and dread any turning in the way of God, these previous clarifications of the aforesaid Pontiffs have not fully quieted the consciences of all the brothers. On the contrary, as repeatedly brought to our ears from quite a few persons in both public and private consistories, certain doubts are beginning to arise and surge among them concerning points of their *Rule* and state of life. For this reason the brothers themselves have humbly entreated us to clarify opportunely the doubts which have arisen and those which may arise in the future, thus applying a remedy through the kindness of the Apostolic See.

³We have from a tender age had a heartfelt devotion for those who profess the aforesaid *Rule* and the whole Order as such. Now that, through no merit of our own, we bear the office of universal pastoral authority, we are the more roused to cherish them and to honor them more kindly and attentively, the more often we consider and reflect on the abundant harvest reaped continually from their exemplary lives and wholesome teaching for the good of the universal Church. Moved, therefore, by the pious intentions of the petitioners, we have found it right to direct our thoughtful efforts towards satisfying their plea. We have had a careful examination made of their doubts by several archbishops, bishops, masters in theology and other learned, prudent, and discreet men.

Article 1: Observance of the Gospel

¹The first of these doubts arises from the opening passage of the said *Rule,* which says: "The rule and life of the Lesser Brothers is this: to observe the Holy Gospel of our Lord Jesus Christ by living in obedience, without anything of their own, and in chastity." Again, farther on in the said *Rule* there is the passage: "When the year of probation has come to an end, they may be received to obedience, promising always to observe this rule and life." And again, at the end of the *Rule* there are the words: "so that . . . we may observe the poverty, humility, and the Holy Gospel of our Lord Jesus Christ, as we have firmly promised."

LR I 1

LR II 11

LR XII 4

Now, there has been uncertainty whether the brothers of the said Order are obliged to all the precepts and counsels contained in the Gospel by profession of their *Rule*. Some have said they are bound to them all. Others, however, have asserted that they are obliged to three counsels only, that is, "living in obedience, without anything of one's own, and in chastity," and to the other things set down in the said *Rule* in obligatory terms.

²With regard to this article, we follow in the footsteps of our predecessors and giving this article further clarification, we answer the doubt as follows. Since every determinate vow must have a defined object, he who vows to observe the *Rule* cannot be considered obliged by virtue of such vow to those counsels of the Gospel which are not mentioned in the *Rule*. And indeed this is shown to have been the intention of blessed Francis, the author of the *Rule*, from the fact that he laid down certain counsels in the *Rule* while omitting others. For if by those words, "The *Rule* and life of the Lesser Brothers is this," etc., he had intended to oblige them to all the evangelical counsels, it would have been superfluous and pointless to include some of them and not others.

Article 2: The Precepts of the *Rule*

¹However, since the nature of a restrictive term demands the exclusion of everything foreign to it but embraces everything comprised in it, we affirm and declare that the said brothers are bound by the profession of their *Rule* not only to the said three vows in their bare and absolute sense, but also to everything related to them expressed in the *Rule* itself. For if, in their promise to observe the *Rule* "by living in obedience, without property, and in chastity," the brothers were obliged to observe these three vows precisely and no more, and not also to observe everything contained in the *Rule* which gives form to those vows, then the words, "I promise always to observe this *Rule*" would be useless, as implying no obligation.

²Still, it must not be thought that the blessed Francis intended that those who profess this *Rule* should be obligated with equal force as regards everything in the *Rule*, whether giving form to the three vows, or anything else contained in it. Rather, he made a clear distinction: in some matters his words imply that transgression is a mortal sin, in others not, since he employs the word "precept" or its equivalent, while elsewhere he is content to use other expressions.

Article 3: Points Equivalent to a Precept

[1]Furthermore, besides those things laid down in the *Rule* in expressed terms of precept or of exhortation and admonition, there are some things stated in the imperative mood in either a negative or affirmative form. For that reason there has been up to now some doubt as to whether they are of precept. As we understand, this doubt is not lessened but rather increased by the declaration of our predecessor Pope Nicholas III of happy memory, that by virtue of professing their *Rule,* the brothers are obliged to those Gospel counsels "which the *Rule* expresses in form of precept or prohibition or equivalent words," and in addition, that they are "obliged to observe everything the *Rule* imposes on them in terms of obligation."[a] The said brothers have therefore begged that we would, for their peace of conscience, graciously define which of these matters should be considered as equivalent to precepts and therefore obligatory.

[2]Delighted by their sincerity of conscience, and aware that in matters affecting the salvation of the soul one should take the safer path in order to avoid grave remorse of conscience, we affirm that the brothers are not obliged to observe everything expressed by the *Rule* in the imperative mood in the way that they are obliged to observe its precepts and matters equivalent to precepts. Nevertheless, it is the proper course for the brothers, if they are to observe their *Rule* in its purity and rigor, to acknowledge that they are bound to observe in this way [as equivalent to precepts] the injunctions noted below.

In order that the brothers may have in summary form these matters which appear equivalent to precepts, in virtue of the words or at least of the subject matter, or of both, we declare that the following points of their *Rule* must be observed by the brothers as obligatory:

Not having more than one tunic with a hood and another without a hood. — LR II 14

Likewise, not wearing shoes, and not riding horseback, except in case of necessity. — LR II 15; III 11

Likewise, that the brothers are to wear poor clothing. — LR II 16

Likewise, that they are bound to fast from the feast of All Saints until the Lord's Nativity and on Fridays. — LR III 5, 8

Likewise, that the clerics shall celebrate the Divine Office according to the rite of the holy Roman Church. — LR III 1

Likewise, that the ministers and custodians must take solicitous care for the sick and for clothing the other brothers. — LR IV 2

---

a. Nicholas III, *Exiit,* 1:3, 5. Cf. supra 743-4.

LR VI 9   Likewise, that if anyone of the brothers falls ill, the other brothers must serve him.

LR IX 1   Likewise, that the brothers may not preach in the diocese of any bishop when he has opposed their doing so.

LR IX 2   Likewise, that none of them may dare to preach in any way to the people unless he has been examined and approved by the general minister, or by such others as have the authority in keeping with the aforesaid declaration, and the office of preaching has been confirmed upon him.[a]

LR X 4   Likewise, that brothers who find they cannot observe the *Rule* spiritually, can and must have recourse to their ministers.

Likewise, all points set down in the *Rule* regarding the form of the habit of both novices and professed, as also the manner of admittance and profession of the brothers, unless, as the *Rule* says, those who admit the brothers may find something else advisable with regard to the habit of the novices.[b]

Likewise, the Order commonly has believed, now holds, and from the outset has held, that wherever the term *teneantur* ("let them be bound") occurs in the *Rule,* that point has the force of a precept and must be observed as such by the brothers.

Article 4: The Goods of Entrants

[1]Moreover, the aforesaid Confessor of Christ, in prescribing for the brothers and their ministers what should be done in regards to

LR II 7-8   admitting members into the Order, said in the *Rule:* "that the brothers and the Minister be careful not to interfere with their temporal goods that they may dispose of their belonging as the Lord inspires them. If, however, counsel is sought, the minister may send them to some God-fearing persons according to whose advice their goods may be distributed to the poor."

Now, many of the brothers were, and still are, uncertain whether they may accept any of the property of those who enter, if it is donated to them; whether they may without fault persuade them to give anything to individuals or convents; and whether the ministers themselves or the brothers may give advice concerning the distribution of such property, when there are other suitable advisors to whom the entrants can be sent.

---

a. Nicholas III, *Exiit,* 17. Cf. supra 758-9.
b. LR II. Cf. FA:ED I 100-1.

[2]We observe attentively that Saint Francis intended to banish from his disciples, whose *Rule* he had based on the greatest poverty, all affection for the temporal goods of those entering the Order, especially in using the above words, so that admittance to the Order might be a holy and utterly disinterested matter so far as the brothers are concerned. They should be seen plainly to have no eye on the temporal goods of the entrants, but only on giving them over to the service of God.

We declare, therefore, that both the ministers and the rest of the brothers must refrain altogether from any forms of inducement or persuasion to give them any property, and also from advice as to its distribution. They should send those who seek counsel to God-fearing persons of some other walk of life, and not to the brothers. In this way all will see them truly as zealous and perfect observers of their Father's sound tradition.

[3]On the other hand, since the *Rule* itself wishes the entrants to be free as the Lord inspires them concerning their property, it does not seem unlawful for the brothers, duly considering their needs and the conditions laid down in the aforesaid declaration, to accept whatever goods an entrant may of his own accord wish to give by way of an alms to them just as to any other poor people. It behooves the brothers, however, to be on the alert in accepting such offerings, lest in accepting such offerings they create an unfavorable impression by the amount they receive.

Article 5: The Garments of the Brothers

[1]Furthermore, the *Rule* says: "those who have promised obedience may have one tunic with a hood and another, if they wish, without a hood"; likewise, that "all the brothers shall wear poor clothes."   LR II 14-16

We have already declared that the above words are equivalent to precepts. In order to express this more clearly, however, we declare that it is not lawful to have more tunics, except when this is necessary in accordance with the *Rule*, as our said predecessor has more fully explained.[a]

[2]As for the poverty of the garments, however, both of the habit and of the inner tunics, we say that the phrase "poor clothes" has to be understood in relation to the customs or conditions of the respective country, both as to the color of the cloth and the price. For in such matters one specific standard cannot be laid down for all lands.

---

a. Nicholas III, *Exiit*, 14. Cf. supra 756-7.

We therefore think that what constitutes "poor clothes" should be entrusted to the judgment of the ministers, custodians, and guardians; they have to form their own consciences, but they also must see to it that poverty in dress is maintained.

[3]In the same way we leave it to the judgment of the ministers, custodians, and guardians as to when the brothers need to wear shoes.

Article 6: The Fasts

Also, the *Rule* refers to two periods when the brothers are obliged to fast, namely: "from the feast of All Saints until the Lord's Nativity," and "during the greater Lent until the Lord's Resurrection." Then we find inserted in the *Rule:* "At other times they may not be bound to fast except on Fridays." From these statements some have concluded that the brothers are not to observe any other fasts except from propriety.

We therefore declare they are not obliged to fast at other times apart from the fasts established by the church. For it is not probable that either the author of the *Rule* or the pontiff who confirmed it intended to dispense the brothers from observing the fasting days to which the common law of the church obligates other Christians.

LR III 5, 7-8

Article 7: The Prohibition of Money

[1]Again, wishing above all to keep his brothers completely detached from coins or money, the aforementioned Saint commanded all the brothers strictly "not to receive coins or money in any form, either personally or through an intermediary." In clarifying this point, our said predecessor defined the cases and the ways in which the brothers cannot and ought not be regarded as receiving money either in person or through an intermediary, contrary to their *Rule* and the pure ideal of their Order.[a]

LR IV 1

We declare, therefore, that the brothers are bound to use the utmost care against having recourse to donors of money or their deputized agents in ways other than those defined by our said predecessor, lest they justifiably be called transgressors of this precept and the *Rule.* For when there is a general prohibition, anything not expressly granted is understood to be refused. For this reason, all soliciting of money or acceptance of money offerings, boxes or

---

a. Nicholas III, *Exiit,* 6-11. Cf. supra 750-5.

coffers set up in church or elsewhere to receive money deposits from
donors or benefactors, and any other recourse to money or those who
have it which is not conceded in the aforesaid declaration, is, we say,
completely and absolutely forbidden.

²Recourse to spiritual friends is expressly allowed in only two
cases, according to the *Rule,* namely, for the needs of the sick and for   LR IV 2
clothing the brothers. Our said predecessor kindly and wisely
extended this permission, in view of the vicissitudes of life, to other
needs of the brothers which might be occurring at the moment, or
even impending ones, when there are no alms.[a]

The brothers, however, are to take note that they are allowed for
no other reasons except the above or those of a similar kind, to have
recourse to such friends, either on the road or elsewhere, whether
these friends be the donors of the money or persons representing
them, be the latter known as agents or trustees or any other name,
even if the procedures permitted by the said declaration in regards to
money are entirely observed.

³The said Confessor wished above all that those who profess his
Rule should be completely detached from any love or desire for
earthly things, and in particular that they should be total strangers to
money and its use, as is proved by his constantly repeating the *Rule*
the prohibition of accepting money. Whenever, therefore, the brothers need, for the reasons mentioned above, to have recourse to the
persons who possess money destined for their needs, whether they
be the principal benefactors or their representatives, it is imperative
that the brothers be studiously alert to conduct themselves in every
detail toward these persons in such a way that will show everyone
that they have no right whatsoever to this money—as in fact they
have not.

⁴Therefore, such actions as ordering what amount and for what
purpose the money is to be expended; exacting an account of the
expenditures; asking for a return of the money in any way; putting it
away, or having it be put away; and carrying a money-box or its key,
are unlawful for the brothers. These actions are the sole prerogative
of the owners who gave the money and of those whom they may
have delegated for the purpose.[b]

---

a. Nicholas III, *Exiit*, 6-7. Cf. supra 750-3.

b. This article speaks in terms of the traditional office of "agents" allowed to receive money alms by the
prescriptions of Nicholas III's *Exiit;* significantly enough, it does not address directly the use of
procurators appointed by the brothers, permitted by Martin IV's *Exultantes,* who in practice were
increasingly rendering the office of agent obsolete. Thus Clement V's *Exivi* let this privilege stand.
By using a procurator, however, the brothers could order how money alms were to be spent, contrary
to what is stipulated in this paragraph. However, some abuses that arose through the use of
procurators—e.g., accepting income-producing property—are addressed below.

Article 8: Renunciation of Ownership and Abuses Reported

LR VI 1-2

[1]Then also, when the Saint expressed the manner of the brothers' poverty in the *Rule,* he said: "Let the brothers not make anything their own, neither house, nor place, or anything at all. But as pilgrims and strangers in this world, serving the Lord in poverty and humility, let them go seeking alms in confidence." It has been made clear, too, by certain of our predecessors as Roman pontiffs, that this renunciation of ownership must be understood as holding both in particular and in common.[a] These pontiffs have therefore accepted for themselves and for the Roman Church the proprietary right and ownership of everything granted, offered and donated to the brothers, which the Order or the brothers are permitted to have, leaving them simply the right of use. And yet certain things have been reported for our investigation which were said to go on in the Order and seemed repugnant to the said vow and the pure spirit of the Order.

[2]The following are the practices which we believe are in need of correction:[b]

That the brothers not only permit themselves to be named as heirs, but even bring this about.

That they accept annual revenues, indeed sometimes so high that the convents concerned can live completely on them.

That when their affairs, even of a temporal kind, are debated in the courts, they assist the advocates and procurators; in order to encourage them, they appear in court personally.

That they accept the office of executor of wills and carry it out; that such executors sometimes put themselves forward to profit from settlements involving usury or unjust acquisition and the restitution to be made.

That here and there they have not only extensive gardens but also large vineyards, from which they garner such quantities of vegetables and wine that they can put them up for sale.

---

a. Gregory IX, *Quo elongati* 6 (FA:ED I 573); Innocent IV, *Ordinem* 6 (FA:ED II 777), Nicholas III *Exiit*, 2. Cf. supra 744-6.

b. These abuses are precisely those submitted to the papal commission by Ubertino's condemnatory *rotuli* [scrolls].

That at harvest and vintage time they collect such amounts of grain and wine by begging or buying, storing them in their cellars and granaries, that they can live off them without begging for the rest of the year.

That they build churches and other buildings, or have them built, of such size, style, and costliness that they seem to be the abodes of the wealthy, not of the poor.

That the brothers in very many places also have so many church furnishings and so obviously expensive ones as to surpass in this even great cathedral churches.

That they indiscriminately accept horses and arms offered to them at funerals.

Yet the community of brothers, and in particular the superiors of the Order, have kept maintaining that the above abuses, or most of them, did not exist in the Order and any brothers found guilty in such matters are strictly punished. Moreover, from the early days very stringent laws have been repeatedly enacted to prevent such abuses.

[3]Wishing, therefore, to provide for the consciences of the brothers and to remove, as far as we can, all doubt from their hearts, we give the following replies to the aforesaid points.[a] For a way of life to be authentic, outward actions must correspond to the interior attitude of mind. Therefore, it is imperative that the said brothers, who have severed themselves from temporal possessions by such an exceptional renunciation, must abstain from all that is or may seem to be incompatible with this renunciation.

Article 9: Remedies for Abuses: Inheritances Not Be Accepted

Now, heirs acquire not only the use of their inheritance but, in time, ownership also, but the brothers cannot acquire anything for themselves as individuals or for their Order in common. We therefore declare that the absoluteness of their vow renders the brothers altogether incapable of such inheritance, which of its nature extends both to money and to other moveable and immovable goods. Nor may they allow themselves to be left or accept as a legacy the value of

---

a. In articles 9-17 infra. The language used in them clearly indicates that the papal commission agreed with Ubertino's charge in his *rotuli* [scrolls] that these abuses were in fact taking place.

such inheritance, or a great part of it, so that it could be presumed that this was done by deceit; indeed, we absolutely forbid anything of the kind.

Article 10: Fixed Revenues and Estates Prohibited

Since annual revenues are classed by law as immovable property, and are contrary to poverty and the state of mendicancy, there is no doubt that given their state of life the brothers may not accept or retain fixed revenues of this kind, just as they may not have estates or the right to their use, since such use is not granted to them.

Article 11: Brothers' Involvement in Lawsuits Prohibited

Furthermore, men devoted to perfection in particular must avoid not only what is acknowledged to be evil, but also everything that has the semblance of evil. But as people can judge only by external appearances, seeing the brothers thus present in court and urging their case in a matter that might be turned to their advantage, they will in all likelihood conclude that brothers are there to acquire something as their own.

In no way, therefore, ought the brothers who profess this vow and *Rule,* to meddle in such court proceedings and lawsuits. By keeping out of such things they will *be well thought of by outsiders,* and they will live up to the purity of their vow and avoid scandal to their neighbors.

1 Tm 3:7

Article 12: Execution of Wills Not to Be Accepted

Again, since, as our oft-mentioned predecessor in his clarification of the *Rule* plainly stated,[a] the brothers of the Order are to be complete strangers not only to the acceptance, ownership, proprietorship, or use of money, but even to any handling of it. Also, the members of this Order cannot go to law for any temporal thing. The brothers may therefore not lend themselves to the execution of wills or their management, but rather consider them forbidden by the purity of their state, because these activities cannot be concluded without litigation and the handling or administration of money.

Nevertheless, they do not act in a manner contrary to their state if they give advice in the execution of wills, since this advice does not

---

a. Nicholas III, *Exiit,* 6. Cf. supra 750-2.

confer on them any jurisdiction or legal authority or administration with regard to temporal goods.

Article 13: Gardens Must Not Be for Profit

Certainly, it is not only lawful but very reasonable that the brothers, who are busily engaged in the spiritual labor of prayer and study, should have gardens and yards suitable for recollection and relaxation, and sometimes in order to provide a bodily distraction after their spiritual labors, and also to cultivate vegetables for their needs. To keep gardens, however, in order to cultivate vegetables and other garden produce for sale, and vines likewise, is inconsistent with the purity of their *Rule* and Order. Our said predecessor has declared and also ordained that if, for this use, someone were to leave a field or a vineyard or something of this nature to the brothers, they should absolutely refuse from accepting it,[a] since to have such things in order to receive the income on the produce in season approaches the nature and character of fixed revenue.

Article 14: Stores of Food Not to Be Accumulated

Again, the aforesaid Saint has shown, both by the example of his life and by the words of his *Rule,* that he wished his brothers and sons, relying on divine providence, to cast their cares on God, who feeds the *birds of the air* though *they neither sow, nor reap, nor gather into barns.* It is not likely, then, that he would have wished them to have granaries or wine cellars, since they should rather hope to make their livelihood by begging from day to day.

For that reason the brothers should not lay aside accumulations or stores of such kind out of some trifling fear, but only when it is very probable from experience that they would not otherwise find the necessities of life. We therefore consider that this decision should be left to the consciences of the ministers and custodians, jointly or severally, within their provinces or custodies, acting with the advice and consent of the guardian and two discreet older priests of the local convent.

Mt 6:26

---

a. Nicholas III, *Exiit,* 11. Cf. supra 754-5.

Article 15: Buildings to Be Modest

The Saint wished to establish his brothers in the utmost poverty and humility, both in principle and in practice, as virtually the entire *Rule* proclaims. It is only right, then, that they should in no way build, or allow to be built, churches or edifices of any kind which, in relation to the number of brothers living there, might be considered excessive in quantity or size. We therefore wish that, throughout their Order, the brothers should be satisfied with buildings which are modest and humble, lest outward appearances, which strike the eye, should contradict the poverty they have promised.

Article 16: Restriction on Church Furnishings

While it is true that church vestments and vessels are ordained for the honor of God's name, for which purpose God Himself created all things, yet *He who knows what is secret* looks primarily at the heart of those who serve Him, not at their hands. He does not wish to be served with things that would be out of harmony with the condition and state of life of His ministers. Dn 13:42

The brothers therefore should be content with church vestments and vessels that are respectable in appearance and adequate in size and number. Excess, costliness, or over-elaboration in these or in anything else is not consistent with their profession and state in life. For since such things smack of treasure and affluence detracts, in the eyes of people, from the profession of such great poverty, we therefore wish and command the brothers to observe what we have said.

Article 17: Donations of Horses and Arms Forbidden

As to the donation of horses and arms, we decree that everywhere and in everything the aforesaid declaration concerning money alms is to be observed.

Article 18: Question of the Poor Use of Things

[1]From the above matters, however, there has arisen among the brothers a question which is causing no little scruple, namely, whether by professing their *Rule* the brothers are held to a strict and meager or poor use of things. Some among them believe and assert that, just as in virtue of their vow the brothers observe the most strict renunciation of the ownership of things, they are also enjoined the

utmost restraint and meagerness in their use. Other brothers on the contrary assert that by their profession they are not obliged to any poor use that is not expressed in the *Rule;* they are, however, obliged to a temperate use, in the same way as other Christians and even more fittingly.

[2]Wishing, then, to give peace to the brothers' consciences and to put an end to these disputes, we affirm and declare that by the profession of their *Rule* the Lesser Brothers are especially obliged to the strict or poor uses contained in that *Rule,* and bound in the measure in which the *Rule* specifies or sets down these matters. To say, however, as some are reported to assert, that it is heretical to maintain that a poor use of things is or is not included in the vow of evangelical poverty, this we judge to be rash and presumptuous.[a]

Article 19: Election and Confirmation of the Provincial Ministers

[1]Finally, when the *Rule* states by whom and where the general minister should be elected, it makes no mention at all of the election or appointment of provincial ministers. There can arise some uncertainty among the brothers on this point. We wish them to be able to proceed with clarity and assurance in all they do.

We therefore declare, decree, and ordain in this Constitution of perpetual validity, that, when a province is to be provided with a minister, his election belongs to the provincial chapter. It shall hold the election the day after assembling. The power to confirm the said election, however, pertains to the general minister.

[2]Now, if this election is made by ballot, and the votes are divided in such a way that several ballots are made without agreement, then the choice made by the numerical majority of the chapter, without regard for consideration of merit or partisanship, notwithstanding objections of any kind from the other side, is to be confirmed or invalidated by the general minister. Having first given consideration to the matter, in accordance with his office, he shall first take counsel with discreet members of the Order, so that a decision is made which is pleasing to God. If the general minister invalidates the election, the provincial chapter shall vote again. Furthermore, if the provincial chapter fails to elect a minister on the day assigned, the minister general shall freely provide a provincial minister.

[3]There are, however, certain provinces—that of Outremer, Ireland, and Greece or Romania—which are said to have had until now,

---

a. Both sides in the dispute had accused the other of heresy because of their position on the "poor use."

for just reasons, another way of providing the provincial minister.[a] In these cases, if the general minister and the general chapter judge, with good reason, that the provincial minister should be appointed by the general minister with the advice of good religious of the Order, rather than by election of the provincial chapter, this should be done without dispute for the provinces of Outremer, Ireland, and Greece or Romania, when the previous provincial minister dies or is relieved of office on the other side of the sea; there should be no deceit, partiality, or fraud, the burden resting on the consciences of those who decide the appointment.

[4]As for deposing provincial ministers, we wish to retain the procedure that has been customary up to now.

[5]Finally, if the brothers are without a general minister, the vicar of the Order shall carry out his duties until provision has been made to elect a new general minister. Further, if there be any attempted violation of this decree concerning the provincial minister, such action shall be automatically null and void.

Article 20: Conclusion

It is forbidden, therefore, for anyone whomsoever to infringe upon what we have declared, endorsed, charged, responded, prohibited, ordained, commanded, enacted, or set down as our verdict and will, or rashly dare to oppose it. If anyone presume to attempt this, let him know that he shall incur the anger of almighty God and of his holy Apostles Peter and Paul.

Given at Vienne, on the sixth day of May, in the seventh year of our Pontificate (1312).

Constitution *Ad Conditorem* of Pope John XXII (1322)

Clement V used all his power to get the Lesser Brothers to accept the compromise between the Community and the Spirituals that he had worked out in *Exivi*, and the general ministers, both Gonsalvo of Valboa and Alexander of Alessandria, who succeeded him in 1313, cooperated with his plan. However,

---

a. These three provinces presented special problems. The first and the last named were largely missionary provinces, composed of brothers of various nationalities. The province of Syria or, as here, *ultramarina* [Outremer, "the land overseas"] was one of the original ten formed in 1217, cf. ChrJG, 9. At this time, with the loss of the Crusader States, it was confined to the island of Cyprus. The province of Greece or Romania consisted of territories in Greece and the Aegean which were under Latin rulers. In Ireland, the right of the brothers to elect their own minister had been taken away due to ethnic tensions between the Celtic and English members of the province; in 1291 fighting had broken out at the chapter in which a number of brothers were killed.

in 1314 both Clement and Alexander died, and it was two years before either of them was replaced. In the interim, extremists on both sides ruined the compromise: provincials and guardians returned to the practice of harassing the Spirituals, who in turn broke out in open rebellion. The new Pope, an elderly no-nonsense canonist, John XXII, moved quickly to bring order to the situation.[a] He sided with the new general minister, Michael of Cesena, to bring the disobedient Spirituals to heel: in *Quorundam exegit* (October 1317) he demanded their obedience to legitimate superiors, and in *Santa Romana* (December, 1317) he excommunicated and ordered the suppression of dissident Franciscan groups.

However, as the years went by John began to look more closely at the whole claim of absolute poverty by the Franciscan Order. Perhaps influenced by the Papal commission which was examining Peter of John Olivi's *Apocalypse Commentary*,[b] John gradually came to feel that this doctrine, enshrined in *Exiit*, underlay the Spiritual revolt, and would be a perennial source for any other perfectionist group claiming true conformity to Christ over against the institutional church. In March 1322, John issued his decree *Quia nonnumquam*, which lifted the ban imposed by *Exiit* on any further discussion of the poverty of Christ.[c] As the Lesser Brothers believed that *Exiit* had settled this issue once and for all, they were profoundly disturbed by this threat at their very self-identity. When the general chapter met at Perugia two months later, the brothers challenged John's right to change a binding decree of his predecessor and sent out two letters to the whole Christian world defending their position. This only served only to inflame Pope John. He reacted in the strongest way possible in December 1322 by issuing this bull, cutting the ground from under the Franciscan position by reversing eighty years of Papal policy and renouncing Papal dominion over the Order's goods. The style of the bull indicates that it was written personally by the Pope himself; it lacks the florid Latin style of typical Curial documents, but speaks directly in simple and blunt terms to the issue.[d]

> John, Bishop, Servant of the servants of God, for an everlasting record.
>
> [1]There is no doubt that it pertains to the legislator, when he sees statutes issued by himself or his predecessors doing harm rather than being of benefit, to take measures that they have no power to do any more harm. Some time ago our predecessor of happy memory, Pope Nicholas III, was attentively making provision for that passage

---

a. Cf. Moorman, *History*, 307-319; Lambert, *Poverty*, 215-269; Nimmo, *Reform*, 176-201.

b. Cf. infra 812-7.

c. Nicholas III, *Exiit*, 23. Cf. supra 762-3.

d. Actually, there are two versions of the papal document. When Bonagratia of Bergamo, the general procurator of the Order, composed a vigorous appeal against *Ad conditorem*, the Pope re-issued the decree in a much longer version, refraining from some of the more pointed remarks of the first, and strengthening his legal arguments. We have given here the first, shorter version. Text is found in BFr 5:235 b-237 a.

in the *Rule* of the loving confessor of Christ, blessed Francis, which says that the members of his Order "should not make anything their own, neither house, nor place, nor anything at all," and diligently considered that his predecessors of pious memory, Gregory IX and several other Roman pontiffs, had declared that this precept should be observed both individually and in common. He likewise had his attention fixed on the fact that a number of people were slandering the said brothers, making accusations that they could not keep their *Rule* and these declarations in such a way. He devoutly wished to put a stop to this railing against the said brothers, and also to provide for the consciences of those professing the *Rule*. Thus, among other things, he ordained and sanctioned that the property and ownership of all the utensils, books, and other mobile goods both present and future, and of all the churches, oratories, and cemeteries, both present and future, and of all the things bought by various alms, or offered or granted to the said brothers—provided that those making such an offering or cession did not reserve anything thereof to themselves—fully and freely belonged to him and to the Roman Church. He accepted all these things for himself and the said Church, with only the use of fact being reserved to the said brothers in regards to these items and goods.[a]

[2]And because it was sometimes advantageous that such books be sold or exchanged, in the same declaration he granted that with the permission of their general or provincial ministers, they could freely exchange such things for other items which the brothers may use.[b]

[3]And because the same *Rule* strictly forbids the brothers themselves to receive money either personally or through an intermediary, he wished and conceded that if the aforesaid mobile goods should be sold for a certain price, that this profit should be received by a procurator deputized by the same Apostolic See or by the Cardinal protector of the same Order, with the purpose of having it spent by the same procurator for some other thing which is lawful for the brothers to use.[c] Concerning movable goods of low price and value, he added that it was permissible for the brothers to make presents thereof to other persons, both within and without the Order, for the sake of piety or devotion or any other proper and reasonable purpose, after previously obtaining the permission of their superiors.[d]

a. Nicholas III, *Exiit*, 3. Cf. supra 746-8.

b. Nicholas III, *Exiit*, 12.1. Cf. supra 755-6.

c. Nicholas III, *Exiit*, 12.2. Cf. supra 756.

d. Nicholas III, *Exiit*, 13. Cf. supra 756.

LR VI 1

⁴However, although our aforesaid predecessor ordered the above arrangements very conscientiously, we do not perceive that they have profited the same brothers, but have only harmed them and others in a number of ways. Now the perfection of the Christian life consists principally and essentially in charity, which the Apostle calls *the bond of perfection,* for it unites or connects human beings in some way to their final end. The path to it is prepared by the contempt of temporal goods and their renunciation, particularly in order that the anxious care caused by acquiring, maintaining, and administering material goods and which thus militates against the act of charity, is thereby removed.ᵃ It follows, then, that if the same anxious care were to remain in people after having made such a renunciation [of material goods], as was in them before, such a renunciation would be of no value for [achieving] perfection.ᵇ Now it is certain that ever since the Holy See retained ownership of their goods, the brothers of the aforesaid Order have been no less solicitous, in court and out of court, in acquiring and keeping goods than are other mendicant religious, who hold some things in common. That greatest of teachers, experience, has made this fact evident to anyone who considers the situation correctly.

⁴That the Holy See's retention of ownership has been an obstacle for these brothers is obvious from the following examples. Its acceptance of the ownership of their goods has provided an occasion for these brothers to vainly boast of their "highest poverty," rashly claiming that they were superior to all the other mendicant orders because they alone had no ownership or dominion, but simply the "bare use" of things.ᶜ Indeed, if they wished to heed reality as well as words and come to rest in the truth, as they should, and considered the way they are using things and the forbearance of the Roman Church toward this, they would have to claim the opposite: that they have much more than the use of things and that it is the ownership of the Roman Church which is really "bare." Would a lender say that someone was "simply using" his possession if that "user" was allowed to exchange it, or sell it, or give it away? Undoubtedly, he

Col 3:14

a. This is the "instrumentalist" view of poverty taught by Thomas Aquinas, *Summa theologiae*, II.II., q. 188, a. 7. Poverty is not a value in its own right, it is simply a means to the end of achieving charity, and as such the "highest poverty" is the one most appropriate to that end.

b. In this instance John is replying to the encyclical letter "to all the faithful" issued by the general chapter of Perugia the preceding June, challenging his bull *Quia nonumquam,* cf. Introduction supra. The letter had defined the highest and most perfect poverty as that which excludes the greater *sollicitudo,* or anxious care, about temporal goods. Even the holding of goods in common, in its view, ensnared the spirits of those who possessed them. Cf. Lambert, *Franciscan Poverty,* 246-9.

c. This discussion is based on the distinctions made by Nicholas III's *Exiit,* 3, which is based on Bonaventure's *Apologia Pauperum.*

would recognize that this goes beyond the nature of "use," and that such activity is not proper to a "user" at all, but to the one who owns it. So when these brothers themselves make such dispositions about so many mobile goods, claiming that this was conceded to them by this ordinance, such examples clearly argue that such a use is hardly "bare."

[5]They are also not "bare users" of things that are consumable by use, for to say that there could be either a use of law or a use of fact without the rights of dominion over such goods is repugnant to law and to reason.[a] Nor does it seem to have been the intention of our predecessor to reserve the ownership of such things to the Roman Church. For what person in his right mind could believe that it was the intention of so great a father to acquire for the Roman Church the ownership of one egg, one bean, or one loaf of bread, or even a crust of bread, which are often given to the brothers? Or if this was his intention, who could defend this claim as a real form of ownership, when it is simply an empty phrase? Rather, should he not denounce something that is not real but a fiction?

[6]For the kind of use that one has in relation to such things can in no way be said to be a "bare use," because the use of a thing that is consumed by the user is no different from the use by a person who owns it. For it is obvious that this kind of use totally consumes the thing, and therefore it is certain that a use that has such complete control over something cannot be called a "bare use." From such cases it seems to follow that they should not be maintaining that they have only a "bare use" of things. Rather, it is the "ownership" of the Roman Church that appears to be bare, verbal, and mathematical, for no gain has so far resulted from it for that Church, nor is it hoped that any gain might occur in the future. For it is neither the intention of the Church who reserves the ownership of these goods nor of the brothers themselves that the benefit of having these goods should accrue to anyone else but these brothers. It is obvious that such "ownership" neither makes the person who has it richer, nor the person who lacks it poorer. So it is quite apparent that it is an empty boast for these brothers to claim that they have the "highest poverty" of all the mendicant orders [because they do not own their belongings].

[7]Moreover, the aforesaid retention of ownership by the Apostolic See has been the cause of recurring dangerous divisions among the brothers of the same Order, and weighty perils which have followed

---

a. Here the Pope takes up an old argument used against the brothers by Gérard of Abbeville, to which Bonaventure attempted to respond in his *Apologia* XI:7-8 (VIII 312-3) *Defense*, 242-244.

in their wake. It has not been possible to put an end to these up to now, nor is it hopeful that this will happen as long as this procedure continues.

[8]Furthermore, the said reservation is not only harmful to the brothers themselves, but it even detracts and has detracted from the honor of the said Roman Church in a not insignificant way. For how is the honor of the said Church not impugned, when its representatives[a] have to go into one court after another, both ecclesiastical and secular, even before some petty judges to argue over some cheap, insignificant matter? Because under the aforesaid ordinance the ownership of everything that is given, offered, or otherwise acquired by the said brothers is reserved to the Roman Church—unless the donors or those offering reserve ownership for themselves—we see that the procurators set up by the ministers of the said Order in the name of the same church are continually occupied, acting on behalf of or defending everything that belongs to the said Order. What is even more serious a consideration, the brothers are said to improperly bother many of these procurators, harassing them constantly to fight for their rights. All such things are recognized as redounding to the ill fame and injury of the same Roman Church.

[9]Finally, the aforesaid ordinance has been shown to be extremely troublesome for the prelates and rectors of churches . . .[b]

[10]Since we have taken all of these factors into the scrutiny of correct consideration, aroused by the complaints of many persons, and wishing to avoid such evils and to provide for the consciences and the state of life of the said brothers, the honor of the same Roman Church, and the relief of the prelates and rectors of churches, we, in accord with the counsel of our brothers, judge that it is better for the holy Roman Church to be without this ownership, which is so useless and pernicious, than to have it. We therefore issue this edict to be valid forever, that the Apostolic See from now on will possess in law no more ownership over or on behalf of the goods which in the future will be conferred, offered, or in any other way come into the possession of the aforesaid brothers or Order than it does over and on behalf of the goods of any other mendicant order. And we further decree that in the future no procurator may be appointed to receive, request, demand, defend, or administer such goods in the name of the Supreme Pontiff or of the same Roman Church, except by our special license and mandate. And we revoke whatever may have been

---

a. The brothers' procurators.

b. At this point, the pope embarks on a litany of complaints from the secular clergy. It is omitted here as it adds little to the discussion of poverty.

established by anyone, judging it harmful and void, any privileges which may have been conceded by our predecessor of happy memory, Martin IV, or any other of our predecessors to the said brothers or the Order under any form whatsoever notwithstanding.

[11]Through this declaration, however, we do not intend to diminish in any way either the *Rule* of the same Order or the privileges conceded to either the brothers themselves or to their Order by the Apostolic See, unless they touch on the foregoing matters; rather, we wish them to remain in full force.

Given at Avignon, on the eighth day of December, in the seventh year of our pontificate (1322).

Constitution *Cum Inter Nonnullos* of Pope John XXII (1323)

John continued to receive challenges to his position even after issuing *Ad conditorem*. In April 1323, John canonized Thomas Aquinas, whose instrumental view of the nature of poverty John had adopted in his decree. In December, John determined to settle the underlying theological issue of the poverty of Christ with this bull.[a] As John H.R. Moorman maintains: *"Ad conditorem* had turned the brothers into possessors; now *Cum inter nonnullos* threatened to turn them into heretics."[b] The Order was dazed. The struggle between at least a good number of the brothers and John would continue for the rest of his pontificate, but it was clear that, at least officially, Francis would no longer serve as a prophet for a poor church.

John, Bishop, Servant of the servants of God, for an everlasting record.

[1]Since it is the case that among various men of learning it is often doubted whether the persistent assertion—that our Redeemer and Lord Jesus Christ and his apostles did not have anything, either individually or in common[c]—should be deemed heretical, as various people hold different and often contradictory opinions in the matter; we, wishing to put an end to this dispute, in accord with the counsel of our brothers, declare by this everlasting edict that a persistent assertion of this kind shall henceforth be deemed erroneous and heretical, since it expressly contradicts Sacred Scripture, which in a number of places asserts that they did have some things, and openly supposes that the Holy Scripture itself, from which undoubtedly the articles of the orthodox faith draw their authority, contains the seeds of falsehood with regard to the above-mentioned, and in

---

a. Text in BFr 5:256-259, no. 518. We have largely followed the translation of Lambert, *Poverty,* 258-259.

b. Moorman, *History,* 317.

c. A view expressed by a Provençal Beguine brought before the Inquisition in 1321.

consequence, by destroying its authority completely (as far as it can), makes the Catholic faith doubtful and uncertain by removing its basis.

[2]Again, to make a pertinacious assertion that our aforesaid Redeemer and his apostles in no way had the right of using those things which Holy Scripture testifies they had, or that they had no right of selling, giving, or exchanging them[a] (although Holy Scripture does testify that they did do this concerning the aforesaid things or it expressly supposes that they could have done so), since this assertion plainly defines the use and actions of Christ and the apostles in the case of the aforesaid things as unjust (which undoubtedly concerning the use, words, and actions of our Lord the Redeemer, the Son of God, is impious, contrary to the Holy Scripture, and inimical to the catholic faith): we declare, in accordance with the counsel of our brothers, that this same pertinacious assertion shall henceforth rightly be deemed erroneous and heretical.

It is forbidden, therefore, for anyone to tamper with this decree which we have confirmed, or rashly dare to oppose it. If anyone presume to attempt this, let him know that he shall incur the anger of almighty God and of his blessed apostles Peter and Paul.

Given at Avignon, the twelfth of November, in the year of our Lord 1323, and in the eighth year of our pontificate.

---

a. This view was at least implicitly stated in the encyclical letter of the brothers from the chapter of Perugia in 1322.

Miscellaneous Franciscan Sources

Thomas of Pavia (c. 1272-80)

Thomas, generally known to history as *Tuscus* ("the Tuscan") because of his many years of service as provincial minister there, was actually a native of Lombardy, being born in the city of Pavia around the year 1212.[a] As a youth he went to study at the University of Padua, where he entered the Lesser Brothers about 1229. Thomas went on to enjoy a lengthy and many-faceted career in the Order as teacher, writer, and administrator. He was appointed lector of theology in Parma around 1240. "A learned man . . . who was very facile in writing,"[b] Thomas's works were well known in his lifetime. After the chapter of 1244, the general minister, Crescentius of Iesi, commissioned him to compose a collection of small biographies, in which the "deeds" of various early "holy brothers" could be preserved for posterity.[c] Among his other works, the most famous was a massive theological encyclopedia, popularly called "The Ox" because of its size.[d] He remained active in education until he was elected provincial minister of Tuscany in 1258, serving with distinction in that capacity until 1270. For some time he was in the service of Charles I of Anjou, the papally-sponsored King of Naples.

It was during his later years that he worked on a lengthy chronicle, *The Deeds of the Emperors and the Popes*,[e] from which the following selection is taken. Thomas's work is a *florilegium*, a selection of instructive events excerpted from encyclopedic works of history and hagiography. Its nineteenth-century editor, impressed by the contemporary ideal of "objective" historiography, dismissed it as the sloppy and uncritical work of a credulous brother. Such a verdict does not do justice to the reason why Thomas wrote his chronicle. Like other works of its type, it was not meant simply as a book of "facts," but to entertain its readers and provide suitable moral anecdotes for preaching as

---

a. See Pierre Péano, "Thomas de Pavie," *Dictionnaire de Spiritualité Ascetique e Mystique* XV (Paris: Beauchenes, 1991), 867-868.

b. From Salimbene's lengthy and laudatory description of Thomas. Cf. *The Chronicle of Salimbene de Adam*, trans. Joseph L. Baird, Giuseppe Baglivi, John Robert Kane (Binghamton, NY: Medieval & Renaissance Texts and Studies, 1986), 434-5.

c. *Dialogus de Gestis Sanctorum Fratrum Minorum Auctore Thomas de Papia*, ed. F. Delorme, Bibliotheca Franciscana Ascetica Medii Aevi, vol. 5 (Ad Claras Aquas, Quaracchi, Collegium S. Bonaventure, 1923). There are some doubts, however, concerning Thomas's authorship of the *Dialogus*. He is also sometimes credited with composing the first biography of Anthony, the *Legenda Assidua;* since Thomas knew Anthony, being present at his burial in 1231, this is possible, although Thomas would have been very young at the time.

d. *Dictionarium Bovis;* it remains unedited.

e. *Gesta Imperatorum et Pontificium*, partially edited by E. Ehrenfeuchter, *Monumenta Germaniae Historica, Scriptores* 22 (Hanover: Hahn, 1872), 483-528.

well.[a] The following selection mentioning Saint Francis is noteworthy for attesting to the great friendship between him and Brother Pacifico, and the latter's testimony of the stigmata. Thomas died in the early 1280's.[b]

[1]As I saw with my own eyes, Brother Pacifico, a man of such remarkable holiness that he was called "sweet mother" by blessed Francis,[c] used to have a little [writing] board. He had fashioned it out of a piece of wood from a walnut tree he found growing beside the altar of a ruined church. As soon as he had hacked out the piece of wood, the image of a crucifix appeared on it—not in relief, but smooth, as if it were painted on. But this was not the work of the corruptible hand of an artist; it was something naturally impressed on that board by the hand of divine wisdom. And so this brother always used to carry this tablet with him out of reverence for the Crucified Christ, along with a few relics of saints.

[2]This is the same Pacifico who merited seeing those sacred stigmata, which are worthy of the admiration of the whole world, on the body of that most blessed man, Francis, while he was still living in the flesh. This is the same Pacifico who, by means of a pious deception but with the greatest devotion, touched the wound that was in Francis's side. And this is the same Pacifico who, while he was still caught up in the vanity [of the world], saw two swords connected in the form of a cross issuing from the mouth of the most holy father while he was preaching. Terrified by this miracle, he was converted and became one of the outstanding imitators of Saint Francis. It is no coincidence, then, that this man, who was such an ardent lover of the cross, should have discovered a cross which nature had fashioned on a piece of wood.

2C 137

LMj IV 9

Thomas is also the source of more anecdotes about Francis, which do not occur in his own works, but are recalled by an anonymous Tuscan brother who gathered together a large number of early stories.[d] This account, which probably dates to sometime in the later thirteenth or early fourteenth cen-

---

a. See the analysis of this work by Bert Roest, *Reading the Book of History: Intellectual Contexts and Educational Functions of Franciscan Historiography 1226—ca. 1350* (Groningen: Regenboog, 1996), 44, 229-233.

b. Salimbene, writing between 1283-88, speaks of him as deceased. Cf. Salimbene, *Chronicle*, 434-5.

c. This is the opposite of an account in 2C 137 (FA:ED II 336), where it is Pacifico who calls Francis "mother."

d. This account is contained in an important manuscript in the library of the College of San Antonio in Rome that contains many early Franciscan sources. It was thoroughly described and partially edited by Livarius Oliger, "Descriptio codicis Santi Antonii de urbe unacum appendice textuum de Sancto Francisco," AFH 12 (1919): 321-401. The manuscript contains three distinct sections. This selection is from the third section, which was redacted in the region of Arezzo toward the middle of the fourteenth century, pp. 354-357. The text is on pp. 382-384, n. 59.

tury,[a] offers a number of lively details, especially concerning Francis's relation to women's monasteries, not transmitted in other sources.

[1]Brother Thomas of Pavia, provincial minister of Tuscany, said that a certain brother, Stephen by name,[b] a man of such simplicity and purity of heart that one could hardly imagine his saying anything untrue, told him several things which I have written down here.

In the early days of the Order, this Brother Stephen said, when Saint Francis received those coming to live in the Order, it was his custom to clothe them with the habit and cord and then entrust them to some monastery or church, because the brothers as yet had no place of their own to live.[c] He would command such brothers to devotedly serve God and the church in which he had placed them, performing the tasks assigned to them, so as not to eat the bread of idleness.

And so it happened that he received this Brother Stephen into the Order and assigned him with a companion to some monastery. Two years later Saint Francis returned to the monastery to learn about the said brother. He wanted to know if he had remained there, and made a diligent investigation among the monks about his behavior with them. And since everyone there gave such laudatory testimony about that brother's life, Francis took him along with him, and for many years he was his special companion.

[2]One day just the two of them arrived at the home of a noble lady, and with great devotion she offered the blessed Francis some cloth, colored in such a manner that it was good enough to make a priest's chasuble. Accepting it, he went to a monastery to seek hospitality from the monks. While the blessed Francis was enjoying some friendly conversation there with the abbot, a certain lay brother, who had been bedridden for a long time with some illness, began to howl and moan horribly, cursing everyone who lived in the monastery because hardly any of them came to see him while he was enduring such suffering. Blessed Francis, taking along his companion,

---

a. The stories themselves are of an earlier date than the redaction, as Thomas died around the year 1280. It seems likely that he would have related them during his years as minister in Tuscany (1258-70).

b. This Brother Stephen is very probably the lay brother who left Italy for Syria in 1220, without the permission of the superiors, to inform Francis about the changes being made in the Order during his absence (ChrJG 12-3). The name of this brother is given only in an addition to Jordan's *Chronicle* by the Polish historian, John of Komerow, cf. *Chronica fratris Jordani*, ed. H. Boehmer, (Paris: Libraire Fischbacher, 1908), 77.

c. This information, related in no other early source, is of significant importance in understanding the very early years of the brotherhood.

hastened to his side and exhorted him to be patient, praising the providence of God which can turn bad things into blessings. His words calmed the sick man, and he admonished him to recognize his fault, while showing him affection and compassion. And because he saw the poor fellow lying there almost naked, barely modest, he said to Brother Stephen: "Bring me that cloth which the lady gave us. We can always find some cloth for outer tunics, so we really don't need this. Instead, I should clothe this naked man with it, as Christ commanded." "And so I brought the cloth," Brother Stephen said,[a] "and Francis cut and made a habit out of it. And before he left that monastery, he went to see that sick man and clothed him in it."

[3]Brother Stephen also used to say that blessed Francis did not want to be on familiar terms with any woman and he did not permit any woman to become familiar with him; only with the blessed Clare did he seem to show affection. And anytime he spoke with her or spoke about her, he did not refer to her by name, but he called her "the Christian." And he showed great concern for her and her monastery.

[4]Also, he never authorized the establishment of other [women's] monasteries, although some were opened during his lifetime through the involvement of others.[b] When it came to his attention that the women who lived together in these monasteries were called sisters, he was greatly disturbed and it is said that he exclaimed: "The Lord has taken away our wives, but now the devil is providing us with sisters."

Cardinal Hugolino, Bishop of Ostia, who was then the protector of the Order of Minors, looked after these sisters with great affection. One time, when he was taking leave of blessed Francis, he said to him: "I am entrusting these ladies to you." Francis replied with a smile: "Well, Holy Father, from now let them not be called 'Lesser Sisters,'[c] but as you have just said, 'Ladies.' " And from then on they were called Ladies and not Sisters.

---

a. At this point, the narrative changes to direct discourse.

b. As is clear from what follows, "others" refer especially to Cardinal Hugolino. This perspective is given only in this source. It seems to corroborate recent studies that limit Clare's work—and Francis's involvement—to San Damiano and a few other houses that followed his form of life. These studies suggest that most of the other eventual monasteries of the "Order of San Damiano" were actually part of an independent "Order of Poor Cloistered Ladies" founded by Hugolino in 1219. Although he tried unsuccessfully to get the Lesser Brothers, under Philip the Long, to take responsibility for these houses, it was only after Francis's death and his own election as Pope in 1227 that Hugolino was able to accomplish his goal. It was then that he convinced Clare and her Sisters to accept his *Rule* and, through this connection, he entrusted the whole Order to the care of the brothers. Cf. Maria Pia Alberzoni, "San Damiano in 1228: A Contribution to the 'Clare Question,' " GR 13 (1999): 105-123.

c. This corroborates the 1216 letter of Jacques de Vitry which refers to the "Lesser Sisters," cf. FA:ED I 579.

Not long afterwards, Brother Ambrose of the Cistercian Order died. He was a [papal] penitentiary to whom Cardinal Ugolino had entrusted the above-mentioned monasteries, with the exception of the monastery of Saint Clare.[a] Then Brother Philip the Tall saw to it that these monasteries were entrusted to him and that he was granted authorization by the Supreme Pontiff to appoint Lesser Brothers for their service as he saw fit.[b] When the blessed Francis learned of this, he was very upset and cursed Philip as a destroyer of his Order. Indeed, Brother Stephen said that he had heard Saint Francis pronounce these words: "Until now the ulcer has been confined to the flesh and so there remained a hope for a cure; but now it has penetrated to the bone and it will surely be incurable."

One time Brother Stephen went to one of these monasteries of Cloistered Ladies by order of the said Brother Philip. A while later, when he was on a journey with blessed Francis from Bevagna to some other town, he asked his forgiveness for having gone to serve that monastery at Brother Philip's beckoning. Then the saint scolded him harshly and commanded him, as a penance, to plunge fully clothed into the river that ran along the side of the road. Now this was during the month of December. And so, soaking wet and shivering with cold, he accompanied the blessed Francis for two good miles until they reached the brothers' place.

[5]Another time Brother Stephen said that he was staying in a hermitage for a few months with Blessed Francis and some other brothers. While he was there, he did the cooking and took care of the kitchen.[c] By Francis's orders the others devoted themselves to silence and prayer until Brother Stephen gave the signal for dinner by banging on a pan.[d] Now it was Saint Francis's custom to come out of his cell at the hour of terce. If he didn't see the fire lit yet in the kitchen, he would pick some greens with his own hands, saying quietly to Brother Stephen, "Go now, and cook up these greens, and it will go well with the brothers." Now many times, if he had also cooked some eggs or cheese that had been offered to the brothers, Blessed Francis would be totally happy, eating with the others and

---

a. Another indication that San Damiano was not yet under Hugolino's Form of Life, cf. *Clare of Assisi: Early Documents*, 2nd ed., trans. and ed. Regis J. Armstrong (St. Bonaventure, NY: Franciscan Institute Publications, 1992), 89-102.

b. This was during Francis's absence in the East in 1219-20. This sentence seems to confirm the identity of this Brother Stephen with the brother who traveled to Syria, as this is precisely one of the things that he reported to Francis, cf. ChrJG 12.

c. It appears that Stephen served as one of the "mothers" mentioned by Francis in RH. These brothers took the role of "Martha," providing the material needs of the community so the others would be free for contemplation. Cf. FA:ED I 61-2.

d. The word is *tegula;* in Latin it means a roof-tile, but it seems more likely in the context that Thomas was using the emerging Italian *teglia,* a pan.

praising the skill of his cook. But other times, with a frown on his face, he would say: "You made too much today, Brother. Tomorrow I don't want you to cook anything." And since Brother Stephen was a little afraid of Saint Francis, he carried out his wishes. When he did so, the next day Francis would see the table with only a few motley pieces of bread and would sit down with the other brothers delighted. But now and then he would say: "Brother Stephen, why haven't you made us anything to eat"? And he would respond: "Because that's what you ordered me to do." And then Saint Francis would answer: "Discretion is a good thing, for we shouldn't always do what the superior says!"

Brother Thomas claimed that he heard Brother Stephen tell him these things. May Christ be praised!

A Book of Exemplary Stories (c. 1280-1310)

In the later thirteenth century a number of brothers attempted to put together collections of edifying stories about their brothers. These loosely organized works, providing instructive models of Franciscan life, seem to have been intended primarily for communal and private reading in the convent. However, they also served another purpose, for they provided a handy source for *exampla,* the illustrative anecdotes that preachers employed in their sermons. Franciscan preachers especially favored such popular stories, and they had the natural tendency to substitute traditional materials with new legends and anecdotes connected with holy men of their own Order.[a]

One such collection was assembled by some anonymous Italian brothers at the end of the thirteenth or early fourteenth century; its modern editor called it *A Book of Exemplary Stories about Thirteenth Century Lesser Brothers.*[b] There is no real order to the collection; most of the stories seem to have originated in either Paris or Assisi, the two locations in the thirteenth century where there was a constant coming and going of a large number of Lesser Brothers from all over Europe. Some of the stories in this collection also occur in the treatise of Thomas of Eccleston and the later *Chronicle of the Twenty-Four Generals.* Most of these *exempla* seem to go back to the period 1260-1280, so it would appear there was some initial attempt to assemble them during the generalate of Saint Bonaventure. The latest dateable reference is during the pontificate of Gregory XI (1271-6). Francis is the subject of twenty of the 146 stories in the collection. Some of these occur almost verbatim in Thomas of Celano's *The Remembrance of the Desire of a Soul,* so we include here only those that offer different perspectives on Francis.[c]

---

a. See Roest, *Reading,* 218-221.
b. "Liber exemplorum Fratrum Minorum Saeculi XII," ed. Livarius Oliger, *Antonianum* 2 (1927): 203-276.
c. Francis is the subject of *exempla* 3, 17, 20, 21, 24, 31, 46, 50, 67-70, 98, 99, 110, 116, 123-23, and 134.

[50]Saint Francis was animated by a burning desire to offer God a worship that would be pleasing to Him. One night, being unable to fall asleep because of the intensity of this preoccupation and his prayer, he begged God insistently to reveal some signs through which he could tell if his life were pleasing to God. Finally, after many such devout supplications, he heard the voice of Christ the Lord saying to him: "Francis!" Recognizing this voice and knowing that it was the Lord, Francis was filled with joy. And the voice continued, "You want to know [what you should do]. Behold, you will know that you can be and are pleasing to Me by these indications. When you are thinking and saying and doing what is just, then know that you are enjoying My good favor. Are you content with these signs?"

Francis responded: "O good Lord, I want to be content with these and I accept this response with immense gratitude."

Then Saint Francis called Brother Leo, a holy man whom he had chosen to be his guardian and his confessor, and told him: "I command that any time you see me failing to do these three just things, you should correct me." But Brother Leo answered: "Father, from this moment I will do what you wish in regards to your words and your actions, but I cannot correct your thoughts!" And Francis responded: "You don't have to worry about my thoughts, my son. Leave that between God and me. I hope that I will put them in order before Him. But in regard to the other things, by no means fail to do what I ask." And what I am telling you, I heard from the companions of Saint Francis.[a]

[70]Brother Peter recounts this incident which Brother Leo, the companion of Saint Francis, had told him. "When I was newly ordained," he said, "I was accustomed to spend a long time celebrating Mass. I used to experience divine consolations, and so I wanted to dwell on them. One day Saint Francis called me, and speaking to me affectionately, said: 'Brother Leo, my son, do what I say. Celebrate your Mass with devotion, but without pausing too much while you are celebrating; rather, conform yourself to the other priests. If the Lord should give you some grace, wait until Mass is finished and go into your cell; there you can meditate and enjoy the divine consolations, if these are given you from heaven. I think that this way of acting is better and more secure. Indeed, because of those assisting at Mass, some temptation of vainglory or something else inordinate

---

a. *Liber exemplorum*, n. 50, p. 231. This incident is also in 2C 159, cf. FA:ED II 350, but this text has several important differences.

might overcome you, and then the devil will rapidly snatch away any merit of such apparent devotion. But in your cell, where no one can see you, you can more securely abandon yourself to prayer, and the devil cannot easily find an occasion to tempt you. In addition, it can happen that some of those assisting at such a drawn-out Mass might be led to make some negative judgment about you, perhaps thinking that a priest who celebrates with such outward devotion does so in order to show off or to wear out the congregation.' "[a]

[71]And Brother John, a companion of Brother Leo, who in his turn was the companion of Saint Francis, tells the following story. Brother Leo used to have an old winter tunic made out of sackcloth, which he had worn for more than four years. So I said to him one day: "Brother Leo, let me get a better tunic for you. That one isn't going to do you much good, if any, keeping out the cold!" But he answered me: "I know that I am getting weaker, and I think it may please God to soon bring an end to my labors. And so I don't want another tunic now. I want death to find me a poor man." And within that very year he died, a little poor man, wearing that same old tunic. And I believe that devout and "poor, he entered heaven a rich man."[b]

[98]The General Minister [Bonaventure] said to us that Brother Illuminato,[c] who was the companion of Saint Francis when he went to visit the Sultan of Babylon, used to recount the following anecdotes.[d]

While Francis was at the Sultan's court, the latter wanted to test the faith and devotion that Francis showed to our Crucified Lord. So one day he had a beautiful multicolored carpet laid out in his audience hall; it was almost entirely decorated with a geometric pattern of crosses. He said to his attendants: "Now fetch this man who seems to be an authentic Christian. If he comes toward me, he will have to tread on the crosses that cover this carpet, so then I will accuse him of insulting his Lord. But if he is unwilling to come toward me, I will ask him why he is insulting me by refusing to approach me."

So Francis was called in. Now he was filled with [the Spirit of] God, and from this plenitude he was well instructed on what he should do and say, so he walked across the carpet to greet the Sultan. Then the Sultan, thinking he had good reason to berate the man of God for showing disrespect for his Lord, Jesus Christ, said to him: "You Christians adore the cross as a special sign of your God. Why

a. *Liber exemplorum*, n. 70, 239-240.
b. Ibid., n. 71, 240.
c. Cf. FA:ED II 633 b.
d. *Liber exemplorum*, nn. 98-99, 250-51.

then do you have the audacity to tread on those crosses?" Saint Francis replied, "You should know that along with our Lord, two thieves were also crucified. We possess the cross of our God and Savior Jesus Christ, and that cross we adore and surround with total devotion. So, while that true cross of God has been entrusted to us, you have been left with the crosses of the thieves. That is why I did not fear to walk on the signs of the thieves. For among you there is nothing of the sacred cross of the Savior."

[99]The Sultan also posed another question to Francis: "Your God teaches in the Gospel that you should not render evil for evil, that you should not refuse anyone who wants to take your cloak, and so on. So how much more should you Christians not invade our land!" Saint Francis replied: "It seems that you haven't read the whole Gospel of our Lord Christ. For he says in another place, *If your eye is an occasion of scandal, pluck it out, and cast it away.* With this he wanted to teach us that even if a man should be a friend or a relative, perhaps as dear to us as the eye of our head, we should not hesitate to break off relations with him, to destroy, or even eradicate him, if he should try to separate us from our faith and our love for God. It is for this reason that Christians have acted justly when they invade your land and fight against you, because you blaspheme the name of Christ and you have tried to keep people from worshiping him. But if you wish to recognize, confess, and adore the Creator and Redeemer of the world, we would love you as ourselves."

And all the Sultan's attendants were amazed at Francis's answers.[a]

[110]Brother John, a man of great holiness who was the special companion and confessor of Brother Giles until the latter's death, used to recount this story.[b] He heard it from Brother Giles himself, who was the fourth brother to enter the Order. Brother Giles said: "When there were only seven of us brothers in the Order—no more than that—the blessed father Francis gathered us together one day at Saint Mary of the Portiuncula in the woods that used to come right up to the place. And there, celebrating the first council meeting or holding the first chapter, as it were, he spoke thus: 'I know, my dearest brothers, that the Lord has called us not only for our own salvation. Therefore, I want us to scatter among the nations, going about

Mt 5:40

Mt 5:29

---

a. Bonaventure did not include these stories in his account of Francis's visit to the Sultan in the LMj IX 7-9 (FA:ED II: 601-4), but he does relate another such episode derived from the same source, Brother Illuminato, in his *Collationes in Hexaemeron* XIX 14 (V 422); English translation *The Works of Bonaventure V*, trans. José da Vinck, (Paterson: St. Anthony Guild Press, 1970), 291.

b. This Brother John is the same one mentioned in the Letter of the Three Companions to Cresentius of Iesi, cf. FA:ED II 67.

the world spreading the word of God and giving an example of virtue.'

"We humbly responded: 'We are illiterate lay brothers. What can we do for the salvation of the world?' He answered: 'Go forth, secure of the help of God. And you have written on our hearts these two assurances that the Lord himself gave us: *Cast your care upon the Lord* *and he will sustain you!* He said this to remove any hesitancy we might have, since he was sending us without any provisions into unknown regions. And he also quoted that saying from the Gospel: *Do not worry* *about what you are to eat or what you are to say. It will not be you that are* *speaking, but the Spirit of your Father speaking in you.'* And this he said in answer to those of us who said, 'We are illiterate,' wanting by these words to comfort and strengthen our hearts to be confident that our God the Most High would make up for our defects, when we act in a spirit of compassion and hope in him.'"[a]

[116]Brother Nicholas of Assisi recounted the following incident: "My father's house was attached to the house of Blessed Francis.[b] My mother told me this story. When Saint Francis's mother was resting in her bed after having given him birth, as women are accustomed to do after their labor, with some of the women of the neighborhood there with her, a pilgrim came to the door as if he were seeking alms. But when he had taken the piece of chicken that Francis's mother sent out to him, he began to beg with great insistence that he wanted to see the newborn child. The women tried to send him away, but he kept insisting that he would not leave until he had first seen the baby boy. Then Lady Pica, the mother of Saint Francis, said: 'Take the baby out so he can see it.' As soon as he saw the child, he embraced it, saying: 'Two babies were born the same day on this street, this one and another. One of them, this one here, will be one of the best men in the world, the other will be one of the worst.' " The passage of the years proved what he said to be true.[c]

[123]The bishop of Assisi, our brother, relates the following story recounted to him by Brother Bonaparte,[d] a holy man who is still

Ps 55: 23

Mt 10:19-20

---

a. This episode is similar to 1C 27-9 and L3C 36; but this redaction is distinguished by its simplicity and naturalness, cf. FA:ED I 205-7; FA:ED II 89-90.

b. Arnaldo Fortini has identified this brother as Nicola di Giacomo, a prominent notary in Francis's day who joined the Order later in life after a successful professional career. His house was next to the church of San Nicolo, and a number of his notary documents were drawn up there, cf. Arnaldo Fortini, *Francis of Assisi*, trans. Helen Moak, (New York: Crossroad, 1981), 90.

c. A slightly different version of this episode is contained in some older editions of the L3C 2, which were based on Vatican Latin codex 7739, where it is certainly an interpolation. It is not included in the modern critical edition of that text. It should be noted that this is the only early source that mentions the name of Francis's mother, Lady Pica.

d. Probably Nicholas of Corbario or Carbio, the confessor of Innocent IV, whom the latter installed as bishop of Assisi (1251 to 1274). This brother Bonaparte is otherwise unknown.

alive, who used to be the cook in a place where Saint Francis was staying with a few brothers. When Saint Francis sat down at table, he used to pour ashes or cold water or something else like that over his food, making it virtually tasteless. This used to upset this brother very much, so one day he said to the blessed Francis: "Look, father, I work hard to prepare a good meal so that you might find a little enjoyment, and you ruin it right away, which makes me feel very bad." The saint responded: "You do well, and you will have your reward with God. You do what you should with a good intention; but I too do with a good intention what I think I should do."[a]

[134]At the time of Saint Francis, when the divine goodness laid the first foundation of our Order, one of the brothers was tempted to return to the world. So he approached Saint Francis and began to ask him to release him from the bond of religion, for he could in no way remain in the Order. But when the blessed Francis said that he was both unwilling and unable to grant his request, he approached the Lord of Ostia but met the same response. Seeing that there was no way he could get a dispensation, impelled by the spirit of temptation, his feet slipped. But when he had only gone a short distance, he came across a young man who asked him where he was going. He replied to him angrily: "What do you care about my business?" Then the young man bared his chest and extended his hands, on which there were wounds that only recently had shed a good deal of blood, and said to him: "You are reopening my wounds, you are crucifying me a second time." Terrified by what he saw, the brother threw himself at his feet, tearfully begging his forgiveness. But as soon as this was disclosed to him, the young man disappeared from sight. Then he went back to Saint Francis and recounted what he had seen. And he remained devotedly in the Order for the rest of his life.[b]

Donation of La Verna (1274)

This document, once deposited in the archives of Borgo San Sepulchro, is a deed giving the mountain of La Verna for the use of the Lesser Brothers by

---

a. This penitential practice of Saint Francis is noted also in the official sources, cf. 1C 51 (FA:ED I 227), LMj V 1 (FA:ED II 561), but this story adds an eyewitness testimony.

b. There is a slightly different version of this story in manuscript 529 of Assisi, cf. Ferdinand Delorme, "Un recueil de miracles ou exempla, " *Studi Francescani* 12 (1926): 366ff., where it is ascribed to a sermon of Brother Luke of Bitonto, Apulia, whom Salimbene mentions as a great preacher around 1233, cf. Salimbene, *Chronicle*, 64-5, 172.

Count Orlando of Chiusi and his brothers.[a] They belonged to a branch of the noble family of the Caetani or Gaetani, who were among the most important feudal landowning families of central Italy. The deed ratifies an oral donation made in the year 1213 to Saint Francis by their father, Count Orlando the Elder. According to a later tradition, this took place at the castle of the counts of Montefeltro, where Francis came to a family celebration at which Count Orlando was a guest. The mountain was a favorite hermitage of Saint Francis, and was first mentioned several years after his death in *The Life of Saint Francis,* 94, by Thomas of Celano.

In the name of God, Amen. In the year of our Lord 1274, while Pope Gregory was reigning and the throne of the Roman Empire was vacant, on Monday, the ninth of July, in the presence of the priests, Giles, rector of the church of Trameggiano, and John, rector of the church of Campo; and of Cambio Catozzi of Chitignano; the Lord Guidone, son of Lord Rainerio of Gufaria, and Bernardino his son; and many other witnesses who were summoned for this purpose, etc. Orlando dei Caetani, son of the late Lord Orlando, Count of Chiusi; and Cungio, Bandino, and Guglielmo, brothers and sons of the said Lord Orlando; by his word and authority, and some of these from certain knowledge, and not through some error of law or fact, admitting that they live by Roman law, and are more than twenty-five years of age, acknowledged that the said Lord Orlando, Count of Chiusi, a most valiant knight of the Emperor and father of the above, in the year of our Lord 1213, on the eighth day of May, solely for reason of devotion, orally gave, bequeathed, and conceded, freely and without any restriction, to Brother Francis and his companions and to the brothers both present and future, the mountain of La Verna, so that the said Father Francis and his brothers might live there. And by the said mountain of La Verna we understand, and the said witnesses also understand, [to include] all the land, whether wooded, rocky, or meadow, without any exception, from the brow of the said mountain to the bases surrounding it on every side, together with everything attached to them. And because this gift was made to the blessed Father Francis and to his companions by word of mouth only and without anything in writing, therefore the said Orlando, most loving father of the younger Orlando and his

a. Text in *Testimonia Minora Saeculi XIII de S. Francisco Assisiensi Collecta Edidit ad VII a Transitu Sancti Completa Saecula,* ed. Leonardus Lemmens (Ad Claras Aquas, Quaracchi: Collegium S. Bonaventurae, 1926), 36-37 (hereafter TM). It was still in the archives at Borgo San Sepulchro in the eighteenth century when it was later edited by Joanne H. Sbaralea, cf. BFr 4:156. See also S. Menerchini, *Codice diplomatico della Verna a delle Stigmate di San Francesco d'Assisi* (Florence: Tipografia Gualandi, 1924), 38-39; Zepherinus Lazzeri, "L'Atto di Conferma della Donazione della Verna," *La Verna* 11 (1913): 101-105.

brothers, when on his deathbed charged and ordained his said sons to renew the gift [of the said mountain] to the said brothers. Wherefore, desiring to carry out each and every command of their late beloved father, so that everything might be done according to his mind, with none of them dissenting or of a different opinion, they have now approved, confirmed, and ratified through this present document each and every thing bequeathed by their father. And they will and declare that the said fathers shall always live there, and that no one shall be able to turn them out or molest them, so that the said bequest of the said mountain [of La Verna] with its approaches shall be valid for all time and that [through this deed] it will stand as valid forever.

Further, by order of the said Lord, the elder Count Orlando, they gave to these same brothers the following items: a cloth, which the said Father Francis used at table with the Lord Count Orlando and his children whenever he was staying with them; also a certain wooden cup or bowl, in which the said Father Francis used to prepare his bread and wine; also a leather belt that belonged to their most beloved father, the Count of Chiusi, which the said Saint Francis blessed and with which he himself girt the same Count Orlando when he received the habit, which has also shown miraculous powers for women in labor pains. The Lord Count Orlando dei Caetani and his brothers have bequeathed and handed over in perpetuity this mountain and every single thing mentioned above, not by force, fraud, or fear, but freely and willingly, and they have confirmed and do confirm these things as conceded and handed over etc., renouncing etc., promising that they, their heirs and successors, will give heed to and observe in perpetuity each and every thing contained therein without any exception etc. The foregoing negotiations took place at the Rocca di Chiusi, in the palace of the aforesaid Count Orlando and his aforesaid brothers, on the day and year stated above.

Jerome of Ascoli (1276)

Jerome was born in 1227 in the city of Ascoli Piceno in the Marches and entered the Lesser Brothers at a young age. We know little of his early career. He emerged into prominence during his years as provincial minister of Dalmatia. His conspicuous abilities in that position led Bonaventure to suggest Jerome's name to the newly-elected Gregory X to head the Papal embassy sent in 1272 to the Byzantine Emperor, Michael Palaeologus, to discuss a reunion of the Eastern and Western church. While yet on route with the Greek delegation to the Second Council of Lyons in 1274, Jerome was unanimously chosen to succeed Bonaventure as general minister at the chapter held at the time of the council.

Unfortunately, Jerome was able to spend little time on the business of governing the Order.[a] His diplomatic abilities made him indispensable to Gregory X, who continued to employ him in the task of shoring up the fragile union with the Eastern Church. A general chapter was scheduled for Padua in the summer of 1276, but Jerome was not able to be present, as he was again going on a Papal embassy to Constantinople. Prior to his departure, he wrote the following letter to be read at the chapter.

As the number of persons who knew Francis or his early companions were quickly passing from the scene, Jerome was anxious to collect and preserve any previously unknown stories about the founder of the Order. One such story, concerning Francis's initial visit to the Papal court, had been brought to Jerome's attention by the elderly Cardinal Riccardo degli Annibaldi, a great-nephew of Pope Innocent III.[b] In this letter Jerome offered another example, which had come to light only recently. Because it involved a dramatic miracle, Jerome felt it should be broadcast to the chapter; it would add an incentive for the delegates to enact a decree ordering that any other such instances to be brought to his attention.[c]

Tb 12:7   A testifying angel said to blessed Tobias: *It is good to conceal the secret of a king, but honorable to acknowledge and reveal the works of God.* And so, wishing to bring joy to your hearts and desiring to increase your devotion, I have striven by means of this letter to unfold the wonderful works of God that were accomplished through the merits of our

1 Jn 1:1-2   Father, blessed Francis. Through the testimony of those people who saw these things with their own eyes and touched them with their own hands, I have ascertained with certainty that they were indeed the works of God.

The lord Gratian, son of Matthew, ruler of the same city arrested a certain man in Assisi, as he was accused of stealing valuables from a church. The sentence of the lord Ottaviani,[d] who was the judge of the same community, was that the eyes of the accused man should be plucked out. This sentence was to be carried out by Otto, the son of Ottaviani, who was a soldier in that same area, and by his assistants, Fringillo, James, and Bartholomew, and by as many others as ordered by the sentence. After the eyes of the accused man were gouged out with a knife, he was led thus blinded to the altar of blessed Francis. The man implored the saint's mercy there, claiming that he had been falsely accused. Through the merits of our blessed

---

a. Cf. Moorman, *History*, 178-9.

b. This cardinal, Riccardo degli Annibaldi, the son of Innocent III's nephew, was made a Cardinal by Gregory IX in 1239 and died in 1274. Jerome added this detail to LMj III 9. Cf. FA:ED II 548 a.

c. Text from Athanasio Lopez, "Litterae ineditae fr. Hieronymi ab Asculo," AFH 1 (1908): 85. A longer version of the same letter was sent out to the provinces the same day, cf. TM, 90-1.

d. The text here actually has Ottoman. This seems to be a transcriber's error, as the longer version of the letter has Ottaviani, and the latter was inserted into the LMj.

Father, within three days, Almighty God gave this blind man new eyes. They were smaller than the eyes that had been cut out with the knife, but his vision was clear. The knight [involved], the lord Otto, bore witness to this miracle under oath in the presence of many witnesses before the lord James, abbot of the monastery of San Clemente, who was investigating the case by authority of the lord bishop, James of Tivoli. In addition, Brother William of Rome was commanded by me under strict obedience, under pain of excommunication to be incurred *ipso facto,* to tell the exact truth about this miracle. He was examined in the presence of Brother Guido, Minister of Rome; Brother Conrad, Minister of Upper Germany; Brother Dominic, penitentiary of the Lord Pope; Brother Bonagratia,[a] and Brother Monaldo, visitator of the monasteries of Saint Clare. Brother William clearly testified that while he was still living in the world, he had seen the blinded man when he still had both his eyes. Then he had watched while his eyes were cut out. Furthermore, while the man's eyes were lying there on the ground, Brother William was curious to see how they were made, so he turned them over quite a few times with a stick. Afterwards, he saw the man, but now he had eyes again. And Brother William saw that the man could see clearly with these new eyes that God had given to him through the merits of blessed Francis—just as well as he could see all of us now, telling us plainly about it. Therefore, it seems to me that such a manifest miracle should be published and be included among the miracles of our holy Father in the recently composed *Legend.*[b] Farewell and pray for me.

Given at Rome on the 5th of May in the year 1276.[c] Amen.

Among its other decisions, the chapter of Padua heeded Jerome's request and issued the following decree:[d]

[9]All [provincial ministers] are hereby charged to carry out diligently the provisions of the letter sent to the ministers assembled in chapter at Padua by the Reverend Father General Minister, entitled "To the venerable brothers, beloved in Christ, etc."[e] The intent of this letter is to have them conduct an investigation into any additional

---

a. Bonagratia of San Giovanni in Persiceto, who was Jerome's vicar at the chapter and who succeeded him as general minister in 1279.

b. That is, LMj. This incident was incorporated into the LMj Mir VII 7, cf. FA:ED II 673 a.

c. The manuscript has 1275, a transcriber's error; the longer version of the letter is dated 1276.

d. Text in Andrew George Little, "Definitiones Capitulorum Generalium Ordinis Fratrum Minorum 1260-1282," AFH 7 (1914): 681.

e. The text of this letter has not survived.

information worthy of remembrance concerning the deeds of the blessed Francis and of other holy brothers, which may have occurred in their provinces. Such instances are to be reported to the general minister in exact language and under the oath of witnesses.

Jerome had offered to submit his resignation to the chapter, but the delegates wished him to continue as general minister. However, in 1278 he was made a cardinal by Nicholas III, and so gave up his office at the chapter of Assisi in 1279. Jerome's career continued to advance at the Roman court; in 1281 he was promoted to Cardinal bishop of Palestrina, and finally, in 1288, he was elected Pope, taking the name of Nicholas IV. As Pope, he promulgated a uniform Rule for the Brothers and Sisters of Penance in his bull *Supra montem* of 1289. He also put pressure on the general minister, Raymond Geoffroi, to crack down on the Spiritual movement.[a] Nicholas IV died on April 4, 1292.

Documents Concerning the Portiuncula Indulgence (1277-1300)

The most significant attestations concerning unrecorded "deeds" of Francis which were submitted in response to Jerome's inquiry of 1276 were those concerning the Portiuncula indulgence. This famous plenary indulgence was offered to all repentant pilgrims who came to the small chapel on August 2nd of each year. The first evidence of any indulgence connected with Assisi is from the mid-thirteenth century: there is no mention of the Portiuncula indulgence in any of the early Franciscan sources or in Papal records before this time.[b] As more and more pilgrims began to stream to Assisi to gain this great "pardon," voices were raised among the clergy who questioned its authenticity.[c] The Lesser Brothers therefore began to collect notarized testimony about the "Pardon of Assisi." The brother Francesco Bartholi around the year 1340 eventually compiled much of this documentation.[d] Although the Papacy has validated and even expanded the Portiuncula Indulgence over the years,[e] its historicity has continued to be a matter of controversy down

---

a. ChrXXIVG 420-2.

b. In 1252 Innocent IV granted an indulgence of one year and a period of forty days to all who visited the Basilica of Saint Francis on the feast of Saint Francis and for two weeks afterwards (BFr 1, p. 594, n. 391); it was only in the 1260's that we also start to hear about the much more generous indulgence connected with the Portiuncula. Bonaventure does not mention such an indulgence in LMj. Some background is given in TM 47-8.

c. At the time, only Crusaders could gain such a plenary indulgence; and only Jerusalem, Rome, and Santiago de Compostella were richly endowed pilgrimage sites.

d. Francesco Bartholi della Rossa, *Tractatus de Indulgentia S. Maria de Portiuncula*, ed. Paul Sabatier (Paris: Fischbacher, 1900).

e. In 1921, the Pardon of Assisi was made what the stories say Saint Francis originally wanted: a plenary indulgence valid every day of the year. The one-day indulgence on August 2 was later extended to all Franciscan churches and, in 1967, to all Catholic churches.

through the ages.[a] The first three of these documents are the earliest of these notarized testimonies.

1

This is a document or public instrument concerning the concession of the indulgence, which was composed and given at Perugia by the Lord Pope Honorius to Saint Mary of the Angels.[b]

In the name of the Lord, Amen. I, Brother Benedict of Arezzo,[c] was at one time with blessed Francis when he was still alive, and, through the working of the God's grace, the most holy Father himself received me into his Order. I was a companion of his companions and often, both during the lifetime of the holy Father and after his death, I had conversations with them concerning the secrets of the Order. I now bear witness that I often heard from one of the companions of blessed Francis, Brother Masseo of Marignano[d] by name—a truthful man who lived a most upright life—that he was with the blessed Francis at Perugia in the presence of the Lord Pope Honorius when he asked for an indulgence for all their sins for those persons who, being contrite and having confessed them, come to Saint Mary of the Angels, otherwise known as the Portiuncula, from first vespers of the first day of August to vespers of the following day. Since this indulgence had been so humbly and yet so earnestly sought by blessed Francis, it was at length most liberally granted by the Supreme Pontiff, although he made it plain that it was not the custom of the Apostolic See to grant such an indulgence.[e]

In a similar manner, I, Brother Rainerio of Mariano of Arezzo,[f] a companion of the venerable Brother Benedict, confess that I have often heard the same thing from the said Brother Masseo, a

---

a. Cf. Raphael Huber, *The Portiuncula Indulgence from Honorius III to Pius XI* (New York: J. Wagner, 1938).

b. *Instrumenta Diversa Pertinentia ad Sacrum Conventum*, Vol. XII, written about 1300; included in Bartholi, 44; TM, 42-43

c. Missionary in the East, minister of Romania, he died in 1282.

d. See Letter of the Three Companions, FA:ED II 66-8.

e. This is certainly true; indeed, the Holy See was trying at the time to restrain the use of indulgences. In 1215, the year before Francis supposedly received the Portiuncula indulgence from Honorius III, the Fourth Lateran Council decreed: "Moreover. Because the keys of the church are brought into contempt and satisfaction when penance loses its force through indiscriminate and excessive indulgences, which certain prelates of the church do not fear to grant, we therefore decreed that when a basilica is dedicated, the indulgence shall not be for more than one year . . . and for the anniversary of the dedication the remission of penances imposed is not to exceed forty days. We order that letters of indulgence, which are granted for various reasons at different times, are to fix this number of days, since the Roman pontiff himself, who possesses the plenitude of power, is accustomed to observe this moderation in such things," DEC vol. 1, 264.

f. Brother Rainerio died in 1302. He is numbered among the blessed of the Order.

companion of blessed Francis; I myself, Brother Rainerio, was one of Brother Masseo's closest friends.

The above statements were read and published in the cell of the [venerable] Brother Benedict of Arezzo in the presence of Brother Compagno of Borgo, Brother Rainaldo of Castiglione, Brother Caro of Arezzo, Brother Homodeo of Arezzo, Brother Aldebrandino of Florence, Brother James of Florence, Brother Tebaldo of Arezzo, Brother Bonaventure of Arezzo, and Massario of Arezzo, who were invited and called for this purpose. This was on Sunday, the last day of October, in the year of our Lord 1277, during the fifth in the cycle of indiction, when the emperor's throne and that of the Roman Church were vacant. I, John, the notary, son of the late Canclias, was present on this occasion, and on the orders of the venerable Brothers Benedict and Rayner I wrote down and published the above.

2[a]

In the presence of Brother Angelo, the Minister,[b] of Brother Guido, Brother Bartholo of Perugia and other brothers at the Portiuncula, Peter Zalfani said that he was present at the consecration of the Church of Saint Mary of the Portiuncula and he heard blessed Francis preaching to the people in front of seven bishops. He had a small sheet of paper in his hand and said: "I want to send you all to paradise and I announce to you an indulgence, which I have from the mouth of the Supreme Pontiff. And may all you who have come here today and all who come yearly on this day, with an upright and contrite heart, have the remission of all their sins. I wanted this for eight days but I was not able to attain it."

3

The testimony of a noble soldier, just as he heard it from the mouth of the confessor of blessed Francis.[c] Which testimony Brother Angelo, the Minister, wrote with his own hand for the remembrance of the ages.

a. In the same Assisi manuscript as the preceding, *Tractatus de Indulgentia S. Maria de Portiuncula*, 54; TM, 43-4.
b. Minister of the province of Assisi, he is mentioned in many of the Papal bulls directed to the Order in the period 1276-79.
c. From manuscript 417 in the library of the Sacro Convento in Assisi, included in Francesco Bartholi della Rossa, *Tractatus de Indulgentia S. Maria de Portiuncula*, ed. Paul Sabatier (Paris: Fischbacher, 1900),135; TM, 44-5.

The Lord James Coppoli of Perugia[a] told me, Brother Angelo, Minister, in the presence of Brother Deodato, Custos of Perugia, and Brother Angelo, my companion, that once in the hearing of his wife and [the priest] Little James [Jacobutio] and another lady, he asked Brother Leo, the companion of Saint Francis, whether the indulgence, which is attached to the Portiuncula, was true or not. He answered in the affirmative, and then related what the blessed Francis had himself told him: namely, that he had petitioned the Pope to attach an indulgence to the Church of the Portiuncula on the anniversary of its consecration. And the Pope asked for how long he wanted this remission to be. For one year? For three years? At length they had gotten as far as seven years, but still Saint Francis was not satisfied. Then the Pope said to him. "Well, for how long then?" And Francis replied: "Holy Father, if it please your Holiness, my wish is that, because of the great benefits which God has distributed there and will yet distribute, all those who come there truly contrite and having confessed their sins may receive the remission of all their sins, so that no further [temporal] punishment is attached to them." The Pope replied: "I grant it; let it be so."

When the Cardinals became aware of this, they told the Pope that he should revoke it, because it would be to the prejudice of the Holy Land [indulgence]. But the Pope said: "I certainly shall not revoke it now that I have promised it." They replied: "Put as much a limit on it as you can." And then the Pope said that it was valid for only the length of one natural day each year.

When blessed Francis left the Pope after the concession of the indulgence, he heard a voice saying to him: "Francis, know that, just as this indulgence has been given on earth, so it also has been ratified in heaven." Then Saint Francis said to Brother Leo: "Keep this secret to yourself and do not divulge it until the time of your death is near, because this is not yet the time for it. This indulgence will be hidden for a time, but the Lord will bring it to light and it will be made manifest."

After a time the Lord James, wishing to have more certainty about this, again questioned Brother Leo. And Brother Leo responded that it was just as he told him. And the Lady Maitana, mentioned above, confirmed before the already mentioned people what Master James said. And the Lord James, a priest of Saint Lucia of Collis, who was called Jacobutio above, confirmed in its entirety what Master James said in the presence of the foregoing people.

---

a. Member of a prominent noble family of Perugia, he gave to the Order in 1276 the hermitage mentioned below, in which Brother Giles died.

All these things took place on the 19th of August (1277) within the Octave of the Assumption of Blessed Mary in the place where Brother Giles used to live.

4

As the controversy about the authenticity of the Portiuncula indulgence continued in the fourteenth century, later accounts of its origin were embellished with accretions of a miraculous nature. The most famous of these is this account recorded in the *Chronicle of the Twenty-four Generals*.[a] According to it, Christ granted the indulgence to Francis directly; the Pope only confirmed it.

In the name of the Holy Trinity, of the blessed Virgin Mary, and of blessed Francis. I, Michael Bernarducci, formerly of Spoleto and now a citizen and inhabitant of the city of Assisi, presently devoted to the Order of blessed Francis, went one day to the place of the Portiuncula. There I found Brother Bernard of Quintavalle, Brother Leo, Brother Peter Catanii, Brother Masseo of Marignano, Brother Angelo of Rieti, Brother Philip the Tall from the coast of San Savino, and Brother William, talking among themselves. When I approached them I saw that they were speaking secretly, so out of embarrassment I wanted to withdraw, but when they called to me I approached them. Now, this conversation was taking place in the garden where the cell of Saint Francis is. One of them, Brother Peter Catanii, turned to me and began to speak thus: "Listen, Michael, to what happened these last few days. Brother Bernard, the companion of Saint Francis, told me this, showing me the place in the cell where it happened, which was this year in the month of January just past, when the great rains and snow poured down.

"One night around midnight Satan came to blessed Francis as he was at prayer next to his cell and said to him: 'Francis, what are you doing? Do you want to die before your time? Why are you doing such things? Don't you know that sleep is the principal nourishment of the body? You are young, so for you sleep and rest are especially necessary. One time I say to you that you are young, and so another time you can do penance for your sins. Why then do you punish yourself so in vigils and prayers?'

"Then blessed Francis took off his tunic and undershorts and left the hut and passed through the large and dense hedge and entered the wildest and thorn-infested woods that belong to Philip Nurbi, adjoining the church of Saint Mary of the Portiuncula. When blessed

a. AF III 632-3.

Francis was in the middle of the woods, his flesh all stained and bloodied from the thorns, he said: 'It is better for me to acknowledge the passion of my Lord Jesus Christ than to give in to the seduction of the deceiver.'

"Then suddenly there was a great light in the midst of the forest and in that time of frost rose blossoms appeared right there where blessed Francis was. And a countless host of angels suddenly appeared both in the woods and in the said church next to the woods, and behold they cried with one voice: 'Blessed Francis, hurry to the Savior and his Mother who await you in the church.' There then appeared to him a straight path as if of decorated silk going up to the church, and blessed Francis took from the rose patch twelve red roses and twelve white roses and entered the church. He proceeded to the altar and placed on it the roses he had brought with him in joined hands. There he saw Jesus Christ standing with his Mother at his right with a great multitude of angels. Then Francis found himself dressed in a very beautiful garment before the Savior and his Mother, and his Savior said to him: 'Francis, ask whatever you will for the enlightenment of the nations and the consolation of souls, to the honor and reverence of God, for you have been designated a light to the nations and the repair of the earthly church, that is the Church Militant.'

"Francis, however, lay as if enraptured in the presence of the Savior and his Mother. Then recovering his senses, he spoke up: 'Our holy Father, I, a sinner, beg you to do me this favor, that you grant an indulgence of all their sins, on one day only, to all who come to this place and enter this church with contrition and confession of their sins, and who have graciously accepted the penance and satisfaction imposed. And I beseech the Virgin Mary your Mother, the advocate of sinners, that she intercede in this regard, for I am unworthy.' Then the Virgin Mary, Queen of heaven, in response to his prayers, begged her Son Jesus Christ saying: 'Most High God, I beg you to grant what your servant requests.' And the Savior replied: 'This is indeed a great thing you have requested, Francis, but you are worthy of even greater, and you shall have a great reward. So I grant your request and prayer. Just name the day when it should happen.'

"Blessed Francis responded: 'Most Holy Father, you who arrange heaven and earth, please, you arrange the day with your Mother.' So the Savior decreed that from the first vespers of the first day of August to vespers of the second day of the same month, whoever comes on that day, having repented and confessed the sins of which they were aware, all the sins they have committed from their baptism up to that day they entered this church would be forgiven. Then blessed Francis added: 'All Holy Father, how will this be known and believed by people?' The Lord Jesus Christ replied: 'Francis, this will be done through my grace; you, however, should go to my Vicar whom I have placed over nations and over kingdoms, and he should make it known as he sees fit.' Then Francis said, 'And how will Your Vicar believe me? Perhaps he won't believe a sinner.' The Savior replied: 'Francis, take with you three of your companions who have heard this, and some of the white and red roses you gathered up in the woods in the month of January. Take with you whatever number seems to you most fitting.' "

Now all these things were heard by Brother Peter Catanii, Brother Rufino Cipii, Brother Bernard of Quintavalle, Brother Masseo of Marignano, and their companions who were in their dwellings, that is, in their cells outside the church in the garden where the cell of blessed Francis is. Then blessed Francis took three white and three red roses in the presence of the Savior and Mary his Mother. Finally the grandest song of the angels was sung: *Te Deum laudamus.*

Peter of John Olivi (c. 1272-97)

Peter of John Olivi (Pierre de Jean Olieu) was one of the most significant and controversial Franciscan thinkers of the last quarter of the thirteenth century.[a] Born around 1248 in Serignan, not far from Béziers in southern France, he entered the Order at the age of twelve. His precocious intelligence quickly came to the attention of his superiors, and he was sent to study theology at Paris in the mid-1260's. For some reason Olivi did not proceed to the doctorate at that point, but shortly after 1270 was recalled to his province to teach.

Within a few years Olivi's inquiring, original mind was getting him into trouble; several brothers in his province reported some of his teachings to Jerome of Ascoli, who censured them.[b] By 1279, Olivi was back enough in favor to be asked by his provincial to write up something on Franciscan poverty for the Papal commission drawing up the bull *Exiit Qui Seminat.*[c] But questions about Olivi's orthodoxy were soon raised again; a number of his teachings were submitted to a panel of Paris theologians who censured him again in 1283; this time he was removed from teaching. One of these censured positions regarded "the poor use." Olivi insisted that a restricted use of things, not simply the renunciation of ownership, was an integral part of the

---

a. For a brief introduction, see Pierre Péano, "Olieu, Pierre Jean," *Dictionnaire de Spiritualité Ascetique e Mystique* 11 (Paris: Beauchesne, 1982), 751-762.

b. Angelo Clareno, *Liber Chronicarum sive Tribulationum Ordinis Minorum, ed. Giovanni Boccali, with introduction by Felice Accroca,* Italian translation by Marino Bigaroni (Sta. Maria degli Angeli, Assisi: Edizioni Porziuncola, 1998), 462-3.

c. Supra 739-64.

Franciscan vow of poverty, a view increasingly unacceptable as the Order made more and more accommodations in its lifestyle.

In 1287 Olivi was rehabilitated by the new general minister, Matthew of Aquasparta, being made lector in the convent of Santa Croce in Florence, a prestigious position. His two years there did a great deal to foster connections between the Italian and Provençal branches of the Spiritual reform. In 1289, Olivi returned to his own province, teaching theology in the convents of Montpellier and Narbonne, where he died in 1298. The following year the general chapter condemned Olivi's teachings because of the influence they were having on dissident Spirituals; the general minister ordered his writings to be burned. On the other hand, many brothers and devout laity venerated Olivi as a saint; his tomb in Narbonne soon became a popular pilgrimage site. But Olivi's persecutors haunted him even after death: in 1318 his body was removed from his tomb and his cult suppressed.

In his voluminous writings, Olivi mentions Francis often; the following selections provide some additional information about the saint and present Olivi's views on Francis's apocalyptic significance. He reports the following historical incident in his *Lectura* on Luke.[a]

> In support of this, I will recount what I myself heard from that most holy, venerable and trustworthy old man, Brother Bernard Barravi, once a canon regular of the Church of Carcassone and later a member of the Order of Minors. In two of the sermons he preached at Béziers to the novices when I was a novice and present there,[b] he said that when he was still a canon and studying theology at Paris he heard from blessed Dominic, whom he had as a friend and fellow canon at Carcassone, that he and his Order had accepted the renunciation of all possessions from the example of blessed Francis and his followers. When Dominic was on his way to Rome and to the Roman Curia for the approbation of his Order, he saw Francis at Assisi with thousands of brothers gathered together in a general chapter. There Dominic was in admiration that without any provision for the next day, all the necessities were sufficiently provided for them each day by the Lord through the devotion of the faithful. Returning to his brothers, he told them that without possessions they would be able to live without anxiety, because he had seen and verified all this in Brother Francis and his Order.

The following selection is from Olivi's Commentary on the *Rule*, written in the latter part of 1288. This was during the time he was teaching theology in

---

a. TM, 97-8. The date of this work, which remains unedited, is uncertain.

b. Olivi was a novice in 1260/61.

Florence; it shows that he had become familiar with the "Leo" sources at this time.[a]

> In the pieces of parchment on which Brother Leo wrote down the things which he, as our Father's special companion, had seen and heard concerning him, one reads that a lay brother once asked the permission of blessed Francis to have and learn the psalter. Our blessed Father replied that at one time he had a similar temptation to learn; and when he prayed to God and in his prayer requested divine counsel, Christ said to him: *"To you it has been given to know the mystery of the kingdom of God, but to the rest in parables."* I think this is the meaning of these words: "To you, as one wholly separated from the world and united to me completely, it is given to learn the naked truth of the virtues and the good things of eternity, and to see into the meaning of these things through your passionate and living experience of them." And what is astonishing if God teaches his own spiritual wisdom to those who have been weaned from the milk of the world and who had fled from the breasts of secular knowledge? I certainly do not believe that without this ray and little fire of divine illumination anyone can perfectly penetrate to the marrow of the letter of Sacred Scripture, nor without some measure of vanity or with cold tastelessness.

Lk 8:10

Olivi's last major work was his *Commentary on the Book of Revelation, composed in 1296/97.* It reflects his growing concern with what he viewed as a crisis confronting both the Church and the Order. In late 1295, his ally Raymond Geoffroi was removed as general minister; his successor was John of Murrovalle, a member of the commission who had censured Olivi's teachings in 1283.[b]

This Apocalypse commentary makes clear Olivi's debt to the ideas of Joachim of Fiore. He accepts the Calabrian abbot's basic premise that salvation history is still unfolding, and in a way that manifests the basic concordance between the Old and the New Testaments. Since there were seven eras of salvation history leading up to the coming of Christ, there will also be seven periods *(status)* in the history of the People of the New Covenant (the church) leading up his second coming.[c] Olivi believed he was living near the end of the fifth of these periods, during which the church had grown in size and

---

a. Translated from the critical edition of David Flood, *Peter Olivi's Rule Commentary* (Wiesbaden: F. Steiner, 1972), 189.

b. Indeed, Olivi's fears were justified: John was the major force behind the general chapter's decision to condemn his writings in 1299.

c. On this work, see David Burr, *Olivi's Peaceable Kingdom: A Reading of the Apocalypse Commentary* (Philadephia: University of Pennsylvania Press, 1993). As Burr comments, *status* is an ambiguous word: it has the qualitative sense of a "state of being" as well as a chronological meaning, cf. supra 145, n. 8.

influence, but also had become corrupted by wealth and power.[a] At the same time, he was convinced that a coming sixth *status* of renewal had already begun in the thirteenth century; Francis was its prophet and poverty its sign. Thus the conflicts Olivi was witnessing were actually the death-throes of the old order: the threatened carnal church, seeing its period of dominion coming to an end, was mounting a fierce battle against the spiritual church of the dawning sixth period.

Olivi's Apocalypse commentary had a major influence on Ubertino of Casale's *Tree of Life*. In 1317, Pope John XXII asked a commission of theologians to investigate its orthodoxy; although the commission suggested in 1319 that the work be condemned, the Pope did not actually carry out this verdict until 1326. The selections that follow are among the excerpts from the work used by the Papal investigating commission.[b]

[1]It should be known that just as our most holy father Francis is, after Christ and under Christ, the first and chief founder, initiator, and exemplar of the sixth *status* and its evangelical rule, so he, after Christ, is primarily designated by this angel. As a sign of this fact, he appeared transfigured *in a fiery chariot* in the sun, so that it might be evident that he has come in the spirit and in the image of Elijah, as well as to bear the perfect image of the true sun, Jesus Christ. He was singularly strong in every virtue and work of God. Through the deepest humility and recognition of the first source of every nature and every grace, coming down always from heaven, and through airy and subtle spiritual lightness free of every earthly weight, he was clothed with a cloud, that is, with the most profound poverty, and was filled with heavenly waters, that is, with the highest possession and draught of celestial riches. He was also clothed with a cloud, that is, the dark cloud of still contemplation, which according to Dionysius in the book entitled *Mystical Theology* is signified by the cloud in which God appeared and spoke to Moses . . .

[2]He has in his hand, that is, in the fullness of work and full possession and power, the open book of the Gospel of Christ, as is evident from the *Rule* that he kept and wrote down, and also from the evangelical way of life that he founded. He placed his right foot upon the sea in that he went to convert the Saracens and labored with the highest energy and fervor to go to them three times to receive martyrdom, as is written in the ninth chapter of his *Legend*. In the sixth year from the time of his conversion he went as the Angel of the

Rv 10:1-3
2 Kgs 2:11
LMj IV 4
LMj IX

---

a. For Olivi, the fifth period is that of Western Christendom, which began with Carolingian times and gave rise to a rich and politicized church.

b. The translation is that of Bernard McGinn, *Visions of the End: Apocalyptic Traditions in the Middle Ages*, rev. ed. (New York: Columbia University Press, 1998), 208-11. We have at times corrected this in light of Burr's study, which used the text of the commentary itself.

Sixth Seal and as a sign that through his Order they would be converted to Christ in the sixth *status* of the Church. Again, he went in the thirteenth year from his conversion as a sign that beginning with the thirteenth century from the Passion and Resurrection of Christ, the Saracens and other infidels are to be converted through his Order and its many martyrs . . .

³These generations [of the New Testament times] begin from the incarnation of Christ and from the beginning parallel the generations of the Old Testament very clearly and with marvelous agreement. Joachim has a full calculation and noteworthy accuracy up to his time. In the sixth year of the forty-first generation, the third age (that still runs along with the second) was fundamentally begun.ᵃ

Rv 7:2 The opening of the sixth seal, still running along with the fifth, was also begun, because Francis, like the angel of the opening of the sixth seal, was converted in that sixth year which was also the sixth year of the thirteenth centenary of the Incarnation of Christ. From that time on, every persecution of his evangelical state anticipates the persecution by the Antichrist. Thus in Paris during the following forty-second generation there was the persecution by those masters who condemned evangelical mendicancy . . . This [is] the error . . . of those who say that having nothing in common does not pertain to evangelical perfection. The declaration or decretal of Lord Nicholas III was issued against them in the same generation . . .ᵇ At the end of this forty-second generation there was the unusual election of Pope Celestine and his successor and other worsening matters . . .

⁴Know that anywhere in this book where it treats of the Great Antichrist in prophetic fashion, it also implies the time of the Mystical Antichrist preceding him. According to this, the beast ascending from the sea signifies the bestial life and race of carnal and worldly Christians which from the end of the fifth period also has many heads made up of worldly princes and prelates.

Rv 13:1-10

The more deeply and broadly evangelical poverty and perfection is impressed and magnified in Christ's church, the stronger the head of earthly cupidity and vile carnality strikes against it. But already this head that was almost dead revives too much, so that all the carnal Christians are in awe of it and follow its earthly and carnal glory.

Rv 13:11-18 When the apostate beast from the land of the religious rises on high

---

a. This is a reference to another of Joachim's attempts to read salvation history; besides the seven parallel *status*, he also viewed history in a three-fold pattern, reflecting an ever-deepening knowledge of God: thus in the age of the Father, humanity knew God primarily through creation; in the age of the Son (the Word), by verbal revelation; in the dawning age of the Spirit, through inner illumination. From this perspective Francis is a harbinger of the contemplative wisdom of the third age.

b. Nicholas III, *Exiit*, cf. supra 739-64.

with its two horns of false religious and false prophets, disguised like the two horns of the Lamb, then will be the strongest temptation of the Mystical Antichrist. *False Christs and false prophets will then arise,* Mt 24:4,11 who will cause all things to adore cupidity and carnality, or the earthly glory of the worldly beast . . . He will set up as Pseudo-Pope a certain false religious who will contrive something against the evangelical rule. . . .[a] Then almost all will depart from the true Pope and will follow the false Pope. He will indeed be false, because he will heretically err against the truth of evangelical poverty and perfection.

Angelo Clareno

Exposition of the *Rule* of the Lesser Brothers
[*Expositio regulae fratrum minorum*] (1321–2)

Written between 1321–2, Angelo Clareno wrote his *Exposition on the Rule of the Lesser Brothers* to clarify ". . . the pure, simple, and final intention that the seraphic man Francis had in the *Rule* divinely inspired by Christ." It must be seen within the context of the struggles among the brothers to observe the *Rule* and, especially its prescription on poverty, in light of the controversial teachings of the popes. In order to defend his positions, Clareno uses his extensive knowledge of the Fathers of the Church, especially the Greeks, and of the early portraits of Francis, those of Thomas of Celano, Bonaventure, and the Companions. He also had access to the fourteenth-century compilations: the *Assisi Compilation,* both editions of *The Mirror of Perfection,* as well as to the commentaries of Hugh of Digne and Peter of John Olivi.

The texts that follow reveal episodes in the life of Francis and the first companions that were unknown or, in certain instances, provide a different perspective. While, outside the context of Angelo's work, it is difficult to appreciate them fully, they nevertheless shed further light on the tensions of these early years of the fourteenth century.

Later Rule I 1: "The rule and life of the Lesser Brothers . . ."

Passages similar to this can be found in the earlier portraits or compilations.[b] This statement of Francis, however, combines elements from many of those earlier passages and is unique to Clareno.[c]

---

a. For some Franciscans this reading of the Apocalypse was fulfilled by John XXII and his bulls against their understanding of poverty, cf. John XXII *Ad conditorem,* supra 784-9.

b. Cf. AC 9, 49, 97 (FA:ED II 123-4, 148-9, 200-2); 2C 148 (FA:ED II 342-3); 1MP 2, 12, 30 (supra 215-7; 223-4; 238-40); 2MP 10, 44 (supra 262-4; 290).

c. Cf. Accrocca, Testimone, 240-1. Cf. Felice Accrocca, "Angelo Clareno, Testimone di S. Francesco. Testi sulla Vita del Santo e dei Primi Frati Contenuti nell'"Espositio Regulae Fratrum Minorum' e Sconosciuti alle Primitive Fonti Francescane," AFH 81 (1988): 225-53.

Therefore Saint Francis used to say that for this reason God wanted them to be called Lesser Brothers, because they should show themselves to be below all by humility of heart, of speech, of external deeds and habit and more humble and poorer, and never presume to be greater ones in the Church, but always seek and thirst for the depths of greater humility.

Later Rule II: 1: "If there are any who wish to accept this life and come to our brothers . . ."

Clareno immediately begins his exposition of the *Later Rule's* second chapter with this statement of Francis, placing it as a description of how the saint understood what it is that draws people to his fellowship and the way in which they are drawn.

When his brothers asked him candidly to encourage a man to enter the religious, Saint Francis answered: "Brothers, it is not for me or for you to induce anyone to take on our life; but it is for us to preach penance to all by the example of our deeds and words, and to attract all to the love and service of Christ and hatred and contempt of the world. It is for the Lord Himself, Who alone knows what people need, to choose and call to this life those He makes suitable, and to whom He will give the grace of taking it on and observing it."

Later Rule II 16: "Let all the brothers wear poor clothes . . ."

Although this passage is attributed to Leo and the companions, it cannot be found among those texts attributed to them and may well be a compendium of Francis's teachings scattered throughout those texts.

And as Brother Leo wrote and other companions of the same Saint testified, who survived many years after his passing from this life, in the desert of this world he taught his brothers to have nothing besides lowly and cheap clothing. And as pilgrims long for their homeland, and those held in prison desire freedom, so the poor of Christ and those who have sworn enmity to the world because of Christ and His kingdom are all the more bound to desire pilgrimage away from the prison of this world and the body.

Later Rule II 5: ". . . let the ministers speak to them the words of the holy Gospel that they go and sell all they have and take care to give it to the poor."

The stories of the minister wanting to keep his books and the novice asking for a psalter appear throughout the earlier texts.[a] This is the only time that it appears in this broader context of entrance into the Order after having given away all of one's possessions.

> Now he answered with great fervor of spirit, according to what he received from God, both to Brother Riccerio and to Brother Masseo and to the minister wanting to have his permission to keep the books which he had, and to the novice who asked him to have a psalter for spiritual comfort by his consent. . . .

Later Rule III 2: ". . . they may have breviaries."

There is no other reference to this practice during the Chapter of Mats.

> Now at the time of Saint Francis up to five thousand brothers gathered at Assisi in a General Chapter, and they placed the breviaries they used in a certain cupboard or wooden box, and none of them took back the breviary he put in, but took the first one his hand touched, even if more battered from use and one of the poorer breviaries, especially exulting in that which was more in keeping with the poverty promised.

Later Rule III 1: "Let the clerical [brothers] recite the Divine Office according to the rite of the Roman Church excepting the psalter . . ."

This episode, absent from the earlier texts, reflects Francis's *Testament* 31 punishing those who may want to change the manner of celebrating the Divine Office. Clareno immediately follows the story with another that took place in the papal court at Avignon, thus accentuating the same tendency plaguing the brothers over a period of time.

> Now when the brothers asked Pope Gregory, who loved the Order very much, for a privilege about this, he, for their own edification and

---

a. Cf. Concerning the minister: AC 103 (FA:ED II 207-9); 2MP 3 (supra 256-7); concerning the novice: AC 105 (FA:ED II 210); 2MP 4 (supra 257-9).

that of others, attempted to convince them by pious exhortations to keep the Office of the Church unchanged, saying to them, "Brothers, if you want to say the Office of the Church without shortening it, I will command all the religious who are in the Church, except the Canons Regular and the monks of Saint Benedict, to say your Office." But the brothers refused to agree, and with pressing requests begged for the privilege of leaving out the "Suffrages of the Saints" at Matins and Vespers, both on feasts and on ferial days and the "Have mercy on me, God" at Matins on ferial days, and the "Gradual Canticle" during the Advent of the Lord and shortening the litanies.

Later Rule IV 1: "I strictly command all my brothers not to receive coins or money in any form, either personally or through intermediaries . . ."

After citing a number of examples in which Francis's brothers ignored this prescription of the *Rule*,[a] Clareno cites this incident:
>   And in the penance that he gave to Brother Agostino, still a novice, because, convinced by the pleas of a certain merchant, he took money which he then carried on a journey through a pass where robbers were suspected.

Later Rule V: "Let the brothers never receive money . . ."

Clareno ends his commentary on the fourth chapter of the *Rule* with this statement which, he claims comes directly from the pen of Brother Leo. The first part of Leo's written statement, at least in this form, is lost. The second part, however, can also be found in AC 15, 2MP 12, and WSF 1.

>   And Brother Leo wrote, "Saint Francis always exhorted and encouraged his brothers by word and example to love of the highest poverty and sharply rebuked in them anything that deviated from its pure observance. And he frequently said these words to the brothers, 'My brothers, I have never been a thief, that is, of alms, which are the inheritance of the poor; I always took less than my due, so that I might not defraud the other poor of their portion, because whoever would do the contrary would be a thief.' "

---

a. AC 27 (FA:ED II 137); 2C 65 (FA:ED II 290); 2MP 14 (supra 266).

Later Rule VI 3: ". . . for the Lord made Himself poor in this world."

As in his commentary on LR I 1, Clareno quotes a saying of Francis, although, in this instance, it cannot be found in any earlier texts.

> Blessed Francis used to say, "It is necessary for every disciple of Christ to look on Christ and His Cross, and to be strengthened in spirit running after Him *by the narrow gate and the hard way*, and to be perfect not only outside love and possession of all things which are under heaven, but forgetful of them, so that he might pass over into the inheritance of Jesus Christ, the Son of God, who humbled Himself and emptied Himself, being *made for us obedient unto death, and to death on the cross.* Mt 7:14 Phil 2:8

Chapter IX Preachers:

After citing ER XVII 17-9, Clareno notes that Francis recognized that, in the future, the brothers would willingly "ascend" to learning, and adds this statement. It can be found in various ways in AC 47, 103; 2C 195, 2MP 69, 72; WSF 8; WBC 10.

> And again [he used to say]: "My brothers who are led by inquisitiveness for knowledge, on the day of tribulation will find their hands empty. Since they preached and knew that some were edified by that or converted to penance, they become puffed up and praise themselves for the gain of another, because the ones they think were edified by their words and converted to penance, the Lord edified and converted by the prayers of the holy brothers, although they do not realize it, because such is the will of the Lord, so that they should not grow proud over this."

Later Rule XI 1: "I strictly command all the brothers not to have any suspicious dealings or conversations with women . . ."

A similar passage can be found in 2C 112 although with significant differences: Thomas does not have the incident take place at the time of Francis's death, uses the verb *recognoscere* [recognize] not *videre* [look], and specifies the women, i.e., his mother and Saint Clare.

> This is what Saint Francis said at his death, so that his brothers would take an example from him: that, from the time that he had

been converted to Christ and renounced the world, he had not looked at the face of any woman, except his mother and Saint Clare.

Chronicles

Chronicle of Erfurt (c. 1275)

This chronicle, written by a Lesser Brother, probably in Erfurt, was one of the Order's first attempts to compose a universal history in the pattern of traditional monastic works of this genre.[a] The author is quite derivative, in that his work is essentially a collection of excerpts from several easily available historical and legal sources, but he has arranged his material around the succession of Popes, beginning with Peter, down to his own day. Although it does treat of secular history, it focuses on the deeds and legislation of the Popes. Because of this distinctly Papalist perspective on history, it was often referred to as the "Roman Chronicle." It proved to be very popular with students and other writers who needed a handy outline of church history.[b]

The author does not show much interest in the details of specifically Franciscan history; he views the Franciscan movement as a divinely inspired development, which was providentially recognized by the Papacy to the benefit of both.

During the tenth year of the pontificate of Pope Innocent III, the 1206th from the Incarnation of the Lord,[c] Francis, as a wise architect, began to do penance, and, through the mercy of God, laid the foundations of the Order of Lesser Brothers. The same Pope, even though he had scarcely seen and heard Saint Francis, was inspired by God to approve the Order and to confer on him and his brothers the office of preaching the Word of God[d] . . .

This Pope, Honorius III, confirmed the way of life and *Rule* of Saint Francis, inserting it in the list of approved rules. . . .[e]

In the year 1227, Pope Gregory IX was elected as the one hundred and eighty-eighth successor of Saint Peter . . . This Pope, in the second year of his pontificate, solemnly canonized the blessed Francis in the city of Assisi. Afterwards, this same Pope canonized three other saints, namely: blessed Dominic of the Order of Preaching

---

a. For an analysis of this work, see Bert Roest, *Reading*, 43, 209-214.

b. *Chronica minor Auctore Minorita Erphordiense*, ed. O. Holder-Egger, Monumenta Germaniae Historica, Scriptores, 24 (Hanover: Hahn, 1879), 172-215.

c. The year 1206 was the ninth year of Innocent's pontificate.

d. Ibid., 194.

e. Ibid., 196.

Brothers, blessed Anthony of the Order of Lesser Brothers, and blessed Elizabeth, the widow of the illustrious prince Louis, Landgrave of Thuringia[a] . . . This same Pope, when he was the Cardinal Bishop of Ostia, supported Saint Francis from the early days of his Order, just as a mother hen cares for her chicks; he was set up as Protector of the Order by Pope Honorius III . . . This same Gregory IX confirmed two orders, which Saint Francis had founded, the one of the Poor Consecrated Ladies, the other of the Penitents. The latter includes people of both sexes: clerics, married folk, virgins, and continent people.[b]

List of the General Ministers (c. 1261-64)

The following brief entry survives in only one German manuscript.[c] Its erroneous title, *The List of Masters General of the Order of Lesser Brothers,* probably betrays a non-Franciscan provenance. It is the earliest known such catalog of the general ministers of the Lesser Brothers.[d] It was drawn up sometime in the generalate of Bonaventure, as he is stated as currently serving in that capacity.[e]

Mt 10:10

In the year 1201,[f] the blessed Francis, putting aside his secular dress, began to walk in God's way. He wore shoes and a leather belt and carried a staff in his hands, and was searching here and there for the way, which he should follow. Then, in the year 1206, hearing one day that the Lord told his disciples that they were to go forth without staff, or traveling bag, or shoes, he immediately cast aside his staff, shoes, and belt, and began to go through the world girded only with a cord, imitating the rule of the Gospels and the life of the apostles. Thus, six years after his conversion, he began the *Rule* and life of the Lesser Brothers, and he governed them as a loving father for twenty years. In the year of the Lord 1226, finishing the course of his life rich

---

a. Clearly showing Gregory's predilection for the Lesser Brothers. Francis died in 1226 and was canonized in 1228; Dominic died in 1221 and was canonized in 1231; Anthony and Elizabeth both died in 1231, Anthony being canonized the following year, Elizabeth in 1235.

b. *Ibid.,* 198. Although clearly indicating Gregory's role, the chronicler sees both the Poor Clares and the Brothers and Sisters of Penance as Francis's inspiration.

c. *Series Magistrorum Generalium Ordinis Fratrum Minorum,* ed. G. Waitz, in Monumenta Germaniae Historica, *Scriptores,* 13: 392.

d. ChrTE 13 has a section treating "The Succession of General Ministers," but does not generally make an attempt to provide dates. Cf. *XIIIth Century Chronicles,* trans by Placid Hermann, with introduction and notes by Marie-Therese Laureilhe (Chicago: Franciscan Herald Press, 1961), 152-62.

e. Some marginal notes inserted in the manuscript following this entry place it in the pontificate of Urban IV (1261-64).

f. One wonders on what basis this author calculated the dates in this paragraph. The standard life at the time this list was composed, Thomas of Celano states that Francis died in 1226 in the twentieth year of conversion, cf. 1C 88 (FA:ED I 258-9).

in abundant fruit, he flew up to heaven, and Brother John Parenti succeeded him.[a]

Brother John Parenti took office in the year of the Lord 1227. He was the first general minister to be elected by a general chapter. After he had served in this capacity for five years, he was released in [the chapter of] 1232, and was succeeded by Brother Elias.

Brother Elias took office in the year 1232 and served for seven years. He was released from office in 1239 and was succeeded by Brother Albert of Pisa.

Brother Albert of Pisa took office in the year 1239 and served for eight months and a few days, when he died. Brother Haymo, an Englishman, succeeded him.

Brother Haymo took office in the year 1240 and served for three and a half years. He died in the year 1244 and was succeeded by Brother Crescentius.

Brother Crescentius took office in the year 1244 and served for three and a half years, being released from office in 1248.[b] Brother John of Parma succeeded him.

Brother John of Parma took office in the year 1248 and served for ten years. He was released from office in 1258 and was succeeded by Bonaventure.

Brother Bonaventure took office in the year 1258, being elected as general in chapter on the Feast of the Purification (2 February). He is the seventh general minister.

Norman Chronicle (1269-1272)

The so-called Norman Chronicle, composed in an undetermined religious house of that region between 1269 and 1272, attests to the striking contrast to traditional monasticism that the new mendicant orders presented to contemporaries. The following entry is under the year 1216, which contains an overview of the pontificate of Honorius III.[c]

In those times there came from the region of Lombardy[d] the Order of Minors, of which the founder was a certain man called Francis, a

---

a. This list does not consider Elias at this point; its author apparently considered him to have been simply a vicar of Saint Francis, rather than a true general minister. This way of numbering the generals was later followed by Jordan of Giano and the influential *Chronicle of the Twenty-Four Generals*. On the other hand, Thomas of Eccleston, Salimbene, and Peregrine of Bologna give the following order of general ministers: Francis, Elias, John Parenti, Elias.

b. This date is erroneous; Crescentius left office at the chapter of 1247. This error throws off the author's succeeding dates. He knew that John of Parma was general for ten years, so he wrongly calculated that he left office in 1258 rather than 1257.

c. *Chronicon Normannie* or *Annales Normannici*, ed. O. Holder-Egger, Monumenta Germaniae Historica, *Scriptores*, 26: 514; cf. TM, 20-21.

d. Often used as a general term for central and northern Italy.

1 Pt 2:11

citizen of Assisi. In the *Rule* which he composed he prescribes that "the brothers may not make anything their own, neither house, nor place, nor anything at all. As *pilgrims and strangers* in this world, serving the Lord in poverty and humility," they are to go about the entire world. The aforesaid Pope Honorius confirmed this *Rule*. At the same time the Order of Jacobites, founded in the region of Spain by a certain man named Dominic, spread throughout the earth; these at a later time chose for themselves the name of Preachers.

LR VI 1-2

These two Orders were received with great joy by both the Church and the people because of the novelty of their way of life, and they began to preach everywhere the name of Christ. The unaccustomed novelty of their life drew many noblemen and young students into these orders, so much so that within a few years they had filled the earth. One can indeed say that there is hardly a city or prominent town in Christendom in which these orders have not erected a house, having thus chosen to lead a religious life in the midst of humanity.

Danish Chronicle (c.1275-1285)

The author of this chronicle, which ends with the year 1282, has the following account under the year 1226. This account attests to the dissemination of the liturgical texts of the Feast of Francis to far-flung regions of Europe, as it is simply a pastiche of quotations from these sources.[a]

In that same year [1226], Saint Francis, freed from the fetters of this mortal life, blessedly departed to Christ, on the fourth day of the Nones of October, a Sunday; by then he had spent twenty years perfectly adhering to Christ.

LCh 17

This saint was a native of the city of Assisi. In the thirteenth year of his conversion, he traveled to the region of Syria, hurrying to the Sultan. Assaulted and beaten he preached Christ; and was sent back by the infidels to the camp of the faithful . . . Filled with the simplicity of a dove, he urged all creatures toward the love of the Creator. He used to preach to the birds, which heard him and allowed him to touch them; nor would they leave until he dismissed them.

LCh 7

LCh 8

Two years before he gave back his soul to heaven, in the vision of God, he saw above him the Crucified One, who clearly impressed on him the signs of his crucifixion, so that Francis, too, appeared crucified. His hands, feet, and side were marked with the stamp of the cross, whose marks were manifest in him.

LCh 11

---

a. *Chronica Danorum et praeciipue Sialandiae*, ed. Langebeck, *Scriptores Rerum Danicarum*, vol. 2 (1772), 626, cited in TM, 22-23.

LCh 15   One reads also that this servant of God *"cleansed* two *lepers,* one of   Mt 11:5
whom was also a paralytic, and he received healing from both afflic-
tions. He healed those afflicted with various diseases—an untold
number of people—all through the power of Christ." That is why it is
sung of him: "Hail, O splendor of the poor," etc.

An Abbreviated Chronicle of the Succession of General Ministers by Peregrine of Bologna (c.1305)

The following document was written by an Italian brother, Peregrine of
Bologna, in the form of a letter to the general minister, Gonsalvo of Balboa,
around 1305. Peregrine was certainly "very elderly," at least in his early 80's,
when he wrote down his reminiscences of the leaders of the Order, for he
had served as a *socius* of Haymo of Faversham sixty years previously. Peregrine rose to some prominence in the Order himself, serving as provincial
minister of both Greece and Genoa. As he mentions here, he served as the
liaison between John of Parma and the provincial ministers at the chapter of
Rome in 1257. Peregrine naturally devotes more space to the ministers of the
1240's and 1250's, with whom he was more familiar personally and who
were simply names for most brothers by the turn of the century. Although
later works, such as the great *Chronicle of the Twenty-Four Generals,* utilized
Peregrine's work, no manuscript of it was known until A. G. Little found a
copy at the turn of the last century.[d]

[1]It is worth transmitting what Brother Peregrine of Bologna, a
very elderly brother, wrote to the general minister, Brother
Gonsalvo, on the succession of the general ministers.

[2]The first general minister was the blessed Francis, of the city of
Assisi, as is narrated in his *Legend.* He was in the Order for seventeen
years;[b] before this he lived for three years as a religious,[c] but with
neither brothers nor places, intent on doing good works, giving alms,
and rebuilding churches, as the Lord inspired him to do these things.

The second was Brother Elias, from the same city, who was in the
office for a number of years. Because the brothers of that time did not
want their ministers to be permanent nor for life, Elias and they
agreed that he should resign his office, which he did.[d]

---

d. Little edited the work in an appendix to his first edition of Thomas of Eccleston's treatise, *Tractatus Thomae Vulgo Dicti de Eccleston, De Adventu Fraturm Minorum in Angliam,* Collection de études et de documents sur l'histoire religieuse et littéraire du Moyen Age, 7 (Paris: Fischbacher, 1909), 141-145. See also John Moorman, *History,* 292.

b. Peregrine calculates from the approval of the primitive way of life in 1209 until Francis's death in 1226.

c. From Francis's break with his father and "renunciation of the world" in 1206.

d. According to Peregrine, Francis resigned at some point, and Elias became general minister. He believes that Elias resigned after Francis's death and called a chapter of election for 1227.

The third was John Parenti, a native of Rome or that region.[a] He had a son in the Order, who behaved badly, and he punished him severely,[b] desiring to spare himself in nothing.

The fourth was the already mentioned Brother Elias, whom the brothers elected a second time with strong pressure.[c] He held office for a long time, and it seemed that he would remain in it for his whole life if the Order had not vigorously risen up against him, removing him from office with the assistance of Pope Gregory IX.[d]

The fifth was Brother Albert of Pisa, a good and holy man, who lived for only six months in office and then returned to the Lord.

The sixth was Brother Haymo, an Englishman, a doctor of sacred theology, who was the first minister general to go about visiting the provinces, even though he was an old man. He showed great concern for the proper celebration of the Divine Office. He also began to limit the authority and the power of the lay brothers, who up to this time had even held the office of superior.[e]

[3]The seventh was Brother Crescentius of Iesi, a city in the Marches of Ancona, who entered the Order when he was already an older man. He was learned in both canon law and the art of medicine. Not long afterwards he was made provincial minister of the Marches of Ancona. He encountered there a superstitious sect who were not walking according to the truth of the Gospel and the institutions of our Order, believing themselves to be more spiritual than the other brothers and wishing to live according to their own will, attributing all this to the Holy Spirit. While he was provincial minister, Brother Crescentius came down on them with a heavy hand. Meanwhile Brother Haymo had died, and when the general chapter was held, he was elected general minister. But once in office he soon proved himself ineffective. For this reason he held office for only three years, that is until the next general chapter, at which he didn't even want to participate. What is more, he was bold enough not to come to the [ecumenical] council, after the Pope had summoned him to it.[f] In both of these cases he sent as his vicar and substitute Brother

---

a. General minister from 1227 to 1232.

b. Perhaps a legend, stemming from the pun of "parent" and Parenti.

c. Does this ambiguous phrase suggest force on Elias's part, pressure from Gregory IX, or simply the popular push of the brothers to have Elias succeed John Parenti when it was clear the latter wished to resign at what was only a cismontane, rather than a general, chapter? See Rosalind Brooke, *Early Franciscan Government* (Cambridge: Cambridge at the University Press, 1959), 143-145.

d. At the chapter of 1239.

e. On Haymo's liturgical contributions and the legislation limiting the authority of lay brothers, see Lawrence Landini, *The Causes of the Clericalization of the Order of Friars Minor* (Chicago, Franciscan Herald Press, 1968), 129-137.

f. The First Council of Lyons, 1245.

Bonaventure of Iseo, a man of great discretion. So at the chapter [of 1247] he was released from office because of his inadequacies and lack of eloquence.

[4]The eighth general minister, John of Parma, was elected at this same general chapter. He held office for nine or ten years. A cultivated and spiritual man, he was sent at that time as an envoy to the Greek emperor with letters of great importance.[a] Because of this mission the Pope called him "the Angel of peace." For when he was there, everyone—not only the emperor, but the patriarch, the princes, the bishops, and all the clergy and people—was greatly edified by him, as much as for his way of life as for his knowledge and learning. He would in no way accept any of the many gifts which were offered him there; this also increased the esteem in which he was held. Having conducted himself so wisely and well in this charge which had been assigned to him, he certainly would have achieved the end for which he was sent, if both the Emperor and the Pope had not died in the Lord the same year.[b] But as the years went by, he had many prominent rivals who accused him before the Pope. They finally swayed the Pope,[c] who ordered him privately to resign from his office; furthermore, he was to refuse absolutely to accept it again, should the ministers choose to re-elect him. Brother Peregrine of Bologna had this from John's own mouth, because he served as the intermediary at this chapter between the ministers and John.

[5]When Brother John was released from office, Brother Bonaventure of Bagnoregio was elected at the same chapter [1257] as the ninth general. He was a great doctor of theology and known by all. He held office for about sixteen years; then he was made a Cardinal, and was poisoned by a certain religious.[d] As a consequence of this poison, he passed to the Lord.

After him, Brother Jerome of Ascoli was elected as the tenth general minister. After completing a diplomatic mission to Greece while still general minister, he was promoted to the cardinalate and then elected Pope.[e]

The eleventh was Brother Bonagratia, who was from a village in the diocese of Bologna called San Giovanni in Persiceto. He lived for only a couple of years in office.[f] The twelfth was Brother Arlotto of

---

a. John was sent on his mission in 1249, returning late in 1250.

b. Pope Innocent IV and the Emperor John III Vatatzes both died in 1254.

c. Pope Alexander IV.

d. This is the only source for the story that Bonaventure was poisoned at the Second Council of Lyons in 1274.

e. For James of Ascoli, cf. supra 25, 803-4.

f. To be exact, four. Bonagratia was elected in May, 1279 and died in October of 1283.

Tuscany, from the noble castle of Prato, who also lived for only a short time in office.[a] The thirteenth was Brother Matthew of Aquasparta; he also was minister for only a brief time, for he was chosen to be a Cardinal in the Roman Curia.[b] The fourteenth was Brother Raymond of the province of Provençe; after some years, because of the suggestion of certain people, he was removed by Pope Boniface VIII.[c] The fifteenth was Brother John of Murrovale, who afterwards was made a cardinal of the Holy Roman Church.[d] The sixteenth was Brother Gonsalvo, a doctor of sacred theology, a Spaniard from the province of Santiago.[e]

On the basis of this calculation, there are fifteen individuals who have been general minister, but there have been sixteen terms of office, because Brother Elias was released from office and later re-elected to it, the only general to which this happened.

Chronicle of Walter of Gisburn (1305-1313)

Walter, an Augustinian canon of Gisburn in Yorkshire, composed a chronicle of the major events of British history in the early years of the fourteenth century. The following account of the new mendicant orders is given under the year 1215.[f]

At that time, during the reign of King John, there arose the two new orders of the Preachers and the Minors . . . The blessed Francis began the Order of Friars Minor in the city of Assisi, where he also was born. Hearing one day what the Lord told his disciples when he sent them forth to preach, Francis got up immediately and began to put into practice with all his strength everything that he had heard. He removed the shoes from his feet and put on a single wretched tunic, taking a cord for a belt.[g] Thus he began his order of brothers near the same city of Assisi, at Saint Mary of the Portiuncula, in the year 1206, which was the fourteenth year of the pontificate of Innocent III,[h] who approved this order.

---

a. Arlotto was elected at the chapter of 1285 and died the following year.

b. Matthew was elected in 1287, and was made a cardinal the following year.

c. Raymond Geoffroi was elected in 1289; he was removed in 1295 because Boniface considered him too sympathetic towards the Spirituals.

d. John was elected in 1296, and made Cardinal Bishop of Porto in 1302.

e. Gonsalvo was elected in 1304, serving until his death in 1313.

f. *Chronica de gestis regum Angliae*, ed. Liebermann, *Monumenta Germaniae Historica, Scriptores*, 28: 631-32; TM, 23-24.

g. Based on 1C 22 cf. FA:ED I 201-2.

h. Perhaps an error in transcribing XIIII for VIIII, as 1206 was the ninth year of Innocent's pontificate.

His brothers had a little house in Riccardina, outside of Bologna, given to them by Signore Accursio Magno, who composed a new Gloss in five volumes on all of civil law.

Many, both noble and ignoble, clerics and laymen, rejecting the pomp of the world, followed this blessed Francis by adhering to his footsteps. Their holy Father taught them how to attain evangelical perfection, to embrace poverty, and to travel the road of holy simplicity. Besides, for himself and for his present and future brothers he wrote a *Rule* based on the Gospel, which the Lord Pope Innocent III confirmed.

After he had been weakened by a long illness and had reached the end of his life, he had himself placed on the bare ground. Then calling his brothers together, he placed his hand on each of them and, after this, he likewise blessed them. Then, in imitation of the Lord's Supper he gave a morsel of bread to each one and, as was his custom, he invited all creatures to praise God. Finally, he ran joyfully to meet death itself and invited it to make its lodging with him, saying: "Welcome, my Sister Death!"[a] She therefore came at that final hour and he fell asleep in the Lord on October 4th, in that same year 1226.

---

a. Closely following here the account of 2C 217, cf. FA:ED II 387-8.

A Liturgical Legend in the Tradition
of the Friars Preacher
(1268)

At the beginning of his *Book of Praises,* Bernard of Besse mentions two lives of Saint Francis written in Italy, one by Thomas of Celano, the other by a Prothonotary, John.[a] In his *Expositio super Regulam* II 124, written in about 1321-22,[b] Angelo Clareno refers to the work, as he does in a letter written to Filippo di Majorca, and in the *Book of Chronicles or Tribulations of the Order of Lesser Ones.* And Arnald of Sarrant in his *The Kinship of Christ* refers to the work,[c] as, in the sixteenth century, does Mariano da Firenze[d] and Peter Rudolph a Tossiniano,[e] in the seventeenth, Luke Wadding.[f] None of these authors quotes the text. Only Bernard of Besse indicates its opening words, *Quasi stella matutina.* And none of the later authors, Mariano or Wadding, indicate where it might be found. Thus questions abound concerning it. Is there any existing manuscript of the work? Did it fall prey to the decision of the Chapter of 1266 to remove all other lives of Saint Francis in favor of that of Bonaventure?[g] Was it absorbed into some other portrait?

Part of the difficulty is the identification of John "the Prothonotary." Bernard of Besse is the first one known to have referred to him as such. Angelo Clareno identifies him as Brother John of Celano, an identification which Arnald of Sarrant rejects in favor of John "the Prothonotary." It is not until the sixteenth century that Mariano of Firenze further complicates the issue by writing of John in the following way: "Brother John of Ceperano, Notary of the Apostolic See, out of the great devotion that he had for Saint Francis, wrote of his life beginning *Quasi stella matutina.*" Wadding accepted this, but added that he wrote because of "the mandate of Gregory IX." Thus more questions arise.

At the turn of the last century, Edouard d'Alençon examined the questions in light of a note made by a Dominican, P. Denifle, who had discovered that the Friars Preacher, after a period of difficulty in determining the texts of their

---

a. Cf. supra BPr I 1.

b. Angelo Clareno, *Expositio Regulae Fratrum Minorum* II, ed. Livarius Oliger (Ad Claras Aquas, Quaracchi: Collegium S. Bonaventurae, 1912), 124.

c. Cf. supra KnSF I 9d.

d. Cf. Giuseppe Abate, "Le fonti storiche della Chronaca di fra Mariano da Firenze," *Miscellanea Francescana* 34 (1934): 46-52; C. Cannarozzi, "Una fonte primaria degli 'Annales' del Wadding (Il 'Fasciculus Chronicarum' di Fra Mariano da Firenze)," *Studi Francescani* 27 (1930): 251-85.

e. Peter Rudolphius a Tossiniano, *Historia Seraphicae Religionis* (Venetiis, 1586), 334.

f. Luke Wadding, *Annales Minorum seu Trium Ordinum a S. Francisco Institutorum,* an. 1230, n.7, t. II (Ad Claras Aquas, Quaracchi: Collegium S. Bonaventurae, 1931), 268.

g. Cf. FA:ED I 18.

liturgical celebrations, accepted in 1268 a text that began *Quasi stella matutina*.[a] While proposing a number of possibilities for the identity of the author, d'Alençon left it an open question. In the final analysis, the Friars Preacher accepted the following set of nine lessons based on Thomas of Celano's *Life of Saint Francis*. The resolution of the question of this being the text of John the Prothonotary remains for future scholars.[b]

Lesson I

1C 7   Blessed Francis was a native of Tuscany, born **of humble origins** in the town of Assisi. After the wantonness **of youthful heat** and the vanities of worldly business, **he was worn down** by the annoyance of a serious **illness** and *the finger of God* brought about his conversion. Lk 11:20 But **one day, when he had invoked the Lord's mercy with his whole** 1C 8   **heart,** it was shown him **what he must do.** He soon changed his life, selling everything that he had acquired with much toil for money. Then one day he entered a church that was falling into ruin. Moved by its distress, he offered the money he was carrying to the priest. 1C 9   Out of fear of his parents he refused to accept it, so Francis threw it away, since he thought it unseemly to possess money and virtues at the same time.

Lesson II

1C 12   His father was in a rage when he saw this and bound him in chains and in prison. His mother intervened, hoping by her coaxing 1C 13   to reverse his decision. But when the man of God could not be softened either by his father's blows or his mother's breasts, he was released at the insistence of his mother's affection. Then having given back all his clothes, even his shorts, to his father's **greed** before **the bishop of the city,** he was **half-clothed,** and a pack of youths pestered him **with mud and stones** as a fool. One day when he heard from the gospel reading that *no staff, nor purse, nor sandals* should *be* Mt 10:9-10 *carried* by the followers of Christ, he put aside his sandals and staff and he dressed with a cord for *a belt* and a poor tunic of scratchy wool.

---

a. Eduard d'Alençon published the work, cf. "Legenda brevis S. Francisci ex gestis ejus quae incipiunt *'Quasi stella,'* " in *Analecta Ordinis Fratrum Minorum Capuchinorum* 14 (1898): 370-3.

b. Cf. Felice Accrocca, "Intorno al Notaio Giovanni Autore della Vita di S. Francesco *Quasi Stella Matutina*," in *Francesco e Le Sue Immagini: Momenti della Evoluzione della Coscienza Storica dei Frati Minori [Secoli XII-XVI]* (Padova: Centro Studi Antoniani, 1997), 37-56. Leonard Lemmens did the same in 1908, cf. "Testimonia minora Saeculi XIII de S. Francisco Assisiensis," in AFH 1 (1908) 259-262; as did the editors of Quaracchi in AF X 533-535.

Lesson III

When more refined food was occasionally brought to him, he
altered it lest they attract his palate, and he rarely took wine. He wore
the same tunic day and night for clothing and for bed;[a] it was covered
with worms, and was made more tolerable by beating with a staff. He
gave much attention to prayers, sacred meditation, dutiful compassion for the unfortunate, wondrous chastity, venerable humility,
and the authority of that saying, to *submit the necks* of the lofty *to the
yoke of discipline.* If ever a spark should leap from the quenched
embers, he would plunge himself naked into a mass of snow or
water. He likewise treated lepers, whom he used to avoid, with
friendly respect. With gentle words he invited animate, as well as
heavenly beings to praise Christ.

1C 51

1C 52

Sir 51:26

1C 17

1C 80-1

Lesson IV

The blessed father Hugolino, while Bishop of Ostia, took him, at
the recommendation of the Supreme Pontiff, under his care. Then
when he was raised to the chair of supreme shepherd, as the same
holy man had predicted, under the name of Gregory IX, he supported
him and the brothers of his Order with loyal affection. He encouraged with great care the Order of Poor Ladies, the slip taken from
their garden. So many began to leave the world and hasten to the
gentle father's guardianship. To them he gave a rule that was unre-
fined in eloquence of speech but effectively eloquent in production of
deeds. He laid out for them a pattern of living in word and deed.

1C 100

1C 37

1C 32

Lesson V

Thus this holy man as one *placed upon a stand* began to shine with a
flash of miracles. Thus he appeared transfigured before the brothers
like solar lightning. He had knowledge of happenings though not
present, the secrets of hearts, and of many future events. Brothers
whom he had sent to diverse parts of the world came together in a
brief time at his bidding, without any human summons, according
to his wish. He set a paralytic free, as well as a certain woman struck
blind, and another possessed by the devil. He also changed water
into wine, and many who touched his cord were healed of their various illnesses.

Mt 5:15

1C 47

1C 48

1C 29-30

1C 66-7; 1C 70

1C 61; 1C 63

---

a. As it is expressed, this is a new piece of information. It rests upon 1C 22: "one tunic," 1C 39, 52. The
following sentence is entirely new. Cf. FA:ED I 201-2, 218, 227-8.

Lesson VI

1C 58

When he once in a certain field preached words of encouragement with his affable naturalness to a flock of birds, they immediately resounded with their melodies the praise of the Creator, their tongues stretched out and their necks extended toward him. And as he walked through their midst, they touched him with their beaks as

1C 59

if to plant kisses. He **likewise imposed silence** on some chattering swallows while he was preaching; they immediately fell silent until

1C 94-5

the preaching was concluded. In a certain hermitage a man in the likeness of a Seraph appeared to him as if affixed to the gibbet of a cross; the figure imprinted on his hands and feet scars like the marks of nails. And in his right side there appeared the scar of the covered wound as if pierced by a lance.

Lesson VII

1C 109

So in the twentieth year of his conversion, when he was aware through divine revelation that his end was near, he announced his imminent death to two brothers. Breaking into the psalm *With a loud* Ps 142 *voice I cry out to the Lord,* **in sackcloth and sprinkled with ashes** at his own request, he forgave the brothers both present and absent their

1C 110

offenses. And thus that holiest of souls was released from the flesh; one of the brothers saw it penetrating the recesses of heaven with the prominence of the moon and not a little of the brilliance of the sun. His sacred body was buried with great respect in the oratory of blessed George alongside the walls of Assisi.

Lesson VIII

1C 112

In the limbs of the deceased, which shone with more brilliance than usual, the imprints of the cross were unveiled. Previously he kept them hidden in his guarded breast. From the imprint of the saving cross, there arose innumerable healthful favors, of which I will state only a few, so that the attention of the audience may not be

1C 139

overburdened. A certain youth lay near death, but recovered with

1C 137

marvelous speed at his mother's prayer. A man troubled by an

1C 138

unclean spirit was freed when he touched his tomb. A woman who had lost her mind was suddenly cured when she received the sign of

1C 136

the cross from him in a vision. A blind man recovered his sight when he touched his tomb.

Lesson IX

Given these prodigious signs and innumerable others proven by   1C 123
the statements of witnesses, Pope Gregory hastened to Assisi, where
Rv 5:9   a multitude *from every nation* had gathered. After the joyous celebra-   1C 126
tion of the holy man, he reverently enrolled blessed Francis, whose
teacher and instructor he had been, in the catalogue of saints. **And in**   LCh 17; LJS 76
his name, he had a church of wonderful grandness built. He laid
the first stone of the foundation, and not long after that, his most
sacred body was buried with marvelous reverence. He died in the   1C 88
one-thousandth, two-hundredth, twenty-sixth year of the Lord.

A Life of Saint Francis by an Anonymous Monk of a German Monastery
(c. 1275)

An anonymous monk of the Benedictine monastery of Oberaltaich, Germany, composed a summary or compilation of the life of Saint Francis. While his portrait is based fundamentally on the writings of Thomas of Celano, it is nuanced by the liturgical texts of Julian of Speyer and the Major Legend of Saint Bonaventure. The author's admiration for Francis is obvious. His verbal tapestry is well crafted: the strands of Thomas's Life and Remembrance are carefully stitched to reveal a portrait that is straight-forward, devoid of the monastic allusions or images one might expect. Yet it is difficult to overlook the author's arrangement of the text and his nuances in this presentation of yet another portrait of Saint Francis.

The oldest manuscript of this text is that of the Manuscript 9533 of the State Library of München, Germany. Its date is sometime in the second half of the thirteenth century. *The Life of Saint Francis* is only part of this manuscript. The other pieces contain *The Lives of the Fathers of Egypt,* John Cassian's *Institutes,* and lives of some monastic saints. When seen from this perspective, the admiration of the anonymous monk casts new light on the document, enabling the reader to appreciate Francis in light of monastic spirituality.

Prologue[a]

To have knowledge of the saints, to know their way of living and the wonderful things which the Lord worked through them, is useful for many reasons, namely, for the teaching of virtue, for their greater veneration and that their prayers be more devoutly invoked. I have, for this reason, striven here to draw out a summary from a life of the most holy Father Francis, for it is burdensome for busy people to read or re-copy in its entirety. I do this so that those who for the preceding reasons desire to have some knowledge, may briefly find what they require in this compilation, although many of his words and deeds, which are most useful for edification, have been omitted here in order to avoid undue length. Those who wish can find these words and deeds more fully in his complete legend.

---

a. This translation is based on the text found in AF X 694-719.

Chapter headings.

The Life of Saint Francis, the Confessor

I: His birth and His Youth

[1]Blessed Francis, the first founder and father of the Order of Lesser Brothers, was born in the city of Assisi in the province of Tuscany. Although he had been raised by his parents to a great degree according to the vanity and arrogance of the age, nevertheless as a young man, he was very refined with good manners, kind, free, humane, affable, removing from himself whatever seemed to him in some manner offensive; he was generous toward the poor, and always devout toward the ministers of God and their ministries.

1C 1

2C 3

2C 3

He Clothes a Poor Man

[2]One day he met a poor half-naked knight. He felt compassion not only for his need but also for his shame. Shedding the finely made clothes he was wearing, he generously gave them to him for the sake of Christ, happy to imitate the example of blessed Martin who clothed a poor man with a part of his cloak. He is known to have

2C 5

LMj I 2; 2C 5

done this not only at that time, but also many times for other **poor people.**

He Prophesies Concerning Himself

2C 4

[3]**Along with a good number of** his **fellow citizens, he was** once **captured in a conflict with the Perugians.** While all his **fellow captives** were grieving, **he was exultant,** and when they wondered about the reason for his joy, he **prophetically answered** in this way:

1C 3

"**I will yet be worshiped as a saint throughout the world."** Divine grace, wishing to draw him to itself more fully, first through **infirmity of body,** then through revelations shown to him from heaven

2C 9

and through divinely infused experiences of internal **sweetness,** rendered the world entirely insipid for him and made him aspire

LMj 1 5

from **his inmost being** for things eternal.

He Greets a Leper with a Kiss

· 2C 9

[4]When he was beginning to be victorious over himself and in order that he might give himself up totally **to divine** service, **one day he met** a filthy **leper** on a road. He jumped down **from the horse on which** he was sitting, offered **money** to the leper and **kissed his hand,** even though earlier there was hardly anything **in the world** which **he abhorred** more than **lepers.** He then immediately **mounted** his **horse** and looked around, but **the leper** was nowhere evident **on the wide field.** This is just like what blessed Gregory has reported as happening to a monk, named Martyrio, who carried Christ on his shoulders, in the appearance of a leper, and when he wanted to detain the leper, he suddenly disappeared.[a] Therefore, Francis, the servant of God, **wondering** at what had been done,

1C 17

began thereafter to be so devoted **to lepers** that, finally renouncing the world, **he sought** them out and washed and **cleaned** the filth **of** their **sores.**

II: The Crucified Speaks to Him

2C 10

[5]He would often **frequent** out-of-the-way **places for the purpose**

Mj II 1; 2C 10

of praying. One day he was devoutly prostrate before **the crucifix in**

LMj II 1

the church of San Damiano when he heard the voice of Christ

2C 10

speaking bodily to him from **the very image of the Crucified: "Francis, go, repair my home which, as you see, is totally falling into**

---

a. Gregory the Great, *Homiliae in Evangelia,* II, hom. 39, 10 (PL 76, 1300). Beyond this story, little is known of this ancient monk. One manuscript has his name as Martin. Cf. AF X 696.

ruins." Stunned by the authority of the voice, he was totally *changed into another man.* He made himself ready to obey, that he might repair that very weakened material church, although the request should rather be understood to refer to the holy Church of the faithful which is the dwelling *of the living God,* and which seemed to be breaking down in many instances on every side, both in faith and in morals, that he would repair it by his example and by the instruction of his holy doctrine. Later, through his servant Francis, the Order of Poor Ladies had its beginning in this same place, of which blessed Clare, that most holy virgin, by God's order, was the primary foundation.

He Sells What He Possesses

[6]Francis, the servant of God, wishing to become the perfect imitator of the evangelical perfection in order to purchase that precious *treasure* and heavenly *pearl, sold everything he possessed,* because he was a salesman by profession, and he dispensed some of that money to repair that church and the rest he set aside for the use of the poor. When his natural father, who loved him according to the flesh, not according to the spirit, understood his son's intention, he tried to recall his son from the good he had begun, first by berating him with abusive words, and then also by molesting him with beatings and chains. But Francis, the man of God who was prepared to suffer these and other things for Christ, rejoiced that he was *accounted worthy to suffer disgrace for* His *name of Jesus.* His father, seeing *that he was doing no good,* was led on by cupidity and tried at length to extort this money from him.

He Restores Everything to His Father.

[7]But he who did not love money, although he decided to spend it on pious uses, carefully weighed in what manner he might licitly rid himself of it. In front of the bishop of the city not only did he cheerfully give up the money, but also the clothes in which he was dressed, down to his trousers. And standing there naked, he demonstrated that he had nothing in common with the world. By embracing the naked Christ on the cross, he was prepared to enter naked into wrestling with the naked devil. It was then discovered, moreover, that he was wearing a hair shirt next to his skin which perfectly shows that he was the victor over the flesh, the world, and the devil, spurning the world, subjecting the flesh to the spirit by chastisement, not acceding to the temptations of the devil, not

1 Sm 10:6

Heb 12:22

Mt 13:44-6

Acts 5:41
Mt 27:24

LMj II 1; 2C 1

LMj II 1; 2C 1
LMj II 1

1C 18

1C 8-9

LJS 1; 1C 8
LMj II 1
2C 12

LJS 8; 1C 12

1C 13

1C 14

1C 14
2C 12
1C 14

1C 15; LJS 9
1C 15

2C 12
LMj II 4
1C 15

heeding the urgings of the demons, suitably attributing what is its own to each of these.[a]

III: He Repairs Three Churches

[LJS 13; 1C 21]
[2C 18]
[1C 22]
[1C 23]
[1C 22]

[8]Therefore, Francis carefully weighed the work in every way to restore the church of San Damiano. In the same way, he rebuilt a second church, and in the same way, with the help of God, also a third one called Saint Mary of the Portiuncula, where he also began to stay frequently, because he was inflamed with a remarkable devotion toward the Mother of all goodness. It was here that on a certain day he heard the Gospel being read during the Mass about how the Lord sent his disciples to preach without *purse,* without *money,* without *shoes* and staff, and *two tunics,* and that they should invoke peace on all, and preach penance. "This is what I desire," he said. And as if these words of the Lord were said especially for him, he strove to implement them all faithfully to the letter.

[Mt 10:10]

He Adopts a Form for the Order

[LJS 14; 1C 23]
[1C 36-7]
[1C 29]
[1C 25-6]
[1C 37]
[1C 26]

[9]At that time he formed for himself the habit of the Order of Lesser Brothers and *began* the Order. From this time on he began to announce to all *the reign of God* and to preach penance, and the fame of his virtue began to call forth many to the contempt of the world and to a desire for a better life. Among these there were first six men of virtue who, instructed by the Holy Spirit, decided to live under his training and followed him. While he formed these men with new instruction, he taught them to walk with steady steps in the way of blessed poverty, holy simplicity, and the entire range of spiritual discipline.

[Lk 4:43]

God Shows Him the Future

[1C 26]
[LJS 18]
[1C 26]

[10]One day when blessed father Francis was at prayer, he recalled before the Lord *in bitterness of his soul the years* he spent in the world. He was divinely infused with an ineffable joy and the guarantee of the remission of all his sins, and caught up above himself *in an excess of mind.* It was revealed to him by the Lord that his new brotherhood would be enlarged into a great multitude and by a divine gift spread to the ends of the earth. When he returned to himself he announced what he had seen and admonished them to have confidence in the

[Is 38:15]
[Ps 31:23]

---

a. The phrase *quod suum est cuique* [what is its own] is taken from Marcus Tullius Cicero (106-43 B.C.) who, in writing of moral goodness and the conservation of organized society, proposes "rendering to every person his/her due." Cf. Cicero *De Officiis, Bk* I, 5, 15.

goodness of God, certain that the Lord would fulfill his promise. Then after certain others joined them, they became **twelve in number.** LMj III 7

IV: The Order Is Confirmed

[11]Therefore, Francis, that man of God, **seeing that** according to His promise **the Lord** was disposed **to increase the number** of the brothers **daily, wrote a rule for himself and his brothers, using primarily** the principles **of the holy Gospel, longing only for its perfection,** although he added **a few other things** which seemed **necessary. He went to Rome to the Lord Pope Innocent III, a man glorious** in all things and remarkably endowed **with a wisdom** both human and divine, and **asked** him **humbly** both to confirm the Order **and approve the** *Rule.* 1C 33 · 1C 32; 1C 33 · LMj III 9

Just a short time before, **the Lord Pope had had a** very memorable **vision.** In it **the Lateran** Church, the mother and nourisher of all the churches in the world, **was on the point of falling down, when a certain religious man, small, scorned, and poor, was propping it up with his bent back so it would not fall.** He was wondering what this vision could mean, when he saw Francis, the man of God, and **after questioning him, he realized his purpose.** Then **he said: "This is truly that** man **who by** his **work** and teaching will shore up the Church which is now slipping." For this reason **that lord easily bowed to his request;** it was also for this reason that, **filled with devotion to God, he always loved** *Christ's servant* with a special love. He granted his requests and promised to grant even more, after **the Lord** increased **the number of brothers** for the salvation of the faithful. 2C 17 · 1C 33 · 2C 17 · Rom 1:1 · 1C 33

He Chooses to Be Useful to Others

[12]Giving thanks to the Lord **for the favor of so great a father,** the brothers began to confer among themselves **whether they should** live **among people or go off to solitary places. But Saint Francis, not** trusting **in his own efforts,** referred such **a matter** to God as **he** devoutly **prayed** together with the brothers that the Lord in his mercy would deem them worthy to communicate His will to them. Therefore, instructed **by** divine **revelation,** he chose to dwell among men for the edification of others, since they had been especially **sent by the Lord to convert very many people.** For this same reason the Son of God left the hidden place of His Father's breast, became man, came to us, and similarly deigned *to associate with men* on earth. For 1C 34; 1C 35 · LMj IV 2 · Bar 3:38

the solitary life teaches to turn one's attention to God and to one's self. But who desires to edify others must necessarily be present to those he ought to benefit.

V: He Preaches Everywhere

1C 36

[13]Francis, the servant of God, went around proclaiming, acting confidently in all matters because of the apostolic authority committed to him. Not fearing anyone's rebuke, he spoke the truth most faithfully so that well-educated men, distinguished by their dignity and fame, were amazed at his words and were frightened

1C 37

in his presence by a salutary fear. The Church was renewed in both sexes at his type of teaching, and he showed the way of salvation to every rank of the faithful.

He Establishes Three Orders

LJS 23

[14]He established three Orders in the Church; he named the first

1C 38

that of Lesser Brothers, using the pretext of the word which Christ will say in judgment to those about to be judged, *"What you did for one of these, the least of my brethren, you did for me,"* whom he holds fast by

Mt 25:40

LJS 23; 1C 38;
1C 18-9

reason of his habit, his profession, and his love. The second, which is called that of Poor Ladies in which Saint Clare is the first stone upon which this Order was divinely founded through the ministry of blessed Francis. It is said that because it had its beginning in the church of San Damiano, it was sometimes called the Order of Saint

LJS 23

Damian. The third is called that of Penitents which comprises both sexes, and is known to have been very fittingly set up both for the married and single, for clerics and lay people, who do not yet presume to renounce their property. Under the symbol of these three Orders, according to the will of God he repaired the three churches.

VI: The Fiery Chariot

1C 47

[15]One night, for the purpose of praying more privately, blessed Francis was away in body from his brothers, from whom, however, he never departed spiritually due to his affective paternal solicitude for them. About midnight some of the brothers were sleeping and others were devoutly praying in silence, when a most brilliant, *fiery*

2 Kgs 2:11-14

chariot entered through the door and moved *here and there* about two or three times. There was a huge ball sitting on the chariot, that looked like the sun and it made the night bright. Those who were awake were astonished; those sleeping awoke in a fright, and they all

wondered what this meant. But by the strength of such a light, by
which not only their bodies but also their hearts had been illuminated, they understood that this was the soul of their holy father,
which because of the grace of his exceptional purity and his concern for great piety in his sons was shown to them in such a won-   LJS 39
derful glory of light while he was still living on earth. For the flame of   1C 47
love, burning like fire, was burning within him due to his devotion,
and shone forth exteriorly in his *word* and *deed, the chariot and chario-*   Off V 3-4
teer of a spiritual army.

Col 3:17; 2 Kgs 2:12

How He Was Affected by the Love of God

[16]How strongly he was affected inwardly by fire of divine love   LMj IX 1
can be gathered from the fact that he could hardly ever hear the   2C 196
words "the love of God" spoken without a change in himself. For as
soon as he heard the words "the love of God," he would suddenly
become excited and on fire, as if the strings of his heart were
inwardly being plucked by the pick of that phrase. "The love" he
said, "of Him, Jesus Christ, who loves us greatly, is intensely to be
loved." He kept unchangeably until his death what he had already
resolved while still in the world, that he would refuse no one who
asked "for the love of God."

Meat Appears as Fish

[17]It happened one time while Francis was at Alessandria in Lom-   2C 78
bardy, he was invited by a devout man to dinner and asked that
according to the Gospel he eat of everything *that was placed before him.*   Lk 10:8
At this time there was a deceitful poor man standing at the door,
asking that for the love of God alms be given to him. Francis, the
friend of God, hearing the man place the words "the love of God" in
his petition, joyfully picked up the capon leg that was placed before
him, put bread with it, and sent it to the man. But that unhappy
man kept what was given to him, in order that by it he might bring
disgrace upon the saint. The next day when the people were gath-   2C 79
ered together, Saint Francis preached with the whole crowd intent
on him. At this point the miserable man arose, looked at Francis
maliciously and, showing everyone the meat which he had saved,
he shouted: "Look, what kind of man this Francis is whom you
honor as a saint! Look at the meat he gave me when he was eating a
short time ago." They all turned on this ill-disposed man and
accused him being possessed by a demon. For what he insisted
was the meat of a capon, appeared to all, by a miracle of God, as a
fish. That wretched man, astounded and confounded by the

miracle, asked the holy man's pardon in front of everyone, exposing what an abominable will he had. After *the rebel turned back* to his senses, the meat returned to its original nature.

Is 46:8

The Ecstasy of His Contemplation

[18]He was moved in a remarkable manner at the name also of our Lord Jesus Christ, and so rather often, sitting at table or doing something else and either hearing, saying, or thinking "Jesus," he forgot what he was doing, and would be suspended and carried away in contemplation. One time, riding on a donkey, he was passing through Borgo San Sepulcro, wishing to go to a certain dwelling of lepers. Men and women from all directions came running to see and touch him, pulling at him with usual devotion and cutting off bits of his tunic. But he seemed insensible to all this and he did not notice any of these things as though he possessed a lifeless corpse. Finally, long past through Borgo, and as if returning from somewhere else, the contemplator of heaven asked whether he was near Borgo yet. For this holy man was living within himself, and therefore the noise outside did not seize his ears, nor did his eyes wander around on things outside. He was intent only on God and himself. Walking, sitting, eating he was always focused on prayer and divine meditation. Nevertheless, he was not reluctant when he recognized the time to be right to involve himself in the spiritual affairs and attend to the salvation of his neighbors.

VII: He Conquers Demons

[19]He very often spent the night alone in prayer in out-of-the-way churches where, with the protection of divine grace, he overcame many terrors and insults of the demons. But the very brave soldier of Christ, knowing that his Lord is present in all places to those who trust in Him, used to say in his heart: "You, evil one, cannot harm me here anymore than if we were in front of a crowd in a public place."

[20]Therefore, spending the night one time in a solitary church, he sensed a crowd of demons running across the roof. He quickly got up, fortified with the sign of the cross, and said to them: "On behalf of Almighty God I order you, demons, do to my body whatever is permitted to you by Him. I gladly bear it, because I do not have a more noxious enemy than my body, so you will be avenging me on my opponent when you will exercise vengeance on him in my

Margin notes:
1C 82
1C 115
2C 98
1C 43
1C 71
1C 71
1C 72
2C 122

place." Confused by shame, the demons immediately fled, amazed   LMj X 3; 2C 12
that in fragile flesh there existed a spirit so constant.   LMj X 3

His Throne in Heaven Is Shown

[21]When morning came, his brother companion came and found   2C 123
him prostrate before the altar in prayer. And when his companion,
who was also a man of great sanctity, gave himself to prayer, he was
rapt in ecstasy and he saw among the many thrones in heaven one
more worthy than the rest, adorned with precious stones and glittering with glory. He wondered whose throne this might be, and
heard a voice saying to him: "This throne belonged to one of the
great ones who fell, and now it is reserved for the humble Francis."
After prayer when they were walking together, the companion said
to Saint Francis: "What is your own opinion of yourself?" The saint
responded: "I see myself as the greatest sinner. For if God had
given such benefits to anyone else that he gave to me, he would have
become much better and more pleasing to God than I." At this
point the Spirit said within that brother's heart: "Now you know
that the vision is true, since humility has preserved for the humblest one this throne that was lost through pride."

VIII: His Humility

[22]In his own opinion he was nothing but a sinner, though he   2C 140
would truly be the model of every kind of holiness. Forgetting what
he had gained, he kept before his eyes only his defects. His only
ambition was to be better, and not satisfied with what he had, he
strove continually to accumulate new virtues and the riches of merits. He was humble in opinion, more humble in manner, and most
humble in the estimation of himself. It could not be discerned that
he was a prelate of the Order and its General Minister, except for this
most sparkling gem, that in virtue of humility he was the least
among the lesser. He preferred that he be disparaged and depreci-
ated, rather than praised and honored. Often honored by all, he suf-   1C 53
fered great sorrow and against their praises he recalled to mind his
humble origins, if there were any. "No one," he said, "should be   2C 133
praised, as long as his end is still uncertain."

His Obedience

[23]In order to preserve the virtue of humility, even though he was   2C 143
the highest prelate in the Order, Francis set up for himself a vicar   2C 144
over the brothers, to whom as his superior he always wished to be   2C 143; 2C 15

subject, like one of the others. "I know," he said, "the fruit of obedience, and that no time passes without fruit for one who by obedience *bends his neck to the yoke* of another." Therefore, he also used to say: "Among the many benefits the Lord gave me this grace, that I would readily obey a novice of one day, if he were put over me as a master, as I would obey the most discerning and oldest. For a subject should not consider his prelate as a human being, but as him whose place he is taking and for love of whom he is subjected to him. The more contemptible is he who presides, the more pleasing to God is the humility of the one who obeys."

Sir 51:26

IX: His Poverty

1C 51

2C 55

[24]He zealously and carefully guarded the holy and evangelical poverty that the Son of God, coming from heaven, taught and observed. He taught that she is the way of perfection and the pledge and guarantee of eternal happiness. No one coveted gold as he this evangelical *pearl*. For content from the beginning until the end of his religious life with a single tunic, cord with breeches, he showed outwardly how his riches were stored. And when he had driven *all envy* from himself, he could not give up his envy for poverty, if he saw anyone poorer than himself, not out of any desire for empty glory but only because from a feeling of simple compassion and his desire for a more sublime poverty. And although he desired all men to be saved, he nevertheless feared that poverty would be diminished for this reason: if many entered religion, since many need more things than a few do, he was afraid to a certain degree of large numbers coming to the Order.

2C 83

1C 76

2C 70

Mt 13:45

1 Pt 2:1

Francis's Begging

2C 74

[25]Training himself sometimes and sparing the embarrassment of his brothers, in the beginning he used to go for alms by himself through the streets. Thus, by his example, he animated others to the humility of begging.

What the World and the Brothers May Owe to Him

2C 71

[26]He used to say: *"In this last hour* of the age the Lesser Brothers have been given to the world as an opportunity for merit, so that through them the elect may be commended to Christ at the judgment, when he says: *'What you did for one of these, the least of my brethren, you did for me.'* There is an exchange," he said, "between the world and the brothers; they owe the world the teaching of salvation and

1 Jn 2:18

Mt 25:45

2C 70

good example; the world owes them the supply of necessities according to the Apostle to the Romans: *'They are debtors to them.'* For if they have been made partakers of their spiritual things, they ought to minister to them the things of the flesh.' And again to the Corinthians: *'The Lord ordained that those who preach the gospel should live by the gospel.'* "

Rom 8:12

1Cor 9:14

The Permanence of the Order

[27]The blessed father Francis **was consoled** by divine revelations, **by which he was made sure that the foundations of his religion would always remain unshaken. He was also promised an indubitable replacement of elect for the number** of those who would fall away. For the institution of the Order is *a work of God,* and *therefore it cannot be dissolved by man.* It has been made clear by very many most excellent signs both in Saint Francis himself and in other very suitable tests that his Order is most certainly *the work of God.*

2C 158

Acts 5:38-9

X: His Compassion for the Poor

[28]As much as the blessed father Francis loved the distress of poverty in himself, so much was he racked **with compassion** for other poor people. **Piety, infused** by grace, **doubled his piety for the poor** which was certainly born in him. For **his soul melted for** the poor, **and to those he could not** give the result of his work, **he extended the affection** of his pious heart, and the indigence of someone else pained him who was in greater need. For **though** he was **content with a ragged tunic,** he often wanted to share **it with some poor person.** Sometimes **during the coldest seasons he used to approach rich people to lend him cloaks or furs. And as they responded ever more gladly to this, he used to say** to them: "I shall accept this from **you** on this condition that **you do not expect to have it returned." And when** he would meet **someone** who in his judgment **was poorer, he would say** to his companion: **"We accepted** this **mantle on loan until someone poorer would come along** to whom we would give it;" many times in cold weather he would deprive himself to help others who were in need. **Frequently he met poor people burdened with wood or other heavy loads. He would then offer his own shoulders to help them, although** they were very weak.

2C 83

1C 76

2C 87

1C 76

His Compassion for the Sick

[29]Great too was his compassion for the sick, great his concern, as though **he were sympathizing for all who were ill, offering words of**

2C 175

compassion, when he could not offer assistance. He sometimes would eat on days of regular fasting, so others who were sick would not be afraid to eat; and he was not embarrassed to go begging through the city's public places for meat for a sick brother.

2C 177   With a greater kindness and patience he would bear those he knew were sick in spirit, those who were fluctuating like children, those agitated by temptations, and also those *faint in spirit.* Avoiding   Ps 77:4
harsh corrections when he saw danger, he *spared the rod* so as *to spare*   Prv 13:24
the soul.

He Is Piously Moved Toward All God's Creatures

1C 77   [30]The saint's compassion **toward humans** is not surprising, **since**
1C 59; 2C 165   he also bore toward **brute animals** a feeling of piety. **He picked up**
little worms from the road so they would not be trampled under
1C 77   foot; he called **all creatures** by a fraternal name, either because all
things came from one father, or because of his estimation of humility, he would not put himself even ahead of vile creatures. **But**
among other animals he **especially loved the meek, in which he**
found some mystical **likeness to the Son of God.** He especially
loved, however, the little lambs, because the gentleness and humility of our Lord Jesus Christ was frequently likened in Scripture and
1C 78-9   **fittingly adapted to the lamb.** Sometimes coming upon **lambs** being   Is 53:7
led *to the slaughter,* he would be sorrowful and **would pay for them**
either **with the mantle he was wearing,** or in whatever way he could
with **the price** asked.

XI: The Cursed Sow

2C 111   [31]**One night** when the man of God **was a guest at the monastery**
of San Verecondo in the diocese of Gubbio, a little sheep gave birth
to a baby lamb which a cruel sow killed with a ravenous bite. When
he heard about this, the saint of God **with admirable compassion**
was very distressed, **and he recalled that the** Immaculate Lamb was
killed by the cruelty of the Jews.[a] Then he said *in front of everyone:*   Gal 2:14
"Cursed be that sow. **Neither man nor beast shall eat of it!"** It is   Jb 24:18
amazing to tell. **Immediately the sow became sick** and died after
three days. Thrown into a nearby ditch, she **was food for no** bird or
beast. **And lying there for a long time,** it was **dried up like a board.**

---

a. This reference to the cruelty of the Jews is a curious, prejudicial addition to the text of 2C 111. Undoubtedly written by the anonymous monk who wrote this text, it is the only such reference in this literature. Cf. FA:ED II 321.

XII: Francis's Severity Toward Himself

³²Even though the Father Francis was most kind towards others, he nevertheless was most strict and severe with himself. **Toward himself** *he had become like a broken vessel,* burdened by no fear or concern for his body. He **hardly or rarely ever ate cooked food, but if he did, he sprinkled it with ashes or he dampened the flavor of spices with cold water.** When he was invited by the important people of the world, **who venerated him with much fondness, he would taste some meat in order to observe the Gospel. The rest, which he** appeared to eat, he dropped in his lap, raising his hand to his mouth so that no one noticed what he was doing. What should I say about drinking wine, when he would not allow himself to drink even enough water when he was burning with thirst? He said that it was impossible to satisfy necessity without bowing to pleasure. As normally happens, sometimes the craving to eat something came upon him, but afterwards he would barely allow himself to eat it, for he feared that pleasure would cunningly be mixed with it.

³³Whenever he received hospitality, he refused to use pillows or **blankets on his bed, but the naked ground, with only his tunic between them, would receive his naked body. Sometimes when he** would refresh his small body with sleep, he would often sleep sitting up, not lying down, using a stone or a piece of wood as a pillow. For from the time of his conversion he did not want to lie on feathers, nor have a pillow for his head, whether he was sick, or receiving hospitality from a stranger.**

³⁴**As if it were a stranger to him, he never spared his body, exposing it to every** hardship and to the afflictions of spiritual exercises. **He was a man, having** *the spirit of God,* ready to endure any suffering of mind and affliction of body as long as *the will of God* **might be fulfilled mercifully** in him.

His Continual Progress

³⁵**He worked with his hands, not allowing any time to go to waste. Always new, he always became more ready for spiritual exercise.** He considered it a great loss not to be doing something good, and in his judgment, he judged not going forward at all times going backward. He considered it an irreparable loss to spend even a little time fruitlessly, since even in a short space of time the faithful servant of God could in the practice of some virtue merit infinite glory without interruption as far as duration is concerned. Hence, just as an hour of time passes by, so also should merit for that time be procured.

Ps 31:13
1C 53
1C 51
1C 52
1C 52
2C 64
2C 21
1 Cor 7:40
Rom 12:2
1C 92
2C 161
2C 159

XIII: The Fight Against Temptation

1C 42

[36]If, as happens, any temptation of the flesh struck him, he would during the winter immerse himself in a ditch filled in winter with ice, or chastise himself with severe scourging, or he would tumble about for a long time in a thicket of briar-bushes or nettles until through the punishment of the body he destroyed this defect of the flesh.[a]

[37]Just as, at one time, powerful struggles with temptations were sometimes placed before blessed Job, so were they placed before holy men. By means of these struggles these people were both purged and merited great glory. They also demonstrated the proof of their virtues by their manful struggles and their steady perseverance. This has also been established as far as Saint Francis is concerned, who certainly withstood many serious assaults of the devil. For struggles of such contests are placed before proven beginners according to the

2C 118

measure of their virtue.[b] Severe struggles **against temptation** are not placed before them, **except before those with the greatest strength.**

2C 116

[38]**One night** when **the man of God was in prayer,** the devil called out to him **three times: "Francis, Francis, Francis!"** And when the man of God *replied to him: "What do you want?"* the devil said to him: "Although God **is forgiving** to all **sinners if they convert,** He will never forgive those who kill themselves by punishing themselves indiscriminately." The **holy** man, therefore, knew that the devil wanted **to recall** him from **the fervor** of devotion **to being** harmfully **lukewarm.**

Mt 9:37; Mt 20:21

Harmony between Body and Soul

1C 97

[39]**There was in the holy man of God such harmony** of body **with spirit, such obedience of flesh, that when he strove to reach all holiness, it did not resist, but even tried to run on ahead,** according to this passage: *For you my soul has thirsted, and my flesh in so many ways.* Continual submission became spontaneous, as the flesh, continually **yielding, reached a place of great virtue, because,** as it is said, **habit often** in some manner **becomes nature.**

Ps 63:2

---

a. The last section of this paragraph is taken from Gregory the Great's *Life of Saint Benedict* II 2, found in his *Dialogues* II, cf. PL 66, 132. In that passage, after a temptation, Benedict "noticing close at hand some thick bushes of nettles and brambles, took off his clothes and threw himself naked among the sharp thorns and fierce nettles." Cf. Gregory the Great, *The Life of Saint Benedict*, trans. Hilary Costello and Eoin de Bhaldraithe, commentary by Adalbert de Vogüe (Petersham, MA: St. Bede's Publications, 1993), 20-9.

b. This reflection on temptation is a condensation of the teaching of Gregory the Great's *Morals on The Book of Job*, Book III, 5-7, cf. PL 75, 602ff.

When Is One a Servant of God?

⁴⁰One night Francis called together all the brothers in the house   2C 159
and said to them: "I prayed to the Lord that He might deign to
show me when I am His servant, since I always desire nothing more
than to be His servant. The most gracious One answered me: 'You
will know that you are my servant when you think, speak, and do
things that are holy.' Therefore, if ever you see me not doing any of
these things, then regard me as not being a servant of Christ."

XIV: His Labors at Preaching

⁴¹Moreover, he was afflicted with frequent infirmities, since for   1C 97
1 Cor 9:27   many years he had completely *chastised his body and brought it into sub-*
jection. For his flesh had hardly any rest at any time as he traveled
around wide and different regions to scatter everywhere the seed of
the word of God, so that in the course of one day he often passed
through four or five villages or cities and preached in each. He so   1C 98
loved the salvation of souls that when he could no longer go on
foot, he traveled around the earth, riding on a little donkey.

The People's Devotion to Him

⁴²On the other hand both men and women had such devotion   1C 62
towards the holy man of God that they mutually pressed against
one another to see and hear him, counting themselves fortunate if
any had been able to touch at least his clothing. In their devotion   1C 63
they often tore at his habit, until he was left almost half-naked.
When he entered a city, the people exulted, the clergy rejoiced with   1C 62
Jn 12:13   them, the bells rang. Often with *palm branches,* singing psalms they
went out to meet him, and as believers rejoiced, heretics hid. The
marks of his holiness were so clear in him, that no one presumed to
Nm 27:22   speak against him, as *the assembly of the people* paid special attention
to him alone.

XV: His Method of Preaching

⁴³Although he proposed simple things when he was among sim-
ple people, nevertheless among spiritual and wise people he uttered
the profound declarations of truth. Though he often preached the   1C 72
Word of God among thousands of people, he was as confident as if
he were speaking with a close friend. He used to view the largest
crowd of people as if it were a single person, and he would preach
fervently to a single person or to a few as if to a large crowd. He

often **uttered the most amazing things** about which he had not pre-viously thought. **Sometimes when he could not remember what he had meditated about and** did not know **what to say, he would con-fess to the people without embarrassment** that he had forgotten what **he intended to say, would give a blessing to the people, and send them away.** His eloquence was inflamed with zeal, **moving** the hearts of his listeners from the depths and ascending by the flame of **compunction. Apostolic authority resided in him, and therefore he altogether refused to flatter** the powerful of the world.

1C 73

1C 43

His Understanding of the Scriptures

2C 102

⁴⁴Although from the beginning he was not given **to the great schol-arly disciplines, still** enlightened by *wisdom from above,* he under-stood the Scriptures deeply. His intellect **penetrated** *hidden mysteries,* and where the knowledge of an educated person remained **outside, the passion of the lover entered. He often untangled** obscurities of **questions, and** in simple **words he brought** into the light the latent power of intelligence. As a result, **one of the cardinals** of the Holy Roman Church **said to him: "I gladly accept your knowledge of the Scriptures, because I know that** *it comes from God alone,* and not from the conjectural subtleties **of humans."**

Col 3:1-3; Jas 1:17

Col 1:26

2C 104

Jn 15:26; Mt 4:4

XVI: He Always Bore Christ in His Heart

1C 84

⁴⁵His highest aim, foremost desire, and most excellent intention was to pay heed to the holy Gospel, to follow the teaching, and to retrace the footsteps of the Lord Jesus Christ. One by one, **the humility of His Incarnation and the** super-eminent **charity of His Passion had occupied his mind so** constantly, **that he scarcely thought of anything** else. **It was his custom** to divide **the time given** to him to acquiring grace, some to what would be profitable **for his** neighbors, and some to the quiet of holy contemplation.

1C 91

Fervor for Martyrdom

1C 55

⁴⁶He desired above all things *to be dissolved and be with Christ;* for it was only there that all his desire reposed. That he might attain this more quickly **he burned with the desire of holy martyrdom** and he attempted for the third time to cross the sea **to the territory of the Saracens** in order **to preach the** Catholic **faith** to them. One time, when **because of the lack of provisions the sailors refused** to accept him **on the ship, he trusted** in the clemency of Almighty God, and **boarded the ship secretly. Immediately, by the provident Lord, a**

Phil 1:23

LJS 34; 1C 55

man bringing food came secretly and gave it to one of the sailors and said: "In their time of need, give it to those poor men hiding in your ship."

Through Francis They Are Freed from the Danger of the Sea

[47]A storm arose for many days, and when all their food had been consumed, only the divine bounty, the food for the poor Francis, multiplied so much, that it sufficed for many days for all those on board until they reached port. The sailors, realizing that they escaped the dangers of the sea through blessed Francis, gave thanks to God, who reveals Himself in his servants as wonderful and worthy of love.

1C 55

[48]Finally, he presented himself in the sight of the Sultan, even though at that time savage battles were being waged daily between the Christians and the Saracens. With what hardships was he weakened, with what injuries and beatings was he afflicted, with what threats was he discouraged before he came into the presence of the Sultan, with what confidence did he speak before him, with what constancy did he defend the faith and reply to those who were insulting the Christian law! It would take too long to mention everything. But in all this the Lord did not fulfill his desire to receive the martyrs' crown but reserved for him the prerogative of a singular glory with which He wished to conform Francis more manifestly to His sufferings and death above other martyrs, as His sacred stigmata, openly exhibited on Francis's body, clearly shows.

1C 57

LMj IX 9; 1C

LJS 36

1C 57

XVII: His Devotion for the Faith and His Reverence for Priests

Heb 10:38

[49]Since *the just one lives by faith,* in a life of grace, the holy father above all things taught that the faith of the Holy Roman Church must be honored and preserved. The salvation of all who would be saved was found in it alone. He venerated priests and every ecclesiastical order with great affection. For he used to say: "If I should happen at the same time to meet any saint *coming from heaven* and some poor little priest, I want to kiss the hands of that priest before those of the saint. For I would say: 'Saint Laurence, wait until I first show due reverence for the priest, because his hands handle bodily the Word of life.' "

1C 62

Jn 3:31; Gal 1:8

2C 201

Peace with Clerics

[50]Although he wanted his sons to keep peace with all, and to show themselves to be humble to everyone, he nevertheless taught

2C 146

them to be particularly humble and devout **towards clerics,** either because of the dignity of the clerical Order or as an example for the laity that these might learn through his sons to be subject to their leaders, or for the purpose **of checking** the malice of **heretics,** who are drawing the faithful away from being devoted to the clergy, so that once the clerics are held in contempt, they can induce the people to follow them.

1C 62

51He used to say: "We have been sent to help clerics promote **the salvation of souls, so that we may make up whatever may be lacking in them.** *Each shall receive a reward,* not on account of authority, but because of the work done. Know, brothers," he said, **"that the good of souls is what pleases God most, and this is more easily obtained through peace with the clergy than by fighting with them. But if** some of them should stand in the way of the people's salvation, *the vengeance of God will be alert to it.* **So,** be humbly **subject to them, so that no jealousy arises in you.** *If you are children of peace,* you will be able **to win over the clergy and people for the Lord,** which *will be* much *more acceptable to God* than only winning over the people while scandalizing the clergy. Cover up their failings," he said, "make up for their many defects, and *when you have done* this, be even more humble!"

2C 146

52The holy Church has been committed to them and the loss of those under their care is exacted from them. Let us therefore participate with them in the harvest of souls, not in their loss. For just as it is not right *to do evil so that some good may result,* such fruit is not pleasing to God which is procured through scandal. He edifies himself and the Church more, who humbly suffers in silence, than if he obstinately raises a clamor in defending his authority, unless it should be openly established that the truth of the faith is endangered. If therefore we are truly seeking gain for God, we should look for it where it can be more securely found, that is, in gentleness.

He Appeases a Bishop by Humility

2C 147

53One time blessed Francis came to the city of Imola and **sought permission from the bishop to preach,** and he heard from him: **"It is enough that I myself preach to my people."** *Bowing his head,* **the** saint left humbly, but after a short time **he came back in** again. **The** bishop was indignant and said: **"What else do you want?" Saint** Francis replied: "My Lord, if a father throws his son out by one door, he should come back in through another." The Bishop was pacified by such **humility. He** embraced the man of God **and said with a smile: "From now on you and all your brothers have my**

1 Cor 3:8

Jer 46:10; 44:27

Lk 10:6
1 Tm 2:3

Lk 17:10

Rom 3:8

Jn 19:30

general permission to preach in my diocese. Holy humility earned this."

XVIII: The Uniformity of the Order

[54]In order that a fellowship of love might be greater **among** his brothers, he wanted his whole Order to be brought together by uniformity, where, by a similar habit and observance of life, **the greater would be united to the lesser,** the educated to the uneducated, and those **far from one another would be held together** by a bond of profound friendship.[a] **"And wherever they are and wherever the brothers find themselves, they should show each other that they are of the same household,"** that they may converse familiarly as though a household family, rejoicing together by the same right according to the institutions of the Order.

2C 191

LR VI 7

Names of the Ministers

[55]In view also of the virtue of humility he did not want in the *Rule* to call the rulers of the Order by names signifying dignity, such as, abbots, presidents, or priors, but ministers and custodians, so that by this the brothers would understand that they were servants of their brothers rather than lords, and preservers of souls and not dispersers of them, according to this passage from Matthew: *He who is the greatest among you shall be your servant,* and this passage from the Song of Songs: *The peaceable one had a vineyard, in that which has people: he let out the same to custodians.* The word "guardian," which has the same meaning as "custodian," is not from the *Rule,* but from its use in the Romance tongue and taken to express a difference of duties.

ER IV 2; LR IV.

Mt 23:11

Sg 8:11

XIX: He Commits the Order to the Care of the Church of Rome

[56]Seeing that, by the providence of God and according to His promise, the Order under his control **was increasing** in the holy Church, and **foreseeing** also in spirit that some inflamed by a malignant spirit would rise up against the Order, as, in the third chapter of Esther, Aman rose up against the people of God in order to dissipate and destroy them, our blessed **Father** Francis approached the Apostolic See and, according to the revelation given to him from heaven,

2C 23

---

a. This is a different perspective on fraternal life, i.e., friendship. It expresses an appreciation of monasticism, especially that accentuated in the twelfth century. Cf. Brian Patrick Mcguire, *Friendship and Community: The Monastic Experience 350-1250* (Kalamazoo: Cistercian Publications, 1988).

2C 24
and not presuming to defend his **sons** by his own strength from the madness of the wicked, **he committed** the Order **to the Holy Roman Church,** that the Order might receive **special** care and be kindly fostered under the wings of its grace.

2C 25
[57]When *the man of God* came to Rome, the Lord Pope Honorius the Third and the cardinals received him with great respect, because **the reputation** of his sanctity made him revered by all. **He preached before** the lord and **the cardinals,** who *marveled at the words of grace that came from his mouth,* and were very edified. **He** then **asked the Lord Pope** that **the Lord Hugo, then the Bishop of Ostia** and later called by divine providence to be the Lord Pope Gregory IX, be set up over the Order in his place, in order that **saving the dignity** and **pre-eminence** of the Apostolic See **the brothers in time of need** might demand from him **the benefits of protection** and **direction. The Lord Pope** looked with pleasure on such **a holy request,** and **soon, just as** the father **had asked, he set the Cardinal** over that Order.

Jgs 13:6

Lk 4:22

The Cardinal

LR XII 3-4
[58]According to the *Rule* and by a commission of the Apostolic See, the Order is now always accustomed to have over it one of the Cardinals of the Holy Roman Church who is requested from the Lord Pope by the Provincial Ministers. The Order is subject to this Bishop as if he were their own, and it is exempt as an Order from the jurisdiction of others, lest the uniformity of the regular observance be disturbed. If the brothers owed obedience in all things to any Bishop where they were staying as if he were their own, different Bishops would be enjoining different things and timid consciences could not easily help themselves out of such a perplexity. Nevertheless, this should be without prejudice to that reverence which, in view of the height of his dignity, should becomingly be shown by all to each bishop without exception. It is right that those whom the Lord has so highly honored be honored punctiliously by the universal family, since the Holy Church has been committed to them, as a bride to bridesmaids, to be protected, to be guided, to be adorned, and to be conducted to the heavenly marriage chamber.

XX [Creatures Obey Hm]

1C 80
[59]It would take **too long** to pursue one by one **all the things which the holy father Francis did and taught.** If anyone wishes to know these things, let him search the entire *Legend* from which these things have been taken in brief form, and to a certain extent his

desire will be satisfied. For hardly anything memorable will be found, by which any of the blessed saints rose to the brilliance of sanctity, for which this saint also did not exemplify brilliantly.

[60] Since **he then subjected himself totally to the will of his Creator,** and most purely **loved all** His **works** because of Him, **those creatures,** therefore, **strove** in their own way **to repay** him **in turn,** as if they were recalling to mind the law of their condition by which they had been so formed, that while man as he ought, should obey God, so should they subject themselves to the will of a human. **They smile at his caress, his requests they grant, they obey his commands, as a few** of many examples illustrate.

Off 1 V
2C 165; 2C 1

He Preaches to the Birds

[61] One time when Saint **Francis was going through the Spoleto Valley near Bevagna** he came upon a great **multitude of different kinds of birds** in a field. **And because** he loved **all creatures out of** love for their Creator, **he approached them and greeted** them **in his usual way.** Seeing that **they did not take flight, he rejoiced,** and he began **to speak to them a word** as though they had the use of reason: "**My** sister **birds, you should greatly love** and **praise your Creator who gave you feathers** for your clothing, **wings for flying,** and a **home in the purity of the air.** And though you *neither sow nor reap* nor possess a storage place for food, **He** feeds **you."** The man of God preached **these and similar words** to the birds, **as those** who were present there with him at that time **have testified. Those birds began to stretch out their necks, open their beaks,** extend their **wings and look attentively at him,** showing in a certain measure by gesture the affection they had for **the holy one of God** and his address. **While Francis walked back and** forth **through their midst, his tunic would touch them,** yet **not** one **of them** left **its place** until, when the sermon was ended, he gave them his **blessing** and **permission** to leave. When this was done, **they** all immediately **flew away** into the heights with a great clamor, as if giving thanks for the favor given to them. Then **the man of God, simple because** of purity, not because of dullness, **began** to censure **himself for negligence, because,** as he had seen, the birds had received the word of God **with such** attention **because until then he had not preached to them.**

1C 58; LJS 37

Lk 12:24

LMj XII 3; 1C

He Restrains the Swallows

[62] Again **one day when** he wanted **to present the word of God to the people** gathered **at Alviano, a very large number of swallows, nesting** in the area, made such **a racket shrieking and chirping that**

1C 59

the man of God **could not be heard** clearly by the people. The holy man **said to them: "My sister swallows, you have spoken enough;** now **be silent and listen to the word of God** in peace!" As if possessing the power of reason the swallows remained silent, nor did they move from the place, until he had finished preaching. Those who were present glorified the Lord when they saw this miracle, and amazed at the sanctity of the blessed man, they desired to touch at least his habit.

Mj XII 4; LJS 38

XXI: He Produces Water from a Rock

2C 46

[63]Once Saint **Francis wanted** to go **to a certain hermitage** of brothers so that he could more freely spend time in contemplation of heavenly things. **Because he was** very **weak, he got a donkey to ride** from a peasant. **It was summer, and as the peasant went up the mountain following the man of God, he was exhausted** from the journey, fainting with a burning thirst. The peasant **urgently cried out** after Saint Francis **and swore he would die if he was not revived by a drink. Saint Francis showed compassion** for his **distress, knelt down on the ground,** and gave himself devoutly **to prayer until he sensed that he was heard** by the Lord. *Rising from his prayer,* **he said** to the man: "**Hurry now, and over there you will find** *water* which at this very hour the Lord, **having mercy** on you, *has brought forth for you from a rock."* The peasant **drank the water** which was produced there **by the power of the prayer** of the holy father, where it never at any time had been found to have flowed before.

Lk 22:45
Is 48:21

He Is Not Injured by Fire

2C 166
LMj V 8
2C 166
LMj V 9
2C 166

[64]At the time the holy Father Francis had contracted an eye disease as a result of frequently shedding **tears,** and had suffered **most severely** from this condition up to the day of his death, he was urged **by Lord Hugo, Bishop of Ostia, to let himself be treated.** When the **surgeon heated the iron** with which he would cauterize the eyes, **and the holy father's body** trembled from this **panic, he began to speak to the fire** in this way: "**My brother fire,** more noble among the other elements, I have always loved you in the Lord! Be tolerant with me now, that I may be strong enough to bear it when you are burning me more gently!" Then, after making the sign of the cross over the fire, he offered himself to be cauterized. The brothers, unable to watch his pain, **ran away.** The iron sunk into his tender flesh and the burn extended from his ear to his eyebrow. When his brothers returned the saint **said with a smile: "Oh, you** *weak souls of*

Mt 14:31

little heart, why did you run away? **Truly** *I say to you,* I did not feel the heat of the iron, nor any pain in my flesh." And to the doctor he also said: **"If the flesh isn't well cooked, try it again!"** The doctor, realizing **that this** was **from God,** said it was **a miracle: "Brothers,** *today I have seen wonderful things."*

Lk 4:2, 5

Lk 5:26

XXII: He Cures a Cleric

1 Cor 12:28-31

[65]Among the charisms of other powers, the holy father possessed *the* unique *gift of healing.* **One time** when he was staying **in the bishop's palace in Rieti, a canon named Gedeone, a lustful and worldly man, who was seized by** a grave **illness, had himself carried** to the man of God, **and tearfully begged him if he** would make **the sign of the cross** over him. He answered: "Since you have followed **the** *desires of the flesh* and have been *an enemy of the cross of Christ,* **how can I make the sign of His** cross **over you?"** Then he added: **"I will sign you in the name of the Lord; but you must know that you will suffer** worse things, if when you are healed **you return to sin." When he made the sign of the cross** over him, **he was immediately restored to health and got up,** saying: "Thanks be to God! **I am free!"** A short **time later** he returned to the same sins as before. **One night when he was sleeping in the house of a** fellow **canon, the roof of the house collapsed on all of them, and while others escaped,** only that man **was killed** according to the prediction of the man of God.

2C 41

Gal 5:16; Phil 3:8

[66]I am purposely passing over many other similar incidents in order to avoid redundancy. For this holy man possessed such *power of the Most High* that the benefits of healing were bestowed not only on **many in his presence** but also **in his absence** by means of articles which **he had touched. Loaves of bread** also **were** rather often **brought** to the saint of God **to be blessed. When those who were sick tasted it,** they were cured of **various diseases.**

Lk 1:35

1C 64

1C 63

Water Is Changed into Wine

[67]Because of his merits **elements** were sometimes changed into **other** natures. **Once when the saint himself was ill at the hermitage of Sant'Urbano, water was miraculously changed into wine** for him. **When he tasted it, he** suddenly **recovered,** and as a result **a double** miracle is demonstrated here. Consult Francis's complete *Legend* for with what power he gave commands to demons and by prayer or command put them to flight from obsessed or tempted people.

1C 61

LJS 40

1C 61; LMj V 10

XXIII: [He Knows Secret Things]

[68]Although because of the pain in his eyes Francis's eyesight was weak toward the end of his life, nevertheless by means of a prophetical illumination he was clear-sighted interiorly so that he manifestly knew by revelation of the Holy Spirit not only the things which pertain to the knowledge of God and of himself, but even secrets of the hearts of others and the nature of future events.

1C 49

His Knowledge of Hidden Things

1C 48

[69]How often he knew by revelation from the Spirit the deeds of absent people and opened up the hidden from view! How many he warned in their dreams, ordering what they should do, or forbidding things to be avoided! The future evil deeds of how many people did he predict, the presence of which were seen somehow or other in good appearances! And so foreseeing the end of evil people, he announced the future grace of salvation for them.

Prophecy

2C 48

[70]One time he spoke prophetically to his brothers about Brother Bernard who, after him, was the second brother in the Order: "I tell you, Brother Bernard has been given the most cunning devils to test him, the worst of among all the other evil spirits. He will be troubled and harassed, but in the end he will triumph over all. Finally, with every temptation overcome, he will enjoy wonderful tranquility and peace. *The race finished,* he will pass happily to Christ." Everything that Saint Francis had predicted was fulfilled. Even his death was lit up with miracles.

Acts 20:24; 2 Tm 4:7

Francis Reads Thoughts

2C 31

[71]Another time the holy father Francis was tired from a journey, and, quite weak, was riding on a donkey. As a traveling companion he had Brother Leonard, a nobleman from Assisi. And since this brother was accompanying the holy father on foot, he became quite tired. Thinking in human terms and moved to impatience by his distress, he began to murmur to himself: "His parents and mine did not socialize as equals, and here he is riding, while I am on foot leading this donkey." While Leonard was thinking about this, Saint Francis immediately got off and said to the companion thinking such things: "It is not right that I should ride while you accompany me on foot, for in the world you were more noble and influential than I." The brother was *completely astonished* and *overcome with*

Est 7:6; Nm 12:14

embarrassment, and he knew the holy father **had caught him. He fell at his feet** and, with **tears in his eyes, he exposed** his thoughts and **begged forgiveness.**

[72]**Another brother named Riccerio, noble by birth,** had such confidence in **the holy man Francis** that he thought **that any person he loved** was also loved **by God, and that someone to whom he showed** himself to be a stranger, would also be considered **a stranger by God. And because he was fearful, he thought** that **the holy man Francis could** not **love** him, and because of this he was terrified for a long time. He did not dare **to reveal** completely to **anyone** what he was suffering internally. **One day,** therefore, **when he was disturbed by this** usual **thought,** he by chance passed by the **holy father's cell,** and he **called** to him, and **said: "Let** no thought **disturb you, son, since you are very dear to me, and I love you with a special love. When you want to be free from anxiety, come to me, and** confer with me **about** anything you wish." **The brother was amazed and he wondered** from what source **the holy father** had received this knowledge, **and, from then on,** he made great progress both in friendship with Francis and **in the grace of God.**

1C 49

LJS 31; 1C 49

1C 50

2C 44a; 1C 50

XXIV: Prophecy

[73]**At the time when the Christian army was besieging Damietta, Saint Francis was there with his companions:** with a desire for martyrdom, **he had sailed across the sea. On the day when the Christians were preparing themselves for battle and he heard about it,** the man of God **was deeply grieved and he said to his companion: "If they come together** now, **the Lord has revealed to me that it will not go well for the Christians.** *But if I say* this, they will take me for a fool. *If I keep silent,* my conscience will torment me." **His companion replied: "Unburden your conscience, and** *don't give the least thought to how people judge you."* Therefore, **Saint Francis forbade the Christians with warnings to save them** from going to **war by announcing what would happen in the future. The truth** of both things which the saint had predicted **became apparent** when they ignored his advice and **the Christians were overcome in battle, so that six thousand** of them were captured and killed. **Compassion** for them **drove the holy man, no less than regret,** for spurning his advice **pressed down upon them more.**

2C 30

LMj XI 3

2C 30

Jb 16:6

1 Cor 4:3

[74]**When Lord Hugo** was still **Bishop of Ostia, the holy father** was made aware through divine revelation that the Bishop would become the Supreme Pontiff of the **future** Church militant. Thus,

1C 100

whenever he sent **private letters** to him, **he would** always **write: "To the Most Reverend Father and Lord Hugo, Bishop of the whole world,"** giving people to understand that by divine dispensation he was chosen to be Pontiff of the whole Church. How Francis, the man of God, had been filled with divine charisms! Let it suffice to have mentioned **these few of many** as examples, so that if anyone desires, he may gather some knowledge from these which are set down here.

XXV: A Description of Him

1C 83

[75]He was **friendly in behavior, affable in speech, faithful in commitment, prudent in advice,** *sober in spirit,* **tireless in prayer, lifted in** contemplation, and fervent in all things. He was quick in pardoning, **difficult to grow angry, free in nature, subtle in discussing, careful in choices, and the same in everything. He was strict with himself and kind with others.**

2 Tm 1:7

1C 83

[76]He was **fluent in eloquence, cheerful in appearance,** mature in character, **of medium height, closer to small. His hair was dark, his beard was black but sparse; he had thin legs, little flesh. His clothing was rough; his sleep was short, his hand was bounteous.** And since he was **very humble, he showed** *meekness to all people,* and duly adapted himself to the behavior of all. Holy among the holy! Among sinners he was as if **one of them,** so that his presence was usefully *gracious in everything.*

Ti 3:2

Est 2:15

XXVI: The Opened Book

1C 91

[77]**And because with all his heart he** always **strove most diligently to conform** himself in all things *to the good pleasure* of the divine **will,** he desired **one time** to be shown **by the Lord** how to serve Him more **perfectly, and what especially would be His will in this regard. He, therefore, went to** the holy **altar, placed the holy book of the Gospels on it, humbly prostrated himself, and prayed to the Lord that at the first opening of the Book, he would deign to show him** what **he had desired,** just as **we read that one of the** earlier **saints had requested. Rising from prayer and** fortifying **himself with the sign of the cross, he opened the book and the first passage he came upon was: "The Passion of the Lord Jesus Christ;" and lest this should be believed to have happened by chance, he** opened the book similarly a second and third time, and the same text or one that was similar occurred to him. Then **this man, filled with God, understood that by the way**

MJ XIII 2; 1C 91

1C 92

1C 93

Lk 12:32; Phil 2:13

LMj XIII 2

of the **Passion** and **trial** he should follow **Christ** to glory, as it is
written, that Christ had to suffer and thus enter into His glory,
although this revelation seems rather to presage another mystery
to be fulfilled in him a little later.

1C 92; LMj

XXVII: The Vision of the Seraph

[78]Two years prior to the time that he returned his soul to heaven,
the blessed man was **staying at the hermitage which is called La
Verna**. While he was giving himself there to the contemplation of
heavenly things, **he saw in a vision a man** of God **above him**, glittering **with remarkable beauty** and whose **hands were extended and
feet joined, affixed to a cross.** He also had **six wings** in the manner
Isaiah describes the Seraphim: *two were over his head, two covered his feet*
and *body,* and *two were stretched out* to the side *for flight.* When the servant and friend of the **Most High saw these things, he was filled
with great awe** and **joy,** both because of **the beauty** of this vision and
also because of **the kind and gracious look that he was observed** by
him. Yet **the bitterness of the seraph's suffering** afflicted him thoroughly with sorrow.

1C 94

LJS 61; 1C 9|

LMJ XIII 3

1C 94

Is 6:2

The Appearance of the Stigmata

[79]And so **while** Saint Francis **was thinking and wondering what
this vision could mean, the marks** of Christ's Passion **began** gradually to be formed **in his hands and feet** and side, **just as a little while
earlier** it had been shown to him in that vision. **Nails** formed out of
his own **flesh** appeared **in his hands and feet,** so that **the heads of
the nails protruded on the inside of the hands and on the top of the
feet, and the points were on the opposite sides.** They seemed to be
like **iron, black,** and hardened like cartilage, and if **they were
pressed on one side,** they responded **on the** other **side.** Yet they
adhered within the skin and could not be extracted. **His right side,**
pierced **as if with a lance, was marked with a thin scar which,** often
opened, discharged **blood, so that his tunic and undergarments
were sprinkled with his holy blood.**

1C 94

1C 95

1C 113; LMj X|

1C 95

[80]Nor was this, as certain ill-disposed people were misrepresent-
ing, the corruption of a scab. But with the rest of the flesh together
with the skin in a healthy condition, those **marks of the nails and the
wound in his side were** wonderfully and very expressively **shown.**
And he bore these in his body up to his death. **And although this servant and friend** of God **saw himself adorned beyond the glory of all
others** by **such pearls, still he did not seek to make himself**

1C 95

LJS 62
1C 95
2C 136

appealing to anyone in a desire for vainglory. And so, he very zealously kept this hidden from all, so that even his closest brothers and companions did not know about it for a long time. For he shrewdly covered his feet with woolen socks and his hands with his sleeves.

The Mystery of the Stigmata in Francis

1C 90
2C 203

[81]What God wished to demonstrate by such a prodigy as this, with which none of the saints before him appeared to be marked and by which he is most expressly likened to the crucified Son of God, has not yet been clearly made known, but it was partly revealed to a particular person by Saint Francis himself that this mystery draws its understanding from the future. For we believe that Christ wished to show how he loved Francis in a special way, or how perfectly Francis followed Christ's ways to sanctity or how deeply was the image of Christ's Passion imprinted on his heart by the pen of Christ's love, or perhaps how properly it represents Christ who is again to be crucified mystically in his members by the faithless in these *last times* according to this passage of the Apostle to the Galatians: *before whose eyes Jesus Christ has been depicted crucified in you?* For whatever is now referred to the members of Christ, is considered imputed to Christ according to what Matthew says: *What you have done for one of my least ones, you did it for me.* Hence, even in those he is depicted and *crucified* by the ungodly even if while *hating them in their heart,* they follow their *words and deeds.*

1 Pt 1:20
Gal 3:1

Mt 25:40
Heb 6:6
Lv 19:17
Col 3:17

Concealing of Secrets

1C 96

[82]It was the custom of the holy father not to reveal his great secrets to anyone, for he feared that by such a revelation some damage would befall *the grace given to him.* For he is not perfect who does not possess intrinsically within himself gifts of virtue and grace which are more perfect than what can from appearance be judged by all. Therefore, he most carefully hid very many revelations and visions made to him by God besides frequent consoling words from saints and angels, since they scarcely came to the knowledge of very few people. He was accustomed always to do this with all his singular gifts of virtue.

Rom 12:3

1C 95

XXVIII: He Experiences More Sickness

1C 97
1C 98

[83]During this same period his body began to be afflicted by different kinds of illnesses, as though *he had not yet filled up in his flesh*

Col 1:24

Gal 6:17   *what was lacking in the sufferings of Christ,* even though *he bore in his body
His* sacred *stigmata* of wounds. **For nearly two years he endured**   1C 102
these things with complete patience, giving thanks to God.

The Newness of Fervor

2 Cor 4:16   [84]**Even though he who was the outer man was decaying due to**   1C 98
the condition of his mortal **nature,** *yet* **he who was the inner man,**
that is, **the mental spirit,** *was being renewed* and **was** always **being**   1C 103
made more fervent in the love of God. To himself he seemed to have
done little and he was always desiring to **begin** a greater and **more**
perfect pursuit of virtue. **But when** the annoyance of **feebleness was**   1C 107
increasing from day to day, **he daily approached his end** little by little. He called these **tribulations his "Sisters"** and setting up the   2C 212; 2C 213
shield of patience against them, he gave himself up totally **by pray-**
Lk 22:43   ing to Christ, from Whom he, *falling* into a struggle, reported that
most certainly he had **the promise of eternal life.**

The Promise of Glory

[85]"Rejoice," He said, "for this **illness of yours is the pledge of my**   2C 213
Kingdom!" It was then that he composed *The Praises* of God in
which he rouses all creatures to His praise. For even death itself,   2C 217
terrible and hateful to everyone, he exhorted to the praise of God;
he eagerly invited her to be his guest, saying: "Welcome, my Sister
Death!" To the doctor he said: "My brother, boldly foretell death is
near, for I believe it will be for me the gate of Life."

XXIX: Francis Blesses His Brothers

[86]**When Saint Francis saw that his final day was drawing near,**   1C 108
as two years before it had been revealed to him, **he called to him the**
Gn 49   **brothers whom he wished,** and **he imposed hands on each of their**
heads, as it was given to him from above, just as long ago the patri-   1C 109
arch Jacob blessed his sons, and in those who were present he   2C 216; 1C 109
blessed them all, both absent and future brothers who would serve
the Lord in the Order **until the end of the world.**
[87]When he approached his last hour **he ordered** that he be placed   2C 214
on the naked ground with sackcloth covering him and sprinkled   1C 110
with ashes. Then turning his attention to heaven, he was totally   2C 214
intent on that glory, to which he was about to depart. He said to his
brothers: **"I have done what was mine; may Christ** bring to comple-
tion **what is yours!"** He then **raised his hands, glorifying Christ,** for   2C 216
free now from all things, he was going to Him free.

His Farewell to His Brothers

2C 216

[88]With words of consolation, he exhorted the brothers to the love of God with fatherly affection; he also spoke at length about patience, poverty, and fraternal charity, and placing the Gospel ahead of other observances. He then said: "Good bye, all you my sons, live in the fear of God and remain in it always, preparing your-

1C 108

selves for the daily approach of trials and tribulations. Happy will they be who persevere in the things they have begun well, for future scandals will separate some from these things."

He Passes to the Lord

1C 110

[89]And so, many brothers gathered, for whom *he was* both father   Acts 14:11
and *leader,* and with tears and many lamentations they awaited the

2C 217

departure of the holy father, and, with all the mysteries of the sacra-

1C 110

ments of Christ fulfilled in him, that most holy soul, released from the flesh, happily rose straight to heaven. And, as his soul was absorbed into the abyss of light, his body fell asleep in the Lord.

His Soul Is Seen Ascending into Heaven

1C 110

[90]One of his brothers and disciples, a man of some fame, but more celebrated before God for his sanctity, whose name he does not wish to be set down here because he does not wish to glory among people in such fame, saw the soul of the most holy father Francis rise straight to heaven, glittering with remarkable splendor and carried up upon a brilliant white cloud, conducted with hymns by choruses of saints and angels to the realms above.

Brother Augustine Goes to Heaven with Francis

2C 218

[91]At that time the minister of the brothers in Terra di Lavoro, Brother Augustine, was also in the last hour of his life. Although he had already lost his speech, *he suddenly cried out* in the hearing of   Acts 23:4; Lk 9:39
those *who were standing by and said:* "Wait for me; Father, wait! Look, I'm coming with you!" The amazed brothers asked him to whom he was speaking. He responded boldly: "Don't you see our father Francis going to heaven?" And immediately his holy soul, released from the flesh, followed the most holy father into heaven. Noting the hour and the day, they found that Saint Francis had passed from this world at the same time and hour.

He Says Farewell to the Bishop of Assisi

2C 220

[92]At that time the Bishop of Assisi had been to the Church of Saint Michael in Apulia because of a pilgrimage. He was returning to

Jn 12:44

Gn 24:54

Benevento where he was lodging, when blessed Francis appeared to him in a vision at night and said: "See, my father, *I am leaving the world and going to* Christ." *When he arose in the morning,* he was flowing with tears because he had lost such a unique father. Then he told his companions what he had seen, had the time and the hour noted. When he returned home, he found that the holy father had died just as he had indicated.

XXX: The Concourse of People

Acts 21:30; Lk 2:13

[93]Then a whole crowd of people *came together praising God* Who had entrusted to them so precious a remnant in the body of the holy father. Still his sons, bereft of so great a father, wept and, from the depths of the heart, produced rivulets of tears. But the joy from the newness of an unheard-of miracle lightened the pain of their sorrow. For they had never read about nor did they ever imagine what was now being presented to their eyes, and they could not have been persuaded to believe if it were not demonstrated by such clear evidence. For the form of the passion of Christ emerged in him, while he appeared as though he had just been taken down from the cross.

1C 112

LMj XV 1
1C 112

His Flesh Appears Dazzling White

Acts 6:15

[94]They saw *his face* like *the face of an angel,* not as if he were dead. They saw his skin, worn out by much hard labor which had been black before and pallid, now shining white and in its beauty promising the glory of the splendor to come. His muscles were not taut like those of the dead; his skin was not hard; his limbs were not rigid, but, because they were soft and delicate as in childhood innocence, they were moved as if flexible.

1C 112

The Stigmata Are Seen

[95]In that glow of his skin, it was more delightful to see in the middle of his hands and feet not the holes of the nails, but the nails themselves formed by his flesh, and thrust through the middle of the hands and feet, and his right side pierced as if with a lance and red with blood. Anyone would rejoice that the greatest favor was shown to him if he could approach to see or kiss the sacred marks of Christ, which Saint Francis was exhibiting in his body. For who would be so dull-witted or stupid that by this obvious truth he would not understand that just as this holy man has been honored by a unique miracle on earth, so also he has been raised on high in heaven to an eminent glory?

1C 113

He Is Buried

⁹⁶Amid hymns and the sound of trumpets and with the people and clergy carrying olive branches and countless lamps the body was carried to the cloister of Saint Clare. There it was shown to her and to her sisters to be viewed and kissed. Then, brought to the Church, it was buried there with the greatest veneration. The most holy Father Francis died on Sunday, the fourth Nones of October, in the year one thousand twelve hundred and twenty-six. He had completed twenty years since his conversion.

XXXI: Famous by His Miracles

⁹⁷At his tomb new miracles were daily multiplied and by his merits very many people were freed from various misfortunes. Blessed Francis, whether he was still living in the flesh or after his death, was famous for so many and such great signs of miracles, that to set them forth fully would demand a much larger work. For besides other innumerable miracles he also marvelously raised many who had died. Even if I am not certain about many of these miracles, nevertheless I am not at present indicating a number, except that we have accepted eleven from trustworthy men, aside from other miracles, knowledge of which has not reached us. For what would he not be able to obtain from the Lord, who exhibits in his hands, feet, and side the sacred wounds, and who *became like Him in his death in the fellowship of* His *sufferings!*

The Lord Pope Visits His Tomb

⁹⁸When the Supreme Pontiff Pope Gregory IX, who had already succeeded Honorius, and who had known Saint Francis most familiarly and, with a remarkable esteem, nurtured him as it were in his bosom, heard about these happenings, he rejoiced exultantly and hastened to Assisi and reverently paid his respects at the tomb of the holy father. After a solemn meeting with the Cardinals and other prelates of the Church was called together and his miracles were approved, he added the holy Francis's name to the catalogue of the saints with the greatest solemnity and to the great joy of all. In addition he set up and ordered that his feast day be solemnly celebrated universally throughout the whole Church on the day of his passing to heaven, that is, on the fourth Nones of October.

To the praise of our Lord Jesus Christ.

The Life of Francis, the Confessor

Phil 3:10

1C 116-8

1C 20-1

LJS 56

1C 119

1C 121

1C 74

1C 123

LJS 74

LJS 71

Vernacular Poetry

Jacopone of Todi (1278-1293)

Jacopo was born into the prominent family of the Benedetti sometime between 1230 and 1236 in the Umbrian hill town of Todi.[a] An ambitious young man, he was settling into a prosperous career as a notary [a profession that combined elements of law and accounting], when his wife died tragically in 1268. This traumatic experience led to a profound religious conversion: totally rejecting his former life, Jacopo became an independent lay penitent (*bizzocone*). His "crazed," unconventional behavior, wandering about the streets as a ragged *giullare di Dio* ("minstrel of God"), gave rise to his popular nickname of Jacopone. In 1278 he entered the Lesser Brothers, where he soon became a vocal spokesman of the Spiritual Franciscans. Like many other Spirituals, Jacopone was distraught at the policies of Pope Boniface VIII, and was one of the signers of the Longhezza Manifesto of 1297, which challenged the validity of the Pope's election. Boniface soon routed the forces opposing him, however, and Jacopone was condemned to life imprisonment in an underground cell in Todi. Released in 1303 by Boniface's successor, Benedict XI, Jacopone spent his last years with the small brother community attached to the monastery of the Poor Clares in Collazzone, where he died in 1306.

Jacopone's fame rests on the prodigious number of devotional poems or lauds which he composed to give expression to his passionate love of God. Collected by admirers later in the century, these lauds, once dismissed by literary critics as rough-hewn, are now generally recognized as one of the greatest manifestations of medieval Italian lyric poetry. The *lauda spirituale* was the major form of non-liturgical religious song in medieval Italy.[b] Its origins probably go back to lay people who were caught up in the reform monastic movements of the late eleventh and twelfth centuries. Wishing to join in the praise of God, they gathered in private homes to sing simplified Latin hymns commemorating the major festivals of the liturgical year. In the thirteenth century, the singing of lauds became a prominent feature of the resurgent lay penitential movement. The form of the laud soon reflected this environment. Now mainly composed in the vernacular rather than in Latin, they expressed themes reflecting popular affective piety rather than more staid liturgical

---

a. See Giulio Silano, "Jacopone of Todi," *Dictionary of the Middle Ages*, vol. 7, ed. Joseph Strayer (New York: Scribner, 1980), 33-35 (hereafter DMA). The best full account is George T. Peck, *The Fool of God: Jacopone of Todi* (University: University of Alabama Press, 1980).

b. Cf. Michael Long, "Lauda," DMA 7: 384-85; John Stevens and William Prizer, "Lauda spirituale," *The New Grove Dictionary of Music and Musicians* (New York: Macmillan Publishers, 1980), 10: 538-543.

patterns. Particularly connected with Franciscan circles,[a] laud-singing marked public religious gatherings, such as sermons and processions. Numerous confraternities devoted to their performance and composition (*laudesi*) sprang up throughout the towns of Italy.

Jacopone was by far the greatest composer of these popular religious lyrics; his lauds are immensely rich in content and display a wide range of themes. Although he undoubtedly wrote some to be sung publicly, others seem to be more introspective and personal compositions. Although Jacopone gives evidence of a wide reading in theology, he tends to express himself in the crude dialect and sharp imagery of a peasant. Of the ninety-three lauds attributed to him, two are devoted to Saint Francis. These express themes common to Jacopone's other lauds: the ecstatic love of God manifest in his self-emptying into human flesh, the madness of God-in-Christ suffering on the cross for ungrateful humanity, the annihilating effect of divine love in the soul who does respond to it. They also voice convictions common to the Franciscan Spiritual tradition. Jacopone believed that he was living in a time of apocalyptic conflict in which the institutional church had fallen to a carnal state in its love of wealth and power, and that the emerging spiritual church, prefigured in Francis, is marked by absolute poverty. Francis, marked with the signs of the crucified Christ, is the herald of the future church; therefore, any deviation from Francis's own practice by his brothers is a betrayal of their prophetic role in the last days.

Although it is extremely difficult to date precisely Jacopone's writings, most authors who have tried to do so suggest that these two lauds are products of the period 1278-93.[b]

Laud 61: "O Francesco Povero"

O poor Francis, new patriarch,
you bear a new standard, emblazoned with the cross.[c]

LMj XIII 10 This cross was manifested through seven signs;
much has been written on the meaning of each.
But I'll spare the reader and try to be brief.

LMj I 3 The first vision, at the beginning of your conversion,
was one of a noble palace. Within, it was filled
with shields marked with the cross—
the shields of those entrusted to you.

---

a. Indeed, musical authorities cite Francis's own *Canticle of the Creatures* as one of the first of the new vernacular lauds.

b. The editors have followed here the translation of Serge and Elizabeth Hughes in *Jacopone of Todi: The Lauds* (New York: Paulist Press, 1982). Although this vividly captures Jacopone's style, it does have a tendency to paraphrase, so the editors have at times corrected it in light of the critical edition of Franca Ageno, *Jacopone da Todi: Laudi, Trattate e Detti* (Florence: Le Monnier, 1953).

c. In his attempt to find a symbol to express Francis's total poverty, the poet views the cross as the fullest expression of his—and God's—total self-renunciation.

Then, as you were absorbed in prayer   LMj I V
(the mere remembrance of that vision
always reduced you to tears), you caught fire
remembering Christ fastened to the cross.

That Christ you saw said to you,
"Come and lovingly embrace this noble cross;
if you would follow Me, become as nothing,
hate yourself and love your neighbor."

Still later, when again you were meditating on the cross,   LMj II 1
in clear, strong tones He called you thrice by name
and then, "My Church has lost its way—
set it once more on the right path."

On the fourth occasion, Brother Sylvester   LMj III 5
saw a golden cross shining from your mouth,
and your blazing words put to rout   LMj XIII 10
the cursed serpent that had encircled Assisi.

In similar fashion, as Brother Pacifico gazed at you,   LMj IV 9
angelic Francis, he saw a cross of two swords—
one reached from your head to your feet,   LMj XIII 10
the other followed the line of your outstretched arms.

As Saint Anthony was preaching, Blessed Brother Monaldo   LMj IV 10
saw a vision of you in the air, on a cross,
in the act of blessing your brothers; and then,
according to the account, you vanished from sight.

The seventh apparition came as you prayed with great devotion   LMj XIII 2-3
on the craggy heights of La Verna—
an awesome vision of a six-winged seraph, crucified,
it sealed you with the stigmata—side, hands, and feet.

The one who hears a brief account finds this hard to believe,
yet many there are who saw these marks
while you were still alive and well,
and on your death, many more came to touch them.

Among others, Saint Clare came,   LMj XV 5
bringing her sisters with her;
greedy for such treasure she tried in vain
to pull out those nails with her teeth:[a]

The nails were made of flesh, hardened like iron,
the flesh was as fair as a child's.
It had lost the traces of many winters;
love had made it radiant, beautiful to gaze on.

LMj XV 2-3 The wound in your side was like a scarlet rose.
All that saw wept at the marvel:
its likeness to that of Christ
made the heart sink into an abyss of love.

O happy weeping, full of wonder—
joyful weeping, full of compassion!
How many tears of love were shed there,
to see and touch the new Christ's wounds!

They flowed freely as folk gazed upon this vision
of fiery love. The precious balm of holiness
that lies hidden in the heart
oozed forth from the wounds of Francis.

That towering palm tree you climbed,[a] Francis—
it was with the sacrifice of Christ Crucified that it bore fruit.
You were so transfixed to Him in love you never faltered,
and the marks on your body attested to that union.

This is the mission of love: to make two one;
Through his prayers it transforms Francis into Christ,
impressing Christ's form which he had in his heart,
that love manifest in his robe streaked with color.[b]

The highest divine love brought you to embrace Christ,
his totally burning affection enfolded you,
to press its stamp on your heart, like a seal in wax.
The impression was His in Whom you are transformed.

I have no words for this dark mystery;
how can I understand or explain
the superabundance of riches,
the disproportionate love of a heart on fire?

Who can measure the force of that fire?
We only know that the body could not contain it

---

a. The fruit-bearing palm is the cross of Christ, which Francis ascended in his love.

b. Love impressed on Francis's body (his "robe" or outer garment) the form of the crucified Christ, which he carried within his heart. The "robe" refers to the coat of many striped colors given to the beloved Joseph by his father (Gn 37:3).

and it burst out through the five wounds,
that all might see that it dwelt therein.

There has never been found a saint who bore such a sign,
A mystery so deep that if God had not revealed it,
it would be better to pass over it in silence, incapable of words.
Let those who have tasted it speak of it.

Wondrous stigmata, workmanship of God,
you demonstrate the great reality behind the awesome sign.
All will be clear at the end, when the last joust is over,
in the presence of those who follow the cross!

O my arid soul, dry of tears, run—
to swallow the bait, to drink at this spring,
to get drunk there, and never leave it again.
Let me die at the fount of love!

Laud 62: "O Francesco, da Dio Amato"

O Francis, beloved of God
Christ has shown himself in you![a]

1 Pt 5:8,9; Eph 6:11

The deceitful Enemy, adversary of the Lord,
dreading that his lost state would devolve to man,
approached him and through fraud led him

Rom 5:12-7

to disobedience and the loss of paradise.
The Adversary gloried in his triumph,
for with man's fall he was raised,

Eph 2:1-2

and became the Prince of the World.

Then God, seeing this fact, became man,
and wounded him mortally,
and wrested that dominion from him.

Phil 2:5-11

God's humility reversed the Enemy's fortunes,
and holy poverty checkmated him.[b]

A long time after his defeat,   ScEx 33-36
the cursed Enemy tried again,
and the world fell into his snares.

---

a. The theme of this apocalyptic laud is that Christ lives again in Francis, taking up the battle against the forces of evil which threaten to overwhelm the church in these last days.

b. It is precisely God's poverty that has overcome the forces of evil.

Seeing the Foe was carrying the day,
the Most High Lord sent in the cavalry
with a well-trained commander.
Saint Francis was chosen as standard-bearer,
but he accepted into his ranks
only those who despised the world.
He wanted no one to ride with him
who did not accept the reins of three bridles:
poverty, obedience, and chastity.

Rv 19:11-21

Francis bore the weapons of his Lord,
Who loved him so greatly
that He marked him with His own coat-of-arms;
So piercing was the love in Francis's heart
that his body was adorned with five pearls.
He was like a fig, whose rich interior
bursts through its skin,
becoming honey sweetness in the mouth.

Gal 6:17

The Lord then showed Francis how to skirmish,
how to deliver blows and how to take them,
and taught his tongue the words of peace.

Test 23

The sight of Francis struck fear into the Foe,
For he resembled the Christ of God,
Who with His cross
Had once before stripped him of his prize.

"If he is the Christ, the victory will be his;
against him there are no defenses.
O misery, to be defeated by such an enemy!
But I will not lose heart, I will tempt him!
Nothing ventured, nothing gained!"

"Francis—what are you doing?
You'd better take care—
that strict fast you've begun will kill you."

2C9

"I fast with discretion,
for the body, properly disciplined,
is a good and useful servant."

"The whole world knows you are holy;
your praises are sung by all.

We've seen in what esteem the Lord holds you,
may His holy name be praised."

> "I want to conceal the good in me,   Adm XXI, XX
> and show the world I am a sinner.
> My heart is with the Lord
> when I bow my head low."

"What do you plan to do? Don't you want to work,   ScEx 45
And with your earnings help those in need?"

> "I shall go about in rags and beg for my bread;
> in my love of God I go about like a drunken man."

"What good will that do, brother?
You will die a miserable death,
and your followers will grieve
that you left them penniless."

> "I will stay on the true path, with neither purse nor bag;   ER VIII 8
> I have told my followers that they must never touch money."

"Go then into that lonely wood
with your ragged band of heroes;
in that solitude you will edify man,
and God from his throne will smile on you."[a]

> "I was not sent into this world to flee it;   LMj IV 2
> rather, I came to hunt for souls.
> Pressing on, I will lay siege,
> pitching my tents around your citadels."

"I fear your tactics: with this Order of yours
you will take many away from me.
At least leave me the women!
You shouldn't be mixing with them."

> "I have upsetting news for you:
> I have founded an order of sisters,
> and they too will wage war on you."

"What woman would ever have the impudence
to move against me, the conqueror of the world?"

---

a. The temptation of many Spirituals to retreat into hermitages, rather than engage in the preaching
   ministry.

"In the valley of Spoleto lives a virgin,
Of sovereign virtue, a temple consecrated to the Lord,
Clare, the daughter of Donna Ortolana."

"But married people should not mix with brothers—
you can let them go, leave them under my patronage."

"I will trouble you even more:
I have founded an order of penitents,
providing a norm for married folk."

"At least leave heresy alone!
It is against your way of life.
If you touch that it will be too great an injury."

"I mean to seek out the heresy that dwells in your mansions,
And those infected with it I'll have thrown into prison."[a]

"Oh, you've left me wretched indeed!
What has happened to that sharp hook of mine?
You've put a bit in my mouth and are reining me in!
Francis, you have crushed me and retaken the world,
so bereaved me that I am utterly destroyed.
But I will suffer no more—
I will turn to the Antichrist!
I will make him come,
For he has been so much prophesied."

Rv 13:11-8

TL V 8

"And I will deal you both the final blow,
And wrench the world completely from you;
I will make peace with your followers,
Whom I will clothe in my striped habit."[b]

"The prophetic texts do me no good;
in the end I am discomfited,
for the victory will be yours,
and I will be cast into the abyss."

Rv 21:10

In this harsh and bitter struggle,
Many shall be wounded unto death,
The one who conquers will have the spoils
And be blessed with all good things.

---

a. Although this is certainly contrary to the methods of Francis himself, this reply reflects the duty of "seeking out" heresy that was entrusted to the Lesser Brothers when Alexander IV put them in charge of the Inquisition in much of central and northern Italy in 1258.

b. Again, as in the previous laud, the true habit marked by conformity to the Crucified Christ.

Dante Alighieri (1315-18)

Universally regarded as the greatest poet of the Middle Ages, Dante Alighieri was born in Florence in 1265 into a family of the lower nobility.[a] He spent his youth acquiring writing skills and serving as a citizen soldier. Although he entered a conventional arranged marriage, Dante was deeply attached to a Florentine lady, Beatrice, whom he idealized as the fulfillment of human love.[b] Her death in 1290 provoked a spiritual crisis in Dante's life. He plunged into the study of theology and philosophy; we know he was taking classes at the Franciscan convent school of Santa Croce in 1291.[c] Dante also became increasingly involved in the political life of the commune, a risky undertaking. During most of the thirteenth century the Guelph (pro-Papal) and Ghibillene (pro-Imperial) parties were engaged in a bitter struggle for control of the city, the Guelphs finally emerging victorious in 1278. However, over time they split into two rival factions: the "White Guelphs," to whom Dante belonged, insisted on maintaining the autonomy of the commune, whereas the "Black" faction wanted Florence to submit to the overlordship of the Papacy. In 1300 Dante was elected as one of the six priors or magistrates of the city, but when the "Blacks" staged a coup in 1302, he was sentenced to perpetual exile.

Although Dante never gave up his attempts to return to Florence, he devoted the last twenty years of his life chiefly to writing. He began his masterpiece, *The Comedy,* given the epithet "divine" by later generations, around 1308. Cantos I-XVII of the *Paradiso* section, in which his portrait of Francis occurs, most likely were composed during Dante's stay in Verona (1315-18). His last years were spent in Ravenna, where he completed *The Comedy* shortly before his death in 1321. Dante was buried in the church of San Francesco in that city.

The Comedy's is the drama of Dante's own personal faith journey, but also the story of Everyman's pilgrimage to God.[d] Dante is first taken to hell, gaining a knowledge of the dimensions of sin; then, in purgatory, he comes to understand the stages of human repentance and conversion. Finally, in the *Paradiso,* as Beatrice guides Dante through the nine heavenly spheres, he describes how the earthly pilgrim comes to center attention on attaining God

---

a. For a good summary of Dante's life and works, see Robert Hollinger, "Dante Alighieri," DMA 4: 94-105.

b. According to the testimony of Boccaccio and others, the woman was Bice, the daughter of Folco Portinari; she married the banker Simone de' Bardi. Dante called her Beatrice, the "bearer of blessings."

c. Robert Davidsohn, *Storia di Firenze,* trans. E. Dupré-Theisider, Vol. 4, pt. 3, *Il mondo della chiesa. Spiritualita ed arte. Vita pubblicca e privata* (Florence: n.p., 1965): 229-230. It is interesting to speculate whether Dante knew of Ubertino of Casale during these years. As a young brother priest, Ubertino was also a student at Santa Croce from 1285 to 1289, for two of these years (1287-89) under Peter of John Olivi. After graduate studies in Paris from 1289 to 1298, Urbertino returned to Tuscany as a lector of theology, probably at Florence, from 1298 to 1302. Dante may have heard Ubertino preach at this time, which was marked by the latter's conversion from a lax brother's life to the position of the Spirituals through the influence of Angela of Foligno. See Gian-Luca Podestà, "Ubertin de Casale," *Dictionnaire de spiritualité* (Paris: Beauchenes, 1994) 16: 3-15.

d. Our treatment here is indebted to the studies of Mark Musa, most readily available in *The Portable Dante* (New York: Penguin Books, 1995), and Allen Mandelbaum, *The Divine Comedy of Dante Alighieri: Paradiso* (Berkeley: University of California Press, 1984).

and thus ultimate happiness. Dante's portrait of Francis is set within the fourth sphere, that of the sun (beginning in Canto X). As Beatrice and Dante enter this realm, they suddenly find themselves surrounded by a circle of brilliant spirits, dancing and singing in their joy. Then the circle pauses in its movement and Thomas Aquinas steps forward to introduce his fellow spirits, all known for their wisdom.

As Canto XI begins, Dante's new position among the truly wise gives him the opportunity to admonish mortals who fail to achieve this wisdom because they seek only earthly satisfaction. At this point, Thomas Aquinas again steps forward to address Dante. He states that the founders of the two great mendicant orders were providentially sent by God to help the church confront the evils presently afflicting it, but as his discourse continues, he does not praise the founder of his own Order of Preachers. Instead, he salutes the contribution of his friendly rivals, the Lesser Brothers, by relating the love story of Francis and Lady Poverty.[a] This magnificent and influential poetic portrait reveals Dante's deep familiarity with Franciscan sources, chiefly *The Major Legend* by Bonaventure of Bagnoregio, but also the *Tree of Life* by Ubertino da Casale[b] and *The Sacred Exchange between Saint Francis and Lady Poverty*. When Thomas concludes his ringing tribute to Francis, he sadly changes tune as he considers the present condition of his own Dominican order. He is forced to lament the fact that too many of his confreres have succumbed to the very temptations of wealth and power which they were called to battle.

Canto XI[c]

> O senseless cares of mortals, how deceiving
> are syllogistic reasonings that bring
> your wings to flight so low, to earthly things![d]
>
> One studied law and one the *Aphorisms*[e]
> of the physicians; one was set on priesthood
> and one, through force or fraud, on rulership;

---

a. Dante's literary device reflects liturgical practice. By this time the Dominicans and Franciscans had the custom of exchanging pulpits on the feasts of their patrons; on the Feast of Francis, a Dominican preached at the Franciscan church, and *vice versa*.

b. On Dante's possible knowledge of Ubertino during his years in Florence, cf. supra 880 c. Ubertino had been banished to LaVerna in 1304 where he composed the *Tree of Life*. After his rehabilitation under Clement V in 1307, Ubertino entered the service of Cardinal Napoleone Orsini, papal legate to Tuscany. During the years 1308-1309 it is possible that he came to know Dante personally, as Ubertino represented the legate at some negotiations with exiled Florentines. Cf. Podestà, *Ubertin*, 4.

c. We have gratefully utilized here the translation of Allen Mandelbaum, *The Divine Comedy of Dante Alighieri: Paradiso* (Berkeley: University of California Press, 1984), with minor alterations.

d. These four opening stanzas may well be a poetical expansion of the opening prayer for the feast of Saint Francis: "Grant, that by imitating him, we may look away from everything on earth, in order to enjoy forever sharing the gifts of heaven," cf. FA:ED I 346.

e. The *Aphorisms* of Hippocrates, the "Father of Medicine" (c. 460-380 B.C.), was a standard medical text at the time of Dante. It contained broad, generally accepted conclusions expressed in compressed, very brief, and easily memorized sentences.

One meant to plunder, one to politic;
one labored, tangled in delights of flesh,
and one was fully bent on indolence;

while I, delivered from our servitude
to all these things, was in the height of heaven
with Beatrice, so gloriously welcomed.

After each of those spirits[a] had returned
to that place in the ring where it had been,
it halted, like a candle in its stand.

And from within the splendor that had spoken
to me before, I heard him,[b] as he smiled—
become more radiant, more pure—begin:

"Even as I grow bright within Its rays,
so, as I gaze at the Eternal Light,
I can perceive your thoughts and see their cause.

You are in doubt; you want an explanation
in language that is open and expanded,
so clear that it contents your understanding

of two points: where I said, 'They fatten well,'
and where I said, 'No other ever rose'[c]—
and here one has to make a clear distinction.

The Providence that rules the world with wisdom
so fathomless that creatures' intellects
are vanquished and can never probe its depth,

so that the Bride of Him who, with loud cries,[d]
had wed her with His blessed blood, might meet
her Love with more fidelity and more

---

a. A reference to the spirits of the great wisdom figures who surround Dante and Beatrice introduced in the preceding Canto.

b. The spirit of Saint Thomas Aquinas again steps forward to address Dante.

c. This is a reference to two enigmatic statements made by Thomas in Canto X which obviously had puzzled Dante. He had referred to Dominic's flock as one where the sheep "may fatten if they do not stray." And when he introduced the members of the circle of the wise, he said "there never arose a second with such a vision" as Solomon. He attempts to explain the first of these remarks in this Canto. The second will be the topic of Canto XIII.

d. Christ cried aloud on the cross (Mt 27:46), at the moment in which he died, thus acquiring his spouse, the Church, with his own blood (Eph 5: 25-27; Rv 21: 2-3).

assurance in herself, on her behalf
commanded that there be two princes, one
on this side, one on that side, as her guides.

One prince was all seraphic in his ardor;
the other, for his wisdom, had possessed
the splendor of cherubic light on earth.[a]

I shall devote my tale to one, because
in praising either prince one praises both:
the labors of the two were toward one goal.

Between Topino's stream and that which flows
down from the hill the blessed Ubaldo chose,
from a high peak there hangs a fertile slope;[b]

from there Perugia feels both heat and cold
at Porta Sole,[c] while behind it sorrow
Nocera and Gualdo under their hard yoke.[d]

From this hillside, where it abates its rise,
a sun was born into the world, much like
this sun when it is climbing from the Ganges.[e]

Therefore let him who names this site not say
Ascesi, which would be to say too little,
but *Orient,*[f] if he would name it rightly.

---

a. Saints Francis and Dominic are the "two princes" sent to guide the Church; Francis is compared to the seraph, Dominic the cherub. Bonaventure described Francis as "totally aflame with seraphic fire" (LMj Prol 1, FA:ED II 526), but Dante seems more indebted here to Ubertino's extended comparison of Francis and Dominic in these angelic terms, cf. TL V 2.

b. A poetic description of the site of Assisi, situated on a spur of Mt. Subasio lying between two rivers: the small Topino in the valley, near the Portiuncola, and the larger Chiascio, flowing from the hill near Gubbio where Saint Ubaldo (d. 1160) had his hermitage. He eventually became bishop of that city.

c. The east gate of Perugia, which felt the changing winds coming off Mt. Subasio.

d. Probably a double allusion here: one geographical, the fact that the "yoke" (shadow) of Mt. Subasio blocked the full light of the sun from these small towns, but the other political, as they were subject to the harsh rule of Perugia.

e. Francis, himself a new spiritual "sun" shining on the darkness of the medieval church, rose in the radiant manner of "this (physical) sun" from the easternmost boundary of the habitable world (India). Cf. LMj Prol, FA:ED II 525-9.

f. The place from which this new Sun rose should be called "Orient" or "Dayspring." The usual form of the name Assisi, in the Tuscan of Dante's day, was Ascesi, which may be interpreted as meaning "I have risen." While this is suggestive, it is inadequate; "Orient" is the only fit word. Dante is making a clear reference here to Francis as the angel of Rv 7:2, "ascending from the rising of the sun, bearing the seal of the living God." Cf. LMj Prol 1, FA:ED II 527..

That sun was not yet very distant from
his rising, when he caused the earth to take
some comfort from his mighty influence;

for even as a youth, he ran to war
against his father, on behalf of her—
the lady[a] unto whom, just as to death,

none willingly unlocks the door; before
his spiritual court *et coram patre*,[b]
he wed her; day by day he loved her more.

She was bereft of her first husband; scorned,
obscure, for some eleven hundred years,
until the sun came, she had had no suitor.[c]

Nor did it help her when men heard that he
who made earth tremble found her unafraid—
serene, with Amyclas[d]—when he addressed her;

nor did her constancy and courage help
when she, even when Mary stayed below,
suffered with Christ upon the cross.[e] But so

that I not tell my tale too darkly, you
may now take Francis and take Poverty
to be the lovers meant in my recounting.

Their harmony and their glad looks, their love
and wonder and their gentle contemplation,
served others as a source of holy thoughts;

so much so, that the venerable Bernard
went barefoot first;[f] he hurried toward such peace;
and though he ran, he thought his pace too slow.

---

a. Dante here takes up the imagery of Francis's seeking Lady Poverty as his bride, first developed in the ScEx 4-5, cf. FA:ED I 530. It seems likely that Dante had only a second-hand knowledge of this work; Ubertino incorporated much of it in TL.

b. *Et coram patre* [in the presence of his father], a reference to Francis' trial before the bishop of Assisi, when he stripped himself, renouncing his possessions and family, cf. LMj II 4, FA:ED II 538.

c. Cf. ScEx, 16-21, 30-31, FA:ED I 534-6, 539.

d. The one "who made earth tremble" was Julius Caesar. At Pharsalis, where he battled Pompey, he entered the house of Amyclas, a poor fisherman, demanding loudly to be ferried across the Adriatic. Amyclas was unperturbed; as a poor man, he had nothing to lose.

e. ScEx 21: "And on that cross, his body stripped, his arms outstretched, his hands and feet pierced, you (Lady Poverty) suffered with Him, so that nothing would appear more glorious in Him than you." Cf. FA:ED I 536. Ubertino says that Poverty was thus able to follow Christ even further than Mary, who had to remain beneath the cross, cf. TL 5, 3, supra 161-2.

f. Francis had begun to go barefoot after hearing the Gospel text (Mt 10:9); the "venerable Bernard" is Bernard of Quintavalle, Francis's first follower, cf. LMj III 1-3, FA:ED II 542-4.

O wealth unknown! O good that is so fruitful!
Giles goes barefoot, and Sylvester,
behind the groom—the bride delights them so.[a]

Then Francis—father, master—goes his way
with both his lady and his family,
the lowly cord already round their waists.

Nor did he lower his eyes in shame because
he was the son of Pietro Bernardone,
nor for the scorn and wonder he aroused;

but like a sovereign, he disclosed in full
to Innocent—the sternness of his rule;
from him he had the first seal of his order.[b]

And after many of the poor had followed
Francis, whose wondrous life was better sung
by glory's choir in the Empyrean,

the sacred purpose of this chief of shepherds[c]
was then encircled with a second crown
by the Eternal Spirit through Honorius.[d]

And after, in his thirst for martyrdom,
within the presence of the haughty Sultan,
he preached of Christ and those who followed Him.[e]

But, finding hearers who were too unripe
to be converted, he—not wasting time—
returned to harvest the Italian fields;

there, on the naked crag between the Arno
and Tiber, he received the final seal
from Christ; and this, his limbs bore for two years.[f]

---

a. Giles and Sylvester also follow Francis, the groom of the bride, Lady Poverty, cf. LMj III 4-5, FA:ED II 544-5.

b. Innocent's oral approval of the primitive brotherhood in 1209/10 is the first "seal" which Francis receives from God in support of his mission. Dante uses the term *religione*, derived from the Latin *religio* [religion], the term the early sources use for the brotherhood in its early days. Cf. FA:ED II 34 a.

c. Dante uses the term *archimandrita* [head of the fold], a term used for a religious superior in the Greek Church.

d. The official "seal" given to the *Rule* in 1223, FA:ED I 99-106.

e. Cf. LMj XIII 6-8, FA:ED II 590-2.

f. The Stigmata, given on La Verna in 1224. Bonaventure views this as a "seal" in LMj XIII 10, FA:ED II 593-4.

When He who destined Francis to such goodness
was pleased to draw him up to the reward
that he had won through his humility,

then to his brothers, as to rightful heirs
Francis commended his most precious lady,
and he bade them to love her faithfully;

and when, returning to its kingdom, his
bright soul wanted to set forth from her bosom,
it, for its body, asked no other bier.[a]

Consider now that man[b] who was a colleague
worthy of Francis; with him, in high seas,
he kept the bark of Peter on true course.

Such was our patriarch; thus you can see
that those who follow him as he commands,
as cargo carry worthy merchandise.

But now his flock is grown so greedy for
new nourishment that it must wander far,
in search of strange and distant grazing lands;

and as his sheep, remote and vagabond,
stray farther from his side, at their return
into the fold, their lack of milk is greater.

Though there are some indeed who, fearing harm,
stay near the shepherd, they are few in number—
to cowl them would require little cloth.

Now if my words are not too dim and distant,
if you have listened carefully to them,
if you can call to mind what has been said,

then part of what you wish to know is answered,
for you will see the splinters on the plant
and see what my correction meant: 'Where one

may fatten well, if one does not stray off.' "

---

a. At his death, Francis commended poverty to his brothers and asked that he lie naked on the naked
earth, cf. LMj XIV 4-5, FA:ED II 642-3.

b. That is, Saint Dominic.

Canto XII

In Canto XII Dante offers an exact counterpart of the preceding one. As soon as Thomas Aquinas concludes his speech, another ring of blessed spirits suddenly joins the first; from this group Bonaventure steps forward, and returns the compliment paid to his own founder by Thomas Aquinas by singing the praises of Saint Dominic. Continuing the nearly line-by-line parallels between the two cantos, when Bonaventure finishes Dominic's story, he comments on the present fallen state of his own order, immersed in temporal cares.

No sooner had the blessed flame[a] begun
to speak its final word than the millstone
of holy lights began to turn, but it

was not yet done with one full revolution
before another ring surrounded it,
and motion matched with motion, song with song—

a song that, sung by those sweet instruments,
surpasses so our Muses and our Sirens
as first light does the light that is reflected.

Just as, concentric, like in color, two
rainbows will curve their way through a thin cloud
when Juno has commanded her handmaid,[b]

the outer rainbow echoing the inner,
much like the voice of one—the wandering nymph[c]—
whom love consumed as sun consumes the mist

(and those two bows let people here foretell,
by reason of the pact God made with Noah,   Gn 9:8-16
that flood will never strike the world again):

so the two garlands of those everlasting
roses circled around us, and so did
the outer circle mime the inner ring.

When the dance and jubilation, festival
of song and flame that answered flame, of light
with light, of gladness and benevolence,

in one same instant, with one will, fell still
(just as the eyes, when moved by their desire,
can only close and open in accord),

---

a. The spirit of Thomas Aquinas, who has been speaking up to this point.

b. Juno's handmaid is Iris, goddess of the rainbow.

c. "The wandering nymph" is Echo, who for love of Narcissus wasted away until only her voice remained.

then from the heart of one of the new lights
there came a voice,[a] and as I turned toward it,
I seemed a needle turning to the polestar;

and it began: "The love that makes me fair
draws me to speak about the other leader[b]
because of whom my own was so praised here.

Where one is, it is right to introduce
the other: side by side, they fought, so may
they share in glory and together gleam.

Christ's army, whose rearming cost so dearly,
was slow, uncertain of itself, and scanty
behind its ensign,[c] when the Emperor

who rules forever helped his ranks in danger—
only out of His grace and not their merits.
And, as was said, He then sustained His bride,

providing her with two who could revive
a straggling people: champions who would
by doing and by preaching bring new life.

In that part of the West where gentle zephyr
rises to open those new leaves in which
Europe appears reclothed,[d] not far from where,

behind the waves that beat upon the coast,
the sun, grown weary from its lengthy course,
at times conceals itself from all men's eyes—

there, Calaroga, blessed by fortune, sits
under the aegis of the mighty shield
on which the lion loses and prevails.[e]

Within its walls was born the loving vassal
of Christian faith,[f] the holy athlete, one
kind to his own and harsh to enemies;

---

a. At this point Bonaventure, the biographer of Francis, steps forward to praise Saint Dominic.

b. Saint Dominic.

c. "Christ's army," humanity, made helpless by sin, had been "rearmed" by Christ's atonement. The "ensign" is the Cross.

d. The region is Spain, near the Bay of Biscay, the area nearest the source of the West wind, or Zephyr.

e. Calaroga or Caleruega, "blest by fortune" because Dominic was born there, is in Old Castile. The arms of the rulers of Castile consisted of two lions and two castles quartered; on one side the lion is below the castle, on the other side, above it. Thus "the lion loses and prevails."

f. The "loving vassal" is Dominic, born there about 1170.

no sooner was his mind created than
it was so full of living force that it,
still in his mother's womb, made her prophetic.

Then, at the sacred font, where Faith and he
brought mutual salvation as their dowry,
the rites of their espousal were complete.

The lady who had given the assent
for him saw, in a dream, astonishing
fruit that would spring from him and from his heirs.

And that his name might echo what he was,
a spirit moved from here to have him called
by the possessive of the One by whom

he was possessed completely.[a] Dominic
became his name; I speak of him as one
whom Christ chose as the worker in His garden.

He seemed the fitting messenger and servant
of Christ: the very first love that he showed
was for the first injunction Christ had given.[b]

His nurse would often find him on the ground,
alert and silent, in a way that said:
"It is for this that I have come." Truly

his father was Felice and his mother
Giovanna if her name, interpreted,
is in accord with what has been asserted.[c]

Not for the world, for which men now travail
along Taddeo's way or Ostian's,[d]
but through his love of the true manna, he

---

a. Dominic (*dominicus*) means "the Lord's" in Latin; it is a possessive adjective of *Dominus*.

b. The "first injunction" may refer to the First Beatitude: "Happy the poor in spirit . . ." (Mt 5:3) or to the injunction Christ gave the rich young man: "Go, sell what you have and give to the poor" (Mt 19:21). Saint Dominic's early biographers relate that during a famine he sold his clothes and books to help feed the poor.

c. His father's name was Felix, which means "happy;" his mother's name, Johanna, comes from the Hebrew and means "the grace of the Lord." Both names would be appropriate to the parents of Dominic.

d. Taddeo d'Alderotto (c. 1235-1295) was the presumed founder of the school of medicine in Bologna. Henry of Susa (1200-1271), cardinal bishop of Ostia (hence his name *Hostiensis*) was an authority on canon law. Those who "travail along Taddeo's way or Ostian's" are those who neglect the study of Scripture and the patristic writings in favor of these other studies.

became, in a brief time, so great a teacher
that he began to oversee the vineyard
that withers when neglected by its keeper.

And from the seat[a] that once was kinder to
the righteous poor (and now has gone astray,
not in itself, but in its occupant),

he did not ask to offer two or three
for six, nor for a vacant benefice,
nor *decimas, quae sunt pauperum Dei*[b]—

but pleaded for the right to fight against
the erring world, to serve the seed from which
there grew the four-and-twenty plants that ring you.

Then he, with both his learning and his zeal,
and with his apostolic office, like
a torrent hurtled from a mountain source,

coursed, and his impetus, with greatest force,
struck where the thickets of the heretics
offered the most resistance.[c] And from him

there sprang the streams with which the Catholic
garden has found abundant watering,
so that its saplings have more life, more green.

If such was one wheel of the chariot
in which the Holy Church, in her defense
taking the field, defeated enemies

within, then you must see the excellence
of him—the other wheel—whom Thomas praised
so graciously before I made my entry.

And yet the track traced by the outer rim
of that wheel is abandoned now—as in
a cask of wine when crust gives way to mold.

---

a. The "seat" is the papacy. Dante distinguishes between the papacy as an institution and the
   degeneracy of recent Popes, especially Boniface VIII, under whom it has "gone astray."

b. Dominic's honesty and love of poverty is shown by his refusal to keep part of the alms for himself or to
   seek a fat benefice (source of income) or to use the "tithes that belong to God's poor" for his own
   benefit.

c. Dominic preached in southern France, the Languedoc, where the Albigensians had their strongest
   foothold.

His family,[a] which once advanced with steps
that followed his footprints, has now turned back:
its forward foot now seeks the foot that lags.[b]

And soon we are to see, at harvest time,
the poor grain gathered, when the tares will be
denied a place within the barn—and weep.[c]

I do admit that, if one were to search
our volume leaf by leaf, he might still read
    one page with, "I am as I always was":

but those of Acquasparta or Casale[d]
who read our *Rule* are either given to
escaping it or making it too strict.

I am the living light of Bonaventure
of Bagnorea; in high offices
I always put the left-hand interests last.[e]

Illuminato and Augustine are here;[f]
they were among the first unshod poor brothers
to wear the cord, becoming friends of God.

---

a. Bonaventure now speaks of his own brothers, who are abandoning the track made by the wheel (Francis).

b. Those who set out to follow in Francis' footsteps are now heading in the opposite direction.

c. An obvious reference to the sorting out of weeds and wheat at the last judgment (Mt 13:30), but probably also an ironic allusion to the Papal decree *Exivi* of 1312, which had forbidden the brothers, as an abuse of their vow of poverty, to store up large quantities of grain (Article 14, p. 780). Thus Dante's seemingly odd remark that the grain is "poor"; the "tares" are the increasingly lax main body of brothers that he criticizes here.

d. Matthew of Aquasparta (1240-1302), a noted theologian, was elected Minister General of the Order in 1287; however, his term in office was brief for he was named a Cardinal by Nicholas IV the following year; a general chapter was held in 1289 to elect a successor. Despite his short term of office, Dante probably singled him out to personify the lax tendencies evident in the Order with such bulls as *Exultantes in Domino* (supra 765-7) because of his own personal experience. As a Cardinal and Papal legate to Tuscany Matthew was a faithful supporter of Boniface VIII; he engineered the Florentine coup of 1302, which sent Dante into exile. "Casale" is of course Ubertino; despite his dependence on Ubertino's literary images, it is clear from this reference that Dante did not follow his views on Franciscan life. By putting these words condemning both the emerging "Conventual" position and the Spiritual reaction into Bonaventure's mouth, Dante seems to be accepting his middle-of-the-road interpretation of the *Rule*, classically embodied in *Exiit Qui Seminat* (pp. 739-64), as normative.

e. The "left-hand interests" are temporal ones, a reference to Prv 3:16: "in her [wisdom's] left hand are riches and honor." So, Bonaventure always gave spiritual matters preference over temporal.

f. Illuminato and Augustine were among the early companions of Francis. On Illuminato, who accompanied Francis on his visit to "the haughty Sultan" (Canto XI:101 supra 885) see LMj IX 8-9; XI 3; XIII 4, FA:ED II 602-4, 614, 633. Augustine was the provincial minister of Campania, who died at the same moment as Francis (LMj XIV 6, FA:ED II 643). It is not clear why Dante places them in the second circle of wisdom figures with Bonaventure.

Hugh of St. Victor,[a] too, is here with them;
Peter of Spain,[b] who, with his twelve books, glows
on earth below; and Peter Book-Devourer,[c]

Nathan the prophet, Anselm, and Chrysostom
the Metropolitan, and that Donatus[d]
who deigned to deal with that art which comes first.

Rabanus,[e] too, is here; and at my side
shines the Calabrian Abbot Joachim,[f]
who had the gift of the prophetic spirit.

To this—my praise of such a paladin[g]—
the glowing courtesy and the discerning
language of Thomas[h] urged me on and stirred,

with me, the souls that form this company.

---

a. Hugh of St. Victor (c.1097-1141) was among the great Parisian theologians of the 12th century whose writings greatly influenced Bonaventure.

b. Peter of Spain (c.1210/15-1277) was actually a native of Portugal. Trained in medicine as well as philosophy, he wrote the *Summulae logicales* (a treatise on logic in "twelve books"). He was elected Pope in 1276, taking the name John XXI; his pontificate lasted just eight months. He is the only contemporary Pope that Dante meets in Paradise.

c. Peter Comestor (+1179), literally Peter "the Eater," an omnivorous reader, became chancellor of the University of Paris in 1164 and canon of the monastery of St. Victor, where he died. His most famous work was *Historia scholastica*, a history of the world up until the time of the Apostles, drawn principally from the Bible.

d. Nathan the prophet was sent by God to rebuke King David for arranging the death of Uriah and taking his wife, Bathsheba, for his own (2 Sm 12:1-15). Anselm (1033-1109) was one of the greatest theologians of the Middle Ages. His most famous work, *Cur Deus homo*, treated of the necessity of the Incarnation. He died as the archbishop of Canterbury. Saint John Chrysostom (c. 345-407), Patriarch of Constantinople and noted for his preaching, was one of the foremost fathers of the Greek Church. Aelius Donatus, Roman scholar and grammarian of the 4th century, was the teacher of Saint Jerome. His *Ars grammatica* became the standard textbook of Latin grammar, "the art which comes first" in the medieval *trivium*, followed by rhetoric and logic.

e. Rabanus Maurus (776-856) was archbishop of Mainz from 847 till his death in 856. He left numerous works of biblical exegesis and theology and was one of Bonaventure's sources.

f. Joachim of Fiore (c. 1145-1202) was the celebrated monastic reformer and Biblical interpreter. Despite the condemnation of his doctrine of the Trinity at the Fourth Lateran Council in 1215, Joachim's prophecies, especially his understanding of the history of salvation, which he saw revealed in Scripture, exercised a compelling influence throughout the thirteenth century, especially among Franciscans. An extreme "Joachite" theology was embraced by many of the more radical elements of the Franciscans, especially Spirituals like Ubertino. Bonaventure accepted some of Joachim's viewpoints, while rejecting others. Bonaventure's praise of him here (like Thomas's of Siger of Brabant, *Paradiso* X:133-38) springs from Dante's spirit of grand conciliation.

g. The "paladin" is Saint Dominic, God's athlete and warrior.

h. In his praise of Saint Francis.

APPENDIX

Explanation of Maps

This geographic supplement is designed to orient the reader—especially those unfamiliar with European geography—to the world of Francis. At its heart is a series of maps, but equally important is the gazetteer, or index of geographic place names, which will allow the reader to find specific locations.

Map one illustrates the European political world in which Francis lived. The political geography of this world was fundamentally different from that of Europe today. That there are many recognizable names of places is deceptive; even though a region may have the same name in the thirteenth century as it does today, its overall political structure was completely different. Nation-states as we know them did not exist in the Middle Ages. Western Europe at this time was organized under a feudal social-political system. Land was controlled by local nobility in the name of a king, or regional ruler. The local nobility swore oaths of fealty to the king, who depended on the cooperation of his nobility to carry out his wishes. No boundaries between regions in Western Europe are shown on Map 1 because they would tend to communicate the notion of a stable, demarked and defended border as is found in Europe today.

Map two illustrates some of these new social realities of the High Middle Ages. The population of Europe had fallen considerably after the fall of Rome and the Germanic invasions, and only began to recover and grow after the tenth century. All population estimates of the Middle Ages can be considered educated guesses at best because the historical data is fragmentary. Geographers estimate that the population between the ninth and fourteenth century doubled, from approximately 45 to 90 million. This increase was not uniformly distributed over the continent, and was frequently interrupted by invasions, wars, plagues, or famines.

The two regions of Europe having the greatest agricultural productivity and the most rapid population increase were the Northern Italian Peninsula and the lowlands of Northwest Europe (modern Belgium, Netherlands, and the Rhine Valley). It is important to distinguish between these regions, however. Although they had suffered a long period of decline in sophistication and population since the fall of the Roman Empire, Northern Italian cities had perdured, and because of their location, when trade with Byzantium and the East began to increase, they were uniquely positioned to become thriving commercial centers. Located at the southern edge of Western Europe and surrounded by the Mediterranean Sea, the cities of Lombardy, the Po Valley, Tuscany and to a lesser extent, the Duchy of Spoleto, had merchants who traded with Byzantium in the east and the rest of Europe in the north. The port cities of Venice, Genoa, and Pisa were some of the largest and wealthiest cities in Europe at this time.

The population growth in Northwest Europe was furthered primarily by the wool industry. The climate and soils are not well suited for crop production, so the region began to specialize in the production of wool and woolen cloth. From the twelfth century onward, agricultural specialization increased, which in turn led to the revival of fairs as a place to exchange goods. These were huge gatherings of merchants from all over Europe lasting about thirty days each. Eventually a pattern of rotation evolved between the various fairs in the two main geographic areas, Flanders (today's Belgium) and Champagne (northern France). The economies of Northern and Southern Europe linked up at these fairs, which fulfilled commercial functions similar to that of the Italian cities.

Map three shows the region of Italy during Francis's era. What we understand to be the modern country of Italy did not exist until the end of the 19th century. During Francis's era, Italy would have been understood to be the area south of the Alps but not extending beyond Rome (on map 3 this is shown as the Holy Roman Empire, Peter's Patrimony and the Papal States). Strong regional contrasts and variations have characterized the Italian Peninsula. Some of these contrasts can be attributed to physical geography, and some to cultural history. Since the fall of Rome, the Italian Peninsula had been divided into numerous political configurations, and there was little expectation that the whole peninsula could be politically united. Extending 700 miles into the Mediterranean and divided into sub-regions by mountains, the peninsula's population identified much more with a local region than with the political aspirations of political leaders. During the Middle Ages, the Byzantine Empire, Moslems, Normans, and the Holy Roman Empire alternately controlled the southern peninsula and the island of Sicily. Lying at the crossroads of the Mediterranean, the Kingdom of Sicily was one of the richest and most civilized states of Europe.

Lombardy and Tuscany grew to be among the most populous and wealthy regions in Europe during the High Middle Ages. The cities in this region benefited from the fertility of the Po Valley, their location as a natural sea-land transfer point for goods between Northern Europe and Byzantium, and the protection of the Alps.

Map four demonstrates how climate and geology combined to impose sharp natural divisions on the Italian Peninsula. The Alps forms a natural barrier to the North, one impenetrable as much as half the year. Over two-thirds of the peninsula may be classified as hill or mountain, and along most of the 100-mile wide peninsula, these are jumbled together in the Apennines. In Lombardy alone there are more variations of elevation, climate, soil and vegetation than in the whole of Germany. The Po Valley is the only expansive fertile plain; in peninsular Italy, fertile lowlands are limited. The ruggedness of the landscape, the unevenness of soil fertility, and the ease of access to the sea led the residents of the Italian Peninsula to become proficient mariners. Trade was much more easily accomplished along the peninsula by sea than by land. There are several physical regions of the northern Italian Peninsula: the greater Po Valley (including Lombardy, Romagna and Venice), the Arno Valley and Tuscany, the more isolated eastern coast of the Marche, Abruzzi (which has historically been the wildest part of the Apennines), the Duchy of Spoleto and Latium (the upper and lower watershed of the Tiber River, respectively).

Map five describes the transportation, religious and social geography of the northern Italian Peninsula at the time of Francis. There is no reliable way to determine the population of cities during the Middle Ages. Map 5 shows Venice, Milan, Genoa and Florence to be larger than other towns. Historians generally agree that Venice was the largest town, and estimate that it had a population of between 50,000 and 100,000. The other three large towns had slightly fewer residents, and overall, the population density in Lombardy and the Po Valley was twice that of the rest of the Italian Peninsula. Rome's population is estimated to have been 30,000. Assisi is estimated to have between 10,000 and 20,000 people at this time, with Perugia about twice as large.

The rise of the city-states and the movement toward urbanization coincided with the heretical movements that began to appear in Western Europe. A proper geography of medieval religious dissent has yet to be undertaken, and a thorough job may be impossible because of the scattered historical record. At the onset of the thirteenth century, there were several heretical movements in Lombardy and the Italian Peninsula, the most significant being the Waldensians, and the Cathars (they were called several other names, including Albigensians and Patarines). The Catholic hierarchy perceived these movements as grave threats because they challenged the official Church authority. Map 5 shows the cities with established communities of these two groups. Other heretical groups may have been present, and these two groups almost certainly had followers in many other cities, but the historical evidence is missing.

Map six details the regions of the Duchy of Spoleto and the Marche of Ancona. The first Franciscans did much of their preaching in the towns and villages shown on this map. Maps 6-9 show all the towns and villages that Francis or the early friars are reported by the early sources to have visited on the Italian Peninsula. There are, of course, many other villages that existed, but in the interest of clarity, they are not shown on the maps. The spine of the Central Apennines separate the Duchy of Spoleto and the Marche of Ancona, with much of Marche oriented toward the Adriatic Sea. Map 6 can be seen as having three sub-regions: the lower Spoleto Valley, where Assisi and Perugia are located, the Rieti Valley, where Francis spent considerable time, and the less-densely settled region of the Marche of Ancona.

Map seven shows the physical relief of the Rieti Valley and the location of the several places of the friars in that region. This map is a good illustration of the geographic relationship between early Franciscan hermitages and an emerging urban center. Francis spent a considerable amount of time in this region.

Map eight illustrates the territories of Assisi and Perugia, its neighbor to the west. Perugia became a papal city and the empire claimed Assisi. Tensions between the two cities dated back centuries, with the Tiber River forming a historical boundary between peoples. Sometime during the eleventh century, Perugia had occupied a strip of land on the east bank near an area called Collestrada. Violence escalated after 1200, resulting in the Battle of Collestrada in 1202. Francis fought in this battle, and when Assisi lost, he was imprisoned in Perugia (2C 4). It seems that Francis's father, Pietro Bernardone, owned some land near the site of the battle.

Map nine shows the first places of the brothers as well as the first two temporary residences of Clare. Also shown are the approximate location of most of the lands which archival records show as belonging to Francis's father, Pietro Bernardone.

Maps ten and eleven show what the city of Assisi looked like at the time of Francis. The walls on this map are essentially the same as those built by the ancient Romans. The locations of the four most important social powers in Assisi are all shown on this map. The Rocca Maggiore was the symbol of Imperial authority, and it dominated the landscape until it was torn down by the Assisians in 1198. The bishop's palace was the seat of Church power, and it was in the Santa Maria Maggiore Piazza (plaza) that Francis shed his clothes, spurning his father and embracing his vocation in a deeper way. Trade and commerce had grown remarkably in the century before Francis's birth and the Market in the town's center became increasingly important. With the emergence of the *commune*, the lesser nobility and merchants organized themselves and established the *Palazzo del Consoli*, or city hall, across from the Basilica of San Rufino. The *Palazzo del Consoli* moved in 1212 to the Tempio di Minerva.

Although Arnaldo Fortini confidently asserts that the paternal house of Francis lies in between the churches of San Paolo and San Nicolo (site #1), the evidence is circumstantial. Other scholars argue that his family home lay on the site now occupied by the Chiesa Nuova (site #2), or the church of San Francesco Piccolo (site #3).

Gazetteer

Place Name	General Location	Type of Feature	Map	Co-ord
Abruzzi	C Italian Peninsula	Region	5	5F
Acquapendente	Tuscany	Town	5	5D
Acquasparta	Sabina	Village	7	1B
Acre	Holy Land	Kingdom/City	1	5H
Adriatic Sea	N Mediterranean	Sea	3	3E
Alessandria	Lombardy	Town	5	2A
Alexandria	Egypt	City	1	6G
Alife	Kingdom of Sicily	Town	5	6F
Almería	Iberian Peninsula	Town	2	4A
Alps	C Europe	Mountains	4	1D
Alviano	SW Duchy of Spoleto	Village	6	7B
Amiterno	Abruzzi	Village	5	5F
Ancona	Marche of Ancona	Town	6	2F
Antioch	Asia Minor	City	1	5H
Antrodoco	Sabina	Village	7	4G
Apennines	Italian Peninsula	Mountains	4	3D
Apulia	S Italian Peninsula	Region	3	5F
Aquitaine	France	Region	1	3B
Aragon	Iberian Peninsula	Kingdom	1	3B
Arezzo	E Tuscany	City	6	3A
Arles	S France	Town	1	3C
Armenia	Asia Minor	Kingdom	1	5G
Ascoli	S Marche of Ancona	Village	6	5F
Assisi	Duchy of Spoleto	Town	6	4C
Asti	Lombardy	Town	5	2A
Atlantic Ocean	W Europe	Ocean	1	2A
Augsburg	Holy Roman Empire	Town	1	2D
Austria	Central Europe	Region	1	2E
Bagnara	Duchy of Spoleto	Village	6	4D
Bagnolo	Lombardy	Town	5	1C
Bagnoregio	Peter's Patrimony	Village	6	7A
Baltic Sea	N Europe	Sea	1	1E
Barcelona	Iberian Peninsula	Town	1	3B
Bari	Apulia	Town	3	4F
Barletta	Apulia	Town	5	6H
Basel	Holy Roman Empire	Town	2	3D
Bastia	Lower Spoleto Valley	Village	9	2A
Bavaria	Holy Roman Empire	Region	1	2D
Benvento	Kingdom of Sicily	Town	3	5D
Bergamo	Lombardy	Town	5	1C
Bettona	Spoleto Valley	Village	8	5E
Bevagna	Spoleto Valley	Village	8	7G
Biscay, Bay of	Atlantic Ocean	Bay	1	2B
Bishop Guido's Palace	Assisi	Bishop's palace	11	5C

Place Name	General Location	Type of Feature	Map	Co-ord
Black Sea	W Asia	Sea	1	3G
Bobbio	Lombardy	Monastery	5	2B
Bologna	Romagna	City	5	3D
Bolsena, Lake	Peter's Patrimony	Lake	4	4E
Bordeaux	France	Town	1	3B
Bovara	Spoleto Valley	Village	6	5C
Bracciano, Lake	Peter's Patrimony	Lake	4	4E
Brenner Pass	Alps	Mountain pass	4	1E
Brescia	E Lombardy	Town	5	1C
Brindisi	Kingdom of Sicily	Town	3	5F
Bruges	Low Countries	Town	1	1C
Buda Petsch	E Europe	Town	1	2E
Bulgaria	Balkan Peninsula	Kingdom	1	3F
Burgundy	France	Region	1	2C
Cadiz	Iberian Peninsula	Town	2	4A
Cairo	Egypt	City	1	6G
Calvi	Sabina	Village	7	5B
Camaldoli	N Marche of Ancona	Monastery	5	3D
Camerino	W Marche of Ancona	Village	6	4D
Campagna	Peter's Patrimony	Region	5	6E
Campiglia	N Tuscany	Village	5	4C
Candia	Cyprus	Town	1	5F
Cannara	Lower Spoleto Valley	Village	8	6F
Canterbury	England	Town	1	1C
Capua	Kingdom of Sicily	Town	5	6F
Carceri	Monte Subasio	Friars' place	9	2E
Carpathians	Eastern Europe	Mountains	2	2E
Castile	Iberian Peninsula	Kingdom	1	3A
Celano	Abruzzi	Village	5	5F
Celle di Cortona	E Tuscany	Friars' place	8	1A
Cerea	Lombardy	Town	5	1D
Cetona	E Tuscany	Friars' Place	6	5A
Champagne	France	Region	1	2C
Chiascio	Lower Spoleto Valley	River	9	1A
Chiusi	E Tuscany	Castle	6	2A
Città della Pieve	W Duchy of Spoleto	Town	6	5A
Città di Castello	N Duchy of Spoleto	Town	6	3B
Cività Castellana	Sabina	Village	7	6A
Civitavecchia	Peter's Patrimony	Town	5	5D
Collestrada	Lower Spoleto Valley	Battle site	8	4F
Collevecchio	Sabina	Village	7	6B
Cologne	Holy Roman Empire	Town	1	2D
Concorezo	Lombardy	Town	5	1B
Constantinople	Asia Minor	City	1	4F
Contigliano	Rieti Valley	Village	7	5D
Coppito	Abruzzi	Village	6	8E
Córdoba	Iberian Peninsula	Town	2	4A
Cori	Peter's Patrimony	Village	5	6E
Corsica	Central Mediterranean	Island	1	3C
Cortona	E Tuscany	Village	8	1A
Cremona	Lombardy	Town	5	2C
Cremona	S Lombardy	City	5	1C

Place Name	General Location	Type of Feature	Map	Co-ord
Cyprus	E Mediterranean	Island	1	5F
Dalmatia	E Europe	Region	1	3E
Damascus	Holy Land	City	1	5H
Damietta	Egypt	City	1	6G
Danube	Hungary	River	2	3E
Denmark	N Europe	Kingdom	1	1D
Dijon	France	Town	2	2C
Durazzo	Bulgaria	Town	1	4E
Egypt	NE Africa	Region	1	6G
Emilia	N Italian Peninsula	Region	5	2B
England	NW Europe	Kingdom	1	1B
Erfurt	Holy Roman Empire	Town	2	2D
Faenza	Romagna	Town	5	3D
Fano	Marche of Ancona	Town	6	1D
Farfa	Peter's Patrimony	Monastery	5	5E
Farneto	Duchy of Spoleto	Friars' Place	8	3F
Fermo	E Marche of Ancona	Village	6	4F
Ferrara	Lombardy	Town	5	2D
Flanders	N Europe	Region	1	1C
Florence	N Tuscany	City	5	3D
Foggia	Kingdom of Sicily	Town	5	6G
Foligno	Duchy of Spoleto	Town	8	6H
Fondi	Kingdom of Sicily	Town	5	6F
Fonte Columbo	Rieti Valley	Friars' place	7	5E
Forano	Marche of Ancona	Friars' place	6	3E
France	W Europe	Kingdom	1	2C
Gaeta	S Italian Peninsula	Town	5	6F
Geneva	Central Europe	Town	2	3C
Genoa	N Italian Peninsula	City	5	3B
Georgia	W Asia	Region	1	3H
Giano	Duchy of Spoleto	Village	6	6C
Granada	Iberian Peninsula	Town	2	4A
Greccio	Rieti Valley	Friars' place	7	4D
Gualdo Tadino	N Duchy of Spoleto	Village	8	2H
Gubbio	NE Duchy of Spoleto	Town	6	3C
Hispania	Iberian Peninsula	Region	1	3A
Hochtor Pass	Alps	Mountain Pass	4	1E
Holy Roman Empire	N Europe	Empire	1	2D
H. of Bernardo di Quintivale	Assisi	House	11	4A
House of Clare	Assisi	House	10	2G
H. Pietro B. (Chiesa Nuova)	Assisi	House	11	3D
H. Pietro B. (Fortini)	Assisi	House	11	2A
H. Pietro B. (S.F. Piccolo)	Assisi	House	11	3D
Hungary	E Europe	Kingdom	1	3E
Iesi	Marche of Ancona	Town	6	2E
Imola	Romagna	Town	5	3D
Ireland	NW Europe	Kingdom	1	1B
Isola Maggiore	Lake Trasimeno	Friars' place	8	3B
Isola Romana	Lower Spoleto Valley	Village	9	2A
Jerusalem	Holy Land	Town	1	6H
Kiev	Russia	Town	1	2G
La Foresta	Rieti Valley	Friars' place	7	4E

Place Name	General Location	Type of Feature	Map	Co-ord
La Verna	N Marche of Ancona	Friars' place	6	2A
Languedoc	France	Region	1	3C
Leon	N Iberian Peninsula	Kingdom	1	3A
Limoges	Touraine	Town	2	3C
Lisbon	W Iberian Peninsula	Town	1	4A
Lisciano	NW Duchy of Spoleto	Village	8	1B
Lombardy	N Italian Peninsula	Region	5	1C
London	England	Town	1	1C
Lubeck	N Germany	Town	1	1D
Lucca	NW Tuscany	City	5	3C
Lugano	Lombardy	Town	5	1A
Lyons	France	Town	1	3C
Machilone	Abruzzi	Village	7	3G
Magliano	Sabina	Village	7	5A
Málaga	Iberian Peninsula	Town	2	4A
Mantova	Lombardy	Town	5	2C
Marche of Ancona	C Italian Peninsula	Region	5	4E
Market (P.d. Commune)	Assisi	Piazza	11	2C
Marseilles	S France	Town	2	3C
Massa Trabaria	N Marche of Ancona	Region	6	2B
Mediterranean Sea	S Europe	Sea	1	4C
Messina	Island of Sicily	Town	3	7E
Milan	Lombardy	City	5	1B
Modena	Lombardy	Town	5	2C
Mogliano	Marche of Ancona	Friars' place	6	4F
Mont Cenis Pass	Alps	Mountain pass	4	2B
Monte Cassino	S Italian Peninsula	Monastery	5	6F
Monte Castrilli	Sabina	Village	7	1B
Monte Gargano	N Apulia	Monastery	5	5H
Monte San Vicino	Marche of Ancona	Friars' place	6	3D
Monte Subasio	Duchy of Spoleto	Mountain	9	3F
Montecasale	W Marche of Ancona	Friars' place	6	2B
Montefalco	Duchy of Spoleto	Village	6	5C
Montefeltro	N Marche of Ancona	Castle	6	1B
Monteluco	Duchy of Spoleto	Friars' place	6	6D
Montenero	Duchy of Spoleto	Village	6	6B
Montenero	Duchy of Spoleto	Village	6	6B
Montepulciano	Tuscany	Town	5	4D
Monteripido	Duchy of Spoleto	Friars' place	8	3D
Monterubbiano	Marche of Ancona	Friars' place	6	4F
Montpellier	Languedoc	Town	2	3C
Morocco	NW Africa	Region	1	5A
Mount Alverna	see: La Verna			
Naples	S Italian Peninsula	Town	3	5D
Narbonne	S France	Town	1	3C
Narni	Duchy of Spoleto	Village	7	3B
Navas de Tolosa	Iberian Peninsula	Town	1	4A
Nera	Duchy of Spoleto	River	7	4A
Nicea	Asia Minor	Kingdom	1	4G
Nocera Umbra	N Duchy of Spoleto	Village	8	4H
Norcia	S. Marche of Ancona	Village	6	6E
North Sea	N Europe	Sea	1	1C

Place Name	General Location	Type of Feature	Map	Co-ord
Nottiano	Duchy of Spoleto	Village	8	4G
Orte	Sabina	Village	7	4A
Orvieto	Duchy of Spoleto	Town	6	6A
Osimo	E Marche of Ancona	Village	6	2F
Ostia	Peter's Patrimony	Town	5	5E
Oxford	England	Town	2	1C
Padua	Lombardy	Town	5	1D
Padua	N Italian Peninsula	City	5	1D
Palazzo dei Consoli	Assisi	Council hall	11	1E
Palermo	Island of Sicily	City	3	7D
Panzo	see: Sant'Angelo di Panzo			
Papal States	Italian Peninsula	Region	5	4E
Paris	France	City	2	2C
Parma	Emilia	Town	5	2C
Pavia	Lombardy	Town	5	2B
Penne	Abbruzzi	Town	5	5F
Perugia	Duchy of Spoleto	Town	6	4B
Peter's Patrimony	C Italian Peninsula	Region	5	5E
Petrella	Sabina	Village	7	6G
Piacenza	Lombardy	Town	5	2B
Piazza del Commune	Assisi	Piazza	11	2C
Piglio nella Campania	Peter's Patrimony	Village	5	5E
Pisa	NE Tuscany	City	5	4C
Po	N Italian Peninsula	River	4	2C
Pofi	Kingdom of Sicily	Village	5	6F
Poggibonsi	Tuscany	Town	5	4C
Poggio Bostone	Rieti Valley	Friars' place	7	3F
Poland	NE Europe	Kingdom	1	1E
Ponte dei Galli	Lower Spoleto Valley	Bridge	9	1D
Ponte San Vettorino	Lower Spoleto Valley	Bridge	9	2C
Porta Antica	Assisi	Gate	10	3C
Porta del Parlascio	Assisi	Gate	10	2H
Porta del Sementone	Assisi	Gate	10	5E
P. Murorupto Inferiore	Assisi	Gate	10	3A
P. Murorupto Superiore	Assisi	Gate	10	2A
Porta Moiano	Assisi	Gate	10	4F
P. qua itur in Marchiam	Assisi	Gate	10	1G
Porta San Giorgio	Assisi	Gate	10	3G
Porta San Rufino	Assisi	Gate	10	3G
Porta Sant'Antimo	Assisi	Gate	10	4D
Portiuncula, S. Maria A.	Spoleto Valley	Friars' place	9	3B
Portugal	W Iberian Peninsula	Kingdom	1	3A
Potenza	Kingdom of Sicily	Town	5	5E
Prague	Holy Roman Empire	Town	1	2D
Preggio	Duchy of Spoleto	Friars' place	8	2C
Provence	France	Region	1	3C
Provins	France	Town, Fair	2	2C
Ragusa	Balkan Peninsula	Town	1	4E
Ratisbon	Holy Roman Empire	Town	2	2D
Ravenna	Lombardy	Town	5	3D
Recanati	Marche of Ancona	Village	6	3F
R. Canons of San Rufino	Assisi	Church residence	10	2G

Place	General Location	Type of Feature	Map	Co-ord
Rhine	Germany	River	2	2D
Rhone	France	River	2	3C
Rieti	Sabina	Town	7	5E
Rieti Valley	Sabina	Region	7	4E
Rimini	SE Romagna	Town	5	3E
Rivo Torto	Spoleto Valley	Stream	9	3D
Rivotorto	Spoleto Valley	Friars' place	9	3D
Rocca	Sabina	Village	7	6F
Rocca Maggiore	Assisi	Castle	10	1D
Romagna	N Italian Peninsula	Region	5	3D
Rome	C Italian Peninsula	City	5	5E
Russia	E Europe	Kingdom	1	1G
Sabina	C Italian Peninsula	Region	5	5E
San Bartolomeo	Lower Spoleto Valley	Priory	9	2C
San Benedetto	Mt. Subasio	Abbey	9	4F
San Bernardo Pass	Alps	Mountain Pass	4	2B
San Damiano	Spoleto Valley	Friars' place	9	2D
San Gemini	Duchy of Spoleto	Village	7	2B
S. Giacomo Murorupto	Assisi	Church	10	2A
San Gimignano	Tuscany	Town	5	4C
San Giorgio	Assisi	Church	10	4G
San Giorgio	Assisi	Piazza	10	4G
San Gottardo	Alps	Mountain pass	4	1C
San Gregorio	Assisi	Church	11	3A
San Gregorio	Assisi	Piazza	11	3A
San Lorenzo	Assisi	Church	10	1G
San Masseo	Lower Spoleto Valley	Church	9	2C
San Nicolo	Assisi	Church	11	2B
San Paolo Abbadesse	Lower Spoleto Valley	Monastery	9	2A
San Paolo di Assisi	Assisi	Church	11	2A
San Pietro della Spina	Lower Spoleto Valley	Church	9	4C
San Quirico	Tuscany	Village	5	4D
San Rufino	Assisi	Basilica	10	2G
San Rufino	Assisi	Piazza	11	1E
San Rufino del Arce	Lower Spoleto Valley	Church	9	3C
San Severino	Marche of Ancona	Village	6	4E
San Stefano	Assisi	Church	10	3D
San Stefano	Marche of Ancona	Village	6	2A
San Verecondo	Duchy of Spoleto	Monastery	8	1G
San Vettorino	Lower Spoleto Valley	Monastery	9	1C
Sansepolcro	E Tuscany	Town	6	2A
Sant' Agata	Assisi	Church	11	2C
Sant' Angelo di Panzo	Spoleto Valley	Church	9	3E
Sant' Annessa	Lower Spoleto Valley	Monastery	9	2D
S. Eleuterio Contigliano	Sabina	Friars' place	7	5D
Sant' Elia	Rieti Valley	Village	7	5E
Sant' Urbano	Sabina	Friars' place	7	4C
S. Maria degli Episcopi	Lower Spoleto Valley	Monastery	9	2D
Santa Maria Maggiore	Assisi	Church	11	4C
Santa Maria Maggiore	Assisi	Piazza	11	4C
Santiago de Compostela	W Iberian Peninsula	Pilgrimage Site	1	3A
Sardinia	C Mediterranean	Island	1	4C

Place Name	General Location	Type of Feature	Map	Co-ord
Sarteano	E Tuscany	Friars' place	6	5A
Satriano	Duchy of Spoleto	Village	8	3G
Saxony	N Germany	Region	1	1D
Sclavonia	E Europe	Region	1	3E
Serbia	Balkan Peninsula	Region	1	3E
Seville	Iberian Peninsula	Town	1	4A
Sicily	C Mediterranean	Island	3	8D
Siena	Tuscany	Town	5	4D
Sirolo	NE Marche of Ancona	Friars' place	6	2F
Soffiano	Marche of Ancona	Friars' place	6	5E
Sora	Kingdom of Sicily	Village	5	6F
Spello	Duchy of Spoleto	Village	8	6G
Spoleto	Duchy of Spoleto	Town	6	6C
Spoleto Valley	Duchy of Spoleto	Valley	9	2B
Spoleto, Duchy of	C Italian Peninsula	Region	5	4D
Subiaco	Peter's Patrimony	Monastery	5	6E
Syracuse	Island of Sicily	Town	3	8E
Syria	Asia Minor	Region	1	5H
Tarano	Sabina	Village	7	5B
Tempio di Minerva	Assisi	Roman temple	11	2B
Terni	Duchy of Spoleto	Village	7	2C
Tescio	Lower Spoleto Valley	River	9	2B
Tiber	C Italian Peninsula	River	4	4E
Tivoli	Campagna	Village	5	5E
Todi	Duchy of Spoleto	Village	6	6B
Toledo	Iberian Peninsula	Town	1	4A
Topino	Spoleto Valley	Stream	9	3B
Torino	Lombardy	Town	5	2A
Torre del Pozzo	Assisi	Tower	11	2D
Toscanella	Sabina	Village	6	8A
Toulouse	S France	Town	2	3C
Touraine	France	Region	1	2B
Tours	France	Town	2	2B
Trapani	Island of Sicily	Town	3	7C
Trasimeno, Lake	Duchy of Spoleto	Lake	8	3B
Trave Bonate	Marche of Ancona	Friars' place	6	4D
Trevi	Spoleto Valley	Village	6	5C
Treviso	N Italian Peninsula	Town	5	1D
Tripoli	Holy Land	Town	1	5H
Tripoli	N Africa	City	1	6D
Troyes	France	Town	2	2C
Tunis	N Africa	Town	2	5D
Tuscany	Central Italian Peninsula	Region	5	4C
Tyrrhenian Sea	C Mediterranean	Sea	4	5D
Valencia	Iberian Peninsula	Town	2	4B
Valfabbrica	Duchy of Spoleto	Monastery	8	3F
Vallombrosa	Tuscany	Monastery	5	4D
Venetian Territories	E Mediterranean	Captured lands	1	5E
Venice	N Italian Peninsula	City	3	1E
Venosa	Kingdom of Sicily	Town	3	5E
Verina	Sabina	River	7	3D
Verona	N Italian Peninsula	Town	5	1C

Place Name	General Location	Type of Feature	Map	Co-ord
Via Aemilia	Lombardy	Roman road	4	3E
Via Antica	Lower Spoleto Valley	Road	9	4E
Via Appia	S Italian Peninsula	Roman road	4	5G
Via Aurelia	C Italian Peninsula	Roman road	4	4D
Via Capobove	Assisi	Street	11	1A
Via d. Ceppo della Catena	Assisi	Street	11	3D
Via dell'Abbadia	Assisi	Street	11	3C
Via di Murorupto	Assisi	Street	10	3B
Via di San Rufino	Assisi	Street	11	2D
Via di Spello	Lower Spoleto Valley	Road	9	4E
Via Flaminia	C Italian Peninsula	Roman road	4	4E
Via Francesca	Lower Spoleto Valley	Road	9	4E
Via per il Collis Infernus	Assisi	Street	10	3B
Via Portica	Assisi	Street	10	3D
Via Sabina	Sabina	Roman road	7	5F
Vicenza	Lombardy	Town	5	1D
Vienna	Holy Roman Empire	Town	2	2E
Viterbo	Peter's Patrimony	Town	6	8A
Volterra	Tuscany	Town	5	4C
Ypres	France	Town, Fair	2	2

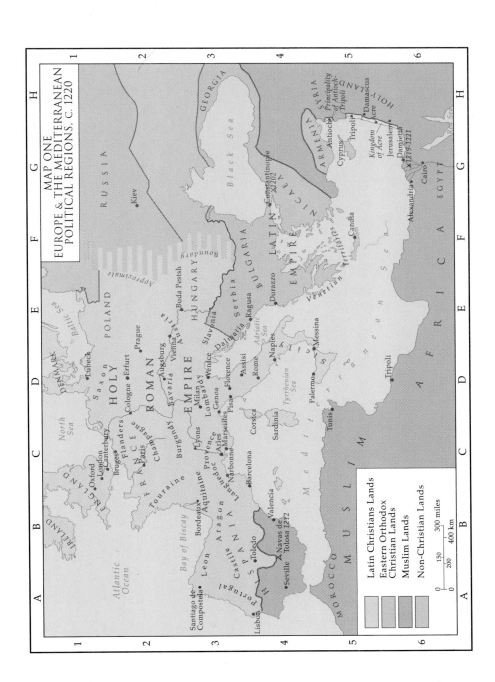

MAP ONE
EUROPE & THE MEDITERRANEAN
POLITICAL REGIONS, C. 1220

Latin Christians Lands

Eastern Orthodox
Christian Lands

Muslim Lands

Non-Christian Lands

0   150   300 miles
0   200   400 km

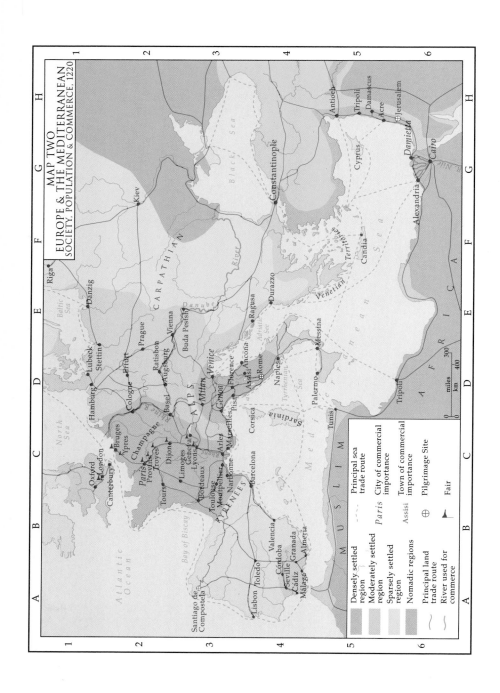

MAP TWO
EUROPE & THE MEDITERRANEAN
SOCIETY, POPULATION & COMMERCE, 1220

Legend:

- Densely settled region
- Moderately settled region
- Sparsely settled region
- Nomadic regions
- Principal land trade route
- River used for commerce
- Principal sea trade route
- *Paris* — City of commercial importance
- Assisi — Town of commercial importance
- ⊕ Pilgrimage Site
- ⚑ Fair

miles 0   300
km   0   400

Places labelled on the map: Riga, Danzig, Stettin, Lubeck, Hamburg, Bruges, Ypres, Cologne, Erfurt, Prague, Ratisbon, Augsburg, Vienna, Buda Pesth, Basel, Milan, Genoa, Venice, Kiev, London, Oxford, Canterbury, Paris, Provins, Troyes, Champagne, Dijon, Geneva, Lyons, Limoges, Tours, Bordeaux, Toulouse, Montpellier, Narbonne, Marseilles, Arles, Barcelona, Valencia, Granada, Almeria, Córdoba, Seville, Cádiz, Málaga, Toledo, Lisbon, Santiago de Compostela, Pisa, Florence, Assisi, Rome, Ancona, Ragusa, Durazzo, Naples, Palermo, Messina, Tunis, Tripoli, Corsica, Sardinia, Constantinople, Cyprus, Candia, Antioch, Tripoli, Damascus, Acre, Jerusalem, Damietta, Cairo, Alexandria

Geographic labels: Atlantic Ocean, North Sea, Baltic Sea, Bay of Biscay, Mediterranean Sea, Black Sea, Adriatic Sea, Tyrrhenian Sea, Venetian Territories, CARPATHIAN, ALPS, PYRENEES, Rhine R., Saone R., Rhone R., Danube River, Dniester River, Nile, MUSLIM, AFRICA

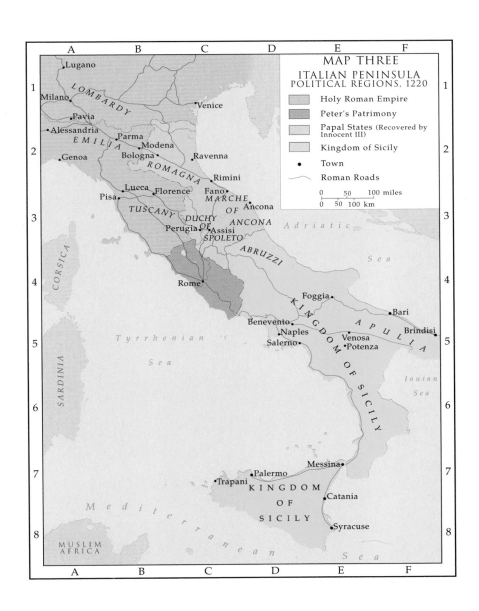

MAP THREE
ITALIAN PENINSULA
POLITICAL REGIONS, 1220

Holy Roman Empire

Peter's Patrimony

Papal States (Recovered by Innocent III)

Kingdom of Sicily

• Town

Roman Roads

0   50   100 miles
0   50   100 km

•Lugano

LOMBARDY

Milano•

•Pavia

•Venice

•Alessandria

EMILIA

•Parma

•Modena

•Genoa

Bologna•

ROMAGNA

•Ravenna

•Rimini

Lucca• •Fano

Pisa•

Florence•

MARCHE

•Ancona

TUSCANY

OF

DUCHY OF ANCONA

Perugia• •Assisi

SPOLETO

Adriatic

Sea

ABRUZZI

Rome•

Foggia•

•Bari

K
I
N
G
D
O
M

APULIA

Benevento•

•Brindisi

•Naples

Venosa

Tyrrhenian

Salerno•

•Potenza

CORSICA

Sea

O
F

S
I
C
I
L
Y

Ionian

Sea

SARDINIA

•Messina

•Trapani

•Palermo

KINGDOM

OF

SICILY

•Catania

Mediterranean

•Syracuse

MUSLIM
AFRICA

Sea

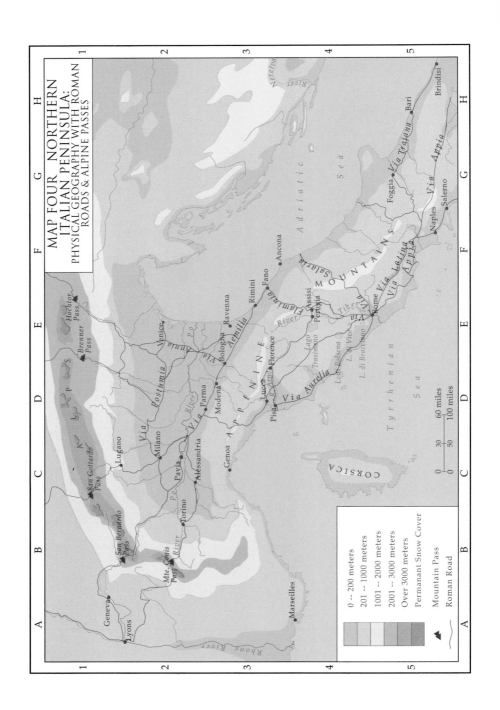

MAP FOUR   NORTHERN
ITALIAN PENINSULA:
PHYSICAL GEOGRAPHY WITH ROMAN
ROADS & ALPINE PASSES

0 -- 200 meters
201 -- 1000 meters
1001 -- 2000 meters
2001 -- 3000 meters
Over 3000 meters
Permanant Snow Cover

Mountain Pass
Roman Road

0   30   60 miles
    50   100 miles

Lyons
Geneva

Rhone River

Marseilles

San Bernardo Pass
Mte. Cenis Pass
Po River
Torino

San Gottardo Pass

Lugano
Milano
Pavia
Alessandria
Po River

Via

Via Postumia

A   L   P   S

Brenner Pass
Hochtor Pass

Venice
Adige

Via Aemilia

Po River
Parma
Modena
Bologna
Ravenna

Genoa

A P E N N I N E

Via Aurelia

Pisa
Lucca
Florence

Lago
Trasimeno
L. di Bolsena
L. di Bracciano

Via Cassia

Via Flaminia

Perugia
Assisi

Rimini
Fano
Ancona

M O U N T A I N S

Tiber River

Via Salaria

Rome
Via Latina
Via Appia

Naples
Salerno

Foggia
Via Trajana
Bari

Via Appia

Brindisi

Netetina River

A d r i a t i c   S e a

T y r r h e n i a n   S e a

CORSICA

A   B   C   D   E   F   G   H

1   2   3   4   5

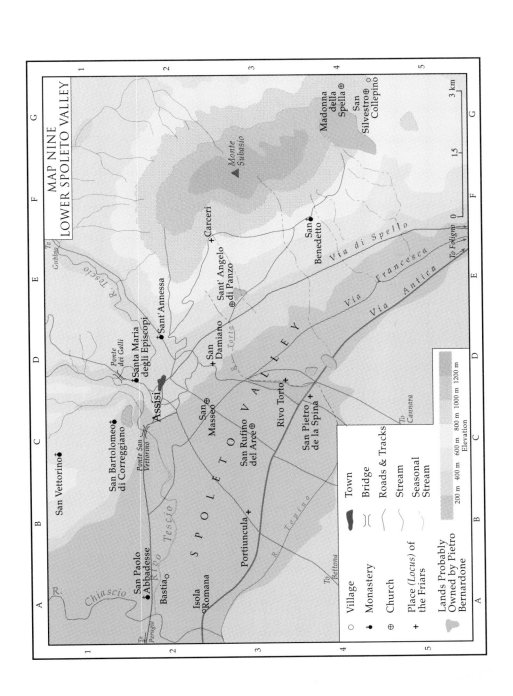

MAP NINE
LOWER SPOLETO VALLEY

Legend:
- ○ Village
- ● Town
- ✚ Monastery
-)(Bridge
- ⊕ Church
- ⟨ Roads & Tracks
- + Place (*Locus*) of the Friars
- ⟨ Stream
- ⟨ Seasonal Stream
- Lands Probably Owned by Pietro Bernardone

Elevation: 200 m · 400 m · 600 m · 800 m · 1000 m · 1200 m

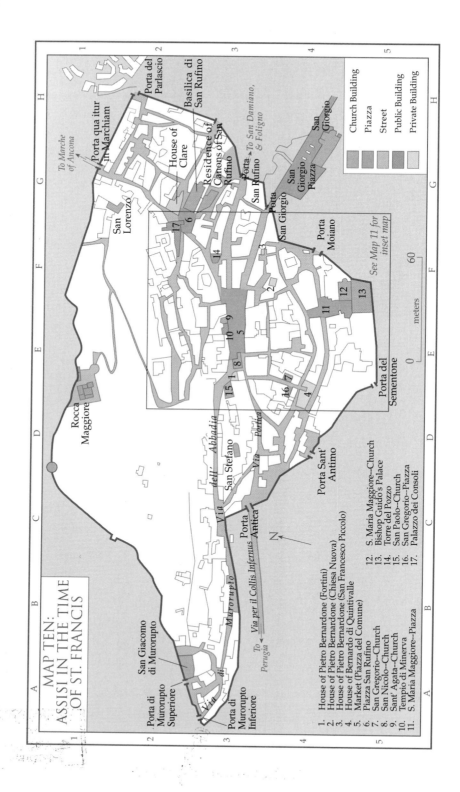

MAP TEN: ASSISI IN THE TIME OF ST. FRANCIS

Church Building
Piazza
Street
Public Building
Private Building

1. House of Pietro Bernardone (Fortini)
2. House of Pietro Bernardone (Chiesa Nuova)
3. House of Pietro Bernardone (San Francesco Piccolo)
4. House of Bernardo di Quintivalle
5. Market (Piazza del Comune)
6. Piazza San Rufino
7. San Gregorio—Church
8. San Nicolò—Church
9. Sant' Agata—Church
10. Tempio di Minerva
11. S. Maria Maggiore—Piazza

12. S. Maria Maggiore—Church
13. Bishop Guido's Palace
14. Torre del Pozzo
15. San Paolo—Church
16. San Gregorio—Piazza
17. Palazzo dei Consoli

Porta del Parlascio
Basilica di San Rufino
House of Clare
Residence of Canons of San Rufino
Porta
San Giorgio
San Giorgio
San Giorgio Piazza
Porta San Rufino
To San Damiano, & Foligno
Porta qua itur in Marchiam
To Marche of Ancona
San Lorenzo
Porta Moiano
See Map 11 for inset map
Rocca Maggiore
San Stefano
Via dell' Abbadia
Via Portica
Porta del Sementone
Porta Sant' Antimo
Porta Antica
San Giacomo di Murorupto
Porta di Murorupto Superiore
Porta di Murorupto Inferiore
Via di Murorupto
Via per il Collis Infernus
To Perugia

meters
0   60

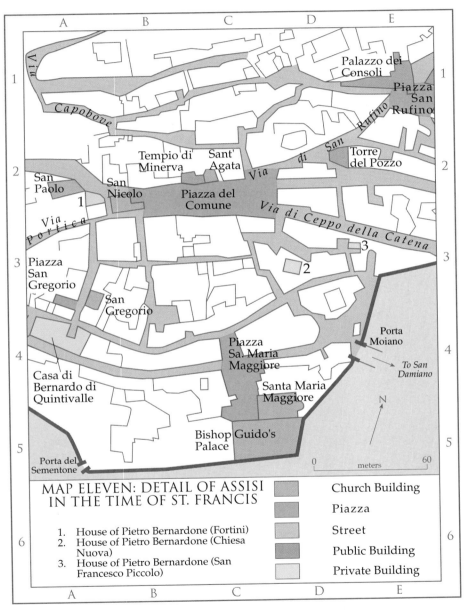

Via Capobove

Palazzo dei Consoli

Piazza San Rufino

San Rufino

Via di San

Tempio di Minerva

Sant' Agata

Torre del Pozzo

San Paolo

San Nicolo

Piazza del Comune

1

Via Portica

Via di Ceppo della Catena

3

Piazza San Gregorio

2

San Gregorio

Porta Moiano

Piazza Sa. Maria Maggiore

To San Damiano

Santa Maria Maggiore

N

Casa di Bernardo di Quintivalle

Bishop Guido's Palace

5

0   meters   60

Porta del Sementone

MAP ELEVEN: DETAIL OF ASSISI
IN THE TIME OF ST. FRANCIS

1. House of Pietro Bernardone (Fortini)
2. House of Pietro Bernardone (Chiesa Nuova)
3. House of Pietro Bernardone (San Francesco Piccolo)

Church Building

Piazza

Street

Public Building

Private Building